THE
ALL ENGLAND
LAW REPORTS
2001

Volume 4

Editor
CRAIG ROSE   Barrister

Butterworths
LexisNexis™

Members of the LexisNexis Group worldwide

United Kingdom	Butterworths Tolley, a Division of Reed Elsevier (UK) Ltd, Halsbury House, 35 Chancery Lane, LONDON, WC2A 1EL, and 4 Hill Street, EDINBURGH EH2 3JZ
Argentina	Abeledo Perrot, Jurisprudencia Argentina and Depalma, BUENOS AIRES
Australia	Butterworths, a Division of Reed International Books Australia Pty Ltd, CHATSWOOD, New South Wales
Austria	ARD Betriebsdienst and Verlag Orac, VIENNA
Canada	Butterworths Canada Ltd, MARKHAM, Ontario
Chile	Publitecsa and Conosur Ltda, SANTIAGO DE CHILE
Czech Republic	Orac sro, PRAGUE
France	Editions du Juris-Classeur SA, PARIS
Hong Kong	Butterworths Asia (Hong Kong), HONG KONG
Hungary	Hvg Orac, BUDAPEST
India	Butterworths India, NEW DELHI
Ireland	Butterworths (Ireland) Ltd, DUBLIN
Italy	Giuffré, MILAN
Malaysia	Malayan Law Journal Sdn Bhd, KUALA LUMPUR
New Zealand	Butterworths of New Zealand, WELLINGTON
Poland	Wydawnictwa Prawnicze PWN, WARSAW
Singapore	Butterworths Asia, SINGAPORE
South Africa	Butterworths Publishers (Pty) Ltd, DURBAN
Switzerland	Stämpfli Verlag AG, BERNE
USA	LexisNexis, DAYTON, Ohio

Any Crown copyright material is reproduced with the permission of the Controller of Her Majesty's Stationery Office. Any European material in this work which has been reproduced from EUR-lex, the official European Union legislation website, is European Union copyright.

A CIP Catalogue record for this book is available from the British Library.

Printed and bound in Great Britain by William Clowes Ltd, Beccles and London

ISBN for the complete set of volumes: 0 406 85159 X
for this volume:

ISBN 0-406-93445-2

9 780406 934451

Visit Butterworths LexisNexis *direct* at www.butterworths.com

House of Lords

The Lord High Chancellor of Great Britain: Lord Irvine of Lairg

Lords of Appeal in Ordinary

Lord Bingham of Cornhill
Lord Slynn of Hadley
Lord Nicholls of Birkenhead
Lord Steyn
Lord Hoffmann
Lord Hope of Craighead
Lord Clyde (retired 30 September 2001)

Lord Hutton
Lord Saville of Newdigate
Lord Hobhouse of Woodborough
Lord Millett
Lord Scott of Foscote
Lord Rodger of Earlsferry (appointed 1 October 2001)

Court of Appeal

The Lord High Chancellor of Great Britain

The Lord Chief Justice of England: Lord Woolf
(President of the Criminal Division)

The Master of the Rolls: Lord Phillips of Worth Matravers
(President of the Civil Division)

The President of the Family Division: Dame Elizabeth Butler-Sloss

The Vice-Chancellor: Sir Robert Andrew Morritt

Lords Justices of Appeal

Sir Paul Joseph Morrow Kennedy
(Vice-President of the Queen's
Bench Division)
Sir Simon Denis Brown
Sir Christopher Dudley Roger Rose
(Vice-President of the Criminal Division)
Sir Peter Leslie Gibson
Sir Denis Robert Maurice Henry
Sir Robin Ernest Auld
Sir Malcolm Thomas Pill
Sir William Aldous
Sir Alan Hylton Ward
Sir Konrad Hermann Theodor Schiemann
Sir Mathew Alexander Thorpe
Sir Mark Howard Potter
Sir Henry Brooke
Sir Igor Judge (Senior Presiding Judge for England
and Wales)
Sir George Mark Waller
Sir John Frank Mummery

Sir Charles Barrie Knight Mantell
Sir John Murray Chadwick
Sir Robert Walker
Sir Richard Joseph Buxton
Sir Anthony Tristram Kenneth May
Sir Simon Lane Tuckey
Sir Anthony Peter Clarke
Sir John Grant McKenzie Laws
Sir Stephen John Sedley
Sir Jonathan Hugh Mance
Dame Brenda Marjorie Hale
Sir David Nicholas Ramsey Latham
Sir John William Kay
Sir Bernard Anthony Rix
Sir Jonathan Frederic Parker
Dame Mary Howarth Arden
Sir David Wolfe Keene
Sir John Anthony Dyson
Sir Andrew Centlivres Longmore

High Court of Justice

The Lord High Chancellor of Great Britain
The Lord Chief Justice of England
The President of the Family Division
The Vice-Chancellor
The Senior Presiding Judge for England and Wales
The puisne judges of the High Court

Chancery Division

The Lord High Chancellor of Great Britain
The Vice-Chancellor

Sir Francis Mursell Ferris
Sir John Edmund Frederic Lindsay
Sir Edward Christopher Evans-Lombe
Sir Robin Raphael Hayim Jacob
Sir William Anthony Blackburne
(Vice-Chancellor of the County Palatine
of Lancaster)
Sir Gavin Anthony Lightman
Sir Robert John Anderson Carnwath
Sir Colin Percy Farquharson Rimer

Sir Hugh Ian Lang Laddie
Sir Timothy Andrew Wigram Lloyd
Sir David Edmund Neuberger
Sir Andrew Edward Wilson Park
Sir Nicholas Richard Pumfrey
Sir Michael Christopher Campbell Hart
Sir Lawrence Anthony Collins
Sir Nicholas John Patten
Sir Terrence Michael Elkan Barnet Etherton

Queen's Bench Division

The Lord Chief Justice of England

Sir Patrick Neville Garland
Sir Michael John Turner
Sir Francis Humphrey Potts (retired 30 September
2001)
Sir Richard George Rougier
Sir Stuart Neil McKinnon
Sir Thomas Scott Gillespie Baker
Sir Douglas Dunlop Brown
Sir Michael Morland
Sir Roger John Buckley
Sir Anthony Brian Hidden
Sir John Michael Wright
Sir John Christopher Calthorpe Blofeld (retired
1 October 2001)
Sir Peter John Cresswell
Dame Ann Marian Ebsworth (retired
30 September 2001)
Sir Christopher John Holland
Sir Richard Herbert Curtis
Dame Janet Hilary Smith

Sir Anthony David Colman
Sir John Thayne Forbes
Sir Michael Alexander Geddes Sachs
Sir Stephen George Mitchell
Sir Rodger Bell
Sir Michael Guy Vicat Harrison
Dame Anne Heather Steel (retired 30 September
2001)
Sir William Marcus Gage
Sir Thomas Richard Atkin Morison
Sir Andrew David Collins
Sir Maurice Ralph Kay
Sir Anthony Hooper
Sir Alexander Neil Logie Butterfield
Sir George Michael Newman
Sir David Anthony Poole
Sir Martin James Moore-Bick
Sir Gordon Julian Hugh Langley
Sir Roger John Laugharne Thomas
Sir Robert Franklyn Nelson

[continued on next page]

Queen's Bench Division *(continued)*

Sir Roger Grenfell Toulson
Sir Michael John Astill
Sir Alan George Moses
Sir Timothy Edward Walker
Sir David Eady
Sir Jeremy Mirth Sullivan
Sir David Herbert Penry-Davey
Sir Stephen Price Richards
Sir David William Steel
Sir Rodney Conrad Klevan
Sir Charles Antony St John Gray
Sir Nicolas Dusan Bratza
Sir Michael John Burton
Sir Rupert Matthew Jackson
Dame Heather Carol Hallett
Sir Patrick Elias
Sir Richard John Pearson Aikens
Sir Stephen Robert Silber
Sir John Bernard Goldring
Sir Peter Francis Crane
Dame Anne Judith Rafferty

Sir Geoffery Douglas Grigson
Sir Richard John Hedley Gibbs
Sir Richard Henry Quixano Henriques
Sir Stephen Miles Tomlinson
Sir Andrew Charles Smith
Sir Stanley Jeffrey Burnton
Sir Patrick James Hunt
Sir Christopher John Pitchford
Sir Brian Henry Leveson
Sir Duncan Brian Walter Ouseley
Sir Richard George Bramwell McCombe
Sir Raymond Evan Jack
Sir Robert Michael Owen
Sir Colin Crichton Mackay
Sir John Edward Mitting
Sir David Roderick Evans
Sir Nigel Anthony Lamert Davis (appointed
1 October 2001)
Sir Peter Henry Gross (appointed 1 October 2001)
Sir Brian Richard Keith (appointed 2 October 2001)
Sir Jeremy Cooke (appointed 2 October 2001)

Family Division

The President of the Family Division

Sir Robert Lionel Johnson
Dame Joyanne Winifred Bracewell
Sir Michael Bryan Connell
Sir Jan Peter Singer
Sir Nicholas Allan Roy Wilson
Sir Nicholas Peter Rathbone Wall
Sir Andrew Tristram Hammett Kirkwood
Sir Hugh Peter Derwyn Bennett
Sir Edward James Holman

Dame Mary Claire Hogg
Sir Christopher John Sumner
Sir Anthony Philip Gilson Hughes
Sir Arthur William Hessin Charles
Sir David Roderick Lessiter Bodey
Dame Jill Margaret Black
Sir James Lawrence Munby
Sir Paul James Duke Coleridge

Official Judgment Numbers
and
Paragraph References

Since 11 January 2001, official judgment numbers have been given to all judgments delivered in the House of Lords, Privy Council, both divisions of the Court of Appeal and the Administrative Court. All such judgments have fixed paragraph numbering, as do judgments delivered on or after 11 January 2001 in divisions of the High Court which have not yet adopted the system of official judgment numbers (see Practice Note (judgments: neutral citation) [2001] 1 All ER 193 for the Court of Appeal and the High Court). We have adopted the following practice in respect of judgments with official judgment numbers and official paragraph numbering:

- The official judgment number is inserted immediately beneath the case name;
- Official paragraph numbers are in bold in square brackets;
- Holding references in the headnotes, and any other cross-references, are to an official paragraph number, not to a page of the report;
- When such a judgment is subsequently cited in another report,

(i) the official judgment number is inserted before the usual report citations in the case lists and on the first occasion when the case is cited in the text. Thereafter, only the report citations are given;

(ii) All 'at' references are to the official paragraph number rather than to a page of a report, with the paragraph number in square brackets but not in bold;

(iii) The 'at' reference is only given in conjunction with the first report cited; eg [2001] 4 All ER 159 at [16], [2001] AC 61. If an 'at' reference is included on the first occasion when the case is cited, it also appears alongside the official judgment number.

For the avoidance of doubt, these changes do not apply to reports of judgments delivered before 11 January 2001 or to the citation of such cases in other reports.

CITATION

These reports are cited thus:

[2001] 4 All ER

REFERENCES

These reports contain references to the following major works of legal reference described in the manner indicated below.

Halsbury's Laws of England

The reference 14 *Halsbury's Laws* (4th edn) para 185 refers to paragraph 185 on page 90 of volume 14 of the fourth edition of *Halsbury's Laws of England*.

The reference 15 *Halsbury's Laws* (4th edn reissue) para 355 refers to paragraph 355 on page 283 of reissue volume 15 of the fourth edition of *Halsbury's Laws of England*.

The reference 7(1) *Halsbury's Laws* (4th edn) (1996 reissue) para 9 refers to paragraph 9 on page 24 of the 1996 reissue of volume 7(1) of the fourth edition of *Halsbury's Laws of England*.

Halsbury's Statutes of England and Wales

The reference 26 *Halsbury's Statutes* (4th edn) 734 refers to page 734 of volume 26 of the fourth edition of *Halsbury's Statutes of England and Wales*.

The reference 40 *Halsbury's Statutes* (4th edn) (2001 reissue) 269 refers to page 269 of the 2001 reissue of volume 40 of the fourth edition of *Halsbury's Statutes of England and Wales*.

Halsbury's Statutory Instruments

The reference 14 *Halsbury's Statutory Instruments* (1999 issue) 201 refers to page 201 of the 1999 issue of volume 14 of the grey volumes series of *Halsbury's Statutory Instruments*.

Cases reported in volume 4

Page

A-G's Reference (No 3 of 2000) [HL] 897
Alam, Sarwar v [CA] 541
Alexander v Arts Council of Wales [CA] .. 205
Al Fawwaz, Re [QBD DC] 149
Allen, R v (No 2) [HL] 768
Ara, DPP v [QBD DC] 559
Arts Council of Wales, Alexander v [CA] .. 205
Ashdown v Telegraph Group Ltd [CA] .. 666
Balbo B & C Auto Transporti Internazionali
(on the application of), R v Secretary of
State for the Home Dept [QBD DC] .. 423
Bank of China v NBM LLC [QBD] 954
Bank of Scotland v Bennett [HL] 449
Banks v Chief Adjudication Officer [HL] .. 62
Barclays Bank plc v Coleman [HL] 449
Bennett, Bank of Scotland v [HL] 449
Beresford (on the application of), R v
Sunderland CC [CA] 565
Bicester Youth Court, R (on the application
of L) v [QBD DC] 411
Callery v Gray (No 2) [CA] 1
Chief Adjudication Officer, Banks v [HL] .. 62
Chief Constable of Greater Manchester
Police, Igwemma v [CA] 751
Chief Constable of the Derbyshire
Constabulary, Gough v [QBD DC] 289
Chief Constable of the Northumbria
Constabulary, R (on the application of
Thompson) v [CA] 354
Chief Constable of the Royal Ulster
Constabulary, McGrath v [HL] 334
Chief Constable of West Yorkshire Police,
Khan v [HL] 834
China National Petroleum Corp, LG Caltex
Gas Co Ltd v [CA] 875
Civil Aviation Authority, Friend v [CA] .. 385
Coleman, Barclays Bank plc v [HL] 449
Colley v Council for Licensed
Conveyancers [CA] 998
Comrs of Customs and Excise, Han v [CA] 687
Comrs of Customs and Excise,
Martins v [CA] 687
Comrs of Customs and Excise,
Morris v [CA] 687
Comrs of Inland Revenue, ex p
Newfields Developments Ltd, R v [HL] .. 400
Cork (as trustee in bankruptcy for
Rawlins) v Rawlins [CA] 50
Council for Licensed
Conveyancers, Colley v [CA] 998
Crown Court at Kingston, R (on the
application of IRC) v [QBD DC] 721
Crown Court at Manchester, R (on the
application of McCann) v [CA] 264

Page

Crown Court at Reading, R (on the
application of Eliot) v [QBD DC] 625
Definitely Maybe (Touring) Ltd v Marek
Lieberberg Konzertagentur GmbH [QBD] 283
Delaware Mansions Ltd v Westminster
City Council [HL] 737
Desmond Banks & Co (a firm),
Kenyon-Brown v [HL] 449
Dimsey, R v (No 2) [HL] 786
Donoghue, Poplar Housing and Regeneration
Community Association Ltd v [CA] .. 604
DPP (on the application of), R v Redbridge
Youth Court [QBD DC] 411
DPP v Ara [QBD DC] 559
DPP, Lilley v [QBD DC] 289
Eliot (on the application of), R v Crown
Court at Reading [QBD DC] 625
Etridge, Royal Bank of Scotland v
(No 2) [HL] 449
Farley v Skinner [HL] 801
Forbes, R v [HL].. 97
Friend v Civil Aviation Authority [CA] .. 385
Goldberg, Liverpool Roman Catholic
Archdiocese Trustees Incorporated v
(No 2) [Ch D] 950
Godwin v Swindon BC [CA] 641
Gough v Chief Constable of the
Derbyshire Constabulary [QBD DC] .. 289
Gray, Callery v (No 2) [CA] 1
Han v Comrs of Customs and Excise [CA] 687
Healy, Murrell v [CA] 345
Hewitt v Wirrall and West Cheshire
Community NHS Trust [CA] 577
Igwemma v Chief Constable of Greater
Manchester Police [CA] 751
Immigration Appeal Tribunal, R (on the
application of the Secretary of State for
the Home Dept) v [QBD] 430
IRC, ex p Newfields Developments
Ltd, R v [HL] 400
IRC (on the application of), R v Crown
Court at Kingston [QBD DC] 721
Kenyon-Brown v Desmond Banks & Co
(a firm) [HL] 449
Khan v Chief Constable of West
Yorkshire Police [HL] 834
L (on the application of), R v Bicester Youth
Court [QBD DC] 411
Leeds Magistrates' Court, R (on the
application of Miller) v [QBD DC] .. 289
Lewis Silkin (a firm), Mortgage
Corporation v [Ch D] 364
LG Caltex Gas Co Ltd v China National
Petroleum Corp [CA] 875

Lichniak (on the application of), R v
  Secretary of State for the Home Dept
  [QBD DC] 934
Lichniak, R v [CA] 934
Lilley v DPP [QBD DC] 289
Liverpool Roman Catholic Archdiocese
  Trustees Incorporated v
  Goldberg (No 2) [Ch D]. 950
London Stock Exchange Ltd, Money
  Markets International Stockbrokers
  Ltd (in liq) v [Ch D] 223
Looseley, R v [HL] 897
Loutchansky v Times Newspapers Ltd [CA] 115
M (a minor) v Secretary of State for Social
  Security [HL].. 41
Marcic v Thames Water Utilities Ltd
  (No 2) [QBD] 326
Marek Lieberberg Konzertagentur GmbH,
  Definitely Maybe (Touring) Ltd v [QBD] 283
Martins v Comrs of Customs and
  Excise [CA] 687
McCann (on the application of), R v Crown
  Court at Manchester [CA] 264
McGrath v Chief Constable of the Royal
  Ulster Constabulary [HL] 334
McPhilemy v Times Newspapers Ltd
  (No 2) [CA] 861
Meade-King (a firm), Official
  Receiver v [CA] 588
Middlesbrough BC v Safeer [QBD DC] .. 630
Miller (on the application of), R v Leeds
  Magistrates' Court [QBD DC] 289
Money Markets International Stockbrokers
  Ltd (in liq) v London Stock Exchange
  Ltd [Ch D] 223
Morris v Comrs of Customs and
  Excise [CA] 687
Mortgage Corporation v Lewis Silkin
  (a firm) [Ch D] 364
Mortgage Corporation v Shaire [Ch D] .. 364
Murrell v Healy [CA]. 345
NBM LLC, Bank of China v [QBD] 954
Newfields Developments Ltd, ex p, R v
  Comrs of Inland Revenue [HL] 400
Official Receiver v Meade-King (a firm) [CA] 588
Pantmaenog Timber Co Ltd (in liq), Re [CA] 588
Petrotrade Inc v Texaco Ltd [CA] 853
Poplar Housing and Regeneration
  Community Association Ltd v
  Donoghue [CA] 604
Practice Direction (criminal proceedings:
  victim personal statements) [CA] .. 640
Practice Note (Crown Court: allocation of
  court business) [CA] 635

Pyrah (on the application of), R v Secretary
  of State for the Home Dept [QBD DC] 934
Pyrah, R v [CA] 934
Quintavalle (on the application of), R v
  Secretary of State for Health [QBD] .. 1013
R v Allen (No 2) [HL] 768
R v Comrs of Inland Revenue, ex p
  Newfields Developments Ltd [HL] .. 400
R v Dimsey (No 2) [HL] 786
R v Forbes [HL] 97
R v IRC, ex p Newfields Developments
  Ltd [HL] 400
R v Lichniak [CA] 934
R v Looseley [HL] 897
R v Pyrah [CA] 934
R (on the application of Balbo B & C Auto
  Transporti Internazionali) v Secretary of
  State for the Home Dept [QBD DC] .. 423
R (on the application of Beresford) v
  Sunderland CC [CA] 565
R (on the application of Eliot) v Crown
  Court at Reading [QBD DC] 625
R (on the application of IRC) v Crown
  Court at Kingston [QBD DC] 721
R (on the application of L) v Bicester Youth
  Court [QBD DC] 411
R (on the application of Lichniak) v
  Secretary of State for the Home
  Dept [QBD DC] 934
R (on the application of McCann) v Crown
  Court at Manchester [CA] 264
R (on the application of Miller) v Leeds
  Magistrates' Court [QBD DC] 289
R (on the application of Pyrah) v Secretary
  of State for the Home Dept [QBD DC] 934
R (on the application of Quintavalle) v
  Secretary of State for Health [QBD] .. 1013
R (on the application of Saadi) v
  Secretary of State for the Home
  Dept [QBD & CA]. 961
R (on the application of the DPP) v
  Redbridge Youth Court [QBD DC] .. 411
R (on the application of the Secretary of
  State for the Home Dept) v Immigration
  Appeal Tribunal [QBD] 430
R (on the application of Thompson) v
  Chief Constable of the Northumbria
  Constabulary [CA] 354
Rawlins, Cork (as trustee in bankruptcy for
  Rawlins) v [CA] 50
Redbridge Youth Court, R (on the
  application of the DPP) v [QBD DC] .. 411
Royal Bank of Scotland v Etridge
  (No 2) [HL] 449

Saadi (on the application of), R v Secretary
of State for the Home Dept [QBD & CA] 961
Safeer, Middlesbrough BC v [QBD DC] 630
Safeway Stores plc v Tate [CA] 193
Saifi, Re [QBD DC] 168
Sarwar v Alam [CA].. 541
Secretary of State for Health, R (on the
application of Quintavalle) v [QBD] .. 1013
Secretary of State for Social Security,
M (a minor) v [HL] 41
Secretary of State for the Home Dept (on
the application), R v Immigration Appeal
Tribunal [QBD] 430
Secretary of State for the Home Dept, R (on
the application of Balbo B & C Auto
Transporti Internazionali) v [QBD DC] 423
Secretary of State for the Home Dept,
R (on the application of Lichniak) v
[QBD DC] 934
Secretary of State for the Home Dept,
R (on the application of Pyrah) v
[QBD DC] 934
Secretary of State for the Home Dept,
R (on
the application of Saadi) v [QBD & CA] 961

Shah v Shah [CA] 138
Shaire, Mortgage Corporation v [Ch D] 364
Skinner, Farley v [HL] 801
Snowden, Totty v [CA] 577
Sunderland CC, R (on the application of
Beresford) v [CA] 565
Swindon BC, Godwin v [CA].. 641
Tate, Safeway Stores plc v [CA] 193
Telegraph Group Ltd, Ashdown v [CA] 666
Texaco Ltd, Petrotrade Inc v [CA].. .. 853
Thames Water Utilities Ltd, Marcic v
(No 2) [QBD] 326
Thompson (on the application of), R v
Chief Constable of the Northumbria
Constabulary [CA] 354
Times Newspapers Ltd,
Loutchansky v [CA] 115
Times Newspapers Ltd,
McPhilemy v (No 2) [CA] 861
Totty v Snowden [CA] 577
W, Re [CA] 88
Westminster City Council, Delaware
Mansions Ltd v [HL] 737
Wirrall and West Cheshire Community
NHS Trust, Hewitt v [CA] 577

Digest of cases reported in volume 4

APPEAL – Statutory appeal – Whether rule of procedure imposing general requirement for permission to appeal in statutory appeals

Colley v Council for Licensed Conveyancers .. .. **CA 998**

ARBITRATION – Award – Whether parties having made ad hoc submissions to arbitrator on question of jurisdiction – Whether appellants entitled to challenge arbitration awards

LG Caltex Gas Co Ltd v China National Petroleum Corp .. .. .. **CA 875**

ARREST – Execution in Northern Ireland of warrant issued in another part of United Kingdom 'for the arrest of a person charged with an offence' – Whether person arrested under warrant having to be a person charged with an offence

McGrath v Chief Constable of the Royal Ulster Constabulary .. .. **HL 334**

CLAIM FORM – Service – Whether court having power to dispense with service of claim form in circumstances where retrospective extension of time prohibited

Godwin v Swindon BC .. .. **CA 641**

——Service – Whether deemed day of service rebuttable by evidence proving that service had actually been effected on different day

Godwin v Swindon BC .. .. **CA 641**

COMMONS – User as of right – Whether implied permission capable of defeating claim to user as of right

R (on the application of Beresford) v Sunderland CC .. .. **CA 565**

COMPANY – Claimant company holding non-transferable share in defendant as stock exchange member firm – Whether transfer of claimant's share offending principle against transactions depriving person of asset on becoming insolvent

Money Markets International Stockbrokers Ltd (in liq) v London Stock Exchange Ltd .. .. **Ch D 223**

——Official Receiver applying for orders for third parties to produce documents relating to company – Whether court having power to make such an order where sole purpose of application was to obtain documents for use in directors disqualification proceedings

Re Pantmaenog Timber Co Ltd (in liq), Official Receiver v Meade-King (a firm) .. .. **CA 588**

CONFLICT OF LAWS – Contract for provision of services of pop group – Whether England or Germany appropriate forum

Definitely Maybe (Touring) Ltd v Marek Lieberberg Konzertagentur GmbH QBD 283

CONTRACT – Damages for breach – Whether non-pecuniary damages only available in cases where object of entire contract was to give pleasure, relaxation or peace of mind – Whether such damages recoverable only in cases where promisor guaranteed achievement of those ends

Farley v Skinner .. .. **HL 801**

COPYRIGHT – Defence – Whether court having to consider facts of individual case when determining whether copyright protection infringing right to freedom of expression under human rights convention

Ashdown v Telegraph Group Ltd .. .. **CA 666**

COSTS – After-the-event (ATE) insurance premium – Own costs insurance – Whether cost of own costs insurance recoverable under order for costs

Callery v Gray (No 2) .. .. CA 1

——Before-the-event (BTE) insurance – Whether passenger entitled to recover after-the-event insurance premium in small personal injury claim where BTE cover available under driver's insurance policy

Sarwar v Alam .. .. CA 541

——Power to award indemnity costs where defendant failing to beat claimant's Pt 36 offer – Principles governing exercise of power

Petrotrade Inc v Texaco Ltd .. .. CA 853

——Power to award indemnity costs where defendant failing to beat claimant's Pt 36 offer – Purpose of power

McPhilemy v Times Newspapers Ltd (No 2) .. .. CA 861

CRIMINAL EVIDENCE – Video recording of child's testimony – Guidance on exercise of court's discretion

R (on the application of the DPP) v Redbridge Youth Court, R (on the application of L) v Bicester Youth Court .. .. QBD DC 411

CRIMINAL LAW – Entrapment – Whether English law on entrapment complying with right to fair trial under human rights convention

R v Looseley, Attorney General's Reference (No 3 of 2000) .. .. .. HL 897

——Extension of custody time limits – Whether Bail Act considerations relevant when court considering whether there was good and sufficient cause to extend custody time limit

R (on the application of Eliot) v Crown Court at Reading .. .. QBD DC 625

——Offender seeking judicial review of sentences of life imprisonment for murder as incompatible with rights under human rights convention – Whether Court of Appeal having jurisdiction to hear matter as appeal against sentence

R (on the application of Lichniak) v Secretary of State for the Home Dept, R v Lichniak, R (on the application of Pyrah) v Secretary of State for the Home Dept, R v Pyrah .. .. QBD DC & CA 934

CROWN COURT – Application for dismissal of charges – Judge concluding that prosecution documentary evidence not giving rise to necessary inferences as to applicant's guilt or to inferences that were compelling – Whether judge usurping role of jury

R (on the application of IRC) v Crown Court at Kingston .. .. QBD DC 721

——Distribution of court business – New directions

Practice Note (Crown Court: allocation of court business) .. .. .. CA 635

CUSTOMS AND EXCISE – Importation of prohibited goods – Whether prosecution having to prove that defendant not only knew goods were prohibited but also nature of goods

R v Forbes .. .. HL 97

DAMAGES – Assessment of damages payable by second tortfeasor to claimant who had previously been injured in earlier unrelated accident – Approach to be adopted

Murrell v Healy .. .. CA 345

EQUITY – Bank charge over matrimonial home – Steps to be taken by bank to avoid having constructive notice of husband's misrepresentation to wife or undue influence over her – Duty of solicitor acting for wife – Principles and guidance

Royal Bank of Scotland v Etridge (No 2), Barclays Bank plc v Coleman, Bank of Scotland v Bennett, Kenyon-Brown v Desmond Banks & Co (a firm)   **HL**   **449**

——Undue influence – Whether 'manifest disadvantage' necessary to give rise to rebuttable evidential presumption of undue influence

Royal Bank of Scotland v Etridge (No 2), Barclays Bank plc v Coleman, Bank of Scotland v Bennett, Kenyon-Brown v Desmond Banks & Co (a firm)   **HL**   **449**

ESTOPPEL – Industrial tribunal upholding complaint of unfair dismissal on procedural grounds but awarding no compensation after concluding that employee's conduct contributing 100% to dismissal – Whether tribunal's decision giving rise to issue estoppel in respect of subject matter of employee's subsequent action for damages arising from dismissal

Friend v Civil Aviation Authority   ..   ..   **CA**   **385**

——Statutory provision requiring deed to be signed in presence of witness who attested signature – Whether statutory requirement for attestation precluding operation of estoppel

Shah v Shah ..   ..   **CA**   **138**

EUROPEAN COMMUNITY – Football banning order – Whether football banning order contravening Community law on freedom of movement

Gough v Chief Constable of the Derbyshire Constabulary, R (on the application of Miller) v Leeds Magistrates' Court, Lilley v DPP   **QBD DC**   **289**

EXTRADITION – Accusation against fugitive not made in good faith in interests of justice – Whether 'accusation' referring to request for extradition or facts supporting request

Re Saifi ..   ..   **QBD DC**   **168**

——Evidence – Whether evidence of anonymous witness inadmissible – Whether use of anonymous witness infringing applicant's right to take proceedings to question lawfulness of detention

Re Al-Fawwaz   ..   ..   **QBD DC**   **149**

——Evidence – Whether magistrate having to determine disputed issues of fact relating to making of statement implicating applicant

Re Saifi ..   ..   **QBD DC**   **168**

——Fugitive offender accused of conspiring with others to murder United States citizens – Whether alleged offence having to be committed within United States territory

Re Al-Fawwaz .   ..   .   **QBD DC**   **149**

HOUSING – Legislative provision requiring court to grant possession if notice to quit given – Whether order for possession contravening right to family life under human rights convention

Poplar Housing and Regeneration Community Association Ltd v Donoghue   **CA**   **604**

HUMAN RIGHTS – Damages – Whether damages recoverable for future infringement of human rights

Marcic v Thames Water Utilities Ltd (No 2)   ..   **Judge Richard Havery QC**   **326**

——Public authority – Test for determining whether private person performing public act

Poplar Housing and Regeneration Community Association Ltd v Donoghue   **CA**   **604**

IMMIGRATION – Detention pending decision on asylum claim – Whether such detention infringing claimants' right to liberty under human rights convention

    R (on the application of Saadi) v Sec of State for the Home Dept .. **QBD & CA**   **961**

——Immigration Appeal Tribunal – Source and nature of tribunal's power to remit appeal to special adjudicator – Whether full tribunal having power to set aside or vary order of chairman of tribunal sitting alone

    R (on the application of the Secretary of State for the Home Dept) v Immigration Appeal Tribunal .. .. **Scott Baker J**   **430**

INCOME TAX – Corporation tax – Whether Revenue having to make statutory attributions if requisite conditions satisfied – Identification of requisite conditions

    R v Comrs of Inland Revenue, ex p Newfields Developments Ltd .. .. **HL**   **400**

——Shadow director – Whether shadow director having same liability to tax as director in respect of provision of living accommodation and benefits in kind

    R v Allen (No 2) .. .. **HL**   **768**

——Statutory provision deeming income of foreign transferee to be that of transferor – Whether provision relieving foreign transferee of normal liability to pay tax on its income

    R v Dimsey (No 2) .. .. **HL**   **786**

INSOLVENCY – Assurance policy – Permanent disablement benefit – Appellant suffering permanent disablement and making claims under policies – Appellant's trustee in bankruptcy claiming policy moneys – Whether policy moneys belonging to bankrupt if contractual claim to them relying on bankrupt's pain and suffering

    Cork (as trustee in bankruptcy for Rawlins) v Rawlins .. .. **CA**   **50**

INTEREST – Power to award enhanced interest on damages and costs where defendant failing to beat claimant's Pt 36 offer – Principles governing exercise of power

    Petrotrade Inc v Texaco Ltd .. .. **CA**   **853**

——Power to award enhanced interest on damages and costs where defendant failing to beat claimant's Pt 36 offer – Whether power to be exercised in relation to jury awards in defamation cases

    McPhilemy v Times Newspapers Ltd (No 2) .. .. **CA**   **861**

JUDICIAL REVIEW – Secretary of State issuing claimant with penalty notice as person responsible for clandestine entrants – Secretary of State upholding notice despite service of notice of objection – Whether judicial review appropriate remedy

    R (on the application of Balbo B & C Auto Transporti Internazionali) v Secretary of State for the Home Dept .. .. **QBD DC**   **423**

JURY – Answers – Whether judge in civil proceedings having discretion to allow discharged jury to alter answer given by them – Guidance on exercise of discretion

    Igwemma v Chief Constable of Greater Manchester Police .. .. .. **CA**   **751**

——Defamation – Proper roles of judge and jury in respect of issues of fact

    Alexander v Arts Council of Wales .. .. **CA**   **205**

——Judge concluding that words complained of were defamatory and giving summary judgment for claimant – Whether judge usurping role of jury

    Safeway Stores plc v Tate .. .. **CA**   **193**

LIBEL AND SLANDER – Judge withdrawing issue of malice from jury – Whether judge in error

    Alexander v Arts Council of Wales .. .. **CA** **205**

——Qualified privilege – Whether defendant entitled to rely on matters not known at time of publication in support of plea of qualified privilege

    Loutchansky v Times Newspapers Ltd .. .. **CA** **115**

LOCAL AUTHORITY – Powers – Whether local authority having power to prosecute for using motor vehicle without insurance

    Middlesbrough BC v Safeer .. .. **QBD DC** **630**

MAGISTRATES – Anti-social behaviour order – Whether proceedings for imposition of anti-social behaviour orders criminal or civil

    R (on the application of McCann) v Crown Court at Manchester .. .. **CA** **264**

MEDICAL TREATMENT – Cell nuclear replacement – Whether organism created by cell nuclear replacement falling within statutory definition of embryo

    R (on the application of Quintavalle) v Sec of State for Health .. ..Crane J **1013**

NUISANCE – Right to sue – Whether reasonable remedial expenditure recoverable by current owner in respect of pre-transfer damage arising from continuing nuisance

    Delaware Mansions Ltd v Westminster City Council .. .. **HL** **737**

PARTICULARS OF CLAIM – Service – Whether court having discretion to grant extension of time for service of particulars of claim

    Totty v Snowden, Hewitt v Wirrall and West Cheshire Community NHS Trust . .. . **CA** **577**

POLICE – Disclosure of information – Whether police having duty to disclose contents of interview to suspect's solicitor for purpose of enabling him to advise on acceptance of caution – Whether failure to give such disclosure rendering subsequent prosecution an abuse of process

    DPP v Ara .. .. **QBD DC** **559**

POWER OF ATTORNEY – Enduring power of attorney – Capacity of donor – Whether burden of proof on attorney to establish donor's capacity if objectors producing evidence that donor lacked capacity

    Re W .. .. **CA** **88**

PRACTICE – Expert witness having long-standing friendship with party proposing to call him – Whether relationship between expert and party rendering expert's evidence inadmissible

    Liverpool Roman Catholic Archdiocese Trustees Incorporated v Goldberg (No 2) .. .. Evans-Lombe J **950**

——Victim personal statements – Procedure

    Practice Direction (criminal proceedings: victim personal statements) .. **CA** **640**

——Worldwide freezing order – Proviso protecting third parties in respect of assets outside the jurisdiction – Appropriate terms

    Bank of China v NBM LLC .. ..David Steel J **954**

PUBLIC ORDER – Football banning order – Whether football banning order constituting a penalty for purposes of human rights convention

    Gough v Chief Constable of the Derbyshire Constabulary, R (on the application of Miller) v Leeds Magistrates' Court, Lilley v DPP **QBD DC** **289**

RACE RELATIONS – Employer refusing to provide employee with reference for fear of prejudicing position in pending discrimination proceedings brought by employee – Whether refusal constituting victimisation 'by reason that' employee had brought discrimination proceedings

    Khan v Chief Constable of West Yorkshire Police .. .. **HL 834**

SENTENCE – Murder – Whether mandatory life sentence for murder incompatible with human rights in cases where convicted person posing no foreseeable risk to public at time of sentence

    R (on the application of Lichniak) v Secretary of State for the Home Dept, R v Lichniak, R (on the application of Pyrah) v Secretary of State for the Home Dept, R v Pyrah .. .. **QBD DC & CA 934**

SOCIAL SECURITY – Disability living allowance – New regulations imposing additional condition on entitlement – Whether transitional provision extending duration of claimant's entitlement to benefit beyond term for which it had been awarded

    M (a minor) v Secretary of State for Social Security .. .. **HL 41**

——Jobseeker's allowance – Method of calculating average weekly number of hours of remunerative work for persons in one-year cycle of work – Whether unpaid holiday periods to be taken into account

    Banks v Chief Adjudication Officer .. .. **HL 62**

SOLICITOR – Before-the-event (BTE) insurance – Steps to be taken by solicitor to discover whether BTE insurance available to client – Guidance

    Sarwar v Alam .. .. **CA 541**

——Deputy chief constable barring probationary solicitor's representative (PSR) from entering any police station in his force's area – Whether imposition of blanket ban on a PSR permissible

    R (on the application of Thompson) v Chief Constable of the Northumbria Constabulary .. .. **CA 354**

TRUST AND TRUSTEE – Application for order for sale by chargee of co-owner's interest in property – Whether new statutory provision changing law on exercise of court's discretion on such an application

    Mortgage Corporation v Shaire, Mortgage Corporation v Lewis Silkin (a firm) .. .. **Neuberger J 364**

VALUE ADDED TAX – Penalty – Whether imposition of penalty for dishonest evasion of value added tax or duty giving rise to criminal charge for purposes of fair trial provisions of human rights convention

    Han v Comrs of Customs and Excise, Martins v Comrs of Customs and Excise, Morris v Comrs of Customs and Excise .. .. **CA 687**

House of Lords petitions

This list, which covers the period 25 April 2001 to 27 November 2001, sets out all cases which have formed the subject of a report in the All England Law Reports in which an Appeal Committee of the House of Lords has, subsequent to the publication of that report, refused leave to appeal. Where the result of a petition for leave to appeal was known prior to the publication of the relevant report a note of that result appears at the end of the report.

Lewis v Commissioner of Inland Revenue [2001] 3 All ER 499. Leave to appeal refused 25 April 2001 (Lord Slynn of Hadley, Lord Hope of Craighead and Lord Hobhouse of Woodborough).

Shah v Shah [2001] 4 All ER 138. Leave to appeal refused 24 July 2001 (Lord Nicholls of Birkenhead, Lord Clyde and Lord Millett).

National Westminster Bank plc v Utrecht-America Finance Co [2001] 3 All ER 733. Leave to appeal refused 16 November 2001 (Lord Nicholls, Lord Hobhouse of Woodborough and Lord Rodger of Earlsferry).

LG Caltex Gas Co Ltd v China National Petroleum Corp [2001] 4 All ER 875. Leave to appeal refused 16 November 2001 (Lord Nicholls, Lord Hobhouse of Woodborough and Lord Rodger of Earlsferry).

Callery v Gray (No 2)

[2001] EWCA Civ 1246

c COURT OF APPEAL, CIVIL DIVISION

LORD PHILLIPS OF WORTH MATRAVERS MR AND BROOKE LJ

24, 31 JULY 2001

Costs – Order for costs – Jurisdiction – After-the-event (ATE) insurance premium – Own
d *costs insurance – Claimant paying premium for ATE insurance in respect of claim*
against defendant – Insurance covering him not only for liability in respect of
defendant's costs but also against risk of paying his own disbursements if claim failed
– Whether cost of own costs insurance recoverable under order for costs – Access to
Justice Act 1999, s 29 – CPR PD 44, section 11.10.

e
The claimant, C, brought a straightforward claim against the defendant, G, for
personal injuries arising out of a road traffic accident. C entered into a conditional
fee agreement (CFA) with his solicitors, and paid a premium of £350 for
after-the-event (ATE) insurance, providing him with cover not only against any
liability to pay his opponent's costs but also against the risk of having to pay
f his own disbursements in the event of the claim failing (own costs insurance).
In subsequent costs-only proceedings under CPR 44.12A, the judge concluded
that the cost of the ATE premium was reasonable and could be recovered as an
item of C's costs. On G's appeal, the Court of Appeal held, inter alia, that there
was jurisdiction, under s 29[a] of the Access to Justice Act 1999, to include in an
award of costs made under CPR 44.12A an insurance premium paid in respect of
g
contemplated proceedings notwithstanding that the claim was subsequently
settled before those proceedings were initiated; s 29 provided that where, in any
proceedings, a costs order was made in favour of any party who had taken out an
insurance policy against 'the risk of incurring a [costs] liability' in those
proceedings, the costs payable to him could include costs in respect of the
h premium of the policy. The court considered, however, that it lacked sufficient
information about ATE insurance to rule on the question of the reasonableness
of the premium, and accordingly directed a costs judge to submit a report on that
matter. At a further hearing subsequent to the receipt of that report,
G contended, inter alia, that the cover in respect of C's own disbursements fell
j outside the scope of s 29 since it was cover not against the 'risk of incurring' the
liabilities, but against the risk of being unable to recover an indemnity in respect
of them consequent upon the failure of the claim. In the course of considering
that submission, the court took into account section 11.10[b] of CPR PD 44

---

a Section 29 is set out at [6], below
b Section 11.10 is set out at [10], below

(the Costs Practice Direction). Section 11.10 provided that in deciding whether a
the cost of insurance cover was reasonable, relevant factors included, where the
insurance cover was not purchased in support of a CFA with a success fee, how
its cost compared with the likely cost of funding the case with a CFA with a
success fee and supporting insurance cover.

Held – On the true construction of s 29 of the 1999 Act, the words 'insurance ... b
against the risk of incurring a [costs] liability' meant 'insurance against the risk of
incurring a costs liability that cannot be passed on to the opposing party'.
Section 29 itself was imprecise, and the provisions of the CPR and the Costs
Practice Direction were of particular importance in clarifying and delimiting the
circumstances in which the cost of an insurance premium could be claimed under c
s 29. Section 11.10 of that practice direction clearly anticipated that insurance
cover which fell within the ambit of s 29 might provide alternative protection to
that provided by a CFA coupled with insurance. Such cover would necessarily
include own costs insurance. Whilst the practice direction could not, of course,
confer on the court a jurisdiction which fell outside that conferred by s 29, the
court's interpretation of that section did no more than give the words in question d
the meaning which would be attributed to them by the reasonable litigant, and
which accorded with the legislative intent and with the overall scheme for the
funding of legal costs. The circumstances in which, and the terms on which, own
costs insurance would be reasonable, so that the whole premium could be
recovered as costs, would have to be determined by the courts when dealing with e
individual cases, assisted, if appropriate, by the Rules Committee. In the instant
case, the right to recover the cost of disbursements was tied to the situations
where the protection afforded by the CFA would come into play. It was arguable
that the disbursements covered were disbursements of a kind that would be
recoverable as costs. There was no objection in principle to that cover forming
part of the cover afforded to C by his legal costs insurance, and the whole of the f
cover could be considered as falling within the description 'insurance ... against
the risk of ... liability' within s 29. The amount of the premium itself did not
appear to be manifestly disproportionate to the risk. Accordingly, the appeal
against the inclusion of the whole of C's insurance premium as an item of his
costs would be dismissed (see [58]–[62], [70], [73], below). g

Notes
For recovery of insurance premiums by way of costs, see 41 *Halsbury's Laws*
(4th edn reissue) para 922.
For the Access to Justice Act 1999, s 29, see 11 *Halsbury's Statutes* (4th edn) h
(2000 reissue) 1514.

Cases referred to in judgment
Callery v Grey, Russell v Pal Pak Corrugated Ltd [2001] EWCA Civ 1117, [2001]
   3 All ER 833. j
Pepper (Inspector of Taxes) v Hart [1993] 1 All ER 42, [1993] AC 593, [1992] 3 WLR
   1032, HL.
*R v Secretary of State for the Environment, Transport and the Regions, ex p Spath Holme
   Ltd* [2001] 1 All ER 195, [2001] 2 WLR 15, HL.
Sarwar v Alam (5 July 2001, unreported), Chester Cty Ct.

Adjourned appeal

a The defendant, Charles Gray, appealed with permission of Hale LJ granted on 16 March 2001 from the decision of Judge Edwards at the Chester County Court on 29 January 2001 dismissing his appeal from the order of District Judge Wallace, made in costs-only proceedings under CPR 44.12A at Macclesfield County Court on 7 November 2000, whereby he allowed the claimant, Stephen Callery, to

b recover from Mr Gray as reasonable costs (i) a success fee uplift of 40% under a conditional fee agreement with his solicitors in respect of a personal injury claim against Mr Gray, and (ii) the premium paid by Mr Callery for after-the-event (ATE) insurance covering him against incurring any liability for Mr Gray's costs and his own disbursements in the event of the claim failing. In a judgment delivered on 17 July 2001 ([2001] 3 All ER 833), the Court of Appeal (Lord Woolf CJ,

c Lord Phillips of Worth Matravers MR and Brooke LJ) allowed the appeal to the extent of reducing the success fee uplift to 20%, but left open the question of the reasonableness of the ATE premium pending the receipt of a report by Master O'Hare. The Association of Personal Injury Lawyers, the Association of British Insurers, the After The Event Insurers' Group, Claims Direct Ltd, the

d Motor Accident Solicitors' Society and the Law Society participated in the adjourned appeal as interested parties. The facts, so far as material, are set out in the judgment of the court.

e *Peter Birts QC* and *David Holland* (instructed by *Beachcroft Wansbroughs*) for Mr Gray.
Geoffrey Nice QC and *Nicholas Bacon* (instructed by *Amelans*, Manchester) for Mr Callery.
Allan Gore (instructed by *Pattinson & Brewer*) for the Association of Personal Injury Lawyers.
John Leighton Williams QC (instructed by *Barlow, Lyde & Gilbert*) for the Association of British Insurers.

f *Timothy Dutton QC* (instructed by *Rowe Cohen*, Manchester) for the After The Event Insurers' Group.
William Norris QC (instructed by *Colman Coyle*) for Claims Direct Ltd.
Cyrus Katrak (instructed by *Andrew Gardner Partnership*, Maidstone) for the Motor Accident Solicitors' Society.

g *Carine Patry* (instructed by the *Solicitor for the Law Society*) for the Law Society.

Cur adv vult

31 July 2001. The following judgment of the court was delivered.

h   *INDEX*

	Paragraphs
Introduction	[1]–[3]
The status of Master O'Hare's report	[4]–[5]
The statutory framework	[6]–[10]
The test of what is reasonable	[11]–[17]
The terms of the ATE cover	[18]–[19]
Issues identified by Master O'Hare	[20]
Costs and expenses	[21]
The burning cost	[22]–[23]
Risk/profit cost	[24]
Administrative costs	[25]

Distribution commission   [26]
Benefits   [27]   a
Costs awarded by the court to the opposing party   [28]–[31]
Collateral benefits   [32]–[33]
Own costs cover   [34]–[47]
Parliamentary material   [48]–[54]
The overall scheme   [55]–[57]   b
The CPR and the Costs Practice Direction   [58]–[62]
The cost of the premium   [63]
Deferred payment of the premium   [64]–[65]
The effect of BTE insurance   [66]
Is £350 too much?   [67]–[73]
                                                                                   c

LORD PHILLIPS OF WORTH MATRAVERS MR.

Introduction

[1] On 17 July this court, presided over by Lord Woolf CJ, gave judgment in this action and in *Callery v Gray, Russell v Pal Pak Corrugated Ltd* ([2001] EWCA Civ d
1117, [2001] 3 All ER 833). Each was an appeal against an order for costs made in costs-only proceedings pursuant to CPR 44.12A. The two appeals were heard together as they raised common issues. Those issues arose out of challenges made by the defendant in each action to the recovery of uplift under a conditional fee arrangement (CFA) and, in this action, to the recovery by way of costs of the e
premium for an after-the-event (ATE) insurance policy.

[2] In that judgment the court ruled that there was jurisdiction, under s 29 of the Access to Justice Act 1999, to include in an award of costs made under r 44.12A an insurance premium paid in respect of contemplated proceedings notwithstanding that the claim was subsequently settled before those proceedings were initiated. The court also ruled that, in principle, in a case such as this it is reasonable for a f
claimant to take out ATE cover at an early stage of the proceedings and before it is known whether the defendant is contesting the claim.

[3] In issue in this appeal was whether the amount of the ATE premium, that is to say £350, was reasonable. The court did not consider that it had sufficient information about ATE insurance to rule on that issue. Accordingly it directed g
that Master O'Hare should, after considering submissions and evidence submitted on behalf of the parties and others with an interest in the issues raised, submit a report to the court. Master O'Hare has now submitted that report, dated 23 July 2001. That report raises issues of general importance in relation to ATE insurance which need to be determined as quickly as possible. For that reason this court has reconstituted, in the absence of Lord Woolf CJ on official duties, in order to give h
judgment before the end of term.

The status of Master O'Hare's report

[4] Master O'Hare's report has been provided to the parties and is thus in the public domain. We have decided to annex it to this judgment but must emphasise j
that, by doing so, we do not confer upon it a status which it does not, in law, enjoy. In the course of his report Master O'Hare has identified a number of issues of principle. He has expressed a provisional view in relation to the answer to some of those issues. His views may prove of assistance to those faced with the task of ruling on the recoverability of ATE premiums, but they cannot be treated

a as definitive. The issues will fall to be judicially determined as and when they arise in individual cases. This court is anxious that issues of general importance should be brought before it for authoritative determination as quickly as possible and will give expedition to cases that raise such issues. The hearing of this appeal exemplifies that policy.

b [5] In the present appeal we propose to address only those issues identified by Master O'Hare which arise on the facts of this case. It would not accord with the interests of justice to express views on other issues without hearing detailed argument on behalf of those directly affected by them in the context of the facts that raise those issues. We shall, in the course of our judgment, identify some of the issues which are not raised by the facts of this case and which remain to be resolved. The principal issue raised by this appeal is whether the cost of insuring against failure to recover one's own costs can be recovered under s 29 of the 1999 Act.

c

The statutory framework

[6] The jurisdiction to include in an award of costs an ATE insurance premium is conferred by s 29 of the 1999 Act, which provides:

d

> '*Recovery of insurance premiums by way of costs.*—Where in any proceedings a costs order is made in favour of any party who has taken out an insurance policy against the risk of incurring a liability in those proceedings, the costs payable to him may, subject in the case of court proceedings to rules of court, include costs in respect of the premium of the policy.'

e

[7] The phrase 'a liability in those proceedings' is imprecise. It does not define the nature of the liability. That the liability is restricted to liability in respect of legal costs is not, however, in issue or in doubt. That restriction can be clearly identified from Parliamentary material admissible under the principle in *Pepper*
f *(Inspector of Taxes) v Hart* [1993] 1 All ER 42, [1993] AC 593. It is also apparent from the rules of court, subject to which s 29 expressly takes effect.

[8] CPR 43.2, which sets out definitions, provides:

> '(1) ... (k) "funding arrangement" means an arrangement where a person has ... (ii) taken out an insurance policy to which section 29 of the Access to Justice Act 1999 (recovery of insurance premiums by way of costs) applies ... (m) "insurance premium" means a sum of money paid or payable for insurance against the risk of incurring a costs liability in the proceedings, taken out after the event that is the subject matter of the claim ...'

g

h It is thus necessary, when considering whether, or to what extent, a premium is recoverable by way of costs to ask the question whether it is consideration paid or payable for insurance against the risk of incurring a costs liability in the proceedings.

[9] The following rule is also relevant to the issues arising on this appeal:

j

> '**44.5 Factors to be taken into account in deciding the amount of costs**
> (1) The court is to have regard to all the circumstances in deciding whether costs were—(a) if it is assessing costs on the standard basis—(i) proportionately and reasonably incurred; or (ii) were proportionate and reasonable in amount...'

[10] The following provisions of the Costs Practice Direction (CPR PD 44) are
also of relevance:

a

'SECTION 11 FACTORS TO BE TAKEN INTO ACCOUNT IN DECIDING THE
AMOUNT OF COSTS: RULE 44.5

11.7 Subject to paragraph 17.8(2), when the court is considering the
factors to be taken into account in assessing an additional liability, it will have
regard to the facts and circumstances as they reasonably appeared to the
solicitor or counsel when the funding arrangement was entered into and at
the time of any variation of the arrangement …

b

11.10 In deciding whether the costs of insurance cover is reasonable,
relevant factors to be taken into account include: (1) where the insurance
cover is not purchased in support of a conditional fee agreement with a
success fee, how its cost compares with the likely cost of funding the case
with a conditional fee agreement with a success fee and supporting insurance
cover; (2) the level and extent of the cover provided; (3) the availability of
any pre-existing insurance cover; (4) whether any part of the premium
would be rebated in the event of early settlement; (5) the amount of
commission payable to the receiving party or his legal representatives or
other agents.'

c

d

The test of what is reasonable

[11] It was common ground, and rightly so, that the court, when considering
whether to award an insurance premium by way of costs, has to consider
whether the premium is reasonable. It was also common ground that, in so far
as the court finds that the premium is not reasonable, it can and should reduce
the amount recoverable in respect of it. There was debate as to the appropriate
approach to the application of the test of what is reasonable.

e

[12] It is important in this context to draw a distinction between two separate
matters. The first is the nature of the benefits to which the litigant is contractually
entitled in exchange for the payment of the premium. This falls to be determined
from the terms of the contract under which the premium is paid. Section 29 of
the 1999 Act permits the recovery of a premium where this is payment for
insurance against the risk of liability for costs. If payment of a so-called premium
buys a contractual entitlement to other benefits it is, to say the least, arguable that
the premium cannot, to that extent, be recovered under s 29. Thus the court has
to consider the terms of the contract under which the premium is paid to see
whether it is simply a contract of insurance against liability for costs or whether
it is something other than, or additional to, that.

f

g

[13] The contractual benefits purchased by the premium must be distinguished
from the use made by the insurer of the premium. An insurer will necessarily
look to premium income to meet the costs of the business. The primary costs are
likely to be those of meeting claims, but the costs will also include matters such
as commissions, advertising and, indeed, refurbishing the insurer's premises.
The court will not be directly concerned with how, or on what, the insurer spends
the premium income. The court will, however, be concerned with the question
of whether the premium is a reasonable price to pay for the benefits that it
purchases. Ultimately, this should be a question to be considered having regard
to experience, or evidence, of the market. If an insurer is conducting his business
in a manner which incurs extravagant, extraneous or otherwise unnecessary
expenditure, which has to be covered by the premiums, those premiums are

h

j

a likely to be uncompetitive. To pay such a premium where other more reasonable premiums are available may disentitle the litigant from making a full recovery of the costs of the premium.

[14] Unfortunately Master O'Hare concluded that the market in ATE insurance was not yet sufficiently developed to enable him to identify standard or average rates of premium for different categories of ATE insurance. He expressed

b doubt as to whether market forces were yet sufficiently compelling. He received a considerable body of evidence of the costs of individual insurers, proffered in confidence, in an endeavour to form a view of the level of premium that was reasonably needed to cover costs. We shall revert to his conclusions in due course. At this point we will confine ourselves to some general observations.

c [15] It is highly desirable in the interests of justice that an effective and transparent market should develop in ATE insurance. If the litigant is not at risk as to the premium, which is a matter that we shall consider in due course, it is less easy for a competitive market to develop. None the less, we consider that the solicitor advising the client should be in a position to assist him in selecting ATE insurance cover that caters for his needs on reasonable terms. Master O'Hare

d informed us that there are at present two sources of information as to availability of ATE cover: the magazine Litigation Funding, published by the Law Society, and the website http://www.thejudge.co.uk. We would encourage solicitors to take advantage of such sources of information and hope that before long the exercise of choice will result in competition for ATE business which establishes transparent market rates.

e [16] In the meantime, where an insurance premium is challenged it must be open to the insurer, whose position is akin to a subrogated underwriter, to place evidence before the court in an attempt to demonstrate that the premium is reasonable having regard to the costs that have to be covered. Satellite litigation involving such an exercise is, however, unsatisfactory. The judge can only be

f expected to give broad consideration to such evidence, for it is not part of the function of a judge assessing costs to carry out an audit of an insurer's business.

[17] Master O'Hare remarked in his report that he expected that fairly quickly courts conducting detailed costs assessments would be able to develop benchmark figures. The sooner that market rates for ATE insurance become recognised the better.

g

The terms of the ATE cover

[18] In order to identify the issues of principle which arise in this case it is necessary to identify the material terms of the policy of insurance to which the disputed premium relates.

h [19] The policy is issued on behalf of Lloyd's underwriters on whose behalf this business is managed by Temple Legal Protection Ltd (Temple). The cover was issued, under the authority of the underwriters, by Legal Protect Assurance Services Ltd, as coverholder. The terms of the cover were set out in a certificate of insurance. This provided by a schedule that the cover was in relation to a

j personal injury action against Charles Gray, that the period of insurance was from 4 May 2000 to the conclusion of the legal action and that the limit of indemnity was £100,000. The certificate went on to provide as follows:

'THE RISKS THAT YOU ARE INSURED AGAINST
Insurers agree to indemnify the Insured up to the Limit of Indemnity; for Opponent's Costs in the event that the Insured becomes liable to pay such

costs whether by order of the Court or because the Legal Action has been *a* withdrawn or discontinued or settled with the prior approval of the Insurers, and, for the Insured's Disbursements in the event that (a) the Insured become liable to pay Opponent's Costs whether by order of the Court or because the Legal Action has, with the prior approval of Insurers been withdrawn or discontinued or, (b) following commencement of proceedings and with the prior approval of the Insurers, the Legal Action is settled *b* without the Insured's Disbursements being payable by the Opponent ...

THE MEANING OF WORDS USED IN THIS INSURANCE ...

Disbursements

Fees and expenses including the premium and mediators fees, which are not the subject of any contingent or conditional fee agreement, paid by the Appointed Legal Representative on behalf of the Insured to any third party, *c* other than to counsel, in connection with the Legal Action but not including (1) any VAT to the extent that the Insured can recover such VAT from H.M. Customs and Excise and (2) any Disbursements which the Court orders the Opponent to pay to the Insured ...

Opponent's Costs   *d*

All costs, expenses and disbursements ordered by the Court to be paid by the Insured to the Opponent in the Legal Action during the Period of Insurance. Where in the Legal Action orders are made both that costs be paid by the Insured to the Opponent and that costs be paid by the Opponent to the Insured, Opponent's Costs shall then be limited to the net sum (if any) payable by the Insured to the Opponent after all costs payable by the *e* Opponent to the Insured have been set off ...

EXCLUSIONS

Insurers shall not be liable under this Certificate in respect of:

6. any Disbursements where an order is made by the Court for the Disbursements to be paid by the Opponent, irrespective of whether or not *f* payment is actually made. If the Insured recovers any monies from the Opponent in the Legal Action, whether described as damages, costs or howsoever described and whether recovered by judgment or settlement, such recovery shall be deemed to include a recovery of Disbursements insofar as the monies payable by the Opponent (whether or not actually paid) are sufficient to do so ...   *g*

6. Assessment of the Premium

If, in any process of assessment, the Opponent is successful in any challenge to the cost of the premium then it is agreed that the premium which was payable at the conclusion of the Legal Action shall be reduced to the amount which was approved or allowed on assessment. It is agreed *h* by the Insured that the Insurer shall have the right to make any representation to the Court or the Opponent as may be necessary in this matter. Any such challenge must be immediately notified by the Insured to the Insurer.'

j

Issues identified by Master O'Hare

[20] Master O'Hare considered the elements that are responsible for the size of the insurance premium, distinguishing between (i) costs and expenses of the insurer funded by the premium and (ii) benefits covered by the premium. He considered whether, and to what extent, a premium covered by s 29 of the 1999 Act should reflect each of these. We shall do likewise.

Costs and expenses

a

[21] Master O'Hare identified four elements of these: the burning cost, the risk/profit cost, administrative costs and distribution commission.

The burning cost

b

[22] This term describes the cost of meeting claims made under policies issued. Overall premium income must suffice to cover claims made, or the insurer's business will not be viable. Master O'Hare learned that, in respect of claims for personal injury, ATE insurers set out to cover this cost on two different bases: (i) an individual premium is assessed for each risk, or each category of risk ('individual assessment'); (ii) a uniform premium is charged in respect of any claim which carries a prospect of success of more than 50% ('block rating').

c

[23] Master O'Hare set out in his report the information supplied by Temple as to the basis upon which the premiums for their policies are determined. Temple has two insurance schemes, one under which a premium is quoted having regard to the facts of the particular case and one under which authority to issue cover is delegated. Under the latter a solicitor is authorised to issue certificates in respect of any case undertaken, rating the case and applying the appropriate premium according to a premium table supplied by Temple. It was on this basis, as we understand it, that Mr Callery's premium was fixed at £350 plus £7·50 insurance premium tax (IPT). Thus on this appeal we are concerned with a premium fixed on an individual assessment basis. Master O'Hare was informed by Accident Group Ltd, which claims to be the market leader in issuing insurance cover in conjunction with CFAs, that, on a block rating basis, Mr Callery would have been charged £997·50 including IPT. The issue of whether it would have been reasonable for Mr Callery to take out insurance for his claim at a much higher premium than £350, costed on a block rating basis, does not arise for determination on this appeal. On the face of it, adoption of such an option would seem hard to justify.

d

e

f

Risk/profit cost

[24] This item will include the cost of laying off risk by way of reinsurance, where this course is adopted. Master O'Hare received widely differing submissions as to the proportion of the premium which should reflect this item. In the longer term market forces ought to constrain it to reasonable proportions. Plainly no objection can be taken to a premium reflecting a reasonable risk/profit cost.

g

Administrative costs

h

[25] These must cover items such as personnel, premises, policy issue and processing and claims administration. No objection could be taken to a premium reflecting costs such as these.

Distribution commission

j

[26] Before Master O'Hare objection was taken in principle in some submissions to premiums being increased to cover advertising and other marketing and commissions. We are not aware of the extent to which these are relevant factors in the case of Temple, but we agree with Master O'Hare that no objection can be taken to these in principle. As he has pointed out, section 11.10 of the Costs Practice Direction provides that 'the amount of commission payable' is one of the factors that should be taken into account when deciding whether the cost of

insurance cover is reasonable. In the longer term, market forces should prevent premiums being unreasonably inflated to reflect extravagant commission payments. *a*

Benefits

[27] We now turn to consider the different types of benefit that Master O'Hare identified may be provided in exchange for the 'premium' paid.

b

Costs awarded by the court to the opposing party

[28] The primary liability covered by Mr Callery's policy was that for opponent's costs as a result of order of the court or withdrawal, discontinuance or settlement of the action with the prior approval of the insurers. Such liability can arise in a number of circumstances, which include: (i) an order of the court to pay the defendant's costs as a result of judgment on liability being given in favour of *c* the defendant, on the normal principle that costs follow the event; (ii) an order of the court to pay the defendant's costs as a consequence of a failure to beat a CPR Pt 36 offer; (iii) an order of the court to pay the defendant's costs as a result of losing an issue, whether at an interim hearing or at the final hearing; and (iv) any other costs order in favour of the defendant made in the exercise of *d* discretion.

[29] All parties were agreed that it is legitimate for ATE insurance to provide cover that falls within the first category set out above. They were right to do so. Such insurance falls fairly and squarely within the meaning of insurance against the risk of incurring a costs liability in the proceedings (see [8], above).

[30] For the defendant, Mr Peter Birts QC objected to the defendant being *e* held liable for that part of the premium which reflects the risk of being ordered to pay costs falling within the second category set out above, and we believe that his argument would naturally extend to the third and fourth categories. In essence this argument was simply that it was unfair to defendants that claimants should be able to pass on to them liability for insuring against costs liabilities of *f* such a type in that those liabilities are likely to have been incurred as a result of failure on the part of claimants to conduct the litigation in a reasonable manner.

[31] It seems to us that such an argument would frequently be open in relation to costs which follow the event after a claim fails. All four categories of risk aptly fall within the words 'risk of incurring a [costs] liability in those proceedings'. *g* In our judgment insurance against such risks falls within the ambit of s 29.

Collateral benefits

[32] The benefits purchased by Mr Callery for his £350 premium were restricted to insurance against the risk of paying legal costs of one kind or another. *h* The contract did not entitle him to any collateral benefits. This position contrasts with that of a litigant who engages the services of an organisation such as Claims Direct Ltd. Master O'Hare received evidence of—

'work done handling and negotiating the claim (whether or not it duplicates what the solicitors may do) and work done to comfort and reassure the *j* insured and/or his family, e g: practical help in the home, counselling, helping in the arrangement of business matters and accompanying the insured on hospital appointments and other appointments.'

[33] If a payment described as a 'premium' entitles the insured to benefits such as these it is, as we have already observed, at least arguable that, to that extent,

a the 'premium' does not fall within the ambit of s 29. Mr Norris QC, who appeared
with our permission to protect the interests of Claims Direct, was concerned that
we might, in this judgment, purport to determine this issue. We do not do so,
but express the hope that it will rapidly be brought before this court in a case
where it is raised on the facts.

b *Own costs cover*

[34] The insurance granted by Temple to Mr Callery entitled him to an indemnity
in respect of his own disbursements, as defined in the cover note, in the event of
the contingencies identified in the cover note. Those contingencies amounted,
in effect, to the failure of Mr Callery's claim.

c [35] Mr Birts contended that an insurance premium that purchases a benefit
of this nature does not fall within the scope of s 29 of the 1999 Act. Section 29
insures against 'the risk of incurring a liability'. The cover provided in relation to
Mr Callery's disbursements was not against the *risk of incurring* those liabilities.
It was against the risk of being unable to recover an indemnity in respect of them
consequent upon the failure of the claim. The liabilities themselves *were incurred*

d voluntarily, not in consequence of a fortuity such as an order of the court.

[36] Mr Nice QC, on behalf of Mr Callery, and those who support his case,
argued that it was necessary to bring own costs insurance within the ambit of s 29
if effect was to be given to the scheme of the legislation, which was to enable
litigants to bring meritorious claims without incurring any significant risk as to
either their own or their opponents' legal costs. They did not, however, attempt

e to explain the precise route of statutory interpretation which would enable own
costs insurance to fall within the definition of 'insurance ... against the risk of
incurring a liability'.

[37] The issue is not one of great significance in the context of this appeal.
Insurance in respect of certain of his own costs constituted a relatively minor

f element of Mr Callery's cover, for most of his own costs were covered by his
CFA. But the issue is one of general importance. Some types of legal costs
insurance, including that offered by Claims Direct, are not designed to be used in
conjunction with a CFA, but provide the litigant with insurance against the risk
of having to pay both sides' costs if the claim fails. This is sometimes referred to
as both sides insurance (BSI), as opposed to conditional fee insurance (CFI). Does

g the part of a BSI premium that reflects the risk that the insured will be left to bear
his own costs fall within the ambit of s 29? The answer to this question turns on
the answer to the issue that arises in respect of Mr Callery's disbursements.

[38] Insurance is the purchase of an indemnity against the risk of loss caused
by a fortuity. A contract that provides for the payment of a sum of money upon

h the occurrence of a fortuitous event will not be insurance unless the sum in question
is intended to indemnify against a consequence of that event. When considering
the nature of 'own costs insurance', it is necessary to identify the fortuity that
triggers liability and to consider the extent to which this fortuity exposes the
insured to the loss against which cover is provided.

j [39] A litigant may be left to bear his own costs in a number of different
circumstances. The costs incurred may be excessive or otherwise unreasonable,
so that they will in no circumstances be recoverable from the litigant's opponent.
Reasonable costs will be recoverable only under a settlement agreement or an
order of the court. A litigant may fail to obtain a court order for payment of costs
for a number of reasons. His claim may fail, so that costs are ordered against him,
rather than in his favour. He may fail on a particular issue at an interlocutory

stage or at the final hearing and, in consequence, fail to obtain a costs order in relation to that issue. If he is successful the costs order made in his favour will not necessarily cover his solicitor and client costs.

[40] If s 29 of the 1999 Act is to be interpreted so as to cover insurance against the risk of the litigant being left to bear his own costs, it is necessary to identify the scope of the cover that is permissible. At the end of the day an interpretation must be given to s 29 that can be applied in practice to different varieties of cover. There are a number of possibilities.

[41] Cover may provide a litigant with an indemnity against his own costs in the event that the claim fails. In such a situation the fortuity of the claim failing is likely, in large measure, to be the reason why the insured fails to obtain an order that his opponent indemnify him in respect of his costs. This will, however, only be true to the extent that he would have obtained an order for those costs had the claim succeeded. To what extent can one say, even speaking broadly, that he has 'incurr[ed] a liability' for his costs as a result of the failure of his claim? Mr Callery's cover does not make it a condition of the recoverability of his disbursements in the event of the failure of his claim that these would have been recoverable had his claim succeeded. In the case of BSI this question is likely to be much more significant.

[42] Even where a litigant's claim succeeds he may not obtain an order requiring the unsuccessful defendant to pay all his costs. Under CPR 44.3 there are many circumstances which may lead a court to exercise its discretion not to award a successful claimant all his costs. We are not aware of the extent to which insurance cover can be obtained which protects a litigant from the risk of failing to obtain an order for the recovery of all his costs when his claim succeeds. It appears, however, that such cover does exist.

[43] Master O'Hare refers in his report to a practice of granting a benefit which consists of 'ring-fencing' the damages; that is providing that unrecovered costs will not reduce the amount of damages below a specified minimum figure. More specifically, some policies provide an indemnity against failing to recover, in whole or in part, the premium paid for the insurance itself. Such an indemnity will apply to the extent that recovery of premium is disallowed because it is excessive, or outside the ambit of s 29.

[44] Master O'Hare was informed that, when Claims Direct decided to 'ring-fence' the first £1,000 of damages recoverable, they added £200 to the premium to cover the cost of assuming this risk. Can the cost of insuring against the risk of having costs disallowed when the claim succeeds be brought within the ambit of 'insurance ... against the risk of incurring a [costs] liability' in s 29?

[45] There is a small element of such cover in the policy issued on behalf of Temple to Mr Callery. Condition 6 provides for a reduction of the premium to the extent that this is disallowed on assessment of costs. This is, on analysis, protection against the failure to recover an element of own legal costs, notwithstanding the success of the claim. On the facts of the present case the extent to which this feature is reflected in the amount of premium must be minimal or non-existent.

[46] The considerations set out above have to be borne in mind when considering what appeared at one time to be the simple submission that the proportion of the premium paid for 'own costs insurance' is recoverable under s 29.

[47] In support of this submission Mr Nice and his supporters made the following points. (1) It was Parliament's intention that the cost of own costs insurance should be recoverable. (2) The overall scheme for funding litigation

a   requires that the cost of own costs insurance should be recoverable. (3) The CPR and the Costs Practice Direction envisage that the cost of own costs insurance will be recoverable.

Parliamentary material

b   [48] The provisions of the 1999 Act that deal with the funding of litigation were preceded and followed by a lengthy and thorough consultation exercise. Counsel referred us to a passage from the Lord Chancellor's Department's explanation of policy published in February 2000, following consultation. It sets out the matters that the court might wish to consider before awarding an insurance premium by way of costs:

c

d

> '... where the insurance cover is purchased in support of a conditional fee agreement with a success fee, the percentage of the premium compared to the level of cover ... where the insurance cover is not purchased in support of a conditional fee agreement with a success fee how its cost compares with the likely costs of a similar case running under a success fee and supporting insurance cover ... the level of cover provided ... the extent of the cover provided, for example against the other side's costs or both sides' costs ... the availability and accessibility of alternative products to the one chosen ...'

This indicates that it was the government's intention that it would be possible to recover the cost of own costs insurance.

e   [49] In June 2000 the government published a consultation paper on collective conditional fees (*Collective Conditional Fees: A Lord Chancellor's Department Consultation Paper*). This included the following statement:

f

> 'Section 29 of the Act allows the court to include in any costs order, any premium paid for an insurance policy against the risk of incurring a liability in those proceedings. The recovery of the insurance premium is not limited to policies backing conditional fee agreements, but covers all after the event policies. The way in which recovery operates is subject to rules of court.'

This indicates that the government believed that it had achieved the intention set out in the previous paragraph.

g   [50] Counsel have not been able to refer us to any authority which supports the use of materials such as those referred to in the previous two paragraphs as an aid to statutory interpretation and we do not consider that they are admissible for this purpose.

h   [51] Of more significance are explanatory notes to the Access to Justice Bill that were provided when this was brought from the House of Lords to the House of Commons on 17 March 1999. The notes explain that they were 'prepared by the Lord Chancellor's Department in order to assist the reader of the Bill and to help inform debate on it. They do not form part of the Bill and have not been endorsed by Parliament.' The notes included the following passage:

j

> 'There are also available insurance policies which can be taken out when someone is contemplating litigation to cover the costs of the other party and the client's own costs (including, if not a conditional fee case, the client's solicitor's fees) if the case is lost. Some of them were developed to support the use of conditional fee agreements but others are used to meet lawyers' fees charged in the more traditional way. For the same reason that the success fee

under a conditional fee is being made recoverable, it is also proposed to make *a* any premium paid for protective insurance recoverable too.'

[52] Counsel were no more successful in referring us to authority on the use of material such as this as an aid to statutory interpretation. They were agreed, however, that it followed logically from *Pepper (Inspector of Taxes) v Hart* [1993] 1 All ER 42, [1993] AC 593 that this material was admissible as an aid to *b* interpretation where the wording of a statute was ambiguous. We were referred to the following passage of the speech of Lord Bingham of Cornhill in *R v Secretary of State for the Environment, Transport and the Regions, ex p Spath Holme Ltd* [2001] 1 All ER 195 at 211, [2001] 2 WLR 15 at 31:

> 'In *Pepper v Hart* the House (Lord Mackay of Clashfern LC dissenting) *c* relaxed the general rule which had been understood to preclude reference in the courts of this country to statements made in Parliament for the purpose of construing a statutory provision. In his leading speech, with which all in the majority concurred, Lord Browne-Wilkinson made plain that such reference was permissible only where: (a) legislation was ambiguous or obscure, or led to an absurdity; (b) the material relied on consisted of one *d* or more statements by a minister or other promoter of the Bill together, if necessary, with such other parliamentary material as might be necessary to understand such statements and their effect; and (c) the effect of such statements was clear (see [1993] 1 All ER 42 at 61, 64, 69, [1993] AC 593 at 631, 634, 640). In my opinion, each of these conditions is critical to the majority *e* decision.'

[53] Mr Birts accepted that explanatory notes provided by the sponsoring department constituted 'parliamentary material' to which reference could be made, although he questioned how much, if any, weight could be attached to it. It seems to us that this concession follows logically from the principle in *Pepper v* *f* *Hart*. We have commented on the enigmatic nature of s 29 of the 1999 Act. In interpreting the section we have derived considerable assistance from this Parliamentary material.

[54] The passage in the explanatory notes suggests that it was the intention of the Lord Chancellor that own costs insurance should be available as an alternative to *g* a CFA as a method of protecting the litigant against the risk, consequent upon the failure of a claim, of having to bear his own legal costs. We have seen nothing to suggest that it was the intention that claimants should be entitled to pass on to defendants the cost of insuring against failure to be awarded costs on the ground that the costs had been unreasonably incurred or were otherwise *h* objectionable.

The overall scheme

[55] Those interests supporting Mr Callery argue that the overall scheme of funding litigation under CFAs and ATE insurance is designed to make it possible *j* for a solicitor to provide the client with a package that will remove any risk as to costs, whether his own or his opponents. This, they argue, cannot be achieved unless the litigant is able to insure against the risk of having to pay his own disbursements. Furthermore, so it is argued, the availability of BSI will increase flexibility and enable the litigant to select the most advantageous means of covering his liability to pay costs.

a **[56]** Mr Birts contended that it is not part of the legislative scheme that litigants should be provided with the opportunity to litigate free of all cost risk. He drew attention to the fact that the consultation paper issued by the Lord Chancellor's Department in September 1999, which sought views on the detailed implementation of the 1999 Act provisions for funding litigation, was entitled *Conditional Fees: Sharing the Risks of Litigation*. He pointed out that under

b the previous legal aid regime a litigant in receipt of legal aid was not shielded from all liability as to costs. There was no warrant for seeking to provide such protection under the new regime. The court should proceed with caution in order to avoid unjustifiable increases in legal costs.

[57] There is some force in Mr Birts' submissions. We observe that the combination of the CFA and the ATE cover available to Mr Callery does not

c afford him complete protection against the risk of liability to pay costs. At the same time we are in no doubt that it is a primary objective of the present scheme that a litigant with an apparently meritorious claim should not be precluded from advancing it by the obligation to pay costs, or the risk of having to do so. If a litigant is precluded from insuring against having to meet his own disbursements,

d there will be occasions when the cost of these will discourage or preclude him from bringing his claim. Furthermore, it does seem clear that it has always been the intention of the Lord Chancellor, as promoter of the legislation, that own cost insurance should be available as an alternative to the CFA.

The CPR and the Costs Practice Direction

e **[58]** As we pointed out at the outset, the provisions of s 29 are imprecise. The September 1999 consultation paper stated:

> '...the Act only provides the legislative framework. The detail of the changes to conditional fees will be provided through secondary legislation, while the operation of the recoverability of the success fee and insurance premium will
f > be informed by Rules of Court and Practice Directions.'

The provisions of the rules and practice directions are of particular importance in clarifying and delimiting the circumstances in which an insurance premium can be claimed under s 29.

g **[59]** The provisions of section 11.10 of the Costs Practice Direction clearly anticipate that insurance cover that falls within the ambit of s 29 may provide alternative protection to that provided by a CFA coupled with insurance. Such cover will necessarily include own cost insurance. That practice direction cannot, of course, confer on the court a jurisdiction that falls outside that conferred by s 29. The question is whether s 29 can and should be interpreted so as to treat the

h words 'insurance ... against the risk of incurring a [costs] liability' as meaning 'insurance against the risk of incurring a costs liability that cannot be passed on to the opposing party'.

[60] We have concluded that s 29 can and should be interpreted in this way. We believe that such an interpretation will do no more than give the words the

j meaning that would be attributed to them by the reasonable litigant. It will also give the words a meaning that accords with the legislative intention and with the overall scheme for the funding of legal costs.

[61] The circumstances in which and the terms on which own costs insurance will be reasonable, so that the whole premium can be recovered as costs, will have to be determined by the courts, when dealing with individual cases, assisted, if appropriate, by the Rules Committee.

[62] In the case of Mr Callery's policy, the right to recover the costs of disbursements is tied to the situations where the protection afforded by the CFA *a* would come into play. It is arguable that the disbursements that are covered are disbursements of a kind that would be recoverable as costs. We cannot see that there is any objection in principle to this cover forming part of that afforded to Mr Callery by his legal costs insurance and consider that the whole of the cover can be considered as falling within the description 'insurance ... against the risk *b* of incurring a liability' within s 29. In this context our only reservation arises in relation to the premium rebate provision in condition 6. As we have indicated, however, this is of no practical significance in the present case and we consider that it is better that the issue of whether the cost of such cover is recoverable under s 29 should be dealt with in a case where this matters.

c

The cost of the premium

[63] The cover provided by the Temple policy, as is usual, includes cover against the risk of being unable to recover the premium as a consequence of losing the action. This item of own cost cover received special consideration by Master O'Hare. *d* We can see no reason, in principle, why this should not form part of the cover provided under insurance that falls within s 29, provided always that any part of the premium attributable to it is reasonable in amount.

Deferred payment of the premium

[64] No challenge to the amount of the premium was made by Mr Birts on the *e* ground that it must include an element to reflect delay in paying it. Indeed, it is not clear to us from the documents precisely what was agreed as to the payment of Mr Callery's premium. Condition 6 of the cover note suggests that the premium was 'payable at the conclusion of the legal action'. If so, this would be typical of ATE insurance and necessarily so if litigants are not going to be discouraged by *f* the obligation of making a substantial payment 'up front'.

[65] CPR 44.3B(1) precludes a solicitor from recovering any proportion of uplift that relates to deferred receipt of fees and expenses. Amelans had added 20% to their uplift to reflect delayed payment and, rightly, did not seek to recover this in these proceedings. Solicitors have always had to wait for payment of legal *g* aid work to a greater or lesser degree, and their fee structure has, no doubt, reflected this. We understand that, in most cases, solicitors do not make any specific addition to uplift to compensate for deferred payment. Nor, so far as we are aware, do they do so in the case of ATE insurance premiums. If and when objection is taken to an insurance premium on the ground that it has been increased to *h* compensate for deferred payment, this issue will have to be addressed. It does not arise in the present case.

The effect of BTE insurance

[66] In the case of *Sarwar v Alam* (5 July 2001, unreported) a claimant passenger *j* took out ATE insurance but was subsequently found to be covered by a policy of BTE (before-the-event) insurance that the defendant driver had taken out. In these circumstances Judge Halbert disallowed the cost of the ATE premium. Permission to appeal against his decision has been given, and the court will expedite the hearing so that the issue can be determined before the end of the vacation. It is not an issue which arises in the present case.

Is £350 too much?

a   [67] We have concluded that there is no reason of principle for refusing to award under s 29 any part of the premium payable for Mr Callery's ATE insurance cover. We have, however, to deal with a challenge made by Mr Birts to the amount of £350 on the ground that it was excessive in the case of a simple passenger claim. His submission was that the maximum premium that would have been

b   reasonable would have been in the region of £160. In support of this figure, he placed before the court a sheet of calculations. Some of the data upon which these were based was not before this court at the substantive hearing of the appeal. None of it had been placed before the judge below. The respondent had been given no advance notice of these calculations. Critically, the calculations depended upon an assumed loss rate of 2·1%, which was not supported by any

c   evidence placed before us. In the circumstances, we did not find it possible to base any conclusions on these calculations.

    [68] Master O'Hare did his best to investigate premium rates in the market. He found that it was not possible to state standard or average premiums for different classes of business. He also found that results over several years had

d   been uniformly poor, leading to several major increases in premium rates over those years. This led him to conclude that it was reasonable to presume as a starting point that a premium was reasonable unless the contrary was shown.

    [69] We do not consider it correct to start with Master O'Hare's presumption. When considering whether a premium is reasonable, the court must have regard to such evidence as there is, or knowledge that experience has provided, of the

e   relationship between the premium and the risk and also of the cost of alternative cover available. As time progresses this task should become easier. In the present case it is not easy as both data and experience are sparse. When considering CFA uplift, we proceeded on the basis that the success rate of claims was at least 90%. Claims that do not succeed will not inevitably be pursued to judgment. Sometimes

f   they will be withdrawn in circumstances that do not involve any liability for defendant's costs. As against this, Mr Callery's cover extended to adverse costs orders after a CPR Pt 36 offer, or an interlocutory defeat. The amount insured was £100,000, but this, of course, was the limit of underwriters' liability and no guide to the much smaller indemnity that is likely to be involved when such a claim fails.

g   [70] In the circumstances, the amount of the premium does not strike us as manifestly disproportionate to the risk. We do not find it possible to be more precise than this. So far as alternatives are concerned, Mr Callery was able to choose, with the assistance of his solicitors, cover at a premium near the bottom of the range of what was available. The premium was one tailored to the risk and

h   the cover was suitable for Mr Callery's needs. The policy terms also had the attractive feature that they gave his solicitors control over the conduct of the proceedings on his behalf, without any involvement by a claims manager until a settlement offer was made. We have concluded that the court below was right to find that the premium was reasonable.

j   [71] Just as in the case of our decision on the CFA uplift, we should emphasise that this judgment should not be treated as determining once and for all that a premium of £350 is reasonable in a case such as this. As further information and experience about the market becomes available it will be possible to found conclusions as to whether premiums are reasonable on a sounder basis.

    [72] We see no reason in principle why the £7·50 IPT should not also be recoverable, and none was suggested.

[73] For these reasons the appeal against the inclusion of the whole of
Mr Callery's insurance premium as an item of his costs will be dismissed.   *a*

Appeal dismissed in respect of the ATE premium. Permission to appeal refused.

Kate O'Hanlon   Barrister.

b

REPORT OF MASTER O'HARE DATED 23 JULY 2001

BACKGROUND
1. In this case, the Court of Appeal has referred to me eleven questions relating
to after-the-event (ATE) insurance in connection with claims for damages for
personal injury in respect of road traffic accidents (RTA). The purpose of the   *c*
inquiry and report is to enable the Court of Appeal to give guidance in its
judgment as to the practice to be adopted in future when taking out such
insurance.
2. In preparing this report, I have received written submissions from twenty
parties and interested parties: their names are set out in annex 1 to this report.   *d*
In many of the submissions there is a request for confidentiality as to the whole
or part of the submission. Written submissions received on or before 29 June 2001
raised in my mind a series of supplementary questions which I communicated to
the parties and interested parties on Tuesday, 3 July 2001. The Court of Appeal
order setting up my inquiry and report had specified Friday, 6 July, as a day upon   *e*
which I would seek clarification of the written submissions received. At that
hearing representations were made by or on behalf of parties and interested
parties whose names are set out in annex 2 to this report. An account of the 6 July
hearing and certain related matters is set out in paras 3 to 8 below. My report on
the submissions on all of the questions, original and supplementary are set out in
paras 9 to 77 below. Some conclusions are set out in paras 78 and 79.   *f*

HEARING ON 6 JULY 2001
3. I began the hearing by making the following preliminary points.
(a) I was keen to include in my final report guidance on reasonable ATE
premiums in pounds and pence for all classes and categories of insurance in
personal injury claims if I could. However, I doubted whether it would be   *g*
practicable to do so and, in any event, I was aware of the limited nature of my
inquiry, which concerns RTA claims.
(b) The guidance I would give would be as to historic cases only, ie policies
taken out before a certain date. I was provisionally of the view that, for the
future, further guidance could be published by the Senior Costs Judge. It might   *h*
be appropriate to publish such guidance, after consultation, every six months
unless and until such guidance became unnecessary. The guidance would be
guidance to judges. The guidance would not fetter the discretion of such judges
and, although given after consultation with interested parties, would not be
intended to regulate interested parties.   *j*
(c) I did not consider it part of my jurisdiction to decide the so-called question
of prematurity, ie is it unreasonable for an intending claimant to take out
insurance before seeking an indication from the defendant as to whether the claim
is to be contested. I would try to give figures for policies taken out at the outset
and also policies taken out after the intended defendant had indicated his
position.

a   (d) I expressed my provisional view that I did not think it part of my jurisdiction to decide whether s 29 of the Access to Justice Act 1999 covers the cost of insurance cover not only in respect of the 'other side's costs' but also in respect of 'both sides' costs'. As with the prematurity issue, I would try to produce figures covering all possibilities.

b   4. Questions were then raised about my jurisdiction to ask supplementary questions, the extremely limited time allowed to answer them and the fears which some of those supplementary questions had raised that I had made preliminary decisions rejecting arguments made in answer made to the original questions. I was addressed on these points particularly by Mr Birts QC (for the appellants), Mr Norris QC (for Claims Direct Ltd) and Mr Langford (group chairman of the Accident Group Ltd). As a result of those submissions I made the

c   following decisions. (a) By Tuesday 10 July 2001 I would deliver my draft report (mainly concerning the original questions) to all parties and interested parties named in annex 1 and 2 of this report. (b) I would take into account for my final report all written submissions received from parties and interested parties on or before Friday 20 July 2001. (c) There would be no further oral hearings in this

d   inquiry.

5. The hearing lasted just over three hours. I will deal with the many submissions made when I deal with the answers to the inquiry questions below. The last persons to make submissions were Mr Norris and Mr Birts. As the hearing developed I had noted down particular questions I would like them or their clients to deal with. Both wanted to give their replies by way of written

e   submissions. Mr Birts also asked me to order the mutual disclosure of all written submissions to the original questions and to the follow-up questions edited as parties wished to remove confidential information. I had no hesitation in refusing that application. It seems to me that this inquiry is only a quasi-judicial inquiry made by a person independent of any interest group who will hear

f   anything which any interest group wishes to say. The importance of confidentiality was referred to in the directions setting up this inquiry.

6. On Tuesday, 9 July 2001, I circulated copies of my draft report to all the parties and interested parties who had contacted me in this matter by that date. The draft report set out the further questions I wished to ask of Claims Direct and of the appellants. Both have supplied answers. For convenience the further

g   questions are set out in annex 3 to this report together with the supplementary questions which I had circulated on 2 July 2001.

7. On 17 July 2001 the Court of Appeal handed down its judgment in *Callery v Gray, Russell v Pal Pak Corrugated Ltd* [2001] EWCA Civ 1117, [2001] 3 All ER 833. I must here draw attention to two paragraphs of that judgment, paras [15] and

h   [65] which are as follows:

'[**15**] The introduction of CFAs in 1995 still left a litigant at risk of having to pay the other side's costs. The Law Society therefore developed the ATE policy, with the help of insurance brokers, as a new form of insurance cover. Since about that time there have also been forms of ATE insurance which

j   provide cover against other risks, but we are not concerned with such cover, whatever form it takes, in this judgment ...

[**65**] We have already observed (see [15] above) that ATE insurance can take a number of quite distinct forms. The major distinction is between the ATE insurers who provide litigation costs insurance cover for personal injury related claims directly through solicitors or through claims management

companies and those who insure non-personal injury or commercial claims. There is also a distinction between ATE cover that is provided only in respect of the "other side's costs" and that provided "for both sides' costs". ATE cover can also be provided for an individual claimant or in standard form by solicitors under delegated authority. As we stated at [15], the only form of ATE insurance to which this judgment relates is insurance providing cover against the other side's costs. We do not deal with the question whether ATE cover against other risks falls within s 29.' (See also [2001] 3 All ER 833 at [78].)

8. Having regard to those paragraphs and to the submissions which have been made to me upon my jurisdiction to decide the question set out in para 3(d) above, I am now of the view that I should not report any conclusions I have reached on ATE insurance covering 'both sides' costs'. I understand that there is to be a hearing tomorrow, 24 July 2001, on the question whether the own costs element in a policy supporting a CFA is recoverable under s 29 of the 1999 Act. Accordingly my conclusions seek to identify as a separate item the reasonable costs incurred in respect of the own costs element. This item may then be stripped out if appropriate.

QUESTION 1

Which firms, organisations and insurers are currently offering ATE insurance and (a) are they all members of the ATE group? (b) If not, are they members of any other group or independent?

9. The ATE group gave me a list of 27 companies and firms currently offering ATE insurance. About twenty of them are members of the ATE group. The list comprises pure risk carriers, brokers and some claims management companies. The ATE group believe that there are at least another 30 claims management companies and/or referral agencies which also have an involvement in offering various types of ATE insurance. Deutsche Automobil Schutz Legal Expenses Insurance Ltd (DAS) have supplied me with a list of over 60 names of insurers, claims management companies and similar bodies all dealing in ATE insurance.

10. Some members of the ATE group are also members of other groups. For example, DAS is also a member of the Association of British Insurers (ABI), the Motor Uninsured Loss Recovery Association (MULRA), the International Association of Legal Expenses Insurance (RIAD), the British Insurance Law Association (BILA) and the ABI Legal Expenses Forum.

11. There are two sources of information for the intending litigant or his solicitor when looking for the most suitable policy: the magazine Litigation Funding published by the Law Society regularly includes charts which compare the various ATE products available. To obtain what may often be the most up-to-date information, it is possible to visit the commonly used website http://www.thejudge.co.uk. It must be said that both of these sources of information are directed towards professionals rather than litigants. Both require the payment of annual subscriptions.

QUESTION 2

What are the different categories or classes of ATE insurance which they are offering?

12. I shall use the term 'category' to refer to the types of risks covered and the term 'class' to refer to the type of cases covered. There are two main categories

a of insurance: conditional fee insurance (CFI) and both sides' costs insurance (BSC). Each category is capable of almost infinite variation. CFI will invariably provide cover for the opponent's costs and the insured's solicitors' disbursements other than counsel's fees. That said, such policies may or may not cover own counsel's fees and adverse orders for costs made at interim hearings. The conditional fee agreements which the CFI supports may or may not require the

b insured to pay a success fee to his solicitor and/or counsel. BSC provides cover for adverse orders for costs and also for the insured's solicitors' costs and disbursements (with or without counsel's fees). It is also possible to obtain a hybrid category, ie a policy which covers adverse orders for costs and also a proportion of the insured solicitors' costs. In theory these categories could equally apply to insurance taken out by defendants. In practice, most insurance

c is taken out only by claimants, and therefore, the rest of this report will be confined to insurance taken out by claimants.

13. As to classes of insurance, some of the claims management companies supply the same policies for all personal injury claims which have a prospect of success which exceeds 50% and in which there is a prospect of recovering

d damages exceeding £1,500. The Accident Group Ltd, which states that it is the market leader, issues CFI policies under which the current premium is £997·50 (including insurance premium tax (IPT)). Another major claims management company, Claims Direct, issues BSC policies in which the current premium is £1,569 (including IPT). In their written submissions on the original questions both of these ATE providers vigorously defended the appropriateness of block

e rating personal injury claims and state that they in fact sell the majority of ATE policies sold in this country.

14. Most other ATE providers classify personal injury claims in at least two ways: different premiums are quoted for fast track cases, and for multi-track cases; each of those classes is further sub-divided into different types of personal

f injury claim. For example, under the Law Society approved Accident Line Protect Scheme (sold by Abbey Legal Protection Ltd (Abbey)) the current premiums (including IPT) for different classes of CFI are as follows: road accident claims (RTA), £315 fast track and £693 multi-track; occupational disease, £892·50 fast track and £3,045 multi-track; other claims, £682·50, fast track and £2,520 multi-track. All of the policies mentioned above, ie Accident Group, Claims

g Direct and Accident Line Protect, are issued prior to communicating with the proposed defendant or his insurer. All of these policies are issued at these premiums for all litigants whose cases are accepted; no distinction is made between litigants who have borderline cases or litigants who have very strong cases.

h 15. In order to investigate the issue of policies which block rate all personal injury claims I raised some supplementary questions about them. None of the answers I received suggested that such policies were inherently wrong. It is true that some of the major players (eg Abbey) do differentiate between types of claim and it may be that, in time, all ATE providers will have better claims statistics

j which will compel them all to differentiate. However, I am persuaded that that time has not arrived yet.

16. Policies which do not differentiate between cases which are strong and cases which are borderline are characteristic of those insurers who give delegated authority to solicitors admitted to their panel (see further, below, question 10). It is often a requirement of such policies that they are issued before sending a letter before claim to the intended defendant. By these means the ATE provider

seeks to obtain a wide basket of cases. Including many good risk cases will lower
the number of claims later made. An all-in approach also reduces the administrative   *a*
cost of risk assessment. There is also the point that risk assessment at the outset
of proceedings may well be imprecise or unreliable.

17. As well as noting the different categories and classes of insurance it is
necessary to observe also that there are two different schemes; standard off-the-peg
policies issued to all cases within the same class (see for example Abbey and the   *b*
Accident Group); and one-off insurance policies (eg policies issued by more
specialist ATE providers such as Saturn). Premiums are lower in standard policies
than they are in one-off policies. This is because the most difficult cases and
therefore the higher risk cases are likely to gravitate towards one-off insurance
policies (although it is not proven before me to what extent this is true of RTA
cases). The most difficult cases are also the ones in which the solicitor will be   *c*
reasonably entitled to a higher than average success fee.

18. I asked a series of supplementary questions and further questions about
different types of policy in an attempt to identify what if any extra cost is involved
in issuing policies which cover all classes of personal injury claim. For example,
what percentage of the cases insured by an ATE provider such as the Accident   *d*
Group are RTA cases or other cases and, with each class, how are they subdivided
between fast track cases and multi-track cases. I had hoped that the answers to
these questions would give me some insight into how much extra it is reasonable
to charge for an all-risks policy. In fact the information produced (for which I am
most grateful) does not enable me to do that.   *e*

QUESTION 3

*What is the standard or average premium for the different classes or categories of
insurance?* (a) *If the insurance is taken out prior to communicating to the
proposed defendant or his insurer?* (b) *After the proposed defendant or his insurer*   *f*
has indicated whether the claim is to be contested? (c) *After the conclusion of the
protocol period?*

19. For several reasons it is not possible to state standard or average premiums
for different classes or categories of ATE insurance. The industry is still immature
and its results over several years have been uniformly poor. Premiums have
undergone several major increases over those years. The range of projects offered   *g*
by the industry and the details of the profit costs and disbursements they cover
are both extremely varied.

20. In the Forum of Insurance Lawyers' (FOIL) submission the wide range of
premiums on offer is evidence that there is no true market for ATE insurance.
If there were, the market pressure would ensure that the premiums on offer were   *h*
broadly in line with other products that offer the same model of insurance cover.
FOIL argues that the published prices of ATE insurance's products show that this
does not occur. On the contrary, it argues that the absence of alignment of
similar products arises from the fact that there is no pressure whatsoever on the
ATE providers to be competitive on price with their rivals. Without this pressure,   *j*
the premiums publicly quoted are, it submits, a flawed basis from which to judge the
reasonableness of the range. APIL challenges FOIL's argument. In their submission
wide ranges of premiums feature in other (established) areas of insurance, for
example motor insurance. On balance I accept what FOIL says on this. There may
well be strong competition between underwriters to supply compulsory insurance
schemes and between different other ATE providers selling standard

a insurance schemes or one-off policies to different solicitors or solicitor groups. However, I am not convinced these market forces impinge upon the premium levied to the ultimate consumer and claimed by him from his unsuccessful opponent.

21. A large majority of ATE insurers and also the appellants (in their oral submissions) urged me not to contemplate favouring or imposing a range of

b standard premiums. The ATE providers fear that, however carefully expressed to indicate judicial discretion, any such guidance will be applied inflexibly and will effectively cap the premiums charged. If that cap does not reflect the commercial realities of the ATE marketplace the market will disappear. That said, some ATE providers gave guarded support to some actual figures which I suggested in my draft report.

c 22. The opposition to guidelines expressed by the appellants derives from their grave disquiet as to the course of this inquiry (their position changed on seeing the judgment in *Callery v Gray*). Giving guidelines would amount to conducting hypothetical detailed assessment without hearing real arguments or evidence as to the policies being assessed. In written submissions made by Temple Legal

d Protection Ltd (Temple) (via counsel for the respondents) it is argued that a regime of standard premiums would inevitably lead defendants to challenge any premium said to fall outside the appropriate standard premium parameters. This, it argues, would inevitably deter insurers like Temple from even contemplating insurance for non-standard risks. It states that the ATE market is sufficiently competitive and difficult that insurers are unlikely to insure a risk where there is

e a high probability of the premium being disputed (a dispute that is itself costly and almost certainly unrewarded). Elsewhere in its submissions Temple states that the court should not arrogate to itself the functions of a financial regulator of the insurance industry.

23. I accept that now is not the time to publish guideline figures for ATE

f premiums but I expect that, fairly quickly, courts conducting detailed assessments will develop individual benchmark figures for major providers such as the Accident Group and Abbey.

If taken out prior to communicating with the proposed defendant or his insurer

24. A search of http://www.thejudge.co.uk conducted by APIL shows the

g range of RTA CFI to be £210 to £1,050 for the fast track and £210 to £1,837 for the multi-track. These figures which are inclusive of IPT are for policies which have differing limits of indemnity. The £210 premiums are for AMICUS policies which have a limit of indemnity of £100,000. The £1,050 premium is for a Wren policy and the £1,837 is for a Temple policy (which is described further in para 65,

h below); both of these policies have a limit of indemnity of £50,000.

25. An ATE provider who requests anonymity describes a fair premium rate for RTA personal injury claims as 6% to 12% (including IPT) based on the level of insurance cover required. In most cases the minimum rate would apply subject to a minimum amount of premium. The 6% rate would produce a premium of £945 (including IPT) for cover of £15,000. This appears to be somewhat higher

j than the rate which most ATE insurers apply for RTA cases.

After it has been indicated that the claim is to be contested

26. The anonymous ATE provider just mentioned would recommend a premium of 12% of the amount of insurance cover required, but states that the defendant's decision to contest the claim would be a vital factor in whether the insurer would

accept the insurance proposal. Other ATE providers make similar points, for example, DAS (the premium should double), X L Brockbank Ltd (the premium should double or treble). Other insurers (eg Keystone) and APIL take the view that many insurers would consider each such case on merit only and may well decline to offer cover once there is a clear indication that the defendant would fight the claim. Alternatively, limited cover might be offered on very expensive terms, eg 15% of the amount of cover required. Temple states that if 'it is clear that the case would be contested' the premiums will be considerably higher than usual; however, a 'clear contest' will lead to cover being refused in approximately 70% of cases. I infer from this that Temple, and perhaps other ATE providers, draw a distinction between court proceedings which are being vigorously defended and court proceedings in which the claimant is merely being put to proof of his claim, possibly as a delaying tactic. Vigorously defended proceedings have less chance of reaching a negotiated settlement. It is said on behalf of the ABI that the distinction these providers draw is out of date: it harks back to a pre-CPR era before the pre-action protocol existed. They say that insurers' claims handling systems are now geared to meeting protocol deadlines in order to settle claims as quickly and as efficiently as possible.

27. Several submissions dwelt upon the long-term effects of the decision of Judge Halbert in the case *Sarwar v Alam* (5 July 2001, unreported). That case concerned a road accident claim in which the claimant was a passenger in the defendant's car. The claimant was disallowed the cost of the ATE insurance he had taken out because the defendant's motor insurance provided before-the-event (BTE) insurance not only for the defendant but also for his passengers. Some commentators may wish to dispute that the judge was right to treat the existence of such insurance as something which the solicitor in that case should have anticipated or dispute that the BTE insurance in that case was suitable for the claimant. However, whether the learned judge was right or wrong on those points it should now be accepted that, unless the case is reversed on appeal, in future, solicitors will have to increase the enquiries they make about existing insurance cover. If that is right this case poses two problems for ATE insurance providers. First, in claims by passengers against drivers, the need to undertake enquiries will postpone the date of issue of the ATE insurance. The case restricts the ability of providers of compulsory insurance schemes to insist that policies be taken out at the outset (see para 16, above). Secondly, the potential for growth of BTE insurance shown by this case may cause immense instability for the ATE insurance providers. The size of the ATE business may diminish so forcing premiums higher. The increasing premiums and the need to make enquiries will encourage more claimants to dispense with insurance altogether, so exacerbating the problem.

28. Other aspects of *Sarwar*'s case which have been dwelt upon at some length in several of the submissions I have received are as follows: a fear which some ATE insurers express that the volume of BTE cover is likely to be increased by one section of the insurance industry (liability insurers) mainly for the purpose of destabilising and destroying another section (the ATE insurers): and arguments about the independence of solicitors acting for BTE insurers and the possibilities of conflict if the same insurer covers both claimant and defendant. Counter-submissions have been made and I have been taken to regs 4 and 5 of the Insurance Companies (Legal Expenses Insurance) Regulations 1990, SI 1990/1159. Interesting as these topics are I am in no doubt that the submissions I have received upon them are not matters which should influence my report. They are not relevant on questions concerning the reasonableness of premiums.

After the conclusion of the protocol period

a

29. Several of the submissions do not distinguish between the commencement of court proceedings and the declaration by a defendant that the claim is to be contested. The willingness to write policies after the commencement of court proceedings must be set against the unwillingness to offer cover at all in contested cases.

b

QUESTION 4

What does the premium cover?

30. In most if not all off-the-peg policies the limit of indemnity cover will be standardised; £25,000, £50,000 or £100,000. Several ATE providers argue that the

c vast majority of cases will not require this level, but a reduction of it would not substantially affect the premiums (see 'burning cost' in para 36, below). Having one limit of indemnity keeps the administrative costs down. Also, I am impressed by the argument (raised by Abbey and Litigation Protection Ltd) that it is a basic premise of good underwriting practice that all risks are adequately insured.

d

31. Most CFI policies provide benefits which are additional to the cover in respect of the other side's costs. Most, but not all, of them are 'own cost' benefits. This raises questions of recoverability which will be affected by any decision made by the Court of Appeal on 24 July 2001. The list of additional benefits I will consider in some detail is as follows:

(a) own counsel's fees;

e

(b) other disbursements (such as court fees and own experts' fees);

(c) cover for appeals;

(d) liability for costs following an offer to settle or CPR Pt 36 payment;

(e) option to buy 'top-up cover' later at the same premium rate;

(f) interest foregone on deferred premiums;

f

(g) full indemnity in respect of the premium if the claim is lost;

(h) partial indemnity in respect of the premium if the full premium is not successfully recovered;

(i) any premium loading because of the claims record of the insured's solicitor;

(j) interest payable on disbursement loans where the claim fails;

(k) advice and help supplied by claims managers.

g

32. As to most of these benefits I have raised supplementary questions as to their recoverability and also enquired into the percentage of a premium which it would be fair to attribute to all or any of them. My purpose in asking these questions was to identify (if I could) a fair discount to make if any of these benefits were included in the policy and are to be regarded as irrecoverable from an

h opposing party ordered to pay costs. Guidance on values would also be of use when comparing different policies which offered different benefits. The third, fourth and final items in the list above were not included in my supplementary questions but were raised in submissions thereon. They indicate that a list such as this can never be exhaustive. The ability of the industry to create new

j additional benefits, whilst not infinite, is extremely great.

33. In their submissions the appellants challenged the recoverability of all of these benefits not only on the grounds that they were 'own costs' benefits but also on the ground that, by purchasing a policy with some or all of these benefits, the insured is purchasing more than just insurance. They place reliance upon the House of Lords decision in *Dimond v Lovell* [2000] 2 All ER 897, [2000] 2 WLR 1121. The opposing argument is that that case is a ruling on damages only and is

therefore irrelevant on this question of costs. I am invited instead to concentrate upon the wording of s 29 of the 1999 Act and upon the definition of 'insurance premium' in CPR 43.2(1)(m). The appellants also rely on those provisions and place emphasis on the words 'insurance [policy] against the risk of incurring a liability in [those the] proceedings'. In my view the provision of the benefit by way of an insurance contract does not by itself make the cost of the benefit recoverable. In my view I ought to look at each benefit in turn and decide (subject to the 'own costs' question) whether it is an item of legal expenses insurance, or is of and incidental to such insurance, or whether it is an extraneous benefit in respect of which some discount should be made. I am in no doubt that a discount would be appropriate in the case of policies which rewarded each insured with valuable gift tokens, discounts on holidays purchased or similar benefits. I note from a Datamonitor report submitted to me by one interested party a suggestion that at least one case management company offers customers a free telephone helpline for advice on any legal question. It seems to me that there is no difference in principle between this benefit and the gift tokens mentioned above but there may obviously be a difference as to the size of the discount appropriate. If the take up rate for a legal telephone helpline were extremely small the cost to the insurer per policy would be negligible.

34. Working through the list of additional benefits I shall, as promised in para 8 above, endeavour to identify the reasonable cost of the item expressed as a percentage of the premium. There are three comments I must make about that by way of explanation and introduction. (a) Many interested parties deny that I have received sufficient information and argument in order to make such assessments. While I accept that that is true I doubt whether, on these topics especially, any court conducting a detailed assessment would be given more information than I have received. Costs judges are frequently left to 'do the best they can' on sketchy information. (b) The discounts I shall identify assume a policy which contains most if not all of the additional benefits listed and no others. Although I shall look at each one separately I believe that, when conducting a detailed assessment, the court should take the so-called broadbrush approach, ie value the collection of relevant items as if they were a single item rather than a collection. (c) Before embarking upon this task it is convenient to report on the next question. My report on the additional benefits therefore begins in para 41.

QUESTION 5

How are premiums in general terms calculated?

35. Several ATE providers identify four main elements in the calculation of the premium: the burning cost, the risk/profit cost, the administrative costs and the distribution commission.

36. The burning cost is the frequency of loss (ie the percentage of policies in which a claim is made) multiplied by the average cost of each claim. If the frequency of loss is 10% and the average cost of each claim is £3,000, the burning cost in each policy is £300. These figures are given for illustration only. They are not intended to represent real figures. Their inclusion in my draft report caused one interested party to describe them as overly optimistic and another interested party to say that, in its opinion, the real figures are 20% and £2,000 (ie a burning cost of £400). £400 exceeds the cost of several total premiums quoted to me.

37. The risk/profit cost is the sum to represent the profit looked for by the underwriter and also a safety margin for the underwriter should the cost of claims

a become higher than the burning cost predicted. There is much dispute about how this should be calculated. Abbey suggests that it is usually calculated as 25% of the burning cost. Litigation Protection suggests that this approach massively underestimates the underwriter's costs and ignores altogether reinsurance costs. They suggest a figure nearer 40%. The appellants submit that it should be calculated as a percentage of the premium income. They then give various worked examples

b in which the largest underwriting profit shown is 10% of the gross premium. X L Brockbank and National Insurance and Guarantee Corp plc (NIG) give it as their opinion that a 10% profit margin is, in all the circumstances, ludicrous.

38. The administrative costs cover items such as personnel, premises, policy issue and processing and claims administration. What if any advertising cost should be included as administrative costs? I shall deal with this question in

c paras 59–63.

39. The distribution commission is a sum payable to brokers and other intermediaries. As with the first two ingredients there is much dispute as to the amount of commissions normally found. I shall give further details when reporting on the answers to question 6 (see para 52, below).

d 40. FOIL and the appellants argue that the distribution commission, although properly regarded as a constituent element in premium calculation, is not something that can be legitimately claimed from an opposing party ordered to pay costs—

'as it is purely a commercial arrangement between the contracting parties' (FOIL).

e 'The court … is respectfully reminded of para 11.10 of the Costs Practice Direction. Costs judges assessing the recoverable premium should obtain details of any commission paid or payable and exclude this from the premium to be paid by the losing party.' (Appellants.)

In my view the arguments raised by FOIL and the appellants on this point are not
f correct. I do not think the Costs Practice Direction (CPR PD 44) provision referred to should normally lead the costs judge to disallow the whole of any commission included in a premium. The paragraph lists 'the amount of commission payable' as one of the factors to be taken into account in deciding whether the cost of insurance cover is reasonable. This factor like the first two mentioned in the paragraph (a comparison with other funding arrangements and the level and

g extent of cover provided) describes matters of degree not items for deletion. Thus, if distribution commissions amounting to, say, 10% of the overall premium were the insurance industry's standard, the Costs Practice Direction enables the costs judge to require a receiving party to justify a commission payment exceeding 10%.

h 41. In the next ten paragraphs I will comment upon each of the additional benefits listed in para 31, above.

(*a*) *Own counsel's fees*
(*b*) *Other disbursements (such as court fees and own experts' fees)*

j 42. There can be little doubt that these are ordinary items of legal expenses insurance and therefore a discount in respect of them will be appropriate only if it is ruled that the own cost element of CFI policies is irrecoverable (see further, para 8, above). In my view, in a claim which fails, the reasonable costs incurred by the claimant on counsel's fees and other disbursements are unlikely to exceed one half of the total costs payable to the opponent. Accordingly, they comprise less than one third of the burning cost of a policy covering both of them. Bearing

in mind the other ingredients in gross premiums, the discount should not exceed
20% of the total. If, as is more usual, the policy does not cover counsel's fees but
does cover other disbursements, the discount would be nominal, a few pounds.

(c) Cover for appeals
(d) Liability for costs following an offer to settle or CPR Pt 36 payment

43. As with the first two, these two are pre-eminently ordinary items of legal
expenses insurance. I do not have sufficient information to make any attempt to
value these benefits. I suspect that the reasonable cost of (c) would be negligible
but the reasonable costs of (d) would be substantial. It should be noted that these
two items, unlike the first two items, may not be limited to own cost protection:
they may include protection in respect of the other sides' costs.

(e) Option to buy top-up cover later at the same premium rate

44. This item, like the first four listed, seems to me plainly a standard ingredient
of legal expenses insurance or at least is plainly of and incidental to such
insurance. Like the last two listed it may well comprise protection not only for
own costs but also in respect of the other sides costs. Top-up cover is the subject
matter of question 8. Such cover is not normally needed in standard insurance
policies (see further, para 30, above). I have received no information upon which
I could base any attempt to put a value on this benefit. Presumably one would
have to start by trying to identify as at the time the policy was taken out, what
premium rate would the insured anticipate as payable had he not had such an
option and then try to identify what was then the reasonable likelihood of his
needing to exercise the option.

(f) Interest foregone on deferred premiums
(g) Full indemnity in respect of the premium if the claim is lost

45. These benefits are to be found in virtually all off-the-peg insurance
policies. Several ATE providers submit that their inclusion in the policy makes
the policies cheaper. In their submission many litigants would be strongly
discouraged from litigating and from buying insurance if they had to pay the
insurance premiums at the outset or if they had to risk paying them (or part of
them) later. Of those who do proceed to litigation the litigants least likely to buy
insurance would be those who have the strongest cases. From this it is argued
that (subject to the ruling upon the own cost question) allowing recovery of these
items falls within the policy underlying the new legislation. This is a matter
discussed in the Court of Appeal judgment ([2001] 3 All ER 833 at [99], note
especially [99](viii)). The opposing argument is that the 'no win no fee' principle
which applies to profit costs and counsel's fees does not apply to insurance
premiums. The new legislation replaces the old legal aid regime. Under that scheme
it was expected that there would be 'legal aid only' items payable by the claimant
out of his compensation. It is said that claimants in the new regime should
similarly expect to shoulder the cost of premium loss cover. There are other
items in the new law which they must shoulder, e g the fee deferment element of
a success fee under a CFA (see CPR 44.3B(1)(a)). In my view if the legislative
policy does not justify the recovery of these items, the effect they are likely to
have on most prospective claimants is such as to make the discount appropriate
to them zero. However, I note that, in some policies premium loss protection is
available on payment of a substantial sum (see, for example, the premiums

a quoted for the following policies issued by Litigation Protection, 'conditional fee protection plan' and 'conditional fee protection plan plus').

(h) *Partial indemnity in respect of the premium if the full premium is not successfully recovered*

46. This benefit covers the insured who obtains an order for costs against his
b opponent but, on detailed assessment, part of the premium is disallowed as unreasonable or the whole premium is disallowed as unreasonable because, for example, of some pre-existing cover which the claimant had. The benefit sometimes takes the form of a ring-fencing of some of the damages recovered.

47. This benefit clearly provides own costs protection and therefore a premium containing it is at risk of discount on that score. In my view a discount
c should be attempted in any event. I do not think the legislative policy argument sought to justify the last two items can be extended to this item. This item protects the policyholder against the risk of loss of taking out insurance which, if he has or might have taken it out, would not have been recoverable from the opposing party. In my view this item is best regarded as extraneous to the legal
d expenses insurance contemplated by s 29.

48. It should be noted that the value of this benefit increases in proportion to the unreasonableness of the sum unrecovered. As to valuation the only information I am aware of relates to the increase in premiums made by Claims Direct (a BSC insurance provider) when it decided to ring-fence the first £1,000 of compensation payable to customers who take out the new policy. In the Datamonitor report
e referred to above (see para 33) the increase is said to have cost over £200 per policy (ie over 15% of the old premium).

(i) *Any premium loading because of the claims record of the insured's solicitor*

49. Whilst the cost of this benefit may have to be discounted as an own costs
f protection, most parties and interested parties submitted that it should be discounted in any event if it can be identified. Like (h) this benefit has a spiralling effect: the worse the solicitor's claims record appears to be, the greater the cost of insurance. Presumably, it is to be excluded as being extraneous to ordinary legal expenses insurance. Several ATE providers commented that rather than load a premium because of perceived incompetence by the solicitor, the insurer
g should not issue the policy in the first place. Indeed, most of the major players operate through panels of solicitors and, presumably, a firm's membership of a panel can be restricted. I am aware that at least one provider does require solicitors to complete a comprehensive proposal form giving details about the firm's past litigation experience and losses.

h
'This enables us to try to match the right premiums to the firm and that firm's profile of risks. We ask the court to not take that ability away from us. The solicitors who have a very low rate of claims against the ATE policy have been snapped up (unfairly we believe) by [other providers].'

j Two other interested parties point out that it is wrong to suggest that a poor claims record reflects poor levels of competence. The claims record is more likely to reflect the type of case taken on. Both of these parties state that it would be contrary to the public interest to discourage solicitors from taking on worthy cases which might adversely affect their claims record. This would mean that potential claimants might be unable to pursue their cases or at least be unable to pursue them with the solicitor of their choice. In my view the public interest they

identify (and which I accept) would not justify the recovery of the cost of this
benefit. The same public interest element arises in respect of the operation of   *a*
panels of solicitors.

(j) Interest payable on disbursement loan where the claim fails

50. Many interested parties, including APIL and several ATE providers, concede
that it is necessary to discount a premium for a policy including this benefit   *b*
whichever way the ruling as to own costs element goes. This benefit is extraneous
to legal expenses insurance. It relates more to funding costs. I am unable to give
guidance on valuation save to say that, in some policies, a price for it may be
shown separately. If it is not, it would presumably be necessary to take into
account the following factors as they reasonably appeared to be at the time the
policy was taken out; the likely rates of interest, the size of the loan in question   *c*
and the likely duration of the proceedings and the risk of loss.

(k) Advice and help supplied by claims managers

51. The work done which I have in mind is work done handling and negotiating
the claim (whether or not it duplicates what the solicitor may do), and work done   *d*
to comfort or reassure the insured and/or his family (eg practical help in the
home, counselling, helping in the arrangement of business matters and accompanying
the insured on hospital appointments and other appointments). In my view these
benefits are extraneous to legal expenses insurance and a substantial discount on
the recoverable premium should be made in respect of them. I have received no   *e*
information or valuation of these services so far as CFI policies are concerned.
This will have to be valued on a case by case basis but, in respect of major ATE
providers, benchmarks will no doubt develop quite quickly.

QUESTION 6

  f

*Of the premium, what percentages are attributable to, administration, advertising
and other matters?*

52. Most of the ATE providers who answered this question have sought
confidentiality as to their answers. Several of them have given me very specific
details of commercially sensitive information including the amount of risk
premiums paid and their commission arrangements. I will not of course repeat   *g*
that information and, indeed will strive to maintain the confidentiality claimed
for it. In respect of question 6 there are five matters upon which I must report:
definition of premium, expenses and commissions, assessment fees, referral fees
and advertising.

  h

Definition of premium

53. In my view the premium to be assessed by the court is that sum paid or
payable by the litigant. The sum to be allowed should include (to the extent that
they are recoverable and reasonable) the four main elements identified in para 35,
above: the first two (burning cost and risk/profit cost) comprise the pure risk   *j*
premium and are usually retained by the underwriter; most if not all of the work
of issuing policies, supervising the conduct of cases and handling claims will be
dealt with by brokers and other intermediaries. Thus they will receive most but
not all of the administrative costs and of course their commissions. The total sum
paid or payable by the insured is the sum upon which insurance premium tax
(IPT) is calculated.

Expenses and commissions

a

54. I have been given a copy of the ABI Insurance Statistics Year Book for 1989–1999 (the latest available) and have been invited to consider four tables setting out average commission and expenses ratios for certain types of insurance. The figures for commissions and expenses which I am about to quote are expressed as percentages of the retained premium, ie that part of the gross

b   premium which is net of reinsurance. For 1999 the commission and expenses ratio for each of the following types of insurance are shown as follows:

UK motor insurance	24·1%
UK accident and health insurance	37·4%
UK general liability insurance	35·8%
UK property insurance	37·3%

c

55. Having now received submissions from other interested parties (in particular, the Accident Group, Claims Direct and DAS) I do not accept that statistics such as these are a useful yardstick to apply. No statistics have yet been given for ATE insurance and I am told that, as a specialist sector of the market, the commission and expenses ratios are likely to be much higher. I am invited

d   instead to treat as a comparable the 'extended warranties' market where, it is said, commission and expenses ratios often equal or exceed 70% of premium. Other specialist areas which are not included in the statistics are said to be 'creditor premiums' and legal expenses insurance which, I am told, have rates much higher than those shown in the yearbook.

e

Assessment fees

56. In policies issued with the delegated authority of the insurer (see question 10) the risk assessment will be made by the solicitor not the insurer and the insurer can therefore make no charge for it. In other cases the underwriter, or, more likely, an intermediary, will make a risk assessment. The cost of that assessment

f   may be included in the premium (when it will bear IPT) or levied as a separate assessment fee. In the latter case the fee may attract VAT. In my view, although such an assessment fee is not a premium, the insured can recover it (subject to assessment) under an order for costs if it is a fee paid or payable by him. The reasonable cost of the policy is itself recoverable. In my view reasonable costs expended in obtaining such a policy are of and incidental to it. I would apply the

g   same approach to time spent by the solicitor in completing the proposal forms and obtaining the policy and also to time spent in complying with policy terms (eg reporting matters or obtaining authority to reject an offer to settle or Pt 36 payment). The compliance work must not, of course, be extraneous to the policy.

h   *Referral fees*

57. The overwhelming majority of parties and interested parties agree that referral fees paid by a solicitor to the ATE provider are not recoverable as such by the solicitor from his client and therefore by the client from an opposing party. The cost to the solicitor is a typical overhead expense of his firm. They replace

j   or comprise part of any budget the solicitor has for advertising and marketing. Being part of the solicitor's overhead costs, it will form a legitimate component in the calculation of hourly rates by that solicitor.

58. Another, and much more contentious, use of the expression 'referral fee' is in the context of fees paid by ATE providers to claims managers. The cost of these fees will be passed to the insured as part of the gross premium he must pay. In my view that part of the premium which is fairly attributable to work which is

extraneous to the legal expenses insurance is not recoverable (see further para 51, above). It is immaterial whether the work is done by an agent of the claims management company or by an employee.

Advertising

59. Many submissions have been made to me in answer to question 6 and a supplementary question I raised about this topic. There is a perception that some market leaders in ATE insurance spend far more than is reasonable on advertising the products they sell. In fairness to the persons attacked, such as the Accident Group, I think I should spell out more exactly what is being said against them.

(i) Abbey acknowledges that it is perfectly reasonable to include in the premium an element for marketing and advertising but implies that the absence of controls may cause advertising budgets to spiral towards infinity.

(ii) APIL express the belief that that part of a premium which is attributable to—

> 'large commissions on sale to the client and the cost of marketing cases (claims farming) should be stripped out from the premium and should not be recovered. Otherwise all insurers could add this to their premium and could all run expensive television advertising campaigns, all ultimately paid for by the liability insurers.'

(iii) The appellants, like Abbey, accept that—

> 'a reasonable premium will include a *modest* percentage in respect of commissions and other payments to brokers and intermediaries, including payments for advertising. However excessive or disproportionate percentages should obviously be irrecoverable. Given the widely differing amounts currently being spent it would not be appropriate to allow or disallow a set percentage in all cases. Rather, a view should be taken now as to the current average percentage in a range of reasonable premiums and that percentage not exceeded when assessing maximum guideline premium figures.'

60. The converse case is put by the Accident Group and Claims Direct. One denies a point (which I do not think has actually been alleged) that any slice or percentage of its premium is calculated specifically to raise an advertising budget. Both emphasise that advertising is a legitimate part of any insurance business and both suspect that the accusations made are—

> 'prompted by the commercial ambitions of our competitors. The small ... providers have every reason to claim that they can prosper without heavy advertising or marketing overheads; they fail to acknowledge that the very market in which they operate has very largely been created, at no cost to them, by the big providers ... the smaller providers are now looking to increase their market share at the expense of those who have created it.'

61. I have set out the arguments as fully as I can so as to enable the Court of Appeal to take this issue from me and make their own ruling upon it if they so wish. I respectfully record here my own view that the court has neither the jurisdiction nor the means by which to regulate the advertising budgets of insurers. If regulation is needed it must be extra-judicial regulation. I respectfully suggest that the proper function for the court when deciding questions of

a   reasonableness concerning insurance premiums, is to consider the conduct of the insured, not the conduct of the insurer. In other words the proper question to ask is whether the choice of policy made by the insured was a reasonable one. If it was the premium paid or payable is recoverable (possibly subject to certain deductions such as those described above). A choice may be regarded as reasonable even if the insured did not in fact make the best choice available.

b   62. There is, however, another aspect to the advertising issue which may merit a reduction in premium recoverability. There are two pre-requisites to the case which I have in mind: (i) the policy in question must have been issued by an ATE insurance provider who, at the time of issue, conducted a high volume advertising and marketing programme in order to attract customers; and (ii) the court must have already decided to make a substantial reduction in the premium

c   recoverable on the basis that it included substantial extraneous benefits, including the non-recoverable benefits of work done by a claims manager or the like.

63. I respectfully suggest that the premium to be allowed should be further reduced to take account of the fact that the advertising costs recouped in the full premium are properly regarded as attributable not only to selling the standard

d   insurance products but also to selling the disallowed extraneous benefits. In the likely absence of evidence of the cost of advertising per policy I would make the reduction the same as the reduction in respect of the extraneous benefits.

QUESTION 7

e   *Is it practicable to obtain a policy in which premiums are rebated in the event of early settlement and are there any policies on the market which provide for this?*

64. The existence or non-existence of rebates is one of the factors listed in section 11.10 of the Costs Practice Direction to be taken into account when considering the reasonableness of insurance. However, the general consensus of most interested parties, including ATE providers, APIL and FOIL is firmly against

f   rebates of premium on early settlement. Such a scheme runs counter to the calculation of 'burning cost' explained in para 36 above. If such policies were introduced it would be necessary to increase the premium in every policy in order to provide for a rebate in some of them. Such a system would also give rise to increased administrative costs and, for the insured or his funder costs increased

g   funding charges. Some parties are unaware of any such policies. Some parties report seeing such policies in some commercial cases. Litigation Protection makes the point that rebates would become viable only in exceptional cases involving very large amounts of indemnity and accordingly a very high level of premium. In RTA claims the average costs of claims rarely exceeds £15,000.

h   65. There is in fact a CFI policy (issued by Temple) which is applicable in RTA cases and which has a three-step premium, ie a premium the amount of which depends on the procedural stage reached by the time the case is concluded. The first stage covers the period up to issue of court proceedings. The second period covers the stage from there to a date at least 45 days before trial. In cases which conclude at stage 1 or stage 2 the policy has a limit of indemnity of £25,000.

j   In cases which do not conclude until stage 3 the highest premium is payable and the limit of indemnity is £50,000. The advantage to the insurer of a reduced limit of indemnity in the earlier stages is obvious. The advantage of the three-step premium to the insured is not obvious to me given that the policy includes premium loss protection.

QUESTION 8

What are the advantages and disadvantages of policies permitting the purchase of further cover as a claim proceeds?

66. Most interested parties felt that the disadvantages would outweigh the advantages. The position is clearly stated by the Law Society, whom I quote in full:

> 'Some policies permit the purchase of further cover as the claim proceeds. It may be that in these cases the cost of the initial cover may be less than if cover is purchased for the maximum reasonable exposure for costs. The disadvantage is that the inception of further cover at a later stage will require reference back to the ATE insurer. There is unlikely to be any guarantee that further cover will be provided. It is likely that the provision of an initial amount of cover followed by the provision of further cover when a claim has not settled at an earlier stage would be considered to be high risk to the insurer. Insurers may fear that claimants will only take out the further cover if the case becomes more complex and more risky. The cost of further cover may therefore be expensive. The *overall* cost of insurance under a model of this sort is likely to be greater than at present because of the administrative costs involved in giving individual consideration to "second stage" cover.'

It was in relation to this question that Litigation Protection made the remark I quoted in para 30 above that it is a basic premise of good underwriting practice that all risks are adequately insured.

67. Two interested parties made submissions which run in favour of 'top-up cover', FOIL and Greystoke Legal Services. As to FOIL I respectfully doubt that the advantages they list do in fact outweigh the disadvantages they note (higher administrative costs for the ATE insurer and the need for more detailed explanation of the policy by the solicitor). I shall state my doubts alongside each of the advantages listed. (a) Ensures that the amount of cover at any stage of the case will relate more closely to the extent of the risks involved (this runs counter to the burning cost principle explained in para 36 above). (b) Encourages the defendant to settle claims where appropriate before the level of premium increases (this assumes that the claimant informs the defendant of the limited cover bought so far; such a disclosure might encourage the defendant to sit tight until the cover was exhausted). (c) Reduces the scope for dispute between the parties in respect of the quantum of the policy taken out (so would not taking out any insurance at all). However, I do find merit in FOIL's suggestion that ATE insurers will not be disinclined to provide further cover unless of course the merits of the claim have substantially deteriorated: they point out that if a claim now has no reasonable prospects of success the insurer would be entitled to cease cover even if a large limit of indemnity had been taken out originally. Nevertheless, it seems to me reasonable for an intending insured to take out adequate cover from the outset of the policy. Delay will not bring peace of mind and, if the defendant is aware of it, may encourage the defendant to play a waiting game. Cover bought late is almost bound to be more expensive than if it had been bought at the outset (cf the policy described in para 65, above).

68. The written submissions made on the original questions by the ABI included a copy of the BSC comparison chart published in Litigation Funding in January 2001. The chart covers 11 ATE providers. In answer to the question 'can limit of indemnity be topped up later?' the answer most frequently given is 'yes, subject to approval'. The exception is at Greystoke where the answer given is

a 'yes, guaranteed option available'. In Greystoke's written submissions on the original questions a brief explanation is given of their 'Lawassist starter policy'. I am told that, for a premium of £175 plus IPT for RTA cases, the initial level of cover is sufficient to investigate the case up to settlement during the protocol period.

b   'If the limit of indemnity is exhausted without the claim being resolved, then it is possible, subject to the continuing merits of the case, to obtain additional ATE cover under our standard Lawassist ATE policy with the option to increase that additional level of indemnity at a later stage.'

So far as I am aware no other insurer offers a similar policy. This policy is not *c* mentioned in the Litigation Funding comparison chart mentioned above but is mentioned in the search result produced to me by APIL from the website http://www.thejudge.co.uk. I presume that a policy such as this would find favour with the liability insurers. If it thrives it may well solve some of the problems raised in this inquiry. However, it is, of course, too early to know whether it will thrive. The policy is a form of BSC although, because it covers the *d* pre-issue period, the question of adverse costs orders does not arise. A CFI version of this policy (which presumably would cover little more than experts' fees) would be even cheaper.

QUESTION 9

e
How is the insurance marketed or sold?

69. ATE policies are sold to policyholders in two main ways: (i) via firms of solicitors throughout the United Kingdom, and (ii) via various claims agencies including claims management companies. In (i) the solicitor meets the intending insured first and introduces him to the insurer. In (ii) the claims agency or claims *f* management company meets the intending insured first and introduces him to a solicitor. I use the term 'claims agency' here to refer to organisations which simply act as the advertising arm of the solicitors they deal with. Claims management companies may investigate and screen cases to a greater or lesser extent and provide supervision and a point of contact for the insured/claimant throughout *g* the litigation (see further, para 51). Some claims agencies and claims management companies charge membership fees and referral fees to the solicitors they deal with (see further, paras 56 and 57).

70. In para 20, above, I have referred to FOIL's submission that there is no true market for ATE insurance. It does seem fair to say that, with policies sold via *h* claims agencies and claims management companies, the intending claimants do not shop around on the basis of premium. Moreover, in those cases and in cases sold via solicitors, clauses in the policies which indemnify the insured for the loss of the premium itself removes any incentive for that insured to seek a reasonably priced policy.

71. In its submissions, Abbey draws attention to the solicitor's professional *j* duties, which include an obligation to examine how the claimant's case can be funded. I am in no doubt that a solicitor must not cause a client to enter into an arrangement which he knows to be unsuitable and must not negligently overlook other forms of funding (eg existing legal expenses cover which the client may have). However, I respectfully doubt whether, in cases in which ATE insurance is appropriate, the solicitor must act as an insurance broker advising his client upon the best deal available.

QUESTION 10

Do any insurers give solicitors delegated authority to issue policies, and, if so, on
what terms?

72. I cannot improve upon the answer given to this question by APIL which I
quote and adopt in full.

'A few insurers give delegated authority to solicitors who have been
admitted to their panel. It will almost certainly be a requirement of
delegated authority that the solicitor puts all his claims through the system
and at the earliest moment, i e receipt of instructions. The following insurers
offer delegated authority. (i) Abbey Legal Protection with accident line
protect relaunched and which came into effect on 1 October 2000. The
membership fee is £3,750 plus VAT. An annual fee [and] a £50 referral fee is
charged. Members have to put all their CFA cases through the Abbey
scheme. This is a common requirement. (ii) DAS/Law Insure. (iii) Claims
Advance. (iv) Law Club Legal Protection. (v) Temple. Temple has two
insurance schemes, one a delegated authority basis and one where premiums
are quoted for individual cases. With the delegated authority scheme (which
is not available for all cases) the solicitor can issue certificates in respect of
any case taken on using a premium table supplied by Temple. The solicitor
rates the case and then applies a corresponding premium. Temple also does
not interfere with the way in which the case is run leaving the solicitor free
to take all decisions.'

QUESTION 11

To what extent are the insured and his lawyers affected by the amount of the
premium payable: (a) in cases which later settle (i e the great majority of cases)?
(b) if the insured succeeds at the trial? (c) if the insured is unsuccessful at the trial?

73. Answers to this question did not make much distinction between (a), (b)
and (c). The real questions here are who pays for the insurance if the insured
loses and who pays in whole or in part if the insured wins. Most considered it
immaterial whether the loss or win occurred at trial or before trial.

74. If the insured loses, the insured must pay the premium unless the policy
contains an indemnity against such loss (as to which, see further para 45).

75. If the insured wins, the opponent will be liable to pay the premium to the
extent that it is reasonable. If some part of it is disallowed as unreasonable,
the insured will suffer the shortfall unless, again, he has some indemnity against
such loss (as to which, see further para 46).

76. Several interested parties have pointed out that the solicitor cannot or, at
any rate, should not make any offer to cover any shortfall or loss on premium
since to do so would breach the indemnity principle. A breach of the indemnity
principle would endanger the recovery of any sum of costs from an opposing
party.

77. It is appropriate to repeat here the submissions made by several interested
parties that one must not overlook the deleterious effect on most litigants which
an obligation to pay or finance any costs will have. Many litigants, including
those with strong claims, would be strongly disinclined to proceed if they had to
pay insurance premiums at the outset (most premiums are funded by disbursement

a loans) or if they had the risk of paying them or part of them later (see further para 45).

CONCLUSIONS

78. The Court of Appeal directions which set up this inquiry stated that its purpose is 'to enable the Court of Appeal to give guidance in its judgment as to *b* the practice to be adopted in future when taking out [ATE] insurance [in RTA cases]'. In the light of the information and submissions which I have received I would respectfully recommend the Court of Appeal to consider what if any guidance to give on the following points. (a) Guidance upon the recoverability of the own cost element in a CFI policy (see paras 8, 31–34). (b) Whether, in future, further guidance should be published by the Senior Costs Judge after *c* arranging consultations with interested parties from time to time unless and until such guidance becomes unnecessary (see para 3(b)). (c) Guidance upon the recoverability of additional benefits included in ATE policies (see paras 31–34, 41–51). (d) Whether it is ever appropriate to reduce the amount claimed for ATE insurance because of the advertising policy of the ATE provider at the time the *d* policy was issued (see paras 59–63). (e) Whether to give guidance to costs judges and district judges now conducting detailed assessments in which claims are made for the recovery of ATE premiums (see below).

79. As to the conduct of detailed assessments I conclude by setting out the approach which I would recommend when determining the reasonableness of an ATE premium claimed in RTA proceedings. (a) The range of variation between *e* policies issued by different providers makes it inappropriate for the time being to think in terms of benchmarks for premiums. However, with more experience of cases, a judge may develop a sufficient feel to set individual benchmarks for policies issued by the major ATE providers (see para 23). (b) In the case of a standard 'off-the-peg' policy, a high limit of indemnity does not by itself indicate *f* that the receiving party paid too much (see para 30). (c) As a general rule the choice of an off-the-peg policy which covers all risks (eg an Accident Group policy) can be regarded as a reasonable choice even though other policies limited to RTA cases may have been cheaper (see para 15). (d) Recent history of the ATE insurance industry makes it reasonable to presume as a starting point that the premium charged is reasonable (subject to any necessary reductions to be *g* made) unless the contrary is shown (see para 19). (e) The premium to be allowed (subject to reasonableness) is the total premium paid or payable by the receiving party, not the pure underwriting risk premium (see para 53). (f) Reasonable sums paid as assessment fees and profit costs in respect of obtaining and complying with the ATE policy may also be recoverable (see para 56). (g) In proving the *h* reasonableness of a premium the receiving party only has to show that he made a reasonable choice. He does not have to show that he made the best choice (see para 61). (h) A paying party who claims that the premium claimed exceeds the maximum premium it was reasonable to pay at the time should make available to the court and the receiving party charts or tables from the relevant *j* issue of Litigation Funding or similar information (see para 11). (i) It may well be reasonable to take out ATE insurance before sending a letter before claim. Also, it is usually reasonable for an intending claimant to delay taking out ATE insurance until the defendant has given an indication whether the claim will be contested. The later the insurance is taken out the more expensive it is likely to be (see para 26). (j) A receiving party who purchased a policy the cost of which

lies at or above the top of the range of other polices available at the time of purchase should explain why (see para 17). (k) A high cost premium is easier to justify in cases in which the court has already held that a high success fee is reasonable (see para 17). (l) Consider what if any reductions should be made in respect of any irrecoverable elements in the premium (see paras 41–51). (m) In valuing any such reductions, adopt a broadbrush approach (see para 34(b)).

Annex 1

List of parties and interested parties who have made written submissions

1. Abbey Legal Protection Ltd
2. Accident Group Ltd
3. Amelans (solicitors for the respondent)
4. Association of Personal Injury Lawyers
5. Association of British Insurers
6. After The Event Insurers' Group
7. Beachcroft Wansbroughs (solicitors for the appellant)
8. Claims Direct Ltd
9. Christian Fisher (solicitors)
10. Deutsche Automobil Schutz Legal Expenses Insurance Ltd
11. Forum of Insurance Lawyers
12. Greystoke Legal Services
13. Keystone
14. Lawclub Legal Protection
15. The Law Society
16. Litigation Protection Ltd
17. National Insurance and Guarantee Corp plc
18. Saturn Professional Risks
19. Temple Legal Protection Ltd
20. X L Brockbank Ltd

Annex 2

List of parties and interested parties who attended the hearing on 6 July 2001

1. Abbey Legal Protection Ltd
2. Accident Group Ltd
3. Amelans (solicitors for the respondent)
4. Association of Personal Injury Lawyers
5. Association of British Insurers
6. After The Event Insurers' Group
7. Beachcroft Wansbroughs (solicitors for the appellant)
8. Claims Direct Ltd
9. Deutsche Automobil Schutz Legal Expenses Insurance Ltd
10. Forum of Insurance Lawyers
11. Greystoke Legal Services
12. Keystone
13. Lawclub Legal Protection
14. The Law Society

a

15. Litigation Protection Ltd
16. Temple Legal Protection Ltd
17. X L Brockbank Ltd

Annex 3

b

Full text of supplementary questions and further questions

Supplementary questions

c

(a) Does the 'many paying for the few' principle justify the spreading of premium costs: over all categories of personal injury claims? Over all cases which are borderline or stronger, without differentiating the strength of each case?

(b) Views are sought on premium protections, ie premium indemnity in respect of loss of claim and premium indemnity in respect of unsuccessful recovery of premium. The latter indemnity sometimes takes the form of a ring-fencing of damages. Should such costs be regarded as additional benefits

d

which are not recoverable against parties ordered to pay costs (cf *Dimond v Lovell* [2000] 2 All ER 897, [2000] 2 WLR 1121)?

(c) Which, if any, of the following should be regarded as additional benefits not recoverable from a party ordered to pay costs: interest payable or interest foregone because the payment of premium was deferred? Interest on other disbursement loans? If the answer to (a) is in the negative, the top slice of the

e

premium paid in an road traffic accident (RTA) case where the same premium applies to all categories of personal injury claim? If the answer to (a) is negative, the top slice of a premium payable in a strong case where the same premium applies to all claims, including borderline claims? Any right to increase cover in certain circumstances? Any premium loading because of the claims record of the

f

insured solicitor?

(d) What percentage of a premium is it fair to attribute to all or any of the benefits listed in (b) and (c) above?

(e) Views are sought upon referral fees, assessment fees and similar expenses. Are these properly regarded as part of the administrative costs of issuing policies?

g

Do they attract insurance premium tax (IPT)? Are they recoverable (subject to assessment) from an opposing party ordered to pay costs?

(f) Views are sought on commissions and other payments made to brokers and intermediaries which include heavy advertising costs. Given the growing market for policies without such payments, is the excess percentage irrecoverable

h

from an opposing party ordered to pay costs? If so, what percentage of the gross premium should be allowed: should it be assessed on a case by case basis, or should there be a percentage reduction (and if so what percentage) in all relevant cases?

(g) Is it appropriate for the court to fix guidelines as to the maximum premium recoverable in all RTA cases where the policy is taken out prior to 2001, and prior

j

to communicating with the proposed defendant or his insurer? If so, are the following guidelines appropriate: fast track £400, multi-track £800? (These figures are proposed as including IPT and the additional benefits described in (b) and (c) above, and it may therefore be appropriate to discount them accordingly. In any particular case, the guidelines may give way to the particular facts of that case.)

(h) If the answer to the first part of (g) is affirmative, what adjustment should
be made to the guidelines in each of the following circumstances: where the
policy relates to other categories of personal injury claim (eg employer liability
claims or slip and trip claims)? Where the policy is taken out in an RTA case after
the proposed defendant or his insurer has indicated that the claim is to be
contested? Where the policy is taken out in an non-RTA case after the proposed
defendant or his insurer has indicated that the claim is to be contested? Where
the policy includes own counsel's fees? Where the policy covers both sides' costs?

(i) Views differ as to whether it would be cheaper for the liability insurance
industry (in overall costs terms as opposed to costs per policy) if fewer policies
were issued at a stage later than the letter before claim stage. Is the economic
advantage of the liability insurance industry (rather than the individual defendant)
an appropriate factor to be taken into account?

Further questions for Claims Direct

(1) Of the 150,000 cases mentioned in your oral submissions, of such of them
as are Claims Direct cases, please classify them by percentage under the following
headings: RTA, slip and trip, injuries at work, occupational disease, clinical
negligence, other personal injury claims.

(2) With each classification, please further classify them into fast track cases
and multi-track cases.

(3) Does Claims Direct accept the submission that, in deciding what
percentage of a premium to allow in respect of expenses and commissions, the
court should have regard to the tables set out in the ABI Insurance Statistics Year
Book for 1989–1999 which are quoted in the draft report (para 25)?

(4) Is it correct to say that when Claims Direct introduced ring-fencing of
damages, it inflated all future premiums in order to off-set the additional burning
costs which the ring fencing would cause?

Further questions for the appellant

(1) Is it accepted that, to date, ATE insurance has not been profitable? Does
this indicate that the premiums charged may be too low?

(2) Is it accepted that many insurers (including Norwich Union) spend
substantial sums on advertising?

(3) Comments are sought on the submissions made orally by Anthony
Mowatt of Keystone that the decision of Judge Halbert in *Sarwar v Alam* (5 July 2001,
unreported) has significantly altered the dynamics of the legal expenses insurance
industry.

a # M (a minor) v Secretary of State for Social Security
[2001] UKHL 35

b HOUSE OF LORDS

LORD BINGHAM OF CORNHILL, LORD NICHOLLS OF BIRKENHEAD, LORD HOBHOUSE OF WOODBOROUGH, LORD MILLETT AND LORD SCOTT OF FOSCOTE

8 MAY, 5 JULY 2001

c *Social security – Disablement benefit – Entitlement – Disability living allowance – Transitional provisions – Appellant awarded disability living allowance for fixed period – New regulations imposing additional condition on entitlement – Appellant unable to satisfy new condition when making further claim for allowance – Regulations containing transitional provision – Whether transitional provision extending duration of claimant's entitlement to benefit beyond term for which it had been awarded – Social* *d* *Security (Persons From Abroad) Miscellaneous Amendments Regulations 1996, reg 12(3).*

The appellant, M, was a severely disabled nine-year old girl. She was born in Pakistan, but was brought to England by her parents in 1993 when she was one year old. In September 1993 she made a claim for disability living allowance. *e* Such an allowance could be awarded either for life or for a fixed period. M satisfied the conditions of residence and presence in Great Britain prescribed by reg 2 of the Social Security (Disability Living Allowance) Regulations 1991. In December 1993 an adjudication officer awarded her an allowance for a period of three years from 27 September 1993 to 26 September 1996. That benefit *f* automatically ceased to be payable at the expiration of the period. In February 1996 reg 4 of the Social Security (Persons From Abroad) Miscellaneous Amendments Regulations 1996 imposed an additional condition of entitlement to the allowance, namely that a claimant's right to reside or remain in Great Britain was not subject to any limitation or condition. M did not satisfy that condition because she had remained beyond the time limited by her leave to enter the United Kingdom. She *g* nevertheless made a claim in June 1996 to an allowance for a further period on the expiry of the award made in 1993. An adjudication officer ruled that M did not satisfy the additional condition imposed by reg 4 of the 1996 regulations and was accordingly not entitled to a further award. That decision was affirmed by another adjudication officer, but M's appeal was allowed by a social security *h* appeal tribunal on the ground that reg 12(3)[a] of the 1996 regulations applied to her claim. Regulation 12(3) provided that where, before the coming into force of the 1996 regulations, a person was receiving disability living allowance under the 1991 regulations, those regulations 'shall, until such time as his entitlement to that benefit is reviewed' under s 30 of the Social Security Administration Act 1992, *j* have effect as if reg 4 of the 1996 regulations had not been made. A social security commissioner, bound by a decision of the Court of Appeal, allowed the Chief Adjudication Officer's appeal, and the Court of Appeal subsequently dismissed M's appeal. On her appeal to the House of Lords, their Lordships were required to determine whether the 1991 regulations applied in their unamended form to a

---

a   Regulation 12, so far as material, is set out at [12], below

claim for disability living allowance made after the date on which the 1996   *a*
regulations came into force by a claimant who had been in receipt of the
allowance immediately before that date under an award for a fixed term which
had since expired.

Held – On its true construction, reg 12(3) of the 1996 regulations did not have the
effect of extending the amount or duration of a claimant's entitlement to benefit   *b*
beyond the amount or term for which it had been awarded. It preserved accrued
rights to benefit under awards which pre-dated the coming into force of the 1996
regulations, but it did not apply to new and repeat claims made after they came
into force. Such claims had to be decided in accordance with the circumstances
obtaining at the time of the new claim and any requirements imposed by the
regulations then in force. That the protection of reg 12(3) ceased on the expiry of   *c*
a fixed term award but continued indefinitely in the case of an award for life was
not an anomaly. In both cases it continued as long as it was needed to preserve
an accrued entitlement, but no longer. The words 'entitlement to that benefit'
referred to the benefit which the claimant was receiving immediately before the
1996 regulations came into force. Transitional provisions such as reg 12(3),   *d*
which came to an end on a specific date or on the occurrence of a specific event,
were sometimes adopted for reasons of administrative convenience rather than
in the interests of claimants. Such provisions enabled the administrative burden
of processing the change to be staggered. Accordingly, the appeal would be
dismissed (see [4]–[6], [25]–[28], [30]–[32], below).

R v Chief Adjudication Officer, ex p B [1999] 1 WLR 1695 approved.   *e*

Notes

For disability living allowance, see 44(2) *Halsbury's Laws* (4th edn reissue)
paras 102–103.

f

Cases referred to in opinions

Bank of Credit and Commerce International SA (in liq) v Ali [2001] UKHL 8, [2001]
   1 All ER 961, [2001] 2 WLR 735.

Maclaine Watson & Co Ltd v Dept of Trade and Industry, Re International Tin Council,
   Maclaine Watson & Co Ltd v International Tin Council, Maclaine Watson & Co Ltd   *g*
   v International Tin Council (No 2) [1988] 3 All ER 257, [1989] Ch 309, [1988]
   3 WLR 1159, CA.

R v Chief Adjudication Officer, ex p B [1999] 1 WLR 1695, CA.

Appeal   *h*

The appellant, M, proceeding by her father and litigation friend, appealed with
permission of the Appeal Committee of the House of Lords given on 4 October
2000 from the order of the Court of Appeal (Peter Gibson, Judge LJJ and Ferris J)
on 30 December 1999 dismissing her appeal from the social security commissioner
(Edward Jacobs) on 21 June 1999 allowing an appeal by the Chief Adjudication   *j*
Officer (for whom was substituted the Secretary of State for Social Security on
8 November 1999) from the decision of Burnley Social Security Appeal Tribunal
on 15 April 1997 allowing the appellant's appeal from the decision of an
adjudication officer on 31 October 1996 affirming on review the decision of
another adjudication officer on 16 August 1996 refusing her claim to disability

a living allowance from 27 September 1996. The facts are set out in the opinion of Lord Millett.

Andrew Nicol QC and *Simon Cox* (instructed by *Luqmani Thompson*) for the appellant.
Richard Drabble QC (instructed by the *Solicitor to the Department of Social Security*)
b for the Secretary of State.

Their Lordships took time for consideration.

5 July 2001. The following opinions were delivered.
c
LORD BINGHAM OF CORNHILL.

[1] My Lords, I have had the advantage of reading in draft the opinion of my noble and learned friend Lord Millett, and gratefully adopt his summary of the relevant facts and submissions.

d [2] Disability benefit is paid out of public funds to those who are severely disabled. The applicant's condition was such that she qualified for and received this benefit. Regulation 4 of the Social Security (Persons from Abroad) Miscellaneous Amendments Regulations 1996, SI 1996/30, introduced a new condition of eligibility for payment of the grant, relating not to an applicant's medical need for assistance but to an applicant's immigration status. The introduction of this new
e condition plainly presented the draftsman with a question to be resolved: how was the new immigration condition to be applied to recipients currently in receipt of the benefit who did not meet the new condition?

[3] One answer would have been to provide that those in receipt of the benefit when the new condition came into effect should continue to be eligible to receive
f it, whether they met the new condition or not, so long as their medical need for assistance persisted. This solution would have had the humanitarian advantage that benefit would not be withdrawn from those who continued to need it on medical grounds and had received it in the past and might have come to depend on it. This is, in effect, the solution which the applicant says was adopted. Another answer would have been to provide that existing recipients should
g continue to be eligible until the period (whether fixed or indefinite) of their current grants of benefit expired or they ceased to need the grant on medical grounds, whichever might be sooner. This solution would have served the ends of greater economy and uniformity. It is, in effect, the solution which the Secretary of State says was adopted. Whatever the answer favoured by the draftsman it
h should not have been hard to express it with enough clarity to avoid argument.

[4] The diversity of opinion among members of the social security appeal tribunal in this case and the Court of Appeal, in the earlier case of *R v Chief Adjudication Officer, Ex p B* [1999] 1 WLR 1695, culminating in this appeal to the House, unhappily shows that such clarity was not achieved. I am not for my part
j persuaded that the Secretary of State's construction favoured by all my noble and learned friends is clearly correct; but equally I find no clear indication that the applicant's construction is to be preferred, and the Secretary of State's construction is somewhat more consistent with the language used. With some misgiving, therefore, and considerable sympathy for the applicant, I am prepared to agree that the decision in *Ex p B* should be affirmed and this appeal dismissed.

LORD NICHOLLS OF BIRKENHEAD.

[5] My Lords, I have had the advantage of reading in draft the speech of my noble and learned friend Lord Millett. For the reasons he gives, and with which I agree, I too would dismiss this appeal.

LORD HOBHOUSE OF WOODBOROUGH.

[6] My Lords, I have had the advantage of reading in draft the speech which my noble and learned friend Lord Millett is about to deliver. I agree that the appeal should be dismissed for the reasons which he has given.

LORD MILLETT.

[7] My Lords, the appellant is a severely disabled child aged nine. She was born in Pakistan and was brought here by her parents in 1993 when she was one year old. She lives with her parents in Lancashire.

[8] On 8 September 1993 she made a claim for disability living allowance. She satisfied the conditions of residence and presence in Great Britain currently prescribed by reg 2 of the Social Security (Disability Living Allowance) Regulations 1991, SI 1991/2890 (the principal regulations). On 16 December 1993 an adjudication officer of the Department of Social Security awarded her an allowance for a period of three years from 27 September 1993 to 26 September 1996.

[9] On 5 February 1996 reg 4 of the Social Security (Persons From Abroad) Miscellaneous Amendments Regulations 1996, SI 1996/30 (the amending regulations) imposed an additional condition of entitlement to the allowance. This required that a claimant's right to reside or remain in Great Britain be not subject to any limitation or condition. The appellant did not satisfy this condition because she had remained beyond the time limited by her leave to enter the United Kingdom. The relevant conditions are now contained in reworded but substantially identical form in s 115 of the Immigration and Asylum Act 1999 which came into force on 3 April 2000. The appellant and her parents were granted indefinite leave to remain in the United Kingdom on 19 July 2000. The appellant thus now satisfies the conditions of the allowance but has done so only since 19 July 2000. The present dispute concerns her entitlement to the allowance between 27 September 1996 and 18 July 2000.

[10] On 7 June 1996 in anticipation of the expiry of the current award the appellant made a claim to an allowance for a further period. On 16 August 1996 an adjudication officer ruled that the appellant did not satisfy the additional condition imposed by reg 4 of the amending regulations and was accordingly not entitled to a further award. On 31 October 1996 another adjudication officer reviewed the decision but affirmed it.

[11] The appellant's appeal was allowed by a social security appeal tribunal (by a majority) on the ground that reg 12(3) of the amending regulations applied to her claim. On 21 June 1999 a Social Security Commissioner, bound by a decision of the majority of the Court of Appeal (Peter Gibson and Schiemann LJJ, Simon Brown LJ dissenting) in *R v Chief Adjudication Officer, Ex p B* [1999] 1 WLR 1695, allowed the appeal of the adjudication officer and restored his decision of 31 October 1996. The Court of Appeal formally dismissed the appellant's appeal from the decision of the Social Security Commissioner.

[12] The present appeal is thus effectively an appeal from the decision of the Court of Appeal in *Ex p B*. It turns on the true construction of reg 12(3) of the amending regulations. Omitting words which relate to other benefits this reads as follows:

a   'Where, before the coming into force of these Regulations, a person is receiving ... disability living allowance ... under ... the ... Disability Living Allowance Regulations ... those Regulations shall, until such time as his entitlement to that benefit is reviewed under section ... 30 of the Social Security Administration Act 1992, have effect as if regulation ... 4 ... of these Regulations had not been made.'

b   The question for decision is whether the principal regulations apply in their unamended form to a claim to disability living allowance made after the date on which the amending regulations came into force by a claimant who was in receipt of the allowance immediately before that date under an award for a fixed term which has since expired.

c   [13] In order that the context in which this question arises may be understood, it is necessary to give a brief description of the structure of the benefit system. Disability living allowance is a non-contributory, non-means-tested benefit for the severely disabled. It comprises two components: a care component and a mobility allowance. Like most benefits, it is calculated at a weekly rate and is d   normally paid weekly. Section 1 of the Social Security Administration Act 1992 provides that (with exceptions which are not material) no person is entitled to any benefit (including disability living allowance) unless he is eligible for such benefit and makes a claim for it in the manner and at the time prescribed by regulations. Save in special circumstances, therefore, every entitlement to benefit is preceded by a claim.

e   [14] A successful claim results in a decision of an adjudication officer under which the claimant is entitled to receive benefit for the duration of the award. In the case of disability living allowance the award must be either for life or for a fixed period (see s 71(2) of the Social Security Contributions and Benefits Act 1992). In the present case it was for a fixed period of three years. Benefit awarded for a f   fixed period automatically ceases to be payable at the expiration of the period. A claimant who wishes to continue to receive benefit after the expiry of the period for which it was awarded must make a further claim and seek a fresh award on that claim. If he is to avoid any discontinuity in the receipt of benefit, he must make the claim before the expiry of the current award.

g   [15] A claimant may also cease to be entitled to benefit if the decision under which it is payable is reviewed pursuant to a statutory provision to that effect. In the case of disability living allowance, s 30(2) of the 1992 Act makes provision for a decision to be reviewed on specified grounds. These include the case where the award was made in ignorance of, or was based on a mistake as to, some material fact; or where there has been any relevant change of circumstances since the h   decision was made; or the decision was erroneous in point of law. At one time the Department took the view that the coming into force of the amending regulations was a change of circumstances capable of justifying a review, but when leave was given to challenge this by judicial review the Department conceded the point. As Simon Brown LJ explained in Ex p B [1999] 1 WLR 1695 j   at 1699, this was not because a change in the law could not be a relevant change of circumstances: it normally would be. It was because reg 12(3) operated to disapply reg 4 only until review, the coming into force of reg 4 could not therefore itself constitute a ground for review.

[16] It is hardly necessary to observe that only a current award is capable of being reviewed. There is neither need nor power to review an award under which the benefit has ceased to be payable by effluxion of time. If the claimant

wishes to continue to receive benefit and makes a further claim, it will be the subject of a fresh determination by reference to the circumstances at the time of the new claim.

[17] After these preliminaries, I turn to reg 12(3) of the amending regulations. It is in three parts: (i) a pre-condition ('Where, before the coming into force of these Regulations, a person is receiving ... disability living allowance ... under ... Disability Living Allowance Regulations'); (ii) an operative part ('those Regulations shall ... have effect as if regulation ... 4 ... of these Regulations had not been made'); and (iii) a cessation provision ('until such time as his entitlement to that benefit is reviewed under section ... 30 of the Social Security Administration Act 1992').

[18] The whole of reg 12 comes under the heading 'Saving'. It contains three paragraphs each of which deals with a different situation. Each takes as its starting point the claimant's position 'before the coming into force of these Regulations', but thereafter the preconditions diverge in matters of detail. Paragraph (1) is concerned with the position of an asylum seeker who was entitled to benefit before the amending regulations came into force, para (2) with the position of a claimant who had made a claim to or was receiving certain specified benefits, and para (3) with a claimant who was receiving other specified benefits. All three paragraphs provide in their operative part that the principal regulations shall apply as if the amending regulations had not been made, but only para (3) contains a cessation provision.

[19] The Court of Appeal considered, rightly in my view, that paras (1) and (2) were of limited assistance in deciphering the meaning of para (3). The most that can be said is that reg 12 is a saving provision which preserves existing entitlements but subject to different preconditions and for different periods in different factual situations. But for reg 12(3), reg 4 would disqualify claimants who were in receipt of disability living allowance when the amending regulations came into force of their entitlement to the allowance. Regulation 12(3) has the effect of disapplying reg 4 in the case of every such claimant until (if ever) his case is reviewed.

[20] It is not easy to discern the policy which dictated that reg 12(3) should cease to have effect on the occasion of a review, whatever the purpose of the review and irrespective of its outcome. As Schiemann LJ observed, this can produce results which appear to be capricious. A review can be initiated by the claimant or by the Department. It can lead to a withdrawal of benefit, but it can also lead to an increase, a reduction or no change in the benefit payable. In the case of a review which resulted in the adjudication officer declining to make any change, the mere fact of the review would deprive someone in receipt of benefit of the protection of reg 12(3) and result in the withdrawal of benefit even though there was no change in his circumstances. In the case of a person with an award for life, the effect could be very significant. Moreover, as the appellant observed, where the review would have resulted in the withdrawal of benefit under the principal regulations in their unamended form, it would cease to be payable irrespective of the application of reg 4. Thus reg 12(3) has effective operation only in a case where the review would otherwise have upheld the claimant's entitlement in whole or part.

[21] The appellant contends that the effect of reg 12(3) is that the principal regulations apply in their unamended form not only to the benefit payable under the award made before the amending regulations came into force but also, in the case of a person who was in receipt of benefit at that date, to a claim for a further award made after that date. She says that this is the effect of the regulation

according to its natural and ordinary meaning. She submits that: (i) she satisfies the precondition in that she was in receipt of disability living allowance immediately before the amending regulations came into force; (ii) the operative part provides that the principal regulations have effect as regards her in their unamended form; (iii) the cessation provision can be disregarded because there has been no review of her entitlement to disability living allowance under s 30; (iv) her application for further benefit ought therefore to have been processed under the principal regulations in their unamended form. The argument has an attractive simplicity, and for the most part is not disputed. The Department accepts that the appellant satisfies the precondition and that there has been no review of her entitlement to benefit. But the logic of the appellant's argument depends on the insertion of the words 'as regards her' in proposition (ii) which do not appear in the regulation itself. That some words need to be implied is not in doubt; but the Department does not accept that 'as regards her' represent the appropriate reading of the regulation.

[22] I would start with the evident purpose of reg 12. As its heading shows, it is a saving or transitional provision. Each of the paragraphs begins with the words 'Where, before the coming into force of these Regulations'. It is common ground that these words are not to be taken literally. They are to be understood as meaning 'immediately before', not 'at any time before'. Regulation 12 is concerned to save or preserve accrued rights to benefit to which the claimant was entitled immediately before the amending regulations came into force.

[23] The fact that reg 12 cannot be read literally in this respect does not, of course, mean that the court is at liberty to depart from the ordinary meaning of the words of the regulation in other respects (see *Bank of Credit and Commerce International SA (in liq) v Ali* [2001] UKHL 8 at [63]–[65], [2001] 1 All ER 961 at [63]–[65], [2001] 2 WLR 735 per Lord Hoffmann). But it does at least serve as a warning that the regulation is drafted in an elliptical style and that its general words are not necessarily to be given their fullest meaning and applied to every case which falls within their literal scope regardless of the context and the object of the regulation (see *Maclaine Watson & Co Ltd v Dept of Trade and Industry, Re International Tin Council, Maclaine Watson & Co Ltd v International Tin Council, Maclaine Watson & Co Ltd v International Tin Council (No 2)* [1988] 3 All ER 257 at 360–361, [1989] Ch 309 at 329–330).

[24] The appellant was in receipt of disability living allowance immediately before the amending regulations came into force. Accordingly, she satisfied the precondition; she possessed accrued rights which it was the purpose of the regulation to preserve. The difficulty is in relation to the operative part, and it is convenient to consider that part in the first instance without reference to the cessation provision.

[25] The material words of the operative part are 'those Regulations shall ... have effect as if regulation ... 4 ... of these Regulations had not been made'. Once again, this is couched in general terms which plainly cannot be taken absolutely literally. Regulation 4 is not disapplied generally. It is not, for example, disapplied in the case of other claimants. Recognising this, the appellant (in her printed case) reads in the words 'as regards [the claimant]'. But this is not enough. Regulation 4 is not disapplied in respect of every benefit to which the claimant may be entitled. In oral argument the appellant narrowed the expression still further by reading in the words 'as regards disability living allowance'. That is better, but in my opinion it is still not enough. The extent of the disapplication must be derived from the terms of the precondition and the evident purpose of the regulation. These limit it to the particular claimant's accrued right to the

particular benefit which she was receiving immediately before the amending
regulations came into force. In the case of the appellant, that was a right to *a*
disability living allowance under an award which entitled her to receive disability
living allowance of a stated amount for a stated period of three years. That was
the full extent of the appellant's accrued entitlement which it was the purpose of
reg 12(3) to save, and in my opinion reg 4 is disapplied only as regards that
entitlement.   *b*

[26] Accordingly, even without the cessation provision, I would hold that
reg 12(3) does not have the effect of extending the amount or duration of a
claimant's entitlement to benefit beyond the amount or term for which it was
awarded. I agree with Peter Gibson LJ in *Ex p B* [1999] 1 WLR 1695 at 1706, where
he said:
                                                                            c
'I do not regard it as a serious anomaly that, on the contention which
I favour, the protection of regulation 12(3) will cease with the expiry of an
award for a fixed period whereas it will continue until death, whenever that
occurs, in the case of an award for life. It is characteristic of transitional relief
that it preserves entitlements existing at the date when the measure comes
into force. It would be uncharacteristic of transitional relief to extend such *d*
relief to new rights coming into existence after the coming into force of the
measure.'

This passage has been criticised on the ground that transitional relief comes in so
many different forms that it is impossible to generalise. But there is no need to
do so. The heading to reg 12 and the terms of the precondition are sufficient to *e*
identify the purpose of the regulation as the saving (and not the enlargement) of
accrued rights. In my opinion there is no anomaly (not merely no serious
anomaly) that the protection of reg 12(3) ceases on the expiry of a fixed term
award but continues indefinitely in the case of an award for life. In both cases it
continues as long as it is needed to preserve an accrued entitlement but no longer. *f*

[27] If there were any remaining doubts on this score they would be laid to
rest by the terms of the cessation provision. This provides that the protection of
reg 12(3) shall continue 'until ... his entitlement to that benefit is reviewed' under
the appropriate section of the 1992 Act. In the Court of Appeal Peter Gibson LJ
held that the words 'entitlement to that benefit' referred to the benefit which the
claimant was receiving immediately before the amending regulations came into *g*
force. The appellant disputed this interpretation, contending that the words
'entitlement to that benefit' merely served to identify the particular benefit, in
this case disability living allowance, rather than the other benefits referred to
in reg 12(3).

[28] I consider that Peter Gibson LJ's construction is correct. Strictly speaking *h*
it is the decision under which the claimant's entitlement arises which falls to be
reviewed, so this is another example of elliptical drafting. The words 'his entitlement
to that benefit' must be understood as a reference to the decision under which the
claimant's entitlement to the particular benefit arose. This brings the cessation
provision into line with the precondition; they are both concerned with the *j*
preservation of accrued rights under an existing award which predated the
coming into force of the amending regulations, but which is subject to review.

[29] I think that too much may be made of the seeming capriciousness of the
cessation provision. A claimant who needs to rely on reg 12(3) will not, if well
advised, seek a review however meritorious his claim to an increase in benefit;
while the Department is unlikely to seek a review unless there is some evidence

a to support the withdrawal or reduction of benefit currently payable. In most cases, therefore, reg 12(3) will cease to apply only when there is some reason to suppose that there has been a change of circumstances which justifies withdrawal of benefit in whole or part. Even where the adjudication officer decides that no change is warranted, his decision is based on the circumstances at the date of the review and not at the date of the original decision; so it is not unreasonable to

b regard it as if it were a decision on a new claim. I agree with Mr Commissioner Rowland in case CFC/1580/1997 (para 34) (which concerned the effect of reg 12(3) on a repeat claim to family credit) when he said: 'It really is quite inconceivable that it should have been intended that the transitional protection should be lost on a review but not on a repeat claim.' For my part I think that the draftsman's thinking was probably the other way round. The preservation of accrued rights

c did not justify their enlargement by disapplying reg 4 to new and repeat claims, and a decision on a review could properly be equated with a decision on a repeat claim.

[30] As the Twelfth Report of the Social Security Advisory Committee (May 1997–March 1999) observed, transitional provisions like the present which

d come to an end on a specific date or on the occurrence of a specific event, such as the renewal of a claim or a change of relevant circumstances, are sometimes adopted for reasons of administrative convenience rather than in the interests of claimants. Such provisions enable the administrative burden of processing the change to be staggered. The introduction of a new 'habitual residence' requirement for income-related benefits, for example, applied only where a claim for income

e support was made or treated as made after the coming into force of the amendment, ie to new and repeat claims (see reg 4(2) of the Income-related Benefits Schemes (Miscellaneous Amendments) (No 3) Regulations 1994, SI 1994/1807). In my opinion reg 12(3) has similar effect: it preserves accrued rights to benefit under awards which pre-dated the coming into force of the amending regulations but it

f does not apply to new and repeat claims made after they came into force. Such claims must be decided in accordance with the circumstances obtaining at the time of the new claim and any requirements imposed by the regulations then in force.

[31] I would affirm the decision in *Ex p B*, and dismiss the appeal.

LORD SCOTT OF FOSCOTE.

[32] My Lords, for the reasons given in the opinion of my noble and learned friend, Lord Millett, with which I agree, I too would dismiss this appeal.

Appeal dismissed.

Celia Fox   Barrister.

Cork (as trustee in bankruptcy for Rawlins) v Rawlins

[2001] EWCA Civ 202

COURT OF APPEAL, CIVIL DIVISION

PETER GIBSON, CHADWICK AND KEENE LJJ

2 FEBRUARY 2001

Insolvency – Bankrupt's estate – Vesting in trustee – Assurance policy – Permanent disablement benefit – Appellant taking out life assurance policies containing provision for earlier payment on receipt of proof of permanent disability – Appellant suffering permanent disablement and making claims under policies – Appellant being made bankrupt – Policy provider accepting claims – Appellant's trustee in bankruptcy claiming policy moneys – Whether policy moneys belonging to bankrupt if contractual claim to them relying on bankrupt's pain and suffering.

The appellant, R, obtained two loans, totalling £70,000, to fund the building of a bungalow. In order to ensure that the loans would be repaid in the event of his death or disability, R took out two assurance policies—a whole life policy and a policy maturing on the expiry of a term of years. Both policies provided for earlier payment, on receipt of proof that R was permanently disabled, of the sum which would otherwise have been payable on his death or on the expiry of the contractual term. Permanent disability was defined as a disability that prevented the assured from carrying out any gainful occupation at any time. R sustained a serious injury that prevented him from working, and he duly made a claim under the policies. He had no claim against anyone else in relation to the accident. Subsequently, R was made bankrupt. Shortly afterwards, R's claim for permanent disablement benefit under both polices was accepted, and a sum of £70,000 became payable. Since the loans had already been repaid from the proceeds of the sale of the bungalow, the policy moneys were no longer required to discharge them. In subsequent proceedings, R's trustee in bankruptcy claimed that he was entitled to the policy moneys. The judge upheld that claim and R appealed, contending that the policy moneys went to the bankrupt, not to his creditors, if the contractual claim to those moneys relied in any way on the bankrupt's pain and suffering. In so contending, he relied by analogy on the common law principle that damages for pain and suffering did not form part of the bankrupt's estate available for distribution to his creditors.

Held – The common law exception from the bankrupt's estate did not include an asset whose only connection with the pain and suffering of the bankrupt was the fact that his disablement was the contractual contingency on which the moneys assured had become payable. The contention to the contrary was not founded directly on any authority, and no assistance was to be found in the suggested analogy between a tortious claim for damages for pain and suffering and a contractual claim for moneys payable under policies of insurance. In the instant case, the policies were assets purchased by R through the payment of premiums which otherwise would have formed part of his estate available for his creditors on his bankruptcy, just as they were available immediately before his bankruptcy commenced, to be disposed of by R for value or seized by his creditors in a execution. It would be surprising if the recognition after the bankruptcy order of R's claim to permanent disablement benefit arising from an accident prior to the bankruptcy made so material a change to the nature of the asset that it no longer was to form part of the bankrupt's estate. In any event, the policy moneys had become payable not because of the satisfaction of a test of pain and suffering, but because of the contractual test of 'employability'. The policy moneys did not

b relate to or represent or compensate for loss or damage to the bankrupt personally, and were not measured by such loss or damage. If the bankrupt's death had been a condition on which the policy moneys became payable, they would have been taken by the trustee. As it was, the payment had merely been triggered by the permanent disablement being proved. Moreover, the right to payment had been purchased so as to provide for the discharge of R's indebtedness to a particular

c creditor who had been paid out of other moneys which would otherwise have come into the bankrupt's estate. In those circumstances, there was no hardship in requiring that the right to payment fell into the estate for the benefit of creditors generally. Accordingly, the appeal would be dismissed (see [25]–[30], [36], [41], [43], [44], below).

d   *Beckham v Drake* (1849) 2 HL Cas 579 applied.
       Ord v Upton (as trustee to the property of Ord) [2000] 1 All ER 193 distinguished.

Notes
For rights of action forming part of the bankrupt's estate, see 3(2) *Halsbury's Laws* (4th edn reissue) para 415.

e

Cases referred to in judgments
Beckham v Drake (1849) 2 HL Cas 579, 9 ER 1213, HL.
Bradburn v Great Western Rly Co (1874) LR 10 Exch 1, [1874–80] All ER Rep 195.
Haig v Aitken [2000] 3 All ER 80, [2001] Ch 110, [2000] 3 WLR 1117.

f *Heath v Tang, Stevens v Peacock* [1993] 4 All ER 694, [1993] 1 WLR 1421, CA.
Ord v Upton (as trustee to the property of Ord) [2000] 1 All ER 193, [2000] Ch 352, [2000] 2 WLR 755, CA.
Parry v Cleaver [1969] 1 All ER 555, [1970] AC 1, [1969] 2 WLR 821, HL.
Rae, Re [1995] BCC 102.

g *Wilson v United Counties Bank Ltd* [1920] AC 102, [1918–19] All ER Rep 1035, HL.

Cases also cited or referred to in skeleton arguments
Campbell (a bankrupt), Re [1996] 2 All ER 537, [1997] Ch 14.
Celtic Extraction Ltd (in liq), Re, Bluestone Chemicals Ltd (in liq), Re [1999] 4 All ER

h 684, [2001] Ch 475, CA.
Cohen (a bankrupt), Re, ex p the bankrupt v Trustee of the property of the bankrupt, ex p Trustee of the property of the bankrupt v the bankrupt [1961] 1 All ER 646, [1961] Ch 246, CA.
Cooke v Gill (1873) LR 8 CP 107.
Glenister v Rowe [1999] 3 All ER 452, [2000] Ch 76, CA.

j *Hussain v New Taplow Paper Mills Ltd* [1988] 1 All ER 541, [1988] AC 514, HL.
Kilvert v Flackett [1998] BPIR 721.
Krasner v Dennison, Lawrence v Lesser [2000] 3 All ER 234, [2001] Ch 76, CA.
Landau (a bankrupt), Re, Pointer v Landau [1997] 3 All ER 322, [1998] Ch 223.
Letang v Cooper [1964] 2 All ER 929, [1965] 1 QB 232, CA.
Morris v Morgan [1998] BPIR 764, CA.

Paragon Finance plc v D B Thakerar & Co (a firm), Paragon Finance plc v Thimbleby &
    Co (a firm) [1999] 1 All ER 400, CA.   *a*
Rayatt (a bankrupt), Re [1998] BPIR 495.
Smith v Lock (a bankrupt) [1998] BPIR 786.
Supperstone v Lloyd's Names Association Working Party [1999] BPIR 832.
Tennant's Application, Re [1956] 2 All ER 753, [1956] 1 WLR 874, CA.

                                                                                             b
Appeal
By notice dated 22 June 2000, Alan James Rawlins appealed with permission of
Judge Weeks QC from his decision, sitting as a judge of the High Court at
Bristol District Registry on 7 April 2000 ([2000] BPIR 654), granting an application
by Mr Rawlins' trustee in bankruptcy, Malcolm Ellis Cork, for a declaration that
sums payable under policies held by Mr Rawlins with Abbey Life Assurance Co Ltd   *c*
had vested in the trustee under s 306 of the Insolvency Act 1986. The facts are set
out in the judgment of Peter Gibson LJ.

Louis Doyle (instructed by *Freeth Cartwright*, Nottingham) for Mr Rawlins.
Stephen Davies QC (instructed by *Osborne Clarke*, Bristol) for the trustee.   *d*

GIBSON LJ.
    [1] This is an appeal by Alan Rawlins, the respondent to an application made
under s 303(2) of the Insolvency Act 1986 by his trustee in bankruptcy, Malcolm Cork.
On 7 April 2000 Judge Weeks QC, sitting as a judge of the High Court in the   *e*
Chancery Division, declared at the hearing of that application that the sums
payable under two assurance policies effected by Mr Rawlins with Abbey Life
Assurance Co Ltd before he became bankrupt became vested in the trustee
pursuant to s 306 of the 1986 Act. The judge gave Mr Rawlins permission to
appeal. The judge's judgment is now reported (at [2000] BPIR 654), and I need
only state such of the background facts as are necessary to make this judgment   *f*
comprehensible.
    [2] Of the two policies, one, called a Living Assurance policy, commenced on
9 October 1987. It was a whole life policy on Mr Rawlins' life and provided for
earlier payment 'on receipt by [Abbey Life] of proof satisfactory to [Abbey Life's]
Chief Medical Officer that the Life Assured had become disabled such that   *g*
entitlement arises to the Permanent Disablement Benefit.' That benefit was 'a
benefit equivalent to the Death Benefit payable if the Life Assured had died on the
date of receipt of such satisfactory proof'. The sum payable was £40,000. The
entitlement to permanent disablement benefit was expressed to arise 'if the Life
Assured has become permanently disabled before his ... 60th birthday through   *h*
sickness or injury contracted after the Commencement Date and is registered
as disabled'. The other policy, called a MortgageMaster Endowment policy,
commenced on 12 November 1990. It had a 23-year term but it provided for
earlier payment on the same contingency as the earlier policy. The sum payable
was £30,000. Thus in the case of the first policy the sum assured did not change,
whether the event on which the sum was payable was the death or the proof of   *j*
disablement. Similarly, in the case of the other policy, the sum assured was the
same whether it became payable at the end of the contractual term or on the
earlier receipt of proof of disablement.
    [3] Mr Rawlins was a self-employed landscape gardener and also carried on a
retail shop business. He specialised in the construction and sale of water features
and ornamental pools. In January 1993 he had an accident whilst engaged in

construction work and sustained a serious injury. He was unable to continue working. He submitted a claim under the policies to Abbey Life in the summer of 1993. On 2 April 1996 a bankruptcy order was made against him on the petition of a trade creditor. On 19 June 1996 he allowed himself to be examined medically for the purpose of his policies. On 16 September 1996 Abbey Life accepted that it had received proof of disablement such that entitlement to the permanent disablement benefit arose under both policies.

[4] On the making of the bankruptcy order the official receiver became the trustee, but Mr Cork was appointed trustee in his place on 4 March 1997. On 27 May 1997 Abbey Life by letter informed the trustee that it accepted that Mr Rawlins was permanently disabled and that £70,000 in total was available to be claimed. The trustee's solicitors on 3 April 1998 wrote asking whether the payment of £70,000 related to compensation for loss of earnings or for pain and suffering. On 27 April 1998 Abbey Life replied:

'The £70,000.00 benefit is neither compensation for loss of earnings nor compensation for pain and suffering. Mr Rawlins purchased life assurance policies with a supplementary sickness benefit attached to the same. The total and permanent disability benefit provides to pay the full sums assured in the event of our Chief Medical Officer being satisfied that the claimant is disabled such that he will never work in any occupation for the remainder of his lifetime. Our Chief Medical Officer was satisfied that Mr Rawlins' medical condition met [these] criteria.'

[5] The trustee claimed that he was entitled to the policy moneys. Mr Rawlins disputed that claim. The trustee therefore made the application which came before the judge. Mr Rawlins was then represented by counsel other than Mr Louis Doyle who appears for Mr Rawlins on this appeal.

[6] The judge first considered whether the rights to the policy moneys were properly comprised in the bankrupt's estate which vested in the trustee. The judge held that the contract between Mr Rawlins and Abbey Life in relation to each policy created one right or bundle of rights which he could have assigned before his bankruptcy and which vested in the official receiver on his bankruptcy. The judge then considered whether the benefits of each policy, or any of them, were to be held for Mr Rawlins. The judge accepted that the events on which the policy moneys were payable included his permanent disablement, which was likely to involve him in pain and suffering. But he said that the moneys payable under the policies were not in any way related or calculated by reference to Mr Rawlins' pain and suffering and that all that permanent disablement did was to advance the date on which the policy moneys were payable. The judge therefore held that the moneys were payable only to the trustee to be divided among the creditors and that no part of them was held by the trustee for Mr Rawlins.

[7] Mr Rawlins on this appeal wishes to challenge the judge's conclusion. He initially acted in person and he has made plain in the various documents which he has submitted to this court his extreme unhappiness with the result. He objects strongly to being denied the policy moneys which might have supported him in coping with his disability, and he has put forward a large number of grounds on which he sought to appeal. But sensibly he has now entrusted this appeal to legal representatives for him.

[8] Mr Doyle in his skeleton argument advanced initially three grounds of appeal, but he has now abandoned two of them, that is to say the submission that

no cause of action existed at the date of the bankruptcy order and that therefore no property vested in the official receiver on the making of that order, and further that the proceeds of the policies constituted income within s 310(7) of the 1986 Act so as not to form property within the bankrupt's estate. In my judgment Mr Doyle was right not to pursue those submissions. That leaves a single ground of appeal, that is to say that the cause of action is personal to Mr Rawlins and did not vest in the trustee by virtue of the payment remaining conditional on his personal pain and suffering.

[9] Before considering that submission it is convenient to go to the relevant provisions of the 1986 Act. Mr Doyle asked us, when considering the statutory provisions, also to take account of the effects of social change since the older authorities were decided and since the Bankruptcy Act 1914 (such as the reforms pursuant to the Beveridge Committee Report and the reforms effected by Acts such as the Welfare Reform Pensions Act 1999). He asks us to take into account the recommendations set out by the Cork Committee in its *Report of the Review Committee on Insolvency Law and Practice* (Cmnd 8558 (1982)) (the Cork Report), the substantial implementation of which was effected by the 1986 Act, and he asks us to take into account the change in the approach adopted by Parliament in enacting it. For my part, I do not doubt that this court can look at the Cork Report to identify the mischief which that Act was intended to obviate, but the intention of Parliament falls to be ascertained primarily from the language used in the 1986 Act, and I cannot accept suggestions, based on other reforms in other fields, as to what was intended to be achieved by that Act. We were asked by Mr Doyle in particular to note from paras 192(a) and 198(c) (pp 53, 54) of the Cork Report that the objectives included: (i) to offer the opportunity for rehabilitation subject to making a contribution to creditors from future earnings without reducing the insolvent and his family to undue and socially unacceptable poverty and without depriving him of the incentive to succeed in a fresh start; and (ii) to relieve the insolvent from harassment and undue demands by creditors whilst taking into account the rights which the individual insolvent and his family should legitimately continue to enjoy.

[10] I have to say that neither of those objectives seem to me to be in point. The first relates to the rehabilitation of the insolvent so that he can earn moneys in the future and so repay creditors out of those earnings. The second relates to creditors harassing the insolvent and making undue demands. Neither seems to me to touch on the question whether an asset of this bankrupt, who cannot work again, in the form of a policy existing at the date of the bankruptcy order, is held for the benefit of creditors.

[11] A further passage from the Cork Report relied on by Mr Doyle is in para 195 (p 53–54), where, after a reference to the insolvency procedures which had been developed over generations, it is said:

'... but it appears to us equally that some of their original objectives and the principles which inspired them have been lost sight of or blurred and there has undoubtedly been in the last half century a failure to keep pace with the needs of our days.'

[12] That is a criticism of the previous insolvency procedures. But that does not seem to me to be in point on this appeal.

[13] The statutory provisions relevant to the issues on this appeal are as follows.

a

[14] Section 306 in Pt IX of the 1986 Act provides for the bankrupt's estate to vest in the trustee 'immediately on his appointment taking effect or, in the case of the official receiver, on his becoming trustee'.

[15] 'The bankrupt's estate' is defined in s 283:

b

'(1) Subject as follows, a bankrupt's estate for the purposes of any of this Group of Parts comprises—(a) all property belonging to or vested in the bankrupt at the commencement of the bankruptcy, and (b) any property which by virtue of any of the following provisions of this Part is comprised in that estate or is treated as falling within the preceding paragraph.

(2) Subsection (1) does not apply to—(a) such tools, books, vehicles and other items of equipment as are necessary to the bankrupt for use personally by him in his employment, business or vocation; (b) such clothing, bedding, furniture, household equipment and provisions as are necessary for satisfying the basic domestic needs of the bankrupt and his family.'

c

[16] Bankruptcy commences on the day on which the bankruptcy order is made (s 278).

d

[17] The term 'property' is given an expanded meaning in s 436:

'... "property" includes money, goods, things in action, land and every description of property wherever situated and also obligations and every description of interest, whether present or future or vested or contingent, arising out of, or incidental to, property ...'

e

[18] Section 307 deals with after-acquired property which the trustee may by notice in writing claim for the bankrupt's estate, that is to say any property which has been acquired by, or has devolved upon, the bankrupt since the commencement of the bankruptcy. But by s 307(5) excluded therefrom is any property which, as part of the bankrupt's income, may be the subject of an income payments order under s 310.

f

[19] Section 310 relates to an income payments order which may be made by the court on the application of the trustee, claiming for the bankrupt's estate so much of the income of the bankrupt during the period for which the order is in force as may be specified in the order.

g

[20] I now turn to Mr Doyle's submission on the footing, as he now accepts, that the rights under each policy vested in the trustee on the commencement of the bankruptcy and that that gave rise to an indivisible claim against Abbey Life.

[21] Mr Doyle submits that the payment of moneys under the policies being conditional on Mr Rawlins' personal disability was therefore conditional on Mr Rawlins' personal pain and suffering, and that, he argues, takes those moneys

h

outside the bankrupt's estate. He suggested that the moneys were intended as a replacement of income. But as he concedes that they do not come within s 310, even if he was right on this characterisation, which I doubt, I do not see how it helps him. Mr Doyle relies on what might be called the common law exception from the statutory definition of 'property' within a bankrupt's estate. Despite the 1986 Act and the wide definition of property, it has been recognised at least twice

j

by this court that an exception exists. In *Heath v Tang, Stevens v Peacock* [1993] 4 All ER 694, [1993] 1 WLR 1421, Hoffmann LJ, when giving the judgment of the court (which included Bingham MR and Steyn LJ), referred to the extended meaning given to 'property' in s 436, and said:

'Despite the breadth of this definition, there are certain causes of action personal to the bankrupt which do not vest in his trustee. These include cases in which—"the damages are to be estimated by immediate reference to pain felt by the bankrupt in respect of his body, mind, or character, and without immediate reference to his rights and property." (See *Beckham v Drake* (1849) 2 HL Cas 579 at 604, 9 ER 1213 at 1222 per Erle J. See also *Wilson v United Counties Bank Ltd* [1920] AC 102, [1918–19] All ER Rep 1035.) Actions for defamation and assault are obvious examples.' (See [1993] 4 All ER 694 at 697, [1993] 1 WLR 1421 at 1423.)

[22] The authorities were recently reviewed by this court in *Ord v Upton* (*as trustee to the property of Ord*) [2000] 1 All ER 193, [2000] Ch 352. In that case a bankrupt after the bankruptcy order issued a writ against a doctor who had treated him before the bankruptcy order, claiming damages for negligence, including damages for pain and suffering as well as damages for loss of earnings. Aldous LJ (with whom Kennedy and Mantell LJJ agreed) referred to some further remarks of Erle J in *Beckham v Drake* (1849) 2 HL Cas 579 at 608–609, 9 ER 1213 at 1224, where the reason for the exception from the property of the bankrupt of certain items was said to be—

'that the creditors cannot legitimately have looked to the pain of the bankrupt from a broken limb, or wounded affection, or blasted character, as a source of profit, they being in their nature casual and unforeseen, and unconnected immediately with property. There is a manifest distinction between damages from such sources as these last mentioned and damages in respect of contracts for labour ...'

[23] This court held that while the action in negligence was a single cause of action and a thing in action which was included in the bankrupt's estate, the trustee held on what would appear to be a remedial constructive trust for the bankrupt the right to recover damages for pain and suffering and other personal losses.

[24] Mr Doyle does not pursue the argument advanced below that the moneys payable under the policies relate to the bankrupt's pain and suffering or were calculated by reference to that pain and suffering. But he submits that where a policy provides that a sum is to be paid by the insurer in the event of the permanent disability of the insured, the circumstances giving rise to the payment are so inherently tied up with the pain and suffering of the insured or his person that it is wholly inequitable and contrary to the principles underpinning the 1986 Act that such moneys should be appropriated by the trustee for the creditors. He prays in aid the approach of Rattee J in *Haig v Aitken* [2000] 3 All ER 80, [2001] Ch 110, where it was held that personal correspondence of the bankrupt was of a nature peculiarly personal to the bankrupt and his life as a human being and as having a nature peculiarly private to the bankrupt. Mr Doyle further relied on the remarks of Warner J in *Re Rae* [1995] BCC 102 at 112 where that judge referred to the retention of an asset (an entitlement to be considered for renewal of a fishing licence) as contrary to the purposes of the 1986 Act without that retention being explicable by reference to the bankrupt's needs as a human being. So, Mr Doyle says, the cause of action triggered by personal disability is of a nature peculiarly personal to the bankrupt, relating to the bankrupt's needs, as his disablement must be assumed to impact on his ability to provide for and maintain himself and his family. He asks this court to go beyond the contractual label of the chose in action and to consider the substance of the claim. He insists that the quantum of the policy moneys has nothing to do with the question whether they fall within the common law exception. He says that the test is whether the

a   contractual claim relies in any way on the pain and suffering of the bankrupt. If so, he says, the policy moneys go to the bankrupt and not to his creditors.

[25] I am unable to accept Mr Doyle's submission for the following reasons.

(1) It is not founded directly on any authority. No case has been drawn to our attention where, on facts in any way comparable to those of the present case, an asset to which the bankrupt was contractually entitled was excepted from the *b*   bankrupt's estate.

(2) As Mr Stephen Davies QC for the trustee rightly stressed, the policies were assets which were purchased by Mr Rawlins through the payment of premiums which otherwise would have formed part of his estate available for his creditors on his bankruptcy, just as they were available immediately before his bankruptcy commenced, to be disposed of by Mr Rawlins for value or to be seized by his *c*   creditors in execution. It would be surprising if the recognition by Abbey Life after the bankruptcy order of Mr Rawlins' claim to permanent disablement benefit arising from an accident prior to the bankruptcy made so material a change to the nature of the asset that it no longer was to form part of the bankrupt's estate.

(3) In *Beckham v Drake* itself (a case involving a contract of service which *d*   provided for the payment of a fixed sum, in the event of default, by the defaulting party), Erle J, being one of the judges giving their opinions for the benefit of the House of Lords, recognised the significance in this area of a contractual right to receive a sum of money. He gave this example:

e   'Thus, in respect of promise, the assignees of a patient, if bankrupt, could not sue a surgeon for a breach of his promise to use due care in treating a wound, because the damages are assessed by reference to bodily annoyance; but the assignees of the same surgeon, if bankrupt, might sue the patient on his promise to pay remuneration for attendance, because the promise relates to property; and the assignees of a bankrupt could not sue on a breach of *f*   promise to marry, but the same assignees might, in my judgment, for the same reason, sue for a breach of promise to pay a given sum in case of refusing, on request, to complete a contract of marriage.' (See (1849) 2 HL Cas 579 at 605, 9 ER 1213 at 1222.)

g   He said ((1849) 2 HL Cas 579 at 606, 9 ER 1213 at 1223): 'The substance of the promise, then, for the breach of which this action was brought, relates immediately to the property of the bankrupt, being for the payment of money …', and:

'Upon the whole then, both because the promise for the breach of which this action was brought appears to me to fall within the class of those relating to property rather than of those relating to the person, and because the *h*   measure of damages appears to me not to have immediate reference to the personal inconvenience of the bankrupt, that is to say, not to any pain to him in respect of his body, mind, or character; and also, if the consideration for his promise is to be considered, because it appears to me in its nature to belong rather to the class relating to property than to the person, I think that the defendant is entitled to the judgment.' (See (1849) 2 HL Cas 579 at 609, *j*   9 ER 1213 at 1224.)

[26] To similar effect was Maule J. He said:

'There is no doubt that the right to bring an action for an injury to the person, character, or feelings, of a bankrupt, does not pass to the assignees, and that the right to bring an action for the payment of money agreed to be

paid to the bankrupt does pass. And it appears to me that the present action
is in effect an action on a contract to pay money.' (See (1849) 2 HL Cas 579
at 621–622, 9 ER 1213 at 1228.)

[27] And a little later:

'Thus, although a right of action for not marrying or not curing, in breach
of an agreement to marry or cure, would not generally pass to the assignees,
I conceive that a right to a sum of money, whether ascertained or not,
expressly agreed to be paid in the event of failing to marry or to cure, would
pass. The agreement of the parties that money shall be paid as compensation
makes, as it seems to me, the right to recover that money a part of the personal
estate of the bankrupt, as much as a recovery, before the bankruptcy, of a
judgment in an action for an injury to the person or character of the
bankrupt, would do.' (See (1849) 2 HL Cas 579 at 622, 9 ER 1213 at 1229.)

[28] The House of Lords accepted the advice of those judges, and Lord Campbell
((1849) 2 HL Cas 579 at 645, 9 ER 1213 at 1237) referred with express approval to
the passage from Maule J's opinion which I have just cited.

(4) In any event the policy moneys became payable not because of the satisfaction
of a test of pain and suffering, but because of the contractual test of what my
Lord, Keene LJ, rightly called 'employability'. The policy moneys do not relate
to or represent or compensate for loss or damage to the bankrupt personally, nor
are they measured by such loss or damage. Had the bankrupt's death been a
condition on which the policy moneys became payable, there is no question but
that the moneys would have been taken by the trustee. In the present case
payment is merely triggered by the permanent disablement being proved,
thereby advancing the date of payment of what otherwise would not have been
payable until death occurred.

(5) To my mind it would involve a considerable extension of the common law
exception from the bankrupt's estate to include within that exception an asset
whose only connection with the pain and suffering of the bankrupt is that his
disablement is the contractual contingency on which the moneys assured have
become payable. If, for social reasons or otherwise, it is thought desirable that
the exception should be extended, in my opinion it is for Parliament, not for the
courts, to make that extension.

[29] I have considerable sympathy with Mr Rawlins, who has suffered so
disastrous an accident that he has not been able to work since. But the policy of
the 1986 Act is to return to the unfortunate creditors who gave credit to the
bankrupt as much of what they are owed as can be realised out of the bankrupt's
estate, subject only to well-recognised exceptions. I am satisfied that on the facts
of this case the policy moneys do not come within any such exception. I therefore
would dismiss this appeal.

CHADWICK LJ.

[30] I agree. I add some words of my own because I recognise that the
outcome of this case is of the greatest importance to Mr Rawlins. It is also, I think,
of some general importance.

[31] The appellant, Mr Alan Rawlins, carried on business on his own account,
in partnership with his wife. In or about 1987 Mr Rawlins obtained a loan from
Nationwide Building Society in order to fund the building of a bungalow on land
which he owned. He was advised to provide for the repayment of that loan, in

a the event of his disability or illness, by an insurance policy. Acting on that advice, he took out a Living Assurance policy with Abbey Life Assurance Co Ltd. The policy (numbered 6222607A) commenced on 9 October 1987. It was a whole of life policy, providing a benefit on the death or disability of the life assured. The sum assured was £40,000. That sum was payable either on Mr Rawlins' death or if he should become disabled such that an entitlement arose under the terms of

b the policy to permanent disablement benefit or living assurance benefit. Entitlement to permanent disablement benefit arose if he became permanently disabled before his sixtieth birthday, through sickness or injury contracted after the policy had commenced, and was registered as disabled. A permanent disablement was defined as to mean such disability as would prevent him from carrying out any gainful occupation at any time during his lifetime, provided that the disability was

c not the result of any of the causes excluded by the policy. Entitlement to living assurance benefit arose on the contraction of a contingent disability after the commencement of the policy. Contingent disability was defined to mean the diagnosis of one or more than a number of medical conditions, of which heart attack, stroke and kidney failure may be given as examples.

d [32] After building work on the bungalow had commenced, Mr Rawlins realised that he would need further funding in order to complete it. He obtained a further loan of £30,000. He was advised to protect the repayment of that loan also, and he did so. He took out a further policy, described as a MortgageMaster Endowment policy, with Abbey Life. That policy (numbered 203863J) commenced on 12 November 1990. It provided endowment assurance at a maturity date; but

e it provided also for payment of benefit in the event of death or disability before that date. The sum assured was the £30,000 needed to repay the loan; and entitlement to permanent disability benefit or living assurance benefit arose under that policy in the same circumstances as under his 1987 Living Assurance policy.

[33] On 18 January 1993 Mr Rawlins fell and injured himself when constructing

f an ornamental fish pond. He was unable to work thereafter. The partnership was dissolved and the assets of the business passed over to his son. The bungalow was sold to his son and daughter. The loans from Nationwide were discharged out of the proceeds of that sale. The policies were no longer required for their original purpose and were released from any claims by Nationwide. Mr Rawlins, however, had made claims for permanent disablement benefit under the two

g policies; and, after some delay, those claims were accepted by Abbey Life on 16 September 1996.

[34] In the meantime, however, Mr Rawlins had been adjudicated bankrupt. The bankruptcy order was made on 2 April 1996. The respondent to this appeal, Mr Malcolm Cork, an insolvency practitioner, was appointed trustee in bankruptcy

h with effect from 4 March 1997. Mr Rawlins has by now been discharged from his bankruptcy under the automatic provisions; but that does not affect the position in the bankruptcy.

[35] The trustee has claimed the moneys payable under the two policies. Following the judge's decision, those moneys have been paid to the trustee; they

j are held by him pending the outcome of this appeal. It is now accepted on behalf of Mr Rawlins that the contractual right to be paid under the two policies did vest in the trustee in bankruptcy under the provisions of s 306 of the Insolvency Act 1986; but it is said that the trustee holds that right on trust, not for the creditors, but for Mr Rawlins personally. It is submitted that the position is analogous to that which was held by this court to exist in *Ord v Upton (as trustee to the property of Ord)* [2000] 1 All ER 193, [2000] Ch 352. It was held, in that case, that a cause

of action in negligence for personal injuries, in which claims were made both for
loss of earnings (as special damages) and for pain and suffering (as general *a*
damages), vested in the trustee; but on terms that he would hold only those
damages awarded in respect of the loss of past and future earnings as part of the
bankrupt's estate distributable amongst creditors. He was to hold damages
awarded for pain and suffering as a constructive trustee for the bankrupt.

[36] For my part, I find no assistance in the suggested analogy between a *b*
tortious claim for damages for pain and suffering and the contractual claim for
moneys payable under policies of insurance.

[37] It is, perhaps, pertinent to keep in mind that if Mr Rawlins had had a claim
for damages for pain and suffering against a third party in respect of the accident
which caused his injury, which on the facts of this case is not suggested, he would *c*
not have been required to bring the moneys payable under the policies into
account when pursuing that claim (see *Bradburn v Great Western Rly Co* (1874) LR
10 Exch 1, [1874–80] All ER Rep 195). The reason was explained by the House of
Lords in *Parry v Cleaver* [1969] 1 All ER 555, [1970] AC 1: see in particular the
speech of Lord Morris of Borth-y-Gest:

  d

> 'If someone makes a purely voluntary and personal decision to insure
> himself against accidents he is choosing to use some of his money or some of
> his savings in a particular way just as he would be doing if he saved some
> of his money and invested it. If he insures against accidents he will hope that
> no accident will befall him and he will be well content to have no return from
> the expenditure which is involved in the payment of premiums. He may be *e*
> one in whose case there is already some provision against sustaining
> economic loss. He may feel that in the event of accident befalling him he
> would welcome the receipt of a sum of money to compensate him in ways
> that would not be possible as a result of a successful claim at law. He may
> contemplate situations in which no claim against anyone would be possible *f*
> or would succeed.' (See [1969] 1 All ER 555 at 572, [1970] AC 1 at 31.)

[38] Although Lord Morris of was in the minority in relation to the result in
Parry's case, that passage fairly reflects the views of all the members of the House.

[39] The position which Lord Morris described reflects what has happened in
this case. Mr Rawlins has provided, by insurance, for the receipt of a sum of *g*
money in the event of an accident in circumstances in which, as it has turned out,
he has no claim against anyone else. That was undoubtedly a prudent provision
for him to make. The provision was made at a time when he could foresee that,
if he became unable to work through disability, he would be unable to make
payments to the building society out of his earnings in respect of the moneys *h*
which he had borrowed.

[40] Mr Rawlins purchased a right to payment from the insurance company,
Abbey Life, so that he could discharge his liability to the building society,
Nationwide, if and when the circumstances arose in which moneys became
payable under the policy. He purchased that right out of his own resources; *j*
resources which he might otherwise have used to make repayments under the
loan, or to invest in a savings account, or in Stock Exchange securities, or in an
endowment policy. Indeed, in the case of the MortgageMaster policy his
purchase of the right to payment in the event of permanent disablement was one
element in an endowment contract under which he purchased a right to payment
on a maturity date for the purpose of discharging the loan.

a [41] The policy moneys are not now required to repay the building society loan. That loan has been repaid out of other assets. But the policy moneys are required for the payment of Mr Rawlins' creditors generally. If they had been received or had become payable before the bankruptcy order was made, there is no doubt that they could, and probably would, have been used for that purpose. The creditors could have taken steps to ensure that they were by obtaining a

b garnishee order or a charging order over the right to receive the moneys from the building society. There is no reason in principle why the position should be different once the bankruptcy order has been made. The right to payment was purchased so as to provide for the discharge of Mr Rawlins' indebtedness to a particular creditor; and, that creditor having been paid out of other moneys which would otherwise have come into the bankrupt's estate, there is no

c hardship in requiring that the right to payment falls into the estate for the benefit of creditors generally.

[42] It is plainly in the general public interest that persons should be encouraged to make provision against the possibility that they will be unable to meet their commitments as a result of misfortune for which they are not responsible. But if

d public policy requires that they should be encouraged to do so by permitting them to shelter that provision from the claims of their creditors, then it is for Parliament to say so. It is not, in my view, for the courts to distort the bankruptcy code in order to achieve that result.

[43] For those reasons, I also would dismiss this appeal.

e **KEENE LJ.**

[44] I agree with both judgments which have been delivered. I too would dismiss this appeal.

Appeal dismissed. Permission to appeal refused.

Gillian Crew   Barrister.

Banks v Chief Adjudication Officer   *a*
[2001] UKHL 33

HOUSE OF LORDS

LORD SLYNN OF HADLEY, LORD COOKE OF THORNDON, LORD HOPE OF CRAIGHEAD,
LORD MILLETT AND LORD SCOTT OF FOSCOTE   *b*

21 MARCH, 28 JUNE 2001

*Social security – Income support – Jobseeker's allowance – Entitlement – Method of
calculating average weekly number of hours of remunerative work for persons in
one-year cycle of work – Whether unpaid holiday periods to be taken into account for* *c*
*purpose of averaging exercise – Income Support (General) Regulations 1987, reg 5 –
Jobseeker's Allowance Regulations 1996, reg 51.*

The appellant, B, was employed as an assistant for children with special needs at a
local authority junior school. He worked for between 20 and 26 hours a week during
term time, but was not required to work during the school holidays and was not *d*
paid for those periods. In 1996 he applied for income support in respect of the
summer holiday, and jobseeker's allowance (which had by then replaced income
support) in respect of the October half-term holiday. Under the relevant legislation,
a person was entitled to those benefits if, inter alia, he was not engaged in remunerative
work. Regulation 5(1)[a] of the Income Support (General) Regulations 1987 (which
corresponded to reg 51(1)[b] of the Jobseeker's Allowance Regulations 1996) defined *e*
remunerative work as work in which a person was engaged, or, where his hours
of work fluctuated, was engaged on average, for not less than 16 hours a week,
being work for which payment was made or which was done in expectation of
payment. In cases where the number of hours for which a person was engaged
fluctuated and there was a recognisable cycle of work, reg 5(2)(b)(i) of the 1987 *f*
regulations (the equivalent of reg 51(2)(b)(i) of the 1996 regulations) provided
that the number of hours for which he was engaged in work was to be
determined by reference to the average of hours worked over the period of one
complete cycle (including, where the cycle involved periods in which the person
did not work, those periods but disregarding any other absences). Regulation 5(2)
of the 1987 regulations was subject to reg 5(3B), a provision which had been *g*
inserted in 1995 and whose equivalent in the 1996 regulations was reg 51(2)(c).
Regulation 5(3B) provided that where, for the purposes of para (2)(b)(i), a person's
recognisable cycle of work at a school, other educational establishment or other
place of employment was one year and included periods of school holidays or
similar vacations during which he did not work, those periods and any other *h*
periods not forming part of such holidays or vacations during which he was not
required to work was to be disregarded in establishing the average hours for
which he was engaged in work. B accepted that his employment constituted a
recognisable cycle of work from the beginning of one school year to the next.
He contended, however, that the 14 weeks of school holidays were not to be *j*
disregarded in calculating the average number of hours worked per week, that
accordingly the denominator was 52 rather than 38 and that he had therefore
worked on average for less than 16 hours a week. The adjudication officer and

---

a   Regulation 5 is set out at [4] and [5], below
b   Regulation 51 is set out at [38], below

a the social security appeal tribunal rejected B's claims, but they were allowed by the social security commissioner. His decision was reversed by the Court of Appeal, and B appealed to the House of Lords.

Held – (Lord Cooke and Lord Scott dissenting) Where an applicant for income support or jobseeker's allowance worked fluctuating hours and had a recognisable
b cycle of work of one year, periods during which he was not required to work, such as school holidays, were to be disregarded in calculating the average number of hours worked per week during that cycle. Regulation 5(2)(b)(i) and (3B) of the 1987 regulations (reg 51(2)(b)(i) and (c) of the 1996 regulations) clearly contemplated that a recognisable yearly cycle of work might include periods in which an employee did no work, and that the averaging for which they provided was part
c of the means of determining whether the employee was engaged in remunerative work for the purpose of reg 5(1) of the 1987 regulations (reg 51(1) of the 1996 regulations). It was difficult to see what point there would be in reg 5(3B) of the 1987 regulations (reg 51(2)(c) of the 1996 regulations) if reg 5(2)(b)(i) of the 1987 regulations (reg 51(2)(b)(i) of the 1996 regulations) applied, contrary to their
d express terms, only to periods of actual work. Regulation 5(2)(b)(i) of the 1987 regulations stated in terms that a person's cycle of work might involve periods when the person did not work. That was why, before the insertion of reg 5(3B) of the 1987 regulations, the averaging exercise was done in all cases by reference to the whole period of the cycle including periods when the person was not required to work during school holidays and similar vacation periods. The effect
e of the insertion was simply to take those periods out of account for the purpose of working out the average. If as a consequence of the calculation directed by reg 5(3B) of the 1987 regulations or reg 51(2)(c) of the 1996 regulations, a claimant's hours were sufficient to place him within the definition of remunerative work in reg 5(1) of the 1987 regulations or reg 51(1) of the 1996 regulations, the
f application of that definition covered the whole period of the cycle which had been identified as the cycle of work in the claimant's contract. That was the result of the averaging exercise which had had to be carried out in the instant case, and accordingly the appeal would be dismissed (see [15], [16], [18], [52]–[55], [65]–[69], below).

Decision of the Court of Appeal [2000] 1 All ER 686 affirmed.
g

Notes

For the meaning of remunerative work for the purposes of income support and jobseeker's allowance, see 44(2) *Halsbury's Laws* (4th edn reissue) paras 179, 262.

For the Income Support (General) Regulations 1987, see 18 *Halsbury's Statutory*
h *Instruments* (2000 issue) 139.

For the Jobseeker's Allowance Regulations 1996, see 18 *Halsbury's Statutory Instruments* (2000 issue) 184.

Case referred to in opinions

j *R v Supplementary Benefits Commission, ex p Lewis* [1982] 1 All ER 680, sub nom *R v Ebbw Vale and Merthyr Tydfil Supplementary Benefits Appeal Tribunal, ex p Lewis* [1982] 1 WLR 420, CA.

Appeal

The appellant, Daniel John Banks, appealed with permission of the Appeal Committee of the House of Lords given on 11 April 2000 from the decision of the

Court of Appeal (Auld, Aldous LJJ and Rattee J) on 29 July 1999, with reasons given on 14 October 1999 ([2000] 1 All ER 686), allowing an appeal by the *a* respondent, the chief adjudication officer (now the Secretary of State for Social Security), from the decision of the social security commissioner (M Rowland) on 24 February 1999 allowing an appeal by Mr Banks from the order of the Doncaster social security appeal tribunal on 10 February 1997 dismissing his appeal from the rejection by an adjudication officer of his claims for income *b* support and jobseeker's allowance. The facts are set out in the opinion of Lord Slynn of Hadley.

Richard Drabble QC and *Helen Mountfield* (instructed by *UNISON*) for Mr Banks.
David Pannick QC and *Nathalie Lieven* (instructed by the *Solicitor to the Department of Social Security*) for the respondent. *c*

Their Lordships took time for consideration.

28 June 2001. The following opinions were delivered.
d

LORD SLYNN OF HADLEY.
[1] My Lords, Mr Banks was employed in a junior school as an assistant for children with special needs. During term time in 1995/1996 he worked for periods of 20 hours a week. He did not work during school holidays and was not paid for those periods. In respect of the summer holidays in 1996 he applied for income *e* support under the Social Security Contributions and Benefits Act 1992 and the Income Support (General) Regulations 1987, SI 1987/1967. On 7 October 1996 income support was replaced by a jobseeker's allowance under the Jobseekers Act 1995 and the Jobseeker's Allowance Regulations 1996, SI 1996/207. For the half-term holiday in October 1996 he applied for the jobseeker's allowance. Although on an earlier occasion a different officer and tribunal had awarded him *f* the earlier benefit the adjudication officer and the social security appeal tribunal rejected these new claims. Special Security Commissioner Rowland allowed his appeal upholding his claims. The Court of Appeal unanimously reversed the commissioner ([2000] 1 All ER 686).
[2] It does not seem that anyone has found this a straightforward or an easy case and there is much sympathy for Mr Banks who was not paid during the not *g* insignificant periods of school holidays and who tried actively but unsuccessfully to obtain other employment during the two relevant periods. The question, however, for your Lordships is whether under these somewhat complex legislative provisions, properly interpreted, he is entitled to the allowances. It is accepted that the conditions of entitlement to the two allowances, though differently *h* structured and sometimes differently phrased, are substantially the same and that on this appeal nothing turns on the difference between them. I accordingly refer to the earlier 1992 Act which covers the first claim. The equivalent provisions of the jobseekers legislation are set out in the judgment of Auld LJ to which reference can be made. *j*
[3] Section 124(1) of the 1992 Act provides that a person is entitled to income support if inter alia '(b) he has no income or his income does not exceed the applicable amount', and '(c) he is not engaged in remunerative work' and '(d) ... he is available for, and actively seeking, employment'. The amount of support is the applicable amount if he has no income and the difference between his income and the applicable amount if higher if he has no income. The manner in which the

a amount payable for a period to which s 124(5) applies is prescribed and that period can be for less than a week by virtue of s 124(6). By s 137(2) of the 1992 Act regulations can be made '(c) as to what is or is not to be treated as remunerative work or as employment' and '(d) as to circumstances in which a person is or is not to be treated as—(i) engaged … in remunerative work'.

[4] Regulation 5 of the 1987 regulations as amended deals with two linked but *b* separate matters. The first is in para (1) which defines remunerative work:

'Subject to the following provisions of this regulation, for the purposes of section 20(3)(c) of the Act (conditions of entitlement to income support), remunerative work is work in which a person is engaged, or, where his hours of work fluctuate, he is engaged on average, for not less than 16 hours a week *c* being work for which payment is made or which is done in expectation of payment.'

The second deals with the method of calculating the number of hours:

'(2) Subject to paragraph (3B), the number of hours for which a person is *d* engaged in work shall be determined—(a) where no recognisable cycle has been established in respect of a person's work, by reference to the number of hours or, where those hours are likely to fluctuate, the average of the hours, which he is expected to work in a week; (b) where the number of hours for which he is engaged fluctuate, by reference to the average of hours worked over—(i) if there is a recognisable cycle of work, the period of one complete *e* cycle (including, where the cycle involves periods in which the person does not work, those periods but disregarding any other absences); (ii) in any other case, the period of five weeks immediately before the date of claim or the date of review, or such other length of time as may, in the particular case, enable the person's average hours of work to be determined more accurately.'

f [5] Regulation 5 further provides:

'(3) A person shall be treated as engaged in remunerative work during any period for which he is absent from work referred to in paragraph (1) if the absence is either without good cause or by reason of a recognised, customary or other holiday.
g (3A) A person shall not be treated as engaged in remunerative work on any day on which the person is on maternity leave or is absent from work because he is ill.
(3B) Where for the purpose of paragraph (2)(b)(i), a person's recognisable cycle of work at a school, other educational establishment or other place of *h* employment is one year and includes periods of school holidays or similar vacations during which he does not work, those periods and any other periods not forming part of such holidays or vacations during which he is not required to work shall be disregarded in establishing the average hours for which he is engaged in work.'

j Paragraph (3B) took effect from 10 April 1995.

[6] The application of these sections and regulations has given rise to sharp differences of opinion. Auld LJ has set out or summarised a number of passages from the decisions of commissioners in England and Scotland reflecting these differences. I refer to and gratefully adopt without repeating those passages from his judgment.

[7] It was and is accepted on behalf of Mr Banks that his employment by the authority even with holiday breaks constituted one 'recognisable cycle of work' from the beginning of one school year to the beginning of the next. Accordingly, since the number of hours for which he was engaged to work fluctuated, para (2)(b)(i) of reg 5 applies subject to para (3B) and the number of hours for which he is engaged in work is to be determined by reference to the average of hours worked over the period of the cycle 'including, where the cycle involves periods in which [he] does not work, those periods'. However, it is said against him that since his recognisable cycle of work is one year at a school and includes periods of school holidays during which he is not required to work, those holidays are to be disregarded in establishing the average hours for which he is engaged in work. On that basis if the total school holidays are 14 weeks the total number of hours worked is divided by 38 and not by 52 to arrive at the average. The average is accordingly higher and in Mr Banks' case took him over the figure of 16 hours which was the cut-off point for both income support and jobseeker's allowance.

[8] The appeal tribunal found that Mr Banks had a continuing contract of employment from 1 September 1995 which was not due to expire at the end of the school year. The tribunal accepted that in 1995/1996 he worked 20 hours a week though initially he was working for 26 hours a week during the term from 3 September 1996. The commissioner found that 'at the material time which I assume to be the term time periods adjacent to the holidays, in respect of which the claims are made, he was working for 20 hours a week'. In the agreed statement of facts it is accepted for the purposes of this appeal that his hours of work fluctuated between about 20 to 26 hours per week during term times. On that agreement and on those facts I think it right to approach the case on the basis that the 'number of hours for which he is engaged fluctuate' for the purposes of reg 5(2)(b) of the 1987 regulations. The alternative approach of the appeal tribunal that the number of hours for which he was engaged 'in work' (para (2)(b) read with the opening words of para (2)) fluctuated between 20 and zero is more debatable since he was engaged to do no hours of work or to be in work in the vacation.

[9] It is accepted that in Mr Banks' case there was 'a recognisable cycle of work' within the meaning of reg 5(2)(b)(i), ie one school year. It follows that 'subject to' para (3B) of reg 5, the number of hours for which he is engaged in work is to be determined by the average of hours worked over the period of the complete cycle including 'where the cycle involves periods in which the person does no work, those periods'. If that were the end of the provisions 52 weeks would be the relevant denominator.

[10] However, by para (3B) his 'recognisable cycle of work at a school ... is one year and includes periods of school holidays ... during which he does not work, those periods ... shall be disregarded in establishing the average hours for which he is engaged in work'. If that applies the total number of hours worked is divided by 38 and not 52. The average is accordingly higher and in Mr Banks' case took him over the 16 hours.

[11] It is said that this result of reading the two paragraphs so as to exclude school holidays in calculating the denominator is inconsistent with the provision of reg 5(1), by which for the purpose of defining remunerative work takes the work in which, because his hours fluctuate, is engaged on average 'for not less than 16 hours a week, being work for which payment is made or which is done in expectation of payment'. In Mr Banks' case he was not paid and did not expect

a to be paid during the vacation. Those 14 weeks must therefore be excluded from the relevant remunerative work.

[12] Paragraph (3) which brings into the concept of being engaged in remunerative work periods of absence by reason of a recognised, customary or other holiday, does not apply because school holidays as such do not fall into those categories of holiday.

b [13] It is obvious that remunerative work indicates in ordinary language that the work is to be the subject of remuneration. If Mr Banks does not work and is not remunerated during the holidays it may sound strange to say that the holidays form part of 'remunerative work'. The question, however, is whether that is the result of the various provisions of reg 5, since in principle it is perfectly possible for Parliament to provide, whether by a deeming provision or otherwise, that a
c person is 'engaged in work' even 'remunerative work', when he is not working and for which he is not being paid.

[14] There does not seem to me any difficulty in reading para (2)(b)(i) together with para (3B) of reg 5. The former is dealing with the generality of workers. The latter takes out of the general category a particular group of workers.

d [15] The objective of reg 5 as the heading shows is to identify 'Persons treated as engaged in remunerative work'. The criterion for being engaged in remunerative work is that a person must be 'engaged in work' for not less than 16 hours a week unless his hours of work fluctuate, when an average has to be taken. Regulation 5(2)(b)(i) identifies the overriding period where there is a recognisable cycle of work. That is a constant when applying sub-para (b)(i) and
e para (3B) which prescribe how the average is to be calculated in order to show whether the individual is engaged in remunerative work within the reg 5(1) definition. Regulation 5(3B) in my opinion requires that in conducting the averaging exercise periods of holiday are to be disregarded. Paragraph (3B) does not say, contrary to para (2)(b)(i), that the cycle is to be reduced from one
f complete cycle to that cycle (here one year) less the holiday period.

[16] It is inherent in the process of averaging that there may be weeks when someone works and is paid for less than 16 hours and in principle there is no reason why throughout the period the average should not take into account a week or weeks in which no work is done or no work for which payment is made. That the week of no work when he is not 'engaged in work' can be included is
g evident from reg 5(2)(b)(i). The fact that the relevant hours for the purposes of reg 5(1) are hours for which payment is made or expected to be made does not prevent the scheme from laying down which weeks are to be taken into account for the purposes of averaging in para (2)(b)(i). The regulation took the whole cycle. In para (3B) it excluded the weeks of holiday. It does not seem to me that
h the fact that the claim here is made in respect of a week in which no work is done and for which he is not remunerated makes the position different from a case in which the claim is sought to be made for a week in which he is employed and remunerated. The averaging is the same in both cases. Accordingly I conclude that the Court of Appeal and the adjudication officer took the right denominator
j by excluding the holiday weeks.

[17] My noble and learned friend, Lord Scott of Foscote, considers for reasons with which I have much sympathy that if the interpretation which he considers right is not accepted 'the sooner the Secretary of State remedies the situation by making appropriate new regulations the better'. But it is to be noticed that Mr Commissioner Rowland, also greatly experienced in this field, in adopting a result in favour of Mr Banks concluded:

'I will add that, while these results are doubtless satisfactory from the point of view of the two claimants before me, I am not sure that the approach I have felt obliged to take is wholly desirable when viewed from a wider perspective and I very much doubt that it was what was intended when reg 5(3B) was introduced. I therefore suspect that there will be further legislation in this field.'

(Semble the other way to that contemplated by Lord Scott.)

[18] If the result arrived at by the Court of Appeal unanimously and by the majority of your Lordships is not a result which is now desired the department will no doubt consider the position. I consider, however, that this appeal must be dismissed.

LORD COOKE OF THORNDON.

[19] My Lords, the issue is whether, during the school holidays when he did not work at or for the school, the appellant, Mr Banks, a special needs assistant in a junior school, was disqualified initially from receiving income support and later from receiving jobseeker's allowance by the statutory condition that he 'is not engaged in remunerative work'. The condition was laid down in turn by the Social Security Contributions and Benefits Act 1992, s 124(1)(c), and the Jobseekers Act 1995, s 1(2)(e). The answer depends on the interpretation of the relevant regulations. It is sufficient to discuss the case in terms of the Income Support (General) Regulations 1987, SI 1987/1967. The Jobseeker's Allowance Regulations 1996, SI 1996/207, are not, I think, significantly different in relation to such an issue as arises in the present case.

[20] Regulation 5 of the 1987 regulations is concerned throughout with defining when persons are to be treated as engaged in remunerative work. This is indicated accurately by its heading 'Persons treated as engaged in remunerative work'. I think that the answer to the issue is to be found by taking four straightforward steps as follows.

[21] The first step is to note that, by reg 5(1), where a person's hours of work fluctuate, remunerative work is work on which he is engaged on average for not less than 16 hours a week being work for which payment is made or which is done in expectation of payment. Thus the average hours are a key part of the criterion for determining whether he is engaged in remunerative work.

[22] The next step is prescribed in the generality of cases of cyclical work by reg 5(2)(b)(i). If there is a recognisable cycle of work, the average hours are to be ascertained by reference to the period of one complete cycle, *including* periods in which the claimant does no work. Thus in general a cyclical worker is to be treated as engaged in work throughout the whole cycle. This is for the purpose of averaging, which itself, as has been seen, is for the purpose of determining whether he is engaged in remunerative work.

[23] But reg 5(2)(b)(i), like the whole of para (2), is expressly made subject to para (3B), which provides:

'Where for the purpose of paragraph (2)(b)(i), a person's recognisable cycle of work at a school, other educational establishment or other place of employment is one year and includes periods of school holidays or similar vacations during which he does not work, those periods and any other periods not forming part of such holidays or vacations during which he is not required to work shall be disregarded in establishing the average hours for which he is engaged in work.'

a This special and overriding provision applies to the present case. For the purpose of determining the average hours, and hence of determining whether Mr Banks is engaged in remunerative work within the meaning of reg 5(1), the school holidays are to be disregarded. That is to say, contrary to the general rule for cyclical workers, he is *not* to be treated as engaged in remunerative work during the school holidays.

b [24] That conclusion accords with the natural and ordinary use of language. One would not normally say that a person is engaged in remunerative work during weeks when he does no work. It is a conclusion which flows, in my view, from the language of these regulations. To the extent, however, that they are ambiguous (as the differences of opinions in this and other cases suggest), I would adopt the approach that if those responsible for the regulations wished to achieve

c a result different from the ordinary and natural one, the public were entitled to clearer language as regards the class of workers covered by reg 5(3B). For other classes of cyclical workers, reg 5(2)(b)(i) is clear enough. The effect of the addition of reg 5(3B) has proved to be obscure; and I respectfully think that the fair and reasonable interpretation is the one that I favour.

d [25] That conclusion is also consistent with the judgments in the Court of Appeal in *R v Supplementary Benefits Commission, ex p Lewis* [1982] 1 All ER 680, sub nom *R v Ebbw Vale and Merthyr Tydfil Supplementary Benefits Appeal Tribunal, ex p Lewis* [1982] 1 WLR 420 (Lord Denning MR, Oliver and Watkins LJJ). But, as the facts and the statutory provisions in that case were different, I have not relied

e on it.

[26] Conscious that the majority of your Lordships' Committee consider the foregoing reasoning simplistic, I respectfully add that as an alternative approach to the present appeal I prefer the opinion of my noble and learned friend Lord Scott of Foscote.

f [27] For these reasons I would allow the appeal.

LORD HOPE OF CRAIGHEAD.

[28] My Lords, on 1 September 1995 the appellant Daniel John Banks began work as a special needs assistant at Denaby Main Junior School under a contract of employment with Doncaster Metropolitan Borough Council. His principal

g duties were to provide support to two children while they were attending the school. During term time Mr Banks worked 20 hours a week. He was not required by his contract to work, nor was he paid by his employer, during the school holidays. At the end of the summer term he applied for and obtained a change of duties under his contract. He undertook to do similar work for the

h same employer but with different children at a different school.

[29] The summer holiday began on 22 July 1996. On that day Mr Banks claimed income support for the period when he was not working during the holiday and for which he was not paid. He then worked from the start of the next term on 3 September 1996 to the start of the autumn half-term holiday. That holiday ran

j from 25 October 1996 to 3 November 1996. This was another period during which he was not required to work and for which he was not paid. On 25 October 1996 he claimed jobseeker's allowance for the period of the holiday. This was because income support had been brought to an end and replaced by the jobseeker's allowance with effect from 7 October 1996. He resumed work at the school on 4 November 1996. His claims were based on the proposition that, although he was in employment under his contract with the education authority during the school

holidays, he was entitled to benefit for the weeks during which he was not
expected to work for his employer and for which he was not paid.

[30] The issue which Mr Banks' claims has raised is one of general public
importance. It relates to the entitlement to the benefit of what is now the
jobseeker's allowance of all part-time and ancillary staff engaged at schools, other
educational establishments or other places of employment under contracts with
an annual cycle of work which includes holiday periods during which they do not
work and for which they are not paid. The question whether the benefits are
payable during these holiday periods is purely and simply one of statutory
entitlement. The answer to it is to be found by construing the statutory and
regulatory provisions which describe the entitlement to the benefit.

[31] On 24 February 1999 Social Security Commissioner Rowland held that
the effect of the regulations was that Mr Banks was entitled to income support
and jobseeker's allowance during the holidays (CIS/3216/1997, CJSA/3218/1997).
On 29 July 1999 the Court of Appeal (Auld, Aldous LJJ and Rattee J) allowed an
appeal against the commissioner's decision by the chief adjudication officer
([2000] 1 All ER 686). An appeal in the case of another claimant to income
support named Frank Stafford, whose wife was employed in a primary school to
assist pupils with special educational needs, was allowed by the Court of Appeal
on 29 July 1999 at the same time and for the same reasons as in Mr Banks' case.
But Mr Stafford, who represented himself in the Court of Appeal, has not appealed
against that decision to your Lordships' House.

[32] Section 124(1) of the Social Security Contributions and Benefits Act 1992
provides that a person is entitled to income support if he satisfies four conditions.
The relevant one for the purposes of this case is that stated in para (c) of the
subsection, which provides: 'he is not engaged in remunerative work and, if he is
a member of a married or unmarried couple, the other member is not so engaged
...' Section 137(2) of that Act provides that regulations may make provision for
the purposes of that Part of the Act: '... (c) as to what is or is not to be treated as
remunerative work or as employment; (d) as to circumstances in which a person
is or is not to be treated as—(i) engaged or normally engaged in remunerative
work ...' The relevant regulations are the Income Support (General) Regulations
1987, SI 1987/1967.

[33] The relevant conditions for entitlement to benefit for income support
are reproduced in similar but not identical terms in the Jobseekers Act 1995.
Section 1(2)(e) of that Act provides that a claimant is entitled to a jobseeker's
allowance if he 'is not engaged in remunerative work.' Paragraph 1 of Sch 1 to
that Act provides:

'(1) For the purposes of this Act, "remunerative work" has such meaning
as may be prescribed.
(2) Regulations may prescribe circumstances in which, for the purposes
of this Act—(a) a person who is not engaged in remunerative work is to be
treated as engaged in remunerative work; or (b) a person who is engaged in
remunerative work is to be treated as not engaged in remunerative work.'

The relevant regulations are the Jobseeker's Allowance Regulations 1996,
SI 1996/207.

[34] It is common ground that, although they differ in some respects both in
wording and layout, the two sets of regulations have the same effect. One of the
basic rules is that only a person who is not engaged in remunerative work is
entitled to benefit. But a person is not denied benefit merely because he does some

a work during the week for which he is paid or is entitled to expect payment. Benefit is denied only to those who are in remunerative work full-time. The dividing line between full-time work and work which is not full-time work for this purpose is set at 16 hours of work each week. As the circumstances in which people work vary from case to case, provision is made as to how the number of hours for which a person is engaged in work is to be calculated.

b [**35**] In cases where the number of hours worked fluctuate the number of hours in which a person is engaged in work is to be determined by reference to the average of hours worked. Provision is made as to how that calculation is to be made in the case of a person who works at a school, other educational establishment or other place of employment whose cycle of work consists of one year but with school holidays or similar vacations during which he does not c work. Mr Banks contends that the effect of the latter provision as to the period over which the hours of work is to be averaged is that the number of hours obtained by means of that calculation is to be applied only to the weeks during which the person is actually working. He maintains that it does not have the effect of deeming the person to be in remunerative employment in weeks during d which he does not work and for which he is not paid.

[**36**] The relevant provisions of the 1987 regulations as amended are to be found in reg 5, which is headed 'Persons treated as engaged in remunerative work.' It provides as follows:

e '(1) Subject to the following provisions of this regulation, for the purposes of section 20(3)(c) of the Act (conditions of entitlement to income support), remunerative work is work in which a person is engaged, or, where his hours of work fluctuate, he is engaged on average, for not less than 16 hours a week being work for which payment is made or which is done in expectation of payment.

f (2) Subject to paragraph (3B), the number of hours for which a person is engaged in work shall be determined—(a) where not recognisable cycle has been established in respect of a person's work, by reference to the number of hours or, where those hours are likely to fluctuate, the average of the hours, which he is expected to work in a week; (b) where the number of hours for which he is engaged fluctuate, by reference to the average of hours worked g over—(i) if there is a recognisable cycle of work, the period of one complete cycle (including, where the cycle involves periods in which the person does no work, those periods but disregarding any other absences) ...

(3) A person shall be treated as engaged in remunerative work during any period for which he is absent from work referred to in paragraph (1) if the h absence is either without good cause or by reason of a recognised, customary or other holiday.

(3A) A person shall not be treated as engaged in remunerative work on any day on which the person is on maternity leave or is absent from work because he is ill.

j (3B) Where for the purpose of paragraph (2)(b)(i), a person's recognisable cycle of work at a school, other educational establishment or other place of employment is one year and includes periods of school holidays or similar vacations during which he does not work, those periods and any other periods not forming part of such holidays or vacations during which he does not work, those periods and any other periods not forming part of such holidays or vacations during which he is not required to work shall be disregarded in establishing the average hours for which he is engaged in work.'

[37] Paragraph (3B) of reg 5 was inserted by reg 19(b) of the Income-related Benefits Schemes (Miscellaneous Amendments) Regulations 1995, SI 1995/516, as from 10 April 1995 in response to a decision by Social Security Commissioner Goodman in R(IS) 15/94, in which he held that the hours of the claimant's wife, a school receptionist who worked an average of about 24 hours in term time but did no work during school holidays, should be averaged under reg 5(2)(b)(i) over the whole of her cycle of work of one year. The result was that the average of her weekly working hours was reduced to less that 16, and the claimant was found entitled to income support throughout the whole year. Mr Pannick QC for the respondent explained that the policy purpose of the insertion of para (3B) was to enable many claimants who had children to claim family credit. He said that it was thought to be right that eligibility to that form of benefit should be calculated by excluding periods of school holidays and similar vacations from the period which was to be taken into account for the purpose of working out the average.

[38] The relevant provisions of the 1996 regulations are to be found in reg 51 which is headed 'Remunerative work' and in reg 52 which is headed 'Persons treated as engaged in remunerative work'. They provide as follows:

'51.—(1) For the purposes of the Act "remunerative work" means—(a) in the case of the claimant, work in which he is engaged or, where his hours of work fluctuate, is engaged on average, for not less than 16 hours per week; and (b) in the case of any partner of the claimant, work in which he is engaged or, where his hours of work fluctuate, is engaged on average, for not less than 24 hours per week; and for those purposes, work is work for which payment is made or which is done in expectation of payment.

(2) For the purposes of paragraph (1), the number of hours in which the claimant or his partner is engaged in work shall be determined—(a) where no recognisable cycle has been established in respect of a person's work, by reference to the number of hours or, where those hours are likely to fluctuate, the average of the hours, which he is expected to work in a week; (b) where the number of hours for which he is engaged fluctuate, by reference to the average of hours worked over—(i) if there is a recognisable cycle of work, and sub-paragraph (c) does not apply, the period of one complete cycle (including, where the cycle involves periods in which the person does not work, those periods but disregarding any other absences) ... (c) where the person works at a school or other educational establishment or at some other place of employment and the cycle of work consists of one year but with school holidays or similar vacations during which he does no work, by disregarding those periods and any other periods during which he is not required to work ...

52.—(1) Except in the case of a person on maternity leave or absent from work through illness, a person shall be treated as engaged in remunerative work during any period for which he is absent from work referred to in regulation 51(1) (remunerative work) where the absence is either without good cause or by reason of a recognised, customary or other holiday.'

[39] Regulation 53 of the 1996 regulations is headed 'Persons treated as not engaged in remunerative work'. It is to be noted that the provision relating to the

a treatment of a person working at a school or other educational establishment or at some other place of work whose cycle of work consists of one year but with school holidays or similar vacations during which he does not work was included in reg 51 (remunerative work) and not in reg 53 (persons treated as not engaged in remunerative work). Nor was it included in reg 52 (persons treated as engaged in remunerative work).

b [40] Mr Drabble QC for Mr Banks laid great stress on the fact that each Act contained distinct and separate empowering provisions for the making of regulations as to the meaning of the expression 'remunerative work' and the circumstances in which a person is or is not to be treated as 'engaged in' remunerative work. He said that Mr Banks was only to be treated as engaged in remunerative work during weeks when he was not in fact working and for which he was not paid if the
c exercise of some deeming provision led to that result. He maintained that the respondent's argument that Mr Banks was to be treated as working throughout the whole cycle of work of which the school holidays formed part was based on a misunderstanding of the regulations, for two reasons. In the first place, the regulations which provided for the treatment of school holidays for the purpose
d of the average were an exercise of the power to define remunerative work, not an exercise of the power to deem persons to be engaged in remunerative work when they were not working. They did not affect the position of a person who was not engaged in remunerative work at all during the holidays. In the second place, if the regulations were to be read as an exercise of the power to deem as well as the power to define, the extent of the deeming should be confined to those
e weeks which were brought into account for the purpose of averaging and should leave out of account those weeks which were directed to be left out of account for the purpose of the averaging exercise.

[41] The argument that the effect of the regulations ought to be determined by reference to the enabling provisions which are to found in the statutes has
f more force in the case of the 1996 regulations than it does in the case of the 1987 regulations. This is because the layout of the 1996 regulations indicates that the draftsman of those regulations was making a conscious attempt to deal separately with the definition of remunerative work on the one hand (in reg 51 of the 1996 regulations) and with persons treated as engaged in, and not engaged in, remunerative work (in regs 52 and 53 of those regulations) on the other hand.
g The draftsmen of the 1987 regulations and of the various amendments which were made to it were not so scrupulous. There is no regulation which is headed simply 'Remunerative work'. Regulation 5 of the 1987 regulations, in which the critical provision about the treatment of holidays and other periods during a cycle of one year during which a person in not required to work is to be found, is
h headed 'Persons treated as engaged in remunerative work'. But it contains within the same regulation a variety of provisions made in the exercise of each of the relevant enabling powers. Paragraph (1) contains a definition of remunerative work. Paragraph (3) provides that a person who is absent from work without good cause or by reason of a recognised, customary or other holiday is to be
j treated as engaged in remunerative work during any such period. Paragraph (3A) provides that a person shall not be treated as engaged in remunerative work on any day when on maternity leave or absent from work when ill. There is a separate list of persons who are not to be treated as engaged in remunerative work in reg 6.

[42] On further examination the precise separation for which Mr Drabble contended is not maintained, even in the case of the 1996 regulations. Where the

definition of remunerative work in reg 51 requires the working out of a number
of hours of work over by reference to an average of hours worked, an element of   *a*
deeming is inherent in the definition of 'work'. The effect of the averaging
exercise is to require it to be assumed that the person is working for the average
numbers of hours for each week in the cycle, even although for some of those
weeks he may be working for far fewer than the 16 hours which disqualifies a
person from benefit. For example a person whose average is, say, 25 hours per   *b*
week but who works for only one hour in a given week in the cycle is deemed, as
a result of the averaging exercise, to be engaged that week in remunerative work
for not less than 16 hours.

[43] I am content to accept, as a general proposition, that guidance as to the
meaning of a provision in a statutory instrument may be obtained from the
wording of the enabling power under which it was made. But the reliability of   *c*
that guidance is diminished if one finds, as one does in this case, that a variety
of enabling powers were available to the draftsman of the statutory instrument
and there were no compelling reasons for maintaining a strict separation between
the exercise of each of them. The fact that it is accepted in this case that both sets
of regulations have the same effect makes Mr Drabble's argument even harder to   *d*
accept. Mr Pannick was entitled to ask that it be tested on the weaker alternative.
When it is applied to the 1987 regulations it is not sustainable.

[44] I see no alternative therefore in this case to the normal approach to the
construction of a statutory instrument, which involves examining the relevant
provisions in the context of the regulations as a whole and determining their
effect according to the ordinary meaning of the words used. For convenience   *e*
I shall conduct my examination under reference to the 1987 regulations, as this
was the regime which was enacted first. I shall give references to the corresponding
1996 regulations where this is appropriate.

[45] The appropriate starting point is reg 5(1) of the 1987 regulations
(reg 51(1) of the 1996 regulations). This provision sets out the requirements   *f*
which must be met with regard to each of the two words in the phrase
'remunerative work'. First there is the work element. This is to be measured by
reference to the number of hours of work a week in which a person is engaged.
Then there is the remuneration element. This is to be determined by reference
to the question whether the work in question is work for which payment is made
or which is done in expectation of payment. The question of remuneration has   *g*
not given rise to any difficulty in this case.

[46] The choice of method which is to be used to determine the number of
hours of work a week in which a person is engaged depends upon whether or not
there is a recognisable cycle of work. The social security appeal tribunal, having
examined Mr Banks' contract of employment, found as a fact that the number of   *h*
hours for which he was engaged fluctuated. This was because in the year
1995/1996 he worked for 20 hours a week for 38 weeks and he did no work at all
for 12 weeks. But the tribunal also held that he had a recognisable yearly cycle of
work. It follows that reg 5(2)(b)(i) of the 1987 regulations (reg 51(2)(b)(i) of the
1996 regulations) applies to this case. The calculation which it lays down is based   *j*
on the average number of hours for the complete cycle.

[47] The regulations do not explain what they mean by the word 'cycle' in this
context. But I think that the concept of a cycle of work in which the number of
hours for which the person is engaged fluctuate necessarily involves the idea that
there will be periods in the cycle when the person works for more hours per week
than the average, and that there will be other periods in the same cycle when he

a   works for fewer hours per week than the average or, it may be, does not work at all. The fact that the cycle may include periods when the person does not work at all is made clear by the words which appear in parenthesis in paras (2)(b)(i) (reg 51(2)(b)(i) of the 1996 regulations) which require there to be included in the period of one complete cycle, 'where the cycle involves periods in which the person does not work', those periods but disregarding any other absences. I do

b   think that it can be doubted therefore that the reason why the periods of school holidays when the person does not work form part of his cycle of work for the purpose of calculating the number of hours for which he is engaged in work is that he is regarded for the purpose of the regulations as engaged in work during those periods even although he is not in fact working. It is on this vital point that I respectfully disagree with my noble and learned friend, Lord Scott of Foscote.

c   To use a colloquial expression, the person is regarded as being 'in work' during the periods of the cycle when he is not working, although he does no work during those periods.

[48] This brings me to para (3B) of reg 5 of the 1987 regulations (reg 51(2)(c) of the 1996 regulations) to which the opening words of reg 5(2) of the 1987 regulations

d   say that para (2) is subject. It provides that for the purposes of reg 5 (2)(b)(i) of the 1987 regulations (calculating the average of hours worked if there is a recognisable cycle of work) a person's recognisable cycle of work at a school, other educational establishment or other place of employment is one year, as it was held to be in this case, and where the cycle includes periods of school holidays or similar vacations when he does not work, as it did in this case also, those periods 'shall

e   be disregarded in establishing the average hours for which he is engaged in work'. The wording of reg 51(2)(b)(i) and (2)(c) of the 1996 regulations is different, but I agree with my noble and learned friend, Lord Millett, for the reasons which he has given that the result is the same.

[49] Two points in particular are to be noted about the wording of the last few

f   words of reg 5(3B) of the 1987 regulations which I have placed between quotation marks. The first is the extent of the disregard which is directed by the paragraph. It extends only to the calculation of the average hours for which the person is engaged in work during the cycle. The period of the cycle of work is not to be treated as having been altered. What is altered is the periods within the cycle which are to be taken into account for the purpose of the averaging exercise.

g   The second point is the use of the phrase 'for which he is engaged in work'. This reflects the wording of reg 5(1) of the 1987 regulations (reg 51(1)(a) of the 1996 regulations) which states that 'remunerative work is work in which a person is engaged' for not less than 16 hours a week. It maintains the distinction which is drawn throughout the regulation between the hours for which a person is engaged

h   in work and the hours for which he is actually working.

[50] For these reasons I am unable to accept Mr Drabble's argument that reg 5 of the 1987 regulations (reg 51 of the 1996 regulations) is designed only to establish how many hours a week a person is to be treated as working in any week in which he does some work and that it does not affect the position of a

j   person who in a given week does no work at all. In my opinion this argument overlooks the fact that, although a recognisable cycle of work may include periods when the person does no work at all, he is nevertheless treated as being 'engaged in work' throughout his cycle of work. Every week is part of the cycle irrespective of whether the person does or does not work during that week. If the intention had been to provide that such a person was to be entitled to benefit during periods of school holidays or similar vacations, I would have expected the regulation to provide, as it does in the case of a person who is on maternity leave or absent from work because he is ill, that the person shall not be treated as engaged in remunerative work during those periods (see reg 5(3A) of the 1987 regulations (reg 52(1) of the 1996 regulations)). The wording of reg 5(3B) of the 1987 regulations (reg 51(2)(c) of the 1996 regulations) appears to me to have deliberately chosen to make it clear that it was not intended that the treatment of school holidays or similar vacations for the purpose of determining the number of hours in which the person is engaged in work should have the effect that the person was to be treated as not engaged in work during those periods simply because he was not required to work during those periods.

[51] I am also unable to accept Mr Drabble's alternative argument that the extent of deeming that a person is engaged in remunerative work during periods when he does not work should be confined to the weeks which are brought into account for the purposes of the averaging exercise, and that it should not extend to those weeks which are directed to be left out of account when the average is being calculated. According to this argument, periods which are disregarded in averaging should be disregarded also in regard to the question whether the person is to be treated as engaged in remunerative work during those periods. In my opinion the concluding words of reg 5(3A) of the 1987 regulations (reg 51(2)(c) of the 1996 regulations) make it clear that the disregard which is directed by that paragraph is for the sole purpose of the averaging exercise. A direction is needed that these periods must be disregarded for this purpose because they are periods which fall within the person's recognisable cycle of work. In the absence of the direction they would, as Mr Commissioner Goodman held in R(IS) 15/94, fall to be taken into account together with all the other periods in the cycle for the purpose of working out the average. But I do not find any words here to indicate that the direction was intended to affect any finding as to the cycle of work to which the result was to be applied after completing the averaging exercise.

[52] It seems to me that Auld LJ stated the position correctly when he said ([2000] 1 All ER 686 at 693) that reg 5(2)(b)(i) and (3B) of the 1987 regulations (reg 51(2)(b)(i) and (c) of the 1996 regulations) clearly contemplate that a recognisable yearly cycle of work may include periods in which an employee does no work, and that the averaging for which they provide is part of the means of determining whether he or she is engaged in remunerative work for the purpose of reg 5(1) of the 1987 regulations (reg 51(1) of the 1996 regulations). As he said, it is difficult to see what point there would be in reg 5(3B) of the 1987 regulations (reg 51(2)(c) of the 1996 regulations) if reg 5(2)(b)(i) of the 1987 regulations (reg 51(2)(b)(i) of the 1996 regulations) applied, contrary to its express terms, only to periods of actual work. Regulation 5(2)(b)(i) of the 1987 regulations states in terms that a person's cycle of work may involve periods when the person does not work. That was why, before the insertion of reg 5(3B) of the 1987 regulations (reg 51(2)(c) of the 1996 regulations), the averaging exercise was done in all cases by reference to the whole period of the cycle including periods when the person was not required to work during school holidays and similar vacation periods. The effect of the insertion is simply to take these periods out of account for the purpose of working out the average.

[53] As Social Security Commissioner May observed in CSJSA/395/98, para 17, if as a consequence of the calculation directed by reg 5(3B) of the 1987 regulations (reg 51(2)(c) of the 1996 regulations) the claimant's hours are sufficient to place the claimant within the definition of remunerative work in reg 5(1) of the 1987

a regulations (reg 51(1) of the 1996 regulations), the application of that definition covers the whole period of the cycle which has been identified as the cycle of work in the claimant's contract. I would hold that that is the result of the averaging exercise which has had to be carried out in this case.

[54] I would dismiss the appeal.

b **LORD MILLETT.**

[55] My Lords, I have had the advantage of reading in draft the speeches of my noble and learned friends, Lord Hope of Craighead and Lord Cooke of Thorndon. I am in full agreement with them that, were it not for reg 5(3B) of the Income Support (General) Regulations 1987, SI 1987/1967 (corresponding to reg 51(2)(c) of the Jobseeker's Allowance Regulations 1996, SI 1996/207), a school ancillary
c worker who does no work during school holidays would nevertheless be treated as being engaged in work throughout the year. The question which has divided their Lordships is whether reg 5(3B) of the former regulations and the corresponding provision of the latter alter this. I agree with Lord Hope that they do not. My reasons are as follows.

d

(1) *The 1987 regulations*

[56] Section 124(1) of the Social Security Contributions and Benefits Act 1992 makes benefit conditional on the claimant (inter alia) not being 'engaged in remunerative work'. This involves two concepts: (i) 'being engaged' in work and (ii) 'remunerative work'. Where necessary the language of the regulations
e distinguishes between the two concepts.

[57] As its heading indicates, reg 5 of the 1987 regulations is concerned with prescribing the circumstances in which a person is to be treated as being 'engaged in remunerative work'. This in turn involves defining the expression 'remunerative work'.

f   [58] Where a person's hours of work fluctuate, reg 5(1) defines 'remunerative work' as work 'in which he is engaged' on average for not less than 16 hours a week. Regulation 5(2)(b)(i) provides that, where there is a recognisable cycle of work, the number of hours for which a person 'is engaged in work' is to be determined by reference to the period of one complete cycle including periods in which the person does no work. This, as Lord Cooke observes, is for the purpose
g of averaging, which in turn is for the purpose of determining whether the claimant is engaged in remunerative work. For these purposes, a person is treated as being engaged in work even during periods when he does no work. The contrast, as Oliver LJ observed in *R v Supplementary Benefits Commission, ex p Lewis* [1982] 1 All ER 680, sub nom *R v Ebbw Vale and Merthyr Tydfil Supplementary*
h *Benefits Appeal Tribunal, ex p Lewis* [1982] 1 WLR 420, is between being 'in work' and being 'at work' (where, however, there was language which indicated that a person was not to be treated as being 'in work' unless he was actually 'at work').

[59] The tribunal found that the work in which the claimant was engaged had a recognisable cycle of one year. Under reg 5(2)(b)(i), therefore, he must be
j treated as being engaged in work throughout the year, including the school holidays when he does no work. Whether the work in which he is to be treated as engaged is remunerative work depends upon the average number of hours per week spread over the whole cycle.

[60] This is not, with respect to my noble and learned friend, Lord Scott of Foscote, to imply a statutory fiction into the regulations. It merely gives effect to the distinction which is drawn in the regulations between being engaged in work

and doing work. It recognises that, if the number of hours for which a person is 'engaged in work' includes periods during which he does no work, it follows that *a* a person can be 'engaged in work' even if he is not working.

[61] There is nothing particularly surprising in this, for were it otherwise the regulations would be open to manipulation. Suppose an employer wished to put his workforce on short time during a recession. He might ask them to work 20 hours a week instead of the usual 40 hours. The unions would ask him to *b* introduce instead a cycle of 80 hours every four weeks, leaving it to the men to decide when to come to work. If they worked 20 hours a week, they would not be entitled to benefit. If they worked 40 hours every other week, they would prima facie be entitled to benefit during the weeks when they did not work. Paragraph (2)(b)(i) prevents this. It does not merely spread the hours when the *c* worker is engaged in work over the four weeks; it also treats him as being engaged in work during the two weeks when he is not working.

[62] Thus far I am in respectful agreement with Lord Cooke. Paragraph (2) is, however, expressly made subject to reg 5(3B) of the 1987 regulations, which applies where a person's cycle of work at a school, other educational establishment or other place of employment is one year and includes periods of school holidays *d* during which he does not work. It provides that, for the purpose of reg 5(2)(b)(i), those periods are to be disregarded in establishing the average hours for which he is engaged in work. Lord Cooke interprets this to mean that, contrary to the general rule for cyclical workers, he is not to be treated as being engaged in remunerative work during the school holidays. *e*

[63] It is at this point that I respectfully part company with him. To my mind the critical point is that para (2)(b)(i) is not replaced by para (3B) but merely made subject to it. Paragraph (2)(b) remains in full force save only to the extent to which it is modified by para (3B). The two paragraphs must be read together. They are both concerned with persons who have a regular cycle of work. Neither *f* of them is concerned with the question when a person is to be treated as being engaged in work, but only with the determination of the average number of hours for which he is engaged in work for the purpose of determining whether the work (in which ex hypothesi he must be treated as being engaged) is remunerative work. Paragraph (2)(b)(i) directs that the average number of hours is to be determined by reference to a complete cycle including periods during *g* which he does no work, and there is nothing in para (3B) which modifies this. It does not affect the duration of the cycle or exclude periods during which he does no work. In the case of the present claimant, therefore, the cycle of work remains the complete year.

[64] This is confirmed by the opening words of para (3B), which applies only *h* where the cycle of work is one year and includes periods of school holidays during which he does no work. Reading para (2)(b)(i) as modified by para (3B) and omitting immaterial words produces the following:

'Where a person's recognisable cycle of work at a school ... is one year and *j* includes periods of school holidays ... during which he does not work, the number of hours for which he is engaged in work shall be determined by reference to the average of hours worked over one complete cycle including periods during which he does not work (ie one year) but so that the school holidays shall be disregarded in establishing the average hours for which he is engaged in work.'

a [65] In my opinion the cycle remains constant at one complete year, and the claimant continues to be treated (by para (2)(b)(i) of the 1987 regulations) as engaged in work throughout the cycle including periods when he does no work. Paragraph (3B) directs that the school holidays are to be disregarded, not for the purpose of determining when a person is to be treated as engaged in work, but merely for the purpose of establishing the average number of hours worked
b during the cycle.

[66] This construction is confirmed by the entirely different approach taken by reg 5(3) and (3A), which unlike para (3B) are concerned with the question when a person is to be treated as being engaged in remunerative work. Paragraph (3A), for example, provides that a person shall not be treated as engaged in remunerative work on any day when the person concerned is on maternity leave or is absent
c from work because he is ill. This displaces para (2) altogether. A claimant is not to be treated as engaged in remunerative work while on maternity leave or absent from work because of illness. But para (3B) does not provide that a claimant to whom it applies is not to be treated as engaged in remunerative work during the school holidays. It does not supplant para (2)(b)(i) which directs that he is to be
d so treated. All it does is direct that the school holidays are to be left out of the calculations which establish the average number of hours worked during the year.

(2) The 1996 regulations

[67] Although the drafting of reg 51 is different, and at first sight critically different, the result is in my opinion the same. The difference is that reg 5(2)(b)(i)
e of the 1987 regulations (which provides for averaging over the whole cycle including periods when the claimant does not work) is not merely subjected to reg 51(2)(c) of the 1996 regulations (which deals with school holidays) but applies only where reg 51(2)(c) does not apply. At first sight, therefore, the two paragraphs are alternatives. But the drafting and the layout of the regulation are inelegant,
f to say the least. Paragraph (2)(c) cannot stand as an independent paragraph; it ought to have been included as reg 51(2)(b)(iii) and expanded since the sense requires the opening words of para (2)(b) and part at least of para (2)(b)(i) to be read into it. Omitting immaterial words, and with as little as possible read in, the regulation reads as follows:

g 'Where a claimant works at a school and the cycle of work consists of one year but with school holidays during which he does no work, the number of hours in which he is engaged in work shall be determined by reference to the average hours worked over the period of one complete cycle but disregarding the periods during which he does no work.'

h [68] Even without the incorporation of the words 'including in the cycle the periods during which he does no work' the effect is tolerably plain. The number of hours for which he engaged in work during the cycle (ie during the year) is to be determined by averaging over the year but disregarding the school holidays. Again this interpretation is confirmed by the way in which periods of illness and
j maternity leave are dealt with in reg 52(1).

[69] I would dismiss the appeal.

LORD SCOTT OF FOSCOTE.

[70] My Lords, the title of these proceedings has become misleading[c]. Mr Stafford has withdrawn his appeal. The only appellant is Mr Banks, anonymously described in the title as 'another'. Mr Banks is, or was at the time when the claims

with which your Lordships are concerned were made, a single man. He was, in
1996, 22 years old. He worked for Doncaster Metropolitan Borough Council as
a special needs assistant. He had entered this employment on 1 September 1995
and from then until the end of the summer term in 1996 he worked at Denaby
Main Junior School. His principal duties were to provide support to two named
children who had special educational needs. From 3 September 1996, the
beginning of the 1996 autumn term, Mr Banks worked at a different school with
different children. But his employer remained the same and his duties and terms
and conditions of employment remained the same. So he had a continuing
contract of employment from 1 September 1995.

[71] Mr Banks' hours of work were defined by the special educational needs of
the particular children he was assisting. His hours were term-time hours only and
amounted to 20 hours per week. He was paid at the rate of £4·43 per hour. His
conditions of employment stated that: 'There is no entitlement to paid annual
leave ...' and that:

> 'As work is available only during the times the pupil attends school other
> than in exceptional circumstances it is expected that holidays and other personal
> commitments are arranged outside of normal working hours.'

[72] It is plain that Mr Banks' hours of work were tied to the actual presence
at school and the educational requirements of specific pupils. There could,
therefore, never be any work for him in school holidays and his pay was not
intended to remunerate him for anything other than the hours of work with the
named pupils that he put in during the school terms. He submitted monthly
returns, detailing the hours he had worked, and, on the basis of the returns, was
paid at monthly intervals. As Mr Commissioner Rowland commented, the
monthly amounts paid to Mr Banks would vary, depending upon the hours
worked from month to month (para 6 of his decision dated 24 February 1999).
But what would not vary would be that during school holidays Mr Banks would
do no work with the special needs children, would not put in any returns and
would be paid nothing.

[73] The Doncaster social security appeal tribunal, in the decision dated
10 February 1997 that was appealed to Special Security Commissioner Rowland,
found that in 1995/1996 Mr Banks worked 20 hours a week for 38 weeks. This gives
a total for the year of 760 hours (not 720 as stated in the decision). So Mr Banks'
remuneration for the year from his employment as a special needs assistant was
around £3,367. Not many people would suppose that an annual income of £3,367
would suffice to keep the recipient out of poverty. So to conclude is not to charge
Doncaster Metropolitan Borough Council with underpaying its special needs
assistants. It is plain that the structure of employment of school ancillary workers,
who include special needs assistants and many other categories, assumes that
they will be available for employment elsewhere during out-of-term periods and
can supplement their income by working during those periods. The reality of
their contracts is that employment is available to them for limited hours during
term time and that they are not employed during out-of-term periods.

[74] This is why it is common ground that reg 5(3) of the Income Support
(General) Regulations 1987, SI 1987/1967, and reg 52(1) of the Jobseeker's Allowance
Regulations 1996, SI 1996/207, do not, so far as school holidays are concerned,

---

c   Editor's note: in the hearing before the House of Lords, the case was referred to as *Stafford and
    another v Chief Adjudication Officer.*

a affect ancillary workers such as Mr Banks. School holidays are holidays for teachers, and, of course, for the children. Teachers receive an annual salary, usually payable monthly. Their remuneration relates to the whole year. Their school employment places them in employment for the year unless earlier terminated. Not so ancillary workers. They are not in employment in any meaningful sense except during school terms.

b [75] It is, as I have said, to be expected that ancillary workers like Mr Banks will make themselves available for employment in out-of-term periods in order to supplement their income, inadequate as it is if viewed on a yearly basis. If they are not able to obtain employment in out-of-term periods, it is to be expected that they will seek to supplement their inadequate income by making a claim for income-related benefit.

c [76] The National Assistance Act 1948, the last of the four major Acts enacted to implement the recommendations of the Beveridge Report on *Social Insurance and Allied Services* (Cmd 6404) (1942) was introduced to take the place of public assistance through the Poor Laws in order to provide a means-tested benefit for the relief of poverty. There have been substantial developments and changes d since 1948 in the social security system of which means-tested benefit for the relief of poverty forms part. The Social Security Act 1986 abolished supplementary benefit and family income supplement and replaced them with 'income support' as the basic safety net benefit and 'family credit' as a progressive benefit for those with family responsibilities. The purpose of this was to counter the 'poverty trap', where the financial disadvantage of losing benefit outweighed the financial e advantages of taking employment. In 1992 the substantive law relating to social security benefits was consolidated in the Social Security Contributions and Benefits Act 1992 which covered, inter alia, income-related benefits such as income support and family credit. The 1992 Act was in force at the time Mr Banks began his employment with Doncaster Metropolitan Borough Council. As from f October 1996, however, in respect of claimants available for work, the Jobseekers Act 1995 replaced income support under the 1992 Act with jobseeker's allowance, also an income-based benefit. Income support under the 1992 Act could be claimed only by those who were not available for work. But none of these legislative changes departed from the fundamental purpose of the social security system, namely, that benefit should be provided in order to keep out of poverty g those whose income was below a minimum poverty level.

[77] My Lords, the statutory provisions in the Acts and regulations made thereunder must be construed, so far as possible, so as to give effect to the fundamental purpose of the legislation to which I have referred. If there are ambiguities or inconsistencies in the statutory language these should, I respectfully h suggest, be resolved in a manner which serves that fundamental purpose and is not inconsistent with it.

[78] The regulations that your Lordships must construe for the purposes of this appeal, namely the 1987 regulations and the 1996 regulations, cannot, in their application to Mr Banks' claims, be presented as models of clarity. Mr Banks' claims j raise the question whether reg 5(2)(b)(i) and (3B) of the 1987 regulations require him to be treated as being in remunerative employment during school holidays. The same question arises under reg 51(2)(b)(i) and (c) of the 1996 regulations.

[79] In the answering of this question there have been disagreements at almost all levels. First, there have been disagreements at the tribunal level. Mr Banks applied for income support in respect of the period 22 December 1995 to 9 January 1996 (the 1995 Christmas school holiday) and for the period 1 April 1996

to 14 April 1996 (the 1996 Easter school holiday). The Doncaster social security appeal tribunal in its decision of 28 May 1996 held that reg 5(2)(b)(i) of the 1987 regulations did not apply because Mr Banks' hours of work did not fluctuate. They said:

> 'He works regular hours during term time and does not work in school holidays. This is not an example of fluctuating hours but of periods of work for non-fluctuating hours followed by periods of no work. We are of opinion that the appellant is engaged in work for a regular number of hours in term time and not so engaged during the holiday periods. The provisions of reg 5(2)(b)(i) do not therefore apply to the appellant's work. As a consequence he is in remunerative work only during the periods when he is working 20 hours per week at the school. During holiday periods he is not in remunerative work. Consequently he is not in remunerative work between 22 December 1995 and 9 January 1996 and between 1 April 1996 and 14 April 1996. The matter should be referred to the adjudication officer to consider whether he was available for work during those periods.'

[80] Presumably the adjudication officer was satisfied about Mr Banks' availability because he was paid income support for the two periods of claim. He was paid £36·80 per week.

[81] Mr Banks made another claim to income support in respect of the 1996 summer holiday, 22 July 1996 to 3 September 1996, and a claim to jobseeker's allowance in respect of the Michaelmas half-term holiday, 25 October 1996 to 4 November 1996.

[82] The Doncaster social security appeal tribunal, in its decision of 10 February 1997, disagreed with the decision of 28 May 1996 that had been reached by a differently constituted tribunal. There was no material difference in the facts but the 1997 tribunal held that reg 5(2)(b)(i) of the 1987 regulations did apply. Since, over the cycle of one year, Mr Banks worked 20 hours a week for 38 weeks and no hours at all for 14 weeks, the tribunal held that 'the number of hours for which Mr Banks is engaged fluctuate'. The difference between the two tribunals was that the 1997 tribunal thought that Mr Banks should be treated as engaged in work during the school holidays. The 1996 tribunal thought he should not be so treated.

[83] Second, there have been disagreements at the commissioner level. In dealing with Mr Banks' appeal against the conclusions of the 1997 tribunal, Mr Commissioner Rowland held that, in a case where a 'recognisable cycle of work' had been established:

> '... a person is engaged in remunerative work during any part of a cycle of work taken into account in establishing the average hours for which he or she is engaged in work ... it would follow that a person to whom reg 5(3B) applies is not to be regarded as engaged in remunerative work during school holidays.'

[84] This is substantially the same approach to construction as that advocated by my noble and learned friend, Lord Cooke of Thorndon.

[85] But, in a decision in Scotland on 18 March 1999 (CSJSA/395/98), Special Security Commissioner May, addressing the 1996 regulations, disagreed with Special Security Commissioner Rowland and held (at para 17):

> '... upon a proper construction of reg 51, when read as a whole, if as a consequence of the calculation in reg 51(2)(c) [the counterpart of reg 5(3B) of the 1987 regulations] the claimant's hours are sufficient to place her within the definition of remunerative work that work covers the whole period of the cycle; namely the calendar year which is clearly the cycle in the claimant's contract.'

[86] The Court of Appeal in dealing with the appeal from Mr Commissioner Rowland's decision, gave a judgment of the court ([2000] 1 All ER 696) which, in effect, preferred Mr Commissioner May's reasoning to that of Mr Commissioner Rowland. But, in your Lordships' House there are again disagreements as to the correct application of the relevant regulations to the facts of Mr Banks' claims.

[87] In these circumstances it can hardly be said that the proper meaning and effect of the regulations is clear. In deciding upon their meaning and effect, and in resolving any ambiguity, the social purpose of the legislation should, in my opinion, be kept in mind and, if possible, given effect to.

[88] Section 124(1) of the 1992 Act entitles a citizen such as Mr Banks to income support if—

> '(b) he has no income or his income does not exceed the applicable amount; (c) he is not engaged in remunerative work ... and (d) except in such circumstances as may be prescribed—(i) he is available for, and actively seeking, employment ...'

[89] Section 1 of the 1995 Act entitles a citizen such as Mr Banks to jobseeker's allowance if he fulfils a number of specified conditions. These conditions include those set out in s 124(1)(b), (c) and (d) as cited above.

[90] This appeal is only concerned with the condition set out in s 124(1)(c) of the 1992 Act (or in s 1(2)(e) of the 1995 Act). It is accepted, at least for the purposes of this appeal, that Mr Banks was able to satisfy all the other conditions.

[91] The condition 'he is not engaged in remunerative work' has two, at least, important elements. First, the expression 'remunerative work' requires definition. It is not a term of art. Second, the question whether and when a person is 'engaged in' remunerative work is, obviously, of importance. The 1992 Act, in s 137(2), provides that:

> 'Regulations may make provision for the purposes of this Part of this Act ... (c) as to what is or is not to be treated as remunerative work ... (d) as to circumstances in which a person is or is not to be treated as—(i) engaged or normally engaged in remunerative work; (ii) available for employment; or (iii) actively seeking employment ...'

[92] The 1995 Act has a regulation-making power in more or less the same language (see s 21 and para (1) of Sch 1).

[93] In reg 5 of the 1987 regulations there is an exercise both of the s 137(2)(c) power and of the s 137(2)(d) power. Paragraph (1) describes the work that is to be treated as 'remunerative work'. And paras (3), (3A) and (4) set out circumstances in which a person is to be 'treated' as engaged in remunerative work (paras (3) and (4)) and 'not treated' as so engaged (para (3A)).

[94] The issues of construction that arise on this appeal relate to paras (2) and (3B) of reg 5. These two paragraphs amplify and supplement para (1). They identify what is or is not 'remunerative work'. They do not purport to, and do not, describe circumstances in which a person who is *not engaged* in remunerative work is to be

treated as so engaged or circumstances in which a person who *is engaged* in remunerative work is to be *treated* as not so engaged. To make good these propositions it is necessary to set out the text of the relevant paragraphs, omitting irrelevant passages:

'(1) Subject to the following provisions of this regulation ... remunerative work is work in which a person is engaged, or, where his hours of work fluctuate, he is engaged on average, for not less than 16 hours a week being work for which payment is made or which is done in   expectation of payment.

(2) Subject to paragraph (3B), the number of hours for which a person is engaged in work shall be determined—(a) where no recognisable cycle has been established in respect of a person's work, by reference to the number of hours or, where those hours are likely to fluctuate, the average of the hours, which he is expected to work in a week; (b) where the number of hours for which he is engaged fluctuate, by reference to the average of hours worked over—(i) if there is a recognisable cycle of work, the period of one complete cycle (including, where the cycle involves periods in which the person does no work, those periods but disregarding any other absences) ...

(3) A person shall be treated as engaged in remunerative work during any period for which he is absent from work referred to in paragraph (1) if the absence is either without good cause or by reason of a recognised, customary or other holiday.

(3A) A person shall not be treated as engaged in remunerative work on any day on which the person is on maternity leave or is absent from work because he is ill.

(3B) Where for the purpose of paragraph (2)(b)(i), a person's recognisable cycle of work at a school ... is one year and includes periods of school holidays ... during which he does not work, those periods and any other periods not forming part of such holidays ... during which he is not required to work shall be disregarded in establishing the average hours for which he is engaged in work.'

[95] As is apparent, para (1) contains a description of the work that for the purposes of s 124(1)(c) of the 1992 Act is 'remunerative work'. It does not set out circumstances in which a person who is not engaged in work at all is to be treated as engaged in work. It is an exercise of the s 137(2)(c) power. If a person *is* engaged in work, para (1) will tell you whether or not the work is 'remunerative work'.

[96] But some amplification of para (1) was plainly necessary. How should the number of 'hours of work', which will determine whether or not the work is 'remunerative work', be calculated? Paragraph (2) provides the answer. It enables the relevant number of hours, for para (1) purposes, to be calculated.

[97] To reprise, a person who is not at or in work at all is, obviously, or so it seems to me, not in 'remunerative work'. If, on the other hand, a person is in work, he may or may not be in 'remunerative work'. Paragraphs (1) and (2) will tell you whether he is or is not.

[98] I now come to reg 5(3B) of the 1987 regulations. Paragraph (3B) qualifies para (2)(b)(i). It only applies if there is a recognisable cycle of work of one year. It alters the 'number of hours' calculation that would otherwise be made under para (2)(b)(i). But no more than para (2)(b)(i) does para (3B) require a person who is not engaged in work at all to be treated as if he was in work. All it does is to

a affect the calculation of the average number of hours 'for which a person is engaged in work' (see the opening words of para (2)).

[99] At [59] above, my noble and learned friend, Lord Millett, says that under para (2)(b)(i) the claimant must be treated as being engaged in work throughout the yearly cycle. Why? The paragraph does not say so. Nowhere are the words '*treated* as being engaged in work', or anything similar, to be found. Those words are,

b by contrast, to be found in paras (3), (3A) and (4), and in other paragraphs as well. But they are absent from para (2), as they are from para (3B).

[100] I would agree, without any difficulty, that the wording of para (2) and of para (3B) does create some problems. For example, there is the parenthetic passage in para (2)(b)(i): '(… including, where the cycle involves periods in which the person does not work, those periods but disregarding any other absences) …'

c What are the 'other absences' to which the passage refers? What are the contrasted 'periods in which a person does not work'? Special Security Commissioner Morcom who decided CIS/261/1990 thought that school holidays were excluded from 'periods in which the person does not work' and, presumably, were included in 'other absences'. Special Security Commissioner Goodman in R(IS)15/94

d disagreed and held that school holidays were, for para (2)(b)(i) purposes, 'periods in which the person does not work'. His decision led to para (3B) being added to reg 5. But whatever the right view on the meaning of the passage, its relevance is to no more than to the calculation of the average number of hours.

[101] Mr Commissioner Goodman in his decision said: '… reg 5(3) is not dealing with the question of hours of work as averaged but is dealing with the

e question of when a person shall be treated as *engaged* in remunerative *work* as defined in reg 5(1).' Similarly, in my opinion, reg 5(2)(b)(i) is dealing with the question of hours of work as averaged and is not dealing with the question of when a person shall be treated as *engaged* in remunerative work.

[102] Paragraph (3) of reg 5 introduces the statutory fiction that a person

f absent from work without good cause or during 'a recognised, customary or other holiday' is in remunerative work although not in fact in work at all. It is accepted that this provision does not apply to Mr Banks during school holidays. School holidays are not holidays for him. It would apply to him during bank holidays. Paragraph (4) of reg 5 says that for the first seven days of a strike, a striker is to be treated as in remunerative work. This is another statutory fiction.

g But there is no provision that, in terms at least, says that ancillary school workers like Mr Banks are to be treated as engaged in remunerative work during out-of-term periods when they are not in work at all. There could easily have been such a provision. Why should the statutory fiction be implied?

[103] This approach to and construction of reg 5 of the 1987 regulation and its

h various paragraphs is, I suggest, confirmed by the language used in the comparable 1996 regulations. It is common ground that the 1996 regulations were intended to produce the same result as the 1987 regulations.

[104] Regulation 51 of the 1996 regulations describes what is meant by 'remunerative work'. It means 'work in which [the claimant] is engaged or, where

j his hours of work fluctuate, is engaged on average, for not less than 16 hours per week' (para (1)(a)). As with reg 5(1) and (2) of the 1987 regulations, reg 51(1) of the 1996 regulations is not expressed to treat anyone as engaged in work who is not in work. But if a person is in work para (1) will tell you whether or not the work is 'remunerative work'.

[105] Paragraph (2) of reg 51 supplements para (1). It tells you how to calculate 'the number of hours in which the claimant … is engaged in work'. As with

paras (2) and (3B) of reg 5 of the 1987 regulations, it is the 'number of hours' on which the paragraph is concentrating. In para (2) of reg 51, as in paras (2) and (3B) of reg 5 of the 1987 regulations, the words 'treated as engaged' nowhere appear. The paragraph does not describe circumstances in which a person not in work is to be treated as being in work. Paragraph (2)(a), (b)(i) and (b)(ii) of reg 51 of the 1996 regulations are in the same terms and serve the same purpose as para (2)(a), (b)(i) and (b)(ii) of reg 5 of the 1987 regulations. Paragraph (2)(c) in reg 51 of the 1996 regulations is in the same terms and serves the same purpose as para (3B) in reg 5 of the 1987 regulations.

[106] The content of reg 51 of the 1996 regulations as a whole makes it, I suggest, clear that it is describing what 'remunerative work' means, and is not dealing at all with the question of who is or is not to be treated as in remunerative work. That is done by reg 52, headed 'Persons treated as engaged in remunerative work', and by reg 53, headed 'Persons treated as not engaged in remunerative work'. It is these two regulations that contain the statutory fictions as to when a person is or is not to be treated as engaged in remunerative work. Regulation 51 does not do so. A construction of reg 51 as requiring a person to be treated as engaged in remunerative work at a time when he is not engaged in work at all is to impute to the draftsman of the regulations an almost impish pursuit of confusion.

[107] I venture to suggest, my Lords, that such a construction of reg 51 of the 1996 regulations or of reg 5 of the 1987 regulations is wrong. At the least it cannot be regarded as a construction that is clearly right. And it is, I suggest, a construction that fails to give effect to the fundamental purpose of the legislation.

[108] The alternative construction, and that which I prefer, is that reg 5 of the 1987 regulations and reg 51 of the 1996 regulations do not require a person to be treated as engaged in remunerative work at a time when he was not engaged in work at all. So, was Mr Banks in work during the periods in respect of which his claims were made? Given the contractual arrangements between him and the Doncaster Metropolitan BC, the answer, in my opinion, is that he was not.

[109] In *R v Supplementary Benefits Commission, ex p Lewis* [1982] 1 All ER 680, sub nom *R v Ebbw Vale and Merthyr Tydfil Supplementary Benefits Appeal Tribunal, ex p Lewis* [1982] 1 WLR 420 the Court of Appeal held that a person who was absent from work through illness was not at the time 'engaged, and normally engaged, in remunerative full time work' for the purposes of the Family Income Supplements Act 1970. Lord Denning MR ([1982] 1 All ER 680 at 683, [1982] 1 WLR 420 at 422) asked the question 'is he engaged in remunerative full-time work during the period when he is sick?' and said: 'The commonsense answer is that he is not engaged in remunerative full-time work at that time.' Oliver LJ agreed. He rejected ([1982] 1 All ER 680 at 684, [1982] 1 WLR 420 at 424) the proposition that 'a person engaged in remunerative full-time work' meant 'simply being engaged under a contract of employment'.

[110] So, in the present case, unless there is some statutory provision that requires Mr Banks to be treated as being engaged in work during school holidays, I would hold on the facts that he was not so engaged. There is no statutory provision that expressly so requires and, in my opinion, no sufficient justification for implying such a provision into reg 5(2)(b)(i) of the 1987 regulations or reg 51 of the 1996 regulations.

[111] If I am wrong about that, I would concur in the opinion of my noble and learned friend, Lord Cooke of Thorndon, and hold that the 'disregard' in reg 5(3B) of the 1987 regulations and in reg 51(2)(c) of the 1996 regulations requires

a that Mr Banks should not be treated as in remunerative work during school holidays.

[112] May I conclude, my Lords, by inviting your Lordships to consider the position that will have been reached if this appeal is to be dismissed.

[113] School ancillary workers who, like Mr Banks, are single and not eligible for family credit will be firmly caught in a 'poverty trap'. Mr Banks' income from
b his employment as a special needs assistant was around £3,367 per annum. This is surely below poverty level. Mr Banks' attempts to supplement this inadequate income by working elsewhere in school holidays failed. This is not surprising. It is not easy to find short-term work. If school ancillary workers like Mr Banks are barred from claiming jobseeker's allowance by being treated as being engaged in work when in fact they are not, what are they to do? They can, I suppose, give
c up their employment as ancillary workers and seek some form of alternative employment where they will not be caught by the construction of the regulations that will have trapped Mr Banks and, pending such re-employment, they can claim benefit. But how will schools and other educational establishments then attract ancillary workers? And if the ancillary work employment is still open to
d them their benefit claim may be barred on the ground that that employment is available to them and they are not actively seeking it. This is a 'poverty trap' sequence that the Social Security Act 1986 was intended to cure. If there had been some express provision in the regulations that made this result unavoidable, then your Lordships would be unable to avoid it. But why should this result be brought about by implying into the regulations a statutory fiction that is not
e expressed? In my opinion, for the reasons I have tried to express, a construction that produces that result is not justified and I would allow the appeal. If that course does not find favour with your Lordships, the sooner the Secretary of State remedies the situation by making appropriate new regulations the better.

Appeal dismissed.

Kate O'Hanlon   Barrister.

Re W

a

COURT OF APPEAL, CIVIL DIVISION

PETER GIBSON, ARDEN LJJ AND SIR CHRISTOPHER STAUGHTON

11 DECEMBER 2000

b

Power of attorney – Enduring power of attorney – Creation – Capacity of donor – Mental capacity of donor when power created – Burden of proof when registration of power opposed – Whether burden of proof on attorney to establish donor's capacity if objectors producing evidence that donor lacked capacity – Enduring Powers of Attorney Act 1985, s 6(6).

c

W, an elderly woman, granted an enduring power of attorney to her eldest child, X. After X gave notice of her intention to register the power under the Enduring Powers of Attorney Act 1985, W's two other children served notice of objection, alleging, inter alia, that the power was not valid because, at the time of its creation, W had lacked the necessary mental capacity and understanding. Under *d* s 6(6)[a] of the Act, the court was required to register the power if it were not satisfied of the grounds of objection. The master upheld the objection, but his decision was reversed on appeal by the deputy judge who held that the objectors had failed to satisfy him that W had lacked the requisite capacity. The objectors appealed, contending that once evidence had been produced which tended to show that the donor lacked the necessary capacity, the burden was on the *e* attorney to prove the contrary.

Held – Where the objectors were seeking to prevent the registration of an enduring power of attorney on the basis that the power was invalid by reason of the donor's lack of capacity, the burden of proof on that issue remained *f* throughout on the objectors. Section 6(6) of the 1985 Act plainly put the burden in the first instance on the objectors. Nor was the burden shifted by the production of evidence tending to show that the donor lacked the necessary capacity. Where there was only one issue in a case and the burden of proof rested on one party, it was wrong to say that the burden of proof shifted after one witness had been called and given evidence which, if believed, would discharge *g* that burden. Unless the burden as to that issue had been discharged, the person on whom it originally rested did not succeed. In the instant case, the judge had been right to treat the burden as resting throughout on the objectors, and he had been entitled to conclude that they had failed to discharge that burden. Accordingly, the appeal would be dismissed (see p 93 *b c j* to p 94 *b* and p 95 *h j* to *h* p 96 *a h*, below).

Dictum of Hoffmann J in *Re K, Re F* [1988] 1 All ER 358 at 363 explained.

Decision of Jules Sher QC [2000] 1 All ER 175 affirmed.

Notes

j

For the court's functions on an application for registration of an enduring power of attorney, see 1(2) *Halsbury's Laws* (4th edn reissue) para 38.

For the Enduring Power of Attorney Act 1985, s 6, see 1 *Halsbury's Statutes* (4th edn) (1998 reissue) 102.

---

a   Section 6(6) is set out at p 91 *c*, below

a   **Cases referred to in judgments**
Beaney (decd), Re [1978] 2 All ER 595, [1978] 1 WLR 770.
Brown v Pourau [1995] 1 NZLR 352, NZ HC.
K, Re, Re F [1988] 1 All ER 358, [1988] Ch 310, [1988] 2 WLR 781.
Peters v Morris (19 May 1987, unreported), NZ CA.
Waring v Waring (1848) 6 Moo PC 341, PC.

b

Appeal
By notice dated 30 October 2000, the appellant objectors, Mrs W and Mr Z, appealed with permission of Robert Walker LJ from the decision of Jules Sher QC, sitting as a deputy judge of the High Court on 8 July 1999 ([2000] 1 All ER 175,
c   [2000] Ch 343), allowing an appeal by the respondent, Mrs X, from the decision of Master Lush on 12 November 1998 refusing to register under the Enduring Powers of Attorney Act 1985 a power of attorney granted to Mrs X by the parties' mother, Mrs W, on 4 July 1996. The facts are set out in the judgment of Sir Christopher Staughton.

d   *David Rees* (instructed by *Gaby Hardwicke Yearwood & Griffiths*, Bexhill-on-Sea) for the objectors.
Adrian Jack (instructed by *Max Barford & Co*, Tunbridge Wells) Mrs X.

PETER GIBSON LJ.
1. I will ask Sir Christopher Staughton to give the first judgment.
e

SIR CHRISTOPHER STAUGHTON.
2. This appeal concerns the affairs of Mrs W, as I shall call her, a widow who is nearly 91 years of age. On 4 July 1996 she granted an enduring power of attorney to her eldest child, Mrs X. Two years later, on 27 April 1998, Mrs X
f   applied for the enduring power of attorney to be registered under the Enduring Powers of Attorney Act 1985. Meanwhile, she had given notice of intention to register on 18 April to the other two children of Mrs W: I will call them Mrs Y, who is now 61, and Mr Z, who is aged 57. They became the objectors. They had already, on 21 February 1997, obtained a report from a Mr Connor on Mrs W's mental health, but no action had been taken on that report in the ensuing year.
g
3. On 13 May 1998 the objectors served notice of objection. That led to the present proceedings. The objections were upheld by Master Lush in the Court of Protection. However, his decision was reached in an unsatisfactory way in that Mrs X had not been notified of the hearing date and was not present. It seems to me, there having been real doubt as to whether she had been notified, that the
h   master would have been wiser not to proceed at that stage. In the event, we should disregard the conclusions of the master. There might have been an order setting his decision aside and directing a fresh hearing before a new master; but the parties instead agreed that on an appeal to a judge of the Chancery Division the matter should be reconsidered (see [2000] 1 All ER 175, [2000] Ch 343). That
j   was done in order to save costs.
4. The assets of the estate are not large. They are somewhat less now than they were before, no doubt, as the master ordered the costs to come out of the estate. So did the judge. In the judge's decision it is said that the assets were a portfolio of investments valued in December 1998 at £211,000, £20,000 in premium bonds and a life policy written in trust of £30,000. At the time Mrs W was in a nursing home, which cost £2,000 a month. She had some other simple

and fairly modest requirements. Of course, she also had on the income side the
old age pension.   *a*

5. The grounds argued before the master were these. First, that the power
purported to have been created by the instrument was not valid as an enduring
power of attorney. The reason put forward for that was that Mrs W did not have
the necessary capacity and understanding at the time when she made it.
Secondly, it was said that undue pressure was used to induce the donor to create   *b*
the power. Thirdly, that having regard to all the circumstances, and in particular
the attorney's relationship to or connection with the donor, the attorney was
unsuitable as an attorney of the donor.

6. The master upheld the first and third grounds, that is to say lack of capacity
and understanding and unsuitability, but not the second ground, which was
undue pressure. The appeal came before Mr Jules Sher QC, sitting as a deputy   *c*
judge of the Chancery Division. Before him only grounds one and three were
argued, the ones upon which the objectors had succeeded before the master. The
deputy judge reversed the master's decision on both points. He had, of course,
additional evidence which was not before the master.

7. There is now an appeal to this court by permission of Robert Walker LJ.   *d*

8. The third ground, unsuitability, is no longer pursued by the objectors. So
the only ground now is that the power of attorney was invalid through want of
capacity.

9. Before the judge the objectors had accepted that the burden of proof as to
that rested on them. The judge accepted that, and there was no challenge to it in
the notice of appeal. But now the objectors seek to amend their notice of appeal   *e*
to say that the burden was on Mrs X, the attorney. There has been no objection
to leave to amend the notice of appeal being granted; and we do grant it.

10. The relevant provisions in the 1985 Act are as follows. Section 4 provides:

'(1) If the attorney under an enduring power has reason to believe that the   *f*
donor is or is becoming mentally incapable subsections (2) to (6) below shall
apply.

(2) The attorney shall, as soon as practicable, make an application to the
court for the registration of the instrument creating the power.'

11. That, of course, was done in this case.   *g*

12. Then s 6 says:

'(1) In any case where—(a) an application for registration is made in
accordance with section 4(3) and (4), and (b) neither subsection (2) nor
subsection (4) below applies, the court shall register the instrument to which
the application relates.'   *h*

13. The provisions there referred to in sub-ss (2) and (4) deal with two cases.
Subsection (2) deals with the case where it appears to the court that there is in
force under Pt VII of the Mental Health Act 1983 an order appointing a receiver.
But that is not this case. In such a case the court can act of its own motion.
Subsection (4) provides: *j*

'If, in the case of an application for registration—(a) a valid notice of
objection to the registration is received [within a certain period]; or (b) it
appears from the application that there is no one to whom notice has been
given under paragraph 1 of [Schedule 1]; or (c) the court has reason to believe
that appropriate inquiries might bring to light evidence on which the court

could be satisfied that one of the grounds of objection set out in subsection (5) below was established, the court shall neither register the instrument nor refuse the application until it has made or caused to be made such inquiries (if any) as it thinks appropriate in the circumstances of the case.'

14. So that deals with two cases: first, whether where there is a valid notice of objection; second, whether the court has reason to believe that appropriate inquiries might bring to light evidence which was relevant.

15. Then sub-s (5) sets out for the purposes of the Act what grounds may be included in the notice of objection. Ground (a) is that the power purported to have been created by the attorney was not a valid and enduring power of attorney. That is the case which now remains to be considered in this court.

16. Then sub-s (6), which is critical for this case, provides:

'If, in a case where subsection (4) above applies, any of the grounds of objection in subsection (5) above is established to the satisfaction of the court, the court shall refuse the application but if, in such a case, it is not so satisfied, the court shall register the instrument to which the application relates.'

17. In this case there was a valid objection under sub-s (4). The question is whether the ground of objection in sub-s (5)(a), that is to say that there was not a valid enduring power of attorney, is established to the satisfaction of the court. If it is, the court must refuse registration. If not, the court shall register the instrument.

18. The law relating to this matter has been considered in two judgments to which we have been referred. First, there is the decision in *Re K, Re F* [1988] 1 All ER 358, [1988] Ch 310. In that case Hoffmann J said:

'The 1985 Act does not specify the mental capacity needed to execute an enduring power and the answer must therefore be found in the common law. It is well established that capacity to perform a juristic act exists when the person who purported to do the act had at the time the mental capacity, with the assistance of such explanation as he may have been given, to understand the nature and effect of that particular transaction: see *Re Beaney (decd)* [1978] 2 All ER 595, [1978] 1 WLR 770. In principle, therefore, an understanding of the nature and effect of the power was sufficient for its validity.' (See [1988] 1 All ER 358 at 361, [1988] Ch 310 at 313.)

19. Later, Hoffmann J referred to what measures should be taken to achieve that:

'Finally I should say something about what is meant by understanding the nature and effect of the power. What degree of understanding is involved? Plainly one cannot expect that the donor should have been able to pass an examination on the provisions of the 1985 Act. At the other extreme, I do not think that it would be sufficient if he realised only that it gave cousin William power to look after his property. Counsel as amicus curiae helpfully summarised the matters which the donor should have understood in order that he can be said to have understood the nature and effect of the power: first, if such be the terms of the power, that the attorney will be able to assume complete authority over the donor's affairs; second, if such be the terms of the power, that the attorney will in general be able to do anything with the donor's property which he himself could have done; third, that the authority will continue if the donor should be or become mentally incapable; fourth, that if he should be or become mentally incapable, the power will be irrevocable without confirmation by the court.' (See [1988] 1 All ER 358 at 363, [1988] Ch 310 at 316.)

20. I would, for my part, agree that those four points are a sound indication of what the donor must understand if the power is to be valid.

21. Hoffmann J went on to say:

'I do not wish to prescribe another form of words in competition with the explanatory notes prescribed by the Lord Chancellor, but I accept the summary of counsel as amicus curiae as a statement of the matters which should ordinarily be explained to the donor whatever the precise language which may be used and which the evidence should show he has understood.' (See [1988] 1 All ER 358 at 363, [1988] Ch 310 at 316.)

22. The last nine words have been relied on as showing that the burden of proof lies on the attorney for the purpose of showing that the instrument is valid. I am unable to reconcile that with the burden provided by s 6(6), which, as is accepted by Mr Rees for the objectors, at any rate imposes prime facie a burden on the objectors. With respect to Lord Hoffmann, I suspect that he did not have in mind the question of the burden of proof when he used those words in the form in which he did.

23. We have also been referred to the case of *Re Beaney (decd)* [1978] 2 All ER 595, [1978] 1 WLR 770. There Mr Martin Nourse QC had something to say about how the requirement of understanding should be put to a donor. He said that the donor in that case was able to give an appearance of understanding that which was not simple, particularly if to the questions he was asked there could be given a Yes or No answer, being the answer which was obviously wanted. That is more concerned with the way that understanding can be tested than with the requirement of understanding itself.

24. The difficulty, as it seems to me, is that old people, as I happen to know, are reluctant to believe that senility is coming upon them and therefore are reluctant to release the powers which they have hitherto enjoyed: hence, I think, the two-stage approach of an enduring power of attorney. Stage 1, the proposed donor is still capable of understanding what she is doing. Stage 2, when the attorney has reason to believe that she is no longer capable, then an application must be made for registration.

25. For my part, I would not be inclined to rely on evidence of one interview, certainly not of the kind described by Mr Nourse. No doubt it is right to ask questions when it is contemplated that a donor shall execute an enduring power; but that is not by any means the final way of determining whether there is the necessary capacity.

26. The argument for the objectors is that the burden of proof in such a case does not necessarily remain on them. It is put in this way in the outline argument on their behalf:

'The initial burden is upon the attorney. At common law the legal burden of proof lies upon the party seeking to establish the validity of a document. This burden of proof is therefore external to the provisions of s 6. Section 6(6) supplements, but does not alter, the common law position by setting out the steps that the court must take once it has reached a decision as to whether a valid ground of objection exists. If it exists, the court must refuse a   registration. Otherwise, the court must register. Section 6(6) does not reverse the burden of proof in relation to any particular ground of objection. If the objection is based on an allegation of fraud, then it is for the party alleging fraud to prove it. If it is based upon a contention that the document itself is invalid, then it is for the party seeking to rely on the document to prove it.'

b   27. That was the way it was put in the outline argument. But before us it seemed to me that Mr Rees was not putting it quite in that way. He was prepared to acknowledge that s 6(6) put a burden in the first instance on the objectors; and if he was not prepared to acknowledge that, for my part I think it is perfectly clear in the section. To take an analogy with computer speak, the way to discover where the burden of proof lies, in my view, is to find the default setting. The default setting is stated quite clearly in s 6(6): if the court is not satisfied on the grounds of objection, then the court shall allow the power of attorney to be registered.

d   28. The way that Mr Rees puts it now is that once evidence had been produced which tends to show that there was not the necessary capacity, then the burden shifts, and it lies with the attorney to show that there was capacity.

29. In support of that he refers to 30 *Halsbury's Laws* (4th edn reissue) para 1387:

e   'Every person is presumed to have mental capacity until the contrary is proved, and this presumption applies in civil as well as in criminal cases. However, it is for the executors or other people seeking to set up a will to show that the testator had capacity at the time.'

30. Mr Rees submits that, just as with wills, so the same is true when somebody proposes an enduring power of attorney for registration. He also
f   referred to a New Zealand case, *Brown v Pourau* [1995] 1 NZLR 352, and particularly to a passage (at 363) where there is cited this passage from the earlier case of *Peters v Morris* (19 May 1987, unreported):

'The approach adopted to the matter of proof in all these cases is the same—that before a will can be admitted to probate it must be shown that
g   the testator was a person of sufficient mental capacity; that in the absence of any evidence to the contrary it will be presumed that the document has been made by a person of competent understanding; that once a doubt is raised as to the existence of testamentary capacity an onus rests on the person propounding the will to satisfy the Court that the testator retained his mental
h   powers to the requisite extent; that in the end the tribunal must be able to declare that it is satisfied of the testator's competence at the relevant time, but that a will will not be defeated merely because a residual doubt remains as to that matter.'

31. It seems to me, if I may say so, that Mr Rees' argument neatly encapsulates
j   what was said in that passage. We were also referred to a case of considerable antiquity, *Waring v Waring* (1848) 6 Moo PC 341.

32. Where there is only one issue in the case and the burden of proof rests on one party, it seems to me wrong to say that the burden of proof shifts after one witness has been called and given evidence which, if believed, would discharge that burden. Courts do not make up their minds on an issue when they have heard only part of the evidence. Surely one can say, if one wishes, 'Well, the

plaintiff is doing quite well. I wonder if there is going to be any evidence from
the defendants?' But to say that the burden of proof has shifted seems to me to
be wrong. One should make up one's mind on that issue having heard all the
evidence on it; and I do not consider that in such a case the burden of proof can
be said to shift. At the end of the day, unless the burden as to that issue has been
discharged, the person on whom it originally rested does not succeed.

33. In this case, I think that the judge was right to treat the burden of proof as
resting throughout upon the objectors. That is what he did. In the result, he did
not feel able to conclude that the objectors had discharged that burden. But,
equally, he did not make an affirmative finding in favour of the attorney, Mrs X.
I reject the argument that he erred in law in that respect.

34. The other ground which has been argued by Mr Rees is that the judge's
decision was wrong on the facts. There were two principal witnesses, with other
evidence as well. The first of the two principal witnesses was a Mr Connor, a
chartered clinical psychiatrist. His evidence came in the form of a report of five
pages. He had carried out tests on Mrs W's mental capacity on two occasions in
November and December 1996. The conclusions that he reached in his report are
these:

'As a final comment, the above detected severity of deterioration across a
number of vital areas of cognitive functioning suggests strongly that for the
past period running into a number of years, Mrs W has not been in a position
to deal properly with the intangible (non-concrete) or hypothetical, or to
correctly comprehend, interpret, see implications in, judge, or direct any
business or operation other than that which does not require weighing up
the pro's and con's, making comparisons, or seeing consequences of action
beyond the immediate step.'

35. Later, in a letter dated 10 July 1998, he said: 'I believe that in no way was
Mrs W in a condition on 4 July 1996 to execute an Enduring Power of Attorney.'

36. There are comments that are made in respect of that evidence: first, that it
was what one might call a theoretical discussion of the effect on comprehension,
rather than a consideration of the actual things which had to be considered or the
actual test for capacity to execute an enduring power of attorney. There was
evidence that at the time of the tests by Mr Connor Mrs W was taking drugs of
several different kinds; and it was acknowledged that drugs might, not necessarily
that they would, affect her capacity. There was also the lapse of time between
the occasion in July when Mrs W executed the power of attorney and November
and December when she was seen by Mr Connor.

37. On the other hand, there is evidence from Mrs W's doctor who had treated
her for some years. He had seen her quite regularly. He was not called as a
witness because by the time the case came on for hearing before the judge he said,
with admirable candour, that he could not now remember any detail whatsoever,
and he was accordingly unable to help the court. But what was available was a
letter that he wrote on 22 June 1996, that is to say about two weeks before the
power of attorney was executed. It was written not to the proposed attorney or
to Mrs W but to the solicitor who eventually witnessed the power of attorney.
The letter said:

'Thank you for your letter about Mrs W I can confirm that I saw her
recently with her daughter and found her to be suffering from a degree of
memory impairment. However in my opinion she still has the necessary

a
mental capacity to sign a Power of Attorney. I would add that her mental abilities are at their best in the early part of the day and tend to deteriorate as the day goes by.'

38. There is also evidence that Mrs W had seen her solicitor alone at some time previously; and it is said that she wished to have an enduring power of attorney.

b
39. There are three letters which are relied on by the objectors as casting doubt on the capacity of Mrs W. In the first letter from Mrs X to her brother, and I take it her sister, dated 31 October 1994, there is this passage: 'Well, she is very confused and one has to organise her very carefully. She does not wake us up because she is used to coming here.'

c
40. This was apparently in answer to the news that when staying with the brother Mrs W had woken them up in the night. That is October 1994. But, in a much later letter which was written to the Public Trust Office, Mrs X wrote this:

'My mother's mental health only started to deteriorate at a stage when she could no longer conduct her affairs when she came out of Eastbourne Hospital

d
having had transfusions for severe anaemia at the end of January 1997.'

41. Mr Rees points to the contrast of what was said there in a later letter dated July 1998 to what had been said in 1994.

42. Third, there is another letter dated 29 October 1998, again to the Public Trust Office. It says:

e
'As I have already stated, my mother was a little confused at times during late 1996. Most of the time she was very logical and she was very much aware of what was happening to her. That is why she previously had got her house in order and told both me and her solicitor what she wanted to happen in the future.'

f
43. That is a brief summary of some points in the evidence. The judge, as I have said, was unable to conclude that it was shown that Mrs W had the necessary capacity. He also did not conclude that she was shown not to have the necessary capacity.

g
44. I can see no ground for interfering with the judge's conclusions on those two points. It may be a simple view, but it seems to me that the general practitioner who saw Mrs W from time to time, and had done so for some time, was in as good a position as anybody to say whether or not she had the necessary understanding. At all events, if the judge reached that conclusion, I would see no reason to differ from him.

h
45. Accordingly, I would dismiss this appeal.

ARDEN LJ.

46. I agree. The Enduring Powers of Attorney Act 1985 established a new mechanism whereby a person could give a power of attorney which would

j
survive his or her incapacity. This was an important innovation because it enabled, among others, elderly people to give powers to attorneys to manage their affairs within the limits permitted by the Act. The Act was passed following a full law reform project by the Law Commission pursuant to the reference under s 3(1)(e) of the Law Commissions Act 1965. The final report is entitled *The Incapacitated Principal* (Law Com no 122, p 63). Accordingly, the policy of the Act was very carefully considered; and it may therefore be taken to have been

very carefully calibrated. In particular, it is evident that the Act provides a
comprehensive set of provisions for registration of the power of attorney and
indeed the effective registration is also dealt with in the Act (see in particular ss 7
and 8).

47. Sir Christopher Staughton has already set out the prescribed procedure for
registration. I agree with him that s 6(6) is the pivotal section. In my judgment
that subsection clearly proceeds on the basis that the grounds of objection have
to be proved. Accordingly, as I see it, the legal burden remains throughout on the
objector, the person presenting the notice of objection. If the objector fails to
establish his objection, the instrument must be registered. The court has no
residual discretion to refuse registration.

48. Mr Rees has submitted that the position should apply as at common law
so that the burden of proof is on the person seeking to uphold a deed or document.
He draws an analogy with wills, as Sir Christopher Staughton has explained. But,
as I see it, it is open to Parliament to change the common law rules for the
purposes of this legislation. In addition Mr Rees accepts that the onus is on the
objector when, for instance, there is a question as to unsuitability of the attorney.
As I see it, the Act must be construed as it stands.

49. The learned master relied on a passage in the judgment of Hoffmann J in
Re K, Re F [1988] 1 All ER 358 at 363, [1988] Ch 310 at 316, namely the words 'and
which the evidence should show he has understood' in the passage cited by
Sir Christopher Staughton. I agree with what Sir Christopher has said about that
passage.

50. Mr Rees has submitted that the situation could arise in which an objector
raises a doubt but fails to show lack of mental capacity. If the respondents to this
appeal are correct and if the learned judge is correct, the court may then be in a
position of registering instruments when it is not satisfied as to the donor's
capacity. But the scheme of the Act does not require the court to be satisfied as
to the donor's capacity. It has a discretion under sub-s (4) to conduct inquiries if
the objection is made on statutory grounds. The Act does not require the court
to carry out those inquiries. Indeed, the court may well take the view that where
there are two parties contesting an issue, there is no need for it to make further
inquiries. Accordingly, in my judgment, Parliament must have envisaged that a
situation could arise in which a power of attorney would be registered where an
objector had failed to discharge the onus of proof. But it should be taken into
account that the Act contains other detailed safeguards for the donor, in
particular the restriction on the attorney's capacity to make gifts on behalf of the
donor without the court's consent.

51. As respects the second ground of appeal (that the judge's conclusions on
the facts were against the weight of the evidence), I agree that, for the reasons
given by Sir Christopher Staughton, that the appeal fails.

PETER GIBSON LJ.

52. I agree with both judgments.

Appeal dismissed.

Gillian Crew   Barrister.

a

R v Forbes
[2001] UKHL 40

HOUSE OF LORDS

b LORD SLYNN OF HADLEY, LORD STEYN, LORD HOPE OF CRAIGHEAD, LORD CLYDE, LORD HUTTON

28 MARCH, 19 JULY 2001

c *Customs and excise – Importation of prohibited goods – Knowingly concerned in fraudulent evasion of prohibition or restriction – Indecent photographs of children under 16 – Whether prosecution having to prove that defendant not only knew goods were prohibited but also nature of goods – Customs and Excise Management Act 1979, s 170(2)(b).*

The defendant, F, was stopped at Heathrow Airport on arrival from Amsterdam.
d He was in possession of two video cassettes which bore the labels of two ordinary films on general release, but which actually contained material whose importation was prohibited, namely indecent photographs of boys under 16. F was charged with two offences of being knowingly concerned in the fraudulent evasion of a prohibition on the importation of goods contrary to s 170(2)(b)[a] of the Customs and Excise Management Act 1979. In his defence, he claimed that he had not
e known that the cassettes had contained indecent photographs of children, and had instead believed them to contain two other films which he thought were prohibited, but were not in fact prohibited. Such a belief, if accepted by the jury as a reasonable possibility, would have required F's acquittal, and the judge directed the jury accordingly. He also directed the jury that the prosecution were
f required to establish that F had been aware that he was importing prohibited material, but that it was not necessary for them to prove that he had known the precise category of goods that had been imported. F was convicted, and his appeal was dismissed by the Court of Appeal. He appealed to the House of Lords, contending that it had been necessary for the prosecution to prove that he had been aware that the cassettes contained indecent photographs of children.

g

Held – Where a defendant was charged with being knowingly concerned in the fraudulent evasion of a prohibition on importation of goods contrary to s 170(2)(b) of the 1979 Act, the prosecution were not required to prove that the defendant had known the precise kind of goods that were being imported.
h Rather, it was sufficient for the prosecution to prove that the defendant had known that the goods were subject to a prohibition on importation and that he had also known that the operation on which he had been engaged was an evasion of that prohibition. A conclusion to the contrary would have highly damaging effects on the systems of prohibition and restriction on the importation of goods
j into the United Kingdom. The essence of the offence created by s 170(2)(b) was being knowingly concerned in the evasion of a prohibition. In many cases a person who, at the request of another and, possibly, in return for payment, brought into the United Kingdom an article, knowing that he was taking part in the fraudulent evasion of a prohibition against importation, would not know the precise nature of

---

a   Section 170, so far as material, is set out at [16], below

the article which he was carrying. In such a case, the task for the prosecution in proving an offence would be virtually impossible if, in addition to having to prove that the article was prohibited and that the defendant knew that he was involved in the evasion of a prohibition, it also had to prove that he knew the precise nature of the article. The application of that principle would give rise to no injustice in a case such as the instant case, as it was open to the defendant to rely on the defence that he had believed that he was carrying an article which in reality, and contrary to his belief, was not prohibited. In the instant case, once the jury had rejected that defence, the only issue for them to decide was whether F had known that the goods that he was carrying were subject to a prohibition. The judge's direction had been correct, and the jury had been fully entitled to find that he had been knowingly concerned in the evasion of a prohibition against importation. Accordingly, the appeal would be dismissed (see [9]–[12], [19], [30], [32]–[34], [53], [56], [57], [61], below).

R v Hussain [1969] 2 All ER 1117 applied.

Notes

For being knowingly concerned in a fraudulent evasion of a prohibition or restriction on importation, see 12(2) *Halsbury's Laws* (4th edn reissue) para 1170.

For the Customs and Excise Management Act 1979, s 170, see 13 *Halsbury's Statutes* (4th edn) (2000 reissue) 289.

Cases referred to in opinions

Conegate Ltd v Customs and Excise Comrs Case 121/85 [1986] 2 All ER 688, [1987] QB 254, [1987] 2 WLR 39, [1986] ECR 1007, ECJ.

R v Bow Street Metropolitan Stipendiary Magistrate, ex p Noncyp Ltd [1990] 1 QB 123, [1988] 3 WLR 827, DC; *affd* [1990] 1 QB 123, [1989] 3 WLR 467, CA.

R v Dunne (1998) 162 JP 399, CA.

R v Hennessey (1978) 68 Cr App R 419, CA.

R v Hussain [1969] 2 All ER 1117, [1969] 2 QB 567, [1969] 3 WLR 134, CA.

R v Shivpuri [1986] 2 All ER 334, [1987] AC 1, [1986] 3 WLR 988, HL.

R v Taaffe [1984] 1 All ER 747, [1984] AC 539, [1984] 2 WLR 326, HL; *affg* [1983] 2 All ER 625, [1983] 1 WLR 627, CA.

Appeal

The appellant, Giles Javen Forbes, appealed with leave of the Appeal Committee of the House of Lords given on 2 November 2000 from the decision of the Court of Appeal (Rose LJ, Alliott and Jackson JJ) on 24 March 2000 dismissing his appeal from his conviction before Judge Evans and a jury in the Crown Court at Isleworth on 23 March 1999 of two offences of being knowingly concerned in a fraudulent evasion of a prohibition on the importation of goods contrary to s 170(2) of the Customs and Excise Management Act 1979. By order of 30 March 2000, the Court of Appeal certified that two points of law of general public importance, set out at [38], below, were involved in its decision. The facts are set out in the opinion of Lord Hutton.

David Lane QC and *Charles Salter* (instructed by *Davis Hanson*) for the appellant.
Martin Field (instructed by the *Solicitor for the Customs and Excise*) for the Crown.

a Their Lordships took time for consideration.

19 July 2001. The following opinions were delivered.

LORD SLYNN OF HADLEY.

b [1] My Lords, I have had the advantage of reading in draft the speech of my noble and learned friend Lord Hutton. I gratefully refer to his recital of the facts, of the relevant statutory provisions and the proceedings at the trial and I do not repeat them.

[2] The puzzlement of the jury, indicated by their questions, the obvious problem the trial judge had in directing the jury and the fact that your Lordships find the
c questions certified by the Court of Appeal to be misconceived, only serve to illustrate the difficulties involved in defining the task of the prosecution in cases of this kind.

[3] One of the problems arises from the fact that in relation to material of this kind there are, as the appellant has stressed, three different categories—(1) obscene
d publications contrary to s 1 of the Obscene Publications Act 1959, (2) an indecent photograph of a child under the age of 16 contrary to s 1 of the Protection of Children Act 1978 and (3) other indecent photographs which fall within the terms of s 42 of the Customs Consolidation Act 1876, but which if they come from another member state of the European Union cannot be the subject matter of a charge of unlawful importation since they can be sold lawfully in the United Kingdom
e (see *Conegate Ltd v Customs and Excise Comrs* Case 121/85 [1986] 2 All ER 688, [1986] ECR 1007). Per contra if they come from outside the Union.

[4] If the charge here were that the defendant was knowingly concerned in the importation of indecent photographs of children it seems plain that the prosecution would have to prove that the photographs were of children and that he knew that
f they were of children. It is really on the basis that that is the charge that the appellant's argument in part proceeds. But that is not the charge. The substance of the charge is that he was 'in any way knowingly concerned in any fraudulent evasion … of any prohibition' on the importation of goods under s 42 of the 1876 Act.

g [5] In *R v Hussain* [1969] 2 All ER 1117 at 1119, [1969] 2 QB 567 at 572 Lord Widgery LJ stressed that the relevant question is whether the accused knows—

'that what is on foot is the evasion of a prohibition against importation and he knowingly takes part in that operation … even if he does not know
h precisely what kind of goods are being imported. It is, of course, essential that he should know that the goods which are being imported are goods subject to a prohibition. It is essential he should know that the operation with which he is concerning himself is an operation designed to evade that prohibition and evade it fraudulently.'

j [6] The correctness of that decision was accepted in *R v Hennessey* (1978) 68 Cr App R 419 at 423 where Lawton LJ said:

'It matters not for the purpose of conviction what the goods were as long as he knew that he was bringing into the United Kingdom goods which he should not have been bringing in.'

[7] The decision in *R v Hussain* was also approved by the House of Lords in *R v Taaffe* [1984] 1 All ER 747 at 749, [1984] AC 539 at 547 and in *R v Shivpuri* [1986] 2 All ER 334, [1987] AC 1.

[8] The decision in *R v Taaffe* also accepted that for the purpose of s 170(2) of the 1979 Act a defendant must be judged on the facts as he believed them to be, such matter being an integral part of the inquiry as to whether he was knowingly concerned in a fraudulent evasion of a prohibition on importation.

[9] In the present case the judge gave a direction in accordance with *R v Hussain*. He told the jury that the prosecution had to prove that the defendant knew that what he was bringing in was prohibited material but that it was not necessary for the prosecution to prove that the defendant knew what the prohibited material was. The prosecution had to prove that—

> 'the defendant knew that the goods which were being imported—and "the goods", of course, are these parts of the video in the middle—are subject to a prohibition. But the Crown do not have to go on to prove that he knew the precise category of goods that were imported.'

[10] There can be no doubt that the jury by their verdict—even if by eleven to one—was satisfied in the present case that the defendant knew that he was bringing in prohibited material and that his behaviour showed that this was part of a fraudulent evasion of a prohibition.

[11] It follows in my opinion that this appeal must be dismissed.

LORD STEYN.

[12] My Lords, I have had the advantage of reading in draft the speeches of my noble and learned friends Lord Hope of Craighead and Lord Hutton. For the reasons they give I would also dismiss the appeal.

LORD HOPE OF CRAIGHEAD.

[13] My Lords, for the good of the country and the health and safety of its inhabitants the importation into the United Kingdom of a wide variety of goods is restricted or prohibited. The categories of prohibited goods include such things as flick knives: s 1 of the Restriction of Offensive Weapons Act 1961; goat hair infected or likely to be infected by anthrax: Anthrax Prevention Order 1971, SI 1971/1234; plants and agricultural products which may lead to the introduction into Great Britain of pests: s 2 of the Plant Health Act 1967; animals, animal carcases and feeding stuffs, the importation of which may introduce disease in people and in animals: ss 24–33 and 35 of the Diseases of Animals Act 1950; indecent or obscene prints, photographs or other articles: s 42 of the Customs Consolidation Act 1876; and controlled drugs: s 3 of the Misuse of Drugs Act 1971.

[14] Some of the prohibitions and restrictions in the older law have had to be modified in order to render them compatible with the principles of European Community law. The importation of goods from other member states must be permitted unless their supply would be unlawful under domestic law (see *R v Bow Street Metropolitan Stipendiary Magistrate, ex p Noncyp Ltd* [1990] 1 QB 123, [1989] 3 WLR 467). But these prohibitions and restrictions continue to apply with regard to the importation of goods from countries outside the European Union.

[15] It is plain that the prohibitions and restrictions would be ineffective unless they were backed up by criminal sanctions in the event of any breach. Their evasion would put at risk the benefits which they were designed to achieve.

a Human nature being what it is, there are bound to be those who with a view to profit or for other ill-founded motives will seek to evade them. There is a market for prohibited goods in this country, such as obscene material and controlled drugs, which some individuals are determined to exploit. Others may seek to import the goods for their own use despite, or perhaps even because of, the risk of harm to the wider community. Those involved may include organised gangs

b or syndicates, and they may go to great lengths to achieve their aims. They commonly resort to the use of couriers, to whom the minimum of information is given to reduce the risk of detection and of tracing the goods back to their source. Sophisticated means of concealment may be employed to ensure that the true nature of the goods is known only to those at each end of the importation process.

c [16] The provision which reinforces these prohibitions and restrictions by subjecting their evasion to a criminal sanction is to be found in s 170(2) of the Customs and Excise Management Act 1979, as amended by s 114(1) of the Police and Criminal Evidence Act 1984, which provides:

d   'Without prejudice to any other provision of the Customs and Excise Acts 1979, if any person is, in relation to any goods, in any way knowingly concerned in any fraudulent evasion or attempt at evasion … (b) of any prohibition or restriction for the time being in force with respect to the goods under or by virtue of any enactment; he shall be guilty of an offence under this section and may be arrested.'

e

[17] This provision extends to all cases involving the evasion or attempted evasion of a prohibition or restriction. It requires proof by the prosecutor of two things. First, he must prove that the goods in question were the subject of a prohibition or restriction under or by virtue of any enactment which was in force

f at the time of the evasion or attempt at evasion. This is an essential element in any prosecution, but its proof in many cases is likely to be a formality. In the present case the fact that the video cassettes contained indecent photographs of children, which is prohibited indecent material, was agreed between the defendant and the prosecutor. The second thing which the prosecutor must prove is that the defendant was knowingly concerned in a fraudulent evasion or attempt at

g evasion of the prohibition or restriction. The question which has been raised by this case is whether it is sufficient for the prosecutor to prove that the defendant knew that the activity in which he was engaged was the evasion of a prohibition or restriction, or whether he must go further and prove that the defendant knew what the goods were.

h [18] The first of the two certified questions asks whether it was sufficient for the Crown to prove that the defendant knew he was importing an indecent photograph or must it be proved also that he knew that it was a photograph of a child. The question is framed in this way because, while s 42 of the 1876 Act provides that the importation of all indecent or obscene photographs is

j prohibited, that prohibition does not extend to the importation from another member state of the European Union of photographs which are neither obscene nor indecent photographs of children. The supply of indecent photographs of adults is not unlawful in this country. Compatibility of the prohibition with Community law requires that it does not extend to the importation of such photographs from another member state—in this case, the Netherlands.

[**19**] But behind this question there is another and logically prior question. For over 30 years it has been the law in this country that, if the defendant knows that what is on foot is the evasion of a prohibition or restriction and he knowingly takes part in that operation, that is sufficient to justify his conviction even if he does not know precisely what kind of goods are being imported. This proposition, which is to be found in 12 *Halsbury's Laws* (4th edn) (1975 issue) para 642, n 2, is attributed to *R v Hussain* [1969] 2 All ER 1117, [1969] 2 QB 567. If it is sound, the certified questions are misconceived. This is because it is not necessary, for the purposes of a prosecution under s 170(2)(b) of the 1979 Act, for the prosecutor to prove that the defendant knew the identity of the goods which were the subject of the prohibition which he was evading or attempting to evade. It is sufficient for him to prove that the defendant knew that the goods, whatever they happened to be, were the subject of a prohibition and that he also knew that the operation on which he was engaged was an evasion of that prohibition. If that is right, the question whether the defendant knew that the photographs which were the subject of the operation were indecent photographs of children does not arise. The prosecutor does not even need to go so far as to prove that the defendant knew that the goods were photographs.

[**20**] *R v Hussain* was a case which concerned the evasion of a prohibition on the importation of controlled drugs. But it is nevertheless instructive as to the extent of and justification for the proposition which it contains. The facts of the case were these. A vessel on which the defendant had been serving as a merchant seaman was searched on its arrival at Liverpool. When the bulkhead of his cabin was removed a number of concealed packages were found behind it which contained cannabis resin. His defence was that a senior member of the crew had entered his cabin during the voyage accompanied by the carpenter who had with him a bucket containing ten packages. They hid these packages behind the bulkhead, threatened to cut his throat if he said anything to anyone about it and promised him a reward if he kept silent. At the trial the jury were directed that it was enough for the Crown to prove that the defendant knew that he was co-operating with smugglers and that it did not matter if he did not know precisely the nature of the goods that they were dealing with. What had to be proved was that he was knowingly, and to that extent consciously and deliberately, concerned in co-operating in what he must have known was an operation of getting prohibited goods into this country.

[**21**] The Court of Appeal rejected the submission that this was a misdirection. The judgment of the court was given by Widgery LJ, who said:

'It seems perfectly clear that the word "knowingly" in s. 304 [of the Customs and Excise Act 1952, which was repealed and replaced by s 170(2)(b) of the 1979 Act] is concerned with knowing that a fraudulent evasion of a prohibition in respect of goods is taking place. If, therefore, the accused knows that what is on foot is the evasion of a prohibition against importation and he knowingly takes part in that operation, it is sufficient to justify his conviction, even if he does not know precisely what kind of goods are being imported. It is, of course, essential that he should know that the goods which are being imported are goods subject to a prohibition. It is essential he should know that the operation with which he is concerning himself is an operation designed to evade that prohibition and evade it fraudulently. But it is not necessary that he should know the precise category of the goods the

a

importation of which has been prohibited.' (See [1969] 2 All ER 1117 at 1119, [1969] 2 QB 567 at 572.)

b

[22] That passage should be read in the light of the argument which was presented to the court. For the appellant it was submitted that the prosecution must prove that the accused knew he was concerned with a prohibited or restricted substance, as against one which merely involved the payment of duty. For the Crown it was submitted that it was not necessary to prove that the accused knew the precise nature of the goods being imported. It was sufficient for the prosecutor to prove that the accused knew that the operation in which he was taking part involved the fraudulent evasion of some kind of prohibition against importation. The point was made that persons involved in operations of this kind frequently do not know the precise nature of the goods involved, and that Parliament cannot have intended that there should be a defence on these grounds.

c

d

[23] The point of law which was established by the decision of the Court of Appeal in that case was expressed in terms which are of general application to all prosecutions brought under s 170(2)(b) of the 1979 Act. It is not possible logically to separate out one category of prohibited goods from the others—indecent photographs, for example, as is being suggested in this case—and say that a different rule should be applied to them. There are only two positions that can logically be adopted. One is to say that the Crown must prove that the defendant knew that the operation on which he was engaged involved prohibited goods because he knew what the *goods* were and that they were prohibited goods. The other is to say that the Crown must prove that the defendant knew that the operation on which he was engaged involved goods which were prohibited because he knew that the *operation* was designed to avoid a prohibition against the importation of those goods.

e

f

[24] The justification for the adoption of the latter position by the Court of Appeal was that to adopt the former position would rob the provision of its effect in those cases, which in this field are likely to be many, which Parliament must have intended to be caught by it. These are cases where the defendant did not know and could not have known what the goods were, because he was merely a courier employed to lend his assistance to those who were engaged in the operation as principals. Nevertheless he was knowingly concerned in the evasion because he was well aware from the nature of the operation that its purpose was to evade a prohibition relating to those goods.

g

h

[25] The law as laid down in *R v Hussain* has not been questioned judicially for over 30 years. It was applied in *R v Hennessey* (1978) 68 Cr App R 419, which was another case involving the fraudulent evasion of the prohibition against the importation of controlled drugs. The trial judge directed the jury in these terms:

j

'"Knowingly" in this section of this statute is concerned with knowing that a fraudulent evasion of a prohibition in respect of goods is taking place. It is not a question of knowing whether you have got a particular commodity in your pocket or container or car and there is quite a considerable amount of legal authority for that proposition. If, therefore, an accused person knows that what is afoot is the evasion of a prohibition against importation and he knowingly takes part in that operation, it is sufficient to justify his conviction

under this section of the Act, even if he does not know precisely what kind
of goods are being imported.'   *a*

[**26**] The defendant appealed against his conviction. He submitted that the
judge should have directed the jury that the prosecution had to prove that the
accused knew what was the subject of the prohibition and that the court had been
wrong to reject that submission in *R v Hussain*. This argument was rejected by
the Court of Appeal. Lawton LJ (at 423), who delivered the judgment of the   *b*
court, said of the decision in *R v Hussain*:

> 'We intend to follow it for the best of reasons—it was correctly decided. On
> his own story Hennessey did know that he was concerned in a fraudulent
> evasion of a prohibition in relation to goods. In plain English he was smuggling
> goods. It matters not for the purpose of conviction what the goods were as   *c*
> long as he knew that he was bringing into the United Kingdom goods which
> he should not have been bringing in.'

Here again the extent of the proposition which was being approved in that case
is significant. It is knowledge of the nature and purpose of the *operation* which has
to be proved, not knowledge of what the *goods* were which were being brought   *d*
in to this country.

[**27**] In *R v Taaffe* [1983] 2 All ER 625 at 627, [1983] 1 WLR 627 at 630 Lord Lane CJ
referred to the decisions in the House of Lords in *R v Hussain* and *R v Hennessey*
without disapproval, and in the same case in the House of Lords Lord Scarman
said that there could be no doubt that *R v Hussain* was rightly decided (see [1984] *e*
1 All ER 747 at 749, [1984] AC 539 at 547). *R v Hussain* was approved again in
R v Shivpuri [1986] 2 All ER 334, [1987] AC 1. Lord Bridge of Harwich said ([1986]
2 All ER 334 at 339, [1987] AC 1 at 14) that, in using the words 'they need not
know precisely what the prohibited goods were, as long as they knew they were
prohibited', the judge in that case had expounded the law to the jury exactly as it
was laid down by the Court of Appeal in *R v Hussain*. He said: *f*

> 'Irrespective of the different penalties attached to offences in connection
> with the importation of different categories of prohibited goods, *R v Hussain*
> established that the only mens rea necessary for proof of any such offence
> was knowledge that the goods were subject to a prohibition on importation.'
> (See [1986] 2 All ER 334 at 341, [1987] AC 1 at 17.)   *g*

[**28**] In *R v Taaffe* the defendant was charged with having been knowingly
concerned in the fraudulent evasion of the prohibition on the importation of
cannabis resin. His defence was that he had been enlisted by a third party to
import the substance in fraudulent evasion of a prohibition on its importation   *h*
into this country but that he believed the substance to be currency which,
contrary to his belief, was not subject to any prohibition on importation. The
recorder ruled that he would be obliged to direct the jury that, even upon the
defendant's version of events, they would be obliged to convict, whereupon he
pled guilty. His appeal against his conviction was allowed by the Court of Appeal
on the ground that, while it was not essential for a conviction for the Crown to *j*
prove that the defendant knew the precise nature of the goods that were being
imported, he was to be judged on the facts as he believed them to be. In the
House of Lords Lord Scarman said ([1984] 1 All ER 747 at 749, [1984] AC 539 at
546) that he agreed with that construction of s 170(2) of the 1979 Act, adding that
the principle that a man must be judged upon the facts as he believed them to be

a was an accepted principle of the criminal law when the state of a man's mind and his knowledge are ingredients of the offence with which he is charged.

[29] In the present case the appellant's defence was based on the decision in *R v Taaffe*. He said that he did not know that the video cassettes contained indecent photographs of children. His explanation for his highly suspicious behaviour at Amsterdam Airport was that he believed that the video cassettes

b contained the films 'The Exorcist' and 'Kidz' and that these films were, contrary to the fact, prohibited in the United Kingdom. The trial judge left it to the jury to decide whether they believed the appellant's explanation. He made it clear that they should judge the appellant's knowledge of the facts as he believed them to be, and that unless they were sure that his defence was untrue they should find him not guilty. Plainly they did not believe his explanation, because they

c convicted him.

[30] The appellant nevertheless says that he was wrongly convicted because the trial judge ought not to have directed the jury that what the prosecution had to establish was simply that he knew that he was importing prohibited material. He maintains that he should have directed them that the prosecution had to

d prove not only that he knew that the videos contained indecent photographs but also that they were indecent photographs of children. I would reject that argument. In my opinion the direction by the trial judge was in accordance with the law as laid down in *R v Hussain* [1969] 2 All ER 1117, [1969] 2 QB 567.

[31] It was, of course, open to the appellant to say, if this was the fact, that he believed the videos to contain indecent photographs of adults and that he acted

e as he did because he believed, contrary to the fact, that they were prohibited. The line of defence which was approved in *R v Taaffe* ensures the acquittal of people who genuinely believe that they are importing indecent photographs of adults which are not obscene, when they are in fact photographs of children. But it is for the defendant to put forward that defence. The prosecution does not have to

f prove what the accused knew the goods were which he was seeking to import knowing that they were prohibited goods.

[32] In many cases, where the goods were placed in sealed or concealed packages and there is no evidence from the accused's own mouth that he knew what was in them, it would be an impossible task for the Crown to have to prove

g that he knew what the goods were. In this case, for example, the evidence showed that the appellant knew that he was importing video cassettes containing photographic material. But there was no evidence that he ever saw what was in the videos which the third party had handed to him or that he had any other means of knowing precisely what they contained. In my opinion the prosecution would have been bound to fail for lack of evidence if the jury had been given the

h direction which, although not asked for at the time, the appellant now says they should have been given.

[33] The importance of this case lies not in the point which the appellant has raised, which I consider to be without merit, but in the highly damaging effects on the systems of prohibition and restriction on the importation of goods into this

j country if his argument were to be upheld. The point had some initial appeal to your Lordships in view of the way in which the certified questions were framed. But on further analysis it can be seen, assuming that *R v Hussain* was correctly decided—as has already been held, in my respectful opinion for sound reasons, on two occasions in this House—that these questions were misconceived. I would dismiss the appeal.

LORD CLYDE.

[34] My Lords, I have had the advantage of reading in draft the speeches of my *a* noble and learned friends Lord Hope of Craighead and Lord Hutton. For the reasons they give I would also dismiss the appeal.

LORD HUTTON.

[35] My Lords, the appellant was stopped at Heathrow Airport on arrival from *b* Amsterdam in possession of two video films. The video films were labelled respectively 'Spartacus' and 'The Godfather Part 2' which are ordinary films on general release. Each film, after beginning as its label indicated, contained footage which included indecent photographs of teenage boys under the age of 16.

[36] Section 42 of the Customs Consolidation Act 1876 provides:

c

'The goods enumerated and described in the following table of prohibitions and restrictions inwards are hereby prohibited to be imported or brought into the United Kingdom ...

A TABLE OF PROHIBITIONS AND RESTRICTIONS INWARDS.   *d*

Goods prohibited to be imported.
... Indecent or obscene prints, paintings, photographs, books, cards, lithographic or other engravings, or any other indecent or obscene articles.'

[37] In considering the application of s 42 it is necessary to have regard to the *e* legislation in England relating to obscene photographs and to indecent photographs of young persons under the age of 16. The Obscene Publications Act 1959 makes it an offence to publish an obscene photograph of a person, whether that person is an adult or a young person. The Protection of Children Act 1978 makes it an offence to have possession of an indecent photograph of a young person under the age of 16. It is not in dispute and is accepted by the Commissioners of *f* Customs and Excise that by reason of arts 30 and 36 of the EEC Treaty (now, after amendment, arts 28 EC and 30 EC) the restriction on the importation of indecent or obscene photographs contained in s 42 of the 1876 Act does not apply unless the publication or possession of such photographs within the United Kingdom is unlawful under domestic law (see *Conegate Ltd v Customs and Excise Comrs* Case *g* 121/85 [1986] 2 All ER 688, [1986] ECR 1007 and *R v Bow Street Metropolitan Stipendiary Magistrate, ex p Noncyp Ltd* [1990] 1 QB 123 at 131, [1988] 3 WLR 827 at 834 per Woolf LJ). Therefore s 42 prohibits the importation of indecent photographs of young persons under the age of 16, but it does not prohibit the importation of indecent photographs of adults if the photographs are not *h* obscene. In the present case it was accepted by the appellant at his trial that the pictures on the two video films were of young persons under the age of 16 and it is not in dispute that their importation was prohibited by s 42.

[38] At Isleworth Crown Court the appellant was convicted on the two counts on which he was indicted under s 170(2) of the Customs and Excise Management Act 1979, as amended, which provides: *j*

'Without prejudice to any other provision of the Customs and Excise Acts 1979, if any person is, in relation to any goods, in any way knowingly concerned in any fraudulent evasion or attempt at evasion ... (b) of any prohibition or restriction for the time being in force with respect to the goods *a* under or by virtue of any enactment; or ... he shall be guilty of an offence under this section and may be arrested.'

The counts were:

'Count 1

b
STATEMENT OF OFFENCE
Being knowingly concerned in a fraudulent evasion of a prohibition on the importation of goods contrary to section 170(2) of the Customs and Excise Management Act 1979.

c
PARTICULARS OF OFFENCE
GILES JAVEN FORBES on or about the 7th July 1998 at London Heathrow Airport and elsewhere within the jurisdiction of the Central Criminal Court, in relation to a certain video cassette labelled "Spartacus" and which contained indecent photographs of children, was knowingly concerned in a fraudulent evasion of the prohibition on importation thereof
d imposed by force of section 42 of the Customs Consolidation Act 1876.

Count 2

STATEMENT OF OFFENCE
e Being knowingly concerned in a fraudulent evasion of a prohibition on the importation of goods contrary to section 170(2) of the Customs and Excise Management Act 1979.

PARTICULARS OF OFFENCE
f GILES JAVEN FORBES on or about the 7th July 1998 at London Heathrow Airport and elsewhere within the jurisdiction of the Central Criminal Court, in relation to a certain video cassette labelled "The Godfather Part 2" and which contained indecent photographs of children, was knowingly concerned in a fraudulent evasion of the prohibition on importation thereof imposed by force of section 42 of the Customs
g Consolidation Act 1876.'

[**39**] The appellant advanced the following defence in giving evidence at his trial. He went to Amsterdam for a break. In a bar in Amsterdam he met a man and they had a talk about London. The man asked him to do him a favour and to take something back for a friend, and he agreed to do so and to meet the man
h the next day. When he met him next day the man gave him two video films 'Spartacus' and 'The Godfather Part 2'. The man told him that the video contained 'The Exorcist' and 'Kidz' and he (the appellant) thought they were prohibited films. The arrangement was that he would hand over the video films to a man whom he was to meet in a cinema in Notting Hill. He received no
j payment for taking the video films to London.

[**40**] The appellant also said in evidence that before he boarded his aeroplane at Amsterdam Airport he went to the airport shop where he bought genuine video films of 'Spartacus' and 'The Godfather Part 2' for which he received receipts. On arrival at Heathrow he left the two genuine video films in a lavatory at Heathrow. He then went through customs with the two video films

containing the indecent pictures, and he was able to produce, and did produce, the receipts for the genuine video films which appeared to relate, by virtue of their external labelling, to the two video films which he was carrying.

[41] The films 'The Exorcist' and 'Kidz', to which the appellant referred in his evidence, were films which were not indecent or obscene and their importation was not prohibited.

[42] It is apparent from the summary of the appellant's evidence, and also from the comments of defence counsel after the trial judge had concluded his summing up to the jury, that the only defence advanced on behalf of the appellant was that he believed that he was carrying two films, 'The Exorcist' and 'Kidz', the importation of which, contrary to his belief, was not prohibited. If the jury had accepted that such a belief was a reasonable possibility they would have had to acquit him on both counts, and in his summing up the trial judge so directed them in accordance with the decision of this House in *R v Taaffe* [1984] 1 All ER 747, [1984] AC 539.

[43] In that case the defendant carried cannabis from Holland into England and his defence was that he believed that he was carrying currency and that the importation of currency was prohibited, but the importation of currency, contrary to his belief, was not prohibited. The Court of Appeal held that on the defendant's version he would not be guilty and this ruling was upheld by this House. In his speech, Lord Scarman cited with approval the following passage from the judgment of Lord Lane CJ in the Court of Appeal and stated that he agreed with it:

'Lord Lane CJ construed the subsection under which the respondent was charged as creating an offence not of absolute liability but as one of which an essential ingredient is a guilty mind. To be "knowingly concerned" meant, in his judgment, knowledge not only of the existence of a smuggling operation but also that the substance being smuggled into the country was one the importation of which was prohibited by statute. The respondent thought he was concerned in a smuggling operation but believed that the substance was currency. The importation of currency is not subject to any prohibition. Lord Lane CJ concluded ([1983] 2 All ER 625 at 628, [1983] 1 627 at 631): "[The respondent] is to be judged against the facts that he believed them to be. Had this indeed been currency and not cannabis, no offence would have been committed." Lord Lane CJ went on to ask this question: "Does it make any difference that the [respondent] thought wrongly that by clandestinely importing currency he was committing an offence?" The Crown submitted that it did. The court rejected the submission: the respondent's mistake of law could not convert the importation of currency into a criminal offence; and importing currency is what it had to be assumed that the respondent believed he was doing. My Lords, I find the reasoning of Lord Lane CJ compelling. I agree with his construction of s 170(2) of the 1979 Act; and the principle that a man must be judged on the facts as he believes them to be is an accepted principle of the criminal law when the state of a man's mind and his knowledge are ingredients of the offence with which he is charged.' (See [1984] 1 All ER 747 at 749, [1984] AC 539 at 546.)

[44] Because of the points raised by the appellant on this appeal it is necessary to describe in a little detail the manner in which the trial judge summed up to the jury. (1) The judge told the jury that the prosecution had to prove that the

a appellant knew that he was importing prohibited material. (2) The judge told the
   jury, in effect, that if the appellant believed that he was importing 'The Exorcist'
   and 'Kidz', then, although he actually thought that he was importing prohibited
   material, he would not be guilty of doing so because those films were not
   prohibited material. (3) Later in the summing up the judge dealt with the matters
   which the prosecution had to prove. He told the jury that the prosecution had to
b prove that there was a deliberate evasion of the prohibition of the importation of
   prohibited material, and he said that it was accepted by the defence that the
   appellant had imported indecent material which was prohibited. He further told
   the jury that the prosecution had to prove that the appellant knew that prohibited
   goods were being imported but that it was not necessary to prove that he knew
   'the very films' that he imported, provided that he knew that he was importing
c indecent material and that he knew that the material was prohibited. (4) The
   judge then summarised the evidence for the prosecution and he concluded that
   summary by stating:

       'Members of the jury, that is the prosecution case. Are you satisfied on that
       case that he was knowingly importing prohibited material? If you are not
d   inclined to be satisfied on that case, or you think it is not good enough, then
       that is the end of the matter. But before you are satisfied, if you are left with
       the view that proves that he imported prohibited matter, before you reach
       that conclusion, you have to reject his defence. That does not mean the
       defence has to prove anything, but it is obvious, is it not, if the prosecution
e   prove the case, on the face of it, and the defendant gives you another
       account, before you can be sure that the prosecution account is right you
       have to reject his account. So let me remind you of what the defence was in
       this case.'

   The judge then summarised the evidence of the defendant and asked the jury to
f retire to consider their verdict.
       [45] Some time after the jury had retired they sent two questions to the judge
   and the following discussion took place in the absence of the jury between the
   judge and Mr Vaudin, counsel for the prosecution, and Miss Black, counsel for the
   defence:

g   'JUDGE EVANS: I have two notes from the jury. The first one is: "Could
       we have clarification if the defendant had brought in the two videos and they
       contained 'The Exorcist' or 'Kidz' which he believed to be prohibited, would
       he be guilty of the charge?" To which the answer is No, is it not? The next
       question is slightly more complicated: "Or does the charge specifically relate
       to child pornography content?" Now, the charge of course is being mainly
h   concerned in the fraudulent evasion of prohibition. And the Crown have
       alleged that it contains indecent photographs of children. They have to prove
       that it contains indecent photographs of children. They do not have to
       prove that he knew that it contained indecent photographs of children, as
       I understand it, but only that he knew that it was prohibited material. In
j   effect, of course, in videos prohibited material would only be indecent or
       violent material, I imagine. Although, I suppose not. It might contain
       instructions such as how to set up bombs and the like. I know not where that
       would come. But the charge does relate specifically to child pornography.
       As laid, the prosecution must prove child pornography. But knowingly?
       They must only prove that he knew that it contained prohibited material. They

do not have to prove he knew exactly what the prohibited material was. Do
you agree with that?   *a*

MR VAUDIN: Yes, I do.

JUDGE EVANS: Yes. What do you say, Miss Black?

MISS BLACK: I agree with your Honour, but I think—the defence is based
around "Kidz" and "The Exorcist".

JUDGE EVANS: Yes. I shall tell them if [he] thought it was "Kidz" and   *b*
"The Exorcist" he would be not guilty.'

[46] The jury then returned to court and the judge told them that the answer
to their first question was No. In reply to the jury's second question the judge
said:

    c

'What the prosecution do have to prove is that he knew he was bringing in
a prohibited substance—I am sorry, I have used the wrong word for this
situation—that he knew that he was bringing in prohibited material; that is,
he knew the video contained prohibited material. Not that he necessarily
knew exactly what the prohibited material was. You can see, it might well
be, especially if a lot is brought in, that someone may well not know exactly   *d*
what is in each item. The prosecution must prove that he knew that he was
bringing in prohibited material. And he, although the burden of proof is on
the prosecution—remember that—he seeks to disprove it by saying,
"I thought I was bringing in 'Exorcist' and 'Kidz', and 'Exorcist' and 'Kidz' is
not banned and indecent material." And if the prosecution have not satisfied
you, as it were, in the first instance, or your first looking at it, that he knew   *e*
he was bringing in prohibited material, that would be the end of it. But if
they do go, as it were, towards satisfying you that he knew that he was
bringing in indecent material, you must remember, before you can reach
that conclusion, you must reject his defence, having listened to his defence
in which he said, "I thought it was 'Exorcist' and 'Kidz'", you must say, Well,   *f*
we just don't believe him. But first you must put with that being sure that
the prosecution have satisfied you by his behaviour, and the situation which
you will find as a matter of fact, that he knew he was bringing in prohibited
photographs. But not necessarily the ones that are there.'

The jury then retired and shortly afterwards the court adjourned for the day.   *g*

[47] Next morning the jury sent further questions to the judge which were:
'Can you reclarify the question on prohibited material? Can you check that we
will understand before we leave?' The judge had a further discussion with
counsel and told them what he intended to say to the jury and defence counsel
agreed that what he was going to say was right. The jury then returned to court   *h*
and in the course of reclarifying his direction to them the judge said:

'Secondly, they must prove that the defendant knew that the goods which
were being imported—and "the goods", of course, are these parts of the
video in the middle—are subject to a prohibition. But the Crown do not
have to go on to prove that he knew the precise category of goods that were   *j*
imported ... So that, taking an example of drugs, if you are asked to import
drugs in a box, or concealed, and you say to the person who asks you, What
are the drugs? And they say, heroin, when it is in fact cocaine, and you bring
it into the country, and that is proved—the prosecution will prove that you
knowingly imported a prohibited material. They won't have proved, of

a course, that you knew it was cocaine, which is what you were told, although in fact it is heroin. That is what you believed, and that is what you will be judged on. They won't have proved either that you knew it was heroin, which is what you did import, because you did not know it was heroin if you believed it was cocaine. But what they will have proved is that you knew, in bringing in the item, you were concerned in bringing in prohibited goods, *b* and evading the customs in doing so.'

After retiring for a further period the jury returned a verdict of guilty on both counts by a majority of eleven to one.

[48] The appellant appealed and Rose LJ stated the point raised before the Court of Appeal as follows:

c   'This appeal, conducted on behalf of the appellant by Mr Salter, who did not conduct the trial below, raises a short and simple question. It is this: when indecent photographs of children are imported, by someone who believes he is importing prohibited material, is it sufficient for the prosecution to prove that the defendant knew he was importing indecent material or *d*   must the prosecution go further and prove that the defendant knew that the indecent material related to children under 16?'

[49] It is clear that in his summing up the trial judge told the jury that they must decide whether the appellant knew that he was importing 'prohibited material', the judge did not refer to 'indecent material' in this context, and *e* therefore I think, with respect, that it would be more accurate to state the question raised before the Court of Appeal as being:

f   'When indecent photographs of children are imported, by someone who believes he is importing prohibited material, is it sufficient for the prosecution to prove that the defendant knew that he was importing [prohibited] material or must the prosecution go further and prove that the defendant knew that the [prohibited] material related to children under 16?'

[50] In its judgment the Court of Appeal, in reliance on the judgment of Widgery LJ in *R v Hussain* [1969] 2 All ER 1117 at 1119, [1969] 2 QB 567 at 572, answered the question in the negative and dismissed the appeal.

g [51] The Court of Appeal then certified two points of law of general public importance:

'1. Where the defendant is charged contrary to section 170(2) of the Customs and Excise Management Act 1979 with being knowingly concerned in the fraudulent evasion of the prohibition imposed by section 42 of the *h*   Customs Consolidation Act 1876 on the importation of an indecent photograph of a child is it sufficient for the Crown to prove that he knew he was importing an indecent photograph or must it be proved also that he knew that it was a photograph of a child?

2. Is the answer to (1) above affected by the defendant's mistaken belief *j*   that what he believes he is importing is subject to a prohibition?'

[52] In delivering the judgment of the Court of Appeal in *R v Hussain* Widgery LJ stated:

'It seems perfectly clear that the word "knowingly" in s 304(b) is concerned with knowing that a fraudulent evasion of a prohibition in respect of goods

is taking place. If, therefore, the accused knows that what is on foot is the
evasion of a prohibition against importation and he knowingly takes part in *a*
that operation, it is sufficient to justify his conviction, even if he does not
know precisely what kind of goods are being imported. It is, of course,
essential that he should know that the goods which are being imported are
goods subject to a prohibition. It is essential he should know that the operation
with which he is concerning himself is an operation designed to evade that *b*
prohibition and evade it fraudulently. But it is not necessary that he should
know the precise category of the goods the importation of which has been
prohibited.' (See *R v Hussain* [1969] 2 All ER 1117 at 1119, [1969] 2 QB 567 at
571–572.)

The principle stated by Widgery LJ in relation to knowledge contains two parts. *c*
The first part is that the prosecution must prove that the defendant knew that the
goods which he is carrying are goods subject to a prohibition. The second part is
that if the prosecution proves such knowledge it is not necessary for it to prove
that the defendant knew what kind of goods he is carrying. The issue for the jury
becomes blurred if they are required to consider the knowledge of the defendant
as to the kind or category of goods which he is carrying. *d*

[53] In the present case it is not in dispute that the goods carried by the appellant
were prohibited goods. Once the jury had rejected (as they did) the '*Taaffe* defence'
advanced on behalf of the appellant that he believed he was carrying two
prohibited video films but that, in reality, those films were not prohibited, the
only issue for the jury to decide was whether the defendant knew that the goods *e*
which he was carrying were subject to a prohibition. The judge on a number of
occasions correctly directed the jury that this was the issue which they had to
decide. He also correctly told the jury that the prosecution had to satisfy them
that the defendant 'by his behaviour, and the situation which you will find as a
matter of fact, that he knew he was bringing in prohibited photographs'.

[54] The submissions advanced to the House on behalf of the appellant by *f*
Mr Lane QC placed reliance on the distinction between three types of indecent
photographs which he categorised as follows:

'(A) An obscene photograph within the meaning of s 1 of the Obscene
Publications Act 1959—where the photograph has a tendency to deprave or
corrupt the viewer. (B) An indecent photograph of a person under the age *g*
of 16 years which contravenes s 1 of the Protection of Children Act 1978.
(C) An indecent photograph which is neither obscene nor an indecent
photograph of a child (e g soft adult pornography); and consequently does
not contravene either of the above statutes.'

Mr Lane relied on the point that there is a prohibition on the importation of *h*
photographs in categories (A) and (B), but there is no prohibition on the
importation of photographs in category (C). He submitted that these differences
have been further emphasised by the Sex Offenders Act 1997 in which a distinction
is drawn between 'child' and 'adult' pornography so that an importer of adult
pornography does not commit a sexual offence and is therefore not required to *j*
notify the police of his name and address, whereas an importer of child
pornography does commit a sexual offence and is so required.

[55] Mr Lane submitted that in this type of case a direction based on the
judgment in *R v Hussain* creates an injustice because: (a) a defendant who believes
(or may believe) that he is importing a photograph in category (C) will be guilty

of an offence; (b) a jury is prevented from determining the defendant's actual knowledge of the facts; (c) it results in the conviction of a defendant whose knowledge of the prohibited import is 'approximate' as opposed to 'actual'; (d) it results in the conviction of a person who knows that the goods are 'indecent' being deemed to know that they were within only categories (A) and (B); (e) it requires a jury to cease their deliberations when they are sure that the defendant knew that he had indecent material in his possession whereas, if they were allowed, they might further conclude that he believed that he was importing material in category (C); (f) the 1997 Act made a distinction between the importation of adult and child pornography and imposed more onerous sanctions for the latter.

[56] I am unable to accept these submissions. The offence created by s 170(2)(b) of the 1979 Act is the offence of being 'knowingly concerned in any fraudulent evasion ... of any prohibition ... with respect to the goods'. The essence of the offence is being knowingly concerned in the evasion of a prohibition. The jury were fully entitled to find that the behaviour of the appellant satisfied them that he was knowingly concerned in the evasion of a prohibition. His behaviour in buying genuine video films of 'Spartacus' and 'The Godfather Part 2' in the airport shop at Amsterdam Airport and obtaining receipts for them, leaving the genuine video films in the lavatory at Heathrow, and then producing the receipts which appeared to relate to the two video films containing indecent material, pointed quite clearly to the conclusion that he knew that he was involved in the evasion of a prohibition against importation.

[57] In many cases a person who, at the request of another and, it may be, in return for a payment, brings into the United Kingdom an article, knowing that he is taking part in the fraudulent evasion of a prohibition against importation, will not know the precise nature of the article which he is carrying. In such a case the task for the prosecution in proving an offence would be virtually impossible if, in addition to having to prove that the article was a prohibited one and that the defendant knew that he was involved in the evasion of a prohibition, it also had to prove that he knew the precise nature of the article. In my opinion the application of the principle stated in *R v Hussain* gives rise to no injustice in a case such as the present one, as it is open to the defendant to seek to rely on the '*Taaffe* defence' if his case is that he believed that he was carrying an article which in reality and contrary to his belief was not prohibited.

[58] Counsel also relied on the judgment of the Court of Appeal in *R v Dunne* (1998) 162 JP 399, but in my opinion the judgment does not support his argument as it was not concerned with the issue which arose in *R v Hussain* but with the issue whether a defendant can know that an article is obscene before a jury has found that it tends to deprave and corrupt.

[59] Counsel advanced an alternative submission that in the present case a strict application of the words of Widgery LJ that the defendant must know 'that the goods ... are subject to a prohibition' means that the prosecution must prove that the appellant knew that the photographs fell into either category (A) or category (B). I am unable to accept that submission. In my opinion there is no reason to qualify Widgery LJ's words and it is sufficient that the prosecution proves that the defendant knew that he was involved in the evasion of a prohibition.

[60] The two certified questions, as they are formulated, do not permit an answer to the issue which arises on this appeal as the first question refers to the

defendant's knowledge of the importation of 'an indecent photograph' rather than to the importation of 'prohibited material' and therefore it is not appropriate to answer them.

[61] For the reasons which I have given I would dismiss the appeal.

Appeal dismissed.

Kate O'Hanlon   Barrister.

Loutchansky v Times Newspapers Ltd and others

[2001] EWCA Civ 536

COURT OF APPEAL, CIVIL DIVISION

THORPE, BROOKE LJJ AND SIR MARTIN NOURSE

12 MARCH, 3 APRIL 2001

Libel and slander – Qualified privilege – Public interest – Duty to communicate information to public – Whether defendant entitled to rely on matters not known at time of publication in support of plea of qualified privilege – Human Rights Act 1998, Sch 1, Pt I, art 10(2).

The claimant brought proceedings for libel against the defendants in respect of two newspaper articles which had accused him of being engaged in international criminal activities of a very serious nature. There was no substantive plea of justification in the defence. Instead, the defendants relied mainly on a defence of qualified privilege, contending that the allegations were of great public interest and concern, such that the public were entitled to know of them. In order to support their contention that they had been under a duty to publish the matters complained of, the defendants applied for permission to amend their defence to include certain facts of which they had been unaware at the time of the publication. The judge refused the application and the defendants appealed.

Held – For the purposes of the defence of qualified privilege, the factors relating to the conduct and decisions of the publisher or journalist were to be considered objectively in the light of the matters known to them at the time and were not to be judged with the benefit of hindsight. Matters such as the steps taken to verify the information, the urgency of the matter and the circumstances of the publication, including the timing, would lose much of their potent effect if the law permitted a publisher to publish untrue defamatory material without sufficient inquiry and then to justify that publication (in the sense of establishing a plea of qualified privilege) by being allowed to rely on after-acquired information. Moreover, it was facile to talk about a 'right to know' if there were no duty to publish. The public had no right to know untrue defamatory matter about which a newspaper had made no sufficient inquiry before deciding to publish it. The right to freedom of expression had never been absolute, whether at common law or under the jurisprudence of the European Convention for the Protection of Human Rights and Fundamental Freedoms 1950 (the convention). Art 10(2)[a] of the convention (as set out in Sch 1 to the Human Rights Act 1998) explicitly stated that the right to freedom of expression carried with it duties and responsibilities, and its jurisprudence showed how the right to freedom of expression was circumscribed by what was strictly necessary and proportionate in a democratic society for the protection of individuals' reputations. If the public 'right to know' were to be adopted as the sole criterion for conferring immunity from liability for damaging and untrue statements, the courts would be turning their back on their duty to prescribe such restrictions on freedom of expression as were needed in order to

---

a   Article 10, so far as material, is set out at [44], below

achieve the public good of protecting an individual's reputation. Some discipline had to be introduced in order to give appropriate effect to the interests recognised as legitimate by art 10(2) of the convention. That discipline involved the court examining the occasion of the publication, and not the circumstances as might have appeared to the publishers weeks or months later if they had waited to make further inquiries, or waited to see if further facts came to light. Accordingly, the appeal would be dismissed (see [40], [41], [44], [45], [78], [80], [83], [84], [87]–[90], below).

Blackshaw v Lord [1983] 2 All ER 311, *Reynolds v Times Newspapers Ltd* [1998] 3 All ER 961 and *GKR Karate (UK) Ltd v Yorkshire Post Newspapers Ltd* [2000] 2 All ER 931 considered.

Notes

For the convention right to freedom of expression and for qualified privilege for communications to the public, see respectively 8(2) *Halsbury's Laws* (4th edn reissue) para 158 and 28 *Halsbury's Laws* (4th edn reissue) para 121.

For the Human Rights Act 1998, Sch 1, Pt I, art 10, see 7 *Halsbury's Statutes* (4th edn) (1999 reissue) 524.

Cases referred to in judgments

Blackshaw v Lord [1983] 2 All ER 311, [1984] QB 1, [1983] 3 WLR 283, CA.
Bladet Tromsø v Norway (1999) 29 EHRR 125, ECt HR.
Cohen v Daily Telegraph Ltd [1968] 2 All ER 407, [1968] 1 WLR 916, CA.
Davies v Snead (1870) LR 5 QB 608.
Gilpin v Fowler (1854) 9 Exch 615, 156 ER 263.
GKR Karate (UK) Ltd v Yorkshire Post Newspapers Ltd (No 2) [2000] EMLR 410.
GKR Karate (UK) Ltd v Yorkshire Post Newspapers Ltd [2000] 2 All ER 931, [2000] 1 WLR 2571, CA.
James v Baird 1916 SC (HL) 158.
London Artists Ltd v Littler [1968] 1 All ER 1075, [1968] 1 WLR 607; *affd* [1969] 2 All ER 193, [1969] 2 QB 375, [1969] 2 WLR 409, CA.
London Association for Protection of Trade v Greenlands Ltd [1916] 2 AC 15, [1916–17] All ER Rep 452, HL.
McCartan Turkington Breen (a firm) v Times Newspapers Ltd [2000] 4 All ER 913, [2000] 3 WLR 1670, HL.
Perera v Peiris [1949] AC 1, PC.
Purcell v Sowler (1877) 2 CPD 215, CA.
Reynolds v Times Newspapers Ltd [1998] 3 All ER 961, [1998] 3 WLR 862, CA; *affd* [1999] 4 All ER 609, [1999] 3 WLR 1010, HL.
Saad Al-Fagih v HH Saudi Research and Marketing (UK) Ltd (28 July 2000, unreported).
Sunday Times v UK (1979) 2 EHRR 245, ECt HR.
Toogood v Spyring (1834) 1 Cr M & R 181, [1824–34] All ER Rep 735, 149 ER 1044.
Watts v Times Newspapers Ltd (Schilling & Lom (a firm), third party) [1996] 1 All ER 152, [1997] QB 650, [1996] 2 WLR 427, CA.
Webb v Times Publishing Co Ltd [1960] 2 All ER 789, [1960] 2 QB 535, [1960] 3 WLR 352.

Cases also cited or referred to in skeleton arguments

Adam v Ward [1917] AC 309, [1916–17] All ER Rep 157, HL.
Derbyshire CC v Times Newspapers Ltd [1993] 1 All ER 1011, [1993] AC 534, HL.
Harrison v Bush (1855) 5 E & B 344, 119 ER 509.
Hashman v UK (2000) 30 EHRR 241, ECt HR.

a *Pullman v Hill & Co* [1891] 1 QB 524, CA.
R v Secretary of State for the Home Dept, ex p Simms [1999] 3 All ER 400, [2000] 2 AC
   115, HL.
Rantzen v Mirror Group Newspapers (1986) Ltd [1993] 4 All ER 975, [1994] QB 670, CA.
Stuart v Bell [1891] 2 QB 341, CA.
Sunday Times v UK (No 2) (1991) 14 EHRR 229, ECt HR.
b *Watt v Longsdon* [1930] 1 KB 130, [1929] All ER Rep 284, CA.

Appeal

The defendants, Times Newspapers Ltd, Peter Stothard, David Lister and
James Bone appealed with permission of May LJ from the decision of Gray J on
22 January 2001 refusing them permission to amend their defence to add certain
c additional paragraphs to their plea of qualified privilege in proceedings for libel
brought against them by the claimant, Grigori Loutchansky. The facts are set out
in the judgment of Brooke LJ.

Richard Spearman QC and *Richard Parkes* (instructed by *Reynolds Porter Chamberlain*)
d   for the defendants.
Desmond Browne QC and *Hugh Tomlinson* (instructed by *Olswang*) for the claimant.

12 March 2001. The appeal was dismissed for reasons to be given later.

e 3 April 2001. The following judgments were delivered.

BROOKE LJ (giving the first judgment at the invitation of Thorpe LJ).
    [1] This is an appeal by the defendants from a decision of Gray J on 22 January 2001
when he refused them permission to amend their defence to add certain additional
paragraphs to their plea of qualified privilege. The issue arises in the context of a
f libel action which started on 19 March 2001 before Gray J and a jury. At the end
of the hearing of the appeal on 12 March we said we were dismissing the appeal
and that we would give our reasons in due course.
    [2] In this action the claimant, who was born in Tashkent and was subsequently
based in Latvia, complains that he was libelled by two publications which
appeared in the columns of The Times on 8 September and 14 October 1999
g respectively. These articles accused him of being engaged in international criminal
activities of a very serious kind. There is no substantive plea of justification in the
defence. Instead the defendants rely mainly on a defence of qualified privilege.
They contend that given the nature and seriousness of the allegations against the
claimant and the evidence to support them, including the claimant's criminal
h conviction and the fact that the allegations had received official endorsement by
public authorities such as the Home Office and the US Department of State, the
allegations were of great public interest and concern, such that the public were
entitled to know of them.
    [3] On 12 January the judge granted the defendants permission to amplify
j their reasons for saying that they were under a duty to publish the articles
complained of, and their grounds for saying that the information available to
them was reliable. He also gave them permission to add various matters to the
existing particulars, including the addition of a fourth source of information of
which no mention had hitherto been made in their statement of case. He
adjourned until 22 January consideration of the question whether he would grant
them permission to add certain additional matters, set out in paras 18.2.1 to 18.2.7

of a draft amended defence, and on that day he refused such permission, setting
out his reasons in a short oral judgment.

[4] It was a feature of these additional matters that none of them were known
to the defendants at the time they published the articles of which complaint is
made. They consisted of reports or views expressed about the claimant by
various governments or governmental bodies in this country, Austria and Israel,
and also by Interpol. It is, for instance, already part of the defendants' case that
the claimant was excluded from the United Kingdom by direction of the Home
Secretary in 1994, and they now wish to rely on an affidavit sworn on behalf of
the Home Secretary in judicial review proceedings in 1996 which sets out the
Home Secretary's reasons for making the exclusion order.

[5] The judge recorded how on a hearing on 23 October 2000 it had been
common ground between the parties that the defendants could not rely on facts
in support of their claim to privilege unless they were known to the journalist
involved with the articles complained of at the time of their publication. He said
that the defendants had now changed their stance. They were now asserting that
they were entitled to rely on facts of which they had been unaware at the material
time in support of their contention that they were under a duty to publish the
matters of which complaint is made.

[6] The judge, who has immense experience in this field of law, took as his
starting point what he called certain basic principles relating to the common law
defence of privilege. He understood these principles to represent common ground
between the parties, and they were not disputed on the appeal to this court. He
expressed them in the following terms. (1) The question is not whether the
publication itself is privileged, but rather whether the occasion of the publication
was privileged. (2) For privilege to obtain, there must be established a duty to
publish on the part of the defendant and a reciprocal interest on the part of those
to whom the words were published in the subject matter of the publication.
(3) The duty must be established to have existed in fact, as must the existence of
the legitimate interest on the part of those to whom the publication was made.
(4) The consequence of an occasion being privileged is that the publisher
acquires an immunity to legal liability for the publication of untrue defamatory
statements about a person, subject always to the question of malice.

[7] The judge then divided his consideration of the matter he had to decide
into two parts. In the first part, in which his conclusions were not challenged by
Mr Spearman QC on this appeal, he said that it appeared beyond doubt that a
defendant pleading qualified privilege could rely only on facts and circumstances
which existed at the time of publication. In the second part, in which his
conclusions are the subject of this appeal, he decided that a defendant could not
pray in aid in support of an alleged entitlement to privilege facts of which it had
been unaware at the time of publication. Referring to the speeches in the House
of Lords in *Reynolds v Times Newspapers Ltd* [1999] 4 All ER 609, [1999] 3 WLR 1010,
he said that it appeared to him that this conclusion provided the certainty which
Lord Steyn ([1999] 4 All ER 609 at 634–635, [1999] 3 WLR 1010 at 1036)
considered to be a desirable objective. He added that this view of the law also
appeared to be productive of the higher standard of journalism mentioned by
Lord Nicholls of Birkenhead ([1999] 4 All ER 609 at 623, [1999] 3 WLR 1010 at 1024).

[8] In so far as the judge was determining the matter as a point of principle, it
was common ground that the point had not been authoritatively determined,
even by the House of Lords in *Reynolds'* case or by this court in *GKR Karate (UK) Ltd v
Yorkshire Post Newspapers Ltd* [2000] 2 All ER 931, [2000] 1 WLR 2571. Indeed, May LJ,

a who gave the leading judgment in the latter case, said when granting permission for the present appeal that the point was an important one, adding that there was a real, if problematic, prospect of success.

[9] In order to resolve this matter, it is necessary to refer to the historical development of the common law defence of qualified privilege. For this purpose there is a very helpful summary of the matter in the judgment of Dunn LJ in

b *Blackshaw v Lord* [1983] 2 All ER 311 at 332–335, [1984] QB 1 at 32–36, in which he referred with approval to the history set out in the argument of Sir Valentine Holmes KC in *Perera v Peiris* [1949] AC 1 at 9. This showed that in the eighteenth century privilege afforded no defence to a defamatory publication. Dunn LJ continued:

c   'During the nineteenth century the judges were using the word "privilege" as meaning the existence of a set of circumstances in which the presumption of malice was negatived. It was said in *Gilpin v Fowler* (1854) 9 Exch 615 at 623–624, 156 ER 263 at 266 that "instead of the expression 'privileged communication' it would be more correct to say that the communication was made on an occasion which rebutted the presumption of malice". The

d   judges, having to face the problem of what would be the circumstances in which the presumption of malice would be negatived, went on two lines, duty and interest, and the public good and for the public interest. By the end of the ensuing 100 years it had been established that certain categories of documents by their very nature rebutted the presumption of malice, and

e   publication of them was accordingly privileged. These included fair and accurate reports of judicial proceedings and of proceedings in Parliament. But the courts stressed that the categories were not closed, and in each case it was necessary to determine whether the occasion was privileged not only by reference to the subject matter of the information published but also to its

f   status, and whether that gave rise to the duty to publish.' (See [1983] 2 All ER 311 at 332–333, [1984] QB 1 at 33–34.)

[10] In *Watts v Times Newspapers Ltd (Schilling & Lom (a firm), third party)* [1996] 1 All ER 152 at 157, [1997] QB 650 at 659 Hirst LJ, who also had vast experience of this branch of the law, said that the general principle on which common law

g qualified privilege was founded was the public interest frequently expressed as 'the common convenience and welfare of society' or 'the general interest of society'. He went on to say that the first classic exposition of the doctrine was to be found in the judgment of Baron Parke in *Toogood v Spyring* (1834) 1 Cr M & R 181 at 193–194, [1824–34] All ER Rep 735 at 737–738, in which he held that a defamatory publication would be protected by common law privilege in cases

h where the occasion of the publication afforded a defence in the absence of express malice. Parke B rationalised the position in these terms:

      'In general, an action lies for the malicious publication of statements which are false in fact, and injurious to the character of another (within the well-known

j   limits as to verbal slander), and the law considers such publication as malicious, unless it is fairly made by a person in the discharge of some public or private duty, whether legal or moral, or in the conduct of his own affairs, in matters where his interest is concerned. In such cases, the occasion prevents the inference of malice, which the law draws from unauthorized communications, and affords a qualified defence depending upon the absence of actual malice. If *fairly* warranted by any reasonable occasion or exigency,

and honestly made, such communications are protected for the common
convenience and welfare of society; and the law has not restricted the right   *a*
to make them within any narrow limits.' (Parke B's emphasis.)

[11] It is not necessary for the purposes of this judgment to trace the later
expositions of the 'duty and interest' formulation. A number of them are
conveniently brought together and discussed in *Duncan and Neill on Defamation*   *b*
(2nd edn, 1983) pp 93–94, paras 14.04 to 14.06. In *James v Baird* 1916 SC (HL) 158
Earl Loreburn described how a court should set about its task of determining
whether the occasion of publication attracted privilege. He said (at 163–164):

> 'If the document is capable of a defamatory meaning, then may be considered
> the point as to whether the occasion was privileged or not. In considering   *c*
> the question whether the occasion was an occasion of privilege, the Court
> will regard the alleged libel and will examine by whom it was published, to
> whom it was published, when, why, and in what circumstances it was
> published, and will see whether these things establish a relation between the
> parties which gives rise to a social or moral right or duty, and the consideration
> of these things may involve the consideration of questions of public policy ...'   *d*

[12] In the same year Lord Buckmaster LC said in *London Association for
Protection of Trade v Greenlands Ltd* [1916] 2 AC 15 at 23, [1916–17] All ER Rep 452
at 456:

> '[It] is, I think, essential to consider every circumstance associated with the   *e*
> origin and publication of the defamatory matter, in order to ascertain whether
> the necessary conditions are satisfied by which alone protection can be
> obtained ...'

[13] In *McCartan Turkington Breen (a firm) v Times Newspapers Ltd* [2000] 4 All ER   *f*
913 Lord Cooke of Thorndon observed that until the decision in *Reynolds'* case it
would seem that the legal profession in England might not have been fully alive
to the possibility of a particular rather than a generic qualified privilege for
newspaper reports where the circumstances warranted a finding of sufficient
general public interest. He mentioned in this context the fact that in *Blackshaw v
Lord* [1983] 2 All ER 311, [1984] QB 1 this court had recognised this possibility,   *g*
although the judgments may have been somewhat discouraging.

[14] Although the nature and extent of the defence in such a case was not fully
explored in this country until *Reynolds'* case, it is worth considering the judgments
of this court in *Blackshaw's* case, which Lord Cooke in his speech in *Reynolds'* case
[1999] 4 All ER 609 at 644, [1999] 3 WLR 1010 at 1046 picked out for specific   *h*
mention as adopting 'substantially the right approach': see also [1999] 4 All ER
609 at 658, [1999] 3 WLR 1010 at 1060 per Lord Hobhouse of Woodborough.

[15] In *Blackshaw's* case the Daily Telegraph had published an article headed
'Incompetence at ministry cost £52 million' in which it recorded that a number of
senior civil servants had been reprimanded following certain investigations by   *j*
the Public Accounts Committee of the House of Commons, and that the plaintiff
had been the official in charge of the office of the relevant department at the
material time. The article also stated that the plaintiff had resigned from the civil
service. The publication of the article followed a press conference at which some
of the evidence had been disclosed, and at which it was revealed that an unnamed
senior department official in Scotland had been reprimanded. The name of the

a official concerned was said to have been subsequently divulged to the journalist (Mr Lord) by one of the department's press officers (Mr Smith) on request.

[16] One of the newspaper's defences was that the publication of the article was protected by common law privilege. It was said that the newspaper had a moral duty to publish information concerning departmental maladministration, the more so since a substantial amount of taxpayers' money was involved.

b [17] Although the appeal was dismissed on other grounds relating to the findings of fact which it was held that the jury was entitled to make, all three members of the court considered the viability of the plea of common law privilege on an occasion in which a newspaper was maintaining that it was under a moral duty to publish information to the world at large, and that the world at large had a corresponding interest in receiving it.

c [18] Stephenson LJ listed the principal authorities on this topic, and then said:

> 'The question here is, assuming Mr Lord recorded Mr Smith's conversation with him fairly and accurately, did Mr Lord (and his newspaper) publish his report of that conversation in pursuance of a duty, legal, social or moral, to persons who had a corresponding duty or interest to receive it … I cannot
> *d* extract from any of those authorities any relaxation of the requirements incorporated in that question. No privilege attaches yet to a statement on a matter of public interest believed by the publisher to be true in relation to which he has exercised reasonable care. That needed statutory enactment which the Faulks Committee refused to recommend (See pp 53–55 paras 211–215). "Fair
> *e* information on a matter of public interest" is not enough without a duty to publish it and I do not understand Pearson J's ruling in *Webb v Times Publishing Co Ltd* [1960] 2 All ER 789, [1960] 2 QB 535, that a plea of a fair and accurate report of foreign judicial proceedings was not demurrable, was intended to convey that it was enough. Public interest and public benefit are necessary (cf s 7(3) of the 1952 Act), but not enough without more. There
> *f* must be a duty to publish to the public at large and an interest in the public at large to receive the publication; and a section of the public is not enough.' (See [1983] 2 All ER 311 at 327, [1984] QB 1 at 25.)

g [19] Dunn LJ, after the historical excursion to which I have already referred (during the course of which he quoted passages from the judgments of Mellish LJ and Bramwell LJ in *Purcell v Sowler* (1877) 2 CPD 215 at 221 and 223), concluded this part of his judgment in these terms:

> 'This review of the authorities shows that, save where the publication is of a report which falls into one of the recognised privileged categories, the
> *h* court must look at the circumstances of the case before it in order to ascertain whether the occasion of the publication was privileged. It is not enough that the publication should be of general interest to the public. The public must have a legitimate interest in receiving the information contained in it, and there must be a correlative duty in the publisher to publish, which depends also on the status of the information which he receives, at any rate where the
> *j* information is being made public for the first time.' (See [1983] 2 All ER 311 at 334, [1984] QB 1 at 35.)

[20] Fox LJ used his own words to reach a similar conclusion. He said:

> 'A wider principle is stated by Pearson J in *Webb v Times Publishing Co Ltd* [1960] 2 All ER 789 at 805, [1960] 2 QB 535 at 570: "As the administration of

justice in England is a matter of legitimate and proper interest to English
newspaper readers, so also is this report [of foreign proceedings], which has   *a*
so much connection with the administration of justice in England. In general,
therefore, this report is privileged." I think that states the principle rather too
widely. It is necessary to a satisfactory law of defamation that there should
be privileged occasions. But the existence of privilege involves a balance of
conflicting pressures. On the one hand there is the need that the press should   *b*
be able to publish fearlessly what is necessary for the protection of the public.
On the other hand there is the need to protect the individual from falsehoods.
I think there are cases where the test of "legitimate and proper interest to
English newspaper readers" would tilt the balance to an unacceptable degree
against the individual. It would, it seems to me, protect persons who
disseminate—"[any] untrue defamatory information of apparently legitimate   *c*
public interest, provided only that they honestly believed it and honestly
thought it was information that the public ought to have." (See *London
Artists Ltd v Littler* [1968] 1 All ER 1075 at 1081, [1968] 1 WLR 607 at 615.) If,
as in my opinion the law requires, it is necessary for the defendants to
establish that they had a duty to publish the article if they are to be entitled   *d*
to common law privilege in respect of it, I do not think that the defendants
have done so. Mr Smith was not prepared to give the authority of the
Department of Energy to the naming of Mr Blackshaw. In so far as the
article implied that Mr Blackshaw had been reprimanded or forced to resign
from the Civil Service it was based on inference or conjecture derived from
insufficient knowledge of the facts. In my opinion the defendants were   *e*
under no duty to the public to publish the article in the form in which it
appeared, having regard to the actual degree of knowledge available to
them. Accordingly, in my view the defence of common law privilege fails.'
(See [1983] 2 All ER 311 at 339, [1984] QB 1 at 42.)

[21] The final part of this extract contains an echo of Lord Buckmaster's   *f*
requirement that a court must examine all the circumstances associated with the
origin and publication of defamatory matter before deciding that its publication
on the particular occasion was privileged. Fox LJ was saying that if a journalist
published information based on inference or conjecture derived from insufficient
knowledge of the facts, he could not successfully assert that he was under a duty   *g*
to publish it.

[22] Although the House of Lords disapproved the three-stage test suggested
by the Court of Appeal in its judgment in *Reynolds v Times Newspapers Ltd* [1998]
3 All ER 961, [1998] 3 WLR 862, that judgment contains a valuable discussion of
earlier English decisions in which courts held that the particular circumstances   *h*
of a publication taken as a whole warranted its dissemination to the public at
large (see [1998] 3 All ER 961 at 990–994, [1998] 3 WLR 862 at 894–899). This
discussion ended with part of the extract from Fox LJ's judgment in *Blackshaw's*
case which I have set out in [20] above.

[23] The House of Lords, like the Court of Appeal, rejected in *Reynolds'* case the   *j*
defendants' contention that the common law should develop a new subject-matter
category of common law privilege whereby the publication of all political
information would attract qualified privilege whatever the circumstances. All five
members of the House, however, stated in clear terms that an occasion of
publication to the world at large would attract qualified privilege if it satisfied
what Lord Nicholls called 'the duty-interest test' (see [1999] 4 All ER 609 at 619,

a   634, 641–642, 654, 658, [1999] 3 WLR 1010 at 1020, 1035–1036, 1046, 1056, 1060). Lord Hobhouse in particular said:

> 'No genus is satisfactory, nor is any genus more satisfactory than the criterion of what it is in the public interest that the public should know and what the publisher could properly consider that he was under a public duty to tell the public.' (See [1999] 4 All ER 609 at 658, [1999] 3 WLR 1010 at 1060.)

b

[24] I have noted how in *Blackshaw*'s case [1983] 2 All ER 311 at 339, [1984] QB 1 at 42 Fox LJ held that the defence of common law privilege failed because the journalist's state of knowledge at the time of publication was based on inference or conjecture derived from insufficient knowledge of the facts. Stephenson LJ touched on the same issue:

c

> 'The general topic of the waste of taxpayers' money was, counsel for the plaintiff concedes, a matter in which the public, including the readers of the Daily Telegraph's first edition, had a legitimate interest and which the press were under a duty to publish; but they had no legitimate interest in Mr Lord's particular inferences and guesses, or even in Mr Smith's, and the
d   defendants had certainly no duty to publish what counsel for the plaintiff unkindly called "half-baked" rumours about the plaintiff at that stage of Mr Lord's investigations. There may be extreme cases where the urgency of communicating a warning is so great, or the source of the information so reliable, that publication of suspicion or speculation is justified; for example,
e   where there is danger to the public from a suspected terrorist or the distribution of contaminated food or drugs; but there is nothing of that sort here. So Mr Lord took the risk of the defamatory matter, which he derived from what he said were Mr Smith's statements and assumptions, turning out untrue.' (See [1983] 2 All ER 311 at 327, [1984] QB 1 at 26–27.)

f   [25] Dunn LJ, for his part, justified his conclusion that The Daily Telegraph were under no duty at common law to publish the article in the form they did by saying:

> 'Taken at its most favourable to Mr Lord, what Mr Smith said about Mr Blackshaw was no more than an ex parte statement based on inference,
g   into the truth of which Mr Smith had made no investigation, and on which Mr Blackshaw had had no opportunity to comment.' (See [1983] 2 All ER 311 at 336, [1984] QB 1 at 38.)

[26] In *Reynolds*' case, Lord Bingham CJ began the process of seeking to identify the circumstances in which a publication to the world at large might
h   attract privilege. He said ([1998] 3 All ER 961 at 994–995, [1998] 3 WLR 862 at 899) that the higher the status of a report, the more likely it was to meet the circumstantial test he proposed. He added:

> 'Conversely, unverified information from unidentified and unofficial sources may have little or no status, and where defamatory statements of fact are to
j   be published to the widest audience on the strength of such sources, the publisher undertakes a heavy burden in showing that the publication is "fairly warranted by any reasonable occasion or exigency".' (See [1998] 3 All ER 961 at 995, [1998] 3 WLR 862 at 899–900.)

He then quoted the examples given by Stephenson LJ in *Blackshaw*'s case which, he said, 'put the requirement quite high'.

[27] Lord Nicholls developed this issue in the guideline passage with which he ended that part of his speech in *Reynolds'* case in which he identified the correct approach to matters of this kind. He dismissed the proposal that 'political information' should become a new 'subject-matter of qualified privilege' on the grounds that this would not provide adequate protection for reputation and that it would be unsound in principle to distinguish political discussion from discussion of other matters of serious public concern. He continued:

'The elasticity of the common law principle enables interference with freedom of speech to be confined to what is necessary in the circumstances of the case. This elasticity enables the court to give appropriate weight, in today's conditions, to the importance of freedom of expression by the media on all matters of public concern. Depending on the circumstances, the matters to be taken into account include the following. The comments are illustrative only. (1) The seriousness of the allegation. The more serious the charge, the more the public is misinformed and the individual harmed, if the allegation is not true. (2) The nature of the information, and the extent to which the subject matter is a matter of public concern. (3) The source of the information. Some informants have no direct knowledge of the events. Some have their own axes to grind, or are being paid for their stories. (4) The steps taken to verify the information. (5) The status of the information. The allegation may have already been the subject of an investigation which commands respect. (6) The urgency of the matter. News is often a perishable commodity. (7) Whether comment was sought from the plaintiff. He may have information others do not possess or have not disclosed. An approach to the plaintiff will not always be necessary. (8) Whether the article contained the gist of the plaintiff's side of the story. (9) The tone of the article. A newspaper can raise queries or call for an investigation. It need not adopt allegations as statements of fact. (10) The circumstances of the publication, including the timing. This list is not exhaustive. The weight to be given to these and any other relevant factors will vary from case to case. Any disputes of primary fact will be a matter for the jury, if there is one. The decision on whether, having regard to the admitted or proved facts, the publication was subject to qualified privilege is a matter for the judge. This is the established practice and seems sound. A balancing operation is better carried out by a judge in a reasoned judgment than by a jury. Over time, a valuable corpus of case law will be built up.' (See [1999] 4 All ER 609 at 625–626, [1999] 3 WLR 1010 at 1027.)

[28] After explaining that a newspaper's unwillingness to disclose the identity of its sources should not weigh against it, he ended by saying:

'Further, it should always be remembered that journalists act without the benefit of the clear light of hindsight. Matters which are obvious in retrospect may have been far from clear in the heat of the moment. Above all, the court should have particular regard to the importance of freedom of expression. The press discharges vital functions as a bloodhound as well as a watchdog. The court should be slow to conclude that a publication was not in the public interest and, therefore, the public had no right to know, especially when the information is in the field of political discussion. Any lingering doubts should be resolved in favour of publication.' (See [1999] 4 All ER 609 at 626, [1999] 3 WLR 1010 at 1027.)

a [29] A little earlier in his speech he had addressed ([1999] 4 All ER 609 at 623, [1999] 3 WLR 1010 at 1024) the problems faced by the media because the outcome of a court decision could not always be predicted with certainty when a newspaper was deciding whether to publish a story. After saying that a degree of uncertainty in borderline cases was inevitable, he added:

b   'However, the extent of this uncertainty should not be exaggerated. With the enunciation of some guidelines by the court, any practical problems should be manageable. The common law does not seek to set a higher standard than that of responsible journalism, a standard the media themselves espouse.'

c [30] In the *GKR Karate* case this court was concerned with a case in which the claimants complained of an article in the Leeds Weekly News which was critical of the way they ran their business of teaching karate. The first and third defendants were the newspaper publishers and the writer of the article (Mrs Holmes) respectively and the second defendant was the general administrator of the English Karate Governing Body (Mr Porch). Each of the defendants pleaded *d* justification, fair comment and qualified privilege. At a pre-trial review held less than a month before the trial was due to start the trial judge ordered that the judge and jury should hear and determine two issues before they went on to the trial of the other issues. The first of these issues was whether the article had been published on an occasion of qualified privilege. If the answer was Yes, the second issue was whether the newspaper defendants or any of them were actuated by *e* express malice. It was believed that the trial of these issues would take three days or so, while a full trial which included the issues of justification would take four to six weeks to try. The case against Mr Porch, which was linked with a separate action against him, would in any event proceed in full whatever the outcome of these preliminary issues. The particulars of malice alleged against him were *f* much more extensive.

[31] The claimants appealed against this order on the grounds that its effect involved a departure from the test of qualified privilege found in *Reynolds'* case and the substitution of a different test. Mr George Carman QC, who presented their case on the appeal, argued that all the circumstances of the publication had to be investigated in order to decide whether the publication of the article was in *g* the public interest, so that the occasion was privileged. These circumstances included the question whether the article was true. He said that the practical effect of the judge's judgment and order was that all that would be considered would be what the journalist knew and what inquiries the journalist should have made. What the journalist would have discovered if she had made further *h* inquiries would be left out. He submitted that the reliability of the journalist's source, objectively determined, was relevant to the issue of privilege.

[32] May LJ, in a judgment with which Tuckey LJ agreed, quoted ([2000] 2 All ER 931 at 937, [2000] 1 WLR 2571 at 2577) that part of Lord Nicholls's speech in *Reynolds'* case in which he said that—

j   'in deciding whether an occasion is privileged the court considers, among other matters, the nature, status and source of the material published and the circumstances of the publication ... These factors are to be taken into account in determining whether the duty-interest test is satisfied or, as I would prefer to say in a simpler and more direct way, whether the public was entitled to know the particular information ... A claim to privilege stands or

falls according to whether the claim passes or fails this test.' (See [1999] 4 All ER
609 at 619, [1999] 3 WLR 1010 at 1020.)

[33] May LJ commented that this passage justified Mr Carman's submission
that the test was whether the public was entitled to know the information, but it
did not support his submission that after-events, including the subsequently
determined truth or falsity of the publication, were relevant. The words 'the
circumstances of the publication' meant in this context the circumstances at the
time of the publication. A little earlier in his speech ([1999] 4 All ER 609 at 615,
[1999] 3 WLR 1010 at 1016) Lord Nicholls had quoted from the judgment of
Blackburn J in *Davies v Snead* (1870) LR 5 QB 608 at 611 where that judge spoke
of circumstances where a person is so situated that it 'becomes right in the
interests of society' that he should tell certain facts to another. Lord Nicholls had
also cited ([1999] 4 All ER 609 at 616–617, [1999] 3 WLR 1010 at 1017) the dictum
of Lord Buckmaster LC in the *Greenlands* case (for which see [12] above).

[34] After quoting the passage of Lord Nicholls's speech which I have reproduced
in [27] of this judgment, May LJ said:

'This passage, in my judgment, clearly supports Mr Moloney's submission
that the existence or otherwise of qualified privilege is to be judged in all the
circumstances at the time of the publication. It is not necessary or relevant
to determine whether the publication was true or not. None of Lord Nicholls'
ten considerations require such a determination and some of them (for
example number 8) positively suggest otherwise. Nor is it necessary or
relevant to speculate (for the purposes, for instance, of considerations 3, 4 or 7)
what further information the publisher might have received if he had made
more extensive inquiries. The question is rather whether in all the
circumstances the public was entitled to know the particular information
without the publisher making further such inquiries. The reliability of the
source of the information is a relevant consideration, but that, in my view, is
to be judged by how objectively it should have appeared to the defendant at
the time. It is to be considered in conjunction with the inquiries which the
defendant made at the time relevant to the reliability of the source. If
the defendant made careful inquiries which, judged objectively, reasonably
justified a conclusion that the source was apparently reliable, that will be a
positive (though not determinative) indication in favour of the occasion
being privileged. If the defendant made no, or only perfunctory, inquiries, a
conclusion that the source was apparently reliable will be less likely. In
neither instance is a subsequent investigation at trial into the actual reliability
of the source relevant. The judge was, in my view, right so to conclude in
the present case. Mr Porch may or may not have had an axe to grind. But,
if he did, what is relevant is whether Mrs Holmes knew it at the time or, if
she did not, whether she made proper inquiries on that subject.' (See [2000]
2 All ER 931 at 938–939, [2000] 1 WLR 2571 at 2578.)

[35] For these and other reasons the court considered that the judge's order,
which involved determining first the issues of privilege and malice in the proceedings
against the newspaper defendants, was fair, sensible and economic. The truth or
falsity of the publication was not relevant to those issues, nor was any present
determination of Mr Porch's reliability in the light of any evidence he might give
in these proceedings.

a

[**36**] The ruling made by the judge, Sir Oliver Popplewell, at the trial of this issue has also been reported: see *GKR Karate (UK) Ltd v Yorkshire Post Newspapers Ltd (No 2)* [2000] EMLR 410. He accepted (at 421) counsel for the defendants' summary of the general principles established by the House of Lords in *Reynolds'* case:

b

'A privileged occasion exists if the public is entitled to know the particular information. That is, if it was the journalist's social or moral duty to communicate it and the interest of the particular public to receive it. This is determined in the light of all the circumstances of the publication and, in particular, whether the sources were, or appeared to be, reliable, to a reasonable and responsible journalist. While Lord Nicholls' ten examples

c

are not to be taken as written in stone, they form the basic framework upon which a judge can do the balancing exercise.'

He then added:

d

'In particular, I am adjured to avoid hindsight, attach importance to the freedom of expression, be slow to conclude that publication was not in the public interest, to resolve any lingering doubts in favour of publication, and to be flexible in my approach.'

[**37**] These appear to me to be useful summaries of the approach which judges should adopt when deciding whether an occasion of publication of this kind

e

attracts qualified privilege.

[**38**] The final case we were invited to consider was the unreported judgment of Smith J in *Saad Al-Fagih v HH Saudi Research and Marketing (UK) Ltd* (28 July 2000, unreported). Smith J had the same task of directing herself on the law she should apply in this libel action against a newspaper publisher in respect of an article of which the claimant made complaint. She referred to the speeches in the House

f

of Lords in *Reynolds'* case and the decision of the European Court of Human Rights in *Bladet Tromsø v Norway* (1999) 29 EHRR 125.

[**39**] In para 50 of her judgment Smith J said:

'Lord Nicholls provided a list, not intended to be exhaustive, of the factors which the court should take into account when carrying out the balancing

g

process. To a very large extent they are the same factors which the European Court of Human Rights discussed in the *Tromsø* case when considering whether the publications in that case, which contained untrue (as it later turned out) allegations of improper conduct by seal hunters, had been in the public interest or whether they had wrongly damaged the reputations of

h

those concerned. The factors considered are relevant to the "duties and responsibilities" referred to in art 10 which Lord Nicholls equates to the standards of responsible journalism. In due course, I shall return to consider such of those factors as appear to me to apply to the circumstances of this case. Some factors relate to the quality, status and importance of the

j

material. Others relate to the conduct and decisions of the publisher or journalist concerned. The factors are to be considered objectively in the light of matters known to the publisher or journalist at the time. In so far as a journalist's conduct and his decision to publish come under scrutiny, he or she should not be judged with the benefit of hindsight. The standards which will be expected of the journalist are no more than is required by responsible and ethical journalism. One of a journalist's duties is to take reasonable care

not to publish false information as the public interest is not served thereby. *a*
This may impose on the journalist a duty to verify information if such
verification is feasible. In some cases, information may come to the journalist
from a source which he reasonably considers to be of sufficient authority and
reliability that he is entitled to rely upon its truth without verification. The
weight to be accorded to each of the various factors will vary according to
the circumstances of the case. If at the end of the balancing exercise, the *b*
court is in doubt, it will resolve the doubt in favour of publication.'

[40] It appears to me that throughout the case law I have considered the judges
are speaking with a single voice. The court has to consider all the circumstances
surrounding a publication when it considers whether the publisher had a duty to
publish the information in question on that particular occasion. I have shown *c*
how Lord Bingham and Lord Nicholls in *Reynolds'* case set out to give guidance
about the kind of matters a publisher should take into account when deciding
whether or not to publish. Lord Nicholls would, I think, have been surprised if
he had thought that a publisher could bolster his contention that he was under a
duty to publish by going out afterwards in search of material which was not to *d*
hand when he took the decision to publish, and there is no sign of this possibility
in his guidelines. Indeed, if that was the law, matters like 'the steps taken to verify
the information', 'the urgency of the matter' and 'the circumstances of the
publication, including the timing' would lose a lot of their potent effect if the law
permitted a publisher to publish untrue defamatory matter without sufficient
inquiry and then to justify that publication (in the sense of establishing a plea of *e*
qualified privilege) by being allowed to rely on after-acquired information.

[41] Mr Browne QC observed, in effect, that, if Mr Spearman's contention
was right, a wealthy newspaper, after complaint was made, could go out to scour
the highways and byways in search of material which it might then call in aid to
justify retrospectively its decision to publish untrue defamatory matter. If it *f*
found material which seemed to provide that retrospective justification it would
add it to its defence. If it found material which appeared to point the other way,
it would be entitled to claim that this material in its hands was privileged from
production, however extensive and persuasive it might be. This appears to me
to be an odd way of setting out to prove that at the time the decision to publish
was made, all the circumstances surrounding that publication, including the *g*
matters known to the publisher, justified publication in the sense that there was
at that time a duty to publish and a correlative interest in the public in receiving
the information published. I agree with Smith J that the factors relating to the
conduct and decisions of the publisher or journalist are to be considered
objectively in the light of the matters known to them at the time and are not to *h*
be judged with the benefit of hindsight.

[42] It appeared to me that in his powerful and well-argued submissions
Mr Spearman was seeking to reopen the issues which have been authoritatively
decided, at any rate for the time being, in *Reynolds'* case. He also appeared to be
contending at the same time for a wider specific genus of information which *j*
should attract qualified privilege automatically than the genus 'political information'
for which Lord Lester QC argued in *Reynolds'* case. As Mr Browne pointed out,
Mr Spearman from time to time elided the distinction between duty and interest,
focused as this distinction should be on the particular occasion of publication. A
typical example of this tendency can be seen in para 17 of his written argument in
which he said:

a

'Whether three questions are asked (as per the Court of Appeal) or whether there is but one test (Lord Nicholls' duty-interest test, tasted in a marinade of nature, status, source and circumstances), the primary issues in each case where the court considers a claim of privilege for publication to the world remain (a) whether the nature of the material is such as to raise issues of legitimate interest and concern (in more traditional language, whether there is a duty to publish and an interest in receiving the information), and (b) whether the circumstances of publication, including the newspaper's conduct, are such as to justify the newspaper in publishing false and defamatory material.'

b

[43] Mr Spearman conceded, as he had before the judge, that most of the illustrative factors mentioned by Lord Nicholls gave rise to questions to be determined in the light of the defendant's state of knowledge at the time of publication. He argued, however, that factor 2 (the nature of the information and the extent to which the subject matter is a matter of public concern) and factor 5 (the status of the information) should be treated differently because they bore directly on the question whether the public had a right to know the information which the defendants published.

c

d

[44] Mr Browne countered this argument, in my judgment convincingly, by submitting that the cases of both *Blackshaw*'s case and *Reynolds*' case demonstrate that if there is no duty to publish, it is facile to talk about a public 'right to know'. The public has no right to know untrue defamatory matter about which a newspaper made no sufficient inquiry before deciding to publish it. The right to freedom of expression has never been absolute, whether at common law or under the jurisprudence of the European Convention for the Protection of Human Rights and Fundamental Freedoms (Rome, 4 November 1950; TS 71 (1953); Cmd 8969) (as set out in Sch 1 to the Human Rights Act 1998) (the convention). In the present context art 10(2) provides:

e

f

'The exercise of these freedoms [freedom of expression etc], since it carries with it duties and responsibilities, may be subject to such ... restrictions ... as are prescribed by law and are necessary in a democratic society ... for the protection of the reputation ... of others ...'

g

[45] The delicate balance between the right to freedom of expression and the individual's right to the protection of his reputation has now been struck by the decision of the House of Lords in *Reynolds*' case. To talk of a public right to know, without more, is misleading. The convention explicitly states that the right to freedom of expression carries with it duties and responsibilities, and its jurisprudence shows how the right to freedom of expression is circumscribed by what is strictly necessary and proportionate in a democratic society for the protection of individuals' reputations. In *Reynolds*' case Lord Nicholls said that 'Reputation is an integral and important part of the individual ... Protection of reputation is conducive to the public good' ([1999] 4 All ER 609 at 622, [1999] 3 WLR 1010 at 1023). If the public 'right to know' was to be adopted, as it has not, as the sole criterion for conferring immunity from liability for damaging and untrue statements, then the courts would be turning their back on their duty to prescribe such restrictions on freedom of expression as are needed in order to achieve that public good.

h

j

[46] In its judgment in *Sunday Times v UK* (1979) 2 EHRR 245, the European Court of Human Rights explained that in determining whether or not an art 10

right was infringed, the court's supervision covered not only 'the basic legislation' but also 'the decision applying it'. The court said (at 281 (para 65)):

> 'It is not sufficient that the interference involved belongs to that class of the exceptions listed in Article 10 which has been invoked; neither is it sufficient that the interference was imposed because its subject-matter fell within a particular category or was caught by a legal rule formulated in general or absolute terms: the Court has to be satisfied that the interference was necessary having regard to the facts and circumstances prevailing in the specific case before it.'

It is therefore necessary to consider the applications of the principles I have been discussing in this judgment in the context of the facts of the present case.

[47] Mr Loutchansky maintains in his statement of case, as re-amended, that he is a well-known international businessman. He was born in Tashkent and was subsequently based in Latvia. He has Russian and Israeli dual nationality. He was a regular visitor to England prior to December 1994, and had numerous personal and business contacts here. In that month the Home Secretary personally directed his exclusion from the United Kingdom on the ground that his presence here would not be conducive to the public good. It appears that this direction has been under challenge ever since, and an appeal is now pending to the new Special Immigration Appeals Commission.

[48] The four defendants are the publishers of The Times newspaper, its editor and two of its journalists. Mr Loutchansky observes that The Times has an enormous circulation and readership throughout this jurisdiction, and a substantial circulation in the countries of the former Soviet Union, Austria, Germany and Switzerland. It is also published on the Internet.

[49] The first article of which he makes complaint was published on p 13 of the issue of The Times dated 8 September 1999. It was in these terms:

> 'Second Russian linked to money-laundering
> British and American investigators are examining the role of an alleged second Russian mafia boss over possible involvement in money-laundering through the Bank of New York. Investigators are understood to be looking at links to Grigori Loutchansky, whose company, Nordex, has been described by the CIA as "an organisation associated with Russian criminal activity". Mr Loutchansky's name surfaced in earlier money-laundering investigations which may have links to the Bank of New York affair in which billions of dollars of Russian money are alleged to have been laundered. The Russian-born businessman came to the attention of European and American investigators in the early Nineties. They suspected Nordex of using its former international base in Vienna as a front for a large-scale money-laundering operation. His name also figured in a British police report in 1995, known as *Operation Ivan*, which looked at the extent of the influence of the Russian mob in London. Mr Loutchansky has repeatedly denied any wrong-doing or links to criminal activity. Nordex, which has since moved out of Vienna, is also alleged to have been involved in the smuggling of nuclear weapons and by the mid-1990s reportedly controlled about 60 businesses in the former Soviet Union and another 40 companies in the West. The Times has learnt that these included between eight and ten offshore companies in British jurisdictions including the Channel Islands and the Isle of Man. They were administered through a chartered accountant in central London whose

a offices and homes were raided in 1996 by officers from the City of London Police. The companies were suspected of being used to help launder money from Russia, which was then channelled through European banks. No charges were ever filed against the accountant. At about the same time, a Yugoslav associate said to have been a front man for Mr Loutchansky was stopped and questioned after arriving at a London airport. No charges were
b filed against him. The British investigation into Nordex is believed to have failed because of the difficulty of establishing that the money funnelled through offshore companies controlled by Nordex was linked to criminal activities. Mr Loutchansky is alleged to be a former business associate of Viktor Chernomyrdin, the former Russian Prime Minister, and in 1995 his name hit the headlines after it emerged that he had been photographed with
c President Clinton at a Democrat fund-raising event in 1993. He is also alleged to have had business dealings with Semyon Mogilevich, the Hungarian-based mafia figure at the centre of the Bank of New York investigation.'

d [50] Mr Loutchansky says that these words in their natural and ordinary meaning meant and were understood to mean: (i) that he was the boss of a major Russian criminal organisation; (ii) that he was involved in the smuggling of nuclear weapons through Nordex, the company he owned and controlled; (iii) that either personally or by means of companies he owned and controlled, he was involved in the criminal laundering of billions of dollars from Russia;
e alternatively, by his conduct, he had given reasonable cause to suspect him or the companies he owned or controlled of such involvement.

[51] Mr Loutchansky also complains of certain further publications in September 1999, by the national Russian television company NTV and by the national Russian newspaper 'Arguments and Facts', which he maintains were
f the natural and probable and/or foreseeable consequence of the words complained of.

[52] The second article of which he makes complaint was published on p 22 of the issue of The Times on 14 October 1999. It was in these terms:

'Trader linked to mafia boss, wife claims
g
A Russian businessman under investigation by Swiss authorities pursuing allegations of money-laundering was a friend of Grigori Loutchansky, a suspected mafia boss, the businessman's wife claims … If Mrs Chernoi's allegations about a connection between her husband and Mr Loutchansky is true, it will raise further questions about Mr Chernoi. In 1996 the CIA
h described Nordex, a company operated by Mr Loutchansky and alleged to have been used to launder money and smuggle nuclear weapons, as an "organisation associated with Russian criminal activity".'

[53] Mr Loutchansky says that these words in their natural and ordinary
j meaning meant and were understood to mean that he was the boss of a major Russian criminal organisation, and that he was involved in the criminal laundering of money and the smuggling of nuclear weapons through Nordex, the company he owned and controlled. He again complains of a re-publication by NTV, on the same day in October, for which he asserted that the defendants were liable.

[54] The matters on which he relies in support of his claim for aggravated damages include a contention that although these allegations were obviously

extremely serious, the defendants made no attempt to contact him to obtain his comments before the articles in The Times were published.   *a*

[55] By their statement of case, as amended on 12 January 2001, the defendants accept that Mr Loutchansky is well known internationally, but say that he is known as a man suspected to be involved in international criminal activity, not as a legitimate businessman. They assert that he has been investigated for criminal activity by the authorities in various countries and excluded from   *b* several jurisdictions, including this one, by reason of strong suspicion as to his involvement in organised crime. These facts, they say, are known publicly because they have been reported in the Western media over about the last decade and published on the Internet.

[56] They have explained that it is at present no part of their case that   *c* Mr Loutchansky is either rightly or reasonably suspected of criminal activity. They do not know at present if such suspicions are justified. Their case is that he has a bad reputation as a man involved in international criminal activity.

[57] They have given the best particulars they can about investigations carried out by investigative authorities in various countries. These are said to have included the CIA, the National Security Agency and the FBI in the United States,   *d* Interpol, and police authorities or intelligence agencies in Switzerland, Germany, Austria, England and Israel. They say that Mr Loutchansky has publicly conceded the fact that he has been investigated on numerous occasions by various authorities. In this context they refer to a television interview with him on CBS in December 1998.   *e*

[58] The defendants were asked on what date and from what source they first became aware of the allegations that Mr Loutchansky had been investigated by these different authorities. In their response they distinguish between the matters of which each of them were aware when the articles were published, the matters of which they were not then aware, and the matters about which they cannot recall their then state of knowledge.   *f*

[59] The defendants refer to Mr Loutchansky's exclusion from this country and say that it was on the grounds that his presence here would not be conducive to the public good. They add that on 13 November 2000 the Home Secretary told Mr Loutchansky's solicitors that he had completed a review of his exclusion and had decided to maintain it.   *g*

[60] There followed, in paras 2–17 of the amended defence, various admissions, non-admissions, averments and/or denials which are not material in the context of this appeal. Paragraph 18 contains a very substantial plea of qualified privilege.

[61] It is not necessary for the purposes of this judgment to describe in any detail the particulars of this plea of qualified privilege, or Mr Loutchansky's reply   *h* to this plea. The nature of the dispute between the parties, on which the judge will in due course have to rule, after the jury has made any necessary findings of fact, is apparent from the pleas and counter-pleas now contained, by amendment, under what is numbered as para 18A. In the defendants' statement of case this contained six averments, which are followed by detailed particulars. The parties'   *j* contentions follow the pattern I set out below.

[62] First, it is common ground that it is the function of a free press in a democratic society to acquire and communicate to the public at large information about matters which are of public interest, and that the public at large has a common and corresponding interest in receiving such information and a right to receive it. Mr Loutchansky would make minor additions to this formulation. He

a adds that the press must exercise this function responsibly and with proper regard to the protection of the reputation and rights of others.

[63] Next, the defendants contend that the information in their articles concerned matters of the greatest general interest and importance to the public at large, and the readership of The Times in particular, that is to say—

b   'the corruption and criminalisation of Russian society since the break up of the USSR, the involvement of Russian organised criminal groups in money laundering through Western banks, the smuggling of nuclear weapons, and the activities of such groups, including the acquisition of businesses, in the West and the United Kingdom in particular.'

c [64] Mr Loutchansky denies that the words published about him concerned matters of general interest or importance. In particular they concerned him and did not involve the provision of any proper information as to the four matters identified by the defendants. The first article contained a speculative and unsubstantiated link between him and the Bank of New York based on manifestly insubstantial sources. Its publication was used as an occasion to repeat false d and obviously unsubstantiated allegations concerning him drawn from other publications. The other article contained an allegation made in pursuance of Mrs Chernoi's own agenda in divorce proceedings, used as an occasion to repeat false allegations concerning him drawn from other publications.

[65] Thirdly, the defendants say that it was particularly their duty to inform the readership of The Times about him. That readership had a particular interest e in knowing about him, and a particular right to know about him, because of the widespread concerns expressed about him and his business activities by and to Western governmental and police authorities (including the British Home Secretary).

[66] Mr Loutchansky denies that it was the defendants' duty to inform the readership of The Times about him by publishing allegations which had the f features set out in [64] above. He denies that 'widespread concerns' had been expressed about him and his business activities by or to Western governments at or around the time of publication, and he puts the defendants to proof as to which allegation they were aware of at the time of publication.

[67] Fourthly, the defendants contend that to the extent that their articles defamed Mr Loutchansky, they were based on sources which they were entitled g to treat as reliable, responsible and authoritative, and on which it was reasonable for them to rely, having regard in particular to the identities of their sources of information. They also rely on the fact that the clandestine nature of the activities described in the articles, and the classified nature of the information and documents available to their sources, had the consequence that corroboration h from primary sources or documents was in practice quite impossible to obtain. Mr Loutchansky puts all these contentions in issue. In particular, he says that the defendants were not entitled to treat their sources as sufficiently reputable, well-informed, reliable and authoritative to justify the publication of defamatory allegations they were unable to verify and which had not been put to him.

j [68] The defendants next contend that the information drawn from their sources was fairly and accurately stated in the words complained of, and that they presented it in a reasonable and responsible manner. They included a statement of Mr Loutchansky's repeated denial of any wrongdoing or any links to criminal activity. Mr Loutchansky puts the first of these propositions in issue. He adds that the defendants' sources did not tell them that there were, in fact, any investigations of links between him and the Bank of New York or state what

those links were. Nevertheless, he complains, the defendants unfairly and
inaccurately reported that 'British and American investigators' were examining
such links. Moreover, he says, the defendants repeated false and unsubstantiated
rumours as to his background without checking the information with him or
with any other source likely to have first-hand knowledge of the events alleged.

[69] Finally, in this context, the defendants maintain that as a consequence
they had a duty to communicate the information set out in the words complained
of to the readership of The Times, and that the readership of The Times had a
corresponding interest in receiving this information and a right to do so. This
contention is denied.

[70] There followed a number of detailed factual averments, to each of which
Mr Loutchansky has responded. In para 18.3 of their statement of case the
defendants set out a quantity of information about Mr Loutchansky which they
said was in the public domain, and they later gave particulars of this assertion. In
para 18.4 they maintain that they relied, and were entitled to rely, on those
publicly-known matters to support the information about Mr Loutchansky
culled from their own sources. They then supply details of the information given
to the third defendant by four sources (whose identity they do not reveal). Three
of these contacts were made in August 1999. The other is undated (save to say
that the contact was made before the first article was published). Mr Loutchansky, for
his part, puts in issue the truth of the matters which have been publicly said about
him, and maintains that the defendants should have been suspicious of each of
their sources.

[71] There followed an assertion by the defendants that the third defendant
attempted to contact Mr Loutchansky. This is put in issue. Finally, the defendants
make the assertion with which I started this judgment (see [2] above), which
Mr Loutchansky disputes. In paras 4.1 and 4.2 of his amended reply he sets out
his positive case in relation to the defendants' claim of qualified privilege. In
particular he maintains that since the allegations were of very serious criminal
wrongdoing, the defendants should have taken great care to ensure that they
were true. They were of a type which were likely to have been made by people
seeking to discredit him for ulterior but undisclosed motives. He said that the
defendants knew or should have known that the sources of information on which
they relied were of poor quality. They took no proper steps to verify the
information the informants provided. They knew (or should have known) that
the criminal allegations against him were unsubstantiated. He adds that there
was no urgency in relation to the publication of these allegations. The defendants
took no proper steps to contact him and seek his comments. The articles did not
contain the gist of his side of the story, but simply stated that he denied
the allegations. The tone of the articles was sensationalist and inappropriate to the
seriousness of the subject matter. And the defendants knew that he had no
involvement in public life in this country.

[72] Mr Loutchansky maintains that if the defendants had taken proper steps
to contact him, he would have been able to deal with and explain the many
misapprehensions and mistakes which they were under (sic) as to his career and
background. He says that on the assumption that the defendants would have
approached his rebuttals in a fair and open way, it could reasonably be inferred
that defamatory allegations in the articles would not have been made.

[73] This, then, was the state of the parties' cases when the judge was invited
to consider whether the defendants should be allowed to add the additional
matter contained in paras 18.2.1 to 18.2.7 of their draft amended pleading. These

a were to follow para 18.2, which in turn formed one of six sub-paragraphs (some of which were fairly expansive) which contained, according to para 18.1.7, details of the facts and matters relied upon in support of the contentions in paras 18A1 to 18A6, which end with the averment that the defendants had a duty to communicate the information in the articles to readers of The Times who had a corresponding interest in receiving this information and a right to do so.

b [74] The context is all-important. The only reason why the defendants wished to rely on the disputed material was to strengthen their case that they had the duty for which they contended.

[75] Paragraph 18.2, in its form permitted by the judge on 12 January 2001, is in the following terms:

c 'As was reported in the articles complained of, for many years the claimant has been suspected of and investigated for very serious crimes with international repercussions by law-enforcement agencies in various jurisdictions. In consequence, he has been excluded from several jurisdictions, including this one. The defendants rely on and repeat paragraph 1.1 above and on the further information supplied under that paragraph.'

d I have summarised this information in [55] and [59] above.

[76] What the defendants sought to achieve by the amendment which was disallowed was to add the following further matters by way of particularisation. (i) The reasons given by the Home Secretary, as set out in an affidavit sworn in July 1996, for the exclusion order he made in December 1994. (ii) Opinions

e expressed by the Home Secretary in a letter sent on his behalf to Mr Loutchansky's solicitors in January 1998. (iii) Comments made by the US Department of State to the US Embassy in Tel Aviv which led to Mr Loutchansky being refused a visa for entry into the United States in July 1995. (iv) References to Mr Loutchansky in a crime intelligence summary produced by the Israeli national police in April 1996.

f (v) References to him and to the Nordex Group in a situation report produced by the Austrian criminal police in December 1996. (vi) References to the Nordex Group in an Interpol intelligence report produced in February 1997. (vii) The contents of an affidavit sworn by a representative of the Israeli Ministry of the Interior in July 1998 setting out the ministry's reasons for opposing the renewal of the validity of Mr Loutchansky's Israeli passport.

g [77] The defendants accept that they did not know of the contents of any of these documents at the time they took the decision to publish their articles, but they maintain that they ought nevertheless to be allowed to rely on them.

[78] It appears to me that if the judge was disposed to find that the defendants should not have published the articles when they did, whether because they

h should have conducted more diligent inquiries, or because they should have made greater efforts to obtain Mr Loutchansky's side of the story, or for whatever other reason, that must be the end of the matter. It was at the moment of publication that the defendants had to decide whether, given the information available to them then and the extent of the inquiries they had then made, they could

j properly consider they were under a duty to tell the public what they wrote about Mr Loutchansky in their articles. They would of course have had to consider whether their sources would have appeared to be reliable to reasonable and responsible journalists (such, indeed, as they claim to be): see [29], [34] and [36] above.

[79] The court has to balance the powerful interests of the media in the right to freedom of expression against the interests of an individual who complains that

he has been wrongfully defamed. Nobody who has lived in this country for the last 50 years, as have most English judges, could possibly be unaware of the great services rendered to the public by skilled and fearless investigative journalists in uncovering fraud and corruption and incompetence, in high places as well as in low. In recent years our higher courts have repeatedly said how important it is that the law should throw its full weight behind the media's right to freedom of expression which is now articulated in a codified form in art 10(1) of the convention.

[80] The House of Lords has ruled in *Reynolds*, however, that the media do not have an unfettered right to publish what they believe to be in the public interest. Some discipline has to be introduced, in order to give appropriate effect to the interests recognised as legitimate by art 10(2). This discipline involves the court examining the occasion of a publication, and not the circumstances as they might have appeared to the publishers weeks or months later if they had waited to make further inquiries, or waited to see if further facts came to light. If they were to be taken to have that additional opportunity, they would by the same token have more time to seek out the complainant and obtain his version of events. It would then be likely that what they then published would be different from what they in fact published, and it is what they in fact published which is the subject of Mr Loutchansky's complaint.

[81] In these circumstances it appears to me that the application of the 'duty-interest' test as articulated by the House of Lords in *Reynolds'* case would work no injustice when applied to the facts of the present dispute, and, following the House of Lords, that there would be no violation of art 10 if the defendants are not permitted to rely on the proposed amendment in support of their plea of qualified privilege.

[82] I would add by way of completeness that we were reminded by counsel of the judgments of this court in *Cohen v Daily Telegraph Ltd* [1968] 2 All ER 407, [1968] 1 WLR 916. These judgments show how the rules about the matters which may be relied upon in support of the defences of justification and fair comment may differ, in the sense that further facts may be pleaded where the defence is justification, whereas only facts existing at the time of the comment may be pleaded where the defence is fair comment. The present appeal provides a good opportunity for this court to make an authoritative statement of the comparable position in relation to a defence of qualified privilege.

[83] These are the reasons why I agreed on 12 March 2001 that this appeal should be dismissed.

SIR MARTIN NOURSE.

[84] I agree.

[85] A publication of an untrue defamatory statement is only protected by the defence of qualified privilege where the defendant is under a duty, legal or moral, to publish it to a person or persons having a corresponding interest in receiving it. The duty must exist at the time of publication and the defendant must have an adequate knowledge of the facts that give rise to it.

[86] This latter requirement, which is most clearly expressed in the judgment of Fox LJ in *Blackshaw v Lord* [1983] 2 All ER 311 at 339, [1984] QB 1 at 42, is part and parcel of the basic principle that the defendant must not only be under a duty to publish the statement but must honestly believe that he is. His belief must be judged at the time of publication and it can only be judged by reference to facts then known to him. It cannot be judged or justified by reference to facts of which he is unaware.

a   **[87]** In para 50 of her judgment in *Saad Al-Fagih v HH Saudi Research and Marketing (UK) Ltd* (28 July 2000, unreported) Smith J said in relation to the ten matters or factors referred to by Lord Nicholls of Birkenhead in *Reynolds v Times Newspapers Ltd* [1999] 4 All ER 609 at 626, [1999] 3 WLR 1010 at 1027:

b   'Some factors relate to the quality, status and importance of the material. Others relate to the conduct and decisions of the publisher or journalist concerned. The factors are to be construed objectively in the light of the matters known to the publisher or journalist at the time. Insofar as a journalist's conduct and his decision to publish come under scrutiny, he or she should not be judged with the benefit of hindsight.'

c   **[88]** I entirely agree with those observations. If a defendant acts on the basis of facts which he honestly and reasonably believes to be true, but which are later found to have been, through no fault of his own, untrue, he will not be deprived of his defence. Equally, facts which are unknown to him at the time of publication cannot have any bearing on the question whether he is under the requisite duty at that time.

d   **[89]** It was for these reasons, as well as for those more fully explained by Brooke LJ and by Gray J at first instance, that I too was of the opinion that the appeal should be dismissed.

THORPE LJ.

e   **[90]** I have had the advantage of reading in draft the judgments of my Lords and I agree that this appeal should be dismissed for the reasons which they have given.

Appeal dismissed. Permission to appeal to House of Lords refused.

Kate O'Hanlon   Barrister.

Shah v Shah
[2001] EWCA Civ 527

COURT OF APPEAL, CIVIL DIVISION

PILL, TUCKEY LJJ AND SIR CHRISTOPHER SLADE

6, 7 MARCH, 10 APRIL 2001

*Estoppel – Representation – Deed – Attestation of signature – Statutory provision
requiring deed to be signed in presence of witness who attested signature – Defendants
and witness signing deed – Defendants knowing that witness had not signed deed in
their presence – Claimant contending that defendants estopped from denying validity of
deed – Whether statutory requirement for attestation precluding operation of estoppel
– Law of Property (Miscellaneous Provisions) Act 1989, s 1.*

The claimant invested £1·5m in a Kenyan bank of which the third defendant was
the chairman and his son, the fourth defendant, was a director. Subsequently, the
bank was placed under statutory management by the Kenyan authorities. It was
unable to pay any part of the claimant's investment, and the sum could not be
found in the records of the bank. The claimant's solicitor went to Nairobi as his
representative and conducted negotiations with the defendants. Those negotiations
resulted in the third and fourth defendants signing a document, which was
governed by English law and described as a deed, in which they made a promise,
unsupported by consideration, to pay the claimant £1·5m. The attesting witness,
an accountant employed by the defendants' companies, signed the document
shortly after the third and fourth defendants had signed it, but not in their
presence. They then took it to the solicitor's hotel where he collected it. When
the claimant subsequently sued upon the document, the third and fourth
defendants contended that it was invalid as a deed, relying on s 1[a] of the Law of
Property (Miscellaneous Provisions) Act 1989. By virtue of s 1(2), an instrument
was not a deed unless, inter alia, it was validly executed by the person making it.
Section 1(3) provided that a lease was validly executed by an individual as a deed
if, and only if, inter alia, it was signed by him in the presence of a witness who
attested the signature. The claimant contended that the defendants were
estopped from denying the validity of the deed. In response, the defendants
contended, inter alia, that a document which was not a deed could not become
one by reliance on estoppel. The judge held that there was an estoppel and gave
judgment for the claimant. The defendants appealed, relying on the proposition
that the doctrine of estoppel could not be invoked to render valid a transaction
which the legislature, on grounds of general public policy, had enacted was to be
invalid. In particular, they contended that the wording of s 1(2) and (3) of the
1989 Act reflected the demands of public policy that there be compliance with the
requirements of the section, and that it did not permit estoppel to be available in
any circumstances.

Held – The principle that an estoppel could not be relied upon in the face of a
statute was not of absolute or universal application. Rather, the court was
entitled to consider the particular statutory provision, its purpose and the social
policy behind it in deciding whether an estoppel was to be allowed. As regards

a   Section 1, so far as material, is set out at [10], below

a s 1 of the 1989 Act, there was no statutory intention to exclude the operation of an estoppel in all circumstances or in the circumstances of the instant case. In laying down a requirement by way of attestation in s 1, Parliament had not excluded the possibility that an estoppel could be raised to prevent the signatory relying upon the need for formalities required by that section. The perceived need for formality in the case of a deed required a signature, and a document could not be

b a deed in the absence of a signature. There was, however, no social policy which required the person attesting the signature to be present when the document was signed. The attestation was at one stage removed from the imperative out of which the need for formality arose. It was not fundamental to the public interest, which was in the requirement for a signature. Failure to comply with the additional formality of attestation should not in itself prevent a party who had

c come into the possession of an apparently valid deed from alleging that the signatory should not be permitted to rely on the absence of attestation in his presence. Indeed, there were policy reasons for preventing a party escaping obligations under the deed by reason of a defect, however minor, in the way his signature had been attested. The possible adverse consequences if a signatory

d could, months or years later, disclaim liability upon a purported deed, which he had signed and delivered, on the mere ground that his signature had not been attested in his presence, were obvious. The lack of proper attestation would be peculiarly within the knowledge of the signatory and would often not be within the knowledge of the other parties. In the instant case, the delivery of the document involved a clear representation that it had been signed by the third and

e fourth defendants in the presence of the witness and had accordingly been validly signed by them as a deed. The defendant signatories had known that it had not been signed in the presence of the witness, but they also had to be taken to have known that the claimant would assume that it had been so signed and that the statutory requirements had accordingly been met so as to render it a valid deed.

f They had intended it to be relied on as such and it had been relied on. The judge had therefore been correct in permitting the estoppel to be raised and in concluding that the claimant could bring an action upon the document as a deed. Accordingly, the appeal would be dismissed (see [30], [31], [33]–[36], below).

Dicta of Robert Walker and Beldam LJJ in *Yaxley v Gotts* [2000] 1 All ER 711 at 719, 734 applied.

g

Notes

For estoppel against statute, see 16 *Halsbury's Laws* (4th edn reissue) para 962.

For the Law of Property (Miscellaneous Provisions) Act 1989, s 1, see 37 *Halsbury's Statutes* (4th edn) (1998 reissue) 658.

h

Cases referred to in judgments

Bankruptcy Notice, Re a [1924] 2 Ch 76, CA.
Godden v Merthyr Tydfil Housing Association [1997] NPC 1, CA.
Kok Hoong v Leong Cheong Kweng Mines Ltd [1964] 1 All ER 300, [1964] AC 993, [1964] 2 WLR 150, PC.

j *TCB Ltd v Gray* [1986] 1 All ER 587, [1986] Ch 621, [1986] 2 WLR 517; *affd* [1988] 1 All ER 108, [1987] Ch 458, [1987] 3 WLR 1144, CA.
Yaxley v Gotts [2000] 1 All ER 711, [2000] Ch 162, [1999] 3 WLR 1217, CA.

Cases also cited or referred to in skeleton arguments

Armitage v Nurse [1997] 2 All ER 705, [1998] Ch 241, CA.
Ashville Investments Ltd v Elmer Contractors Ltd [1988] 2 All ER 577, [1989] QB 488, CA.

Bankers Trust Co v Namdar [1997] EGCS 20, CA.
Barrow Mutual Ship Insurance Co Ltd v Ashburner (1885) 54 LJQB 377, CA.
Eckersley v Binnie (1988) 18 Con LR 1, QBD and CA.
H (minors) (sexual abuse: standard of proof), Re [1996] 1 All ER 1, [1996] AC 563, HL.
Hornal v Neuberger Products Ltd [1956] 3 All ER 970, [1957] 1 QB 247, CA.
Humphries v Humphries [1910] 2 KB 531, CA.
Kaufman v Gerson [1904] 1 KB 591, [1904–7] All ER Rep 896, CA.
King v Jackson [1998] 1 EGLR 30, CA.
Kleinwort Benson Ltd v Malaysia Mining Corp Bhd [1989] 1 All ER 785, [1989] 1 WLR
    379, CA.
McCausland v Duncan Lawrie Ltd [1996] 4 All ER 995, [1997] 1 WLR 38, CA.
Mutual Finance Ltd v John Wetton & Sons Ltd [1937] 2 All ER 657, [1937] 2 KB 389.
Paragon Finance plc v D B Thakerar & Co (a firm), Paragon Finance plc v Thimbleby &
    Co (a firm) [1999] 1 All ER 400, CA.
Penney v East Kent Health Authority (1999) 55 BMLR 63, CA.
Pepper (Inspector of Taxes) v Hart [1993] 1 All ER 42, [1993] AC 593, HL.
Sherratt (W A) Ltd v John Bromley (Church Stretton) Ltd [1985] 1 All ER 216, [1985]
    QB 1038, CA.
United Bank of Kuwait plc v Sahib [1996] 3 All ER 215, [1997] Ch 107, CA.
Vincent v Premo Enterprises (Voucher Sales) Ltd [1969] 2 All ER 941, [1969] 2 QB 609, CA.
Williams v Bayley (1866) LR 1 HL 200, [1861–73] All ER Rep 277, HL.
Zakhem International Construction Ltd v Nippon Kokan KK [1987] 2 Lloyd's Rep 596, CA.

Appeal

The third and fourth defendants, Panachand Jivraj Shah and Dipak Panachand
Shah, appealed with permission of the Court of Appeal from the order of Judge
Crawford QC, sitting as a judge of the High Court on 4 August 2000, giving
judgment for the claimant, Mukesh Zaverchand Shah, against the third and
fourth defendants jointly and severally in the sum of £1·5m plus interest. Judgment
was not given against the first defendant and the second defendant did not appeal.
The facts are set out in the judgment of Pill LJ.

James Bonney QC and *Rupert D'Cruz* (instructed by *Gandecha & Pau*) for the third
    and fourth defendants.
Jonathan Rayner James QC (instructed by *Courtenay van der Borgh Shah*) for the
    claimant.

Cur adv vult

10 April 2001. The following judgments were delivered.

PILL LJ.
    [1] This is an appeal by the third and fourth defendants, Mr Panachand Shah
and Mr Dipak Shah, against an order of Judge Crawford QC, sitting as a deputy
High Court judge, made on 4 August 2000. Judgment was given against the
defendants, jointly and severally, in the sum of £1·5m together with interest of
£170,302·86. The claim by Mr Mukesh Shah (the claimant) was based on a
document headed 'Deed' made on 18 February 1999 and signed by the third and
fourth defendants. Three issues arose at the trial. The defendants alleged, first,
that in signing the deed they did not intend to create legal relations and, second,
that they signed under duress. The third defence was that the claimant could not
sue upon the document in any event because it was not valid as a deed. Sedley LJ

a considered the application for permission to appeal on paper. He refused permission on the first and second grounds and adjourned the issue upon the validity of the deed to the full court.

[2] The application was renewed on all three grounds to the court as now constituted. It had been ordered that, if permission were granted, the hearing of the appeal would follow immediately and counsel addressed the court on the
b application for permission with that in mind. At the hearing, permission was refused on the first two grounds and granted on the third. The reasons why permission was refused on grounds one and two were given in oral judgments at the conclusion of the hearing. The court decided to take time for consideration on ground three, on which permission had been granted.

c [3] On 12 August 1998, the claimant met two cousins of the third defendant at a wedding reception in Hertfordshire. (Judgment was given against one of them, the second defendant, in the action but that is not material for present purposes. He does not appeal.) The claimant told them that he was interested in investing money in a bank in Kenya and one of them made inquiries about interest rates at a Kenyan bank known as Reliance of which the third defendant was chairman and
d his son the fourth defendant was a director. On 14 August, the fourth defendant let it be known that Reliance would repay on 19 April 1999 the sum of £1·665m on an investment by the claimant of £1·5m on 20 August 1998. The claimant accepted that offer and on 20 August 1998 transferred £1·5m to Reliance's account at the Habib Bank at Moorgate, in the City of London, for a sub-account in his name.

e [4] The judge found that both third and fourth defendants played an executive role in the management of the Reliance bank whenever they wished. The judge was satisfied that the third defendant, when necessary, had authority in relation to the management of the bank and that the fourth defendant fulfilled the functions of chief executive. Both defendants were experienced businessmen.

f [5] On 7 September 1998, Reliance was placed under statutory management by the Kenyan authorities. It was unable to repay to the claimant any part of his investment. Moreover, the sum could not be found in the records of the bank.

[6] In February 1999, the claimant's solicitor, Mr Anup Shah, went to Nairobi as the claimant's representative. He conducted negotiations with the defendants
g which resulted in the third and fourth defendants signing a document described as a deed. The judge accepted Mr Anup Shah's evidence as to what happened. On 14 February, he met the second and fourth defendants at the Norfolk Hotel in Nairobi. He expressed to them the claimant's belief that the loan had been made to the defendants personally and that they were personally liable to repay
h the money to him. Mr Anup Shah's evidence was that the second and fourth defendants accepted that they and the other two defendants were personally liable to repay the money. He asked them to sign a simple form of guarantee and was told to prepare a document for them and to fax it to them.

[7] The judge found that the defendants had an incentive to repay the money personally because, if a formal claim was made in the liquidation, it would
j inevitably involve investigation of what had happened to the £1·5m and that would have been at least embarrassing to the defendants. As already stated, the judge rejected arguments that the relevant document was signed without an intention to create legal relations or as a result of duress.

[8] Mr Anup Shah prepared a document in the form of a very short deed. The third and fourth defendants amended the draft in certain respects, had it retyped and signed the document which was in the following form. They took it to

reception at Mr Anup Shah's hotel where it was collected by him. The second
defendant was not contactable and did not sign.

> 'THIS DEED is made the 18th Day of February 1999 BETWEEN A. Mukesh
> Zaverchand Shah of Baytree House, Broomer Place, Cheshunt Herts ("MZ")
> and B. Panachand Shah and Dipak Panachand Shah ("Messrs Shah")
>
> WHEREAS 1. On 20th August 1998 MZ telegraphically transferred the
> sum of £1.5 million into the account of Reliance Bank Ltd at Habib Bank, AG
> Zurich in London (Sort Code 60-91-94) for account of Messrs Shah 2. Messrs
> Shah have jointly and severally agreed to pay the sum of £1.5 million
>
> Now This Deed witnesseth as follows:— 1. Messrs Shah hereby jointly
> and severally agree to pay to MZ the said sum of £1.5 million 2. The provisions
> of this Deed shall be governed by English Law.'

Beneath those words it was stated: 'Signed as a Deed by Panachand Shah in the
Presence of ...' and 'Signed as a Deed by Dipak Panachand Shah in the Presence
of ...' Each of them signed the deed at the appropriate place and the signature of
an attesting witness, the same signature in each case, appears at the appropriate
place. The attesting signature is that of Mr Jaydeep Patel. He is a chartered
accountant employed by the defendants' companies and had an office in the same
building as the defendants. The document was brought to him by the defendants'
secretary after it had been signed by them. The judge found that the signature of
the attesting witness was added to the document shortly after it had been signed
by the parties to the document but not in their presence.

[9] The third and fourth defendants submit that in those circumstances the
document is not valid as a deed. The claimant submits that the defendants are
estopped from denying its validity, to which the defendants reply that estoppel
does not arise on the facts and, even if it does, a document which is not a deed
cannot become a deed by reliance on an estoppel.

[10] Section 1 of the Law of Property (Miscellaneous Provisions) Act 1989
provides, in so far as is material:

> 'Deeds and their execution.—(1) Any rule of law which—(a) restricts the
> substances on which a deed may be written; (b) requires a seal for the valid
> execution of an instrument as a deed by an individual; or (c) requires
> authority by one person to another to deliver an instrument as a deed on his
> behalf to be given by deed, is abolished.
>
> (2) An instrument shall not be a deed unless—(a) it makes it clear on its
> face that it is intended to be a deed by the person making it or, as the case
> may be, by the parties to it (whether by describing itself as a deed or
> expressing itself to be executed or signed as a deed or otherwise); and (b) it is
> validly executed as a deed by that person or, as the case may be, one or more
> of those parties.
>
> (3) An instrument is validly executed as a deed by an individual if, and
> only if—(a) it is signed—(i) by him in the presence of a witness who attests
> the signature; or (ii) at his direction and in his presence and the presence of
> two witnesses who each attest the signature; and (b) it is delivered as a deed
> by him or a person authorised to do so on his behalf.'

[11] Mr Bonney QC, for the third and fourth defendants, submits that the
terms of the statute prevent the document from being a deed. An instrument
shall not be a deed unless it is validly executed as a deed by the parties to it. It can
be validly executed only if it is signed by an individual in the presence of a witness

a   who attests the signature. Since the document was not signed by the defendants in the presence of the attesting witness the instrument is not a deed. It is common ground that, because of the absence of consideration, it cannot be relied on as a contract.

[12] Mr Bonney submits that, in any event, the estoppel which it is sought to set up in order to prevent reliance on the statute, is not established on the facts.
b   Mr Anup Shah, as the claimant's solicitor, was not entitled to rely upon the document as a deed. His fax of 16 February 1999, which accompanied his draft, indicated that 'the witness should also sign where indicated and must add his / her name address and occupation'. That was not done. The signature of the witness, though established in evidence as that of Mr Jaydeep Patel, was not legible.
c   Because of the history of the matter, Mr Anup Shah had reason not to trust the defendants. Moreover, he had no reason to assume their knowledge of the formalities of English law with respect to deeds. In those circumstances, Mr Anup Shah was put on enquiry and was not entitled to rely upon the document as being a deed. It is also submitted that action to the prejudice of the claimant is not established. The judge did not make a finding that, had the
d   defendants been requested upon Mr Anup Shah's receipt of the document to validate it, they would have done so.

[13] I do not accept those submissions. The delivery of the document constituted an unambiguous representation of fact that it was a deed. Mr Anup Shah acted reasonably in relying upon that representation, as in fact he did. The absence of the name and address of the witness, its presence not being a statutory requirement,
e   and the character of the signature did not, in the circumstances, render the reliance unreasonable and there was nothing else in the circumstances which did so.

[14] The judge found—

f   '(i) that the deed was properly signed by the parties with, as I find, full knowledge and understanding of its contents; (ii) that it was apparently validly witnessed, in the sense that the signature of a witness duly appears against the statutory attestation; (iii) that it was put forward by the defendants as a valid and effective document in the knowledge that it was to be relied on and with the intention, as I find, of being bound by it. The
g   intention was expressed to Mr Anup Shah at the meeting the previous day in Nairobi. I have no reason to suppose that that was not a genuine intention held by them at that time.'

Those findings were in my judgment justified. Mr Anup Shah said in evidence
h   that he believed that the third and fourth defendants would have re-executed the document had they been asked to do so. There is no evidence that the formal defect would not have been corrected had Mr Anup Shah been made aware of it upon delivery of the document and the action to the detriment of the claimant is in the loss of the opportunity to go back to the defendants and obtain their signature in accordance with the statute. The judge's finding as to the genuine
j   intention of the defendants amounts to a finding that they would have re-signed had they been asked to do so at the material time so that there was in the event prejudice. I leave open the question whether upon a representation by conduct that it is a valid deed being delivered, it is necessary to establish that the defendants would have cured the defect upon a resubmission to the signatory.

[15] In support of his submission that the doctrine of estoppel does not assist the claimant, Mr Bonney relies upon a statement in 16 *Halsbury's Laws* (4th edn

reissue) para 962, cited by Simon Brown LJ in *Godden v Merthyr Tydfil Housing Association* [1997] NPC 1: 'The doctrine of estoppel may not be invoked to render valid a transaction which the legislature has, on grounds of general public policy, enacted is to be invalid ...' That statement in *Halsbury's Laws* is, however, qualified by a footnote which states: 'As to whether this is the right test see *Kok Hoong v Leong Cheong Kweng Mines Ltd* ([1964] 1 All ER 300 at 308, [1964] AC 993 at 1016).'

[16] In *Yaxley v Gotts* [2000] 1 All ER 711, [2000] Ch 162, Robert Walker LJ cited the relevant passage from *Kok Hoong*'s case, which had not been cited in *Godden*'s case. In *Kok Hoong*'s case the Privy Council decided that there could be no estoppel in face of the Moneylenders Ordinance 1951 of the Federation of Malaya. Delivering the judgment of the Privy Council, Viscount Radcliffe acknowledged ([1964] 1 All ER 300 at 308, [1964] AC 993 at 1015) that there are statutes which 'though declaring transactions to be unenforceable or void, are nevertheless not essentially prohibitory and so do not preclude estoppels'. He referred ([1964] 1 All ER 300 at 308, [1964] AC 993 at 1016) to *Re a Bankruptcy Notice* [1924] 2 Ch 76 at 79 where Atkin LJ referred to 'general public policy' in this context. Viscount Radcliffe thought that 'rather an elusive guide' and stated a more direct test to be applied when it was sought to set up an estoppel in the face of a statute. Where the laws of moneylending were involved the test was—

> 'to ask whether the law that confronts the estoppel can be seen to represent a social policy to which the court must give effect in the interests of the public generally or some section of the public, despite any rules of evidence as between themselves that the parties may have created by their conduct or otherwise.'

[17] Viscount Radcliffe continued with a general statement:

> 'General social policy does from time to time require the denial of legal validity to certain transactions by certain persons. This may be for their own protection, as in the case of the infant or other category of person enjoying what is to some extent a protected status, or for the protection of others who may come to be engaged in dealings with them, as, for instance, the creditors of a bankrupt. In all such cases there is no room for the application of another general and familiar principle of the law that a man may, if he wishes, disclaim a statutory provision enacted for his benefit, for what is for a man's benefit and what is for his protection are not synonymous terms. Nor is it open to the court to give its sanction to departures from any law that reflects such a policy, even though the party concerned has himself behaved in such a way as would otherwise tie his hands.' (See [1964] 1 All ER 300 at 308–309, [1964] AC 993 at 1016–1017.)

[18] In *Godden*'s case, an attempt was made to defeat by an estoppel the provision in s 2(1) of the 1989 Act that 'A contract for the sale or other disposition of an interest in land can only be made in writing and only by incorporating all the terms which the parties have expressly agreed in one document or, where contracts are exchanged, in each'. Simon Brown LJ stated that the argument that 'although Parliament has dictated that a contract involving the disposition of land made otherwise than in compliance with s 2 is void, the defendants are not allowed to say so' was 'an impossible argument'. Simon Brown LJ regarded the principle stated in *Halsbury's Laws* as a 'cardinal rule' the 'absolute nature' of which cannot be 'outflanked by one of the equitable techniques or types of estoppels

a sought to be deployed in the present case'. Thorpe LJ and Sir John Balcombe
agreed with Simon Brown LJ.

[19] The case of *Yaxley v Gotts* was also concerned with s 2 of the 1989 Act.
An oral agreement purporting to grant an interest in land, though void and
unenforceable under s 2 of the 1989 Act, was held still to be enforceable on the
basis of a constructive trust under s 2(5) which provides that 'nothing in this
b section affects the creation or operation of resulting, implied or constructive
trusts'. Robert Walker LJ stated:

> 'Parliament's requirement that any contract for the disposition of an
> interest in land must be made in a particular documentary form, and will
> otherwise be void, does not have such an obviously social aim as statutory
c > provisions relating to contracts by or with moneylenders, infants, or protected
> tenants. Nevertheless it can be seen as embodying Parliament's conclusion,
> in the general public interest, that the need for certainty as to the formation
> of contracts of this type must in general outweigh the disappointment of
> those who made informal bargains in ignorance of the statutory requirement.
d > If an estoppel would have the effect of enforcing a void contract and
> subverting Parliament's purpose, it may have to yield to the statutory law
> which confronts it, except so far as the statute's saving for a constructive trust
> provides a means of reconciliation of the apparent conflict.' (See [2000]
> 1 All ER 711 at 720, [2000] Ch 162 at 175.)

e [20] Clarke LJ stated ([2000] 1 All ER 711 at 726, [2000] Ch 162 at 182) that
where a particular estoppel relied upon would offend the public policy behind a
statute it is necessary to consider the mischief at which the statute is directed.
Where a statute had been enacted as the result of the recommendations of the
Law Commission it is appropriate to consider those recommendations. He stated
f that in his opinion:

> '... the contents of that report [*Transfer of Land: Formalities for Contracts for
> Sale etc of Land* (1987) (Law Com No 164)] will be of the greatest assistance in
> deciding whether or not the principles of particular types of estoppel should
> be held to be contrary to the public policy underlying the Act. In this regard
g > it seems to me that the answer is likely to depend on the facts of the
> particular case.'

Beldam LJ stated ([2000] 1 All ER 711 at 734, [2000] Ch 162 at 191) that: 'The general
principle that a party cannot rely on an estoppel in the face of a statute depends
upon the nature of the enactment, the purpose of the provision and the social
h policy behind it.'

[21] In my judgment, that statement of Beldam LJ, reflecting as it does the
judgment of the Privy Council in *Kok Hoong*'s case, is, with respect, an accurate
statement of the law of England and Wales. The court is entitled to consider the
particular statutory provision, its purpose and the social policy behind it when
j deciding whether an estoppel is to be allowed. Upon such an analysis of s 2 of the
1989 Act, requiring contracts for sale of land to be made by signed writing, I do
not, with respect, question the conclusion of Simon Brown LJ in *Godden*'s case
that the section should not on the facts of that case be 'outflanked' by an estoppel.
I cannot, however, accept that the principle stated in *Halsbury's Laws* is of
absolute or universal application and agree with the comment of Robert
Walker LJ in *Yaxley v Gotts* [2000] 1 All ER 711 at 719, [2000] Ch 162 at 174, and in

the context of s 2, that a general assertion of a 'no-go area' for estoppel would be unmaintainable.

[22] Analysis of s 1 of the 1989 Act is required in the context of general social policy. Though in the same statute as s 2, it has its origins in a different report of the Law Commission (*Deeds and Escrows* (1987) (Law Com No 163)) and requires specific consideration. Policy considerations may apply to s 2 which do not apply to s 1.

[23] I first consider the Law Commission report (No 163). Mr Rayner James QC, for the claimant, relies on para 2.15 headed 'Formalities for Deeds: Failure to comply' (p 388):

> 'It would be undesirable if failure to have just one signature witnessed, perhaps on a deed which had many, were to render the whole deed invalid. We therefore recommend that failure to have a signature witnessed and attested should have the effect that the signatory would not prima facie be bound but that the deed, if capable of operating without that signatory, would still be valid. The signatory should still be bound if he took the benefit of the deed or through estoppel if someone else had acted on the assumption that the deed was properly executed.'

[24] The comment on estoppel is supported by a reference, in a footnote, to *TCB Ltd v Gray* [1986] 1 All ER 587, [1986] Ch 621, a then recent decision of Browne-Wilkinson V-C dealing with a power of attorney expressed to be signed, sealed and delivered but without an indication or evidence that it had ever been sealed. Mr Rayner James relies upon the reference at the end of para 2.15 to estoppel. He submits that the Law Commission must have contemplated in their report that estoppel could be asserted in the face of what became s 1 of the 1989 Act. The draft bill, which accompanied the Commission's report, was not materially different from s 1 as enacted.

[25] I consider the reference in the report to estoppel to be too slender a thread to influence the court's assessment on the effect of s 1 of the statute. The word appears near the end of a paragraph dealing with a different situation. Beyond the reference to the then recent case, the Commission did not consider the type of situation with which the court is now confronted. Had the Commission had the present problem in mind, I would have expected it to be dealt with specifically and expressly, together with an explanation as to how the concept of estoppel fitted with the terminology its members selected for the draft bill. Bearing in mind the court's task, no clear guidance in my view appears in the report as to whether and, if so, to what extent, estoppel can operate. I do, however, add that Browne-Wilkinson V-C's willingness in the *TCB Ltd* case to allow an estoppel, when the then existing requirement to establish that the deed had been sealed was not satisfied, supports the view that neither before nor after the passing of the 1989 Act has there been any general social policy requiring the exclusion of estoppel in all circumstances when the validity of a deed is in issue.

[26] Mr Bonney submits that the wording of s 1(2) and (3) is clear and leaves no room for the operation of an estoppel. Section 1 plainly provides that an instrument shall not be a deed unless it is validly executed and it is validly executed only if signed in the presence of a witness who attests the signature. He submits that the wording reflects the demands of public policy that there is compliance with the requirements of the section so that the doctrine of estoppel may not be invoked to render valid a transaction which the legislature has enacted to be invalid. It is formality which distinguishes a deed from other

a documents. As to the aims of formality, Mr Bonney adopts the criteria set out by the Law Commission in their Working Paper No 93 (*Transfer of Land: Formalities for Deeds and Escrows*) issued in 1985 (pp 4–5):

b '3.2 ... (a) cautionary: that is, trying to ensure that the maker does not enter into a transaction without realising what he is doing; (b) evidential: providing evidence that the maker did enter into a transaction and evidence of its terms; (c) labelling: making it apparent to third parties what kind of a document it is and what its effect is to be.'

[27] The wording of the section does not permit estoppel to be available in any circumstances, it is submitted. It does not permit a consideration of the facts of c the particular case such as would allow estoppel to operate in limited circumstances, as for example in the present case, where the signature on the deed is admitted and only the manner of attestation is defective. Mr Bonney adopts propositions which, for the purposes of argument, Sir Christopher Slade put to him: in many cases the formality of a deed will operate in law to confer privileges or benefits on persons which they would not receive under a mere written instrument. The price d to be paid for those privileges or benefits is that compliance with the statutory formalities must be established.

[28] For the claimant, Mr Rayner James accepts that an estoppel could not defeat the absence of a signature, as distinct from a defect in or the absence of its attestation. The signature is fundamental to the validity of the deed. The absence of attestation e in the manner required by s 1 does not, he submits, subvert the policy of the 1989 Act. That policy seeks to ensure that signatures on deeds are authentic and to limit the possibility of disputes as to authenticity. There may, however, be cases, such as the present case, where the authenticity of the signatures is not in question and public policy need not and does not go so far as to prevent the raising of an estoppel where there is a defect in the manner of attestation.

f [29] I bear in mind the clarity of the language of s 1(2) and (3) and also that the requirement for attestation is integral to the requirement for signature in that the validity of the signature is stipulated to depend on the presence of the attesting witness. I also accept that attestation has a purpose in that it limits the scope for disputes as to whether the document was signed and the circumstances in which it g was signed. The beneficial effect of the requirement for attestation of the signature in the manner specified in the statute is not in question. It gives some, but not complete, protection to other parties to the deed who can have more confidence in the genuineness of the signature by reason of the attestation. It gives some, but not complete, protection to a potential signatory who may be under a disability, either h permanent or temporary. A person may aver in opposition to his own deed that he was induced to execute it by fraud, misrepresentation or (as was unsuccessfully alleged in the present case) duress and the attestation requirement is a safeguard.

[30] I have, however, come to the conclusion that there was no statutory intention to exclude the operation of an estoppel in all circumstances or in circumstances such as the present. The perceived need for formality in the case of a deed requires a
j signature and a document cannot be a deed in the absence of a signature. I can detect no social policy which requires the person attesting the signature to be present when the document is signed. The attestation is at one stage removed from the imperative out of which the need for formality arises. It is not fundamental to the public interest, which is in the requirement for a signature. Failure to comply with the additional formality of attestation should not in itself prevent a party into whose possession an apparently valid deed has come from

alleging that the signatory should not be permitted to rely on the absence of attestation in his presence. It should not permit a person to escape the consequences of an apparently valid deed he has signed, representing that he has done so in the presence of an attesting witness, merely by claiming that in fact the attesting witness was not present at the time of signature. The fact that the requirements are partly for the protection of the signatory makes it less likely that Parliament intended that the need for them could in all circumstances be used to defeat the claim of another party.

[31] Having regard to the purposes for which deeds are used and indeed in some cases required, and the long-term obligations which deeds will often create, there are policy reasons for not permitting a party to escape his obligations under the deed by reason of a defect, however minor, in the way his signature was attested. The possible adverse consequences if a signatory could, months or years later, disclaim liability upon a purported deed, which he had signed and delivered, on the mere ground that his signature had not been attested in his presence, are obvious. The lack of proper attestation will be peculiarly within the knowledge of the signatory and, as Sir Christopher Slade observed in the course of argument, will often not be within the knowledge of the other parties.

[32] In this case the document was described as a deed and was signed. A witness, to whom the third and fourth defendants were well known, provided a form of attestation shortly afterwards and the only failure was that he did so without being in the presence of the third and fourth defendants when they signed.

[33] Having considered the wording of s 1 of the 1989 Act in the context of its purpose and the policy consideration which apply to deeds, I am unable to detect a statutory intention totally to exclude the operation of an estoppel in relation to the application of the section or to exclude it in present circumstances. The section does not exclude an approach such as that followed by Browne-Wilkinson V-C in the *TCB Ltd* case. For the reasons I have given, the delivery of the document in my judgment involved a clear representation that it had been signed by the third and fourth defendants *in the presence of the witness* and had accordingly been validly executed by them as a deed. The defendant signatories well knew that it had not been signed by them in the presence of the witness, but they must be taken also to have known that the claimant would assume that it had been so signed and that the statutory requirements had accordingly been complied with so as to render it a valid deed. They intended it to be relied on as such and it was relied on. In laying down a requirement by way of attestation in s 1 of the 1989 Act, Parliament was not in my judgment excluding the possibility that an estoppel could be raised to prevent the signatory relying upon the need for the formalities required by the section. In my judgment, the judge was correct in permitting the estoppel to be raised in this case and in his conclusion that the claimant could bring an action upon the document as a deed.

[34] I would dismiss this appeal.

TUCKEY LJ.

[35] I agree.

SIR CHRISTOPHER SLADE.

[36] I also agree.

Appeal dismissed.

Gillian Crew   Barrister.

Re Al-Fawwaz

a

QUEEN'S BENCH DIVISION, DIVISIONAL COURT

BUXTON LJ AND ELIAS J

b   25, 26, 27 OCTOBER, 30 NOVEMBER 2000

Extradition – Fugitive offender – Relevant offence – Extra-territorial offence – Fugitive offender accused of conspiring with others to murder United States citizens – Whether alleged offence having to be committed within United States territory – Extradition Act 1989, Sch 1 – United States of America (Extradition) Order 1976.

c

Extradition – Committal – Evidence – Sufficiency – United States government relying on evidence of anonymous witness in extradition proceedings – Magistrate admitting evidence even though not satisfied that witness's creditworthiness had been investigated and disclosed – Whether evidence of anonymous witness inadmissible –

d Whether use of anonymous witness infringing applicant's right to take proceedings to question lawfulness of detention – Human Rights Act 1998, Sch 1, Pt I, art 5(4).

The applicant, F, was accused in proceedings before a United States district court of conspiring with others to murder American citizens in the United States and

e elsewhere. The United States government claimed that F was the head of, or strongly involved in, ARC, a body which was alleged to be the London organisation of the conspiracy and a front for the terrorist organisation behind that conspiracy. It was further alleged that F, who had never himself visited the United States, had set up a secure telephone line and purchased a satellite phone system in that country, and that the conspiracy had resulted in the bombing of

f the United States embassies in Kenya and Tanzania. The United States government sought F's extradition under Sch 1 to the Extradition Act 1989 and the United States of America (Extradition) Order 1976. At the committal hearing, the United States government relied on the evidence of an anonymous witness. Although the stipendiary magistrate was not satisfied that the witness'

g creditworthiness had been fully investigated and disclosed by the United States government, he admitted the evidence and concluded that there was a prima facie case against F. Accordingly, the magistrate committed him to await the decision of the Secretary of State. On F's subsequent application for habeas corpus, the question arose whether, as F contended, the relevant legislation

h required the crime in respect of which extradition was sought to have been committed within the territory of the United States, or whether, as the United States government contended, it was sufficient that the conduct alleged was governed by its extra-territorial jurisdiction and would in similar circumstances be governed by the extra-territorial jurisdiction of the United Kingdom. F further

j contended that the evidence of the anonymous witness was inadmissible as a matter of law since the magistrate had not been satisfied that the creditworthiness of the witness had been fully investigated and disclosed. Alternatively, he contended, inter alia, that the use of an anonymous witness had infringed his right to take proceedings to question the lawfulness of his detention under art 5(4)[a] of the European Convention for the Protection of Human Rights and Fundamental Freedoms 1950 (as set out in Sch 1 to the Human Rights Act 1998).

Held – (1) In cases governed by Sch 1 to the 1989 Act, the extradition crime had
to be committed within the territory of the requesting state so that it would, as
transposed, be committed within the territory of England and Wales. It was not
enough that the latter crime would be indictable under the extra-territorial
jurisdiction of the United Kingdom. Furthermore, the concept of jurisdiction in
art 1 of the treaty annexed to the 1976 order was subject to the same limitation.
It followed in the instant case that F was correct in arguing that jurisdiction had
to be established on a territorial basis. However, provided that a prima facie case
of conspiracy could be established, the acts alleged by the United States
government were sufficient to establish territorial jurisdiction (see p 158 *j* to p 159 *a*
and p 160 *f g*, below); *Schtraks v Government of Israel* [1962] 3 All ER 529 and *R v
Governor of Pentonville Prison, ex p Osman* [1989] 3 All ER 701 considered.

(2) A magistrate had a discretion to admit the evidence of an anonymous
witness, even though the requesting state had not satisfied him that the
creditworthiness of the witness had been fully investigated and disclosed. There
was no rule of law governing the admissibility of the evidence of an anonymous
witness. Like most or all 'rules of evidence', those relating to anonymous evidence
were simply rules of practice, guiding or controlling the discretion of the trial
judge in the fair conduct of the trial. Moreover, the position in domestic law was
unaffected in the instant case by art 5(4) of the convention. The protection given
by art 5(4) was that detainees should have the assurance of judicial supervision of
their detention. That was provided in the English extradition procedure by the
magistrate's supervision. Before such a procedure could be said not to meet the
requirements of art 5(4), it would have to be so defective as not to be
characterisable as judicial at all. The broad question was whether the detention
was lawful. Neither in domestic law nor in the convention jurisprudence did that
entail a full trial of the issues at that stage, bearing in mind that a full trial was to
follow. In the instant case, it could not be said that the way in which the
magistrate had dealt with the anonymity of the witness made the proceedings so
unfair as to render them invalid as a control over F's continued detention. It
followed that the magistrate had not erred either in domestic law or under the
convention in acting on the evidence of the anonymous witness. That evidence
was conclusive in establishing a prima facie case against F. Accordingly, the
application would be dismissed (see p 162 *g* to *j*, p 165 *c* to *h* and p 167 *c*, below);
R v Taylor (1994) Times, 17 August explained; *De Wilde, Ooms and Versyp v Belgium
(No 1)* (1971) 1 EHRR 373 considered.

Notes

For the right to liberty, see 8(2) *Halsbury's Laws* (4th edn reissue) para 127, and for
jurisdiction and committal in extradition proceedings, see 17(2) *Halsbury's Laws*
(4th edn reissue) paras 1198, 1213.

For the Extradition Act 1989, Sch 1, see 17 *Halsbury's Statutes* (4th edn)
(1999 reissue) 732.

For the Human Rights Act 1998, Sch 1, Pt I, art 5, see 7 *Halsbury's Statutes*
(4th edn) (1999 reissue) 522.

---

a   Article 5(4) provides: 'Everyone who is deprived of his liberty by arrest or detention shall be entitled
to take proceedings by which the lawfulness of his detention shall be decided speedily by a court
and his release ordered if the detention is not lawful.'

Cases referred to in judgments

a
Associated Provincial Picture Houses Ltd v Wednesbury Corp [1947] 2 All ER 680, [1948] 1 KB 223, CA.

De Wilde, Ooms and Versyp v Belgium (No 1) (1971) 1 EHRR 373, ECt HR.

DPP v Doot [1973] 1 All ER 940, [1973] AC 807, [1973] 2 WLR 532, HL.

Gross, Re [1998] 3 All ER 624, [1999] QB 538, [1998] 3 WLR 1420, DC.

b
Kirkwood v UK (1984) 37 DR 158, E Com HR.

Lamy v Belgium (1989) 11 EHRR 529, ECt HR.

Liangsiriprasert v United States Government [1990] 2 All ER 866, [1991] 1 AC 225, [1990] 3 WLR 606, PC.

R v Bow Street Metropolitan Stipendiary Magistrate, ex p Pinochet Ugarte (No 3) [1999] 2 All ER 97, [2000] 1 AC 147, [1999] 2 WLR 827, HL.

c
R v Governor of HM Prison, Brixton, ex p Minervini [1958] 3 All ER 318, [1959] 1 QB 155, [1958] 3 WLR 559, DC.

R v Governor of Pentonville Prison, ex p Osman [1989] 3 All ER 701, [1990] 1 WLR 277, DC.

R v Naini [1999] 2 Cr App Rep 398, CA.

d
R v Taylor (1994) Times, 17 August, CA.

R v Watford Magistrates' Court, ex p Lenman [1993] Crim LR 388, DC.

Rees v Secretary of State for the Home Dept [1986] 2 All ER 321, [1986] AC 937, [1986] 2 WLR 1024, HL.

Sanchez-Reisse v Switzerland (1986) 9 EHRR 71, ECt HR.

e
Schtraks v Government of Israel [1962] 3 All ER 529, [1964] AC 556, [1962] 3 WLR 1013, HL; *affg* [1962] 2 All ER 176, [1963] 1 QB 55, [1962] 2 WLR 976, DC.

Cases also cited or referred to in skeleton arguments

Alves v DPP [1992] 4 All ER 787, [1993] AC 284, [1992] 3 WLR 844, HL.

Government of Denmark v Nielsen [1984] 2 All ER 81, [1984] AC 406, [1984] 2 WLR 737, HL.

f
Kossekechatkov v A-G for Trinidad [1932] AC 78, PC.

Kostovski v Netherlands (1989) 12 EHRR 434, ECt HR.

R v Governor of Pentonville Prison, ex p Chinoy [1992] 1 All ER 317, DC.

R v Governor of Pentonville Prison, ex p Fernandez [1971] 2 All ER 24, [1971] 1 WLR 459, DC; *affd* sub nom *Fernandez v Government of Singapore* [1971] 2 All ER 691, [1971] 1 WLR 987, HL.

g
R v Governor of Pentonville Prison, ex p Naghdi [1990] 1 All ER 257, [1990] 1 WLR 317, DC.

Royal Government of Greece v Brixton Prison Governor [1969] 3 All ER 1337, [1971] AC 250, [1969] 3 WLR 1107, HL.

h
Smith v Illinois (1968) 390 US 129, US SC.

Soering v UK (1989) 11 EHRR 439, ECt HR.

Tzu-Tsai Cheng v Governor of Pentonville Prison [1973] 2 All ER 204, [1973] AC 931, [1973] 2 WLR 746, HL.

United States Government v McCaffery [1984] 2 All ER 570, [1984] 1 WLR 867, HL.

j

Application for habeas corpus

By application dated 22 September 1999 Khalid Al-Fawwaz applied for a writ of habeas corpus ad subjiciendum directed to the governor of HM Prison, Brixton. Mr Al-Fawwaz had been committed on 8 September 1999 by Nicholas Evans, a stipendiary magistrate sitting at Bow Street Magistrates' Court, pending the decision of the Secretary of State for the Home Department on the request of the

government of the United States of America for his extradition to the United
States. The facts are set out in the judgment of the court.   *a*

Edward Fitzgerald QC and *Keir Starmer* (instructed by *Raja & Partners*) for
    Mr Al-Fawwaz.
James Lewis and *Saba Naqshbandi* (instructed by the *Treasury Solicitor*) for the
    United States government.   *b*

Cur adv vult

30 November 2000. The following judgment of the court was delivered.

BUXTON LJ.   *c*
    1. This is the judgment of the court, to which both members have made
substantial contributions.

The basic facts and the issues
    2. The applicant Mr Al-Fawwaz is accused in proceedings before the United   *d*
States District Court for the Southern District of New York of conspiring with
Usama bin Laden and others between 1 January 1993 and 27 September 1998 by
agreeing that: (a) citizens of the United States would be murdered in the United
States and elsewhere; (b) bombs would be planted and exploded at American
embassies and other American installations; (c) American officials would be killed   *e*
in the Middle East and Africa; (d) American soldiers deployed in the United
Nations peacekeeping missions would be murdered; (e) American diplomats and
other internationally protected persons would be murdered.
    3. The category referred to of Internationally Protected Persons (IPP) is
recognised by the United Kingdom Act of Parliament, the Internationally   *f*
Protected Persons Act 1978. That provides that any murder of an IPP outside the
United Kingdom is justiciable within the United Kingdom, even if the accused is
not a United Kingdom citizen.
    4. The United States government's case alleges as follows. Bin Laden was the
moving force in an Islamic terrorist organisation called Al-Qaida, devoted to
violent opposition to, in particular, the United States. The organisation issued   *g*
various *fatwahs* or rulings, which members were obliged to obey, including
rulings requiring the pursuit of *jihad* (holy war) against the United States. Since
1993 Al-Qaida had operated a cell in Kenya. In 1994 it created an organisation in
London called the Advice and Reform Committee (ARC), which purported to be
devoted to peaceful activities against breaches of human rights in Arab countries,   *h*
but which was in fact the London organisation of the conspiracy. Amongst the
alleged fruits of this conspiracy was the bombing on 7 August 1998 of the
embassies of the United States in Nairobi and Dar-es-Salaam. Many persons were
killed, including American diplomats who were IPPs.
    5. So far as Mr Al-Fawwaz is concerned, it is alleged against him that he was a   *j*
participant in the cell in Kenya. He lived in London from 1994, at a house at 94
Dewsbury Road. It is further alleged that he had clear links during that period
with the premises in London at which ARC was operated, at 1a Beethoven Street,
and with a man called Adel Barry who is another alleged conspirator, and that
Mr Al-Fawwaz was the head of or strongly involved in ARC. Claims of
responsibility for the bombings in Nairobi and Dar-es-Salaam, allegedly originating

a   from before the time of the bombings and thus demonstrating knowledge of what was planned, were said to be traceable or attributable to him.

6. Mr Al-Fawwaz was arrested and is currently detained in England. The United States seeks his extradition. An order to proceed was issued on 9 December 1998 in terms that Mr Al-Fawwaz—

b   'is accused of offences which, had they occurred in the United Kingdom, would have constituted the offence of conspiracy to murder, within the jurisdiction of the United States of America.'

7. At a hearing in 1999 Mr Evans, Metropolitan Stipendary Magistrate, found that there was a prima facie case against Mr Al-Fawwaz, and committed him to await the decision of the Secretary of State. Mr Al-Fawwaz now moves an
c   application for habeas corpus before this court.

8. The application as it now stands gives rise to three issues: (i) Do the governing provisions of English law require the crime in respect of which extradition is sought to have been committed within the territory of the United States, or is it sufficient that conduct alleged is governed by the extra-territorial
d   jurisdiction of the United States and would in similar circumstances be governed by the extra-territorial jurisdiction of the United Kingdom? (ii) Did the magistrate err in law in admitting the evidence of two anonymous witnesses, 'CS/1' and 'CS/2'? (iii) Was the magistrate correct in finding that there was a prima facie case against Mr Al-Fawwaz?

e   *Jurisdiction: summary*

9. Extradition, affecting as it does the liberty of the subject, can only take place by statutory authority. The present statute, the Extradition Act 1989, contains two separate regimes. The first, 'Part III extradition', relates to extradition to countries in respect of which the procedures under Pt III of the 1989 Act are
f   available. The latter countries consist mainly of designated Commonwealth countries and countries that are signatory to the European Convention on Extradition 1957 (Paris, 13 December 1957; TS 97 (1991); Cmnd 1762). They do not include the United States. The second category, 'Schedule 1 cases', are referred to in s 1(3) of the 1989 Act:

g   'Where an Order in Council under section 2 of the Extradition Act 1870 is in force in relation to a foreign state, Schedule 1 to this Act (the provisions of which derive from that Act and certain associated enactments) shall have effect in relation to that state, but subject to the limitations, restrictions, conditions, exceptions and qualifications, if any, contained in the Order.'

h   10. The relevant Order in Council in respect of the United States is the United States of America (Extradition) Order 1976, SI 1976/2144. By para 1 of Sch 1 to the 1989 Act, 'fugitive criminals' are liable to be surrendered. By para 20 of that Schedule fugitive criminals are persons 'accused or convicted of an extradition crime committed within the jurisdiction of' the relevant foreign state. The
j   concept of an 'extradition crime' is to be construed according to the terms of the Order in Council as it had effect at the date of coming into force of the 1989 Act. By art III of the Schedule to the 1976 Order extradition was available for an offence of (as in the case of Mr Al-Fawwaz, conspiracy to murder) if it were one for which extradition might be granted under the laws of both parties; and by the 1870 Act extradition could take place of fugitive criminals who had committed crimes that, by s 26 of the 1870 Act, 'if committed in England or within English

jurisdiction' would be one of a specific list of crimes, including conspiracy to murder.

11. We would not pretend that these provisions are pellucidly clear in their meaning. However, their effect is that before an offence can be a relevantly extraditable offence in a Sch 1 case it must be recognised as extraditable by the relevant laws both of the requesting state (in this case, the United States) and of England. The law of England is applied on the hypothesised basis that the acts that took place in the requesting state, but no other acts, took place in England (see *R v Governor of Pentonville Prison, ex p Osman* [1989] 3 All ER 701 at 713, [1990] 1 WLR 277 at 290). Mr Lewis, counsel for the government of the United States, accepted for present purposes that that decision bound us; though he wished to reserve for another day the possibility that what is transposed to England is not merely the acts done in the requesting state, but all the acts wherever done that constituted the offence charged. And because of the provisions set out in para 10 above, that crime, with elements of it transposed to England, has to be one that, so transposed, would have been committed within the 'jurisdiction' of the English court. This latter was the crucial issue, because we were told that it was common ground that the offence was within the jurisdiction of the United States.

12. Mr Al-Fawwaz has never been in the United States, and it is disputed whether any of the acts in pursuit of the conspiracy have taken place there. We shall have to return to that factual matter. The immediate importance of the general facts of the case is that, by the combined terms of Sch 1 to the 1989 Act and the Order in Council, the question of the English court's 'jurisdiction' has to be determined according to the law as it stood immediately before the coming into force of the 1989 Act: that is, as provided by the law under the 1870 Act.

13. These considerations give rise to the issue posed in question (i) above. The two competing contentions were as follows. Mr Fitzgerald QC, for Mr Al-Fawwaz, contended that (save where extended by specific statutory provisions) the relevant jurisdiction was 'territorial': that is, that the transposed offence had to be committed within the territorial jurisdiction of England and Wales. Mr Lewis contended the only question was whether the offence would be indictable in England and Wales, even if on an extra-territorial basis. Mr Lewis further contended that, even if jurisdiction was to be judged on a territorial basis, this case fulfilled that requirement, since overt acts in furtherance of the alleged conspiracy had taken place in the United States. We deal with that contention at the end of this part of the judgment. First, we address a series of issues to which the principal question in the case gives rise.

Authority

14. It is surprising that, as we were told, what appears to be a fundamental and long-standing question is not concluded by authority. It seemed to us, however, that such authority as there was, and in particular two decisions of the House of Lords, pointed in the direction of territorial jurisdiction.

15. In *Rees v Secretary of State for the Home Dept* [1986] 2 All ER 321, [1986] AC 937 the issue was whether evidence from other than the requesting state was admissible in extradition proceedings under s 14 of the 1870 Act. The possibility appears to have been raised in argument that the construction of the words 'depositions ... taken in a foreign state' in s 14 might be illuminated by the reach of other provisions in the 1870 Act that spoke of foreign states, including the definition of 'fugitive criminal' in s 26 of the 1870 Act, which is continued in para 20 of Sch 1 to the 1989 Act. In that connection, Lord Bridge of Harwich

a   during argument raised in terms a question plainly highly relevant to that facing us:

> 'Does "jurisdiction of any foreign state" in the definition of "fugitive criminal" in section 26 of the Act of 1870 mean its territorial jurisdiction or its jurisdiction, if any, over the crime wherever committed?' (See [1986] AC 937 at 946.)

b

16. The question does not appear to have received a clear answer. However, in the leading speech, concurred in by the whole House, Lord Mackay of Clashfern returned to the subject:

c   > 'When the 1870 Act was passed it dealt only with crimes committed within the territorial jurisdiction of a state with whom an extradition arrangement had been made: see, for example, *Schtraks v Government of Israel* [1962] 3 All ER 529 at 532, [1964] AC 556 at 579 per Lord Reid. Although the Taking of Hostages Act 1982 has now enlarged that jurisdiction, it has done so, in s 3(4), by deeming an offence committed under the 1982 Act which is also an offence against the law of any state in the case of which the 1870 Act is
d   > applied by an Order in Council to be an offence committed within the jurisdiction of that state. In any event when the 1870 Act was passed it was dealing only with crimes committed within the territorial jurisdiction of the states that are parties to an extradition agreement.' (See [1986] 2 All ER 321 at 327, [1986] AC 937 at 955.)

e   17. Lord Mackay did not then use these observations directly to decide the issue in the case, and they cannot therefore be said to form part of the House's ratio. They were, however, considered observations on an issue that had been squarely raised before the House, and as such demand, at the very least, serious attention.

f   18. Some assistance can also be gained from the further House of Lords case referred to by Lord Mackay, *Schtraks v Government of Israel* [1962] 3 All ER 529, [1964] AC 556. The accused contended that he could not be extradited to Israel for offences committed in Jerusalem, over which Israel had de facto control but not sovereignty. That contention was rejected by the whole House, Lord Reid saying that—

g

> 'In my judgment neither the Extradition Act, 1870, nor the [Israel (Extradition) Order 1960] ... is concerned with sovereignty; they are concerned with territory in which territorial jurisdiction is exercised.' (See [1962] 3 All ER 529 at 532, [1964] AC 556 at 579.)

h   19. Mr Lewis said, rightly, that this observation was in strict terms obiter; and also that the House had approved a passage in the judgment of Lord Parker CJ in the Divisional Court which had taken a wider view of the concept of jurisdiction (see [1962] 2 All ER 176 at 181, [1963] 1 QB 55 at 75). It is true that in that passage Lord Parker CJ relied on his conclusion in *R v Governor of HM Prison, Brixton, ex p*
j   *Minervini* [1958] 3 All ER 318, [1959] 1 QB 155 to the effect that, in the Anglo-Norwegian Extradition Treaty, 'territory' meant 'jurisdiction' (and not vice versa). But that case concerned a murder on board a Norwegian ship, a situation that has always been regarded as a legitimate extension of the territorial jurisdiction of the state of the ship's flag. Had Lord Parker CJ indeed sought to apply the theory of jurisdiction urged by Mr Lewis, he would have expressed himself differently and in much wider terms.

20. That latter point is also relevant in relation to s 25 of the 1870 Act, which provides that:

> 'For the purposes of this Act, every colony, dependency, and constituent part of a foreign state, and every vessel of that state, shall (except where expressly mentioned as distinct in this Act) be deemed to be within the jurisdiction of and to be part of such foreign state.'

21. Mr Fitzgerald submits that unless the concept of jurisdiction were territorial, it would not be necessary to extend jurisdiction by extending what appeared to be the (notional) territorial extent of the state. We see some force in that argument; but it should be noted that the extending provision 'deems' *the vessel, etc*, to be within the jurisdiction of the state. That would seem to suggest that, first, these cases are not seen as true examples of the concept of jurisdiction, it would seem because the latter is territorial in nature; and second that events on the vessel, etc, are brought under the Act by that vessel, and not in terms the events that take place on it, being deemed to be within the state's 'jurisdiction'. That indicates that the latter concept when employed elsewhere in the 1870 Act (for instance, in the definition of fugitive criminal referred to in para 15 above) is indeed based on territoriality.

22. None of these authorities are conclusive, but in our view they demonstrate an underlying assumption that jurisdiction for the purposes of the 1870 Act was indeed territorial in nature.

Special cases

23. In a number of cases special rules have been introduced to give the courts of England and Wales jurisdiction over crimes of an international nature: usually, in implementation of an international treaty or convention. Reference was made in the speech of Lord Mackay in *Rees's* case [1986] 2 All ER 321, [1986] AC 937 to s 3(4) of the Taking of Hostages Act 1982. Our attention was also drawn, with particular relevance to the present case, to the 1978 Act. Section 1(3) of that Act makes it an offence under the domestic law of all parts of the United Kingdom for any person anywhere in the world to do one of a series of prohibited acts in relation to an IPP. Paragraph 15 of Sch 1 to the 1989 Act, under the general heading of 'Deemed extension of jurisdiction of foreign states', provides, in relation to that and a long series of other United Kingdom offences of a broadly international character, that such offence, if also an offence against the law of a Sch 1 state, 'shall be deemed to be an offence committed within the jurisdiction of that state'.

24. We understood Mr Fitzgerald to say that that provision was not relevant to our present problem. We do not agree. Just as Lord Mackay pointed out in *Rees'* case that the extra-territorial provisions of the 1982 Act had only been extended to the jurisdiction of foreign states by a deeming provision, so in this case also the acts are deemed to be, not are provided for the avoidance of doubt to be, committed within the 'jurisdiction' of that foreign state. That provision also seems to point in the direction of jurisdiction being regarded as a territorial concept.

Comparison with Pt III extradition

25. Section 2 of the 1989 Act extensively defines 'extradition crime' for the purposes of Pt III cases. That definition specifically includes reference to 'extra-territorial' offences under the laws of foreign states, provided that what is

a described as 'equivalent conduct' would constitute an extra-territorial offence against the law of the United Kingdom.

26. We were not specifically addressed on this provision, and the specific exclusion that it makes, at the beginning of s 2(1) of the 1989 Act, of extra-territorial crime from the regime under Sch 1. We mention it here, first because it is of some relevance to arguments to which we are about to come; and

b second because the perceived need to make specific provision in respect of extra-territoriality in the new and different regime under Pt III of the 1989 Act is a further pointer to the limited nature of 'jurisdiction' as it was understood under the 1870 Act.

The speech of Lord Hope of Craighead in R v Bow Street Metropolitan Stipendiary
c *Magistrate, ex p Pinochet Ugarte (No 3)*

27. The offence with which Mr Al-Fawwaz is charged is conspiracy to murder. The courts of England and Wales have jurisdiction to try a charge of conspiracy where the conspiracy was entered into abroad, if the conspiracy was to do something in England and Wales or that might be done there, even if no overt act

d pursuant to the conspiracy was done in England and Wales (see *R v Naini* [1999] 2 Cr App Rep 398). In *Ex p Pinochet Ugarte (No 3)* [1999] 2 All ER 97 at 142, [2000] 1 AC 147 at 236, Lord Hope accepted that that rule extended to conspiracies to commit offences that were offences under the law of England and Wales by reason of special provisions as to extra-territoriality: that is, where under the relevant substantive offence nothing was to or need occur in England and Wales,

e but our courts take jurisdiction none the less. Lord Hope then applied that principle to the (alleged) facts of *Ex p Pinochet Ugarte (No 3)*:

'Accordingly the courts of this country could try Senator Pinochet for acts of torture in Chile and elsewhere ... because they are extra-territorial offences under s 134 of the [Criminal Justice Act 1988]. They could also try him here for
f conspiring in Chile or elsewhere ... to commit torture, wherever the torture was to be committed, because torture ... is an extra-territorial offence and the courts in England have jurisdiction over such a conspiracy at common law.' (See [1999] 2 All ER 97 at 142, [2000] 1 AC 147 at 236.)

g 28. In our case, the English courts would have jurisdiction over some or all of the acts in relation to which Mr Al-Fawwaz was alleged to have conspired, had those acts actually taken place, by reason of a different extra-territorial provision, s 1(3) of the 1978 Act. In relation to a conspiracy to commit those acts it was therefore argued that, following the same approach as in *Ex p Pinochet Ugarte (No 3)*, the English court would have jurisdiction over the conspiracy alleged to murder

h IPPs, even though no part of that conspiracy had occurred or was intended to occur in England. This argument, however, begs the question of the extradition regime that was in issue in *Ex p Pinochet Ugarte (No 3)*. Lord Hope's exposition of the position in English law, and his emphasis on the date at which torture became an extra-territorial crime, was relevant only because, Spain being a 'Part III'

j country, there had to be applied the definition of 'extradition crime' in s 2 of the 1989 Act (see [1999] 2 All ER 97 at 135–136, [2000] 1 AC 147 at 229–230 per Lord Hope, and the very clear summary in para (1) of the headnote ([2000] 1 AC 147 at 148). But, as we have seen, Sch 1 cases are specifically excluded from the s 2 definition, and in particular from its express reference to extra-territorial offences. *Ex p Pinochet Ugarte (No 3)* therefore in our view takes the present inquiry no further.

The advice of the Privy Council in Liangsiriprasert v United States Government

29. Lord Hope in *Ex p Pinochet Ugarte (No 3)* adopted the view of the law of
extra-territorial conspiracy that was taken in *Liangsiriprasert v United States
Government* [1990] 2 All ER 866, [1991] 1 AC 225. Mr Lewis said that the latter was
his best, indeed a conclusive, case. If the applicant in the present case were right,
then *Liangsiriprasert's* case was wrongly decided. It was sought to extradite L
from Hong Kong to the United States on a charge of conspiring in Thailand to
import drugs into the United States. No overt acts had been done in the United
States, and thus in the offence transposed to Hong Kong it was to be assumed that
no overt acts were done in Hong Kong. The Privy Council applied the then
English law, assumed to be governed by the 1870 Act. The only question debated
in this part of the case was whether the transposed conspiracy was justiciable in
Hong Kong. The Privy Council, in the advice delivered by Lord Griffiths, held
that—

> 'a conspiracy entered into in Thailand with the intention of committing the
> criminal offence in Hong Kong is justiciable in Hong Kong even if no overt
> act pursuant to the conspiracy has yet occurred in Hong Kong. This then is
> a sufficient reason to justify the magistrate's order [to commit the applicant
> to await extradition].' (See [1990] 2 All ER 866 at 878, [1991] 1 AC 225 at 251.)

30. This, Mr Lewis argues, makes it clear that the concept of 'jurisdiction' in
s 26 of the 1870 Act, and by the same token in para 20 of Sch 1 to the 1989 Act,
cannot mean 'territory'. If it had that meaning, the Privy Council could not have
decided the matter as it did. That would be a very powerful argument, albeit
raising questions as to its relationship to *Rees's* case [1986] 2 All ER 321, [1986] AC
937, had the point been in issue in *Liangsiriprasert's* case. It is, however, clear that
it was not in issue. Leading counsel agreed that in relation to the extradition issue
the only question was whether the accused's conduct would constitute a crime
under the law of Hong Kong (see [1991] 1 AC 225 at 229, 231 per Mr Martin
Thomas QC, and Mr Alun Jones QC respectively). The Board adopted this
agreement, saying:

> 'It is common ground that [the alleged] crimes are all extradition crimes
> and that the task of the magistrate was to apply Hong Kong law and to
> consider whether the evidence disclosed a prima facie case against the
> appellant on the assumption that the drugs were to be imported into Hong
> Kong rather than into the United States: see s 10 of the Extradition Act 1870
> and *Government of Denmark v Nielsen* [1984] 2 All ER 81, [1984] AC 406.'
> (See [1990] 2 All ER 866 at 871, [1991] 1 AC 225 at 241.)

31. It is plain from this statement of its task that the Board simply assumed,
rather than decided, the issue of jurisdiction. The advice cannot, therefore, have
the import for which Mr Lewis contends. Nor is the position improved by the
reliance placed on *Liangsiriprasert's* case by Lord Hope in *Ex p Pinochet Ugarte
(No 3)* since, as we have seen, that was a Pt III case, to which the approach of the
Privy Council in *Liangsiriprasert's* case was entirely appropriate.

Conclusion as to the jurisdiction of the English court

32. We conclude that in cases governed by Sch 1 to the 1989 Act the
extradition crime has to be committed within the territory of the requesting state
so that it would, as transposed, be committed within the territory of England and

a Wales. It is not enough that the latter crime would, as in Pt III cases as recognised in *Ex p Pinochet Ugarte (No 3)*, be indictable under the extra-territorial jurisdiction of the United Kingdom. We also think that the concept of jurisdiction in art 1 of the treaty annexed to the 1976 Order is subject to the same limitation. Whether this is a sensible rule in a world of major international crime and of the regular passage of persons involved in such crime between different jurisdictions is no *b* doubt not for us to say.

Did overt acts take place in the territory of the United States?

33. As we have seen, Mr Lewis argued that even if the basis of the English court's jurisdiction was limited to territoriality, none the less there was a prima facie case that overt acts relevant to the conspiracy had occurred in the United *c* States. This argument involves, first, looking at the criteria for determining what events are relevant to the territorial commission of the crime of conspiracy; and second, at whether such events are manifested in this case.

34. First, however, we dispose of a separate argument advanced by Mr Lewis which we do not accept. He said that since by para 15 of Sch 1 to the 1989 Act, *d* set out in para 23 above, offences under the 1978 Act were 'deemed' to be offences committed within the jurisdiction of the requesting state, so it was to be assumed, without further argument, that overt acts constituting those offences had taken place within the United States. That was an ingenious attempt to circumvent the territoriality rule, but it plainly fails. Paragraph 15 is indeed what it says it is, a deeming provision. That locution is the very reverse of a provision establishing *e* as a matter of fact that anything actually did occur in the requesting state.

35. We therefore turn to the two live issues under this part of the case.

Overt acts in conspiracy

36. We assume that this question is to be determined according to English *f* domestic law, since the issue as to what occurred in the United States is relevant to the transposition of the offence to this jurisdiction. That law provides that, although conspiracy is complete as a crime as soon as the forbidden agreement is made, the crime continues to be committed so long as there are two or more parties to the agreement intending to carry out the design. And it is continued in a particular jurisdiction if acts in pursuit of the conspiracy are carried out in that *g* jurisdiction. That was decided by the House of Lords in *DPP v Doot* [1973] 1 All ER 940, [1973] AC 807. It is necessary only to cite a short passage from the speech of Lord Pearson:

h '... a conspiracy to commit in England an offence against English law ought to be triable in England if it has been wholly or partly performed in England. In such a case the conspiracy has been carried on in England with the consent and authority of all the conspirators. It is not necessary that they should all be present in England. One of them, acting on his own behalf and as agent for the others, has been performing their agreement, with their consent and authority, in England. In such a case the conspiracy has been *j* committed by all of them in England.' (See [1973] 1 All ER 940 at 951, [1973] AC 807 at 827.)

37. The government of the United States submits that such acts did take place within the United States, and indeed were committed by Mr Al-Fawwaz himself. We now examine that claim.

Overt acts in the United States

38. We are concerned with whether there is a prima facie case of there having *a* been such acts, and if so whether there is a prima facie case that they were conspiratorial in nature. Mr Fitzgerald contends that there is no prima facie case of conspiracy at all. We consider that contention in the next part of this judgment. If it were right, then of course the present issue does not arise. However, we assume for present purposes that the claim of conspiracy is made *b* out on a prima facie basis.

39. The acts relied on by the government of the United States are, first, the setting up and operating of a secure telephone line in the United States by Mr Al-Fawwaz through an organisation called MCI; the purchase by Mr Al-Fawwaz of a satellite phone system in the United States; and the issuing of *fatwahs* and *jihads* in pursuit of the conspiracy, allegedly prepared with the concurrence of Mr Al-Fawwaz, in *c* various countries, including the United States. Mr Al-Fawwaz says as to the last of these that he had no involvement in the *fatwahs* and *jihads*. As to the two first events, they are both said to have an innocent explanation. The secure communication link was intended for proper use by Saudi dissidents to communicate with ARC in London. Its routing through the United States was for security *d* reasons, to conceal that the calls were coming from Saudi Arabia. The satellite phone system was not in itself sinister; though the United States government contended that it was intended for use by bin Laden when he removed his operations to Afghanistan.

40. These are plainly matters for argument at the trial. We did not, however, accept Mr Fitzgerald's submission that since each alleged act taken alone could *e* not be shown to be conspiratorial in nature, therefore they could not be relied on to found jurisdiction. If there is a prima facie case of conspiracy in the terms alleged by the United States government, then the acts set out in para 39 were, on the basis argued by the United States government, done in pursuit of that conspiracy. That in our view is enough to establish territorial jurisdiction, in the *f* terms recognised by the House of Lords in *Doot's* case.

Conclusion on the issue of jurisdiction

41. We conclude that Mr Al-Fawwaz is correct to argue that in Sch 1 cases jurisdiction has to be established on a territorial basis. We further conclude, however, that provided a prima facie case of conspiracy can be established the *g* acts set out as alleged in para 39 above suffice to establish that territorial jurisdiction. We accordingly need to pass to issues (ii) and (iii), which involve reviewing the decision of the magistrate that a prima facie case has been established against Mr Al-Fawwaz.

h

Prima facie case: preliminary

42. The magistrate identified two questions. First, whether the evidence established a case to answer that there was an agreement between bin Laden and others to pursue the course of conduct alleged in the charge as set out in para 2 above. Second, whether the evidence established a case to answer that *j* Mr Al-Fawwaz was a party to that agreement. We did not understand the first issue to be seriously contested. The argument before the magistrate and before us concentrated on the second issue, the case against Mr Al-Fawwaz.

43. Mr Al-Fawwaz's argument that the requirements of a case to answer had not been met had two limbs. First, issue (ii) above, the magistrate had erred as a matter of law in admitting and acting upon the evidence of two anonymous

a witnesses, called in the case CS/1 and CS/2. Second, (issue (iii) above) if the evidence of the anonymous witnesses had been excluded the magistrate was not, and could not properly have been, satisfied on the basis of the remaining evidence that there was a case to answer against Mr Al-Fawwaz. To these arguments based upon English domestic law were added further and different arguments based on the European Convention for the Protection of Human Rights and Fundamental

b Freedoms (Rome, 4 November 1950; TS 71 (1953); Cmd 8969 (the convention)).

The role of the magistrate and of this court

44. It was confirmed by this court in *Re Gross* [1998] 3 All ER 624, [1999] QB 538 that despite recent amendments to para 7(1) of Sch 1 to the 1989 Act the task of the magistrate remains to determine whether sufficient evidence exists as

c would in a domestic case justify a committal for trial; he does not have to approach the matter as he would approach an actual trial in the magistrates' court. How he should discharge that task was explained by this court in *R v Governor of Pentonville Prison, ex p Osman* [1989] 3 All ER 701 at 721, [1990] 1 WLR at 299–300:

d   '... it was the magistrate's duty to consider the evidence as a whole, and to reject any evidence which he considered worthless ... He was neither entitled nor obliged ... to compare one witness with another. That would be for the jury at the trial. It follows that the magistrate was not concerned with the inconsistencies or contradictions in [a given witness's] evidence, unless they

e   were such as to justify rejecting or eliminating his evidence altogether ... As a working guide, we could not do better than adopt the language of the magistrate'

—his duty is to consider the evidence to see whether that evidence is such that upon it a reasonable jury properly directed could convict.

f 45. *Ex p Osman* also decided that the task of this court in reviewing the decision of the magistrate is best defined in *Wednesbury* terms (see *Associated Provincial Picture Houses Ltd v Wednesbury Corp* [1947] 2 All ER 680, [1948] 1 KB 223). As it was put in *Ex p Osman*:

g   '... the court was justified in interfering either because there was no evidence to support the committal or because no reasonable magistrate would commit on that evidence or because the magistrate must have been guilty of an error of law.' (See [1989] 3 All ER 701 at 722–723, [1990] 1 WLR 277 at 301.)

h *Anonymous witnesses: the evidence of CS/1*

46. Although two anonymous witnesses were relied on by the government of the United States, by far the most significant of them was CS/1, and the argument concentrated on his position. Mr Al-Fawwaz argues that in this case the magistrate has been guilty of an error of law, and not just of an error of judgment,

j since it was not open to him as a matter of law to admit the evidence of an anonymous witness.

47. CS/1 claims to have been directly involved in the conspiracy and to be in mortal fear by reason of his co-operation with the authorities. He needs anonymity at this stage to protect himself, though it is envisaged that he will give evidence revealing his identity at the trial in the United States. His evidence is of the first importance, because it directly involves Mr Al-Fawwaz in the conspiracy.

Mr Fitzgerald was careful not to concede that CS/1's evidence, if admitted, concluded the issue of whether there was a prima facie case, since he said that the *a* evidence was open to criticism on grounds of imprecision. In reality, however, it is impossible to conclude that a magistrate who acted on the evidence of CS/1 to commit Mr Al-Fawwaz, as the magistrate acted in this case, would be acting irrationally in *Ex p Osman* terms.

b

Anonymous witnesses: the English law

48. Mr Fitzgerald's argument was based strongly on a decision of the Court of Appeal (Criminal Division) as to the hearing of anonymous witnesses at trial, *R v Taylor* (1994) Times, 17 August. Having said that the matter was pre-eminently one for the trial judge's discretion, the court then set out various factors that were *c* relevant to the exercise of that discretion. One was that there must be real grounds for fear of the consequences if the identity of the witness was revealed, a factor that was effectively not in issue in our case. The court then continued to say, inter alia, that: (a) The evidence must be sufficiently relevant and important to make it unfair to make the Crown proceed without it. (b) The Crown must satisfy the court that the creditworthiness of the witness had been fully *d* investigated and disclosed. (c) The court must be satisfied that there would be no undue prejudice to the accused, although some prejudice was inevitable, even if it was only the qualification placed on the right to confront a witness as an accuser. (d) The court could balance the need for protection of the witness, including the extent of that protection, against unfairness or the appearance of *e* unfairness.

49. The same general approach, though without such specific formulation of the considerations to be taken into account, had previously been applied to committal proceedings by this court in *R v Watford Magistrates' Court, ex p Lenman* [1993] Crim LR 388 at 389, Beldam LJ being reported as saying:

f

'It was difficult to think of a decision more dependent on the exercise of discretion that the magistrate's decision in this case. The Court would not interfere with such a decision unless it was shown that it was so unreasonable that no magistrate properly considering it and properly directing himself could have reached that conclusion.'

g

50. Mr Fitzgerald argued that the *R v Taylor* criteria, and in particular item (b) in para 49 above, were mandatory. Unless anonymous evidence fulfilled the requirements set out in *R v Taylor* it was, as a matter of law, inadmissible. That submission was incorrect on two, related, grounds.

51. First, there are very few categories of evidence in English law in respect of *h* which there are rules of *law* relating to their admissibility as a *category* of evidence. After the abolition of the corroboration rules by s 32 of the Criminal Justice and Public Order Act 1994, it is difficult to think of any such case other than that of hearsay evidence. In truth, most or all of the 'rules of evidence' are in fact rules of practice, guiding or controlling the discretion of the trial judge in the fair *j* conduct of the trial. There is no reason to think that anonymous witnesses are treated by the law any differently from that. Second, that approach to anonymous witnesses is strongly underlined by the emphasis placed in both the authorities relied on upon the discretion of the trial judge. If the criteria set out in *R v Taylor* were indeed rules of law, the trial judge would not have a discretion whether to apply them or not. In particular, it would have been impossible for Beldam LJ to

a have expressed himself as set out in para 49 above if there were rules of law governing the admissibility of the evidence of an anonymous witness.

52. The apparently mandatory language used in one part of the judgment in *R v Taylor* must be read in that context. In respect of that issue, investigation of the creditworthiness of the witness as set out in para 48(b) above, and generally in respect of CS/1, the magistrate said this:

b ' ... the government seeks to satisfy this court that the creditworthiness of CS/1 has been fully investigated and disclosed. I am not so satisfied. Perhaps that is because no attempt was made in the preparation of this extradition request to focus on that one issue. The time when it is most important that the court is so satisfied on these issues is at the effective trial. No doubt more *c* information will be put before the trial judge in the event of extradition taking place. I know nothing to the detriment of CS/1's creditworthiness. What I do know is that the cumulative effect of all the circumstantial evidence is such that CS/1's evidence cannot be described as so inherently incredible that no jury properly directed could convict on it. The remaining evidence is exactly what one would expect to find if all that CS/1 says is true *d* ... The fact that one of the [*R v Taylor*] "principles" to be followed in this situation may not be satisfactorily met does not mean that this court is automatically bound to rule the evidence inadmissible. There are rare and exceptional circumstances in existence in this case. In all the circumstances, I am satisfied that there would be no undue prejudice to Mr Al-Fawwaz by *e* my admitting the evidence of CS/1 and CS/2.'

53. Mr Fitzgerald argued that the fact that the magistrate was not satisfied as to the fulfilment of the *R v Taylor* principle relating to the investigation of credibility meant that the evidence was necessarily inadmissible as a matter of law. For the reasons that we have already set out, that submission was *f* misconceived. Mr Fitzgerald, however, had further objections to the use of CS/1's evidence. They were, first, that even if the issue were one of the magistrate's discretion and judgment, his decision and the way in which he reached it was so unfair as to be irrational; and second that in any event the process, and in particular the use of an anonymous witness, had involved a breach of the guarantees of the Convention. We deal with those issues in turn.
g

Irrationality

54. Once we pass from the argument that the use of the evidence of CS/1 was the breach of a rule of law, we are governed by the rule expounded in *Ex p Osman* (see para 45 above). Mr Fitzgerald argued that the magistrate's decision was *h* unfair to the point of irrationality for two reasons: first, if the United States authorities had not fully investigated creditworthiness, there might be information that they had not found, or alternatively that they had found but withheld, that would undermine CS/1's credit; second, that if Mr Al-Fawwaz did not know who CS/1 was, he could not himself adduce, or alternatively look for, *j* matter that undermined CS/1's evidence.

55. There are substantial difficulties in both of these arguments. In extradition proceedings it would not avail Mr Al-Fawwaz simply to produce evidence that cast doubt on CS/1's creditworthiness. Investigation of that question is a matter for the trial, and for cross-examination there. The only material that could assist Mr Al-Fawwaz before the magistrate was material that showed that, because of previous contradictory statements or behaviour by Mr Al-Fawwaz, his evidence

was worthless, in the terms used in *Ex p Osman* (see para 44 above). It will be
noted that that is a much more demanding test than the test of whether there is a
material that casts doubt on the witness's credibility. We very much doubt
whether we should assume that the United States government is in possession of,
undisclosed, material so extreme as to make CS/1's evidence plainly worthless.
However, looking narrowly at matters as they stood before the magistrate, we
acknowledge that on the evidence before him there was a theoretical possibility b
that if more were known about CS/1 it might be established that his evidence was
indeed worthless. We cannot, however, agree that the magistrate acted irrationally
in not treating that consideration, in the absence of further evidence about CS/1
from the United States government, as compelling the exclusion of CS/1's
evidence.

56. The reasoning of the magistrate is set out in para 52 above. First, he was c
justified in placing weight on the fact that he was dealing with committal or
extradition proceedings, and not with a trial. That did not mean, as Mr Fitzgerald,
argued, that he held that the *R v Taylor* principles do not apply to extradition;
rather, the magistrate realistically acknowledged that the effect and application of
those principles, and the weight that he should give to different elements within d
them, varied according to the nature of the issues that the court had to decide.
Second, the magistrate did not take CS/1 at face value. It was relevant for the
magistrate to take into account evidence that he was given that CS/1's statement
was corroborated from other sources, and in particular that he had provided
evidence that proved to be accurate before it was publicly known or known from
other sources. Third, the magistrate was plainly entitled to test CS/1's evidence e
against the other evidence in the case. And, as we shall see when we come to
review the other evidence, he was plainly right to find that CS/1's account fitted
in to that other evidence.

57. The magistrate did properly consider CS/1's evidence in the context of an
extradition proceeding, and did not simply accept it as gospel. He adopted the f
right approach, and was not irrational in his conclusions.

The Convention on Human Rights and Fundamental Freedoms
58. It was, however, further argued that, whatever might be the position in
English domestic law, the extradition process was now governed by the rules of
the Convention. It was a breach of the Convention to have committed g
Mr Al-Fawwaz, that is, to have refused him his liberty, on the basis of the process
in this case, and in particular when CS/1 remained anonymous.

59. This complaint was originally formulated in terms of a breach of art 6 of
the Convention. Mr Fitzgerald, however, recognised that it was difficult to sustain
that argument in the face of the ruling by the Commission in *Kirkwood v UK* (1984) h
37 DR 158 to the effect that it would be 'wholly inappropriate to accord the full
panoply of rights contemplated in art 6 to an accused in committal proceedings'.
It will only be very rarely that a national court feels able to rule on the meaning
and reach of an article of the Convention in terms different from those adopted,
on the identical question, by one of the Convention organs, and Mr Fitzgerald did j
not ask us to do so in this case. Rather, he argued that the procedure offended
against art 5(4) of the Convention (right to take proceedings to question
lawfulness of detention): as indeed the Commission had envisaged as a possibility
in *Kirkwood*'s case.

60. It is therefore the Commission's view that art 5(4) does potentially apply,
but that the process is not subject to the full requirements of art 6. Mr Fitzgerald

submitted that when a court was, in our case, reviewing the legality of a
detention under art 5(4), the basic principle of fairness still applied. We will be
forgiven for commenting that it does not require recourse to the Convention to
establish that proposition. The difficulty lies in deciding the content of the duty
in any given case. The only authority that we were shown was *Lamy v Belgium*
(1989) 11 EHRR 529, a bail case far removed from our present facts, where there
had been serious failure in permitting the detainee to know even the nature of the
case that was put against him; and, as the argument developed, we increasingly
formed the view that Mr Fitzgerald, having disclaimed recourse to the full
panoply of rights under art 6, was none the less seeking to reintroduce those
rights under the rubric of art 5(4). That would be plainly contrary to the guidance
given by the Commission in *Kirkwood*'s case.

61. The correct position in our view is as follows. The protection given by art
5(4) is that detainees should have the assurance of judicial supervision of their
detention (see e g *De Wilde, Ooms and Versyp v Belgium (No 1)* (1971) 1 EHRR 373
at 407 (para 76)). That is certainly provided in English extradition procedure by
the supervision by the magistrate. We incline to think that, before such a
procedure could be said not to meet the requirements of art 5(4), it would have
to be so defective as not to be characterisable as 'judicial' at all. But we need not
go so far. The broad question is whether the detention is lawful. Neither in
domestic law nor in the jurisprudence of the Convention does that entail a full
trial of the issues at that stage: bearing in mind that a full trial is to follow. The
question is rather whether the anonymity of CS/1, and the way in which the
magistrate dealt with that anonymity, made the proceedings so unfair as to
render them invalid as a control over Mr Al-Fawwaz's continued detention. For
the reasons that we have already set out at length in analysing the magistrate's
ruling, we cannot so find.

62. We are fortified in that conclusion by reference to cases on detention in
connection with deportation, where the Strasbourg court has accepted the
lawfulness of modified procedures to review detention under art 5(1)(f), which
deals indifferently with detention pending deportation and detention pending
extradition (see for instance *Sanchez-Reisse v Switzerland* (1986) 9 EHRR 71 at 83
(para 51)). This particular line of authority was not ventilated before us, and we
therefore do not act on it. We are, however, bound to remark that it is in line
with the conclusion that we had already reached on other grounds.

Conclusion on the decision of the magistrate

63. We conclude that the magistrate did not err either in domestic law or
under the law of the Convention in acting on the evidence of CS/1. That
evidence is conclusive in establishing a prima facie case against Mr Al-Fawwaz.

64. If, however, we are wrong about that, we should go on to review the
contention of the United States government that there is a prima facie case
against Mr Al-Fawwaz even without relying on CS/1.

The other evidence

65. It is not entirely clear how the magistrate viewed the force of the other
evidence. He of course did not need to enter upon that question in order to reach
his decision. In our view, however, irrespective of whether the matter is
addressed in the magistrate's ruling, it is open to this court to conclude on the
basis of the other evidence that the magistrate's actual decision that there was a

prima facie case was not irrational in the *Wednesbury* sense, even if he had been wrong to take the evidence of CS/1 into account.

66. Detailed submissions were made by both parties. In assessing those submissions we have reminded ourselves of two things. First, an atmosphere of suspicion must not be mistaken for proof. Second, however, in a case such as the present a prima facie case may be demonstrated from a series of pieces of evidence, no one of which, taken in isolation, might be conclusive in that regard. The approach of Mr Al-Fawwaz tended to be to take each piece of evidence separately, and say that it was inconclusive. That is not the right approach; but for purposes of exposition only it will be convenient to review in series each of the main pieces of evidence relied on by the prosecution.

67. (1) Documents were discovered in Kenya at premises associated with Al-Qaida and with a man called El Hage, indicted in relation to the bin Laden conspiracy, which included business documents relating to Mr Al-Fawwaz and a 'security report' which is alleged to have been prepared on Mr Al-Fawwaz's instructions, and to refer to activities by another cell of Al-Qaida in killing Americans in Somalia. Mobile phone bills in Mr Al-Fawwaz's name were also found. The defence contends in relation to all of these documents that they postdate Mr Al-Fawwaz's removal from Kenya.

68. (2) It appears to be accepted that Mr Al-Fawwaz purchased the satellite phone in the United States, and set up the secure telephone link through the United States. The innocent explanation given by the defence of these acts has been set out in paras 39 and 40 above. As we there said, these are issues for argument at the trial.

69. (3) In London, Mr Al-Fawwaz was the original signatory of the lease of the premises of ARC at Beethoven Street, and remained such until February 1998. Various documents were discovered in a search of Beethoven Street, of which the most important for present purposes are claims of responsibility for the embassy bombings on 7 August 1998, which the prosecution alleges were in all probability received there before the bombings took place, and then distributed by post by conspirators working from that address. There is no evidence directly demonstrating Mr Al-Fawwaz's performance of those acts, which took place after he had relinquished the lease. However, the prosecution case is that he remained closely involved with events at Beethoven Street, as evidenced by a volume of telephone calls between that address and his residence at Dewsbury Street.

70. (4) When Dewsbury Street was searched a booklet relating to the use of scrambler telephones for secure communications was found, as was, in a concealed place, a copy of one of the documents from Beethoven Street.

71. We have no hesitation in saying that this evidence, taken together, and in the context of the overall evidence about the cell in Kenya and about the nature of ARC, calls for an explanation by Mr Al-Fawwaz. Each item separately may be susceptible of an innocent explanation. The whole taken together may be equally susceptible. But in its present state the evidence points sufficiently strongly to Mr Al-Fawwaz's involvement in the conspiracy to amount to a prima facie case, which will have to be met at the trial.

72. We conclude, therefore, that even if the magistrate had refused to act on the evidence of CS/1 he would not have acted irrationally in finding a prima facie case to exist against Mr Al-Fawwaz.

a

Article 3 of the United States Supplementary Treaty

73. It was originally intended to be argued on Mr Al-Fawwaz's part that the requisition was discriminatory on grounds of race, and that no fair trial could be obtained by Mr Al-Fawwaz in the United States: thus engaging the provisions of the treaty referred to above. At the end of the second day of the hearing, but not before that, Mr Fitzgerald applied for that part of the proceedings to be

b adjourned, so that he could consider and reply to the evidence of the United States government. That evidence had been lately served, but that was because it was in reply to evidence on behalf of Mr Al-Fawwaz that itself had been served very late, in proceedings that had been in hand for some two years. We refused the application for the adjournment, and Mr Fitzgerald then withdrew that part of the habeas corpus application. We therefore say no more about it.

c

Conclusion

74. The application for habeas corpus is dismissed.

Application dismissed.

Dilys Tausz   Barrister.

Re Saifi

QUEEN'S BENCH DIVISION, DIVISIONAL COURT
ROSE LJ AND NEWMAN J
20–23 NOVEMBER, 21 DECEMBER 2000

*Extradition – Committal – Evidence – Evidence sufficient to justify committal –
Admissibility – Exclusion of evidence – Indian government seeking applicant's extradition
and relying on English-language deposition made in India by alleged accomplice –
Deposition purporting to be translation by Indian magistrate of evidence given on oath
in Hindi – Whether secondary evidence admissible in extradition proceedings –
Whether magistrate having to determine disputed issues of fact relating to making of
statement implicating applicant – Police and Criminal Evidence Act 1984, s 78 –
Extradition Act 1989, s 27(1).*

*Extradition – Discharge of fugitive – Circumstances rendering it unjust or oppressive to
return fugitive – Accusation against fugitive not made in good faith in interests of
justice – Whether 'accusation' referring to request for extradition or facts supporting
request – Extradition Act 1989, s 11(3)(c).*

The Indian government sought the extradition of the applicant for murder and
conspiracy to murder. At the hearing before the stipendiary magistrate, the
government relied on a deposition in English, implicating the applicant, which
purported to be a translation by an Indian magistrate of evidence given on oath
in the Hindi language by an alleged accomplice, AS. By virtue of s 27(1)[a] of the
Extradition Act 1989, a document, duly authenticated, which purported to set out
evidence given on oath in a designated Commonwealth country was admissible
as evidence of the matters stated in it. Although the document was signed by AS
and properly authenticated, he had subsequently given evidence on oath in India
retracting the statements implicating the applicant and alleging that they had
been extracted by police torture and intimidation and by the promise of bail. The
applicant challenged the admissibility of the deposition and also argued that it
should be excluded under s 78[b] of the Police and Criminal Evidence Act 1984.
The stipendiary magistrate declined to exclude the evidence, found that there
was sufficient evidence to establish a prima facie case against the applicant and
committed him to await the Secretary of State's decision as to his return. On a
subsequent application for habeas corpus, the applicant contended, inter alia,
(i) that the English-language deposition constituted secondary evidence, and that
s 27 of the 1989 Act did not permit such evidence to be admitted in extradition
proceedings; (ii) that the magistrate should have made various findings of fact on
disputed issues relating to AS's evidence and that, if had done so, the evidence
would have been excluded under s 78 of the 1984 Act; (iii) that in any event the
evidence before the stipendiary magistrate was insufficient to justify committal;
and (iv) that it would be unjust or oppressive to return the applicant because 'the
accusation against him was not made in good faith in the interests of justice'
within the meaning of s 11(3)(c) of the 1989 Act. Evidence was presented to the
Divisional Court, inter alia, that the police commissioner in India had asserted

---

a   Section 27, so far as material, is set out at p 172 *g* to *j*, below
b   Section 78, so far as material, is set out at p 187 *b*, below

a that there was evidence of the applicant's guilt at a time when no legally admissible evidence was available; that there had been a failure to disclose AS's retractions until part of the way through the committal proceedings; that AS could not write in any language; and that accordingly he could not have written a statement in Hindi purportedly stating his willingness to confess. The Indian government submitted that the word 'accusation' in s 11(3)(c) of the 1989 Act related to

b the state which made the request for extradition, not to those involved in the investigation or prosecution or the witnesses, and that there was no basis for concluding that the request for extradition was made for a collateral purpose or improper motive.

c **Held** – (1) On its true construction, s 27 of the 1989 Act did not permit secondary evidence to be admitted. Section 27(1) dealt with evidence contained in depositions or in affidavits and enabled a deposition or affidavit to be given in evidence, thus obviating the necessity to call the maker. To that extent the subsection created an exception to the rule that evidence was given orally in court. It did not, however, create any wider exception to the hearsay principle. Having regard

d to the nature of extradition proceedings, it was unlikely that the defendant would be present when a deposition was taken, nor, generally, would his advocate be there to question the witness, or challenge the accuracy of any translation. In order for the document to be admissible, the evidence it recorded had to be given on oath and the document authenticated. Furthermore, fairness required that

e the actual evidence of the witness should be available to the defendant, otherwise a case could proceed to trial without the defendant ever having an opportunity of seeing a record of the evidence of the witness and his ability to demonstrate inconsistencies could be significantly affected. In the instant case, the Indian government relied on AS's signature on the deposition, but that added nothing to the character of the deposition. AS could not have adopted the deposition as a

f record of his evidence, because he did not know what the English record set out. There was therefore no record of the evidence given by AS, and his deposition in the English language was inadmissible (see p 185 *b d j* and p 186 *g*, below).

(2) When considering whether to exclude evidence under s 78 of the 1984 Act in extradition proceedings, a magistrate was simply required to carry out an

g evaluation of the evidence tendered, both by the government and the accused, as to the circumstances in which the evidence was obtained and to decide, on that evidence, whether its admission would have such an adverse effect on the fairness of the proceedings that it should be excluded. There was no need for the magistrate to make a specific finding in relation to every issue raised. The

h absence from the section of words suggesting that facts were to be established or proved to any standard was deliberate. It left the matter open and untrammelled by rigid evidential considerations. In the instant case, the magistrate had been entitled to conclude that the circumstances did not outrage civilised values and that accordingly the evidence should not be excluded under s 78. However,

j his review of the evidence bearing on the issue of sufficiency was not comprehensive enough. He should have considered all the circumstances surrounding the making of AS's confession, its content and the ambit and character of the retractions. If he had done so, he would have been bound to conclude that no judge, properly directing himself, could convict on that evidence, because it was worthless (see p 182 *g* to p 183 *a*, p 188 *g* and p 189 *e f*, below); *Union of India v Narang* [1977] 2 All ER 348 and *Re Proulx* [2001] 1 All ER 57 considered.

(3) On the true construction of s 11(3) of the 1989 Act, the word 'accusation' did not refer to the request for extradition notwithstanding that the nexus between accusation and request might be obvious. A request for extradition was not in character an accusation. Section 11(3)(c) referred to 'good faith in the interests of justice' in relation to the accusation, not the request. Moreover, 'accusation' was broad enough to encompass the accusation of a witness or witnesses and the offence charged in consequence. The protection afforded by sub-s (3) would be rendered sterile if the issue of bad faith could be divorced from the underlying facts supporting the request. In the instant case, the accusation of murder and conspiracy made against the applicant had not been made in good faith and in the interests of justice. Moreover, it would be unfair and unjust to return the applicant, because of the appearance of misbehaviour by the police in pursuing their inquiries and the significant risk that the activities surrounding that misbehaviour had so tainted the evidence as to render a fair trial impossible. Accordingly, the application for habeas corpus would be allowed (see p 190 *d* to p 191 *j* and p 192 *b*, below).

Per curiam. The fact a deposition is recorded in a foreign language, but unaccompanied by a certified translation, may not necessarily lead to the deposition being inadmissible, although, generally speaking, certified translation is necessary (see p 186 *f g*, below).

Notes

For evidence from Commonwealth countries in extradition proceedings and for circumstances rendering it unjust or oppressive to return a person, see 17(2) *Halsbury's Laws* (4th edn reissue) paras 1119, 1183.

For the Police and Criminal Evidence Act 1984, s 78, see 17 *Halsbury's Statutes* (4th edn) (1999 reissue) 236.

For the Extradition Act 1989, ss 11, 27, see 17 *Halsbury's Statutes* (4th edn) (1999 reissue) 703, 721.

Cases referred to in judgment

Alves v DPP [1992] 4 All ER 787, sub nom *R v Governor of Pentonville Prison, ex p Alves* [1993] AC 284, [1992] 3 WLR 844, HL.
Ashley Riddle, Re (22 November 1993, unreported), DC.
Associated Provincial Picture Houses Ltd v Wednesbury Corp [1947] 2 All ER 68, [1948] 1 KB 223, CA.
Calis, Re (19 November 1993, unreported), DC.
Dokleja, Re, R v Stipendiary Magistrate, ex p Dokleja (31 January 1994, unreported), DC.
Fernandez v Government of Singapore [1971] 2 All ER 691, [1971] 1 WLR 987, HL.
Kakis v Government of the Republic of Cyprus [1978] 2 All ER 634, [1978] 1 WLR 779, HL.
Kruger v Northward Prison (Director), Government of Switzerland and A-G [1996] CILR 157, Cayman Is Grand Ct.
Lloyds Bank Ltd v Marcan [1973] 2 All ER 359, [1973] 1 WLR 339; *affd* [1973] 3 All ER 754, [1973] 1 WLR 1387, CA.
Osman, Re [1992] Crim LR 741, DC.
Propend Finance Pty Ltd v Sing (1997) 111 ILR 611, CA.
Proulx, Re, R v Bow Street Magistrates' Court, ex p Proulx [2001] 1 All ER 57, DC.
R v Christou [1992] 4 All ER 559, [1992] QB 979, [1992] 3 WLR 228, CA.
R v Cooke [1995] 1 Cr App R 318, CA.

a *R v Delaney* (1988) 88 Cr App R 338, CA.

R v Galbraith [1981] 2 All ER 1060, [1981] 1 WLR 1039, CA.

R v Governor of Brixton Prison, ex p Levin [1997] 3 All ER 289, [1997] AC 741, [1997] 3 WLR 117, HL.

R v Governor of Pentonville Prison, ex p Chinoy [1992] 1 All ER 317, DC.

R v Governor of Pentonville Prison, ex p Kirby [1979] 2 All ER 1094, [1979] 1 WLR 541, DC.

b *R v Governor of Pentonville Prison, ex p Osman* [1989] 3 All ER 701, [1990] 1 WLR 277, DC.

R v Hughes [1988] Crim LR 519, CA.

R v Keenan [1989] 3 All ER 598, [1990] 2 QB 54, [1989] 3 WLR 1193, CA.

R v Khan (Sultan) [1996] 3 All ER 289, [1997] AC 558, [1996] 3 WLR 162, HL.

R v O'Leary (1988) 87 Cr App R 387, CA.

c *R v Raynor* (2000) 165 JP 149, CA.

R v Shannon [2001] 1 WLR 51, CA.

Schmidt v Federal Republic of Germany [1994] 3 All ER 65, [1995] 1 AC 339, [1994] 3 WLR 228, HL.

Union of India v Narang [1977] 2 All ER 348, [1978] AC 247, [1977] 2 WLR 862, HL.

d

Cases also cited or referred to in skeleton arguments

Chatenay v Brazilian Submarine Telegraph Co Ltd [1891] 1 QB 79, [1886–90] All ER Rep 1135, CA.

Farinha (Antonio da Costa), Re [1992] Imm AR 174, DC.

R (on the application of Kashamu) v Governor of Brixton Prison (6 October 2000,
e unreported), DC.

R v Bow Street Metropolitan Stipindiary Magistrate, ex p Government of the United States of America, R v Governor of Brixton Prison, ex p Allison [1999] QB 847, [1998] 3 WLR 1156, DC; *rvsd* [1999] 4 All ER 1, [2000] 2 AC 216, HL.

R v Ewing [1983] 2 All ER 645, [1983] QB 1039, CA.

f *R v Governor of Brixton Prison, ex p Lennon* [1963] Crim LR 41, DC.

R v Governor of Brixton Prison, ex p Percival [1907] 1 KB 696, DC.

R v Governor of Brixton Prison, ex p Sadri [1962] 3 All ER 747, [1962] 1 WLR 1304, DC.

Schtraks v Government of Israel [1962] 3 All ER 529, [1964] AC 556, HL.

Tomasi v France (1992) 15 EHRR 1, [1992] EHRR 12850/87, ECt HR.

Trendtex Trading Corp Ltd v Central Bank of Nigeria [1977] 1 All ER 881, [1977]
g QB 529, CA.

Application for habeas corpus

By notice of motion dated 20 October 1999 the applicant, Nadeem Akhtar Saifi, applied for a writ of habeas corpus ad subjiciendum directed to the first respondent,
h the governor of HM Prison, Brixton following his committal to that prison by Christopher Pratt, a stipendiary magistrate sitting at Bow Street Magistrates' Court, pending the decision of the Secretary of State for the Home Department on the request for his extradition by the second respondent, the Union of India. The facts are set out in the judgment of the court.

j *Clive Nicholls QC*, *James Lewis* and *Clair Dobbin* (instructed by *Henri Brandman & Co*) for the applicant.

Paul Garlick QC, *David Perry* and *Adina Ezekiel* (instructed by the *Crown Prosecution Service*) for the respondents.

Cur adv vult

21 December 2000. The following judgment of the court was delivered.

a

ROSE LJ.

1. The applicant, an Indian Muslim who came to this country with his pregnant wife and child in July 1997, applies for habeas corpus. The second respondent, the Union of India, seeks his extradition for the murder of Gulsham Kumar on 12 August 1997 and conspiracy to murder.

b

2. By rulings on 25 February, 30 June and 21 September 1999 the Metropolitan Stipendiary Magistrate at Bow Street, Mr Christopher Pratt, declined to exclude the evidence relied on by the Union of India, found that there was sufficient evidence to establish a prima facie case against the applicant and ordered, under s 9(8) of the Extradition Act 1989, that he be committed to await the Secretary of State's decision as to his return.

c

3. The applicant challenges these decisions on five grounds. First, the evidence of Ali Shaikh, on which the prosecution rely, proffered to the Bow Street magistrate in English, was inadmissible in extradition proceedings because Ali Shaikh had given his evidence in India in Hindi. Secondly, Ali Shaikh's evidence should have been excluded under s 78 of the Police and Criminal Evidence Act 1984. Thirdly, the evidence was insufficient to justify committal and the magistrate's analysis of it was inadequate. Fourthly, it would be unjust or oppressive to return the applicant because, pursuant to s 11(3)(c) of the 1989 Act, 'the accusation against him is not made in good faith in the interests of justice'. Fifthly, the applicant might, if returned, 'be prejudiced at his trial or punished, detained or restricted in his personal liberty by reason of his ... religion' (s 6(1)(d) of that Act).

d

e

4. As to the first ground, Mr Clive Nicholls QC, for the applicant, submitted that there should have been primary evidence from Ali Shaikh before the Bow Street magistrate, that is a record in Hindi, together with an independent expert translation into English. Instead, although there may have been primary evidence before the Indian magistrate, all that was before the Bow Street magistrate was a statement in English which was the product of non-independent, unchallengeable translation from Hindi by the Indian magistrate or his clerk: this was inadmissible, secondary, hearsay evidence.

f

5. Section 27 of the 1989 Act provides:

> '(1) In any proceedings under this Act in relation to a person whose return has been requested by a designated Commonwealth country or a colony, including proceedings on an application for habeas corpus in respect of a person in custody under this Act—(a) a document, duly authenticated, which purports to set out evidence given on oath in a designated Commonwealth country or a colony shall be admissible as evidence of the matters stated in it ...
>
> (2) A document shall be deemed to be duly authenticated for the purposes of this section—(a) in the case of a document purporting to set out evidence given as mentioned in subsection 1(a) above, if the document purports to be certified by a judge or magistrate or officer in or of the country or colony in question to be the original document containing or recording that evidence or a true copy of such a document ...'

g

h

j

6. Mr Nicholls did not suggest that, in the present case, there is any want of authentication of the document. He submitted that the rationale of s 27 is to provide an exception to the hearsay rule, by avoiding the need for oral evidence to be given before the English magistrate by the maker of the statement relied on. It is for the Union of India to establish admissibility. And, in the present case, the

a Bow Street magistrate fell into error. In particular, having rightly concluded that the document setting out evidence given in India was authenticated in accordance with s 27(2) and admissible as a document, he failed to consider the implications of *R v Governor of Pentonville Prison, ex p Kirby* [1979] 2 All ER 1094, [1979] 1 WLR 541 where, giving the Divisional Court's judgment, Croom-Johnson J, referring to s 11(1)(a) of the Fugitive Offenders Act 1967 (which is in identical terms to s 27(1)(a)

b of the 1989 Act), said:

> 'This section is dealing with procedure and method but not admissibility … this is an enabling provision allowing documents with due authentication to be put before the magistrate … it does not mean that anything which is in that document, regardless of whether or not it complies with the ordinary
> c rules of evidence which would be applied in the committing court, shall be considered by the magistrate.' (See [1979] 2 All ER 1094 at 1099, [1979] 1 WLR 541 at 544.)

Mr Nicholls submitted, accordingly, that s 27 does not make otherwise inadmissible evidence admissible. The Bow Street magistrate should have concluded that, in
d order to be admissible in the English extradition proceedings, the Indian depositions had to comply with English rules of admissibility requiring the statement of a witness to be in his own language. By asking himself whether, if he had done what the Indian magistrate did, the evidence would be admissible in England, he asked the wrong question. He should have asked whether, sitting in Bow Street, the evidence was admissible before him. Had he done so, he would have
e concluded that it was not, because the English translation was not the statement of the witness. Mr Nicholls submitted that the practical importance of the witness' Hindi evidence being before the English magistrate is amply demonstrated in the present case by the crucially different translations of an alleged telephone conversation in Hindi on 9 August 1997 between the murdered man and a
f newspaper editor relating to threats made to the former: the purported English translation before the court includes a reference to the applicant, whereas the correct translation does not.

7. Mr Nicholls referred to *R v Raynor* (2000) 165 JP 149, where it was concluded that the translation placed before a magistrate of statements made to a police officer were not 'statements of the witness' within the meaning of s 5A of the
g Magistrates' Courts Act 1980 but, rather, the interpreter's translation of what had been said. Mr Nicholls also referred to *Kruger v Northward Prison (Director), Government of Switzerland and A-G* [1996] CILR 157 where Harre CJ held that there was no basis on which a prima facie case could be found when, on an extradition request by Switzerland to the Cayman Islands, statements in German were submitted to
h the Cayman court without any translation into English.

8. As to s 78 of the 1984 Act, Mr Nicholls submitted that, in the light of *R v Hughes* [1988] Crim LR 519, the correct approach for the magistrate was a two-stage process. First, determination of the circumstances, including the primary facts, and then a decision in the light of the primary facts as to whether
j admitting the evidence would have such an adverse effect on the fairness of the committal proceedings that it ought not to be admitted. In determining the primary facts, there is an evidential burden on the defendant and then a burden to the criminal standard on the prosecution ie the prosecution must rebut the facts raised by the defence beyond reasonable doubt. Accordingly, he submitted that there is no difference in this respect between ss 78 and 76 of the 1984 Act which expressly confer such a burden on the prosecution in relation to

confessions. Mr Nicholls referred to *R v Keenan* [1989] 3 All ER 598 at 604–605,
[1990] 2 QB 54 at 63–64 and a reference therein to *R v Delaney* (1988) 88 Cr App R *a*
338 and submitted that those judgments contemplated the prosecution having to
disprove allegations under s 78 to the criminal standard. This, in our judgment,
is an impossible contention. An examination of these decisions shows that the
passage relied on by Mr Nicholls relates to breaches of the Code of Practice in
relation to confessions and s 76.   *b*

9. The second stage, he submitted, involved the court forming an opinion,
without reference to the burden or standard of proof. In the present case, if the
police had acted in bad faith the evidence should have been excluded. He
accepted, in the light of Lord Hoffmann's speech in *R v Governor of Brixton Prison,
ex p Levin* [1997] 3 All ER 289 at 295, [1997] AC 741 at 748, that the proceedings *c*
here relevant for the purposes of s 78 are the extradition proceedings rather than
the trial of the accused and that the scope of the application of the section is more
limited than in relation to a trial. But, he submitted, evidence had been obtained
in the present case in a way which, in the words of Lord Hoffmann, 'outrages
civilised values'. As in extradition proceedings there is no opportunity to cross-
examine and accomplice evidence may be sufficient to establish a case to answer, *d*
a police officer in the requesting state can disproportionately influence the decision
to commit if he produces evidence obtained in bad faith. Therefore, the consequence
of admitting improperly obtained evidence is more profound at committal than
at trial. The court must have regard to its obligations under the Human Rights
Act 1998 when considering s 78 of the 1984 Act. Furthermore, breaches of
international and foreign law and rules designed for the protection of an accused *e*
or a witness in the country where evidence was gathered can be taken into
account (see *R v Governor of Pentonville Prison, ex p Chinoy* [1992] 1 All ER 317 at
332 per Nolan J). Regard should also have been paid to the Convention against
Torture and Other Cruel, Inhuman or Degrading Treatment or Punishment 1984
(10 December 1984; UN General Assembly Resolution 39/46, Doc A/39/51; Cmnd *f*
9593) (the Torture Convention). Accordingly, the magistrate should have asked
himself whether he was sure that the police did not coerce Ali Shaikh to give his
evidence: if the answer was 'No' the evidence of Ali Shaikh should have been
excluded.

10. Mr Nicholls submitted that the Bow Street magistrate failed to make any
finding of primary facts from which he could form an opinion. He was wrong to *g*
say that he did not have to determine every factual issue and that he need not
determine a number of issues which remained unanswered. He was wrong to
rule that the arguments on burden of proof had no application in relation to s 78
and that, in relation to committal proceedings, there was a lesser test than at trial
for determining the circumstances relevant to a s 78 application.   *h*

11. In support of his submission that the Bow Street magistrate's s 78 decision
was perverse, Mr Nicholls identified many facts in dispute and not in dispute. He
also relied on these facts in support of his submissions as to the sufficiency of the
evidence and under s 11(3) of the 1989 Act to which we will come later. It is
convenient at this stage to summarise these facts.   *j*

12. In outline, the applicant's case is that Ali Shaikh is an uncorroborated
accomplice, who made statements implicating the applicant in return for a pardon
for a capital offence, which subsequently he retracted on more than one occasion.
His statements were the result of physical and mental ill-treatment and coercion
arising during his unlawful detention between 25 and 31 August, and from
pressure on his family, as confirmed by sworn evidence from his wife and daughter

a on 26 September 1997. Mr Mokashi, an advocate compliant to the police, was foisted on him so that he made the confession which implicated the applicant.

13. The Bow Street magistrate should have made findings about a number of disputed matters. These included: the date and time of Ali Shaikh's arrest; whether his wife and children were also arrested with him; whether he was physically or mentally tortured; whether the stress which he was under on 18 and

b 20 September 1997 as observed by the magistrate at Ballard Pier was the consequence of police activity; whether his wife and daughter were required by the police on 21 September to change his lawyer from Sutrali to Mr Mokashi; whether the police engineered a false confession before Magistrate Palnitkar on or after 1 October; whether his statements of 27 and 28 November inculpating Javed Fawda were falsely contrived by the police; whether Insp Bagadi and/or Assistant Commissioner

c Rao fabricated evidence thereby undermining the integrity of the investigation; whether the name 'Nadeem' was properly added to the charge sheet under the guise of a purportedly accurate translation; and whether the evidence of Prison Officer Wankhede and Mr Mokashi, that Ali Shaikh wrote the Hindi text in the document ABB 10 appointing Mr Mokashi as his advocate and asking to give

d evidence for the prosecution, is false. Mr Nicholls submitted that, if the Bow Street magistrate had resolved any of these issues, as he ought to have, adversely to the prosecution, this should have led to the exclusion of Ali Shaikh's evidence under s 78 of the 1984 Act, a consequential insufficiency of evidence and a refusal to commit.

14. Furthermore, Mr Nicholls submitted that a number of undisputed facts

e were themselves sufficient to lead to exclusion of the evidence under s 78. These are: breaches of Indian law, in particular the Maharashtra Police Manual and rules in relation to the keeping of a diary concerning the arrest and detention of Ali Shaikh; the lack of any written notes or statements in relation to Ali Shaikh's alleged admissions prior to 1 October 1997; up to 3 October, and in particular during a

f bail application on 14 September, Ali Shaikh was still protesting his innocence; the Ballard Pier magistrate on 18 and 20 September recorded Ali Shaikh as saying that he was in danger if he did not give a statement; the incriminating statement was only given after Ali Shaikh's lawyer had been changed and his wife and daughter threatened; the offer and acceptance of a free pardon in relation to a capital offence in return for making the statement; the signs of fear and intimidation

g on 1 October before Magistrate Palnitkar; the fact that, despite being in judicial custody supposedly without police contact, Ali Shaikh was brought to court without a court order on 5 November; the introduction of Javed Fawda as a co-conspirator for the first time in Ali Shaikh's evidence on 27 November; internal inconsistencies in Ali Shaikh's account, in particular as to whether he was

h inside or outside the cabin in which the conspiratorial conversation allegedly took place; Ali Shaikh's subsequent retraction of his evidence and the issue of a writ petition, not only retracting the evidence but making allegations against the police of being threatened and tortured to give the evidence implicating the applicant and Javed Fawda; and the omission of any reference in the extradition process to

j the Ballard Pier hearings on 18 and 20 September.

15. Mr Nicholls also relied on the findings of Judge Aguiar that Javed Fawda was never involved in this murder and was deliberately killed by the police by a shot at close range. This decision has been appealed to the High Court and there is a further appeal pending to the Supreme Court.

16. Finally, in relation to s 78, Mr Nicholls complained that the Bow Street magistrate gave no reason for not heeding the Torture Convention.

17. As to sufficiency, it is common ground that the prosecution case against *a* the applicant depends on the evidence of Ali Shaikh. It is also common ground that his statements, taken at face value, provide a case to answer. For they describe in detail visits by the applicant to Dubai in May 1997, during the first of which he says there was a discussion involving the applicant and others to the effect that Gulsham Kumar was troubling the applicant in his business and was therefore to be killed. Thereafter two guns and a car were acquired and used in *b* the killing.

18. Mr Nicholls submitted, in reliance on *Alves v DPP* [1992] 4 All ER 787, sub nom *R v Governor of Pentonville Prison, ex p Alves* [1993] AC 284 that it was the Bow Street magistrate's duty to weigh the evidence before him, rejecting that which was inherently incredible or worthless. Lord Goff of Chieveley said:

c

'If the magistrate concludes, on the evidence before him, that the previous evidence is such that a jury properly directed could not properly convict upon it, then, on the principle stated in *R v Galbraith* ([1981] 2 All ER 1060, [1981] 1 WLR 1039), he should not commit. This was the approach approved by the Divisional Court in *R v Governor of Pentonville Prison, ex p Osman* [1989] 3 All ER 701 at 721, [1990] 1 WLR 277 at 299–300, where it was stated that *d* the magistrate should reject any evidence which he considers to be worthless.' (See [1992] 4 All ER 787 at 793, [1993] AC 284 at 292.)

In *Alves v DPP* the House of Lords held that the retraction by a witness in extradition proceedings of evidence previously given in the requesting state did *e* not, in itself, discredit that evidence and, unless it was worthless, the magistrate was entitled to act upon it in deciding whether there was sufficient evidence to justify an order for committal. But subsequent retraction of itself does not render previous evidence worthless, because it may be that the later retraction is not worthy of belief. Mr Nicholls distinguished the facts of the present case from those in *Alves v DPP* in a number of respects. In that case, the magistrate saw *f* the witness, who had a motive to help the accused, retracting his evidence. In the present case, the original evidence was motivated by promise of pardon for a capital offence; and it contained inconsistencies as to whether Ali Shaikh was inside or outside the room at the time of the crucial conversation, as to the date when he was arrested and in relation to the late introduction of the name Javed Fawda. Furthermore, Ali Shaikh's evidence against the applicant came *g* after he had protested his innocence until the failure of his 14 September bail application and there was sworn evidence from his family on 26 September tending to support his claim of police coercion.

19. In the evidence on oath given by Ali Shaikh in his writ petition and to the National Human Rights Commission from March 1998 onwards, he claims to *h* have been arrested on 25 not 31 August 1997, to have been tortured and intimidated by the police, to have been deceitfully induced to change his lawyer to another chosen by the police, to have been promised bail if he implicated the applicant and to have been tortured and intimidated to introduce the name Javed Fawda, which had not appeared earlier, into his final statements to the magistrate in late *j* November 1997. Mr Nicholls submitted that, if he had lied about any of these matters, his evidence was worthless. If, on the other hand, his retraction is not worthy of belief, so, equally, is his earlier evidence implicating the applicant. His later account is confirmed, in part, by the evidence of his wife and daughter on 26 September 1997 that they had been arrested with him and that, contrary to Mr Mokashi's evidence, they had not instructed Mr Mokashi to represent Ali Shaikh.

a   Furthermore, there was evidence from Mr Vanjara, the highly respected lawyer who later represented him on his writ petition, that Ali Shaikh could not read or write. Even if it was not necessary for the Bow Street magistrate to make specific findings for the purpose of the s 78 submission, it was necessary for him to do so when looking at sufficiency. In *Ex p Osman* [1989] 3 All ER 701 at 721, [1990] 1 WLR 277 at 299–300 in the passage approved in *Alves v DPP* Lloyd LJ said:

b
> 'In our judgment, it was the magistrate's duty to consider the evidence as a whole and to reject any evidence which he considered worthless. In that sense it was his duty to *weigh up* the evidence. But it was not his duty to *weigh* the evidence. He was neither entitled or obliged to determine the amount of weight to be attached to any evidence or to compare one witness with
c
> another. That would be for the jury at trial. It follows that the magistrate was not concerned with the inconsistencies or contradictions in Jaafar's evidence, unless they were such as to justify rejecting or eliminating his evidence altogether.' (Lloyd LJ's emphasis.)

Accordingly, Mr Nicholls submitted that the Bow Street magistrate's reasons in
d relation to the sufficiency of the evidence are inadequate. No reasonable jury properly directed on such evidence could convict upon it.

    20. As to s 11(3) of the 1989 Act, this provides, omitting immaterial words:

> '… the court shall order the applicant's discharge if it appears to the court in relation to the offence, or each of the offences, in respect of which the
e applicant's return is sought, that … (c) because the accusation against him is not made in good faith in the interests of justice, it would, having regard to all the circumstances, be unjust or oppressive to return him.'

It is common ground that this confers original jurisdiction on this court.

    21. Mr Nicholls again relied on the facts referred to in his submissions in
f relation to s 78. He submitted that, even if the Bow Street magistrate did not have to come to any conclusion in relation to those facts, this court must. He also relied on material subsequent to the magistrate's decision, namely the evidence bearing on the genuineness or otherwise of ABB 10 given in India in July and October 2000 by Ali Shaikh's wives and daughters, Prison Officer Wankhede and Mr Mokashi and the further affidavits from Ali Shaikh's relations on 2 November
g 2000. Mr Nicholls relied on a number of matters as demonstrating bad faith on the part of the police and the prosecution authorities in relation to the applicant. First, as appears from newspaper reports, on 31 August 1997 the Mumbai Police Commissioner and on 2 September the Mumbai Deputy Chief Minister asserted that there was evidence of the applicant's guilt, at a time when no legally
h admissible evidence was available. Secondly, in relation to extradition proceedings, neither the first request in November 1997 nor the second in January 1998 made any reference to the pressure and tension exhibited by Ali Shaikh and recorded by the magistrate on 18, 20 and 26 September. Nor were Ali Shaikh's retractions of his evidence in his petition to the National Human Rights Commission in
j March 1998 and his writ petition in April 1998 disclosed to the applicant until part way through the committal proceedings in the summer of 1999, although the prosecution were well aware of those matters from the spring of 1998. In consequence, there was a failure properly to present Ali Shaikh 'warts and all' to the Bow Street magistrate to enable a proper assessment of his credibility to be made. Thirdly, the original of ABB 10, the authority to Mr Mokashi to act and the expressed wish to give evidence for the prosecution, has never been produced

and the explanations for its non-production, proffered by the prosecution, conflict. In July 2000 Mr Nikkam, the prosecutor, claimed that Mr Mokashi had refused to hand it over; in October 2000 Mr Mokashi said he had never been asked for it by the police and he failed to produce it to the court. Ali Shaikh's family denied ever instructing Mr Mokashi to act for him. Fourthly, the literacy of Ali Shaikh has been challenged by the defence ever since a copy of ABB 10 was produced, but the prosecution have refused requests for an independent investigation of his literacy. Furthermore, ABB 10 was never mentioned by Mr Mokashi to the magistrate on 26 September 1997, in the pardon order on 27 November, in the request for extradition, or by Insp Bagadi in his affidavit in response to Ali Shaikh's writ petition in April 1998. Fifthly, there was evidence before the Bow Street magistrate from Mr Vanjara, that Ali Shaikh signed instructions to act in broken Urdu, did not read any of the documents which Mr Vanjara showed him and said that he could not write in any language. There is also evidence before this court from Ali Shaikh's educated daughter Shabnam that her father can write his signature in Urdu but cannot write in Hindi. In addition, there is expert evidence before us that the signature on ABB 10 in broken Urdu was not written by the educated writer of the Hindi text and was made on a blank sheet of paper before the text was written. Sixthly, there was a breach of the Maharashtra Prison Rules, in that no records were made, or if made kept, in the gate register or otherwise, of the visit to the prison of Mr Mokashi and his alleged interview there with Ali Shaikh, with Prison Officer Wankhede 10 to 15 feet away; it was also inappropriate for Prison Officer Wankhede to countersign ABB 10 on the basis that it had been voluntarily made. Seventhly, as to the date and circumstances of Ali Shaikh's arrest, during a bail application on 14 September 1997 it was claimed he had been illegally detained, on 20 September 1997 he broke down in the presence of the magistrate and said he was in danger that, if he did not give a statement, he might be 'sent somewhere very long' and he requested to be kept away from 'gangsters'. The magistrate recorded that he appeared to be under tremendous pressure. On 1, 3 and 4 October 1997 he said he had been arrested on 25 August 1997 and he did not change that date to 31 August until making amendments to his October statements on 5 November. There are also discrepancies in the remand sheet as to the time of Ali Shaikh's arrest. Finally, it was Assistant Commissioner Rao who applied for extradition.

22. Mr Nicholls submitted that if, on the balance of probabilities, it is established that Ali Shaikh is illiterate or that Prison Officer Wankhede and Mr Mokashi may be lying in relation to ABB 10 there has been a want of good faith requiring the applicant's discharge under s 11(3). He relied on observations of Woolf LJ in Re Osman [1992] Crim LR 741:

'"Good faith" has to be given a reasonably generous interpretation so that if the proceedings were brought for a collateral purpose or with an improper motive and not for the purposes of achieving the proper administration of justice they would not be regarded as complying with the statutory requirement. Likewise, accusations would not be made in good faith and in the interests of justice if the prosecution deliberately manipulates or misuses the process of the court to deprive the defendant of the protection to which he is entitled by law.'

In *Union of India v Narang* [1977] 2 All ER 348 at 379, [1978] AC 247 at 293–294 Lord Keith of Kinkel said it would be sufficient to establish the primary facts on *a* the balance of probabilities and for the court to form an opinion upon the facts established. Furthermore, Mr Nicholls submitted that it would be unjust or oppressive to return the applicant because of the circumstances in which he came to be charged in India and the conduct of the Indian authorities in the extradition process both in India and the United Kingdom. The word 'accusation' in s 11(3)(c) of the 1989 Act is apt to embrace not only the state which prosecutes but those

b involved in the investigation and the witnesses relied on: in *Re Calis* (19 November 1993, unreported) the court held that a complainant's corrupt motive in continuing to press a complaint demonstrated want of good faith in the accusation.

23. As to s 6 of the 1989 Act, omitting immaterial words, it provides as follows: '(1) A person shall not be returned ... if it appears to an appropriate authority ...

c (d) that he might, if returned, be prejudiced at his trial or punished, detained or restricted in his personal liberty by reason of his ... religion ...'

24. Mr Lewis, for the applicant, submitted that the voluminous material before this court, in particular the reports from Mr Martin Lau dated 17 April 1998, 19 May 2000, and 17 November 2000 (which, he said, should be preferred to the reports

d of Dr Chitnis for the respondents), demonstrate that, although in general the judiciary in Maharashtra is independent, the Mumbai Police are biased against Muslims. The words of s 6(1)(d) are not limited to the trial process but embrace the investigatory and prosecuting processes as well. He relied on the 1994 Amnesty International Report, the Indian People's Human Rights Commission Report into the December 1992 and January 1993 Bombay riots and the Shri Krishna

e Commission Report into the same riots which was, initially, repressed by the Maharashtra government. Those reports catalogue an appalling series of incidents in which Muslims were killed or injured and their property destroyed in circumstances demonstrating active participation, acquiescence, or conspicuous failure to intervene, by the Bombay police. Mr Lau, in his report of 17 April 1998

f expressed the view, in reliance upon the Human Rights Watch World Report 1997, that the situation in relation to Muslims had worsened in 1996. In February 1998 Mr Lau went to Bombay and, in the light of the interviews which he then had with a number of witnesses, concluded that the then ruling coalition of BJP and Shiv Sena created a situation where the authorities were demonstrably anti-Muslim. In consequence, the legal system was not able to protect the Muslim

g minority adequately or at all: the problem is not that the trial judge himself would be prejudiced against a Muslim but that the investigatory process is so tainted by anti-Muslim bias that a Muslim might not receive a fair trial. He also added that it was 'extremely unlikely that an accused persons and witnesses who make statements before a magistrate have not been tortured or otherwise intimidated

h by the police'. (It is to be noted that the BJP/Shiv Sena coalition came to an end in October 1999.) Mr Lewis invited us to find, on the basis of Mr Lau's report, that it is more likely than not that the applicant will be discriminated against by the Mumbai Police because he is a Muslim; the legal theory adumbrated by Dr Chitnis does not coincide with the reality in Mumbai as identified by Mr Lau,

j so that it is likely that discrimination will not be eradicated by the higher judiciary. In this respect, Mr Lewis took us to the judgment of the High Court, on appeal from Judge Aguiar, in relation to the alleged extra-judicial murder of Javed Fawda by the police. The High Court preferred eyewitness police accounts claiming that Javed Fawda was shot from a distance, in the teeth of expert forensic evidence that the fatal shot was delivered at close range within one or two feet. That decision is currently the subject of an appeal to the Supreme Court.

25. For the respondents, Mr Garlick QC did not seek to diminish the significance of the human rights complaints, but urged that they be put in context *a* with reference to the specific aspects of the applicant's case. He submitted that this is not an appropriate forum to determine the wide-ranging issues involved. He stressed that, since the murder, there has been a change of government in India and in Maharashtra.

26. With regard to the background, Mr Garlick stressed that, following his *b* arrest, Ali Shaikh was taken, in the presence of independent witnesses, to his flat where he retrieved a set of car keys. Thereafter he took the police to the firearms and car used in the killing, which at least confirmed *his* participation in these events. On 1 and 14 September 1997, when he appeared in court represented by his chosen lawyer Mr Sutrali, no complaint was made about his treatment while in custody. Also, on the latter occasion, he was permitted to telephone his wife *c* who was in hospital for an operation and the prosecution placed no obstacle in the way of him communicating with the outside world. On 18 September, when asked by the magistrate, he said in terms that he had no complaints against the police, expressed his willingness to make a confession, and was given 24 hours for reflection. There was no evidence of any injury to him at that time. On *d* 20 September, when he was clearly under pressure and asked to be kept away from gangsters, he made no complaint of mistreatment by the police. On 25 September, he wrote ABB 10 appointing Mr Mokashi as his lawyer and indicated he wished to confess. When he appeared in court on 26 September represented by Mr Mokashi and Mr Sutrali both said they jointly represented Ali Shaikh and there was no dispute between them, which is inconsistent with the *e* claim that he had been forced to change his advocate. No complaint was made about his treatment. He spoke to the magistrate in private in the absence of his lawyers. On 1, 3 and 4 October 1997, he appeared before a different magistrate, said that he had not been pressurised or ill-treated and provided a confession statement. On 5 November, he gave additional details of events leading to the *f* murder and he gave evidence on oath on 27 and 28 November, repeating his earlier evidence implicating the applicant in the murder. It is against this background, Mr Garlick submitted, that the retraction first made in March 1998 should be viewed. Further, the writ petition to set aside his confession was dismissed by the Mumbai High Court in April 1999—a matter to which the Bow Street magistrate attached importance in assessing Ali Shaikh's credibility. *g*

27. As to the translation challenge, Mr Garlick submitted that what s 27 of the 1989 Act requires is, first, a document, secondly that it be authenticated and thirdly that it purport to set out evidence given on oath. The section contains no requirement that the evidence be set out in the language of the witness. The document is a deposition made on oath by Ali Shaikh on 27 and 28 November *h* taken before Magistrate Palnitkar.

28. Mr Garlick submitted that s 27 distinguishes between documents and depositions. Proceedings in India are habitually conducted in more than one language and the magistrate was entitled to receive the evidence in the local language and to translate and record it in English. He submitted that the position *j* is no different from proceedings in Wales where a Welsh-speaking magistrate receives evidence in Welsh and records it in English without the assistance of an interpreter. Ali Shaikh's evidence was read over to him in Hindi. He admitted it was correct and the deposition was then signed by him as well as by the magistrate. Mr Garlick submitted that evidence of translation is only required

a where the document setting out the evidence on oath is in a language other than English, because an English court is not entitled to translate a foreign language. Accordingly, submitted Mr Garlick, the magistrate's ruling on 25 February 1999 was correct. He directed himself properly in accordance with *Ex p Kirby* [1979] 2 All ER 1094, [1979] 1 WLR 541. He was entitled to draw an analogy with old-style committal proceedings where the evidence of a non-English speaking

b witness would be translated by an interpreter into English and recorded by the court clerk in English, after which the deposition would be read back in English by the clerk and translated by the interpreter in order to obtain the witness' assent. Such a deposition would not refer to the existence of the interpreter. Accordingly, the Bow Street magistrate was entitled to conclude that there was 'little difference between a deposition prepared under the rules of the English

c courts and six depositions prepared in India'.

29. As to s 78 of the 1984 Act, Mr Garlick submitted that the Bow Street magistrate's function was to consider the circumstances and give a reasoned decision, but this did not involve an obligation to make findings of fact upon every issue: the state of the evidence might make this impossible. The magistrate

d correctly drew a distinction between the terms of ss 76 and 78. He dealt with the evidence of Ali Shaikh's wife and daughter and with the literacy issue. He was not in a position to make findings, because he had not seen the witnesses or heard any cross-examination on the voir dire or otherwise. He bore in mind the circumstances and reached a reasoned conclusion.

30. The burden of persuading the court to exclude evidence was on the

e defence (see *R v Cooke* [1995] 1 Cr App R 318 at 328 per Glidewell LJ). The Bow Street magistrate's decision could only be challenged on *Wednesbury* principles (*Associated Provincial Picture Houses Ltd v Wednesbury Corp* [1947] 2 All ER 68, [1948] 1 KB 223) (see *R v O'Leary* (1988) 87 Cr App R 387 at 391 and *R v Christou* [1992] 4 All ER 559 at 565, [1992] QB 979 at 989). Mr Garlick also referred to *R v*

f *Khan (Sultan)* [1996] 3 All ER 289, [1997] AC 558 in which Lord Nolan, having referred to an apparent breach of the law of a foreign country being a matter which may be relevant to the exercise of the s 78 power, said:

'This does not mean that the trial judge is obliged to decide whether or not there has been a breach of the convention or of the foreign law. That is not

g his function, and it would be inappropriate for him to do so ... But if the behaviour of the police in the particular case amounts to an apparent or probable breach of some relevant law or convention, common sense dictates that this is a consideration which may be taken into account for what it is worth. Its significance, however, will normally be determined not so much by its apparent unlawfulness or irregularity, as upon its effect, taken as a

h whole, upon the fairness or unfairness of the proceedings.' (See [1996] 3 All ER 289 at 301, [1997] AC 558 at 581–582.)

In *R v Shannon* [2001] 1 WLR 51 at 67–68 Potter LJ said, in relation to a s 78 application to exclude evidence on the ground of entrapment:

j '... the principal focus of the judge's attention must be upon the procedural fairness of the proceedings, the nature and reliability of the prosecution evidence and the fullness and fairness of the opportunity available to the defendant to deal with the evidence which the prosecution seeks to adduce.'

He said (at 68):

'... the ultimate question is not the broad one: is the bringing of proceedings
fair (in the sense of appropriate) in entrapment cases. It is whether the   *a*
fairness of the proceedings will be adversely affected by admitting the evidence
of the agent provocateur ... So, for instance, if there is good reason to
question the creditability of evidence given by an agent provocateur ... and
that question is not susceptible of being properly or fairly resolved in the
course of the proceedings from available, admissible and "untainted" evidence,   *b*
then the judge may readily conclude that such evidence should be excluded.
If, on the other hand, the unfairness complained of is no more than the
visceral reaction that it is in principle unfair ... for a person to be prosecuted
for a crime which he would not have committed without the incitement or
encouragement of others, then that is not itself sufficient, unless the behaviour
of police ... and/or the prosecuting authority has been such as to justify a   *c*
stay on grounds of abuse of process.'

31. Mr Garlick relied on the observations of Lord Hoffmann in *Ex p Levin*
[1997] 3 All ER 289 at 295, [1997] AC 741 at 748:

'... it must be borne in mind that when the section is being applied to   *d*
committal or extradition proceedings, the question is whether the admission
of the evidence would have such an adverse effect on the fairness of *those*
proceedings that the court ought not to admit it. This is not at all the same
thing as the question of whether the admission of the evidence at the trial
would have an adverse effect on the fairness of the trial. On the contrary, the   *e*
magistrates should ordinarily assume that the powers available to the judge
at the trial will ensure that the proceedings are fair. The question is,
therefore, whether the admission of the evidence would have an adverse
effect on the fairness of the decision to commit or extradite the accused for
trial, even if the trial is a fair one ... In extradition proceedings there is even
less scope for the exercise of the discretion because ... extradition procedure   *f*
is founded on concepts of comity and reciprocity. It would undermine the
effectiveness of international treaty obligations if the courts were to
superimpose discretions based on local notions of fairness upon the ordinary
rules of admissibility. I do not wish to exclude the possibility that the
discretion may be used in extradition proceedings founded upon evidence
which, though technically admissible, has been obtained in a way which   *g*
outrages civilised values. But such cases are also likely to be very rare.'

32. Mr Garlick submitted that the magistrate was correct in concluding that
there was no obligation on the prosecution to disprove matters raised by the
defence beyond reasonable doubt and that he correctly identified his role as being   *h*
to—

'carry out an evaluation of the evidence tendered by both the government
and the accused as to the circumstances in which the evidence was obtained
and ultimately to decide on that evidence whether its admission would have
such an adverse effect on the fairness of these proceedings that I should   *j*
exclude it.'

Mr Garlick submitted it would be entirely inappropriate, in the absence of the
principal witnesses, for the magistrate to make specific findings of fact on every
issue. The disputed facts were properly for determination at trial and not on the
extradition application.

a
33. Accordingly, submitted Mr Garlick, the magistrate did not err in his approach to s 78 of the 1984 Act. He did not misdirect himself and his decision was not perverse. Furthermore the magistrate specially referred to the Torture Convention which raised precisely the same factual issues as under s 78.

34. As to sufficiency, Mr Garlick submitted, in reliance on *Alves v DPP,* that retraction in itself did not discredit Ali Shaikh's evidence. Sufficiency was
b essentially a matter for the decision for the magistrate whose decision is only susceptible to challenge on *Wednesbury* grounds. The magistrate considered *Alves v DPP* and accepted that it was necessary to look at the evidence with great care. He commented that if the original evidence was the product of inducement by way of pardon it was curious 'that he would wish to retract his evidence, lose the offer of a free pardon and place himself once again in jeopardy of the severest
c penalty'. The magistrate considered the possibility that it might be the retraction rather than the original evidence which was false, as a result of Ali Shaikh's fear of gangsters. He referred to the remarkably detailed account which Ali Shaikh gave over a three-day period. He concluded, applying the *Galbraith* test (*R v Galbraith* [1981] 2 All ER 1060, [1981] 1 WLR 1039) set out in *Alves v DPP,* that a
d properly directed tribunal could find Ali Shaikh's evidence capable of belief. This approach, submitted Mr Garlick, cannot effectively be challenged.

35. As to s 11(3) of the 1989 Act, Mr Garlick submitted that there is no basis for concluding that the requisition for extradition was made for a collateral purpose or improper motive. It comes, he said, from the Union of India, not the police, the prosecutor or the state. He accepted this did not end the matter. But the
e burden is on the applicant to show that the accusation was not made in good faith and, because of this, it would be unjust to return him. He referred to the well-known observations of Lord Diplock in *Kakis v Government of the Republic of Cyprus* [1978] 2 All ER 634 at 638, [1978] 1 WLR 779 at 782–783, in the context of delay, he said:

f
'"Unjust" I regard as directed primarily at the risk of prejudice to the accused in the conduct of the trial itself, "oppressive" as directed to hardship to the accused resulting from changes in his circumstances that have occurred during the period to be taken into consideration; but there is room for overlapping, and between them they would cover all cases where to
g return him would not be fair.'

He pointed out that Judge Aguirar, who had concluded that Javed Fawda was executed by the police, is one of the judges at an appropriate level in Maharashtra to try the applicant if he is returned.

h
36. He submitted that the 'accusation' in the present case is made by the state of Maharashtra. He accepted that if the state were tainted this would taint the accusation. But he submitted that 'accusation' in s 11(3) refers to the state, not those involved in investigation or prosecution or the witnesses. He sought to distinguish *Re Calis* (19 November 1993, unreported) on the basis that in that case
j it was a complainant rather than a witness whose motive was tainted. In the present case, he pointed out, it was not until March 1998, after the request for extradition had been made, that the retraction occurred and serious allegations were made against the independent prosecutor. There is no suggestion that the judiciary is partial and every indication that they are vigorous in investigating impropriety, so there will be no injustice in the trial process: this is particularly so as the applicant is very well known and there has been much publicity in relation

to the case already, so the judiciary will be particularly alert to investigate matters thoroughly.

37. In relation to the evidence of impropriety, Mr Garlick submitted that this is far from conclusive. Ali Shaikh's statements have not been tested in cross-examination. On the literacy point, Prison Officer Wankhede and Mr Mokashi are both credible witnesses who have given evidence and been thoroughly cross-examined. Their account gainsays that of Ali Shaikh and the conflict should properly be resolved by an impartial, competent, vigilant judiciary in India. A trial in such circumstances will avoid any possibility of prejudice from the prior investigation and prosecution. In this respect, Mr Garlick made the separate submission that, even if the accusation were made in bad faith, it would not, as s 11 requires, cause injustice because of the Indian judiciary's rigorous examination of the matter. He referred to a judgment of Sedley J in *Re Ashley Riddle* (22 November 1993, unreported) where, in relation to s 11(3)(b), there is reference to the need for a link between delay and whether return would be unjust or oppressive.

38. Mr Garlick referred to *Schmidt v Federal Republic of Germany* [1994] 3 All ER 65, [1995] 1 AC 339 and the speech of Lord Jauncey of Tullichettle ([1994] 3 All ER 65 at 70, [1995] 1 AC 339 at 371) where he refers to the majority view in the House of Lords in *Narang*'s case that the powers of the court to discharge a person are restricted to situations falling within the three categories identified in s 11(3). Although the Secretary of State has a wider discretion, unfettered by the words of s 11(3), the Divisional Court, although its jurisdiction is wider than that of the magistrate, 'has no inherent common law supervisory power' ([1994] 3 All ER 65 at 77, [1995] 1 AC 339 at 379 per Lord Jauncey).

39. As to s 6(1)(d) of the 1989 Act, Mr Garlick submitted, by reference to the speech of Lord Diplock in *Fernandez v Government of Singapore* [1971] 2 All ER 691, [1971] 1 WLR 987 that the proper test is whether there is 'reasonable chance', 'substantial ground for thinking' or 'serious possibility' that the applicant will be detained or restricted by reason of his religion if returned. There is, he submitted, no basis on which it can be said that the applicant will be prejudiced at his trial in the light of Mr Lau's acceptance that the judiciary is not prejudiced and the report and evidence of retired Pendse CJ, who, referring to the state of Maharashtra, said that 'it is impossible to even consider the suggestion that the legal system is unable to protect the Muslim minority adequately or at all'. Mr Garlick also relies on the expert evidence of Dr Chitnis that, since the BJP/Shiv Sena government was replaced in 1999 by the government of the Congress Party and its secular allies, a minorities commission for the protection and interests of minorities and a state Human Rights Commission have been established. Furthermore, there are now openly pro-Muslim parties in the government. The high profile of the applicant will ensure particular vigilance by the judiciary at trial and there can be no possibility of further questioning if the applicant is returned, because he will be taken before a magistrate.

40. Accordingly, Mr Garlick submitted that this court should take the view that there is no reason under s 6(1)(d) for the applicant not to be returned.

41. In his reply, Mr Nicholls submitted that, if Mr Garlick's construction of 'accusation' in s 11(3) were correct, the section would be sterile: the word must extend to persons responsible for presenting and maintaining prosecutions including the police: he referred to *Propend Finance Pty Ltd v Sing* (1997) 111 ILR 611 where, in relation to s 14(1) of the State Immunity Act 1978, the Court of

a Appeal held that the activity of a police superintendent involved acts of a sovereign or governmental nature.

42. In the light of these competing submissions we turn to our conclusions.

SECTION 27(1) OF THE EXTRADITION ACT 1989

43. Section 27 of the 1989 Act is an enabling provision. Section 27(1) deals
b with evidence contained in depositions or in affidavits and enables a deposition or affidavit to be given in evidence, thus obviating the necessity to call the maker. To that extent the subsection creates an exception to the rule that evidence is given orally in court. But we reject the submission that it creates any wider exception to the hearsay principle. Nor can the distinction between documents and depositions assist the respondent. In the normal course, where a magistrate
c or an examiner takes a deposition he records the evidence of the witness, given on oath, in response to questions. Frequently the deposition takes the form of a narrative and does not record the question and the answer in verbatim form, although it has been said that the better course is that the question and answer should be recorded verbatim (see *Lloyds Bank Ltd v Marcan* [1973] 2 All ER 359 at
d 371, [1973] 1 WLR 339 at 348).

44. At the conclusion of taking the evidence the record is read to or by the witness and, if accepted, signed by the witness as the record of his evidence. It purports to be his evidence. Having regard to the nature of extradition proceedings, it is unlikely that the defendant will be present when a deposition is taken, nor, generally, will his advocate be there to question the witness, or challenge the
e accuracy of any translation. The precise circumstances in which depositions are taken in foreign jurisdictions will vary according to the procedures of the jurisdiction but in order for the document to be admissible, the evidence it records must be given on oath and the document authenticated. Such requirements go to the admissibility of the document, not its contents.

f 45. In the present case, after the magistrate (or his clerk) had taken the deposition, by translating Ali Shaikh's evidence into English, he translated it back into Hindi to secure Ali Shaikh's agreement to the terms of what was written in English. Ali Shaikh then signed the deposition and the respondent relies upon this signature. But in our judgment the signature adds nothing to the character of the deposition. Ali Shaikh could not adopt the deposition as a record of his
g evidence, because he did not know what the English record set out. There is therefore no record of the evidence given by Ali Shaikh. Nor, contrary to the submission of Mr Garlick, does the deposition 'purport to set out evidence given on oath'. It purports to set out an English version of what was said on oath. In our judgment the word 'purports' cannot bear the weight of the argument and
h introduce a further exception to the hearsay rule, by enabling what purports to be secondary evidence of a witness's evidence to be admissible in extradition proceedings.

46. Furthermore, if the interpretation of s 27(1)(a) were as Mr Garlick contends, there would be nothing in the section to limit the admissibility of secondary
j evidence to instances of translation. In any event, we are satisfied that, in the case of unchallengeable translation, errors could arise causing real prejudice. We have already drawn attention to an error in the translation of a telephone call on 9 August 1997. In our judgment, fairness requires that the actual evidence of the witness should be available to the defendant, otherwise a case could proceed to trial without the defendant ever having an opportunity of seeing a record of the evidence of the witness and his ability to demonstrate inconsistencies could be

significantly affected. The analogy with proceedings in Wales before a Welsh-speaking magistrate is not in point because the defendant or his lawyers are present and can challenge the accuracy of the translation. As Mr Garlick recognised, faced with clear authority (*Ex p Kirby* [1979] 2 All ER 1094, [1979] 1 WLR 541, *R v Governor of Pentonville Prison, ex p Osman* [1989] 3 All ER 701, [1990] 1 WLR 277, *Re Dokleja, R v Stipendiary Magistrate, ex p Dokleja* (31 January 1994, unreported)) that the substantive rules of evidence apply to the contents of a document admitted under s 27(1)(a), the resolution of the issue turns upon whether the proper construction of the section permits secondary evidence to be admitted. As we have stated, we reject his submission that it does.

47. This conclusion is consistent with other statutory provisions. Although hearsay was made more widely admissible in criminal cases by the Criminal Justice Act 1988, that Act nevertheless contained protective provisions (see ss 23, 24 and 25) enabling the court to control the admissibility of such evidence. Again, under the provisions of the Criminal Justice (International Co-operation) Act 1990, where international co-operation is achieved by a letter of request, the admission of the evidence is subject to the discretion conferred by s 25 of the 1988 Act (see s 3(8) of the 1990 Act), the court being required to have regard—

'(a) to whether it was possible to challenge the statement by questioning the person who made it; and (b) if proceedings have been instituted, to whether the local law allowed the parties to the proceedings to be legally represented when the evidence was being taken.'

Where a deposition or affidavit tendered under s 27(1)(a) of the 1989 Act contains the first-hand evidence of the witness, no equivalent discretionary basis for exclusion is available. A defendant in extradition proceedings would be in a peculiarly disadvantageous position if this procedure could be adopted to render secondary evidence admissible.

48. Mr Nicholls placed some store by the fact that the magistrate was someone who was not independent and not qualified to act as an interpreter. It is not in dispute that in India, judges and magistrates conduct their proceedings in English as well as in such local language as may be necessary. We incline to the view, without deciding the point, that the fact that a deposition is recorded in a foreign language but unaccompanied by a certified translation may not necessarily lead to the deposition being inadmissible although, generally speaking, certified translation is necessary.

49. But, in our judgment, the proffered deposition of Ali Shaikh in the English language is not admissible.

SECTION 78 OF THE POLICE AND CRIMINAL EVIDENCE ACT 1984

50. The purpose of the section is to enable the court to achieve fairness in the conduct of its proceedings, not by reference to the particular character or type of evidence but by having 'regard to all the circumstances'. The exercise of the power is unlikely to achieve its aim if encased in a rigid framework. That said, the outcome of the argument depends upon the proper interpretation of the section.

51. It is obvious that, since the court cannot infer there would be unfairness without having regard to all the circumstances, there are in our judgment two aspects, rather than two stages, to the exercise of the power, namely consideration of the circumstances and assessment of their impact on fairness. But the words of the section provide no support for the applicant's contention as to onus and

a standard of proof. The enactment in s 76(2) of the 1984 Act of a burden on the prosecution to prove beyond reasonable doubt that a confession was not obtained by oppression or other circumstances affecting its reliability is a clear pointer against the validity of the argument. The operative words of s 78(1) are:

b 'In any proceedings the court may refuse to allow evidence on which the prosecution proposes to rely to be given if it appears to the court that, having regard to all the circumstances ... the admission of the evidence would have such an adverse effect on the fairness of the proceedings that the court ought not to admit it.'

52. Section 78 confers a power in terms wide enough for its exercise on the court's own motion. The power is to be exercised whenever an issue appears as *c* to whether the court could conclude that the evidence should not be admitted. The concept of a burden of proof has no part to play in such circumstances. No doubt it is for that reason that there is no express provision as to the burden of proof, and we see no basis for implying such a burden. The prosecution desiring to adduce and the defence seeking to exclude evidence will each seek to persuade *d* the court about impact on fairness. We regard the position as neutral and see no reason why s 78 should be understood as requiring the court to consider upon whom the burden of proof rests.

53. In this case it is said that the magistrate should have made findings of fact. If the section places a burden of proof upon the prosecution this would advance the applicant's fundamental attack on the magistrate's refusal to make specific *e* findings and his failure to apply the criminal standard of proof to the prosecution's rebuttal of issues raised by the defence. In our judgment these submissions are inconsistent with the breadth of purpose of s 78. Unlike the words of s 76(2), where the burden and standard of proof is directed towards a specific issue, namely whether or not the prosecution has proved that the confession was not *f* obtained by oppression, or in circumstances rendering it unreliable, the reach of the protection provided by s 78 is broader, namely the prevention of unfairness from the admission of any evidence, not just a confession. The objective being broader, so also is the range of circumstances having a bearing on it. The ambit is not confined to what emanates from the defence. Circumstances may appear to the court other than those raised by the defendant. In this instance, issues of *g* fact were raised by the defence as to whether Ali Shaikh had been coerced, and whether the police had perverted the course of justice by falsifying evidence. But findings on these issues were not a pre-condition to the proper exercise of the s 78 power.

54. The magistrate stated his reasons for rejecting the submission as follows:

h 'I share the view expressed by the Government that my role in deciding whether to exclude evidence under s 78 is to carry out an evaluation of the evidence tendered by both the Government and the accused, to the circumstances in which the evidence was obtained and, ultimately, to decide on that evidence whether its admission would have such an adverse effect on *j* the fairness of these proceedings that I should exclude it. I do not accept, in relation to every issue raised, that I need to make a specific finding.'

For the reasons we have given we consider this direction impeccable.

55. The words in s 78 of the 1984 Act 'if it appears to the court' are also found in s 11(3) of the 1989 Act (and in s 6(1) of that Act there is a similar phrase 'if it appears to an appropriate authority').

56. In *Narang's* case, s 8(3) of the Fugitive Offenders Act 1967, the precursor of *a* s 11(3), was considered. The material conclusions were as follows. (1) The task for the court is to consider all the materials before it and then to decide whether or not the inference is to be drawn that return would be unjust or oppressive (see [1977] 2 All ER 348 at 363, [1978] AC 247 at 273). This chimes harmoniously with our view as to the correct approach under s 78. (2) The words 'having regard to all the circumstances' enjoin the court to have 'regard' to all the circumstances *b* which reasonably can have a bearing on the question whether 'by reason of the passage of time' an order to return would be unjust (see [1977] 2 All ER 348 at 368, [1978] AC 247 at 280). Similarly, under s 78, it is all the circumstances which could reasonably have a bearing on the issue of fairness to which the court must have regard. (3) In extradition proceedings there is no proof of fact, in the proper sense of the word, and in certain cases there might be difficulty in deciding as to *c* the primary facts upon which the court should proceed ([1977] 2 All ER 348 at 359–380, [1978] AC 247 at 259–296). Exactly the same consideration applies to s 78 in extradition proceedings.

57. In *R v Khan (Sultan)* [1996] 3 All ER 289, [1997] AC 558, which was concerned with s 78, two separate acts were said to constitute invasions of *d* privacy, namely fixing a device to the wall of the flat of an occupier and recording what was said. Ultimately the argument for exclusion depended upon the alleged breach of privacy, the absence of statutory authorisation and an alleged infringement of art 8 of the European Convention for the Protection of Human Rights and Fundamental Freedoms (Rome, 4 November 1950; TS 71 (1953); Cmd 8969) (as set out in Sch 1 to the 1998 Act) (the ECHR). In the passage already set out at *e* para 30 above, Lord Nolan rejected the need for the judge to determine whether a breach of the ECHR had occurred or that criminal damage had been caused, and emphasised the significance of the conclusion to which the court was required to come rather than the character of findings of fact upon which that conclusion had to be based ([1996] 3 All ER 289 at 301, [1997] AC 558 at 581–582). *f*

58. Under s 78 any circumstance which can reasonably have a bearing on fairness should be considered. The weight to be attached to an individual circumstance may increase or decrease because of the presence of other related or unrelated circumstances. The preponderance of all the circumstances may show that the admission of the evidence would have such an adverse effect on fairness as to require its exclusion. *g*

59. The absence from s 78 of words suggesting that facts are to be established or proved to any particular standard is, in our judgment, deliberate. It leaves the matter open and untrammelled by rigid evidential considerations. It may well be impossible for a court to make a finding on the issues raised. For example, the contention that the magistrate should have found as a fact either that the prosecution *h* had proved to the criminal standard that Ali Shaikh was arrested on 31 August 1997 or that, on the balance of probabilities, he was arrested on 25 August was, as the magistrate said, not something that he could decide without having Ali Shaikh before the court and questioned. The undesirability of such an approach is demonstrated by the purpose for which this specific submission was raised. It *j* was but a step towards another stage of fact-finding. If it could be established that Ali Shaikh was arrested on 25 August, then, according to relevant Indian law, a presumption was raised that Ali Shaikh had been intimidated. But this stage, even if it had been reached, would have simply raised another issue for the magistrate to resolve, namely whether that presumption was to be rebutted, or could be rebutted by any other evidence in the case. In our judgment,

a investigation in the nature of a full trial to determine such facts is not practical, desirable or intended by the terms of s 78.

60. The magistrate considered *Ex p Levin* [1997] 3 All ER 289, [1997] AC 741 and referred to the dictum of Lord Hoffmann to the effect that the exclusion of evidence under s 78 is likely to occur very rarely. Before embarking upon a consideration of the circumstances which the magistrate regarded as bearing
b upon the fairness of the proceedings before him, he referred to the objective background material received from the experts. He rightly regarded it as providing an important contextual framework in which to consider the circumstances. He summarised those circumstances comprehensively, weighing conflicting accounts. He dealt first with the question of Ali Shaikh's literacy, on which he heard evidence from an Indian lawyer now representing Ali Shaikh. He
c weighed and considered the impact of that evidence. He next turned to the manner in which Ali Shaikh came to make a confession. He concluded:

> 'When considering the manner in which Magistrates Garde and Palnitkar dealt with the hearings between 18 September 1997 and 25 November 1997 and bearing in mind the purpose of those hearings, I find it impossible to say
d that they were not conducted other than in a completely fair and exemplary manner.'

Thereafter he concluded that, whilst some questions remained unanswered, the admission of Ali Shaikh's evidence would not have such an adverse effect on the proceedings before him as to merit exclusion either under s 78 of the 1984 Act or
e art 15 of the Torture Convention. In our judgment reference to the Torture Convention adds nothing to the case. The intent of art 15 has been ensured in our law, by the common law and statute.

61. Although there were a number of circumstances which would cause considerable difficulty for the prosecution if the issue under s 78 fell to be decided
f in trial proceedings in this country (see *Re Proulx, R v Bow Street Magistrates' Court, ex p Proulx* [2001] 1 All ER 57), in our judgment, for the magistrate to conclude that the circumstances did not 'outrage civilised values' was one which was within the margin of opinion open to him and is not susceptible to challenge on *Wednesbury* grounds.

g INSUFFICIENCY

62. The magistrate correctly regarded *R v Galbraith* as the authority which laid down the proper approach. He was taken to *Alves v DPP*. He concluded:

> 'I have considered its reliability along with the later retraction but have
h come to the conclusion, applying the *Galbraith* test as set out in *Alves v DPP*, that a properly directed tribunal could find Ali Shaikh's original evidence capable of belief.'

We accept the submissions of Mr Nicholls summarised in paras 18 and 19 above. In particular we consider there is considerable force in the submission that
j Ali Shaikh's retraction has been repeated on four occasions, including on oath in his writ petition to the National Human Rights Commission, and that his retraction placed him in jeopardy of being convicted of a capital offence. In our judgment, the magistrate's review of the evidence bearing on the issue of sufficiency was not comprehensive enough. He was not dealing with the mere retraction of a confession. He should have considered all the circumstances surrounding the making of the original confession and its content, which, on the

critical issue as to the applicant's involvement, contained a significant internal
inconsistency as to whether Ali Shaikh was inside or outside the room at the time
of the alleged conversations. He made no reference to the protestations of
innocence up to the failure of the bail application on 14 September. He did not
consider the evidence from Ali Shaikh's wife and daughter. In addition to their
evidence, there was cogent evidence that, before the magistrate, Ali Shaikh felt
intimidated, whether by gangsters or the police. Had he considered all the
circumstances of the original confession and the ambit and character of the
retraction, the magistrate would, in our judgment, have been bound to conclude
that no judge, properly directing himself, could convict on Ali Shaikh's evidence,
because it was worthless.

SECTION 11(3) OF THE EXTRADITION ACT 1989

'Accusation'

63. Mr Garlick submitted that since 'accusation' referred to the request for
extradition and the request was being made by the Union of India on behalf of the
state of Maharastra and the state was acting through an independent public
prosecutor, there was no evidence that any party who could properly be regarded
as making the request had acted in bad faith. We do not consider that the
ordinary meaning of the word 'accusation' is a request, notwithstanding that the
nexus between accusation and request may well be obvious. Such a nexus
appears from the terms of s 11(3) of the 1989 Act because the subsection refers in
turn to the following: (1) 'the offence, or each of the offences'; (2) the request,
namely 'in respect of which the applicant's return is sought'; and (3) 'the
accusation against him'. But the words of the subsection are against the accusation
meaning the request because sub-s (3)(c) refers to 'good faith in the interests of
justice' in relation to the accusation not the request. A request for extradition is
not in character an accusation. It is an exercise of sovereign power pursuant to a
treaty in respect of an alleged offence. Whether or not it could ever be regarded
as an 'accusation', for the purposes of an allegation that such an exercise of power
was not in good faith, does not arise in this case. But we are satisfied that, even
if it could be so regarded, that is not the limit of the meaning of accusation nor
the most obvious reflection of what is referred to in the subsection. Accusation
is broad enough to encompass the accusation of a witness or witnesses and the
offence charged in consequence. By making a request for extradition, reliance is
placed upon the evidence of any witness and the offence disclosed thereby. The
protection afforded by the subsection would be rendered 'sterile', as Mr Nicholls
submitted, if the issue of bad faith could be divorced from the underlying facts
supporting the request. Certainly Sedley J in *Re Calis* (19 November 1993,
unreported) examined the good faith of the complainant to determine the issue
under s 11(3). No one appears to have argued to the contrary. Having heard such
argument we reject it.

64. We turn to our conclusion on s 11(3). This court has received evidence on
this issue over and above that which was before the magistrate. We find the
following circumstances bear upon whether the accusation is made in good faith
and in the interests of justice, and whether it would be unjust or oppressive to
return him. (1) There was no legally admissible material available to the Mumbai
Police Commissioner to provide reasonable grounds for his statements that
witnesses 'quite clearly indicated that Nadeem (the applicant) hired Abu Salem
gang's services to eliminate Kumar' and 'we have ample evidence to prove

a Nadeem's involvement'. This court is placed on inquiry as to what motive there could have been for such an unsubstantiated statement to be made at a press conference. Indeed, even if grounds existed for such a belief, the making of such a statement would raise questions about its underlying motive. (2) The assertion of the Mumbai Deputy Chief Minister gives rise to like concern. (3) Having regard to the vital importance to be attached to the circumstances surrounding

b the confession made by Ali Shaikh, the absence of any reference in the requests for his return to the pressure recorded by the magistrate on 18, 20 and 26 September 1997, is remarkable. This non-disclosure on such a central feature of the case has not been explained. It is to be inferred that it was deliberate and calculated to leave those considering the case with the impression that it was stronger than the true facts merited. (4) Equally, the failure to disclose Ali Shaikh's retractions until

c part way through the committal proceedings causes this court astonishment. No explanation has been provided. It is to be inferred that it, too, was deliberate and calculated to leave the impression that the case against the applicant was stronger than the true facts merited. (5) The above circumstances have to be considered in the light of the further evidence, since the committal, about the obtaining of

d Ali Shaikh's confession, his literacy and the genesis of ABB 10. In our judgment a pattern of events emerges, which is consistent with (a) a pre-conceived desire to blame the applicant when no evidence existed; and (b) the use of improper pressure to obtain a statement from Ali Shaikh to make good the allegations. Whereas the evidence of Ali Shaikh's lawyers may have provided some reassurance about the propriety of what happened, the evidence of Prison Officer

e Wankhede and Mr Mokashi give added cause for anxiety. Further, we note, so far as these two witnesses are concerned, that the police plainly disregarded Mr Garlick's direction that no approach should be made to them before they gave evidence. We infer that the police have an improper interest in interfering with the evidence in this case. (6) The expert evidence points to ABB 10 as having

f been signed by Ali Shaikh in blank. The language of the document shows that, unless he is more educated than anyone suggests, it could not be his own confession. We infer that this document could not have been created without interference from those responsible for holding Ali Shaikh. (7) The evidence of Mr Vanjara supports the conclusion that Ali Shaikh is illiterate. His daughter's evidence is consistent with the document being the construct of another, placed

g above his signature after this had been obtained from him on a blank sheet of paper. (8) The inclusion of Javed Fawda's name in Ali Shaikh's deposition, at a late stage and where there are grounds to connect it with unlawful and unjustified action by the police requiring false justification, leads us to question the role of the police in relation to the appearance of Javed Fawda's name.

h 65. The cumulative effect of all these circumstances causes us to infer that the accusation of murder and conspiracy made against this applicant is not made in good faith and in the interests of justice.

66. Having reached this conclusion we are also satisfied that it would not be fair and would be unjust to return the applicant, because of the appearance of

j misbehaviour by the police in pursuing their inquiries and the significant risk that the activities surrounding that misbehaviour have so tainted the evidence as to render a fair trial impossible.

SECTION 6(1) OF THE 1989 ACT

67. In view of our other conclusions in this case, it is unnecessary to reach any decision on this aspect. It suffices to say that the background material to which

we were referred does not establish that every Muslim on trial in Mumbai, at the
suit of a prosecution instigated by the Mumbai police, is at risk of being *a*
prejudiced by reason of his religion and we are not satisfied that the bad faith,
which we have found to be present in the accusation, has a religious basis or
motive.

CONCLUSION   *b*
68. We therefore order that a writ of habeas corpus issue to procure the
production before this court of the applicant, Nadeem Akhtar Saifi, and that he
be discharged forthwith in relation to the offences in respect of which his return
is sought by the Union of India.

Application allowed. Permission to appeal refused.

                                                    Dilys Tausz   Barrister.

Safeway Stores plc v Tate

a

COURT OF APPEAL, CIVIL DIVISION

OTTON, MANTELL LJJ AND SIR RONALD WATERHOUSE

2 NOVEMBER, 18 DECEMBER 2000

b

Jury – Trial by jury – Defamation – Summary judgment – Claimant bringing proceedings for libel against defendant – Judge concluding that words complained of were defamatory and giving summary judgment for claimant – Whether judge usurping role of jury – Supreme Court Act 1981, s 69(1) – Civil Procedure Act 1997, ss 1(3), 4 –
c *CPR 24.2.*

The claimant, S plc, brought proceedings for libel against the defendant, T. By the time the case reached trial in June 1999, the only defence was a general traverse whose effect was to put S plc to proof that the words complained of bore a defamatory meaning. Due to an administrative error, no jury panel had been
d arranged on the date fixed for the hearing. S plc therefore applied for summary judgment under CPR 24.2[a] on the ground that T had no defence of any substance. Under the former Rules of the Supreme Court, actions for libel or slander were expressly excluded from the court's jurisdiction to grant summary judgment, but there was no such exclusion under the CPR. Instead, r 24.2 gave the court a
e general discretion to grant summary judgment if the defendant had no real prospect of successfully defending the claim, and there was no other compelling reason why the case should be disposed of at a trial. The CPR themselves had been made under s 1[b] of the Civil Procedure Act 1997 which, in sub-s (3), provided that the power to make procedural rules was to be exercised with a view to securing that the civil justice system was accessible, fair and efficient. Under
f s 4[c] of that Act, the Lord Chancellor had the power to amend, repeal or revoke any enactment to the extent he considered necessary or desirable. At the hearing, the judge directed himself that he only had to consider whether the words complained of were defamatory. He concluded that T had no real prospect of success on that issue, and that in the circumstances it was right to avoid a trial.
g Accordingly, he gave summary judgment for S plc, even though s 69(1)[d] of the Supreme Court Act 1981 provided that an action 'shall be tried with a jury' where the court was satisfied that there was in issue a claim in respect of libel or slander. On appeal, T contended that CPR 24.2 could not deprive a party in a defamation suit of his fundamental right to trial by jury, and that only a jury could decide if
h the words complained of were actually defamatory. In seeking to uphold the judge's decision, S plc attacked the contention that the right to trial by jury was a fundamental right, and relied on the rule-making power in the 1997 Act.

---

a   Rule 24.2 is set out at p 198 *e f*, below
b   Section 1, so far as material, provides: '… (3) The power to make Civil Procedure Rules is to be
j   exercised with a view to securing that the civil justice system is accessible, fair and efficient.'
c   Section 4, so far as material, provides: '(1) The Lord Chancellor may by order amend, repeal or
        revoke any enactment to the extent he considers necessary or desirable in consequence
        of—(a) section 1 or 2, or (b) Civil Procedure Rules.
            (2) The Lord Chancellor may by order amend, repeal or revoke any enactment passed or made
        before the commencement of this section to the extent he considers necessary or desirable in order
        to facilitate the making of Civil Procedure Rules … '
d   Section 69(1) is set out at p 198 *d*, below

Held – Although an application under CPR 24.2 could properly be made in order
to determine certain questions which fell within the jurisdiction of the judge in a
libel action, that rule did not permit a judge alone to determine questions of fact
which Parliament had determined should be decided by a jury, and in particular
whether the words complained of were defamatory. The right to trial by jury, and
in particular the right to have the jury determine the question 'libel or no libel', was
not a matter of mere procedure, but an important and substantive legal right. As
such, that right was beyond the power of the Civil Procedure Rules Committee to
abolish or limit by its general powers to reform the rules of practice and procedure.
Thus although the right might be amended by statute, that could not be achieved
by subordinate legislation founded on an Act conferring a broad general power.
Since neither the 1997 Act nor CPR 24.2 made express reference to defamation
actions, the general provision in the CPR did not override the specific provisions of
s 69(1) of the 1981 Act. That was so notwithstanding the terms of s 1(3) of the 1997
Act. Nor did the wide power in s 4 of that Act enable delegated legislation to repeal
or amend primary legislation which embodied a fundamental (as opposed to
procedural) right such as trial by jury. Even if that power were wide enough, it was
intrinsically unlikely that delegated legislation which purported to abolish such a
fundamental right would do so without express reference to the statutory right. To
do so would be to remove the right by a casual change or mere sidewind. That was
particularly so where the right was intertwined with the defendant's freedom of
speech. In the instant case, the judge had fallen into error in assuming that he had
the power to assume the role of the jury when, due to administrative error, there
was none available. The issue whether the words complained of were defamatory
was a question of fact to be determined by a jury. Accordingly, the appeal would
be allowed (see p 202 *b* to *g* *j* to p 203 *a g h* and p 204 *c* to *f,* below).

Notes

For the judge's duty as to questions to be left to the jury, see 28 *Halsbury's Laws*
(4th edn reissue) para 238.

For the Supreme Court Act 1981, s 69, see 11 *Halsbury's Statutes* (4th edn) (2000
reissue) 1107.

For the Civil Procedure Act 1997, ss 1, 4, see 11 *Halsbury's Statutes* (4th edn)
(2000 reissue) 1472, 1475.

Cases referred to in judgments

Broome v Agar (1928) 44 TLR 339, CA.
Capital and Counties Bank Ltd v George Henty & Sons (1882) 7 App Cas 741, [1881–5]
   All ER Rep 86, HL.
Goldsmith v Pressdram Ltd [1987] 3 All ER 485, [1988] 1 WLR 64, CA.
Jones v Skelton [1963] 3 All ER 952, [1963] 1 WLR 1362, PC.
Mulligan v Cole (1875) LR 10 QB 549.
Nevill v Fine Art and General Insurance Co Ltd [1897] AC 68, [1895–9] All ER Rep 164, HL.
R v Shipley (1784) 4 Doug KB 73.
Ward v James [1965] 1 All ER 563, [1966] 1 QB 273, [1965] 2 WLR 455, CA.
William Coulson & Sons v James Coulson & Co (1887) 3 TLR 846, CA.

Cases also cited or referred to in skeleton arguments

Aitken v Preston [1997] EMLR 415, CA.
Bairstow v Queens Moat Houses plc [1998] 1 All ER 343, CA.
Berkoff v Burchill [1996] 4 All ER 1008, CA.

a   *Beta Construction Ltd v Channel Four Television Co Ltd* [1990] 2 All ER 1012, [1990] 1 WLR 1042, CA.

British Data Management plc v Boxer Commercial Removals plc [1996] 3 All ER 707, CA.

Broadmoor Special Hospital v Robinson [2000] 2 All ER 727, [2000] QB 775, CA.

D & L Caterers Ltd v D'Ajou [1945] 1 All ER 563, [1945] 1 KB 364, CA.

Evans v Davies [1991] 2 Qd R 498, Qld Full Court.

b   *Ford v Blurton* (1922) 38 TLR 801, CA.

General Mediterranean Holdings SA v Patel [1999] 3 All ER 673, [2000] 1 WLR 272.

Hayward v Thompson [1981] 3 All ER 450, [1982] QB 47, CA.

Hough v London Express Newspaper Ltd [1940] 3 All ER 31, [1940] 2 KB 507, CA.

Hubbard v Pitt [1975] 3 All ER 1, [1976] QB 142, CA.

c   *Inco Europe Ltd v First Choice Distribution (a firm)* [1999] 1 All ER 820, [1999] 1 WLR 270, CA; *affd* [2000] 2 All ER 109, [2000] 1 WLR 586, HL.

James Gilbert Ltd v MGN Ltd [2000] EMLR 680.

Jenkins v Bushby [1891] 1 Ch 484, CA.

John v MGN Ltd [1996] 2 All ER 35, [1997] QB 586, CA.

Jozwiak v Sadek [1954] 1 All ER 3, [1954] 1 WLR 275.

d   *Lewis v Daily Telegraph Ltd* [1963] 2 All ER 151, [1964] AC 234, HL.

Lockhart v Harrison (1928) 139 LT 521, [1928] All ER Rep 149, HL.

Looker v Halcomb (1827) 4 Bing 183.

Lucas-Box v News Group Newspapers Ltd, Lucas-Box v Associated Newspapers Group plc [1986] 1 All ER 177, [1986] 1 WLR 147, CA.

e   *Mahon v Rahn (No 2)* [2000] 4 All ER 41, [2000] 1 WLR 2150, CA.

Mapp v News Group Newspapers Ltd, Gillian v News Group Newspapers Ltd, Goscomb v News Group Newspapers Ltd, Watton v News Group Newspapers Ltd [1998] QB 520, [1998] 2 WLR 260, CA.

McDonald's Corp v Steel [1995] 3 All ER 615, CA.

f   *McKiernon v Chief Adjudication Officer* (1989) Times, 1 November, CA.

Mehmet Dogan Bey v GG Abdeni & Co Ltd [1951] 2 All ER 162, [1951] 2 KB 405.

Mineral Resources Ltd, Re, Environment Agency v Stout [1999] 1 All ER 746.

Mitchell v Book Sales Ltd (1994) Independent, 25 March, CA.

Morgan v Odhams Press Ltd [1971] 2 All ER 1156, [1971] 1 WLR 1239, HL.

Palmer (decd) (a debtor), Re [1993] 4 All ER 812, [1994] Ch 316; *rvsd* [1994] 3 All ER 835, [1994] Ch 316, CA.

g   *R v Battle Justices, ex p Shepherd* (1983) 147 JP 372, DC.

R v Broadcasting Standards Commission, ex p British Broadcasting Corp [2000] 3 All ER 989, [2000] 3 WLR 1327, CA.

R v Lord Chancellor, ex p Witham [1997] 2 All ER 779, [1998] QB 575, DC.

h   *R v Secretary of State for the Home Dept, ex p Hickey* [1995] 1 All ER 479, [1995] QB 43, CA.

R v Secretary of State for the Home Dept, ex p Leech [1993] 4 All ER 539, [1994] QB 198, CA.

R v Secretary of State for the Home Dept, ex p Simms [1999] 3 All ER 400, [2000] 2 AC 115, HL.

j   *R v St Albans Juvenile Court, ex p Godman* [1981] 2 All ER 311, [1981] QB 964, DC.

Racz v Home Office [1994] 1 All ER 97, [1994] 2 AC 45, HL.

Rantzen v Mirror Group Newspapers (1986) Ltd [1993] 4 All ER 975, [1994] QB 670, CA.

Raymond v Honey [1982] 1 All ER 756, [1983] 1 AC 1, HL.

Red Man's Syndicate Ltd v Associated Newspapers Ltd (1910) 26 TLR 394.

Regan v Taylor [2000] EMLR 549, CA.

Rothermere v Times Newspapers Ltd [1973] 1 All ER 1013, [1973] 1 WLR 448, CA.

S v Gloucestershire CC, L v Tower Hamlets LBC [2000] 3 All ER 346, [2001] 2 WLR
    909, CA.
S v Newham LBC (5 November 1999, unreported).
Seward v The Vera Cruz (owners), The Vera Cruz (1884) 10 App Cas 59, [1881–5]
    All ER Rep 216, HL.
Slim v Daily Telegraph Ltd [1968] 1 All ER 497, [1968] 2 QB 157, CA.
South Hetton Coal Co Ltd v North-Eastern News Association Ltd [1894] 1 QB 133, CA.
Sutcliffe v Pressdram Ltd [1990] 1 All ER 269, [1991] 1 QB 153, CA.
Swain v Hillman [2001] 1 All ER 91, CA.
Tancic v Times Newspapers Ltd (2000) Times, 12 January, CA.
Telnikoff v Matusevitch [1990] 3 All ER 865, [1991] 1 QB 102, CA; *rvsd in part* [1991]
    4 All ER 817, [1992] 2 AC 343, HL.

Appeal
The defendant, Albert Tate, appealed with permission of Roch LJ granted on
17 March 2000 from the decision of Judge Green QC at Central London County
Court on 10 June 1999 giving summary judgment to the claimant, Safeway
Stores plc, in its action for libel against Mr Tate. The facts are set out in the
judgment of Otton LJ.

Harry Boggis-Rolfe (instructed through the *Bar Pro Bono Unit* by *Lovells* through the
    Solicitors' Pro Bono Scheme) for Mr Tate.
Adam Wolanski (instructed by *Lawrence Jones*) for Safeway.
Victoria Sharp (instructed by the *Treasury Solicitor*) as amicus curiae.

Cur adv vult

18 December 2000. The following judgments were delivered.

OTTON LJ. This an appeal by the defendant, Mr Tate, against the decision on
10 June 1999 of Judge Barry Green QC in the Central London County Court to
award summary judgment under CPR Pt 24 to the claimant, Safeway Stores plc
(Safeway). The action was brought by Safeway against Mr Tate for damages and
an injunction for libel. On 17 March 2000 Roch LJ granted permission to appeal
on one of Mr Tate's proposed grounds; namely that he was denied the right to a
jury trial.

At the hearing before Judge Green Mr Tate appeared in person. For the
purposes of this appeal Mr Harry Boggis-Rolfe appears through the Bar Pro Bono
Unit instructed by Lovells through the Solicitors' Pro Bono Scheme. The court
would wish to record their gratitude to both for undertaking this task and thus
providing the court with invaluable assistance.

Background
The libel action arose out of a boundary dispute between the parties. Mr Tate
lives at 24 Weymouth Street, Warminster, Wiltshire one of four dwelling houses
known collectively as Hall's Terrace. Mr Tate has a grievance against Safeway in
relation to the alleged encroachment by Safeway on 24 Weymouth Street by means
of a 'fraudulent boundary' to the rear of Hall's Terrace.

A further complaint arose in relation to the rebuilding of a wall. Mr Tate claims
that a wall forming part of 24 Weymouth Street was damaged and then demolished
during construction works on what was to become Safeway land. An offer was

a made by the developers involved to rebuild the wall. Mr Tate was aggrieved at the location of the foundations of this wall and possibly about the fact that the wall was never in fact rebuilt. These matters are peripheral to this appeal.

As a result of these grievances Mr Tate produced a leaflet containing his understanding of the boundary dispute with the headline 'Safeway: where fraud ideas come naturally'. These leaflets do not form part of Safeway's case. Mr Tate

b subsequently produced a placard with only the words of the headline written on it and displayed the placard in the garden of his house where it was plainly visible to customers of the adjacent Safeway store. Additionally, he erected a different sign (with identical content) on his car and parked the car in the car park of six other Safeway stores. On one occasion he displayed the sign at the end of the Warminster carnival procession, where it was again plainly visible to customers. Judge

c Green QC proceeded on the basis of these facts which were apparently not challenged by Mr Tate at the hearing on 10 June 1999.

On 3 December 1992, Safeway issued a writ for libel, claiming damages and an injunction. On 4 December 1992 Blofeld J ordered that Mr Tate 'be restrained from further publishing pending further order'. There appear to have been breaches of

d the order and a suspended sentence for contempt. Mr Tate commenced his own action for trespass which was automatically struck out on 12 September 1996.

On 8 September 1997 Judge Simpson ordered that Mr Tate's purported defence of justification be struck out. On 8 May 1998 Mr Tate applied for permission to appeal which was granted whereupon the court allowed the appeal and remitted the matter to the trial judge. Evans LJ said:

e

> 'The defendant has sought to justify the claim, but has so far failed to set out in his pleadings the reason why he says that that allegation, that serious allegation, was justified … It may be that … the judge will see his way to his making an order which will permit the defendant at least the minimum of scope for manoeuvre so that the issue can be dealt with and put to rest by a

f proper adjudication at the trial.'

An ineffectual attempt was made to put the pleadings in order but on 10 August 1998 Judge Simpson struck out those paragraphs of the defence alleging justification. The matter proceeded to trial.

On 1 June 1999 (the date fixed for the hearing) due to a lamentable administrative

g error no jury panel had been arranged. Mr Tate applied for the trial to be adjourned on the ground of ill-health. Without any proper notice, Safeway applied for summary judgment on the ground that 'There is no defence of any substance to the claimant's case.' Both applications were heard by Judge Green on 10 June. Mr Tate's application to adjourn on the ground of ill-health was dismissed. The

h judge entered a judgment for Safeway for damages for libel to be assessed by a jury and granted an injunction to restrain Mr Tate from publication of the words 'Safeway: where fraud ideas come naturally'. He ordered Mr Tate to pay Safeway costs and refused leave to appeal.

The learned judge found that—

j

> 'after no less than four attempts to amend his defence to plead justification, the only live defence is … a general traverse or general denial, the effect of which is that the claimant is put to proof that the words bear a defamatory meaning and that they were published as above.'

Mr Tate has never denied publication and accordingly the learned judge directed himself that he had only to consider whether the words complained of 'tend to

lower a person or a company in the estimation of other people'. Safeway submitted
that Mr Tate stood no real prospect of success on this point and the learned judge   *a*
acceded to that submission. He held that 'the power to give summary judgment is
discretionary', and considered that the costs of a jury trial, and the unfair adverse
publicity which Safeway would suffer even on a successful trial, left him in 'no
doubt' that it was right to avoid a jury trial. The learned judge considered the effect
of s 69 of the Supreme Court Act 1981 which provides for an unqualified right to a   *b*
jury, but held that the plain wording of CPR 24.3 made no exception for libel to a
right to summary judgment.

As indicated, on 17 March 2000 Roch LJ ordered that permission to appeal be
granted but limited to the ground that Mr Tate was denied the right to a jury trial.
Roch LJ also invited the Attorney General to appoint an amicus curiae to assist the
court with the point in issue. Victoria Sharp was so appointed and she prepared a   *c*
skeleton argument and appeared before us. In the meantime Mr Boggis-Rolfe
undertook to appear for Mr Tate.

Section 69 of the 1981 Act provides:

> 'Trial by jury.—(1) Where, on the application of any party to an action to be
> tried in the Queen's Bench Division, the court is satisfied that there is in   *d*
> issue—(a) a charge of fraud against that party; or (b) a claim in respect of libel,
> slander, malicious prosecution or false imprisonment; or (c) any question or
> issue of a kind prescribed for the purposes of this paragraph, the action shall be
> tried with a jury, unless the court is of opinion that the trial requires any
> prolonged examination of documents or accounts or any scientific or local   *e*
> investigation which cannot conveniently be made with a jury.'

CPR 24.2 provides:

> **'Grounds for summary judgment**
> The court may give summary judgment against a claimant or defendant on
> the whole of a claim or on a particular issue if—(a) it considers that—(i) that   *f*
> claimant has no real prospect of succeeding on the claim or issue; or (ii) that
> defendant has no real prospect of successfully defending the claim or issue; and
> (b) there is no other compelling reason why the case or issue should be
> disposed of at a trial.'

g

Mr Tate's case

Mr Boggis-Rolfe conceded that on its face and as worded CPR 24.2 enables
summary judgment to be given in appropriate circumstances even in defamation
cases and if there is no other reason for trial. He points out that although the
present matter was decided under CPR 24.2 in its original form, the proviso in   *h*
CPR 24.2(b) now reads 'other *compelling* reason' by amendment from July 2000.
Thus CPR 24.2 in its modified form is wider in applicability than it was.

He submitted that although this provision reflects the overriding objectives of
the CPR to enable litigation to be resolved proportionately and expeditiously and
to save costs it is not sufficient to deprive a party in a defamation suit of his   *j*
fundamental right to trial by jury. This right is so engrained in our constitution that
only a jury can decide if the words complained of actually are defamatory and what
they mean. The now extinct RSC Ord 14 did not apply to actions for libel and
slander. RSC Ord 18, r 19 and the court's inherent powers in cases of abuse of
process did not enable a plaintiff to obtain summary judgment because meaning
was always for the jury even if the court was persuaded to strike out other defences.

a Moreover RSC Ord 82, r 3A which provided for preliminary rulings on meanings is still preserved by CPR PD 53. Thus the court can still non-suit a plaintiff and deprive him of trial by jury if the judge found that the words were incapable of a defamatory meaning. It could also deprive a defendant of a particular defence of justification, but only in relation to a meaning that the words were incapable of bearing. Thus the statutory right to a jury trial, and in particular that of a defendant, *b* was recognised in the procedural limitations.

It follows that CPR 24.2 is ultra vires s 1(3) of the Civil Procedure Act 1997 in so far as it purports to deprive or impinge upon the right to trial by jury. If CPR 24.2 is not ultra vires then it has to be read, as suggested by the editors of the White Book (*Civil Procedure* (Autumn 2000), vol 1, p 383, para 24.2.4), to mean that the fact that a respondent may have a right to trial by jury may, of itself, be a reason for a trial. *c* Extreme caution is appropriate before removing such a fundamental right.

Safeway's case

Mr Adam Wolanski (on behalf of Safeway) contended that CPR 24.2 removes the express exclusion of defamation claims from the summary judgment regime *d* which existed under RSC Ord 14. The learned judge was correct in holding that there was a discretion to give summary judgment against Mr Tate and he did not err in principle in exercising his discretion in Safeway's favour.

Counsel mounted a spirited attack upon the concept that the right to trial by jury is a fundamental right. He submitted that this right is not (and never has been) an *e* unqualified or absolute right, it is subject to significant limitations. A party to a libel action has never had the right to have a jury return a perverse verdict in his favour. In support of this proposition he cited *Gatley on Libel and Slander* (9th edn, 1998) pp 890–891 (para 36.20):

f 'Where the words are obviously incapable of any but a defamatory meaning, and there is no question but that they were published of the plaintiff, and the jury have nevertheless found a verdict for the defendant, the court will set aside the verdict as perverse and unreasonable and order a new trial.'

Counsel also cited *Broome v Agar* (1928) 44 TLR 339 at 341 per Sankey LJ:

g 'It is not, however, open to the Judge to say that the words do bear a defamatory meaning, that is for the jury, but the jury must have evidence upon which they can found their verdict and if there is no evidence upon which they can find that the words were not defamatory, or if it can be conclusively proved that they have not exercised any reasonable discretion at all, an appellate court may grant a new trial.'

h

Moreover, the Court of Appeal has the power to make an award of damages where it decides that the jury's verdict in favour of the defendant is perverse. CPR 52.10(3) provides that the court may, instead of ordering a new trial, make an award of damages or vary an award of damages made by the jury.

j Mr Wolanski's argument that the claimant is never entitled to a 'perverse verdict' can be disposed of briefly. The issue of whether a verdict is perverse can only be raised after a jury's verdict has been given. The decisions cited by counsel in support of his proposition are all decisions of the Court of Appeal. None is authority for the proposition which he states or that the judge is entitled to take away an issue of fact from the jury merely because he considers that the jury might reach a perverse verdict.

Mr Wolanski also advanced a novel argument that when granting the injunction
Blofeld J must have concluded that the words complained of were 'unarguably
defamatory'. In support he cited *Gatley on Libel and Slander* pp 633–634 (para 25.2)
and *William Coulson & Sons v James Coulson & Co* (1887) 3 TLR 846 where Lord
Esher MR, when considering the court's power to grant an interim injunction,
stated:

> '... the jurisdiction was of a delicate nature. It ought only to be exercised in
> the clearest cases, where any jury would say that the matter complained of was
> libellous, and where if the jury did not so find the Court would set aside the
> verdict as unreasonable. The Court must also be satisfied that in all probability
> the alleged libel was untrue, and if written on a privileged occasion that there
> was malice ... It followed ... that the Court could only on the rarest occasions
> exercise their jurisdiction. In the present case his Lordship could not go to the
> length of saying that it would be unreasonable in the jury to find that this was
> not a libel, therefore ... the Court ought not to grant an interim injunction.'

I was not impressed by this argument. Suffice it to say that these observations were
made in the context of interlocutory injunctions and have no bearing on the
particular circumstances of this case where an application was made ex parte, the
defendant was a litigant in person who disregarded the injunction and made no
application to discharge it before trial.

Counsel further submitted that the limitations on the right to a jury trial are
intended to ensure that the correct balance is struck between the efficient
administration of justice, ensuring that proceedings are conducted rationally and in
a manner which is acceptable to public opinion, and a party's right to a jury trial.
Section 69 of the 1981 Act, whilst preserving the pre-existing right, nevertheless
created exceptions. The word 'conveniently' makes it clear that the efficient
administration of justice is a significant fact to be taken into consideration by the
court in exercising its discretion as to whether to order trial by judge alone.
Slade LJ in *Goldsmith v Pressdram Ltd* [1987] 3 All ER 485 at 496, [1988] 1 WLR 64 at
74 stated:

> 'I infer that the legislature, in using the particular word "conveniently" in
> the context of the subsection, was directing its attention to the efficient
> administration of justice, rather more than the probable difficulty or
> otherwise of the issues involved.'

In giving the Rules Committee the power to make rules 'with a view to
ensuring the civil justice system is accessible, fair and efficient' the 1997 Act was
providing a wide power to reform the procedural code in its entirety.
Consequently the judge exercised his discretion correctly. The judge's finding
that the defendant had 'no prospect *at all*' of successfully defending the claim was
amply justified in the circumstances of the case.

The submissions of the amicus curiae

Ms Sharp submitted that the learned judge was wrong to give summary
judgment for the complainant under CPR 24.2 for three reasons: (1) defendants in
libel actions had at that time a statutory right to have the material question
answered by the learned judge (ie that the words complained of were in fact
defamatory of the complainant) determined by the jury; (2) the statutory and
specific right had not been impliedly amended by the general permissive words of
the 1997 Act, nor of the CPR 24.2, delegated legislation under the Act; (3) the right

a to trial by jury is a substantive and important legal right, which it is beyond the power of the Civil Procedure Rules Committee to abolish or limit by its general powers to reform the rules of practice and procedure of the courts. Such a right may be amended by statute, indeed has since been amended by a provision of the Defamation Act 1996, not then in force, but not by subordinate legislation founded on an Act conferring a broad general power.

b She further submitted that in the particular circumstances of this case, there existed 'a reason' why the case or issue raised by the defendant should have been disposed of at a trial, and the learned judge should have exercised his power to make that direction under CPR 24.2(b).

Discussion and conclusion
c I take as my starting point the history and development of the statutory provision of trial by jury in defamation. Originally the question 'libel or no libel'—whether the words were defamatory of the plaintiff—was a question of law for the court (see *R v Shipley* (1784) 4 Doug KB 73 at 169). The Libel Act passed in 1792 (Fox's Act) is still in force; its title is 'An Act to remove doubts respecting function of juries in *d* cases of libel'. Although the Act was confined to criminal proceedings, the rules as to the respective functions of judge and jury in civil and criminal proceedings became assimilated. The effect of the Act was that the court could still give judgment for the defendant if in law the words complained of could not be a libel (see *Mulligan v Cole* (1875) LR 10 QB 549 cited and approved in *Capital and Counties Bank Ltd v George Henty & Sons* (1882) 7 App Cas 741 at 782, [1881–5] All ER Rep 86 *e* at 102). If the words were capable of being defamatory and of bearing the meaning complained of by the plaintiff, the question whether the publication complained of was *in fact* libellous was for the jury (see *Nevill v Fine Art and General Insurance Co Ltd* [1897] AC 68 at 72, [1895–9] All ER Rep 164 at 165 et seq).

All counsel contributed to the history of the material enactments leading up to *f* the 1981 Act. It is clear that the right to trial by jury in libel actions is preserved, save in special circumstances which are identified in the 1981 Act and which are not relevant here. The right is indelibly enshrined in statute and can only be removed or modified by subsequent Act of Parliament. Thus either party to an action for libel or slander in the High Court can claim as of right to have the action tried by a jury, unless the court or judge is of the opinion that the trial *g* requires any prolonged examination of documents or accounts or any specific or local investigation which cannot conveniently be made with a jury. Section 69(1) is mandatory in its terms:

> 'Where, on the application of any party to an action ... the court is satisfied
> that there is in issue ... (b) a claim in respect of libel, slander ... the action *shall*
h > be tried with a jury unless ...' (My emphasis.)

Moreover the concept of 'convenience' is confined to the three express statutory exceptions. These cannot be relevant to the determination of the ambit of the right given under s 69(1) or even how the right should be construed in the light *j* of subsequent legislation (as Ms Sharp succinctly put it).

I now turn to consider the effect upon this right of the 1997 Act and CPR 24.2 and whether the right already identified, which existed prior to the introduction of the CPR, has been removed by CPR 24.2.

Under the former regime there were limited circumstances in which libel actions could be determined under RSC Ord 18, r 19 and RSC Ord 82, r 3A. However, summary judgment could not be obtained by a plaintiff in any action

which included a claim for libel or slander (see RSC Ord 14, r 1(2)(a)). The *a*
commentary on RSC Ord 14 stated in terms:

> 'The Order does not apply to any actions specified in r.1(2) which are those
> in which there is a *right* to trial by jury (see O.33, r.5(1) and [Supreme Court
> Act] 1981, s.69) ...'

CPR 24.2 is in general terms only: '(a) it considers that ... (ii) that defendant has *b*
no prospect of successfully defending the claim or issue'. I am satisfied that an
application under CPR 24.2(a) can properly be made in order to determine certain
questions which fall within the jurisdiction of the judge in a libel action. These
include, for example, whether the words complained of were published on an
occasion of absolute privilege. On the other hand, the rule does not permit a judge
alone to determine questions of fact which Parliament has determined should be *c*
decided by a jury, and in particular, whether the words complained of are
defamatory of the claimant.

In my judgment, the right to trial by jury, and in particular to have the jury
determine the question 'libel or no libel' is not a matter of mere procedure, but an
important and substantive legal right. As such it is beyond the power of the Civil *d*
Procedure Rules Committee to abolish or limit by its general powers to reform the
rules of practice and procedure. Thus although the right may be amended by
statute this cannot be achieved by subordinate legislation founded on an Act
conferring a broad general power.

Since neither the 1997 Act nor CPR 24.2 makes express reference to defamation
actions, I am satisfied that the general provision in the CPR does not override the *e*
specific provisions of s 69(1) of the 1981 Act. This is so notwithstanding the terms
of s 1(3) of the 1997 Act which creates the power to make procedural rules with a
view to securing that the civil justice system is accessible, fair and efficient.
Section 4 enables the Lord Chancellor to amend, repeal or revoke any enactment
to the extent he considers necessary or desirable. This is a very wide power and is *f*
not confined to amendments etc which are merely consequential. In my judgment
it does not enable delegated legislation to repeal or amend primary legislation
which embodies a fundamental (as opposed to a procedural) right such as trial by
jury. Even if this power were wide enough it is intrinsically unlikely that delegated
legislation which purports to abolish such a fundamental right would do so without
express reference to the statutory right. To do so would be to remove the right by *g*
a casual change or a mere sidewind. This is particularly so where the right is
intertwined with a defendant's freedom of speech.

In reaching this conclusion I derive support from the structure of the 1996 Act
which came into force on 28 February 2000 together with its subordinate legislation
for summary disposal provided by CPR 53.2. The Act specifically provides for the *h*
summary disposal of libel actions and for that disposal to be determined without a
jury, albeit subject to specific limitations on the amount of damages which can be
recovered under this procedure. If the application for summary judgment had
come before Judge Green on or after 28 February 2000 it would have been within
his power to determine that the words were defamatory of the complainant, to give *j*
summary judgment for Safeway, to award damages up to £10,000 and to issue an
injunction. The fact that Parliament considered it necessary to make such separate
provision for defamation claims is an indicator that the CPR did not have the effect
contended for by Safeway.

In summary therefore it is beyond the power of the Civil Procedure Rules
Committee to limit the right to trial by jury or the right to have the question 'libel

a   or not libel' determined by the jury, by its general powers to reform the rules of practice in procedure of the courts. As the editor of Bennion *Statutory Interpretation* (3rd edn, 1997) p 627 states: 'The more fundamental the change, the more thoroughgoing and considered should be the provisions by which it is implemented.'

b   Finally, I return to consider the functions of the judge and jury in a defamation action. As Lord Denning MR said in *Ward v James* [1965] 1 All ER 563 at 571, [1966] 1 QB 273 at 295:

> 'It [trial by jury] has been the bulwark of our liberties too long for any of us to seek to alter it. Whenever a man is on trial for serious crime, or when in a civil case a man's honour or integrity is at stake ... then trial by jury has no
c   > equal.'

This recognition of the importance which English law has ascribed to trial by jury over the centuries has been frequently endorsed at the highest level before Blackstone and after Lord Devlin (see Devlin *Trial by Jury*, *The Hamlyn Lectures* (8th series, 1956) pp 164–165, 'Jury as Lamp of Freedom'). This is still as true
d   today as it has ever been.

The determination as to whether the words are defamatory normally involves a two-stage process: first, deciding what the words mean, second, deciding whether the meaning is defamatory of the claimant (see *Gatley on Libel and Slander* p 22 (para 2.1)). Thus unless there is any amendment express or implied of Fox's Act or the subsequent legislation it is for the jury to decide whether the facts are
e   in fact defamatory, and what meaning the words in fact bear. Thus the jury has an exclusive role and is subject only to the restriction that it is for the judge to rule whether the words are capable of defamatory meaning. The seminal statement of this principle is to be found in *Jones v Skelton* [1963] 3 All ER 952 at 958, [1963] 1 WLR 1362 at 1370 where Lord Morris of Borth-Y-Gest said:

f   > 'It is well settled that the question whether the words complained of are capable of conveying a defamatory meaning is a question of law and is therefore one calling for decision by the court. If the words are so capable it is a question for the jury to decide whether the words do in fact convey a defamatory meaning.'

g   It may be that the learned judge overlooked the distinction between the roles of the judge and jury in this respect. Alternatively he was not reminded of the distinction when the application was made. Whatever the cause, the learned judge unfortunately fell into error in assuming that he had the power to assume the role of the jury, when due to administrative error there was none available. The
h   position created by ss 8 and 9 of the 1996 Act apart, the issue of whether the words complained of are defamatory is still a question of fact to be determined by a jury because the question is reserved by Fox's Act and because actions for libel must, save in special circumstances which do not apply to this case, be tried by a jury. In this regard, I accept Mr Boggis-Rolfe's submission that meaning and damages are
j   connected and that it is not sensible to separate them and both ought to be before the jury. He cited in support the Supreme Court Procedure Committee's Report on Practice and Procedure in Defamation (1991) XXIV 5–6, pp 196–197. The fact that the plaintiff in the instant case did not seek damages but merely an injunction did not permit the judge to usurp unwittingly the jury's function in the way that he did.

I wish to conclude by expressing considerable sympathy for the learned judge, and, indeed, Mr Tate, the defendant. They both anticipated that there would be a trial by jury on the date fixed for trial. The jury had not been summoned and thus a gap appeared in the judge's busy schedule. Without prior notice Safeway sprang the application upon both of them. The absence of the jury did not create a situation to enable such an application to be made. Even if it did exist, it had existed from some time since the strike out of the purported defence of justification and should have been made on proper notice under the County Court Rules. There was no skeleton argument from Safeway. Mr Tate was a litigant in person without access to legal advice or assistance. It is perhaps not surprising that even this experienced judge acceded to the application without the assistance from counsel that he would normally be entitled to expect. The law of defamation is a specialised field and he may not have had readily to mind the distinct roles of judge and jury (or have had them pointed out to him). This is in sharp contrast to the assistance we have received in this court from counsel who are specialists in this field. Thus, although I can well understand the temptation to the learned judge to dispose of what might well have proved an expensive and time-consuming piece of litigation, it was not open to him to rule that the words complained of were defamatory of the complainant and to enter judgment for Safeway.

I would allow this appeal, set aside the judgment in favour of Safeway and discharge the injunction granted by Judge Green. As suggested by Mr Boggis-Rolfe, I would remit the case to the county court for a short jury trial at which the issues of meaning and damage can be decided by the jury. If a proper application or notice is made by the defendant that the words complained of are not capable of being defamatory this should be decided by the judge before the jury is empanelled. If the jury decides in favour of Safeway it will then be appropriate for the judge to consider the need for an injunction. In the meantime, in the absence of an undertaking by Mr Tate, the injunction of Blofeld J must remain.

MANTELL LJ. I agree.

SIR RONALD WATERHOUSE. I agree that this appeal should be allowed for the reasons stated by Otton LJ.

Appeal allowed.

Gillian Crew   Barrister.

a Alexander v Arts Council of Wales and another

[2001] EWCA Civ 514

b COURT OF APPEAL, CIVIL DIVISION
LORD WOOLF CJ, MAY AND JONATHAN PARKER LJJ
6 MARCH, 9 APRIL 2001

*Libel and slander – Qualified privilege – Malice avoiding privilege – Judge withdrawing
issue of malice from jury – Whether judge in error.*
c

*Jury – Trial by jury – Defamation – Proper roles of judge and jury in respect of issues of
fact – Supreme Court Act 1981, s 69 – CPR Pt 24.*

The claimant, A, was the director of a charity which owned and operated an arts
d centre in Cardiff. The charity formulated plans to build a new arts centre, and
asked ACW, a non-departmental public body which distributed National Lottery
grants and other funding from public sources to arts organisations in Wales, to
provide a commitment in principle to contribute to the funding of the project.
After ACW declined to give such a commitment, A issued a press release
criticising its decision. At a subsequent press briefing, ACW's chief executive, W,
e responded to questions on the subject. A alleged that W's reported comments
were defamatory, and he brought proceedings for libel and slander against her
and ACW. The defendants relied, inter alia, on the defence of qualified privilege.
In response, A claimed, inter alia, that W, and therefore ACW, were actuated by
express malice. Following submissions at the end of the evidence, the trial judge
f concluded that there was no evidence upon which a reasonable jury, properly
directed, could hold that W had been malicious. He therefore withdrew the issue
of malice from the jury and gave judgment for the defendants. On appeal, A
submitted that the case of malice depended on findings of fact which the judge
ought not to have withdrawn from the jury.

g **Held** – It was open to the judge in a libel case to conclude that a jury, properly
directed, could not properly reach a necessary factual conclusion, or that the only
jury decision capable of supporting the case in question would be bound to be set
aside on appeal as perverse. In those circumstances, it was the judge's duty, upon
a submission being made to him, to withdraw that issue from the jury. In the
h instant case, A's case on malice was unsound and artificial, without any proper
evidential basis. If the judge had left the issue of malice to the jury and they had
found in A's favour, the decision would have been set aside on appeal as perverse.
Accordingly, the judge had reached an entirely supportable conclusion, and the
appeal would therefore be dismissed (see [37], [38], [41], [44]–[47], below);
j *Kingshott v Associated Kent Newspapers Ltd* [1991] 2 All ER 99 considered.
  Per curiam. (1) If there is a material issue of fact in a libel case, s 69[a] of the
Supreme Court Act 1981 entitles a party to have that issue decided by the jury. It
is, however, for the judge to decide whether there really is such an issue. Just as
it is open to the judge to decide that a publication is incapable of bearing a

---

a   Section 69, so far as material, is set out at [48]–[49], below

defamatory meaning, so it is open to him to decide in an appropriate case that a
publication is incapable of not bearing a particular defamatory meaning and that   *a*
a jury's verdict to the contrary will be perverse. In those circumstances, there will
be nothing 'in issue' on which s 69 of the 1981 Act can operate. Conversely,
although the court has power under CPR Pt 24 to grant summary judgment in
defamation actions, Pt 24 does not give a right to summary judgment in such
actions where there are issues fit to be placed before a jury (see [39], [46], [47],   *b*
[51], [59], below); *Safeway Stores plc v Tate* [2001] 4 All ER 193 explained.

(2) It may be appropriate in a case such as the instant case to leave questions
to the jury, notwithstanding a judge's view on matters of law, in order to obviate
or mitigate the risk of an expensive new trial, should the judge's decision be
overturned on appeal (see [45]–[47], below).

c

Notes

For the judge's duty where malice is in issue, see 28 *Halsbury's Laws* (4th edn
reissue) para 243.

For the Supreme Court Act 1981, s 69, see 11 *Halsbury's Statutes* (4th edn) (2000
reissue) 1107.   *d*

Cases referred to in judgments

Adam v Ward [1917] AC 309, [1916–17] All ER Rep 157, HL.
Broadway Approvals Ltd v Odhams Press Ltd [1965] 2 All ER 523, [1965] 1 WLR 805, CA.
Colchester Oyster Fishery Ltd v Purslow (10 June 1997, unreported).   *e*
Heath v Humphreys (21 May 1990, unreported), CA.
Horrocks v Lowe [1974] 1 All ER 662, [1975] AC 135, [1974] 2 WLR 282, HL.
Kingshott v Associated Kent Newspapers Ltd [1991] 2 All ER 99, [1991] 1 QB 88, [1990]
   3 WLR 675, CA.
Loveless v Earl [1999] EMLR 530, CA.   *f*
R v Galbraith [1981] 2 All ER 1060, [1981] 1 WLR 1039, CA.
Safeway Stores plc v Tate [2001] 4 All ER 193, [2001] 2 WLR 1377, CA.
Somerville v Hawkins (1851) 10 CB 583, 138 ER 231.
Telnikoff v Matusevitch [1990] 3 All ER 865, [1991] 1 QB 102, [1990] 3 WLR 725, CA.
Turner (otherwise known as Robertson) v Metro-Goldwyn-Mayer Pictures Ltd [1950]   *g*
   1 All ER 449, HL.

Cases also cited or referred to in skeleton arguments

Cannock Chase DC v Kelly [1978] 1 All ER 152, [1978] 1 WLR 1, CA.
Daley v R [1993] 4 All ER 86, [1994] 1 AC 117, PC.   *h*
H (minors) (sexual abuse: standard of proof), Re [1996] 1 All ER 1, [1996] AC 563, HL.
R v Barker (1975) 65 Cr App R 287, CA.
Reynolds v Times Newspapers Ltd [1999] 4 All ER 609, [2000] 2 AC 127, HL.
Riches v News Group Newspapers Ltd [1985] 2 All ER 845, [1986] QB 256, CA.

j

Appeal

The claimant, Janek Alexander, appealed with permission of Simon Brown LJ
granted on 31 August 2000 from the decision of Eady J on 20 July 2000 whereby
he withdrew from the jury the claimant's action for libel and slander against the
defendants, the Arts Council of Wales and Joanna Weston, and gave judgment
for the defendants. The facts are set out in the judgment of May LJ.

a   *Patrick Milmo QC* and *William Bennett* (instructed by *Reynolds Porter Chamberlain*) for the claimant.

   Thomas Shields QC and *Timothy Atkinson* (instructed by *Edwards Geldard*) for the defendants.

Cur adv vult

b
9 April 2001. The following judgments were delivered.

MAY LJ.

Facts
c   **[1]** The Arts Council of Wales (ACW), the first defendant, is a non-departmental public body which distributes National Lottery grants and other funding from public sources to arts organisations in Wales. The second defendant, Joanna Weston, was until September 2000 ACW's chief executive. The claimant, Jan Alexander, is the director of Chapter Ltd (Chapter), a charity
d   which owns and runs the Chapter Arts Centre in Cardiff. Chapter is chiefly concerned with the promotion and performance of contemporary art. The claimant's position is equivalent to that of a chief executive. Over a number of years, ACW has made substantial grants of public money to Chapter both towards the cost of particular projects and also for revenue funding.

   [2] In about 1996, Chapter formulated plans to build a new arts centre on a
e   new site in Cardiff Bay. The estimated cost of this project was in excess of £5m. The claimant and Chapter were hoping to obtain a lottery grant to meet most of the cost. In September 1996, Chapter made a formal application to ACW for funds in the order of £60,000 for a feasibility study into this proposed project. The application was not promptly dealt with, but was deferred for various reasons.
f   After more than a year without progress, the claimant in exasperation appealed under the ACW code of practice and sought a finding of maladministration. This complaint was rejected in April 1998, but the hope was expressed that it might be possible for an urgent decision to be made by ACW in July 1998 at least as to its priorities. The hope was also expressed that ACW's strategy for lottery funding might soon be in place.

g   **[3]** The National Lottery Act 1998 received the royal assent at the beginning of July 1998 after which ACW received its detailed instructions from the government in relation to the distribution of lottery money. They had to develop a strategy for this. At one stage it was apparently envisaged that the strategy might be in place by the autumn of 1998. It was in fact finally in place by early
h   1999.

   [4] From September 1997, ACW had introduced a three-stage process for grant applications. This was well publicised in a document which stated that ACW would not consider large applications for grants towards construction projects until design plans had reached RIBA (Royal Institute of British
j   Architects) stage D. It was usual for applications for large projects to have three stages: (1) feasibility; (2) development; and (3) main project.

   [5] Chapter had sought additional funds from elsewhere and by March 1998 had obtained conditional offers of funding in excess of £1m. The main source of these funds was to be the European Regional Development Fund (ERDF). These funds would not be available indefinitely and the ERDF offer would lapse unless Chapter could be assured by the autumn of 1998 that lottery funds would be available.

[6] In June 1998, Chapter withdrew its original application for money to support a feasibility study. Instead it made a request in correspondence for ACW's capital committee to approve a commitment in principle to Chapter's project. The request was for a commitment in principle to a grant of £4·1m towards an estimated project cost of £5·8m, or £3·6m if the eventual total cost was £4·8m. Chapter's request meant that ACW were being asked to commit an amount that would be well in excess of half the funds available to it for the year for spending on the arts in Wales. It was also an unusual, if not unique, request because it asked for a commitment in principle in advance of the three-stage process to which I have referred. It appears, however, that Chapter may have received some encouragement to make a request of this kind.

[7] The request was considered by the capital committee of ACW on 25 June 1998. The second defendant was present at the meeting. The request was in effect rejected although, since it was not a formal application, it was not dealt with in the same way as other applications. The minutes of the meeting record that members did not feel able to make the requested commitment in advance of an agreed strategy giving a clearer indication of the priority to be given to Chapter's request. The recommendation of the capital committee was considered at a meeting of ACW itself at Llandudno on 17 July 1998, at which the recommendation of the capital committee was accepted. The second defendant was present at that meeting also. The claimant was told about this on 20 July 1998 and was clearly upset. One consequence of the decision was that the conditional ERDF funding would be lost.

[8] On 21 July 1998, the claimant issued a press release strongly critical of ACW's decision. This led to an article in the Western Mail of 22 July 1998 under the headline 'Anger as Arts Centre bid for Lottery cash rejected'. The article said that ACW had turned down a £3·6m lottery application; that it meant that more than £1m of European money would be lost and hundreds of jobs could be put at risk; that the claimant had described the decision as 'crazy' and accused members of living in a world of their own; and that it was understood that the application was rejected because ACW had decided to put a freeze on lottery applications from arts organisations based in Cardiff.

[9] The second defendant regarded this article as misleading, in particular because it gave the impression that ACW had turned down a normal application rather than an unusual request to commit funds in principle; and because it did not say that ACW were being asked to commit well over half its annual available funds. The second defendant was giving a press briefing, as it happened, on the morning of 22 July 1998. She expected to be asked questions on the subject, and she was. She spoke for several minutes and some of those present took notes. There were subsequent press and broadcast publications of what she said.

The proceedings

[10] In these proceedings, ACW and the second defendant are sued for slander and libel contained in those publications. There is a dispute as to precisely what she said and as to the accuracy of the reports of what she said. In his amended statement of claim, the claimant complains of the following words spoken by the second defendant at the press briefing:

'In this case we were asked to make a commitment in principle by the administrator/administrators of Chapter to a very large sum of money, and it was without that request being supported by a detailed development and *a*   business plan and all of the details that we always ask for before making a commitment to a large capital sum. It simply would not be a priority use of public money or accountable to make that commitment in principle. We have never done so, did not do so in this case and would not in the future.'

b   [11] The claimant attributes two possible meanings to that passage. The first is essentially innocuous and was scarcely supported at the trial as capable of carrying a serious defamation claim. The second meaning was as follows:

c   'In making such an application the plaintiff has shown himself to be reckless and/or negligent and/or incompetent in the performance of his job at Chapter and also as an arts administrator. Furthermore, it demonstrates that his attitude to the use of public funds is cavalier making him an unworthy custodian of them in his role as director of Chapter.'

d   [12] The claimant also relies on five further press or broadcast publications deriving from the press briefing. The content of the reports vary somewhat in detail and in some instances have additional material from an interview of the second defendant by a BBC journalist, Nick Palit; and from Emyr Williams, press officer of ACW. For present purposes, these publications are, with one qualification, essentially the same and essentially the same meanings are attributed to them.

e   [13] The qualification relates to a television broadcast on BBC Wales on 22 July 1998. The claimant by amendment alleges that, after the press briefing, the second defendant spoke with a BBC interviewer, Nick Palit, and that she said words to the effect that Chapter had not been given the money because they did not fill out the forms properly. The broadcast began with an introduction, written by Mr Palit, which ended with the words: 'However, the Arts Council say that they won't

f   contribute because the grant application wasn't submitted properly.'

[14] This sentence is relied on as conveying what the second defendant had said and consequently as being a defamatory publication by her. The broadcast continued with Mr Palit saying that the ACW had refused to contribute, as they said they had received no formal application. The second defendant then said:

g   'What they were asking [ACW] to do was to make a commitment in principle to an amount of £3·8m. Now it would not be a proper use of public funds for the Arts Council to say: "In principle we'll give you nearly four million pounds, and then come back and tell us what you're doing with it."'

h   [15] In their defence, the defendants deny that the claimant has accurately recorded the substance of what the second defendant said. They deny the meanings contended for by the claimant. They plead that the publications were on occasions of qualified privilege. By his reply, the claimant disputed that the occasions were privileged and contended in the alternative that the second defendant, and therefore ACW, were actuated by express malice.

j   [16] The action came for trial before Eady J and a jury and the hearing lasted for about eight days. At the end of the evidence, the judge heard submissions as a result of which, on 20 July 2000, he withdrew the case from the jury and gave judgment for the defendants. This is the claimant's appeal against that decision. Simon Brown LJ gave permission to appeal.

The judge's decision

[17] It was submitted to the judge that none of the words relied on were capable of bearing a defamatory meaning. The judge considered that there were powerful arguments to that effect and to the effect that the second defendant would not be held responsible for any inaccurate summaries in subsequent publications of what she had said. However, since what she had said was in a number of respects in dispute, the judge did not think that it would be right for him to pre-empt the jury's decision on what she did say and as to the meaning of what she said. He observed that he was not the judge of fact in the case. He reached a similar conclusion on a contention that there was no evidence capable of establishing that what the second defendant said referred to the claimant. But he concluded, without any hesitation at all, that the occasion on which the second defendant was speaking on 22 July 1998 and the subsequent publication did attract the defence of qualified privilege. He gave extended reasons for this, which it is not necessary to rehearse in detail since the finding is not challenged on this appeal. In short summary, he concluded that the second defendant was speaking on a topic of public interest and that she had a duty to communicate a response to a published attack that the claimant had made on ACW; and that the media recipients of what she said and the public generally had an interest to receive her response. The judge expressed his conclusion in these terms:

'It seems to me that the matter can be put on both bases, that is to say the general duty/interest test and the "reply to an attack" test. I prefer to place the matter on the more general footing by saying that this was a matter concerning public funding and decisions made in relation to it which were likely to have a considerable impact on the arts in South Wales. It seems to me to be clear that someone in Miss Weston's position had a duty to explain, as far as she could, the nature of the decision and, if pressed upon it, the reasons for the decision. That is particularly so in a case where the matter had been placed in the public domain very recently and had thereby become a matter of legitimate interest.'

[18] The judge then turned to the issue of malice. He said that this had to be seen against the background that ACW had supported Chapter very substantially over a number of years. The allegation was that the second defendant was malicious in what she said at the press briefing. The judge referred to long-established principles and particularly the exposition of the law by Lord Diplock in *Horrocks v Lowe* [1974] 1 All ER 662, [1975] AC 135, from which it was clear that malice is a very serious allegation and generally tantamount to dishonesty. The case was either that the second defendant had no honest belief in the words she spoke or that she had ulterior dominant motives to blame the claimant and thus to divert critical attention away from herself and ACW. The judge understood the main case to be the first of these, that is that the second defendant told the assembled journalists on 22 July 1998 something which she knew to be false.

[19] The judge cited very well-known passages from the speech of Lord Diplock in *Horrocks'* case. He said that it was rare for malice to be found at all, but that he had never known a case in which malice had been found without there being dishonesty on the part of the defendant.

[20] The essence of the claimant's case, as advanced by Mr Milmo QC on his behalf, was that the second defendant was saying that 'the grant *application* was not submitted properly'. The judge emphasised the word 'application' because Chapter had not in fact made a formal application, only a request for a commitment

a in principle. The form of expression derived from Nick Palit's introduction to a BBC Wales broadcast—one of the subsequent publications relied on. Mr Milmo relied on the fact that the second defendant had admitted that, if she had said that the grant application was not submitted properly, it was not true and she would have known that it was not true. It was, of course, her evidence that she had not said this. Mr Milmo's submission was that there was substantial evidence that the

b reasons given at the press briefing, according to the evidence of the claimant and Mr Palit, were not the true reasons for ACW's decision nor for the decision of its capital committee. The minutes of the capital committee meeting only record as a reason the absence of a finalised funding strategy. The judge regarded this as an artificial division into watertight compartments. The fact that this was a unique request for commitment of funds in principle was obviously a factor that would

c have been in the minds of those considering it. Mr Edge, Mr Roberts and the second defendant had all given evidence to that effect. The judge considered evidence which in his view made it clear that there was no attempt by ACW to hide the fact that the lottery capital strategy was not in place in the summer of 1998 and he did not see how the omission by the second defendant to mention this at the

d press briefing on 22 July 1998 was capable of amounting to malice.

[21] The judge referred to submissions by Mr Shields QC on behalf of the defendants to substantially the same effect as those which he advances in opposition to this appeal. The judge reminded himself of the important distinction between his role and that of the jury in relation to malice. He observed that only the second defendant remained in contention in the context of malice. He said that

e for his present purposes he had to make certain assumptions. The first was that the claimant succeeded in proving that the second defendant spoke the words attributed to her at the press briefing. The second assumption was that a jury might possibly infer that there was an implication in those words to reasonable listeners that the claimant had failed to supply all the information for which he had been

f asked. The judge also assumed that the words were free standing, in the sense that they were not prefaced by a detailed explanation emphasising the distinction between the unique request for a commitment in principle and the usual circumstances in which a formal application is made to ACW for funding. He reminded himself that he was concerned with the second defendant's state of mind—he had previously referred to what Hirst LJ had said in *Loveless v Earl* [1999]

g EMLR 530 at 538–539—this in contrast with the objective test to be applied in determining what a publication means. The judge then said:

> 'It is to my mind manifest that Miss Weston was saying that at least one reason why the request could not be accepted was that the ACW did not have
>
> *h* the information that usually accompanies a commitment to funding of this order; ie in the case of an application. There is no evidence from which it could be inferred that she was *intending* to convey the idea that Mr Alexander had failed to provide what he was asked for. There are three messages contained in the words alleged to have been spoken and I will identify them as follows:
>
> *j* (1) that ACW were being asked to make a commitment "in principle" to a very large sum of money; (2) the request was made without being supported by a detailed development and business plan and all of the details that ACW always ask for before making a commitment to a large capital sum; (3) it would not be a proper use of public money to make a commitment in principle and, what is more, ACW had never done so and was unlikely to do so in the future. It is possible always to criticise ex tempore words on the basis that they could have

been better drafted or expressed. It may be, for example, that if Miss Weston had inserted after the words "the details that we always ask for" an additional phrase along the lines of "on a standard application", it might have been clearer to listeners unfamiliar with ACW procedures, but what matters in this context is what she *intended* to convey.'

[22] The judge said that if there was evidence to justify any other intention, he should obviously leave it to the jury. Mr Milmo had placed considerable reliance on what the second defendant was supposed to have said to Mr Palit after the conclusion of the press briefing. The judge said that, on the face of it, this would appear not to be relevant to what the second defendant was saying at the press briefing. Mr Milmo's submission, however, was that this demonstrated and the jury might conclude that what she said to Mr Palit was her state of mind throughout. It was submitted that the effect of that evidence was that the second defendant had been telling Mr Palit that Chapter's request had been rejected simply because Chapter did not fill out the forms properly. The judge referred in detail to Mr Palit's written and oral evidence. He emphasised that the written statement was made just over 18 months after the events in question and that the evidence was at a number of points imprecise as to what the second defendant had said. The judge observed that, if the second defendant had actually said that the forms had not been filled out properly, that would have been an astonishing lie because there were no forms for the unique situation of a request for a commitment in principle. He said that, if there was evidence upon which a reasonable person could conclude that she had spoken such a lie, then he should obviously leave it to the jury for their consideration. He set alongside Mr Palit's evidence the evidence given by the second defendant, which he referred to in detail. He said that the passages to which he had referred from Mr Palit's evidence, when set alongside her clear denials, were so unclear and equivocal that they could not be relied on for the purpose of concluding that the second defendant said anything to the effect that the forms had not been filled out properly.

[23] The judge accordingly concluded that there was no evidence upon which a reasonable jury, properly directed, could hold that the second defendant was malicious in either of the senses for which Mr Milmo contended. On this basis he withdrew the issue of malice from the jury.

Grounds of appeal and submissions

[24] The grounds of appeal are limited to contending that the judge was wrong not to leave the issue of malice to the jury. It is said that the judge should not have concluded that Mr Palit's evidence was unclear and equivocal. It is said that an issue relevant to malice was what words the second defendant actually spoke at the press briefing, their context and their meaning; and that the judge had correctly decided that these questions were for the jury to decide. In concluding that there was no evidence from which it could be inferred that the second defendant was intending to convey the idea that the claimant had failed to provide what he was asked for, the judge contradicted one of his own assumptions and made a decision of fact which ought to have been left to the jury. The judge was wrong to conclude that the fact that no mention was made at the press briefing of the only recorded reason for rejecting Chapter's request was not capable of contributing to a finding of malice. Further, the judge was wrong to rely on his own experience that an allegation of malice very rarely succeeds.

a   [25] Mr Milmo submits that, although the claimant's case on ulterior motive was not withdrawn, his primary case was that the second defendant had no honest or positive belief in the truth of what she said. The suggested ulterior motive—to divert attention from the embarrassing true reason for rejecting Chapter's request—supported and explained the primary case. Mr Milmo submits that the strongest evidence in support of this came from Mr Palit's evidence. In both his
b   written statement and oral evidence, Mr Palit said that the second defendant had told him in the course of the conversation preceding her filmed statement to be shown on television that 'Chapter did not fill in the forms correctly'. From this, Mr Palit derived the introductory words which he spoke on the BBC Wales programme that ACW would not contribute 'because the grant application wasn't submitted properly'. The second defendant had admitted that, if she had said this,
c   it would have been untrue and she would have known it to be untrue. If the jury had accepted Mr Palit's evidence, there would be direct and conclusive evidence of malice for the BBC Wales broadcast and a strong inference of malice for what she had said at the press briefing. There was an issue of fact as to what she had said to Mr Palit and the judge was wrong to withdraw this question from the jury. The
d   critical facts were (a) the statement to Mr Palit, which was according to his evidence untrue; (b) the part of the BBC Wales broadcast deriving from this spoken by the introducer, which was the most serious libel; and (c) the second defendant's concealment of the only or principal reason for ACW's decision to reject Chapter's request. Mr Milmo submits that if these facts were proved, they were capable of amounting to malice.

e   [26] Mr Milmo submits that the judge's reasons for concluding that Mr Palit's evidence was unclear and equivocal were sparse and unsound. He ignored the fact that the introductory words to the broadcast were written within hours of the conversation. The judge had concluded that issues as to what was said and as to meaning should be left to the jury. Yet when it came to the question of malice, he
f   withdrew from the jury what was in effect an issue as to what was said which, on the claimant's case, found its way into Mr Palit's introduction to the broadcast and contained the alleged sting of the defamation. Further, the judge made conclusions as to what the second defendant intended to say, but in the course of doing so himself made a finding about what she said which ought to have been left to the jury. In *Loveless'* case, the Court of Appeal said that the subjective intention of a
g   defendant was an issue for the jury. The judge concluded that there was no evidence from which it could be inferred that the second defendant was intending to convey that the claimant had failed to provide what he was asked for. But Mr Palit's evidence would, if it were accepted, be cogent evidence that she was intending to give a false and misleading reason for the rejection by ACW of
h   Chapter's request for funding in principle. Mr Milmo further submits that, in failing to include at the press briefing the sole reason recorded in the minutes for the decision of ACW's capital committee, it was open to the jury to conclude that the second defendant had intended to mislead and misinform the public. In summary, the submission is that the case of malice depended on findings of fact which the
j   judge ought not to have withdrawn from the jury.

[27] Mr Shields submits that the claimant's essential case on malice depended on establishing that the second defendant gave dishonest reasons at the press briefing for ACW's decision to reject the request for funding in principle. He submits that the case on malice advanced by the claimant at trial fell apart for the reasons given by the judge and that it is a travesty to suggest that the whole case of malice depended upon Mr Palit's evidence. Mr Shields submits that the crux of the

claimant's original case on malice was that the second defendant, on behalf of
ACW, published or caused to be published the words complained of as part of a
dishonest scheme, in which others participated, to promote a cynical agenda of
misinformation designed to divert criticism from ACW in relation to its rejection of
Chapter's request and the reasons for it. In essence, this case fell apart because the
facts supporting the ulterior motive—that is, that ACW did not have in place a
strategy for lottery funding—were made known publicly and known to Chapter
before the events giving rise to the publications complained of; and because a case
of dishonesty by anyone other than the second defendant was not maintained.
Mr Shields submits that the claimant has attempted to construct an artificial case of
malice where none existed. He refers to *Broadway Approvals Ltd v Odhams Press Ltd*
[1965] 2 All ER 523 at 534, [1965] 1 WLR 805 at 815, where Sellers LJ said that malice
was not to be established by forensic imagination however eloquently and subtly
expressed. The claimant had accepted that there was no previous history of
animosity or ill will by the second defendant towards the claimant.

[28] Mr Shields submits that there was no case based upon improper motive.
Instead the claimant attempted to rely on the assertion that the second defendant
had no honest belief in the words she is alleged to have spoken at the press briefing
by elevating the evidence of Mr Palit to a status which it did not deserve. Mr Palit
did not sign a written witness statement until nearly 18 months after the press
briefing. The claimant's reliance on the conversation which was said to have taken
place before the press briefing was not pleaded as a particular of malice until four
months after that. Mr Palit admitted that he knew almost nothing about Chapter's
request before the press briefing. As a busy journalist, he was inherently unlikely
to have any reliable memory of a short conversation with the second defendant
immediately following the press briefing. There was no indirect corroboration of
the conversation because Eleri Morgan, the Welsh-speaking BBC Wales journalist
who accompanied Mr Palit and was present throughout, was not called to give
evidence. Mr Shields submits that the judge's approach towards Mr Palit's evidence
was both careful and consistent with authority and that his decision that the
evidence was unclear and equivocal was correct. The judge correctly applied the
principles in *Loveless'* case. He accepted for the purpose of his ruling that the
claimant's version of the publication of the press briefing was established and to be
taken as free-standing. He analysed the words complained of against the evidence
properly capable of establishing directly or by inference the second defendant's
state of mind and he then applied the proper test. He correctly found in the light of
all the evidence that it would be utterly fanciful for a jury, properly directed, to
conclude that the second defendant had any dishonest intention.

[29] As to the law, Mr Shields submits that it was for the judge to decide whether
there is any evidence of express malice fit to be left to the jury—that is, whether
there is any evidence on which a reasonable man could find malice (see *Adam v
Ward* [1917] AC 309 at 318, [1916–17] All ER Rep 157 at 162). He submits that it is
not enough, in order to prove malice, for the claimant to show that the defendant
published words which objectively bore a meaning which the defendant did not
believe to be true, if the defendant did not subjectively intend to convey that
meaning. As Hirst LJ said in *Loveless'* case [1999] EMLR 530 at 538–539:

'Here, it is very important to contrast the test for meaning on the one hand
and the test for malice on the other. Meaning is an objective test, entirely
independent of the defendant's state of mind or intention. Malice is a
subjective test, entirely dependent on the defendant's state of mind and

a　　intention. Thus, in a case where words are ultimately held objectively to bear meaning A, if the defendant subjectively intended not meaning A but meaning B, and honestly believed meaning B to be true, then the plaintiff's case on malice would be likely to fail.'

[30] Hirst LJ then referred to the judgment of Lord Donaldson MR in *Heath v Humphreys* (21 May 1990, unreported), in which Lord Donaldson quoted from the
b　speech of Lord Diplock in *Horrocks's* case [1974] 1 All ER 662, [1975] AC 135, and then continued:

'I think that this passage requires some qualification by the addition of a further exceptional case. Since, as Lord Diplock emphasised, the public interest essentially requires protection for freedom of communication honestly
c　　exercised, what matters is that the publisher shall believe in the truth of what he intends to say. If, from his viewpoint, his remarks are misconstrued, he would be likely to be the first to say "I never believed in the truth of that" or "I never considered whether or not that was true". If such an answer would take him outside the protection of qualified privilege, its purpose would on
d　　occasion be wholly undermined. Putting it another way, in such circumstances the defamer cannot be said to be "telling deliberate and injurious falsehoods". At worst, he is doing so unintentionally.'

[31] Mr Shields submits that the present is a paradigm case of inducing the second defendant to accept that, if she had said what she denies saying, it would
e　have been untrue; and then constructing a case of malice, based on forensic ingenuity but no substance, on the contention that the jury might find that she said that which she denies saying. Mr Shields submits that the essential question is what subjectively she intended to say.

[32] Mr Shields submits that the correct legal test is that a case of malice should
f　be withdrawn from the jury if the evidence does not raise a probability of malice. He refers to *Gately on Libel and Slander* (8th edn, 1981) p 349 (paras 794 and 795). He relies in particular on para 795, which stated as follows:

'*Plaintiff must adduce probability of malice at least.* In order to enable the plaintiff to have the question of malice submitted to the jury, it is necessary that
g　　the evidence should raise a probability of malice and "be more consistent with its existence than with its non-existence." "It is not sufficient if it falls short of that and is consistent only with a *mere* possibility. To direct a jury to consider mere possibilities in such a case would be practically to destroy the protection which the law throws over privileged communications."'

h　　[33] There is now a 9th edition of *Gatley on Libel and Slander* (1998), which, at para 34.18 (p 863), states the law in slightly different terms. But the two paragraphs from the 8th edition were referred to with approval by this court in *Telnikoff v Matusevitch* [1990] 3 All ER 865 at 879, [1991] 1 QB 102 at 120, with reference to *Somerville v Hawkins* (1851) 10 CB 583 at 590, 138 ER 231 at 234 and *Turner (otherwise
j　known as Robertson) v Metro-Goldwyn-Mayer Pictures Ltd* [1950] 1 All ER 449 at 455; and see also *Colchester Oyster Fishery Ltd v Purslow* (10 June 1997, unreported), Eady J.

Discussion and conclusions

[34] The classic passage from the speech of Lord Diplock in *Horrocks'* case [1974] 1 All ER 662 at 668–670, [1975] AC 135 at 149–150, in which he enunciates the law relating to malice in libel cases, is too well known to require extended citation. For

present purposes the essential features are as follows. To entitle a person to the protection of qualified privilege, he has to have a positive belief in the truth of what he published. Such a belief is presumed unless the contrary is proved, and so the burden of establishing malice lies on the person who asserts it, in this instance the claimant. What the claimant has to establish is a dominant and improper motive on the part of the defendant comprising a desire to injure the claimant. This dominant motive can only be inferred from what the defendant did or said or knew. If it is proved that he did not believe that what he published was true, that is generally conclusive evidence of express malice. But a person may have an honest belief in what he publishes despite imperfection of the mental process by which the belief is arrived at. To this may be added the important clarification that, to establish malice, what has to be inferred is the defendant's subjective state of mind and intention (see the passage from the judgment of Hirst LJ in *Loveless'* case, to which I have already referred). There is also the point made by Lord Donaldson MR in *Heath's* case that malice is not to be inferred from the hypothetical untruth of a proposition derived from a misconstruction of a publication. In my view, it is important to emphasise in the present context that the essential question is necessarily one of inference; and that the motive which the claimant has to establish relates to the defamatory publication. In the present case, as I shall indicate, the evidence which Mr Milmo relies on as containing an issue of fact fit to go before the jury did not directly relate to the publications which the claimant had to rely on.

[35] The respective functions of judge and jury in libel actions have recently been considered by this court in *Safeway Stores plc v Tate* [2001] 4 All ER 193, [2001] 2 WLR 1377. In that case, there was a boundary dispute between the parties. Arising out of this, the defendant placed placards in the garden of his house and elsewhere containing the words 'Safeway: where fraud ideas come naturally'. Safeway brought libel proceedings. Mr Tate represented himself. A defence of justification was struck out. The remaining defence only put the claimant to proof that the words bore a defamatory meaning and were published as alleged. Mr Tate had never denied publication, and so the only question was whether the words published were defamatory. The judge gave summary judgment for the claimant under CPR Pt 24. The defendant appealed. It was submitted that, under s 69 of the Supreme Court Act 1981, a defendant in a libel action had a statutory right to have the material question determined by a jury and that CPR Pt 24 either had not removed that right or, if it purported to do so, had no power to remove it.

[36] The leading judgment was given by Otton LJ with whom Mantell LJ and Sir Ronald Waterhouse agreed. Otton LJ considered the historical antecedents of s 69 of the 1981 Act and the extent to which, under the former Rules of the Supreme Court, it was open to the judge to determine questions of law or abuse of process. He observed that the court had formerly no power to give summary judgment in favour of a plaintiff; although by contrast the court did have power under RSC Ord 18, r 19 and RSC Ord 82, r 3A to make determinations which could have the effect of giving summary judgment for the defendant. He was satisfied that under the CPR, an application under CPR 24.2(a) could properly be made in order to determine questions which fall within the jurisdiction of a judge in a libel action. On this basis, therefore, it is now possible in an appropriate case for a claimant to obtain summary judgment in a libel action under CPR Pt 24—in addition to the possibility of doing so under the special provisions of the Defamation Act 1996. This would be so if there were no issues other than those which fall within the jurisdiction of the judge. Otton LJ considered, however, that it was beyond the power of the Civil Procedure Rules Committee to limit the right to trial by jury or

a the right to have the question 'libel or not libel' determined by the jury. He also declined to anticipate the possibility that the verdict of a jury on this or other matters within the province of the jury might be perverse and such that it would be reversed on appeal.

[37] There is of course a variety of possible circumstances in libel cases in which issues of law may arise for decision by the judge. In so far as questions of this kind

b properly depend on an evaluation of evidence so as to determine material questions of disputed fact, these are matters for the jury. But, as Mr Milmo accepted in the present appeal, it is open to the judge in a libel case to come to the conclusion that the evidence, taken at its highest, is such that a jury properly directed could not properly reach a necessary factual conclusion. In those circumstances, it is the judge's duty, upon a submission being made to him, to withdraw that issue from

c the jury. This is the test applied in criminal jury trials (see *R v Galbraith* [1981] 2 All ER 1060 at 1062, [1981] 1 WLR 1039 at 1042). In my view, it applies equally in libel actions. It is in substance the test which the judge set himself to apply in the present case.

[38] Mr Milmo also drew our attention to the judgment of Bingham LJ in

d *Kingshott v Associated Kent Newspapers Ltd* [1991] 2 All ER 99 at 107, [1991] 1 QB 88 at 99. In that case, a question arose under s 7 of the Defamation Act 1952 whether a newspaper article was a fair and accurate report of proceedings at a local public inquiry. The judge ruled that no reasonable jury properly directed could conclude that the words complained of were other than a fair and accurate report of the proceedings. Bingham LJ accepted that this was the correct test, but was not

e persuaded that the jury could not attach decisive weight to any of the plaintiff's points or to those points cumulatively. Relevantly for present purposes, he asked himself whether, if the issue were left to the jury and the jury found for the plaintiffs, that verdict would be set aside as perverse. His answer in that appeal was that he did not think it would. His judgment, however, shows that, if in a libel

f action a party's case depends on a finding of fact by the jury which, if it were so found, is bound to be set aside on appeal as perverse, the judge should withdraw that issue from the jury in the first place. In my view, this is not, as was suggested in the *Safeway* case, speculating that the jury *might* reach a perverse decision: rather that the only jury decision capable of supporting the case in question would be bound to be set aside on appeal.

g [39] As is evident from Otton LJ's judgment, the first instance judge had decided that Mr Tate had no real prospect of success on the question whether the words complained of were defamatory ([2001] 4 All ER 193 at 198, [2001] 2 WLR 1377 at 1381). He had held that the power to give summary judgment was discretionary. He had accordingly made an evaluative decision on an issue which Otton LJ held

h should have been left to the jury. The *Safeway* case is thus a decision binding on this court to the effect that, if there is a material issue of fact in a libel case, s 69 of the 1981 Act entitles a party to have that issue decided by the jury. It is, however, for the judge to decide whether there really is such an issue. In my view, just as it is open to the judge to decide that a publication is not capable of bearing a defamatory

j meaning, so it is open to the judge to decide in an appropriate case that a publication is not capable of not bearing a particular defamatory meaning and that a jury's verdict to the contrary would be perverse. In those circumstances, there would be nothing 'in issue' on which s 69 of the 1981 Act could operate.

[40] I agree with Mr Milmo that the principles to which I have just referred apply to questions of primary fact. I agree with Mr Shields that the crucial question in this case of the second defendant's subjective state of mind is a matter of inference. It

was a question for the judge to decide whether available primary facts were capable
of supporting the necessary inference. The authorities to which Mr Shields referred
overlay this question with a further question whether the evidence raises a
probability of malice, rather than a mere possibility. But I do not think that it is
necessary, in order to resolve this appeal, to extend the inquiry that far.

[41] In my judgment, the claimant's case on malice is an unsound and artificial
one, forensically constructed without any proper evidential basis. The artificiality
starts with the meanings of the publications for which the claimant contends.
Although the judge decided, with evident lack of enthusiasm, that what the second
defendant said at the press briefing and subsequently was in issue, and that the
terms of the publications, their meanings and whether they were defamatory
should be left to the jury, I am far from convinced that this was a correct decision.
Mr Milmo correctly points out that this part of the judge's decision is not subject to
appeal. But it is necessary to explain briefly how, in my view, this contributes to the
artificiality of the claimant's case on malice. I leave aside disputes as to what the
second defendant said at the press briefing. It is sufficient to concentrate on the
publications for which the claimant contends. These are set out in para 7 of the
amended statement of claim, which I have set out earlier in this judgment, and the
relevant parts of the transcript of the BBC Wales broadcast which, assuming they
are correctly transcribed, are not amenable to dispute. As to the publication
contended for in para 7 of the amended statement of claim, it seems to me that this
means what it says—an expression which libel pleaders never seem to use—and
that the meaning attributed to it in para 9.2 of the amended statement of claim,
which I have already set out, is scarcely capable in any context of being its meaning.
The fact that the judge was persuaded to assume that this was its meaning
contributed to the artificial submission that the second defendant may have
intended that meaning and that, if she did, she knew that it was untrue. The same
essentially applies to the terms of the transcript of the BBC Wales broadcast. The
sentence at the end of the announcer's introduction, taken by itself, is a much
modified version of that which Nick Palit said in evidence the second defendant had
said to him. But that single sentence, taken together with and in the context of what
the second defendant herself said in the broadcast almost immediately after it
(which Mr Milmo accepts was not defamatory), is scarcely capable of supporting
the defamatory meaning contended for.

[42] The critical question for the judge was whether there was any evidence,
taken at its highest, on which a jury properly directed could properly infer that the
second defendant subjectively did not honestly believe that what she intended to
say in the publications relied on was true. In substance, what she may or may not
have said to Nick Palit was not part of the publications relied on other than to the
extent that it may have found its way into the BBC Wales broadcast itself. (Mr
Milmo did not suggest that oral publication to Nick Palit alone would sustain a
serious defamation case.) Thus, although there may have been a vestige of a case
that the publications contended for might objectively have had the meanings
contended for, there was no proper inferential case that the second defendant
subjectively intended that meaning.

[43] This was essentially what the judge decided. He understood the case to be
primarily that the second defendant told the assembled journalists on 22 July 1998
something she knew to be false in order to deflect criticism from ACW. He was
thus, correctly in my view, concentrating on her state of mind as to the publications
relied on. He examined the case for ulterior motive, which he found to be
insubstantial for reasons which I have already described. He referred to the reason

a recorded in the minutes of the capital committee meeting of 25 June 1998. He was entitled, in my view, in the light of the uncontradicted evidence of Mr Edge, Mr Roberts and the second defendant to conclude that the fact that it was a unique request for commitment of funds in principle was obviously a factor that would have been in the minds of those considering it. Importantly, the judge was correct to conclude that there was no evidence from which it could be inferred that the

b second defendant was intending to convey the idea that the claimant had failed to provide what he was asked for. He was correct to conclude that there was no alternative interpretation than that the second defendant was intending to point out the contrast between the information sought when there was a formal application and that which was provided on this unique occasion.

[44] Mr Milmo concentrated his submissions in this appeal on the divergent
c evidence of Mr Palit and the second defendant in relation to what she may have said to him after the press briefing. This tends to overlook the fact that the judge introduced his consideration of this evidence by saying that, on the face of it, it would appear not to be relevant to what she was saying at the press briefing. In my view, the judge was correct here. As I have already indicated, the critical first
d question was to determine what subjectively the second defendant intended to convey by the publications relied on. In the circumstances of this case, where the *objective* meaning contended for is scarcely supportable, a *subjective* dishonest intention is not in my view reasonably capable of being sustained by what she is alleged to have said on another occasion, but which she denies saying. The claimant's artificial case on malice is yet further undermined by the critique of
e Mr Palit's evidence which the judge undertook. As a matter of objective fact, Chapter's request was not rejected because they did not fill in forms properly, and the judge was correct to conclude that the second defendant cannot have intended to say this in the publications relied on. I am satisfied that, if the judge had left the issue of malice to the jury and they had found in the claimant's favour, this court
f would have set that decision aside as being perverse.

[45] For these reasons, in my judgment the judge reached an entirely supportable conclusion which I would not disturb on appeal. I would, however, wish to add a note of caution. The judge made his ruling after about eight days of evidence in what must have been a very expensive trial. As has appeared, there was a risk of his decision being overturned on appeal, in which event this court would
g probably have had to order a new trial. On the face of it, that would have been disproportionately expensive but may have been unavoidable. The word of caution is simply to draw attention to the possibility in cases such as this of leaving questions to the jury, notwithstanding a judge's view on matters of law, to obviate or mitigate the risk of an expensive new trial. That possibility was discussed by
h Bingham LJ in *Kingshott's* case [1991] 2 All ER 99 at 108, [1991] 1 QB 88 at 101. Having said that, I acknowledge that the possibility was not debated before this court and that there may have been complications in the present case arising from the judge's other decisions which would have made the course there suggested inappropriate.

j **JONATHAN PARKER LJ.**
[46] I agree with the judgments of both May LJ and Lord Woolf CJ.

LORD WOOLF CJ.
[47] I have read the judgment of May LJ and I agree with it and the result he proposes. In those circumstances I would not normally have given a judgment.

However, I do so because of the case of *Safeway Stores plc v Tate* [2001] 4 All ER 193, [2001] 2 WLR 1377 to which May LJ refers. The result of the judgment of Eady J in the court below was to withdraw from the jury the issue as to whether the second defendant was malicious in making the publication complained of. His view as to malice, that a jury could not make a finding that the second defendant made the publications maliciously, was fatal to the claimant's case since unless she was malicious, the claimant could not succeed in his action.

[48], [49] The decision in the *Safeway* case was concerned with the circumstances in which it would be appropriate for a court to give summary judgment to a claimant under CPR 24.2 in a defamation action bearing in mind the provisions of s 69 of the Supreme Court Act 1981 which provides:

> 'Trial by Jury.—(1) Where, on the application of any party to an action to be tried in the Queen's Bench division, the court is satisfied that there is in issue ... (b) a claim in respect of libel, slander, malicious prosecution or false imprisonment ... the action shall be tried with a jury, unless the court is of opinion that the trial requires any prolonged examination of documents or accounts or any scientific or local investigation which cannot conveniently be made with a jury.'

[50] CPR 24.2 provides:

> **'Grounds for summary judgment**
> The court may give summary judgment against a claimant or defendant on the whole of a claim or on a particular issue if—(a) it considers that—(i) that claimant has no real prospect of succeeding on the claim or issue; or (ii) that defendant has no real prospect of successfully defending the claim or issue; and (b) there is no other compelling reason why the case or issue should be disposed of at a trial.
>
> (Rule 3.4 makes provision for the court to strike out a statement of case or part of a statement of case if it appears that it discloses no reasonable grounds for bringing or defending a claim.)'

[51] The terms of CPR 24.3 make clear that the CPR intended to give the court power to grant a summary judgment in defamation actions. This is because CPR 24.3 specifically states: '[t]he court may give summary judgment against a claimant in any type of proceedings'. (The power is then expressly excluded in relation to a limited group of proceedings against a defendant and CPR 24.1 recognises that summary disposal is also available in the case of defamation claims in accordance with the 1996 Act.)

[52] The fact that summary judgment can be given in defamation proceedings distinguishes the position under the CPR from that which existed under RSC Ord 14. As the White Book (*Civil Procedure* (2001), vol 1, p 399, para 24.4.2) points out, '[t]he question whether summary judgment should be granted may be raised at trial'.

[53] The relevance of the *Safeway* case to the present proceedings is that, in the *Safeway* case, this court, in a decision which is binding upon us, decided that the circuit judge in that case had been wrong to give summary judgment to a claimant under CPR Pt 24 since this would deprive a defendant of his right to trial by jury. In a judgment, with which the other members of the court agreed, Otton LJ concluded—

> 'that CPR 24.2 is ultra vires s 1(3) of the Civil Procedure Act 1997 in so far as it purports to deprive or impinge upon the right to trial by jury. If CPR 24.2 is

not ultra vires then it has to be read, as suggested by the editors of the White Book (*Civil Procedure* (Autumn 2000), vol 1, p 383, para 24.2.4), to mean that the fact that the respondent may have a right to trial by jury may, of itself be a reason for a trial. Extreme caution is appropriate before removing such a fundamental right.' (See [2001] 4 All ER 193 at 199, [2001] 2 WLR 1377 at 1383.)

[54] The problem arises because in the *Safeway* case the circuit judge had previously struck out Mr Tate's purported defence of justification. This left whether the words were defamatory as the only issue which remained to be determined. As to this, a different circuit judge who, as Otton LJ points out had to reach a decision in difficult circumstances, came to the conclusion that he was entitled to give summary judgment under CPR Pt 24. Otton LJ's judgment explains why the judge was not entitled to reach this decision.

[55] The reasoning of Otton LJ could be interpreted as indicating that the right of a judge to withdraw a decision from a jury was not as wide as hitherto had been thought to be the case. Prior to the CPR there were well-recognised situations where a judge was entitled to withdraw issues from the jury because a jury could not properly come to a decision in favour of a claimant. This would be the situation if the proceedings were vexatious or an abuse of process or for some other reason they could not succeed. An example would be where the words relied on were not capable of being defamatory or, as here, where it was not possible for the defendant to rely on malice in a case where the claimant is entitled to qualified privilege.

[56] In the course of argument Mr Milmo, who appears on behalf of the claimant, was referred by the court to the decision in the *Safeway* case but he did not rely upon it. In my judgment he was right not to do so. To have relied on the *Safeway* case would have been to misunderstand that decision in the way some litigants have misunderstood it since it was decided.

[57] In considering Otton LJ's judgment, it is important to have in mind that, in the *Safeway* case, the judge did not expressly ask himself the question whether the words complained of were only capable of having a defamatory meaning. Instead he appears to have given judgment having evaluated the issue himself. If the judge had asked himself that question and properly come to the conclusion that the words were only capable of having a defamatory meaning, then it is difficult to see what objection there could be to his giving summary judgment on an issue on which there was no room for argument. The judge would have been doing no more than what the trial judge could have done if the action had proceeded to trial. The court, that is the judge, would not be 'satisfied that there is in issue', whether the words were defamatory, as required by s 69 of the 1981 Act. So here the trial judge was entitled to rule on the question of whether it was possible to make a finding of malice. In so doing he would not be interfering with a party's right in a defamation action to have a jury trial.

[58] In the *Safeway* case, the counsel appearing for Safeway in the Court of Appeal, so far as can be gathered, sought to justify the decision of the judge without suggesting the case was one where the words were only capable of having a defamatory meaning. Unless the words were only capable of having a defamatory meaning then the issue of whether they are in fact defamatory must be left to the jury. If the words were capable of being defamatory or not defamatory, the decision is for the jury and a judge should not himself perform the task of evaluating the evidence so as to decide that the 'defendant has no reasonable prospect of defending the claim or issue'. Instead the judge should conclude that there is 'compelling reason why the case or issue should be disposed of at a trial'.

[59] CPR Pt 24 does not and should not be regarded as giving a right to summary judgment in a defamation case where there are issues fit to be placed *a* before a jury. In saying this, I am reflecting what Otton LJ said in the *Safeway* case. In his judgment, Otton LJ made this clear. He said:

> 'I am satisfied that an application under CPR 24.2(a) can properly be made in order to determine certain questions which fall within the jurisdiction of the *b* judge in a libel action. These include, for example, whether the words complained of were published on an occasion of absolute privilege. On the other hand, the rule does not permit a judge alone to determine questions of fact which Parliament has determined should be decided by a jury, and in particular, whether the words complained of are defamatory of the claimant.' (See [2001] 4 All ER 193 at 202, [2001] 2 WLR 1377 at 1386.) *c*

[60] The only passage in the judgment of Otton LJ to which I would draw attention is a passage which was not necessary for the decision of the court. Otton LJ said:

> 'The issue of whether a verdict is perverse can only be raised after a jury's *d* verdict has been given. The decisions cited by counsel in support of his proposition are all decisions of the Court of Appeal. None is authority for the proposition which he states or that the judge is entitled to take away an issue of fact from the jury merely because he considers that the jury might reach a perverse verdict.' (See [2001] 4 All ER 193 at 199, [2001] 2 WLR 1377 at 1383.) *e*

[61] I have no problem with what Otton LJ states in so far as he is indicating (which I believe was all that he was doing) that in a case in which a jury can come to a proper verdict you cannot assume they are going to come to an improper verdict. Otton LJ's statement does not, however, mean that in determining an issue on which the judge is entitled to rule, a judge cannot consider whether a particular *f* conclusion would be perverse. If it would be perverse then that would indicate the way the judge should rule as a matter of law on that issue. To take an obvious example, if the jury could not come to the conclusion that the words were defamatory then it would inevitably be perverse for them to do so. It would be an indication that the words were not capable of being defamatory.

[62] Properly understood the decision of this court in the *Safeway* case has not *g* altered what has hitherto been regarded as the proper role of the CPR.

Appeal dismissed.

Kate O'Hanlon   Barrister.

Money Markets International Stockbrokers Ltd (in liquidation) v London Stock Exchange Ltd and another

CHANCERY DIVISION

NEUBERGER J

12–14 JUNE, 10 JULY 2001

Company – Compulsory winding up – Distribution of assets – Defendant mutual company owning and operating stock exchange – Claimant company holding non-transferable share in defendant as stock exchange member firm – Defendant's articles of association requiring shareholder to transfer share on ceasing to be member firm – Member firms ceasing to be members on declaration of default – Defendant declaring claimant to be defaulter – Claimant going into insolvent liquidation – Defendant transferring claimant's share – Whether transfer of claimant's share offending principle against transactions depriving person of asset on becoming insolvent.

In 1992 the claimant Irish company, MMI, became a member firm of the London Stock Exchange (the stock exchange). As such, it was required to obtain a 'B' share in the first defendant, LSE, a mutual company which owned and operated the stock exchange. LSE duly arranged for a 'B' share to be transferred to MMI. Such a share carried voting rights and, in the event of LSE's dissolution, participation rights, but no dividend, bonus, distribution or payment of any kind was payable in respect of it. Under art 8.03 of LSE's articles of association, 'B' shares were only to be transferable to, and held by, member firms or the share trustee (the second defendant company, HSE), and no consideration was to be paid or given for the transfer of any such share except as the directors might from time to time require. Article 8.03 further provided that a 'B' shareholder which ceased for any reason to be a member firm, or its trustee in bankruptcy, was bound, when called upon by the directors to do so, to transfer the 'B' share. Under the rules of the stock exchange, a member firm which was unable to fulfil it obligations in respect of one or more stock exchange market contracts, or appeared to be or to be likely to become so unable, could be declared a defaulter and thereupon ceased to be a member firm. On 18 February 1999 MMI petitioned the Irish High Court for its own winding up on the ground that it was unable to pay its debts. The next day, the directors of LSE declared MMI a defaulter and accordingly it ceased to be a member firm of the stock exchange. On 18 March 1999, three days after MMI had been put into compulsory liquidation, LSE asked the liquidator to transfer MMI's 'B' share (the disputed share). It repeated that request on three other occasions up to 1 February 2000, with the final request, at least, being made in the proper form. The liquidator failed to comply, and on 14 February 2000 LSE purported to transfer the disputed share to HSE for no consideration. A few weeks earlier, on 27 January 2000, the LSE board had decided to demutualise LSE. The shareholders gave their approval on 15 March 2000, and demutalisation was completed on 12 April 2000 when each member firm received 100,000 ordinary shares in return for each 'B' share. On the same day, the disputed share was purportedly transferred by HSE to LSE and then cancelled. Subsequently, LSE registered as a public company and its shares began trading at a price which valued the former 'B' shares at £2.8m each.

In proceedings brought by it against LSE and HSE, MMI contended that LSE was
not entitled to deprive it of the disputed share to the detriment of its creditors. *a*
In so contending, MMI invoked the principle under which the court regarded as
void, where a person was insolvent, a provision that his property was to be
confiscated or pass to another (the anti-deprivation principle). MMI further relied
on the right to the peaceful enjoyment of possessions under the European
Convention for the Protection of Human Rights and Fundamental Freedoms *b*
1950 (as set out in Sch 1 to the Human Rights Act 1998), and the convention's
prohibition of discrimination.

Held – Although the transfer of an asset on the condition that it would revest in
the transferor in the event of the transferee's insolvency was generally invalid, a
deprivation provision which might otherwise be invalid in light of the *c*
anti-deprivation principle could be held to be valid if the asset concerned was
closely connected with or, more probably, subsidiary to, a right or other benefit
in respect of which a deprivation provision was valid. If such a provision did not
offend against that principle, then (subject to there being no other objection to it)
it would be enforceable against a trustee in bankruptcy or on a liquidation just as *d*
much as it would have been enforceable in the absence of an insolvency. In the
instant case, a member firm's ownership of a 'B' share in LSE could not realistically
be treated as ownership of a free-standing asset, at least until demutualisation. A
member firm's principal or real asset was membership of the stock exchange, and
its ownership of a 'B' share in LSE was effectively ancillary to that membership.
Such membership was a personal thing, incapable of uncontrolled transfer, and *e*
expulsion from membership would normally follow default. Upon expulsion, all
interest of the defaulting member in the property of the organisation ceased.
Thus although the disputed share was a thing separate altogether from LSE's
property, the nature and character of LSE and the stock exchange was such that
in the case of a defaulting member who was expelled from membership, no *f*
interest in his share remained in himself and none could pass to his assignee. Once
LSE had demutualised, so that its shares were effectively independent of
membership and not subject to restrictions on disposal by the owner, the exercise
of the deprivation provision would probably have fallen foul of the anti-deprivation
principle. However, although the directors had approved the proposal to
demutualise before 1 February 2000, the structure enshrined in the stock exchange *g*
rules and the LSE articles was in place until at least 15 March 2000 when the
shareholders approved the proposal. In those circumstances, there could have
been no infringement of the anti-deprivation principle when the disputed share
was transferred to HSE on 14 February 2000. That conclusion was not affected
by the convention rights invoked by MMI. Accordingly, LSE and HSE had no *h*
liability to MMI (see [118], [124], [125], [129], [132], [134], [135], [141]–[143], [145],
[146], below); *Bombay Official Assignee v Shroff* (1932) 48 TLR 443 applied; *Borland's
Trustee v Steel Bros & Co Ltd* [1901] 1 Ch 279 distinguished; *British Eagle International
Airlines Ltd v Cie Nationale Air France* [1975] 2 All ER 390 considered.

Per curiam. In deciding whether a deprivation provision exercisable other than *j*
on insolvency offends against the anti-deprivation principle, the court is primarily
concerned with the effect of the provision and not with the intention of the
parties, but it may be that, if the deprivation provision is exercisable for reasons
which are not concerned with the owner's insolvency, default or breach, then its
operation will fall outside the principle. However, if the intention of the parties
when agreeing the deprivation provision was to evade the insolvency rules, then

a that may invalidate a provision which would otherwise have been valid, and if the
intention of the parties was not to evade the insolvency laws, the court will be
more ready to uphold the deprivation provision if it provides for compensation
for the deprivation. The court will scrutinise with particular care a deprivation
provision which would have the effect of preferring the person to whom the asset
reverted or passed, as against other unsecured creditors of the insolvent person
b whose estate is deprived of the asset pursuant to the provision. Where, however,
a deprivation provision relates to an asset which has no value, or is incapable of
transfer, or depends on the character or status of the owner, it will normally be
enforceable on insolvency (see [118], below).

Notes

c For the insolvency of a shareholder, see 3(2) *Halsbury's Laws* (4th edn reissue)
para 411.

Cases referred to in judgment

A-G v Guardian Newspapers Ltd (No 2) [1988] 3 All ER 545, sub nom *A-G v Observer Ltd,*
d   *A-G v Times Newspapers Ltd* [1990] 1 AC 109, [1988] 3 WLR 776, HL.
Balfour's Settlement, Re, Public Trustee v Official Receiver [1938] 3 All ER 259, [1938]
      Ch 928.
Barter, Ex p, ex p Black, ex p Walker (1884) 26 Ch D 510, CA.
Bombay Official Assignee v Shroff (1932) 48 TLR 443, PC.
e *Borland's Trustee v Steel Bros & Co Ltd* [1901] 1 Ch 279.
British Eagle International Airlines Ltd v Cie Nationale Air France [1975] 2 All ER 390,
      [1975] 1 WLR 758, HL.
Cowan v Trésor public Case 186/87 [1989] ECR 195.
Detmold, Re, Detmold v Detmold (1889) 40 Ch D 585.
f *EC Commission v France* Case 270/83 [1986] ECR 273.
Felixstowe Dock & Rly Co v US Lines Inc [1988] 2 All ER 77, [1989] QB 360, [1989]
      2 WLR 109.
Fitzgerald v Williams, O'Regan v Williams [1996] 2 All ER 171, [1996] QB 657, [1996]
      2 WLR 447, CA.
Grant, Ex p, re Plumbly (1880) 13 Ch D 667, CA.
g *Higinbotham v Holme* (1812) 19 Ves 88, [1803–13] All ER Rep 504, 34 ER 451.
IRC v Crossman, IRC v Mann [1936] 1 All ER 762, [1937] AC 26, HL.
Jay, Ex p, re Harrison (1880) 14 Ch D 19, CA.
Mackay, Ex p, ex p Brown, re Jeavons (1873) LR 8 Ch App 643, LJJ.
h *Newitt, Ex p, re Garrud* (1881) 16 Ch D 522, [1881–5] All ER Rep 1039, CA.
Official Custodian for Charities v Parway Estates Development Ltd [1984] 3 All ER 679,
      [1985] 1 Ch 151, [1984] 3 WLR 525, CA.
Pye, J A (Oxford) Ltd v Graham [2001] EWCA Civ 117, [2001] 2 WLR 1293.
R v Secretary of State for the Home Dept, ex p McQuillan [1995] 4 All ER 400.
j *Sharp's Settlement Trusts, Re, Ibbotson v Bliss* [1972] 3 All ER 151, [1973] Ch 331,
      [1972] 3 WLR 765.
Whitmore v Mason (1861) 2 J & H 204, 70 ER 1031.
*Williams & Humbert Ltd v W & H Trade Marks (Jersey) Ltd, Rumasa SA v Multinvest
      (UK) Ltd* [1986] 1 All ER 129, [1986] AC 368, [1986] 2 WLR 24, HL.
Wilson v First County Trust Ltd [2001] EWCA Civ 633, [2001] 3 All ER 229, [2001]
      3 WLR 42.

Cases also cited or referred to in skeleton arguments

Ashby, Re, ex p Wreford [1892] 1 QB 872.

Bramelid v Sweden (1982) 5 EHRR 249, E Com HR.

Brind v Secretary of State for the Home Dept [1991] 1 All ER 720, sub nom *R v Secretary of State for the Home Dept, ex p Brind* [1991] 1 AC 696, HL.

Keen & Keen, Re, ex p Collins [1902] 1 KB 555.

Gasus Dosier-und Fördertechnik GmbH v Netherlands (1995) 20 EHRR 403, [1995] ECHR 15375/89, ECt HR.

Gustafsson v Sweden (1996) 22 EHRR 409, [1996] ECHR 15573/89, ECt HR.

Mateos v UK (1988) 57 DR 268, E Com HR.

Hentrich v France (1994) 18 EHRR 440, [1994] ECHR 13616/88, ECt HR.

Iraqi Ministry of Defence v Arcepey Shipping Co SA (Gillespie Bros & Co Ltd intervening), The Angel Bell [1980] 1 All ER 480, [1981] QB 65.

James v UK (1986) 8 EHRR 123, [1986] ECHR 8793/79, ECt HR.

Krasner v Dennison, Lawrence v Lesser [2000] 3 All ER 234, [2001] Ch 76, CA

National & Provincial Building Society v UK (1997) 25 EHRR 127, [1997] ECHR 21319/93, ECt HR.

Pender v Lushington (1877) 6 Ch D 70.

R v International Stock Exchange of the UK and the Republic of Ireland Ltd, ex p Else (1982) Ltd [1993] 1 All ER 420, [1993] QB 534, CA.

Action

By claim form issued on 4 April 2000, the claimant, Money Markets International Ltd (in liquidation) (MMI), brought proceedings against the defendants, London Stock Exchange Ltd (LSE) and London Stock Exchange (Holdings) Ltd (Holdings), arising from the purported transfer from LSE to Holdings of a 'B' share in LSE formerly held by MMI. By order of Deputy Master Hoffmann made on 21 August 2000, the court was required to determine first the issue of liability. The facts are set out in the judgment.

Andrew Hochhauser QC and *Salim Moollan* (instructed by *Stephenson Harwood*) for MMI.

Anthony Mann QC and *John Nicholls* (instructed by *Herbert Smith*) for the LSE and Holdings.

Cur adv vult

10 July 2001. The following judgment was delivered.

NEUBERGER J.

INTRODUCTION

[1] The issue in this case concerns the extent and applicability of the principle 'that there cannot be a valid contract that a man's property shall remain his until his bankruptcy, and on the happening of that event shall go over to some one else, and be taken away from his creditors' (*Ex p Jay, re Harrison* (1880) 14 Ch D 19 at 26 per Cotton LJ). The principle is not in doubt, but, as the arguments in this case have demonstrated, the breadth of the principle and the circumstances in which it applies are not entirely clear.

THE FACTS

a

The structure of the London Stock Exchange

[2] The London Stock Exchange (the Stock Exchange) was originally formed as an incorporated association constituted by a deed of 27 March 1802, which was later replaced by a deed of 31 December 1875 (the 1875 deed). It carried on

b business for the benefit of its proprietors, each of whom had unlimited liability for its obligations. In July 1965, the Federation of Stock Exchanges in Great Britain and Ireland was formed, comprising the various Regional Stock Exchanges (including the Stock Exchange) in those territories, and in March 1973 these various Stock Exchanges in the United Kingdom, the Republic of Ireland, the Isle of Man and the Channel Islands were amalgamated. In November 1986,

c the Stock Exchange merged with the International Securities Regulatory Organisation to form the International Stock Exchange of the United Kingdom and the Republic of Ireland Ltd, which was registered as a private limited company, and which changed its name to London Stock Exchange Limited (LSE) following separation of the Irish Stock Exchange on 9 December 1995.

d   [3] In 1948, the 1875 deed had been varied so that the category of potential membership of the Stock Exchange was more limited and ownership of the Stock Exchange became formally vested in its members. From that time, the business of the Stock Exchange itself was not to be carried on with a view to making a profit. The incorporation in November 1986 enabled the shareholders to enjoy the usual benefits of limited liability in respect of the debts and obligations of the

e Stock Exchange, but the company retained for a time as its constitutional document an amended version of the 1875 deed.

[4] The 1875 deed provided that only individuals who were members of the Stock Exchange could be proprietors of its business assets. The rights of members were reorganised on the incorporation of the LSE in 1986; its shares were

f classified into 'A' and 'B' shares. Only proprietors who were 'Member Firms' (as subsequently defined in the LSE's articles of association) were thereafter able to control the Stock Exchange, and they were each allocated a 'B' share, which, in short, carried voting rights and, albeit only on the dissolution of LSE, participation rights. Each Member Firm was normally required to acquire a 'B' share on becoming a Member Firm of the Stock Exchange, and to surrender that

g share on ceasing to be a Member Firm.

[5] Proprietors who in 1986 were individual or external members (ie not Member Firms) were each to be allocated one 'A' share. Such a share carried no voting rights or participation rights, but, by way of compensation for the loss of such rights, the holder of an 'A' share was entitled to £10,000 on redemption of

h that share, and there was provision for the circumstance in which redemption would occur. Eventually, it was envisaged that all the 'A' shares would be redeemed.

[6] On 9 July 1991, the LSE approved the replacement of the 1875 deed (as amended) by a more modern memorandum and articles of association which led

j to the demise of the LSE's previous governing body, the Council of the Stock Exchange, and its replacement by a Board of Directors.

[7] As described in its memorandum of association, the main object of the LSE is to carry on the business of an investment exchange and to provide, manage and regulate markets in a variety of investments, in the Stock Exchange. Comprehensive and detailed rules (the LSE rules) governing the running of the Stock Exchange have always existed, although they have inevitably been varied

from time to time. Importantly, the LSE only allows its facilities to be utilised by Member Firms, and a person who wishes to acquire that status has to go through *a* an application process set out in ch 1 of the LSE rules which require the LSE to be satisfied as to the suitability of the applicant.

[8] London Stock Exchange (Holdings) Ltd (Holdings) is a company formed, under a different name, on 4 October 1948 with objects which included that of acting as share trustee for what was then the Council of the London Stock *b* Exchange. Holdings adopted new articles of association on 17 December 1985, but they retained the object to which I have referred. With effect from 15 October 1948, all the assets then owned by the Stock Exchange were transferred to Holdings, as custodian trustee. Under its articles of association, LSE's directors are empowered to nominate a body corporate for the purpose of holding its assets, including any shares in LSE pending their transfer to Member Firms. *c*

[9] Until the recent comprehensive reorganisation of the statutory arrangements for regulating the provision of financial services, LSE was the competent authority in the United Kingdom for the purpose of the official listing of securities by virtue of the Financial Services Act 1986. Probably, LSE's most important remaining function is to provide, through the Stock Exchange, a recognised *d* investment exchange, affording facilities for dealing in quoted securities between its members. An entity (which would include a limited or unlimited company, a partnership or even an individual) is allowed to deal directly on the Stock Exchange provided that it becomes a Member Firm.

e
LSE's articles of association

[10] This case has been argued by reference to the articles of association of LSE (the LSE articles) immediately following an amendment passed on 8 July 1999 and effective from that date. There has been no suggestion that any other relevant version of the LSE articles differs in any respect material for the purpose of the resolution of the dispute between the parties, and accordingly I shall *f* confine myself to the terms of the LSE articles as they stood on that date.

[11] Article 2 was concerned with interpretation, and contains the following relevant definitions:

'"Bankruptcy" includes liquidation by arrangement and in relation to a *g* body corporate the winding up thereof and references to "bankruptcy" or "trustee in bankruptcy" shall be construed accordingly ... "Member" means the registered holder of one or more shares in the Company [sc LSE] ... "Member Firm" means a[n] entity ... elected as such in accordance with Article 26.01 ... "Rules" includes rules made pursuant to Article 18.01 and regulations and bye-laws and decisions or directions intended to have the *h* force of Rules.'

[12] Article 3 was concerned with share capital and provided so far as relevant:

'3.01 ... any share may be issued with such rights or restrictions as the *j* Company [sc LSE] may by ordinary resolution determine.

3.02 ... shares may be issued which are to be redeemed or are to be liable to be redeemed at the option of the Company or the holder on such term and in such manner as may be provided by the Articles ...

3.04 ... the Company shall not be bound by or recognise any interest in any share except an absolute right to the entirety thereof in the holder.'

[13] Article 4 was concerned with 'Share Rights and their variation', and provided for 'A' and 'B' shares. Articles 4.02 and 4.04 stipulated that 'A' shareholders had no right to be notified of, attend, or vote at, any general meeting, nor to any payment or distribution save £10,000 redemption payment on liquidation if a share had not already been redeemed. Article 4.03 provided that a 'B' shareholder (other than Holdings) had 'The right (in the case of each holder so long as it is a

b Member Firm) to receive notice of (and to attend and vote at any general meeting'.

[14] Article 4.11 provided: 'Save on dissolution or as provided in Article 27.02 no dividend, bonus, distribution or payment of any kind shall be paid on or in respect of any "B" share.'

[15] Article 27.02 stipulated that, save in relation to redeeming the 'A' shares:

c

'The Company shall not be carried on with a view to earning profits for distribution to the members. Accordingly ... the net revenues of the Company shall be applied solely towards the promotion of the objects or purposes of the Company and no portion thereof shall be paid or transferred directly or indirectly by way of dividend bonus or otherwise by way of profit
d to the members as such.'

[16] Article 8 is of central relevance to these proceedings. It was headed 'Transfer or Transmission of Shares'. Articles 8.01 and 8.02 were concerned with the 'A' shares. Articles 8.03 and 8.04 provided:

e '8.03 The "B" shares shall only be transferable to and held by Member Firms or the share Trustee and no consideration shall be paid or given for the transfer of any "B" share except as the directors may from time to time require. The directors may also direct that a Member Firm shall dispose of all (or such number as the directors may direct) of its "B" shares. Accordingly: (a) Every "B" Shareholder ceasing for any reason to be a Member
f Firm or the personal representatives or trustee in bankruptcy of any "B" Shareholder dying or becoming bankrupt or any "B" Shareholder being directed under the provisions of this article shall be bound, when called upon by the directors in writing at any time thereafter so to do, to transfer all (or such number as the directors may specify) of the "B" shares registered in the name of such "B" Shareholder or deceased or bankrupt "B" Shareholder; and
g (b) All [entities] becoming Member Firms shall be entitled and bound to acquire such numbers of "B" shares in the Company by such respective dates or within such respective periods as the directors may prescribe and the directors shall, if requested in writing by any such Member Firms so to do, take all necessary steps, by notices to "B" shareholders who are not Member
h Firms or to the personal representatives or trustees in bankruptcy of deceased or bankrupt "B" Shareholders or by directions to the share Trustee, to enable it to do so. Any Member Firm hereby required to acquire and failing by the date or within the period prescribed as aforesaid to acquire the shareholding prescribed as aforesaid shall on the relevant date or at the
j expiration of the relevant period cease to be a Member Firm except as may otherwise be determined by the directors from time to time.

8.04 Every notice given by the directors pursuant to this article calling upon a member or personal representatives or trustee in bankruptcy of a deceased or bankrupt member (hereinafter collectively referred to as 'the retiring member') to transfer any share shall be accompanied by an instrument of transfer of the share for execution by the retiring member and shall refer to this article and require him to return the transfer duly executed to the Secretary within such period, not being less than seven days, as the directors may determine. If in any case the retiring member shall make default in executing and returning the transfer so sent to him within the period so fixed the directors may at any time after the expiration of that period authorise some person to transfer the share to the transferee named in the transfer so sent and shall thereupon cause the name of such transferee to be registered as the holder of the share, and after the name of the said transferee has been so registered in purported exercise of the aforesaid power the validity of the proceedings shall not be questioned by any person.'

[17] I should also refer to art 8.14 which stated that:

'The personal representatives of any deceased member and the trustee in bankruptcy of any member who shall become bankrupt shall not be entitled to be registered as members in respect of the shares of such deceased or bankrupt members, but may transfer such shares subject to, and shall be bound to transfer such shares if and when called upon to do so in accordance with, the provisions of this article.'

[18] Article 14 was concerned with voting, and effectively entitled every 'B' shareholder to a single vote at every general meeting or poll.

[19] Article 18 was headed 'Rules'. Article 18.01 provided:

'The directors may from time to time make Rules for any object of the Company including ... Rules respecting, inter alia ... (d) the election, expulsion, suspension and conduct of Member Firms and their respective rights and obligations.'

[20] Article 26 was headed 'Election of Member Firms etc.'. So far as relevant it provided:

'26.01 The directors may elect such [entities] (whether or not members of the Company) as they think proper to be Member Firms ... Member Firms shall be subject to the Rules and shall enjoy such rights and privileges as may from time to time be provided by the articles and by the Rules.

26.02 All rights conferred by election as aforesaid shall be personal to those elected and shall not be transferable.

26.03 A Member Firm shall cease to be a Member Firm if it shall resign ... or in such other circumstances as may from time to time be provided for in the Rules ...'

The rules of the Stock Exchange

[21] The LSE rules are a long and detailed document, as one might expect in the present legislative and regulatory climate. Fortunately, it is not necessary to refer to many of the rules.

[22] Rule 1.8 provides that a Member Firm shall be limited to a person authorised for membership; for instance, he must be authorised or exempt under the Financial Services Act. It also provides that if a Member Firm is not so authorised, it may be suspended from trading without prior notice. Rule 1.11 provides that: 'A Member Firm shall be bound by and observe the Rules of the Exchange for the time being in force and any decision or direction of the Exchange.'

[23] Rule 1.18 provides for resignation of a Member Firm on three months notice, and the following rule entitles the Stock Exchange to refuse to accept such

a notice. Rule 1.20 entitles the Stock Exchange to determine the membership of
a Member Firm that 'has ceased to carry on business on the Exchange … for a
period of six months or more'. Rule 1.24 requires a Member Firm 'so far as it is
able' to notify the Stock Exchange of any change in control, and r 1.7 similarly
requires notification 'immediately' on the occurrence of certain events, including
the presentation of a petition for the winding up of the Member Firm, or of any
subsidiary or holding company.

[24] Of central relevance are rr 15.5 to 15.8 which are headed 'Declaration of
defaulters'. I set them out in full:

> '15.5 A member firm which: (a) is unable to fulfil its obligations in respect
> of one or more Stock Exchange market contract(s); or (b) appears to be or to
> be likely to become so unable; may, and shall if the Exchange is so directed
> pursuant to section 166 or 167 Companies Act 1989, be declared a defaulter
> by direction of the Chairman of Deputy Chairman or by direction of two
> members of the Board. Thereafter, the default rules shall apply to any Stock
> Exchange market contract to which the defaulter is at the time of default a
> party.
>
> 15.6 Upon a declaration of default the default official shall, as soon as is
> reasonably practicable: (a) notify the defaulter of the declaration; (b) in
> relation to any unsettled or any unexercised relevant contracts notify the
> parties to such contracts of the default and of any decision taken under the
> default rules in relation to those contracts; and (c) in relation to any unsettled
> or any unexercised relevant agency contracts notify the parties to such
> contracts of the default and the identity of the other party to the contract.
>
> 15.7 Declaration of default shall be made in such manner as the Exchange
> shall decide.
>
> 15.8 Any member firm declared a defaulter shall thereupon cease to be a
> member firm but shall nevertheless be bound to take or refrain from taking
> all such action and suffer all such things to be done as this chapter requires in
> the case of a defaulter and shall continue to be bound by this chapter in
> relation to all matters, transactions and circumstances arising while it was a
> member firm.'

[25] As with the LSE articles, I have quoted from the edition of the LSE rules
by reference to which the argument on each side proceeded, namely the January
2001 edition. Although the LSE rules have obviously been amended from time
to time, both before and after that edition, there has been no suggestion that
there has been any amendment of substance so far as the current dispute is
concerned.

Money Markets International Stockbrokers Ltd

[26] Until 20 March 1992, a partnership trading under the name of Doak & Co
(Doak) was a Member Firm of the Stock Exchange and the holder of a 'B' share
in LSE. On 20 March 1992, Doak agreed to sell its stockbroking business to
Money Markets International Stockbrokers Ltd (MMI), a company incorporated
in the Republic of Ireland the previous day, presumably for the purpose of
completing this transaction. Mr Thomas Kavanagh, a chartered accountant and
the liquidator of MMI, says that he was informed by Mr Adrian Doak that 'the
reason that MMI purchased the firm … was because MMI wished to expand its
then existing business of money broking into stockbroking'. He also states that
he was told by Mr John Curran, a director of MMI, that 'the easiest way to

achieve this was to purchase an existing stockbroking firm with a seat on the London Stock Exchange'. Mr Kavanagh further says that Mr Curran informed him that Doak's 'main asset of value was [its "B"] share and that later MMI made its own application for membership of the London Stock Exchange'. He states that Mr Curran told him that the purchase of Doak—

> 'was made so that trading could begin at once in the name of that firm to save time before MMI's own application [for membership of the Stock Exchange] could be approved and the application itself be easier to make as MMI had acquired [Doak].'

[27] Having acquired Doak's business, MMI applied to LSE to become a Member Firm, and it was formally elected as such on 6 August 1992. Pursuant to art 8.03, LSE then arranged for a 'B' share to be transferred to MMI. In practice, it is clear that MMI replaced Doak as a Member Firm. While it is not entirely clear from the evidence, it seems likely that Doak's 'B' share was effectively transferred to MMI. MMI carried on a stockbroking business successfully until 1998. Unfortunately as it transpired, MMI engaged in considerable margin trading activity, and due to a substantial fall in the value of shares in certain sectors of the stock market in September 1998, it found itself in financial difficulties owing to the fact that some of its clients were unable to meet substantial debts which they owed to MMI. Accordingly, pursuant to a shareholders' resolution, on 18 February 1999, MMI presented a petition to the High Court in Dublin to be wound up. That petition (the petition) was presented pursuant to s 213(e) of the Irish Companies Act 1963 which, in similar terms to its English equivalent, provides that: 'A company may be wound-up by the Court if ... the company is unable to pay its debts ...' On the same day, the Irish High Court appointed Mr Kavanagh as the provisional liquidator of MMI. On 15 March 1999, the Irish High Court put MMI into compulsory liquidation and confirmed Mr Kavanagh as liquidator.

[28] Before the presentation of the petition, MMI informed LSE that it was insolvent and that it was unable to meet a substantial number of market contracts to other Member Firms. Although LSE initially wished to declare MMI a defaulter before 18 February 1999, it agreed to hold off from doing so until the appointment of the provisional liquidator. The day following Mr Kavanagh's appointment, ie on 19 February 1999, the directors of LSE declared MMI a defaulter pursuant to r 15.5. MMI thereupon ceased to be a Member Firm in accordance with r 15.8. The evidence establishes that there were a number of grounds for LSE's decision, in addition to the fact that MMI was in default under its Stock Market contracts. These, in brief were as follows: the cash flow position of MMI, the insolvency of MMI, the Central Bank of Ireland's suspension of MMI from carrying on business, the appointment of a provisional liquidator and intended winding up of MMI, and the termination of an earlier moratorium agreement between MMI and some of its major creditors.

[29] After the declaration of default, LSE sought to invoke r 15.3 to obtain access to MMI's books and records so as to be able to notify MMI's clients of the identity of counterparties to unsettled market contracts, with a view to facilitating the completion of such contracts. Mr Kavanagh, the liquidator of MMI, apparently felt unhappy about acceding to this without the protection of a court order, and accordingly on 15 March 1999 LSE applied to the Irish High Court, which declared that LSE was entitled to implement the default provisions set out in ch 15 of the rules against MMI.

a **[30]** On 18 March 1999, LSE's registrar wrote to Mr Kavanagh referring to MMI's 'B' share (the disputed share), stating that:

'After the conclusion of the resignation process it will be necessary, in accordance with the Exchange's articles of association to transfer the ... "B" share back to the Exchange. I would be grateful if you would assist with the transfer of the "B" share and attach a stock transfer form for this purpose.'

b

[31] It is MMI's case that this request did not comply with the requirements of art 8.03(b), and indeed that two subsequent requests to MMI to transfer the disputed share, dated 21 October and 15 November 1999, similarly failed to comply with that article. However, a fourth such request, dated 1 February 2000, clearly complies with the requirements of art 8.03(b), at least so far as its

c contents were concerned. Between March 1999 and February 2000, there were communications between LSE and MMI which suggested that one department within the LSE considered that MMI was still entitled to retain the disputed share. However, it is not argued that MMI or Mr Kavanagh acted, let alone reasonably acted, in reliance on any such indication, and therefore it seems to me that

d nothing hangs on that. On 14 February 2000, the LSE purported to transfer the disputed share to Holdings for no consideration.

Evidence relating to LSE

[32] According to the evidence of Lisa Condron, the company secretary of LSE, the reason that Member Firms were members of LSE—

e

'was to allow [them] for as long as they retained that status (and therefore retained an interest in the operation of the Stock Exchange Markets) to participate in the ownership and the management of the LSE (as the company which controls the Stock Exchange Markets).'

f The purpose of Member Firm status is and was to allow any suitable company or firm to become a Member Firm and thereby to utilise the facilities provided by LSE and to trade on the Stock Exchange. In return, the LSE was able to collect fees from Member Firms.

[33] The possibility of 'demutualising' LSE was apparently first formally raised at a board meeting on 29 July 1999, and it was canvassed with members on

g 21 October 1999. The formal decision to demutualise LSE was taken at a board meeting on 27 January 2000. On 15 March 2000, at a general meeting, the shareholders in LSE decided to demutualise. The demutualisation was completed on 12 April 2000 by each Member Firm receiving 100,000 ordinary shares in return for each 'B' share. On the same day, the disputed share was purportedly

h transferred by Holdings to LSE and cancelled by LSE. On 8 June 2000 LSE was registered as London Stock Exchange plc and on 24 July 2000. Shares in that company started trading at a price of £28 each. This valued each of the former 'B' shares at £2·8m.

[34] The evidence of Ms Condron shows that the directors of LSE normally

j exercised their powers under arts 8.03 and 8.04 in cases where entities lose Member Firm status for reasons other than default, e g by breach of the LSE rules, loss of authorised status under the Financial Services Act, resignation, lack of activity or expulsion. It appears that Member Firm status is lost on grounds other than default more than 20 times a year on average. Since March 1989, only ten Member Firms, other than MMI, have been declared in default. In none of those cases, has the Member Firm been permitted to retain its 'B' share. In some cases

not involving default, there may well have been occasions where a Member Firm
who has become insolvent have not been required to relinquish their 'B' share.   *a*
The evidence on this topic was very limited, but in so far as there was any such
indulgence, it never involved a Member Firm which was a defaulter. There has
been no occasion to which I have been referred when the transfer of a 'B' share
for value has been permitted by the directors of LSE.

                                                                                    b
SUMMARY OF THE ARGUMENTS

MMI's case

[35] These proceedings were issued by MMI against LSE and Holdings on
4 April 2000. As amended and re-amended, MMI's CPR Pt 8 claim seeks various
declaratory and injunctive orders, which are directed either to its reinstatement   *c*
as a member of LSE, or to enabling it to obtain compensation for the loss of the
disputed share. By virtue of an order made on 21 August 2000, I am only
concerned at this stage with liability, not with remedy.

[36] MMI's case is that LSE was not entitled to deprive MMI of the disputed
share to the detriment of MMI's creditors, on the basis of the principle, that a   *d*
provision that, a person's property shall pass to another, is regarded by the court,
where the person concerned is insolvent, as being contrary to insolvency
principles or, to use the expression adopted from some of the cases by
Mr Andrew Hochhauser QC (who appears with Mr Salim Moollan for MMI) a
fraud upon the bankruptcy laws and void. I shall refer to this as 'the principle'.

[37] In essence, MMI's case is that, subject to one or two exceptions, a   *e*
contractual provision which requires a person who has become insolvent to be
deprived of property or a right ('an asset') will be treated by the court as
unenforceable on the ground that it conflicts with well established principles
equally applicable to bankruptcy or liquidation ('insolvency'), namely, that, on
insolvency, the insolvent's assets are to be available for distribution amongst its   *f*
creditors in accordance with primary and delegated legislation, in this country the
Insolvency Act 1986 and the Insolvency Rules 1986, SI 1986/1925. The exceptions
to this principle accepted by MMI are where the asset is inherently determinable
or where there is some sort of superior or reversionary interest, and the terms
under which the asset was created or granted include a provision for its
determination in the event of insolvency, or indeed, on the happening of any   *g*
other event. The obvious examples of such interests are a protective trust or a
lease. A person's rights under a protective trust are automatically determined on
his bankruptcy; under a lease, there is always a reversioner with a superior
interest, and there is very frequently a proviso for forfeiture in the event of the
lessee's insolvency, or breach of covenant.   *h*

[38] On MMI's case, the provisions of art 8.03, in so far as they fell to be
applied where the Member Firm was insolvent, fall foul of the principle.
There is no question of the disputed share being inherently determinable, and it
cannot sensibly be said that the disputed share is, as it were, carved out of some
superior interest which survives. Although it is property of which MMI could   *j*
lawfully be required to divest itself in certain circumstances (e g if it sold its
stockbroking business to a third party in the same way as Doak sold its business
to MMI) that does not, it is argued, undermine the point that LSE's invocation of
art 8.03 in the present case was triggered by MMI's inability to meet its liabilities,
and/or was sought to be enforced when MMI was insolvent. The fact that
art 8.03 appears to entitle LSE to require MMI to transfer the disputed share to

a Holdings, rather than simply to forfeit the disputed share, is said to underscore the inherent difference between this case and the operation of a protective trust or a proviso in a lease for forfeiture in the event of insolvency. The difference between determination or forfeiture, on the one hand, and requirement to transfer, on the other, is said not merely to be a difference of remedy: it is a difference which, claims MMI, demonstrates the essential distinction between

b ending an inherently determinable interest, such as a protective trust or a lease, and requiring the transfer to a third party of an inherently non-determinable interest, such as a share.

[**39**] MMI seeks to bolster its case by reference to the European Convention for the Protection of Human Rights and Fundamental Freedoms (Rome, 4 November 1950; TS 71 (1953); Cmd 8969), now enshrined in the Human Rights

c Act 1998. In this connection, MMI is not relying on the new remedy created by s 7(1)(a) of the 1998 Act; indeed, given that the action it complains of took place, at the latest, on 12 April 2000 (when the disputed share was purportedly transferred by Holdings to LSE and cancelled) and the 1998 Act came into force on 2 October 2000, it could not do so in light of s 22(4) of the 1998 Act.

d However, what is said on behalf of MMI in this connection is that, particularly given that its case rests on a principle based on public policy, the court should lean heavily in favour of a conclusion which does not involve infringing MMI's rights under the convention.

LSE's case

e [**40**] For LSE, Mr Anthony Mann QC (who appears with Mr John Nicholls) initially contended that the principle could not be relied on by MMI, because it is based upon English insolvency law, and MMI is an Irish company being wound up in Ireland. However, after evidence that Irish insolvency law, at least so far as the treatment of the assets on insolvency is concerned, is effectively identical to

f English law, LSE did not press that particular argument.

[**41**] Although any view I express on the point must therefore be strictly obiter, and it is inappropriate to discuss it in detail, I consider that LSE was right not to pursue the point. First, although comity is, as Mr Mann rightly says, a concept which is much easier to invoke than to analyse in any particular case, I take the view that it does apply in relation to the principle relied upon by MMI,

g at least in a case such as the present. Given that the relevant Irish statutory rules relating to insolvency are effectively identical to those in this jurisdiction, it would seem to me unduly insular for this court not to apply the principle in connection with an asset in this jurisdiction, simply because the insolvent is an Irish company being wound up in Ireland rather than in England. All the more

h so when many (I suspect most) of the creditors will be English entities. I draw indirect support in reaching this conclusion from observations in *Williams & Humbert Ltd v W & H Trade Marks (Jersey) Ltd, Rumasa SA v Multinvest (UK) Ltd* [1986] 1 All ER 129 at 134–135, [1986] AC 368 at 429–431 and *Felixstowe Dock & Rly Co v US Lines Inc* [1988] 2 All ER 77 at 89–91, [1989] QB 360 at 373–376. I note

j also the attitude of the Irish Court on 15 March 1999, redolent of comity, which permitted enforcement of the LSE rules against MMI.

[**42**] Quite apart from this, it seems to me that, if comity cannot be relied on, there is a pretty strong case for saying that, in relation to an asset or potential asset in this jurisdiction, arts 52 and 59 of the EC Treaty (now arts 43 and 49 EC) (read together with arts 6 and 65 (now arts 12 and 54 EC)) would require this court to treat an Irish company being wound up in Ireland in the same way, so

far as common law or public policy is concerned, as an English company being
wound up here. I accept that this argument involves giving a relatively wide
meaning to art 52 and/or art 59 of the EC Treaty, but that may very well be
justified in light of decisions such as that of the Court of Appeal in *Fitzgerald v
Williams, O'Regan v Williams* [1996] 2 All ER 171, [1996] QB 657 at 681–687 and of
the Court of Justice of the European Communities in *Cowan v Trésor public* Case
186/87 [1989] ECR 195 at 220 (para 14) and *EC Commission v France* Case 270/83
[1986] ECR 273 at 302–303, 305 (paras 13, 16, 21).

[43] I now turn to LSE's case on the main issue, that is, the application of the
principle to the instant facts. While accepting that there is a principle that certain
transactions will be held invalid or unenforceable in so far as they may result in
an asset being taken away on insolvency, Mr Mann contends on behalf of LSE
that it does not apply to a provision inherent in the asset which provides for its
forfeiture or removal, even in the event of an insolvency; alternatively, he
contends that such a provision will be valid provided it can be implemented other
than on insolvency. He contends that an arrangement, whereby A divests himself
of an asset in favour of B on terms, or in such a way, that the ownership of the
asset is forfeited or lost in a certain event is enforceable even if B becomes
insolvent. He says that it is permissible to create a property, an interest or a right
which is, in effect, validly limited in a certain event (including insolvency),
provided that it is so limited at the outset, ie so that it never existed free from that
limitation. By way of illustration, he refers to leases with provisos for re-entry in
the event of insolvency (or on other grounds), and protective trusts, which are
expressly condoned by s 33 of the Law of Property Act 1925.

[44] On this analysis as put forward by LSE, the terms and implementation of
art 8.03 of LSE's articles are said not to offend against the principle. This is
because it had always been an integral feature of the disputed share (as with every
other 'B' share in LSE) that it is subject to a compulsory transfer away at no
consideration, at the suit of the directors of LSE, in the event of the shareholder's
ceasing to be a Member Firm, which will occur if the shareholder is in default.
Accordingly, contend LSE, the principle does not apply.

[45] Over and above this, LSE contends that, in the circumstances of this case,
the terms and implementation of art 8 of LSE's articles are unexceptionable,
given that art 8 is part of a fair overall commercial scheme, with no intention of
defrauding creditors in the event of a shareholder's insolvency. The disputed
share was accorded to MMI as an integral part of its membership of the Stock
Exchange, and when that membership determined, its need for the share, the
reason for its owning the share, indeed the appropriateness of its ownership of
the share, effectively disappeared.

[46] The parties referred to a number of cases in connection with their
arguments, and I shall start by discussing the authorities, and shall then turn to
consider the principles to be derived from the cases. I shall then seek to apply
those principles to the present case. I shall finally deal with the convention point
raised by MMI.

THE AUTHORITIES

[47] The law on protective trusts is helpfully summarised in *Snell's Equity*
(30th edn, 2000) pp 160–161 (para 7-69):

'Although a condition or proviso against alienation, or for forfeiture on
bankruptcy, is void, a limitation until bankruptcy or attempted alienation is
valid. The difference is between giving the beneficiary, *e.g.* a complete life

interest with a condition against alienating that interest, and giving him a limited life interest, *i.e.* a life interest until attempted alienation; the limitation in the latter case marks the bounds or compass of the interest, whereas the condition in the former case attempts to defeat the interest before it attains its boundary. A person cannot, however, make use of the rules governing determinable interests in order to defeat the bankruptcy laws as regards his own property.'

[48] To the same effect, *Underhill's and Hayton's Law Relating to Trusts and Trustees* (15th edn, 1995) pp 184–185, say:

'A trust with a conditional proviso that the interest of the beneficiary shall not be liable to the claims of creditors, is void so far as the condition or proviso is concerned … Similarly a man cannot make a settlement of his own property upon *himself* until bankruptcy, and then over … On the other hand, a trust created by a third party, to pay the income to A until he dies or becomes bankrupt … and then over to B, is perfectly good, and may even take effect in respect of bankruptcy or alienation preceding the settlement. The distinction between this valid determinable interest and the void conditional interest is that the determinable limitation is allowed since the limitation merely sets a natural limit to the interest whilst a condition or proviso cuts down the interest before it reaches its natural limit.'

[49] As the editors of *Underhill and Hayton* immediately go on to point out (p 185):

'A trust creating a determinable life interest determining naturally upon bankruptcy or alienation (… "a protected life interest") is equally good where the trustee is, upon bankruptcy of or alienation by the beneficiary, given a discretion to apply the income for the benefit or maintenance of the bankrupt or his wife or issue … Such trusts are now so common that the Trustee Act 1925, in section 33, contains … provisions intended to shorten wills and settlements by substituting a reference to "protective trusts" for the rather lengthy clause formerly employed.'

[50] In his book *Principles of Corporate Insolvency Law* (2nd edn, 1997) Professor Roy Goode expressed the principle a little more widely at 147:

'The transfer of property in an asset to a company upon the condition that the asset is to revest in the transferor if the company goes into liquidation is void … Forfeiture clauses of this kind … will almost invariably be struck down. On the other hand, there is no objection to a disposition by which property is transferred to the company for an interest coming to an end on winding up …'

[51] I have not been referred to any case where the principle has been invoked to challenge the enforceability of a proviso in a lease, which often provide for forfeiture in the event of the insolvency of the lessee, where the proviso is sought to be enforced after the lessee has become insolvent. Such provisos are, of course, frequently to be found in leases, although well-advised lessees (and their mortgagees) seek to exclude or limit them in drafting negotiations, at least where the lease is to be granted for a substantial premium. The legislature has impliedly sanctioned such provisions in s 146(9) of the Law of Property Act 1925.

[52] I now turn to consider a number of cases, decided over the past 150 years or so, where the court has had to consider the applicability of the principle upon which MMI's case relies.

[53] *Whitmore v Mason* (1861) 2 J & H 204, 70 ER 1031 was a decision of Page Wood V-C (later Lord Hatherley) in 1861. Mr Mason had been granted a mining lease which he held on trust for himself and four partners in shares based on the amounts they each had subscribed to the capital of the partnership. The partnership deed included a provision that in the event of the bankruptcy of any of the partners his share of the assets would be forfeited to the remaining partners, but that he or his representatives would be paid out his share on the basis of a valuation which was not, however, to include the lease, on the basis that 'the value of the ... lease ... is not to be taken into account'. The question was whether this provision was enforceable as regards his share of the lease on Mr Mason's bankruptcy.

[54] Page Wood V-C said:

'... I apprehend that the law is too clearly settled to admit of a shadow of doubt, that no person possessed of property can reserve that property to himself until he shall become bankrupt, and then provide, that, in the event of his becoming bankrupt, it shall pass to another, and not to his creditors.' (See (1861) 2 J & H 204 at 212, 70 ER 1031 at 1034.)

He then said:

'But it was argued ... that, in forming a partnership, each partner is making a bargain with the rest, and has a right to stipulate for such privileges as he can obtain; that, by contributing his share to the common fund, and thereby giving the advantage of that share to the other persons entering into the partnership, he acquires the right to stipulate, that, in the event of the others becoming bankrupt, their shares shall not pass to their creditors, but shall remain the property of the partnership. And it was said, that the case resembled the ordinary condition of a demise of land, that, in the event of the tenant becoming bankrupt, the land shall revert to the landlord. The principle upon which such a condition as last mentioned has been upheld in the case of a demise of land, is expressed in the maxim, "cujus est dare ejus est disponere." The question is, whether that question is applicable to a partnership deed of this description.' (See (1861) 2 J & H 204 at 212–213, 70 ER 1031 at 1034–1035.)

[55] The Vice Chancellor continued:

'Consistently with the authorities, it seems to me impossible to hold that this can be done ... The rule is clearly laid down by Lord *Eldon* in the case of *Higginbotham* v. *Holme* ((1812) 19 Ves 88, [1803–13] All ER Rep 504), that no one can be allowed to derive benefit from a contract that is in fraud of the bankrupt laws.' (See (1861) 2 J & H 204 at 213, 70 ER 1031 at 1035.)

[56] Towards the end of his judgment, Page Wood V-C said:

'It was argued, that, the limitation to take effect in the event of "bankruptcy *or insolvency*"—in the alternative, it took effect in this case immediately the partner was unable to pay his debts and consequently before any act of bankruptcy under which his assignees could claim. But it would be impossible to allow that argument to prevail. A bankrupt is usually a insolvent before he commits an act of bankruptcy ... Besides, I observe that in several cases before Lord *Redesdale* the limitation is worded in the same alternative form ...' (See (1861) 2 J & H 204 at 215, 70 ER 1031 at 1035.)

[57] In *Ex p Mackay, ex p Brown, re Jeavons* (1873) LR 8 Ch App 643, A sold a patent to B in consideration of (i) B lending A £12,500 and (ii) B paying royalties
b to A. It was agreed that B should retain half the royalties towards satisfaction of the debt, but the arrangement was subject to a proviso that if A became insolvent B could retain the whole of the royalties in satisfaction of the debt. The Court of Appeal unanimously held that the proviso was ineffective. James LJ said (at 647):

c 'If it were to be permitted that one creditor should obtain a preference in this way by some particular security, I confess I do not see why it might not be done in every case—why, in fact, every article sold to a bankrupt should not be sold under the stipulation that the price should be doubled in the event of his becoming bankrupt. It is contended that a creditor has the right to sell on these terms; but in my opinion a man is not allowed ... to provide for a different distribution of his effects in the event of bankruptcy from that
d which the law provides. It appears to me that this is a clear attempt to evade the operation of the bankruptcy laws.'

[58] Having referred to, and quoted from, *Higinbotham v Holme* (1812) 19 Ves 88, [1803–13] All ER Rep 504, Mellish LJ said (at 648): '[A] person cannot make it
e part of his contract that, in the event of bankruptcy, he is then to get some additional advantage which prevents the property being distributed under the bankruptcy laws.'

[59] Similar views were expressed in the Court of Appeal in *Ex p Jay, re Harrison* (1880) 14 Ch D 19. In that case, a building agreement provided that the contractor was to erect 40 houses and was to be granted leases as and when the houses were
f completed. The agreement stated that, in the event of his insolvency, all the improvements on the land not demised to the builder as well as all the building materials which had been placed upon that land by the builder should become absolutely forfeited to the landlord. The Court of Appeal held that the agreement was unenforceable so far as it related to the building material.
g James LJ said (at 25):

'[A] simple stipulation that, upon a man's becoming bankrupt, that which was his property up to the date of the bankruptcy should go over to some one else and be taken away from his creditors, is void as being a violation of the policy of the bankrupt law ... I think we cannot escape from applying
h that principle to the present case.'

Brett LJ agreed, as did Cotton LJ who, after referring to *Higinbotham v Holme*, summarised the law in the passage I have quoted at the beginning of this judgment.

j [60] In *Ex p Newitt, re Garrud* (1881) 16 Ch D 522, [1881–5] All ER Rep 1039, the Court of Appeal again considered the efficacy of a provision in a building agreement. In that case, the provision in question provided that, if the builder was in default, the land owner could re-enter on the land, expel the builder, and forfeit any materials on the land, which materials would become the property of the land owner 'as and for liquidated damages'. The land owner purported to exercise his right under this provision, and it was argued that the provision was unenforceable because, prior to the land owner seizing the goods, the builder had gone bankrupt. That argument failed. James LJ said (at 531):

> 'The broad general principle is that the trustee in a bankruptcy takes all the bankrupt's property, but takes it subject to all the liabilities which affected it in the bankrupt's hands, unless the property which he takes as the legal personal representative of the bankrupt is added to by some express provision of the bankrupt law. There is no such provision applicable to the present case. The building agreement provides, in effect, that in a certain event certain property of the builder may be taken by the landowner in full satisfaction of the agreement. It appears to me analogous to a sale of property with a power of repurchase in a certain event.'

[61] Cotton LJ said (at 534):

> '[I]f ... the rights of the landowner under the agreement could not have been defeated by a transfer of the chattels for value, so long as they remained on the land, by what provision of the *Bankruptcy Act* is the landowner placed in a worse position as against the trustee? None has been pointed out to us.'

[62] In *Ex p Barter, ex p Black, ex p Walker* (1884) 26 Ch D 510, a shipbuilding contract provided that if the builder should cease working on the ship for 14 days, or should be late in delivering the ship, or should become bankrupt, the buyer was entitled to have the ship completed by a third party and should be entitled to employ such of the builder's materials as were on the premises where the ship was being constructed, which premises belonged to the buyer. The Court of Appeal held that, at least so far as the clause applied on the bankruptcy of the builder, it was void. Fry LJ, giving the judgment of the court, said (at 519–520):

> '[I]n our opinion, a power upon bankruptcy to control the user after bankruptcy of property vested in the bankrupt at the date of the bankruptcy is invalid. The general rule on this subject was thus expressed many years ago ... in language which was adopted as accurate by Lord *Hatherley* in *Whitmore* v. *Mason* ((1861) 2 J & H 204 at 210, 70 ER 1031 at 1033): "The general distinction," he says, "seems to be that the owner of property may, on alienation, qualify the interest of his alienee by a condition to take effect on bankruptcy; but cannot, by contract or otherwise, qualify his own interest by a like condition, determining or controlling it in the event of his own bankruptcy, to the disappointment or delay of his creditors ..."'

[63] The next case, which I must consider is *Borland's Trustee v Steel Bros & Co Ltd* [1901] 1 Ch 279, a decision of Farwell J. The detailed facts set out at 280 to 284 reveal that the case involved a private company with a capital of £400,000 of which Mr Borland had contributed £20,000. Following a dispute about the share of the profits between employees and shareholders, the company adopted new articles of association in 1897. Those new articles included: (1) art 47 which entitled each of the holders of the shares to continue to hold his shares until he should die, voluntarily transfer the shares, or become bankrupt; (2) arts 49ff which prevented any shareholder selling his shares without first offering them to employees of the company at a 'fair price' to be assessed in accordance with principles set out in art 53; (3) art 58 which entitled the directors to require a shareholder (other than an employee shareholder) to transfer all or any of his shares at a fair value to be determined in accordance with art 53. Mr Borland went bankrupt, and the directors served notice on him pursuant to art 58.

a [64] Mr Borland's trustee in bankruptcy challenged the validity of the notice served upon him under art 58 of the company's articles of association on various grounds. Farwell J rejected two of those grounds (namely that art 58 was repugnant to absolute ownership and that it offended the rule against perpetuities) and offered a classic definition of the nature of a share, which has perhaps some relevance to the present case. He said (at 288):

b 'A share is the interest of a shareholder in the company measured by a sum of money, for the purpose of liability in the first place, and of interest in the second, but also consisting of a series of mutual covenants entered into by all the shareholders inter se ... The contract contained in the articles of association is one of the original incidents of the share. A share is not a sum
c of money settled in [any] way, but is an interest measured by a sum of money and made up of various rights contained in the contract, including the right to a sum of money or for more or less amount.'

This description was endorsed by the House of Lords in *IRC v Crossman, IRC v Mann* [1936] 1 All ER 762 at 769, 781–782, 787, [1937] AC 26 at 40–41, 58–59, 66
d per Viscount Hailsham LC, Lord Blanesburgh and Lord Russell of Killowen respectively.

[65] Farwell J ([1901] 1 Ch 279 at 290) turned to 'the question whether or not these provisions constitute a fraud on the bankruptcy law'. He cited and adopted 'the principle as stated by James LJ in (*Ex p Jay, re Harrison* (1880) 14 Ch D 19 at 25)' which I have quoted, and continued (at 290–291):
e
'There is no idea of preferring any one person to another, except so far as is pointed by art. 47, under which by contract the original shareholders, at the time of the passing of the special resolution for the new articles, retained for themselves the right to refuse the compulsory sale of their shares until they should die, or voluntarily transfer the same, or should become
f bankrupt.'

[66] Farwell J (at 291) rejected the contention that the references to becoming bankrupt in art 47 'constitute a fraud on the bankruptcy law, and are void', and he said:

g 'If I once arrive at the conclusion that these provisions were inserted bonâ fide—and that is not contested—and if I also come to the conclusion that they constitute a fair agreement for the purpose of the business of the company, and are binding equally upon all persons who come in, so that there is no suggestion of fraudulent preference of one over another, there is
h nothing obnoxious to the bankruptcy law in a clause that provides that if a man becomes a bankrupt he shall sell his shares.'

[67] Later on the same page, Farwell J said:

'If I came to the conclusion that there was any provision in these articles
j compelling persons to sell their shares in the event of bankruptcy at something less than the price that they would otherwise obtain, such a provision would be repugnant to the bankruptcy law; but it is not so. They all stand on the same footing, and the proper value is to be ascertainable for all alike.'

[68] He then went on to consider in a little more detail the basis upon which Mr Borland's shares were to be paid for under art 53. He then said:

'These shares can have no value ascertainable by any ordinary rules, because having held ... that the restrictive clauses are good, it is impossible to find a market value. There is no quotation. It is impossible, therefore, for any one to arrive at any actual figure, as to which it may be said it is clear that that it is the value, or something within a few pounds of the value.'

[69] Towards the end of his judgment (at 292–293) Farwell J referred to *Whitmore v Mason* (1861) 2 J & H 204, 70 ER 1031, and said:

'In that case Page Wood V.-C. had before him a partnership deed which contained an article under which, in case of bankruptcy, the partners were to forfeit the whole value of a certain lease. That was held to be bad, and if there had been anything of the sort here I should, of course, have held it bad too. But there was also a provision, which was held to be good, that there was to be valuation of the share of the bankrupt partner ... I think I am following that case when I hold that there is no fraud on the bankruptcy law here.'

[70] I must next refer to a decision of the Privy Council, *Bombay Official Assignee v Shroff* (1932) 48 TLR 443. In that case, a Mr Madhavji had been a registered broker in the Bombay Brokers' Hall, an unincorporated association. The rules of that association permitted only those 'holding ... a card' to enter the hall and conduct business. The rules also provided for an initial payment 'for admission into the Hall' and thereafter for an annual subscription. The rules were not drafted with conspicuous clarity, but they clearly entitled the directors to declare a member who failed to meet obligations to other members of the association a defaulter. Under r 56Kh, a member declared a defaulter: '... shall cease to derive any benefit as a member of the Association and the amount paid by him as entrance fee to the Association shall be forfeited.'

[71] Under r 62 of the association, a person becoming a defaulter:

'... his card shall be cancelled in accordance with the rules of the Association. If he fails to pay in full his creditors within a period of six months then his card shall be sold and the amount realized on the sale thereof shall be distributed among his creditors in proportions [to their claims] and if on such distribution being made any balance remains over then the same shall remain credited to the account of the fund in respect of the hall.'

[72] Following Mr Madhavji's failure to pay funds owing to other members, he was declared a defaulter and he went bankrupt. The official assignee, whose status was effectively equivalent to that of a modern trustee in bankruptcy, contended that his card and/or right of membership of the association or the value thereof, vested in him as the assignee in the insolvency. The argument on behalf of the association was that, having been declared a defaulter, his card and right of membership of the association had been validly forfeited in accordance with the rules of the association.

[73] Giving the judgment of the board, Lord Blanesburgh said (at 445):

'[A]s to the nature of the association in point of law. It is, of course, not a company. Nor is it a partnership. It is not formed for profit of its members as associates in business. It is merely a voluntary association, resembling a members' club, perhaps, more closely than anything else. It has been formed in order that its members, share and stock brokers ... might have for their use

a   a hall for the transaction of their business with one another ...   The
     transactions of the members *inter se* are for the benefit or burden of the
     several participants and of them only.'

     [74] He then continued on the same page:

b   'Now if such an organization is to attain its ends membership must plainly
     be a personal thing, incapable of uncontrolled transfer: expulsion from
     membership must normally follow default or misconduct: upon expulsion
     all interest of the defaulting member in the property of the organization
     must cease.'

c   [75] Lord Blanesburgh (at 445–446) then went on to explain the nature of the
     interest enjoyed by a member of the association:

     'It may not, of course, be said that the members of the association, so long
     as they remain members, are interested in its hall and other property. On the
     contrary, that hall and property are theirs collectively, although held, on
d   their account, for the purposes of the association and with no right in any
     member or any majority of members to have any realization for individual
     benefit. Only if and when all the members have agreed to put an end to the
     association will they ... be entitled to have a division among themselves of
     what remains ... It may well be that the remoteness of the individual interest
     possessed by any member in the property such an association is the effective
e   reason why forfeiture or abandonment of all interest therein naturally
     follows expulsion, resignation, or death ...'

     [76] Lord Blanesburgh turned to consider the two grounds upon which the
     official assignee put his case. The first was simply on the basis of the rules of
f   the association. Lord Blanesburgh (at 446) had no difficulty in concluding that,
     as a matter of construction, 'the insolvent's interest in the association, whether in
     respect of his card or otherwise, became, under the rules, extinguished'. In that
     passage, he appears to have recognised that the interest that member had in the
     property of the association on dissolution could be treated as a separate interest
     from his ownership of the card, a point which he emphasised a little later, where
g   he said: 'In relation to his card, which is a thing separate altogether from the
     property of the association, certain rights are reserved to a member his
     representatives on death or retirement.'

     [77] Lord Blanesburgh then considered the second way in which the official
     assignee put his case, namely that: '... if the effect of the rules be that the proceeds
h   of sale of the insolvent's card do not enure for the benefit of the general body of
     his creditors the rules are contrary to the law of insolvency ...'

     [78] He then said that the official assignee relied on *Borland*'s case and
     Whitmore v Mason and continued:

     'It being agreed ... that the rules of this association are entirely innocent of
j   any design to evade the law of insolvency, it may be that even these cases,
     although cases of a company and a partnership, are more favourable to the
     [association] than to the [official assignee].'

     [79] Lord Blanesburgh then referred to *Ex p Grant, re Plumbly* (1880) 13 Ch D
     667, which he described as 'a Stock Exchange case ... more germane to the
     present ... case'. It seems to me reasonably clear, from the way in which he

expressed himself, that the immediately following paragraph encapsulates Lord
Blanesburgh's reason for rejecting the official assignee's second point:

> 'But their Lordships find the real answer to this contention of the [official
> assignee] in the nature and character of the association as they have
> described it whereby in the case of a defaulting member who is expelled from
> the association no interest in his card remains in himself, and none can pass
> to his assignee, whether his expulsion does or does not take place before the
> commencement of his insolvency.'

[80] The most recent case to which I must refer is *British Eagle International
Airlines Ltd v Cie Nationale Air France* [1975] 2 All ER 390, [1975] 1 WLR 758.
In that case, the plaintiff and defendant, together with many other airline
operators, were members of IATA, which established a clearing house
arrangement contractually binding on all its members, with the object of
providing machinery for the settlement of debits and credits arising where
members performed services for one another, as they very frequently did.
Under those regulations, the members could not claim payment directly from
one another, and could only claim from IATA on the basis of the balances due to
them under the clearing house scheme, pursuant to which the closure was
effected at the end of the month following that in which any debits or credits
were paid, and the net balance due to or from a member was ascertained and
notified to that member within five days of closure. In IATA's clearing house
manual of procedure, it was expressly stated that it was to 'be deemed to be an
express term of every contract agreement or arrangement for the time being
subsisting between any two members' that any 'debit or credit shall be payable
or receivable by and through the medium of the clearing house in accordance
with the regulations and current clearing procedure and not otherwise in any
manner' (see [1975] 1 WLR 758 at 760).

[81] The plaintiff company ceased trading and went into liquidation on 8 November
1968, and its liquidator claimed from the defendant a sum equal to the difference
between the value of services rendered by the plaintiffs to the defendant and the
value of services rendered by the defendants to the plaintiffs, after 1 September
1968. Differing from the courts below, the House of Lords, by a bare majority,
held that the liquidator of the plaintiff succeeded, on the basis that, in so far as the
IATA clearing house regulations effected a different setting of procedure from
that provided for in insolvency liquidation (then s 302 of the Companies Act 1948)
after the liquidation in respect of debts which had accrued before the liquidation,
it was contrary to public policy.

[82] Lord Cross of Chelsea ([1975] 2 All ER 390 at 409–410, [1975] 1 WLR 758
at 779), giving the reasons for the majority view, referred to *Ex p Mackay, ex p
Brown, re Jeavons* (1873) LR 8 Ch App 643 and the observations of James LJ which
I have quoted above. He accepted that the facts in the *British Eagle* case were
distinguishable, in the sense that 'there was no change whatever on the
winding-up; the same "clearing house" provisions applied both before and after
8th November' (see [1975] 2 All ER 390 at 410, [1975] 1 WLR 758 at 780). He then
stated that the clearing house arrangements did not give one member a charge
over the book debts of another, saying:

> 'The documents were not drawn so as to create charges but simply served
> to set up by simple contract a method of settling each other's mutual
> indebtedness at monthly intervals ... The "clearing house" creditors ... are

a claiming ... that they ought not to be treated in the liquidation as ordinary
unsecured creditors but that they have achieved by the medium of the
"clearing house" agreement a position analogous to that of secured creditors
without the need for the creation and registration of charges on the book
debts in question ... [and that this] is not forbidden by any provision in the
1948 Act, and that the power of the court to go behind agreements, results
b of which are repugnant to our insolvency legislation, is confined to cases in
which the parties' dominant purpose was to evade its operation. I cannot
accept this argument.' (See [1975] 2 All ER 390 at 410–411, [1975] 1 WLR 758
at 780.)

[83] Lord Cross then went on to explain:

c
'The court [was entitled to go behind the arrangement in *Ex p Mackay, ex p
Brown, re Jeavons* (1873) LR 8 Ch App 643 because] it was satisfied ... that [the
relevant charge on the royalties] had been created deliberately in order to
provide for a different distribution of the insolvent's property on his bankruptcy
from that prescribed by the law.' (See [1975] 2 All ER 390 at 411, [1975] 1
d WLR 758 at 780.)

He then continued:

'But what Air France are saying here is that the parties to the "clearing
house" arrangements by agreeing that simple contract debts are to be
e satisfied in a particular way have succeeded in "contracting out" of the
provision contained in s 302 of the 1948 Act for the payment of unsecured
debts "pari passu". In such a context it is to my mind irrelevant that the
parties to the "clearing house" arrangement had good business reasons for
entering into them and did not direct their minds to the question of how the
arrangements might be affected by the insolvency of one or more of the
f parties. Such a "contracting out" must, to my mind, be contrary to public
policy.'

[84] The minority view in the *British Eagle* case was explained most fully by
Lord Morris of Borth-y-Gest. His analysis of the position relevant to these
g proceedings is perhaps best expressed:

'When one airline effects a transportation in respect of a contract entered
into by another airline an obligation results. It might be called a debt owed
by one operator to another but more accurately it is that which would be a
debt but for the agreement made; by the scheme there is an agreement that
in lieu of there arising a debtor/creditor relationship between members
h there will be debits or credits in account with the clearing house.
Alternatively the effect of the scheme is that when a debtor/creditor
relationship arises it is by agreement superseded so that only a debt to or
from the clearing house can result. On either view the only "property"
owned by British Eagle on 8th November 1968 was the right (if on balance
j they proved to be in credit) to receive a payment from the clearing house. In
my view the effect of the scheme was that if on clearance a member proved
to be in credit with the clearing house such member in default of receiving
payment could sue IATA. Similarly IATA could sue a member who on
clearance proved to be in debit and failed to pay the clearing house.' (See
[1975] 2 All ER 390 at 400, [1975] 1 WLR 758 at 768.)

[85] Lord Morris said:

   'I see no reason to think that the contracts which were entered into by the members of the clearing house offended against the principles of our insolvency laws ... Services rendered during October and the first few days of November were in my view rendered under perfectly lawful contracts which were made in the same way as contracts had been made for years past. Because of the terms of the contracts which were made British Eagle had no claims against and no rights to sue other individual members of the clearing house. It is a general rule that a trustee or liquidator takes no better title to property than that which was possessed by a bankrupt or a company. In my view the liquidator in the present case cannot remould contracts which were validly made.' (See [1975] 2 All ER 390 at 401, [1975] 1 WLR 758 at 769.)

[86] Lord Morris ([1975] 2 All ER 390 at 401, [1975] 1 WLR 758 at 770) went on to refer to *Ex p Mackay*, and said that it was of no relevance because there was 'no stipulation which came within the principles' expressed in the judgment of James LJ (see [1975] 2 All ER 390 at 402, [1975] 1 WLR 758 at 770).

THE PRINCIPLES AS DERIVED FROM THE AUTHORITIES

Introduction

[87] MMI relies on the principle that 'there cannot be a valid contract that a man's property shall remain his until his bankruptcy, and on the happening of that eventual go over to someone else, and be taken away from his creditors', which as already mentioned I call 'the principle'. As a number of the cases to which I have referred show, there is no doubt that the principle exists, and has been applied to defeat provisions which have that purported effect. However, it is equally clear from the authorities that there are occasions where a provision which, at least on its face, appears to offend the principle has been upheld. I do not find it easy to discern any consistent approach in the authorities as to the application of the principle. In this, I do not appear to be alone. The difference of outcome in *Ex p Jay, re Harrison* (1880) 14 Ch D 19 and *Ex p Newitt, re Garrud* (1881) 16 Ch D 522, [1881–5] All ER Rep 1039 has been described as 'rather [surprising]' by Dr Fidelis Oditah in an article entitled 'Assets and the Treatment of Claims in Insolvency' (1992) 108 LQR 459 at 476. 'The result in *British Eagle* ... has not been the subject of universal approbation' according to Gerard McCormack *Proprietary Claims and Insolvency* (1997) p 18. The—

   'distinction between a determinable interest and an interest forfeitable on a condition subsequent has rightly been characterised ... as "little short of disgraceful to our jurisprudence" when applied to "a rule professedly founded on considerations of public policy," a view endorsed in *Re Sharp's Settlement Trusts* ([1972] 3 All ER 151 at 156, [1973] Ch 331 at 340).' (See *Principles of Corporate Insolvency Law* (2nd edn, 1997) p 148 per Professor Roy Goode.)

[88] It is not, however, my function to criticise the law. I have to decide whether the principle applies to invalidate the purported exercise by the directors of LSE of their rights under art 8 of the LSE articles in relation to the disputed share, bearing in mind the facts of this case, the guidance given by the authorities as to the circumstances in which the principle applies, and, to the extent that it is relevant, the convention. Having considered the authorities, it seems to me

a convenient to proceed to deal with the various ways to which the application of the principle has been analysed in the present case. This course has its dangers, because it may be that one has to look at the position 'in the round', given that the principle is essentially one of public policy, and it therefore could be said to be inappropriate to compartmentalise features. However, to justify the applicability or non-applicability of a particular principle by reference to 'public *b* policy', without considering the specific ground or grounds upon which it is said that public policy requires a particular result is even more dangerous. Public policy has been famously described as 'an unruly horse', and, therefore, at least to my mind, when considering an argument based on public policy, the court should analyse each of the arguments advanced to explain it. In the present, because it is accepted on behalf of LSE that the principle exists, and that it is based *c* on public policy, it seems to me that this reasoning indicates that I should consider each of the arguments as to the proper approach to the principle, in turn.

Established categories

[**89**] Although I have already mentioned them, it is right to start with two *d* established categories where the principle does not apply. It does appear well established that an interest granted on the basis that is inherently limited on insolvency is recognised by the court. In other words, a determinable interest, that is an interest with a limitation until insolvency, is valid, see the discussions in *Snell's Equity, Underwood and Hayton*, and Professor Goode's book and the passage quoted above from Fry LJ in *Ex p Barter, ex p Black, ex p Walker* (1884) 26 Ch D 510 *e* at 519–520. It must, I think, follow that an interest granted on the basis that it is inherently limited on some other event is effective, even if that event occurs on or after an insolvency.

[**90**] Secondly, a lease can be validly forfeited, ie determined by the lessor in the event of the lessee or tenant becoming insolvent. As I have mentioned, that *f* has never been challenged and appears to have been impliedly sanctioned by the legislature in s 146(9) of the 1925 Act. For some reason, a lease liable to forfeiture on grounds other than insolvency will be determinable on any of those grounds notwithstanding that the lessee is insolvent.

An inherent proviso

g [**91**] Mr Mann argues on behalf of LSE that, where, as the original part of the arrangement pursuant to which a right or property (an 'asset') is granted, there is a provision under which the grantor can in some way confiscate the asset ('a deprivation provision'), on an insolvency or otherwise, it is enforceable even if the grantee is insolvent. Another way of putting the same point, possibly in a *h* more limited way, is that, where it is an inherent feature of an asset from the inception of its grant that it can be taken away from the grantee (whether in the event of his insolvency or otherwise), the law will recognise and give effect to such a provision. A property or right subject to removal in the event of insolvency has been described by Oditah ((1992) 108 LQR 459 at 474) as a 'flawed' *j* asset.

[**92**] This has the merit of being a simple and readily comprehensible proposition, and one which is easy to apply. However, it does not seem to me to be correct. First, it would represent such an easy way of avoiding the application of the principle, that it would be left with little value. In other words, it seems to me that, if I accepted Mr Mann's simple proposition, the effect would be to emasculate the principle which, at least to Professor Goode, is one which should

be more widely, rather than more narrowly, applied. In his book (p 150) he not
only described '[t]he distinction between recapture of an [interest] transferred
outright and termination of a limited interest' as 'redolent of [a] highly artificial
distinction'. He went on to describe as 'sound' s 541(c)(i) of the US Bankruptcy
Code which he said, 'roundly declares *ipso facto* termination clauses ineffective,
however they are formulated'. Professor Goode also suggested that this 'is a
sound rule and one which English courts could sensibly follow'. I appreciate that
there is a real argument to support the contrary view, namely that the principle
should be abrogated on the basis that it is not for the courts but for the legislation
to override contractual terms. This argument could be said to have particular
force in light of the sophisticated and detailed legislative apparatus enshrined in
the Insolvency Act 1986 , and Insolvency Rules 1986. However, that is not an
approach open to me in view of the authorities to which I have referred.

[93] Secondly, it would be inconsistent with the apparently well established
principle referred to by *Snell's Equity, Underwood and Hayton,* and Professor
Goode. That principle, to quote from Professor Goode, is that 'the transfer of an
asset ... upon the condition that the asset is to revest [on] liquidation [of the
transferee] is void'. It is true that this rule can in some cases (especially relating
to real property) be explained by reference to the provision being repugnant or
offending the rule against perpetuities. However, such arguments do not apply
to personal property, see, for instance, *Borland's Trustee v Steel Bros & Co Ltd* [1901]
1 Ch 279 at 288–290 per Farwell J.

[94] Thirdly, it appears to me that an analysis of the authorities undermines
the notion that the initial inclusion, and subsequent operation, of a deprivation
provision in the event of insolvency is ipso facto effective in an insolvent
situation. In *Whitmore v Mason* (1861) 2 J & H 204, 70 ER 1031, there was a single
contract pursuant to which Mr Mason had paid his share of capital into a
partnership, had acquired his interest in the partnership assets, including the
mining lease, and had agreed that, in the event of his bankruptcy, his interest in
that lease would effectively be forfeited for no consideration to his partners.
The deprivation provision was thus an inherent part of the bargain pursuant to
which he obtained his interest in the lease; the beneficial interest which was
accorded to him by the partner who acquired the lease contained what amounted
to a provision for forfeiture in favour of the surviving partners in the event of
the bankrupt's insolvency. In my judgment, if LSE's first argument is correct,
Page Wood V-C ought to have concluded that the effective confiscation of the
bankrupt's equitable interest was effective, and yet he did not.

[95] I consider that the decision in *Borland's* case is also difficult to reconcile
with LSE's first argument. It was an inherent term of the contract between the
members of the company inter se and with the company (by virtue of articles of
association) that, from the moment the shares in question were issued to Mr Borland,
they were subject to the directors of the company being entitled to require him
to transfer them away. As Farwell J made clear in passages in his judgment
(at 291–293), in so far as the articles entitled the directors to require the shares to
be transferred away on the shareholder's insolvency, they would have offended
against the principle, were it not for the fact that they provided for compensation.
Apart from being, at least in some respects, pretty similar to the present case,
there is force in the contention that Farwell J should have decided otherwise if
LSE's first argument is correct.

[96] However, Mr Borland originally had shares in the company which were
not, it would appear from the report, subject to such a potential direction from

a the directors. Accordingly, Mr Mann contends that *Borland's* case was a case where the bankrupt had had shares which were not 'flawed', but subsequently voluntarily agreed to their becoming flawed. Properly understood, he therefore contends that the decision in *Borland's* case was really based on the well-established proposition that, having acquired assets which were not subject to being confiscated in the event of bankruptcy, a provision which rendered the

b assets subject to such deprivation agreed to after they had been acquired would not be enforceable. I accept that principle is correct, see the passages I have quoted from *Snell's Equity* and from *Underwood and Hayton* and the decision in *Ex p Mackay,* may well be explicable on this basis. Although the argument has some force, it does not seem to me that it can be fairly said to have been the basis from which Farwell J reached his conclusion. It is true that, in at least two places

c in his judgment, he did make reference to the fact that the potentially offending provision was to be found only in the new articles, but it does not seem to me that that fact formed part, let alone an essential part, of his reasoning.

[97] In what amounts to something of a refinement or narrowing of the proposition, Mr Mann suggests that the principle applies not only in those cases

d where a bankrupt agrees the deprivation provision subsequent to his acquisition of the property or right, but also where he acquires the property or right subject to a deprivation provision for consideration which was not subject to a deprivation provision. Thus, in *Borland's* case, the bankrupt acquired the shares which were subject to the deprivation provision in exchange for shares which were not subject to such a provision; in *Whitmore v Mason*, the acquisition of the interest in

e the lease subject to the deprivation provision was for a sum of money which, ex hypothesi, was itself not subject to any deprivation provision. That argument could be said to tie in the decisions in *Whitmore v Mason* and *Borland's* case with cases such as *Ex p Mackay.* However, as I have mentioned, it does not seem to be the basis upon which Farwell J decided *Borland's* case; nor do I think that it was

f the basis upon which Page Wood V-C decided *Whitmore v Mason.*

[98] Furthermore, if this alternative way of putting LSE's first point was correct, it would mean that a deprivation provision was unenforceable even in a case where it was an inherent part of the asset or a term pursuant to which the asset was originally acquired, unless the asset was obtained gratuitously or in return for another asset which was itself subject to a deprivation provision. That is

g not a test propounded in any textbook, article or case on the topic, save, possibly, *Whitmore v Mason*. In any event, if that was indeed the proper formulation of the principle, it would mean that a proviso for re-entry in the event of insolvency, was unenforceable in the case of a lease granted for a premium. While I know of no authority where that point has been specifically considered, it would appear

h to be inconsistent with what has always been understood to be the law (see for instance *Official Custodian for Charities v Parway Estates Development Ltd* [1984] 3 All ER 679, [1985] 1 Ch 151 where the consideration for the grant of a lease was not a capital sum, but substantial building works). Quite apart from this, in *Bombay Official Assignee v Shroff* (1932) 48 TLR 443, it is clear that Mr Madhavji

j paid for his membership of the Bombay Broker's Hall, and for his membership card; yet, as I have mentioned, the Privy Council held cancellation of his membership and the forfeiture of his card subsequent on his bankruptcy was effective.

[99] It also appears to me that, whether expressed in the broader or narrower way, LSE's contention is difficult to reconcile with the majority view of the House of Lords in *British Eagle International Airlines Ltd v Cie Nationale Air France*

[1975] 2 All ER 390, [1975] 1 WLR 758. At the time that the plaintiff agreed to
render the relevant services to the defendant, both of them were bound by the a
IATA clearing house arrangements, and accordingly at the very moment they
entered into their agreement, it was an inherent part of their contractually
enforceable arrangement that, in due course, when the clearing house accounts
came to be drawn up, there would be no debts as between the plaintiff and the
defendant, merely debits or credits as between each of them and IATA. Mr Mann b
argues that the difference between the majority view expressed by Lord Cross
and the minority view expressed by Lord Morris was attributable to the
difference between their respective juridical analyses of the interrelationship
between the agreement between the plaintiff and the defendant for the provision
of specific services, and the over-arching arrangement between various airlines,
including the plaintiff and the defendant, and IATA. I am not persuaded that that c
is correct. The point is perhaps most graphically illustrated in the passage I have
quoted from the judgment of Lord Morris ([1975] 2 All ER 390 at 400, [1975] 1 WLR
758 at 768) where he expressly reached his conclusion '[o]n either view'.

[100] Accordingly, convenient and simple though it may be, I do not consider
that the suggestion that a deprivation provision on insolvency or otherwise is d
valid provided it is included as part of the initial bargain (or as an inherent part of
the asset) is correct; nor do I consider that the more refined version of this
analysis, involving a super added requirement that the asset in question must
have been acquired for no consideration or for consideration which was itself
subject to a deprivation provision, can be supported. However, as is common e
ground, it seems that the converse proposition is correct: if a person has a specific
asset which is not subject to a deprivation provision, then a deprivation provision
to which he subsequently agrees to make it subject is unenforceable in the event
of insolvency (see the passages quoted above from *Snell's Equity*, and from
Underwood and Hayton).

f

No intention to prejudice

[101] Mr Mann contends that an important validating feature of any
deprivation provision is that it was not entered into with the intention of
disadvantaging creditors on a bankruptcy. It may be that, at one time, the fact
that there was no intention to interfere with, or to override that pari passu rules g
on bankruptcy would have been a reason for holding a deprivation provision
valid. However, in light of the observations of Lord Cross in the *British Eagle* case
(see [1975] 2 All ER 390 at 411, [1975] 1 WLR 758 at 780), I consider that that
contention is no longer maintainable: he said that it was 'irrelevant' the parties to
the arrangements in that case 'had good business reasons for entering into them h
and did not direct their minds to the question of how the arrangements might be
affected [on] insolvency'. To my mind, he was indicating that one must look at
the effect of the deprivation provision, and whether, if it applies in the context of
an insolvency, it is contrary to public policy in light of the bankruptcy laws.

[102] Further, I would refer to the observations I have quoted of Farwell J in j
Borland's case ([1901] 1 Ch 279 at 290–291) and of Lord Blanesburgh in *Shroff*'s
case ((1932) 48 TLR 443 at 446). In my judgment, they are difficult to marry up
with the view that the absence of any intention to evade the insolvency rules is a
factor, or at any rate a major factor, which assists the court in concluding that
a deprivation provision should be effective on an insolvency. Certainly, the
reasoning in those two cases is very hard to reconcile with the view that the

a absence of intention to evade would render a provision effective if it would otherwise have been held to have been unenforceable.

[**103**] Once again, however, it seems to me that the converse of the proposition upon which LSE relies is correct. If a deprivation provision, which might otherwise be held to be valid, can be shown to have been entered into by the parties with the intention of depriving creditors their rights on an insolvency, *b* then that may be sufficient to justify holding invalid the provision when it would not otherwise have been held invalid. Support for that may be found in *Borland's* case ([1901] 1 Ch 279 at 290) where Farwell J referred to there being no question of the article in question 'preferring any one person to another', and in *Shroff's* case where Lord Blanesburgh ((1932) 48 TLR 443 at 446) referred to the fact that the rules of the association were 'entirely innocent of any design to evade the law *c* of insolvency'. Further, it seems to me that the judgment of Farwell J in *Borland's* case indicates that, if it is clear that there was no intention to evade the bankruptcy law, then the court will tend to lean in favour of upholding a deprivation provision (which otherwise be invalid) on the ground that it entitles the person so deprived to a reasonable sum in respect of the asset concerned.

d
The provision applies on an event other than insolvency

[**104**] It is also argued on behalf of LSE that the fact that a deprivation provision falls to be operated on the happening of an event or events not being the insolvency of the transferee, is at least a factor which is to be taken into account as a factor upholding the provision. That may be the ground for *e* justifying the fact that the deprivation provision was effective in *Ex p Newitt, re Garrud* (1881) 16 Ch D 522, [1881–5] All ER Rep 1039, in contrast with the striking down of the provision in *Ex p Jay, re Harrison* (1880) 14 Ch D 19. As I see it, in *Ex p Newitt*, the essential points were that the landowner's right to take possession of the builder's materials was not dependent on the builder being *f* bankrupt, but being in default, and the materials were specifically to become the property of the landowner on the basis that they represented liquidated damages in respect of the builder's breach of contract.

[**105**] In light of the reasoning of the majority of the House of Lords in the *British Eagle* case, there must be real doubt as to whether that reasoning can now be sustained. First, it appears clear from the speech of Lord Cross that it is the *g* effect of a deprivation provision in the event of insolvency with which one is ultimately concerned, and not, so much whether or not the deprivation provision is expressed to apply on insolvency or not (see [1975] 2 All ER 390 at 411, [1975] 1 WLR 758 at 780). Further, it is clear from the facts of the *British Eagle* case itself: the deprivation provision, or its equivalent, was in no way concerned with *h* insolvency, and was intended to apply automatically to what would otherwise be sums due under contracts between IATA members. Secondly, the effect of the arrangement in *Ex p Newitt* was to render the landowner a secured creditor (at least to the value of the builder's materials on the premises) so far as his claim for damages was concerned. In part of his reasoning, Lord Cross considered that this *j* represented an objectionable feature of the arrangement from the point of view of bankruptcy principles (see [1975] 2 All ER 390 at 411, [1975] 1 WLR 758 at 780).

[**106**] None the less, it appears to me that, particularly when one bears in mind that a forfeiture clause in a lease is binding on a trustee in bankruptcy or liquidator, even if the forfeiture is triggered by the bankruptcy or liquidation itself, there is something to be said for the logic of the view expressed in *Ex p Newitt*, namely that the forfeiture proviso in respect of the builders materials was

enforceable against the builder, and therefore his trustee in bankruptcy could not avoid it. However, I find it hard to see how the reasoning in *Ex p Newitt* can stand in light of the reasoning of the majority of the House of Lords in the *British Eagle* case. It is not as if the forfeiture arrangement in *Ex p Newitt* was akin to a forfeiture provision in a lease, because, other than the right to forfeit, the landowner had no interest whatever in the materials: as between him and the builder, they were the builder's property and the builder encumbered them with a deprivation provision. On the other hand, at least with a forfeiture clause in a lease, it can be said that the landlord always retains the reversionary interest to the land the subject of the lease.

[107] However, there are problems with applying the principle if *Ex p Newitt* is wrong. Would a purported forfeiture of the materials by the landowner after the builder had actually gone bankrupt have been ineffective, if the principle had applied? Whether a purported forfeiture of the materials before the bankruptcy, and if so for how long before the bankruptcy, would have been valid, it is hard to say. After all, in the *British Eagle* case, the clearing house arrangement would only have taken effect after the plaintiff had gone into liquidation, and there was no criticism of the effect of clearing house arrangements prior to the liquidation. It may be that, if the deprivation provision can be activated in an event other than bankruptcy or liquidation (irrespective of whether those events could also activate the provision) then, provided the right to implement the provision has arisen before the bankruptcy or liquidation, and provided that the deprivation has been completed by the date of the bankruptcy or liquidation, then it will not fall foul of the principle. Some support for this view is to be found in cases such as *Re Detmold, Detmold v Detmold* (1889) 40 Ch D 585, and *Re Balfour's Settlement, Public Trustee v Official Receiver* [1938] 3 All ER 259, [1938] Ch 928. However, in *Ex p Newitt* itself, James LJ said ((1881) 16 Ch D 522 at 531): 'To my mind it is immaterial at what particular moment the seizure was made'. Similarly, Lord Blanesburgh in *Bombay Official Assignee v Shroff* (1932) 48 TLR 443 at 446 reached his conclusion 'whether [or not the] expulsion [takes] place before the commencement of ... insolvency'.

[108] There is attraction in the argument that a deprivation provision which engages on an event other than insolvency will be enforceable notwithstanding the insolvency of the owner of the asset concerned. There is also authority to support that view, namely *Ex p Newitt*, as I have mentioned. However, I think the argument is difficult to reconcile not only with the view of Lord Cross in the *British Eagle* case, but also with the way Lord Blanesburgh (at 446) expressed himself in *Shroff*'s case. The deprivation provision in that case was exercisable on default not on bankruptcy; if that alone had been enough to validate the provision even on a Member's bankruptcy, it is hard to see why there was any necessity to justify the decision by reference to 'the nature and character of the Association'. It also may be that this argument on behalf of LSE is difficult to reconcile with *Borland*'s case.

[109] The alternative approach is to analyse cases such as *Shroff*'s case as involving a deprivation provision which is exercisable on an event which is so similar to insolvency, namely default, that it falls within the basic principle as described in the earlier cases. Such an approach could be said to be consistent with the last of the passages I quoted from the judgment in *Whitmore v Mason* (1861) 2 J & H 204 at 215, 70 ER 1031 at 1035. If this alternative approach is correct then it would validate some deprivation provisions in the event of an

a insolvency (ie those triggered by events not akin to insolvency) but it would not
assist LSE in the instant case.

Valueless assets etc

[110] Clearly, there must be cases where, for one reason or another, not so far
considered, a deprivation provision will be upheld. There may in exceptional
b cases be a public policy reason for upholding a deprivation provision. Cases which
would more frequently occur are those where the right or property subject to the
deprivation provision has no value, or (in many cases) if it is incapable of
assignment, or depends on the character or status of the owner. In such cases, a
deprivation provision would, as I see it, normally be enforceable in the event of
the insolvency of the owner. If the asset has no value, or if it is incapable of transfer,
c then it could scarcely be said to be to the detriment of the creditors of the owner
if he was deprived of the asset. Similarly, if the ownership of the asset depends
on the personal characteristics of the owner, it is difficult to see how objection
could be taken to a power to take away the asset, not least because it would be
inherently unsuitable to be retained for the benefit of his creditors. An example
d which springs to mind would be membership of a club. Coming closer to the
facts of the present case, the loss of membership of a financial institution, such as
a stock exchange, where one has failed to meet one's debts or has gone bankrupt
cannot, in my view, be said to fall foul of the principle. Membership of such an
exchange turns on the personal attributes and acceptability of a particular
individual, and expulsion of the grounds of not honouring financial obligations
e (or, indeed, insolvency) would seem to be almost an inevitable incident of
membership.

[111] It is presumably for this sort of reason that no argument was advanced
in *Shroff*'s case, or indeed in this case, to support the contention that loss of
membership of a stock exchange on the grounds of failure to honour obligations,
f or bankruptcy, could be challenged. In the instant case, and, I think, in *Shroff*'s
case, it was accepted that a person's membership of such an exchange depends on
his personal characteristics, and is in any event not transferable.

Ancillary assets

[112] On behalf of LSE, it is contended that the decision in *Shroff*'s case goes
g rather further than this. Having accepted that a member of the association had
two separate interests, namely an interest in his card and a contingent interest in
the property of the association, the Privy Council concluded that 'the nature and
character of the association' was such that, if a defaulting member was expelled
from the association 'no interest in his card remains in himself, and none that can
h pass to his assignee'. In other words, although a member's interest in his card was
a proprietary right, separate from his right as a member of the association, it
was effectively ancillary to his membership of the association, and if he was
validly expelled from the association (which, for the reasons which I have been
discussing, he had been), the principle could not be applied so as to invalidate the
j deprivation of his card.

[113] In agreement with this contention, it seems to me that the reasoning of
the Privy Council was effectively that the membership of the association and the
ownership of the card, although separate rights, were so inextricably linked, that
a valid deprivation of the former right justified a deprivation of the latter
property, notwithstanding the principle. It is not entirely clear from the reasoning
of Lord Blanesburgh whether one looks to see which is the main asset,

membership of the association or ownership of the card, or whether one looks at the composite arrangement. I suspect that in most cases, these would come to the same thing.

[114] It is contended on behalf of MMI that this is not the right analysis of *Shroff*'s case, and, if it is, I should not follow it. So far as the first component of that argument is concerned, I do not agree with it. As I have already said, it appears to me that the analysis I have been considering is to be found in the passage in Lord Blanesburgh's judgment ((1932) 48 TLR 443 at 446) which opens with the words 'But their Lordships find the real answer to this contention': as a matter of ordinary language, one would expect what follows to encapsulate the essential reasoning for rejecting the contention he has been considering, which is, in effect, the application of the principle to the facts of that case.

[115] As to the argument that I should not follow this reasoning, I accept that a decision of the Privy Council is not technically binding on me; I also accept that Lord Blanesburgh's apparent reliance on *Ex p Grant, re Plumbly* (1880) 13 Ch D 667 is a little mystifying, and Mr Mann did not seek strenuously to justify or even explain it. It is further the fact that the decision in *Shroff*'s case does not appear to have been considered, or even cited, in any subsequent cases on the topic. On the other hand, it would obviously be wrong to adopt a cavalier approach to a decision of the Privy Council; perhaps the most directly relevant case, namely *Borland*'s case, was cited to, and distinguished by, the board, and there is nothing in any previous or subsequent authority which can fairly be said to call into question the reason given by the board for rejecting the contention that the principle applied on the facts of that case. Over and above that, it seems to me that both the result and the reasoning, at least as I understand it, in *Shroff*'s case were correct. The essential right or interest enjoyed by a member of the association was the right to be a broker and conduct business as such, which involved coming into the Bombay Broker's Hall, because that is where the business was carried on. The rights and obligations, such as the ownership of the card and the contingent right to share in the assets of the association if and when it was dissolved, as well as the obligation to make payments pursuant to, and to abide by, the rules of the association, were all incidental to that basic right and were unassignable. If a member was justifiably deprived of that right in circumstances where he was bankrupt, then public policy would not require application of the principle to invalidate the deprivation or removal of the other ancillary rights, even if the principle would have invalidated the deprivation of one or more of those ancillary rights if they had been rights which, as it were, stood alone.

Conclusion

[116] I am here concerned with a claim to rely on 'the principle' ie that a provision that a person's property shall pass to another or be confiscated is regarded by the court as void where the person concerned is insolvent. Having considered a number of authorities concerned with the application of the principle, and the analysis of those authorities, it seems to me that the position may be summarised as follows.

[117] First, there is no doubt that the principle exists: it has been applied or approved in a number of cases, and fairly recently in the House of Lords. Secondly, the principle is essentially based on a common law rule of public policy, which is itself based on the long-established approach of the English law to the treatment of assets and creditors on insolvency. Thirdly, there are circumstances

a in which the principle does not apply. Fourthly, it is not possible to discern a coherent rule, or even an entirely coherent set of rules, to enable one to assess in any particular case whether such a provision (a 'deprivation provision') falls foul of the principle. Fifthly, and perhaps not surprisingly, it is not entirely easy to reconcile the conclusions, and indeed the reasoning, in some of the cases. Sixthly, there are some rules, of a somewhat 'piecemeal' nature which can be derived

b from the cases.

[118] It seems to me that one can extract the following rather limited propositions from the cases. (1) A person cannot validly arrange his affairs so that what is already his own property becomes subject to being taken away in the event of his insolvency. (2) Subject to the first proposition, the transfer of an asset for an interest coming to an end on the transferee's insolvency (or on some

c other event) is apparently effective even if the transferee is insolvent. (3) Subject to the following propositions, the transfer of an asset on the condition that the asset will revest in the transferor in the event of the transferee's insolvency is generally invalid. (4) A proviso in a lease for determination, i e for forfeiture or re-entry, even in the event of the lessee becoming insolvent, is enforceable where

d the lessee is insolvent. (5) In deciding whether a deprivation provision exercisable other than on insolvency offends against the principle, one is primarily concerned with the effect of the provision and not with the intention of the parties, but it may be that, if the deprivation provision is exercisable for reasons which are not concerned with the owner's insolvency, default or breach, then its operation will not be within the principle. (6) However, if the intention of the parties when

e agreeing the deprivation provision was to evade the insolvency rules, then that may invalidate a provision which would otherwise have been valid, and if the intention of the parties was not to evade the insolvency laws, the court will be more ready to uphold the deprivation provision if it provides for compensation for the deprivation. (7) The court will scrutinise with particular care a deprivation

f provision which would have the effect of preferring the person to whom the asset reverts or passes, as against other unsecured creditors of the insolvent person whose estate is deprived of the asset pursuant to the provision. (8) Where the deprivation provision relates to an asset which has no value, or which is incapable of transfer, or which depends on the character or status of the owner, then it will normally be enforceable on insolvency. (9) A deprivation provision which might

g otherwise be invalid in light of the principle may be held to be valid if the asset concerned is closely connected with or, more probably, subsidiary to, a right or other benefit in respect of which a deprivation provision is valid. (10) If the deprivation provision does not offend against the principle then (subject to there being no other objection to it), it will be enforceable against a trustee in

h bankruptcy or on a liquidation just as much as it would have been enforceable in the absence of an insolvency.

APPLICATION OF THE PRINCIPLES TO THIS CASE

[119] If the disputed share had been, as it were, free-standing, in the sense of
j being unconnected with MMI's membership of the Stock Exchange, there would obviously be a powerful argument open to MMI to the effect that a provision such as art 8.03 of the LSE articles was unenforceable in the event of a 'B' shareholder being insolvent. On that assumption, it seems to me that, subject to one point, it would be difficult to distinguish the case from *Borland's Trustee v Steel Bros & Co Ltd* [1901] 1 Ch 279, where, had there not been reasonable provision for compensation for the deprivation, Farwell J would have held the deprivation

provision unenforceable, in light of the shareholder's bankruptcy, by virtue of
application of the principle. In this case, as in that case, the company's articles of *a*
association gave the directors the power to require a shareholder (or his trustee
in bankruptcy) to transfer his shares to a third party. The fact that the power is
contained in the articles of the company concerned, and the fact that they were
freely agreed by the company's members, would not appear to be enough to
justify the principle not applying. Not only does that appear to be the view of *b*
Farwell J, but, as I have mentioned, it is, as I see it, consistent with the view of the
majority of the House of Lords in *British Eagle International Airlines Ltd v Cie
Nationale Air France* [1975] 2 All ER 390, [1975] 1 WLR 758. Further, there is
reason to believe, as Mr Hochhauser argues, that, even without the relatively
near possibility of demutualisation, a 'B' share would have had value. He relies
on common sense, the fact that each 'A' share was valued at £10,000 in 1986 and *c*
the substantial value on demutualisation

[120] On the face of it, therefore, and assuming that the disputed share is a
free-standing asset, art 8.03 of the LSE articles represents a term providing that
the transfer of the asset, namely a 'B' share in LSE, is vested in the shareholder
subject to a condition that the asset will revest, or at least be capable of being *d*
compulsorily revested, in someone, for no consideration, and this condition can
be operated in the event of the shareholder's insolvency. On the basis that the
disputed share was either issued to MMI by or at the direction of LSE, or was
transferred to MMI with the consent, even at the direction, of LSE, it can be said
that the arrangement embodied in art 8 effectively entitles the transferor, or at
least a person involved in the transfer, of the disputed share, to get it back, or at *e*
least to direct its transfer away, for no consideration. This would appear to
represent what, at least on the face of it, is a classic deprivation provision which
offends against the principle, at least if it is activated on the insolvency of the
owner of the asset.

[121] However, even on the basis that the disputed share should be treated as *f*
a free-standing asset, there is a real argument to support the implementation of
art 8 in the event of a shareholder's insolvency. It can be said that a 'B' share in
LSE, even treated as a free-standing asset, had no real value, because it could never
be transferred away for consideration, unless the directors otherwise agreed, and
there is no way in which the directors of LSE could be compelled to agree. It is at
this point that it perhaps becomes unrealistic to consider the disputed share as a *g*
free-standing asset, because, if the 'B' shares were free-standing assets, a provision
that they could not be transferred away for any consideration whatever without the
consent of the LSE directors would be a somewhat surprising provision. In
practice, as I understand it, up to and including the compulsory transfer of the
disputed share in the present case, the directors of LSE have insisted on the transfer *h*
of any 'B' share being for no consideration, and that is consistent with how the first
sentence of the article is worded. If the 'B' shares were free-standing assets, then it
is conceivable that the court would be prepared to take the unusual course of
implying into the first sentence of art 8.03 a provision to the effect that the directors
of LSE would act reasonably when considering whether to permit a shareholder to *j*
transfer his share for the consideration he was able to obtain, subject to their
approval. The court is slow to imply terms into articles of association, and it is right
to say that there was no argument on this point. However, it seems to me that, in
the context of free-standing shares, the court might take the view that a provision
in articles of association such as that in the first sentence of LSE art 8.03 would,
exceptionally, require some sort of implied term.

a [122] At this point it is therefore unhelpful to proceed further on the counter-factual assumption that the 'B' shares in LSE can be treated as free-standing. As is clear from the first sentence of art 8.03, it is intended that 'B' shares are only capable of being held by Member Firms and, by virtue of art 26, it is up to the directors of LSE as to who to elect as a Member Firm, and, as that article goes on to make clear, Member Firms are bound by the LSE rules.

b Mr Hochhauser contends that the LSE articles and the LSE rules should be treated as a single contract. I do not think that the resolution of the issue in this case is asserted by the determination of that contention. The LSE articles and rules were clearly closely connected, and it would be unrealistic to look at a Member Firm's rights under the articles without taking into account his rights and liabilities under the LSE rules. However, in case it is relevant, I do not

c consider that the LSE articles and the LSE rules constituted a single contract.

[123] I accept that it is possible for the court to 'conflate' two apparently separate contractual documents, and treat them as constituting a single agreement, but, as I see it, if parties have chosen to embody their relationship in two separate contractual documents, the court can only treat them as having entered into a

d single contract if there is some good reason for doing so. Far from that being the case here, it seems to me that there are good reasons for treating them as having entered into two separate contractual arrangements. The function of the LSE articles and the LSE rules are different. The articles effectively govern the running of LSE as a company, and are contractually binding as between LSE and its members, and the members inter se; on the other hand, the LSE rules govern the

e way in which the Stock Exchange is to be run, and are binding, like the rules of a proprietary club, between the proprietor, LSE, and its members, but they are not contractually enforceable as between the members. Furthermore, there will be shareholders who are not members, for instance entities that have left or have been expelled from the Stock Exchange, but who are still recorded as 'B'

f shareholders. None the less, this does not mean that the LSE rules have to be construed disregarding the LSE articles or, indeed, vice versa. However, given that the LSE rules and the LSE articles were, inevitably, subject to a different regime so far as variation is concerned (another good reason as to why they represent separate contracts) care must obviously be taken in relying on any provision in one of them when construing the other.

g [124] However one looks at the LSE rules and articles, it appears to me that, at least until demutualisation, a Member Firm's ownership of a 'B' share could not be realistically treated as representing ownership of a free-standing asset. Subject to a few exceptions, membership of the Stock Exchange and ownership of a 'B' share went together. Inevitably, there would be occasions when a 'B'

h share was vested in someone who was not a Member Firm; not only would that occur during the inevitable hiatus between death, bankruptcy, resignation or expulsion, and art 8.03 being invoked. Further, as I have mentioned, it may well have been the case that the directors were prepared to permit an insolvent, but non-defaulting, former Member Firm to hold onto its 'B' share for a time,

j presumably for the better realisation of its business. However, I do not think that calls into question the essential point that membership of the Stock Exchange and ownership of a 'B' share went together. First, the former Member Firm would only have acquired and owned the 'B' share in the first place because it was a Member Firm. Accordingly, it would only have been in exceptional cases, and for a relatively short time, that a 'B' share would be owned by someone who was not a Member Firm. Thirdly, even where, as an indulgence, a Member Firm, which

wished to do so, was entitled to retain its 'B' share, that could only have been to
enable it to find a purchaser who was prepared to take over the business, and who   *a*
would hope to obtain a transfer of the 'B' share. Fourthly, even then, it would be
a matter for the directors whether, in accordance with the LSE articles and the
LSE rules, that purchaser should be elected as a Member Firm, and should be
permitted to acquire the 'B' share in question. Fifthly, assuming that purchaser
was permitted to acquire the 'B' share, it would have been for no consideration.   *b*

[125] Indeed, that analysis suggests to me that it went rather further than
Member Firm status and ownership of a 'B' share being closely connected or, in
effect, part and parcel of the same overall asset. As I see it, a Member Firm's
principal or real asset was membership of the Stock Exchange, and its ownership
of a 'B' share in LSE was effectively ancillary to that membership. That conclusion
appears to me to be supported by a number of factors. First, there is the history   *c*
of the change in structure of the Stock Exchange which I have described earlier.
For the majority of its life, it was an unincorporated association, rather like a club.
Although it may be involve a slight over-simplification, if one wanted to trade in
quoted shares, one had to become a member of the Stock Exchange, and
membership of the Stock Exchange involved owning a share in what amounted   *d*
to an unincorporated association. The incorporation in 1986 enabled members,
in their capacity as owners of the Stock Exchange, to have the benefit of limited
liability, but it led to membership and ownership being separated, because of the
need for formal shares in the company and articles of association governing the
same. However, apart from representing a significant restructuring and modernising,
the fundamental nature of the commercial and financial benefits and incidents of   *e*
Stock Exchange membership did not really change.

[126] Secondly, the view that ownership of a 'B' share was effectively ancillary
to membership status is supported by the terms of art 8 itself, and the way in
which it has been implemented. It is not merely that the article indicated that
ownership of a 'B' share is linked to Member Firm status; it is also the fact that,   *f*
subject to the powers of the directors to require otherwise, the 'B' share itself
could not be transferred for value, and, indeed, it could not be transferred other
than to a person who was approved by the directors, because it was up to them
whether a person could become a Member Firm, and only Member Firms could
hold 'B' shares. On the other hand, there was nothing in the LSE articles, or the
LSE rules, which imposed any restriction on the freedom of a Member Firm to   *g*
sell its stockbroking business for the best price it could obtain; indeed, it would be
surprising if there was any such provision. Accordingly, in their governing
contractual documentation, namely the LSE articles and the LSE rules, the
parties themselves have indicated that the 'B' share is, in financial and practical
terms, very much an ancillary asset compared with the right to be a stock   *h*
exchange member, to carry on stockbroking business, and to sell that business.

[127] Thirdly, there is the way in which one would expect a purchase to
proceed, as exemplified by MMI's purchase of Doak's stockbroking business.
The business was acquired for a payment in anticipation of the vendor's 'B' share
being transferred. The purchaser (presumably with the vendor) then would   *j*
apply, ie after the acquisition of the business, or at any rate after agreeing to
acquire the business, for election as a Member Firm and thereafter for what
amounts to a transfer of the vendor's 'B' share. Assuming all went according to
plan, the 'B' share is then transferred to the purchaser, for no consideration.

[128] Quite apart from this, as a matter of commercial common sense,
supported by the observations of Lord Blanesburgh in *Bombay Official Assignee v*

a *Shroff* (1932) 48 TLR 443, the entitlement to a distribution of the assets of LSE only arose 'if and when all the members have agreed to put an end to [LSE]' as a mutual company. In other words, the 'B' share itself, quite apart from the provisions of art 8.03 of the LSE articles, had no or little inherent present value. Bearing in mind that LSE could not trade at a profit in light of art 27.02, the only inherent value of a 'B' share was in the event of the demutualisation of LSE.

b [129] In my opinion, subject to one point, this case is really governed by the reasoning in *Shroff*'s case. Membership of the Stock Exchange was and 'must plainly be a personal thing, incapable of uncontrolled transfer: expulsion from membership must normally follow default or misconduct' (at 445 per Lord Blanesburgh). If that is so, then 'upon expulsion all interest of the defaulting member in the property of the organization must cease'. Although the disputed

c share was 'a thing separate altogether from the property of [LSE]', ' the nature and character' of LSE and the Stock Exchange was such that 'in the case of a defaulting member who is expelled from [membership] no interest in his [share] remains in himself and none can pass to his assignee'. It is true that in *Shroff*'s case, expulsion from membership ipso facto resulted in loss of the card,

d whereas in this case expulsion from the Stock Exchange, and consequent loss of Member Firm status, did not automatically lead to loss of the 'B' share. However, given the way in which art 8.03 of the LSE articles was worded, given the way in which art 8.03 had been operated by the directors consistently in relation to Member Firms who were expelled and in default, given that in practice the ownership of a 'B' share and membership status went so closely together, and

e given that the directors are entitled to control the identity of any transferee of a 'B' share and to insist on the 'B' share being transferred for no consideration, it seems to me that this is no satisfactory basis for distinguishing the present case from *Shroff*'s case.

[130] Further, bearing in mind that the principle upon which MMI relies is

f ultimately based on public policy, it seems to me that where the basis for concluding that the deprivation provision is effective in relation to an asset is founded on the proposition that the asset is inextricably linked with a right which has been validly determined, it is appropriate to consider the rationale behind the deprivation provision. The idea that ownership of a 'B' share in LSE should be limited to members of the Stock Exchange appears to me to have been a

g reasonable and coherent policy, and one which reflected the basis upon which the Stock Exchange had been owned and managed for over a hundred years, and possibly longer. While LSE is now demutualised, one can well see the attraction of members effectively owning the entity which owned and ran the exchange. The idea that the company which owned the Stock Exchange, namely LSE,

h should not only be a mutual company, but one which should not trade at profit, and the notion that ownership of its shares should be limited to Member Firms also appears to be readily understandable. That a Member Firm should be expelled from membership in the event of failing to meet its Stock Exchange liabilities seems to me to be more than understandable. While there may well be

j exceptional cases, I can see a great deal to be said for the view that any self-respecting Stock Exchange would not want to retain as a member anyone who had not honoured his commitments to other members of the exchange. Quite apart from anything else, one can also see that it would be regarded as undesirable that such a person should in any circumstances be permitted to enjoy any say, indeed any vote, in the running of the Stock Exchange, through the rights enjoyed under his 'B' share in LSE. The terms of arts 8.03 and 8.04 of the

LSE articles were only not agreed with a view to evading any insolvency
principles. Indeed, as is pointed out on behalf of LSE in the present case, the LSE
rules do not enable a Member Firm to be expelled simply on the grounds of
insolvency.

[131] It is also worth mentioning that this is not a case where a creditor of the
insolvent is receiving any preference, or some sort of de facto security, as against
other unsecured creditors of an insolvent, which was a concern of Lord Cross on
the facts in the *British Eagle* case (see [1975] 2 All ER 390 at 410–411, [1975] 1 WLR
758 at 780). Indeed, the person responsible, LSE, for ordering the transfer of the
asset, the 'B' share, is not getting any benefit from it at all. Of course, in light of
Borland's case, that does not of itself validate the deprivation provision in this
case. However, given the reason why I think the provision is enforceable, and
given Lord Cross' remarks, I believe that this is a factor which assists LSE's case.

[132] The point which none the less gives rise to concern in the present case,
and indeed the point which has no doubt given rise to MMI's application, is that,
at the time that the relevant events occurred, demutualisation of LSE was under
consideration, and, within a relatively short time of the matters complained of by
MMI, the disputed share would have been worth nearly £3m. Accordingly, it can
be said that, unlike in *Shroff*'s case, this is not a case where one could refer to the
indirect interest of the owner of the disputed share in the assets of LSE as being
one of 'remoteness'. Further, it seems to me that, once LSE had demutualised,
so that its shares were effectively independent of membership and not subject to
restrictions or disposal by the owner, the exercise or deprivation provision would
very probably fall foul of the principle. Certainly, I am prepared to proceed on
that assumption.

[133] In connection with this aspect, I think it is important to bear in mind the
dates. MMI lost its membership of the Stock Exchange, and therefore its Member
Firm status, on 19 February 1999. Quite rightly to my mind, it does not challenge
the validity of its expulsion. On 18 March 1999, it was made quite clear to MMI
that, pursuant to art 8.03, the directors of LSE were requiring a transfer of the
disputed share away from MMI. It may well be that the first time that this was
requested in appropriate form was on 1 February 2000. From MMI's point of
view, the later the date one takes for the operation of the deprivation provision,
the stronger its case that there may be a breach of the principle. On the facts as I
have described them, it seems to me that the latest date one can take is 1 February
2000, because, if on that date there was a valid and enforceable implementation
of the directors' powers under art 8.03, then it is not open to MMI to rely on its
wrongful failure to comply with the request and thereby to raise a case based on
a later date. If that is wrong, then the latest date must be 14 February 2000 when
the 'B' share was transferred away to Holdings.

[134] The directors of LSE had approved the proposal to demutualise a few
days before 1 February 2000, namely 27 January 2000. However, that was not a
decision which could have been implemented without more. Any such decision
required the approval the shareholders in general meeting, and such a meeting
approved the proposal on 15 March 2000. In my judgment, if, as I believe, the
implementation of art 8 of the LSE articles did not offend against the principle
so long as the structure enshrined in the LSE rules and the LSE articles were in
place, then, as I see it, that position would have obtained at least until 15 March 2000.
The choice of any particular date, before which implementation of art 8 of the
LSE articles would not offend the principle, but after which such implementation
would offend, could be said to be somewhat arbitrary.

a [135] However, if it is accepted that implementation of art 8 in the event of a Member Firm's insolvency would not be objectionable so long as LSE was a mutual company with no prospects of demutualisation, but that such implementation would offend against the principle once demutualisation had occurred, then one has to find a point in time between the moment when demutualisation was first mooted (July 1999) and the moment when it occurred

b (8 June 2000), in order to decide at what point the principle is engaged. There can be arguments as to the right date to choose, but my view is that commercial common sense and certainty suggest that it should be no earlier than the point at which the equivalent of a binding and enforceable decision to demutualise had been reached. That date would in my view be 15 March 2000, when the decision of the LSE members to demutualise was formally taken, and following which

c there were no further barriers to demutualisation. If, as I believe, 15 March 2000 is the earliest date at which the principle would have applied, then, even when the disputed share was actually transferred to Holdings, 14 February 2000, there could have been no infringement of the principle.

d THE CONVENTION POINT

[136] MMI contends that an acceptance of LSE's case would involve a breach of art 1 of the First Protocol to the European Convention for the Protection of Human Rights and Fundamental Freedoms (Rome, 4 November 1950; TS 71 (1953); Cmd 8969) (as set out in Sch 1 to the Human Rights Act 1998), which provides that: 'No one shall be deprived of his possessions except in the public

e interest and subject to the conditions provided for by law and by the general principles of international law.' MMI further contends that, depriving it of the disputed share would involve a breach of art 14 of the convention which provides that: 'The enjoyment of the rights and freedoms set forth in this Convention shall be secured without discrimination ...'

f [137] MMI do not rely on any specific provision of the 1998 Act, but contend that the fact that there would be a breach of art 1 of the First Protocol to the convention and/or art 14 of the convention itself must be taken into account when considering LSE's case. In effect, this submission involves two stages. First, it relies on the principle enshrined in what Lord Goff of Chieveley said in *A-G v Guardian Newspapers Ltd (No 2)* [1988] 3 All ER 545 at 660, sub nom *A-G v*

g *Observer Ltd, A-G v Times Newspapers Ltd* [1990] 1 AC 109 at 283: '... I conceive it to be my duty, when I am free to do so, to interpret the law in accordance with the obligations of the Crown under [the convention].' Specifically in connection with the common law, this is echoed by what was said by Sedley J in *R v Secretary of State for the Home Dept, ex p McQuillan* [1995] 4 All ER 400 at 422:

h
> 'Once it is accepted that the standards articulated under the convention are standards which both march with those of the common law and inform the jurisprudence of the European Union, it becomes unreal and potentially unjust to continue to develop English public law without reference to them.'

j Secondly, it is said that, given that that was the position before the convention was formally recognised in domestic legislation, namely by the 1998 Act, it must apply with all the more force to a case which has to be considered after the 1998 Act has come into force. I see the force of those points.

[138] As to the fact that the 1998 Act only came into force after the relevant events in the present case, MMI rely on two decisions of the Court of Appeal. First, in *Wilson v First County Trust Ltd* [2001] EWCA Civ 633 at [22], [2001] 3

All ER 229 at [22], [2001] 3 WLR 42, it was held that infringements of convention rights (as defined in the 1998 Act) which occurred before the 1998 Act came into force do not give a separate cause of action under s 7(1) thereof, but that the court is under an obligation pursuant to s 6(1) of the 1998 Act to act in a way which is compatible with convention rights, in so far as it is possible. That seems to be consistent with the view of the Court of Appeal in *J A Pye (Oxford) Ltd v Graham* [2001] EWCA Civ 117, [2001] 2 WLR 1293 at 1309, albeit by implication.

[139] I have difficulty with the notion of applying the convention to the common law, save to the extent explained by Lord Goff and Sedley J in the passages I have briefly quoted. Further, while there will no doubt be exceptions, it seems to me that it will be a rare case where the convention and the common law conflict. Bearing in mind the basis of the common law, the way in which it has developed over the centuries, and the continuing ability of the courts to adapt it with the passage of time, it would be surprising if it were otherwise.

[140] In the present case, given that the basis of the principle upon which MMI relies is public policy, it seems to me particularly difficult to contend that consideration of the convention should lead to the conclusion that the principle does apply, if, without having so far considered the effect of the convention, I have reached the view that it should not apply. That is all the more true in light of the particular features which, when taken together, appear to me to render the enforcement of art 8 of the LSE articles permissible as against MMI in relation to the disputed share, notwithstanding MMI's insolvency.

[141] Assuming that the convention could none the less be relied on by MMI in relation to the present claim, LSE argues that there can be no question of a breach of art 1 of the First Protocol, given that the 'property' in question has an in-built mechanism for its deprivation, namely pursuant to art 8 of the LSE articles, and/or that the mechanism pursuant to which the disputed share was taken was one which was agreed as a matter of contract. Accordingly, LSE contends that MMI cannot say that it has been 'deprived of [its] possession' other than in accordance with 'the conditions provided for by law and by the general principles of international law'. If that is right, then no question of breach of art 14 of the convention can arise, because, contends LSE, there can be no breach of art 14 unless art 1 applies.

[142] Unless it can be contended that the provisions of art 8 of the LSE articles were unfairly 'thrust on' MMI, it appears to me that LSE's argument is well founded. It seems to me almost self-evident that, at least in the absence of special circumstances, a person cannot be said to have been deprived of a possession other than 'subject to the conditions provided for by law', or, indeed, 'by the general principles of international law' if the manner and circumstances in which he was so deprived were pursuant to the very agreement under which he acquired the property, or, to put it another way, were an integral part of that property, provided, of course, that those provisions were enforceable according to the domestic law in the country concerned.

[143] Essentially for the same reasons which satisfy me that the deprivation provision in the present case did not offend the principle, it appears to me that the imposition or enforcement of the provisions of art 8 of the LSE articles was not oppressive in the circumstances of this case. In my judgment, it cannot sensibly be said to have been oppressive to require a person who wished to become a Member Firm of the Stock Exchange to acquire for nothing a share in LSE which was liable to be taken away for nothing on his ceasing to be a Member Firm. It is true that, when acquiring the goodwill of a Member Firm, a purchaser would no

a doubt take into account the value of becoming a member of the Stock Exchange, but, as I have explained, the acquisition of the 'B' share would have been for no consideration and would have been incidental or ancillary to the acquisition of the business and of the right to be a member of the Stock Exchange. Of course, all this would have changed on demutualisation of LSE, but that was not even contemplated at the time that MMI acquired the business of Doak, and in due

b course acquired the disputed share. I cannot see how, in these circumstances, it can be contended that the 'imposition' or indeed implementation of the deprivation provision in arts 8.03 and 8.04 of the LSE articles was an infringement of MMI's rights under the First Protocol.

[144] It should be added that Mr Mann contends that MMI's argument based

c on the convention could not have succeeded in any event because LSE was not or is not a public authority for the purposes of the 1998 Act. He contends that LSE is no longer a public authority (now that it has lost its listing function) and that, even if it was or is a public authority, it status as such does not extend to the way in which it governs its membership, and that it should be treated for the purposes of the human rights legislation as a private body. I do not need to decide

d that point, and do not propose to do so as it is by no means straightforward.

[145] As to art 14 of the convention, Mr Mann also contends that it could not apply because the evidence shows that in every case where a Member Firm was expelled on the ground that it was unable to meet its liabilities to other Member Firms, the LSE directors required the share of the Member Firm to be transferred

e to the trustee for no consideration. Accordingly, he says that the fact that insolvent Member Firms are not always required to dispose of their respective share for no consideration was not discriminatory, because it was only in those cases where the Member Firm met its liabilities to other Member Firms in full that the directors may sometimes not have required the 'B' share to have been

f relinquished. In my judgment, that is a good point. In other words, even if art 14 of the convention is engaged (which I do not believe to be the case in light of the fact that art 1 of the First Protocol is not engaged) it still would not assist MMI, because the provisions of art 8 of the LSE articles have not been invoked by the directors in a way which could be said to be discriminatory.

g
CONCLUSION

[146] In these circumstances, I am of the view that there has in this case been no infringement of the principle which is relied on by the claimant, and that the issue of liability must therefore be determined in favour of the defendants.

h Subject to further argument, I believe that it would follow that the claim must be dismissed.

Order accordingly.

Celia Fox   Barrister

R (on the application of McCann and others) v Crown Court at Manchester

[2001] EWCA Civ 281

COURT OF APPEAL, CIVIL DIVISION

LORD PHILLIPS OF WORTH MATRAVERS MR, KENNEDY AND DYSON LJJ

26 FEBRUARY, 1 MARCH 2001

Magistrates – Proceedings – Anti-social behaviour order – Whether proceedings for imposition of anti-social behaviour orders criminal or civil – Crime and Disorder Act 1998, s 1 – Human Rights Act 1998, Sch 1, Pt I, art 6.

A chief constable applied to the magistrates under section 1(1)[a] of the Crime and Disorder Act 1998 (CDA) for the making of anti-social behaviour orders against three brothers. Such an order could be made against a person if he had acted in a manner that caused or was likely to cause harassment, alarm or distress to one or more persons not in the same household as himself (sub-s (1)(a)), and it was necessary to protect persons in the local government area in which the harassment, alarm or distress was caused from further anti-social acts by that person (sub-s (1)(b)). The order could prohibit that person from doing anything described in the order, but the prohibition had to be necessary for the purpose of protecting persons in the relevant local government area from further anti-social acts by him. By virtue of s 1(10), the breach of such an order was punishable by a maximum of five years' imprisonment. In accordance with s 1(3), the chief constable's applications against the brothers were made by complaint, the method for commencing civil proceedings in magistrates' courts. The applications were granted, and the brothers appealed to the Crown Court. In the course of dismissing the appeal, which took the form of a rehearing, the Crown Court held that an application under s 1 of the CDA was a civil proceeding both in domestic law and under the jurisprudence of the European Court of Human Rights on art 6[b] of the European Convention for the Protection of Human Rights and Fundamental Freedoms 1950 (as set out in Sch 1 to the Human Rights Act 1998) (the convention). The brothers challenged that decision in judicial review proceedings, contending that applications for anti-social behaviour orders were criminal proceedings, and that the Crown Court's decision to the contrary had resulted in the admission of inadmissible hearsay evidence. The Divisional Court dismissed the application, and the brothers appealed to the Court of Appeal.

Held – Proceedings for the imposition of anti-social behaviour orders under s 1 of the CDA constituted civil proceedings, subject to the more relaxed rules of evidence applicable to such proceedings, both as a matter of domestic law and under the jurisprudence of the European Court of Human Rights. The statutory form of procedure laid down by the CDA in relation to such orders was the procedure appropriate for civil rather than criminal proceedings, and that was a powerful indication of Parliament's intention as to the nature of the proceedings. It could not, however, be conclusive, and it was therefore necessary to look at the

---

a   Section 1 is set out at [6], below
b   Article 6 is set out at [15], below

a substance of the proceedings, asking whether the two essential elements of criminal proceedings under English law, a criminal offence and a punishment, could be identified in proceedings for anti-social behaviour orders. In respect of the first element, the wide description of anti-social behaviour in s 1(1)(a) did not carry sufficient certainty to form a satisfactory definition of a criminal offence. Moreover, the requirement in s 1(1)(b) was at odds with the thesis that s 1(1) was

b concerned with the definition of a criminal offence in the context of dealing with crime and punishment. Furthermore, when considering whether an order imposed a penalty or punishment, it was necessary to look beyond its consequence and to consider its purpose. An order which was restricted to the prohibition necessary to protect persons in a defined area from anti-social behaviour was manifestly an order to protect in the future and not to punish for past misconduct. It followed

c that proceedings leading to the imposition of an anti-social behaviour order, when considered in isolation, contained neither of the essential elements of criminal proceedings under English law and did not themselves constitute a criminal cause or matter. That conclusion was not affected when the order was considered in the context of the consequences that might flow from its breach.

d As regards the jurisprudence of the European Court of Human Rights, that court had identified three principal criteria which it considered when deciding whether proceedings had a criminal character, namely the manner in which the domestic state classified the proceedings; the nature of the offence; and the character of the penalty to which the proceedings might give rise. Applications for anti-social behaviour orders had the procedural form of civil proceedings under English law,

e and neither of the other two criteria could satisfactorily be demonstrated. Offensive conduct was a pre-requisite for proceedings, but was not the only one, and the order, whilst impacting adversely on the defendant, was not imposed as a punishment. Anti-social behaviour orders were not about crime and punishment, but about protection of an identified section of the community. Accordingly, the

f appeal would be dismissed (see [21]–[23], [31], [32], [35], [39], [40], [42], [47], [52], [63],[68], below).

B v Chief Constable of the Avon and Somerset Constabulary [2001] 1 All ER 562 approved.

Notes

g For criminal charges in the context of the right to a fair hearing and for anti-social behaviour orders, see respectively 8(2) *Halsbury's Laws* (4th edn reissue) para 136 and Supp to 11(2) *Halsbury's Laws* (4th edn reissue) para 1262E.

For the Human Rights Act 1998, Sch 1, Pt I, art 6, see 7 *Halsbury's Statutes* (4th edn) (1999 reissue) 523.

h
Cases referred to in judgments

A-G for Ontario v Hamilton Street Rly Co [1903] AC 524, PC.
Amand v Secretary of State for Home Affairs [1942] 2 All ER 381, [1943] AC 147, HL.
B v Chief Constable of the Avon and Somerset Constabulary [2001] 1 All ER 562, [2001]
j   1 WLR 340, DC.
Benham v UK (1996) 22 EHRR 293, [1996] ECHR 19380/92, ECt HR.
Botross v Hammersmith and Fulham London BC (1994) 93 LGR 268, DC.
Customs and Excise Comrs v City of London Magistrates' Court [2000] 4 All ER 763, [2000] 1 WLR 2020, DC.
Engel v Netherlands (No 1) (1976) 1 EHRR 647, [1976] ECHR 5100/71, ECt HR.
Lauko v Slovakia [1998] ECHR 26138/95, ECt HR.

Özturk v Germany (1984) 6 EHRR 409, [1984] ECHR 8544/79, ECt HR.

Proprietary Articles Trade Assocn v A-G for Canada [1931] AC 310, [1931] All ER Rep a
277, PC.

Steel v UK (1998) 5 BHRC 339, ECt HR, (1998) 28 EHRR 603, E Com HR and ECt HR.

Woodhall, Ex p (1888) 20 QBD 832, CA.

Cases also cited or referred to in skeleton arguments   b

Albert v Belgium (1983) 5 EHRR 533, [1983] ECHR 7299/75, ECt HR.

Allenet de Ribemont v France (1995) 20 EHRR 557, [1995] ECHR 15175/89, ECt HR.

Campbell and Fell v UK (1984) 7 EHRR 165, [1984] ECHR 7819/77, ECt HR.

Clingham v Kensington and Chelsea London BC (2001) Times, 20 February, DC.
                                                                                    c
Demicoli v Malta (1991) 14 EHRR 47, [1991] ECHR 13057/87, ECt HR.

Deweer v Belgium (1980) 2 EHRR 439, [1980] ECHR 6903/75, ECt HR.

Garyfallou AEBE v Greece (1997) 28 EHRR 344, [1997] ECHR 18996/91, ECt HR.

McIntosh v Lord Advocate [2001] UKPC D1, [2001] 2 All ER 638, [2001] 3 WLR 107, PC.

Kolompar v Belgium (1992) 16 EHRR 197, [1992] ECHR 1163/85, ECt HR.   d

Lee v UK [2001] ECHR 25289/94, ECt HR.

Minelli v Switzerland (1983) 5 EHRR 554, [1983] ECHR 8660/79, ECt HR.

Pine Valley Developments Ltd v Ireland (1991) 14 EHRR 319, [1991] ECHR 12742/87,
ECt HR.

R v Benjafield [2001] 2 All ER 609, [2001] 3 WLR 75, CA.   e

R v Hull Prison Board of Visitors, ex p St Germain, R v Wandsworth Prison Board of
Visitors, ex p Rosa [1979] 1 All ER 701, [1979] QB 425, CA.

Société Stenuit v France (1992) 14 EHRR 509, [1992] ECHR 11598/85, ECt HR.

Appeal   f

The appellants, Sean, Joseph and Michael McCann, proceeding by their mother
and litigation friend, Margaret McCann, appealed with permission of Lord
Phillips of Worth Matravers MR granted on 2 January 2001 from the decision of
the Divisional Court (Lord Woolf CJ and Rafferty J) on 22 November 2000
([2001] 1 WLR 358) dismissing their application for judicial review of the decision
of the Crown Court at Manchester (Judge Rhys Davies QC sitting with justices) g
on 17 May 2000 to make anti-social behaviour orders against them under s 1 of
the Crime and Disorder Act 1998. Those orders were made on appeals by the
appellants from the anti-social behaviour orders imposed upon them at Manchester
City Magistrates' Court on 15 December 1999 by a stipendiary magistrate
(Alan Berg) on the application of the Chief Constable of Greater Manchester.   h
The National Council for Civil Liberties (Liberty) was given permission to
intervene on the appeal. The facts are set out in the judgment of Lord Phillips of
Worth Matravers MR.

Adrian Fulford QC and James Stark (instructed by Burton Copeland, Manchester) for j
the appellants.

Charles Garside QC and Peter Cadwallader (instructed by Peter Scofield, Head of Legal
Services for the Greater Manchester Police, Manchester) for the chief constable.

Jessica Simor (instructed by Liberty) for Liberty.

Cur adv vult

a 1 March 2001. The following judgments were delivered.

LORD PHILLIPS OF WORTH MATRAVERS MR.

[1] This is an appeal from the judgment of Lord Woolf CJ and Rafferty J sitting in the Administrative Court ([2001] 1 WLR 358). It was delivered on 22 November 2000 and dismissed an application for judicial review made by the three

b appellants. That application sought to quash anti-social behaviour orders made against each of the appellants on 17 May 2000 under s 1 of the Crime and Disorder Act 1998 (the CDA). The orders were made by Judge Rhys Davies, the Recorder of Manchester, sitting with lay magistrates in the Crown Court.

[2] The ground for the application was that the recorder wrongly treated the applications for the orders as being made in civil proceedings when in fact they

c were made in criminal proceedings. It was contended that this resulted in the admission of hearsay evidence under the Civil Evidence Act when, under the rules of evidence that should have been applied to criminal proceedings, this evidence was inadmissible.

d *Jurisdiction*

[3] After judgment was given in the Administrative Court, the appellants asked for permission to appeal to this court on the premiss that, as the Administrative Court have held this is a civil cause or matter, that was the correct avenue of appeal. The appellants seek to establish, however, that these are

e criminal proceedings. If that contention is correct, the Court of Appeal has no jurisdiction to entertain the appeal.

[4] Although the Administrative Court recognised this paradox, they did not refuse permission to appeal because of it. They refused permission because they considered that the position in law was clear. Equally, when the paper application for permission to appeal came before me, I did not think it right to refuse

f permission on this technical point. I gave permission to appeal because the case raises a point of general importance which merits consideration by this court. Mr Adrian Fulford QC, for the appellants, accepted that, if his argument succeeded, the fruits of his success would be a declaration that this court had no jurisdiction to entertain his appeal.

g [5] Anti-social behaviour orders are a recent arrival on the English legal scene. Whether the proceedings in which they are sought are criminal or civil is a question of general public importance. If they are criminal, the criminal rules of evidence and the criminal standard of proof apply and they attract the protection of arts 6(2) and (3) of the European Convention for the Protection of Human Rights and Fundamental Freedoms (Rome, 4 November 1950; TS 71 (1953);

h Cmd 8969) (as set out in Sch 1 to the Human Rights Act 1998).

[6] Provision for making anti-social behaviour orders is made by s 1 of the CDA. That provides:

j '(1) An application for an order under this section may be made by a relevant authority if it appears to the authority that the following conditions are fulfilled with respect to any person aged 10 or over, namely—(a) that the person has acted, since the commencement date, in an anti-social manner, that is to say, in a manner that caused or was likely to cause harassment, alarm or distress to one or more persons not of the same household as himself; and (b) that such an order is necessary to protect persons in the local government area in which the harassment, alarm or distress was caused or

was likely to be caused from further anti-social acts by him; and in this
section "relevant authority" means the council for the local government area
or any chief officer of police any part of whose police area lies within that
area.

(2) A relevant authority shall not make such an application without
consulting each other relevant authority.

(3) Such an application shall be made by complaint to the magistrates'
court whose commission area includes the place where it is alleged that the
harassment, alarm or distress was caused or was likely to be caused.

(4) If, on such an application, it is proved that the condition mentioned in
subsection (1) above are fulfilled, the magistrates' court may make and order
under this section (an "anti-social behaviour order") which prohibits the
defendant from doing anything described in the order.

(5) For the purpose of determining whether the condition mentioned in
subsection (1)(a) above is fulfilled, the court shall disregard any act of the
defendant which he shows was reasonable in the circumstances.

(6) The prohibitions that may be imposed by an anti-social behaviour
order are those necessary for the purpose of protecting from further
anti-social acts by the defendant—(a) persons in the local government area;
and (b) persons in any adjoining local government area specified in the
application for the order; and a relevant authority shall not specify an
adjoining local government area in the application without consulting the
council for that area an each chief officer of police any part of whose police
area lies within that area.

(7) An anti-social behaviour order shall have effect for a period (not less
than two years) specified in the order or until further order.

(8) Subject to subsection (9) below, the applicant or the defendant may
apply by complaint to the court which made an anti-social behaviour order
for it to be varied or discharged by a further order.

(9) Except with the consent of both parties, no anti-social behaviour order
shall be discharged before the end of the period of two years beginning with
the date of service of the order.

(10) If without reasonable excuse a person does anything which he is
prohibited from doing by an anti-social behaviour order, he shall be
liable—(a) on summary conviction, to imprisonment for a term not
exceeding six months or to a fine not exceeding the statutory maximum, or
to both; or (b) on conviction on indictment, to imprisonment for a term not
exceeding five years or to a fine, or to both.

(11) Where a person is convicted of an offence under subsection (10)
above, it shall not be open to the court by or before which he is so convicted
to make an order under subsection (1)(b) (conditional discharge) of section
1A of the Powers of Criminal Courts Act 1973 ("the 1973 Act") in respect of
the offence.'

[7] Section 2 makes similar provisions in relation to convicted sex offenders.
It provides for the making of sex offender orders and sub-ss (1) to (4) read as
follows:

'(1) If it appears to a chief officer of police that the following conditions are
fulfilled with respect to any person in his police area, namely—(a) that the
person is a sex offender; and (b) that the person has acted, since the relevant
date, in such a way as to give reasonable cause to believe that an order under

a this section is necessary to protect the public from serious harm from him, the chief officer may apply for an order under this section to be made in respect of the person.

(2) Such an application shall be made by complaint to the magistrates' court whose commission area includes any place where it is alleged that the defendant acted in such a way as is mentioned in subsection (1)(b) above.

b (3) If, on such an application, it is proved that the conditions mentioned in subsection (1) above are fulfilled, the magistrates' court may make an order under this section (a "sex offender order") which prohibits the defendant from doing anything described in the order.

(4) The prohibitions that may be imposed by a sex offender order are those necessary for the purpose of protecting the public from serious harm

c from the defendant.'

The facts

[8] Sean McCann was aged 16, Joseph McCann was aged 15 and Michael McCann was aged 13 at the time that the orders under challenge were made. All three of

d them live at 29A Ardwick Green North, Ardwick, Manchester. On 22 October 1999 the Chief Constable for Greater Manchester made an application under s 1(1) of the CDA in relation to each youth. Pursuant to s 1(3) of the CDA, that application was made by complaint to the Manchester City Magistrates' Court.

[9] The application in relation to each of the brothers was in the following identical terms:

e
'The respondent has acted on various dates between 1 April 1999 and 22 October 1999 in the Beswick area of Manchester in an anti-social manner, that is to say, in a manner that caused, or was likely to cause, harassment, harm or distress to one or more persons not of the same household as himself.'

f
Each application averred:

'That an anti-social behaviour order is necessary to protect persons in the City of Manchester local government area in which the harassment, alarm or distress was caused, or was likely to be caused by anti-social acts by him.'

g [10] On 15 December 1999 the applications were heard before Mr Alan Berg, a stipendiary magistrate. Mr Berg granted the applications and made orders against each applicant.

[11] The McCann brothers appealed to the Crown Court, pursuant to s 4 of the CDA, on 16 and 17 May. The appeal, in the form of a rehearing, was heard

h by the Recorder of Manchester sitting with justices. The appeal was dismissed. The terms of the order made by the court prohibited each appellant:

'(1) From entering the Beswick area as defined, edged in red on the map attached; (2) from using or engaging in any abusive, insulting, offensive, threatening or intimidating language or behaviour in any public place in the

j City of Manchester; (3) from threatening or engaging in violence or damage against any person or property within the City of Manchester; (4) from encouraging any other person to engage in any of the acts described in paras (2) and (3) within the City of Manchester.'

[12] Before hearing the evidence, the Crown Court heard argument and made rulings on preliminary issues. These were: (1) were the proceedings under

English domestic law to be regarded as civil or criminal proceedings? (2) If the proceedings were to be regarded as civil under English domestic law, should they, nevertheless, be treated as criminal proceedings by virtue of the application of art 6 of the convention which was about to be incorporated into English domestic law by the Human Rights Act?

[13] The Crown Court held that, as a matter of domestic law, an application under s 1 of the CDA was a civil proceeding. The court further held that the application was a civil proceeding under the jurisprudence of the European Court of Human Rights. Those findings were upheld by the Administrative Court.

[14] This appeal raises two closely interrelated questions: (i) how does our domestic law classify these proceedings? (ii) How would the European Court classify these proceedings?

[15] Article 6 of the convention provides:

'1. In the determination of his civil rights and obligations or of any criminal charge against him, everyone is entitled to a fair and public hearing within a reasonable time by an independent and impartial tribunal established by law. Judgment shall be pronounced publicly but the press and public may be excluded from all or part of the trial in the interests of morals, public order or national security in a democratic society, where the interests of juveniles or the protection of the private life of the parties so require, or to the extent strictly necessary in the opinion of the court in special circumstances where publicity would prejudice the interests of justice.

2. Everyone charged with a criminal offence shall be presumed innocent until proved guilty according to law.

3. Everyone charged with a criminal offence has the following minimum rights: (a) to be informed promptly, in a language which he understands and in detail, of the nature and cause of the accusation against him; (b) to have adequate time and facilities for the preparation of his defence; (c) to defend himself in person or through legal assistance of his own choosing or, if he has not sufficient means to pay for legal assistance, to be given it free when the interests of justice so require; (d) to examine or have examined witnesses against him and to obtain the attendance and examination of witnesses on his behalf under the same conditions as witnesses against him ...'

[16] The question of whether particular proceedings are criminal or civil in character is one that has arisen often at Strasbourg in the context of art 6. The first question that the European Court asks is how the relevant domestic law of the country concerned classifies the proceedings? Conversely, under the Human Rights Act, it is the duty of this court to interpret the CDA in accordance with the convention and to have regard to the Strasbourg jurisprudence in so doing. In these circumstances, I propose to approach the issue, first, having regard to considerations of our domestic law before turning to consider the implications of the Strasbourg jurisprudence.

Domestic law

[17] In the court below, Lord Woolf CJ said ([2001] 1 WLR 358 at 359–360 (para 3)):

'The significance of whether the proceedings are civil or criminal arises because of the difficulty that exists in relation to the proof of the sort of conduct against which section 1 is designed to provide protection.

a   Understandably, those who are subject to anti-social behaviour are chary about giving evidence in criminal proceedings. It is in particular because of those difficulties that, after a consultation process, the legislation which is contained in Part I of the Crime and Disorder Act 1998 was passed. The object of making the proof of conduct which is anti-social more easy to prove would be defeated if in fact the proceedings were criminal. Then the normal

b   rules of evidence which apply to criminal proceedings would have to be complied with and furthermore the proceedings would be subject to the additional protection provided by article 6(2) of the European Convention in relation to criminal proceedings.'

[18] The Home Office has published a guidance document which, it emphasises,
c   is non-statutory and should not be regarded as authoritative legal advice. This includes the following commentary:

'The order making process itself is a civil one akin to that for an injunction. The order is aimed at deterring anti-social behaviour and preventing escalation of the behaviour, without recourse to criminal sanctions. Breach

d   of the order, however, is a criminal offence. The process is not suitable for private disputes between neighbours (which are usually civil matters), but is intended to deal with criminal or sub-criminal activity which, for one reason or another, cannot be proven to the criminal standard, or where criminal proceedings are not appropriate. The orders are not intended to replace existing criminal offences, for example in the Public Order Act 1986, but

e   there may be circumstances where they provide alternative means to deal with such behaviour.'

[19] It may be that Lord Woolf CJ had this passage in mind when he spoke of an object of the legislation as being to make anti-social behaviour easier to prove.
f   It may be that he had in mind the legislative history. No evidence has been put before us in relation to this, but it is apparent from the CDA itself that its purpose is to adopt a novel method of attacking anti-social behaviour. It can properly be implied that the reason for so doing was that the existing provisions of the criminal law were not proving adequate for this purpose.

[20] So far as domestic law is concerned, the first argument advanced by the
g   respondent in support of the proposition that the proceedings are civil proceedings relates to the form of procedure laid down by the CDA. Criminal proceedings are begun by arrest, charge and production at court or by the laying of information followed by summons or warrant. Applications for anti-social orders are begun by complaint. That is the method for commencing civil

h   proceedings in magistrates' courts (see s 51 of the Magistrates' Courts Act 1980). This is a simple point, swiftly made, but it is a cogent one. The fact that the statutory form is that appropriate for civil rather than criminal proceedings is a powerful indication of Parliament's intention as to the nature of the proceedings.

[21] Mr Fulford submitted that the form of the proceedings cannot be
j   conclusive of their nature. In support of this submission he referred us to *Botross v Hammersmith and Fulham London BC* (1994) 93 LGR 268 where the Divisional Court held that proceedings for committing a nuisance under s 82(1) of the Environmental Protection Act 1990 were criminal in character, although commenced by way of complaint. This case does not take Mr Fulford far, however, for the court held (at 278), after considering the legislative history, that the use of the word 'complaint' had been incorporated in the legislation by an

oversight. None the less, I would accept that the statutory form of the procedure cannot be conclusive even under English law. One must look at the substance. What are the substantive elements of the proceedings that are said to give them a criminal character?

[22] Mr Fulford first referred us to a statement in the opinion of the Privy Council, delivered by Lord Atkin in *Proprietary Articles Trade Assocn v A-G for Canada* [1931] AC 310 at 324, [1931] All ER Rep 277 at 283:

'"Criminal law" means "the criminal law in its widest sense": *Attorney-General for Ontario* v. *Hamilton Street Ry. Co* ([1903] AC 524). It certainly is not confined to what was criminal by the law of England or of any Province in 1867. The power must extend to legislation to make new crimes. Criminal law connotes only the quality of such acts or omissions as are prohibited under appropriate penal provisions by authority of the State. The criminal quality of an act cannot be discerned by intuition; nor can it be discovered by reference to any standard but one: Is the act prohibited with penal consequences?'

[23] I accept the relevance of this reference. It requires one to look for (i) a prohibited act which has (ii) penal consequences.

[24] Mr Fulford next referred us to two cases (*Ex p Woodhall* (1888) 20 QBD 832 and *Amand v Secretary of State for Home Affairs* [1942] 2 All ER 381, [1943] AC 147), each of which raised the question of whether a decision whether to issue a writ of habeas corpus was given in a criminal cause or matter. Mr Garside QC, for the respondent, sought to brush these cases aside on the basis, as I understood him, that the issue in the present case is not whether an application for an anti-social behaviour order is a step in a criminal cause or matter, but whether it is a criminal proceeding. He relied before us, as he had before the Administrative Court, on a passage in the judgment of Lord Bingham of Cornhill CJ in *Customs and Excise Comrs v City of London Magistrates' Court* [2000] 4 All ER 763 at 768, [2000] 1 WLR 2020 at 2025. In this passage Lord Bingham CJ drew a distinction between criminal proceedings and a criminal cause or matter. I do not find this distinction helpful in the present case. In the *Customs and Excise* case the court was concerned with a proceeding which was an incident in a wider cause or matter. In the present case the application for, and making of, the anti-social behaviour orders have so far constituted discrete proceedings. There has been no sequel to these proceedings. There may never be a sequel to them. On the other hand, they may prove to be a precursor to further proceedings, criminal proceedings for breach of the anti-social behaviour orders.

[25] In the Administrative Court Lord Woolf CJ held that where the making of an anti-social behaviour order is followed by proceedings for breach of the order, the two sets of proceedings fall to be separately classified. He held that the proceedings in which the order is made constitute civil proceedings and the proceedings for breach of the order constitute criminal proceedings. He did not expressly consider the question of whether the first set of proceedings was, or was part of, a criminal cause or matter. Had he considered it was, the appropriate response to the request for permission to appeal to this court would have been to refuse it on that ground. It is implicit in his judgment that he did not consider the proceedings that led to the making of the anti-social behaviour orders to be either criminal proceedings or proceedings constituting or forming part of a criminal cause or matter.

[26] Mr Fulford has launched a two-stage attack on the judgment of the Administrative Court: (1) if the proceedings leading to the making of anti-social behaviour orders fall to be considered as separate proceedings, they have the character of criminal proceedings and of a criminal cause or matter; but (2) those proceedings should not be considered as separate proceedings but as an initial step in a criminal cause or matter, thereby reinforcing the conclusion that they are criminal proceedings. I propose to consider each stage in turn.

The order considered in isolation

[27] I agree with Lord Woolf CJ that certain passages in *Amand*'s case are of assistance in considering whether an application for an anti-social behaviour order is a criminal proceeding or a criminal cause or matter.

[28] The first is a passage from the judgment of Lord Wright where he said:

'... if the cause or matter is one which, if carried to its conclusion, might result in the conviction of the person charged and in a sentence of some punishment, such as imprisonment or fine, it is a "criminal cause or matter". The person charged is thus put in jeopardy. Every order made in such a cause or matter by an English court, is an order in a criminal cause or matter ...' (See [1942] 2 All ER 381 at 388, [1943] AC 147 at 162.)

[29] And the further passage in the speech of Lord Porter:

'This does not mean that the matter in order to be criminal must be criminal throughout: it is enough if the proceeding in respect of which *mandamus* is asked is criminal, e.g., the recovery of a poor rate is not of itself a criminal matter, but its enforcement by magistrates by warrant of distress is; and, if a case be stated by them as to their right to enforce it and that case is determined by the High Court, no appeal lies ... The proceeding from which the appeal is attempted to be taken must be a step in a criminal proceeding, but it need not itself necessity end in a criminal trial or punishment. It is enough if it puts the person brought up before the magistrate in jeopardy of a criminal charge ...' (See [1942] 2 All ER 381 at 389, [1943] AC 147 at 164.)

[30] These passages emphasise that if a proceeding is to rank as criminal cause or matter the proceeding must have as its possible culmination a punishment such as imprisonment or fine. The same message is given by a passage in the judgment of Lord Bingham CJ in the *Customs and Excise* case:

'It is in my judgment the general understanding that criminal proceedings involve a formal accusation made on behalf of the state or by a private prosecutor that a defendant has committed a breach of the criminal law, and the state or the private prosecutor has instituted proceedings which may culminate in the conviction and condemnation of the defendant.' (See [2000] 4 All ER 763 at 767, [2000] 1 WLR 2020 at 2025.)

[31] Can one identify in the anti-social behaviour order proceedings the two elements of (i) a criminal offence and (ii) a punishment? Mr Fulford submits, first, that the element of a criminal offence is present. An application for an order involves, first, alleging and proving that a person has been guilty of conduct which almost certainly amounts to offences under criminal law. In so submitting, Mr Fulford drew attention to s 4A of the Public Order Act 1986, as inserted by s 154 of the Criminal Justice and Public Order Act 1994, which provides:

'(1) A person is guilty of an offence if, with intent to cause a person harassment, alarm or distress, he—(a) uses threatening, abusive or insulting words or behaviour, or disorderly behaviour, or (b) displays any writing, sign or other visible representation which is threatening abusive or insulting, thereby causing that or another person harassment, alarm or distress.'

[32] These ingredients of a criminal offence under the 1986 Act mirror, to a significant degree, the conduct which has to be proved before an anti-social behaviour order can be imposed. But the express ingredient of 'threatening, abusive or insulting words or behaviour' does not form part of the definition of anti-social behaviour in the CDA, nor does the express requirement of intent. The range of conduct which can lead to the imposition of an anti-social behaviour order is consequently wider, indeed, so it seems to me, potentially much wider, than that which constitutes a criminal offence under the 1986 Act. Nor does the wide description of anti-social behaviour carry sufficient certainty to form a satisfactory definition of a criminal offence.

[33] In this context I note that the original order imposed by the stipendiary magistrate included a prohibition on engaging or threatening to engage in 'any other anti-social behaviour or other conduct to the annoyance of any person or which is likely to cause alarm, harassment or distress'. This part of the order was not reproduced in the order imposed by the Crown Court. I suspect that this was because it was appreciated that this language was not sufficiently specific to identify conduct forming the actus reus of a criminal offence.

[34] There is, moreover, a further matter relevant in this context to which Mr Garside has drawn attention. Proof of the conduct specified in s 1(1)(a) of the CDA is not the only precondition to the imposition of an anti-social behaviour order. The applicant also has to prove that 'such an order is necessary to protect persons in the local government area in which the harassment, alarm or distress was caused or was likely to be caused from further anti-social acts by him' (see s 1(1)(b)).

[35] This requirement is at odds with the thesis that s 1(1) of the CDA is concerned with the definition of a criminal offence in the context of dealing with crime and punishment.

[36] This observation leads me to the consideration of the other limb of criminal proceedings; the question of whether they are liable to culminate in the imposition of a punishment. At this point of the argument I am concerned only with the immediate consequences of the imposition of an anti-social behaviour order, not with the consequences of breach of such an order.

[37] Section 1(4) of the CDA provides that an anti-social behaviour order may prohibit the defendant from doing anything described in the order. The width of that provision is, however, restricted by s 1(6), which provides that the prohibition must be necessary for the purpose of protecting persons in the relevant local government area from further anti-social acts by the defendant.

[38] Mr Fulford submitted that the prohibitions imposed by an anti-social behaviour order can have severe consequences to a defendant. In the present case the order prohibits the appellants from going into an area of Manchester where they have family and friends. Mr Fulford submitted that such a restriction of liberty operates as a penalty.

[39] Many injunctions in civil proceedings operate severely upon those against whom they are ordered. In matrimonial proceedings a husband may be ordered to leave his home and not to have contact with his children. Such an order may

a be made as a consequence of violence which amounted to criminal conduct. But such an order is imposed not for the purpose of punishment but for protection of the family. This demonstrates that, when considering whether an order imposes a penalty or punishment, it is necessary to look beyond its consequence and to consider its purpose.

b [40] An order which is, in terms, restricted to the prohibition necessary to protect persons in a defined area from anti-social behaviour, is manifestly an order designed to protect in the future, not to punish for past misconduct.

[41] The imposition by s 1(6) of an additional obligation to consult before making an order in relation to an adjoining local government area underlines the fact that we are not here dealing with the imposition of penal sanctions.

c [42] For these reasons, I find that proceedings leading to the imposition of an anti-social behaviour order, when considered in isolation, contain neither of the essential elements of criminal proceedings under English law and do not themselves constitute a criminal cause or matter.

[43] I am supported in this conclusion by the observations of Lord Bingham CJ, sitting in the Divisional Court, in *B v Chief Constable of the Avon and Somerset Constabulary* [2001] 1 All ER 562, [2001] 1 WLR 340. That case concerned a sex offender order made under s 2 of the CDA. One issue was whether the justices had erred in applying the civil rather than the criminal standard of proof when making the order. In relation to this issue, Lord Bingham CJ said:

e '23. ... I turn to the first issue, which concerns the standard of proof. It is common ground between the parties that Parliament intended an application for a sex offender order in the magistrates' court to be a civil proceeding and intended the civil standard of proof to apply. But Miss Booth QC for the appellant submits: (1) that, whatever its intention, Parliament has failed to express in the statute as enacted any stipulation that

f the civil standard of proof shall apply; (2) that, as a matter of domestic law, an application for a sex offender order is to be regarded as a criminal proceeding; (3) that if it is not as a matter of domestic law to be regarded as a criminal proceeding, it is a civil proceeding of such a character that the criminal standard of proof should be applied; and (4) that, whatever the position in domestic law, this proceeding would for purposes of the

g European Convention for the Protection of Human Rights and Fundamental Freedoms (Rome, 4 November 1950; TS 71 (1953); Cmd 8969) (the convention) be regarded as a criminal proceeding and so should attract the criminal standard of proof. 24. As to the first point Miss Booth is correct. Parliament has not expressly enacted what standard of proof shall be applied on an

h application for a sex offender order. In relation to her second point Miss Booth relies on the severe consequences which may follow for the defendant on the making of a sex offender order: the duty to notify under the 1997 Act on pain of criminal penalty; the restriction on a defendant's freedom of movement and activity; and the possible penalty of up to five

j years' imprisonment on proof that the order has been broken. These are all important and legitimate considerations, but they do not persuade me that, as a matter of English domestic law, this is to be regarded as a criminal proceeding. Under that law a criminal proceeding is one in which a prosecutor accuses a defendant of committing a specific crime, on conviction of which the defendant will be susceptible to punishment. Here the application is made by a chief officer of police, but he is not acting as a prosecutor. The defendant is not accused of committing any specific crime. If the outcome of the application is adverse to the defendant, he does not become susceptible *a* to punishment. It is true that in s 18(1)(a) of the Supreme Court Act 1981 the expression "criminal cause or matter" has been interpreted more widely, so as to cover matters such as extradition. In my judgment, however, to assess the character of the present proceedings it is necessary to look more closely into the nature of the issue to be decided by the magistrates' court. Part I of *b* the 1998 Act is concerned with the prevention of crime and disorder, not the trial and punishment of those convicted. Magistrates' court proceedings are initiated under the section by complaint, which is the initiating process for civil matters in the magistrates' court (see s 51 of the Magistrates' Courts Act 1980). The condition provided in s 2(1)(b) of the 1998 Act is in my judgment appropriate as a basis for administrative action, not criminal conviction. *c* Furthermore, the problem to which s 2 is directed is not the detection, apprehension, trial and punishment of those who have committed crimes, but the restraint of those who have a proven record of sex offending and whose conduct founds a reasonable belief that a measure of restraint is necessary to protect members of the public against the risk of serious harm *d* caused by further sex offending. 25. There is no room for doubt about the mischief against which this legislation is directed, which is the risk of re-offending by sex offenders who have offended in the past and have shown a continuing propensity to offend. Parliament might have decided to wait until, if at all, the offender did offend again and then appropriate charges could be laid on the basis of that further offending. Before 1998 there was *e* effectively no choice but to act in that way. But the obvious disadvantage was that, by the time the offender had offended again, some victim had suffered. The rationale of s 2 was, by means of an injunctive order, to seek to avoid the contingency of any further suffering by any further victim. It would also of course be to the advantage of a defendant if he were to be *f* saved from further offending. As in the case of a civil injunction, a breach of the court's order may attract a sanction. But, also as in the case of a civil injunction, the order, although restraining the defendant from doing that which is prohibited, imposes no penalty or disability upon him. I am accordingly satisfied that, as a matter of English domestic law, the application is a civil proceeding, as Parliament undoubtedly intended it to *g* be.' (See [2001] 1 All ER 562 at 571–572, [2001] 1 WLR 340 at 351–352.)

[44] Mr Fulford sought to distinguish this decision. He pointed out that the first precondition for the imposition of a sex offender order is that the defendant should be a convicted sex offender. I am not sure which way this distinction cuts *h* when the issue is whether the proceedings constitute a criminal cause or matter. What is more pertinent is that the nature and potential consequences of a sex offender order closely mirror those of an anti-social behaviour order. I consider that the observations of Lord Bingham CJ can properly be applied to the present case. Mr Fulford stated that, if necessary, he would argue that B's case was wrongly decided. In my judgment it was correctly decided. *j*

The order in its wider context

[45] Mr Fulford submitted that the anti-social behaviour order should not be considered in isolation, but in the context of the consequences that might flow from the breach of the order by virtue of s 1(10) of the CDA. These were

a undoubtedly penal, with a maximum sentence of five years' imprisonment. Furthermore, s 1(11) precluded, when there was a breach of the order, the imposition of a conditional discharge. Mr Fulford submitted that the effect of the legislative scheme was that the original anti-social behaviour was an element, indeed the most significant element, of the criminal conduct leading to a conviction under s 1(10).

b [46] To my mind, this was the most cogent argument advanced in support of this appeal. Orders such as those imposed under ss 1 and 2 of the CDA make those against whom they are made subject to the risk of criminal sanctions in respect of conduct which would not otherwise be criminal. In this respect there is an analogy, as Lord Bingham CJ observed in *B's* case, with an injunction ordered in civil proceedings, but the analogy is not exact. Are these potential *c* criminal consequences such that s 1(1) of the CDA must be interpreted as giving rise to a criminal process subject to the criminal rules of evidence? No precedent drives one to this conclusion. There is no precedent to an anti-social behaviour order.

[47] I return full circle to the intention of Parliament as deduced from the *d* statutory language and the object of the legislation. My conclusion from these is that it was the intention of Parliament that an application for an anti-social behaviour order should be a civil proceeding, subject to the more relaxed rules of evidence applicable to such proceedings. That intention of Parliament is consistent with the substantive provisions of the CDA that I have just analysed. Thus, looking at the matter through the eyes of English domestic law, I conclude *e* that these proceedings are civil proceedings.

[48] That conclusion, however, now has to be tested for compatibility with the convention in the light of the Strasbourg jurisprudence.

Human rights

f [49] In relation to this area of the appeal, I acknowledge the assistance that the court has received from Miss Simor, instructed by the National Council for Civil Liberties (Liberty), to whom we gave permission to intervene. I would observe at the outset that the exercise of the powers conferred by s 1(1) of the CDA carries with it the risk of infringing a number of articles of the convention. If this risk is *g* to be avoided, the principle of proportionality must be carefully observed. But we are here concerned not with a wider attack on the order made, but with a question whether art 6(2) and (3) of the convention applied to the proceedings in which the order was made.

[50] Mr Fulford and Miss Simor referred us to a substantial volume of *h* Strasbourg jurisprudence in relation to this issue. As is the practice in this jurisprudence, principles once established tend to be re-enunciated verbatim in subsequent decisions. I propose to be eclectic in my reference to these authorities.

[51] The line of authorities starts with *Engel v Netherlands (No 1)* (1976) 1 EHRR 647. There the relevant issue was whether proceedings in a military court against *j* soldiers for disciplinary offences involved criminal charges within the meaning of art 6(1). In respect of this issue, the court held (at 678–679):

'82. … In this connection, it is first necessary to know whether the provision(s) defining the offence charged belong, according to the legal system of the respondent State, to criminal law, disciplinary law or both concurrently. This however provides no more than a starting point. The

indications so afforded have only a formal and relative value and must be
examined in the light of the common denominator of the respective *a*
legislation of the various Contracting States. The very nature of the offence
is a factor of greater import. When a serviceman finds himself accused of an
act or omission allegedly contravening a legal rule governing the operation
of the armed forces, the State may in principle employ against him
disciplinary law rather than criminal law. In this respect, the court expresses *b*
its agreement with the Government. However, supervision by the court
does not stop there. Such supervision would generally prove to be illusory
if it did not also take into consideration the degree of severity of the penalty
that the person concerned risks incurring. In a society subscribing to the rule
of law, there belong to the "criminal" sphere deprivations of liberty liable to
be imposed as a punishment, except those which by their nature, duration or *c*
manner of execution cannot be appreciably detrimental. The seriousness of
what is at stake, the traditions of the Contracting States and the importance
attached by the Convention to respect for the physical liberty of the person
all require that this should be so. 83. It is on the basis of these criteria that
the court will ascertain whether some or all of the applicants were the *d*
subject of a "criminal charge" within the meaning of Article 6(1).'

[52] This decision identified three principal criteria which it has become the
European Court's practice to consider when deciding whether proceedings have
a criminal character: (1) the manner in which the domestic state classifies the
proceedings; (2) the nature of the offence; and (3) the character of the penalty to *e*
which the proceedings may give rise.

[53] As far as the first criterion is concerned, this normally carries
comparatively little weight. As the European Court observed in *Özturk v Germany*
(1984) 6 EHRR 409 at 421 at 422:

'49. ... if the Contracting States were able at their discretion, by classifying *f*
an offence as "regulatory" instead of criminal, to exclude the operation of the
fundamental clauses of Articles 6 and 7, the application of these provisions
would be subordinated to their sovereign will. A latitude extending thus far
might lead to results incompatible with the object and purpose of the
Convention ... 52. ... the indications furnished by the domestic law of the
respondent State have only a relative value ... the very nature of the offence, *g*
considered also in relation to the nature of the corresponding penalty—
represents a factor of appreciation of greater weight.'

[54] When one examines the cases that followed *Özturk v Germany*, it becomes
apparent that neither the offence nor the penalty has to be particularly serious for *h*
the European Court to classify the proceedings as criminal. In *Benham v UK* (1996)
22 EHRR 293, the court held that the proceedings for non-payment of the
community charge were criminal.

[55] The court noted (at 323–324 (para 56)):

'... the law concerning liability to pay the community charge and the *j*
procedure upon non-payment was of general application to all citizens, and
that the proceedings in question were brought by a public authority under
statutory powers of enforcement. In addition, the proceedings had some
punitive elements. For example, the magistrates could only exercise their
power of committal to prison on a finding of wilful refusal to pay or of
culpable neglect. Finally, it is to be recalled that the applicant faced a

a   relatively severe maximum penalty of three months' imprisonment, and was in fact ordered to be detained for 30 days. Having regard to these factors, the Court concludes that B was "charged with a criminal offence" for the purposes of Article 6(1) and (3). Accordingly, these two paragraphs of Article 6 are applicable.'

b   [56] In *Lauko v Slovakia* [1998] ECHR 26138/95, of which the provisional report is in Reports 1998-VI, the court observed that the three criteria were not cumulative and that it sufficed that the offence in question should, by its nature, be criminal from the point of view of the convention, or should have made the person concerned liable to a sanction which, by its nature and degree of severity, belonged in general to the criminal sphere. At the same time a cumulative

c   approach could be adopted where the separate analysis of each criterion did not make it possible to reach a clear conclusion as to the existence of a criminal charge.

[57] That case concerned proceedings in Slovakia against a man for making an accusation against a family of causing a nuisance without justification. This was classified as a minor offence under the relevant statute in Slovakian law, namely,

d   'a wrongful act which interferes with or causes danger to the public interest and is expressly classified as a minor offence'. The sanctions that could be imposed were: (a) reprimand; (b) fine; (c) prohibition on the exercise of a certain activity; or (d) confiscation of an object or a combination of (b), (c) and (d). The court held that the general character of the legal provision infringed, together with the

e   detriment and punitive purpose of the penalty, sufficed to show that the offence was criminal in nature so that the relative lack of seriousness of the penalty was not material.

[58] The case that comes closest to the present case is *Steel v UK* (1998) 5 BHRC 339, (1988) 28 EHRR 603, where a number of applicants had been arrested in different circumstances and each charged with breach of the peace contrary to

f   common law. Under the 1980 Act, the court can bind over a defendant to keep the peace, if the defendant consents, and impose a sentence of up to six months' imprisonment if the defendant refuses to consent to a bind over. The procedure is initiated by a complaint and a bind over order does not constitute a criminal conviction.

g   [59] The opinion of the European Commission of Human Rights (1998) 28 EHRR 603 at 616:

'67. The proceedings brought against the first applicant for breaching the peace also display these characteristics: their deterrent nature is apparent from the way in which a person can be arrested for breach of the peace and

h   subsequently bound over "to keep the peace or be of good behaviour", in which case no penalty will be enforced, and the punitive element derives from the fact that if a person does not agree to be bound over, he will be imprisoned for a period of up to 6 months. 68. In these circumstances, the Commission considers the charge of breach of the peace to be a criminal

j   offence and binding over proceedings to be "criminal" in nature, for the purposes of Article 6 of the Convention.'

[60] The court agreed:

'48. Breach of the peace is not classed as a criminal offence under English … law. However, the court observes that the duty to keep the peace is in the nature of a public duty; the police have powers to arrest any person who has breached the peace or who they reasonably fear will breach the peace; and the magistrates may commit to prison any person who refuses to be bound over not to breach the peace where there is evidence beyond reasonable doubt that his or her conduct caused or was likely to cause a breach of the peace and that he or she would otherwise cause a breach of the peace in the future ... 49. Bearing in mind the nature of the proceedings in question and the penalty at stake, the court considers that breach of the peace must be regarded as an "offence" within the meaning of art 5(1)(c) ...' (See (1998) 5 BHRC 339 at 351, (1998) 28 EHRR 603 at 635–636.)

[61] On behalf of Liberty, Miss Simor made the following written submission:

'Liberty submits that the position under section 1 of the Act is indistinguishable from proceedings in which an individual is bound over to keep the peace. A finding of anti-social behaviour leading to the imposition of an ASBO [anti-social behaviour order] is a finding of a breach of a "public duty". It would be considered by the public at large to be a finding of culpability for "criminal" conduct. The police have power of arrest in respect of anti-social conduct; put at its lowest the power to arrest for breach of the peace or risk of causing breach of the peace. The risk of "arrest" for such conduct and subsequent proceedings has a "deterrent" effect. The punitive element is arguably greater than in the case of a bind over to keep the peace because an ASBO can extend beyond a prohibition of anti-social behaviour and include additional prohibited conduct that would otherwise be lawful. Moreover, a refusal to comply with an ASBO can result in imprisonment for up to five years, while a refusal to be bound over can only result in imprisonment for six months. Its "criminal nature" can also be seen in the fact that failure to attend the hearing before the magistrates renders the defendant liable to arrest.'

[62] I do not agree that proceedings under s 1 of the CDA are indistinguishable from those in which an individual is bound over to keep the peace for the following reasons. (1) There is no power to arrest for the purpose of proceedings under s 1. The fact that the failure to respond to a summons to attend the hearing before the magistrates can render a defendant liable to arrest, does not demonstrate the criminal nature of the proceedings. It demonstrates the appropriate response to a failure to comply with a court summons. (2) While the anti-social conduct that is one precondition to proceedings under the CDA can be categorised as a breach of public duty, that conduct does not of itself justify the commencement of proceeding under s 1. The necessity to protect persons in a particular local government area also has to be demonstrated. (3) Proceedings under s 1 of the CDA cannot, themselves, result in the imposition of a sentence of imprisonment or of any penalty. Contrast proceedings for breach of the peace in which, as the commission remarked in *Steel v UK*, the punitive element derives from the fact that if a person does not agree to be bound over he will be liable to be sent to prison for a period of up to six months.

[63] Applications for anti-social behaviour orders have the procedural form of civil proceedings under English law. Neither of the other two criminal criteria for which the Strasbourg jurisprudence looks can be satisfactorily demonstrated. Offensive conduct is a prerequisite to proceedings under s 1, but not the only one. The order, while impacting adversely on the defendant, is not imposed as a punishment. In short, anti-social behaviour orders are not about crime and

a punishment, they are about protection of an identified section of the community. I do not consider that, applying the Strasbourg jurisprudence, they are criminal proceedings.

[64] Lord Bingham CJ in B's case dealt with art 6 of the convention somewhat more briefly than have I. He said:

b '28. ... Miss Booth submitted, rightly, that the European Court of Human Rights does not regard itself as bound by the classification of proceedings in domestic law. In deciding whether there is a criminal charge for purposes of art 6 of the convention the court has regard to the classification of proceedings in domestic law, but also to the nature of the offence itself and the severity of the penalty which may be imposed (see Lester and Pannick

c *Human Rights Law and Practice* (1999) p 138 para 4.6.13). Here the proceedings are in my judgment classified as civil in domestic law. No offence is charged and the making of an order does not depend on proof of any offence. No penalty may be imposed. I am aware of no case in which the European Court has held a proceeding to be criminal even though an

d adverse outcome for the defendant cannot result in any penalty.' (See [2001] 1 All ER 562 at 573, [2001] 1 WLR 340 at 353.)

Lord Bingham CJ's reasoning reflects my own.

[65] Anti-social behaviour orders have serious implications. While, technically, the civil standard of proof applies to applications for them, that standard is a

e flexible one. In B's case Lord Bingham CJ observed:

'31. In a serious case such as the present the difference between the two standards is, in truth, largely illusory. I have no doubt that, in deciding whether the condition in s 2(1)(a) is fulfilled, a magistrates' court should apply a civil standard of proof which will for all practical purposes be

f indistinguishable from the criminal standard. In deciding whether the condition in s 2(1)(b) is fulfilled the magistrates' court should apply the civil standard with the strictness appropriate to the seriousness of the matters to be proved and the implications of proving them.' (See [2001] 1 All ER 562 at 573–574, [2001] 1 WLR 340 at 354.)

g [66] In his judgment in the present case, the Recorder of Manchester referred to this passage in Lord Bingham CJ's judgment. He commented:

'Having considered this authority and the arguments, we are satisfied that the standard to be applied is the civil standard, but how are we to give effect

h to the guidance of the Chief Justice, that is to apply the civil standard with the strictness appropriate to the seriousness of the matters to be proved and the implications of proving them. This is not an easy task and we have brought to bear the judicial experience of all three of us which, it has to be said, is considerable, and we have concluded that in reality it is difficult to

j establish reliable gradations between a heightened civil standard commensurate with seriousness and implications of proving the requirements, and the criminal standard. And we have concluded that for the purposes of this particular case, and we do not intend to lay down any form of precedent, so I emphasise that for the purposes of this particular case, we will apply the standard of being satisfied so that we are sure that the conditions are fulfilled before we would consider the making of an order in the case of each appellant severally, because, of course, each case must be considered separately.'

a

[67] I believe that the course followed by the Crown Court in this case is likely to be appropriate in the majority of cases where an anti-social behaviour order is sought and I would commend it.

[68] For the reasons that I have given, I would dismiss this appeal.

b

KENNEDY LJ.

[69] I agree.

DYSON LJ.

[70] I also agree.

Appeal dismissed. Permission to appeal refused.

Kate O'Hanlon   Barrister.

Definitely Maybe (Touring) Ltd v Marek Lieberberg Konzertagentur GmbH

QUEEN'S BENCH DIVISION (COMMERCIAL COURT)

MORISON J

27, 30 MARCH 2001

Conflict of laws – Contract – Proper law of contract – Contract for provision of services of pop group – Claimant managers based in England – Defendant concert organiser based in Germany – Defendant refusing to pay full price for services of pop group – Claimant issuing proceedings in England – Whether England or Germany appropriate forum – Contracts (Applicable Law) Act 1990, Sch 1, art 4.

The claimant, DM Ltd, a company based in England, contracted with the defendant, M, a German company, to provide the services of a pop group, O, at two pop festivals in Germany. N, the talented lead guitarist of O, did not play in Germany. M argued that O without N was not the group contracted for and refused to pay the full price agreed for O's services. DM Ltd issued proceedings in England for the balance of the moneys said to be owing. M contended that the proper place for the proceedings was Germany, not England, and its application for service of the writ to be set aside was granted. DM Ltd appealed, submitting that the court was required to give full effect to the presumption in art 4(2) of the Rome Convention on the Law Applicable to Contractual Obligations 1980 (OJ 1998 C27 p 34) (the convention) (as set out in the Contracts (Applicable Law) Act 1990) that the country with the closest connection with the contract was to be determined by identifying the place where the party which effected or was to effect the characteristic performance of the contract was located. It was common ground that the characteristic performance was to be performed by the claimant, as the substantive obligation under the contract was for O to play at the festivals. Article 4(5) of the convention provided that the presumption was to be disregarded 'if it appears from the circumstances as a whole that the contract is more closely connected with another country.' M argued that the presumption in art 4(5) should be disregarded where, as in the instant case, there was a divergence between the place of business of the principal performer and the place of performance and the circumstances of the contract showed a closer connection with the place of performance.

Held – The proper approach to the interpretation of art 4(2) of the convention and its interrelationship with art 4(5) was to stay with the words and to apply them as best as possible. On that basis, the presumption in art 4(2) would be 'disregarded' in the instant case if it appeared from the circumstances as a whole that the contract was more closely connected with Germany rather than England. M had, on the facts, established that the contract between the parties had a closer connection with Germany than England, and, even recognising the convention's emphasis on England as the place of the performer's business, having regard, inter alia, to the place of performance by both parties, Germany had more attachment to or connection with the contract than England. Aside from any other consideration, the centre of gravity of the dispute was Germany, which would provide the more convenient forum for deciding to what extent O without N was worth anything and, if so, how much. Accordingly, the appeal would be dismissed (see [15]–[17], below).

Credit Lyonnais v New Hampshire Insurance Co [1997] 2 Lloyd's Rep 1 considered.

Notes

For the applicable law where the law has not been expressly chosen, see 8(1) *Halsbury's Laws* (4th edn reissue) para 847.

For the Contracts (Applicable Law) Act 1990, Sch 1, art 4, see 11 *Halsbury's Statutes* (4th edn) (2000 reissue) 251.

Cases referred to in judgment

Credit Lyonnais v New Hampshire Insurance Co [1997] 2 Lloyd's Rep 1, CA.
Société Nouvelle des Papéteries de l'Aa SA v BV Machinefabriek (25 September 1992, unreported), Holland Superior Ct.

Cases also cited or referred to in skeleton arguments

Bank of Baroda v Vysya Bank Ltd [1994] 2 Lloyd's Rep 87.
Bank of Credit and Commerce Hong Kong Ltd (in liquidation) v Sonali Bank [1995] 1 Lloyd's Rep 227.
Bastone & Firminger Ltd v Nasima Enterprises (Nigeria) Ltd [1996] CLC 1902.
Canada Trust Co v Stolzenberg (No 2) [1998] 1 All ER 318, [1998] 1 WLR 547, CA; *affd* [2000] 4 All ER 481, HL.
Offshore International SA v Banco Central SA [1976] 3 All ER 749, [1977] 1 WLR 399.

Appeal

The claimants, Definitely Maybe (Touring) Ltd, appealed from the order of Master Foster made on 1 November 2000 whereby he granted an application made by the defendants, Marek Lieberberg Konzertagentur GmbH, to set aside service of a writ served on them by the claimants for a sum said to be owing in respect of the provision of the services of a pop group by the claimants to the defendants. The facts are set out in the judgment.

David Wolfson (instructed by *Statham Gill Davies*) for the claimants.
David Waksman (instructed by *Eversheds*) for the defendants.

Cur adv vult

30 March 2001. The following judgment was delivered.

MORISON J.

[1] This is an appeal from a decision of Master Foster given on 1 November 2000. He acceded to the defendants' application to set aside service of the writ issued against them by the claimants.

[2] The brief facts relevant to this appeal are these. The claimants, who are based in England, provide the services of the pop group called Oasis to those who organise live concerts. The defendants are a German-based company which organised two pop festivals in Germany in June of last year and contracted with the claimants for live performances by Oasis. Unfortunately, there was apparently a rift between the two Gallagher brothers and Noel, the talented lead guitarist, did not play in Germany. The defendants say that Oasis without Noel Gallagher is not really the group contracted for. Thus, they have refused to pay

a   the full price. The claimants, by these proceedings issued in this jurisdiction, claim the balance of the moneys they say are owing.

[3] The sole question at issue is whether the English court has or should take jurisdiction over the dispute. The defendants say that the proper place for these proceedings is Germany and not England, and it was the master's decision upholding that contention that is the subject of the appeal.

b   [4] In order to resolve the jurisdiction issue the court must, initially, turn to the Convention on Jurisdiction and the Enforcement of Judgments in Civil and Commercial Matters 1968 (as set out in Sch 1 to the Civil Jurisdiction and Judgments Act 1982) (the Brussels Convention), to which both countries have acceded. Under that convention, the normal rule is that a person, including, of course, a corporate entity, should be sued in the place where he is domiciled; in

c   other words, Germany. But the normal rule is displaced if the place of performance of the obligation in question, namely the duty to pay, is England. But the place of performance of an obligation such as this may, and in this case does, depend upon which system of law governs the contract. Under German law the place of performance of an obligation to pay is the domicile of the debtor,

d   namely Germany. Under English law the place of performance of the defendant's obligation to pay is England, the place where the money is to be received. Thus, the question as to whether these proceedings can continue in this jurisdiction is dependent upon the answer to the question: what is the governing law of the contract? If the answer is English law, then the proceedings can continue here and the appeal must be allowed. Conversely, if the answer is German law then

e   the appeal must be dismissed and the stay of proceedings in this jurisdiction continued.

[5] The answer to the question comes from a proper interpretation of the Rome Convention on the Law Applicable to Contractual Obligations 1980 (OJ 1998 C27 p 34) (set out in the Contracts (Applicable Law) Act 1990) adopted by

f   both countries. Article 3 of the convention gives effect to parties' own choice of law. There is no express or implied choice of law clause in this case and, therefore, one must turn to art 4. Paragraph 1 of that article directs that a contract is governed by the law of the country with which it is most closely connected. Paragraph 2 provides, subject to the provisions of para 5, that the country with the closest connection with the contract is to be determined by

g   identifying the place where the party who effects or is to effect the characteristic performance of the contract is 'located' (has its central administration or principal place of business). Thus, subject to para 5, there are two questions to be answered: which party effects the characteristic performance of the contract, and where is that party located (in the sense used above). Here, it is common ground

h   that the claimants have the characteristic performance of the contract, in the sense that the substantive obligation under the contract was for Oasis to perform in two concerts in Germany. The claimants are located in England, and hence, by virtue of art 4(2), English law would be the governing law of the contract.

[6] But art 4(2) is expressly made subject to the provisions of para 5 of the

j   same article. Paragraph 5 displaces the presumption in para 2 'if it appears from the circumstances as a whole that the contract is more closely connected with another country'. In such a case, para 5 provides that para 2 shall be disregarded.

[7] The real issue between the parties centres on the relationship between these two paragraphs of art 4. Whilst para 2 looks to the location of the principal performer, para 5 looks more widely to a connection between the contract and a country. If there is a divergence between the location of the principal performer

and the place of substantial or characteristic performance, what then? On the one hand, were the presumption to be displaced whenever such divergence existed, the presumption would be of little weight or value. Paragraph 2 must have been inserted to provide a 'normal' rule which is simple to apply. Giving wide effect to para 5 will render the presumption of no value and represent a return to the English common law test of ascertaining the proper law, which places much less weight on the location of the performer and much more on the place of performance, and the presumed intention of the parties.

[8] Rather than seeking to find an answer to this issue, I turn to those factors which are said to show a closer connection between the contract and Germany than with England. The contract provided for Oasis to perform live in Germany; that was the place of the characteristic or substantial performance of the contract. The defendants were obliged to make arrangements in Germany to enable the performances to take place (for example, marketing and promotion) and to provide facilities such as security and bits of equipment. Thus, the contract required performance of contractual obligations in Germany by both parties. For what it is worth, the defendant company is German and payment was to be made in Deutschmarks and subject to deduction for German tax. Apart from the location of the claimants and the group, and the place of payment, there is no other connection between England and the contract. The centre of gravity of the dispute is, I think, Germany. Therefore, if the test were simply that laid down in para 5, namely, to say with which country was the contract most closely connected, I would have said Germany, rather than England.

[9] But I return to the issue of the relationship between paras 2 and 5 of art 4 and the legal effect of the presumption. There are, I think, two schools of thought. The first is to say that the presumption in para 2, which is expressly made subject to para 5, is weak and will more readily be displaced where the place of performance differs from the place of business of the performer. The second, adopts a narrower view of the 'exception' to the presumption in para 5 and gives firm dominance to the presumption.

[10] In relation to the first approach, the editors of *Dicey and Morris* (13th edn, 2000) vol 2, p 1240, para 32-124 state that—

> 'the presumption may most easily be rebutted in those cases where the place of performance differs from the place of business of the party whose performance is characteristic of the contract.'

That is this case. In *Credit Lyonnais v New Hampshire Insurance Co* [1997] 2 Lloyd's Rep 1 at 5, the Court of Appeal noted that art 4(5) 'formally makes the presumption very weak'.

[11] In support of the more restricted view, the claimants rely upon a Dutch case: *Société Nouvelle des Papéteries de l'Aa SA v BV Machinefabriek* (25 September 1992, unreported) where the court gave a most restrictive interpretation to para 5. It appears that the Superior Court in Holland concluded that—

> 'this exception to the main rule of section 2 [paragraph 2] has to be applied restrictively, to the effect that the main rule should be disregarded only if, in the special circumstances of the case, the place of business of the party who is to effect the characteristic performance has no real significance as a connecting factor.'

[12] The problem is caused, I think, by the fact that the factor which identifies the governing law in para 2 (namely the location of the principal performer) may

a well not play an important part in determining the closest connection between country and contract. Thus, the presumption to which it gives rise is likely to be capable of being rebutted in most cases, and as such the presumption may be worthless. Yet, if para 2 has the dominance suggested by the Dutch Court, the presumption becomes a rule of law to which para 5 must be treated as an exception, and that is not the language of the convention.

b [13] In well-presented and interesting submissions counsel concentrated on this problem. Mr David Wolfson for the claimants adopted the Dutch position although he said that he did not need to go that far. He submitted that the court was required to give full effect to the presumption and to the thinking behind it. The scheme of art 4 was to provide a simple and easily applied test. If, as was said in an obiter remark, the presumption was weak, then parties would not know
c where they stood and the convention would not work as it was intended. He said that there were many cases where para 5 might apply; for example, those cases where there was a link between one contract and another. Thus, he accepted as an archetype, the case where the court accepted that the rights of the beneficiary against the confirming bank were governed by the same law as his rights against
d the issuing bank. Or, he said, a case of a guarantee being construed as being subject to the same governing law as that which applied to the contract between debtor and creditor. For the defendant, it was submitted that the Dutch case was wrong in law, in that it added words which were not in art 4 and that I should not follow it. He submitted that it was not necessary to adopt any extreme position in relation to art 4. The presumption would do its work in the majority of cases,
e but where there was a divergence between the place of business of the principal performer and the place of performance it was right that the presumption should be displaced if the factors showed a closer connection with the place of performance. But if the factors were evenly balanced, then the place of business of the principal performer would be decisive. In that way, the presumption had
f some meaning, yet it was rebuttable where appropriate.

[14] I must confess that I have not found this an easy case to decide. To some extent the court must recognise, I think, a natural tendency to wish to maintain the old, well-developed common law position where factors were weighed and attempts were made to ascertain the true intention of the parties. Intention does not appear to exist as a factor any more, save in an art 3 context. Although art 18
g of the Rome Convention encourages a uniform interpretation of the convention, that is less easy to achieve than to say. The importance attached to the location of the principal performer stems from Swiss law. The provisions of art 4 have been the subject of much criticism by academics; it is rightly pointed out that the Giuliano-Lagarde report (to which reference may be made) does not provide
h much useful guidance as to the interpretation of art 4 although the authors accept that judges have been left with a measure of discretion or judgment. It may be that the convention represents a compromise between different positions adopted by different countries during the negotiation of its terms.

[15] It seems to me not to be helpful to characterise art 4 by asking whether
j there is a one, two or three-stage test. Nor am I attracted to the notion that the words of the article should be twisted so as to accord with what is thought to be the intention of the draftsman. With an international convention of this sort, I prefer to stay with the words and apply them as best as possible. On that basis, it seems to me that the presumption in art 4.2 'shall be disregarded' (not rebutted) if it appears from the circumstances as a whole that the contract is more closely connected with Germany rather than England. I accept that it is for the defendant

to show that the presumption should be disregarded, by establishing factors which point to Germany. I accept that this will be more readily achievable where *a* the place of performance is different from the place of the performer's business. But in carrying out what must be regarded as a comparative exercise, due weight must be given to the factor identified in art 4.2.

[16] Here, the defendants have established to my satisfaction that, overall, the contract between the parties has a closer connection with Germany than with *b* England. Even recognising the convention's emphasis on England as the place of the performer's business, having regard to the place of performance by both parties and the other factors referred to above, Germany has more attachment to or connection with the contract than England. Aside from any other consideration, the centre of gravity of the dispute is Germany, which will provide the more convenient forum for deciding to what extent Oasis without Noel *c* Gallagher was worth anything, and, if so, how much.

[17] Thus, in the result, I endorse the decision of Master Foster and dismiss the appeal.

Appeal dismissed.

James Wilson   Barrister (NZ).

^a # Gough and another v Chief Constable of the Derbyshire Constabulary

R (on the application of Miller) v Leeds Magistrates' Court

^b # Lilley v Director of Public Prosecutions

[2001] EWHC Admin 554

^c QUEEN'S BENCH DIVISION, DIVISIONAL COURT

LAWS LJ AND POOLE J

1, 2, 3 MAY, 13 JULY 2001

^d *Public order – Football – Football banning order – Whether football banning order constituting a penalty for purposes of human rights convention – Football Spectators Act 1989, ss 14A, 14B – Human Rights Act 1998, Sch 1, Pt I, art 7.*

European Community – Freedom of movement – Persons and services – Restriction on freedom – Football banning order – Whether football banning order contravening Community law on freedom of movement – Football Spectators Act 1989, s 14B – EC
^e *Treaty, art 49 – Council Directive (EEC) 64/221.*

In various cases heard together by the Divisional Court—an application for judicial review by M and appeals by way of case stated by G, S and L—questions arose as to the legality of banning orders made under ss 14A[a] and 14B[b] of the Football Spectators Act 1989, as amended by the Football (Disorder) Act 2000.
^f Section 14A, which applied where a person (the offender) was convicted of a relevant offence, required the court to make a banning order if it were satisfied that there were reasonable grounds to believe that making such an order would help to prevent violence or disorder at or in connection with a regulated football match. An order under s 14A could only be made, inter alia, in addition to a sentence imposed in respect of the relevant offence (sub-s (4)(a)). Under s 14B(1),
^g a chief officer of police could apply to a magistrates' court for a banning order in respect of any person residing in his area if it appeared to him that the condition in sub-s (2) was met, namely that the respondent had at any time caused or contributed to any violence or disorder in the United Kingdom or elsewhere. The court was required by s 14B(4) to make the banning order if it were proved
^h that that condition had been met (sub-s (4)(a)) and the court was satisfied that there were reasonable grounds to believe that making such an order would help to prevent violence or disorder at or in connection with any regulated football matches (sub-s (4)(b)). 'Banning order' itself was defined by s 14(4)[c] as an order which (a) in relation to regulated football matches in England and Wales,
^j prohibited the person subject to the order from entering any premises for the purpose of attending such matches, and (b) in relation to such matches outside England and Wales, required that person to report to a police station. The court

---

a Section 14A, so far as material, is set out at [10], below
b Section 14B is set out at [10], below
c Section 14, so far as material, is set out at [10], below

could vary such an order (s 14G[d]) or terminate it early in the light of all the
circumstances (s 14H[e]). Breach of a banning order constituted a criminal offence   *a*
(s 14J[f]). M and L had both pleaded guilty to relevant offences for the purposes of
s 14A, and had been made subject to banning orders under that section for
6 years, even though the maximum length of such an order had only been three
years at the time of the acts that had led to the imposition of the banning orders.
They therefore contended that the orders breached art 7[g] of the European   *b*
Convention for the Protection of Human Rights and Fundamental Freedoms
1950 (as set out in Sch 1 to the Human Rights Act 1998), which prohibited the
imposition of a 'penalty' heavier than the one that was applicable at the time the
criminal offence was committed. G and S, who had been made subject to orders
under s 14B of the 1989 Act preventing them from travelling to football matches   *c*
abroad for two years, contended that banning orders under s 14B were contrary
to the right of freedom of movement within the European Union under art 49[h]
of the EC Treaty. In particular, they contended that, save in certain inapplicable
circumstances, there was no derogation on grounds of public policy for
restrictions on the rights of EU citizens to leave a member state. Alternatively,
they submitted, inter alia, that the material provisions of the 1989 Act were   *d*
disproportionate to the end sought to be achieved, and that they could not be
justified under Council Directive (EEC) 64/221 (on the co-ordination of special
measures concerning the movement and residence of foreign nationals which
were justified on grounds of public policy, public security or public health).

          e

Held – (1) A football banning order, whether made under s 14A or s 14B of the
1989 Act, was not a penalty for the purposes of art 7 of the convention. It was no
part at all of the purposes of any such order to inflict punishment. The fact that
it imposed a detriment on its recipient no more demonstrated that it possessed a
punitive element than in the case of a freezing order. The purpose was to protect   *f*
the public, here and abroad, from the evil of football violence and the threat of it.
That was clear from the whole scheme of the Act. Moreover, the order was not
made as part of the process of distributive criminal justice. Under s 14B there was
no requirement of a criminal conviction. In s 14A, the existence of a relevant
conviction was no more than a gateway criterion for the making of the order.   *g*
Indeed s 14A(4)(a) contrasted the banning order with the sentence imposed for
the relevant offence. In other more detailed respects the order's characterisation
under national law told against its being treated as a penalty, namely the
provisions contained in s 14G relating to the alteration of the requirements
imposed; the power to terminate the order in the light of all the circumstances in   *h*
s 14H; and the provision in s 14J which treated breach of the order's requirements
as a separate criminal offence, rather than a default for which a penalty was made.
Although the restrictions imposed by the banning orders were more than trivial,
severity alone could not be decisive and the burdens or detriments involved
could not conceivably confer the status of penalty on banning orders if otherwise   *j*
they did not possess it, which they did not (see [42], [43], [95], below); *Welch v UK*

d   Section 14G, so far as material, is set out [10], below
e   Section 14H is set out at [10], below
f   Section 14J is set out at [10], below
g   Article 7 is set out at [29], below
h   Article 49 is set out at [45], below

a (1995) 20 EHRR 247 and *R (on the application of McCann) v Crown Court at Manchester* [2001] 4 All ER 264 considered.

(2) Section 14B of the 1989 Act was not contrary to art 49 of the EC Treaty. In a proper case, a member state of the European Union could be justified on public policy grounds in preventing a citizen of the Union from leaving its shores, and its right to do so was not limited to any narrow conception of 'abuse of rights'.

b Moreover, the prevention or diminution of violence associated with international football matches constituted a legitimate aim of public policy which in principle could properly be furthered by deployment of a member state's power to confine citizens of the Union (including its own citizens) within its borders. Nor was s 14B of the 1989 Act disproportionate to that legitimate aim. The state was entitled to conclude that very firm measures were justified to confront the various sickening

c ills of football violence, and the terms of s 14B(4)(b) were amply justified in the light of Council Directive (EEC) 64/221, the relevant case law and the general law relating to proportionality. Accordingly, the appeals and the application for judicial review would be dismissed (see [61], [62], [81], [94], [95], below); *Criminal proceedings against Calfa* Case C-348/96 [1999] All ER (EC) 850 and *R v Secretary of*

d *State for the Home Dept, ex p Daly* [2001] UKHL 26, [2001] 3 All ER 433 considered.

Notes

For the prohibition on retrospective penalties and for derogations on treaty provisions on freedom of movement, see respectively 8(2) *Halsbury's Laws* (4th edn reissue) para 148 and 52 *Halsbury's Laws* (4th edn) para 16.23.

e   For the Human Rights Act 1998, Sch 1, Pt I, art 7, see 7 *Halsbury's Statutes* (4th edn) (1999 reissue) 523.

Cases referred to in judgments

Adamson v UK (1999) 28 EHRR CD 209, E Com HR.

f *Alpine Investments BV v Minister van Financiën* Case C-384/93 [1995] All ER (EC) 543, [1995] ECR I-1141, ECJ.

Associated Provincial Picture Houses Ltd v Wednesbury Corp [1947] 2 All ER 680, [1948] 1 KB 223, CA.

B v Chief Constable of Avon and Somerset Constabulary [2001] 1 All ER 562, [2001]

g 1 WLR 340, DC.

Brown v Stott (Procurator Fiscal, Dunfermline) [2001] 2 All ER 97, [2001] 2 WLR 817, PC.

Calfa, Criminal proceedings against Case C-348/96 [1999] All ER (EC) 850, [1999] ECR I-11, ECJ.

h *Centros Ltd v Erhvervs-Org Selskabsstyrelsen* Case C-212/97 [2000] Ch 446, [2000] 2 WLR 1048, [1999] ECR I-1459, ECJ.

Etablissements Delhaize Freres v Promalvin Case C-47/90 [1992] ECR I-3669.

Hudson County Water Co v McCarter (1908) 209 US 349, US SC.

Ibbotson v UK (1998) 27 EHRR CD 332, ECt HR.

j *Kremzow v Austria* Case C-299/95 [1997] ECR I-2629.

Pharmacia and Upjohn SA (formerly Upjohn SA) v Paranova A/S Case C-379/97 [1999] All ER (EC) 880, [2000] Ch 571, [2000] 3 WLR 303, ECJ.

R (on the application of Mahmood) v Secretary of State for the Home Dept [2001] 1 WLR 840, CA.

R (on the application of McCann) v Crown Court at Manchester [2001] EWCA Civ 281, [2001] 4 All ER 264, [2001] 1 WLR 1084.

R v Bouchereau [1981] 2 All ER 924n, [1978] QB 732, [1978] 2 WLR 250, [1977] ECR
  1999, ECJ.   *a*
R v Lord Saville of Newdigate, ex p A [1999] 4 All ER 860, [2000] 1 WLR 1855, CA.
*R v Minister of Agriculture, Fisheries and Food and the Secretary of State for Health,
  ex p Fedesa* Case C-331/88 [1990] ECR I-4023.
R v Ministry of Defence, ex p Smith [1996] 1 All ER 257, [1996] QB 517, [1996] 2 WLR
  305, CA.   *b*
R v Secretary of State for Health, ex p Eastside Cheese Co [1999] 3 CMLR 123.
R v Secretary of State for the Home Dept, ex p Daly [2001] UKHL 26, [2001] 3 All ER
  433, [2001] 2 WLR 1622.
R v Secretary of State for the Home Dept, ex p Launder [1997] 3 All ER 961, [1997]
  1 WLR 839, HL.
Raimondo v Italy (1994) 18 EHRR 237, ECt HR.   *c*
Rutili v Minister for the Interior [1975] ECR 1219.
Sporrong v Sweden (1983) 5 EHRR 35, ECt HR.
*Union Nationale des Entraîneurs et Cadres Techniques Professionnels du Football
  (UNECTEF) v Heylens* Case 222/86 [1987] ECR 4097.
Welch v UK (1995) 20 EHRR 247, ECt HR.   *d*

Cases stated and application for judicial review

Gough and anor v Chief Constable of the Derbyshire Constabulary
The appellants, Carl Gough and Gary Smith, appealed by way of case stated from
banning orders of two years under s 14B of the Football Spectators Act 1989   *e*
imposed on them by a deputy district judge at Derby Magistrates' Court on
2 October 2000 on the application of the respondent, the Chief Constable of the
Derbyshire Constabulary. The facts are set out in the judgment of Laws LJ.

R (on the application of Miller) v Leeds Magistrates' Court   *f*
The claimant, Nathan Frederick Miller, applied for judicial review of the banning
order of six years under s 14A of the Football Spectators Act 1989 imposed on him at
Leeds Magistrates' Court on 20 October 2000. The facts are set out in the judgment
of Laws LJ.

Lilley v DPP   *g*
The appellant, Mark Lilley, appealed by way of case stated from the decision of the
Crown Court at Leeds on 1 December 2000 dismissing his appeal from the banning
order of six years under s 14A of the Football Spectators Act 1989 imposed on him at
Leeds Magistrates' Court on 12 October 2000. The facts are set out in the judgment
of Laws LJ.   *h*

Rhodri Thompson and *Jessica Simor* (instructed by *Timms*, Derby) for Gough and Smith.
Alan Newman QC and *Timothy Maloney* (instructed by *Cousins Tyrer*, Leeds) for Miller.
Alan Newman QC and *Scott Wilson* (instructed by *Lester Morrill*, Leeds) for Lilley.
Philip Havers QC and *Simon Davenport* (instructed by *Weightmans*, Leicester) for the *j*
  chief constable.
Philip Havers QC and *Simon Davenport* (instructed by the *Crown Prosecution Service*) for
  the DPP.
David Pannick QC and *Mark Hoskins* (instructed by the *Treasury Solicitor*) for the
  Secretary of State.

Cur adv vult

a 13 July 2001. The following judgments were delivered.

LAWS LJ.

INTRODUCTORY

[1] These cases are about statutory measures enacted by Parliament in
b primary legislation to confront the shame and menace of football hooliganism.
The three sets of proceedings before the court, which we heard together, raise
important questions as to the legality of 'banning orders' made under the Football
Spectators Act 1989 (the 1989 Act) as amended by the Football (Disorder) Act 2000.
In *Miller v Leeds Magistrates' Court* the claimant seeks a judicial review (permission
c to apply having been given by Richards J on 4 April 2001) to quash a banning
order made against him under s 14A of the 1989 Act at the Leeds Magistrates'
Court on 20 October 2000. The other two sets of proceedings are appeals by way
of case stated. In *Lilley v DPP* the decision under challenge was made by the Crown
Court at Leeds on 1 December 2000, when the court on appeal upheld a banning
order under s 14A made against Lilley at the Leeds Magistrates' Court on
d 12 October 2000. In *Gough and Smith v Chief Constable of Derbyshire* the composite
appeal is directed to banning orders made against both appellants under s 14B of
the 1989 Act on the same occasion at the Derby Magistrates' Court on 2 October
2000. I shall set out the relevant legislation below.

[2] The appellants Gough and Smith take a series of far-reaching points which
e their counsel Mr Thompson encapsulated in five propositions, to which I shall
come. Their principal content consisted in arguments of European Community
law, though there was also a submission based on art 8 of the European
Convention for the Protection of Human Rights and Fundamental Freedoms
(Rome, 4 November 1950; TS 71 (1953); Cmd 8969) (the Convention). It is to be
f noted in their case that the date of the hearing, 2 October 2000, was also the date
when the principal provisions of the Human Rights Act 1998 took effect.
Mr Newman QC for the other two claimants adopted Mr Thompson's
submissions so far as they might be applied to banning orders made under s 14A
(as I have said the orders against Mr Thompson's clients were made under s 14B),
but his primary argument was that the orders made against his clients fell foul of
g art 7 of the convention.

THE DOMESTIC LEGISLATION

[3] Before turning to the facts it will make for clarity if I first explain and set
out the relevant provisions of domestic legislation. The starting point is to be
h found in Pt IV of the Public Order Act 1986. This was the first measure taken by
the legislature specifically to address the evils of hooliganism at football matches.
Section 30(1) empowered a court 'by or before which a person is convicted of an
offence to which s 31 applies' to make an 'exclusion order', that is an order
'prohibiting him from entering any premises for the purpose of attending any
j prescribed football match there'. I will not take time with the meaning of 'prescribed
football match': it is enough to say that it did not include any matches played
abroad. Section 30(2) provided:

> 'No exclusion order may be made unless the court is satisfied that making
> such an order in relation to the accused would help to prevent violence or
> disorder at or in connection with prescribed football matches.'

Section 31 applied to any offence which fulfilled one or more of three conditions
set out in s 31(2)–(4). I will summarise them briefly, omitting some of the detail. *a*
The first was that the offence was committed within a defined period of time
starting not long before and ending not long after the match, and while the
accused was at or entering or leaving the football ground concerned. The second
was (essentially) that the offence involved violence or the threat of violence on
the way to or from the match. The third was that the offence was one committed *b*
in breach of other statutory measures designed to control the consumption of
alcohol on the way to or from football matches. Section 32(2) provided that the
duration of an exclusion order should be not less than three months. Section 33(1)
enabled a person in relation to whom an exclusion order had been made to apply
to the court to terminate it.

[4] Next in time comes the 1989 Act, as originally enacted. Section 14(1) *c*
provided in part:

'This Part of this Act applies in relation to football matches in any country
outside England and Wales which are designated football matches …'

Here, then, is the first statutory measure to regulate attendance at matches *d*
abroad; and this Act, in its original form, dealt *only* with matches played abroad.
Section 14(4) defines a 'restriction order' as 'an order of a court under ss 15 or 22
below requiring the person to whom the order applies to report to a police station
on the occasion of designated football matches'. Section 15 provided in part:

'(1) A court by or before which a person is convicted of a relevant offence *e*
… may make a restriction order in relation to him.
(2) No restriction order may be made unless the court is satisfied that
making such an order in relation to the accused would help to prevent
violence or disorder at or in connection with designated football matches.
[Effectively the same language as that of s 30(2) of the Act of 1986.] *f*
(3) A restriction order may only be made—(a) in addition to a sentence
imposed in respect of the offence of which the accused is (or was) convicted;
or (b) in addition to a probation order …
16.—(1) … the period for which a restriction order has effect in relation to
a person convicted of a relevant offence is—(a) in a case where he was
sentenced in respect of that offence to a period of imprisonment taking *g*
immediate effect, five years, and (b) in any other case, two years, beginning
with the date of the making of the order.'

A failure without reasonable excuse to comply with the duty to report to a police
station imposed by a restriction order is made a summary criminal offence *h*
(s 16(4) and (5)). Section 17 allows a person 'in relation to whom a restriction
order has had effect for at least one year' to apply to the court to terminate it.
'Relevant offence' is defined in great detail in Sch 1. I may deal with it very
broadly: it covers a whole series of statutory offences involving violence or the
threat of violence, or drunkenness at, near, or on the way to or from a designated
football match. Section 22 made provision for offences under the law of countries *j*
outside England and Wales to be treated as if they were Sch 1 offences. I need
not set out the mechanics.

[5] Here, then, were two statutory regimes, respectively constituted by the
1986 and 1989 Acts, made by Parliament to respond to what was plainly an

a increasing barbarism. The later Act recognised the particular evil of violence and drunkenness by British fans abroad.

[6] The Football (Offences and Disorder) Act 1999 amended both the 1986 Act and the 1989 Act. The 1986 Act was amended by ss 6–8. A 'domestic football banning order' was substituted for an exclusion order. A new s 30(2) was enacted as follows:

b
> 'Subject to subsection (4), it shall be the duty of the court to make a domestic football banning order in relation to the accused if it is satisfied that there are reasonable grounds to believe that making the order would help to prevent violence or disorder at or in connection with prescribed football matches.'

c Section 30(4) as substituted provided:

> 'A domestic football banning order may only be made—(a) in addition to a sentence imposed in respect of the offence of which the accused is (or was) convicted; or (b) in addition to an order discharging him absolutely or conditionally.'

d Section 32(2) as substituted provided that the duration of a domestic football banning order should be not less than one year and not more than three years.

[7] The 1989 Act was amended so that the following substitute provisions were made in s 15:

e
> '(1) Subject to subsection (3) below—(a) a court by or before which a person is convicted of a relevant offence, or (b) [the Crown Court where the person has been committed there] shall have the power to make an international football banning order in relation to him.

> (2) Subject to subsection (3) below, it shall be the duty of the court to
f make an international football banning order in relation to the accused if it is satisfied that there are reasonable grounds to believe that making the order would help to prevent violence or disorder at or in connection with designated football matches.' [Effectively the same language as is used in the new s 30(2) of the 1986 Act.]

g The new s 15(3) replicates precisely the new s 30(4) of the 1986 Act.

[8] Now I may come to the 1989 Act (that is, the 1989 Act as amended by the Football (Disorder) Act 2000). It will be clearest if I set out the relevant provisions in full, though there is some replication of what has gone before.

[9] Given the arguments in the case I should first cite part of the long title of
h the 1989 Act in its original form:

> 'An Act... to provide for the making by courts and the enforcement of orders imposing restrictions on persons convicted of certain offences for the purpose of preventing violence or disorder at or in connection with designated football matches played outside England and Wales.'

j The long title of the 2000 Act was in these terms:

> 'An Act to make further provision for the purpose of preventing violence or disorder at or in connection with association football matches; and for connected purposes.'

[10] Then the relevant provisions in the body of the statute are as follows.

'14 ... (2) "Regulated football match" means an association football match (whether in England and Wales or elsewhere) which is a prescribed match or a match of a prescribed description.

(3) "External tournament" means a football competition which includes regulated football matches outside England and Wales.

(4) 'Banning order' means an order made by the court under this Part which—(a) in relation to regulated football matches in England and Wales, prohibits the person who is subject to the order from entering any premises for the purpose of attending such matches, and (b) in relation to regulated football matches outside England and Wales, requires that person to report at a police station in accordance with this Part.

(5) "Control period", in relation to a regulated football match outside England and Wales, means the period—(a) beginning five days before the day of the match, and (b) ending when the match is finished or cancelled.

(6) "Control period", in relation to an external tournament, means any period described in an order made by the Secretary of State—(a) beginning five days before the day of the first football match outside England and Wales which is included in the tournament, and (b) ending when the last football match outside England and Wales which is included in the tournament is finished or cancelled, but, for the purposes of paragraph (a), any football match included in the qualifying or pre-qualifying stages of the tournament is to be left out of account ...

(8) "Relevant offence" means an offence to which Schedule 1 to this Act applies.

14A.—(1) This section applies where a person (the "offender") is convicted of a relevant offence.

(2) If the court is satisfied that there are reasonable grounds to believe that making a banning order would help to prevent violence or disorder at or in connection with any regulated football matches, it must make such an order in respect of the offender.

(3) If the court is not so satisfied, it must in open court state that fact and give its reasons.

'(4) A banning order may only be made under this section—(a) in addition to a sentence imposed in respect of the relevant offence, or (b) in addition to an order discharging him conditionally ...

(6) In this section, "the court" in relation to an offender means—(a) the court by or before which he is convicted of the relevant offence, or (b) if he is committed to the Crown Court to be dealt with for that offence, the Crown Court.

14B.—(1) An application for a banning order in respect of any person may be made by the chief officer of police for the area in which the person resides or appears to reside, if it appears to the officer that the condition in subsection (2) below is met.

(2) That condition is that the respondent has at any time caused or contributed to any violence or disorder in the United Kingdom or elsewhere.

(3) The application is to be made by complaint to a magistrates' court.

(4) If—(a) it is proved on the application that the condition in subsection (2) above is met, and (b) the court is satisfied that there are reasonable grounds to believe that making a banning order would help to prevent

a   violence or disorder at or in connection with any regulated football matches, the court must make a banning order in respect of the respondent.

14C.—(1) In this Part, "violence" means violence against persons or property and includes threatening violence and doing anything which endangers the life of any person.

b   (2) In this Part, "disorder" includes—(a) stirring up hatred against a group of persons defined by reference to colour, race, nationality (including citizenship) or ethnic or national origins, or against an individual as a member of such a group, (b) using threatening, abusive or insulting words or behaviour or disorderly behaviour, (c) displaying any writing or other thing which is threatening, abusive or insulting.

c   (3) In this Part, "violence" and "disorder" are not limited to violence or disorder in connection with football.

(4) The magistrates' court may take into account the following matters (among others), so far as they consider it appropriate to do so, in determining whether to make an order under section 14B above—(a) any decision of a court or tribunal outside the United Kingdom, (b) deportation or exclusion

d   from a country outside the United Kingdom, (c) removal or exclusion from premises used for playing football matches, whether in the United Kingdom or elsewhere, (d) conduct recorded on video or by any other means.

(5) In determining whether to make such an order—(a) the magistrates' court may not take into account anything done by the respondent before the beginning of the period of ten years ending with the application under

e   section 14B(1) above, except circumstances ancillary to a conviction ...

14D.—(1) An appeal lies to the Crown Court against the making by a magistrates' court of a banning order under section 14B above ...

14E.—(1) On making a banning order, a court must in ordinary language explain its effect to the person subject to the order.

f   (2) A banning order must require the person subject to the order to report initially at a police station in England and Wales specified in the order within the period of five days beginning with the day on which the order is made.

(3) A banning order must, unless it appears to the court that there are exceptional circumstances, impose a requirement as to the surrender in

g   accordance with this Part, in connection with regulated football matches outside the United Kingdom, of the passport of the person subject to the order.

(4) If it appears to the court that there are such circumstances, it must in open court state what they are ...

h   **14F.**—(1) Subject to the following provisions of this Part, a banning order has effect for a period beginning with the day on which the order is made.

(2) The period must not be longer than the maximum or shorter than the minimum.

(3) Where the order is made under section 14A above in addition to a sentence of imprisonment taking immediate effect, the maximum is ten

j   years and the minimum is six years; and in this subsection "imprisonment" includes any form of detention.

(4) In any other case where the order is made under section 14A above, the maximum is five years and the minimum is three years.

(5) Where the order is made under section 14B above, the maximum is three years and the minimum is two years.

14G.—(1) A banning order may, if the court making the order thinks fit, impose additional requirements on the person subject to the order in relation to any regulated football matches.

(2) The court by which a banning order was made may, on an application made by—(a) the person subject to the order, or (b) the person who applied for the order or who was the prosecutor in relation to the order, vary the order so as to impose, replace or omit any such requirements ...

14H.—(1) If a banning order has had effect for at least two-thirds of the period determined under section 14F above, the person subject to the order may apply to the court by which it was made to terminate it.

(2) On the application, the court may by order terminate the banning order as from a specified date or refuse the application.

(3) In exercising its powers under subsection (2) above, the court must have regard to the person's character, his conduct since the banning order was made, the nature of the offence or conduct which led to it and any other circumstances which appear to it to be relevant.

(4) Where an application under subsection (1) above in respect of a banning order is refused, no further application in respect of the order may be made within the period of six months beginning with the day of the refusal ...

14J.—(1) A person subject to a banning order who fails to comply with—(a) any requirement imposed by the order, or (b) any requirement imposed under section 19(2B) or (2C) below, is guilty of an offence ...

19.—(1) The enforcing authority ["enforcing authority" means a police organisation prescribed by the Secretary of State: s 22A(1)] and the officer responsible for the police station at which he reports initially shall have the following functions as respects any person subject to a banning order.

(2) On a person reporting initially at the police station, the officer responsible for the station may make such requirements of that person as are determined by the enforcing authority to be necessary or expedient for giving effect to the banning order, so far as relating to regulated football matches outside England and Wales.

(2A) If, in connection with any regulated football match outside England and Wales, the enforcing authority is of the opinion that requiring any person subject to a banning order to report is necessary or expedient in order to reduce the likelihood of violence or disorder at or in connection with the match, the authority must give him a notice in writing under subsection (2B) below.

(2B) The notice must require that person—(a) to report at a police station specified in the notice at the time, or between the times, specified in the notice, (b) if the match is outside the United Kingdom and the order imposes a requirement as to the surrender by him of his passport, to surrender his passport at a police station specified in the notice at the time, or between the times, specified in the notice, and may require him to comply with any additional requirements of the order in the manner specified in the notice.

(2C) In the case of any regulated football match, the enforcing authority may by notice in writing require any person subject to a banning order to comply with any additional requirements of the order in the manner specified in the notice.

(2D) The enforcing authority may establish criteria for determining whether any requirement under subsection (2B) or (2C) above ought to be imposed on any person or any class of person.

(2E) A notice under this section—(a) may not require the person subject to the order to report except in the control period in relation to a regulated football match outside England and Wales or an external tournament, (b) may not require him to surrender his passport except in the control period in relation to a regulated football match outside the United Kingdom or an external tournament which includes such matches ...

(6) A person who, without reasonable excuse, fails to comply with any requirement imposed on him under subsection (2) above shall be guilty of an offence ...

20.—(1) A person who is subject to a banning order may—(a) as respects a particular regulated football match, or (b) as respects regulated football matches played during a period, apply to the authority empowered to grant exemptions under this section ... to be exempt from the requirements imposed by or under this Part, or any of them as respects that match or matches played during that period ...

(4) The exempting authority shall exempt the applicant from the requirements imposed by or under this Part, or any of them, as respects any match or matches to which the application relates if he shows to the authority's satisfaction—(a) that there are special circumstances which justify his being so exempted; and (b) that, because of those circumstances, he would not attend the match or matches if he were so exempted ...

(7) A person who is aggrieved by the refusal of the exempting authority to grant him an exemption under subsection (4) above may ... appeal to a magistrates' court ...

21.—(1) The Secretary of State may issue to the enforcing authority such guidance as he considers appropriate for the purposes of the exercise of their functions under sections 19 and 20 above ...

(3) The Secretary of State may make regulations regulating the giving by the enforcing authority to persons subject to banning orders of notices under section 19 above ... and it shall be the duty of the enforcing authority to comply with the regulations.

21A.—(1) This section and section 21B below apply during any control period in relation to a regulated football match outside England and Wales or an external tournament if a constable in uniform—(a) has reasonable grounds for suspecting that the condition in section 14B(2) above is met in the case of a person present before him, and (b) has reasonable grounds to believe that making a banning order in his case would help to prevent violence or disorder at or in connection with any regulated football matches.

(2) The constable may detain the person in his custody (whether there or elsewhere) until he has decided whether or not to issue a notice under section 21B below, and shall give the person his reasons for detaining him in writing ...

21B.—(1) A constable in uniform may exercise the power in subsection (2) below if authorised to do so by an officer of at least the rank of inspector.

(2) The constable may give the person a notice in writing requiring him—(a) to appear before a magistrates' court at a time, or between the times, specified in the notice, (b) not to leave England and Wales before that time (or the later of those times), and (c) if the control period relates to a

regulated football match outside the United Kingdom or to an external tournament which includes such matches, to surrender his passport to the constable, and stating the grounds referred to in section 21A(1) above ...

(4) For the purposes of section 14B above, the notice is to be treated as an application for a banning order made by complaint by the constable to the court in question and subsection (1) of that section is to have effect as if the references to the chief officer of police for the area in which the person resides or appears to reside were references to that constable.

21C.—(1) The powers conferred by sections 21A and 21B above may only be exercised in relation to a person who is a British citizen.

(2) A person who fails to comply with a notice given to him under section 21B above is guilty of an offence...

21D.—(1) Where a person to whom a notice has been given under section 21B above appears before a magistrates' court and the court refuses the application for a banning order in respect of him, it may order compensation to be paid to him out of central funds if it is satisfied—(a) that the notice should not have been given, (b) that he has suffered loss as a result of the giving of the notice, and (c) that, having regard to all the circumstances, it is appropriate to order the payment of compensation in respect of that loss.

(2) An appeal lies to the Crown Court against any refusal by a magistrates' court to order the payment of compensation under subsection (1) above.

(3) The compensation to be paid by order of the magistrates' court under subsection (1) above or by order of the Crown Court on an appeal under subsection (2) above shall not exceed £5,000 (but no appeal may be made under subsection (2) in respect of the amount of compensation awarded).'

Schedule 1 ('relevant offences') lists a large number of statutory offences. I do not think it necessary to set them all out. They replicate and update the list contained in Sch 1 to the 1989 Act in its original form.

THE FACTS

[11] I will first deal very shortly with the facts in *Lilley's* and *Miller's* case. The distinct point taken by Mr Newman QC on their behalf, arising as I have said under art 7 of the Convention, requires no elaboration of factual detail.

Lilley's case

[12] On 20 April 2000 the UEFA Cup semi-final between Leeds United and Galatasaray was held at Leeds. After the game there was an ugly episode of public disorder. Lilley took part. He appears on a video recording of the scene near the football ground, hurling two missiles at the police in quick succession. He was charged with an offence of using threatening, abusive or insulting words or behaviour contrary to s 4(1) of the 1986 Act. He pleaded guilty at the Leeds Magistrates' Court on 21 September 2000, and after an adjournment for pre-sentence reports he was sentenced on 12 October 2000 to eight weeks' imprisonment, and was made the subject of a football banning order for six years under s 14A of the 1989 Act. As I have shown, that is the minimum period in such a case (s 14F(3)). His appeal (brought against the banning order only) was dismissed by the Crown Court at Leeds on 1 December 2000.

Miller's case

[13] Miller also attended the Leeds United v Galatasaray match on 20 April 2000. Like Lilley, he was involved in the disorder and was charged with an offence

a contrary to s 4(1) of the 1986 Act. On 21 September 2000 he pleaded guilty and on 20 October 2000 was sentenced to eight weeks' imprisonment and made the subject of a banning order for six years. In his case there was no appeal to the Crown Court.

[14] In each of these cases, it was argued below (in *Lilley*'s case, at least in the Crown Court) that there was a violation of art 7 of the Convention because at the

b time when the appellants did the acts which led to the banning orders—20 April 2000—the permissible duration of a domestic football banning order was no more than three years (s 32(2) of the 1986 Act as amended by the 1999 Act), so that the imposition of a banning order for six years was in breach of the rule, enshrined in art 7, against the imposition of a heavier penalty than was applicable when the offence was committed. The lower courts in both cases rejected that

c contention, and, as the case stated in *Lilley* and the judicial review grounds in *Miller*'s case both demonstrate, its correctness is the issue for decision in this court. I propose to address it before the other arguments which arise in *Gough*'s case and *Smith*'s case, but before doing so I must set out the facts in those cases, and also some more general factual considerations.

d
Gough and Smith

[15] As I have said the orders in these cases were made under s 14B of the 1989 Act, and not s 14A. Considerable emphasis was placed on the differences between these provisions in the course of argument. On 18 September 2000 the Chief Constable of Derbyshire preferred complaints against Gough and Smith (and others)

e under s 14B(3) with a view to seeking orders under s 14B(4) in the magistrates' court. The complaints alleged in each case that the condition stipulated in s 14B(2)—that 'the respondent has at any time caused or contributed to any violence or disorder in the United Kingdom or elsewhere'—was fulfilled: in *Gough*'s case specifically by a conviction on 17 March 1998 for common assault,

f and in *Smith*'s case specifically by a conviction on 26 November 1990 for assault with intent to resist arrest. However, it is plain from the terms of the case stated that the court attached greater importance to the 'profile' prepared by the police in respect of each man, and I must explain what these are and how they come into existence.

[16] As a matter of background it is important to recognise, as appears from

g the witness statement made by Supt Wright on 18 September, that violence connected with football matches has become organised, even sophisticated. Groups of men who associate themselves with particular clubs use mobile phones and the Internet to arrange fights with other such groups. These men are not ordinary football club supporters. The fights, at which weapons are often

h used, generally take place away from the football ground. Specifically as regards Derby County matches, with which Gough and Smith were associated, Supt Wright says this:

> 'There is currently a group of males that can number between 40 and 60 for high profile games who come under the banner of the media term
j "football hooligans". The policing term for these people is "football prominents". In the Derby group they are males aged from 18 to 40. The group is commonly referred to by the public and themselves as the DLF (Derby Lunatic Fringe).'

[17] The tactics of the police have had to respond to this developing phenomenon. There is a Football Intelligence System co-ordinated by the

National Criminal Intelligence Service. Each club has a Football Intelligence
Officer, who is known to the prominents as they are known to him. In relation
to each match—certainly as regards Derby, for it is what was done in these
cases—information is collected by police 'spotters' who watch the prominents.
The information is collated in an information/intelligence report. The profiles
are prepared in reliance on the contents of such reports, and consist in short
notes, each giving an outline description of the particular prominent's
involvement in actual or threatened trouble in relation to any given match.
15 profiles for Gough were put before the magistrates' court, describing incidents
from 14 September 1996 to 29 April 2000; 21 for Smith, from 14 September 1996
to 17 June 2000. Within these there appear to be eight incidents in which both
appellants participated. I will not set out all the profiles. The following convey
the flavour:

'8/3/97. Derby v Middlesborough, 70 of the Derby prominent group were
involved in disturbances with Middlesborough prominents both before and
after this game. Gough was part of the Derby group.'

There is an identical profile for Smith, referring to the same occasion. There are
two profiles which make no reference to disorder or to prominents:

'7/8/99. Leeds v Derby, Gough seen leaving the stadium with three other
males.'
'11/12/99. Smith seen sitting in the South East corner of the ground
during the Derby v Burnley FA Cup game.'

The deputy district judge in the magistrates' court referred to this profile in
particular:

'29/4/00. Tottenham v Derby, Gough attended London on this day on a
rogue coach with 40 other Derby prominents. This coach was stopped and
searched and was found to contain DLF calling cards, drugs and tickets for
the game, all had been secreted on the coach. The group were allowed by
police to walk into central London where they later became involved in
slight disorder with West Brom prominents.'

Again there is an identical profile for Smith. I should explain what is meant by a
'rogue' coach. Apparently a system exists by which coach trips to away matches
are notified to the police. A coach not so notified is a 'rogue' coach. However,
the police have no powers to prevent a rogue coach from travelling, nor indeed
(as I understand it) to require the notification procedure to be followed. Then
lastly:

'17/6/00. England v Germany Euro 2000 Championships. Smith was seen
in the square in Charleroi after the disorder had occurred corralled by the
Belgian riot police with around 15 other Derby prominents and 1,500 other
England supporters.'

[18] At the hearing Gough, then aged 36, gave unchallenged evidence that he
suffered from a brain tumour; that his last football-related conviction had been
18 years previously; that he had never been to a football match outside the
United Kingdom; and that he regularly took his children to the Derby town
centre for shopping as well as football matches. Smith was 38. He had had no
convictions of any kind since November 1990. He said that his last 'football-related
incident' had happened nearly 15 years previously.

a
[19] Mr Thompson's submissions for Gough and Smith were largely directed to the legality of the material provisions of the 1989 Act as a matter of principle. But the case stated raises questions as to the adequacy of the evidence in these instances to justify the making of banning orders under s 14B, and it was part of Mr Thompson's argument that evidence of the kind contained in the profiles was generally inadequate or unjustified: a submission which straddles the ground

b between the general law and the facts of the case. In these circumstances it is appropriate to see what challenge was offered in the court below to the material contained in the profiles, such as it was.

[20] There was no suggestion in the magistrates' court that the profiles were not admissible evidence. Rather, Mr Thompson took a few narrow, specific

c points in relation to them. On behalf of Gough and Smith respectively he challenged the relevance of the profiles of 7 August 1999 and 11 December 1999 (these I have set out: they are the ones which make no reference to prominents or to disorder). Moreover both appellants disputed the evidence of the 'rogue coach' trip to London on 29 April 2000, or rather the inferences to be derived from it: they asserted that they were going to London 'in relation to the death of

d a friend': this seems to have been a claim that the visit was for a fund-raising event. As regards the incident at Charleroi on 17 June 2000, Smith's evidence was that he was not in the square at the time of the disorder, although he had arrived there shortly afterwards.

[21] There was thus in truth no challenge to the primary facts very shortly

e stated in the profiles. The deputy district judge rejected in terms the appellants' account of why they had gone to London in the rogue coach on 29 April 2000. He found that their evidence was 'of little assistance to the court'. He concluded as regards each appellant that the matters set out in s 14B(4)(a) and (b) were established and so proceeded to make banning orders, for two years in each case. That was the minimum period permitted by the statute: (s 14F(5)). The orders as

f made curtailed the appellants' freedom of movement to a lesser extent than had been sought by the police. As the deputy district judge made clear by reference to a map before him, there was no restriction placed upon their going into the city of Derby within the inner ring road.

g *Matches played outside England and Wales*

[22] There was some uncertainty at the Bar during the course of argument as to the likely real impact of a banning order, in terms of the length of time for which it might effectively prevent its recipient from travelling abroad, especially having regard to s 14(3) and (6) of the 1989 Act which respectively define 'external

h tournament' and 'control period' in relation to external tournaments. An agreed note was placed before us. It describes the three European football club competitions presently existing, namely the Champions League, the UEFA Cup and the Intertoto Cup (whose winner qualifies for the UEFA Cup). As must be obvious, the involvement of English and Welsh sides in these competitions, and

j therefore the impact on any individual of a banning order in terms of the period(s) of time in which he may not travel abroad, depends on the clubs' success rates at all the earlier stages in the process. I do not think it necessary to go into the minutiae, not least since the note helpfully includes a table showing how the reporting and passport surrender requirements of the 1989 Act have in practical terms affected all four appellants in 2000/2001. From this I shall only take the data relating to Gough and Smith. Each has so far been prevented from travelling abroad for three periods: 6–11 October 2000, 10–15 November 2000, and 23–28 March 2001.

The Secretary of State's evidence

[23] The Secretary of State put in two witness statements. The first was made by Mr Bohannan, who is head of the Home Office section with responsibility for football-related disorder. The second was by Mr Jaglall who is an officer of the Football Banning Orders Authority (FBOA), an enforcing authority within the meaning of s 22A(1) of the 1989 Act. Mr Bohannan gives some of the melancholy history of the involvement of Englishmen in violence and disorder at football matches held abroad. The main focus of his statement, however, is directed to the police preparations for the Euro 2000 finals, the events which happened at Euro 2000 at Charleroi and Brussels, and the legislature's response to those events contained in the amending 2000 Act. Euro 2000 took place after the coming into effect of the amending legislation of 1999 but before that of 2000. Mr Jaglall deals with the procedures adopted by his authority in relation to the giving of notices under s 19 of the 1989 Act, and its treatment of applications for exemption under s 20. In light of various aspects of the argument before us (not least that contained in Mr Thompson's critical note on the Secretary of State's evidence), it is necessary to give some account of this material.

[24] In the run-up to Euro 2000 there was mounted what Mr Bohannan called 'the most extensive United Kingdom policing operation ever for an overseas football tournament'. He gives details, which include many measures of co-operation with police services on the Continent. I need not set them out. Despite these extensive precautions, 'English fans were still involved in significant disturbances in both Charleroi and Brussels'. He continues:

'In total, 965 England followers were arrested during the tournament. Only one was convicted of an offence. Police checks on the individuals concerned revealed that only one of those arrested was subject to a football banning order and only 35 were known to the National Criminal Intelligence Service as prominent football hooligans. However, further analysis revealed that 391 (40%) of the 965 individuals arrested had non-football-related criminal records. Of this number 133 had convictions for violence, 200 for ... offences under the Public Order Act 1986 ... 38 for offensive weapons, and 122 for criminal damage (Some had records in more than one category) ... the profile of the England following, compared to the support of other competing nations, was disproportionately young white males (aged 20–35) with a propensity to "herd" together in large groups, consume excessive quantities of alcohol and in many cases adopt an overtly racist, xenophobic and threatening demeanour ... This sort of behaviour is consistent with the high proportion of those arrested who had previous convictions for such offences, even although those offences had not necessarily been committed in a football context.'

[25] Mr Bohannan proceeds to refer to the heavy criticisms directed to the United Kingdom for its perceived failure to protect European centres from the activities of English hooligans, and in particular to a threat issued by UEFA on 18 June 2000 to expel the English team from Euro 2000 if there were further outbursts of disorder involving English supporters. Mr Bohannan says in terms: 'The 2000 Act was adopted in response to the lessons learned from Euro 2000';

a and this same point was made by the Secretary of State in addressing the House of Commons on the occasion of the Bill's second reading.

[26] Mr Bohannan describes the changes to the previous regime made by the amending legislation of 2000. These, of course, may be gathered from the statutes themselves. I will not therefore set out Mr Bohannan's account save for this short passage which, I think, is of some significance in light of the arguments as to
b proportionality which have been addressed to us:

> 'The first key change was that the distinction between domestic and international football banning orders was abolished. This was done as only 106 of the 560 individuals who were subject to football banning orders as a result of conviction of a football-related offence could be prevented from
> c travelling to Euro 2000, because most of those who were the subject of banning orders were only the subject of a domestic order.'

[27] Mr Jaglall's description of the procedures adopted by the FBOA in relation to the giving of notices under s 19 of the 1989 Act is to be found in his statement:

d
> 'The FBOA issue individual notices to those made subject to an order setting out the conditions and reporting requirements in each case. Notices are sent to all subjects prior to the control period for an England international match played overseas and, where appropriate, prior to the control period for an international club match involving the club that the subject supports. Each
> e club match is looked at individually with a risk assessment made at that particular time. The risk of disorder at some club matches abroad is considered minimal and no reporting requirements are imposed. Exceptionally, where intelligence is received that attaches a greater degree of risk to a particular match, notices may be sent to subjects who do not have an allegiance to that club.'
f

He proceeds to explain that applications for exemptions under s 20 are considered on an individual basis. 26 exemptions had been granted since Euro 2000.

[28] That is a sufficient account of the facts for the purpose of deciding the issues which have been argued before us. I turn next to Mr Newman's argument
g on art 7 of the Convention. It was specifically disavowed by Mr Thompson. The orders in his clients' case were of course made under s 14B of the 1989 Act, whereas those against Mr Newman's clients were made under s 14A.

ARTICLE 7 OF THE CONVENTION

[29] Article 7(1) of the Convention provides:

h
> 'No one shall be held guilty of any criminal offence on account of any act or omission which did not constitute a criminal offence under national or international law at the time when it was committed. Nor shall a heavier penalty be imposed than the one that was applicable at the time the criminal offence as committed.'
j

Mr Newman's submission is that a banning order, at least one made under s 14A of the 1989 Act, is a 'penalty' within the meaning of this provision. If that is right, it is argued (as I have indicated) that in the cases of Lilley and Miller there was a violation of art 7 because at the time when they did the acts which led to the banning orders—20 April 2000—the permissible duration of a domestic football banning order was no more than three years (s 32(2) of the 1986 Act as

amended by the 1999 Act), so that the imposition in October 2000 of a banning
order for six years was a heavier penalty enacted with retroactive effect.

[30] In *Welch v UK* (1995) 20 EHRR 247 the European Court of Human Rights
had to consider the nature of a confiscation order made under the Drug
Trafficking Offences Act 1986, it being argued that such an order constituted a
'penalty' within the meaning of art 7. The court held that 'penalty' in that context
was an autonomous Convention concept; and it set out the approach to be taken
to the question whether, in any given case, a measure amounted to such a penalty.
In its unanimous judgment the court stated (at 262 (para 28)):

> 'The wording of Article 7(1), second sentence, indicates that the starting
> point in any assessment of the existence of a penalty is whether the measure
> in question is imposed following conviction for a "criminal offence". Other
> factors that may be taken into account as relevant in this connection are the
> nature and purpose of the measure in question; its characterisation under
> national law; the procedures involved in the making and implementation of
> the measure; and its severity.'

[31] The court in *Welch's* case concluded that a confiscation order was a
'penalty' within art 7. It considered, however, that such an order had a preventive
as well as a punitive purpose (at 262 (para 30)), and in addressing the art 7 issue in
the present case I think it of some importance to recognise that many orders
made by courts may possess both these characteristics. It is important also to
have in mind the fact, obvious as it is, that there are various instances in which a
familiar form of order may bear with great severity on the person against whom
it is made without there being the least question of its amounting to a 'penalty'
for the purposes of art 7: what were previously known as Mareva injunctions and
Anton Pillar orders (now freezing injunctions and search orders) are plain
examples.

[32] Our duty is to take account of the Strasbourg jurisprudence, not
necessarily to apply it: see s 2 of the Human Rights Act 1998. But given the
Strasbourg Court's judgment that 'penalty' within art 7 is an autonomous
Convention concept, I am clear that we should in any event follow the guidance
given in *Welch's* case.

[33] In conducting that exercise, I would make two linked points at the outset.
First, the question whether the proceedings in which the relevant order is made
fall to be classified as 'criminal' proceedings or not is, in my judgment, very
largely unhelpful in relation to the 'penalty' issue under art 7. Plainly, the
proceedings in which an order under s 14A is imposed are necessarily criminal,
since it is made in the very proceedings and by the very court in and before which
the person in question is convicted of the 'relevant offence': s 14A(6). I venture
to suppose that such a state of affairs is likely to arise in cases where there is a live
issue as to 'penalty' within art 7, since if the order in question is made in civil
proceedings it may be doubted whether it is much of a candidate for the status of
'penalty' in any event. But none of this throws useful light on the question
whether the order in any given instance *is* in truth a penalty. There are various
circumstances in which criminal courts are empowered to make orders which
would not be classed as penalties.

[34] Secondly, I cannot think that there could be different answers to the art 7
question as between ss 14A and 14B. I say at once that Mr Newman did not
submit as much; he was, understandably, at pains to emphasise that he was
concerned only with s 14A. However, a major theme in his argument was that a

a   banning order under s 14A can only follow conviction of a criminal offence—the starting point in *Welch's* case—and as I understood him he would not accept that orders under ss 14A and 14B necessarily fall to be classified in the same way for the purposes of art 7. (Indeed the skeleton argument in *Lilley's* case, drafted by junior counsel Mr Scott Wilson, comes close to suggesting the contrary.) I recognise the differences between the structure of ss 14A and 14B respectively,

b   and also the differences in the potential duration of ss 14A and 14B orders (see s 14F(3)–(5)). But a single definition of 'banning order' applies to both: s 14(4); and the provisions of ss 14E, 14G, 14H and 14J, and the regimes of ss 19–21, apply to both without distinction. In my judgment it would simply be absurd to hold that one constituted a penalty within art 7 and the other did not. It follows that the nature of an order made under s 14A cannot be examined and

c   categorised without regard to that of an order under s 14B.

[**35**] Although I have said that the categorisation of the proceedings in which the order is made as 'criminal' is of itself very largely unhelpful in relation to the 'penalty' issue under art 7, there is jurisprudence concerning the classification of proceedings, as opposed to orders made in proceedings, in which as it seems to

d   me the reasoning offers assistance on the art 7 question. *R (on the application of McCann) v Crown Court at Manchester* [2001] EWCA Civ 281, [2001] 4 All ER 264, [2001] 1 WLR 1084 concerned the making of 'anti-social behaviour orders' under s 1 of the Crime and Disorder Act 1998. The Crown Court had treated applications for such orders as being made in civil proceedings. In consequence evidence was admitted under the Civil Evidence Act 1968 which would have

e   been inadmissible in criminal proceedings. An anti-social behaviour order (like a banning order under s 14B) may be sought by complaint to a magistrates' court. It must be shown (s 1(1)(a)) that the respondent to the application has acted in a manner which caused or was likely to cause harassment, alarm or distress, and (s 1(1)(b))—

f   'that such an order is necessary to protect persons in the local government area in which the harassment, alarm or distress was caused or was likely to be caused from further anti-social acts by him ...'

Section 1(6):

g   'The prohibitions that may be imposed by an anti-social behaviour order are those necessary for the purpose of protecting from further anti-social acts by the defendant—(a) persons in the local government area; and (b) persons in any adjoining local government area specified in the application for the order ...'

h   Lord Phillips of Worth Matravers MR said this:

'[38] Mr Fulford [counsel for the applicants] submitted that the prohibitions imposed by an anti-social behaviour order can have severe consequences to a defendant. In the present case the order prohibits the applicants from going

j   into an area of Manchester where they have family and friends. Mr Fulford submitted that such a restriction of liberty operates as a penalty.

[39] Many injunctions in civil proceedings operate severely upon those against whom they are ordered. In matrimonial proceedings a husband may be ordered to leave his home and not to have contact with his children. Such an order may be made as a consequence of violence which amounted to criminal conduct. But such an order is imposed not for the purpose of

punishment but for protection of the family. This demonstrates that, when considering whether an order imposes a penalty or punishment, it is necessary to look beyond its consequence and to consider its purpose.

[40] An order which is, in terms, restricted to the prohibition necessary to protect persons from anti-social behaviour is manifestly an order designed to protect in the future not to punish for past misconduct.'

[36] In my view this reasoning serves to emphasise the difference between a punitive order and one whose purpose is to offer future protection to the public or a section of it (and one may compare para 63 of the judgment, and the Master of the Rolls' citations from the judgment of Lord Bingham CJ as he then was in *B v Chief Constable of Avon and Somerset Constabulary* [2001] 1 All ER 562, [2001] 1 WLR 340).

[37] As I have acknowledged, many court orders may serve both a punitive and a preventive or protective purpose. The use of imprisonment in criminal cases is itself a prime example; and a community sentence is no less a penalty by reason of the fact that its principal focus may be rehabilitative. In truth, a just and humane system for the punishment of criminals is bound to have all these different ends in view. It follows that a punitive or retributive purpose no more marks an order as a penalty than a protective order serves to take it out of such a category. That being so the court is, as it seems to me, likely to be assisted by considering whether, in the statutory scheme before it, the predominant purpose of the measure under scrutiny is punitive, or for the protection of the public at large or a section of it.

[38] In line with this, it is I think possible to give a little more focus to the art 7 issue, penalty or no, than is afforded by the list of considerations provided in *Welch's* case (1995) 20 EHRR 247. As it seems to me, the more closely an order is related, or under the regime in question falls to be related, to the commission of a particular offence or offences, the more likely it is that the order should fall to be treated as a penalty. The reason is that the very idea of a penalty—albeit that in the particular case its imposition may be to protect, prevent, or rehabilitate—takes its place within a distinct scheme or philosophy of distributive justice. There is a principled distinction between distributive justice and social betterment simpliciter, however much the former may advance the latter.

[39] The primacy of distributive justice in the steps toward a conclusion that a measure amounts to a penalty in my judgment marches with the Strasbourg Court's insistence in *Welch's* case that the starting point is the measure's being shown to follow a criminal conviction. More than this; it stands in line with the Court of Human Rights' reasoning on the particular facts in *Welch's* case (at 263):

'33. However, there are several aspects of the making of an order under the 1986 Act which are in keeping with the idea of a penalty as it is commonly understood even though they may also be considered as essential to the preventive scheme inherent in the 1986 Act. The sweeping statutory assumptions in section 2(3) of the 1986 Act that all property passing through the offender's hands over a six-year period is the fruit of trafficking unless he can prove otherwise; the fact that the confiscation order is directed to the proceeds involved in drug dealing and is not limited to actual enrichment or profit; the discretion of the trial judge, in fixing the amount of the order, to take into consideration the degree of culpability of the accused; and the possibility of imprisonment in default of payment by the offender—are all a   elements which, when considered together, provide a strong indication of *inter alia* a regime of punishment.'

It is useful to compare the Commission decision in *Ibbotson v UK* (1998) 27 EHRR CD 332, which was concerned with the registration requirements imposed by the Sex Offenders Act 1997. The Commission stated (at 334):

b   '... the measures complained of are imposed as a matter of law: no procedure whatever is involved ... Whilst the Commission accepts that failure to comply with a measure is a criminal offence, it considers that the position is different from that in the case of *Welch*, where periods of imprisonment in default of payment were fixed at the sentencing stage ... In

c   the case of the [Sex Offenders Act 1997], independent criminal proceedings would have to brought against a defaulter ... Overall, the Commission considers that, given in particular the way in which the measures imposed by the Act operate completely separately from the ordinary sentencing procedures, and the fact that the measures do not, ultimately, require more than mere registration, it cannot be said that the measures imposed on

d   the applicant amounted to a "penalty" within the meaning of Article 7 of the Convention.'

See also *Adamson v UK* (1999) 28 EHRR CD 209, which was again concerned with the sex offenders register.

[40] It seems to me with respect that this learning tends to underline the

e   importance of the role of the mechanisms of distributive criminal justice in ascertaining whether a measure amounts to a penalty within art 7; and with all these considerations in mind, I address that question as it arises in these cases.

[41] As I have said Mr Newman sought to emphasise the fact that under s 14A the order must follow conviction of a criminal offence. He was also at pains to

f   draw attention to the potential severity, particularly in terms of duration, of orders under s 14A in comparison with the earlier statutory regimes. The details, canvassed by Mr Newman with inexhaustible thoroughness, appear in the legislation as I have set it out and I will not repeat them. Mr Newman also had a point concerning certain statutory appeal rights to the Court of Appeal (Criminal Division).

g   **[42]** In my judgment it is plain that a football banning order, whether made under s 14A or s 14B, is not a penalty within the autonomous sense of the term for the purposes of art 7.

(1) In my judgment it is no part *at all* of the purpose of any such order to inflict punishment. The fact that it imposes a detriment on its recipient no more

h   demonstrates that it possesses a punitive element than in the case of a Mareva injunction. The purpose is to protect the public, here and abroad, from the evil of football violence and the threat of it. So much is plain from the whole scheme, but in particular the preamble to the 1989 Act and the condition 'that there are reasonable grounds to believe that making a banning order would help to prevent

j   violence or disorder at or in connection with any regulated football matches' (ss 14A(2), 14B(4)(b)).

(2) The order is not made as part of the process of distributive criminal justice. Under s 14B there is no requirement of a criminal conviction, so that the *Welch* starting point is not met. In s 14A, the existence of a relevant conviction is in my judgment no more than a gateway criterion for the making of the order, equivalent to the provision in s 14B(4)(a) where no conviction is involved.

Section 14A(4)(a) actually *contrasts* the banning order with the sentence imposed for the relevant offence.

(3) (Plainly this overlaps with (2).) In other more detailed respects the order's characterisation under national law tells against its being treated as a penalty. I have in mind the provisions relating to the alteration of requirements imposed (s 14G); the power to terminate the order in light of all the circumstances (s 14H); the provision in s 14J which treats breach of the order's requirements as a separate criminal offence, rather than a default for which a penalty is fixed when the order is made: cf the Commission's reasoning in *Ibbotson's* case; and all the regimes established by ss 19–21B. Sections 19–21 in particular provide for pragmatic administrative measures, whose good sense is plain but which by their nature are not about or within the ordinary framework of criminal justice.

(4) As for the orders' severity, I would accept that the restrictions they impose are more than trivial; and under the 1989 Act they are potentially more burdensome than previously. How harshly they might bear on any individual must, I would have thought, be largely subjective. However that may be, it is clear from the Strasbourg jurisprudence, not least *Welch's* case itself, that severity alone cannot be decisive; and in my judgment the burdens or detriments involved cannot conceivably confer the status of penalty on banning orders if otherwise they do not possess it, which in my judgment plainly they do not. I have in mind also the right to seek exemption (s 20); and this will be of some relevance to Mr Thompson's submissions on proportionality to which I will come in due course.

[43] For these reasons I would hold that banning orders under ss 14A and 14B of the 1989 Act do not constitute penalties within the meaning of art 7 of the convention. I would have come to the same conclusion in relation to s 14A even had I not been of the clear view that the result must be the same as between the two sections. I hope I do no injustice to Mr Newman if I say that none of his detailed submissions, so far as I have not expressly dealt with them, began to persuade me to the contrary.

GOUGH AND SMITH: MR THOMPSON'S FIVE PROPOSITIONS

[44] These were helpfully put in writing. The first four assert by one route or another that the regime of banning orders under s 14B is contrary to Community law. The first three engage European provisions and principles relating to freedom of movement. The fourth concerns procedural standards under Community law. The last asserts a violation of art 8 of the convention. As Mr Thompson articulated them the five are as follows:

'(1) There is no derogation, in particular on grounds of public policy, for restrictions on the rights of EU citizens to leave a Member State, other than: (a) those implicit in domestic criminal and public order legislation (for example, imprisonment); and (b) those recognised by the Court of Justice as a general principle of Community law precluding abuse of rights conferred by Community law.

(2) Even if a public policy derogation exists, it is limited to cases where it can be *proved*, to a fair standard, that the departure of an individual from the Member State would constitute a genuine, present and sufficiently serious threat to one of the fundamental interests of society in that Member State.

(3) Even if a broader public policy derogation exists, it is not necessary or appropriate to impose a 2-year *international* banning order on an individual: (a) who is proved on the balance of probabilities to have been involved in

a violence or disorder in the past 10 years; and (b) in respect of whom it is found, again on the balance of probabilities, that there are reasonable grounds to believe that the imposition of such an order would reduce the risk of violence or disorder at any matches, without any need for such matches to include international matches.

b (4) The procedures and evidential rules under section 14B and 14C are incompatible with Community law standards of procedural fairness, as provided for in Articles 6 ff. of Directive 64/221 and Articles 6 and 13 of the Convention, whether or not the section 14B procedure is a "criminal charge" for the purposes of Article 6.

c (5) Section 14B banning orders, including the ancillary powers conferred on the Secretary of State, magistrates, police and the enforcing authority, are incompatible with Article 8.'

THE FIRST PROPOSITION

[45] In order to understand this and the next two following propositions it is
d necessary to set out the relevant European materials. Mr Thompson first referred to general provisions contained in arts 10, 14(2) and 18 of the EC Treaty, and also to the Protocol on the Application of Certain Aspects of art 14 of the Treaty to the United Kingdom and to Ireland. Of these texts I need only cite art 18:

e 'Every citizen of the Union shall have the right to move and reside freely within the territory of the Member States, subject to the limitations and conditions laid down in this Treaty and by the measures adopted to give it effect.'

Then art 49 of the EC Treaty provides:

f 'Within the framework of the provisions set out below, restrictions on freedom to provide services within the Community shall be prohibited in respect of nationals of Member States who are established in a State of the Community other than that of the person for whom the services are intended ...'
g
By force of art 55, art 46 is applied to art 49, and provides in part:

'1. The provisions of this Chapter and measures taken in pursuance thereof shall not prejudice the applicability of provisions laid down by law,
h regulation or administrative action providing for special treatment for foreign nationals on grounds of public policy, public security or public health.'

Council Directive (EEC) 73/148 (OJ 1973 L172 p 14) gives effect to art 49. I note
j first the last recital:

'Whereas the coordination of special measures concerning the movement and residence of foreign nationals, justified on grounds of public policy, public security or public health, is already the subject of the Council Directive of 25 February 1964 [viz Council Directive (EEC) 64/221 (OJ 1964 L56 p 850), to which I will refer below]'.

Then:

'*Article 1*

1. The Member States shall, acting as provided in this Directive, abolish restrictions on the movement and residence of ... (b) nationals of Member States wishing to go to another Member State as recipients of services ...

Article 2

1. Member States shall grant the persons referred to in Article 1 the right to leave their territory. Such right shall be exercised simply on production of a valid identity card or passport. Members of the family shall enjoy the same right as the national on whom they are dependent.

2. Member States shall, acting in accordance with their laws, issue to their nationals, or renew, an identity card or passport, which shall state in particular the holder's nationality ...

Article 3

1. Member States shall grant to the persons referred to in Article 1 right to enter their territory merely on production of a valid identity card or passport ...

Article 8

Member States shall not derogate from the provisions of this Directive save on grounds of public policy, public security or public health.'

In light of Mr Thompson's argument I should refer also to Directive 64/221 'on the co-ordination of special measures concerning the movement and residence of foreign nationals which are justified on grounds of public policy, public security or public health'.

'*Article 1*

1. The provisions of this Directive shall apply to any national of a Member State who resides in or travels to another Member State of the Community, either in order to pursue an activity as an employed or self-employed person, or as a recipient of services ...

Article 2

1. This directive relates to all measures concerning entry into their territory, issue or renewal of residence permits, or expulsion from their territory, taken by Member States on grounds of public policy, public security or public health ...

Article 3

1. Measures taken on grounds of public policy or of public security shall be based exclusively on the personal conduct of the individual concerned.

2. Previous criminal convictions shall not in themselves constitute grounds for the taking of such measures ...

Article 6

The person concerned shall be informed of the grounds of public policy, public security, or public health upon which the decision ... is based, unless this is contrary to the interests of the security of the State involved.'

a   **[46]** It is common ground that banning orders impose, at least are capable of imposing, restrictions on an individual's right to travel to another member state to provide or receive services. That being so I think it right to proceed on the basis that the orders made against Gough and Smith prima facie violate their rights under art 49 of the Treaty and art 2 of Directive 73/148. Mr Thompson's argument under proposition 1 is that the Treaty neither enacts nor allows for any

b   right of derogation from the free movement provisions such that a member state might, on public policy grounds, prohibit a citizen of the Union (including its own nationals) from leaving its territory.

    [47] Upon analysis this argument rests essentially on two steps. (1) No such derogation is given or allowed for by the terms of art 46 of the Treaty (nor by any other Treaty provision). (2) Article 8 of Directive 73/148 must be read

c   conformably with art 46, and cannot extend its scope (and the terms of Directive 64/221 are said to confirm that the public policy exception contained in art 8 of 73/148 has the same scope as art 46).

    [48] I would first draw attention to a characteristic of Mr Thompson's submission which, though in other more municipal debates it may possess a

d   robust and traditional attraction, in the arena of Community law represents a potential Trojan Horse. It consists in the argument's tight dependence on a literal interpretation of the Treaty. Article 46 is the *fons et origo* of his proposition 1. It refers to 'special treatment for *foreign* nationals on grounds of public policy, public security or public health' (my emphasis). Upon the adjective *foreign*

e   Mr Thompson must build an edifice of legislative intent, sure and sound, to demonstrate that the Community lawmakers intended in this context that a member state should enjoy far richer powers of derogation as regards entry to its territory by nationals of other member states than it may possess as regards its own citizens leaving its shores.

f   **[49]** That, I think, would be a heroic labour. And at the very level of literal interpretation, which must be Mr Thompson's password, his argument is pressed with difficulty: here is the Trojan Horse. It will be recalled that art 8 of Directive 73/148 provides: 'Member States shall not derogate from the provisions of this Directive save on grounds of public policy, public security or public health'. Now, Directive 73/148 is plainly concerned with EU citizens' rights to leave their

g   home member state; one needs only to recall the first sentence of art 2(1). Mr Thompson is driven to submit that the Community legislature intended by art 8 no implication that member states might derogate from art 2(1) (and all the associated provisions) on the public interest grounds to which art 8 specifically refers. But that requires a grossly restrictive reading of art 8, for which the terms

h   of Directive 73/148 offer no perceptible support.

    [50] There is more to be said about the language of the relevant legislation. Mr Thompson's submission tends to conflate the subject matter of Directives 64/221 and 73/148. Desiring to avoid the error of over-literal interpretation, which I think confounds Mr Thompson's approach, I put the matter very broadly.

j   Directive 64/221 is generally concerned with the rights of EU citizens to *enter* a member state other than their home state: see arts 1(1), (2)(1). Directive 73/148 is, by contrast, first concerned with the rights of EU citizens to *leave* their home state for another member state: see arts 1(1)(b), 2(1); though it deals also with rights of entry (see for example arts 3 and 4). These considerations seem to me to undermine such support for his position relating to art 46 and Directive 73/148 as Mr Thompson seeks to derive from Directive 64/221.

[51] Now, I of course accept (for it is elementary) that legislation by Directive
must be intra vires the Treaty; and that, accordingly, subordinate Community
legislation must not break ground where the Treaty gives no power to tread.
Mr Thompson cites *Pharmacia and Upjohn SA (formerly Upjohn SA) v Paranova A/S*
Case C-379/97 [1999] All ER (EC) 880, [2000] Ch 571 and *Etablissements Delhaize
Freres v Promalvin* Case C-47/90 [1992] ECR I-3669 which with respect I need not
set out. Neither is authority for so literal a reading of art 46 of the Treaty as is
required by Mr Thompson's argument. In my judgment, given the points as to
the legislation's language to which I have drawn attention, the words of art 46
provide no sufficient foundation for proposition 1.

[52] However, Mr Pannick QC for the Secretary of State did not rest on the coils
of the legislation's language. He submitted in addition that Mr Thompson was
fixed with a reductio ad absurdum: though a member state may on Mr Thompson's
argument prohibit citizens of other member states from entering its territory on
proper public interest grounds, upon the very same argument it has no shred of
power to prohibit a citizen of its own from leaving its territory on *any* public
interest ground whatever.

[53] Mr Thompson accepted that his argument was far-reaching to this extent:
it would mean that restriction orders provided for by the 1989 Act as originally
enacted were repugnant to Community law. But he sought to disavow so
extreme a conclusion as was attributed to his argument by Mr Pannick. Here is
the basis on which he did so.

[54] Mr Thompson conceded, first, that a member state's internal criminal
jurisdiction is in the ordinary way unaffected by the requirements of Community
law, so that a lawful sentence of imprisonment, which obviously stops the
prisoner's free movement, cannot be said to infringe Treaty rights (see *Kremzow v
Austria* Case C-299/95 [1997] ECR I-2629, a case about a retired Austrian judge
convicted of murder). I need not go into the details. He accepts, secondly, that
Community law recognises an emerging principle, which he named 'abuse of
rights'. Its effect is that where an EU citizen purports to exercise a right such as
freedom of movement, but is actually intent upon some ulterior and alien
purpose for which the Community right is nothing but false cover, Community
law will not protect him. For this position he cited *Centros Ltd v Erhvervs-Org
Selskabsstyrelsen* Case C-212/97 [2000] Ch 446, [1999] ECR I-1459. In that case two
Danish residents had formed a company in the United Kingdom with the express
purpose of avoiding the effects of Danish legislation which required (in contrast
to the British position) that a minimum amount of the share capital of a Danish
company be paid up. They promptly applied to register a branch of the company
in Denmark. The application was refused on the ground that the true intention
was to set up a principal trading establishment in Denmark while circumventing
the rules as to paid-up shares. In subsequent proceedings there was a reference
to the Court of Justice.

[55] In its judgment in *Centros'* case the court said:

'24 ... according to the case law of the court a member state is entitled to
take measures designed to prevent certain of its nationals from attempting,
under cover of the rights created by the Treaty, improperly to circumvent
their national legislation or to prevent individuals from improperly or
fraudulently taking advantage of provisions of Community law [and authority
is then set out].

a   25 ... However, although, in such circumstances, the national courts may, case by case, take account—on the basis of objective evidence—of abuse or fraudulent conduct on the part of the persons concerned in order, where appropriate, to deny them the benefit of the provisions of Community law on which they seek to rely, they must nevertheless assess such conduct in the light of the objectives pursued by those provisions ...' (See [2000] Ch 446 at

b   480, [1999] ECR I-1459 at 1492–1493.)

[56] In light of *Kremzow's* case and more particularly *Centros'* case, Mr Thompson accepted in terms that were it shown that Gough or Smith, or anyone else, proposed to travel to the Continent for the purpose of perpetrating (or presumably inciting or encouraging) acts of violence and hooliganism the United Kingdom

c   authorities would be wholly entitled to stop them at the point of departure, and nothing in the law of Europe would gainsay their right so to confine them. It would be a case of abuse of Community law rights.

[57] If that concession is correctly made, as surely it is, I think it undermines Mr Thompson's proposition 1. It implies at once that the language and structure

d   of the Treaty and Directives are perfectly consistent with such a right, to confine their citizens at least in *some* circumstances, in the hands of the member states. In face of that the edifice of Mr Thompson's argument based on the language of art 46 of the Treaty, art 8 of Directive 73 / 148, and the terms of Directive 64/221 is in my judgment turned into a house of cards. He is driven to espouse the proposition that whereas nothing in those materials impedes the member state's

e   right to confine within its territory those of its nationals who can be proved to be bent on hooliganism in connection with football matches elsewhere in Europe, these same provisions, by contrast, render the member state absolutely powerless so to restrict any of its nationals where a court is satisfied that there are reasonable grounds to believe that to do so would help to prevent just such hooliganism: it

f   lacks only distinct proof of the individual's subjective intentions – proof which will often be hard or impossible to find. In my view such a distinction could only be sustained by acceptance of a subjection of the public interest to private rights so abject and supine as to be alien to the civilised balances struck by the common law and the law of Europe alike. It cannot, in my judgment, represent the law. Mr Pannick's reductio ad absurdum remains intact. (I shall have more to say

g   about these balances in the next section of the judgment, dealing with Mr Thompson's second and third propositions.)

[58] Given all these factors I prefer Mr Pannick's submission, first, that in the ordinary way one would expect Community law to confer or allow the same or greater powers upon a member state as regards restrictions upon its own

h   nationals in contrast with the powers it may exercise in relation to nationals of other member states. It is difficult to see a rational basis for any other position. Secondly, the express reference to *foreign* nationals in art 46 is no more than an implicit recognition of an obvious and prior truth, that as regards its own nationals a member state may of course impose restrictions; and so far as a

j   question then arises whether the state may impose equivalent restrictions on foreign nationals, Directive 73 / 148 shows that the same principles apply to both.

[59] Mr Pannick is supported, moreover, by the decision of the Court of Justice in *Alpine Investments BV v Minister van Financiën* Case C-384/93 [1995] ECR I-1141. The case concerned the practice of a company established in the Netherlands of 'cold-calling', by telephone, clients or potential clients in other member states. Such cold-calling was prohibited by Dutch law. In reference

proceedings before the Court of Justice the company argued that the prohibition
contravened art 59 (now 49) of the Treaty. The court rejected that submission
on the facts of the case, and said (at 1179):

> '43. Although the protection of consumers in the other Member States is
> not, as such, a matter for the Netherlands authorities, the nature and extent
> of that protection does none the less have a direct effect on the good
> reputation of Netherlands financial services
>
> 44. Maintaining the good reputation of the national financial sector may
> therefore constitute an imperative reason of public interest capable of
> justifying restrictions on the freedom to provide public services.'

[60] The *Alpine Investments* case could hardly be further distant from the
present case on its facts. But Mr Pannick's point is that the court's reasoning
recognises that in principle, subject always to the particular circumstances, a
member state may on public policy grounds be justified in imposing restrictions
on those within its territory to prevent their conducting themselves elsewhere in
the Union in such a way as to damage the home state's reputation in some
concrete respect. Mr Thompson is of course entitled to point out that it is one
thing to ban telephone calls to another member state, and something quite
different to prohibit a person from travelling from one state to another. However,
Mr Pannick seeks no more than broad support from the *Alpine Investments* case,
and that I think it provides.

[61] For all these reasons I would hold that Mr Thompson's proposition 1 is
false. In a proper case a member state may be justified on public policy grounds
in preventing a citizen of the Union from leaving its shores, and its right to do so
is not limited to any narrow conception of 'abuse of rights'. I should add that in
reply Mr Thompson submitted that were I against him on proposition 1, I should
nevertheless refer it in the form of a question to the Court of Justice under art 234
of the Treaty, the matter not being acte clair. I decline to do so. I consider that
this point is acte clair.

THE SECOND AND THIRD PROPOSITIONS

[62] Given the shape of Mr Thompson's argument, it is convenient to take
these two together. This part of the case of course proceeds on the footing that
proposition 1 is wrong, as I would hold it is. Indeed the argument recognises
that the prevention, more realistically the diminution, of violence associated with
international football matches constitutes a legitimate aim of public policy which
in principle may properly be furthered by deployment of a member state's power
to confine citizens of the Union (including its own citizens) within its borders.
The overall submission is that the material provisions of the 1989 Act as they
were framed in 2000 are disproportionate to this legitimate aim. At para 9 of his
note on propositions 2–5 Mr Thompson says: 'The basic defect of s 14B(4)(b) is
that there is no necessary connection between the public policy objective of the
legislation as drafted and the matters that form the basis of international banning
orders.'

[63] Mr Thompson first points to the fact that it is effectively common ground
that the scope of the power to derogate on public policy grounds from the
Treaty's free movement rights is to be derived from the jurisprudence of the
Court of Justice relating to Directive 64/221, and the terms of the Directive itself.
As for the latter, art 3(1) and (2) (which I have set out) are the salient provisions. As
for the authorities, particular emphasis was laid on *Criminal proceedings against*

a *Calfa* Case C-348/96 [1999] All ER (EC) 850, [1999] ECR I-11. That case concerned a Greek law by which a foreign national convicted of a drugs offence in Greece was to be expelled from the country for life unless there were compelling reasons to the contrary. The Court of Justice referred to Directive 64/221 and stated:

b   '24 ... It follows that the existence of a previous criminal conviction can, therefore, only be taken into account in so far as the circumstances which gave rise to that conviction are evidence of personal conduct constituting a present threat to the requirements of public policy.

    25. It follows that an expulsion order could be made against a Community national such as Ms Calfa only if, besides her having committed an offence
c   under drugs laws, her personal conduct created a genuine and sufficiently serious threat affecting one of the fundamental interests of society.' (See [1999] All ER (EC) 850 at 863, [1999] ECR I-11 at 30–31.)

The judgment of the Court of Justice in *Rutili v Minister for the Interior* [1975] ECR 1219 is further authority for the requirement that the concept of public policy be
d interpreted strictly, where it is advanced as the justification for a derogation from core Community rights. In particular there is some emphasis placed on the need for any restrictive decision to be based on the individual circumstances of the person concerned.

    [64] Mr Thompson submits that the regime of the 1989 Act, so far from being concerned with the individual conduct of persons against whom orders might be
e made, lacks entirely any requirement to prove that the individual in question presents an actual risk or threat to public order. He says that so far as personal conduct seemingly plays a part in the scheme, Mr Bohannan's evidence (and a statement made by the Secretary of State to Parliament) shows that it figures only in the sense and to the extent that the individual is shown to be a member of a
f class: that is, the class of persons with some propensity for disorder and some connection with football. And the policy adopted in relation to the issues of notices under s 19, as disclosed by Mr Jaglall, shows also that restrictions are imposed on a class basis.

    [65] But, so the argument runs, it is much worse than that. Under the regime as it stands an order under s 14B *must* be made, if the statutory conditions are met,
g even in the case of a subject who on the evidence has never been to a football match abroad and in respect of whom there is nothing to show that he intends to do so. Yet the order covers domestic and international matches alike. Mr Thompson says that this argument is well illustrated by the case of Mr Gough. He submits that there exists a mismatch both between the scope of an order made under
h s 14B and the statutory basis for making it, and between the objective of the order and the nature of the restrictions which it imposes. The bite of Mr Thompson's argument on this part of the case, I think, is well displayed by his acceptance, rather his positive submission, that s 15(2) of the 1989 Act in its original form satisfied the requirements of Directive 64/221. As will be recalled the terms of
j s 15(2) were:

    'No restriction order may be made unless the court is satisfied that making such an order in relation to the accused would help to prevent violence or disorder at or in connection with designated football matches.'

That provision required the court to be satisfied that the order would have the desired effect *in relation to the particular accused*.

[66] In relation to proportionality more generally Mr Thompson submitted
that there were various possible measures to which recourse might be had which *a*
(this is necessarily implicit in the argument) would fulfil the public policy aim in
question, but whose effects would be less draconian than the measures actually
in place. These included notification to other national authorities of persons
against whom orders might be made; restricting the scope of international
banning orders so as only to prevent attendance at the ground, or at least only *b*
travel to the country where the match or tournament was to take place; and
limiting the requirement to report at a police station to the day of the match.

[67] Mr Thompson had two further submissions on this part of the case.
Neither in my judgment can carry the case standing alone, and I summarise them
very briefly. First, it is not the business of the United Kingdom to enact legislation
to repair what it may perceive as the failure of other member states to act in the *c*
field in question (I do not of course suggest that there has been any such actual or
perceived failure). Secondly, even though Mr Newman's arguments as to art 7 of
the Convention are wrong, the retrospectivity inherent in the scheme of the 1989
Act is material to the judgment to be made as to proportionality.

[68] To the battery of all these submissions Mr Pannick responds thus. (1) An *d*
order under s 14B(4)(b) must indeed be based on the magistrates' perception of
the conduct of the particular individual. And that is what happens, as the course
of the proceedings below in *Gough's* and *Smith's* case demonstrate. (2) The case
of *Calfa* shows that derogations from free movement rights may be permitted to
counter what are no more than risks or threats (see [1999] All ER (EC) 850 at 862,
863, [1999] ECR I-11 at 30, paras 21 and 24 of the court's judgment). (3) As regards *e*
Mr Thompson's strictures relating to the use of the notice provisions under s 19,
the magistrates' court will already have made a decision based on personal
conduct, under s 14B(4)(b); and in relation to enforcement, the subject can apply
for exemption under s 20 and such an application will be considered on its
individual merits. *f*

[69] As for the requirement of proportionality more generally, first it is plain
from Mr Bohannan's evidence that the measures in place before the amendments
made in 2000, and the implementation of those measures, had proved woefully
inadequate; and 'the United Kingdom was heavily criticised for not taking more
radical steps to protect host cities and citizens from other European countries
from English hooligans'. Secondly Mr Pannick submitted that in practice the *g*
effect of the restrictions imposed by banning orders was distinctly limited, given
their scope under the scheme and the number of matches played abroad that are
likely to be involved, and the opportunity to seek exemption. There can be no
question (as at one stage had been suggested) that the Secretary of State might
make an order under s 14(6) by force of which an individual may be required to *h*
surrender his passport in September and have it kept from him until the following
May, simply because certain isolated matches were to be played within the
period.

[70] Both Mr Pannick and Mr Havers QC for the Chief Constable of
Derbyshire advanced particular submissions intended to demonstrate that the *j*
less draconian measures suggested by Mr Thompson in the course of argument
would be ineffective or in other respects undesirable or counter-productive.
Thus for example: notification to other states' authorities of the identities of
possible subjects had been tried before Euro 2000 and proved a failure (Bohannan
paras 13(h), 16). Barring entry to the ground only would fail to meet the plain fact
that hooligans riot in town squares and streets. Banning subjects only from travel

a to the country where the match is to take place does not engage with the
likelihood of their congregating just across the border. Limiting the requirement
to report at a police station to the day of the match fails to confront the fact that
violence may erupt on days before or after the game.

[71] I should briefly record arguments of Mr Pannick and Mr Havers advanced
to counter Mr Thompson's submissions (a) that it must be disproportionate to
b impose a banning order potentially having effect to prohibit travel abroad upon
someone as regards whom there is nothing to show he has ever been to a football
match in another country or intends to do so, and (b) that the issue of notices
under s 19 is not done by reference to the individual's circumstances. Mr Havers
said that it cannot nowadays be supposed that football hooligans, with a history
of involvement in ugly incidents at home, will necessarily intend to restrict their
c activities to domestic matches; and he referred to Supt Wright's evidence as to
the orchestrated nature of football violence. Mr Pannick said that the scheme
would be frankly unworkable if there were a requirement to establish whether or
not any given person proposed to travel abroad. Likewise Mr Havers submitted
that it would be unreal, at the s 19 stage, to insist that the enforcing authority,
d before it serves a notice, should distinctly discover in every individual case
whether the subject intends to travel to the relevant match or matches overseas.

[72] By what kind of yardstick is the court to judge these competing
arguments? It is time to turn to the law. The idea of proportionality mediates the
tension between private right and public interest, where enacted law proposes to
prefer the latter over the former. In *R v Minister of Agriculture, Fisheries and Food*
e *and the Secretary of State for Health, ex p Fedesa* Case C-331/88 [1990] ECR I-4023 at
4063 (para 13) it was described thus (the passage is cited at para 41 in the judgment
of Lord Bingham CJ as he then was in *R v Secretary of State for Health, ex p Eastside
Cheese Co* [1999] 3 CMLR 123 at 142):

f   'By virtue of that principle [sc proportionality], the lawfulness of
the prohibition of an economic activity is subject to the condition that the
prohibitory measures are appropriate and necessary in order to achieve
the objectives legitimately pursued by the legislation in question; when
there is a choice between several appropriate measures recourse must be had
to the least onerous, and the disadvantages caused must not be disproportionate
g   to the aims pursued.'

However, it is plain on European and domestic authority alike that when in any
given case the court's duty is to decide whether a legislative measure or
administrative decision is in truth proportionate to the aim in view, the judge
does not stand in the shoes of the first decision-maker and retake the decision for
h himself on the merits. Rather he will exercise a secondary judgment, there being
a margin of discretion in the original decision-maker which the court respects:
indeed the court confers it. Upon this aspect I have in mind the learning to be
found in *R v Bouchereau* [1981] 2 All ER 924n at 940, [1977] ECR 1999 at 2013–2014,
paras 34–35 of the judgment; *Ex p Eastside Cheese* [1999] 3 CMLR 123 at 145
j (para 48); *Brown v Stott (Procurator Fiscal, Dunfermline)* [2001] 2 All ER 97 at 114,
[2001] 2 WLR 817 at 834–835 per Lord Bingham; these materials were cited by
counsel before us. There is also important further authority (which with great
respect I need not cite), including authority of their Lordships' House, to which
I referred in *R (on the application of Mahmood) v Secretary of State for the Home Dept*
[2001] 1 WLR 840 (an immigration case in which were raised arguments founded
on art 8 of the Convention): *R v Ministry of Defence, ex p Smith* [1996] 1 All ER 257,

[1996] QB 51, *R v Lord Saville of Newdigate, ex p A* [1999] 4 All ER 860, [2000] 1 WLR 1855, and *R v Secretary of State for the Home Dept, ex p Launder* [1997] 3 All ER 961, [1997] 1 WLR 839. Since the target of Mr Thompson's submissions had been the 1989 Act itself, it is no surprise that Mr Pannick was at pains to emphasise a particular feature of the jurisprudence, namely that the margin of discretion accorded by the courts will be the greater where the decision-maker in question is the primary legislator (see *Ex p Eastside Cheese* [1999] 3 CMLR 123 at 145 (para 48)).

[73] The legal security of the principle of proportionality must be made consistent with the public decision-maker's margin of discretion. The means of doing it can be found in closer scrutiny of the tension between private right and public interest. This case is about the scope or reach of rights of free movement given by the EU Treaty. Now, there exists a great danger in allowing any pride of place to rights. Once a right is established in the state, it will by force of human nature be asserted to the uttermost. There is a dictum of the great American jurist, Holmes J, that is very much in point:

> 'All rights tend to declare themselves absolute to their logical extreme. Yet all in fact are limited by the neighborhood of principles of policy which are other than those on which the particular right is founded, and which become strong enough to hold their own when a certain point is reached.' (See *Hudson County Water Co v McCarter* (1908) 209 US 349 at 355.)

To give effect to the right's uttermost assertion—its logical extreme—would alike confound the right's moral credentials and its practical utility. The reason is, first, that the claim of moral authority for any right given by the general law rests upon the fact that the right belongs to every citizen, as do all other rights thus given; so that in any particular case, where there is a clash of interests, it is inherent *in the nature of the right itself* that the individual who claims its benefit may have to give way to the supervening weight of other claims. And secondly, the right's practical utility rests upon the fact that there can be no tranquillity in the state without a plethora of unruly individual freedoms, which will be measured in the language of rights; anything else looks tyranny in the face without blinking; so that in any particular case, to crown the possessors of one such right and consign the others beneath the throne, will sooner or later undercut the community fabric.

[74] Here I would respectfully emphasise what was said by Lord Steyn in *Brown's* case [2001] 2 All ER 97 at 118, [2001] 2 WLR 817 at 839:

> 'The fundamental rights of individuals are of supreme importance but those rights are not unlimited: we live in communities of individuals who also have rights. The direct lineage of this ancient idea is clear: the convention is the descendant of the Universal Declaration of Human Rights (Paris, 10 December 1948; UN TS 2 (1949); Cmd 7226) which in art 29 expressly recognised the duties of everyone to the community and the limitation on rights in order to secure and protect respect for the rights of others.'

As it seems to me this passage points to the same essential truth as is reflected in what was said by the European Court of Human Rights in *Sporrong v Sweden* (1983) 5 EHRR 35 at 52 (para 69):

> '... the Court must determine whether a fair balance was struck between the demands of the general interest of the community and the requirements

a   of the protection of the individual's fundamental rights. *The search for this balance is inherent in the whole of the Convention ...*' (My emphasis.)

Such texts, I think, reflect the same idea as Holmes J's 'neighborhood of principles of policy which are other than those on which the particular right is founded'. Also they reflect ancient good sense: it was the Preface to the Book of Common
b   Prayer that declared the wisdom of the Church of England 'to keep the mean between the two extremes'; it is a wisdom which travels far beyond this local context of the English Church. It is in my judgment clear that the balance of private right and general interest falls to be struck, no less surely than at Strasbourg, also in the field of Community law where, as in this very case, a judgment must be made whether considerations of the public interest should
c   override the individual's enjoyment of a right which prima facie the Treaty accords to him.

[75] It is inherent, then, in any principled approach to rights enjoyed by the individual under the general law that the right's very justification, and its consistency with the state's sound fabric, critically depend upon its being subject
d   to limits imposed to protect the public interest: to protect, compendiously, the rights of others. If there are absolute untrammelled rights, they are very few and far between. The right not to be tortured, the right to think whatever one likes, and the right to a fair trial are candidates, but it is difficult to think of others. Otherwise rights are divisive, harmful, ultimately worthless, unless their possession is conditional upon the public good.
e
[76] The importance of these points for present purposes is that the doctrine of proportionality is what translates this philosophical truth into practical reality. It provides the means by which the balance between private right and public interest is weighed and fulfilled. Now, the balance between the individual's right, which is conditional, and the general public good, which is often amorphous and
f   arguable, is frequently difficult and frequently delicate. It is always so where there is a clash between values none of which is absolute. And if the possession of rights is conditional upon the public good, nothing is more important than that the public good should not itself be usurped, deployed as a means of suppressing liberty by spurious excuses for the extinguishment or diminution of individual rights. In my judgment, this difficult trade between private right and public good
g   is regulated by the idea of proportionality.

[77] Thus the doctrine of proportionality in general, and the jurisprudence exemplified in *Calfa*'s case [1999] All ER (EC) 850, [1999] ECR I-11 in particular, recognise in terms that it is not legitimate for the state decision-maker (legislature or executive) to override an established Community right on any grounds
h   whatever which it might choose, even granted that the grounds would be reasonable. Where the restriction of such a right is in contemplation, the doctrine insists that the state recognise a principle which, certainly, was not earlier insisted on by the domestic law of England as exemplified in *Associated Provincial Picture Houses Ltd v Wednesbury Corp* [1947] 2 All ER 680, [1948] 1 KB 223. The principle
j   is that the right in question, which possesses an independent value calling for respect by virtue of the very fact that it is guaranteed by the European legislature, is not to be interfered with save on substantial and objective grounds of public interest. This principle necessarily gives rise in practice to a further requirement: that the state, if it decides that the right must be interfered with, has to choose a means judged to constitute the least interference consistent with the public policy aim in view. Anything else overweens the state to the citizen's cost and would

usurp the public good; it upsets the balance between private right and public *a*
interest.

[78] And so the law demands that the state respect and adhere to this principle,
and its consequent requirement, as I have described them. No less important,
however, the state enjoys a margin of discretion. That does not extend so as to
entitle the state to question the principle, nor yet to question the need to judge
what is the least intrusive interference. Those are mandatory; fixed points in the *b*
constellation of the state's authority. The margin of discretion goes rather to the
assessment on the merits as to what interference *is*, in truth, required; and to that
extent it regulates the trade between private right and public interest. This is a
discretion of ample scope; it is demanded alike by the imperative of respect due
to the democratic arm of the state, and as an antidote to the dreary solipsism of
rights asserted to the uttermost. The state decision-maker is free—indeed, by his *c*
public responsibilities may be obliged—to judge the degree of importance
possessed by the public interest in question, to which it is proposed that the
private right be subordinated. He will judge whether it is necessary to take
measures to avoid the certainty, or only the probability, or only the risk, of
damage to the public interest in whatever sphere is in contemplation. He will *d*
judge the gravity of the interference with the private right which the measures he
propounds may involve. His respect for the principle, and his observation of the
requirement, which I have sought to formulate, should suffice to give effect to
the ideal of proportionality. His judgment thereafter as to the measures required
to save the public interest will be subjected to a judicial scrutiny that may be close
to the conventional *Wednesbury* test if the decision maker is the primary *e*
legislature. So far as he sits lower in the hierarchy of public power, it may be the
court's judgment will be more intrusive. But the first protections of proportionality
are the law's insistence on the principle, and the requirement, which I have
discussed. They are the weights in the balance scales; and they will measure,
broadly at least, where Holmes J's 'certain point is reached'. *f*

[79] Since this case was argued, their Lordships' opinions have been delivered
in *Ex p Daly* [2001] UKHL 26, [2001] 3 All ER 433, [2001] 2 WLR 1622, which
concerned a challenge to the Secretary of State's policy relating to the searching
of prison cells. Counsel have had no opportunity to advance submissions before
us about it; but it does not alter my view of the right result in the case before us, *g*
and I think it appropriate to refer to what was said by Lord Steyn:

'... there is an overlap between the traditional grounds of review and the
approach of proportionality. Most cases would be decided in the same way
whichever approach is adopted. But the intensity of review is somewhat
greater under the proportionality approach. Making due allowance for *h*
important structural differences between various convention rights ... a few
generalisations are perhaps permissible. I would mention three concrete
differences without suggesting that my statement is exhaustive. First, the
doctrine of proportionality may require the reviewing court to assess the
balance which the decision maker has struck, not merely whether it is within *j*
the range of rational or reasonable decisions. Secondly, the proportionality
test may go further than the traditional grounds of review in as much as it
may require attention to be directed to the relative weight accorded to
interests and considerations. Thirdly, even the heightened scrutiny test
developed in ... *R v Ministry of Defence, ex p Smith* [1996] 1 All ER 257 at 263,
[1996] QB 517 at 554 is not necessarily appropriate to the protection of

a human rights. [His Lordship proceeded to refer to the Strasbourg Court's decision in *Ex p Smith*, which criticised the domestic judgments as having effectively excluded a "pressing social need" or proportionality test.] In other words, the intensity of the review, in similar cases, is guaranteed by the twin requirements that the limitation of the right was necessary in a democratic society, in the sense of meeting a pressing social need, and the question
b whether the interference was really proportionate to the legitimate aim being pursued.' (See [2001] UKHL 26 at [27], [2001] 3 All ER 433 at [27], [2001] 2 WLR 1622.)

[80] With deference I believe that what I have said in the foregoing paragraphs as to the nature of proportionality, and its application, is in line with this reasoning.
c It seems to me that the principle which I have suggested reflects the first, and the requirement which I have asserted reflects the second, of Lord Steyn's three propositions; and the third of them provides critical guidance to the intensity of review where the right in question is one guaranteed by the Convention (no doubt subject, as Lord Steyn said, to the structural differences between Convention rights).

[81] Applying this approach to the present case yields a plain answer. The
d state was entitled to conclude that very firm measures were justified to confront the various sickening ills of football violence. The principle and the requirement which must be respected and followed have clearly been so: the progressive nature of the succeeding measures from 1986 onwards, and the safeguards clearly established in the 1989 Act, demonstrate as much. In short the terms of
e s 14B(4)(b) are amply justified in light of Directive 64/221, the *Calfa* jurisprudence, and the general law relating to proportionality.

THE FOURTH PROPOSITION

[82] There is no doubt, and I understand it to be common ground, that where an established Community law right is to be restricted by a member state on
f public interest grounds, appropriate procedural protections must be provided: *Rutili's* case [1975] ECR 1219, to which I have already referred, shows as much. It is no less clear that the Court of Justice has regarded arts 6 and 13 of the Convention as providing particular substance to this general proposition.

[83] In this context Mr Thompson submits first, by reference to art 6 of Directive 64/221 and *Union Nationale des Entraîneurs et Cadres Techniques*
g *Professionnels du Football (UNECTEF) v Heylens* Case 222/86 [1987] ECR 4097, that decisions made under the 1989 Act carry a duty to give reasons to the affected party. Mr Pannick accepts as much. But of course the magistrates' court in this case gave reasons for imposing banning orders under s 14B. As regards decisions taken by the enforcing authority under s 19, Mr Pannick points to the fact that
h before us there are no judicial review proceedings of any such decision: we are concerned (in the case of Mr Thompson's clients) solely with an appeal by way of case stated against the magistrate's orders. He adds that if reasons had been sought, they would have been given; in any event the reasons are obvious—to prevent disorder; and there is nothing to show that either appellant has sought an
j exemption under s 20. In my judgment there is no live issue in this case arising from any obligation to give reasons.

[84] In support of his general argument that there are no adequate procedural protections built into the regime of the 1989 Act, Mr Thompson next submitted that no sufficient standard of proof is insisted on. He was disposed to say that the formula in s 14B(4)(b) imposes (as regards any individual who is in contemplation for a banning order) a requirement as to what must be proved, effectively no

greater than what must be shown to justify a public decision when it is assaulted   *a*
on traditional judicial review grounds; this, he suggested, was inherent in the
language of the subsection. And he submitted that the inadequacy of the statute's
requirements as to proof is graphically illustrated by the fact that the magistrate
might perfectly logically hold that there existed 'reasonable grounds to believe
that making a banning order would help to prevent violence or disorder [etc]',
but yet not himself believe that it would do so.   *b*

[85] This last seems to me to be a wholly artificial point. The 'reasonable
grounds' test assumes that the magistrate does not know whether the result will
be achieved or not. The magistrate may be sceptical, or optimistic; but if he were
actually to conclude that the order *would not* achieve the desired result, that could
in reality only be on the footing that the reasonable grounds test was not made
out on the evidence before the court.   *c*

[86] On the more general issue as to standard of proof, Mr Thompson did not
go so far as to argue that an application under s 14B is made in criminal proceedings
for the purpose of art 6 of the Convention. He accepts that the procedures under
s 14B are 'civil in form'. However, he submitted that 'applications under s 14B are
in substance criminal charges for the purposes of Art. 6 [of the convention]'.   *d*
Accordingly, the rights and safeguards provided for by art 6(2) and (3) should
effectively be applied; or (I think he would say) they should at least be reflected
in the statutory procedures.

[87] That approach seems to me entirely misconceived. An application under
s 14B is, categorically, *not* a criminal charge, and no amount of special pleading
will make it so. Mr Pannick referred to *Raimondo v Italy* (1994) 18 EHRR 237. In   *e*
that case the applicant was placed under special police supervision in the course
of certain criminal proceedings against him. The court said (at 264 (para 43)):

'... special supervision is not comparable to a criminal sanction because it is
designed to prevent the commission of offences. It follows that proceedings
concerning it did not involve "the determination ... of a criminal charge".'   *f*

[88] In any event, it seems to me that Mr Pannick was right to submit that
Mr Thompson's true complaint was not so much a procedural one, but rather to
the effect that in substance the s 14B(4)(b) criterion is of itself offensive. However,
such a complaint in essence replicates Mr Thompson's propositions 2 and 3 by
another name; and these propositions I have already rejected. Mr Thompson was   *g*
at pains to draw a contrast between the requirements of s 14B and the emphasis
of the Court of Appeal in *R (on the application of McCann) v Crown Court at Manchester*
[2001] EWCA Civ 281 at [65]–[67], [2001] 4 All ER 264 at [65]–[67], [2001] 1 WLR
1084 per Lord Phillips MR upon the need for rigorous proof of relevant facts
against the individual in question in the context of the making of anti-social   *h*
behaviour orders. I have referred to this case in dealing with Mr Newman's
argument. The contrast urged by Mr Thompson is misplaced. The legislation
relating to such orders is framed so as distinctly to require proof of matters relating
wholly to the individual in question. There is no analogue to s 14B(4)(b) of the 1989
Act. The suggestion that s 14B should have been drafted so as to constitute an   *j*
analogue (or at least a reflection) to the Crime and Disorder Act 1998 lacks any
foundation if I am right as to Mr Thompson's propositions 2 and 3 (and, indeed,
proposition 1). In fact Mr Pannick accepts (rightly) that the standard of proof
required for s 14B(4)(a) will be practically indistinguishable from the criminal
standard; and that the standard for s 14B(4)(b) will be appropriate to the gravity of
what is asserted.

a

[89] Once these matters are clear, there is in my judgment nothing in Mr Thompson's submissions as to the *procedures* of s 14B. There is nothing to suggest that an affected person will not get a fair trial before the magistrate. There is nothing objectionable in the measures, relating to evidence, provided for by s 14C(4). As regards the particular evidence which was admitted in the cases of Mr Thompson's clients—the profiles—there was no challenge to their admissibility,

b nor to the primary facts asserted in them. In those circumstances I cannot see what complaint can run here.

[90] There were some subsidiary arguments advanced by Mr Thompson which, with respect, I will not set out in what is already a very long judgment. None of them could carry the day alone.

[91] I conclude against Mr Thompson on his proposition 4.

c

THE FIFTH PROPOSITION

[92] I mean no disrespect to Mr Thompson in dealing very shortly with this last argument. Mr Pannick suggests that any issue as to violation of the Convention rights in the context of the case would in truth call up, not art 8, but art 2 of the Fourth Protocol to the Convention, which guarantees the right to leave one's own

d country but allows (art 2(3)) restrictions on the right to be imposed on a series of public interest grounds—the very kind of grounds as justify derogations from the rights given by arts 8–11 of the Convention. The United Kingdom has not ratified art 2 of Protocol 4. Mr Pannick's point is that it cannot sensibly be supposed that the right given by art 2 of Protocol 4 is for all the world already conferred, at least

e for some situations, by art 8; and in truth, art 8 has nothing to do with the case.

[93] I think this argument is correct. But even if it were not, once given my conclusions as to proportionality upon propositions 2 and 3, there is no perceptible basis on which s 14B, while proportionate to its aim as a matter of Community law, may be said to be disproportionate in the context of art 8 of the Convention and therefore not justified within art 8(2). In my judgment this part of Mr Thompson's

f argument is not even a makeweight.

[94] In my judgment these appeals, and Miller's application for judicial review, should all be dismissed. If my Lord agrees, we should hear counsel as to the proper form of our answers to the questions posed by the courts below, and the orders which we ought to make.

g

POOLE J.

[95] I agree.

Appeals and application for judicial review dismissed.

Dilys Tausz   Barrister.

Marcic v Thames Water Utilities Ltd (No 2) *a*

QUEEN'S BENCH DIVISION (TECHNOLOGY AND CONSTRUCTION COURT)

JUDGE RICHARD HAVERY QC

5, 6 JUNE, 10 JULY 2001

b

Human rights – Infringement of human rights – Damages – Whether damages recoverable for future infringement of human rights – Human Rights Act 1998, s 8(4) – European Convention for the Protection of Human Rights and Fundamental Freedoms 1950, art 41.

c

The claimant, M, brought proceedings for nuisance against the defendant statutory sewerage and water undertaker, TWUL, in respect of the latter's failure to carry out works necessary to prevent repeated flooding to his property from overloaded drains. The judge held that TWUL's failure to carry out those works was incompatible with certain of M's rights under the European Convention for the Protection of Human Rights and Fundamental Freedoms 1950 (as set out in Sch 1 to the Human Rights Act 1998); that TWUL had no intention to carry out the works in the future; that, as a public authority for the purposes of the 1998 Act, TWUL's inactivity had become unlawful when that Act came into force on 2 October 2000; and that accordingly M had a cause of action against TWUL for a continuing nuisance from that date. At a subsequent hearing, the judge was *e* required to determine the proper measure of damages. By virtue of s 8(4)[a] of the 1998 Act, the court was required, in determining the amount of an award of damages against a public authority under the Act, to take into account the principles applied by the European Court of Human Rights in relation to an award of compensation under art 41[b] of the convention. Article 41 provided that *f* if the internal law of a contracting party allowed only partial reparation to be made, the European Court of Human Rights would, if necessary, afford just satisfaction to the injured party. TWUL contended, inter alia, that an award of damages for future wrongs would be contrary to the Strasbourg jurisprudence and that the judge should follow the common law in not awarding damages for future wrongs.

g

Held – An award of damages for future wrongs would not be contrary to the Strasbourg jurisprudence, and the court would make such an award in the instant case. The common law would not afford M just satisfaction. He would have to bring onerous proceedings from time to time to enforce his rights and he would *h* be unable to recover any damages for the diminution in the value of the property caused by the prospect of future wrongs. The measure of damage itself had to reflect the difference between M's hypothetical situation in the absence of infringement of his rights and his actual situation given those infringements. Accordingly, damages would be assessed as the difference between (i) the value of M's property at the date on which TWUL would have completed works to put *j* an end to the nuisance if those works had been commenced on 2 October 2000 and (ii) the value of the property on the notional completion date in the absence of those works. If that date was in the past when the damages were awarded, they

---

a　Section 8, so far as material, is set out at [16], below

b　Article 41, so far as material, is set out at [16], below

a should reflect additionally an element of interest. Similarly, if the completion date was in the future when the damages were awarded, an appropriate discount should be made (see [16], [17], below).

Notes

b For relief in respect of the infringement of human rights by a public authority, see 17(2) *Halsbury's Laws* (4th edn reissue) para 1268.

For the Human Rights Act 1998, s 8, see 7 *Halsbury's Statutes* (4th edn) (1999 reissue) 507.

Cases referred to in judgment

c *Baron v Portslade UDC* [1900] 2 QB 588, CA.

Bybrook Barn Garden Centre Ltd v Kent CC [2001] BLR 55, CA.

Glossop v Heston and Isleworth Local Board [1879] 12 Ch D 102, [1874–80] All ER Rep 836, CA.

Hole v Chard Union [1894] 1 Ch 293, CA.

Hooper v Rogers [1974] 3 All ER 417, [1975] Ch 43, [1974] 3 WLR 329, CA.

d *Jaggard v Sawyer* [1995] 2 All ER 189, [1995] 1 WLR 269, CA.

Marcic v Thames Water Utilities Ltd [2001] 3 All ER 698.

Pride of Derby and Derbyshire Angling Association Ltd v British Celanese Ltd [1953] 1 All ER 179, [1953] Ch 149, [1953] 2 WLR 58, CA.

Robinson v Workington Corp [1897] 1 QB 619, CA.

e *S v France* (1990) 65 D & R 250, E Com HR.

Shelfer v City of London Electric Lighting Co, Meux's Brewery Co v City of London Electric Lighting Co [1895] 1 Ch 287, [1891–4] All ER Rep 838, CA.

Smeaton v Ilford Corp [1954] 1 All ER 923, [1954] Ch 450, [1954] 2 WLR 668.

f **Remedies hearing**

Following the decision of Judge Richard Havery QC on 14 May 2001 ([2001] 3 All ER 698) by which he found that the defendant, Thames Water Utilities Ltd, was liable to the claimant, Peter Marcic, from 2 October 2000 in respect of its failure to prevent flooding to Mr Marcic's property at 92 Old Church Lane, Stanmore, Middlesex, the judge ordered the hearing of a further preliminary issue

g on the proper measure of damages. The facts, so far as material, are set out in the judgment, but are more fully set out in the judgment delivered on 14 May 2001.

Peter Harrison (instructed by *South & Co*) for Mr Marcic.

Michael Daiches (instructed by *Simon Byrne*) for the defendant.

h
                                                                    Cur adv vult

10 July 2001. The following judgment was delivered.

JUDGE RICHARD HAVERY QC.

j [1] In the light of my judgment on liability dated 14 May 2001 (*Marcic v Thames Water Utilities Ltd* [2001] 3 All ER 698), I ordered a further preliminary issue to be heard, namely the proper measure of damages. At the hearing of that issue, Mr Daiches at the outset applied to me to reconsider my judgment on liability. It was open to me to change my decision, since no order of the court had been drawn up. Since the judgment on liability involved new law, I acceded to that application. This judgment relates principally to the measure of damages, but I shall start by considering the submissions of Mr Daiches that I should change my judgment on liability.

[2] The starting point for Mr Daiches' submissions was that a failure to act, such as to give rise to liability under s 6(1) of the Human Rights Act 1998, must involve the concept that the defendant could reasonably have acted so as to prevent or put an end to the infringement of the claimant's human rights (see [2001] 3 All ER 698 at [60], [107]). Thus in substance the court had held that the duty on a public authority under the 1998 Act was a duty to do what was reasonably practicable to abate the nuisance which gave rise to the infringement. Mr Daiches submitted that it was not reasonably practicable for the defendant to carry out the necessary works.

[3] Mr Daiches submitted that my judgment on liability was erroneous. He based his argument on para [104] of the judgment, in which I said:

> 'Mr Marcic seeks a mandatory injunction requiring one of the proposed schemes to be carried out. In my judgment, there can be no question of a mandatory injunction. Any scheme would require the purchase of land, and the preferred scheme would require the co-operation of the Environment Agency.'

Mr Daiches submitted that para [104] showed that I had decided that I had no power to grant an injunction. It followed that I had found that it was not reasonably practicable for the defendants to carry out the necessary works. Both those propositions are wrong. My decision to refuse a mandatory injunction was made in the exercise of my discretion. My reasons were expressed briefly since it seemed obvious that in the exercise of my discretion I should refuse a mandatory injunction. And I did consider it reasonably practicable for the works to be carried out (see [2001] 3 All ER 698 at [24], [86]). After all, the works are no different in principle from the kind of works that the defendant is regularly carrying out.

[4] Mr Daiches submitted that even if he were wrong in his submission that I had found that it was not reasonably practicable to carry out the works, nevertheless it was not reasonably practicable to carry out the works. He submitted that I was wrong to 'hold' the contrary. It was, he said, a question of mixed fact and law, since he was tying his submission to an argument that the whole line of cases at common law on nuisance in relation to sewage were explicable on the basis that an injunction would be granted where it was reasonably practicable to carry out the work (see *Pride of Derby and Derbyshire Angling Association Ltd v British Celanese Ltd* [1953] 1 All ER 179, [1953] Ch 149, *Baron v Portslade UDC* [1900] 2 QB 588, *Hole v Chard Union* [1894] 1 Ch 293), but not otherwise (see *Glossop v Heston and Isleworth Local Board* [1879] 12 Ch D 102, [1874–80] All ER Rep 836, *Robinson v Workington Corp* [1897] 1 QB 619, *Smeaton v Ilford Corp* [1954] 1 All ER 923, [1954] Ch 450). The old distinctions between feasance and non-feasance and between discharge of effluent and escape of effluent were not conclusive, but were generally related to reasonable practicability. Doing what was reasonably practicable to abate a nuisance involved the concept that the public authority had an immediate ability to abate the nuisance, rather than an ultimate ability. Another way of putting it was that the public authority must have immediate control, rather than ultimate control, over the events which were necessary to abate the nuisance. Mr Daiches submitted that the dichotomy between immediate control and ultimate control was broadly coincidental with that between ownership of the land on which the works are required and the absence of such ownership, though there could be exceptions not relevant to the instant case. Since the defendant did not own the relevant land, its control was ultimate, not immediate. It seemed remarkable that in none of the many authorities in this area of the law was there any express reference to the dichotomy between immediate

a control and ultimate control. In support of his submission, Mr Daiches relied on the observations of Waller LJ in *Bybrook Barn Garden Centre Ltd v Kent CC* [2001] BLR 55 at 61 (para 24):

b '... it will be a relevant consideration as to whether a defendant should be liable for "continuing" a nuisance created by forces for which that defendant is not responsible, whether it is reasonably practicable for that person to prevent the nuisance continuing.'

Thus the immunity at common law which I had found to exist was in truth based on the fact that it was not reasonably practicable to carry out the works. And since it was not reasonably practicable to carry out the works, there was no 'act' falling

c within s 6(1) of the 1998 Act.

[5] I reject those submissions of Mr Daiches. He seeks to work back from my holding that the defendant has immunity at common law, through a theory which, as a justification of old decisions, is absent from their reasoning and is based on a decision of the Court of Appeal (the *Bybrook Barn* case) in which the sewage cases are expressly distinguished (see [2001] BLR 55 at 65 (para 46)), to a conclusion which in

d my judgment is clearly one of fact and is contrary to my finding.

[6] Notwithstanding those submissions, Mr Daiches said that the defendant would be content to submit to an injunction to do specific works. But it was for the claimant to provide the necessary specification of the works, since it was for the claimant to tell the court what order he wanted. No such specification is before

e the court.

[7] Of my own motion, I shall amend para [104] of my judgment on liability in order to clarify the position. Otherwise, that judgment stands. Paragraph [104] will read:

f 'Mr Marcic seeks a mandatory injunction requiring one of the proposed schemes to be carried out. In the exercise of my discretion, I refuse that injunction on the grounds that: (1) the injunction would have to specify the required works precisely; (2) the specification would be a matter of engineering expertise that is not before the court; and (3) performance of the injunction would require the co-operation of third parties, albeit that the defendant has

g powers of compulsory purchase of land.'ᶜ

[8] Mr Harrison submitted that Mr Marcic was entitled under the provisions of s 50 of the Supreme Court Act 1981 to damages for future infringements of his rights in substitution for an injunction. Mr Harrison was content not to argue that I should

h alter my earlier judgment by ordering a mandatory injunction. Mr Marcic would prefer damages. He had had the problem of flooding for long enough. I dare say that Mr Marcic would like to have an award of damages in order to buy another house and move away from the flooding. However that may be, Mr Marcic's own preference is for an award of damages. Mr Harrison submitted that the damages should include the difference between the value of the property as it would be if and

j when works necessary to prevent the flooding were completed, and its actual value. The damages would thus represent not a diminution in value, but a failure to achieve an increase in value. Mr Daiches rightly made no submission that that was not a proper measure of damages in principle. For convenience, I shall nevertheless call it a diminution in value.

c   Editor's note: this amendment was incorporated in the report published at [2001] 3 All ER 698.

[9] Mr Daiches submitted on several grounds that this was not an appropriate case for damages in lieu of an injunction. First, he submitted that the measure of damages would produce a result that fell foul of the rules in *Shelfer v City of London Electric Lighting Co, Meux's Brewery Co v City of London Electric Lighting Co* [1895] 1 Ch 287, [1891–4] All ER Rep 838. He relied on passages in the judgments in the Court of Appeal in *Jaggard v Sawyer* [1995] 2 All ER 189, [1995] 1 WLR 269. Bingham MR ([1995] 2 All ER 189 at 197, [1995] 1 WLR 269 at 277) said that *Shelfer's* case was chiefly notable for the guidance given by AL Smith LJ on the circumstances in which damages may properly be awarded in lieu of an injunction. That guidance included the following:

> '... a person by committing a wrongful act ... is not thereby entitled to ask the Court to sanction his doing so by purchasing his neighbour's rights, by assessing damages in that behalf, leaving his neighbour with the nuisance, or his lights dimmed, as the case may be. In such cases the well-known rule is not to accede to the application, but to grant the injunction sought, for the plaintiff's legal right has been invaded, and he is *primâ facie* entitled to an injunction. There are, however, cases in which this rule may be relaxed, and in which damages may be awarded in substitution for an injunction ... In my opinion, it may be stated as a good working rule that—(1.) If the injury to the plaintiff's legal rights is small, (2.) And is one which is capable of being estimated in money, (3.) And is one which can be adequately compensated by a small money payment, (4.) And the case is one in which it would be oppressive to the defendant to grant an injunction:—then damages in substitution for an injunction may be given.' (See [1895] 1 Ch 287 at 322–323, [1891–4] All ER Rep 838 at 847–848.)

Mr Daiches submitted that if the damages were to reflect compensation to Mr Marcic for all flooding which was ever likely to occur to the property in perpetuity, the injury to Mr Marcic's legal rights could not be described as 'small'. Nor would it be capable of being estimated in money. Nor would the injury be one which could be adequately compensated 'by a small money payment'.

[10] I reject Mr Daiches' submission that the damages would not be capable of being estimated in money. The 'difference in value' measure contended for by Mr Harrison would reflect the view of the market on the prospects of flooding. A valuation would indeed be hypothetical, but not incapable of being carried out. I accept, however, that the injury would not be small, nor could it be adequately compensated by a small money payment. It does not fall within the rules in *Shelfer's* case. But in my judgment the rules in *Shelfer's* case do not apply here. Those rules apply where it is the defendant who is seeking to avoid being enjoined. That is apparent from what AL Smith LJ himself said. In the passage cited above he referred to the defendant's asking the court to sanction his committing a wrongful act. And later on he said this:

> 'There may also be cases in which, though the four above-mentioned requirements exist, the defendant by his conduct ... has disentitled himself from asking that damages may be assessed in substitution for an injunction.' (See [1895] 1 Ch 287 at 323, [1891–4] All ER Rep 838 at 848.)

And in *Jaggard's* case [1995] 2 All ER 189 at 208, [1995] 1 WLR 269 at 287, Millett LJ said that AL Smith LJ's 'working rule' applied to the exercise of discretion to withhold injunctive relief when the plaintiff claimed an injunction and the defendant asked the court to award damages instead. AL Smith LJ's checklist was only a working rule and did not purport to be an exhaustive statement of the circumstances a in which damages might be awarded instead of an injunction. Here, the defendant is not asking the court to award damages instead of an injunction. It is the claimant that is doing that. Mr Daiches told me that the defendant would prefer an injunction to an award of damages against it. In my judgment, the wording of s 50 of the 1981 Act does not trammel the power of the court to award damages in lieu of an injunction.

b [11] Mr Daiches next submitted that I could not award damages in lieu of an injunction, since an injunction did not lie. My decision to refuse an injunction on the basis that the court would not supervise the works was a holding that I had no jurisdiction to grant an injunction. I reject that submission. My decision was based on an exercise of discretion. I am satisfied that I have jurisdiction to award damages in lieu of an injunction. As Millett LJ said in *Jaggard*'s case [1995] 2 All ER 189 at 205,

c [1995] 1 WLR 269 at 285: 'The question is whether, at the date of the writ, the court *could* have granted an injunction, not whether it *would* have done ...' Mr Daiches submitted that in the above passage 'could' meant 'could in the exercise of the normal discretion', and that 'it would have done' meant 'having decided it could, it would do so on *Shelfer* principles'. I reject that submission. It defies analysis, but I

d shall do my best. The question to which Millett LJ was referring was the question whether, as at the date of the writ, the court had jurisdiction to grant an injunction. If so, it had to decide, by reference to the circumstances existing at the date of the hearing, whether to grant an injunction or award damages instead. The interpretation for which Mr Daiches contended implies that Millett LJ was saying something very odd. It is this: that in deciding, by reference to circumstances

e existing at the date of the hearing, whether or not to grant an injunction, the court does not decide whether it has jurisdiction to do so by reference to whether at the date of the writ it would have exercised that jurisdiction. That statement is no doubt true, but it is devoid of useful content and is manifestly not the true interpretation. Moreover, Mr Daiches' interpretation of the word 'could' is problematical. At most

f it can mean '*might* in the exercise of the normal discretion', otherwise the reference to discretion is irrelevant. Yet in the next sentence of his judgment, Millett LJ approved a remark of Russell LJ in *Hooper v Rogers* [1974] 3 All ER 417 at 419, [1975] Ch 43 at 48 that the question was "whether ... the judge could have (however unwisely ...) made a mandatory order". Mr Daiches' submission implies that in considering whether he has jurisdiction to award damages in lieu of an injunction,

g the question the judge has to decide is whether another judge, or perhaps himself, might, however unwisely, have exercised his discretion in a particular way at the date of the writ. If 'might' should read 'would', the implication is even more absurd.

[12] Mr Daiches submitted that it would be wholly oppressive and unjust to the defendant not to grant an injunction, since in the event of an award of damages to

h the claimant, the defendant would be under a continuing liability to pay damages to every successive occupier of the claimant's property until the crack of doom. Such damages would be in respect of the same loss and damage as that suffered by the claimant. I reject that submission. So far as successors in title are concerned, the matter would be res judicata (see *Jaggard*'s case [1995] 2 All ER 189 at 206, [1995]

j 1 WLR 269 at 286 per Millett LJ). And as regards all occupiers, if a person chooses to go into occupation of a property known to be subject to flooding, I do not think that failure to alleviate the flooding could be regarded as an infringement of his human rights. Moreover, as Mr Harrison submitted, s 8(3) of the 1998 Act covers the situation. That subsection provides:

'No award of damages is to be made unless, taking account of all the circumstances of the case, including—(a) any other relief or remedy granted, or

order made, in relation to the act in question (by that or any other court), and
(b) the consequences of any decision (of that or any other court) in respect of
that act, the court is satisfied that the award is necessary to afford just
satisfaction to the person in whose favour it is made.'

[13] Mr Daiches submitted that damages for future wrongs ought not to be
awarded. His first ground was as follows. Even if the defendant had embarked
upon the processes necessary to lead to the construction of the necessary drainage
works immediately upon the coming into force of the 1998 Act on 2 October 2000,
those works would not yet be completed. Mr Marcic's property would still be liable
to flooding. No actionable damage could accrue until those works could
reasonably have been completed. It was premature to award damages now.
Mr Marcic's human rights had been vindicated by the court, and he was entitled to
his costs. That entitlement was just satisfaction at this stage. If he suffered damage
in the future, he should bring further proceedings then. It was not certain that
infringement of Mr Marcic's human rights would continue. The defendant might
change its system of priorities so as to avoid such infringement. Or further
proceedings might give the defendant an opportunity to adduce further evidence in
support of its existing system. The present claim involved new law, and it was only
fair to give the defendant an opportunity to defend its system in the light of the
existing judgment.

[14] There is force in that last point, but it is outweighed in my judgment by the
heavy burden that would be imposed on Mr Marcic by his having to bring
proceedings all over again. As to the argument generally, I have made a finding not
only that the defendant intends not to carry out the works necessary to remedy the
nuisance, but also that it intends to continue to operate its existing system of
priorities (see [2001] 3 All ER 698 at [106]). An argument of counsel that the
defendant might change its mind does not affect that finding. I have held that the
claimant's rights have been infringed, and that the defendant intends to continue
the state of affairs that leads to that holding. If that intention is fulfilled, Mr Marcic's
human rights will continue to be infringed. Given that I have exercised my
discretion against granting an injunction, justice requires that Mr Marcic should
have an award of damages now. Such an award is necessary to afford him just
satisfaction.

[15] Mr Daiches' second argument in support of the proposition that damages
for future wrongs ought not to be awarded was that such an award would be
contrary to the Strasbourg jurisprudence. So far as he was aware, there was no case
in the Strasbourg jurisprudence where an applicant had been awarded damages in
respect of future wrongs. In *S v France* (1990) 65 D & R 250 the complaint had been
declared inadmissible on the basis inter alia that the applicant had been reasonably
compensated by the domestic courts in respect of past wrongs. Mr Harrison
submitted that in *S v France* compensation in respect of future infringement was
recognised by the European Commission of Human Rights. The Conseil d'Etat
had awarded the claimant compensation for diminution in the value of her
property arising out of nuisance by noise. That must have been compensation for
future noise, as I accept. The Commission, in reaching its conclusion that the
interference complained of did not go beyond what was necessary in a democratic
society, bore that compensation in mind.

[16] Section 8(4) of the 1998 Act provides:

'In determining ... the amount of an award, the court must take into account
the principles applied by the European Court of Human rights in relation to

_a the award of compensation under Article 41 of the [European Convention for the Protection of Human Rights and Fundamental Freedoms (Rome, 4 November 1950; TS 71 (1953); Cmd 8969].'

Article 41 provides that 'if the internal law of the High Contracting Party concerned allows only partial reparation to be made, the Court shall, if necessary, afford just satisfaction to the injured party'. I conclude that an award of damages for future

_b wrongs is not contrary to the Strasbourg jurisprudence.

[17] Mr Daiches further submitted that I should follow the common law in not awarding damages for future wrongs. In my judgment, I should not do so. The common law would not afford the claimant just satisfaction. He would have to bring onerous proceedings from time to time to enforce his rights. Nor would he

_c be able to recover any diminution in the value of his property caused by the prospect of future wrongs.

[18] My conclusions as to the measure of damages are these: (1) If the defendant had on 2 October 2000 put in hand the processes necessary to bring the nuisance to an end, and diligently pursued them, it would have avoided infringing s 6(1) of the 1998 Act. It would have completed those processes on some date that I shall call

_d the completion date. On the completion date, Mr Marcic's property would have had some value X. That value would doubtless reflect any unrepaired damage caused by flooding occurring before the completion date. Mr Marcic would in those circumstances have no cause of action against the defendant. (2) In fact, on the completion date Mr Marcic's property will have some value Y. That value will probably be less than X, since, unlike X, it will reflect the prospect of future flooding.

_e (3) The measure of damage must reflect the difference between the hypothetical situation of Mr Marcic in the absence of infringement of his rights, and his actual situation given those infringements. (4) Thus, as of the completion date, Mr Marcic will have suffered damage by reason of diminution in the value of his property in the sum of X minus Y. (5) If the completion date is in the past when the damages

_f are awarded, the damages should reflect additionally an element of interest. By the same token, if the completion date is in the future when the damages are awarded, an appropriate discount should be made. (6) The only other head of damage claimed is damage for inconvenience, distress and vexation arising out of the flooding. That again can be claimed only in respect of the future from the

_g completion date, and will not include any element arising from damage to the property caused by events occurring before then. But in my judgment it will be reflected in the value of the house, and accordingly no additional sum will be awarded in respect of it.

[19] If necessary I shall decide an appropriate completion date after hearing evidence on the point.

_h [20] In arriving at the above conclusions, I have borne in mind the voluminous report of the Law Commission (Law Com no 266) and the Scottish Law Commission (Scot Law Com no 180) entitled *Damages under the Human Rights Act 1998*, put before me by Mr Daiches.

Order accordingly.

Martyn Gurr   Barrister.

McGrath v Chief Constable of the Royal Ulster Constabulary and another

[2001] UKHL 39

a

HOUSE OF LORDS

LORD STEYN, LORD BROWNE-WILKINSON, LORD COOKE OF THORNDON, LORD CLYDE
AND LORD HUTTON

2 APRIL, 12 JULY 2001

b

Arrest – Warrant – Execution – Execution in Northern Ireland of warrant issued in
another part of United Kingdom 'for the arrest of a person charged with an offence' –
Claimant being impersonated by acquaintance – Acquaintance being prosecuted and
convicted in Scotland under claimant's name – Acquaintance absconding before
sentence and Scottish court issuing warrant for claimaint's arrest – Northern Ireland
police arresting claimant under warrant – Whether person arrested under warrant
having to be a person charged with an offence – Criminal Law Act 1977, s 38(3).

c

d

DM was arrested for stealing a car by officers of the Dumfries and Galloway
Constabulary. On his arrest, DM gave the police, as his own personal details, the
name, Belfast address and date of birth of an acquaintance, TM. DM persisted in
the deception throughout the subsequent proceedings for theft in the sheriff
court at Stranraer. The charge ran in the name of TM and a schedule of his
previous convictions was prepared in connection with the charge. DM eventually
pleaded guilty, and signed his plea using TM's name. He was granted bail, but
subsequently failed to attend court for sentencing. The sheriff therefore granted
a warrant for the arrest of TM. That warrant was a proper and valid one under
the law of Scotland, and authorised police officers to search for and arrest the
persons named in it. Subsequently, a constable of the Royal Ulster Constabulary
(RUC), who was aware that a warrant had been issued for TM's arrest, saw TM
in Belfast and asked for his personal details. Those given precisely fitted the
details which had been passed to the constable relating to the warrant. He
arrested TM who was transferred into the custody of two officers of the Dumfries
and Galloway Constabulary to be taken to Stranraer. On arrival in Stranraer, it
was discovered that TM was not the person who had been detained for the theft
of the car, and he was released. TM subsequently brought an action in Northern
Ireland against the chief constables of the RUC and the Dumfries and Galloway
Constabulary, claiming that he had been arrested wrongfully, unlawfully and
without reasonable cause. The chief constables contended that the arrest was
lawful, relying on s 38(3)[a] of the Criminal Law Act 1977 which provided that a
warrant issued in England, Wales or Scotland 'for the arrest of a person charged
with an offence' could be executed in Northern Ireland by any member of the
RUC. The judge dismissed the claim, and TM appealed. The Court of Appeal in
Northern Ireland allowed the appeal, holding that TM was not a 'person charged
with an offence' for the purposes of s 38(3) because he was not the person who
had been before the court and whom the sheriff had intended to have arrested.
The chief constables appealed to the House of Lords.

e

f

g

h

j

---

a   Section 38(3) is set out at [8], below

a **Held** – On its true construction, s 38(3) of the 1977 Act did not require the person arrested pursuant to the warrant to have been a person charged with an offence. The phrase 'for the arrest of a person charged with an offence' was not detailing the substance of the warrant so as to require the person arrested to have been charged with an offence. Rather, it simply described the kind of warrant with which s 38(3) was concerned, namely a warrant to arrest as distinct from a

b warrant to search or any other kind of warrant. Even if that construction were incorrect and the critical phrase was to be understood as requiring the warrant, in its substance, to be for the arrest of the person who had been charged with an offence, the situation in the instant case was that TM had been, albeit mistakenly, charged with an offence. The indictment had been issued against TM by name. He could thus qualify as a person 'charged with an offence' for the purposes of

c s 38(3). Contrary to the Court of Appeal's view, there was no requirement that the warrant could only be executed against TM if he had in fact been the person who had actually appeared before the sheriff and whom the sheriff had intended to be arrested. That construction would involve questioning what appeared clearly, even although mistakenly, on the face of the warrant. Where there was

d no reason to question what appeared on the face of the warrant, the constable enforcing it had no obligation to do so. On the contrary, he had the duty to enforce it. If in executing it he complied with the terms of the instruction embodied in the warrant, he should not be regarded as having acted unlawfully. The alternative view involved penalising the officers engaged in the enforcement of the warrant where they had acted reasonably and in perfect good faith. It would impose an

e unfair burden upon the police in acting responsibly and honestly in carrying out what was a ministerial function. If that left an innocent third party without a remedy, that was not because the law had deprived him of any right to a remedy, but because the circumstances of the person who had caused the mistake to be made by his own deliberate deception might be such that the remedy was not

f worth pursuing. Accordingly, the appeal would be allowed (see [1]–[3], [21]–[26], [30], below).

Hoye v Bush [1835–42] All ER Rep 286 applied.

Notes

For the execution of a warrant of arrest, see 11(1) *Halsbury's Laws* (4th edn

g reissue) para 700.

The Criminal Law Act 1977, s 38, has been repealed by the Criminal Justice and Public Order Act 1994, s 168(3), Sch 11, and replaced with effect from 3 February 1995 by s 136 of the 1994 Act. For s 136, see 12 *Halsbury's Statutes* (4th edn) (1997 reissue) 1451.

h
Cases referred to in opinions

Bell v HM Advocate 1988 JC 69, HC of Just.
Chuck v Cremer (1846) 1 Coop *temp* Cott 338, 47 ER 884, LC.
Cole v Hindson (1795) 6 TR 234, 101 ER 528.

j *Hadkinson v Hadkinson* [1952] 2 All ER 567, [1952] P 285, CA.
Henderson v Preston (1888) 21 QBD 362, CA.
Horsfield v Brown [1932] 1 KB 355, [1931] All ER Rep 469.
Hoye v Bush (1840) 1 Man & G 775, [1835–42] All ER Rep 286, 133 ER 545.
IRC v Rossminster Ltd [1980] 1 All ER 80, [1980] AC 952, [1980] 2 WLR 1, HL.
Metropolitan Police Comr v Hammond [1964] 2 All ER 772, [1965] AC 810, [1964] 3 WLR 1, HL.

Mullady v DPP (3 July 1997, unreported), DC.

O'Hara v Chief Constable of the Royal Ulster Constabulary [1997] 1 All ER 129, [1997]
AC 286, [1997] 2 WLR 1, HL.

Olotu v Home Office [1997] 1 All ER 385, [1997] 1 WLR 328, CA.

R v Governor of Brockhill Prison, ex p Evans (No 2) [2000] 4 All ER 15, [2001] 2 AC 19,
[2000] 3 WLR 843, HL.

R v Manchester Stipendiary Magistrate, ex p Granada Television Ltd [2000] 1 All ER 135,
[2001] 1 AC 300, [2000] 2 WLR 1, HL.

R v Oldham JJ, ex p Cawley [1996] 1 All ER 464, [1997] QB 1, [1996] 2 WLR 681, DC.

Shadgett v Clipson (1807) 8 East 328, 103 ER 368.

Appeal

The defendants, the Chief Constable of the Royal Ulster Constabulary and the
Chief Constable of the Dumfries and Galloway Constabulary, appealed with
leave of the Appeal Committee of the House of Lords given on 29 June 2000 from
the order of the Court of Appeal in Northern Ireland (Carswell LCJ, Nicholson
and McCollom LJJ) on 28 October 1999 ([2000] NI 56) allowing an appeal by
the plaintiff, Terence Joseph McGrath, from the decision of MacDermott LJ on
6 February 1998 dismissing his action for wrongful arrest against the defendants.
The facts are set out in the opinion of Lord Clyde.

Nicolas Hanna QC and *Gerald Simpson QC* (both of the Northern Ireland Bar)
(instructed by the *Treasury Solicitor*) for the defendants.

James McNulty QC and *Nigel McCombe* (both of the Northern Ireland Bar)
(instructed by *James Doran & Co,* Belfast) for the plaintiff.

Their Lordships took time for consideration.

12 July 2001. The following opinions were delivered.

LORD STEYN.

[1] My Lords, I have had the advantage of reading in draft the speeches of my
noble and learned friends, Lord Clyde and Lord Hutton. For the reasons they
have given I would allow the appeal.

LORD BROWNE-WILKINSON.

[2] My Lords, I have had the advantage of reading in draft the speech prepared
by my noble and learned friend, Lord Clyde. For the reasons he gives I too would
allow the appeal.

LORD COOKE OF THORNDON.

[3] My Lords, I have had the advantage of reading in draft the speeches of my
noble and learned friends, Lord Clyde and Lord Hutton. For the reasons they
have given I would allow the appeal.

LORD CLYDE.

[4] My Lords, various provisions exist for the enforcement in one part of the
United Kingdom of warrants granted in another part and the statutory provisions
enabling such enforcement have sometimes given rise to problems. One recent
example is *R v Manchester Stipendiary Magistrate, ex p Granada Television Ltd* [2000]
1 All ER 135, [2001] 1 AC 300. Another example is *O'Hara v Chief Constable of the
Royal Ulster Constabulary* [1997] 1 All ER 129, [1997] AC 286. The present case is,

a however, somewhat exceptional on its facts. The plaintiff, the respondent in the present appeal, was arrested in Northern Ireland by virtue of a warrant granted by a sheriff in Scotland. He has raised proceedings in Northern Ireland against the appellant defendants claiming damages for wrongful arrest. The defendants are the chief constables respectively of the Royal Ulster Constabulary and of the Dumfries and Galloway Constabulary. The case came before MacDermott LJ

b and after hearing the evidence he gave judgment for the defendants. The plaintiff then appealed to the Court of Appeal in Northern Ireland ([2000] NI 56) who allowed the appeal and awarded a sum of damages against both the defendants. They have now appealed to this House. It is necessary at the outset to narrate the facts.

[5] On 24 January 1991 Dominic Mackin and William John Joseph Barker stole

c a car in Stranraer. The following day, after Barker had been seen driving the car in a reckless manner, they were both arrested by officers of the Dumfries and Galloway Constabulary. Mackin told the police that he was Terence Joseph McGrath of 29 Distillery Street, Belfast and that his date of birth was 15 July 1970. He had given those details to the harbour police at Stranraer when he came

d ashore from the Larne ferry two days earlier. That name, address and date of birth related not to Mackin but to the plaintiff. Mackin knew the plaintiff because they had been at school together. Mackin persisted in this deception throughout the subsequent proceedings in the Sheriff Court at Stranraer. He appeared, along with Barker, at the Sheriff Court in Stranraer on 25 January 1991 and was then remanded in custody to Dumfries prison. He was charged, along with Barker,

e with the theft. So far as Mackin was concerned the charge ran in the name of Terence Joseph McGrath and a schedule of previous convictions of Terence Joseph McGrath was prepared in connection with the charge against him. On 11 February 1991 he pleaded guilty to the charge of theft. Barker also pleaded guilty to the theft and to a number of offences under the Road Traffic Act 1988.

f In accordance with practice Mackin was asked to sign his plea of guilt and he did so using the name Terence McGrath. The case was then adjourned for reports and sentence. On 13 February 1991 Mackin, under the name of McGrath, and Barker were granted bail.

[6] On 25 February 1991 they both failed to appear at court for sentencing. The sheriff accordingly on that day, on the application of the procurator fiscal,

g granted a warrant for the arrest of both men. The sheriff's direction was issued orally and he signed a manuscript record of it made by the sheriff clerk. That record read:

> 'The court on the motion of the prosecutor granted warrant to apprehend
h and commit the accused Terence Joseph McGrath and William John Joseph
> Barker to any lawful prison until liberated in due course of law.'

An 'extract of warrant' was then prepared by the sheriff clerk and signed by the sheriff. That was sent to the procurator fiscal so that the police might enforce it. It was confirmed by a Scottish advocate who gave evidence before the court in

j Northern Ireland that the warrant which was issued was a proper and valid warrant under the law of Scotland and that its effect was to authorise police officers to search for and arrest the persons named therein.

[7] On 25 September 1991 a constable of the Royal Ulster Constabulary, who was aware that a warrant had been issued for the arrest of Terence Joseph McGrath, date of birth 1970, of 29 Distillery Street, Belfast, saw the plaintiff standing on a footpath in Belfast. He asked the plaintiff for his personal details. These precisely

fitted the details which had been passed to him relating to the warrant. He accordingly checked with his base by radio and then arrested the plaintiff. Later on that day the plaintiff was transferred into the custody of two officers of the Dumfries and Galloway Constabulary and was taken to Stranraer. It was then discovered that he was not the person who had been detained in January 1991. He was released and given some money for his fare to travel back to Belfast.

[8] The plaintiff claims that he was arrested wrongfully, unlawfully and without reasonable cause. The defendants contend that the arrest was lawful. The authority on which the defendants rely for making the arrest is to be found in s 38(3) of the Criminal Law Act 1977. Section 38 of that Act was repealed by s 168(3) of and Sch 11 to the Criminal Justice and Public Order Act 1994 and replaced by s 136 of that Act. But it was s 38(3) which was in force at the period with which we are concerned and it ran as follows:

'A warrant issued in England, Wales or Scotland for the arrest of a person charged with an offence may be executed in Northern Ireland by any member of the Royal Ulster Constabulary or the Royal Ulster Constabulary Reserve; and subsections (4) and (5) of section 159 of the Magistrates' Courts Act (Northern Ireland) 1964 (execution without possession of the warrant and execution on Sunday) shall apply to the execution in Northern Ireland of any such warrant.'

[9] The intention of the sheriff in granting the warrant to arrest Terence McGrath was no doubt to have the man who had appeared before him in court to be arrested and brought back for sentence. That that was his intention was recognised both by the trial judge and the Court of Appeal. The Court of Appeal, however, considered the terms of s 38(3) and took the view that the subsection did not avail the defendants because the plaintiff was not 'a person charged with an offence' for the purposes of the subsection. The person charged with an offence was Mackin. The warrant 'was for the arrest of Mackin, the person who had been before the sheriff and whom the latter intended to have brought back to his court' ([2000] NI 56 at 60). The court (at 61) did not think it possible 'to construe the phrase "person charged" as meaning the person whose name is set out in the warrant if he was not the person who had been before the court and whom the sheriff intended to have arrested'. The court continued:

'We recognise that this penalises a police officer who has acted in good faith and who has been misled by the deception perpetrated by the accused, but we think that it would be less than just if a third person who has been arrested and detained, although innocent of any wrongdoing, were left without a remedy.'

[10] The question in the case comes eventually to be one of the construction of s 38(3). Before I turn to that question, however, it is convenient to mention certain other lines of argument which were raised during the course of the hearing and to make some more general observations about the granting and execution of warrants.

[11] Some attempt at the hearing before us was made to resurrect an argument that a defence was open to the appellants under s 50 of the Constabulary (Ireland) Act 1836. According to MacDermott LJ counsel had conceded that they were not entitled to rely on that section, and counsel did not rely on it before the Court of Appeal. On the view which I am taking of the case it is not necessary to consider this argument. However, it is not immediately evident that the section extends

a not only to warrants granted by a magistrate within the jurisdiction of the Northern Irish courts but also to a warrant granted by a sheriff in Scotland. We were not addressed in detail on the point and I remain doubtful whether such a construction would be possible.

[12] Section 50 of the 1836 Act provides a protection to the constable in respect of an irregularity in the issuing of a warrant or for any want of jurisdiction
b in the magistrate who has issued it. A protection comparable with that provided in s 50 of the 1836 Act was afforded to a constable in England under s 6 of the Constables Protection Act 1750. As is pointed out in *Clerk and Lindsell on Torts* (18th edn, 2000) p 912 (para 17-128), at one time a constable was exposed to a double danger, namely that the warrant might have been issued without jurisdiction and so was a nullity; or that it was issued with jurisdiction but the
c constable did something not covered by its authority. The 1750 Act provided protection against the former danger. As Macnaghten J observed in *Horsfield v Brown* [1932] 1 KB 355 at 369, [1931] All ER Rep 469 at 476:

> 'If the constable acts in obedience to the warrant, then, though the warrant be an unlawful warrant, he is protected by the statute of 1750, but if the
d warrant be a lawful warrant, and he executes it in an unlawful way, then no action is maintainable against the magistrate, but an action is maintainable against the constable.'

In the present case, however, the argument is that the warrant was lawful and was executed lawfully. The defendants' claim is that they were acting in the lawful
e exercise of a statutory provision, s 38(3) of the 1977 Act, in the enforcement of a warrant which had been regularly issued by a sheriff acting within his jurisdiction. If that was the case, the defendants would have a sound defence against a claim of wrongful arrest (see *Archbold's Criminal Pleading, Evidence and Practice* (2001 edn) p 1745 (paras 19-339, 19-340)).

f [13] Another line of argument was presented under reference to art 5 of the European Convention for the Protection of Human Rights and Fundamental Freedoms (Rome, 4 November 1950; TS 71 (1953); Cmd 8969) (as set out in Sch 1 to the Human Rights Act 1998). But it was not made clear how this could constitute a distinct argument in its own right. It was not suggested that the provisions of the 1998 Act should apply. It was not suggested that the article should be invoked
g as a consideration in the construction of s 38 of the 1977 Act. Regard must certainly be paid to the basic right to liberty and security of a person, but beyond that general consideration it is not easy to discern what further weight reference to art 5 adds to the argument. The question still remains whether the execution of the warrant was lawful.

h [14] One of the cases to which counsel referred us was *R v Governor of Brockhill Prison, ex p Evans (No 2)* [2000] 4 All ER 15, [2001] 2 AC 19. But that case was very different from the present. It was held there that the applicant was entitled to damages for false imprisonment. She had been sentenced to various concurrent terms of imprisonment. But she was entitled to a reduction in the actual period
j to be served. The court did not specify the date of release. That was for the governor of the prison to calculate. The governor of the prison had calculated her release date on a basis which was subsequently held to be unsound. On the correct calculation she should have been released 59 days earlier than the date of her actual release. Thus she had been unlawfully detained for that period. It was held that the fact that the governor had acted in accordance with the law as it was at the time when he made his calculation was not sufficient justification for

a false imprisonment, which is a tort of strict liability. That case concerned a
mistake as to the law, committed by the governor in calculating the period for *a*
release under a sentence of the court which had left that calculation as matter
for him. Once the calculation had been corrected it followed that there was a
period of unlawful imprisonment. The present case concerns a mistake of fact in
the identity of the person named in the order of the court. The order was not
unlawful. The only issue is whether its execution upon the person named in it *b*
constituted an unlawful arrest. I do not consider that *Ex p Evans* is of direct
assistance to the resolution of the present case.

[15] If reference is to be made to the situation of a gaoler acting under a
warrant a closer example would be that of *Henderson v Preston* (1888) 21 QBD 362,
which represents a line of authority which was distinguished in *Ex p Evans*. In
Henderson v Preston an action for false imprisonment failed where the warrant *c*
ordered the prison governor to receive the plaintiff and keep him for the space of
seven days. The sentence ran from 24 August but the plaintiff was only lodged in
prison on 25 August. The governor detained him until and including 31 August
and was held to be protected by the warrant. Lindley LJ stated (at 366):

> 'All that one has to do is to read the warrant. What is a governor of a gaol *d*
> who receives such a warrant to do except to obey it? It is perfectly valid and
> correct, and is authorized by the Act of Parliament, and issued by persons
> who have jurisdiction to issue it. It appears to me that the governor by
> obeying that warrant has simply done his duty, and the warrant protects him
> and is an answer to the action.' *e*

Another example can be found in *Olotu v Home Office* [1997] 1 All ER 385, [1997]
1 WLR 328.

[16] Of more direct relevance is one of the other cases to which we were
referred, *Hoye v Bush* (1840) 1 Man & G 775, [1835–42] All ER Rep 286. It was held
in that case that an arrest was wrongful where the constable had applied for a *f*
warrant to arrest Richard Hoye, the warrant had been mistakenly issued in the
name of John Hoye and the constable had arrested Richard Hoye. Thus a police
officer cannot under a warrant arrest someone who is not named in it even
although he knows the person intended to be covered by it. Tindal CJ observed:
'It would be dangerous if a person whose office is wholly ministerial, were *g*
allowed to sit in judgment, and say who is the unnamed person intended by the
warrant which he is required to execute.' (See (1840) 1 Man & G 775 at 786,
[1835–42] All ER Rep 286 at 288.) One principle which can be found in *Hoye v Bush*
is that the person executing a warrant should follow and be entitled to rely on the
face of the warrant. He may not act outside the terms of the warrant. That was
what happened in *Hoye v Bush*. But he should not be held to have acted unlawfully *h*
if he carries out the instruction which appears from the face of the warrant. It is
not for him to question that instruction if it is clear.

[17] Warrants issued by a court of law require to be treated with the same
respect as must be accorded to any order of the court. The general rule was
stated by Romer LJ in *Hadkinson v Hadkinson* [1952] 2 All ER 567 at 569, [1952] *j*
P 285 at 288:

> 'It is the plain and unqualified obligation of every person against, or in
> respect of, whom an order is made by a court of competent jurisdiction to
> obey it unless and until that order is discharged. The uncompromising
> nature of this obligation is shown by the fact that it extends even to cases

a where the person affected by an order believes it to be irregular or even void. LORD COTTENHAM, L.C., said in *Chuck* v. *Cremer* ((1840) 1 Coop *temp* Cott 338 at 342–343, 47 ER 884 at 885): "A party, who knows of an order, whether null or valid, regular or irregular, cannot be permitted to disobey it … It would be most dangerous to hold that the suitors, or their solicitors, could themselves judge whether an order was null or valid—whether it was

b regular or irregular. That they should come to the court and not take upon themselves to determine such a question. That the course of a party knowing of an order, which was null or irregular, and who might be affected by it, was plain. He should apply to the court that it might be discharged. As long as it existed it must not be disobeyed."'

c That passage was followed in *R v Oldham JJ, ex p Cawley* [1996] 1 All ER 464, [1997] QB 1, where it was held that a prison governor did not require to question the order contained in a warrant of committal.

[18] If warrants which are apparently valid are to be taken at their face value and justify the action taken in conformity with them it is necessary that there be

d strict controls governing the granting and the execution of them. In so far as warrants may authorise what would otherwise be an unlawful invasion of private rights, there are various safeguards which accompany the granting and execution of them. Whether or not they are granted under statutory provision the procedures required for the granting of them must be carefully followed. They must state whatever the particular statutory provision under which they are issued requires

e them to state (e g *IRC v Rossminster Ltd* [1980] 1 All ER 80, [1980] AC 952). The warrants must be sufficiently clear and precise in their terms so that all those interested in their execution may know precisely what are the limits of the power which has been granted. As Coltman J stated in *Hoye v Bush*: 'It is of the essence of a warrant that it should be so framed, that the officer should know whom he

f is to take, and that the party upon whom it is executed should know whether he is bound to submit to the arrest.' (See (1840) 1 Man & G 775 at 788, [1835–42] All ER Rep 286 at 289.) To take an example from Scots law, a search warrant must clearly identify the premises which the constable has power to search (see *Bell v HM Advocate* 1988 JC 69). Compliance with the proper procedure is particularly important where the liberty of the subject is concerned (see *Metropolitan*

g *Police Comr v Hammond* [1964] 2 All ER 772 at 783, [1965] AC 810 at 837). Where legislation requires particular information to be given to the arrested person, as in s 28(3) of the Police and Criminal Evidence Act 1984, the failure to give the information will make the arrest unlawful (e g *Mullady v DPP* (3 July 1997, unreported)).

h [19] So far as the present case is concerned it has to be noted that the warrant was lawfully and validly issued under the law of Scotland. The evidence to that effect was not disputed. The sheriff was acting within his jurisdiction in directing that the order be issued. One starts then with the basis that there was a valid warrant granted by the sheriff in Scotland. It may be that that did not in fact achieve what the sheriff had presumably intended, that the warrant should enable

j the arrest of the man who had appeared before him in court. But, albeit mistakenly, it was on the face of it a valid warrant for the arrest of the plaintiff. It was not a warrant for the arrest of Mackin. If a constable had attempted to arrest Mackin on the strength of the warrant the arrest would have been as unlawful as was the arrest in *Hoye v Bush*. That it might be possible to strike it down on the ground of the mistake did not render it a nullity. The granting of

the warrant was a lawful judicial act and the validity of the warrant would remain
until it was recalled or cancelled. While the granting of a warrant is a judicial act,
an endorsement of the warrant is merely a ministerial act (see *Metropolitan Police
Comr v Hammond* [1964] 2 All ER 772 at 783, [1965] AC 810 at 837) and, as was
noticed in *Hoye v Bush*, the execution of it is correspondingly also a ministerial act.

[20] The plaintiff makes no other complaint about the lawfulness of the arrest
than that the constable was not acting within the scope of s 38(3). We are not
concerned with any lack of formalities in the way the arrest was made. As regards
possession of the warrant, s 159(4) of the Magistrates' Courts Act (Northern
Ireland) 1964 is expressly made applicable to s 38(3). That section provides:

> 'Any warrant lawfully issued for the arrest of any person in connection
> with proceedings before a magistrates' court may be executed by any
> constable at any time notwithstanding that the warrant is not in his
> possession at that time ...'

But it is unnecessary to explore any such considerations regarding the manner or
procedure of the arrest. The only question is whether its execution was in
conformity with s 38(3) of the 1977 Act.

[21] I turn next to the question of the construction of s 38(3). There can be no
doubt that the warrant was 'a warrant issued in Scotland'. Indeed, as I have
already said, the warrant was validly issued, even although it was directed against
a person who was in fact not the person who had earlier appeared before the
sheriff and whom the sheriff intended should be returned for sentence. The problem
then arises regarding the following phrase 'for the arrest of a person charged with
an offence'. On the view which the Court of Appeal took, these words require
that the person named in the warrant is a person who has actually been charged
with an offence. But that is not the only possible construction. It is also possible
that they are simply describing the kind of warrant with which the subsection is
concerned, namely a warrant to arrest, as distinct from a warrant to search, or
any other kind of warrant. On this approach the words are not detailing the
substance of the warrant so as to require that the person arrested has in fact been
charged with an offence.

[22] In my view counsel for the defendants was correct in submitting that the
latter construction is to be preferred. As he pointed out, if the plaintiff had been
in Scotland and the warrant had been executed in Scotland the arrest in conformity
with the warrant would have been lawful. That position should still be the same
when by virtue of the legislation the power is given to execute it in Northern
Ireland. Section 38(3) simply gives the power to execute the warrant within
another jurisdiction. If the execution is lawful in the one country, then it should
be lawful in the other. The purpose of the section is to enable warrants granted
in one of the stated jurisdictions to be readily enforceable in another within the
United Kingdom. Endorsation of the warrant is expressly declared in sub-s (4)
not to be required. The phrase 'for the arrest of a person charged with an offence'
appears in all of the first three subsections, covering the three jurisdictions in
which the warrants in question may be executed. In each case it seems to me that
the words have no greater significance than to denote that the warrants are, to
use the language of the sidenote, 'warrants of arrest'. The construction adopted
by the Court of Appeal would have more weight if the subsection had read 'may
be executed against that person'. But those last three words do not appear in the
legislation and there is no obvious reason for construing the subsection as if they
were there.

a

[23] Even if the construction which I prefer was incorrect and the critical phrase should be understood as requiring that the warrant should in its substance be for the arrest of a person who has been charged with an offence, the situation here was that the plaintiff had been, albeit mistakenly, charged with an offence. It was against the plaintiff by name that the indictment had been issued. The plaintiff can thus qualify as a person 'charged with an offence' for the purposes of

b the subsection. While I prefer to base my decision on the construction of the critical phrase, this alternative approach also seems to me to be acceptable. But I do not consider that the Court of Appeal was correct in requiring that the warrant could only be executed against the plaintiff if he had in fact been the person who actually appeared before the sheriff and whom the sheriff intended to be arrested. That construction involves a questioning of what appeared clearly, even although

c mistakenly, on the face of the warrant. Where there is no reason to question what appears on the face of the warrant, the constable enforcing it has no obligation to do so: indeed on the contrary he has the duty to enforce it. And if in executing it he complies with the terms of the instruction embodied in the warrant he should not be regarded as having acted unlawfully.

d [24] The alternative view involves, as the Court of Appeal recognised, penalising the officers engaged in the enforcement of the warrant where they had acted reasonably and in perfect good faith. It would impose an unfair burden upon the police in acting responsibly and honestly in carrying out what is a ministerial function. The Court of Appeal considered it would be unjust that the third party who had been arrested without any evident wrongdoing on his part

e should be without a remedy. But if he is without a remedy that is not because the law deprives him of any right to a remedy but because the circumstances of the person who caused the mistake to be made by his own deliberate deception may be such that the remedy is not worth pursuing.

[25] For the foregoing reasons I would allow the appeal.

f

LORD HUTTON.

[26] My Lords, I have had the advantage of reading in draft the speech of my noble and learned friend Lord Clyde, and I am in general agreement with his reasons for concluding that the appeal should be allowed. However, because we are differing from the decision of the Court of Appeal I wish to state briefly the

g considerations which have led me to conclude that the decision of MacDermott LJ sitting at first instance should be restored.

[27] The central issue in the case relates to the construction of the words 'a person charged with an offence' in s 38(3) of the Criminal Law Act 1977. The argument advanced on behalf of the appellant defendants, the Chief Constable of

h the Royal Ulster Constabulary and the Chief Constable of the Dumfries and Galloway Constabulary, is that those words mean the person whose name is set out in the warrant. The argument advanced on behalf of the respondent plaintiff, Mr McGrath, is that the words mean the person who has actually been charged with an offence, and that person was Dominic Mackin, not the plaintiff.

j [28] The Court of Appeal ([2000] NI 56 at 60–61) accepted the plaintiff's argument and stated:

'It is true to say that the object of the legislation concerning warrants is to confine the police to following strictly the terms of the warrants which they are executing and to give them protection if they do so. But we do not think it possible to construe the phase "person charged" as meaning the person whose

name is set out in the warrant if he was not the person who had been before
the court and whom the sheriff intended to have arrested.'

[29] There is considerable force in this reasoning, but I think that guidance can
be obtained from the principle that a statutory provision is to be construed in its
context, which includes the common law context. In *Hoye v Bush* (1840) 1 Man & G
775, [1835–42] All ER Rep 286 a constable applied for a warrant for the arrest of
Richard Hoye, but the justice mistakenly issued a warrant for the arrest of John Hoye,
which was the name of Richard Hoye's father. The constable arrested Richard Hoye,
who sued for false imprisonment, and he was held to be entitled to recover.
Tindal CJ stated:

> 'The question in this case is, whether the defendant was justified in arresting
> the plaintiff under a warrant, describing him as *John Hoye*, his real name being
> *Richard Hoye*. On the part of the defendant it is contended that the justification
> was sufficient, inasmuch as an officer is protected, where the party arrested
> is the person really intended to be taken. Such a qualification is not allowed
> by law. In civil process you could not justify taking a person by the name
> mentioned in the warrant, his real name being different. The case of *Cole v
> Hindson* ((1795) 6 TR 234, 101 ER 528) is precisely upon that point. That case
> is stronger than the present, because there the plea averred that *Aquila Cole*
> and *Richard Cole* were the same person. So in *Shadgett v Clipson* ((1807) 8 East
> 328, 103 ER 368), it was held that a sheriff's officer could not justify an
> imprisonment of *A. B.* under a *latitat* against *C. B.*, though it was averred that
> *A. B.* and *C. B.* are one and the same person, there being no averment that *A. B.*
> was known by the name of *C. B.* Then what distinction can be made between
> civil and criminal process? If the warrant of the sheriff will not justify the
> officer, why should a magistrate's warrant? In either case the object of
> the warrant is to identify the party who is to be arrested.' (See (1840) 1 Man & G
> 775 at 784–785, [1835–42] All ER Rep 286 at 287–288.)

And: 'It would be dangerous if a person whose office is wholly ministerial, were
allowed to sit in judgment, and say who is the unnamed person intended by the
warrant which he is required to execute.' (See (1840) 1 Man & G 775 at 786,
[1835–42] All ER Rep 286 at 288.) Coltman J stated: 'It is of the essence of a
warrant that it should be so framed, that the officer should know whom he is to
take, and that the party upon whom it is executed should know whether he is
bound to submit to the arrest.' (See (1840) 1 Man & G 775 at 788, [1835–42]
All ER Rep 286 at 289.) See also the judgment of Lindley LJ in *Henderson v Preston*
(1888) 21 QBD 362 at 366 cited by my noble and learned friend, Lord Clyde.

[30] Therefore it is clear that the common law placed emphasis on the
importance of a warrant of arrest or commitment being precise in its terms, and
on the need for a police officer or prison governor, given the duty of executing a
warrant, to comply with its terms and not to exercise his own discretion as to
whether or not he should enforce it. Construing s 38(3) of the 1977 Act against
that background I consider that it is right to construe it as the defendants contend
and accordingly I would allow the appeal.

Appeal allowed.

Dilys Tausz   Barrister.

Murrell v Healy and another
[2001] EWCA Civ 486

COURT OF APPEAL, CIVIL DIVISION

WALLER AND DYSON LJJ

31 JANUARY, 5 APRIL 2001

Damages – Personal injury – Amount of damages – Subsequent further injury to claimant – Assessment of damages payable by second tortfeasor to claimant who had previously been injured in earlier unrelated accident – Approach to be adopted.

The claimant, M, was a manual labourer. In May 1995 he was injured in a car accident (the first accident), and subsequently claimed damages for personal injury. In November 1995, after M had begun to pursue that claim, he was injured in a second unrelated car accident (the second accident). In February 1996, during settlement discussions in relation to the first accident, M's solicitors informed the defendant's insurers that it was feared that M might never work again. He was eventually paid a sum in settlement of the claim relating to the first accident. In 1998 M brought proceedings in relation to the second accident. Those proceedings included a claim for loss of earnings, made on the basis that M was unable to work again as a result of the second accident and quantified by reference to the wages he would have expected to earn as a manual worker. On an assessment of damages in July 2000, the judge concluded that the first accident had removed M's ability to do heavy manual work, but would not have precluded him from doing light work; that the second accident had prevented M from doing any work; that a condition, which was not caused by either accident, would have prevented him from doing any work from the date of trial; that the settlement of the claim in respect of the first accident had included two years' loss of earnings; and that he was therefore entitled to loss of earnings only from 1 March 1998 until the date of the trial. In reaching that conclusion, the judge's starting point was that it would not be just for M to receive double compensation by obtaining damages from one tortfeasor on the basis that he would be unable to work during a specific period, and to obtain the same damages against the second tortfeasor on the basis that he would in fact have worked. M appealed, inter alia, against the judge's assessment of his pre-trial loss of earnings, contending that he was entitled to be compensated for the fact that the second accident had prevented him from doing light work and that the sum he had received in compensation for the first accident was irrelevant.

Held – When assessing damages against a second tortfeasor, the court had to ask what damage had been suffered as a result of that tort by the already injured victim. If, in the instant case, the answer was that M would in fact have been able to work following the first accident, but was prevented from working by the second accident, that would have to be the basis on which damages were to be assessed. Equity did not enter into that calculation. In answering the critical question, the court should start by asking in a much more focused way than the judge had done, not only whether M would have been fit for light work but whether he would in fact have found such work after the first accident if the second had not taken place. Indeed, the question to be posed included whether, even if M would have found light work for some period, he would always have been in light work. Although he had tried some light work after the first accident, he was basically a manual worker. Having regard to the way he had put his claim as against the first tortfeasor, it hardly lay in his mouth to say that he would have found light work even as at 1 January 1996. It certainly seemed against all probability that he would always have been in light work following the first accident, even if the second accident had not happened. It was not unfair to conclude against him, and the judge should have so concluded, that there would have been a period or periods when he would not, as a result of the first accident, have in fact worked. Nor was it unfair to conclude that the periods for which he would not have worked would have been of at least two years duration in the period from 1 January 1996 until the trial of the action. In that way, the decision reached by the judge could, and should, be upheld by a more orthodox route. Accordingly, the appeal against the assessment of pre-trial loss of earnings would be dismissed (see [22]–[24], [31], [32], below).

Notes
For damages in respect of successive torts in personal injury claims, see 12(1) *Halsbury's Laws* (4th edn reissue) para 855.

Cases referred to in judgments
Baker v Willoughby [1969] 3 All ER 1528, [1970] AC 467, [1970] 2 WLR 50, HL.
Jobling v Associated Dairies Ltd [1981] 2 All ER 752, [1982] AC 794, [1981] 3 WLR 155, HL.
Muller v Linsley & Mortimer [1996] 1 PNLR 74, CA.
Pickett v British Rail Engineering Ltd [1979] 1 All ER 774, [1980] AC 136, [1978] 3 WLR 955, HL.
Rush & Tompkins Ltd v Greater London Council [1988] 3 All ER 737, [1989] AC 1280, [1988] 3 WLR 939, HL.

Appeal and cross-appeal
The claimant, Gordon Murrell, appealed with permission of Judge Coates from the assessment of damages for loss of earnings made by her at Brighton County Court on 31 July 2000 in Mr Murrell's action for personal injury against the first defendant, Ivan Derek Healy, an uninsured driver whose liability to Mr Murrell was met by the second defendant and respondent to the appeal, the Motor Insurers' Bureau. The respondent cross-appealed against the judge's assessment of general damages. The facts are set out in the judgment of Waller LJ.

Charles Taylor (instructed by *Richard Thorn & Co*, Brighton) for Mr Murrell.
Ian Ashford-Thom (instructed by *Barlow Lyde & Gilbert*) for the respondent.

Cur adv vult

5 April 2001. The following judgments were delivered.

WALLER LJ.
[1] This is an appeal from Judge Coates who assessed damages in the following sums in relation to an injury which Mr Murrell suffered in a road accident on 29 November 1995. The judge awarded £25,000 general damages; £1,000 for psychiatric treatment; and special damages of £25,000 loss of earnings,

a and other items for care, etc at £4,114. The relevant background to the issues that arise on this appeal is as follows.

[2] During 1995, the appellant, Mr Murrell, was involved in two car accidents. The first was on 22 May and the second was on 29 November 1995. In relation to the first accident he was already pursuing a claim, and indeed had obtained medical reports, before the second accident occurred. In relation to the first accident
b a settlement was reached under which: (1) he was paid £58,500; (2) Compensation Recovery Unit payments were made; and (3) Mr Murrell's costs of those proceedings were paid.

[3] It would seem that although those defending the first claim became aware of the second accident before finally concluding the settlement, the aim of Mr Murrell and his advisors, once the second accident had occurred, was to settle
c the first claim as quickly as possible. No further medical examination took place prior to the settlement, so that the defence insurers on the first accident did not appreciate the full extent of any injury from the second accident before settling. Indeed, on the evidence of one file note recording what was said by the solicitor acting for Mr Murrell during the settlement negotiations, the solicitor was playing
d down the consequences of the second accident and playing up the likely effects of the first. When Mr Murrell's advisors came to plead the claim on the second accident, they reversed the position, saying as little as possible about the first accident and enhancing the effects of the second.

[4] I have to say that I for my part have some disquiet about the way the
e negotiations were conducted between the solicitor acting for Mr Murrell and the insurers in settling the first accident, and some disquiet about the way in which the schedule of special damages was originally drafted in relation to the second accident by, as I understand it, the same solicitor. One letter from Richard Thorn & Co to the insurers of the defendant in the first accident case in discussing settlement of that claim dated 29 February 1996 says: 'We fear that our client's
f condition is such that he may never be able to work again. If you are prepared to concede this point we see no reason why settlement should not be discussed as soon as possible.' The claim with three medical reports and a schedule of special damages was issued and served in October 1998, and, although the particulars of claim referred to pre-existing injury and the reports dealt with both accidents, the
g schedule of special damages stated 'at the time of the accident [I emphasise the second accident] the plaintiff was unemployed but he expected to return to work within approximately two months'. There is thus a significant inconsistency between the apparent presentation of the first and second accident claims. Claims for loss of earnings up to the date of the pleading, and for future losses of earnings, are then made on the basis that he was unable to work again as a result
h of that accident, quantified by reference to wages he would have expected to earn as a manual labourer.

[5] On any view Mr Murrell's claim in relation to his injuries in the second accident should never have been quantified, other than on the basis that some damage to his ability to work resulted from the first accident. The fact that it was
j not was in my view regrettable.

[6] It is fair however to say that ultimately the assessment of damages was conducted on the basis that he had suffered an injury in the first accident, which did affect his ability to work, but that he had suffered a great deal more serious injury in the second accident. But the complications which have arisen in this case might well have been avoided if once the second accident had taken place

the full details of both accidents and the injuries suffered had been fully disclosed
to both defendants. Any settlement could then have been negotiated on a basis
that fairly divided up the liability for Mr Murrell's injuries between the two
tortfeasors who had injured Mr Murrell.

[7] Not only did that not happen, but at the hearing of the assessment of the
damages with which we are concerned, the advisors for Mr Murrell sought to
persuade the judge that the documents including the letter above quoted
obtained from the insurers' file in relation to the claim made in relation to the first
accident, should not be admitted in evidence. The judge ruled they were admissible
on the basis that she had to determine the relevant level of compensation in
relation to the second accident, and that she needed to have the best evidence
available showing for what Mr Murrell had already been compensated. This ruling
of the judge is one matter raised on the appeal.

[8] The main point on the appeal relates to the assessment of damages for
that second accident. Not surprisingly one of the major points which arises
relates to the effect on that assessment of the injuries already suffered in, and
compensation received for, the first accident.

[9] Further complications in making a proper assessment relate to the fact
that the most serious physical injury from each accident was to Mr Murrell's
back, but before either accident occurred he had symptomatic back problems
likely to reduce the period of his working life, at least for the heavy manual work
he had performed, up until the accidents.

[10] A further complication is produced by the fact that it was common
ground between the experts, and established by a video covertly taken, that
Mr Murrell undoubtedly exaggerated what he was alleging were the consequences
of the second accident. That exaggeration has complicated matters in two ways.
It made the assessment of what injury had in fact been caused by each accident
more difficult, but it is also now relied on in Mr Murrell's favour as being a reason
why the judge should not have accepted certain of Mr Murrell's answers at their
face value. Mr Murrell's evidence was to the effect that he had suffered injury to
his hips and knees as a result of the second accident, and that by the date of trial
they prevented him carrying out any kind of work. The experts were agreed that
neither accident caused any injury to his knees or hips. The judge concluded thus
in the light of Mr Murrell's answers that since he would not have worked from
the date of trial because of the condition of his knees or hips, he had no
entitlement to future loss of earnings at all. That deprived him of what was a very
substantial part of his claim to damages.

[11] Mr Taylor, on his behalf, says that this evidence from Mr Murrell relating
to the effect of his knees and hips on his working life was clearly Mr Murrell
exaggerating, and that the judge should have found that but for the second
accident Mr Murrell would have continued to work in light employment for
many years after the date of the trial. He submits that finding was supported by
the evidence of Mr Wynn-Davis, the medical expert called on Mr Murrell's behalf,
which Mr Taylor told us was to the effect that Mr Murrell was physically fit to do
light work even after the second accident, and that it was his psychiatric injuries
which ultimately prevented him working after the second accident.

[12] It should be said that the second accident was a much more serious
accident than the first. Mr Murrell was hit head-on by a driver on the wrong side
of the road seeking to escape from the police. The medical evidence accepted by
the judge showed that in addition to inflicting on him a lumbar flexion strain,

a thereby causing further damage to an already damaged back, it caused mild to moderate post-traumatic stress disorder.

[13] The issues that arise on the appeal I can thus summarise as follows. (i) The assessment of Mr Murrell's loss of earnings up to the date of trial; Mr Taylor, for Mr Murrell, submitted they were too low on the basis that the judge (a) should not have admitted in evidence the details of the settlement of
b the first accident; and (b) should not then have deducted from the damages being awarded for loss of earnings, the figure assessed as already recovered for loss of earnings in the settlement relating to the first accident. Mr Ashford-Thom, for the defendant, submitted that the loss of earnings figure assessed by the judge was too high, because she should have concluded that Mr Murrell had agreed to settle any claim that he had for loss of earnings in settling the claim on the first accident.
c It is under this heading that the admissibility of the documents obtained in relation to the first accident arises. He also takes a point on mitigation. (ii) The refusal to award any damages for loss of earnings from the trial date onwards. Mr Taylor argued that the judge placed too much weight on the answers given by Mr Murrell about his ability to work as a result of pain in his hips and knees, while
d Mr Ashford-Thom submitted there was no basis for reversing the judge on this finding of fact. (iii) General damages, which are the subject of a respondent's notice; it is submitted by Mr Ashford-Thom that they are too high, and Mr Taylor submitted that the award should not be interfered with.

e *Loss of earnings to the date of trial*

[14] So far as loss of earnings is concerned, the judge's findings can be summarised in this way. The judge awarded Mr Murrell two years four months loss of earnings for the period 1 March 1998 until 31 July 2000 (the date of trial). She did not find expressly that after the first accident Mr Murrell would have been fit for light work, *nor that he would have found light work, despite his previous working life*
f *being that of a manual worker.* It can be argued that by implication she must have so found, but the reality is that she did not need to address the point because of the deduction she in any event made. In particular she did not focus on the point whether Mr Murrell could in fact have found light work. The two years four months period was calculated on the following basis: (1) that the first accident
g removed Mr Murrell's ability to do heavy manual work, but would not have precluded him doing light work; (2) the second accident with its combination of further physical injury to Mr Murrell's back and the mild to moderate post traumatic stress disorder prevented Mr Murrell doing any work; (3) Mr Murrell's hips and knees would have prevented Mr Murrell doing any work as from the date
h of trial and that condition was not due to either accident; but (4) since he had been compensated for two years of that working period (1 March 1996 to 1 March 1998) by the settlement in respect of the first accident, two years should be deducted from the damages awarded for the second accident; (5) in making that assessment the judge allowed into evidence the documents obtained from the insurers of the tortfeasor in the first accident case and analysed the settlement figures being
j proposed by the insurers on their internal file notes so as to conclude that two years loss of earnings was paid in that settlement.

[15] Both sides criticise the judge. For Mr Murrell, Mr Taylor submitted that it was wrong to admit into evidence the documents relating to the settlement of the first claim. He submitted they were part of a record of without prejudice negotiations and inadmissible; alternatively he submitted they were simply irrelevant

to any issue in the second accident case. He submitted that on the evidence
following the first accident Mr Murrell was fit to do light work, and that accordingly
Mr Murrell was entitled to be compensated for the fact that the second accident
prevented him from doing that work. The submission was simple, that what
Mr Murrell received in compensation for the first accident was irrelevant.

Admissibility of documents

[16] Mr Ashford-Thom's submission was that the documents showed how the
settlement was reached in relation to the first accident and were clearly
admissible in order to provide the judge with a full picture as to what injuries had
been caused by the first accident and for what he had already been compensated.
He submitted that if Mr Murrell had been compensated for being unable to work
during the period up until the trial, it would be wrong that he should receive
further compensation for the same damage. He submitted that the documents
were relevant to that point.

[17] I have no doubt that the documents produced from the insurers' file were
admissible. It seems to me that the circumstances of this case are a long way from
Rush & Tompkins Ltd v Greater London Council [1988] 3 All ER 737, [1989] AC 1280.
The evidence was relevant to an inquiry as to what injury the plaintiff had
suffered in the first accident. *Muller v Linsley & Mortimer* [1996] 1 PNLR 74 is
the more relevant authority, and the reasoning of Hoffmann LJ would lead to the
conclusion that this file was admissible. He said as follows (at 80):

> '... the public policy rationale [for the without prejudice privilege] is, in my
> judgment, directed solely to admissions. In a case such as this, in which the
> defendants were not parties to the negotiations, there can be no other basis
> for the privilege. If this is a correct analysis of the rule, then it seems to me
> that the without prejudice correspondence in this case falls outside its scope.
> The issue raised by paragraph 17 of the statement of claim is whether the
> conduct of the Mullers in settling the claim was a reasonable mitigation of
> damage. That conduct consisted in the prosecution and settlement of the
> earlier action. The without prejudice correspondence forms part of that
> conduct and its relevance lies in the light it may throw on whether the
> Mullers acted reasonably in concluding the ultimate settlement and not in its
> admissibility to establish the truth of any express or implied admissions it may
> contain. On the contrary, any use which the defendants may wish to make
> of such admissions is likely to take the form of asserting that they were not
> true and that it was therefore unreasonable to make them.'

Assessment of loss of earnings to trial

[18] This case has disquieting features, because it certainly appears that
Mr Murrell was not suggesting to the insurers after the first accident that he could
or would return to light work even if heavy manual work was impossible; the
thrust of his case was that the injury precluded heavy manual work and that was
the only work for which Mr Murrell was suitable (see Mr Wynn-Davies' report
dated October 1995, and the solicitors' letter already quoted). The importance of
putting the case that way at that stage was that if a concession had been made that
he could perform light work and would find light work, his earnings would
apparently be close to those he could have made as a manual worker. His case
against the respondent to this appeal, so far as the effects of the first accident were
concerned, was always quite inconsistent with the above case.

[19] I would emphasise thus this is not simply a case where a person has been
injured by one tortfeasor to an extent which would have precluded him from
working and then injured by another tortfeasor which injury would also have
precluded him from working quite independently of the first injury. In such a
situation the decisions of *Baker v Willoughby* [1969] 3 All ER 1528, [1970] AC 467
and *Jobling v Associated Dairies Ltd* [1981] 2 All ER 752, [1982] AC 794 would be
relevant. Those decisions demonstrate the difficulty of making an assessment as
against each tortfeasor in such cases. In *Baker v Willoughby* the question was how
the injury at the hands of a second tortfeasor affected the calculation of damage
as against the first, to which the answer in *Baker v Willoughby*, putting it shortly,
was that it did not. In *Jobling's* case the question was how the discovery that a
plaintiff was suffering from myellopathy at a date after he had been seriously
injured at work affected the calculation of damage as against the employer, to
which the answer was that it did with serious criticisms being made of the
reasoning in *Baker v Willoughby*. But neither in fact considered the position of
the assessment of damages as against the second tortfeasor, and it would seem to
be accepted even in *Baker v Willoughby* that the second tortfeasor is only responsible
for the additional damage that the second tortfeasor has caused (see [1969] 3 All ER
1528 at 1533, [1970] AC 467 at 493, per Lord Reid with which Lord Guest,
Viscount Dilhorne and Lord Donovan agreed, and the speech of Lord Pearson at
[1969] 3 All ER 1528 at 1535, [1970] AC 467 at 496.)

[20] I am sympathetic with the judge's starting point which is that it hardly
seems just that Mr Murrell should receive double compensation by obtaining
damages from one tortfeasor on the basis he would be unable to work during a
specific period, and against the second tortfeasor the same damages on the basis
that he would in fact have worked. That would have been the effect of
Mr Taylor's submission.

[21] On the other hand it is hardly attractive that because Mr Murrell made a
claim against the first tortfeasor that he could not work but was compensated on
the basis that he would ultimately find work, the second tortfeasor should not be
liable at all. This seemed to be the effect of Mr Ashford-Thom's submission.

[22] What then is the solution? The question for the court assessing the
damages against the second tortfeasor must be: what damage was suffered as
the result of that tort to an already injured victim? If the answer to that was that
Mr Murrell would in fact have been able to work following the first accident, but
was prevented from working by the second accident, that would have to be the
basis on which the damages should be assessed. Equity would not seem to me to
enter into that calculation. But in answering the critical question, it would seem
to me that the court should start by asking in a much more focused way than the
judge did, not only whether Mr Murrell would have been fit for light work but
would in fact have found light work after the first accident if the second accident
had not taken place. Indeed the question to be posed included whether, even if
he would have found light work for some period, he would always have been in
light work. He had tried some light work after the first accident, but he was
basically a manual worker. It hardly lies in his mouth, having regard to the way
in which he put his claim as against the first tortfeasor, to say that he would have
found light work even as at 1 January 1996. But it certainly seems against all
probability that he would always have been in light work following the first
accident, even if the second accident had not happened.

[23] In my view it is not unfair to conclude against him, and in my view the judge should have concluded against him, that there would have been a period a or periods when he would not, as a result of the first accident, have in fact worked. It further does not seem to me unfair to conclude against Mr Murrell that the periods for which he would not have worked would have been of at least two years duration during the period 1 January 1996 until the trial of the present action. In that way, it seems to me that the decision actually reached by the judge b can, and should, in fact be upheld by a more orthodox route.

[24] Thus I would dismiss the appeal on this aspect of the case.

Future earnings—knees and hips point

[25] I should say straight away that my initial reaction to this aspect of the case c was that it is unattractive in the extreme for an appellant to complain in the Court of Appeal that the judge should not have accepted the evidence he was giving and that his damages should be increased as a result. It seems to me that if a claimant is exaggerating, and in effect bringing a false claim, he or she is not entitled to have the court bend over backwards in his or her favour. That would simply be an encouragement to bring false claims on the basis that if the d exaggeration does not work the court will still help out.

[26] But Mr Taylor, in a very persuasive argument, sought to dismiss those initial reactions. He submitted that it was common ground that Mr Murrell was exaggerating. He pointed to the finding of the judge that the exaggeration 'may, on the balance of probabilities, be partly due to his depression'. He also relied on e the evidence of Mr Wynn-Davies that as at the date of trial Mr Murrell was in the view of that doctor fit to do a number of pieces of light work, which contradicts Mr Murrell's own evidence that because of his hips and knees he would not be able to do any work at all as at the date of trial.

[27] I have considered Mr Taylor's submission with care, but his difficulty is f this. First, any disability being caused by the psychiatric injury did not *compel* Mr Murrell to act in any particular way. It is clear from the video evidence that Mr Murrell acted differently when he did not know he was being watched. His exaggeration was not thus compulsive, and something he could not help. Second, the judge realised the importance of the answer that Mr Murrell was giving and gave him a chance to think about it carefully as spelt out in her g judgment. Third, it really cannot be right to disturb a finding of fact made by a judge on the basis of the claimant's own evidence, and admission.

General damages

[28] Mr Ashford-Thom did not begin to persuade me that the award of h general damages should be disturbed. Mr Taylor reminded us of the well known passages in *Pickett v British Rail Engineering Ltd* [1979] 1 All ER 774, [1980] AC 136 cited in paras 19-003 and 19-004 of *Kemp and Kemp on the Quantum of Damages*, vol 2. He also referred to a number of authorities relating to the award of damages for physical injury where there was also psychiatric damage. Here the post traumatic j stress disorder was plainly due to the second accident and an important element in the assessment of damages. In my view even if it might have been better to try and calculate the damages in the way I have previously identified, on this aspect the conclusion would not seem to me to be any different.

[29] I would thus uphold the judge's assessment of the general damages.

Mitigation

a

[**30**] The judge did not expressly deal with the question of mitigation, but by implication must have found that Mr Murrell was not able to work at all for the period up until the trial by virtue of his physical and psychiatric injuries. In truth the question of mitigation does not in those circumstances arise.

b *Conclusion*

[**31**] I would dismiss the appeal in those circumstances.

DYSON LJ.

[**32**] I agree.

Appeal and cross-appeal dismissed.

Alex Horne   Barrister.

R (on the application of Thompson) v Chief Constable of the Northumbria Constabulary

[2001] EWCA Civ 321

COURT OF APPEAL, CIVIL DIVISION

LORD WOOLF CJ, MAY AND JONATHAN PARKER LJJ

20 FEBRUARY, 8 MARCH 2001

Solicitor – Access to – Right of person in custody – Access by probationary solicitor's representative (PSR) – Applicant being dismissed by police for alleged misconduct but lodging appeal – Applicant obtaining employment as PSR – Deputy chief constable barring applicant as PSR from entering any police station in his force's area – Whether imposition of blanket ban on a PSR permissible – Police and Criminal Evidence Act 1984 – Code of Practice for the Detention, Treatment and Questioning of Persons by Police Officers, paras 6.12, 6.13.

In August 1999 T, an officer in the Northumbrian Constabulary, was dismissed from the force following allegations that he had made sexually discriminatory comments. He denied the allegations and had an appeal to the Home Office pending. Following his dismissal, T obtained employment with a firm of solicitors as a probationary solicitor's representative (PSR), and was included on the Legal Aid Board's register of PSRs. In September 1999 T, in his capacity as a PSR, attended with his supervising solicitor the police station where he had been based for the last eight years of his service in order to represent a client in custody. Under para 6.12[a] of the Code of Practice for the Detention, Treatment and Questioning of Persons by Police Officers (Code C), issued under the Police and Criminal Evidence Act 1984, a PSR had to be admitted to a police station for that purpose unless an officer of the rank of inspector or above considered that such a visit would hinder the investigation of crime. Paragraph 6.13[b] provided that, in exercising that discretion, the officer should take into account, inter alia, whether the PSR was of suitable character to provide legal advice. T was refused access to interview the client and was required to leave the police station. Shortly afterwards, the deputy chief constable, acting on behalf of the chief constable, decided that T should not be admitted to any police station in Northumbria to act as a PSR. Among the reasons given for that decision were T's outstanding appeal which, if successful, could result in his being reinstated as a police officer, thereby rendering it inappropriate for him to act for suspects; the fact that he had indicated his personal feelings towards the police, which created a real risk of an investigation being prejudiced as a result; and the lack of trust between investigating officers and T in his capacity as legal advisor. It was also stated that, in view of his outstanding appeal, T's personal interest conflicted with the independence required to give advice to a client in custody. T challenged that decision in judicial review proceedings, but his application was dismissed by the judge who held that the deputy chief constable had been justified in concluding

---

a Paragraph 6.12 is set out at [9], below
b Paragraph 6.13 is set out at [14], below

a that the investigation of crime would be hindered by giving T access to police stations. T appealed.

Held – It was inappropriate to impose a blanket ban on a particular PSR having access to persons in police custody. The whole focus of Code C was on a particular investigation of a crime rather than the hindering of the investigation
b of crime generally. The officer involved in a specific case would know whether there was, in fact, any risk of interference. Whilst it was important that the advice given to a client should be independent, the responsibility of providing independent advice was that of the solicitor, the responsibility of the police being to ensure access to such advice. The quality of the legal advice was not the concern of the police. It was for the person in custody to decide from which solicitor he wished
c to obtain advice and it was for the solicitor, subject to the requirements of the 1984 Act, to decide whether he would give the advice personally and, if not, who should do so on his behalf. Although it might make obvious good sense that someone who was seeking to be reinstated as a police officer could not properly be regarded as independent of the police, it was the responsibility of T's employer
d rather than that of the police to form a judgment as to whether he was sufficiently independent. Moreover, although it might be uncomfortable both for T and for his former fellow officers if he returned as a solicitor's representative to the police station where he had served, unless interference with the investigation of a crime was likely, that did not entitle the police to object to his attendance as long as he was otherwise properly qualified and behaved appropriately when he did attend.
e Whilst a chief constable could give advice as to the character of a representative, in the light of which the appropriate officer could reach a decision as to whether his attendance was likely to interfere with a particular investigation, he was not entitled to make a blanket direction such as that made in the instant case. Accordingly, the appeal would be allowed (see [17], [19], [22]–[27], below).
f   *R v Chief Constable of Avon and Somerset Constabulary, ex p Robinson* [1989] 2 All ER 15 approved.

Notes
For the right to legal advice, see 11(1) *Halsbury's Laws* (4th edn reissue) para 727.
    For the Police and Criminal Evidence Act 1984, see 12 *Halsbury's Statutes*
g (4th edn) (1997 reissue) 801.

Case referred to in judgments
R v Chief Constable of Avon and Somerset Constabulary, ex p Robinson [1989] 2 All ER 15, [1989] 1 WLR 793, DC.
h

Cases also cited or referred to in skeleton arguments
Murray v UK (1996) 22 EHRR 29, ECt HR.
Schiesser v Switzerland (1979) 2 EHRR 417, ECt HR.

j ### Appeal
By notice dated 1 August 2000, Alan Thompson appealed with permission of Potter LJ from the decision of Gibbs J on 20 July 2000 dismissing his application for judicial review of the decision of the Deputy Chief Constable of the Northumbria Constabulary, acting on behalf of the respondent chief constable, on 23 September 1999 barring Mr Thompson from admission to any police station

within the force's area for the purpose of carrying out duties as a probationary solicitor's representative. The facts are set out in the judgment of Lord Woolf CJ. *a*

Gavin Millar QC and *Ben Cooper* (instructed by *Hindle Campbell*, North Shields) for Mr Thompson.
John Milford QC and *Michael Ditchfield* (instructed by *Denise Aubrey*, Newcastle-upon-Tyne) for the chief constable.   *b*

Cur adv vult

8 March 2001. The following judgments were delivered.

LORD WOOLF CJ.   *c*

[1] This is an appeal from the decision of Gibbs J given on 20 July 2000. Gibbs J dismissed the application of Mr Thompson for judicial review of a decision dated 23 September 1999 taken by the Deputy Chief Constable of the Northumbria Constabulary on behalf of the chief constable. The decision was to ban Mr Thompson, who is appealing against his dismissal from the force, from *d* attending as a probationary solicitor's representative (PSR) at any police station within the area of the force. Permission to appeal was granted by Potter LJ.

[2] Although similar facts to those giving rise to this appeal are unlikely to occur often, the appeal does raise issues of general significance. The issues are: first the extent to which the police are entitled to object to a particular PSR giving advice to a person detained in a police station on the grounds that he is not a suitable person *e* to act as an advisor. Second, whether the chief constable can make a blanket as opposed to a specific order excluding a PSR from attending police stations within the area for which he is responsible.

Facts   *f*

[3] For the purpose of this judgment, the facts can be stated very shortly. Mr Thompson is a former officer of the Northumbria Constabulary. He served as a constable for approximately 18 years and for the last eight years of his service he was based at Pilgrim Street police station, Newcastle. On 26 August 1999 he was dismissed from the force following allegations that he had made sexually discriminatory comments. Mr Thompson has consistently denied the allegations *g* and is pursuing an appeal to the Home Office against the finding and punishment. Mr Thompson's wife, a former police officer, has made serious allegations of impropriety in connection with the conduct of the disciplinary case against her husband. These allegations have been investigated and this has resulted in a report being submitted to the Crown Prosecution Service. Pending the outcome of the *h* investigation, Mr Thompson's appeal has not been heard. Following his dismissal Mr Thompson obtained employment with a firm of solicitors as a PSR. From 15 September 1999 he was included on the Legal Aid Board's Register of PSRs.

[4] On 20 September 1999 Mr Thompson, as a PSR, attended Pilgrim Street police station with his supervising solicitor to represent a client in custody. *j* Mr Thompson was refused access to interview the client and required to leave the police station. The decision that this should happen was taken by a police sergeant.

[5] On 23 September the deputy chief constable, on behalf of the chief constable, decided at a meeting attended by the legal advisor of the force, that Mr Thompson was not to be admitted to any police station in Northumbria to act as a PSR. The reason for the deputy chief constable's decision was set out in writing in an

a
attendance note dated 23 September 1999 prepared by the force's solicitor. The decision was in these terms:

> 'A decision was made by the Deputy Chief Constable that Mr Thompson would not be admitted to any police stations in the Northumbria Police area to act as a solicitor's representative. Mr Brown [the deputy chief constable] concluded that it would be inappropriate to do so and that he would review his decision once the Home Office had determined the appeal.'

b

Reasons were then given for the decision:

> '(i) Mr Thompson has an outstanding Home Office Appeal against finding and punishment.

c

> (ii) If successful, Mr Thompson could be reinstated as a police officer. It was therefore inappropriate for him to be acting for suspects.
> (iii) He was dismissed from the Force on a serious charge of misconduct. In giving his reasons for his decision, the Chief Constable had stated that he had found the allegations specified by the female officer to have been proved. This

d

> means that he preferred the evidence of the female officer to that of PC Thompson, which by implication means that PC Thompson was not telling the truth. There is serious question therefore as to the officer's honesty, and therefore whether he is a suitable character to provide legal advice.
> (iv) If admitted to police stations he will have access to witnesses who gave evidence against him. There is a risk of prejudice to the appeal process by

e

> Mr Thompson having access to prosecution witnesses.
> (v) Mr Thompson has indicated his personal feelings towards the Force. It is therefore felt that there is a real risk of an investigation being prejudiced as a result.
> (vi) As a man dismissed from the Force for misconduct, there is unlikely to

f

> be any trust or respect between investigating officers and Mr Thompson in his capacity as a legal advisor, particularly in view of the proximity of the disciplinary hearing.
> (vii) The risk of prejudice is the greater where police officers who gave evidence against him are the officers in charge of an investigation against the suspect.

g

> (viii) The decision to exclude Mr Thompson from police stations in the Force area is consistent and in the spirit with the Police and Criminal Evidence Act 1984, Code of Practice C, paragraph 6.12 and 6.13.'

There were then set out the following 'Other Observations':

h

> 'The question of a conflict of interest is for the solicitor and/or his representative. However, it is the first rule of professional practice that a solicitor must not act where there is a conflict of interest. There can be no bigger conflict of interest than when one's personal interest conflicts with one's professional responsibilities. It is believed that Mr Thompson's personal

j

> interest, bearing in mind his Appeal is outstanding, conflict with the independence required to give advice to a client in custody. There is a real risk that a suspect in custody will not get independent advice.'

[6] Gibbs J felt that it was entirely reasonable for the deputy chief constable to conclude that is was inappropriate for Mr Thompson to act as a PSR. He stated that in his judgment, reasons (i), (ii), (v), (vi), (vii) and (viii) justified this conclusion and

'taken together support the view that the investigation of crime would be hindered'.

[7] Gibbs J added that the distinguishing factor of this case is—

'the fundamental inability of a person in the applicant's position from fulfilling that independent role for the benefit of suspects to which they are entitled. The question, therefore, is whether the admission of the applicant can reasonably have been said to hinder the investigation of crime.'

Gibbs J also rejected the submission made on behalf of Mr Thompson that it was not lawful to make a blanket exclusion of a former police officer until his appeal was heard.

The law

[8] In considering the legal position of the chief constable, the starting point is s 10 of the Police Act 1996 which provides that a police force 'shall be under the direction and control of the chief constable'. It is accepted on behalf of the police that this wide power has to be exercised in accordance with the Police and Criminal Evidence Act 1984 (PACE) and the Code of Practice issued by the Secretary of State under ss 66 and 67 of PACE.

[9] Section 58 of PACE gives a person arrested and held in custody in a police station or other premises the right to consult a solicitor privately at any time subject to certain specified limitations. The right to legal advice is amplified by Code C of the Code of Practice. It is relevant to refer to the following provisions of the Code: C3.1 which sets out the information which must be given to a person brought to a police station under arrest or who is arrested at the police station. He must be told clearly by the custody officer that he has '(ii) the right to consult privately with a solicitor and the fact that *independent legal advice is available free of charge*' (my emphasis). The position as to legal advice is amplified in C6. C6 points out that it is only in limited circumstances that access to advice can be delayed (C6.5) and if a person wants legal advice, he cannot be interviewed or continued to be interviewed until he has received that advice except in restricted circumstances (C6.6). Furthermore after an interview begins or while it is in progress the solicitor must be allowed to be present (C6.8). A solicitor may only be required to leave the interview if his conduct is such that the investigating officer is unable properly to put questions to the suspect (C6.9). The powers of the investigating officer are therefore precisely constrained. C6.11 provides:

'The removal of a solicitor from an interview is a serious step and, if it occurs, the officer of superintendent rank or above who took the decision will consider whether the incident should be reported to the Law Society. If the decision to remove the solicitor has been taken by an officer below the rank of a superintendent, the facts must be reported to an officer of superintendent rank or above who will similarly consider whether a report to the Law Society would be appropriate. Where the solicitor concerned is a duty solicitor, the report should be both to the Law Society and to the Legal Aid Board.'

C6.12 contains a broad definition of 'solicitor' for the purposes of the Code of Practice and sets out the status of a PSR:

'... "solicitor" means a solicitor who holds a current practising certificate, a trainee solicitor, a duty solicitor representative or an accredited representative included on the register of representatives maintained by the Legal Aid Board.

a
If a solicitor wishes to send a non-accredited or probationary representative to provide advice on his behalf, then that person shall be admitted to the police station for this purpose unless an officer of the rank of inspector or above considers that such a visit will hinder the investigation of a crime and directs otherwise. (Hindering the investigation of a crime does not include giving proper legal advice to a detained person in accordance with Note 6D.) Once admitted to the police station, the provisions of paragraphs 6.6 to 6.10 apply.'

b

[10] As I have pointed out Mr Thompson, the appellant, is a 'non-accredited or probationary representative' referred to in C6.12. Although he attends the police station as a representative of a solicitor, he does not fall within the wide definition of a 'solicitor' in the Code.

c
[11] There are other provisions of the Code to which it is necessary to refer, but before I do so, it is convenient at this stage to turn to the one relevant authority, namely *R v Chief Constable of Avon and Somerset Constabulary, ex p Robinson* [1989] 2 All ER 15, [1989] 1 WLR 793. In this Divisional Court case Watkins and Mann LJJ and Auld J had to consider the legality of general instructions which a deputy chief constable had given to his force as to clerks whose character, antecedents and behaviour were such as to make their presence at an interview of a person in custody undesirable. A challenge to the validity of the instructions was unsuccessful. This was because the court was of the opinion that the instructions were advisory and left it to the officer in charge to decide whether to allow a particular clerk to be present. The court decided that there was no reason why senior police officers should not advise their subordinates as to what action they should consider taking as to the activities of clerks as long as the instructions were advisory and did not pre-empt the actual decision of the appropriate officer based on a particular investigation of a crime. The instructions were accordingly intra vires PACE and the Code.

d

e

[12] In the course of giving the judgment of the court, Mann LJ said:

f

'It is apparent that there is only one ground on which the clerk or legal executive can be excluded from the police station and that is that his visit would hinder the investigation of crime. That, of course, is a matter for the subjective judgment of the officer being an officer of the rank of inspector or above. However, although there is but one express reason justifying exclusion there is a prefatory question which must be asked, that is to say is the person who seeks admission "a clerk or legal executive"? There should be no difficulty in identifying a legal executive, but who is a "clerk"? The expression "clerk to a solicitor" occurs in the Solicitors Act 1974 (see for example s 43) but nowhere in either statute or case law is the expression "clerk" defined. Leaving aside for the moment the question whether the inspector may not be entitled to exclude an obviously incompetent person on the basis that he is likely to "hinder", it seems to us that there are certain matters which are necessarily implicit in the words of para 6.9. The first of those implicit matters is that the clerk must be sent by the solicitor to provide "advice on his behalf", and if the police know or believe that the person is not capable of providing advice on behalf of the solicitor, whether because of his appearance, his age, his mental capacity or because of the police knowledge of him, they are entitled to refuse to allow him to enter the police station. The second implicit matter, which is perhaps the same point differently expressed, is that the person must be a "clerk" genuinely so-called and not someone recruited, so to speak, off the streets masquerading as a clerk. In this case also, if the police know or believe that the

g

h

j

person is merely a colourable pretence of a clerk, they are entitled to exclude
him from the station. We return to the hindering point. There may be *a*
circumstances where the police know that the person has a record of
convictions, they may know that he is criminally orientated if unsullied by
detection. In those circumstances, likewise, they will be entitled to conclude
that to admit such a person to the station to tender advice would hinder the
investigation of crime. If a person is ostensibly capable of giving advice then *b*
we do not think that the police could refuse admission on the basis that the
quality of the advice would be poor. We see no objection to the police forming
a view on capacity but we think it would be unfortunate if the police were also
to form a view on quality. That being said, we are anxious about quality.'
(See [1989] 2 All ER 15 at 17–18, [1989] 1 WLR 793 at 795.)

c

[13] Mr Gavin Millar QC drew attention to the importance that Mann LJ, in this
passage of his judgment, attached to the fact that the only basis upon which the clerk
or legal executive could be excluded was that 'his visit would hinder the investigation
of crime'. He also drew attention to the matters which Mann LJ regarded as
implicit in what was C6.9 of the Code (now C6.12 of the Code). In addition
Mr Millar referred to the final sentence of the passage which has been quoted and *d*
submitted that it made it clear that the question of the quality of advice which was
given was not an issue about which the police should be directly concerned.

[14] Mr Millar also submitted that it was this part of Mann LJ's judgment which
caused the Code to be amended by the insertion of what is now C6.13. This could
well be the case since C6.13 reads: *e*

'In exercising his discretion under paragraph 6.12, the officer should take into
account in particular whether the identify and status of the non-accredited or
probationary representative have been satisfactorily established; whether he is
of suitable character to provide legal advice (a person with a criminal record
is unlikely to be suitable unless the conviction was for a minor offence and is *f*
not of recent date); and any other matters in any written letter of authorisation
provided by the solicitor on whose behalf the person is attending the police
station.'

There are notes to Code C. For example, in relation to C6.9, which deals with the
police's ability to require a solicitor to leave an interview if as result of the solicitor's *g*
conduct the investigating officer is unable to put properly questions to the suspect,
one of the notes (Note 6D) reads:

'Paragraph 6.9 will only apply if the solicitor's approach or conduct prevents
or unreasonably obstructs proper questions being put to the suspect or his
response being recorded.' *h*

Again in relation to C6.13, the note (Note 6F) reads:

'If an officer of at least the rank of inspector considers that a particular
solicitor or firm of solicitors is persistently sending non-accredited or
probationary representatives who are unsuited to provide legal advice, he *j*
should inform an officer of at least the rank of Superintendent who may wish
to take the matter up with the Law Society.'

[15] This last note is particularly relevant because it relates to the quality of the
advice which a person in custody receives. The police's response if a solicitor
persistently behaves improperly should be indirect. The police should involve the

a Law Society. Looking at the provisions of the Code as it has been amended subsequent to the judgment of Mann LJ, it is striking the extent to which the amendments have made explicit what was previously implicit.

[16] There is another passage of Mann LJ's judgment to which I should refer. It is in these terms:

b 'We regard the general and particular instructions as paying scrupulous regard to the 1984 Act and to Code C. As is recognised in the instructions it is a matter for the individual police officer to decide in regard to admission but we see no reason why senior officers should not advise their subordinates of the activities or proclivities of clerks. That advice must not and cannot derogate from the individual responsibilities of the officer concerned with the
c investigation. He must make his own decision within the area with which he is empowered to do so and which we have endeavoured to describe earlier in this judgment. There was in this case no complaint by any suspect. There was in this case no direction how a discretion in regard to presence at interview should be exercised. It is quite plain on the evidence that police officers concerned with interview have been exercising an individual discretion in each
d case which comes before them because there has been no blanket ban on the clerks in question. The same or different officers have made the same or different decisions on different occasions, having regard, no doubt, to the information about the clerk in question to hand and the nature and circumstances of the investigation. We would accordingly and do dismiss this
e application.' (See [1989] 2 All ER 15 at 21, [1989] 1 WLR 793 at 799.)

[17] In this passage of his judgment, Mann LJ makes it abundantly clear that it was the view of that court that although senior officers can give advice, the Code gives the responsibility to the officer concerned with the individual investigation. Unless Mann LJ was in error in his approach, it follows that the whole focus of the
f Code is on a particular investigation of a crime rather than the hindering of the investigation of crime generally. Furthermore, the second citation from Mann LJ's judgment makes it clear that that court was firmly of the view that a blanket ban was inappropriate, but that advice of a general nature, which preserved the discretion of the officer in charge of an investigation, was in order.

[18] This examination of the changes to the Code, introduced after Mann LJ's
g judgment, suggests that the Home Secretary accepted that the judgment was correct and by amending the Code was seeking to give effect to it. As amended the Code recognises that it will be an unusual and significant step for the police to interfere in the relationship between a person in custody and his legal advisor. How a legal advisor chooses to provide advice is primarily for him to determine. It is only
h where there is significant interference with an investigation that the police should intervene. Generally, it is for the solicitor to deal with any faults on the part of his representative. If he does not take the necessary action then it is primarily for the profession to ensure that proper standards are maintained.

[19] In general, I would accept Mr Millar's submission as to the respective duties
j which are in play here. It is the duty of the police to ensure access to independent legal advice. It is the solicitor's duty to ensure that independent advice is provided. The interest of the police is however catered for by the police being able to make a complaint to the Law Society.

[20] The advice is provided free and this meant that the Legal Aid Board used to be involved before its demise. The Legal Advice and Assistance Regulations 1989, SI 1989/340 made provision for advice and assistance at police stations. This was

provided regardless of the resources of the person held in custody. The *a* arrangements made were contained in the Legal Advice and Assistance at Police Stations Register Arrangements 1995. Paragraph 1 of the Arrangements identifies an accredited representative as a representative whose name is included on the police station register as having passed the relevant test. It also refers to the requirement of a 'certificate of fitness', that is a certificate given by the supervising solicitor that the representative 'is of suitable character to provide legal advice at *b* police stations ... and that the applicants should be so regarded by the police in accordance with paragraph 6.13 of the Code of Practice'. The certificate of fitness is a form signed by the supervising solicitor (para 3.1). No one could be registered as a probationary or accredited representative without submitting a properly completed application incorporating a certificate of fitness (para 3.2). The board was given powers to suspend and remove probationary representatives (para 4.1). *c*

[21] The arrangements, if the board received a complaint as to the suitability of the character of a representative, were that the board should respond by requesting the representative to obtain from the supervising solicitor a certificate of fitness. If, notwithstanding the receipt of that certificate of fitness, the board was not satisfied as to the fitness of the representative the board was able to refer the matter to the *d* Solicitors' Complaints Bureau (para 6). So again the remedy was to be by a complaint to the professional body.

Conclusion

[22] Although I was initially of the view that the approach of the judge had *e* much to commend it, having examined the regulatory framework under which advice is given by a PSR more closely, I am satisfied that his decision cannot be supported. It is inconsistent with the judgment of Mann LJ in *Ex p Robinson*. Mr Milford QC on behalf of the chief constable was not able to explain convincingly how the decision of the deputy chief constable in this case could be supported if Mann LJ's reasoning was correct. He therefore submitted that Mann LJ's decision *f* was wrong in so far as it conflicted with Gibbs J's decision. In fact, in my judgment far from Mann LJ being wrong, he was clearly right. There is very good reason for the decision as to whether the investigation of crime has been hindered by a PSR being taken in relation to a specific case rather than on a blanket basis. The officer involved in a specific case will know whether in fact there was any risk of interference. If, for example, no further investigation was required in a specific case *g* then there could be no question of interference with the investigation. The question of interference or no interference can only be determined properly by examining the issue in the factual context of a particular investigation of crime.

[23] Mr Milford and the judge attached great importance to the advice having to be independent. I agree that this is important. However, the responsibility for *h* providing independent advice, as already indicated, is that of the solicitor and not the police. The responsibility of the police is to provide access to that advice. Gibbs J was correct to say that the right to independent legal advice exists for the benefit of suspects, not for solicitors and their representatives. The framework within which the advice is given makes it clear that while this is so, the quality of *j* the legal advice is not the concern of the police. It is for the person in custody to decide the solicitor from whom he is to obtain advice and it is for the solicitor, subject to the requirements of PACE, to decide whether he will give the advice personally and if not who should do so on his behalf. Mr Milford urged and the judge accepted that someone who was seeking to be reinstated as a police officer could not be properly regarded as independent of the police. This makes obvious

a good sense. However it was not the police's responsibility to form a judgment as to whether Mr Thompson was sufficiently independent. This was Mr Thompson's employer's responsibility. Mr Milford made the point that if the advice was not independent, at the trial a defendant could seek to rely on this. I appreciate this could happen but the Code limits the ability of the police to intervene to situations where the investigation is being hindered. The interference relied on by Mr Milford

b would not be with the investigation of crime but the prosecution of crime. Furthermore the fact that a defendant may make a complaint of this sort underlines the importance of the police having no responsibility for the quality of the advice.

[24] I also recognise that particularly at the police station at which he had been serving, for Mr Thompson to return as a solicitor's representative could be uncomfortable for his fellow officers as well as himself. He could also come into

c contact with potential witnesses in relation to his appeal. However, unless interference with the investigation of a crime is likely, this does not entitle the police to object to his attendance as long as the PSR is otherwise properly qualified and behaves appropriately when he does attend.

[25] The framework within which the Duty Solicitor Scheme operates does not

d entitle a deputy chief constable to make a blanket direction such as was made here. *Advice* can be given as the Divisional Court held in *Ex p Robinson*. When giving advice the character of the representative can be taken into account. The character of the representative will not vary from day to day and if, because of his character, a representative is likely to hinder an investigation, then advice can be given as to this. The appropriate officer can then reach a decision in the light of the advice as

e to whether the attendance of a representative is likely to interfere with a particular investigation. The advice can provide guidance as to what the decision should be but the decision must still be in relation to the individual case. However, although this is the legal position, I recognise that where advice is given because of the character of a PSR within the terms of C6.13, in practice there is likely to be little

f difference between advice and a blanket ban. Any officer is likely to consider the PSR would hinder an investigation.

[26] As to this appeal, however, my decision is that the appeal must be allowed and the direction of the deputy chief constable quashed.

[27] Mr Thompson is making a claim for damages. For my part, I find it difficult

g to see any basis for this claim but I am prepared to hear argument as to what is to be done about this claim.

MAY LJ.
I agree.

h **JONATHAN PARKER LJ.**
I also agree.

Appeal allowed.

Kate O'Hanlon   Barrister.

Mortgage Corporation v Shaire and others   *a*
Mortgage Corporation v Lewis Silkin (a firm) and another

CHANCERY DIVISION   *b*

NEUBERGER J

21, 22, 23, 25 FEBRUARY 2000

Trust and trustee – Trust of land – Order for sale – Application for order for sale by chargee of co-owner's interest in property – Whether new statutory provision changing *c*
law on exercise of court's discretion on such an application – Trusts of Land and Appointment of Trustees Act 1996, s 15.

Section 15[a] of the Trusts of Land and Appointment of Trustees Act 1996 has
changed the law on the way in which the court will exercise its power to order a
sale at the suit of a chargee of the interest of one of the owners of the beneficial *d*
interest in a property. Under s 30 of the Law of Property Act 1925, which has
effectively been replaced by the 1996 Act, the normal rule in such cases was that,
save in exceptional circumstances, the wish of the chargee would prevail, and the
interests of children and families in occupation would be unlikely to prevail. As
a result of s 15 of the 1996 Act, however, the court now has greater flexibility as *e*
to how it exercises its jurisdiction in such cases on an application for an order for
sale of land subject to a trust of land. There are certain factors that must be taken
into account under s 15(1) and (3), and there may be other factors in a particular
case that the court can, indeed should, take into account. Once the relevant
factors have been identified, the weight to be given to each factor in a particular
case is a matter for the court. Accordingly, although it would be wrong to throw *f*
over all the earlier authorities without paying them any regard, they must be
treated with caution, in light of the change in the law, and in many cases they are
unlikely to be of great, let alone decisive, assistance (see p 377 *c e*, p 378 *b d*, and p
380 *b d h*, below).

    Re Citro (a bankrupt) [1990] 3 All ER 952 and *Lloyds Bank plc v Byrne* [1993] 2 FCR *g*
41 not followed.

Notes

For powers of court in relation to trusts of land, see 48 *Halsbury's Laws* (4th edn)
(2000 reissue) para 934.

    For the Trusts of Land and Appointment of Trustees Act 1996, s 15, see 37 *h*
Halsbury's Statutes (4th edn) (1998 reissue) 703.

Cases referred to in judgment

Abbey National plc v Moss [1994] 2 FCR 587, CA.
Ahmed v Kendrick [1988] 2 FLR 22, CA.   *j*
Banker's Trust Co v Namdar [1997] CA Transcript 349.
Barclays Bank plc v Hendricks [1996] 1 FCR 710.

---

a   Section 15 is set out at p 377 *h* to p 378 *b*, below

a
Citro (a bankrupt), Re [1990] 3 All ER 952, [1991] Ch 142, [1990] 3 WLR 880, CA.
Dennis v McDonald [1982] 1 All ER 590, [1982] Fam 63, [1982] 2 WLR 275, CA.
Goodman v Gallant [1986] 1 All ER 311, [1986] Fam 106, [1986] 2 WLR 236, CA.
Lloyds Bank plc v Byrne [1993] 2 FCR 41, CA.
Lloyds Bank plc v Rosset [1990] 1 All ER 1111, [1991] 1 AC 107, [1990] 2 WLR 867, HL.

b
Midland Bank plc v Cooke [1995] 4 All ER 562, CA.
Penn v Bristol and West Building Society [1997] 3 All ER 470, [1997] 1 WLR 1356, CA.
Roberts v Johnstone [1989] QB 878, [1988] 3 WLR 1247, CA.
Stokes v Anderson [1991] FCR 539, CA.
Thames Guaranty Ltd v Campbell [1984] 2 All ER 585, [1985] QB 210, [1984] 3 WLR
c
109, CA.
TSB plc v Marshall [1998] 2 FLR 769.
Zandfarid v Bank of Credit and Commerce International SA (in liq) [1996] 1 WLR 1420.
Zwebner v Mortgage Corp Ltd [1998] PNLR 769, CA.

d
Cases also cited or referred to in skeleton arguments

Birmigham Midshires Mortgage Services Ltd v Phillips [1998] PNLR 468.
Bristol and West Building Society v Fancy & Jackson (a firm) [1997] 4 All ER 582.
Firbank's Exors v Humphreys (1886) 18 QBD 54, CA.
First National Securities Ltd v Hegerty [1984] 1 All ER 139, [1985] QB 850, [1984]
e
3 WLR 769, CA.
Midland Bank plc v Cox McQueen [1999] Lloyd's Rep PN 223, CA.
Portman Building Society v Bevan Ashford [2000] 1 EGLR 81.
*Taylor Fashions Ltd v Liverpool Victoria Trustees Co Ltd, Old & Campbell v Liverpool
Victoria Trustees Co Ltd* [1981] 1 All ER 897, [1982] QB 133, [1981] 2 WLR 576.
f
Westdeutsche Landesbank Girozentrale v Islington LBC [1996] 2 All ER 961, [1996] AC
669, [1996] 2 WLR 802, HL.

Consolidated actions

g
In the first of two actions consolidated by order of Master Winegarten on 7 June 1999, the claimant, the Mortgage Corporation (TMC), sought possession against the defendants, Marsha Shaire, Adam Shaire and the personal representatives of David Barry Fox (deceased), of a property known as 74 Winchmore Hill Road, London N14. In the second action, TMC sought damages against the defendant solicitors, Lewis Silkin (a firm) and Michael Edgar Blaxill, in respect of a transaction by which TMC acquired a charge over the property. The second and
h
third defendants in the first action took no active part in the proceedings. By the agreement of the parties, the issues between TMC and the defendant solicitors were adjourned pending the resolution of the issues between TMC and Mrs Shaire. The facts are set out in the judgment.

j
Timothy Harry (instructed by *Salans Hertzfeld Heilbronn HRK*) for TMC.
Jalil Asif (instructed by *Traymans*) for Mrs Shaire.
Patrick Lawrence (instructed by *Pinsent Curtis*) for the defendant solicitors.

Cur adv vult

25 February 2000. The following judgment was delivered.

a

NEUBERGER J.

INTRODUCTION

This case concerns the extent and nature of the interests enjoyed by Mrs Marsha Shaire and the Mortgage Corporation (TMC) in 74 Winchmore Hill Road, London *b* N14, and what order should be made in relation to that house. It raises issues as to the basis upon which unmarried parties own beneficial interests in their home or former home, and also the way in which the court should exercise its powers under the provisions of s 15 of the Trusts of Land and Appointment of Trustees Act 1996.

c

THE BASIC FACTS

In 1976 Mrs Shaire married Mr Marvin Shaire and they acquired 74 Winchmore Hill Road (the house) as their matrimonial home. It cost £18,750, which was mostly provided with the assistance of a mortgage in their joint names in the sum of £15,000 from the Abbey National Building Society (the Abbey *d* National mortgage), for which they were jointly responsible. The balance consisted of a gift of £2,000, to both of them from Mr Shaire's parents, and £1,750 which came from sources which, due to the passing of time, have become unclear.

From the entries at HM Land Registry (the Registry) it appears that Mr Shaire was initially the sole proprietor (and that he may even have initially taken out the *e* Abbey National mortgage alone) but it is clear that on 20 January 1977 both Mr and Mrs Shaire were entered at the Registry as joint proprietors.

A son, Adam, was born in 1977, but unfortunately the marriage did not prosper, and Mr Shaire left the house in 1980. He continued to provide Mrs Shaire with the funds to make the Abbey National mortgage repayments, as well as the other bills *f* in relation to the house. After Adam started school in 1985, Mrs Shaire began work in a local chemist's shop where she still works most mornings, and one afternoon, a week.

In early 1986 Mrs Shaire started a relationship with a Mr David Fox. In May 1986 she and Mr Fox told Mr Shaire that Mr Fox had moved into the house and was *g* living with Mrs Shaire. Mr Fox and Mr Shaire then discussed matters in the absence of Mrs Shaire. Following that, on 6 March 1987 a transfer of the house was executed by Mr and Mrs Shaire to Mrs Shaire and Mr Fox. This transfer (the 1987 transfer) was said to be made 'pursuant to an agreement made in divorce proceedings between the parties in the Divorce Registry ... and in consideration of £15,000'. Clause 4 of the 1987 transfer provided: 'The transferees declare that *h* the survivor of them can give a valid receipt for capital money arising on a disposition of the land.' The reference to the Divorce Registry arose from the fact that Mrs Shaire had begun divorce proceedings against Mr Shaire, and, by an order made by consent in the Divorce Registry on 16 March 1987, it was ordered that 'The respondent [ie Mr Shaire] had transferred all of his interests in the *j* [house] to the petitioner [ie Mrs Shaire] and Mr David Barry Fox.' It was stated to be in consideration for this transfer, according to the order, that Mrs Shaire and Mr Fox paid to Mr Shaire the lump sum of £15,000. In consideration for this, the order recited, all claims for periodical payments, lump sum payments or property adjustment orders would be dismissed.

a   Partly in order to pay Mr Shaire the £15,000, Mrs Shaire and Mr Fox raised a sum of £43,750 from the Chase Manhattan Bank (Chase), secured by way of a mortgage (the Chase mortgage) over the house. The offer of the Chase mortgage, dated 24 November 1986, recorded that the house had a value at that time of £87,500. The Chase mortgage was duly completed on 15 January 1987. Of the £43,750, £15,000 went to Mr Shaire pursuant to the agreement to which I have
b   referred, £15,000 went to redeem the Abbey National mortgage, and it is unclear what happened to the £13,750.

Thereafter Mr Fox and Mrs Shaire lived in the house together with Adam. She continued to earn comparatively modestly through her work at the chemist shop. Mr Fox appeared to earn money from his clothing import business. According to
c   Mrs Shaire's evidence, the payments due under the Chase mortgage were all provided by Mr Fox as were the household expenses and other outgoings. Mr Fox died of a heart attack on 25 May 1992. At least according to Mrs Shaire's evidence, it then came to light for the first time that he had forged her signature on a number of documents of which she had previously had no knowledge. They
d   included two relevant documents. Firstly, a further charge over the house dated 25 August 1988 in favour of First National Bank (the FNB mortgage) registered on 6 September 1988 at the Registry, which was to secure the sum of £52,439. Secondly, a charge on the house dated 17 January 1990 in favour of TMC and registered on 27 February 1990 at the Registry, which was to secure the sum of
e   £118,000. The £118,000 raised by the latter mortgage (the TMC mortgage) was used to pay off the Chase mortgage and the FNB mortgage, the balance of the money being retained by Mr Fox.

Although Mrs Shaire accepts that she signed and knew about the Chase mortgage at the time it was granted, she denies any liability under, or knowledge
f   of, the FNB mortgage or the TMC mortgage.

On 22 November 1994 TMC began proceedings in the Barnet County Court for possession of the house. Exactly one year later, TMC began proceedings in the High Court for damages against two firms of solicitors (the solicitors). First, against Lewis Silkin on the grounds that they acted for TMC in connection with
g   the TMC mortgage and had stated that 'All appropriate documentation would be properly executed and will be produced on completion.' Secondly, against a Mr Michael Blaxill, the solicitor who had acted for Mr Fox and purportedly for Mrs Shaire in connection with the TMC mortgage, for breach of warranty of authority.

h   The two actions have been consolidated and now come before me. Although the two firms of solicitors have taken part in the proceedings through their counsel, Mr Patrick Lawrence, it has been agreed between the parties that I should deal with the issues between TMC and Mrs Shaire, and that the issues between TMC and the solicitors will be adjourned on the basis that either they will be
j   compromised or that a further hearing will take place. This is because both firms of solicitors accept liability in light of decisions of the Court of Appeal: *Zwebner v Mortgage Corp Ltd* [1998] PNLR 769, in the case of Lewis Silkin, and *Penn v Bristol and West Building Society* [1997] 3 All ER 470, [1997] 1 WLR 1356, in the case of Mr Blaxill. It is right to add that each solicitor has reserved its position in connection with taking the matter to the House of Lords.

THE ISSUES

(1) Is Mrs Shaire bound by the TMC mortgage on the grounds of agency or *a* estoppel?

(2) What is Mrs Shaire's share of the house?

(3) What is the consequence in terms of the interests which TMC and Mrs Shaire have in the house?

(4) Ought I to make an order for the sale of the house and, if not, what order *b* ought I to make?

Issue 1 turns solely on the facts. Issue 2 turns on the application of principles to be derived from a number of authorities to the facts of this case. Issue 3 is effectively agreed. Issue 4 turns on the effect of s 15 of the 1996 Act. This appears to be the first time when a court of record has had to consider this new provision. I will deal with the issues in that order. *c*

ISSUE 1

This issue is whether Mrs Shaire is bound by the TMC mortgage. It is accepted by TMC that what appears to be Mrs Shaire's signature on the TMC mortgage, and indeed on the FNB mortgage, is a forgery. The overwhelming likelihood is *d* that it was forged by, or with the authority of, Mr Fox. Accordingly, on the face of it, Mrs Shaire cannot be bound by the TMC mortgage, or, indeed, by the FNB mortgage. However, it is contended by TMC, supported by the solicitors, that, on the evidence, it should be concluded either that she authorised Mr Fox to enter into the TMC mortgage on her behalf, or that, by her conduct she is estopped from denying that she is bound by the TMC mortgage. *e*

The matters relied on by Mr Timothy Harry, who appears on behalf of TMC, are, in summary form, as follows. Firstly, Mrs Shaire said that she left all financial matters and dealings to Mr Fox. Secondly, Mrs Shaire signed, and accepts that she signed, together with Mr Fox, an application to TMC for the grant of the TMC mortgage. Thirdly, Mrs Shaire has given inconsistent explanations of the *f* circumstances in which she signed the TMC mortgage. Fourthly, it is likely that Mrs Shaire knew what was going on in terms of a new mortgage being granted over the house before it was granted. For instance, TMC relies on the fact that a valuation surveyor must have visited the house and a doctor gave a medical report on Mrs Shaire to support an insurance policy on her life as further security for the loan from TMC. Fifthly, Mrs Shaire must have been put on inquiry when, *g* as she accepts she did, she learned that the payments to Chase in respect of the Chase mortgage were not being paid after 1990. Sixthly, TMC sent a large number of letters in connection with the TMC mortgage, both before and after it was granted. These letters were sent to the house and Mrs Shaire must have seen at least some of them, and appreciated their effect. A few of these letters sent *h* to the house in connection with the TMC mortgage were addressed to Mrs Shaire, as well as to Mr Fox. Seventhly, there was a telephone conversation recorded in TMC's records with Mrs Shaire in connection with the TMC mortgage and another telephone conversation with her son, Adam. Eighthly, after the death of Mr Fox, correspondence between Mrs Shaire's solicitors and *j* TMC suggests that Mrs Shaire must have known of the TMC mortgage prior to his death, contrary to what she now says.

Although it would be wrong to pretend that these points, particularly when taken together, are not without force, I am firmly of the view that the case against Mrs Shaire on this issue, whether put in terms of authority or estoppel, has not been made out. The very fact that Mr Fox forged her signature, or had her a signature forged, on the TMC mortgage speaks for itself. This is particularly so, given that Mrs Shaire was plainly prepared to sign some documents such as the Chase mortgage and the application for the TMC mortgage. The fact that Mr Fox had to forge her name on the TMC mortgage, and indeed on the FNB mortgage, suggests that he knew that she would not be prepared to execute the TMC mortgage or indeed the FNB mortgage.

b Then there is Mrs Shaire's evidence relating to the circumstances in which she signed the application for the TMC mortgage. She said that Mr Carle-Tide, a mortgage broker, called on Mr Fox at the house, and, after they had been talking for some time, Mr Fox called her and asked her to sign a document which was mostly hidden. She says that she signed it and then asked what it was. On being told that it was an application for a substantial further mortgage on the house, she said that she stated that she wanted nothing more to do with it and would be not prepared to enter into such a mortgage. As far as she was concerned, that was the end of the matter.

c Albeit not without hesitation, I accept this evidence. Mr Carle-Tide was called, but there are two problems about his evidence. Firstly, I regret to say that I found him a thoroughly unreliable witness of fact even in so far as his evidence went. Secondly, his recollection of the meeting was, even on his own evidence, very slender indeed. I have to say that I am left with the impression that he may well remember more than he suggested. If that is wrong and he does not remember anything much about the meeting, then there is no specific evidence to contradict Mrs Shaire. If he does remember more than he says, then I suspect that the reason that he has not given the full version of what he recollects is that it is not to his advantage. The most obvious reason for that is that something along the lines of what Mrs Shaire suggests did indeed happen, and yet he none the less went along with the execution of the TMC mortgage. In this connection, it is right to mention that it appears that Mr Carle-Tide did purport to witness signatures of Mrs Shaire on other documents, which signatures appear to have been clearly forged.

d It also seems to me that Mrs Shaire's evidence is consistent with what she says about the fact that she actually signed the application for the TMC mortgage but did not sign the TMC mortgage itself. Mrs Shaire's evidence is not by any means wholly improbable and, while she was not a particularly good witness, there are no grounds, in my judgment, for not accepting her evidence.

e It is unfair to make too much of the inconsistencies in her explanations. In an early affidavit she gives a somewhat different explanation, but I am satisfied that that was due to casualness and hurry when she swore that affidavit. Now that privilege has been waived, she has produced a copy of notes taken in 1993 of discussions (before the affidavit) with her solicitor in which what she said appears to have been consistent with what she says now. Additionally, there is a letter sent by her solicitor shortly after Mr Fox died; this appears somewhat inconsistent with what she now says, but, to my mind, bearing in mind the distress that she must have suffered at the time, and the uncertainties and surprises that she was encountering, it is not surprising that the letter was inaccurate.

f As to the other points which I have mentioned, I do not want to deal with them in great detail. I am not satisfied that Mrs Shaire saw any of the letters sent to the house in connection with the mortgage. Almost all of them were addressed to Mr Fox alone. Given that, on her evidence, on most days she left the house before Mr Fox, the two letters which were addressed to both of them could easily have been opened by him. The fact that the documentation shows that there might have been opportunities for her to have discovered what was going on, for *a* instance, when the surveyor inspected the house for the purpose of advising TMC as to its value, or her doctor talking about the medical report he was asked to give, does not greatly impress me. Mr Fox was prepared, it would seem, to take risks and no doubt would have tried to come up with a plausible explanation if she had met the surveyor in the house or had talked to the doctor about the medical report. *b*

So far as the telephone calls are concerned, I am not satisfied that the note of the telephone call with Mrs Shaire shows that there was any discussion other than TMC seeking to talk to Mr Fox, who was their point of contact. It is by no means clear that anything else was or would have been said. I am wholly unsatisfied that any assistance can be derived from a conversation which apparently took place with Adam when he was 13 or 14. *c*

Realistically, Mr Lawrence and, as I understand it, Mr Harry, accepted that if I thought that Mrs Shaire's version of what happened when she signed the mortgage application form was correct, then any case on authority was in difficulties. I do not think she can be criticised for not tearing up the mortgage application form which she had signed on discovering what it was. At that time, *d* and indeed until his death, from what I have heard, Mrs Shaire had no reason to believe Mr Fox was dishonest.

ISSUE 2

The principles   *e*
What is Mrs Shaire's share of the house? When determining the respective beneficial interests of two persons who are living in a house together, either as man and wife or in a close relationship, the law appears to be as follows:

(1) Where parties have expressly agreed the shares in which they hold, that is normally conclusive (see *Lloyds Bank plc v Rosset* [1990] 1 All ER 1111 at *f* 1118–1119, [1991] 1 AC 107 at 132, and *Goodman v Gallant* [1986] 1 All ER 311, [1986] Fam 106).

(2) Such an agreement can be in writing or oral (see *Rosset's* case [1990] 1 All ER 1111 at 1118–1119, [1991] 1 AC 107 at 132).

(3) Where the parties have reached such an agreement, it is open to the court to depart from that agreement only if there is very good reason for doing so, for *g* instance, a subsequent renegotiation or subsequent actions which are so inconsistent with what was agreed as to lead to the conclusion that there must have been a variation or cancellation of the agreement.

(4) Where there is no express agreement the court must rely on the contemporary and subsequent conduct of the parties (see *Rosset's* case [1990] 1 All ER 1111 at 1119, *h* [1991] 1 AC 107 at 132, and *Midland Bank plc v Cooke* [1995] 4 All ER 562).

(5) In this connection one is not confined to the conduct of the parties at the time of the acquisition or the time of the alleged creation of the alleged interest. The court can look at subsequent actions (see *Stokes v Anderson* [1991] FCR 539 at 543). *j*

(6) The extent of the respective financial contributions can be, and normally is, a relevant factor although it is by no means decisive (see for instance in *Cooke's* case where the wife's contribution was 7% and yet she was held to have a 50% interest).

(7) Further, the extent of the financial contribution is perhaps not as important an aspect as it was once thought to be. It may well carry more weight in a case

a   where the parties are unmarried than when they were married (see *Cooke's* case
[1995] 4 All ER 562 at 576, and the closing part of *Stokes'* case [1991] FCR 539 at
544).

(8) None the less, subject to other factors, relevant payments of money
should, or at least can, be 'treated as illuminating the common intention as to the
extent of the beneficial interest' (see *Stokes'* case [1991] FCR 539 at 543 per

b   Nourse LJ).

(9) As the same case demonstrates (at 543), where there is no evidence of a
specific agreement 'the court must supply the common intention by reference to
that which all the material circumstances show to be fair'.

(10) Only at the last resort should the court resort to the maxim that equality
is equity (see *Cooke's* case [1995] 4 All ER 562 at 574).

c   (11) It may well be of significance whether the property is in joint names (as here)
or in the name of one party, as in *Rosset's* case and *Cooke's* case, and as appears to
have been in *Stokes'* case [1991] FCR 539 at 542. In this connection see the
discussion in *Rosset's* case [1990] 1 All ER 1111 at 1115, 1119, [1991] 1 AC 107 at
128, 133, which is not directly in point but tends to support that view.

d
Mr and Mrs Shaire
The first issue which has to be determined is the shares in which Mr and
Mrs Shaire held the beneficial interest in the house before the events of 1986–87.
In my judgment, what appears to have been the common view of counsel in this
case, namely that they shared the beneficial interest in equal proportions, is

e   correct.

Firstly, the cost of £18,500 was funded as to £17,000 equally in the sense that
£2,000 was, according to Mrs Shaire's uncontradicted evidence, a wedding
present from Mr Shaire's parents to both of them (in this connection, see *Cooke's*
case [1995] 4 All ER 562 at 575), and £15,000 was provided by a mortgage under

f   which Mr and Mrs Shaire were both liable. The balance, of £1,500, came from
sources which are a matter of speculation.

Secondly, the house was held in joint names.

Thirdly, until the marriage broke up, Mr and Mrs Shaire were a married couple
who lived together in the house and, for most of the period they lived there, they
did so with a young child of the marriage.

g   Fourthly, Mrs Shaire seems to have been brought up in an environment which
led her to believe and assume that, where a husband and wife owned a house
jointly, they held it in equal shares, and there is no reason to think that Mr Shaire
(who did not give evidence) thought differently.

Fifthly, perhaps of slight value, by permitting Mrs Shaire to stay in the house

h   after the marriage broke up in 1980, Mr Shaire has given some support to this
conclusion.

Sixthly, there is the fallback presumption that equality is equity.

It is true that there is evidence upon which one could mount an argument that
Mr Shaire's proportion was more than 50%. In particular there is the fact that he

j   paid the instalments on the Abbey National mortgage and all the outgoings of the
household. However, on the facts of this case, it seems to me that that is not
nearly enough to depart from the view that there was effectively a 50/50 split in
the beneficial interest between Mr Shaire and Mrs Shaire, not least because I have
virtually no evidence as to what was said and done between Mr and Mrs Shaire
(save the matters to which I have referred) between their marriage and their
divorce.

This conclusion is reinforced by a further point made by Mr Jalil Asif, who appears on behalf of Mrs Shaire. Had the ancillary relief proceedings not been compromised as I have described, Mr and Mrs Shaire's interests in the property would have been at large and the court would have had a wide power under s 24 of the Matrimonial Causes Act 1973 to adjust their respective interests in the house in any event. Mr Shaire had left the house; indeed he had walked out on the marriage. There is no reason to think in those circumstances that Mrs Shaire would not have had at least a 50% interest in the house as a result.

On the basis that Mr and Mrs Shaire each had a 50% share in the house, what was the effect of the arrangements between Mr Shaire, Mr Fox and Mrs Shaire in 1986 and 1987? The main argument was directed to the issue of whether Mr Fox in effect took over Mr Shaire's 50% so that he had 50% and Mrs Shaire had 50% (as Mr Harry, with the support of Mr Lawrence, contends), or whether (as Mr Asif contends) Mr Shaire's 50% was shared equally between Mrs Shaire and Mr Fox so that she had a 75% share. I describe this as the main argument, as it was accepted by all parties that the law was flexible, and that it would be possible for me to determine a figure between 50% and 75% or even, Mr Asif suggested, higher than 75%.

Mrs Shaire and Mr Fox: was there an agreement?

The first question is whether this is a case where there was an agreement between the parties as to how they would hold the beneficial interest. Two possible bases for such an agreement have been put forward. The first is the conversation between Mr Fox and Mr Shaire. I do not think I can make any finding about that conversation, although Mr Lawrence invited me to. Mrs Shaire was not present, Mr Fox has died and left no evidence of the conversation, and Mr Shaire was not called as a witness. Mr Lawrence very properly referred me to an observation of Lord Bridge of Harwich in *Rosset's* case [1990] 1 All ER 1111 at 1118, [1991] 1 AC 107 at 132:

'The finding of an agreement or arrangement to share in this sense can only, I think, be based on evidence of express discussions between the partners, however imperfectly remembered and however imprecise their terms may have been.'

I have no evidence of the content of the conversation. The only evidence which throws light on the conversation are the other matters which I will refer to, and they speak for themselves.

A second argument was raised by Mr Harry. He contended that cl 4 of the 1987 transfer is either an agreement, or a strong indication that Mr Fox and Mrs Shaire intended, to share the beneficial interest in the house equally. I do not accept that contention. It seems to me that cl 4 was included in the 1987 transfer in light of the provisions of s 58(3) of the Land Registration Act 1925. Section 58 is concerned with restrictions on the register, and s 58(3) provides as follows:

'In the case of joint proprietors the restriction may be to the effect that when the number of proprietors is reduced below a certain specified number no disposition shall be registered except under an order of the court, or of the registrar after inquiry into title, subject to appeal to the court, and, subject to general rules, such an entry under this subsection as may be prescribed, shall be obligatory unless it is shown to the registrar's satisfaction that the joint

a   proprietors are entitled for their own benefit, or can give valid receipts for
     capital money, or that one of them is a trust corporation.'

     In my judgment, the purpose of including a provision such as cl 4 in a transfer,
     where the property is held by two individuals, is to avoid the need to register a
     restriction on the register where the parties have agreed among themselves that,
b   on the death of one of them, the survivor 'can give valid receipts for capital
     money'. In other words, it seems to me that a provision such as cl 4, while
     consistent with the view that the two owners (as it is in this case) were intending
     to share the beneficial interest equally, is equally consistent with the view that
     they were merely concerned to ensure that when one of them died the survivor
     could effectively sell the property to a third party without the problem of having
c   to appoint another trustee or a trust corporation. Accordingly, I am of the view
     that cl 4 of the 1987 transfer is perfectly capable of being explained by the fact that
     it is included merely to assist the disposal of the property after one of the two
     co-owners has died.

     I am supported in that view by a passage in *Megarry & Wade on the Law of Real
d   Property* (6th edn, 2000) p 486 (para 9-026), which deals with the possible wording
     of a conveyance or transfer. There is no suggestion there that a provision such as
     cl 4 of the 1987 transfer operates to indicate how the beneficial interests in the
     property are owned.

     Furthermore, I am here concerned with what two individuals, neither of
     whom are lawyers, intended. To hold that two non-lawyers, Mrs Shaire and
e   Mr Fox, would have appreciated that a provision such as cl 4 of the 1987 transfer
     operated to indicate, at least in the absence of supporting evidence, that the
     beneficial interest in the property was held equally, in circumstances where there
     may be factors pointing the other way, seems to me to be unrealistic. It is one
     thing for the transfer, whose main function is to operate to transfer property to
f   two parties, to contain a provision in clear terms which ordinary people would
     understand as dealing with their respective interests in the property. It is another
     thing for a provision such as cl 4 of the 1987 transfer to be invoked as a clear
     indication, by reference to the esoteric law relating to restrictions on transfers and
     the rights of one or more persons to give a valid receipt for payments overreaching
     beneficiaries, as to how the beneficial interest is to be shared.

g   Accordingly, to my mind this is not a case where there is any express agreement,
     or anything which can fairly be construed as an express agreement, between the
     parties as to how the beneficial interest is shared.

Mrs Shaire and Mr Fox: discussion

h   I turn, first, to consider the main question, namely whether Mrs Shaire has 50%
     of the beneficial interest in the house or 75%. To my mind, the arguments in
     favour of 75% are compelling. Mrs Shaire owned 50% of the house (if I can put
     it in those terms) at the time that Mr Shaire divested himself of his 50%. I think
     there are a number of reasons for thinking that she and Mr Fox, and indeed
j   Mr Shaire, intended that Mr Shaire's share should be distributed between
     Mrs Shaire and Mr Fox equally.

     Firstly, Mrs Shaire and Mr Fox both took on liability under the Chase mortgage
     in respect of which they both benefited from £30,000—£15,000 going to buy out
     Mr Shaire and £15,000 to buy out the Abbey National mortgage. In so far as the
     £13,750 is concerned, I suspect that some of it went to Mr Fox's benefit in
     connection with his business, and some of it went to the household expenses.

Secondly, Mr Shaire's interest in the house was worth about £36,000. I assess *a* that by assuming that he owned half of the freehold interest in a house worth £87,500, and over which there was a £15,000 mortgage. He sold that interest worth £36,000, for £15,000. Subject to the next point, there was thus a large element of gift. It seems to me that it is very unlikely that he intended all that gift to go to Mr Fox. It is far more likely that he intended at least part of that gift to go to his former wife, particularly in light of the fact that the evidence shows that *b* even now (and possibly while Mr Fox was alive) Mr Shaire had behaved very generously to his former wife.

Thirdly, it may be that Mr Shaire's apparent generosity in this connection can be explained by reference to the fact that Mrs Shaire, as part of the overall transaction under which Mr Shaire sold his interest in the house, gave up any money claims she might otherwise have had against Mr Shaire in the Divorce *c* Registry order. By giving up any such potential claim against Mr Shaire it seems to me that, if anything, she contributed more than Mr Fox to buying out Mr Shaire because he made no such contribution.

Fourthly, if he acquired a 25% interest in the house, Mr Fox roughly got what he paid for in the sense that he took on a shared liability for £43,750 under the *d* Chase mortgage, ie just under £22,000; in return, he acquired a 25% interest in the house which was also worth just under £22,000. In fact, he probably did better in that I suspect that he received a significant share of the £13,750, received from Chase (after deducting the payments of £15,000 to Abbey National and Mr Shaire).

Fifthly, there are the actual terms on which the divorce proceedings were *e* settled. It seems to me that, reading them naturally, they tend to suggest that Mrs Shaire and Mr Fox were together buying out Mr Shaire's interest in the house, in return for a payment of £15,000 and taking on the Chase mortgage. This, to my mind, is the nearest thing there is to evidence of an agreement, and it suggests that Mrs Shaire and Mr Fox were each acquiring half of Mr Shaire's *f* interest.

Lastly, I draw some comfort from the decision of the Court of Appeal in *Stokes'* case, which has features of similarity to the present case, in that the defendant in that case went to live with the claimant and helped buy out the claimant's former wife's half-interest in the property. The Court of Appeal held on those facts that the fair result was that the claimant and the defendant each acquired half of the *g* claimant's former wife's interest. However, each case in this field turns very much on its own facts, and it can be dangerous to rely upon a not dissimilar case when arriving at a conclusion on another case.

I must deal with the arguments in favour of the contention that Mrs Shaire only has a 50% interest in the house.   *h*

First, it is said that the sensible conclusion is simply that, following the discussions between them, Mr Fox stepped into Mr Shaire's shoes. It seems to me, with respect, that that is merely another way of stating the proposition, and does not of itself take matters any further.

Secondly, there is Mrs Shaire's view to which I have referred, namely that, if a *j* husband and wife live together and the house is jointly owned, they would each own half equally. To my mind, that is a perfectly natural and understandable view where a married couple, having no previous interest in the house, acquire a house in joint names. In this case, Mrs Shaire already had a 50% interest and she and Mr Fox never got married. Therefore the fact that I am departing from Mrs Shaire's normal assumption does not cause me concern.

a Thirdly, and perhaps most significantly, Mrs Shaire said in her witness statement: 'I imagine that Mr Fox took over Mr Shaire's half of the house, and that Mr Fox and I each own 50% of the house.' She seems also to have said to her solicitor in the conversation to which I have referred (in respect of which privilege was waived) in 1993: 'Effectively he owned half the house for no capital outlay.' These observations are significant because they show what was in her
b mind. First, what is in someone's mind is not by any means necessarily determinative as to what the agreement or understanding, whether expressed or inferred from actions and statements, actually was. It is trite law that what is locked away in the mind of one party to a contract has no bearing on the terms or effect of the contract. Secondly, what is said in her witness statement (and was
c said to her solicitor in 1993) is in the present tense and appears only to be an indication of what she thought at the time she made the witness statement (or spoke to her solicitor). Thirdly, as to the solicitor's note of the conversation in 1993, it could be either consistent with what she was told by her solicitor or even could be what the solicitor was noting for his own benefit. What neither
d observation establishes is that there was any agreement or understanding between Mrs Shaire and Mr Fox to indicate that the division of the beneficial interest was to be in equal shares.

Fourthly, there is the point that Mr Fox paid the instalments on the Chase mortgage. I have already dealt with that. Fifthly, it is said that although Mr Fox and Mrs Shaire were not married, they were apparently contemplating marriage.
e I am not convinced that they did seriously contemplate marriage: they lived together for some five or six years and at no time does it seem that there were serious preparations for marriage.

Sixthly, while it is true that Mr Fox was taking on primary liability, as between himself and Mrs Shaire, for repayments under the Chase mortgage, there are two
f points that should be made. First, there is Mrs Shaire's more substantial contribution towards buying out Mr Shaire's interest, namely by giving up her right to any repayments in the Divorce Registry. Secondly, it is not as if Mr Fox has actually paid off the Chase mortgage; indeed, in the events that have happened, the idea that Mr Fox has shouldered the burden in respect of the
g mortgages on the house would understandably be greeted by Mrs Shaire with something of a hollow laugh.

Lastly, Mrs Shaire and Mr Fox were both registered as proprietors at the Registry. That is of some significance but not of central significance.

h Accordingly, subject to the second argument on this issue, I conclude that Mrs Shaire has a 75% interest in the house.

As I have mentioned, the notion that I could determine a figure other than 50% or 75% was canvassed. However, I do not think it is appropriate to treat the court's role, in deciding in what shares the beneficial interest in a property is held, as involving some sort of roving commission. In this case it seems to me that in
j reality the first battle ground is the only real battle ground: is Mrs Shaire's share 75% or is it 50%? For the reasons I have given, I think it is 75%.

Another way of reaching the same conclusion is that some of the factors I have mentioned which have weight could be said to point to a figure of lower than 75% and others could be said to point to a figure of higher than 75%. I conclude that there is no reason to depart from the 75%.

ISSUE 3

As I have indicated, the parties are agreed on this aspect. TMC contends, and *a*
Mrs Shaire accepts, the following. Firstly, the TMC mortgage is valid as against
Mr Fox's share in the house and is therefore valid against his estate's interest in
the house (see Fisher and Lightwood *Law of Mortgage* (10th edn, 1988) p 255,
Thames Guaranty Ltd v Campbell [1984] 2 All ER 585 at 595, [1985] QB 210 at 234
and *Ahmed v Kendrick* [1988] 2 FLR 22 at 29–30). Secondly, given that Mr Fox's *b*
estate is effectively insolvent, TMC is in practice the owner of the 25% beneficial
interest in the house previously owned by Mr Fox. Thirdly, while the TMC
mortgage is not binding on Mrs Shaire, TMC is subrogated to the Chase mortgage
in relation to Mrs Shaire's 75% share in light of the fact that the moneys secured
by the TMC mortgage were used to pay off the moneys secured by the Chase
mortgage (see *Snell's Equity* (13th edn, 2000) p 513). Fourthly, the extent of the *c*
subrogation is 75% of the Chase mortgage, as Mrs Shaire has 75% of the equity in
the house. This is based on the nature of subrogation, which is to be applied
according to broad equitable principles. Fifthly, the amount owing on the Chase
mortgage is around £46,653, so the extent of TMC's share over Mrs Shaire's share
of the house is £34,240-odd.
d

ISSUE 4

Introductory

The question here is ought I to make an order for sale of the house and, if not,
what order ought I to make? Until the 1996 Act came into force on 1 January *e*
1997, property owned by more than one person, not held on a strict settlement,
was held on trust for sale, and s 30 of the Law of Property Act 1925 applied. In
that connection the law had developed in the following way. In *Re Citro*
(*a bankrupt*) [1990] 3 All ER 952 at 961–962, [1991] Ch 142 at 157 Nourse LJ said:
f
'Where a spouse who has a beneficial interest in the matrimonial home has
become bankrupt under debts which cannot be paid without the realisation
of that interest, the voice of the creditors will usually prevail over the voice
of the other spouse and a sale of the property ordered within a short period.
The voice of the other spouse will only prevail in exceptional circumstances.
No distinction is to be made between a case where the property is still being *g*
enjoyed as the matrimonial home and one where it is not. What then are
exceptional circumstances? As the cases show, it is not uncommon for a wife
with young children to be faced with eviction in circumstances where the
realisation of her beneficial interest will not produce enough to buy a
comparable home in the same neighbourhood, or indeed elsewhere; and, if *h*
she has to move elsewhere, there may be problems over schooling and so
forth. Such circumstances, while engendering a natural sympathy in all who
hear of them, cannot be described as exceptional. They are the melancholy
consequences of debt and improvidence with which every civilised society
has been familiar.'
j

In *Lloyds Bank plc v Byrne* [1993] 2 FCR 41 the Court of Appeal had to consider
a number of grounds advanced for distinguishing between a case (such as *Re Citro*)
where the trustee in bankruptcy of one of the owners of a beneficial interest in
the property, wanted to sell, and a case (such as *Byrne's* case) where a mortgagee
or chargee of the one of the parties' beneficial interests wished to sell. Those
differences were recorded, including lastly:

'…"a trustee in bankruptcy is under a statutory duty to realize the assets of the bankrupt whereas there is no such duty upon a chargee under a charging order."' (See [1993] 2 FCR 41 at 44–45.)

Parker LJ went on to say (at 45):

'I accept these are differences and as to the last I accept that the statutory duty of a trustee was stressed in *Citro*'s case. None of the others appears to me to be significant. As to the last, I accept that the statutory duty of the trustee is a powerful factor to be borne in mind when considering the exercise of discretion, but I cannot accept that it justifies any change in approach. Moreover the position of a chargee may well be more powerful. If the sale is postponed the chargee creditor will suffer a postponement of the full amount of what may be a very large and increasing debt, whereas on a bankruptcy each individual creditor may suffer very little. In addition, it must be remembered that where the creditor is a company, the directors of that company owe a duty to its shareholders and it cannot be consistent with that duty to allow a debt, which already exceeds the security held, to continue to mount up save perhaps where to enforce the debt would, or might, damage any public goodwill.'

Accordingly, there was, in relation to trusts for sale and before the 1996 Act came into force, no difference between the two types of case considered in *Re Citro* and *Byrne*'s case. The normal rule in such cases was that, save in exceptional circumstances, the wish of the person wanting the sale, be it a trustee in bankruptcy or a chargee, would prevail, and that the interests of children and families in occupation would be unlikely to prevail. These conclusions were applied in a number of cases at first instance, including *Barclays Bank plc v Hendricks* [1996] 1 FCR 710 (Laddie J), and *Zandfarid v Bank of Credit and Commerce International SA (in liq)* [1996] 1 WLR 1420 (Jonathan Parker J).

However, trusts for sale and s 30 have now been effectively replaced by the 1996 Act. Section 1 of the 1996 Act has the effect of rendering trusts for sale obsolete, including those in existence on 1 January 1997, and replacing them with the less arcane and simpler trusts of land. Sections 6 to 11 are concerned with the powers and duties of trustees. Sections 12 and 13 are concerned with the rights of beneficiaries to occupy the trust property. I must set out s 14(1) and (2) in full:

'(1) Any person who is a trustee of land or has an interest in property subject to a trust of land may make an application to the court for an order under this section.

(2) On an application for an order under this section the court may make any such order—(a) relating to the exercise by the trustees of any of their functions (including an order relieving them of any obligation to obtain the consent of, or to consult, any person in connection with the exercise of any of their functions), or (b) declaring the nature or extent of a person's interest in property subject to the trust, as the court thinks fit.'

I must also set out the whole of s 15:

'(1) The matters to which the court is to have regard in determining an application for an order under section 14 include—(a) the intentions of the person or persons (if any) who created the trust, (b) the purposes for which the property subject to the trust is held, (c) the welfare of any minor who occupies or might reasonably be expected to occupy any land subject to the trust as his home, and (d) the interests of any secured creditor of any beneficiary.

(2) In the case of an application relating to the exercise in relation to any land of the powers conferred on the trustees by section 13, the matters to which the court is to have regard also include the circumstances and wishes of each of the beneficiaries who is (or apart from any previous exercise by the trustees of those powers would be) entitled to occupy the land under section 12.

(3) In the case of any other application, other than one relating to the exercise of the power mentioned in section 6(2), the matters to which the court is to have regard also include the circumstances and wishes of any beneficiaries of full age and entitled to an interest in possession in property subject to the trust or (in case of dispute) of the majority (according to the value of their combined interests).

(4) This section does not apply to an application if section 335A of the Insolvency Act 1986 (which is inserted by Schedule 3 and relates to applications by a trustee of a bankrupt) applies to it.'

Two questions of principle have been canvassed. First, as a result of the 1996 Act, has the law, relating to the way in which the court will exercise its power to order a sale at the suit of a chargee of the interest of one of the owners of the beneficial interest in property, changed? In other words, does s 15 change the law from how it had been laid down in *Re Citro* and *Byrne*'s case? Secondly, does s 15(3) apply in the present case?

The effect of the 1996 Act

To my mind, for a number of reasons, Mr Asif is correct in his submission, on behalf of Mrs Shaire, that s 15 has changed the law.

First, there is the rather trite point that if there was no intention to change the law, it is hard to see why Parliament has set out in s 15(2) and, indeed, on one view, s 15(3), the factors which have to be taken into account specifically, albeit not exclusively, when the court is asked to exercise its jurisdiction to order a sale.

Secondly, it is hard to reconcile the contention that Parliament intended to confirm the law as laid down in *Byrne*'s case with the fact that, while the interest of a chargee is one of the four specified factors to be taken into account in s 15(1)(d), there is no suggestion that it is to be given any more importance than the interests of the children residing in the house (see s 15(1)(c)). As is clear from the passage I have quoted from the judgment of Nourse LJ in *Re Citro* as applied to a case such as this in light of *Byrne*'s case, that would appear to represent a change in the law.

Thirdly, the very name 'trust for sale' and the law as it has been developed by the courts suggests that under the old law, in the absence of a strong reason to the contrary, the court should order sale. Nothing in the language of the new code as found in the 1996 Act supports that approach.

Fourthly, it is clear from the reasons in *Byrne*'s case and indeed the later two first instance cases to which I have referred, that the law, as developed under s 30 of the Law of Property Act 1925, was that the court should adopt precisely the same approach in a case where one of the co-owners was bankrupt (*Re Citro*) and a case where one of the co-owners had charged his interest (*Byrne*'s case). It is quite clear that Parliament now considers that a different approach is appropriate in the two cases—compare ss 15(2) and 15(3) of the 1996 Act with s 15(4) and the new s 335A of the Insolvency Act 1986.

a Fifthly, an indication from the Court of Appeal that the 1996 Act was intended to change the law is to be found in (an albeit plainly obiter) sentence in the judgment of Peter Gibson LJ in *Banker's Trust Co v Namdar* [1997] CA Transcript 349. Having come to the conclusion that the wife's appeal against an order for sale had to be refused in light of the reasoning in *Re Citro* and *Byrne's* case, Peter Gibson LJ said:

b 'It is unfortunate for Mrs Namdar, that the very recent Trusts of Land and Appointment of Trustees Act 1996 was not in force at the relevant time [ie at the time of the hearing at first instance] ...'

Of course it would be dangerous to build too much on that observation, but it is an indication from the Court of Appeal and indeed from a former chairman of the Law Commission, as to the perceived effect of the 1996 Act.

c Sixthly, the leading textbooks support the view that I have reached. In *Megarry & Wade on the Law of Real Property* p 510 (para 9-064) one finds this:

'Although the authorities on the law prior to 1997 will therefore continue to provide guidance, the outcome will not in all cases be the same as it would have been under the previous law. This is because the legislature was much *d* more specific as to the matters which a court is required to take into account.'

Emmet on Title (19th edn, January 1999 release) para 22-035, contains this:

'Cases decided on pre-1997 law may be disregarded as of little, if any, *e* assistance ... because the starting point ... was necessarily a trust for sale implied or expressed as a conveyancing device enabling the convenient co-ownership of the property ...'

Seventhly, the Law Commission report which gave rise to the 1996 Act, *Transfer of Land, Trusts of Land* (Law Com No 181, 8 June 1989), tends to support *f* this view as well. It is fair to say that the Law Commission did not propose a new section in a new Act such as s 15 of the 1996 Act, but a new s 30 of the Law of Property Act 1925. It is also fair to say that the terms of the proposed new s 30 were slightly different from those of s 15. However, in my judgment, the way in which the terms of the 1996 Act, and in particular s 15, have been drafted suggests *g* that the Law Commission's proposals were very much in the mind of, and were substantially adopted by, the legislature. In para 12.9 of the report, the Law Commission describe the aim as being to 'consolidate *and rationalise*' (my emphasis) the current approach. When commenting on the proposed equivalents of what are now s 15(2) and (3), the Law Commission said (note 143):

h 'Clearly, the terms of these guidelines may influence the exercise of the discretion in some way. For example, it may be that the courts' approach to creditors' interests will be altered by the framing of the guideline as to the welfare of children. If the welfare of children is seen as a factor to be considered independently of the beneficiaries' holdings, the court may be *j* less ready to order the sale of the home than they are at present.'

Finally, the Law Commission said (para 13.6):

'Within the new system, beneficiaries will be in a comparatively better position than beneficiaries of current trusts of land. For example, given that the terms governing applications under section 30 will be less restrictive than they are at present, beneficiaries will have greater scope to challenge the decisions of the trustees and generally influence the management of the trust land.'

Eighthly, to put it at its lowest, it does not seem to me unlikely that the legislature intended to relax the fetters on the way in which the court exercised its discretion in cases such as *Re Citro* and *Byrne's* case, and so as to tip the balance somewhat more in favour of families and against banks and other chargees. Although the law under s 30 was clear following *Re Citro* and *Byrne's* case, there were indications of judicial dissatisfaction with the state of the law at that time. Although Bingham LJ agreed with Nourse LJ in *Re Citro*, he expressed unhappiness with the result ([1990] 3 All ER 952 at 965, [1991] Ch 142 at 161), and Sir George Waller's dissatisfaction went so far as led him to dissent ([1990] 3 All ER 952 at 965–966, [1991] Ch 142 at 161–163). Furthermore, there is a decision of the Court of Appeal in *Abbey National plc v Moss* [1994] 2 FCR 587, which suggests a desire for a new approach.

All these factors, to my mind, when taken together point very strongly to the conclusion that s 15 has changed the law. As a result of s 15, the court has greater flexibility than heretofore, as to how it exercises its jurisdiction on an application for an order for sale on facts such as those in *Re Citro* and *Byrne's* case. There are certain factors which must be taken into account (see s 15(1) and, subject to the next point, s 15(3)). There may be other factors in a particular case which the court can, indeed should, take into account. Once the relevant factors to be taken into account have been identified, it is a matter for the court as to what weight to give to each factor in a particular case.

The only indication the other way is a decision of Judge Wroath in the Newport, Isle of Wight, County Court in *TSB plc v Marshall* [1998] 2 FLR 769 at 771–772, where he said this, having referred to *Byrne's*, *Moss'*, and *Hendricks'* cases:

'Those three cases were all decided where the applications to the court were under s 30 of the Law of Property Act. However, it has been submitted that the principles established are applicable to an application under s 14, and I accept that submission.'

It does not appear clear to what extent the matter was argued before him, or, indeed, whether it was argued before him. With all due respect to Judge Wroath, I disagree with his conclusion.

A difficult question, having arrived at this conclusion, is the extent to which the old authorities are of assistance, and it is no surprise to find differing views expressed in the two textbooks from which I have quoted. On the one hand, to throw over all the wealth of learning and thought given by so many eminent judges to the problem which is raised on an application for sale of a house where competing interests exist seems somewhat arrogant and possibly rash. On the other hand, where one has concluded that the law has changed in a significant respect so that the court's discretion is significantly less fettered than it was, there are obvious dangers in relying on authorities which proceeded on the basis that the court's discretion was more fettered than it now is. I think it would be wrong to throw over all the earlier cases without paying them any regard. However, they have to be treated with caution, in light of the change in the law, and in many cases they are unlikely to be of great, let alone decisive, assistance.

Section 15(3)

a

The second question of principle can be dealt with more shortly. The question is whether s 15(3) applies in a case such as this. That turns on the meaning of the words: 'In the case of any other application'. Mr Harry, for TMC, said that those words mean any application which does not fall within sub-ss (1) or (2) and, as the present application falls within sub-s (1), sub-s (3) does not apply. Mr Asif, for

b   Mrs Shaire, contended that the reference to 'any other application' is to any application not falling within sub-s (2), and given that the present application falls within sub-s (1), sub-s (3) applies.

Looking at the matter as one of pure language, either construction appears to me to be acceptable and, if anything, I would tend to favour that preferred by Mr Harry. However, once one looks at the matter more widely in the context of

c   the 1996 Act as a whole, it seems to me clear that Mr Asif is right and sub-s (3) does apply to a case such as this. In my judgment, the essential clue is that s 14 is the only section specifically dealing with applications to the court for an order. Many of the other sections are, as I have mentioned, concerned with exercise of powers of duties by trustees, and certain other sections are concerned with the

d   rights of beneficiaries. However, s 14 is the section which deals with the rights of the parties to make applications to the court. If one reads sub-s (3) in the way for which Mr Harry contends, it seems to me very difficult to give it any meaning at all in those circumstances, because any application would seem to be governed by s 14 and therefore to fall within sub-s (1).

e   In my judgment, therefore, the position is as follows. When considering any application under the 1996 Act, sub-s (1) always applies. When considering any application made under the 1996 Act relating to s 13, sub-s (2) applies. When considering any application other than one made under s 13 or one made under s 6(2), sub-s (3) applies. It also seems to me that, bearing in mind the factors which the legislature has said should be taken into account, on any view, when

f   considering an application for sale such as the present, namely the four matters specified in sub-s (1), it would be surprising if the legislature intended the factor identified in sub-s (3) to be ignored.

An order for sale?

g   Bearing in mind these conclusions as to the effect of the 1996 Act, ought I to make an order for sale? I consider, first, the matters to which I am specifically required to have regard in s 15(1) and (3). So far as s 15(1)(a) is concerned, the house was acquired in 1987 as a home for Mr Fox, Mrs Shaire and Adam, and Mrs Shaire and Adam still live there and still want to live there. It is also true that Mrs Shaire has lived there since 1976, on her own since 1980. However,

h   there is no evidence as to the intention of Mrs Shaire and Mr Fox as to what would happen to the house if Mr Fox died. Furthermore, Mr Fox changed the basis on which he held his interest when, albeit unknown to Mrs Shaire, he charged that interest first to FNB and then to TMC for a large sum to assist his business.

j   In *Namdar's* case [1997] CA Transcript 349, Evans-Lombe J, at first instance, is quoted in the judgment of Peter Gibson LJ as saying:

> 'The subsistence of that purpose [to provide a matrimonial home for the family] depended on the continuation of their joint ownership of the property and was brought to an end by the alienation by Mr Namdar of his interest in it by charging that interest to the bank. It may also have been brought to an

end by his leaving the property and his wife in circumstances in which it is plain that their marriage was at an end.'   *a*

In *Hendricks'* case [1996] 1 FCR 710 at 715, Laddie J said:

> '... the only collateral purpose upon which Mrs. Hendricks could rely, namely that the house was to be retained as the matrimonial home, had ceased to exist both because Mr. Hendricks was no longer living there and,   *b* more importantly, because Mr. Hendricks' interest as co-owner had been charged to the bank. He had therefore alienated his interest in the home.'

Secondly, there is s 15(1)(b). It is difficult to say for what purposes the house is held. So far as Mrs Shaire is concerned, it is primarily a home for her to live in, but also an asset as she has 75% of the beneficial interest. So far as TMC is concerned,   *c* it is partly security for the loan for which Mrs Shaire is liable, and it is an asset, as it has 25% of the beneficial interest which it is naturally anxious to sell to realise as much as it can from the mess it has got into through Mr Fox's dishonesty.

Section 15(1)(c) does not apply. Section 15(1)(d), concerned, as it is, with the interests of any secured creditor of any beneficiary, requires one to have regard to   *d* TMC's interest, which I have already described.

As to s 15(3), the major part of the beneficial interest is held, I have concluded, by Mrs Shaire and she obviously wishes to remain in occupation.

Having gone through the statutory required factors, I stand back to look at the position of the two parties. TMC do not want to be tied into a 25% equity in a property producing no income and with no certainty when it will be   *e* realised. Mrs Shaire is 48 and there is no reason to think that she will sell, let alone in the foreseeable future. TMC will also have no control over the state of the house or whether it is properly insured, save through the medium of the subrogated Chase mortgage which it currently has over Mrs Shaire's 75% interest. However, that mortgage could be redeemed at any time, for   *f* instance by Mrs Shaire remortgaging.

Thirdly, TMC point out that Mrs Shaire does not appear to need a house with three bedrooms, as she lives there alone with her son. If the house is sold, she will have between £105,000 and £145,000. Those figures are based on the value of the house; I currently have evidence of a value between £190,000 and £240,000.

Fourthly, TMC also contend that if Mrs Shaire stayed in the house she should   *g* have to pay not only the instalments on the Chase mortgage, but also a fair sum to compensate TMC for being kept out of any benefit from its quarter share in the house, and that, in light of the evidence she has given as to her means, she could not pay.

So far as Mrs Shaire's son, Adam, is concerned, he is earning and of age, and his   *h* interest, argue TMC (to my mind quite rightly), is not something which I should take into account.

So far as Mrs Shaire is concerned, she says, perfectly reasonably, that she does not want to leave the house. It has been her home since 1976 with Mr Shaire, then on her own, then with Mr Fox and now again on her own. She has 75% of the equity in the house as against TMC's 25%, and therefore she says that her wishes should   *j* be given greater weight. She contends that she has perfectly satisfactorily, albeit with the assistance of the Department of Social Security, been meeting payments due under the subrogated Chase mortgage. She also has some earnings, and says she could earn more, from her job in the chemist's shop; that she has some money from a PEP and that, consistent with my view that he is a generous man, Mr Shaire has been giving her assistance.

a Mr Asif made three points which do not impress me. First, that TMC are more to blame than Mrs Shaire for the present situation because they delayed in proceeding with this case. I think that Mrs Shaire and TMC are both victims of Mr Fox's deception. Secondly, delay. Although there are grounds for thinking that TMC did delay unreasonably, albeit that there may be an explanation, I would have thought that the disadvantage that that produced, in the sense of further interest accruing, has been very much more than offset by the fact that the house must have

b appreciated in value substantially over the past few years. Thirdly, it is said that I should take into account the fact that TMC's ultimate interest is financial, and that, if it is worse off as a result of any order I make, it will recover from the solicitors. I do not regard that as a good argument. It seems to me that, although not precisely the same, it is similar to the position if TMC had mortgage insurance. It is res inter

c alios acta and should not be, indeed cannot be, taken into account, when considering what is the correct order to make as between Mrs Shaire and TMC.

Quite apart from this, although the solicitors in each case have been constrained by decisions of the Court of Appeal to accept liability, it may be that they will successfully avoid liability in the House of Lords. Neither decision of the Court of

d Appeal upon which TMC relies against the solicitors is without critics, and it is not inconceivable that either or both decisions will be disapproved in the House of Lords if and when they are considered there.

To my mind, for Mrs Shaire to have to leave her home of nearly a quarter of a century would be a real and significant hardship, but not an enormous one. She would have a substantial sum that she could put towards a smaller home. Even if

e Adam continued to live with her, she would only need a two-bedroom house. On the other hand, I have no evidence as to what properties might be available for the sort of money which she would be able to pay. For TMC to be locked into a quarter of the equity in a property would be a significant disadvantage unless they had a proper return and a proper protection so far as insurance and repair is concerned.

f It seems to me that if (a) TMC can be protected by sorting out the equitable interest providing for a proper return and ensuring that the house is repaired and insured, and (b) Mrs Shaire can really pay a proper return, it would be right to refuse to make an order for possession and sale primarily because Mrs Shaire has a valid interest in remaining in the house and has a 75% interest in it, and because TMC is

g ultimately in the business of lending money on property in return for being paid interest.

What is suggested in relation to the 25% interest is either that Mrs Shaire is ordered to pay 3% pa on the value of that 25% interest based on the reasoning of the Court of Appeal in cases such as *Roberts v Johnstone* [1989] QB 878 at 892–893, [1988] 3 WLR 1247 at 1257–1258 as suggested by Mr Asif, or a quarter of the rental

h value of the house based on the fair rent of the house, in line with the approach of the Court of Appeal in *Dennis v McDonald* [1982] 1 All ER 590, [1982] Fam 63. I do not find either course entirely satisfactory. It seems to me that the first course would be quite unfair on TMC and that the suggested analogy with *Roberts'* case is not sound. Landlords of residential property would not regard themselves as

j having a satisfactory return if it were based on the sort of approach in *Roberts'* case. In any event, whichever of the two options one takes, TMC is not in the business of owning shares in property; it is in the business of lending on property.

An idea which attracts me is that put forward by Mr Lawrence on behalf of the solicitors, and accepted by Mr Harry, if there is no order for sale. This idea is that the house is valued at a specific figure (rather than the range I have mentioned) and that TMC is effectively taken out by having its equity converted into loan, and

Mrs Shaire then has to pay interest on that loan. In my judgment, unless Mrs Shaire is in a position to agree that course and to meet the payments which that course would involve, I would not be prepared to refuse the order for sale. If she is prepared to agree that course and she is in a position to meet the repayments as and when they fall due, then I would be prepared to refuse an order for sale.

To go into a little more detail, what the course would involve would be as follows. One would have to value the house; TMC's share would be worth a quarter of that value. The beneficial interest would then be vested in Mrs Shaire alone and TMC's mortgage would be increased from the 75% of the subrogated Chase mortgage to take into account the additional 25% of the value of property. Mrs Shaire would then have to pay interest on the Chase mortgage by reference, I think, to Chase rates of interest. On the 25% converted loan she would have to pay interest which, to my mind, should be 3% above an appropriate bank base rate. It seems to me it would be wrong for her to pay interest at base rate or lower. She clearly could not borrow at that level. On the other hand, because of the special facts of this case, I believe that she should not be paying at a rate which was TMC's normal market rate.

If, on reflection, this would involve Mrs Shaire taking on a liability she cannot meet, or if TMC satisfied me that this is a liability that Mrs Shaire could not fairly meet, then I do not think it would be right to refuse an order for sale. It seems to me that the furthest I can go to help Mrs Shaire, if I can put it that way, is to make an order in the terms I have indicated. If TMC cannot enjoy such terms, then I think, bearing in mind that the hardship on Mrs Shaire would not be enormous, it would be wrong for me to refuse an order for sale. If I make an order along the lines I have indicated and Mrs Shaire is currently in a position to pay interest but subsequently fails to do so for any reason, then TMC would have the right to apply for an order to me seeking sale of the property in these proceedings rather than having to start originating proceedings.

I appreciate that this leaves matters slightly up in the air, but I do not believe that I should make an order without a little more information. At the risk of adding further to the time and costs of this case, I would rather make the order on the basis of the parties having an opportunity to consider my conclusions, work out their consequences and, if necessary, argue about their consequences.

One final point. If TMC decide, in light of what I have said and in light of what Mrs Shaire says, to press for an order for possession now, then it seems to me that both TMC and Mrs Shaire would be very well advised to file evidence, as to the type of property which might be available to Mrs Shaire, and as to the money which would be realised on the sale of the house.

Judgment accordingly. Mrs Shaire to have 80% of her costs.

Celia Fox   Barrister.

a

Friend v Civil Aviation Authority
[2001] EWCA Civ 1204

COURT OF APPEAL, CIVIL DIVISION
SIMON BROWN, CHADWICK AND TUCKEY LJJ
b   17, 18 JULY 2001

Estoppel – Issue estoppel – Issue – Relationship between employer and employee breaking down over dispute about safety of instructions given to employee – Employee being dismissed and complaining of unfair dismissal on procedural grounds – Industrial tribunal upholding complaint but awarding no compensation after concluding that
c   *employee's conduct contributing 100% to dismissal – Employee bringing action based on safety issues against employer for damages arising from his dismissal – Whether tribunal's earlier decision giving rise to issue estoppel in respect of subject matter of employee's action – Employment Protection (Consolidation) Act 1978, s 74(1), (6).*

d   F, a former pilot of fixed-wing aircraft, was employed by the Civil Aviation Authority (CAA) as a flight operations inspector. He was subsequently transferred to a different group, the operating standards appraisal programme. In the latter capacity, he was required to take part in helicopter inspections to ensure compliance with safety standards. F objected to participating in such inspections on the ground that the inspection team did not include a helicopter pilot, which
e   he maintained was essential for reasons of safety. F's view, which was not shared by his senior officers, was the source of growing friction, and he was eventually dismissed. F brought industrial tribunal proceedings for unfair dismissal, based solely on allegations of procedural unfairness. The tribunal upheld F's complaint, and then considered the amount of any compensatory award under s 74[a] of the
f   Employment Protection (Consolidation) Act 1978 (now s 123 of the Employment Rights Act 1996). Section 74(1) provided that the amount of a compensatory award was to be such amount as the tribunal considered just and equitable in all the circumstances, having regard to the loss sustained by the complainant in consequence of the dismissal in so far as that loss was attributable to action taken by the employer. Where, however, the tribunal had found that the dismissal was
g   to any extent caused or contributed to by any action of the complainant, s 74(6) required it to reduce the amount of the compensatory award by such proportion as it considered just and equitable, having regard to that finding. The tribunal concluded that the manner in which F had pursued the matter had inevitably led to the situation whereby he could no longer continue to be employed by the
h   CAA, that he had contributed 100% to his dismissal and that in those circumstances there would be no compensatory award. On appeal to the Employment Appeal Tribunal (EAT), F alleged for the first time in the proceedings that the CAA had embarked on a deliberate campaign of harassment and victimisation against him for refusing to put helicopter safety in jeopardy,
j   and that it had sought to coerce him into complying with unreasonable and unlawful instructions (the safety issue). The EAT dismissed the appeal, holding, inter alia, that the safety issue could not be raised on appeal because it had not been put before the tribunal. Subsequently, F brought an action against the CAA for malicious falsehood, conspiracy, breach of contract and inducing breach of

---

a   Section 74, so far as material, is set out at [33], [36], below

contract (the 1996 action). In that action, he sought to have the safety issue
adjudicated upon and claimed damages of up to £1m for the loss of his
employment. The CAA applied for the 1996 action to be struck out on the
ground of issue estoppel. It contended that, since the tribunal had decided that
F's conduct was entirely the cause of his own dismissal, no conduct on behalf of
the CAA had caused or contributed to that dismissal, and that accordingly any
damage resulting from his dismissal had been caused by F himself, not the CAA
or its employees. That contention was accepted by the judge who duly struck out
the claim. F appealed.

Held – Although the concept of issue estoppel was a useful tool, to which the
court could have recourse in order to prevent issues being relitigated in
circumstances in which to relitigate them would be abusive, it had to be used
with caution. Before a claimant was prevented from bringing his claim before the
court on the ground of issue estoppel, the court had to be satisfied after careful
examination of all the circumstances that the issue on which he had to succeed in
the claim he was seeking to bring was indeed the same issue that had been
considered and decided in earlier proceedings. That test had not been met in the
instant case as the tribunal had never considered or decided the safety issue. Set
in its statutory framework, a decision under s 74(6) of the 1978 Act that the
complainant's conduct had contributed to his dismissal, and that it would be just
and equitable to reduce compensation by 100%, could not be regarded as a
decision that the loss about which F complained in the 1996 action had not been
caused by any of the actions on the part of the CAA, or its employees, of which
he had complained in his statement of claim. A tribunal should not embark on a
consideration of the questions posed by s 74(6) unless it had satisfied itself, under
s 74(1), that some part of the loss sustained by the complainant in consequence of
his dismissal was attributable to action taken by the employer. It was not
surprising that the tribunal had concluded that F had pursued the matter in a way
that inevitably led to a situation in which he could no longer continue to be
employed by the CAA, but that decision implied no judgment on the lawfulness
or otherwise of the instructions that he had received. Nor did the case fall within
the *Henderson v Henderson* form of estoppel. Accordingly, the appeal would be
allowed (see [18]–[21], [24], [37], [40]–[44], below).

Henderson v Henderson [1843–1860] All ER Rep 378 distinguished.

Johnson v Gore Wood & Co (a firm) [2001] 1 All ER 481 considered.

Notes

For issue estoppel and for contributory fault in respect of unfair dismissal, see
respectively 16 *Halsbury's Laws* (4th edn reissue) para 953 and 16 *Halsbury's Laws*
(4th edn) (2000 reissue) para 532.

Section 74 of the Employment Protection (Consolidation) Act 1978 has been
replaced by s 123 of the Employment Rights Act 1996. For s 123, see 16 *Halsbury's
Statutes* (4th edn) (2000 reissue) 727.

Cases referred to in judgments

Arnold v National Westminster Bank plc [1991] 3 All ER 41, [1991] 2 AC 93, [1991]
2 WLR 1177, HL.

Gibson v British Transport Docks Board [1982] IRLR 228, EAT.

Henderson v Henderson (1843) 3 Hare 100, [1843–1860] All ER Rep 378, 13 ER 301.

Johnson v Gore Wood & Co (a firm) [2001] 1 All ER 481, [2001] 2 WLR 72, HL.

a Kumchyk v Derby City Council [1978] ICR 1116, EAT.
Malik v Bank of Credit and Commerce International SA (in liq), Mahmud v Bank of
   Credit and Commerce International SA (in liq) [1997] 3 All ER 1, [1998] AC 20,
   [1997] 3 WLR 95, HL.
Thoday v Thoday [1964] 1 All ER 341, [1964] P 181, [1964] 2 WLR 371, CA.

b **Cases also cited or referred to in skeleton arguments**
Allders International Ltd v Parkins [1981] IRLR 68, EAT.
Ashingdane v UK (1985) 7 EHRR 528, [1985] ECHR 8225/78, ECt HR.
Ashmore v British Coal Corp [1990] 2 All ER 981, [1990] 2 QB 338, CA.
Barber v Staffordshire CC [1996] 2 All ER 748, CA.
Barrow v Bankside Members Agency Ltd [1996] 1 All ER 981, [1996] 1 WLR 257, CA.
c Brown v Stott (Procurator Fiscal, Dunfermline) [2001] 2 All ER 97, [2001] 2 WLR 817, PC.
Chatterton v Secretary of State for India in Council [1895] 2 QB 189, [1895–9] All ER
   Rep 1035, CA.
Christy (Thomas) Ltd (in liq), Re [1994] 2 BCLC 527.
Dawkins v Lord Paulet (1869) LR 5 QB 94.
d Delcourt v Belgium (1970) 1 EHRR 355, [1970] ECHR 2689/65, ECt HR.
Divine-Bortey v Brent LBC [1998] ICR 886, CA.
Dowson v Queen (1981) 124 DLR (3d) 260, Can Fed Ct.
Fayed v Al-Tajir [1987] 2 All ER 396, [1988] QB 712, CA.
Fayed v UK (1994) 18 EHRR 393, [1994] ECHR 17101/90, ECt HR.
Fidelitas Shipping Co Ltd v V/O Exportchleb [1965] 2 All ER 4, [1966] 1 QB 630, CA.
e Friend v Institution of Professional Managers and Specialists [1999] IRLR 173.
Galoo Ltd (in liq) v Bright Grahame Murray (a firm) [1995] 1 All ER 16, [1994] 1 WLR
   1360, CA.
Golder v UK (1975) 1 EHRR 524, [1975] ECHR 4451/70, ECt HR.
Green v Hampshire CC [1979] ICR 861.
f Greig v Insole [1978] 3 All ER 449, [1978] 1 WLR 302.
Grovit v Doctor [1997] 2 All ER 417, [1997] 1 WLR 640, HL.
H v UK (1985) 45 DR 281, E Com HR.
Hancock v Doncaster Metropolitan BC [1998] ICR 900, EAT.
Hollier v Plysu [1983] IRLR 260, CA.
Hunter v Chief Constable of the West Midlands [1981] 3 All ER 727, [1982] AC 529, HL.
g Isaacs (M) & Sons Ltd v Cook [1925] 2 KB 391.
James v UK (1986) 8 EHRR 123, [1986] ECHR 8793/79, ECt HR.
Joyce v Sengupta [1993] 1 All ER 897, [1993] 1 WLR 337, CA.
Ladd v Marshall [1954] 3 All ER 745, [1954] 1 WLR 1489, CA.
Lonrho plc v Fayed (No 2) [1991] 4 All ER 961, [1992] 1 WLR 1.
h Lonhro plc v Fayed (No 5) [1994] 1 All ER 188, [1993] 1 WLR 1489, CA.
Mahon v Rahn (No 2) [2000] 4 All ER 41, [2000] 1 WLR 2150, CA.
Mallenash Ltd v Hussein (12 October 1998, unreported), EAT.
Mann v O'Neill (1997) 191 CLR 204, Aust HC.
Manson v Vooght [1999] BPIR 376, CA.
j McCarthy v City of Regina (1921) 60 DLR 205, Sask KB.
Merricks v Nott-Bower [1964] 1 All ER 717, [1965] 1 QB 57, CA.
Nelson v BBC (No 2) [1980] ICR 110, CA.
O'Laoire v Jackel International Ltd [1991] ICR 718, CA.
Osman v UK (1998) 5 BHRC 293, ECt HR.
Parker Foundry Ltd v Slack [1992] ICR 302, CA.
Peerless Bakery Ltd v Watts [1955] NZLR 339, NZ SC and CA.

Reichel v Magrath (1889) 14 App Cas 665, HL.
Richards v Naum [1966] 3 All ER 812, [1967] 1 QB 620, CA.
Stephenson v Garnett [1898] 1 QB 677, CA.
Szalatnay-Stacho v Fink [1946] 2 All ER 231, [1947] KB 1, CA.
Taylor v Serious Fraud Office [1998] 4 All ER 801, [1999] 2 AC 177, HL.
Tinnelly & Sons Ltd v UK [1998] 4 BHRC 393, ECt HR.
Tolstoy v UK (1995) 20 EHRR 442, [1995] ECHR 18139/91, ECt HR.
Turner v London Transport Executive [1977] ICR 952, CA.
X v Sweden (1982) 31 DR 223, E Com HR.

a

b

Appeal

The appellant claimant, Brian Leonard Friend, appealed with permission of Brooke LJ granted on 22 February 2001 from the decision of Sir Oliver Popplewell, sitting as a deputy judge of the High Court, on 21 December 2000 whereby he (i) struck out on the grounds of issue estoppel the appellant's action (the 1996 action) for malicious falsehood, conspiracy, breach of contract and inducing breach of contract against the respondent defendants, the Civil Aviation Authority (the CAA), Kenneth J Anderson, John G Impriss, Patricia A Richardson, John E Page, John W Saull and Russell Williams, and (ii) struck out on the grounds of absolute privilege, alternatively abuse of process, the appellant's action for defamation against the CAA (the 1997 action). The facts are set out in the judgment of Simon Brown LJ.

c

d

Paul Garlick QC and Nathan Tavares (instructed by Baker & Duke, Ilminster) for the appellant in the 1996 action.
The appellant in person in the 1997 action.
Patrick Moloney QC and Andrew Tabachnik (instructed by Rupert Britton, Head of the Civil Aviation Authority Legal Department) for the respondents.

e

f

SIMON BROWN LJ.

[1] Captain Brian Leonard Friend appeals with the permission of Brooke LJ against the order of Sir Oliver Popplewell, sitting as a deputy High Court judge on 21 December 2000, striking out two actions (which I shall call respectively the 1996 action and the 1997 action) brought against the Civil Aviation Authority (the CAA) and, in the case of the 1996 action, also against a number of their senior employees, following upon Captain Friend's employment by the CAA between April 1987 and March 1993. The 1996 action, which is for malicious falsehood, conspiracy, breach of contract and inducing breach of contract, was struck out on the ground that it was barred by issue estoppel following upon a 1994 industrial tribunal decision on the appellant's complaint of unfair dismissal. The 1997 action, a claim for defamation, was struck out on the ground of absolute privilege, alternatively as an abuse of process.

g

h

[2] The appellant is represented by counsel, Mr Paul Garlick QC and Mr Tavares, in the 1996 action but not in the 1997 action.

[3] Although the papers in the case are voluminous (the dispute between the parties having ranged far and wide over many years and involved several other actions), the background to the present appeal can be briefly stated. The CAA is a statutory corporation created by the Civil Aviation Act 1971 which, by reason of s 3 of the Civil Aviation Act 1982, is concerned with the regulation and safety of air transport. The appellant is a former Royal Navy and airline pilot, whose

j

a   initial employment with the CAA was as a flight operations inspector (FOI) but who was then transferred to a different group, the operating standards appraisal programme (OSAP). In this latter capacity he was required to take part in helicopter inspections to ensure compliance with safety standards. He strongly objected to this on the ground that the inspection team did not include a helicopter pilot, which he maintained was essential for reasons of safety.

b   [4] Sir Oliver Popplewell spoke of the appellant's 'unswerving view ... that to require him, who was a fixed-wing pilot to monitor the safety of helicopters was an unsafe practice, resulting in a large number of fatalities'. This vehemently and repeatedly expressed view was not shared by his senior officers at the CAA and was the source of acute and growing friction between them. Such was the

c   strength of Captain Friend's expression of his views that a formal complaint was laid before the CAA's internal disciplinary panel, contending that his conduct in the course of his employment had disrupted his working relationship with his colleagues. After a four-day hearing, ending on 1 October 1992, the panel recommended that the complaint be dismissed. They held that, while good relations between the appellant and his managers had broken down, the fault was

d   not clearly attributable to one side and they recommended that he and another senior manager should work together on a rehabilitation programme. The panel's recommendations were rejected by the head of the operating standards division, Mr Saull, and in the result the appellant was dismissed by letter dated 1 December 1992.

e   [5] Having failed in two internal appeals brought under the CAA's disciplinary procedure, the appellant then complained to an industrial tribunal (IT) (as I shall continue call it, although of course it is now renamed an employment tribunal). The complaint was one of unfair dismissal and was based solely on allegations of procedural unfairness. Following a six-day hearing in May 1994 the IT, by their

f   decision dated 22 June 1994, upheld the appellant's contention that he had been unfairly dismissed due to a number of procedural shortcomings, but went on to hold that he had contributed 100% to his dismissal. They said that it was clear from the evidence and the documents which the IT had seen that he had pursued his grievance as to the constitution and the procedures of inspection teams in a

g   way and to an extent that inevitably led to the situation whereby he could no longer continue to be employed by the CAA. The IT also noted that he himself had accepted in evidence that trust had broken down irretrievably. As a result, applying s 74(6) of the Employment Protection (Consolidation) Act 1978, they concluded that it would not be appropriate to make any award of compensation.

h   [6] The appellant appealed to the Employment Appeal Tribunal (the EAT) and sought before it to pursue his complaint about the safety aspects of the inspection procedures. In reply to the CAA's pleaded case before the IT that he had contributed to his own dismissal, the appellant had put in a 76-page document making his detailed case on the safety issue and further contending that the CAA

j   had embarked on a deliberate campaign of harassment and victimisation against him for refusing to put helicopter safety in jeopardy, and had sought to coerce him into complying with their unreasonable and unlawful instructions. That case, however, ('the safety case', as it came to be called) had not been heard by the IT and this it was that decided the EAT to refuse to allow it to be advanced on appeal.

[7] In giving the judgment of the EAT on 24 July 1995, Tuckey J, as he then was, said:

'In his IT1 [his claim form to the IT] Captain Friend only complained of procedural unfairness. He has told us that in subsequent correspondence he made it clear to the tribunal that he was contending (among other things) that the instructions that he had been given by the CAA were unlawful because it was necessary, as a matter of law, for helicopters to be inspected in the way that he was saying they should be. This is what has been called the safety case. Captain Friend also told us that in the run-up to the hearing he attempted to obtain witness orders from the tribunal which were directed to proving that the instructions he had received were unlawful. But at the hearing before the industrial tribunal where he was represented by counsel and solicitors Captain Friend's case was expressly limited to one of procedural unfairness. So the tribunal were not concerned with the safety case and it is apparent from the reasons which they gave for their decision that they did not address that issue. The respondents object to the "safety case" being resurrected before us on the well known grounds set out in *Kumchyk v Derby City Council* [1978] ICR 1116. The passage often cited in decisions of this tribunal is to be found at 1123–1124. Usually, this appeal tribunal will not hear new points. It will certainly not hear new points which would require further findings of fact to be made if they are to be resolved. Here the respondents say that this is a new point; that it is a point which requires much further evidence before it could be resolved and, therefore, it is not open to Captain Friend to raise the safety case before us on appeal. We agree.'

[8] In seeking permission to appeal from that decision to the Court of Appeal the appellant again sought to pursue the safety issue but again was refused permission to do so. In dismissing the application on 22 February 1996 Waite LJ, with whom Millett LJ agreed, said:

'Turning finally to the proposed main ground of appeal, the sole basis for it is Captain Friend's frequently repeated complaint that he was not allowed to bring onto the stage of the industrial tribunal hearing the merits of the helicopter safety issue. It is obviously a topic on which he feels strongly. I have not the least doubt myself, having listened to all he has had to say to us and having read all that is relevant in the substantial body of documents he has laid before us for the purpose of these applications, that he sincerely holds the opinion that if this issue had been allowed to have been investigated his own views would have emerged as fully vindicated, and that the views of others would have been found to be lax and ill-informed. The question for the industrial tribunal, however, was not whether he was right or wrong, reasonable or unreasonable, in the views he expressed; but whether his way of expressing them, and the steps he took, or omitted to take, as a means of emphasising them, amounted to action which caused or contributed to his dismissal for the purposes of s 74(6) of the Employment Protection (Consolidation) Act 1978. The industrial tribunal had every justification, in my view, for adopting the attitude that for the purpose of answering that question it was unnecessary to enlarge the ambit of an already long hearing by going into the rights and wrongs of the controversy engendered by the helicopter safety issue.'

a   **[9]** The 1996 action followed. Deploying a variety of causes of action, the appellant is striving finally to have the safety issue adjudicated on and (if he succeeds upon it) to recover substantial damages, claimed at up to £1m, for the loss of his employment by the CAA. It is this case, however, which the respondents contend and the judge below held is now barred on the ground of issue estoppel as a result of the IT's determination. Having concluded as they did that the cause

b   of the appellant's dismissal was entirely his own conduct, it follows, submits Mr Moloney QC for the respondent, that no conduct on behalf of the CAA or its employees caused or contributed to that dismissal, and consequently that all damages resulting from the dismissal resulted not from anything done by the CAA or its employees but, on the contrary, was entirely caused by the appellant's own behaviour.

c   **[10]** This argument, which was accepted below, was effective to dispose of the 1996 action in all its various manifestations. It defeated all the claims in tort, advanced variously by way of conspiracy, inducing breach of contract and malicious falsehood, because damage is an essential element of each, and damage was the one thing that the IT had decided the appellant could not prove to have been

d   caused other than by his own conduct. True, s 3 of the Defamation Act 1952 provides:

'(1) In an action for ... malicious falsehood, it shall not be necessary to allege or prove special damage—(a) if the words upon which the action is founded are calculated to cause pecuniary damage to the plaintiff and are

e   published in writing or other permanent form ...'

[11] But, the judge held, the claim for malicious falsehood amounts effectively to a claim for damages arising from the appellant's dismissal and, this issue having been determined by the IT in favour of the CAA, the published words were not calculated (that is, likely) to cause the appellant pecuniary damage, so that s 3

f   could not in the event avail him.

[12] As for the claims made in the 1996 action against the personal defendants, albeit strictly the plea of issue estoppel could not arise since they were not themselves directly party to the IT proceedings (although three of them gave evidence to the IT), these claims clearly involved a collateral attack on the IT's decision and thus on the authorities constituted a plain abuse of process.

g   **[13]** For my part I have not the least doubt that the judge was correct in all these conclusions, provided only and always that he was right to accept that the IT had, as the judge put it in his judgment, 'clearly concluded that the cause of the dismissal was entirely the claimant's fault and that no responsibility in any shape or form lies on the CAA'. That then is the crucial issue on this appeal: is

h   this truly a case of issue estoppel? Mr Moloney submits that it is. Indeed he describes it as 'a pure, classic substantive issue estoppel'. The IT, he argues, decided as between the same parties, Captain Friend and the CAA, precisely the same issue as the appellant now seeks to have litigated afresh in his 1996 action; the issue as to who caused the appellant's dismissal and his consequential loss

j   and, more particularly, as to whether the employers' conduct played any part in it. The IT's decision, he submits, is fatal to the appellant's proposed civil claim on the issue of causation. Only by seeking to impeach the IT's conclusion that the appellant contributed 100% to his own dismissal can the appellant hope to succeed in his 1996 action, and that he is not allowed to do. Mr Moloney characterises the argument as one of 'brutal simplicity but irresistible logic'. This was the argument that came to be accepted below.

[14] Sir Oliver Popplewell noted the appellant's submission that the proceedings before the IT had been 'simply confined to procedural matters' but rejected it: 'This I fear is wholly to misunderstand the nature of the proceedings before the IT.' He said:

> 'The issues which this industrial tribunal had to consider were firstly whether there had been a dismissal and that was plainly not in dispute and secondly whether it was fair and thirdly, if it were unfair, whether the amount of compensation should be affected by the conduct of the claimant.'

[15] The judge then set out ss 73(7) and 74(1) and (6) of the 1978 Act, which I do not propose to repeat. He continued:

> 'Thus a finding of unfair dismissal by a tribunal does not bring the proceedings to an end. The other part of the equation is to consider compensation either as a basic award or compensatory award, which is subject to a reduction, having regard to the claimant's conduct. The burden is on the CAA to show that the dismissal was fair and they were entitled to say and were saying (as many other employers said) that even if the procedure was unfair it "would have made no difference". The "would have made no difference" argument was a regular one and necessarily required the tribunal to look at all the circumstances relating to the conduct of the employee.'

[16] A little later he said:

> '[The IT] were not concerned with the safety issue, which it was impossible for them to resolve. They were, however, plainly concerned with the conduct of the claimant. It had been raised by the CAA, it was a necessary inquiry into the reason for dismissal and before making any deduction in the award, it was necessary for them to hear evidence and effectively to make findings. Six working days in a case as comparatively simple as this, showed that the tribunal had investigated the relevant issues in very considerable detail. To make a finding of 100% contribution against a claimant was, in my experience [Sir Oliver Popplewell was a past President of the EAT], a very rare occurrence and this view was expressed in a number of authorities.'

[17] The judge then considered the authorities, both as to the nature of the conduct on the part of an employee apt to justify a reduction in his compensation (including, one may note, 'bloody-mindedness') and as to what is required to support a finding of 100% contribution. Such a finding, said Browne-Wilkinson J, as the then President of the EAT in *Gibson v British Transport Docks Board* [1982] IRLR 228 at 232 (para 30), could not in that case be justified since the complainant's conduct was not 'the sole cause of the dismissal'. Logically, runs the respondent's argument, it must follow that the determination of 100% contribution carries with it a finding that the employee's conduct is the sole effective cause of dismissal.

[18] Ably though the argument was advanced, and persuasively though at first blush the judgment below reads, to my mind it just cannot be right. One central difficulty it faces is how to reconcile, on the one hand, the judge's conclusion that the appellant's contention that the IT had been purely concerned with procedural matters was wholly to misunderstand the nature of IT proceedings with, on the other hand, the EAT's reasoning, supported by the Court of Appeal, that the IT hearing had indeed been expressly limited to procedural unfairness and the

a IT had simply not been concerned with the safety issue. In this regard Waite LJ's words are worth repeating:

'The question for the industrial tribunal, however, was not whether he was right or wrong, reasonable or unreasonable, in the views he expressed; but whether his way of expressing them, and the steps he took, or omitted to take, as a means of emphasising them amounted to action which caused or
b contributed to his dismissal for the purposes of s 74(6) of the Employment Protection (Consolidation) Act 1978.'

[19] The Court of Appeal in the unfair dismissal proceedings took the view that it was unnecessary to decide who was right on the safety issue and whether, therefore, the CAA were acting unlawfully in requiring the appellant to participate
c in what he strongly maintained were unsafe inspection procedures. This view to my mind necessarily postulates that in applying the contribution/reduction provisions of the 1978 Act, the IT was concerned only with the complainant's conduct immediately precipitating the dismissal, and not at all with the employer's conduct, quite possibly itself tortious or in breach of contract, which
d may have led the complainant to act as he did. Certainly it would seem to me quite impossible to say of any court that comes to hear the 1996 action, as Waite LJ was saying of the IT, that it would be irrelevant for it to address the question whether the appellant was right or wrong, reasonable or unreasonable in the view he held and expressed on the helicopter safety issue. Rather this issue would lie at the very heart of the claim for wrongful, as opposed to unfair,
e dismissal. If the appellant could prove in his civil action that he was being unlawfully instructed to carry out unsafe procedures, that must inevitably affect the court's reaction to his attitude and behaviour whilst refusing to be coerced into such action, for example his bloody-mindedness. It is one thing to say that the appellant's conduct contributed 100% to the dismissal, in so far as his
f complaint is merely that it was unfairly effected—that is, procedurally unfair. It is quite another thing to say that this conclusion applies equally to the appellant's substantive complaint that it was his employer's breach of contract in requiring him to work unlawfully which in reality underlay the breakdown of their relationship and ultimately made his dismissal, whether it be viewed as actual or constructive, inevitable. True, as the IT's determination noted, 'the appellant
g himself accepted that trust had broken down irretrievably'. That, however, said nothing as to where the blame for that breakdown lay.

[20] It is plain beyond argument that the IT never did consider the safety issue, including therefore whether the appellant was being required to follow unsafe procedures. If this issue was not considered, by definition it cannot have been
h decided. If it was not litigated and decided, then it cannot properly be the subject of issue estoppel strictly so called. The highest the respondents' case could then be put would be that the issue should have been pursued before the IT but was not. Some hint of that indeed is to be found in the judgment below:

<blockquote>

j 'It necessarily follows in my judgment from the finding of 100% contribution, that the allegations of victimisation etc, if raised before the industrial tribunal, had been rejected by them or if not afford the claimant no assistance; see *Henderson v Henderson* (1843) 3 Hare 100 at 114, [1843–1860] All ER Rep 378 at 381, per Wigram V-C.'

</blockquote>

[21] To my mind, however, the *Henderson v Henderson* form of estoppel could not possibly run in the circumstances of the present case. The words already

quoted from Waite LJ's judgment in the Court of Appeal sufficiently indicate that
the appellant and/or his then advisors cannot properly be criticised for failing to
urge yet more strongly that they be allowed to canvas the safety issue before the
IT. The recent decision of the House of Lords in *Johnson v Gore Wood & Co (a firm)*
[2001] 1 All ER 481, [2001] 2 WLR 72 cautions against too ready an application of
the *Henderson v Henderson* principle to stifle legitimate claims on abuse of process
grounds. I have no doubt that to prevent the appellant yet again from ventilating
his case on the safety issue, including the contention that it was his justifiable
stance upon this which ultimately led to his dismissal, would work injustice
rather than justice, and cannot therefore be permitted.

[22] None of this, of course, is to say that the appellant will in the end succeed
in his 1996 action. He may or he may not. The respondents accept neither the
sincerity nor the merits of his objections to the OSAP system. They suggest that
his real objection to his transfer to OSAP duties was that it severely disrupted his
existing domestic arrangements, and they contend that his stated objections to
the system are based on a wilful misunderstanding of the different roles of OSAP
and FOI inspections in achieving safety. None of that, however, is for decision on
this appeal. For the purposes of the present strike out proceedings the appellant
must be assumed to have a worthwhile case on the merits.

[23] Having indicated at the conclusion of the argument on the 1996 action
that we proposed to allow that part of the appeal, we suggested that in those
circumstances Captain Friend might think it unprofitable to pursue his appeal
with regard to the subsequent 1997 libel action, an action which in any event
appeared to us to face very real difficulties. The appellant readily, and, as I think,
wisely, indicated that (subject only to further appeal by the respondent) he no
longer sought the reinstatement of that separate action. I need accordingly say
no more about it.

[24] In the event I would allow the appeal to the extent of reinstating the 1996
action.

CHADWICK LJ.

[25] The issue on this appeal is whether the statement of claim in proceedings
brought by the appellant, Captain Brian Friend, against the Civil Aviation
Authority (the CAA) and others should be struck out, and the action dismissed,
on the ground that the claim has no reasonable prospects of success.

[26] The basis for the contention that the claim is bound to fail is that the
appellant cannot be permitted to attempt to establish an issue which is essential
to his cause of action in these proceedings—namely that the respondents'
conduct of which he complains was the cause of the loss which he seeks to
recover. It is said that that issue has already been decided against him in earlier
proceedings before an industrial tribunal.

[27] The principle relied upon by the respondents is that described by Diplock LJ,
in *Thoday v Thoday* [1964] 1 All ER 341 at 352, [1964] P 181 at 198, as 'issue estoppel'.
In *Arnold v National Westminster Bank plc* [1991] 3 All ER 41 at 47, [1991] 2 AC 93
at 105, Lord Keith of Kinkel put the point in these terms:

'Issue estoppel may arise where a particular issue forming a necessary
ingredient in a cause of action has been litigated and decided and in
subsequent proceedings between the same parties involving a different cause
of action to which the same issue is relevant one of the parties seeks to
reopen that issue.'

a The starting point, as it seems to me, is to identify the issue in the present proceedings in relation to which there is said to be an estoppel. These proceedings were commenced by the issue of a writ on 2 July 1996 under the reference 1996 F 428. A statement of claim, first served on 10 January 1997, was amended and re-served on 31 March 1999. At this stage of the proceedings it is to the amended statement of claim that the court must look in order to identify the issues which

b the appellant must establish in order to succeed in his action. In para 2 of the amended statement of claim, the appellant asserts that he was employed by the CAA from April 1987 until 1 March 1993 as a fixed-wing flight operations inspector. That is not in dispute. He goes on to set out certain of the terms of his employment contract—in particular those relating to disciplinary procedure. Paragraph 2A of the amended statement of claim contains an assertion that his contract of

c employment contained an implied term that the employer would not, without reasonable and proper cause, conduct itself in a manner calculated and likely to destroy or seriously damage the relationship of confidence and trust between itself and the appellant as its employee. It may be assumed that that allegation is based on the decision of the House of Lords in *Malik v Bank of Credit and*

d *Commerce International SA (in liq), Mahmud v Bank of Credit and Commerce International SA (in liq)* [1997] 3 All ER 1, [1998] AC 20 (see, in particular, the speech of Lord Nicholls of Birkenhead [1997] 3 All ER 1 at 4, 5, [1998] AC 20 at 33, 34). In paras 4 and 5 of the amended statement of claim the appellant alleges that, with effect from April 1990, he was required by his employer to carry out safety inspections of helicopters, in relation to which he had no experience or

e expertise; and that he objected to that. In para 6 he asserts that he was correct to refuse, on safety grounds, to comply with his employer's instructions to inspect helicopters; and that, in persisting in its instructions the CAA was in disregard of its statutory duties. As a result of his stance, as he says, complaints were made against him by his line managers. Disciplinary proceedings were instituted, which

f led to his dismissal on three months' notice, by letter dated 1 December 1992 (see paras 8 to 13 of the amended statement of claim). Paragraph 14 refers to subsequent proceedings before the industrial tribunal in which his dismissal was found to be unfair, on procedural grounds. No compensatory award was made to him on the grounds, as found by the tribunal, that his own contribution to his dismissal should be assessed at 100%. Paragraph 15 of the amended statement of claim

g contains specific complaints of bias against the sixth respondent, Mr John Saull, who had taken the decision to dismiss the appellant notwithstanding a recommendation to the contrary by the internal disciplinary panel of the CAA, and against the seventh respondent, Mr Russell Williams, who had made an adverse report about him. Paragraph 16 is in these terms:

h

'It is averred that the conspiracy, malicious falsehoods, breaches of contract and attempts to induce breaches of contract caused the plaintiff's dismissal and the industrial tribunal's finding of 100% contribution to dismissal. In making its said finding the industrial tribunal did not engage in any

j determination of the existence of any conspiracy or the cause or motivation behind it.'

[28] Paragraphs 17 and 18 set out, in some detail, particulars of the malicious falsehoods which are alleged to have been published by, amongst others, the sixth and seventh respondents. Paragraph 19 contains an allegation of malice; para 20, an allegation that the representations made were calculated to cause the appellant

pecuniary loss; and para 21, allegations of harassment and discrimination.
Paragraph 22 is in these terms, so far as material:

> 'The defendants in making the above representations and acting as referred
> to in paras 15 and 21 above were in breach of their contract terms ... in that
> such representations/actions had an adverse effect on their relationship with
> the plaintiff, was not maintaining a good relationship with the plaintiff and
> not an acceptable standard of conduct. Those actions/representations
> induced the first defendant's breach of contract with the plaintiff referred to
> in para 15 above the defendants all knowing of the plaintiff's contractual
> terms referred to above and acting as described deliberately to breach those
> terms.'

[29] Paragraph 22A of the amended statement of claim contains an allegation
that, further or in the alternative, the CAA was in breach of the implied term of
trust and confidence pleaded in para 2A and that, by their actions, the sixth and
seventh respondents procured or induced that breach. In para 23 it is alleged that,
'By reason of the matters aforesaid the plaintiff has suffered loss and damage'.
The particulars of loss alleged include loss of future income, loss of pension, loss
of reputation and a position of disadvantage on the labour market.

[30] The issue on which it is said that an estoppel arises by reason of the
finding by the industrial tribunal in the proceedings mentioned in para 14 of
the amended statement of claim was identified by Mr Moloney QC, counsel for
the respondents to this appeal, in these terms: 'What caused the claimant's
dismissal and consequent pecuniary loss?' The point had been put in much the
same terms at the hearing in the High Court before Sir Oliver Popplewell. It is
said that the effect of the industrial tribunal's decision to refuse a compensatory
award is that that issue has been decided against the appellant; in the sense that
the industrial tribunal has decided that his own conduct was the sole cause of his
dismissal. That submission was accepted by the judge.

[31] Before examining the decision of the industrial tribunal, it is convenient
to refer to the legislative framework within which that decision was reached.
The statute in force at the relevant time was the Employment Protection
(Consolidation) Act 1978. That Act has now been replaced by the Employment
Rights Act 1996, but the relevant provisions are substantially unchanged.
Section 54 of the 1978 Act conferred on an employee a statutory right not to be
unfairly dismissed by his employer. Section 57 set out the basis upon which the
question whether or not dismissal was unfair should be determined. It was for
the employer to show what was the reason for the dismissal; and to show either
that that was a reason which fell within s 57(2) or that it was some other reason
justifying dismissal of an employee holding the position which the employee
himself held. But that did not, of itself, resolve the question whether the dismissal
was unfair. The tribunal had to determine that matter in accordance with s 57(3)
of the 1978 Act. Those provisions are now contained in s 98(4) of the 1996 Act:

> 'Where the employer has fulfilled the requirements of subsection (1), the
> determination of the question whether the dismissal is fair or unfair (having
> regard to the reasons shown by the employer)—(a) depends on whether in
> the circumstances (including the size and administrative resources of the
> employer's undertaking) the employer acted reasonably or unreasonably in
> treating it as a sufficient reason for dismissing the employee, and (b) shall be
> determined in accordance with equity and the substantial merits of the case.'

a [32] 'Equity', in that context, is not used in any technical sense. It is plain, therefore, that the question whether or not a dismissal is unfair is not determined by a decision that the dismissal was not in breach of contract or otherwise wrongful. A dismissal which involves no breach of contract by the employer may still be unfair.

b [33] Where the tribunal finds that a complaint of unfair dismissal is well founded, it is required either to make an order for reinstatement or re-employment or (if it does not make such an order) to make an award of compensation for unfair dismissal (see s 68 of the 1978 Act, now re-enacted as s 112 of the 1996 Act). An amount of compensation for unfair dismissal is to consist of a basic award and a compensatory award (see s 72 of the 1978 Act, now s 118 of the 1996 Act). The compensatory award is to be calculated in accordance with s 74 of the 1978 Act,
c now s 123 of the 1996 Act. Section 74(1) of the 1978 Act was in these terms:

> 'Subject to sections 75 and 76, the amount of the compensatory award shall be such amount as the tribunal considers just and equitable in all the circumstances having regard to the loss sustained by the complainant in consequence of the dismissal in so far as that loss is attributable to action
d taken by the employer.'

[34] Section 75 imposed a financial limit on the amount of compensation which could be awarded to a claimant, including the amount by way of compensatory award. Section 76 contained provisions where the compensation fell to be awarded in respect of an act which would attract compensation, also, under the Sex
e Discrimination Act 1975 or the Race Relations Act 1976. Those statutes are not relevant in this context.

[35] Section 74(1) of the 1978 Act required the tribunal to identify what loss had been sustained by the complainant in consequence of the dismissal and whether any of that loss (and if so, what part of that loss) was attributable to
f action by the employer. It must be kept in mind that the exercise in which a tribunal is engaged under s 74 is the calculation of one element ('the compensatory award') in an award of compensation for unfair dismissal (see s 72 of the 1978 Act). It is, to my mind, plain that it is only if some part of the loss sustained in consequence of the dismissal—which, in this context, means the dismissal which has been found to be unfair—is attributable to action taken by the employer, that
g any amount can be awarded by way of compensatory award under s 74(1). If no part of the loss which the complainant has sustained in consequence of the dismissal is attributable to action taken by the employer, then s 74 is not engaged and the complainant is limited to the basic award, calculated under s 73.

[36] If the tribunal is satisfied that, prima facie, some amount is to be awarded
h by way of compensatory award under s 74(1) of the 1978 Act, then it is required to go on to consider whether the dismissal was, to any extent, caused or contributed to by any action of the complainant. It is required to do that by the provisions of s 74(6) of the 1978 Act, now re-enacted in s 123(6) of the 1996 Act. The subsection is in these terms:

j > 'Where the tribunal finds that the dismissal was to any extent caused or contributed to by any action of the complainant it shall reduce the amount of the compensatory award by such proportion as it considers just and equitable having regard to that finding.'

[37] That subsection requires the tribunal to address the questions: (i) whether or not the dismissal was to any extent caused or contributed to by any action of

the complainant; and if so, (ii) to what extent (if any) it is just and equitable to
reduce the amount of the compensatory award in the light of that finding. *a*
For the reasons that I have already sought to explain, it seems to me that the
tribunal is not required to (and should not) embark on a consideration of the
questions posed by s 74(6), unless it has satisfied itself, under s 74(1), that some
part of the loss sustained by the complainant in consequence of the dismissal is
attributable to action taken by the employer. It is for that reason, if for no other, *b*
that a decision that the reduction under s 74(6) should be 100% can be appropriate
only in exceptional circumstances. Such a decision requires the tribunal to satisfy
itself that, although some part of the loss sustained is attributable to action taken
by the employer, nevertheless the complainant's contribution to the dismissal
makes it just and equitable that he should receive no compensatory award.

[38] In the present case, the tribunal addressed the questions posed by s 74(6) *c*
of the 1978 Act, in a short passage which appears in its reasons and to which
Simon Brown LJ has already referred. The tribunal said: 'Having invited submissions
from counsel on the issue of contribution, we find that the applicant contributed
to his dismissal and assess that contribution as being 100%.'

[39] They went on to say that it was clear from the evidence and the *d*
documents that the appellant had pursued the matter in a way, and to an extent,
which must inevitably have led to the situation where he could no longer
continue to be employed by the respondents.

[40] In the circumstances set out in the statement of claim, it is a matter of no
surprise that the tribunal should come to the conclusion that the appellant had *e*
pursued the matter in a way which must inevitably have led to a situation in
which he could no longer continue to be employed by the respondents. An
employee, who takes the view, for reasons sincerely held, that what his employer
is requiring him to do is unsafe and unlawful, and who raises that contention
with the employer in forceful terms, makes it impossible, unless the employer
accepts the employee's contention, for the employment relationship to *f*
continue. If the employer does not accept the employee's contention, then the
employment relationship is inevitably doomed. The employee cannot continue
in an employment under which he refuses to comply with his employer's
instructions; nor can it be expected that he will comply with instructions which
he believes are unlawful and will lead to unsafe results. That implies no judgment
on the lawfulness or otherwise of the instructions. It does no more than recognise *g*
that, if the employee sincerely believes that the instructions are unlawful, the
employment will, inevitably, come to an end either by resignation or by dismissal.

[41] Set in its statutory framework, a decision under s 74(6) of the 1978 Act,
that the complainant's conduct contributed to his dismissal, and that it would be
just and equitable to reduce the amount of the compensatory award by 100% *h*
cannot be regarded as a decision that the loss about which the appellant
complains in these proceedings was not caused by any of the actions on the part
of the CAA, or of its employees, of which complaint is made in the statement of
claim.

[42] As has been said in earlier authority, the concept of 'issue estoppel' is a *j*
useful tool, to which the court can have recourse in order to prevent issues being
relitigated in circumstances in which to relitigate them would be abusive. But it
is a tool which must be used with caution. It is essential that, before a claimant is
prevented from bringing his claim before the court on the ground of issue estoppel,
the court must be satisfied after careful examination of all the circumstances that

a the issue on which he has to succeed in the claim which he seeks to bring is indeed the same issue as that which has been considered and decided in earlier proceedings.

[43] For the reasons given by Simon Brown LJ and for the reasons which I have sought to set out, I am satisfied that that test is not met in this case. The question whether or not the actions by the respondents of which Captain Friend complains

b in this action led to the loss which he asserts, in these proceedings, that he has suffered is not one which has already been determined against him. I too would allow this appeal.

TUCKEY LJ.

[44] I agree for the reasons given in both judgments that the appeal in the 1996

c action should be allowed.

Appeal allowed in the 1996 action. Appeal in the 1997 action withdrawn. Permission to appeal refused.

Dilys Tausz   Barrister.

R v Inland Revenue Commissioners, ex parte Newfields Developments Ltd

[2001] UKHL 27

HOUSE OF LORDS

LORD BINGHAM OF CORNHILL, LORD STEYN, LORD HOFFMANN, LORD COOKE OF THORNDON AND LORD SCOTT OF FOSCOTE

25, 26 APRIL, 23 MAY 2001

Income tax – Corporation tax – Small companies' relief – Associated company – Control – Attributions – Whether Revenue having to make statutory attributions if requisite conditions satisfied – Identification of requisite conditions – Income and Corporation Taxes Act 1988, ss 13, 416.

The issued share capital of the taxpayer company was held by the trustees of the will of W. Under the trusts of the will, W's widow had a life interest. As a result, she was a 'participator' in the taxpayer for the purposes of s 417(1)(c)[a] of the Income and Corporation Taxes Act 1988, and the trustees were her 'associates' within the meaning of s 417(3)(c). The trustees had power to 'control' the taxpayer within the definitions set out in s 416(2)[b] and (3) of the 1988 Act, while W's widow would be taken to have control of the taxpayer if that power were attributed to her under s 416(6). Subsection (6) provided that, for the purposes of sub-ss (2) and (3), 'there may also be attributed' to any person all the rights and powers of any company of which he had, or he and his associates had, control or any two or more such companies, or of any associate of his or of any two or more associates of his. In its concluding words, sub-s (6) further provided that 'such attributions shall be made under this subsection as will result in the company being treated as under the control of five or fewer participators if it can be so treated'. Subject to certain exceptions, a company that was under the control of five or fewer participators constituted a close company for the purposes of other provisions of the 1988 Act. The taxpayer claimed that it was entitled, under s 13[c] of the 1988 Act, to small companies' relief from corporation tax in respect of its profits for certain accounting periods. Its entitlement to relief depended upon whether another company, L Ltd, was an associated company of the taxpayer. That in turn depended on whether both companies were under the same person's 'control'—a word which, by virtue of s 13(4), was to be construed in accordance with s 416(6). The issued share capital of L Ltd was held by the trustees of a discretionary settlement which had been established by W in his lifetime. W's widow had no interest under that settlement, and was therefore not a participator. Nevertheless, under s 417(3)(b), the trustees of that settlement were her associates since she was a relative of the settlor. Accordingly, if the trustees' powers were attributed to W's widow under s 416(6), she would have to be taken as having control of L Ltd as well as the taxpayer. The two companies would thus have been under the control of the same person and they would therefore have been associated companies. Relying, however, on the use of the word

---

a Section 417, so far as material, is set out at [8] and [10], below
b Section 416, so far as material, is set out at [9], below
c Section 13, so far as material, is set out [39], below

a 'may' in sub-s (6), the taxpayer contended that the Revenue had a discretion as to whether to make an attribution, that that discretion was to be exercised to prevent taxpayers from abusing s 13 relief, and that there was no abuse in the instant case since W's widow had no interest in L Ltd and no real control over its affairs. The Revenue concluded that it had no discretion, and the taxpayer applied for judicial review of that decision. The application was dismissed by the judge

b who held that an attribution had to be made if it would result in two companies being under the control of the same person for the purposes of s 416(2) and (3). On the taxpayer's appeal, the Court of Appeal agreed with the judge that there was no discretion and that an attribution had to be made if the requisite conditions were satisfied. It further held, however, that the concluding words of s 416(6) laid down exhaustively the conditions under which the attributions

c should be made, that accordingly they could not be made unless they would result in a company being under the control of five or fewer participators and that an attribution in the instant case would not have produced such a result since W's widow was not a participator in L Ltd. Accordingly, the taxpayer's appeal was allowed, and the Revenue appealed to the House of Lords.

d
Held – (1) On the true construction of s 416(6) of the 1988 Act, the Revenue had no discretion as to the making of the attributions. Such a construction was supported not only by the absence of any person identified as entrusted with a discretion but also by the absence of any grounds upon which a discretion should be exercised. Even without sub-s (6), the definition of control was wide and could

e apply to people who had no real control over a company's affairs. That made it difficult to apply the reality of control as a criterion for exercising a discretion. As for the word 'may', it appeared in an impersonal construction—'there may also be attributed'—and its force was not facultative but conditional, as in 'VAT may be chargeable'. The question whether VAT was chargeable did not depend

f upon anyone's choice but upon whether the conditions for charging VAT were satisfied. Likewise, the question whether rights or powers should be attributed depended upon whether the necessary conditions had been satisfied. It was therefore necessary to identify the conditions under which an attribution had to be made (see [1], [2], [19], [20], [23], [34], [35], [43], below).

g (2) The conditions for attribution under s 416(6) of the 1988 Act were whether or not attribution resulted in the person or persons under consideration being treated as being in control. That was the only intelligible construction once the notion of a discretion had been rejected. Nor was that conclusion displaced by the concluding words of sub-s (6). Section 416(2) to (6), up to those words, provided a definition of control. The concluding words did not form part of

h definition of control which was applied by s 13(4) and other sections. Rather, they were a special qualification of that definition for the specific purpose of deciding whether one limb of the definition of a close company was satisfied. They took effect only when one had applied the general definition of control in sub-ss (2) or (3), as extended by the preceding part of sub-s (6), and found that it

j could yield groups of participators of varying numbers who could each be treated as being in control. The concluding words then required the making only of such attributions as would result in the company being treated as under the control of five or fewer participators. However, that qualification had no relevance to any case in which the general definition of control, as set out in the rest of s 416(2) to (6), was sufficient to answer the statutory question, namely whether a person or persons had to be treated as having control of a given company. In the instant

case, the general definition was sufficient to answer that question, and
accordingly the appeal would be allowed (see [1], [2], [29], [30], [32]–[35], [40],   *a*
[43], [44], below).

Notes
For small companies' relief and the meaning of control, see 23 *Halsbury's Laws*
(4th edn reissue) paras 845, 1295.   *b*

For the Income and Corporation Taxes Act 1988, ss 13, 416, 417, see 44
Halsbury's Statutes (4th edn) (1996 reissue) 45, 676, 677.

Appeal
The Commissioners of Inland Revenue appealed with permission of the Appeal
Committee of the House of Lords given on 22 June 2000 from the decision of the   *c*
Court of Appeal (Peter Gibson, Sedley LJJ and Sir Christopher Staughton) on
21 December 1999 ([2000] STC 52) allowing an appeal by the respondent,
Newfields Developments Ltd, from the decision of Moses J on 17 February 1999
([1999] STC 373) dismissing its application for judicial review of the decision of
the commissioners, contained in a letter dated 22 September 1997, that no   *d*
discretion was conferred on them by s 416(6) of the Income and Corporation
Taxes Act 1988. The facts are set out in the opinion of Lord Hoffmann.

Lord Goldsmith QC and *Timothy Brennan QC* (instructed by the *Solicitor of the Inland
Revenue*) for the Crown.
Kevin Prosser QC and *Elizabeth Wilson* (instructed by *Allen & Overy*) for Newfields.   *e*

Their Lordships took time for consideration

23 May 2001. The following opinions were delivered.   *f*

LORD BINGHAM OF CORNHILL.
[1] My Lords, for reasons given by my noble and learned friends, Lord Hoffmann
and Lord Scott of Foscote, which I have had the benefit of reading in draft,
I would allow this appeal and restore the order of the judge.

          g
LORD STEYN.
[2] My Lords, I have had the advantage of reading in draft the speeches of my
noble and learned friends, Lord Hoffmann and Lord Scott of Foscote. For the
reasons which they have given I would also allow the appeal.

LORD HOFFMANN.   *h*
[3] My Lords, the Finance Act 1972 introduced a relief for small companies
in the form of a reduced rate of corporation tax. The full relief can be claimed
if the company's profits in the relevant accounting year do not exceed one
specified amount and partial relief can be claimed if they do not exceed
another specified amount. The conditions for obtaining the relief and the   *j*
specified amounts are now contained in s 13 of the Income and Corporation
Taxes Act 1988 as amended. The reduced rate is 20%, as against the full rate of
30%.
[4] The relief would be open to obvious abuse if a business could be divided
among two or more companies so that each earned profits below the specified

a amount. Section 13(3) therefore provides that if a company has one or more associated companies, the relevant specified amount shall be divided by the number of associated companies plus one. Thus a company with one associated company can claim the relief in full or in part only if its profits in the relevant accounting period do not exceed half the relevant specified amount.

[5] The question in the present appeal is whether the taxpayer company
b (Newfields Developments Ltd, which I shall call Newfields) has an associated company or not. The Revenue contend that it has an associated company as defined in the 1988 Act, namely a company called Lawrek Properties Ltd (Lawrek). I shall in due course describe what the Revenue say is the relevant relationship between the two companies but, in order to explain why the Revenue say that their relationship is relevant, I must first go into the details of
c the rather complicated definition of an associated company.

[6] Associated companies are defined in s 13(4) as companies of which one controls or is controlled by the other or which are both under the control of the same person or persons. Crucial to this definition is therefore the concept of control, which the subsection says 'shall be construed in accordance with section
d 416'.

[7] The primary purpose of s 416 of the 1988 Act is to define the expressions 'associated company' and 'control' for the purposes of Pt XI of that Act, which deals with close companies. The term 'close company' appeared for the first time in the Finance Act 1965, which introduced the corporation tax, but had its roots in earlier concepts: the company 'under the control of not more than five
e persons' in respect of which income could be apportioned to its members for surtax purposes under s 21 of the Finance Act 1922 and the 'company whereof the directors have a controlling interest therein' which was limited in the deductions it could make in respect of directors' salaries for the purposes of profits tax by para 11 of Sch 4 to the Finance Act 1937. The close company is
f defined by s 414(1) of the 1988 Act, subject to exceptions, as 'one which is under the control of five or fewer participators, or of participators who are directors'. Part XI provides that in certain respects close companies are to be subject to a special fiscal regime. Thus the definition of control in s 416, which originally appeared in para 3 of Sch 18 to the 1965 Act, was for a purpose quite different from its use in s 13(4), which made its first appearance in the Finance Act 1972.

g [8] The definition of a close company made it necessary to provide definitions of 'participator' and 'control'. Participator is defined by s 417(1) of the 1988 Act:

'For the purposes of this Part, a "participator" is, in relation to any company, a person having a share or interest in the capital or income of the company, and, without prejudice to the generality of the preceding words,
h includes—(a) any person who possesses, or is entitled to acquire, share capital or voting rights in the company; (b) any loan creditor of the company; (c) any person who possesses, or is entitled to acquire, a right to receive or participate in distributions of the company (construing "distributions" without regard to section 418) or any amounts payable by the company (in
j cash or in kind) to loan creditors by way of premium on redemption; and (d) any person who is entitled to secure that income or assets (whether present or future) of the company will be applied directly or indirectly for his benefit. In this subsection references to being entitled to do anything apply where a person is presently entitled to do it at a future date, or will at a future date be entitled to do it.'

[9] Control is defined in s 416, of which the relevant subsections are (2) to (6):

'(2) For the purposes of this Part, a person shall be taken to have control of a company if he exercises, or is able to exercise or is entitled to acquire, direct or indirect control over the company's affairs, and in particular, but without prejudice to the generality of the preceding words, if he possesses or is entitled to acquire—(a) the greater part of the share capital or issued share capital of the company or of the voting power in the company; or (b) such part of the issued share capital of the company as would, if the whole of the income of the company were in fact distributed among the participators (without regard to any rights which he or any other person has as a loan creditor), entitle him to receive the greater part of the amount so distributed; or (c) such rights as would, in the event of the winding-up of the company or in any other circumstances, entitle him to receive the greater part of the assets of the company which would then be available for distribution among the participators.

(3) Where two or more persons together satisfy any of the conditions of subsection (2) above, they shall be taken to have control of the company.

(4) For the purposes of subsection (2) above a person shall be treated as entitled to acquire anything which he is entitled to acquire at a future date, or will at a future date be entitled to acquire.

(5) For the purposes of subsections (2) and (3) above, there shall be attributed to any person any rights or powers of a nominee for him, that is to say, any rights or powers which another person possesses on his behalf or may be required to exercise on his direction or behalf.

(6) For the purposes of subsections (2) and (3) above, there may also be attributed to any person all the rights and powers of any company of which he has, or he and associates of his have, control or any two or more such companies, or of any associate of his or of any two or more associates of his, including those attributed to a company or associate under subsection (5) above, but not those attributed to an associate under this subsection; and such attributions shall be made under this subsection as will result in the company being treated as under the control of five or fewer participators if it can be so treated.'

[10] It will be seen that although this definition starts in sub-s (2) with a concept of control which reflects its meaning in ordinary speech ('a person shall be taken to have control of a company if he exercises, or is able to exercise or is entitled to acquire, direct or indirect control over the company's affairs'), that fairly simple notion is enormously widened by subsequent subsections. Subsection (4) deems the person in question to already have interests which have not yet vested and sub-s (5) attributes to him the rights or powers of his nominees. Subsection (6) goes much further in providing that for the purposes of deciding whether a person falls within the definition in sub-s (2) (or the definition of joint control in sub-s (3)) any person may have attributed to him the rights or powers of any associate or of any company which he or his associates or both have control. The full breadth of this extension can be seen from the definition of 'associate' in s 417(3):

'For the purposes of this Part "associate" means, in relation to a participator—(a) any relative or partner of the participator; (b) the trustee or trustees of any settlement in relation to which the participator is, or any

a relative of his (living or dead) is or was, a settlor ("settlement" and "settlor" having here the same meaning as in section 681(4)); and (c) where the participator is interested in any shares or obligations of the company which are subject to any trust, or are part of the estate of a deceased person—(i) the trustee or trustees of the settlement concerned or, as the case may be, the personal representatives of the deceased; and (ii) if the participator is a
b company, any other company interested in those shares or obligations; and has a corresponding meaning in relation to a person other than a participator.'

[11] 'Relative' is defined in s 417(4) to mean 'husband or wife, parent or remoter forebear, child or remoter issue, or brother or sister'. The effect of these cumulative definitions is that for the purpose of deciding whether a person 'shall
c be taken to have control of a company' under s 416(2), it may be necessary to attribute to him the rights and powers of persons over whom he may in real life have little or no power of control. Plainly the intention of the legislature was to spread the net very wide.

[12] Against this statutory background one can turn to what the Revenue say
d is the relevant relationship between Newfields and Lawrek. The issued share capital of Newfields is held by the trustees of the will of the late Mr Walker. Under the trusts of that will, his widow Mrs Walker has a life interest. Her life interest in the shares means that she is a 'participator' in Newfields (s 417(1)(c)) and, more to the point, the trustees are her 'associates' (s 417(3)(c)). The trustees
e plainly have power to control Newfields and if that power is attributed to Mrs Walker under s 416(6), she must be taken under s 416(2) to have control of Newfields.

[13] The issued share capital of Lawrek is held by the trustees of a discretionary settlement established by the late Mr Walker in his lifetime. Mrs Walker has no interest under that settlement: to avoid the income being deemed to be that of
f Mr Walker, she was expressly excluded from taking any benefit. She is therefore not a participator. Nevertheless, she is a relative of the settlor and therefore it is said that under s 417(3)(b), as applied to non-participators by the concluding words of the subsection, the trustees of that settlement are also her associates. If their powers are attributed to her under s 416(6), then she must be
g taken to have control of Lawrek as well. It follows that Newfields and Lawrek are under the control of the same person and are associated companies.

[14] The first ground upon which the taxpayer objected to this conclusion was that s 416(6) does not say that the powers of associates must be attributed to Mrs Walker. The subsection says 'may'. Therefore the taxpayer submits that the
h Revenue has a discretion as to whether to make an attribution or not. The discretion should be exercised to prevent taxpayers from abusing the relief under s 13 of the 1988 Act. In this case, however, the taxpayer says that it would be unfair to make an attribution because there is no abuse. Mrs Walker has no interest in Lawrek and no real control over its affairs. It and Newfields are quite separate
j companies.

[15] The Revenue denied that s 416(6) conferred a discretion. They said that the word 'may' merely indicated that such an attribution would not always be made. It should be made if the result was that a given person or persons would be taken to have control within the meaning of s 416(2) or (3). Otherwise not. But this depended upon the consequences of the attribution and not upon the discretion of the Revenue. On 22 September 1997 the inspector wrote to the

taxpayer's accountant saying that the Revenue had no discretion and proposed to refuse small companies' relief.

[16] Newfields issued proceedings for judicial review of this decision. It sought a declaration that there was a discretion and an order of mandamus requiring it to be exercised.

[17] Moses J held ([1999] STC 373) that the Revenue were right. He recorded (at 377) that both parties had agreed that 'the opening words of sub-s (6) of s 416 confer a power and not a duty'. But he said (at 380) that the Revenue were obliged to exercise the power for the purpose for which it was conferred. That purpose was 'to ascertain whether, in the instant case, two companies are under the control of the same person'. If an attribution will produce an affirmative answer, an attribution should be made.

[18] The taxpayer appealed to the Court of Appeal ([2000] STC 52), where a majority (Peter Gibson and Sedley LJJ) agreed on this point with the judge. Sir Christopher Staughton, on the other hand, thought that the Revenue had a discretion which ought to have been exercised. In rejecting the notion of a discretion, Peter Gibson LJ said that it was significant that no one was designated as the person in whom the discretion was vested. Was it the inspector, the commissioners or the taxpayer? It seemed to him (at 59) to 'provide an instruction to the Revenue and the taxpayer alike as to how control of a company for the purposes of s 416(2) and (3) is to be determined'. Sedley LJ said that, although he was tempted by the notion of discretion, he agreed that the absence of anyone upon whom it purported to be conferred was an irremovable objection.

[19] In my opinion the judge and the majority in the Court of Appeal were right. In addition to the absence of any person identified as entrusted with a discretion, there is the absence of any grounds upon which the discretion should be exercised. Even without s 416(6) of the 1988 Act, the definition of control is wide and can apply to people who have no real control over the company's affairs. This makes it difficult to apply the reality of control as a criterion for exercising a discretion. If real control were to be the test, the opening words of s 416(2) would be enough. The purpose of the extended definition appears to be to make it unnecessary for the Revenue to have to make detailed factual enquiries.

[20] Sir Christopher Staughton, in taking the opposite view, naturally attached importance to the word 'may'. But the word appears in an impersonal construction—'there may also be attributed'—and I think that its force is not facultative but conditional, as in 'VAT may be chargeable'. The question of whether VAT is chargeable does not depend upon anyone's choice but on whether the conditions for charging VAT are satisfied: are the goods or services subject to VAT, is the trader registrable and so on. Likewise, the question of whether rights or powers should be attributed depends upon whether the necessary conditions have been satisfied. As Peter Gibson LJ pointed out (at 59) the draftsman could not sensibly have said 'there shall also be attributed' because s 416(6) permits a wide range of attributions. Some will result in a given person or persons being in control within the meaning of sub-ss (2) or (3) and others will not.

[21] It should be noted that while sub-s (2) of s 416 specifies the conditions under which 'a person' shall be taken to have control, sub-s (6) says that for the purposes of sub-s (2), there may be attributed to 'any person' all the rights and powers of companies under his control, associates and so forth. The possible subject of attribution is therefore not confined to the candidate for control.

a Thus, while sub-s (6) would permit the attribution to the candidate of powers exercisable by his wife, it would also permit the attribution to his wife of powers exercisable by him. In the first case, the result might be to treat the candidate as being in control when otherwise he would not be. In the second, it might be to treat him as not being in control when otherwise he would be. If all the attributions possible under sub-s (6) were mandatory, it could not be applied
b without absurdity and contradiction.

[22] Although the point may be merely verbal, I do not think that it is right to say, as the parties appear to have done before Moses J, that 'may' confers a 'power'. It is true that there are powers which in certain circumstances must be exercised. But I think it is clearer, having regard to the impersonal use of 'may' in the subsection, to say that it expresses conditionality.
c
[23] If the force of the word 'may' is conditional, the next stage in the argument is to identify the conditions under which an attribution must be made. The argument before the judge seems to have proceeded on the basis that although the conditions were not spelled out in sub-s (6), they could be inferred from the purpose of sub-s (6) as an adjunct to sub-ss (2) and (3), namely to specify
d what counts as being in control of a company. In the same way, if it said in a catalogue 'VAT may be chargeable', it would not be necessary to spell out that it would be chargeable if the conditions for charging VAT were satisfied. That would be obvious from the nature of VAT.

[24] The judge therefore concluded, as I have already stated, that an attribution
e should be made if the result would be to treat the candidate or candidates as being in control of the company, but not otherwise. He did say at one point ([1999] STC 373 at 380) that the purpose of s 416(6) was to 'ascertain whether … two companies are under the control of the same person pursuant to s 13(4)'. Mr Prosser objected that this involved illegitimately reading the purpose of
f s 13(4) of the 1988 Act into a general definition of control which served a number of different provisions, each having its own purpose. But I do not think that the judge meant to say more than that the general purpose of s 416 of the 1988 Act was to tell one whether a given person could be said to be in control of a given company and that sub-s (6) was part of the hypothesis on which one answered that question. Section 13(4) requires one only to ask whether an affirmative
g answer can be given in respect of both companies.

[25] On this point, however, the Court of Appeal disagreed. They said that one could not treat sub-s (6) of s 416 as subject to conditions which could be inferred from sub-ss (2) and (3) because the conditions under which attributions should be made were already spelled out in the concluding words of the
h subsection itself: '… such attributions shall be made under this subsection as will result in the company being treated as under the control of five or fewer participators if it can be so treated.'

[26] The Court of Appeal treated these words as laying down exhaustively the conditions under which attributions could and should be made. It followed that
j unless the attributions would result in the company being treated as under the control of five or fewer participators, they could not be made at all. Mrs Walker was not a participator in Lawrek and the effect of an attribution would therefore not result in Lawrek being under the control of five or fewer participators. On the other hand, if coincidentally it would have had that effect, the attribution could have been made for the purposes of refusing small companies' relief.

[27] This construction produces a very arbitrary result and would appear to make s 416(6) an unsuitable element in any definition of control for the purposes of s 13(4). Small companies' relief does not depend upon whether the company is a close company or not. No doubt most companies which qualify for the relief will be close companies, but that is not essential. The question, or rather one of the questions, raised by s 13(4) is whether a person who controls a company applying for relief also controls one or more other companies. In deciding what counts as controlling another company, it would be illogical to attribute additional powers only if the effect was to bring that other company within the definition of a close company. That would seem an irrelevant consideration. Mr Prosser said that one could avoid this illogicality by treating the whole of sub-s (6) as applicable only to the question of whether a company was a closed company. But this would leave it open to anyone to claim small companies' relief by dividing his business between companies controlled by himself and his wife, or himself and the trustees of discretionary settlements for the benefit of his family. The absence of the attribution provisions of sub-s (6) would leave a large gap in the defence which s 13(4) provides for the public revenue.

[28] The Court of Appeal were fully aware that their construction produced a rather odd result. Peter Gibson LJ spoke of unease and discomfort and Sedley LJ said he reached the answer with considerable diffidence.

[29] In my opinion, if the concluding words were not there, one would have no difficulty in inferring from s 416(2) and (3) that the conditions for attribution are whether or not it resulted in the person or persons under consideration being treated as being in control. Once one has rejected the notion of a discretion, there can be no other intelligible construction. The question is whether this conclusion is displaced by the concluding words or whether those words serve some other purpose.

[30] In my opinion, they do serve another purpose. Section 416(2) to (6), up to the commencement of the concluding words, provides a definition of control. If one wants to know of any person or persons whether he or they must be treated as having control of a given company, those parts of the section will provide the answer. For many of the purposes for which the concept of control is used, that is all that one requires. In the present case, for example, all one wants to know is whether Mrs Walker can be said to be in control of Newfields and of Lawrek. But there are cases in which it is not enough to know that it can be said of a certain person, or certain people, that they control company A. An example is the question of whether company A is a close company, which involves not only asking whether participators control the company but also whether they are directors or number five or fewer.

[31] There is no difficulty about applying the definition to answer the question of whether the company is controlled by participators who are directors. If one or more people who answer that description control the company within the meaning of s 416(2) or (3), as extended if necessary by the other subsections including sub-s (6), the definition is satisfied. But the question of whether the controlling participators are five or fewer is different. If one simply said that an attribution should be made under sub-s (6) if it resulted in a given participator or participators being treated as in control, it could yield the result that various numbers of participators were in control. With some attributions it could be five or fewer, without them or with others, more.

[32] In my opinion, therefore, the concluding words of sub-s (6) do not form part of the definition of 'control' which is applied by s 13(4) and other sections.

a They are a special qualification of that definition for the specific purpose of deciding whether one limb of the definition of a close company is satisfied. The concluding words take effect only when one has applied the general definition of control in s 416(2) or (3) as extended by the preceding part of the subsection and found that it can yield groups of participators of varying numbers who can each be treated as being in control. The concluding words then require
b one to make only such attributions as will result in the company being treated as under the control of five or fewer participators. But this qualification has no relevance to any case in which the general definition of control, as set out in the rest of s 416(2) to (6), is sufficient to answer the statutory question.

[33] In the present case, as I have said, the general definition is sufficient to answer the question. I would therefore allow the appeal and restore the order of
c Moses J.

LORD COOKE OF THORNDON.

[34] My Lords, I have had the advantage of reading in draft the speech of my noble and learned friends Lord Hoffmann and Lord Scott of Foscote. For the
d reasons which they have given I would also allow the appeal.

LORD SCOTT OF FOSCOTE.

[35] My Lords, I have had the advantage of reading in advance the opinion of my noble and learned friend, Lord Hoffmann. I agree with his analysis of the
e relevant statutory provisions and with his reasons for allowing the appeal.

[36] One of the issues of construction that was debated before the Court of Appeal was whether or not s 416(6) of the Income and Corporation Taxes Act 1988 should be treated as a single provision. The relevance of this issue was that if it were to be treated as a single provision, then, so it was argued, the whole of the subsection, including the passage after the semicolon, ie 'and such
f attributions shall be made' etc, would have to be applied when answering the question whether Mrs Walker was to be treated as in control of Lawrek. If that were right, the passage would then have a limiting effect, preventing the attributions prescribed by the subsection from having any function other than to allow a company to be treated as under the control of five or fewer participators
g and, consequently, a close company. Peter Gibson LJ concluded ([2000] STC 52 at 59) that the subsection should be treated as a single provision:

'On its natural construction it seems to me to be a single provision, the second half closely related to the first as can be seen by the conjunction "and" following the semi-colon and the reference to the attributions under he
h subsection which are to be made.'

[37] He held that, since Mrs Walker was not a participator vis-à-vis Lawrek, none of the sub-s (6) attributions could be used in order to treat her as in control of Lawrek and to enable Newfields and Lawrek to become, for s 13(4) of the
j 1988 Act purposes, associated companies.

[38] The purpose of sub-s (6) when originally enacted in para 3 of Sch 18 to the Finance Act 1965 was to enable such attributions to be made as would result in a company becoming a close company for the purposes of that Act. In that context it seems to me accurate to treat the subsection as a single provision. It required, and still does require, to be applied as a single provision for the purpose of enabling a company to be treated as a close company.

[39] But s 13(4) of the 1988 Act has nothing to do with close companies. It is concerned with whether or not companies are 'associated' with one another. They are to be treated as associated if 'one of the two has control of the other or both are under the control of the same person', and, s 13(4) declares, '"control" shall be construed in accordance with section 416'.

[40] In applying s 416 in order to construe 'control' in s 13(4) and to determine whether or not companies are 'associated', the whole of s 416 must be applied. To omit sub-s (6) would make no sense and defeat an important part of the statutory intention underlying s 13. But, in applying sub-s (6), the passage after the semicolon, which has relevance only to the identification of close companies and no relevance to whether or not companies are 'associated', should simply be ignored. It has no part to play.

[41] Subsection (2) of s 416 provides: '... a person shall be taken to have control of a company if he exercises, or is able to exercise or is entitled to acquire, direct or indirect control over the company's affairs ...' The words I have cited prescribe a test of actual control. But s 416 goes on, in the remaining part of sub-s (2) and in sub-ss (4), (5) and (6), to describe circumstances in which, whether or not a person has actual control, the person 'shall be taken to have control'. It is worth emphasising the word 'shall' in sub-s (2). There is no element of discretion.

[42] Subsection (6) describes a number of circumstances in which, for the purposes of sub-s (2), control 'may ... be attributed' to a person. The particular circumstances that permit an attribution of control to a person are not necessarily exclusive of the circumstances that permit an attribution of control of the same company to some other person. The facts relating to two companies may, under sub-s (6), permit the attribution of control to several different people.

[43], [44] This, in my opinion, explains the use of the word 'may' in sub-s (6) of s 416. The use of the word 'may' does not lead to the conclusion that the subsection creates a discretionary power. The absence of any indication of the criteria by which the discretion is to be exercised or any identification of the person by whom the discretion is to be exercised seems to me to make that plain. In my opinion, the use of the word 'may' was an acceptable linguistic means of indicating that not every permutation of control thrown up by sub-s (6) attributions has to be applied when the question whether a particular person has control of a particular company is being considered. Subsection (6) supports sub-s (2). Subsection (2) says that 'a person *shall* be taken to have control of a company if ...' (my emphasis). This mandatory provision supplemented by sub-s (6) attributions requires, in my opinion, that when the circumstances of a particular person are being examined in order to determine whether that person has control of a particular company, that person 'shall be taken' to have control if any of the possible sub-s (6) attributions give him or her control.

[45] For these reasons and those given by Lord Hoffmann I, too, would allow this appeal.

Appeal allowed.

Celia Fox   Barrister.

a
R (on the application of the Director of Public Prosecutions) v Redbridge Youth Court

b
R (on the application of L) v Bicester Youth Court

[2001] EWHC Admin 209

QUEEN'S BENCH DIVISION, DIVISIONAL COURT

c LATHAM LJ AND ASTILL J

8, 22 MARCH 2001

Criminal evidence – Child – Video recording of testimony – Application to admit video recording of testimony of child – Application for evidence to be given by live television
d *link – Exercise of court's discretion – Guidance – Criminal Justice Act 1988, ss 32, 32A.*

In two separate applications for judicial review, issues arose as to the exercise of court's powers to hear a child's evidence by live television link under s 32[a] of the Criminal Justice Act 1988 and to receive in evidence a video recording of an
e interview with a child as that child's evidence in the proceedings under s 32A[b] of the Act. In the first case, a 14-year-old boy was charged with an indecent assault on two 14-year-old girls. The prosecution applied for orders under both s 32 and s 32A, contending that the complainants would be caused embarrassment if they were required to give live evidence. There was no evidence of intimidation or any suggestion that the complainants would refuse to give evidence if they were
f required to give it in court. The justices refused the applications, and the Director of Public Prosecutions (DPP) applied for judicial review. In the second case, the prosecution applied for orders under s 32 permitting three boys, aged 10, 11 and 13 respectively, to give evidence by live television link against L, a 14-year-old boy charged with causing grievous bodily harm, who had allegedly threatened the two younger boys with a gun at the time of the incident. The district judge
g allowed the applications, concluding that the vulnerability of the two younger boys justified the making of orders in relation to them and citing, in relation to the older boy, 'the ease with which his presence in court to give evidence is achieved'. L applied for judicial review. On the applications, the Divisional Court considered whether there was any difference in the approach to be applied by the
h courts to the exercise of their discretion under the two sections, particularly in light of s 32A(3). That subsection required the court to permit a video recording of an interview with a child to be given in evidence unless, inter alia, the court was of the opinion, having regard to all the circumstances of the case, that the recording ought not to be admitted in the interests of justice (sub-s (3)(c)). There
j was no such provision in s 32.

Held – (1) Although ss 32 and 32A of the 1988 Act had the same general legislative purpose—namely to provide, in relation to a child, conditions which

---
a   Section 32, so far as material, is set out at [6], below
b   Section 32A, so far as material, is set out at [6], below

were most conducive to ensuring that a child was able to give as full an account as
possible of the events in question—a distinction was to be made between the
approach of the court under the two sections. The procedures were intended to
provide a mechanism whereby a child witness who might otherwise be upset,
intimidated or traumatised by appearing in court was not, as a result, inhibited from
giving a full and proper account of the events of which he was a witness. It followed
that orders under either section were appropriate where there was a real risk that
the quality of evidence given by a child would be so affected or that it might even
be impossible to obtain any evidence from that child. Fairness to the defendant was
achieved by enabling him to see the witness giving evidence in interview, or by a
television link, and having a full opportunity to cross-examine by way of a television
link. In relation to s 32A, however, there was a further purpose, namely that the
evidence of a child should be the child's account given as contemporaneously as
possible, so that evidence-in-chief was not a memory test. If, under s 32A(3)(c), the
question was raised whether or not in the interests of justice the recording should
be excluded, the court was required to carry out a balancing exercise bearing in
mind the legislative purposes. It had to consider on the one hand the extent to
which the witness's evidence would be so affected if the video recording was not
admitted in evidence, and on the other the prejudice to the defendant if the video
recording were to be admitted in evidence. In carrying out that exercise, the court
had to bear in mind that Parliament had determined that the primary method by
which a child witness's evidence should be given to the court was by means of the
video interview, and it seemed to follow that it was for a defendant to establish that
any prejudice to him displaced that parliamentary intention. In relation to s 32 the
position was different. Parliament had provided no presumption one way or the
other as to the way in which the evidence should be given. It was necessary
therefore to consider in every case the extent to which justice was best achieved by
making or not making the order sought. In doing so, the court would bear in mind
that the paradigm or norm was that a witness should give evidence in court in the
presence of the defendant. It followed that some good reason had to be shown in
accordance with the legislative purpose if an order were to be made under s 32.
The court was therefore required to strike a balance between the right of the
defendant to have a hearing in accordance with the norm and the need to provide
protection in accordance with the legislative purpose, in the interests not only of
the child witness but also of justice, to ensure that the witness would be able to give
evidence unaffected by the stress of appearing in court itself (see [15]–[17], [22],
below).

(2) In the first of the instant cases, the justices had been entitled to refuse to make
the orders sought, and accordingly the DPP's application would be dismissed. In
the second case, the district judge had been entitled to take the view that the fear
expressed by the two younger boys justified making an order under s 32 that they
should give their evidence by live television link. However, he should not have
made such an order in relation to the older boy. The district judge had not been
concerned about the quality of that boy's evidence. Nor had he expressed any
concern about the boy's willingness to give evidence once he was at court. The
justification for making the order was the ease with which the witness might be
brought to court, and that was not in itself a justifiable reason for making the order.
Accordingly, the order would be quashed in so far as it related to the older boy (see
[20]–[22], below).

a
Notes
For evidence through television link, see 11(2) *Halsbury's Laws* (4th edn reissue) paras 1169–1170.
  For the Criminal Justice Act 1988, ss 32, 32A, see 17 *Halsbury's Statutes* (4th edn) (1999 reissue) 260, 262.

b **Cases referred to in judgments**
Doorson v Netherlands (1996) 22 EHRR 330, [1996] ECHR 20524/92, ECt HR.
R v McAndrew-Bingham [1999] 1 WLR 1897, CA.

Cases also cited or referred to in skeleton arguments
Associated Provincial Picture Houses Ltd v Wednesbury Corp [1947] 2 All ER 680,
c   [1948] 1 KB 223, CA.
Baegen v Netherlands [1995] ECHR 16696/90, ECt HR.
Barberà v Spain (1988) 11 EHRR 360, [1988] ECHR 10588/83, ECt HR.
Brown v Stott (Procurator Fiscal, Dunfermline) [2001] 2 All ER 97, [2001] 2 WLR 817, PC.
Delcourt v Belgium (1970) 1 EHRR 355, [1970] ECHR 2689/65, ECt HR.
d *G v DPP* [1997] 2 All ER 755, [1998] QB 919, DC.
Jasper v UK (2000) 30 EHRR 441, ECt HR.
Khan v UK (2000) 8 BHRC 310, ECt HR.
MK v Austria (1997) 24 EHRR CD 59, E Com HR.
R v Acton Youth Court, ex p DPP (10 May 2000, unreported), DC.
e *R v Greenwood* [1993] Crim LR 770, CA.
R v Lee [1996] Crim LR 412, CA.
R v Schaub, R v Cooper [1994] Crim LR 531, CA.
R v X (1989) 91 Cr App R 36, CA.
Rowe v UK (2000) 8 BHRC 325, ECt HR.
f *Teixeira de Castro v Portugal* (1998) BHRC 533, ECt HR.
Trivedi v UK [1997] EHRLR 521, E Com HR.
Unterpertinger v Austria (1986) 13 EHRR 175, [1986] ECHR 9120/80, ECt HR.
Van Mechelen v Netherlands (1997) 2 BHRC 486, ECt HR.

Applications for judicial review
g
R (on the application of the DPP) v Redbridge Youth Court
The claimant, the Director of Public Prosecutions (DPP), applied for judicial review of the decision of justices sitting at Redbridge Youth Court on 27 October 2000 refusing the Crown's application, in proceedings for indecent assault against a
h 14-year-old boy, for video recordings of interviews of the two 14-year-old complainants to be admitted in evidence under s 32A of the Criminal Justice Act 1988 and for the remainder of their evidence to be given by way of live television link under s 32 of the Act. The facts are set out in the judgment of Latham LJ.

j
R (on the application of L) v Bicester Youth Court
The claimant, L, applied for judicial review of the decision of District Judge Wicks, sitting at Bicester Youth Court on 8 November 2000, granting an application by the Crown for three boys to give evidence by live television link under s 32 of the Criminal Justice Act 1988 in proceedings against L for inflicting grievous bodily harm contrary to s 20 of the Offences Against the Person Act 1861 and for

firearms offences contrary to ss 16A and 19 of the Firearms Act 1968. The facts
are set out in the judgment of Latham LJ.   *a*

David Perry (instructed by the *Crown Prosecution Service*) for the DPP.
Hugo Keith (instructed by the *Treasury Solicitor*) as amicus curiae in the DPP's
   application.
Julian Knowles (instructed by *Arnold du Feu*, Oxford) for L.   *b*
Peter Ross (instructed by the *Crown Prosecution Service*, Abingdon) for the Crown
   in L's case.

Cur adv vult

22 March 2001. The following judgments were delivered.   *c*

LATHAM LJ.
[1] These two applications raise different, but overlapping questions in relation
to ss 32 and 32A of the Criminal Justice Act 1988. These two sections are
concerned with the court's powers to hear evidence by live television link and to
receive in evidence a video recording of an interview with a child as the child's   *d*
evidence in the proceedings. The facts of each case are as follows.

REDBRIDGE YOUTH COURT
[2] The defendant before the youth court was a 14-year-old youth, who had
been charged with three offences of indecent assault on two girls both of whom   *e*
were, at the relevant time, 14 years of age. It was alleged that on 18 August 2000
he, together with other youths, approached the girls, one of whom was known
to him, produced a sum of money and stated that he wished to have sex. After a
number of requests of a sexual nature, the defendant was alleged to have
assaulted both girls by slapping their bottoms over their clothes. The two girls
were interviewed on video tape. An application was made for the video   *f*
recordings in respect of both girls to be admitted in evidence, under s 32A of the
1988 Act, and for the remainder of their evidence to be given by way of a live
television link under s 32 of that Act.
[3] The application was heard on 27 October 2000 by three justices. The Crown
relied on the age of the girls and evidence to the effect that to require them to give   *g*
live evidence would cause them embarrassment. There was no evidence before
the court of intimidation, nor was there any suggestion at that time that they
would refuse to give evidence if they were required to give evidence in the
courtroom itself. The justices refused the applications. Their reasons are set out
in an affidavit from Michael Batten, their chairman dated 23 January 2001:   *h*

   '5. The court carefully considered the purpose behind the Crown's
   application of seeking to reduce the risk of embarrassment to child witnesses
   giving evidence in a reasonably formal setting. Section 32A of the 1988 Act
   clearly sought to reduce any harm suffered by a child witness when
   ascertaining the facts of a case without unfairly interfering with the rights of   *j*
   the parties to a fair trial.
   6. It was considered by the court that in exercising its discretion it must
   balance the interests of both parties in a criminal trial. The need to save the
   child as much trauma as possible and to improve his or her ability to give
   evidence in ascertaining the true facts of the case had to be balanced against
   the need to safeguard the interest of the accused. The interest of the accused

to have a fair trial generally included the right to be present whilst the case against him was being expounded, to be represented by counsel of his choosing and to test the evidence against him such as by cross-examining the child witnesses and observing the demeanour of the witness during testimony.

7. The court considered that it must exercise its discretion as to when and how the video link procedure is used, so as to ensure that all interests are

b carefully and independently taken into account. The prosecution may not always be in the best position to assess the likely effect on a child witness. It is difficult to define proceedings in which the procedure would operate fairly in all circumstances and the flexibility and ability to choose to use the procedure for a particular child witness in a particular case is paramount.

c 8. In exercising its discretion the court considered the following factors. (a) The fact that the defendant and the witnesses were of similar age, thus eliminating the potential for any intimidation by an older defendant in a position of authority. The Crown offered no evidence to suggest that there were any additional factors of relevance including personality, intelligence and immaturity in assessing if the witnesses would be competent to give live

d evidence or disability to which the child may or may not be subject. The court considered both witnesses to be competent to give evidence. (b) The nature and importance of the matters on which the witnesses were being called to give evidence. The allegations related to slapping the girls' bottoms whilst fully clothed. The court considered that the allegation of indecent assault fell

e towards the lower end of the scale of seriousness. (c) The court noted that the Crown at no stage asserted that either witness would suffer trauma or intimidation by giving live evidence but claimed that the Crown witnesses would suffer embarrassment, which although not conclusive, was a relevant factor for consideration in all the circumstances of this case. The court

f concluded that neither witness would suffer emotional harm or significant embarrassment if required to give live evidence in camera, in a relatively informal court setting accompanied by an appropriate adult who would offer support. (d) The court was concerned to ensure that as far as possible both prosecution and defence should be afforded an opportunity to present their evidence under conditions that did not substantially advantage or disadvantage

g either party, thus ensuring equality of arms. (e) The court considered the issue of the quality of evidence and if such evidence would be more reliable if adduced by way of video link, the court concluded that it would not. The impact of the witnesses' evidence through an electronic medium may be lessened and the circumstances in which the recorded interview was made

h may affect the quality and reliability of evidence. Moreover, the best evidence rule would be breached and the accused may be disadvantaged by being unable to confront the witness in the court room. (f) The court considered that additional complications could arise as an interpreter was required for the defendant who spoke little English.

j 9. The court in exercising its discretion balanced the nature of the allegation, the proximity in age of the parties, the characteristics of the witnesses, the potential risk of embarrassment or intimidation (although not asserted by the Crown) which may have been occasioned by the witness giving evidence in camera supported by an appropriate adult, against the risk of prejudice to the defendant, the detraction of the immediacy of live testimony in the courtroom which would provide the court with the best opportunity to test

the credibility of the witnesses prior to cross-examination and the desire for
equality of arms to be preserved and a fair trial to be secured.

10. The court concluded having regard to all the above factors that in the
particular circumstances of this case it was not in the interests of justice that
evidence by video recording and live TV link should be admitted in
accordance with s 32A(3)(c) of the 1988 Act.'

b

BICESTER YOUTH COURT

[4] In this case the claimant is also 14 years of age. He was charged with inflicting
grievous bodily harm contrary to s 20 of the Offences Against the Person Act 1861
and firearms offences contrary to ss 16A and 19 of the Firearms Act 1968. On
8 August 2000 the adult complainant was crossing a playground in Banbury on
which a number of children were playing. His account was that two of the boys
pulled out air guns and began shooting at tin cans. Then one of the boys, who
was alleged to be the claimant, pointed the gun at him and shot him in the face
from a short distance, hitting him in his cheek.

[5] The incident was witnessed by a number of children who made witness
statements. Perhaps not surprisingly, these statements disclose considerable
discrepancies. On 25 October 2000, the Crown applied for the use of a live
television link in relation to the evidence of three of the boys, a 10-year-old, an
11-year-old, and two 13-year-olds. The application was not ultimately pursued in
relation to one of the 13-year-olds. The basis of the application was that each of
the witnesses was vulnerable and that in relation to the two younger ones, that
they were threatened by the claimant with the air gun at the time of the incident.
The applications were ultimately heard by District Judge Wicks who gave his
decision on 8 November 2000. We have been provided with a note of his reasons.
The relevant parts are as follows:

'My decision is as follows and I believe that the factors that I can properly
take into account have to be geared to ensuring that justice is achieved to the
maximum extent possible as this requires a very careful balancing of interests
of the defendant that a fair and just outcome ensuring that the witnesses who
might otherwise not be available to give evidence at all are capable of giving
evidence if that is achieved. Of course it does not mean any person under the
age of 14 who has to give some evidence should not automatically give their
evidence through video link. *There has to be some factor from which a court can
deduce the witness is potentially so vulnerable for whatever reasons may be
applicable that without video link they either would not appear at all or their
evidence would be affected by factors of stress which would adversely affect the value
of the evidence* [original emphasis]. Taking the three children in turn.

SH 10 years of age ... His father says he is extremely frightened at the
prospect of giving evidence and a police officer indicates willingness may
turn on video evidence. My view in his case is that the exercise of the court's
discretion should result in my saying that he has a degree of vulnerability
that justifies me to ensure that justice in the widest sense authorising TV link
for his evidence ... I am satisfied in the case of SH the fear I anticipate is fear
going beyond mere giving evidence.

BO'N aged 11 He is personally threatened by the defendant according to
the evidence "Do you want a pellet in your mouth?" and threatened to get
one if he doesn't shut up. He is very frightened by the experience and is
described as a crucial witness although not subsequently alleged to have

a been threatened by the defendant. He is scared and apprehensive. I believe I can properly say that in the case of a child of 11 he shares characteristics I have attributed in more detail to the other and permit his evidence also by video link.

b *AA Born 8 April 1987* Is 13 and a half-years-old, very fact that he is that much older makes the application more difficult to resolve ... I am told he is very frightened and I find that to be not simply the fact of giving evidence but of the whole surrounding circumstances he finds himself in following the incident and the stress of giving evidence. I am told his willingness and ability to come to court and provide evidence the court regards as important more persuasive (sic). If the video link is available, not to the quality of the evidence but the ease with which his presence in court to give evidence is

c achieved. I have considered with the greatest care whether the anxiety of the witness and the Crown can be sufficiently alleviated behind the screens, after long and careful consideration I am mindful that the paramount outcome the court strives to achieve is that of justice in its widest sense. I have concluded that I should permit the evidence of this witness also to be given

d by video link. I am satisfied that the tribunal hearing this case will be able to accord the evidence of the witness whatever is the appropriate weight and the fears Mrs Conway understandably expressed of the witness giving less than full and proper evidence will not arise and the tribunal will be able to protect itself from any wrong assessment. I have decided in reaching my conclusion I had at all times had paramount in mind that the defendant must

e receive a fair trial and I am satisfied the order I am making will not in any way preclude this.'

THE STATUTORY PROVISIONS

[6] The relevant provisions of the 1988 Act, as amended, are as follows:

f
'32. *Evidence through television links.*—(1) A person other than the accused may give evidence through a live television link in proceedings to which subsection (1A) below applies if ... (b) the witness is a child, or is to be cross-examined following the admission under section 32A below of a video recording of testimony from him, and the offence is one to which subsection (2)

g below applies, but evidence may not be so given without the leave of the court.

(1A) This subsection applies ... (b) to proceedings in youth courts ...

(2) This subsection applies—(a) to an offence which involves an assault on, or injury or threat of injury to, a person ... (c) to an offence under the

h Sexual Offences Act 1956 ...

32A. *Video recordings of testimony from child witnesses.*—(1) This section applies in relation to the following proceedings, namely ... (c) proceedings in youth courts [for any offence to which s 32(2) above applies] ...

(2) In any such proceedings a video recording of an interview

j which—(a) is conducted between an adult and a child who is not the accused or one of the accused ("the child witness"); and (b) relates to any matter in issue in the proceedings, may, with the leave of the court, be given in evidence in so far as it is not excluded by the court under subsection (3) below.

(3) Where a video recording is tendered in evidence under this section, the court shall (subject to the exercise of any power of the court to exclude

evidence which is otherwise admissible) give leave under subsection (2) above
unless—(a) it appears that the child witness will not be available for cross-
examination; (b) any rules of court requiring disclosure of the circumstances
in which the recording was made have not been complied with to the
satisfaction of the court; or (c) the court is of the opinion, having regard to
all the circumstances of the case, that in the interests of justice the recording
ought not to be admitted ...'

[7] The issues and arguments in relation to the two cases are as follows.

REDBRIDGE YOUTH COURT

[8] In this application we heard submissions from Mr Perry on behalf of the
Director of Public Prosecutions (DPP) and Mr Keith as amicus curiae. We are very
grateful to them both. Neither the defendant in the criminal proceedings nor the
justices were represented, although as I have already indicated, the chairman of
the justices provided us with an affidavit, and a full acknowledgment of service
was filed giving more detail of the nature of the argument before the justices
upon which they came to the decision which is the subject of challenge. An
acknowledgment of service was also filed on behalf of the defendant in the
criminal proceedings supporting the justices' decision.

[9] On behalf of the DPP Mr Perry submitted that s 32A sets out a scheme for
the purposes of protecting child witnesses in which the primary rule is that where
there has been a video interview, that shall be admitted as the evidence of that
witness. The statutory purpose is, he submitted, to encourage witnesses to come
forward knowing that there is a presumption in favour of their evidence being
presented to the court in video form, to improve the quality and reliability of such
evidence, and to reduce the trauma to a child of appearing in court. He accepts
that the court has to exercise a discretion if it is submitted under s 32A(3)(c) that
the video adduced should not be received in the interests of justice, that the court
then has to carry out a discretionary exercise, which he submitted is restricted to
issues of competence and reliability. He submitted that those are the only relevant
issues which could give rise to prejudice to a defendant. The statutory presumption
which he submitted is contained within s 32A, namely that such a video interview
is to be admitted, precludes any argument that such a procedure in some way
prejudices a defendant. Parliament has determined that this procedure is appropriate
in the case of child witnesses and therefore it cannot, of itself, be said to amount
to injustice to the defendant. He submitted that the justices were wrong as a
matter of law in inquiring into the nature of the objection that the girls had to
giving evidence in court. If a court is required to make such inquiries, he
submitted that that could result in the court becoming embroiled in a difficult
exercise in establishing the state of mind of the child in question.

[10] He further submitted that the justices wrongly imported into the resolution
of the issue the concept of equality of arms, alternatively misunderstood its effect.
He submitted that what is necessary in order to meet the obligations of the
European Convention for the Protection of Human Rights and Fundamental
Freedoms (Rome, 4 November 1950; TS 71 (1953); Cmd 8969) (as set out in Sch 1
to the Human Rights Act 1998) is that the proceedings, taken as a whole, are fair
and that the rights of the parties adequately respected. He referred us to *Doorson v
Netherlands* (1996) 22 EHRR 330 at 358 (para 70), where the court held:
'... principles of fair trial also require that in appropriate cases the interests of the
defence are balanced against those of witnesses or victims called upon to testify.'

a [11] He submitted that the defendant in the present case would have a full opportunity to see and hear the evidence and to cross-examine the witnesses, so that his rights were properly respected. In these circumstances, he submitted that the justices were clearly wrong in the way they carried out the exercise under s 32A(3)(c) of the 1988 Act.

b [12] Mr Keith did not accept that the court was only concerned with competence and reliability. He submitted that the purpose of the statutory provisions was to provide protection for child witnesses so that their evidence was not affected by any stress or fear engendered by having to give evidence in court. He submitted that in every case the statute effectively provided a presumption that this would be achieved by the admission of a video interview, and that it would be for a defendant to show that in any given case the interests of justice would not be best

c served by taking that course. He further submitted that it is unlikely that a defendant could, save in an exceptional case, be prejudiced by the use of a videoed interview. He would be free to identify and challenge the witness by way of cross-examination; and the court itself would be helped by an account given by a witness, as is usually the case in videoed interviews, close to the time of the

d alleged offence. He submitted that the justices erred in carrying out the balancing exercise which he accepts they were required to do by failing to consider the extent to which the girl's testimony would be less reliable by reason of their expressed embarrassment, as against the contents of the interviews, and to determine precisely what prejudice would be suffered by the defendant if the video interviews were admitted.

e

BICESTER YOUTH COURT

[13] Mr Knowles on behalf of the claimant, and Mr Ross on behalf of the defendant, also made helpful submissions to the court in the different context of s 32 of the 1988 Act. Mr Knowles submitted that unlike s 32A of the 1988 Act, the

f court's discretion is not affected by any presumption as to the admissibility of evidence which is sought to be tendered through a live video link. He submitted that the primary rule is that evidence should be given in court in the presence of a defendant. Any special measures taken to protect a witness whether by the use of a live television link, or by any of the other measures which a court can take to protect a witness detract from that principle to the potential prejudice of a

g defendant. It deprives both the court and the defendant of the opportunity to see most clearly the demeanour of the witness and avoids the inherent discipline of having to give evidence openly and not in artificially protected circumstances. He submitted that a youth court is in particular required to take into account the fact that the procedure and the layout of the court are all designed to minimise

h the stress imposed not only on a defendant, but also on witnesses. Accordingly, he submitted, the use of a live television link is only justified if the quality of the evidence would be substantially impaired if such a link were not used. The court is also required, he submitted, to consider any steps short of a television link which could make it easier for a witness to give evidence on the basis that the

j court should only interfere with the normal process of the court to the minimum extent necessary. In relation to the facts of the case itself, he submitted that the district judge was wrong in principle in using the provisions of s 32 as an alternative to the issue of a witness summons. This was particularly clear in the case of AA, where it would appear that the district judge was of the view that if the witness was brought to court, the lack of a television link would not affect the quality of his evidence.

[14] Mr Ross submitted that the fact that a witness indicated a reluctance to come to court in the absence of a television link was not irrelevant. It was a fact from which the court could infer that the witness would be sufficiently affected by the stress of the process of giving evidence that the quality of his evidence would be affected, or that he may not be ultimately able to give any evidence to the court. In relation to SH and BO'N he submitted that the district judge was entitled to take the view that the evidence before him was such as to justify the conclusion that their evidence would be affected particularly because of the intimidation to which it was said they had been subjected. As far as AA was concerned, he accepted that the evidence was not so compelling, nor were the district judge's conclusions as clear. None the less, he submitted that a fair reading of the district judge's reasons shows that he was satisfied that AA was frightened, which would of itself have justified the inference that there was a real risk that the quality of his evidence would be affected.

CONCLUSION

[15] In my judgment, there is a distinction to be made between the approach of the court under s 32 and 32A of the 1988 Act. In the case of video interviews, Parliament has provided that the primary method of presenting evidence of a child witness where there is a video interview is by means of such an interview. There is no such presumption in s 32. But the general legislative purpose of both sections is the same, namely to provide, in relation to a child, conditions which are most conducive to ensuring that a child is able to give as full an account as possible of the events in question. The procedures are intended to provide a mechanism whereby a child witness who might otherwise be upset, intimidated or traumatised by appearing in court is not as a result inhibited from giving a full and proper account of the events of which he or she was a witness (see *R v McAndrew-Bingham* [1999] 1 WLR 1897). It follows that orders under either section are appropriate where there is a real risk that the quality of the evidence given by that child would be so affected or that it might even be impossible to obtain any evidence from that child. Fairness to the defendant is achieved by enabling the defendant to see the witness giving evidence in interview, or by a television link, and having a full opportunity to cross-examine by way of the television link.

[16] In relation to s 32A, there is a further purpose, namely that the evidence of a child should be the account of the child given as contemporaneously as possible, so that evidence-in-chief is not a memory test. The wording of sub-s (3) makes it clear that leave must therefore be granted for a video recording of an interview to be given in evidence, unless any of the exceptions are established. If the exceptions in sub-paras (a) or (b) are established leave must be refused. If under sub-para (c) the question is raised whether or not in the interests of justice the recording should not be admitted, the court is required to carry out a balancing exercise bearing in mind the legislative purposes to which I have referred. This requires the court to consider whether there will be any arguable injustice in admitting the video. If the injustice alleged is simply the fact that the witness will not be giving live evidence, it is unlikely that that could ever prevail if there was material which established that the witness could be upset, intimidated or traumatised by appearing in court as a result of which there was a real risk that the quality of the child's evidence would be affected or that no evidence would be forthcoming. To permit such an argument to succeed would defeat the legislative purpose. This principle in my view applies whatever the age of the defendant. It follows that the court is required to consider on the one hand

a the extent to which the witness's evidence would be so affected if the video recording was not admitted in evidence, and on the other the prejudice to the defendant if the video recording were to be admitted in evidence. In carrying out that exercise, the court must bear in mind that Parliament has determined that the primary method by which a child witness's evidence should be given to a court is by means of the video interview. It seems to me to follow that it is for a
b defendant to establish that any prejudice to him displaces this parliamentary intention.

[17] In relation to s 32, as I have said, the position is different. Parliament has provided no presumption one way or the other as to the way in which the evidence should be given. It is necessary therefore to consider in every case the extent to which justice is best achieved by making or not making the order
c applied for. In doing so the court will bear in mind that the paradigm or norm in our courts is that a witness should give evidence in court in the presence of the defendant. It follows that some good reason must be shown in accordance with the legislative purpose if an order is to be made under s 32. Again the court is required to strike a balance, on this occasion between the right of the defendant
d to have a hearing in accordance with the norm and the need to provide protection in accordance with the legislative purpose, in the interests not only of the child witness but also of justice, to ensure that the witness will be able to give evidence and give evidence unaffected by the stress of appearing in court itself.

[18] In the instant cases, the only prejudice suggested by the defendants to the criminal proceedings is that they would be deprived of the benefits of seeing and
e hearing the witnesses live in court. Whilst there is no doubt that this procedure has the advantage of enabling a defendant and the court to see directly the demeanour of the witness and the way in which his or her evidence is given, the court must bear in mind the fact that both the video recording and a television link provide an opportunity, albeit in an indirect form, to carry out
f that same exercise. The court should also bear in mind that although there may be disadvantages in the indirect method of giving evidence, they do not necessarily disadvantage only the defendant. The impact of evidence given directly to the court is likely to be greater whether it be in favour of the prosecution or the defence.

[19] Article 6 of the convention does not, in my judgment, provide any further assistance in resolving the difficult question which the court has to answer under
g either section. As the European Court of Human Rights recognised in *Doorson v Netherlands*, it is appropriate to provide protection to certain classes of witness. It seems to me to be clear that child witnesses fall into a category of witness which is entitled to such protection. Provided that a decision of a court is based on the purpose for which such protection is provided, steps taken to provide that
h protection cannot result in unfairness to a defendant provided always that the defendant is given a fair opportunity both to test that evidence and to answer it. The procedures under ss 32 and 32A of the 1988 Act provide that opportunity.

THE INDIVIDUAL CASES

j *Redbridge Youth Court*

[20] I pay tribute to the care with which the justices considered what was a difficult question in this case in the absence of any guidelines. It seems to me that in essence the justices determined that the embarrassment which they accepted would be suffered by the complainants, was not such as to give rise to a real risk that the quality of their evidence would be affected (see para 8(c) and (e) of

Michael Batten's affidavit). That being the conclusion of the justices, it follows that the defendant had discharged the burden of establishing that the legislative purpose would not be compromised by not making the order. In those circumstances, the justices were entitled to take the view that fairness, and therefore justice, required that the complainants' evidence be given live in court. The disadvantages to the defendant, and to the court's ability to assess the quality of a witness's evidence, were the evidence to be given by way of a video recorded interview or by a video link could properly be said to justify that conclusion. Accordingly the justices were entitled to refuse to make the orders applied for in this case; and the application must therefore be refused.

Bicester Youth Court

[21] The district judge in this case was simply dealing with applications under s 32 of the 1988 Act. It is apparent from the extract from the notes of his reasons to which I have already referred that he applied the correct burden of proof. He directed himself that there had to be some factor from which a court could deduce that the witness would either not appear at all or the quality of the evidence would be adversely effected. I have no doubt that he was correct in taking the view that if there was evidence that by reason of the witness's vulnerability he might not appear at all were there no live television link, that was a fact which he was entitled to take into account. If a child witness is so frightened that he is unwilling to come to court unless his evidence is given by live television link, the likelihood is that were he to be forced to come to court he would either give no evidence, or the quality of his evidence would be affected by his fear. In relation to SH and BO'N, who are respectively 10 and 11 years of age, the district judge was clearly entitled to take the view that the fear that they were expressing, based partly on the threats to which each said he was subjected, justified the making of the order. AA is in a different position. Doing the best one can from the note of the judgment, it would appear that the district judge was not concerned about the quality of his evidence, nor did he express any concern about the witness's willingness to give evidence once he got to court, but justified the making of the order on the 'ease' with which he might be brought to court. That is not, in itself, a justifiable reason for making the order. As Mr Knowles submitted, a witness summons could achieve that objective. It is only if the district judge came to the conclusion that the use of that method of ensuring his presence at court would not ensure that he was either willing to give evidence or to give evidence of value, that an order would have been justified. For this reason, I consider that the order so far as it relates to AA should be quashed, and the application remitted to the district judge for further consideration.

ASTILL J.

[22] I agree.

The DPP's application dismissed. L's application allowed in part.

Dilys Tausz   Barrister.

a
R (on the application of Balbo B & C Auto Transporti Internazionali) v Secretary of State for the Home Department
[2001] EWHC Admin 195

b

QUEEN'S BENCH DIVISION, DIVISIONAL COURT
BROOKE LJ AND POTTS J
8 FEBRUARY, 15 MARCH 2001

c
Judicial review – Availability of remedy – Alternative remedy available – Clandestine entrants – Penalty for carrying clandestine entrants – Secretary of State issuing claimant with penalty notice as person responsible for clandestine entrants – Secretary of State upholding notice despite service of notice of objection – Claimant applying for judicial review – Whether judicial review appropriate remedy – Immigration and Asylum Act 1999, ss 32, 34, 35, 37.

d

Immigration service officials found 11 persons inside a transporter on its arrival by ferry from Calais. Those persons were clandestine entrants within the meaning of s 32[a] of the Immigration and Asylum Act 1999, and the owners of the transporter were the persons responsible for them for the purposes of that section. As such, the owners were liable to penalties under s 32(2) of the 1999 Act,

e
subject to any defences they might have under s 34[b]. Such a penalty could be recovered by the Secretary of State as a debt due to him. Under s 37[c], the court had power to release a vehicle detained under s 36 if, inter alia, it considered that satisfactory security had been tendered in place of the transporter for the payment of the penalty alleged to be due. If the court had not ordered the release

f
of the transporter and the penalty had not been paid within a period of 84 days beginning with the date of its detention, the Secretary of State could, with leave of the court, sell the transporter. The Secretary of State duly issued the owners with a penalty notice pursuant to s 35[d], requiring payment of the penalty within the period prescribed by the Act. The owners served a notice of objection under s 35(7), but the Secretary of State concluded that the owners had not made out a

g
valid defence under s 34 and accordingly he decided that the penalty notice should stand. The owners applied for judicial review. At the hearing, the Secretary of State raised as a preliminary point the question whether there was not a more convenient alternative remedy available to the owners, namely the right to raise any arguments they wished when he issued proceedings for

h
_____

a   Section 32, so far as material, is set out at [6], below
b   Section 34 is set out at [8], below
c   Section 37, so far as material, provides:
    '(1) This section applies if a transporter is detained under section 36.
    (2) The person to whom the penalty notice was addressed ... may apply to the court for the
j   transporter to be released.
    (3) The court may release the transporter if it considers that—(a) satisfactory security has been tendered in place of the transporter for the payment of the penalty alleged to be due and connected expenses ...
    (4) If the court has not ordered the release of the transporter, the Secretary of State may sell it if the penalty in question and connected expenses are not paid before the end of the period of 84 days beginning with the date on which the detention began ...'
d   Section 35, so far as material, is set out at [10], below

recovery of the penalty. The owners contended that if an owner had tendered
satisfactory security to obtain the release of a transporter detained under s 36, he
would have to wait, perhaps indefinitely, for the Secretary of State to initiate
proceedings in order to obtain the release of his security.

Held – Where the Secretary of State had upheld a penalty notice under s 35 of the
1999 Act following the service of a notice of objection under s 35(7), judicial
review was not the appropriate remedy for the person who was the subject of the
penalty notice. Rather, he should wait until the Secretary of State sued him in
the ordinary courts after the expiry of the time prescribed for payment. In such
proceedings, the Secretary of State would be alleging that the owner of the
transporter was liable to a penalty under s 32, and the owner would be able, if so
advised, to assert in those proceedings any of the defences available to him under
s 34. Court proceedings of that kind, not judicial review proceedings, would be
the natural forum for a trial of disputed fact, such as would arise when the
viability of a s 34 defence was in issue. If the responsible persons were found not
to be liable to a penalty under s 32, whatever might have happened under the s 35
procedure would fall away. Similarly, if the Secretary of State sought the leave of
the court to sell the transporter, it would be open to the owner to assert in such
proceedings that he was not liable to pay the penalty because he had a valid s 34
defence. Moreover, an owner who had tendered satisfactory security for a
transporter detained under s 36 would not have to wait for the Secretary of State
to initiate proceedings in order to obtain the release of his security. It would
always be open to him to seek a declaration that he was not a person liable to a
penalty under s 32, and an order restoring to him, or cancelling, the security that
he had tendered. Accordingly, the appropriate venue for the dispute in the
instant case was an ordinary court (almost certainly a county court), and the
application would therefore be dismissed (see [14]–[16], [18], below).

Notes
For alternative remedies to judicial review, see 1(1) *Halsbury's Laws* (4th edn)
(2001 reissue) para 67.

For the Immigration and Asylum Act 1999, ss 32, 34, 35, 37, see 31 *Halsbury's
Statutes* (4th edn) (2000 reissue) 305, 307, 309.

Cases cited or referred to in skeleton arguments
Boddington v British Transport Police [1998] 2 All ER 203, [1999] 2 AC 143, HL.
Booth v Trail (1883) 12 QBD 8.
Cannock Chase DC v Kelly [1978] 1 All ER 152, [1978] 1 WLR 1, CA.
Council of Civil Service Unions v Minister for the Civil Service [1984] 3 All ER 935,
    [1985] AC 374, HL.
Kruse v Johnson [1898] 2 QB 91, [1895–9] All ER Rep 105, DC.
Luby v Newcastle-under-Lyme Corp [1964] 1 All ER 84, [1964] 2 QB 64; *affd* [1964]
    3 All ER 169, [1965] 1 QB 214, CA.
R v Birmingham City Council, ex p Ferrero Ltd [1993] 1 All ER 530, CA.
R v Lincoln City Council, ex p Wickes Building Supplies Ltd (1993) 92 LGR 215, DC.
R v Secretary of State for Social Services, ex p Association of Metropolitan Authorities
    [1986] 1 All ER 164, [1986] 1 WLR 1.
R v Secretary of State for the Environment, ex p Fielder Estates (Canvey) Ltd (1988) 57
    P & CR 424.

a R *(on the application of Alconbury Developments Ltd) v Secretary of State for the Environment, Transport and the Regions* [2001] 2 All ER 929, DC; *rvsd* [2001] UKHL 23, [2001] 2 All ER 929, [2001] 2 WLR 1389.

Application for judicial review

b By notice dated 10 August 2000, the claimants, Balbo B & C Auto Transporti Internazionali, applied for judicial review of the decision of the defendant, the Secretary of State for the Home Department, on 12 June 2000 that a notice of liability to civil penalty served on the claimant under s 35 of the Immigration and Asylum Act 1999 should stand. The facts are set out in the judgment of the court.

c *Nevil Phillips* and *Nicholas Craig* (instructed by *Holmes Hardingham Walser Johnston Winter*) for the claimants.

John Howell QC and *Robin Tam* (instructed by the *Treasury Solicitor*) for the Secretary of State.

d At the conclusion of argument the court announced that the application would be dismissed for reasons to be given later.

15 March 2001. The following judgment of the court was delivered.

BROOKE LJ.
e [1] This is the judgment of the court.

[2] This is an application by Balbo B & C Auto Transporti Internazionali for judicial review of a decision by the Secretary of State on 12 June 2000 whereby he decided that a notice of liability to civil penalty issued pursuant to s 35 of the Immigration and Asylum Act 1999 in respect of 11 persons being clandestine *f* entrants should stand.

[3] The brief history of the matter is that on 6 June 2000 a transporter owned by the claimants was searched by immigration service officials on its arrival by ferry from Calais. When the trailer was opened, 11 clandestine entrants (including six children) were found within it. Since the claimants were the persons responsible for the clandestine entrants found in the transporter they owned they were prima *g* facie liable to the penalties (being 11 times the prescribed amount) mentioned in s 32(2) of the 1999 Act. On the same day the Secretary of State served a penalty notice in accordance with that Act, and on 9 June 2000 solicitors acting for the claimants served a notice of objection pursuant to s 35(7) of the same Act. Three days later the Secretary of State made the decision whose validity is impugned in *h* these proceedings. He said that in his view the penalty was payable and he gave his reasons for this decision.

[4] On the hearing of this application the Secretary of State raised as a preliminary point the question whether there was not a much more suitable alternative remedy available to the claimants. He was referring to their right to *j* raise any arguments they wished when the Secretary of State issued proceedings against them in court to recover the penalty.

[5] We decided to hear argument on this point as a preliminary issue. At the end of the argument we said that we were satisfied that there was a more convenient alternative remedy and that the application would therefore be dismissed. In this judgment we are setting out our reasons for this decision.

[6] The relevant statutory provisions are contained in Pt II of the 1999 Act. Because they are relatively new, we will set them out in some detail, so far as is material:

'**32.**—(1) A person is a clandestine entrant if—(a) he arrives in the United Kingdom concealed in a vehicle, ship or aircraft, (b) he passes, or attempts to pass, through immigration control concealed in a vehicle, or (c) he arrives in the United Kingdom on a ship or aircraft, having embarked—(i) concealed in a vehicle; and (ii) at a time when the ship or aircraft was outside the United Kingdom, and claims, or indicates that he intends to seek, asylum in the United Kingdom or evades, or attempts to evade, immigration control.

(2) The person (or persons) responsible for a clandestine entrant is (or are together) liable to—(a) a penalty of the prescribed amount in respect of the clandestine entrant; and (b) an additional penalty of that amount in respect of each person who was concealed with the clandestine entrant in the same transporter.

(3) A penalty imposed under this section must be paid to the Secretary of State before the end of the prescribed period.

(4) Payment of the full amount of a penalty by one or more of the persons responsible for the clandestine entrant discharges the liability of each of the persons responsible for that entrant.

(5) In the case of a clandestine entrant to whom subsection (1)(a) applies, each of the following is a responsible person ... (b) if it is a vehicle (but not a detached trailer), the owner, hirer or driver of the vehicle ...

(7) Subject to any defence provided by section 34, it is immaterial whether a responsible person knew or suspected—(a) that the clandestine entrant was concealed in the transporter; or (b) that there were one or more other persons concealed with the clandestine entrant in the same transporter.'

[7] On the facts of the present case, the application of s 32 creates no difficulty. The 11 persons concealed in the trailer were clandestine entrants because they arrived in the United Kingdom concealed in a vehicle and one of the other conditions at the end of s 32(1) was fulfilled. The owners of the vehicle were among the persons responsible for these clandestine entrants (s 32(5)(b)), and as such they were liable to the penalties referred to in s 32(2), which must be paid to the Secretary of State before the end of 'the prescribed period' (being 60 days from the service of the penalty notice which informs the person served that the Secretary of State has decided that he is liable, not counting 'any period during which the Secretary of State considers any objection notice'): see s 32(3), and regs 4(1) and (2) of the Carriers' Liability (Clandestine Entrants and Sale of Transporters) Regulations 2000, SI 2000/685. Subject to any defence provided by s 34, it is immaterial whether the owners knew or suspected any of the matters set out in s 32(7).

[8] Nothing in this judgment turns on any of the provisions of the code of practice provided for in s 33 of the 1999 Act, but we need to set out s 34 in full:

'(1) This section applies if it is alleged that a person ("the carrier") is liable to a penalty under section 32.

(2) It is a defence for the carrier to show that he, or an employee of his who was directly responsible for allowing the clandestine entrant to be concealed, was acting under duress.

a

(3) It is also a defence for the carrier to show that—(a) he did not know, and had no reasonable grounds for suspecting, that a clandestine entrant was, or might be, concealed in the transporter; (b) an effective system for preventing the carriage of clandestine entrants was in operation in relation to the transporter; and (c) that on the occasion in question the person or persons responsible for operating that system did so properly.

b

(4) In determining, for the purposes of this section, whether a particular system is effective, regard is to be had to the code of practice issued by the Secretary of State under section 33.

(5) If there are two or more persons responsible for a clandestine entrant, the fact that one or more of them has a defence under subsection (3) does not affect the liability of the others.

c

(6) But if a person responsible for a clandestine entrant has a defence under subsection (2), the liability of any other person responsible for that entrant is discharged.'

[9] The normal meaning of such a provision, coupled with the liability-creating provisions of s 32, is that s 32 creates an absolute legal liability in the sense that no mens rea has to be proved. This legal liability will, however, be negated if the responsible person in question can prove on the balance of probabilities one of the matters set out in s 34(2) or (3).

d

[10] Section 35 of the 1999 Act provides, so far as is material:

e

'(1) If the Secretary of State decides that a person ("P") is liable to one or more penalties under section 32, he must notify P of his decision.

(2) A notice under subsection (1) (a "penalty notice") must—(a) state the Secretary of State's reasons for deciding that P is liable to the penalty (or penalties); (b) state the amount of the penalty (or penalties) to which P is liable; (c) specify the date before which, and the manner in which, the penalty (or penalties) must be paid; and (d) include an explanation of the steps—(i) that P must take if he objects to the penalty; (ii) that the Secretary of State may take under this Part to recover any unpaid penalty …

f

(6) If a person on whom a penalty notice is served, or who is treated as having had a penalty notice served on him, alleges that he is not liable for one or more, or all, of the penalties specified in the penalty notice, he may give written notice of his allegation to the Secretary of State.

g

(7) Notice under subsection (6) ("a notice of objection") must—(a) give reasons for the allegation; and (b) be given before the end of such period as may be prescribed.

(8) If a notice of objection is given before the end of the prescribed period, the Secretary of State must consider it and determine whether or not any penalty to which it relates is payable …

h

(10) Any sum payable to the Secretary of State as a penalty under section 32 may be recovered by the Secretary of State as a debt due to him.'

j

[11] In the present case an immigration officer acting on behalf of the Secretary of State served a penalty notice in the requisite form (Form IS 11) on 6 June, requiring payment of £22,000 not later than 5 August 2000. The notice ends as follows:

'Any sum payable to the Secretary of State as a penalty under section 32 of the Act may be recoverable by the Secretary of State through the Courts. In addition, if payment in full is not received, the Secretary of State may apply to the court for leave to sell the transporter if 84 days have elapsed since it was detained.'   *a*

[12] Solicitors acting for the owners served a notice of objection pursuant to s 35(6), giving reasons for their objection, by a letter dated 9 June 2000. By a letter dated 12 June an inspector at the United Kingdom Immigration Service Headquarters responded to the objection, and stated why he did not consider that a valid   *b* defence under s 34 had been made out. He therefore told them that the liability under the penalty notice stood, and extended the time for payment to allow for the time taken to reply to the letter of objection. He enclosed with his letter Form IS 11B, which was signed by an immigration officer on behalf of the Secretary of State. This form is entitled 'Clandestine Entrants—Determination of Notice of Objection and Demand for Penalty', and demands the sum of £22,000,   *c* to be paid not later than 9 August 2000. On this occasion the form repeats the final sentence of the earlier form, but says nothing about the penalty being recoverable by the Secretary of State through the courts.

[13] It was this omission, no doubt, and the emphasis contained in the form on the fact that this civil penalty must be paid by 9 August, which led the owners' *d* solicitors to believe that the only means of challenging the lawfulness of this notice was by way of judicial review. As the argument proceeded, it appeared increasingly odd that this should have been Parliament's intention, because if the Secretary of State were to be the sole arbiter of the question whether a person served with a penalty notice had a viable defence under s 34 he would be acting *e* as judge in his own cause. Since the issue between the Secretary of State and the owners related to the determination of the owners' civil obligations, such an interpretation of the provisions would immediately fall foul of the 'fair trial' requirement of art 6(1) of the European Convention for the Protection of Human Rights and Fundamental Freedoms (Rome, 4 November 1950; TS 71 (1953); Cmd 8969) (as set out in Sch 1 to the Human Rights Act 1998).   *f*

[14] In our judgment the 1999 Act should not be interpreted in this way. If the owners consider they have a valid defence to the penalty notice, notwithstanding the Secretary of State's rejection of their objection, they should wait until the Secretary of State sues them, which he will be able to do as soon as the time prescribed for payment has expired. In such proceedings the Secretary of State *g* will be alleging that the owners are liable to a penalty under s 32 (s 34(1)), and the owners will be able, if so advised, to assert in those proceedings any of the defences available to them under s 34. Court proceedings of this kind would be the natural forum for a trial of disputed fact, such as would arise when the viability of a s 34 defence is in issue. Judicial review proceedings would not.   *h*

[15] It should be noted in this context that the draftsman deliberately chose the words 'liable to a penalty under section 32'. The issue in the proceedings will be whether a successful s 34 defence will mean that the responsible persons are not liable to a penalty under s 32 after all, because they can show that they were acting under duress, or that an effective system for preventing the carriage of *j* clandestine entrants was in operation, and so on. If they are found not to be liable to a penalty under s 32, then whatever may have happened under the s 35 procedure will fall away. Similarly if the Secretary of State seeks the leave of the court to sell the transporter pursuant to s 37 and para 1(1) of Sch 1 to the 1999 Act, the court is not to give its leave except on proof that the penalty was due and that the person liable to pay it has failed to do so (para 1(2)(a) and (b) of Sch 1). It will be

a open to the owner of the transporter in such proceedings to assert that he was not liable to pay the penalty because he had a valid s 34 defence.

[16] Mr Phillips suggested that if an owner tendered satisfactory security to obtain the release of a transporter detained under s 36 of the 1999 Act (see s 37(3)(a)) he would have to wait, perhaps indefinitely, for the Secretary of State to initiate proceedings in order to obtain the release of his security. We do not understand

b why this necessarily follows, because it would always be open to the owner in such circumstances to seek a declaration that he was not a person liable to a penalty under s 32 and an order restoring to him, or cancelling, the security he tendered.

[17] We are sure that unnecessary difficulties have arisen in this case because the statutory provisions are rather dense, and because Forms IS 11 and IS 11B do

c not state with the clarity that one would expect from government forms the right of a person served with a penalty notice to rely on the statutory defences in court proceedings whether or not he has availed himself of the administrative objection procedure open to him under s 35. We hope that consideration may be given to the redrafting of these forms in order to set the position out with greater clarity.

d [18] However that may be, we are satisfied that the appropriate venue for this dispute is an ordinary court (almost certainly a county court), and we therefore dismiss this application for judicial review on the grounds that a far more convenient alternative forum is available.

Application dismissed.

Dilys Tausz   Barrister.

R (on the application of the Secretary of State for the Home Department) v Immigration Appeal Tribunal

[2001] EWHC Admin 261

QUEEN'S BENCH DIVISION (ADMINISTRATIVE COURT)

SCOTT BAKER J

12 MARCH, 9 APRIL 2001

Immigration – Appeal – Immigration Appeal Tribunal – Appeal from special adjudicator – Source and nature of tribunal's power to remit appeal to special adjudicator – Whether full tribunal having power to set aside or vary order of chairman of tribunal sitting alone – Immigration Act 1971, ss 19, 20, 22 – Immigration Appeals (Procedure) Rules 1984, rr 21, 38 – Asylum Appeals (Procedure) Rules 1996, r 17(2).

Z, an asylum seeker, successfully appealed to a special adjudicator under s 19[a] of the Immigration Act 1971 against the refusal of his application for asylum. The Secretary of State was granted leave to appeal to the Immigration Appeal Tribunal. Under r 21[b] of the Immigration Appeals (Procedure) Rules 1984, the tribunal could, if it thought it appropriate to do so, remit an appeal to an adjudicator for determination by him in accordance with any directions given to him by the tribunal. Rule 17(2)[c] of the Asylum Appeals (Procedure) Rules 1996 required the tribunal to determine the appeal itself unless it considered that it was desirable in the interests of justice and would save time and expense to remit the case to a special adjudicator for determination in accordance with any directions given to him by the tribunal. Those remittal rules had both been made under s 22(2)(a)[d] of the 1971 Act which provided that rules of procedure could include provision enabling the tribunal, on an appeal from an adjudicator, to remit an appeal to an adjudicator for determination by him in accordance with any directions of the tribunal. The Secretary of State's appeal was listed for mention before a tribunal chairman sitting alone. Z's solicitors wrote to the tribunal saying that they did not intend to appear at the mention and asking for the appeal to be listed for hearing. However, the chairman took the view that the adjudicator's decision was flawed and that the case should be remitted to be heard afresh by a different adjudicator. He persuaded Z, who had attended in person, to agree, and accordingly made an order under r 17(2) of the 1996 rules. Z's solicitors applied for the order to be set aside and for the appeal to be determined. The application was heard by a full tribunal which held that it had jurisdiction to set aside the chairman's order and that the appeal should be listed for hearing in the normal way. In the course of reaching its decision, the tribunal concluded that it had two separate powers to remit a case to an adjudicator, namely (i) an express power granted under r 21 of the 1984 rules and r 17(2) of the 1996 rules; and (ii) an implied power to be found in s 20[e] of the 1971 Act which provided that any party

---

a   Section 19, so far as material, is set out at [7], below
b   Rule 21 is set out at [10], below
c   Rule 17(2) is set out at [11], below
d   Section 22, so far as material, is set out at [9], below
e   Section 20 is set out at [8], below

a to an appeal to an adjudicator could, if dissatisfied with his determination, appeal to the tribunal and that the latter could affirm the determination or make any other determination that could have been made by the adjudicator. The tribunal further concluded that the express power involved the tribunal delegating to the adjudicator its function of deciding the appeal from the adjudicator, thereby precluding any further appeal to the tribunal, while the implied power

b involved the tribunal disposing of the appeal by allowing it and ordering a rehearing by the adjudicator of the appeal to him. On his application for judicial review, the Secretary of State did not seek to quash the full tribunal's decision since he accepted that the circumstances of the chairman's decision would have entitled Z to have had that decision quashed on judicial review. He nevertheless sought clarification of the law by means of declaratory relief in two areas, namely

c the source and nature of the tribunal's power to remit a case for rehearing by an adjudicator and the circumstances in which an order made by a chairman of the tribunal sitting alone might be varied or set aside by the full tribunal. The tribunal contended that s 22(2)(a) covered only 'procedural' remittals where the adjudicator acted on behalf of the tribunal, and did not extend to 'substantive' remittals where

d the adjudicator considered the matter afresh, giving rise to a further right of appeal to the tribunal. The Secretary of State contended that a remittal decision, even when made by a single member tribunal, could not be set aside by the tribunal since that decision was the tribunal's decision on the appeal to it from the adjudicator. That submission led the court to consider r 38[f] of the 1984 rules which provided that any irregularity resulting from a failure to comply with

e the rules before the tribunal had reached its decision did not by itself render the proceedings void, but the tribunal could before reaching its decision take steps to cure the irregularity.

Held – (1) The tribunal had a single power to remit a case to an adjudicator and it

f was neither necessary nor appropriate to speak of substantive remittals and procedural remittals. That power arose by virtue of s 20 of the 1971 Act, read together with ss 19 and 22, and the remittal rules made under s 22(2)(a) had to be read compatibly with it. Section 22(2)(a) itself regulated and reflected, but did not confer, the jurisdiction. It was subservient to s 20 from which the jurisdiction

g emanated. When they were read together, s 22(2)(a) clearly recognised that s 20 was intended to include a power of remittal. That power did not involve the tribunal delegating to the adjudicator the tribunal's function of deciding an appeal from an adjudicator. Rather, it involved disposing of the appeal to the tribunal and ordering a rehearing by the adjudicator of the appeal to him. Adjudicators never determined appeals to the tribunal. Adjudicators decided appeals to them,

h and there was always a right of further appeal to the tribunal (see [20], [22], [23], [46], [47], below).

(2) The tribunal had no power to rescind its own decision or that of another tribunal. What was critical was that the decision to remit the appeal to an adjudicator for determination was a decision which disposed of the appeal to the

j tribunal, after which the power to cure irregularities given by the rules could no

---

f Rule 38 provides: 'Any irregularity resulting from failure to comply with these Rules before an appellate authority has reached its decision shall not by itself render the proceedings void, but the appellate authority may, and shall if it considers that any person may have been prejudiced, take such steps as it thinks fit before reaching its decision to cure the irregularity, whether by amendment of any document, the giving of any notice or otherwise.'

longer be exercised. It was therefore of no significance in the instant case that the
remittal decision had been made by a chairman of a tribunal sitting alone, rather
than by a full tribunal. The appellate authority had reached its decision within
the meaning of r 38 of the 1984 rules and it could not thereafter be corrected as
an irregularity. Accordingly, judgment would be given for the Secretary of State
(see [64], [67], below); dicta of Sedley LJ in *Akewushola v Secretary of State for the
Home Dept* [2000] 2 All ER 148 at 153–154 applied.

Notes

For procedure on an appeal to the tribunal from an adjudicator, see 4(2)
Halsbury's Laws (4th edn reissue) para 138.

    For the Immigration Act 1971, ss 19, 20, 22, see 31 *Halsbury's Statutes* (4th edn)
(2000 reissue) 92, 93, 94. Sections 19, 20 and (for certain purposes) s 22 have been
repealed with effect from 2 October 2000 by the Immigration and Asylum Act
1999, s 169(1), (3), Sch 14, paras 43, 49, Sch 16.

    For the Immigration Appeals (Procedure) Rules 1984, rr 21, 38, see 14
Halsbury's Statutory Instruments (1999 issue) 173, 178.

    For the Asylum Appeals (Procedure) Rules 1996, r 17, see 14 *Halsbury's Statutory
Instruments* (1999 issue) 188.

Cases referred to in judgment

Ahmed v Entry Clearance Officer, Islamabad, Taj Bibi v Entry Clearance Officer, Islamabad
    [1977] Imm AR 25, IAT.
Akewushola v Secretary of State for the Home Dept [2000] 2 All ER 148, [2000] 1 WLR
    2295, CA.
Barnard v Gorman [1941] 3 All ER 45, [1941] AC 378, HL.
Borissov v Secretary of State for the Home Dept [1996] Imm AR 524, CA.
Kara v Secretary of State for the Home Dept [1995] Imm AR 584, CA.
R v Immigration Appeal Tribunal, ex p Wanyoike [2000] Imm AR 389.
Salter Rex & Co v Ghosh [1971] 2 All ER 865, [1971] 2 QB 597, [1971] 3 WLR 31, CA.
Secretary of State for the Home Dept v Zengin [2000] Imm AR 518, IAT.

Cases also cited or referred to in skeleton arguments

Casella London Ltd v Banai [1990] ICR 215, EAT.
Charman v Palmers Scaffolding Ltd [1979] ICR 335, EAT.
R (Kadhim) v Brent London BC Council Housing Benefit Review Board [2001] 2 WLR
    1674, CA.
*R v Immigration Appeal Tribunal, ex p Jeyeanthan, Ravichandran v Secretary of State for
    the Home Dept* [1999] 3 All ER 231, [2000] 1 WLR 354, CA.
R v Immigration Appeal Tribunal, ex p S [1998] Imm AR 252.
R v Secretary of State for the Home Dept, ex p Isiko [2001] 1 FCR 633, CA.

Application for judicial review

By notice dated 20 October 2000, the claimant, the Secretary of State for the
Home Department, applied by way of judicial review for a declaration that the
defendant, the Immigration Appeal Tribunal (Collins J, chairman, P Moulden
and G Warr) ([2000] Imm AR 518), erred in law in its decision of 8 June 2000,
promulgated on 27 July 2000, setting aside the order of another tribunal chairman,
J R A Fox, dated 6 March 2000, remitting the asylum appeal of Musa Zengin to a
special adjudicator for rehearing. The facts are set out in the judgment.

a Michael Fordham (instructed by the *Treasury Solicitor*) for the Secretary of State.
Robin Tam (instructed by the *Treasury Solicitor*) for the tribunal.

Cur adv vult

9 April 2001. The following judgment was delivered.

b
SCOTT BAKER J.

[1] The claimant in this claim for judicial review is the Secretary of State for
the Home Department. The defendant is the Immigration Appeal Tribunal
(the tribunal). The underlying litigation concerned Musa Zengin, an asylum
seeker, who is an interested party but who has taken no part in the present
c application which raises two points of law: (i) the tribunal's power to remit a case
for rehearing by an adjudicator, and (ii) the circumstances in which an order
made by a chairman of the tribunal sitting alone may be varied or set aside.

[2] The facts are very simple; the law much more difficult. On 20 October 1998
Mr Zengin's claim for asylum was refused. He appealed to a special adjudicator
who allowed his appeal on 27 August 1999. The Secretary of State was granted
d leave to appeal and on 6 March 2000 the appeal was listed for mention before a
tribunal chairman sitting alone (Mr Fox). Mr Zengin's solicitors wrote to
the tribunal saying they did not intend to appear at the mention and asked for the
appeal to be listed for hearing. This was an entirely proper course to save costs,
and the tribunal was aware that the appeal was resisted. Mr Fox took the view
e that the special adjudicator's decision was flawed and that the case should be
remitted to be heard afresh by a different adjudicator. He persuaded Mr Zengin,
who had attended in person, to agree and accordingly made an order under
r 17(2) of the Asylum Appeals (Procedure) Rules 1996, SI 1996/2070.

[3] Mr Zengin's solicitors were not surprisingly upset and wrote complaining
f that such an order should not have been made in their absence when all they had
expected to happen was for a hearing date to be fixed. They applied for Mr Fox's
order to be set aside and for the appeal to be determined. They wished to argue
that the special adjudicator's decision should be upheld and the Secretary of
State's appeal dismissed. The application was listed before a full tribunal presided
over by Collins J on 10 May 2000, but it was adjourned for legal argument until
g 8 June 2000 when the tribunal decided it did have jurisdiction to set aside Mr Fox's
order and that the appeal should be listed for hearing in the normal way as soon as
possible (see *Secretary of State for the Home Dept v Zengin* [2000] Imm AR 518).

[4] The relief sought by the claimant in the present proceedings is limited to
declaratory relief. No quashing order is sought, because the claimant accepts that
h the circumstances of Mr Fox's decision would have entitled Mr Zengin to have
that decision quashed by the Administrative Court on judicial review. Whilst it
is important for the law to be clarified, Mr Zengin ought not to be deprived of the
benefit of the order of 8 June 2000, nor should further delay and uncertainty be
injected into his case.

j
Introduction

[5] Both Mr Tam, supporting the tribunal's decision, and Mr Fordham for the
claimant, contend that the tribunal has power to remit to a special adjudicator for
a rehearing, but they spell out that power from the legislation in very different
ways. I have to consider the possibility that neither is right and that there is no
such power of remittal. That is a conclusion I would only reach with the greatest

reluctance. Everybody is agreed that such a power is an important tool in the tribunal's armoury and furthermore that over a number of years many remittals have been ordered on the basis that such a power does exist. For example the existence of such a power is crucial to meet the case where an adjudicator hears an appeal in the appellant's absence but the tribunal learns that there was a good reason for his absence of which the adjudicator was unaware. The tribunal referred to this as the paradigm case.

[6] This case is concerned with what I shall call the old law, that is the Immigration Act 1971 and the Asylum and Immigration Appeals Act 1993 and various rules that predate the Immigration and Asylum Appeals (Procedure) Rules 2000, SI 2000/2333. The Immigration and Asylum Act 1999 and the 2000 rules (the new law) are not materially different for the purposes of the present questions before the court. For convenience, there is annexed to this judgment a table that shows the corresponding provisions in the old and new law.

[7] The key statutory provisions are ss 19, 20 and 22 of the 1971 Act. Section 19 covers determination of appeals by adjudicators. It provides, so far as material:

'(1) Subject to sections 13(4) and 16(4) above, and to any restriction on the grounds of appeal, an adjudicator on an appeal to him under this Part of this Act—(a) shall allow the appeal if he considers—(i) that the decision or action against which the appeal is brought was not in accordance with the law or with any immigration rules applicable to the case; or (ii) where the decision or action involved the exercise of a discretion by the Secretary of State or an officer, that the discretion should have been exercised differently; and (b) in any other case, shall dismiss the appeal …

(3) Where an appeal is allowed, the adjudicator shall give such directions for giving effect to the determination as the adjudicator thinks requisite, and may also make recommendations with respect to any other action which the adjudicator considers should be taken in the case under this Act; and, subject to section 20(2) below, it shall be the duty of the Secretary of State and of any officer to whom directions are given under this subsection to comply with them.'

[8] Sections 20 and 21 are together headed 'Appeals from adjudicator to Tribunal, and review of decisions'. Section 20 is headed 'Appeal to Tribunal from determination of adjudicator'. It provides:

'(1) Subject to any requirement of rules of procedure as to leave to appeal, any party to an appeal to an adjudicator may, if dissatisfied with his determination thereon, appeal to the Appeal Tribunal, and the Tribunal may affirm the determination or make any other determination which could have been made by the adjudicator.

(2) Directions given by an adjudicator under section 19(3) above need not be complied with so long as an appeal can be brought against his determination and, if such an appeal is duly brought, so long as the appeal is pending; and if the Tribunal affirm his determination allowing the appeal, they may alter or add to his directions and recommendations under section 19(3) or replace them with their own directions and recommendations, and the provisions of that subsection shall apply to directions given by them accordingly.

(3) Where an appeal is dismissed by an adjudicator but is allowed by the Tribunal, section 19(3) above shall apply with the substitution of references to the Tribunal for references to the adjudicator.'

[9] Sections 22 and 23 are headed 'Supplementary' and s 22 itself is headed 'Procedure'. Section 22(1) contains the rule-making power. Section 22(2) provides:

'Rules of procedure may include provision—(a) enabling the Tribunal, on an appeal from an adjudicator, to remit the appeal to an adjudicator for determination by him in accordance with any directions of the Tribunal, or for further evidence to be obtained with a view to determination by the Tribunal; or (b) enabling any functions of the Tribunal which relate to matters preliminary or incidental to an appeal, or which are conferred by Part II of Schedule 2 to this Act, to be performed by a single member of the Tribunal ...'

[10] The relevant rules are r 21 of the Immigration Appeals (Procedure) Rules 1984, SI 1984/2041, and r 17(2) of the 1996 rules. Rule 21 is headed 'Remittal of appeal for determination by adjudicator'. It provides:

'(1) The Tribunal may, if in the circumstances of a particular appeal it thinks it appropriate to do so, remit that appeal to an adjudicator for determination by him in accordance with any directions given to him by the Tribunal.
(2) The adjudicator to whom an appeal is remitted under this Rule may be either the adjudicator whose determination is the subject matter of the appeal or some other adjudicator.
(3) Subject to any necessary adaptations, Rules 17, 18 and 19 shall apply in relation to any proceedings on an appeal remitted to an adjudicator under this Rule as they apply in relation to proceedings before the Tribunal.'

[11] Rule 17 of the 1996 rules is headed 'Deciding an appeal'. Rule 17(2) provides:

'Unless it considers—(a) that it is necessary in the interests of justice, and (b) that it would save time and avoid expense to remit the case to the same or another special adjudicator for determination by him in accordance with any directions given to him by the Tribunal, the Tribunal shall determine the appeal itself.'

[12] The tribunal, in my judgment quite correctly, pointed out that it has only those powers that are given to it by the statutes and rules that govern its jurisdiction and procedure. It has no inherent powers save those which enable it to prevent its processes being abused. Without these it could not function properly as a tribunal. What, in particular, it does not have is power to deal with appeals in a way which is not permitted by the governing statutes or rules.

[13] The tribunal found that it had two separate powers to remit a case to an adjudicator. First an express power granted under r 21 of the 1984 rules and r 17(2) of the 1996 rules, made under s 22(2)(a) of the 1971 Act, and second an implied power to be found in s 20 of the 1971 Act, but nowhere mentioned in the rules. I should add that there were under the old rules, but are no longer under the new rules, separate rules dealing with asylum and non-asylum immigration cases.

[14] The two powers of remittal are, so the tribunal held, functionally different. The express remittal power involves the tribunal delegating to the adjudicator the tribunal's function of deciding the appeal from the adjudicator. As a result there can be no further appeal to the tribunal, but only direct from the adjudicator to the Court of Appeal. In exercising this power the tribunal is, as it were, delegating its job to the adjudicator. The implied power of remittal, on the other hand, involves the tribunal disposing of the appeal to it by allowing it and ordering a rehearing by the adjudicator of the appeal to him. During argument, for convenience the express power of remittal has been referred to as procedural remittal and the implied power as substantive remittal. I have adopted the same description.

[15] The conclusion envisaged by the tribunal is, on the face of it, surprising. Why should Parliament spell out with some care in s 22(2)(a) a power to make rules for one kind of remittal (which incidentally the tribunal said in its determination ([2000] Imm AR 518 at 526 (para 14)) should only rarely, if ever, be used) and yet remain completely silent about the other kind of remittal, the one of which frequent use is to be made?

[16] Furthermore, absent any assistance from s 22(2)(a) (because, on the tribunal's finding, it deals with an entirely different kind of remittal), it is not easy to extract the implied power to order substantive remittal from s 20. Section 20 says the tribunal may affirm the determination or make any other determination which could have been made by the adjudicator. One determination which the adjudicator cannot make is to direct that the matter be reheard by himself.

[17] If Mr Tam, who has appeared on behalf of the tribunal, is right about the true construction of s 22(2)(a) of the 1971 Act, ie that it covers only procedural remittals where the adjudicator acts on behalf of the tribunal, and does not include substantive remittals where the adjudicator considers the matter afresh giving rise to a further right of appeal to the tribunal, then my inclination is that there is probably no power to order a substantive remittal because it cannot in those circumstances be found within s 20 of the 1971 Act. This appears to have been the position of Mr Henderson who argued the case for Mr Zengin before the tribunal.

[18] Mr Tam's argument is that s 22(2)(a) recognises that the tribunal has the power to order remittal even though it cannot itself give the tribunal such power, because it is a provision which deals only with procedural matters regulating the exercise of a jurisdiction that is found elsewhere. The provision must, therefore, he argues have something to regulate. What it regulates is the power to order a remittal of any kind which is contained in s 20, the section creating the jurisdiction of the tribunal to deal with appeals from adjudicators. Properly understood, therefore, s 22(2)(a) regulates part (but only part) of the remittal jurisdiction conferred by s 20.

[19] The next stage in his argument is that once it is accepted that the tribunal has a power to remit which is contained in s 20 (albeit not expressly mentioned) there is no reason to limit it to the type of procedural remittal envisaged by s 22(2)(a). There is no statutory limitation on the remittal power. There will plainly be situations in which the tribunal considers that the justice of the case requires that it should allow the appeal from the adjudicator to the tribunal, but also that it should order some disposal other than giving a final decision on the case itself. This need can be met by an exercise of the s 20 remittal power in the form of a substantive remittal. I am not attracted by this somewhat convoluted route

a to establish an implied power to order the one kind of remittal that is most critically and frequently required in the interest of justice. Also there is no rule under which to exercise this power for the rules relate only, on Mr Tam's argument, to the procedural remittals envisaged by s 22(2)(a).

[20] In my judgment a better approach is along the following lines. The tribunal has a single power to remit a case to an adjudicator and it is neither necessary nor
b appropriate to speak of substantive remittals and procedural remittals. The power arises by virtue of s 20 of the 1971 Act read together with ss 19 and 22 of that Act. It is with this power that the remittal rules, r 21 of the 1984 rules and r 17(2) of the 1996 rules, made under s 22(2)(a), must be read compatibly. The question then is the extent and nature of the remittal power. It is on this issue that there is fundamental disagreement between the tribunal and the Secretary of State.
c

The tribunal's powers under s 20

[21] The express words of s 20(1) of the 1971 Act say the tribunal can affirm the adjudicator's decision or make any other decision he could have made. It is not, however, expressed in exhaustive terms. It does not say the tribunal's powers
d are limited in this way. The draughtsman could easily have said the tribunal may *either* affirm the determination or make any other determination which could have been made by the adjudicator. Nor does it contain an equivalent provision to that in s 19(1)(b), which says 'and in any other case, shall dismiss the appeal'. Remittal is thus not on the face of the words excluded. Parliament has clearly in
e mind some form of remittal, because it refers to it in s 22.

[22] Section 20 mirrors s 19 and is directed towards the underlying issue which the adjudicator was considering. The overturning or upholding of the adjudicator's determination of that issue is what is expressly described in s 20. In one sense remittal is a step towards that conclusion. I agree with Mr Fordham that s 22(2)(a) regulates and reflects, but does not confer, jurisdiction. It is subservient to s 20
f from where the jurisdiction emanates. Section 22 is the torch that casts light on s 20.

[23] The only modes of dealing with an appeal expressly referred to in s 20 are by affirming the adjudicator's determination or by making any other determination which he could have made. But when ss 20 and 22(2)(a) are read together the latter clearly recognises that the former was intended to include a power of
g remittal and I agree that s 20 should be so construed. Mr Fordham submits that this can, if necessary, be seen as a form of 'allowing the appeal', a view with which the tribunal concurred.

The meaning of s 22(2)(a)

h [24] I therefore turn to s 22(2)(a) of the 1971 Act to see whether it must be interpreted in such a way as to conclude that Parliament intended to exclude substantive remittals. Is it to be construed as permitting only what Mr Tam has called procedural remittals?

[25] The cornerstone of the argument of Mr Fordham for the Secretary of
j State is that the tribunal's jurisdictional powers to decide appeals are to be found in s 20 whereas the adjudicator's jurisdictional powers are in s 19. The adjudicator's function is to decide appeals to *him*; the tribunal's function is to decide appeals to *it*. Section 22(2) reflects a particular situation that crosses the boundary between the adjudicator and the tribunal and spells out the procedure for coping with it. But it must be read and construed against the power-giving ss 19 and 20.

[**26**] Difficulty arises because on a literal reading s 22(2)(a) suggests that *the adjudicator* is being required to determine *the appeal from an adjudicator.* It says: 'Rules ... may include provision ... enabling the Tribunal, *on an appeal from an adjudicator,* to remit *the appeal* to an *adjudicator for determination by him* ...' (My emphasis.)

[**27**] In other words the tribunal gets the adjudicator to do its job for it, namely decide the appeal that was sent to it. Mr Fordham submits that such a construction, although supported by the way the subsection reads, is manifestly absurd. It does not fit with the statute as a whole; it produces an unjust result and it cannot have been Parliament's intention. The court is not obliged to adopt this construction and should not do so. The adjudicator only has jurisdiction to decide *an appeal to him.* He has no jurisdiction to decide an appeal *to the tribunal.* Rules of procedure cannot confer such a jurisdiction. When s 22(2)(a) is read with s 19 remittal must mean that the adjudicator becomes seised of the appeal 'to him'. He then exercises the jurisdiction he has been given by s 19. If s 22(2)(a) is not read in this way and it is treated as having jurisdictional implications, albeit it is a mere procedural provision, four problems arise. (i) Where is the tribunal's jurisdiction to delegate its function to an adjudicator? (ii) Where does one find the adjudicator's jurisdiction to determine the appeal to someone else? His jurisdiction is to determine appeals to him. (iii) Where is the right of appeal from the adjudicator's decision? (iv) How does s 9 of the Asylum and Immigration Appeals Act 1993 fit?

[**28**] The first two problems require no further elaboration. As to the others, there are real difficulties in the paradigm case (see [5] above). Such an appellant effectively loses a layer in the appeal process. I am not persuaded that these difficulties can be overcome by exercise of the tribunal's factual jurisdiction on appeal which, in any event, is only to be used sparingly (see *Borissov v Secretary of State for the Home Dept* [1996] Imm AR 524). Because the adjudicator's decision on remittal is effectively that of the tribunal, any right of appeal lies, if anywhere, to the Court of Appeal. But until 1993 there was no appeal from the tribunal to the Court of Appeal. An error of law could be corrected by judicial review; but that was it. I am unconvinced by Mr Tam's response that an appeal to the Court of Appeal from a first instance decision of the tribunal was contemplated by statute (see s 15(7) and (8) of the 1971 Act) and there is therefore nothing unusual in the concept of an appeal to the Court of Appeal from an adjudicator's determination of an appeal at tribunal level.

[**29**] Thus Mr Fordham's case is that there is only one kind of remittal and it is impossible to believe that Parliament intended two, one express the other implied, one via jurisdictional powers the other via procedural powers with the express one being little used and yielding in significance to the implied one.

[**30**] The tribunal found it impossible to accept that the word 'appeal' is being used in two different senses in the same sentence and this is obviously a very formidable point against the way Mr Fordham primarily put his case before the tribunal. However, Mr Fordham frankly admitted that he had developed and refined his case in argument before me. Whereas before the tribunal his primary point was that it is possible albeit unusual for a draughtsman to use the same word with two different meanings in the same section, this is no longer in the forefront of his argument now that he has developed his argument about jurisdiction.

[**31**] Mr Fordham's primary argument before me is that where the word 'appeal' is used in the subsection the focus in on appeal to the tribunal. Once the

a appeal is sent back to the adjudicator he has back what he originally had. Accordingly, he submits, the subsection should be read as follows, i e that rules of procedure may include provision—

> 'enabling the tribunal, on an appeal from an adjudicator, to remit the appeal to an adjudicator for (a) determination by him in accordance with any directions of the tribunal, or for (b) further evidence to be obtained with a view to determination by the tribunal ...'

b

Mr Tam's reading on the other hand is:

> '... enabling the tribunal, on an appeal from an adjudicator, (a) to remit the appeal to an adjudicator for determination by him in accordance with any directions of the tribunal, or (b) to remit the appeal to an adjudicator for further evidence to be obtained with a view to determination by the tribunal ...'

c

[32] If Mr Fordham's submission is accepted the difficulty of attributing different meanings to the word 'appeal' does not arise. His fall back position is *d* that even if it is necessary to read 'appeal' in two different senses in the subsection the court should not, in the particular circumstance, shrink from doing so.

[33] Mr Fordham submitted that even approaching the problem linguistically there are three points that militate against Mr Tam's interpretation. First, the natural meaning of 'remit' is to 'send back'. Sending back should be seen in the context of sending back to a lower level in the appellate structure rather than sending *e* across to someone at the same level. What is 'sent back' to the adjudicator is the appeal 'to the adjudicator'. The tribunal has an appeal from an adjudicator; it sends it *back* 'to an adjudicator'. What the adjudicator has and receives back is the appeal 'to an adjudicator'. Secondly the subsection uses the phrases 'appeal *from* an adjudicator' and 'appeal *to* an adjudicator'. Thus it can be said that the tribunal *f* has 'an appeal from an adjudicator' but it remits an 'appeal to an adjudicator'. It remits that appeal for 'determination by him'. Thirdly, even if the tribunal remits (*sends*) the appeal *to it* that is because the tribunal necessarily has the function of dealing with the appeal *to it*. It does not follow that what the adjudicator *receives* is an appeal *to the tribunal*. The adjudicator necessarily has the function of deciding appeals *to him*. Each deals with the appeal with which it is empowered *g* to be seised.

[34] In the course of argument I asked counsel whether they could provide any examples of instances where Parliament had used the same word with two different meanings in the same section. My attention was drawn to *Bennion on Statutory Interpretation* (3rd edn, 1997) p 942 and also to words of Lord Romer in *h* *Barnard v Gorman* [1941] 3 All ER 45 at 57, [1941] AC 378 at 397:

> 'My Lords, it very often happens that a word is used in more than one section in an Act of Parliament, and that it bears one meaning in one section and a different meaning in another. It may even happen that a word is used in different senses in the same section of an Act, but to arrive at the *j* conclusion that the noun "offender," which appears only once in the section under consideration, has one meaning when applied to the verb "detain" and a different meaning when applied to the words "proceed against by summons" requires a feat of mental gymnastics of which I personally am quite incapable.'

[35] It is very difficult to see linguistically why the second reference to 'appeal' in s 22(2)(a) is not referring back to the first mention of 'appeal' earlier in the sentence. The linguistic point is strengthened by yet further mention of 'appeal' in s 22(2)(b) where is it plainly being used in the sense of appeal to the tribunal. Although this point is a formidable one it is not in my judgment determinative. There is no absolute rule that one word cannot have two different meanings within the same section or subsection. True, it will only rarely occur but the ultimate question is what did Parliament intend. To determine this it is necessary to look at the 1971 Act as a whole. When one looks at s 22(2) in the context that the 1971 Act gives the adjudicator power to hear appeals *to* him it seems to me that Parliament cannot have intended the linguistic construction submitted by Mr Tam.

[36] The tribunal said that if there was any doubt that it was the appeal to the tribunal of which the section was speaking throughout it was put beyond doubt by r 21 of the 1984 rules which refers to remitting *that* appeal to an adjudicator. The answer in my judgment is that r 21 cannot be used to construe s 22(2)(a). If the true construction of s 22(2)(a) is that the tribunal is not being empowered to delegate to the adjudicator the function of deciding appeals to the tribunal, then any rule made under s 22 must be read down so as to be compatible. To the extent that it cannot be, it is ultra vires.

[37] Mr Tam contends that the legislative history strongly supports his case that s 22(2)(a) is limited to procedural remittals. Adjudicators and the tribunal were first created by the Immigration Appeals Act 1969 (see s 1). Section 7 provided for an appeal from an adjudicator to the tribunal. Section 8(4) was the forerunner of s 20 of the 1971 Act and used similar wording.

[38] Section 11 contained the rule-making power and provided:

'(2) Rules made under this section may in particular make provision ... (f) in the case of an appeal to the Tribunal under section 7 of this Act, for enabling evidence to be given otherwise than orally and for an appeal to be remitted to an adjudicator for further evidence to be obtained ...'

[39] Thus any remittal was for the express purpose of obtaining further evidence. There was no other reference in the Act to remittals to an adjudicator and no provision corresponding to the words 'for determination by him in accordance with any directions of the Tribunal' which were introduced by s 22(2)(a) of the 1971 Act.

[40] The relevant rule was r 16(2)(b) of the Immigration Appeals (Procedure) Rules 1970, SI 1970/794, which made provision for the tribunal to remit the appeal to the same or another adjudicator 'for such further evidence as the Tribunal may require to be obtained'. Subparagraph (c) provided for a record of the evidence received by the adjudicator to be received as evidence by the tribunal. The rule, like the statute, did not appear to contemplate a remittal for a rehearing by the adjudicator.

[41] The first rules under the 1971 Act appear to have been the Immigration Appeals (Procedure) Rules 1972, SI 1972/1684, which were in identical terms to the 1984 rules. Mr Tam, as I have said, relies strongly on the reference to 'a particular appeal' and remitting 'that appeal' as entirely consistent with his construction of s 22(2)(a). The rules, he argues, have provided throughout procedures to regulate procedural remittals because that was all s 22, and earlier to an even lesser extent its predecessor s 11(2)(f) of the 1969 Act, provided for. If the tribunal's analysis is correct, the power to order substantive remittal has

a always existed quite independently of the rules. If the power is to be found in s 20 of the 1971 Act it must also, because of the similarity of language, have existed in s 8(4) of the 1969 Act.

[**42**] However, if the power existed, its existence may not have been appreciated. At any rate there is no reported instance of it having been used until *Ahmed v Entry Clearance Officer, Islamabad, Taj Bibi v Entry Clearance Officer, Islamabad* [1977]
b Imm AR 25. In that case the tribunal purported to remit for a full oral hearing under r 21 of the 1972 rules.

[**43**] Interestingly, r 17(2) of the 1996 rules (which were introduced to replace the Asylum Appeals (Procedure) Rules 1993, SI 1993/1661, and, like those, dealt separately with asylum appeals) speaks of remitting *the case* rather than the appeal. This broader language suggests the draughtsman envisaged Mr Fordham's
c construction rather than Mr Tam's.

[**44**] Mr Tam spelt out a number of reasons why in his submission the new words introduced into s 22(2)(a) can only refer to procedural remittals. I shall deal with each in turn. (i) They appear in a section which, like its predecessor s 11(2)(f) of the 1969 Act, deals only with the procedures which could be laid
d down to regulate the exercise of the tribunal's jurisdiction, and which could not itself create a jurisdiction which the tribunal did not otherwise have. Mr Fordham's answer is that if it is correct that there is within s 20 a jurisdiction to remit, s 22(2)(a) recognises and reflects it but does not create it. (ii) It is natural to read the new words in s 22(2)(a) as an extension in substance of what went
e before, namely the tribunal calling on the adjudicator to assist the tribunal in its determination of the case. There is obvious force in this point. The question is whether the main thrust of Mr Fordham's submission overrides it. (iii) The word 'remit', going back to s 11(2)(f) of the 1969 Act, is used more in the sense of sending from one court to another than sending back by an appeal court to an inferior court. I have already referred to Mr Fordham's response and I do not
f think too much weight should be attached to the fact that the word 'remit' first appeared in the predecessor provision in the 1969 Act. The natural meaning of 'remit' is send back rather than across. (iv) Although the word 'appeal' could be used in more than one sense in these statutory provisions, s 22(2)(a) of the 1971 Act is concerned only with proceedings in which the tribunal reviews the soundness of the adjudicator's determination. The statutory scheme is that each successive
g level of challenge is treated as a separate appeal. (v) In s 22(2)(a) the words 'to remit the appeal' appear only once. They apply to both limbs of s 22(2)(a) ie 'for determination by him' and 'for further evidence to be obtained', that is to the new words and to the re-enacted words. The words 'to remit the appeal' must therefore have the same meaning in respect of both limbs. So, if in the second
h limb it is the appeal *before the tribunal* which is remitted to adjudicator for further evidence to allow the *tribunal* to determine the appeal, it must be the same in the first limb. The wording of r 21(1) of the 1984 rules is even clearer because it makes it clear that what the adjudicator is to determine is the particular appeal before the tribunal. (vi) The terms 'on an appeal from an adjudicator' and 'to remit
j the appeal' are immediately adjacent to each other in s 22(2)(a) and the word 'appeal' cannot sensibly refer to two different things, even if elsewhere the word is capable of bearing other meanings. Mr Fordham accepts that there is some force in these three points if his primary argument is overcome. His case is that in both instances where the word 'appeal' appears the subsection is focussing on the appeal to the tribunal and what the tribunal is doing. 'Determination by him' should be read as shorthand for 'determination by him of an appeal to him'.

He has to determine something and he can only determine that which the 1971
Act by s 19 gives him power to determine. But, he says, even if Mr Tam is right
in his construction, the first limb is looking at the adjudicator determining
something and the second limb is looking at the tribunal determining something.
It is possible to give the same word a different meaning if you focus on what the
adjudicator is doing as against what the tribunal is doing. (vii) Rule 42 of the
1984 rules, like its predecessor in the 1972 rules, permitted the president or a
chairman acting alone to remit an appeal to an adjudicator under r 21(1) but only
(see s 22(2)(b) of the 1971 Act) if doing so was preliminary or incidental to
determination of an appeal at tribunal level. It is difficult, says Mr Tam, to imagine
how the disposal of the appeal at tribunal level by an order that there be a retrial
by an adjudicator could properly be regarded as preliminary or incidental to an
appeal. Mr Fordham points to the fact that the same rule permits the president
or a chairman to determine a preliminary issue. That, like a substantive remittal,
may be dispositive of the appeal, and the mere fact that it is preliminary does not
mean it cannot be dispositive. (viii) Rule 21(3) of the 1984 rules brings in rr 17,
18 and 19 of those rules on an appeal remitted to an adjudicator which, Mr Tam
says, is inconsistent with a substantive remittal. Mr Fordham's response is that there
is no inconsistency. All it means is that the evidential starting point for the fresh
hearing is the evidence before the tribunal. But the tribunal can direct the adjudicator
either to allow further evidence or to take some other course as the circumstances
demand. All this does is to give the tribunal a measure of control over what the
adjudicator is required by the tribunal to do, whether it is a substantive or
procedural remittal.

[45] Mr Tam has produced a compelling argument in support of his construction
of the subsection, namely that it provides only for procedural remittals. If he is
correct, the legislation leaves what Mr Fordham calls a black hole in the form of
the absence of any rule describing the circumstances in which a tribunal can
exercise the implied power in s 20 to order a substantive remittal ie in effect a
retrial. In my judgment, if Mr Tam's construction of s 22(2)(a) is correct, the
logical conclusion is that the tribunal is unable to order a substantive remittal, for
there is no rule enabling it to do so. This is a conclusion to which I would only
be driven with the greatest reluctance. It is a strong pointer in my view that
Mr Tam's construction is not correct for it is difficult to conclude that Parliament
did not intend the tribunal to have the use of the power of substantive remittal.

[46] Whilst I can see the force of Mr Tam's arguments and in particular that
the historical development of this legislation supports his construction of s 22(2)(a),
I prefer the view that the subsection reflected for the first time the power
contained in s 20 of the 1971 Act so that rules could be made for its use. That is
what the additional words 'for determination by him in accordance with any
directions of the Tribunal' achieved. It was obviously sensible that there should
be a wider power of remittal than had hitherto been available. Here was the
opportunity for the rules to reflect the underlying power of s 20 and it is
unthinkable that Parliament should only have allowed the adjudicator to rehear
the case as the agent for the tribunal. In no case is an adjudicator seised of an
appeal to the tribunal, albeit he does his job under the directions of the tribunal.
The adjudicator never determines appeals to the tribunal. Adjudicators decide
appeals to them; the tribunal decides appeals to it.

[47] In my judgment there is no remittal power involving a tribunal
delegating to the adjudicator its function of deciding the appeal from the
adjudicator. Substantive remittal always involves the disposing of the appeal to

a   the tribunal and ordering a rehearing by the adjudicator of the appeal to him. There is always a right of further appeal to the tribunal.

Mr Fox's decision

[48] The tribunal decided the order of Mr Fox could be set aside because it was an interlocutory order. Mr Fox had decided to order a substantive remittal in
b   circumstances in which he should not have done so. On the tribunal's case that was under the implied power to be found in s 20, but in my judgment it was under the procedural rule made under s 22(2)(a). It involved a rehearing by an adjudicator with a further right of appeal, if appropriate, to the tribunal. The tribunal took the entirely understandable view that it was much better to put matters right within its own procedure rather than that expense be incurred in
c   applying for judicial review or appealing to the Court of Appeal. The question is whether it had the power to do so.

[49] The tribunal's submission is that substantive remittals are final determinations and that the position is as follows. (i) Any determination by which an appeal from an adjudicator to the tribunal is effectively brought to an
d   end is a final determination. This includes: (a) dismissing the appeal and affirming the adjudicator's decision; (b) allowing the appeal but substituting the opposite decision; (c) allowing the appeal by ordering a substantive remittal. (ii) The tribunal will then normally have the opportunity of considering that party's application for leave to appeal. (iii) If the tribunal thinks that there is, at least arguably, merit in the grounds of appeal and is thus minded to grant leave to
e   appeal, it may hear representations from all parties on whether it should exercise its power under r 27(5) of the 2000 rules to set aside its own determination and order a rehearing by itself of the appeal. This is a new power that has recently been introduced to avoid unnecessary litigation and speed up disposal of cases.

[50] Section 9 of the Asylum and Immigration Appeals Act 1993 provides:

f   '(1) Where the Immigration Appeal Tribunal has made a final determination of an appeal brought under Part II of the 1971 Act ... any party to the appeal may bring a further appeal to the appropriate appeal court on any question of law material to that determination.

        (2) An appeal under this section may be brought only with the leave of
g   the Immigration Appeal Tribunal or, if such leave is refused, with the leave of the appropriate appeal court.'

'Appropriate appeal court' means in England the Court of Appeal.

[51] The tribunal's submission is that a substantive remittal is a final determination but a procedural remittal is not. If the procedural remittal is for the adjudicator
h   to determine the appeal to the tribunal on the tribunal's behalf, then when the adjudicator makes that determination there will be a 'final determination' from which an appeal to the Court of Appeal may be brought. Similarly, if the order for a procedural remittal is for an adjudicator to obtain further evidence, the tribunal will thereafter have the case back to determine the appeal itself. At that
j   point there will be a 'final determination'.

[52] Save in the case of substantive remittals there is no difficulty in the tribunal following the above procedure. But in the case of substantive remittals the tribunal is faced with the decision in *Kara v Secretary of State for the Home Dept* [1995] Imm AR 584 which decided that a remittal of a case for a hearing de novo is not a 'final determination' within s 9(1) of the 1993 Act, and that accordingly no appeal lay to the Court of Appeal. The tribunal concluded that *Kara*'s case was

wrongly decided and should not be followed. The decision is not binding because it was based on a concession by counsel; the point was not fully argued. I accept that I am not absolutely bound by the decision but it nevertheless warrants close examination. In *Kara's* case the remittal had been after a full hearing by the tribunal. Swinton Thomas LJ said (at 586) that the Immigration Appeal Tribunal allowed the appeal from the adjudicator substantially on the basis that he was wrong not to have granted the adjournment sought by the Secretary of State and that accordingly it directed that the appeal should be remitted to a different adjudicator for a rehearing. The issue before the Court of Appeal was whether the tribunal had made an error of law in ordering that the matter be remitted for a hearing de novo. When she realised that the Court of Appeal had no jurisdiction to entertain an appeal, counsel for Mr Kara changed her tack and sought leave to apply for judicial review. Interestingly, the single Lord Justice who refused leave to appeal said that if there was a statutory right of appeal against the decision he would have granted leave, since the issues raised in the grounds were arguable; but he refused because the tribunal's decision was not a final determination. Swinton Thomas LJ said (at 586):

'The Immigration Appeal Tribunal in this case neither confirmed the determination, nor made a determination which could have been made by the adjudicator. As I have said, the matter was remitted to the adjudicator for a new hearing.'

[53] He then quoted r 17(3) of the 1993 rules and went on (at 587):

'That is the course taken by the Tribunal in this case. Accordingly the issue arose as to whether this court had any jurisdiction to entertain this appeal. [Counsel for Mr Kara] has conceded that the court does not have jurisdiction because the Tribunal has not determined the appeal. In those circumstances, we have not heard any argument on the issue. Certainly, rule 17(3) would tend to indicate no determination has taken place. The rules cannot govern the meaning of the primary legislation but they have persuasive effect. However, albeit that we have not heard argument on this point, it does seem to me that there has not been a final determination of the appeal pursuant to the 1993 Act, with the result that no appeal can lie to this court from the order of the Tribunal.'

[54] The tribunal in the present case posed the question: when, if the remittal is not a determination, is the appeal determined and by whom? The appeal cannot be left in the air. It must be finally determined by the tribunal at some point. It drew attention to a statement by Professor Jackson in *Immigration: Law and Practice* (2nd edn, 1999) p 732 (para 22-86):

'A determination ... to remit the matter for rehearing ... is "final" in relation to the proceedings before the Tribunal but not "final" of the issue to be decided on the appeal. After some uncertainty it is accepted that in the statute "final" refers to the appeal issue.'

This is in my view a helpful analysis. One has to distinguish between the underlying issue and the vehicle by which disposal of that issue is transmitted from one level of hearing to another. This is material not only to understanding the meaning of 'final determination of an appeal' in s 9 of the 1993 Act but also to the true construction of s 22(2)(a) of the 1971 Act. What s 9 is aimed at is the issue between the parties. Only when that has been finally resolved will it be

a   relevant for the case to proceed to the Court of Appeal. Remittal is but a step on
the way to resolution. Viewed in this light, Mr Tam's conceptual problem about
what becomes of the appeal disappears.

[55] Mr Tam submits that 'final determination' should be given its ordinary
meaning. If the tribunal has disposed of the case before it by remitting it to an
adjudicator for re-determination at first instance level, with a further right of
b   appeal back to the tribunal thereafter, the tribunal is no longer seised of the case;
it has no further function in relation to it. It will never see it again unless it comes
back on a further appeal. In ordinary language it has made a final determination
of the appeal before it, even if that decision has not yet produced a definitive
answer to the individual's underlying challenge to the original administrative
decision.

c   [56] Furthermore, he argues, there is no logical or linguistic or legal reason
why this meaning should not be adopted. In my judgment, however, there is no
reason to open up orders for remittal to scrutiny by the Court of Appeal. There
is, of course, always the remedy of judicial review in appropriate circumstances.

[57] I accept the submission of Mr Fordham. There was no final determination
d   of the appeal in the present case. What s 9 envisages is the outcome of the case,
whether the Secretary of State's decision remains intact or is overturned.
Section 9, he points out, requires (i) a determination (ii) *of* not *on* the appeal
which must (iii) be final. Such a description is not applicable to a remittal, which
by its very nature is designed to leave open the outcome of the case. The emphasis
in my judgment of *finality* is important as is the reference to a determination of
e   an appeal under Pt II of the 1971 Act which of course contains ss 19 and 20 as well
as the procedural s 22. The tribunal does not determine the case; rather it remits
it. Remittal is an option not expressly described in s 20 and therefore does not fall
within the expression final determination of the appeal. Remittal is an alternative
to final determination by the tribunal; it is for a final determination by the
f   adjudicator.

[58] Further help is to be found in r 21 of the 1984 rules and r 17 of the 1996
rules. In particular r 17 refers to remitting the case to a special adjudicator for
determination by him. It is perfectly possible, it seems to me, for the tribunal to
make a decision that is not a final determination; a remittal is one such. In my
judgment there is no good reason not to follow the decision in *Kara*'s case which
g   I believe to be good law.

[59] I was also referred to s 33(4) of the 1971 Act, as amended by s 9(5) of the
1993 Act and by s 7(4) of the Special Immigration Appeals Commission Act 1997,
which provides:

h   '... an appeal ... shall ... be treated as pending during the period
beginning when notice of appeal is duly given and ending when the appeal is
finally determined or withdrawn; and an appeal shall not be treated
as finally determined so long as a further appeal can be brought by virtue of
section 20 [of the 1971 Act] or section 9 of the Asylum and Immigration Appeals
Act 1993 ... nor, if such an appeal is duly brought, until it is determined or
j   withdrawn.'

[60] Initially Mr Fordham sought to place great reliance on this subsection but
having seen Mr Tam's response (para 7.13 of his skeleton) he accepted that his
argument that s 33(4) disposed of the point in his favour was misconceived,
because it led to the absurd conclusion that there could never be a final
determination of an appeal when there remained a possibility that an appeal to

the Court of Appeal could be brought under s 9 of the 1993 Act. In other words
his argument was circular.

[61] The purpose of s 33(4) was in my judgment to define the period during
which a person is protected from enforcement action if he is seeking to challenge
the administrative decision. This it did by defining 'pending appeal', rather than
'finally determined'. Section 33(4) is of little value to Mr Fordham's arguments.
All it does is underline that available appeals should first be pursued and
concluded before an appeal can be determined.

[62] Given that Mr Fox did not make a final determination when he remitted
the case to an adjudicator was there power for the full tribunal to set his order
aside? Mr Fordham's submission is that it makes no difference who makes the
order for the tribunal. Whether it is a single member or the full tribunal the nature
of the application, the power and the legal consequences are the same. In neither
case can the remittal decision be set aside by the tribunal, because it is the
tribunal's decision on the appeal to it.

[63] There are two rules that are relevant, r 38 of the 1984 rules and r 44 of the
1996 rules. They are in almost identical terms. The differences are immaterial
for present purposes. These rules provide that any irregularity resulting from
failure to comply with the rules before the tribunal has reached its decision shall
not by itself render the proceeding void, but the tribunal can before reaching its
decision take steps to cure the irregularity.

[64] The position was considered in *Akewushola v Secretary of State for the Home
Dept* [2000] 2 All ER 148, [2000] 1 WLR 2295. Sedley LJ ([2000] 2 All ER 148 at 153,
[2000] 1 WLR 2295 at 2300) asked the question: can even a full tribunal rescind its
own or another tribunal's decision? He said he could find no explicit power to do
so in the rules and that he could see a number of reasons why no such power
should be inferred or implied. Then he quoted r 38 before he said ([2000] 2 All ER
148 at 153, [2000] 1 WLR 2295 at 2301): 'The limit in point of time of this power
to cure irregularities is thus the point at which a decision is reached.' Then:

> 'For my part I do not think that, slips apart, a statutory tribunal—in
> contrast to a superior court—ordinarily possesses any inherent power to
> rescind or review its own decisions. Except where the High Court's
> jurisdiction is unequivocally excluded by privative legislation, it is there that
> the power of correction resides.' (See [2000] 2 All ER 148 at 153–154, [2000]
> 1 WLR 2295 at 2301.)

And a little later ([2000] 2 All ER 148 at 154, [2000] 1 WLR 2295 at 2301): 'If
something has gone procedurally wrong which is capable of having affected the
outcome, it is to the High Court—if necessary on a consensual application—that
recourse must be had.'

[65] Tucker J followed this approach in *R v Immigration Appeal Tribunal, ex p
Wanyoike* [2000] Imm AR 389 but the tribunal in the present case distinguished
the observations of Sedley LJ (with whom Peter Gibson and Laws LJJ agreed) on
the ground that they did not apply to interlocutory orders, because if they did it
would be impossible for the tribunal to manage cases before it.

[66] Mr Tam's argument in support of the tribunal's decision was on the
following lines. Mr Fox had a choice between ordering a substantive remittal or
leaving the appeal to continue on to a full hearing before the tribunal. This was
a classic interlocutory order regardless of whether the order he actually made was
or was not a 'final determination'. The distinction drawn in *Salter Rex & Co v
Ghosh* [1971] 2 All ER 865, [1971] 2 QB 597 between interlocutory and final orders

a applies to statutory tribunals as well as to the High Court and county court. It was the possibility that the proceedings would not be terminated by Mr Fox's decision that made it an interlocutory order. So, submits Mr Tam, Mr Fordham's argument that it makes no difference whether it was the chairman alone or the full tribunal is wrong. If the full tribunal had considered this question at the full hearing of the appeal to the tribunal it would not have had the option of leaving
b the appeal to continue on to a full hearing by the tribunal.

[67] I cannot accept that the distinction between interlocutory and final orders has any relevance to proceedings in statutory tribunals such as the Immigration Appeal Tribunal. The relevant rules expressly provide for self-correction by the tribunal at any time before it reaches a decision. It matters not whether the decision was taken at a preliminary hearing or before a single chairman. Where a legislative
c scheme provides express powers of self-correction one does not expect to find an implied power to revoke decisions. In my judgment the law is as stated by Sedley LJ in *Akewushola*'s case. What is critical is that the decision to remit the appeal to an adjudicator for adjudication is a decision which disposes of the appeal to the tribunal, after which the power to cure irregularities given by the rules can
d no longer be exercised.

Conclusion

(i) The tribunal has a single power to remit a case to an adjudicator and not two separate powers, one express and one implied as found by the tribunal. The power is exercised under rules made under s 22(2)(a) of the 1971 Act. (ii) There
e is no remittal power involving the tribunal delegating to the adjudicator the tribunal's function of deciding an appeal from an adjudicator. Remittal involves disposing of the appeal to the tribunal and ordering a rehearing by the adjudicator of the appeal to him. There is always a right of further appeal to the tribunal. (iii) Remittal is never a final determination within the meaning of s 9 of the 1993
f Act. (iv) It is of no significance that the remittal decision was made by Mr Fox rather than a full tribunal. The appellate authority had reached its decision within the meaning of r 38 of the 1984 rules and it could not thereafter be corrected as an irregularity. There will in the circumstances be judgment for the Secretary of State and I shall hear further argument as to the appropriate declarations to reflect the tribunal's errors of law.

Application allowed. Permission to appeal granted.

Dilys Tausz   Barrister.

ANNEXE

COMPARATIVE TABLE OF LEGISLATIVE PROVISIONS

SUBJECT	OLD LAW	NEW LAW
Adjudicator	Section 19 of the Immigration Act 1971	Paragraph 21 of Sch 4 to the Immigration and Asylum Act 1999
Tribunal	Section 20 of the 1971 Act	Paragraph 22 of Sch 4 to the 1999 Act
Remittal	Section 22(2)(a) of the 1971 Act Rule 21 of the Immigration Appeals (Procedure) Rules 1984 Rule 17(2) of the Asylum Appeals (Procedure) Rules 1996	Paragraph 4(1)(d) of Sch 4 to the 1999 Act Rule 23 of the Immigration and Asylum Appeals (Procedure) Rules 2000
Single member	Section 22(2)(b) of the 1971 Act Rule 42 of the 1984 rules Rule 37 of the 1996 rules	Paragraph 6(3) and (4) of Sch 2 to the 1999 Act
Irregularities	Rule 38 of the 1984 rules Rule 44 of the 1996 rules	Rule 49 of the 2000 rules
Final determination	Section 33(4) of the 1971 Act Section 9(1) of the Asylum and Immigration Appeals Act 1993	Section 58(6) and (7) of the 1999 Act Paragraph 23(1) of Sch 4 to the 1999 Act

Royal Bank of Scotland v Etridge (No 2) and other appeals

Barclays Bank plc v Coleman

Bank of Scotland v Bennett

Kenyon-Brown v Desmond Banks & Co (a firm)

[2001] UKHL 44

HOUSE OF LORDS

LORD BINGHAM OF CORNHILL, LORD NICHOLLS OF BIRKENHEAD, LORD CLYDE, LORD HOBHOUSE OF WOODBOROUGH AND LORD SCOTT OF FOSCOTE

14–17, 21–24 MAY, 11 OCTOBER 2001

Equity – Undue influence – Presumption of undue influence – Manifest disadvantage – Whether 'manifest disadvantage' necessary to give rise to rebuttable evidential presumption of undue influence.

Equity – Undue influence – Presumption of undue influence – Husband and wife – Constructive notice of undue influence – Bank charge over matrimonial home – Steps to be taken by bank to avoid having constructive notice of husband's misrepresentation to wife or undue influence over her – Duty of solicitor acting for wife – Principles and guidance.

(1) A transaction that is not readily explicable by the relationship of the parties remains one of the two elements necessary to give rise to a rebuttable evidential presumption of undue influence, shifting the evidential burden of proof from the party who is alleging undue influence to the party who is denying it. However, the term 'manifest disadvantage', as used to describe that element, has been causing difficulty, can give rise to misunderstanding and should be discarded. Moreover, in the ordinary course, a wife's guarantee of her husband's business debts is not to be regarded as a transaction which, failing proof to the contrary, is explicable only on the basis that it has been procured by the exercise of undue influence by the husband. Such transactions as a class are not to be regarded as prima facie evidence of the exercise of undue influence by husbands, though there will be cases which call for an explanation (see [3], [14], [16], [21]–[26], [29]–[31], [91], [100], [153], [156], [159]–[162], [192], below); *Allcard v Skinner* [1886–90] All ER Rep 90 and *National Westminster Bank plc v Morgan* [1985] 1 All ER 821 considered.

(2) Where a wife proposes to charge the matrimonial home as security for a bank loan to her husband or to a company through which he operates his business, the following principles and guidance apply with regard to the position of the bank and the duty of the solicitor acting for the wife in the transaction—

(i) A bank is put on inquiry whenever a wife offers to stand surety for her husband's debts (or vice versa). On its face, such a transaction is not to the financial advantage of the wife and there is a substantial risk in such transactions that, in procuring the wife to act as surety, the husband has committed a legal or equitable wrong that entitles the wife to set aside the transaction. Although those two factors constitute the underlying rationale

for the bank being put on inquiry, they do not have to be proved in each case
before the bank is put on inquiry. Nor is it essential that the bank is aware *a*
that the parties are cohabiting or that the particular surety places implicit
trust and confidence in the principal debtor in relation to her financial affairs.
The bank is also put on inquiry in cases where the wife becomes surety for
the debts of a company whose shares are held by her and her husband, even
when the wife is a director or secretary of the company. Such cases cannot *b*
be equated with joint loans to a husband and wife, where the bank is not put
on inquiry unless it is aware that the loan is being made for the husband's
purposes, as distinct from their joint purposes. The shareholding interests,
and the identity of the directors, are not a reliable guide to the identity of the
persons who actually have the conduct of the company's business (see [3], [44],
[46]–[49], [91], [100], [110], [192], below); dictum of Lord Browne-Wilkinson in *c*
Barclays Bank plc v O'Brien [1993] 4 All ER 417 at 429 explained.

(ii) Where a bank has been put on inquiry, it need do no more than take
reasonable steps to satisfy itself that the practical implications of the proposed
transaction have been brought home to the wife, in a meaningful way, so
that she enters into the transaction with her eyes open so far as its basic *d*
elements are concerned. The bank is not required to discharge that obligation
by means of a personal meeting with the wife, provided that a suitable
alternative is available. Ordinarily, it will be reasonable for the bank to rely
upon confirmation from a solicitor, acting for the wife, that he has advised
her appropriately. The position will be different if the bank knows that the
solicitor has not duly advised the wife or the bank knows facts from which it *e*
ought to have realised that she has not received appropriate advice. In such
circumstances, the bank proceeds at its own risk. In the ordinary case,
however, deficiencies in the advice are a matter between the wife and the
solicitor, and the bank is entitled to proceed in the belief that a solicitor
advising the wife has done so properly. In giving such advice, the solicitor is *f*
acting not as the bank's agent but solely for the wife (see [3], [54]–[57], [77],
[78], [91], [100], [192], below).

(iii) The scope of the responsibilities of the solicitor acting for the wife is
dictated by a retainer which stems from the bank's concern to receive
confirmation from him that he has brought home to the wife the risk
involved in the proposed transaction. As a first step, he will need to explain *g*
to the wife the purpose for which he has become involved at all. He should
explain that, if it ever becomes necessary, the bank will rely upon his
involvement to counter any suggestion that the wife has been overborne by
her husband or that she has not properly understood the implications of the
transaction. The solicitor will need to obtain confirmation from the wife *h*
that she wishes him to act for her in the matter and to advise her on the legal
and practical implications of the proposed transaction. When such an
instruction is forthcoming, the content of the advice required from the solicitor
will, inevitably, depend on the facts of the case. Typically, the advice that a
solicitor can be expected to give should cover the following matters as a core *j*
minimum. First, he will need to explain the nature of the documents and the
practical consequences they will have for the wife if she signs them. Secondly,
he will need to point out the seriousness of the risks involved. The wife
should be told the purpose of the proposed new facility, its amount and
principal terms, and that the bank may increase the amount of the facility, or
change its terms, or grant a new facility, without reference to her. She should

a be told the amount of her liability under the guarantee. The solicitor should discuss the wife's financial means, including her understanding of the value of the property being charged. He should discuss whether the wife or her husband have any other assets out of which repayment can be made if the husband's business fails. Thirdly, the solicitor will need to state clearly that the wife has a choice. The decision is hers and hers alone. Explanation

b of the choice facing the wife will call for some discussion of the present financial position, including the amount of the husband's present indebtedness, and the amount of his current overdraft facility. Fourthly, the solicitor should check whether the wife wishes to proceed. She should be asked whether she is content that the solicitor should write to the bank confirming that he has explained to her the nature of the documents and the

c practical implications they may have for her, or whether, for instance, she would prefer him to negotiate with the bank on the terms of the transaction. Matters for negotiation may include the sequence in which the various securities will be called upon or a specific or lower limit to her liabilities. The solicitor should not give any confirmation to the bank without the wife's

d authority. The solicitor's discussion with the wife should take place at a face-to-face meeting, in the absence of the husband, and should be couched in suitably non-technical language. He should obtain from the bank any information he needs. If the bank fails for any reason to provide the information requested, the solicitor should decline to provide the confirmation sought by the bank (see [3], [64]–[67], [91], [100], [116], [120], [192], below).

e (iv) As a general rule, however, it is not for a solicitor to veto the transaction by declining to confirm to the bank that he has explained the documents to the wife and the risks she is taking upon herself. If the solicitor considers the transaction not to be in the wife's best interests, he should give her reasoned advice to that effect. However, the decision on whether to proceed is the

f client's, not the solicitor's, and a wife is not to be precluded from entering into a financially unwise transaction if, for her own reasons, she wishes to do so. There may, of course, be exceptional circumstances where it is glaringly obvious that the wife is being grievously wronged. In such a case, the solicitor should decline to act further (see [3], [61], [62], [91], [100], [192], below); *Powell v Powell* [1900] 1 Ch 243 and *Re Coomber, Coomber v Coomber* [1911] 1 Ch

g 723 considered.

(v) The solicitor advising the wife may also act for her husband or the bank, provided that he is satisfied that that is in the wife's best interests and will not give rise to any conflicts of duty or interest. If he decides to accept instructions from the wife, his assumption of legal and professional responsibilities to her ought, in

h the normal course of things, to provide sufficient assurance that he will give the requisite advice fully, carefully and conscientiously. If at any stage the solicitor becomes concerned that there is a real risk that other interests or duties may inhibit his advice to the wife, he must cease to act for her (see [3], [73], [74], [91], [96], [100], [116], [192], below).

j (vi) With regard to future transactions, a bank should take the following steps once it has been put on inquiry and is looking for protection to the fact that the wife will be advised independently by a solicitor. First, it should communicate directly with the wife, informing her that for its own protection it will require written confirmation from a solicitor acting for her, to the effect that the solicitor has fully explained to her the nature of the documents and the practical implications they will have for her. She should be told that the purpose of that requirement is that thereafter she should not be able to dispute that she is legally bound by the documents once she has signed them. She should be asked to nominate a solicitor whom she is willing to instruct to advise her, separately from her husband, and act for her in giving the bank the necessary confirmation. She should be informed that, if she wishes, the solicitor may be the same solicitor who is acting for her husband in the transaction. If a solicitor is already acting for the husband and the wife, she should be asked whether she would prefer a different solicitor to act for her regarding the bank's requirement for confirmation from a solicitor. The bank should not proceed with the transaction until it has received an appropriate response directly from the wife. Secondly, if the bank is unwilling to undertake the task of explaining the husband's financial affairs to the wife, it must provide the solicitor with the financial information he needs for that purpose. The information required will depend on the facts of the case. Ordinarily, it will include information on the purpose for which the proposed new facility has been requested, the current amount of the husband's indebtedness, the amount of his current overdraft facility, and the amount and terms of any new facility. If the bank's request for security arises from a written application by the husband for a facility, a copy of the application should be sent to the solicitor. The bank will, of course, need to obtain the consent of its customer to that circulation of confidential information. If that consent is not forthcoming, the transaction will not be able to proceed. Thirdly, where, exceptionally, the bank believes or suspects that the wife has been misled by her husband or is not entering into the transaction of her own free will, it must inform the wife's solicitor of the facts giving rise to its belief or suspicion. Fourthly, the bank should in every case obtain from the wife's solicitor a written confirmation to the effect mentioned above. In respect of past transactions, the bank will ordinarily be regarded as having discharged its obligations if a solicitor who is acting for the wife in the transaction has given it confirmation to the effect that he has brought home to her the risks she was running by standing as surety (see [3], [79], [80], [91], [100], [116], [120], [192], below).

(3) In future, banks should regulate their affairs on the basis that they are put on inquiry in every case where the relationship between the surety and the debtor is non-commercial. The creditor must always take reasonable steps to bring home to the individual guarantor the risks that he is running by standing as surety. That constitutes a modest burden for banks and other lenders, being no more than is reasonably to be expected of a creditor who is taking a guarantee from an individual. If the bank or other creditor does not take those steps, it will be deemed to have notice of any claim the guarantor may have that the transaction was procured by undue influence or misrepresentation on the part of the debtor (see [3], [87], [89], [91], [100], below); *Credit Lyonnais Bank Nederland NV v Burch* [1997] 1 All ER 144 approved.

Decision of the Court of Appeal in *Royal Bank of Scotland plc v Etridge (No 2)* [1998] 4 All ER 705 reversed in part.

Decision of the Court of Appeal in *Barclays Bank plc v Coleman* [2000] 1 All ER 385 affirmed.

Notes

For constructive notice of undue influence in cases where a wife charges property to secure her husband's debts, see 32 *Halsbury's Laws* (4th edn reissue) paras 349–353.

Cases referred to in opinions

a

Allcard v Skinner (1887) 36 Ch D 145, [1886–90] All ER Rep 90, CA.

Bainbrigge v Browne (1881) 18 Ch D 188.

Banco Exterior Internacional SA v Thomas [1997] 1 All ER 46, [1997] 1 WLR 221, CA.

Banco Exterior Internacional v Mann [1995] 1 All ER 936, CA.

Bank of Baroda v Rayarel [1995] 2 FCR 631, CA.

b *Bank of Credit and Commerce International SA v Aboody* [1992] 4 All ER 955, [1990] 1 QB 923, [1989] 2 WLR 759, CA.

Bank of Montreal v Stuart [1911] AC 120, PC.

Barclays Bank plc v O'Brien [1993] 4 All ER 417, [1994] 1 AC 180, [1993] 3 WLR 786, HL.

Barclays Bank plc v Thomson [1997] 4 All ER 816, CA.

c *CIBC Mortgages plc v Pitt* [1993] 4 All ER 433, [1994] 1 AC 200, [1993] 3 WLR 802, HL.

Cobbett v Brock (1855) 20 Beav 524, 52 ER 706.

Commission for the New Towns v Cooper (GB) Ltd [1995] 2 All ER 929, [1995] Ch 259, [1995] 2 WLR 677, CA.

d *Coomber, Re, Coomber v Coomber* [1911] 1 Ch 723, CA.

Craig (decd), Re [1970] 2 All ER 390, [1971] Ch 95, [1970] 2 WLR 1219.

Credit Lyonnais Bank Nederland NV v Burch [1997] 1 All ER 144, CA.

Forsyth v Royal Bank of Scotland plc 2000 SLT 1295, Ct of Sess, OH.

Hamilton v Watson (1845) 12 Cl & Fin 109, 8 ER 1339, HL.

e *Huguenin v Basely* (1807) 14 Ves Jun 273, [1803–13] All ER Rep 1, 33 ER 526, LC.

Inche Noriah v Shaik Allie Bin Omar [1929] AC 127, [1928] All ER Rep 189, PC.

Kempson v Ashbee (1874) LR 10 Ch App 15, LC and LJJ.

Lloyds Bank Ltd, Re, Bomze v Bomze [1931] 1 Ch 289.

London General Omnibus Co Ltd v Holloway [1912] 2 KB 72, [1911–13] All ER Rep 518, CA.

f *Massey v Midland Bank plc* [1995] 1 All ER 929, CA.

Midland Bank plc v Serter [1995] 3 FCR 711, CA.

National Westminster Bank plc v Morgan [1985] 1 All ER 821, [1985] AC 686, [1985] 2 WLR 588, HL.

Pooraka Holdings Pty Ltd v Participation Nominees Pty Ltd (1989) 52 SASR 148, S Aust Full Ct.

g

Powell v Powell [1900] 1 Ch 243.

Seaton v Heath, Seaton v Burnand [1899] 1 QB 782, CA; *rvsd* [1900] AC 135, HL.

Smith v Bank of Scotland 1997 SC (HL) 111.

Turnbull & Co v Duval [1902] AC 429, PC.

h *Wright v Carter* [1903] 1 Ch 27, [1900–3] All ER Rep 706, CA.

Yerkey v Jones (1939) 63 CLR 649, Aust HC.

Zamet v Hyman [1961] 3 All ER 933, [1961] 1 WLR 1442, CA.

Appeals

j

Royal Bank of Scotland plc v Etridge (No 2)

The appellant, Susan Rosemary Etridge, appealed with permission of the Appeal Committee of the House of Lords given on 22 July 1999 from the order of the Court of Appeal (Stuart-Smith, Millett and Morritt LJJ) on 31 July 1998 ([1998] 4 All ER 705) dismissing her appeal from the order of Judge Behrens, sitting as a judge of the High Court on 26 February 1998, giving the respondent, Royal Bank of Scotland plc, possession of a property known as Laverstoke Rectory, Laverstoke, Hampshire. The facts are set out in the opinion of Lord Scott of Foscote.   *a*

Barclays Bank plc v Harris

By petition of reviver granted on 9 May 2001, Sidney Thomas Harris, as executor of the estate of Beryl Iris Harris (deceased), appealed with permission of the Appeal Committee of the House of Lords given to Mrs Harris on 16 May 1999   *b* from the order of the Court of Appeal (Stuart-Smith, Millett and Morritt LJJ) on 31 July 1998 ([1998] 4 All ER 705) dismissing her appeal from the decision of Judge Alton at Birmingham County Court on 12 January 1998 dismissing her appeal from the order of Deputy District Judge Hilton on 29 May 1997, as amended on 9 August 1997, (i) striking out her defence to proceedings brought   *c* by the respondent, Barclays Bank plc, for possession of a property known as the Old Rectory, Nether Whitacre, Warwickshire, and (ii) giving the bank posession of the property. The facts are set out in the opinion of Lord Scott of Foscote.

Midland Bank plc v Wallace   *d*

The appellant, Anna Maria Wallace, appealed with permission of the Appeal Committee of the House of Lords given on 14 June 1999 from the order of the Court of Appeal (Stuart-Smith, Millett and Morritt LJJ) on 31 July 1998 ([1998] 4 All ER 705) dismissing her appeal from the order of Lloyd J on 24 October 1996 allowing an appeal by the respondent, Midland Bank plc, from the order of   *e* Master Barratt on 24 July 1996 dismissing the respondent's application for summary judgment in its proceedings for possession of a property known as the ground floor flat, 91 Priory Road, Hampstead, London NW3. The facts are set out in the opinion of Lord Scott of Foscote.

f
National Westminster Bank plc v Gill

The appellant, Marie Irene Gill, appealed with permission of the Appeal Committee of the House of Lords given on 19 May 1999 from the order of the Court of Appeal (Stuart-Smith, Millett and Morritt LJJ) on 31 July 1998 ([1998] 4 All ER 705) dismissing her appeal from the order of Mr Recorder Paulusz made   *g* at Bournemouth County Court on 19 September 1997 giving the respondent, National Westminster Bank plc, possession of a property known as 60A Queen's Park Avenue, Bournemouth, Dorset. The facts are set out in the opinion of Lord Scott of Foscote.

h
UCB Home Loans Corp Ltd v Moore

The appellant, Judit Moore, appealed with permission of the Appeal Committee of the House of Lords given on 19 May 1999 from the order of the Court of Appeal (Stuart-Smith, Millett and Morritt LJJ) on 31 July 1998 ([1998] 4 All ER 705) dismissing her appeal from the order of Judge Holden made at Reading   *j* County Court on 6 May 1997 whereby he (i) allowed an appeal by the respondent, UCB Home Loans Corp Ltd (UCB), from the order of District Judge Sparrow on 5 December 1996 dismissing UCB's application to strike out Mrs Moore's defence to proceedings for possession of a property known as Pangbourne Lodge, Tidmarsh Road, Pangbourne, Berkshire, and (ii) gave UCB possession of the property. The facts are set out in the opinion of Lord Scott of Foscote.

Barclays Bank plc v Coleman

The appellant, Miriam Mara Coleman, appealed with permission of the Appeal Committee of the House of Lords given on 26 October 2000 from the order of the Court of Appeal (Nourse, Pill and Mummery LJJ) on 21 December 1999 ([2000] 1 All ER 385, [2001] QB 20) dismissing her appeal from the order of Judge Wakefield made at Central London County Court on 27 July 1998 giving the respondent, Barclays Bank plc, possession of a property known as 52 Ashtead Road, Clapton, London E5. The facts are set out in the opinion of Lord Scott of Foscote.

Bank of Scotland v Bennett

The appellant, Jane Christine Bennett, appealed with permission of the Appeal Committee of the House of Lords given on 9 July 1999 from the order of the Court of Appeal (Auld, Chadwick LJJ and Sir Christopher Staughton) on 21 December 1998 ([1999] 1 FCR 641) allowing an appeal by the respondent, the governor and company of the Bank of Scotland, from the order of James Munby QC, sitting as a deputy judge of the High Court on 7 February 1997 ([1997] 3 FCR 193), dismissing its proceedings for possession of a property known as 15 Elthiron Road, Fulham, London SW6. The facts are set out in the opinion of Lord Scott of Foscote.

Kenyon-Brown v Desmond Banks & Co (a firm)

The appellant firm of solicitors, Desmond Banks & Co, appealed with permission of the Appeal Committee of the House of Lords given on 22 June 2000 from the decision of the Court of Appeal (Peter Gibson and Mance LJJ, Wilson J dissenting) on 16 November 1999 ([2000] PNLR 266), given effect in its order dated 14 March 2000, allowing an appeal by the respondent, Jessica Kenyon-Brown, from the order of Peter Leaver QC, sitting as a deputy judge of the High Court on 5 June 1998, dismissing her action for breach of duty against the firm. The facts are set out in the opinion of Lord Scott of Foscote.

Richard Mawrey QC and *Simon Wheatley* (instructed by *Collins*, Watford) for Mrs Etridge.

Michael Briggs QC and *Amanda Harrington* (instructed by *Fladgate Fielder*) for the Royal Bank of Scotland.

Jules Sher QC and *Stephen Whitaker* (instructed by *Evans Derry Binnion*, Birmingham) for the estate of Mrs Harris.

John Jarvis QC and *David Wolfson* (instructed by *Salans Hertzfeld & Heilbronn Hrk*) for Barclays Bank in the Harris appeal.

Jules Sher QC and *Mark Lyne* (instructed by *Keppe Shaw*, Twickenham) for Mrs Wallace.

Michael Briggs QC and *Clive H Jones* (instructed by *Tarlo Lyons*) for Midland Bank.

Jules Sher QC and *Teresa Rosen Peacocke* (instructed by *Baxter & Co*, Bournemouth) for Mrs Gill.

Michael Lerego QC and *Nicholas Briggs* (instructed by *Osborne Clarke,* Bristol) for National Westminster Bank.

Jules Sher QC and *Bernard Devlin* (instructed by *Richard Wilson & Co*, Pangbourne) for Mrs Moore.

Michael Briggs QC and *Christopher Coney* (instructed by *Copley Clark & Bennett*, Sutton) for UCB.

Jules Sher QC and *Helena Pines Richman* (instructed by *Waller & Co*) for Mrs Coleman.

John Jarvis QC and *David Wolfson* (instructed by *Nicholson Graham & Jones*) for Barclays Bank in the Coleman appeal.   *a*

Nicholas Yell (instructed by *Trevor Jenkin & Co*, Reading) for Mrs Bennett.

John Jarvis QC (instructed by *Underwood & Co*) for the Bank of Scotland.

Jonathan Sumption QC and *Ben Hubble* (instructed by *Henmans*, Oxford) for Desmond Banks & Co.

Julia Smith (instructed by *Neilson & Co*) for Mrs Kenyon-Brown.   *b*

Jonathan Sumption QC (instructed by *Pinsent Curtis Biddle*) for the Law Society as intervenors in all the appeals save for the Desmond Banks & Co appeal.

Their Lordships took time for consideration.

c

11 October 2001. The following opinions were delivered.

LORD BINGHAM OF CORNHILL.

[1] My Lords, I have had the great advantage of reading in draft the opinions prepared by each of my noble and learned friends.

[2] The transactions which give rise to these appeals are commonplace but of *d* great social and economic importance. It is important that a wife (or anyone in a like position) should not charge her interest in the matrimonial home to secure the borrowing of her husband (or anyone in a like position) without fully understanding the nature and effect of the proposed transaction and that the decision is hers, to agree or not to agree. It is important that lenders should feel *e* able to advance money, in run-of-the-mill cases with no abnormal features, on the security of the wife's interest in the matrimonial home in reasonable confidence that, if appropriate procedures have been followed in obtaining the security, it will be enforceable if the need for enforcement arises. The law must afford both parties a measure of protection. It cannot prescribe a code which will be proof against error, misunderstanding or mishap. But it can indicate minimum *f* requirements which, if met, will reduce the risk of error, misunderstanding or mishap to an acceptable level. The paramount need in this important field is that these minimum requirements should be clear, simple and practically operable.

[3] My Lords, in my respectful opinion these minimum requirements are clearly identified in the opinions of my noble and learned friends Lord Nicholls of Birkenhead and Lord Scott of Foscote. If these requirements are met the risk that *g* a wife has been misled by her husband as to the facts of a proposed transaction should be eliminated or virtually so. The risk that a wife has been overborne or coerced by her husband will not be eliminated but will be reduced to a level which makes it proper for the lender to proceed. While the opinions of Lord Nicholls and Lord Scott show some difference of expression and approach, I do not myself *h* discern any significant difference of legal principle applicable to these cases, and I agree with both opinions. But if I am wrong and such differences exist, it is plain that the opinion of Lord Nicholls commands the unqualified support of all members of the House.

[4] In agreement with all members of the House, I would allow the appeals of *j* Mrs Wallace, Mrs Bennett and Desmond Banks & Co and dismiss those of Mrs Etridge and Mrs Gill, in each case for the reasons given by Lord Scott. I would allow the appeal of Mrs Harris, bearing in mind that this is an interlocutory case, for the reasons given by Lord Hobhouse of Woodborough. I would allow the appeal of Mrs Moore and dismiss that of Mrs Coleman, in each case for the reasons given by Lord Scott.

LORD NICHOLLS OF BIRKENHEAD.

[5] My Lords, before your Lordships' House are appeals in eight cases. Each case arises out of a transaction in which a wife charged her interest in her home in favour of a bank as security for her husband's indebtedness or the indebtedness of a company through which he carried on business. The wife later asserted she signed the charge under the undue influence of her husband. In *Barclays Bank plc v O'Brien* [1993] 4 All ER 417, [1994] 1 AC 180 your Lordships enunciated the principles applicable in this type of case. Since then, many cases have come before the courts, testing the implications of the *O'Brien* decision in a variety of different factual situations. Seven of the present appeals are of this character. In each case the bank sought to enforce the charge signed by the wife. The bank claimed an order for possession of the matrimonial home. The wife raised a defence that the bank was on notice that her concurrence in the transaction had been procured by her husband's undue influence. The eighth appeal concerns a claim by a wife for damages from a solicitor who advised her before she entered into a guarantee obligation of this character.

UNDUE INFLUENCE

[6] The issues raised by these appeals make it necessary to go back to first principles. Undue influence is one of the grounds of relief developed by the courts of equity as a court of conscience. The objective is to ensure that the influence of one person over another is not abused. In everyday life people constantly seek to influence the decisions of others. They seek to persuade those with whom they are dealing to enter into transactions, whether great or small. The law has set limits to the means properly employable for this purpose. To this end the common law developed a principle of duress. Originally this was narrow in its scope, restricted to the more blatant forms of physical coercion, such as personal violence.

[7] Here, as elsewhere in the law, equity supplemented the common law. Equity extended the reach of the law to other unacceptable forms of persuasion. The law will investigate the manner in which the intention to enter into the transaction was secured: 'how the intention was produced', in the oft repeated words of Lord Eldon LC, from as long ago as 1807 (*Huguenin v Basely* (1807) 14 Ves Jun 273 at 300, [1803–13] All ER Rep 1 at 13). If the intention was produced by an unacceptable means, the law will not permit the transaction to stand. The means used is regarded as an exercise of improper or 'undue' influence, and hence unacceptable, whenever the consent thus procured ought not fairly to be treated as the expression of a person's free will. It is impossible to be more precise or definitive. The circumstances in which one person acquires influence over another, and the manner in which influence may be exercised, vary too widely to permit of any more specific criterion.

[8] Equity identified broadly two forms of unacceptable conduct. The first comprises overt acts of improper pressure or coercion such as unlawful threats. Today there is much overlap with the principle of duress as this principle has subsequently developed. The second form arises out of a relationship between two persons where one has acquired over another a measure of influence, or ascendancy, of which the ascendant person then takes unfair advantage. An example from the nineteenth century, when much of this law developed, is a case where an impoverished father prevailed upon his inexperienced children to charge their reversionary interests under their parents' marriage settlement with payment of his mortgage debts (see *Bainbrigge v Browne* (1881) 18 Ch D 188).

[9] In cases of this latter nature the influence one person has over another provides scope for misuse without any specific overt acts of persuasion. The relationship between two individuals may be such that, without more, one of them is disposed to agree a course of action proposed by the other. Typically this occurs when one person places trust in another to look after his affairs and interests, and the latter betrays this trust by preferring his own interests. He abuses the influence he has acquired. In *Allcard v Skinner* (1887) 36 Ch D 145, [1886–90] All ER Rep 90, a case well known to every law student, Lindley LJ ((1887) 36 Ch D 145 at 181, [1886–90] All ER Rep 90 at 98) described this class of cases as those in which it was the duty of one party to advise the other or to manage his property for him. In *Zamet v Hyman* [1961] 3 All ER 933 at 936, [1961] 1 WLR 1442 at 1444–1445 Lord Evershed MR referred to relationships where one party owed the other an obligation of candour and protection.

[10] The law has long recognised the need to prevent abuse of influence in these 'relationship' cases despite the absence of evidence of overt acts of persuasive conduct. The types of relationship, such as parent and child, in which this principle falls to be applied cannot be listed exhaustively. Relationships are infinitely various. Sir Guenter Treitel QC has rightly noted that the question is whether one party has reposed sufficient trust and confidence in the other, rather than whether the relationship between the parties belongs to a particular type (see Treitel, *The Law of Contract* (10th edn, 1999) pp 380–381). For example, the relation of banker and customer will not normally meet this criterion, but exceptionally it may (see *National Westminster Bank plc v Morgan* [1985] 1 All ER 821 at 829–831, [1985] AC 686 at 707–709).

[11] Even this test is not comprehensive. The principle is not confined to cases of abuse of trust and confidence. It also includes, for instance, cases where a vulnerable person has been exploited. Indeed, there is no single touchstone for determining whether the principle is applicable. Several expressions have been used in an endeavour to encapsulate the essence: trust and confidence, reliance, dependence or vulnerability on the one hand and ascendancy, domination or control on the other. None of these descriptions is perfect. None is all embracing. Each has its proper place.

[12] In *CIBC Mortgages plc v Pitt* [1993] 4 All ER 433, [1994] 1 AC 200 your Lordships' House decided that in cases of undue influence disadvantage is not a necessary ingredient of the cause of action. It is not essential that the transaction should be disadvantageous to the pressurised or influenced person, either in financial terms or in any other way. However, in the nature of things, questions of undue influence will not usually arise, and the exercise of undue influence is unlikely to occur, where the transaction is innocuous. The issue is likely to arise only when, in some respect, the transaction was disadvantageous either from the outset or as matters turned out.

BURDEN OF PROOF AND PRESUMPTIONS

[13] Whether a transaction was brought about by the exercise of undue influence is a question of fact. Here, as elsewhere, the general principle is that he who asserts a wrong has been committed must prove it. The burden of proving an allegation of undue influence rests upon the person who claims to have been wronged. This is the general rule. The evidence required to discharge the burden of proof depends on the nature of the alleged undue influence, the personality of the parties, their relationship, the extent to which the transaction cannot readily be

a accounted for by the ordinary motives of ordinary persons in that relationship, and all the circumstances of the case.

[14] Proof that the complainant placed trust and confidence in the other party in relation to the management of the complainant's financial affairs, coupled with a transaction which calls for explanation, will normally be sufficient, failing satisfactory evidence to the contrary, to discharge the burden of proof. On proof

b of these two matters the stage is set for the court to infer that, in the absence of a satisfactory explanation, the transaction can only have been procured by undue influence. In other words, proof of these two facts is prima facie evidence that the defendant abused the influence he acquired in the parties' relationship. He preferred his own interests. He did not behave fairly to the other. So the evidential burden then shifts to him. It is for him to produce evidence to counter the inference

c which otherwise should be drawn.

[15] The case of *Bainbrigge v Browne* (1881) 18 Ch D 188, already mentioned, provides a good illustration of this commonplace type of forensic exercise. Fry J held (at 196) that there was no direct evidence upon which he could rely as proving undue pressure by the father. But there existed circumstances 'from

d which the court will infer pressure and undue influence'. None of the children were entirely emancipated from their father's control. None seemed conversant with business. These circumstances were such as to cast the burden of proof upon the father. He had made no attempt to discharge that burden. He did not appear in court at all. So the children's claim succeeded. Again, more recently, in *Morgan*'s case [1985] 1 All ER 821 at 829, [1985] AC 686 at 707, Lord Scarman

e noted that a relationship of banker and customer may become one in which a banker acquires a dominating influence. If he does, and a manifestly disadvantageous transaction is proved, 'there would then be room' for a court to presume that it resulted from the exercise of undue influence.

[16] Generations of equity lawyers have conventionally described this

f situation as one in which a presumption of undue influence arises. This use of the term 'presumption' is descriptive of a shift in the evidential onus on a question of fact. When a plaintiff succeeds by this route he does so because he has succeeded in establishing a case of undue influence. The court has drawn appropriate inferences of fact upon a balanced consideration of the whole of the evidence at the end of a trial in which the burden of proof rested upon the plaintiff. The use, in the

g course of the trial, of the forensic tool of a shift in the evidential burden of proof should not be permitted to obscure the overall position. These cases are the equitable counterpart of common law cases where the principle of res ipsa loquitur is invoked. There is a rebuttable evidential presumption of undue influence.

[17] The availability of this forensic tool in cases founded on abuse of

h influence arising from the parties' relationship has led to this type of case sometimes being labelled 'presumed undue influence'. This is by way of contrast with cases involving actual pressure or the like, which are labelled 'actual undue influence' (see *Bank of Credit and Commerce International SA v Aboody* [1992] 4 All ER 955 at 964, [1990] 1 QB 923 at 953, and *Royal Bank of Scotland plc v Etridge (No 2)*

j [1998] 4 All ER 705 at 711–712 (paras 5–7)). This usage can be a little confusing. In many cases where a plaintiff has claimed that the defendant abused the influence he acquired in a relationship of trust and confidence the plaintiff has succeeded by recourse to the rebuttable evidential presumption. But this need not be so. Such a plaintiff may succeed even where this presumption is not available to him; for instance, where the impugned transaction was not one which called for an explanation.

[18] The evidential presumption discussed above is to be distinguished
sharply from a different form of presumption which arises in some cases. The law
has adopted a sternly protective attitude towards certain types of relationship in
which one party acquires influence over another who is vulnerable and
dependent and where, moreover, substantial gifts by the influenced or vulnerable
person are not normally to be expected. Examples of relationships within this
special class are parent and child, guardian and ward, trustee and beneficiary,
solicitor and client, and medical advisor and patient. In these cases the law presumes,
irrebuttably, that one party had influence over the other. The complainant need not
prove he actually reposed trust and confidence in the other party. It is sufficient
for him to prove the existence of the type of relationship.

[19] It is now well established that husband and wife is not one of the
relationships to which this latter principle applies. In *Yerkey v Jones* (1939) 63 CLR
649 at 675 Dixon J explained the reason. The Court of Chancery was not blind to
the opportunities of obtaining and unfairly using influence over a wife which a
husband often possesses. But there is nothing unusual or strange in a wife, from
motives of affection or for other reasons, conferring substantial financial benefits
on her husband. Although there is no presumption, the court will nevertheless
note, as a matter of fact, the opportunities for abuse which flow from a wife's
confidence in her husband. The court will take this into account with all the
other evidence in the case. Where there is evidence that a husband has taken
unfair advantage of his influence over his wife, or her confidence in him, 'it is not
difficult for the wife to establish her title to relief' (see *Re Lloyds Bank Ltd, Bomze v
Bomze* [1931] 1 Ch 289 at 302, per Maugham J).

INDEPENDENT ADVICE

[20] Proof that the complainant received advice from a third party before
entering into the impugned transaction is one of the matters a court takes into
account when weighing all the evidence. The weight, or importance, to be attached
to such advice depends on all the circumstances. In the normal course, advice
from a solicitor or other outside advisor can be expected to bring home to a
complainant a proper understanding of what he or she is about to do. But a person
may understand fully the implications of a proposed transaction, for instance, a
substantial gift, and yet still be acting under the undue influence of another.
Proof of outside advice does not, of itself, necessarily show that the subsequent
completion of the transaction was free from the exercise of undue influence.
Whether it will be proper to infer that outside advice had an emancipating effect,
so that the transaction was not brought about by the exercise of undue influence,
is a question of fact to be decided having regard to all the evidence in the case.

MANIFEST DISADVANTAGE

[21] As already noted, there are two prerequisites to the evidential shift in the
burden of proof from the complainant to the other party. First, that the complainant
reposed trust and confidence in the other party, or the other party acquired
ascendancy over the complainant. Second, that the transaction is not readily
explicable by the relationship of the parties.

[22] Lindley LJ summarised this second prerequisite in the leading authority
of *Allcard v Skinner* (1887) 36 Ch D 145, [1886–90] All ER Rep 90, where the donor
parted with almost all her property. Lindley LJ pointed out that where a gift of a
small amount is made to a person standing in a confidential relationship to the

a donor, some proof of the exercise of the influence of the donee must be given. The mere existence of the influence is not enough. He continued:

'But if the gift is so large as not to be reasonably accounted for on the ground of friendship, relationship, charity, or other ordinary motives on which ordinary men act, the burden is upon the donee to support the gift.' (See (1887) 36 Ch D 145 at 185, [1886–90] All ER Rep 90 at 100–101.)

b

In *Bank of Montreal v Stuart* [1911] AC 120 at 137 Lord Macnaghten used the phrase 'immoderate and irrational' to describe this concept.

[23] The need for this second prerequisite has recently been questioned: see Nourse LJ in *Barclays Bank plc v Coleman* [2000] 1 All ER 385 at 397–399, [2001] QB 20 at 30–32, one of the cases under appeal before your Lordships' House. Mr Sher QC
c invited your Lordships to depart from the decision of the House on this point in *Morgan*'s case.

[24] My Lords, this is not an invitation I would accept. The second prerequisite, as expressed by Lindley LJ, is good sense. It is a necessary limitation upon the width of the first prerequisite. It would be absurd for the law to presume that
d every gift by a child to a parent, or every transaction between a client and his solicitor or between a patient and his doctor, was brought about by undue influence unless the contrary is affirmatively proved. Such a presumption would be too far-reaching. The law would be out of touch with everyday life if the presumption were to apply to every Christmas or birthday gift by a child to a parent, or to an agreement whereby a client or patient agrees to be responsible
e for the reasonable fees of his legal or medical advisor. The law would be rightly open to ridicule, for transactions such as these are unexceptionable. They do not suggest that something may be amiss. So something more is needed before the law reverses the burden of proof, something which calls for an explanation. When that something more is present, the greater the disadvantage to the vulnerable person, the more cogent must be the explanation before the presumption
f will be regarded as rebutted.

[25] This was the approach adopted by Lord Scarman in *Morgan*'s case [1985] 1 All ER 821 at 826–829, [1985] AC 686 at 703–707. He cited Lindley LJ's observations in *Allcard v Skinner* (1887) 36 Ch D 145 at 185, [1886–90] All ER Rep 90 at 100, which I have set out above. He noted that whatever the legal
g character of the transaction, it must constitute a disadvantage sufficiently serious to require evidence to rebut the presumption that in the circumstances of the parties' relationship, it was procured by the exercise of undue influence. Lord Scarman concluded:

h '... the Court of Appeal erred in law in holding that the presumption of undue influence can arise from the evidence of the relationship of the parties without also evidence that the transaction itself was wrongful in that it constituted *an advantage taken of the person subjected to the influence which, failing proof to the contrary, was explicable only on the basis that undue influence had been exercised to procure it.*' (See [1985] 1 All ER 821 at 827, [1985] AC 686
j at 704; my emphasis.)

[26] Lord Scarman attached the label 'manifest disadvantage' to this second ingredient necessary to raise the presumption. This label has been causing difficulty. It may be apt enough when applied to straightforward transactions such as a substantial gift or a sale at an undervalue. But experience has now shown that this expression can give rise to misunderstanding. The label is being

understood and applied in a way which does not accord with the meaning
intended by Lord Scarman, its originator.

[27] The problem has arisen in the context of wives guaranteeing payment of
their husband's business debts. In recent years judge after judge has grappled
with the baffling question whether a wife's guarantee of her husband's bank
overdraft, together with a charge on her share of the matrimonial home, was a
transaction manifestly to her disadvantage.

[28] In a narrow sense, such a transaction plainly ('manifestly') is disadvantageous
to the wife. She undertakes a serious financial obligation, and in return she personally
receives nothing. But that would be to take an unrealistically blinkered view of
such a transaction. Unlike the relationship of solicitor and client or medical advisor
and patient, in the case of husband and wife there are inherent reasons why such
a transaction may well be for her benefit. Ordinarily, the fortunes of husband and
wife are bound up together. If the husband's business is the source of the family
income, the wife has a lively interest in doing what she can to support the
business. A wife's affection and self-interest run hand-in-hand in inclining her to
join with her husband in charging the matrimonial home, usually a jointly-owned
asset, to obtain the financial facilities needed by the business. The finance may
be needed to start a new business, or expand a promising business, or rescue an
ailing business.

[29] Which, then, is the correct approach to adopt in deciding whether a
transaction is disadvantageous to the wife: the narrow approach, or the wider
approach? The answer is neither. The answer lies in discarding a label which
gives rise to this sort of ambiguity. The better approach is to adhere more directly
to the test outlined by Lindley LJ in *Allcard v Skinner*, and adopted by Lord Scarman
in *Morgan's* case, in the passages I have cited.

[30] I return to husband and wife cases. I do not think that, *in the ordinary course*,
a guarantee of the character I have mentioned is to be regarded as a transaction
which, failing proof to the contrary, is explicable only on the basis that it has been
procured by the exercise of undue influence by the husband. Wives frequently
enter into such transactions. There are good and sufficient reasons why they are
willing to do so, despite the risks involved for them and their families. They may
be enthusiastic. They may not. They may be less optimistic than their husbands
about the prospects of the husbands' businesses. They may be anxious, perhaps
exceedingly so. But this is a far cry from saying that such transactions as a class
are to be regarded as prima facie evidence of the exercise of undue influence by
husbands.

[31] I have emphasised the phrase 'in the ordinary course'. There will be cases
where a wife's signature of a guarantee or a charge of her share in the
matrimonial home does call for explanation. Nothing I have said above is
directed at such a case.

A CAUTIONARY NOTE

[32] I add a cautionary note, prompted by some of the first instance judgments
in the cases currently being considered by the House. It concerns the general
approach to be adopted by a court when considering whether a wife's guarantee
of her husband's bank overdraft was procured by her husband's undue influence.
Undue influence has a connotation of impropriety. In the eye of the law, undue
influence means that influence has been misused. Statements or conduct by a
husband which do not pass beyond the bounds of what may be expected of a
reasonable husband in the circumstances should not, without more, be castigated

a as undue influence. Similarly, when a husband is forecasting the future of his business, and expressing his hopes or fears, a degree of hyperbole may be only natural. Courts should not too readily treat such exaggerations as misstatements.

[33] Inaccurate explanations of a proposed transaction are a different matter. So are cases where a husband, in whom a wife has reposed trust and confidence for the management of their financial affairs, prefers his interests to hers and *b* makes a choice for both of them on that footing. Such a husband abuses the influence he has. He fails to discharge the obligation of candour and fairness he owes a wife who is looking to him to make the major financial decisions.

THE COMPLAINANT AND THIRD PARTIES: SURETYSHIP TRANSACTIONS

[34] The problem considered in *Barclays Bank plc v O'Brien* [1993] 4 All ER 417,
c [1994] 1 AC 180 and raised by the present appeals is of comparatively recent origin. It arises out of the substantial growth in home ownership over the last 30 or 40 years and, as part of that development, the great increase in the number of homes owned jointly by husbands and wives. More than two-thirds of householders in the United Kingdom now own their own homes. For most home-owning
d couples, their homes are their most valuable asset. They must surely be free, if they so wish, to use this asset as a means of raising money, whether for the purpose of the husband's business or for any other purpose. Their home is their property. The law should not restrict them in the use they may make of it. Bank finance is in fact by far the most important source of external capital for small businesses with fewer than ten employees. These businesses comprise about
e 95% of all businesses in the country, responsible for nearly one-third of all employment. Finance raised by second mortgages on the principal's home is a significant source of capital for the start-up of small businesses.

[35] If the freedom of home-owners to make economic use of their homes is not to be frustrated, a bank must be able to have confidence that a wife's
f signature of the necessary guarantee and charge will be as binding upon her as is the signature of anyone else on documents which he or she may sign. Otherwise banks will not be willing to lend money on the security of a jointly owned house or flat.

[36] At the same time, the high degree of trust and confidence and emotional interdependence which normally characterises a marriage relationship provides
g scope for abuse. One party may take advantage of the other's vulnerability. Unhappily, such abuse does occur. Further, it is all too easy for a husband, anxious or even desperate for bank finance, to misstate the position in some particular or to mislead the wife, wittingly or unwittingly, in some other way. The law would be seriously defective if it did not recognise these realities.

h [37] In *O'Brien's* case this House decided where the balance should be held between these competing interests. On the one side, there is the need to protect a wife against a husband's undue influence. On the other side, there is the need for the bank to be able to have reasonable confidence in the strength of its security. Otherwise it would not provide the required money. The problem lies
j in finding the course best designed to protect wives in a minority of cases without unreasonably hampering the giving and taking of security. The House produced a practical solution. The House decided what are the steps a bank should take to ensure it is not affected by any claim the wife may have that her signature of the documents was procured by the undue influence or other wrong of her husband. Like every compromise, the outcome falls short of achieving in full the objectives of either of the two competing interests. In particular, the steps required of banks

will not guarantee that, in future, wives will not be subjected to undue influence
or misled when standing as sureties. Short of prohibiting this type of suretyship
transaction altogether, there is no way of achieving that result, desirable although
it is. What passes between a husband and wife in this regard in the privacy of their
own home is not capable of regulation or investigation as a prelude to the wife
entering into a suretyship transaction.

[38] The jurisprudential route by which the House reached its conclusion in
O'Brien's case has attracted criticism from some commentators. It has been said
to involve artificiality and thereby create uncertainty in the law. I must first
consider this criticism. In the ordinary course a bank which takes a guarantee
security from the wife of its customer will be altogether ignorant of any undue
influence the customer may have exercised in order to secure the wife's
concurrence. In *O'Brien's* case Lord Browne-Wilkinson prayed in aid the doctrine
of constructive notice. In circumstances he identified, a creditor is put on inquiry.
When that is so, the creditor 'will have constructive notice of the wife's rights'
unless the creditor takes reasonable steps to satisfy himself that the wife's
agreement to stand surety has been properly obtained (see [1993] 4 All ER 417 at
429, [1994] 1 AC 180 at 196).

[39] Lord Browne-Wilkinson would be the first to recognise this is not a
conventional use of the equitable concept of constructive notice. The traditional
use of this concept concerns the circumstances in which a transferee of property
who acquires a legal estate from a transferor with a defective title may none the
less obtain a good title, that is, a better title than the transferor had. That is not
the present case. The bank acquires its charge from the wife, and there is nothing
wrong with her title to her share of the matrimonial home. The transferor wife
is seeking to resile from the very transaction she entered into with the bank, on
the ground that her apparent consent was procured by the undue influence or
other misconduct, such as misrepresentation, of a third party (her husband). She
is seeking to set aside her contract of guarantee and, with it, the charge she gave
to the bank.

[40] The traditional view of equity in this tripartite situation seems to be that
a person in the position of the wife will only be relieved of her bargain if the other
party to the transaction (the bank, in the present instance) was privy to the
conduct which led to the wife's entry into the transaction. Knowledge is required
(see *Cobbett v Brock* (1855) 20 Beav 524 at 528, 531, 52 ER 706 at 707, 708, per
Romilly MR, *Kempson v Ashbee* (1874) LR 10 Ch App 15 at 21, per James LJ, and
Bainbrigge v Browne (1881) 18 Ch D 188 at 197, per Fry J). The law imposes no
obligation on one party to a transaction to check whether the other party's
concurrence was obtained by undue influence. But *O'Brien's* case has introduced
into the law the concept that, in certain circumstances, a party to a contract may
lose the benefit of his contract, entered into in good faith, if he *ought* to have
known that the other's concurrence had been procured by the misconduct of a
third party.

[41] There is a further respect in which *O'Brien's* case departed from conventional
concepts. Traditionally, a person is *deemed* to have notice (that is, he has 'constructive'
notice) of a prior right when he does not actually know of it but would have
learned of it had he made the requisite inquiries. A purchaser will be treated as
having constructive notice of all that a reasonably prudent purchaser would have
discovered. In the present type of case, the steps a bank is required to take, lest it
have constructive notice that the wife's concurrence was procured improperly by
her husband, do not consist of making inquiries. Rather, *O'Brien's* case envisages

a that the steps taken by the bank will reduce, or even eliminate, the risk of the wife entering into the transaction under any misapprehension or as a result of undue influence by her husband. The steps are not concerned to discover whether the wife has been wronged by her husband in this way. The steps are concerned to minimise the risk that such a wrong may be committed.

b [42] These novelties do not point to the conclusion that the decision of this House in *O'Brien*'s case is leading the law astray. Lord Browne-Wilkinson ([1993] 4 All ER 417 at 430, [1994] 1 AC 180 at 197) acknowledged he might be extending the law. Some development was sorely needed. The law had to find a way of giving wives a reasonable measure of protection, without adding unreasonably to the expense involved in entering into guarantee transactions of the type under consideration. The protection had to extend also to any misrepresentations made
c by a husband to his wife. In a situation where there is a substantial risk the husband may exercise his influence improperly regarding the provision of security for his business debts, there is an increased risk that explanations of the transaction given by him to his wife may be misleadingly incomplete or even inaccurate.

d [43] The route selected in *O'Brien*'s case ought not to have an unsettling effect on established principles of contract. *O'Brien*'s case concerned suretyship transactions. These are tripartite transactions. They involve the debtor as well as the creditor and the guarantor. The guarantor enters into the transaction at the request of the debtor. The guarantor assumes obligations. On the face of the transaction the
e guarantor usually receives no benefit in return, unless the guarantee is being given on a commercial basis. Leaving aside cases where the relationship between the surety and the debtor is commercial, a guarantee transaction is one-sided so far as the guarantor is concerned. The creditor knows this. Thus the decision in *O'Brien*'s case is directed at a class of contracts which has special features of its own. That said, I must at a later stage in this speech return to the question of the
f wider implications of the *O'Brien* decision.

THE THRESHOLD: WHEN THE BANK IS PUT ON INQUIRY

[44] In *O'Brien*'s case the House considered the circumstances in which a bank, or other creditor, is 'put on inquiry'. Strictly this is a misnomer. As already noted,
g a bank is not required to make inquiries. But it will be convenient to use the terminology which has now become accepted in this context. The House set a low level for the threshold which must be crossed before a bank is put on inquiry. For practical reasons the level is set much lower than is required to satisfy a court that, failing contrary evidence, the court may infer that the transaction was procured by undue influence. Lord Browne-Wilkinson said:
h

'Therefore, in my judgment a creditor in put on inquiry when a wife offers to stand surety for her husband's debts by the combination of two factors: (a) the transaction is on its face not to the financial advantage of the wife; and (b) there is a substantial risk in transactions of that kind that, in procuring the
j wife to act as surety, the husband has committed a legal or equitable wrong that entitles the wife to set aside the transaction.' (See [1993] 4 All ER 417 at 429, [1994] 1 AC 180 at 196.)

In my view, this passage, read in context, is to be taken to mean, quite simply, that a bank is put on inquiry whenever a wife offers to stand surety for her husband's debts.

[45] The Court of Appeal, comprising Stuart-Smith, Millett and Morritt LJJ, interpreted this passage more restrictively. The threshold, the court said, is somewhat higher. Where condition (a) is satisfied, the bank is put on inquiry if, but only if, the bank is aware that the parties are cohabiting or that the particular surety places implicit trust and confidence in the principal debtor in relation to her financial affairs (see *Royal Bank of Scotland plc v Etridge (No 2)* [1998] 4 All ER 705 at 719).

[46] I respectfully disagree. I do not read (a) and (b) as factual conditions which must be proved in each case before a bank is put on inquiry. I do not understand Lord Browne-Wilkinson to have been saying that, in husband and wife cases, whether the bank is put on inquiry depends on its state of knowledge of the parties' marriage, or of the degree of trust and confidence the particular wife places in her husband in relation to her financial affairs. That would leave banks in a state of considerable uncertainty in a situation where it is important they should know clearly where they stand. The test should be simple and clear and easy to apply in a wide range of circumstances. I read (a) and (b) as Lord Browne-Wilkinson's broad explanation of the reason why a creditor is put on inquiry when a wife offers to stand surety for her husband's debts. These are the two factors which, taken together, constitute the underlying rationale.

[47] The position is likewise if the husband stands surety for his wife's debts. Similarly, in the case of unmarried couples, whether heterosexual or homosexual, where the bank is aware of the relationship (see *O'Brien's* case [1993] 4 All ER 417 at 431, [1994] 1 AC 180 at 198, per Lord Browne-Wilkinson). Cohabitation is not essential. The Court of Appeal rightly so decided in *Massey v Midland Bank plc* [1995] 1 All ER 929 at 933, per Steyn LJ.

[48] As to the type of transactions where a bank is put on inquiry, the case where a wife becomes surety for her husband's debts is, in this context, a straightforward case. The bank is put on inquiry. On the other side of the line is the case where money is being advanced, or has been advanced, to husband and wife jointly. In such a case the bank is not put on inquiry, unless the bank is aware the loan is being made for the husband's purposes, as distinct from their joint purposes. That was decided in *CIBC Mortgages plc v Pitt* [1993] 4 All ER 433, [1994] 1 AC 200.

[49] Less clear cut is the case where the wife becomes surety for the debts of a company whose shares are held by her and her husband. Her shareholding may be nominal, or she may have a minority shareholding or an equal shareholding with her husband. In my view the bank is put on inquiry in such cases, even when the wife is a director or secretary of the company. Such cases cannot be equated with joint loans. The shareholding interests, and the identity of the directors, are not a reliable guide to the identity of the persons who actually have the conduct of the company's business.

THE STEPS A BANK SHOULD TAKE

[50] The principal area of controversy on these appeals concerns the steps a bank should take when it has been put on inquiry. In *O'Brien's* case Lord Browne-Wilkinson ([1993] 4 All ER 417 at 429–430, [1994] 1 AC 180 at 196–197) said that a bank can reasonably be expected to take steps to bring home to the wife the risk she is running by standing as surety and to advise her to take independent advice. That test is applicable to past transactions. All the cases now before your Lordships' House fall into this category. For the future a bank satisfies these requirements if it insists that the wife attend a private meeting with

a a representative of the bank at which she is told of the extent of her liability as surety, warned of the risk she is running and urged to take independent legal advice. In exceptional cases the bank, to be safe, has to insist that the wife is separately advised.

[51] The practice of the banks involved in the present cases, and it seems reasonable to assume this is the practice of banks generally, is not to have a
b private meeting with the wife. Nor do the banks themselves take any other steps to bring home to the wife the risk she is running. This has continued to be the practice since the decision in O'Brien's case. Banks consider they would stand to lose more than they would gain by holding a private meeting with the wife. They are, apparently, unwilling to assume the responsibility of advising the wife at such a meeting. Instead, the banking practice remains, as before, that in general the
c bank requires a wife to seek legal advice. The bank seeks written confirmation from a solicitor that he has explained the nature and effect of the documents to the wife.

[52] Many of the difficulties which have arisen in the present cases stem from serious deficiencies, or alleged deficiencies, in the quality of the legal advice given
d to the wives. I say 'alleged', because three of the appeals before your Lordships' House have not proceeded beyond the interlocutory stage. The banks successfully applied for summary judgment. In these cases the wife's allegations, made in affidavit form, have not been tested by cross-examination. On behalf of the wives it has been submitted that under the current practice the legal advice is often perfunctory in the extreme and, further, that everyone, including the banks,
e knows this. Independent legal advice is a fiction. The system is a charade. In practice it provides little or no protection for a wife who is under a misapprehension about the risks involved or who is being coerced into signing. She may not even know the present state of her husband's indebtedness.

[53] My Lords, it is plainly neither desirable nor practicable that banks should
f be required to attempt to discover for themselves whether a wife's consent is being procured by the exercise of undue influence of her husband. This is not a step the banks should be expected to take. Nor, further, is it desirable or practicable that banks should be expected to insist on confirmation from a solicitor that the solicitor has satisfied himself that the wife's consent has not been procured by undue influence. As already noted, the circumstances in which banks are put on
g inquiry are extremely wide. They embrace every case where a wife is entering into a suretyship transaction in respect of her husband's debts. Many, if not most, wives would be understandably outraged by having to respond to the sort of questioning which would be appropriate before a responsible solicitor could give such a confirmation. In any event, solicitors are not equipped to carry out such
h an exercise in any really worthwhile way, and they will usually lack the necessary materials. Moreover, the legal costs involved, which would inevitably fall on the husband who is seeking financial assistance from the bank, would be substantial. To require such an intrusive, inconclusive and expensive exercise in every case would be an altogether disproportionate response to the need to protect those
j cases, presumably a small minority, where a wife is being wronged.

[54] The furthest a bank can be expected to go is to take reasonable steps to satisfy itself that the wife has had brought home to her, in a meaningful way, the practical implications of the proposed transaction. This does not wholly eliminate the risk of undue influence or misrepresentation. But it does mean that a wife enters into a transaction with her eyes open so far as the basic elements of the transaction are concerned.

[55] This is the point at which, in *O'Brien's* case, the House decided that the balance between the competing interests should be held. A bank may itself provide the necessary information directly to the wife. Indeed, it is best equipped to do so. But banks are not following that course. Ought they to be obliged to do so in every case? I do not think Lord Browne-Wilkinson so stated in *O'Brien's* case. I do not understand him to have said that a personal meeting was the only way a bank could discharge its obligation to bring home to the wife the risks she is running. It seems to me that, provided a suitable alternative is available, banks ought not to be compelled to take this course. Their reasons for not wishing to hold a personal meeting are understandable. Commonly, when a bank seeks to enforce a security provided by a customer, it is met with a defence based on assurances alleged to have been given orally by a branch manager at an earlier stage: that the bank would continue to support the business, that the bank would not call in its loan, and so forth. Lengthy litigation ensues. Sometimes the allegations prove to be well founded, sometimes not. Banks are concerned to avoid the prospect of similar litigation which would arise in guarantee cases if they were to adopt a practice of holding a meeting with a wife at which the bank's representative would explain the proposed guarantee transaction. It is not unreasonable for the banks to prefer that this task should be undertaken by an independent legal advisor.

[56] I shall return later to the steps a bank should take when it follows this course. Suffice to say, these steps, together with advice from a solicitor acting for the wife, ought to provide the substance of the protection which *O'Brien's* case intended a wife should have. Ordinarily it will be reasonable that a bank should be able to rely upon confirmation from a solicitor, acting for the wife, that he has advised the wife appropriately.

[57] The position will be otherwise if the bank knows that the solicitor has not duly advised the wife or, I would add, if the bank knows facts from which it ought to have realised that the wife has not received the appropriate advice. In such circumstances the bank will proceed at its own risk.

THE CONTENT OF THE LEGAL ADVICE

[58] In *Royal Bank of Scotland plc v Etridge (No 2)* [1998] 4 All ER 705 at 715 (para 19), the Court of Appeal set out its views of the duties of a solicitor in this context:

'A solicitor who is instructed to advise a person who may be subject to the undue influence of another must bear in mind that [it] is not sufficient that she understands the nature and effect of the transaction if she is so affected by the influence of the other that she cannot make an independent decision of her own. It is not sufficient to explain the documentation and ensure she understands the nature of the transaction and wishes to carry it out: see *Powell v Powell* [1900] 1 Ch 243 at 247, approved in *Wright v Carter* ([1903] 1 Ch 27, [1900–3] All ER Rep 706). His duty is to satisfy himself that his client is free from improper influence, and the first step must be to ascertain whether it is one into which she could sensibly be advised to enter if free from such influence. If he is not so satisfied it is his duty to advise her not to enter into it, and to refuse to act further for her in the implementation of the transaction if she persists. In this event, while the contents of his advice must remain confidential, he should inform the other parties (including the bank) that he has seen his client and given her certain advice, and that as a result he has declined to act for her any further. He must in any event advise her that she

a
is under no obligation to enter into the transaction at all and, if she still wishes to do so, that she is not bound to accept the terms of any document which has been put before her: see *Credit Lyonnais Bank Nederland NV v Burch* [1997] 1 All ER 144.'

b
[59] I am unable to accept this as an accurate formulation of a solicitor's duties in cases such as those now under consideration. In some respects it goes much too far. The observations of Farwell J in *Powell v Powell* [1900] 1 Ch 243 at 247, should not be pressed unduly widely. *Powell v Powell* was a case where strong moral pressure was applied by a stepmother to a girl who was only just 21. She was regarded as not really capable of dealing irrevocably with her parent or guardian in the matter of a substantial settlement. Farwell J's observations cannot be
c
regarded as of general application in all cases where a solicitor is giving advice to a person who may have been subject to undue influence.

[60] More pertinently, in *Re Coomber, Coomber v Coomber* [1911] 1 Ch 723 at 730, Fletcher Moulton LJ summarised the general rules applicable to cases of persons who are competent to form an opinion of their own:

d
'All that is necessary is that some independent person, free from any taint of the relationship, or of the consideration of interest which would affect the act, should put clearly before the person what are the nature and the consequences of the act. It is for adult persons of competent mind to decide whether they will do an act, and I do not think that independent and competent advice
e
means independent and competent approval. It simply means that the advice shall be removed entirely from the suspected atmosphere; and that from the clear language of an independent mind, they should know precisely what they are doing.'

[61] Thus, in the present type of case it is not for the solicitor to veto the
f
transaction by declining to confirm to the bank that he has explained the documents to the wife and the risks she is taking upon herself. If the solicitor considers the transaction is not in the wife's best interests, he will give reasoned advice to the wife to that effect. But at the end of the day the decision on whether to proceed is the decision of the client, not the solicitor. A wife is not to be precluded from entering into a financially unwise transaction if, for her own reasons, she wishes
g
to do so.

[62] That is the general rule. There may, of course, be exceptional circumstances where it is glaringly obvious that the wife is being grievously wronged. In such a case the solicitor should decline to act further. In *Wright v Carter* [1903] 1 Ch 27 at 57–58, [1900–3] All ER Rep 706 at 717, Stirling LJ approved Farwell J's
h
observations in *Powell v Powell* [1900] 1 Ch 243 at 247. But he did so by reference to the extreme example of a poor man divesting himself of all his property in favour of his solicitor.

[63] In *Etridge*'s case ([1998] 4 All ER 705 at 722 (para 49)), the Court of Appeal said that if the transaction is 'one into which no competent solicitor could
j
properly advise the wife to enter', the availability of legal advice is insufficient to avoid the bank being fixed with constructive notice. It follows from the views expressed above that I am unable to agree with the Court of Appeal on this point.

[64] I turn to consider the scope of the responsibilities of a solicitor who is advising the wife. In identifying what are the solicitor's responsibilities the starting point must always be the solicitor's retainer. What has he been retained to do? As a general proposition, the scope of a solicitor's duties is dictated by the

terms, whether express or implied, of his retainer. In the type of case now under consideration the relevant retainer stems from the bank's concern to receive confirmation from the solicitor that, in short, the solicitor has brought home to the wife the risks involved in the proposed transaction. As a first step the solicitor will need to explain to the wife the purpose for which he has become involved at all. He should explain that, should it ever become necessary, the bank will rely upon his involvement to counter any suggestion that the wife was overborne by her husband or that she did not properly understand the implications of the transaction. The solicitor will need to obtain confirmation from the wife that she wishes him to act for her in the matter and to advise her on the legal and practical implications of the proposed transaction.

[65] When an instruction to this effect is forthcoming, the content of the advice required from a solicitor before giving the confirmation sought by the bank will, inevitably, depend upon the circumstances of the case. Typically, the advice a solicitor can be expected to give should cover the following matters as the core minimum. (1) He will need to explain the nature of the documents and the practical consequences these will have for the wife if she signs them. She could lose her home if her husband's business does not prosper. Her home may be her only substantial asset, as well as the family's home. She could be made bankrupt. (2) He will need to point out the seriousness of the risks involved. The wife should be told the purpose of the proposed new facility, the amount and principal terms of the new facility, and that the bank might increase the amount of the facility, or change its terms, or grant a new facility, without reference to her. She should be told the amount of her liability under her guarantee. The solicitor should discuss the wife's financial means, including her understanding of the value of the property being charged. The solicitor should discuss whether the wife or her husband has any other assets out of which repayment could be made if the husband's business should fail. These matters are relevant to the seriousness of the risks involved. (3) The solicitor will need to state clearly that the wife has a choice. The decision is hers and hers alone. Explanation of the choice facing the wife will call for some discussion of the present financial position, including the amount of the husband's present indebtedness, and the amount of his current overdraft facility. (4) The solicitor should check whether the wife wishes to proceed. She should be asked whether she is content that the solicitor should write to the bank confirming he has explained to her the nature of the documents and the practical implications they may have for her, or whether, for instance, she would prefer him to negotiate with the bank on the terms of the transaction. Matters for negotiation could include the sequence in which the various securities will be called upon or a specific or lower limit to her liabilities. The solicitor should not give any confirmation to the bank without the wife's authority.

[66] The solicitor's discussion with the wife should take place at a face-to-face meeting, in the absence of the husband. It goes without saying that the solicitor's explanations should be couched in suitably non-technical language. It also goes without saying that the solicitor's task is an important one. It is not a formality.

[67] The solicitor should obtain from the bank any information he needs. If the bank fails for any reason to provide information requested by the solicitor, the solicitor should decline to provide the confirmation sought by the bank.

[68] As already noted, the advice which a solicitor can be expected to give must depend on the particular facts of the case. But I have set out this 'core minimum' in some detail, because the quality of the legal advice is the most

a disturbing feature of some of the present appeals. The perfunctory nature of the advice may well be largely due to a failure by some solicitors to understand what is required in these cases.

INDEPENDENT ADVICE

[69] I turn next to the much-vexed question whether the solicitor advising the
b wife must act for the wife alone. Or, at the very least, the solicitor must not act for the husband or the bank in the current transaction save in a wholly ministerial capacity, such as carrying out conveyancing formalities or supervising the execution of documents and witnessing signatures. Commonly, in practice, the solicitor advising the wife will be the solicitor acting also for her husband either in the particular transaction or generally.

c [70] The first point to note is that this question cannot be answered by reference to reported decisions. The steps a bank must take once it is put on inquiry, if it is to avoid having constructive notice of the wife's rights, are not the subject of exposition in earlier authority. This is a novel situation, created by the *O'Brien* decision.

d [71] Next, a simple and clear rule is needed, preferably of well-nigh universal application. In some cases a bank deals directly with a husband and wife and has to take the initiative in requiring the wife to obtain legal advice. In other cases, a bank may deal throughout with solicitors already acting for the husband and wife. The case of *Bank of Baroda v Rayarel* [1995] 2 FCR 631 is an example of the latter type of case. It would not be satisfactory to attempt to draw a distinction
e along these lines. Any such distinction would lack a principled base. Inevitably, in practice, the distinction would disintegrate in confusion.

[72] Thirdly, here again, a balancing exercise is called for. Some features point in one direction, others in the opposite direction. Factors favouring the need for the solicitor to act for the wife alone include the following. Sometimes a wife
f may be inhibited in discussion with a solicitor who is also acting for the husband or whose main client is the husband. This occurred in *Banco Exterior Internacional v Mann* [1995] 1 All ER 936: see the finding of the judge (at 941). Sometimes a solicitor whose main client is the husband may not, in practice, give the same single-minded attention to the wife's position as would a solicitor acting solely for the wife. Her interests may rank lower in the solicitor's scale of priorities, perhaps
g unconsciously, than the interests of the husband. Instances of incompetent advice, or worse, which have come before the court might perhaps be less likely to recur if a solicitor were instructed to act for the wife alone and gave advice solely to her. As a matter of general understanding, independent advice would suggest that the solicitor should not be acting in the same transaction for the person who, if there
h is any undue influence, is the source of that influence.

[73] The contrary view is that the solicitor may also act for the husband or the bank, provided the solicitor is satisfied that this is in the wife's best interests and satisfied also that this will not give rise to any conflicts of duty or interest. The principal factors favouring this approach are as follows. A requirement that a
j wife should receive advice from a solicitor acting solely for her will frequently add significantly to the legal costs. Sometimes a wife will be happier to be advised by a family solicitor known to her than by a complete stranger. Sometimes a solicitor who knows both husband and wife and their histories will be better placed to advise than a solicitor who is a complete stranger.

[74] In my view, overall the latter factors are more weighty than the former. The advantages attendant upon the employment of a solicitor acting solely for

the wife do not justify the additional expense this would involve for the husband. When accepting instructions to advise the wife the solicitor assumes responsibilities directly to her, both at law and professionally. These duties, and this is central to the reasoning on this point, are owed to the wife alone. In advising the wife the solicitor is acting for the wife alone. He is concerned only with her interests. I emphasise, therefore, that in every case the solicitor must consider carefully whether there is any conflict of duty or interest and, more widely, whether it would be in the best interests of the wife for him to accept instructions from her. If he decides to accept instructions, his assumption of legal and professional responsibilities to her ought, in the ordinary course of things, to provide sufficient assurance that he will give the requisite advice fully, carefully and conscientiously. Especially so, now that the nature of the advice called for has been clarified. If at any stage the solicitor becomes concerned that there is a real risk that other interests or duties may inhibit his advice to the wife he must cease to act for her.

AGENCY

[75] No system ever works perfectly. There will always be cases where things go wrong, sometimes seriously wrong. The next question concerns the position when a solicitor has accepted instructions to advise a wife but he fails to do so properly. He fails to give her the advice needed to bring home to her the practical implications of her standing as surety. What then? The wife has a remedy in damages against the negligent solicitor. But what is the position of the bank who proceeded in the belief that the wife had been given the necessary advice?

[76] Mr Sher contended that, depending on the facts, the solicitor should be regarded as the agent of the bank. Commonly, what happens is that the bank asks the solicitor acting for the husband to undertake the conveyancing formalities on behalf of the bank. The bank also asks the solicitor to undertake the further task of explaining the nature and effect of the documents to the wife, and then confirming to the bank that he has done so. In carrying out these requested tasks, it was submitted, the solicitor is acting for the bank. The bank requires the solicitor to advise the wife, not for her benefit, but for the benefit and protection of the bank. Any deficiencies in the advice given to the wife should be attributed to the bank. In this regard, it was submitted, the solicitor's knowledge is to be imputed to the bank. A certificate furnished by the solicitor to the bank should not prejudice the position of the wife when, as happened in several cases, the contents of the certificate are untrue. If the solicitor has not given the wife any advice, her rights should not be diminished by the solicitor telling the bank that she has been fully advised.

[77] I cannot accept this analysis. Confirmation from the solicitor that he has advised the wife is one of the bank's preconditions for completion of the transaction. But it is central to this arrangement that in advising the wife the solicitor is acting for the wife and no one else. The bank does not have, and is intended not to have, any knowledge of or control over the advice the solicitor gives the wife. The solicitor is not accountable to the bank for the advice he gives to the wife. To impute to the bank knowledge of what passed between the solicitor and the wife would contradict this essential feature of the arrangement. The mere fact that, for its own purposes, the bank asked the solicitor to advise the wife does not make the solicitor the bank's agent in giving that advice.

[78] In the ordinary case, therefore, deficiencies in the advice given are a matter between the wife and her solicitor. The bank is entitled to proceed on the assumption that a solicitor advising the wife has done his job properly. I have

a already mentioned what is the bank's position if it knows this is not so, or if it knows facts from which it ought to have realised this is not so.

OBTAINING THE SOLICITOR'S CONFIRMATION

[79] I now return to the steps a bank should take when it has been put on inquiry and for its protection is looking to the fact that the wife has been advised
b independently by a solicitor. (1) One of the unsatisfactory features in some of the cases is the late stage at which the wife first became involved in the transaction. In practice she had no opportunity to express a view on the identity of the solicitor who advised her. She did not even know that the purpose for which the solicitor was giving her advice was to enable him to send, on her behalf, the
c protective confirmation sought by the bank. Usually the solicitor acted for both husband and wife. Since the bank is looking for its protection to legal advice given to the wife by a solicitor who, in this respect, is acting solely for her, I consider the bank should take steps to check *directly with the wife* the name of the solicitor she wishes to act for her. To this end, in future the bank should communicate directly with the wife, informing her that for its own protection it
d will require written confirmation from a solicitor, acting for her, to the effect that the solicitor has fully explained to her the nature of the documents and the practical implications they will have for her. She should be told that the purpose of this requirement is that thereafter she should not be able to dispute she is legally bound by the documents once she has signed them. She should be asked
e to nominate a solicitor whom she is willing to instruct to advise her, separately from her husband, and act for her in giving the necessary confirmation to the bank. She should be told that, if she wishes, the solicitor may be the same solicitor as is acting for her husband in the transaction. If a solicitor is already acting for the husband and the wife, she should be asked whether she would
f prefer that a different solicitor should act for her regarding the bank's requirement for confirmation from a solicitor. The bank should not proceed with the transaction until it has received an appropriate response directly from the wife. (2) Representatives of the bank are likely to have a much better picture of the husband's financial affairs than the solicitor. If the bank is not willing to undertake the task of explanation itself, the bank must provide the solicitor with
g the financial information he needs for this purpose. Accordingly it should become routine practice for banks, if relying on confirmation from a solicitor for their protection, to send to the solicitor the necessary financial information. What is required must depend on the facts of the case. Ordinarily this will include information on the purpose for which the proposed new facility has been
h requested, the current amount of the husband's indebtedness, the amount of his current overdraft facility, and the amount and terms of any new facility. If the bank's request for security arose from a written application by the husband for a facility, a copy of the application should be sent to the solicitor. The bank will, of course, need first to obtain the consent of its customer to this circulation of
j confidential information. If this consent is not forthcoming the transaction will not be able to proceed. (3) Exceptionally there may be a case where the bank believes or suspects that the wife has been misled by her husband or is not entering into the transaction of her own free will. If such a case occurs the bank must inform the wife's solicitors of the facts giving rise to its belief or suspicion. (4) The bank should in every case obtain from the wife's solicitor a written confirmation to the effect mentioned above.

[**80**] These steps will be applicable to future transactions. In respect of past *a* transactions, the bank will ordinarily be regarded as having discharged its obligations if a solicitor who was acting for the wife in the transaction gave the bank confirmation to the effect that he had brought home to the wife the risks she was running by standing as surety.

THE CREDITOR'S DISCLOSURE OBLIGATION *b*

[**81**] It is a well-established principle that, stated shortly, a creditor is obliged to disclose to a guarantor any unusual feature of the contract between the creditor and the debtor which makes it materially different in a potentially disadvantageous respect from what the guarantor might naturally expect. The precise ambit of this disclosure obligation remains unclear. A useful summary of *c* the authorities appears in O'Donovan and Phillips *The Modern Contract of Guarantee* (3rd edn, 1996) pp 122–130. It is not necessary to pursue these difficult matters in this case. It is sufficient for me to say that, contrary to submissions made, the need to provide protection for wives who are standing as sureties does not point to a need to revisit the scope of this disclosure principle. Wives require a different form of protection. They need a full and clear explanation of the risks *d* involved. Typically, the risks will be risks any surety would expect. The protection needed by wives differs from, and goes beyond, the disclosure of information. The *O'Brien* principle is intended to provide this protection.

A WIDER PRINCIPLE *e*

[**82**] Before turning to the particular cases I must make a general comment on the *O'Brien* principle. As noted by Professor Peter Birks QC, the decision in *O'Brien*'s case has to be seen as the progenitor of a wider principle (see 'The Burden on the Bank' in *Restitution and Banking Law*, ed Rose (1998) p 195). This calls for explanation. In *O'Brien*'s case the House was concerned with formulating a fair *f* and practical solution to problems occurring when a creditor obtains a security from a guarantor whose sexual relationship with the debtor gives rise to a heightened risk of undue influence. But the law does not regard sexual relationships as standing in some special category of their own so far as undue influence is concerned. Sexual relationships are no more than one type of relationship in which an individual may acquire influence over another *g* individual. The *O'Brien* decision cannot sensibly be regarded as confined to sexual relationships, although these are likely to be its main field of application at present. What is appropriate for sexual relationships ought, in principle, to be appropriate also for other relationships where trust and confidence are likely to exist. *h*

[**83**] The courts have already recognised this. Further application, or development, of the *O'Brien* principle has already taken place. In *Credit Lyonnais Bank Nederland NV v Burch* [1997] 1 All ER 144 the same principle was applied where the relationship was employer and employee. Miss Burch was a junior employee in a company. She was neither a shareholder nor a director. She provided security *j* to the bank for the company's overdraft. She entered into a guarantee of unlimited amount, and gave the bank a second charge over her flat. Nourse LJ (at 146) said the relationship 'may broadly be said to fall under [*O'Brien*'s case]'. The Court of Appeal held that the bank was put on inquiry. It knew the facts from which the existence of a relationship of trust and confidence between Miss Burch and Mr Pelosi, the owner of the company, could be inferred.

a   [84] The crucially important question raised by this wider application of the O'Brien principle concerns the circumstances which will put a bank on inquiry. A bank is put on inquiry whenever a wife stands as surety for her husband's debts. It is sufficient that the bank knows of the husband/wife relationship. That bare fact is enough. The bank must then take reasonable steps to bring home to the wife the risks involved. What, then, of other relationships where there is an

b   increased risk of undue influence, such as parent and child? Is it enough that the bank knows of the relationship? For reasons already discussed in relation to husbands and wives, a bank cannot be expected to probe the emotional relationship between two individuals, whoever they may be. Nor is it desirable that a bank should attempt this. Take the case where a father puts forward his daughter as a surety for his business overdraft. A bank should not be called upon

c   to evaluate highly personal matters such as the degree of trust and confidence existing between the father and his daughter, with the bank put on inquiry in one case and not in another. As with wives, so with daughters, whether a bank is put on inquiry should not depend on the degree of trust and confidence the particular daughter places in her father in relation to financial matters. Moreover, as with

d   wives, so with other relationships, the test of what puts a bank on inquiry should be simple, clear and easy to apply in widely varying circumstances. This suggests that, in the case of a father and daughter, knowledge by the bank of the relationship of father and daughter should suffice to put the bank on inquiry. When the bank knows of the relationship, it must then take reasonable steps to ensure the daughter knows what she is letting herself into.

e   [85] The relationship of parent and child is one of the relationships where the law irrebuttably presumes the existence of trust and confidence. Rightly, this has already been rejected as the boundary of the O'Brien principle. O'Brien's case was a husband/wife case. The responsibilities of creditors were enunciated in a case where the law makes no presumption of the existence of trust and confidence.

f   [86] But the law cannot stop at this point, with banks on inquiry only in cases where the debtor and guarantor have a sexual relationship or the relationship is one where the law presumes the existence of trust and confidence. That would be an arbitrary boundary, and the law has already moved beyond this, in the decision in the Credit Lyonnais case. As noted earlier, the reality of life is that relationships in which undue influence can be exercised are infinitely various.

g   They cannot be exhaustively defined. Nor is it possible to produce a comprehensive list of relationships where there is a substantial risk of the exercise of undue influence, all others being excluded from the ambit of the O'Brien principle. Human affairs do not lend themselves to categorisations of this sort. The older generation of a family may exercise undue influence over a younger member, as

h   in parent/child cases such as Bainbrigge v Browne (1881) 18 Ch D 188 and Powell v Powell [1900] 1 Ch 243. Sometimes it is the other way round, as with a nephew and his elderly aunt in Inche Noriah v Shaik Allie Bin Omar [1929] AC 127, [1928] All ER Rep 189. An employer may take advantage of his employee, as in the Credit Lyonnais case. But it may be the other way round, with an employee taking

j   advantage of her employer, as happened with the secretary/companion and her elderly employer in Re Craig (decd) [1970] 2 All ER 390, [1971] Ch 95. The list could go on.

[87] These considerations point forcibly to the conclusion that there is no rational cut-off point, with certain types of relationship being susceptible to the O'Brien principle and others not. Further, if a bank is not to be required to evaluate the extent to which its customer has influence over a proposed

guarantor, the only practical way forward is to regard banks as 'put on inquiry' in
every case where the relationship between the surety and the debtor is ᵃ
non-commercial. The creditor must always take reasonable steps to bring home
to the individual guarantor the risks he is running by standing as surety. As a
measure of protection, this is valuable. But, in all conscience, it is a modest
burden for banks and other lenders. It is no more than is reasonably to be
expected of a creditor who is taking a guarantee from an individual. If the bank ᵇ
or other creditor does not take these steps, it is deemed to have notice of any
claim the guarantor may have that the transaction was procured by undue
influence or misrepresentation on the part of the debtor.

[88] Different considerations apply where the relationship between the debtor
and guarantor is commercial, as where a guarantor is being paid a fee, or a
company is guaranteeing the debts of another company in the same group. ᶜ
Those engaged in business can be regarded as capable of looking after themselves
and understanding the risks involved in the giving of guarantees.

[89] By the decisions of this House in *O'Brien*'s case and the Court of Appeal in
the *Credit Lyonnais* case, English law has taken its first strides in the development of
some such general principle. It is a workable principle. It is also simple, coherent ᵈ
and eminently desirable. I venture to think this is the way the law is moving, and
should continue to move. Equity, it is said, is not past the age of child-bearing.
In the present context the equitable concept of being 'put on inquiry' is the parent
of a principle of general application, a principle which imposes no more than a
modest obligation on banks and other creditors. The existence of this obligation
in all non-commercial cases does not go beyond the reasonable requirements of ᵉ
the present times. In future, banks and other creditors should regulate their
affairs accordingly.

THE PARTICULAR CASES

[90] I have had the advantage of reading in draft a copy of the speech of my ᶠ
noble and learned friend Lord Scott of Foscote. He has summarised the facts in
the eight appeals. My views on the particular cases are as follows.

(1) *Midland Bank plc v Wallace*

I would allow this appeal. The bank was put on inquiry, because this was a case
of a wife standing as surety for her husband's debts. As the evidence stands at ᵍ
present, Mr Samson's participation in the transaction does not assist the bank. He
was not Mrs Wallace's solicitor. Deficiencies in the advice given by a solicitor do
not normally concern the bank. That is the position where the solicitor is acting
for the wife, or where the solicitor has been held out by the wife to the bank as
her solicitor. But where the solicitor was not acting for the wife, the bank is in ʰ
the same position as any person who deals with another in the belief that the
latter is acting on behalf of a third party principal when in truth he is not. Leaving
aside questions of ostensible authority or the like, the alleged principal is not
bound or affected by the acts of such a stranger. The remedy of the bank lies
against the (unauthorised) 'agent'. If the bank has suffered provable loss, it has a ʲ
claim for damages for breach of implied warranty of authority. This action
should go to trial.

(2) *Barclays Bank plc v Harris*

This is another interlocutory appeal, against an order striking out Mrs Harris'
defence. It is common ground that for striking out purposes Mrs Harris has an

a arguable case on undue influence. The bank was put on inquiry, because Mrs Harris was standing as surety for the debts of the company, S T Harris (Powder Coatings Consultant) Ltd. I consider Mrs Harris has an arguable case that Wragge & Co never acted for her. In this respect the case is similar to *Wallace*'s case. This case should go to trial.

b (3) *UCB Home Loans Corp Ltd v Moore*
    This is another interlocutory appeal. For the reasons given by my noble and learned friend Lord Hobhouse of Woodborough, I would allow this appeal.

(4) *Royal Bank of Scotland v Etridge (No 2)*, (5) *National Westminster Bank plc v Gill*, (6) *Barclays Bank plc v Coleman*, (7) *Bank of Scotland v*
c *Bennett, and* (8) *Kenyon-Brown v Desmond Banks & Co*
    I agree with Lord Scott that, for the reasons he gives, the appeals of Mrs Bennett and Desmond Banks & Co should be allowed. The appeals of Mrs Etridge, Mrs Gill and Mrs Coleman should be dismissed.

d **LORD CLYDE.**
    [91] My Lords, I have had the opportunity of reading in draft the speech of my noble and learned friend Lord Nicholls of Birkenhead and agree with it. I add a few observations of my own because of the importance of the appeals which we have heard.
e [92] I question the wisdom of the practice which has grown up, particularly since *Bank of Credit and Commerce International SA v Aboody* [1992] 4 All ER 955, [1990] 1 QB 923 of attempting to make classifications of cases of undue influence. That concept is in any event not easy to define. It was observed in *Allcard v Skinner* (1887) 36 Ch D 145 at 183, [1886–90] All ER Rep 90 at 99 (per Lindley LJ) that 'no Court has ever attempted to define undue influence'. It is something
f which can be more easily recognised when found than exhaustively analysed in the abstract. Correspondingly the attempt to build up classes or categories may lead to confusion. The confusion is aggravated if the names used to identify the classes do not bear their actual meaning. Thus on the face of it a division into cases of 'actual' and 'presumed' undue influence appears illogical. It appears to confuse definition and proof. There is also room for uncertainty whether the
g presumption is of the existence of an influence or of its quality as being undue. I would also dispute the utility of the further sophistication of subdividing 'presumed undue influence' into further categories. All these classifications to my mind add mystery rather than illumination.
    [93] There is a considerable variety in the particular methods by which undue
h influence may be brought to bear on the grantor of a deed. They include cases of coercion, domination, victimisation and all the insidious techniques of persuasion. Certainly it can be recognised that in the case of certain relationships it will be relatively easier to establish that undue influence has been at work than in other cases where that sinister conclusion is not necessarily to be drawn with such ease.
j English law has identified certain relationships where the conclusion can prima facie be drawn so easily as to establish a presumption of undue influence. But this is simply a matter of evidence and proof. In other cases the grantor of the deed will require to fortify the case by evidence, for example, of the pressure which was unfairly applied by the stronger party to the relationship, or the abuse of a trusting and confidential relationship resulting in for the one party a disadvantage and for the other a collateral benefit beyond what might be expected from the

relationship of the parties. At the end of the day, after trial, there will either be
proof of undue influence or that proof will fail, and it will be found that there was *a*
no undue influence. In the former case, whatever the relationship of the parties
and however the influence was exerted, there will be found to have been an
actual case of undue influence. In the latter there will be none.

[94] The second point relates to the steps which were suggested in *Barclays
Bank plc v O'Brien* [1993] 4 All ER 417, [1994] 1 AC 180 as being appropriate for the *b*
lender to escape constructive notice of the wrongdoing in question. I agree that
what was suggested in the case was not intended to be prescriptive. So far as past
cases were concerned it was said that the creditor 'can reasonably be expected to
take steps to bring home to the wife the risk she is running by standing as surety
and to advise her to take independent advice' (see [1993] 4 All ER 417 at 429,
[1994] 1 AC 180 at 196, per Lord Browne-Wilkinson). Those two courses of action *c*
were reflected in the Scottish case of *Smith v Bank of Scotland* 1997 SC (HL) 111 at
122 by the suggestion which I made in relation to the corresponding situation
under Scots law that 'it would be sufficient for the creditor to warn the potential
cautioner of the consequences of entering into the proposed cautionary obligation
and to advise him or her to take independent advice'. That statement echoed *d*
what was understood to be the existing practice recognised by banks and building
societies and it seemed to me that steps of that kind ought to be enough to enable
the creditor to counter any allegation of bad faith. But Lord Browne-Wilkinson
proposed more stringent requirements for the avoidance of constructive notice
in England for the future. These were that the creditor should insist—

e

> 'that the wife attend a private meeting (in the absence of the husband) with
> a representative of the creditor at which she is told of the extent of her
> liability as surety, warned of the risk she is running and urged to take
> independent legal advice.' (See [1993] 4 All ER 417 at 429–430, [1994] 1 AC
> 180 at 196.)

f

He also recognised ([1993] 4 All ER 417 at 430, [1994] 1 AC 180 at 197) that there
might be exceptional cases where undue influence was not simply possible but
was probable and advised that in such cases the 'the creditor to be safe will have
to insist that the wife is separately advised'.

[95] One course is for the lender himself to warn the surety of the risk and to
recommend the taking of legal advice. But there may well be good reasons, *g*
particularly for banks, to feel it inappropriate or even unwise for them to be
giving any detailed form of warning or explanation, and to take the view that it
is preferable for that matter to be managed by a solicitor acting for the wife. It is
certainly possible to suggest courses of action which should be sufficient to
absolve the creditor from constructive notice of any potential undue influence. *h*
Thus in the summary at the end of his speech Lord Browne-Wilkinson said:

> '... unless there are special exceptional circumstances, a creditor will have
> taken such reasonable steps to avoid being fixed with constructive notice if
> the creditor warns the surety (at a meeting not attended by the principal
> debtor) of the amount of her potential liability and of the risks involved and *j*
> advises the surety to take independent legal advice.' (See [1993] 4 All ER 417
> at 431–432, [1994] 1 AC 180 at 199.)

But matters of banking practice are principally matters for the banks themselves
in light of the rights and liabilities which the law may impose upon them. I would
not wish to prescribe what those practices should be. One can only suggest some

a courses of action which should meet the requirements of the law. These are not matters of ritual, the blind performance of which will secure the avoidance of doom, but sensible steps which seek to secure that the personal and commercial interests of the parties involved are secured with certainty and fairness. Necessarily the precise course to be adopted will depend upon the circumstances. In the Scottish case of *Forsyth v Royal Bank of Scotland plc* 2000 SLT 1295 it appeared to

b the creditor that the wife had already had the benefit of professional legal advice. In such a case, it may well be that no further steps need be taken by the creditor to safeguard his rights. Of course if the creditor knows or ought to know from the information available to him that the wife has not in fact received the appropriate advice then the transaction may be open to challenge.

c [96] Thirdly, I agree that it is not fatal that the solicitor is also the solicitor who acts for the party for whose benefit the guarantee or the charge is being effected, that is to say the husband in cases where the wife is granting the deed in question. If there is any question of any conflict of interest arising, or if the solicitor feels that he cannot properly act for the wife in the matter of giving the advice, then he will be perfectly able to identify the difficulty and withdraw. Again it should

d be stressed that the wife's consultation with her solicitor is a serious step which is not to be brushed off as a mere formality or a charade. It is in the interests of all the parties involved that the wife should appreciate the significance of what she has been asked to sign so that the transaction may not only appear to be fair but also in fact to be freely and voluntarily undertaken.

e [97] I agree that the appeals in the cases of Mrs Wallace, Mrs Bennett, Mrs Moore and Desmond Banks & Co be allowed. I have had some hesitation about the case of Mrs Harris but following in particular the view expressed by Lord Scott of Foscote I consider that the appeal in her case should also be allowed. I consider that the other appeals should be dismissed.

f **LORD HOBHOUSE OF WOODBOROUGH.**

INTRODUCTION

[98] My Lords, these appeals have come before your Lordships in order to enable the workings of the judgments of your Lordships' House in *Barclays*

g *Bank plc v O'Brien* [1993] 4 All ER 417, [1994] 1 AC 180 and *CIBC Mortgages plc v Pitt* [1993] 4 All ER 433, [1994] 1 AC 200 to be considered. The leading speech in both of those cases was, with the agreement of the House, that of Lord Browne-Wilkinson. His speeches are in my respectful opinion a masterly exposition of principles designed to give structure to this difficult corner of the law and to

h provide practical solutions to the problems to which it gives rise whilst recognising the conflict between the interests of the commercial community and the need to protect vulnerable members of society from oppression or exploitation. These problems and conflicts are real and should not be ignored. The value of the transactions takes them outside the scope of the existing statutory protection

j and the solution therefore has to be found in the application of equitable principles formulated by judges. Experience in litigation since 1993 has not been encouraging. Disputes have continued to come before the courts; the determination of those disputes has not always carried conviction. Before your Lordships no party has sought to challenge the authority of Lord Browne-Wilkinson's speeches, subject to the criticism of one point of categorisation derived from *Bank of Credit and Commerce International SA v Aboody* [1992] 4 All ER 955, [1990] 1 QB 923, criticism which I, like the rest of your Lordships, consider to be justified; the point of categorisation has been the source of much of the confusion which has ensued.

[99] I therefore propose to take the speech of Lord Browne-Wilkinson in *O'Brien's* case as my starting point. Some of what he said was novel. Some has been criticised as departing from fully conventional equitable principle. It is true that other approaches had been adopted in other cases, including in the Court of Appeal in that case. But the purpose of such judgments of this House is to settle the law and enable certainty to be re-established. That should again be the objective of your Lordships on these appeals. Doubt should not be cast upon the authority of *O'Brien's* case. There is a need for some clarification and for the problem areas to be resolved as far as possible. But the essential structure of *O'Brien* is in my view sound and Lord Browne-Wilkinson fully took into account the practical implications.

[100] To the end that lenders, those advising parties and, indeed, judges should have clear statements of the law on which to base themselves, I will state at the outset that in this speech I shall agree with my noble and learned friend Lord Nicholls of Birkenhead and, specifically, the guidance which he gives concerning the role of the burden of proof, the duties of solicitors towards their clients (see [64]–[68] and [74], above), and the steps which a lender which has been put on inquiry should take (see [79], above). I would stress that this guidance should not be treated as optional, to be watered down when it proves inconvenient (as may be thought to have been the fate of Lord Browne-Wilkinson's equally carefully crafted scheme). Nor should it be regarded as something which will only apply to future transactions; it has represented, and continues to represent, the reasonable response to being put on inquiry. The purpose of guidance is to provide certainty for those who rely upon and conform to the requirements of that guidance: it is not a licence to excuse unreasonable conduct on the ground that no judge had previously told them in express terms what was not an adequate response. If the relevant solicitor was not in fact acting for the wife and had not been held out by the wife as doing so, the conduct of that solicitor will not avail the lender. Once a lender has been put on inquiry, mere assumptions on the part of the lender will not assist him. I will, in the course of this speech and without qualifying the scope of my agreement with Lord Nicholls, mention certain points in the hope that it will add to the clarity and accuracy of the analysis. I must also express my gratitude to my noble and learned friend Lord Scott of Foscote, whose speech I have read in draft, for his summary of the facts of the eight individual cases before the House.

BARCLAYS BANK PLC v O'BRIEN

[101] The speech of Lord Browne-Wilkinson followed a four part scheme. First, he characterised the law of the enforceability of suretyship contracts and security as between lenders to a husband or his company and a wife as being an application of the equitable principle of undue influence. Secondly, he sought to categorise the undue influence into classes drawn from *Allcard v Skinner* (1887) 36 Ch D 145, [1886–90] All ER Rep 90, *Turnbull & Co v Duval* [1902] AC 429 and *Aboody's* case giving rise to presumptions. Thirdly, he provided a formulation to answer the question whether the lender had been put on inquiry as to the risk of undue influence:

'... a creditor is put on inquiry when a wife offers to stand surety for her husband's debts by the combination of two factors: (a) the transaction is on its face not to the financial advantage of the wife; and (b) there is a substantial risk in transactions of that kind that, in procuring the wife to act as surety, the husband has committed a legal or equitable wrong that entitles the wife to set aside the transaction.' (See [1993] 4 All ER 417 at 429, [1994] 1 AC 180 at 196.)

Fourthly, he laid down steps which if taken would enable the lender to say that he had taken reasonable steps to satisfy himself that the 'surety entered into the obligation freely and in knowledge of the true facts' ([1993] 4 All ER 417 at 431, [1994] 1 AC 180 at 198). His speech thus provides a structured scheme for the decision of cases raising the issue of enforceability as between a lender and a wife. It can be expressed by answering three questions. (1) Has the wife proved what is necessary for the court to be satisfied that the transaction was affected by the undue influence of the husband? (2) Was the lender put on inquiry? (3) If so, did the lender take reasonable steps to satisfy itself that there was no undue influence? It will be appreciated that unless the first question is answered in favour of the wife neither of the later questions arise. The wife has no defence and is liable. It will likewise be appreciated that the second and third questions arise from the fact that the wife is seeking to use the undue influence of her husband as a defence against the lender and therefore has to show that the lender should be affected by the equity—that it is unconscionable that the lender should enforce the secured contractual right against her.

[102] Difficulties have arisen in relation to each of these three questions. I will take the questions in turn. The most important difficulties relate to the first and third questions.

(1) PRESUMED UNDUE INFLUENCE

[103] The division between presumed and actual undue influence derives from the judgments in *Allcard v Skinner*. Actual undue influence presents no relevant problem. It is an equitable wrong committed by the dominant party against the other which makes it unconscionable for the dominant party to enforce his legal rights against the other. It is typically some express conduct overbearing the other party's will. It is capable of including conduct which might give a defence at law, for example, duress and misrepresentation. Indeed many of the cases relating to wives who have given guarantees and charges for their husband's debts involve allegations of misrepresentation. (*O'Brien's* case was such a case.) Actual undue influence does not depend upon some pre-existing relationship between the two parties though it is most commonly associated with and derives from such a relationship. He who alleges actual undue influence must prove it.

[104] Presumed undue influence is different in that it necessarily involves some legally recognised relationship between the two parties. As a result of that relationship one party is treated as owing a special duty to deal fairly with the other. It is not necessary for present purposes to define the limits of the relationships which give rise to this duty. Typically they are fiduciary or closely analogous relationships. A solicitor owes a legal duty to deal fairly with his client and he must, if challenged, be prepared to show that he has done so. In *CIBC Mortgages plc v Pitt* [1993] 4 All ER 433 at 439–440, [1994] 1 AC 200 at 209, Lord Browne-Wilkinson referred to—

'the long standing principle laid down in the abuse of confidence cases, viz the law requires those in a fiduciary position who enter into transactions

with those to whom they owe fiduciary duties to establish affirmatively that
the transaction was a fair one ...'

Such legal relationships can be described as relationships where one party is
legally presumed to repose trust and confidence in the other, the other side of the
coin to the duty not to abuse that confidence. But there is no presumption
properly so-called that the confidence has been abused. It is a matter of evidence.
If all that has happened is that, say, a client has left a small bequest to his family
solicitor or that a solicitor has made a reasonable charge for professional services
rendered to the client, no inference of abuse or unfair dealing will arise. But if a
solicitor has bought property from his client and it is properly put in issue that the
purchase was at an undervalue or that the client's consent may have been
improperly obtained, the solicitor will have to show that the price was fair and
that the client's consent to the transaction was freely given in knowledge of the
true facts. The solicitor has to justify what he has done. He has a burden of proof
to discharge and if he fails to discharge it he will not have succeeded in justifying
his conduct. Thus, at the trial the judge will decide on the evidence whether he
is in fact satisfied that there was no abuse of confidence. It will be appreciated that
the relevance of the concept of 'manifest disadvantage' is evidential. It is relevant
to the question whether there is any issue of abuse which can properly be raised.
It is relevant to the determination whether in fact abuse did or did not occur. It
is a fallacy to argue from the terminology normally used, 'presumed undue
influence', to the position, not of presuming that one party reposed trust and
confidence in the other, but of *presuming* that an abuse of that relationship has
occurred; factual inference, yes, once the issue has been properly raised, but not
a *presumption*.

[105] The Court of Appeal in *Aboody*'s case and Lord Browne-Wilkinson
classified cases where there was a legal relationship between the parties which the
law presumed to be one of trust and confidence as 'presumed undue influence:
class 2A'. They then made the logical extrapolation that there should be a class 2B
to cover those cases where it was proved by evidence that one party had in fact
reposed trust and confidence in the other. It was then said that the same
consequences flowed from this factual relationship as from the legal class 2A
relationship. Lord Browne-Wilkinson said:

'In a class 2B case therefore, in the absence of evidence disproving undue
influence, the complainant will succeed in setting aside the impugned
transaction merely by proof that the complainant reposed trust and confidence
in the wrongdoer without having to prove that the wrongdoer exerted actual
undue influence or otherwise abused such trust and confidence in relation to
the particular transaction impugned.' (See *O'Brien*'s case [1993] 4 All ER 417
at 423, [1994] 1 AC 180 at 189–190.)

There are difficulties in the literal application of this statement. It describes the
other party as a 'wrongdoer' without saying why when it is expressly postulated
that no wrongdoing may have occurred. He treats trust and confidence as
indivisible. His actual words are: '... a relationship under which the complainant
generally reposed trust and confidence in the wrongdoer ...' (my emphasis). But
a wife may be happy to trust her husband to make the right decision in relation
to some matters but not others; she may leave a particular decision to him but
not other decisions. Nor is it clear why the mere 'existence of such relationship
raises the presumption of undue influence'. Where the relevant question is one

a of fact and degree and of the evaluation of evidence, the language of presumption is likely to confuse rather than assist and this is borne out by experience.

[106] That there is room for an analogous approach to cases concerning a wife's guarantee of her husband's debts is clear and no doubt led to Lord Browne-Wilkinson saying what he did. The guarantee is given by the wife at the request of the husband. The guarantee is not on its face advantageous to the wife,
b doubly so where her liability is secured upon her home. The wife may well have trusted the husband to take for her the decision whether she should give the guarantee. If he takes the decision in these circumstances, he owes her a duty to have regard to her interests before deciding. He is under a duty to deal fairly with her. He should make sure that she is entering into the obligation freely and in knowledge of the true facts. His duty may thus be analogous to that of a class 2A
c fiduciary so that it would be appropriate to require him to justify the decision. If no adequate justification is then provided, the conclusion would be that there had been an abuse of confidence. But any conclusion will only be reached after having received evidence. This evidence will inevitably cover as well whether there has in fact been an abuse of confidence or any other undue influence. The
d judge may have to draw inferences. He may have to decide whether he accepts the evidence of the wife and, if so, what it really amounts to, particularly if it is uncontradicted. Since there is no legal relationship of trust and confidence, the general burden of proving some form of wrongdoing remains with the wife, but the evidence which she has adduced may suffice to raise an inference of wrongdoing which the opposite party may find itself having to adduce evidence
e to rebut. If at the end of the trial the wife succeeds on the issue of undue influence, it will be because that is the right conclusion of fact on the state of the evidence at the end of the trial, not because of some artificial legal presumption that there must have been undue influence.

[107] In agreement with what I understand to be the view of your Lordships,
f I consider that the so-called class 2B presumption should not be adopted. It is not a useful forensic tool. The wife or other person alleging that the relevant agreement or charge is not enforceable must prove her case. She can do this by proving that she was the victim of an equitable wrong. This wrong may be an overt wrong, such as oppression; or it may be the failure to perform an equitable duty, such as a failure by one in whom trust and confidence is reposed not to
g abuse that trust by failing to deal fairly with her and have proper regard to her interests. Although the general burden of proof is, and remains, upon her, she can discharge that burden of proof by establishing a sufficient prima facie case to justify a decision in her favour on the balance of probabilities, the court drawing appropriate inferences from the primary facts proved. Evidentially the opposite
h party will then be faced with the necessity to adduce evidence sufficient to displace that conclusion. Provided it is remembered that the burden is an evidential one, the comparison with the operation of the doctrine res ipsa loquitur is useful.

(2) PUT ON INQUIRY

j [108] However described, this is an essential step in the reasoning of Lord Browne-Wilkinson. The wife becomes involved at the request of her husband. It is he who, in these types of case, is the source of the undue influence and commits the equitable wrong against her. But the party with whom the wife contracts and to whom the wife accepts obligations is the lender. It is the lender who is seeking to enforce those obligations. Therefore there has to be some additional factor before the lender's conscience is affected and he is to be restrained from enforcing his legal rights. The solution adopted by Lord Browne-Wilkinson was to formulate a principle of constructive notice. He did so in terms which were not as restrictive as the established principles of constructive knowledge. However, there is a structural difficulty in his approach. Notice of the risk of undue influence is not an all or nothing question. Situations will differ across a spectrum from a very small risk to a serious risk verging on a probability. There has to be a proportionality between the degree of risk and the requisite response to it. Lord Browne-Wilkinson expressed it in terms of a 'substantial risk' (see *O'Brien's* case [1993] 4 All ER 417 at 429, [1994] 1 AC 180 at 196). But, then, in describing the requisite response he stated ([1993] 4 All ER 417 at 430, [1994] 1 AC 180 at 197) that he had been considering 'the ordinary case where the creditor knows only that the wife is to stand surety for her husband's debts'. This is, as my noble and learned friend Lord Nicholls has said, a low threshold. There are arguments which would favour a higher threshold. It would enable a more positive approach to be taken to the response. It would avoid calling for a response when the level of risk did not really justify it. But the advantage of this low threshold is that it assists banks to put in place procedures which do not require an exercise of judgment by their officials and I accept Lord Nicholls' affirmation of the low threshold. This, however, is not to say that banks are at liberty to close their eyes to evidence of higher levels of risk or fail to respond appropriately to higher risks of which they have notice.

[109] Needless to say the question whether the bank has been put on inquiry has to be answered upon the basis of the facts available to the bank. Does the bank know that the wife is standing surety for her husband's debts? This should be an easy question for the bank to answer. The bank should know who the principal debtor is and what is the purpose of the facility. Likewise the bank should know of any factors which are likely to aggravate the risk of undue influence. Paradoxically the best place at which to start to assess the risk of undue influence is to consider the true nature of the transaction and examine the financial position of the principal debtor and the proposal which he is making to the bank. These are the facts which the bank has most readily to hand and, if it finds that it lacks relevant information, it is in a position to get it and has the expertise to assess it. A loan application backed by a viable business plan or to acquire a worthwhile asset is very different from a loan to postpone the collapse of an already failing business or to refinance with additional security loans which have fallen into arrears. The former would not aggravate the risk; the latter most certainly would do so. The bank is as well placed as anyone to assess the underlying rationality of the debtor's proposal. It will be the bank that will have formed the view that it is not satisfied with the debtor's covenant and the security he can provide and it will be the bank that has called for additional security. The bank will also probably be aware what has been the previous involvement, if any, of the wife in the husband's business affairs.

[110] The position therefore is that in relation to any guarantee by a wife of her husband's debts (or those of his company) the bank is put on inquiry and accordingly will have to respond unless it is to run the risk of finding that the guarantee and other security provided by the wife are unenforceable. If it becomes aware of any aggravation of the risk of undue influence, its response must take that into account. More will be required to satisfy it that the wife's agreement has been properly obtained.

The practical situation

a

[111] Before turning to discuss what are the reasonable steps to be taken by a lender who had been put on inquiry, I will pause to look at some of the practical aspects. Lord Browne-Wilkinson clearly regarded these as important ([1993] 4 All ER 417 at 430–431, [1994] 1 AC 180 at 197–198). He drew attention to the report of the *Review Committee on Banking Services: Law and Practice* (Cm 622) under the chairmanship of Professor Jack which reported in 1989 which noted that 'there are cases of guarantors losing their houses because of open ended commitments that they entered into, without understanding or advice' (para 13.22) and recommended that banks should adopt a standard of best practice which would require them to—

b

c

'ensure that prospective guarantors, whether or not they are not customers, are adequately warned about the legal effects and possible consequences of guarantees, and about the importance of receiving independent advice ...' (Recommendation 13(5).)

The committee was concerned with the lack of the understanding on the part of guarantors of the onerous contractual obligations arising from the signature of the forms used by banks for guarantees or charges. The printed documentation used by banks is of such length, complexity and obscurity that it is unlikely to be read let alone understood by private guarantors who lack legal training or appropriate business experience. They are treated by banks as contracts of adhesion discouraging any attempt to modify any of their terms. They are often unduly favourable to the bank and excessively onerous to the surety. The surety will probably be made a principal debtor and liable without limit for very onerous rates of interest and charges. The liability may be an 'all moneys' guarantee covering without limit any future advances not merely the advances intended to be guaranteed. Thus, quite apart from the question of undue influence, the signature of such documents may not represent any reality of informed consent. The need to guard against lack of comprehension is important and applies in any event to a non-business surety. But it is not the same as guarding against undue influence. It may be a first step but it is a fallacy to confuse the two. Comprehension is essential for any legal documents of this complexity and obscurity. But for the purpose of negativing undue influence it is necessary to be satisfied that the agreement was, also, given freely in knowledge of the true facts. It must be remembered that the equitable doctrine of undue influence has been created for the protection of those who are sui juris and competent to undertake legal obligations but are nevertheless vulnerable and liable to have their will unduly influenced. It is their weakness which is being protected not their inability to comprehend. I regret that I must specifically disagree with my noble and learned friend Lord Scott when (in his summary) he treats a belief on the part of a lender that the wife has understood the nature and effect of the transaction as sufficient to exonerate the lender from inquiry or as treating this as the effect of the scheme laid out by Lord Nicholls in the paragraphs to which I have referred earlier.

d

e

f

g

h

j

[112] A further point of relevance which has been commented on in the past and should be commented upon again has been the use by banks of forms under which the surety gives an unlimited guarantee or charge. This was what banks ordinarily asked for. Indeed, the guarantees obtained in the cases from which these appeals arise, are unlimited. Banks have acknowledged that such guarantees are likely to be unnecessary and unjustifiable where private sureties are sought. They should be subject to a stated monetary limit on the surety's liability and any

legal advisor should so advise a private client. Where a bank has nevertheless
obtained an unlimited guarantee from a wife, it should ask itself how that can be
if the wife has in truth been independently advised. Would anyone who had a
proper regard to the wife's interests ask her to sign an unlimited guarantee or
charge?

[113] Lord Browne-Wilkinson stressed the need for the wife to be seen and
communicated with *separately* from her husband. This was clearly appropriate
since, if the purpose is to satisfy oneself that the wife is acting freely in knowledge of
the true facts, an interview in the presence of the husband is unlikely to achieve this
objective if she has been improperly influenced by him. Lord Browne-Wilkinson
concluded that the requirement of a personal interview did not impose such an
additional administrative burden as to make the bank's position unworkable
(*O'Brien*'s case [1993] 4 All ER 417 at 431, [1994] 1 AC 180 at 198). What the banks
appear to find difficult is entrusting the conduct of such an interview to one of
their own officers as opposed to entrusting it to an outside agent. This is sad but
probably derives from a wish to avoid getting directly involved in imparting
information and maybe opinions to an individual whose interests are likely to
conflict with their own and with whom they may subsequently be in dispute.
Lord Browne-Wilkinson contemplated that the banks might use a representative
to do what he considered necessary and this would imply that they would be
responsible for their representative. The banks have not done this. They have
used solicitors. They have denied any responsibility even for a complete failure
of the solicitor whom they have instructed to carry out their instructions and
have nevertheless sought to hold the wife to her signature so obtained. I doubt
that this is what Lord Browne-Wilkinson had in mind.

[114] The use of solicitors has given rise to further practical (and, to a limited
extent, legal) problems. The first is ensuring that the solicitor is in possession of
the relevant facts as known to the bank. The advantage of an officer of the bank
conducting the interview with the wife is that he has the file and access to
the relevant facts. The solicitor on the other hand may have nothing except the
documents which are to be signed. It is within the control of the bank what it
sends to the solicitor. If the solicitor is to conduct the interview with the wife, the
bank must give him the information. The next difficulty is that the bank's
information about the affairs of its customer is confidential and the bank may
need to obtain the husband's consent to give this information to the solicitor and
the wife. However, if the husband refuses to give his consent, this would be a
clear indication to the bank and the solicitor that something may be amiss and
that it ought not to rely upon the wife being bound. A further point is that
contracts of suretyship are not contracts of the utmost good faith. There is no
general duty of disclosure: see the authorities cited by my noble and learned
friends in their speeches, to which I would add the speech of Lord Clyde in *Smith v
Bank of Scotland* 1997 SC (HL) 111. Seeing that the solicitor is adequately informed
is not the performance of a *duty* owed by the bank to the wife. It is simply a
necessary step to be taken by the bank so that it may be satisfied that the wife
entered into the obligation freely and in knowledge of the true facts.

[115] Another consequence of using solicitors is the risk of confusion about
what the solicitor's role is to be. The solicitor will normally have been instructed
by the bank to act for it. The solicitor will often already be acting for the husband.
The solicitor may not be acting for the wife at all, let alone separately and
independently from the solicitor's other clients. Similarly, the solicitor's instructions
may simply be to explain to the signatories the character and legal effect of the

a documents. This is a low order of advice which can be given solely by reference to the formal documents to be signed. It is also important to appreciate that the solicitor's role may simply be to witness a signature. Such a role involves no necessary relationship whatsoever between the solicitor and the signatory. Indeed they may have or represent conflicting interests. The solicitor may simply have been instructed by one party to see and be prepared to provide evidence that

b the relevant document was signed and delivered by the other party. Seeing that a solicitor has witnessed a signature itself means nothing. Even when a solicitor is instructed to explain the character and legal effect of a document, he will not without more concern himself at all with the interests of the wife or whether she is accepting the obligations freely and with knowledge of the true facts. Under these circumstances it is scarcely surprising, as the facts of these cases and many

c others show, that wives are still signing documents as a result of undue influence. The involvement of a solicitor has too often been a formality or merely served to reinforce the husband's wishes and undermine any scope for the wife to exercise an independent judgment whether to comply. Lord Browne-Wilkinson observed:

d 'The number of recent cases in this field shows that in practice many wives are still subjected to, and yield to, undue influence by their husbands. Such wives can reasonably look to the law for some protection when their husbands have abused the trust and confidence reposed in them.' (See *O'Brien*'s case [1993] 4 All ER 417 at 422, [1994] 1 AC 180 at 188.)

e The result of the practice of relying upon solicitors' certificates has been described by Sir Peter Millett (as he then was) in his lecture to the Chancery Bar Association ('Equity's Place in the Law of Commerce' (1998) 114 LQR 214 at 220), referring to an article by Sir Anthony Mason ('The Place of Equity and Equitable Remedies in the Contemporary Common Law World' (1994) 110 LQR 238):

f 'What Sir Anthony Mason has described as "ritual reliance on the provision of legal advice" is foreign to the traditional approach of a court of equity and is manifestly failing to give adequate protection to the wife or cohabitant who acts as surety. We have substituted an inappropriate bright line rule for a proper investigation of the facts and have failed the vulnerable in the process. The Australians are turning to the jurisdiction to relieve against

g harsh and unconscionable bargains as an alternative, and there is much merit in this approach. It is certainly better than allowing the bank to assume that the surety has received adequate legal advice, an assumption which the bank almost always knows to be false.'

h The crux of this situation is that the bank requests the solicitor to give a certificate which the bank then treats as conclusive evidence that it has no notice of any undue influence which has occurred. But the wife may have no knowledge that this certificate is to be given and will not have authorised the solicitor to give it and, what is more, the solicitor will deny that he is under any obligation to the wife (or the bank) to satisfy himself that the wife is entering into the obligations

j freely and in knowledge of the true facts. The law has, in order to accommodate the commercial lenders, adopted a fiction which nullifies the equitable principle and deprives vulnerable members of the public of the protection which equity gives them.

[116] Lord Browne-Wilkinson contemplated a two-stage exercise, the first stage being an interview between the lender and the wife (for which the lender would be responsible) and the second being the wife taking independent advice

from a solicitor (for which the lender would not be responsible). The practice of
banks has been to run these two stages together, thus creating confusion about *a*
the role of the solicitor. I accept that the best solution is that adopted by
Lord Nicholls in his speech. The solicitor in communicating with and advising
the wife should be doing so solely as her solicitor. The solicitor's certificate
which the bank asks for is something which the bank is asking the wife to procure
and which the solicitor is providing as her solicitor. I am satisfied that, provided *b*
that the guidance which Lord Nicholls gives (in the paragraphs which I have
identified at the outset of this speech) is complied with, the wife will have a
reasonable chance of receiving the protection she may need. But it will be
appreciated that an essential feature of the scheme is that the wife has to be aware
of what is going on, that the bank is asking for the certificate and why, that she is
being asked to instruct a solicitor to advise her and that she is being asked to *c*
authorise the solicitor to provide the certificate. This is a far cry from the situation
which has been tolerated in the past where the wife has not appreciated that she
had any solicitor or was being advised and did not know of the existence of the
certificate or its significance; indeed it has been that type of situation which has
given rise to the most scandalous cases. *d*

[117] Illuminating evidence was given at the trial of the *Gill* action relevant to
what was practical from the bank's point of view. The bank there was the
National Westminster Bank. The bank manager gave evidence. In answer to
direct questions he accepted without qualification that he foresaw the potential
for undue influence by a husband where his wife is being asked to stand surety for
the debts of her husband's business. His solution was to procure that the wife *e*
received *separate* legal advice. In saying this he was following the practice of his
bank as set out in a document (which he produced during his evidence-in-chief)
with which he said he was already familiar in December 1988 (that is to say well
before *O'Brien's* case in the House of Lords) headed 'CHARGED
SECURITY—Separate Legal Advice—Action Sheet'. It includes the following *f*
passages:

'The security may be voidable if **undue influence** can be established.
Therefore, great care is needed when there is any likelihood that a potential
guarantor or third-party chargor may be unduly influenced by a borrower.
Undue influence may exist where there is a special relationship between the *g*
parties, e g: husband and wife ... Do not regard the above list as exhaustive.
The background always requires careful thought ... (ii) where the
guarantor/chargor is a customer of the Bank ... **the Bank has a duty, where
any doubts exist, to INSIST that independent legal advice is given
regarding**: (a) the nature of the guarantee/charge (b) the viability of the *h*
underlying proposition—advise the guarantor/chargor to obtain full details
from the principal debtor, whose consent is required before disclosures, as to
the underlying transaction, can be made to the grantor/chargor or legal
advisor. Always consider, in detail, the circumstances surrounding a transaction,
as undue influence may arise where **direct** security is taken for joint *j*
borrowing, e g: (i) joint borrowing for purposes ostensibly in the interest of
only one of the borrowers ... Where there is any suspicion of undue
influence, the Manager must ensure that all guarantors/third-party chargors
take separate legal advice from a firm of solicitors **nominated by the
guarantor/chargor. Send the charge form directly to the solicitor
concerned** ... To avoid a conflict of interest, ensure that the witnessing

a
solicitor is not also acting for the borrower. In such circumstances another solicitor, who may be a partner in the same firm, must be used.'

[118] My Lords, I have quoted from this document because it discloses the response of a major high street bank to the question of undue influence. It does not seek to play down the risk. It puts husbands and wives at the top of the list. It requires that independent/separate legal advice be taken by the guarantor/chargor. It stresses the importance of having regard to the viability of the underlying proposition or transaction and where necessary obtaining full details from the principal debtor. It requires that the solicitor be the solicitor nominated by the guarantor/chargor and that the actual solicitor must not be acting for the borrower as well. These points are all of practical as well as legal importance. Banks were prepared to accommodate them. They did not need to be told that they had to by Lord Browne-Wilkinson. It represented a pragmatic response to the practical as well as the legal questions. In some respects, the National Westminster Bank 'Action Sheet' goes quite a bit further than what is required by Lord Nicholls. It shows that the speech of Lord Nicholls does not require banks to go further than they had already been prepared to go before *O'Brien's* case and that what Lord Nicholls requires is and was in fact reasonable and practical.

(3) REASONABLE STEPS

[119] Lord Browne-Wilkinson favoured a personal interview with the wife conducted in the absence of the husband by a representative of the bank. The wife would then be urged to take independent/separate legal advice. It followed that the bank would be responsible for the first of these steps but not the second. The banks were not following this course. They were not doing anything themselves. They were instructing a solicitor, asking him to supply a formal certificate limited to comprehension and that is all. This is what had given rise to the fiction of free and informed consent where none existed and no steps had been taken to discover the true position.

[120] Given the state of the authorities since the speeches in *O'Brien's* case and *Pitt's* case were delivered and the need to provide fresh guidance, I agree that your Lordships should adopt the scheme spelled out by Lord Nicholls. The central feature is that the wife will be put into a proper relationship with a solicitor who is acting for her and accepts appropriate duties towards her. Likewise the bank or other lender must communicate directly with the wife to the end that that relationship is established and that any certificate upon which it may seek to rely is the fruit of such a professional relationship.

[121] If the bank follows this procedure then the fiction of independent advice and consent should be replaced by true independent advice and real consent. It will probably be less onerous for the lender than what was required by Lord Browne-Wilkinson and the National Westminster Bank 'Action Sheet'. It will also be observed that it is consistent with the duty of the solicitor towards his client, the wife. He will appreciate that he cannot give the statement and certificate unless it conforms to the reality. Similarly, the wife will not be left in ignorance of what has been going on and will know what she is entitled to get from the solicitor.

[122] It also resolves the question of what knowledge of the solicitor will affect the bank either under the common law or under s 199 of the Law of Property Act 1925. The solicitor in question will not be acting for the bank. Any knowledge the solicitor acquires from the wife will be confidential as between the two of them. If it renders untruthful the statement or certificate, the solicitor cannot

sign them without being in breach of his professional obligation to the wife and
committing a fraud on the bank. The wife's remedy will be against the solicitor   *a*
and not against the bank. If the solicitor does not provide the statement and
certificate for which the bank has asked, then the bank will not, in the absence of
other evidence, have reasonable grounds for being satisfied that the wife's
agreement has been properly obtained. Its legal rights will be subject to any
equity existing in favour of the wife.   *b*

INDIVIDUAL CASES

[123] Turning to the individual appeals, the cases fall into three different
categories. There are three cases—*Barclays Bank plc v Harris, Midland Bank plc v
Wallace* and *UCB Home Loans Corp Ltd v Moore*—which have not got beyond the
interlocutory stage, the wives' pleadings having been struck out as disclosing no *c*
defence to the banks' claims for possession. There are four cases—*Royal Bank of
Scotland plc v Etridge (No 2), National Westminster Bank plc v Gill, Barclays Bank plc v
Coleman* and *Bank of Scotland v Bennett*—which have proceeded to trial and in
which, at trial and/or on appeal, the wife has been unsuccessful. Finally there is
a single case—*Kenyon-Brown v Desmond Banks & Co (a firm)*—in which the wife   *d*
was suing her solicitor for damages for breach of duty. Your Lordships are in
favour of allowing the appeals in *Kenyon-Brown, Harris, Wallace, Moore* and
Bennett: I agree. I also agree that the appeals in *Etridge, Gill* and *Coleman* should
be dismissed. There is an important distinction to be drawn between cases which
have been tried where the parties have been able to test the opposing case and the
trial judge was able to make findings of fact having seen the critical witnesses and *e*
evaluated the evidence. By contrast, in those cases where the lender is applying
for an immediate possession order without a trial or to have the defence struck
out, the court is being asked to hold that, even if the wife's allegations of fact be
accepted, the wife's case is hopeless and bound to fail and that there is no reason
why the case should go to trial. This conclusion is not to be arrived at lightly nor *f*
should such an order be made simply on the basis that the lender is more likely
to succeed. Once it is accepted that the wife has raised an arguable case that she
was in fact the victim of undue influence and that the bank had been put on
inquiry, it will have to be a very clear case before one can say that the bank should
not have to justify its conduct at a trial.

g

Kenyon-Brown v Desmond Banks & Co (a firm)

[124] I take this case first because it falls into a different category to the others.
The wife was claiming damages against a firm of solicitors on the basis that, under
the undue influence of her husband, she had entered into an adverse suretyship
transaction for the benefit of her husband, which also involved charging a cottage *h*
which they jointly owned, and that the solicitors had failed to give her
appropriate advice to prevent this happening. The guarantee was unlimited. The
wife was unable to give specific or reliable evidence in support of her case against
the solicitors but relied upon the fact that the transaction was manifestly
disadvantageous to her and upon the duty of the solicitor, as stated by the Court *j*
of Appeal in *Royal Bank of Scotland plc v Etridge (No 2)* [1998] 4 All ER 705 at 715
(para 19), to satisfy himself that she was free from improper influence. The
certificate which the solicitor gave to the lender was that he had given her legal
advice. In *Kenyon-Brown*, the majority of the Court of Appeal ([2000] PNLR 266),
in disagreement with the trial judge, considered that this led inexorably to the
conclusion that the solicitor must have been negligent. I agree with your

a Lordships that the conclusion of the Court of Appeal was not justified upon the evidence adduced at the trial. The burden of proof was upon the wife to establish that the solicitor had been negligent. She could not say that she had not been given comprehensive advice which included a full warning of the consequences of her entering into the transaction. She could not contradict that he had told her specifically that the mortgage would only benefit her husband and was without

b limit. He was her solicitor and advised her as his client. The judge was right: she failed to make out her case against the solicitor on the facts. If she had been able to give reliable evidence and be clearer about what she said had happened and had been in a position to challenge the solicitor's attendance note, she might have succeeded. The solicitor's duty towards her was as stated by my noble and learned friend Lord Nicholls. It seems that it was substantially observed and in so

c far as the solicitor might be criticised, no causative relevance was established.

Midland Bank plc v Wallace

[125] This was an interlocutory case. The bank claimed the possession of a flat in Priory Road, Hampstead, which was jointly owned by Mr and Mrs Wallace.

d The bank claimed possession on the basis of an all moneys legal charge signed by the husband and the wife against which the bank had advanced money to the husband. It was accepted that she had an arguable case that she had been unduly influenced to sign by her husband. The bank did not at any stage communicate with the wife or anyone acting for her. It sent the charge to its own solicitor with instructions to attend to the necessary formalities in the signing of the charge.

e The husband and wife went together to the bank's solicitor's office. The wife's case was that she was there three or four minutes at most; she signed as directed by the solicitor; there was no other discussion; her impression was that the solicitor had been instructed by the bank merely to take and witness her signature. On this case the bank had no basis for rebutting the risk that her signature had not been

f properly obtained. It had no basis for any belief that she had been separately advised by a solicitor who was acting for her. The only solicitor of which the bank knew was a solicitor acting for itself alone which had in a side letter to the bank, of which the wife knew nothing, told the bank no more than that the documents had been explained. The wife clearly had an arguable case for defending the possession action. The reasoning of the Court of Appeal ([1998]

g 4 All ER 705) in arriving at the contrary conclusion was that the bank was (or, perhaps, would have been) entitled to assume that the solicitor had been acting as the wife's solicitor and had discharged his duty to her as her solicitor. As stated, this assumption would have been without foundation. I agree that this appeal should be allowed.

h

Barclays Bank plc v Harris

[126] This was also an interlocutory case. The judge struck out her defence and counterclaim as disclosing no arguable defence to the bank's action for the possession of the house owned jointly by the husband and wife where they lived.

j The husband had, through the medium of two companies, two businesses one of which had effectively failed leaving him with a heavy personal liability. He consulted solicitors, Wragge & Co, to find a way of carrying on his other business. They advised him to negotiate a new facility with the bank with new security. The outcome was an offer from the bank of new finance for the second company secured by unlimited guarantees from both the husband and wife and a legal charge on their house. The bank was clearly put on inquiry. It was

accepted that for striking out purposes the wife had an arguable case on undue
influence. The relevant question was therefore whether the bank took reasonable *a*
steps to satisfy itself that the wife's agreement had not been improperly obtained.
Wragge & Co were only known to the bank as the husband's solicitors. The bank
took no steps to communicate with the wife who was allowed to remain in
ignorance of what precisely was the position between her husband and the bank.
The wife was never told that she would be required to be separately advised nor *b*
that she should instruct a solicitor to certify to the bank that she had been so
advised. In her pleading the wife had pleaded that the solicitors were acting for
the bank, her husband and herself. However before the judge the affidavit sworn
by her solicitor in the action (Mr Holt of Evans Derry Binnion) in response to the
bank's striking out application deposed:

c

> 'It is important to note that in so far as my client is concerned Wragge &
> Co were not her solicitors. Wragge & Co were solicitors who had been
> instructed by Mr Harris personally previously and he had a personal
> connection with one of the partners at that [firm].'

The wife therefore has an arguable case that Wragge & Co were never her *d*
solicitors and that the case is in this respect the same as *Wallace's* case. There is
however a further feature of this case. The bank wrote to Wragge & Co,
knowing them only as the husband's solicitors, asking them, among other things,
'to explain the nature of the document to both parties and confirm to us that
independent legal advice has been given'. The letter in reply from Wragge & Co
did not give the bank that confirmation, a fact which the bank did not pick up *e*
until about nine months later. The bank then wrote to Wragge & Co pointing
this out and asking for confirmation that independent legal advice had nevertheless
been given. On receiving this further letter, the partner at Wragge & Co
commented: 'I do not think that independent legal advice was given.' On this, it
would appear that the bank appreciated that it needed confirmation that the wife *f*
had been independently advised. Patently it did not get it. The bank realised that
it had not got it and that she may well never have been independently advised.
This was clearly a case where the judge should have allowed the case to go to
trial. The wife had an arguable defence on more than one ground. The Court of
Appeal dismissed the wife's appeal giving only brief reasons:

g

> 'The solicitors were acting for Mrs Harris in the transaction and the bank
> were entitled to assume that they had given appropriate advice and were
> entitled to accept the solicitors' letter as confirmation that this had been
> done.' (See [1998] 4 All ER 705 at 730.)

These reasons fly in the face of the evidence and cannot be supported. This *h*
appeal should be allowed.

UCB Home Loans Corp Ltd v Moore

[127] This is the third of the interlocutory cases. It is less clear cut than the
other two. But it is not a case in which it should be said, in my judgment, that no *j*
trial is justified and that, on the basis of her pleaded case, the wife is bound to fail
in her defence of the possession action. It is accepted for present purposes that
she has an arguable case of undue influence and misrepresentation by her
husband. Her case is that she had in fact instructed no solicitors to act for her and
received no advice whatsoever. The charge was unlimited in amount. The loan
transaction was not wholly straightforward in that, whilst it included the

a refinancing of indebtedness which was already secured on the matrimonial home in Pangbourne, it was as to three-fifths composed of a substantial additional advance to the company run by the husband which was already in financial trouble (and was to fail within two years). In this connection, the company and the husband used an independent insurance broker, Mr Zerfahs and his brother (a credit broker), as a go-between with the lender. The lender had no direct

b communication with the wife, nor did Mr Zerfahs communicate with her. Were it not for one fact, this would be a case which fell into the same category as *Wallace's* case. The potential saving fact for the lender was that the husband had started his deception by persuading his wife to sign the mortgage application form in blank. One of the boxes in the form was 'solicitor's details'. The husband, who was the primary applicant, filled this in with the name of the

c solicitors who had been instructed by Mr Zerfahs without informing the wife or obtaining her authority: 'Quiney & Harris (Nigel Whittaker)' and their address in Wootton Bassett near Swindon. As a result, on the face of the form sent to the lender there was a single solicitor who was to act on behalf of both applicants. The wife says that the husband had not obtained her authority to fill in the form

d in this way; it is agreed that the husband undoubtedly filled in other parts of the form fraudulently. Having received instructions from Mr Zerfahs, the solicitors, without obtaining confirmation from the wife, referred to her and her husband in correspondence as 'our clients'. The lender did not obtain any assurance that the wife had received independent advice before signing. It is the wife's case that

e she received no advice at all. This is a disturbing case. It may turn out (if there is a trial) that the wife is an unreliable witness and that her case cannot be accepted. But, for present purposes, the lender's case has to depend wholly upon an estoppel arising from her having signed the application form in blank and, it is argued, an inference that she had been separately advised as an independent client by the solicitor. I do not believe that this is a sound basis for disposing of

f this case without a trial. The true facts need to be known. She was the victim of misrepresentation; the solicitors purported to act on her behalf without any authority to do so; the only document which the lender saw did not suggest anything other than a joint retainer; the lender never checked the position with the wife or sought any confirmation that she was being separately advised.

g Discovery of documents and a morning in the county court would have sorted the matter out more expeditiously and cheaply. I agree that this appeal should be allowed.

Royal Bank of Scotland plc v Etridge (No 2)

h [128] This is a case which, after some delay and contested interlocutory proceedings, went to a trial before Judge Behrens. The wife gave evidence. The judge found that, on the evidence, she had not been the victim of any actual undue influence. However he went on to deal with the case on the basis of *presumed* undue influence. On appeal, the Court of Appeal ([1998] 4 All ER 705) upheld the

j judge's finding of no actual undue influence; nor did she at either level obtain a finding in her favour that she had been induced to sign by any misrepresentation. Accordingly, on the correct view of the law, her case failed in limine and none of the other points arose. Judgment was rightly entered for the bank. On this ground, I agree that this appeal should be dismissed. This case provides an object lesson in the dangers of attempting a summary resolution of issues of mixed law and fact without having ascertained the facts.

National Westminster Bank plc v Gill

[129] This too is a case which went to trial. The evidence discloses what might have been a case of misrepresentation which possibly could have led to the wife succeeding. The transaction was presented in a fashion which may have led the wife and the solicitors mistakenly to believe that only an advance of £36,000 was involved, not a probable £100,000. However, be that as it may, the case advanced by the wife at the trial was that she had been the victim of actual undue influence. This case was rejected by the judge and, in any event, there was evidence that the extended scope of the transaction is something which she would in fact have supported and was not causative. Therefore this case is, in the critical respect, similar to *Etridge's* case. She failed to prove the allegation necessary to found her case. I agree that this appeal should be dismissed.

Barclays Bank plc v Coleman

[130] In this case there was a trial which was not confined to a simple claim by the bank against the wife; it involved also her husband (who in addition counterclaimed against the bank) and third parties joined by the wife. With some reluctance I agree that the wife's appeal should be dismissed. This is not because of any inherent lack of merit in her case; she has been appallingly badly served. It is because to set aside the judgments entered against her below would be contrary to the grounds upon which her case was conducted at the trial and in the Court of Appeal ([2000] 1 All ER 385, [2001] QB 20). The wife and her husband were members of the Hasidic Jewish community. This factually involved a relationship of complete trust and confidence between the wife and her husband in relation to financial matters. I agree with Lord Scott that it is a case where, having drawn the appropriate inferences, actual undue influence was in fact established. The wife was being asked to charge her home to secure advances to her husband for the purpose of enabling him to engage in property speculation, he being unable to offer the bank adequate other security. It was also a case where the bank was clearly put on inquiry. The relevant point which should have been considered was therefore whether the bank took steps of the kind referred to by Lord Nicholls (see [79], above) (or in the National Westminster Bank document) in order to protect itself from being affected by any such undue influence. But at the trial the dealings between the bank and the wife and the solicitor were not covered by documentary evidence and seem not to have been the subject of direct oral evidence either. The wife simply said that she went to the solicitor's office at the request of her husband and that all the managing clerk, whom they saw there, did before witnessing her signature was to ask her in the presence of her husband if he, her husband, had explained the documents to her. Her account (which the judge accepted) gives a pertinent reminder of the gap between theory and reality and illustrates the type of charade which, as Sir Peter Millett has observed, lenders well know may occur and should not be tolerated or sanctioned by equity. However, at the trial, the wife's case was that the elderly solicitor for whom the managing clerk worked was acting as her solicitor. She joined what she thought were the appropriate persons as third parties suing them for breach of professional duty. The elderly solicitor had died. The trial judge dismissed her claim against the third parties, holding that she had sued the wrong persons. There was a further unusual feature of the case. The bank had asked for a certificate in the unusual terms: 'I confirm that this document was signed in my presence and that the full effect of its contents have been explained to and were understood by Miriam Mara Coleman, *and she has signed this document of her own*

a *free will.'* It was this certificate that the managing clerk signed. If the bank were entitled to believe that this certificate was supplied by the wife's own solicitor instructed by her, the bank might have had a basis for believing that the wife's consent had been properly obtained. I venture to doubt whether any reasonable banker would have put this construction upon the available evidence but in view of the course of the proceedings before the trial judge and the basis upon which

b the wife's case was then put it would not be permissible now to allow this appeal upon an inconsistent and untested basis. The greater part of the time at the trial seems to have been taken up with the dispute between the husband and the bank. As between the wife and the bank, the judgments in the courts below were primarily concerned with aspects of the problem of *presumed* undue influence which do not now arise and with the question of the adequacy of a certificate

c signed by a legal executive as opposed to a solicitor which must depend on the facts of each case.

Bank of Scotland v Bennett

d [131] I agree that this appeal should be allowed. The existence of the ranking agreement was important and qualified the transaction as it was disclosed to the surety. I do not wish to add anything to what is to be said about this point by Lord Scott. This suffices for the allowing of the appeal. It is accordingly unnecessary to say anything about the undue influence issues.

e **LORD SCOTT OF FOSCOTE.**

Introduction

[132] My Lords, eight appeals have been heard together. In seven of these appeals, the appellant is a wife who agreed to subject her property, usually her

f interest in the matrimonial home, to a charge in favour of a bank in order to provide security for the payment of her husband's debts, or the debts of a company by means of which her husband carried on business. In each of these cases the bank has commenced proceedings for possession of the mortgaged property with a view to its sale and the wife has defended the claim by alleging, first, that her agreement to grant the charge to the bank was brought about by

g undue influence or misrepresentation, or both, on the part of her husband, and, secondly, that, in the circumstances, the chargee bank ought not to be allowed to enforce the charge against her. In each of these cases the question has been raised whether the bank should be treated as having had notice of the impropriety, or alleged impropriety, of the husband. In each of these cases the bank has had some

h reason to believe that a solicitor had acted for the wife in the transaction in question. So the question has arisen as to the extent to which the solicitor's participation, or believed participation, has absolved the bank of the need to make any further inquiries about the circumstances in which the wife was persuaded to agree to grant the charge, or to take any further steps to satisfy itself

j that her consent to do so was a true and informed consent.

[133] Four of these seven cases, *Royal Bank of Scotland plc v Etridge (No 2), National Westminster Bank plc v Gill, Barclays Bank plc v Coleman* and *Bank of Scotland v Bennett* went to a full trial, with evidence and cross-examination. The other three, *Barclays Bank plc v Harris, Midland Bank plc v Wallace* and *UCB Home Loans Corp Ltd v Moore,* have come to your Lordships' House as a result of interlocutory applications; in *Harris'* case and in *Moore's* case, an application to strike

out the relevant parts of the wife's defence; in *Wallace*'s case, an application by
the bank for summary judgment for possession.

[134] In each of these seven cases, the submissions on behalf of the wife have
been based upon the principles expressed by Lord Browne-Wilkinson in *Barclays
Bank plc v O'Brien* [1993] 4 All ER 417, [1994] 1 AC 180 and, to a lesser extent, in
CIBC Mortgages plc v Pitt [1993] 4 All ER 433, [1994] 1 AC 200.

[135] The eighth appeal before the House, *Kenyon-Brown v Desmond Banks &
Co (a firm)*, is a case in which the wife is suing the solicitor who acted for her in
such a transaction as I have described. She alleges breach of duty by the solicitor.
One of the issues in the seven wife v bank appeals that your Lordships are invited
to consider relates to the extent of the duty lying upon a solicitor who acts for a
wife who is proposing to grant a charge over her property as security for her
husband's, or his company's, debts. It was, therefore, thought convenient to add
the *Kenyon-Brown* appeal to the seven other appeals so that all could be heard
together.

[136] Five of the seven wife v bank appeals, namely, *Etridge*, *Harris*, *Moore*,
Wallace and *Gill*, were heard together by the Court of Appeal (*Royal Bank of
Scotland plc v Etridge (No 2)* [1998] 4 All ER 705, Stuart-Smith, Millett and
Morritt LJJ). In each, the Court of Appeal dismissed the wife's appeal against the
order for possession made by the court below. In *Bennett*'s case, the Court of
Appeal (Auld, Chadwick LJJ and Sir Christopher Staughton) ([1999] 1 FCR 641)
allowed the bank's appeal against the judgment below ([1997] 3 FCR 193) in
favour of the wife and made an order for possession. The Court of Appeal placed
strong reliance on passages in the judgment of the court given by Stuart-Smith LJ
in *Etridge*'s case. In *Coleman*'s case, the Court of Appeal (Nourse, Pill and
Mummery LJJ) ([2000] 1 All ER 385, [2001] QB 20) dismissed the wife's appeal
against the possession order made below.

[137] In *Kenyon-Brown*'s case, the Court of Appeal (Peter Gibson and
Mance LJJ, Wilson J dissenting) ([2000] PNLR 266) allowed the wife's appeal and,
in expressing the extent of the defendant solicitor's duty to her, placed strong
reliance on *Etridge*'s case.

[138] In deciding these appeals it is necessary in my opinion, first, to analyse
and explain the principles formulated by Lord Browne-Wilkinson in *O'Brien*'s
case. The case law since *O'Brien*'s case has, in my view, disclosed some
misconceptions about these principles.

The O'Brien principles

[139] It is convenient to start with a look at the problems that had to be
addressed in *O'Brien*'s case and at Lord Browne-Wilkinson's solution to them.

[140] There had been an increasing number of cases in which wives had
sought to avoid the charges they had given to banks or finance houses in support
of their husbands' debts. In many, probably in most, of the cases that had come
to court, the wives had not read, or, if they had, had not understood the
document they had signed. Many of the wives protested that they had signed
because excessive pressure to do so had been brought to bear on them by their
husbands; others said that their husbands had misrepresented the amount of the
secured debts, the time during which the charge would remain in force or some other
material matter. In most cases the wife emphasised, in explaining her willingness to
sign the charge, the trust and confidence she had had in her husband. This trust and
confidence, it was said, had led her to succumb to his pressure to sign and to be

a the more easily misled by his misrepresentations. Lord Browne-Wilkinson in O'Brien's case said:

> '... although the concept of the ignorant wife leaving all financial decisions to the husband is outmoded, the practice does not yet coincide with the ideal ... In a substantial proportion of marriages it is still the husband who has the business experience and the wife is willing to follow his advice without
b> bringing a truly independent mind and will to bear on financial decisions. The number of recent cases in this field shows that in practice many wives are still subjected to, and yield to, undue influence by their husbands. Such wives can reasonably look to the law for some protection when their husbands have abused the trust and confidence reposed in them.' (See [1993]
c> 4 All ER 417 at 422, [1994] 1 AC 180 at 188.)

[141] Lord Browne-Wilkinson emphasised, however, the importance of keeping a sense of balance in deciding what degree of protection should be afforded. He pointed out that 'a high proportion of privately owned wealth is invested in the matrimonial home' and referred to 'the need to ensure that the
d wealth currently tied up in the matrimonial home does not become economically sterile'. He added:

> 'If the rights secured to wives by the law renders vulnerable loans granted on the security of matrimonial homes, institutions will be unwilling to accept such security, thereby reducing the flow of loan capital to business
e> enterprises. It is therefore essential that a law designed to protect the vulnerable does not render the matrimonial home unacceptable as security to financial institutions.'

Each of these considerations is as relevant and important today as it was when O'Brien's case was decided.
f [142] One of the difficulties is that the protection the wife needs in these cases is a remedy against the bank, or other lender, to whom she is offering the suretyship security. It is not protection against her husband, who has allegedly procured her to do so by some wrongdoing, that is the problem. The law has no difficulty in providing an oppressed or deceived wife with a remedy against the
g wrongdoing husband. But, in most of the cases with which the House is now concerned, the husband is supporting his wife in her attempt to prevent the bank from enforcing its security. They stand together in attempting to save the family home. In these circumstances, Lord Browne-Wilkinson held that the requisite protection for wives against the banks should be provided by the application of the doctrine of constructive notice. He had in mind that in certain circumstances
h constructive notice of the husband's impropriety towards his wife could be imputed to the bank.
[143] The doctrine of notice is a doctrine that relates primarily and traditionally to the priority of competing property rights.   Lord Browne-Wilkinson described the operation of the doctrine in this way:
j
> '... the earlier right prevails against the later right if the acquirer of the later right knows of the earlier right (actual notice) or would have discovered it had he taken proper steps (constructive notice). In particular, if the party asserting that he takes free of the earlier rights of another knows of certain facts which put him on inquiry as to the possible existence of the rights of that other and he fails to make such inquiry or take such other steps as are

reasonable to verify whether such earlier right does or does not exist, he will
have constructive notice of the earlier right and take subject to it.'
(See [1993] 4 All ER 417 at 429, [1994] 1 AC 180 at 195–196.)

This is a classic statement of the operation of the doctrine of notice in order to
determine the priority of property rights.

[144] Banks and other lenders who take charges from surety wives are
certainly purchasers of property rights. But they acquire their rights by grant
from the surety wives themselves. The issue between the banks and the surety
wives is not one of priority of competing interests. The issue is whether or not
the surety wife is to be bound by her apparent consent to the grant of the security
to the bank. If contractual consent has been procured by undue influence or
misrepresentation for which a party to the contract is responsible, the other
party, the victim, is entitled, subject to the usual defences of change of position,
affirmation, delay etc, to avoid the contract. But the case is much more difficult
if the undue influence has been exerted or the misrepresentation has been made
not by the party with whom the victim has contracted, but by a third party. It is,
in general, the objective manifestation of contractual consent that is critical.
Deficiencies in the quality of consent to a contract by a contracting party, brought
about by undue influence or misrepresentation by a third party, do not, in general
allow the victim to avoid the contract. But if the other contracting party had had
actual knowledge of the undue influence or misrepresentation the victim would
not, in my opinion, be held to the contract (see *Commission for the New Towns v
Cooper (GB) Ltd* [1995] 2 All ER 929 at 943–946, [1995] Ch 259 at 277–280 and *Banco
Exterior Internacional SA v Thomas* [1997] 1 All ER 46 at 54, [1997] 1 WLR 221 at
229). But what if there had been no actual knowledge of the third party's undue
influence or misrepresentation but merely knowledge of facts or circumstances that,
if investigated, might have led to actual knowledge? In what circumstances does the
law expect a contracting party to inquire into the reasons why the other party is
entering into the contract or to go behind the other party's apparent agreement,
objectively ascertained, to enter into the contract? These are the questions that
Lord Browne-Wilkinson had to answer in *O'Brien*'s case. They are contractual
questions, not questions relating to competing property interests.

[145] Care must, in my opinion, be taken in applying principles evolved in cases
in which the issue has been whether a purchaser was bound by some pre-existing
equitable interest in the purchased property to cases in which the issue is whether
a contracting party can safely rely on the other contracting party's apparent
consent. Among other things, the onus is different. If a purchaser acquires property
over which there is an existing equitable interest, for example, an equitable charge,
it is up to the purchaser to show that he is a purchaser without notice and so is not
bound by the equitable interest. He must show that his conscience is clear. But if
a contracting party, A, acquires an interest under a contract with another
contracting party, B, and B wishes to escape from the contract on the ground that
his consent to it was procured by the undue influence or a misrepresentation of a
third party, A can rely on B's apparent consent to the contract and it is for B to show
that A had actual or constructive notice of the undue influence or misrepresentation.
It is, in my opinion, important to recognise that constructive notice, in cases
such as those now before the House, is serving a different function from that
served by constructive notice in its traditional role and is not necessarily subject
to the same rules.

[146] In particular, it must be recognised that in the bank v surety wife cases the constructive notice that is sought to be attributed to the bank is not constructive notice of any pre-existing prior right or prior equity of the wife. The husband's impropriety, whether undue influence or misrepresentation, in procuring his wife to enter into a suretyship transaction with the bank would not entitle her to set it aside unless the bank had had notice of the impropriety. It is notice of the husband's impropriety that the bank must have, not notice of any prior rights of the wife. It is the notice that the bank has of the impropriety that creates the wife's right to set aside the transaction. The wife does not have any prior right or prior equity.

[147] In a case where the financial arrangements with the bank had been negotiated by the husband, no part in the negotiations having been played by the wife, and where the arrangements required the wife to become surety for her husband's debts, the bank would, or should, have been aware of the vulnerability of the wife and of the risk that her agreement might be procured by undue influence or misrepresentation by the husband. In these circumstances the bank would be 'put on inquiry', as Lord Browne-Wilkinson put it. But 'on inquiry' about what? Not about the existence of undue influence, for how could any inquiry reasonably to be expected of a bank satisfy the bank that there was no undue influence? 'On inquiry', in my opinion, as to whether the wife understood the nature and effect of the transaction she was entering into. This is not an 'inquiry' in the traditional constructive notice sense. The bank would not have to carry out any investigation or to ask any questions about the reasons why the wife was agreeing to the transaction or about her relationship with her husband. The bank would not, unless it had notice of additional facts pointing to undue influence or misrepresentation, be on notice that undue influence or misrepresentation was to be presumed. It would simply be on notice of a risk of some such impropriety. What Lord Browne-Wilkinson had in mind was that the bank should be expected to take reasonable steps to satisfy itself that she understood the transaction she was entering into. If the bank did so, no longer could constructive notice of any impropriety by the husband in procuring his wife's consent be imputed to it. The original constructive notice would have been shed. If, on the other hand, a bank with notice of the risk of some such impropriety, failed to take the requisite reasonable steps, then, if it transpired that the wife's consent had been procured by the husband's undue influence or misrepresentation, constructive knowledge that that was so would be imputed to the bank and the wife would have the same remedies as she would have had if the bank had had actual knowledge of the impropriety.

[148] Under Lord Browne-Wilkinson's scheme for the protection of vulnerable wives it is the bank's perception of the risk that the wife's consent may have been procured by the husband's misrepresentation or undue influence that is central. The risk must be viewed through the eyes of the bank. Some degree of risk can, usually, never be wholly eliminated. But it can be reduced to a point at which it becomes reasonable for the bank to rely on the apparent consent of the wife to enter into the transaction and to take no further steps to satisfy itself that she understood the transaction she was entering into. Lord Browne-Wilkinson thought that, in order to reach this point, the bank should itself give the wife an explanation of the nature and effect of the proposed transaction and should advise her to take independent legal advice. The function of these steps would be to try and ensure that the wife understood what she was doing in entering into the proposed transaction and that her consent to do so was an informed consent. But whether

these steps would always be necessary, or would always be sufficient, would
depend on the facts of the particular case. Lord Browne-Wilkinson was not a
legislating; he was suggesting steps that, if taken, would in the normal case entitle
a bank to rely on the wife's apparent consent, evidenced by her signature to the
document or documents in question.

[149] In each of the wife v bank appeals now before your Lordships, the
transactions pre-dated O'Brien's case and the bank did not have the advantage of b
the guidance provided by Lord Browne-Wilkinson. The question to be asked in
each of these cases, therefore, is whether at the time the security was granted to
the bank, the bank's perception of the risk that the grant might have been
procured by the husband's impropriety was such as to have required the bank to
take some additional steps to satisfy itself that she understood the nature and
effect of the transaction. c

[150] Since Lord Browne-Wilkinson's constructive notice route for providing
protection to vulnerable wives who agree to become sureties for their husband's
debts was substantially based on the risk that the wife might have been subjected
to undue influence by her husband, it is necessary to review the principles of
undue influence on which he built that protection. d

Undue influence

[151] Undue influence cases have, traditionally, been regarded as falling into
two classes, cases where undue influence must be affirmatively proved (class 1)
and cases where undue influence will be presumed (class 2). The nature of the
two classes was described by Slade LJ in *Bank of Credit and Commerce International* e
SA v Aboody [1992] 4 All ER 955 at 964, [1990] 1 QB 923 at 953:

'Ever since the judgments of this court in *Allcard v Skinner* (1887) 36 Ch D
145, [1886–90] All ER Rep 90 a clear distinction has been drawn between (1)
those cases in which the court will uphold a plea of undue influence only if
it is satisfied that such influence has been affirmatively proved on the f
evidence (commonly referred to as cases of "actual undue influence" ...
"class 1" cases); (2) those cases (commonly referred to as cases of "presumed
undue influence" ... "class 2" cases) in which the relationship between the
parties will lead the court to presume that undue influence has been exerted
unless evidence is adduced proving the contrary, eg by showing that the g
complaining party has had independent advice.'

[152] This passage provides, if I may respectfully say so, an accurate summary
description of the two classes. But, like most summaries, it requires some
qualification.

[153] First, the class 2 presumption is an evidential rebuttable presumption. It h
shifts the onus from the party who is alleging undue influence to the party who
is denying it. Second, the weight of the presumption will vary from case to case
and will depend both on the particular nature of the relationship and on the
particular nature of the impugned transaction. Third, the type and weight of
evidence needed to rebut the presumption will obviously depend upon the j
weight of the presumption itself. In *Allcard v Skinner* the presumption was a very
heavy one. Correspondingly strong evidence would have been needed to rebut
it. Even independent legal advice would not necessarily have sufficed. Lindley LJ
((1887) 36 Ch D 145 at 184, [1886–90] All ER Rep 90 at 100) made clear his view
that without legal independent advice the presumption could not have been
rebutted but went on to doubt whether independent legal advice would have

a   sufficed 'unless there was also proof that she was free to act on the advice which might be given to her'. And in *Inche Noriah v Shaik Allie Bin Omar* [1929] AC 127 at 135, [1928] All ER Rep 189 at 193 Lord Hailsham LC said: '... their Lordships are not prepared to accept the view that independent legal advice is the only way in which the presumption can be rebutted ...'

b   [154] The onus will, of course, lie on the person alleging the undue influence to prove in the first instance sufficient facts to give rise to the presumption. The relationship relied on in support of the presumption will have to be proved.

[155] In *National Westminster Bank plc v Morgan* [1985] 1 All ER 821 at 827, [1985] AC 686 at 704 Lord Scarman, referring to the character of the impugned transaction in a class 2 case, said:

c   '... it must constitute a disadvantage sufficiently serious to require evidence to rebut the presumption that in the circumstances of the relationship between the parties it was procured by the exercise of undue influence.'

Lord Scarman went on:

d   'In my judgment, therefore, the Court of Appeal erred in law in holding that the presumption of undue influence can arise from the evidence of the relationship of the parties without also evidence that the transaction itself was wrongful in that it constituted an advantage taken of the person subjected to the influence which, failing proof to the contrary, was explicable
e   only on the basis that undue influence had been exercised to procure it.'

With respect to Lord Scarman, the reasoning seems to me to be circular. The transaction will not be 'wrongful' unless it was procured by undue influence. Its 'wrongful' character is a conclusion, not a tool by which to detect the presence of undue influence. On the other hand, the nature of the transaction, its inexplicability
f   by reference to the normal motives by which people act, may, and usually will, constitute important evidential material.

[156] Lord Browne-Wilkinson in *CIBC Mortgages plc v Pitt* [1993] 4 All ER 433, [1994] 1 AC 200 pointed out, plainly correctly, that if undue influence is proved, the victim's right to have the transaction set aside will not depend upon the disadvantageous quality of the transaction. Where, however, a class 2 presumption
g   of undue influence is said to arise, the nature of the impugned transaction will always be material, no matter what the relationship between the parties. Some transactions will be obviously innocuous and innocent. A moderate gift as a Christmas or birthday present would be an example. A solicitor who is appointed by a client as his executor and given a legacy of a moderate amount if he consents
h   to act, is not put to proof of the absence of undue influence before he can take the legacy. If the nun/postulant/novice in *Allcard v Skinner* had given moderate Christmas presents to the mother superior, or to the sisterhood, no inference that the gifts had been procured by undue influence could be drawn and no presumption of undue influence would have arisen. It is, in my opinion, the
j   combination of relationship and the nature of the transaction that gives rise to the presumption and, if the transaction is challenged, shifts the onus to the transferee.

[157] In *Aboody*'s case Slade LJ split the class 2 cases into two sub-divisions. He categorised ([1992] 4 All ER 955 at 964, [1990] 1 QB 923 at 953) the 'well-established categories of relationship, such as a religious superior and inferior and doctor and patient where the relationship as such will give rise to the presumption' as class 2A cases, and confirmed that neither a husband/wife relationship nor a

banker/customer relationship would normally give rise to the presumption.
(See also *Morgan's* case [1985] 1 All ER 821 at 826, [1985] AC 686 at 703 and
O'Brien's case [1993] 4 All ER 417 at 424, [1994] 1 AC 180 at 190.) He continued:

> 'Nevertheless, on particular facts (frequently referred to in argument as
> "class 2b" cases) relationships not falling within the "class 2a" category may
> be shown to have become such as to justify the court in applying the same
> presumption ...'

In *O'Brien's* case Lord Browne-Wilkinson adopted Slade LJ's class 2B category for
the purpose of the surety wife cases that he was considering. He said:

> 'Even if there is no relationship falling within class 2A, if the
> complainant proves the de facto existence of a relationship under which
> the complainant generally reposed trust and confidence in the wrongdoer,
> the existence of such relationship raises the presumption of undue influence.
> In a class 2B case therefore, in the absence of evidence disproving undue
> influence, the complainant will succeed in setting aside the impugned
> transaction merely by proof that the complainant reposed trust and
> confidence in the wrongdoer without having to prove that the wrongdoer
> exerted actual undue influence or otherwise abused such trust and confidence
> in relation to the particular transaction impugned.' (See [1993] 4 All ER 417
> at 423, [1994] 1 AC 180 at 189–190.)

[158] In my respectful opinion, this passage, at least in its application to the
surety wife cases, has set the law on a wrong track. First, it seems to me to lose
sight of the evidential and rebuttable character of the class 2 presumption. The
presumption arises where the combination of the relationship and the nature of
the transaction justify, in the absence of any other evidence, a conclusion that the
transaction was procured by the undue influence of the dominant party. Such a
conclusion, reached on a balance of probabilities, is based upon inferences to be
drawn from that combination. There are some relationships, generally of a
fiduciary character, where, as a matter of policy, the law requires the dominant
party to justify the righteousness of the transaction. These relationships do not
include the husband/wife relationship. In the surety wife cases, the complainant
does have to prove undue influence: the presumption, if it arises on the facts of a
particular case, is a tool to assist him or her in doing so. It shifts, for the moment,
the onus of proof to the other side.

[159] Second, the passage cited appears to regard a relationship of trust and
confidence between a wife and husband as something special rather than as the
norm. For my part, I would assume in every case in which a wife and husband
are living together that there is a reciprocal trust and confidence between them.
In the fairly common circumstance that the financial and business decisions of the
family are primarily taken by the husband, I would assume that the wife would
have trust and confidence in his ability to do so and would support his decisions.
I would not expect evidence to be necessary to establish the existence of that trust
and confidence. I would expect evidence to be necessary to demonstrate its
absence. In cases where experience, probably bitter, had led a wife to doubt the
wisdom of her husband's financial or business decisions, I still would not regard
her willingness to support those decisions with her own assets as an indication
that he had exerted undue influence over her to persuade her to do so. Rather
I would regard her support as a natural and admirable consequence of the
relationship of a mutually loyal married couple. The proposition that if a wife,

a who generally reposes trust and confidence in her husband, agrees to become surety to support his debts or his business enterprises a presumption of undue influence arises is one that I am unable to accept. To regard the husband in such a case as a presumed 'wrongdoer' does not seem to me consistent with the relationship of trust and confidence that is a part of every healthy marriage.

[160] There are, of course, cases where a husband does abuse that trust and b confidence. He may do so by expressions of quite unjustified over-optimistic enthusiasm about the prospects of success of his business enterprises. He may do so by positive misrepresentation of his business intentions, or of the nature of the security he is asking his wife to grant his creditors, or of some other material matter. He may do so by subjecting her to excessive pressure, emotional c blackmail or bullying in order to persuade her to sign. But none of these things should, in my opinion, be presumed merely from the fact of the relationship of general trust and confidence. More is needed before the stage is reached at which, in the absence of any other evidence, an inference of undue influence can properly be drawn or a presumption of the existence of undue influence can be said to arise.

d [161] For my part, I doubt the utility of the class 2B classification. Class 2A is useful in identifying particular relationships where the presumption arises. The presumption in class 2B cases, however, is doing no more than recognising that evidence of the relationship between the dominant and subservient parties, coupled with whatever other evidence is for the time being available, may be e sufficient to justify a finding of undue influence on the balance of probabilities. The onus shifts to the defendant. Unless the defendant introduces evidence to counteract the inference of undue influence that the complainant's evidence justifies, the complainant will succeed. In my opinion, the presumption of undue influence in Class 2B cases has the same function in undue influence cases as res ipsa loquitur has in negligence cases. It recognises an evidential state of affairs in f which the onus has shifted.

[162] In the surety wife cases it should, in my opinion, be recognised that undue influence, though a possible explanation for the wife's agreement to become surety, is a relatively unlikely one. O'Brien's case itself was a misrepresentation case. Undue influence had been alleged but the undoubted pressure which the husband had g brought to bear to persuade his reluctant wife to sign was not regarded by the judge or the Court of Appeal as constituting undue influence. The wife's will had not been overborne by her husband. Nor was O'Brien's case a case in which, in my opinion, there would have been at any stage in the case a presumption of undue influence.

h
The steps to be taken by the creditor bank

[163] The protection that Lord Browne-Wilkinson proposed for the vulnerable surety wives is based upon the undoubted risk that in procuring his wife's consent to the transaction the husband might have used undue influence or made some j material misrepresentation and upon the proposition that the bank must be taken to be aware of the existence of the risk. So the bank should take reasonable steps to satisfy itself that the wife understands what she is doing. The protection is not based upon the bank's knowledge of facts from which a presumption of undue influence arises. If, of course, a bank is aware of such facts, the steps the bank will then have to take in order to be able with safety to rely on the wife's apparent consent to the transaction may be considerable. In his dissenting

judgment in *Banco Exterior Internacional v Mann* [1995] 1 All ER 936 at 948, Hobhouse LJ (as he then was) said:

> 'It must be remembered that the starting point of this exercise is that the wife's will is being unduly and improperly influenced by the will of her husband. The steps taken have to be directed to freeing her of that influence or, at the least, providing some counterbalance.'

[164] I respectfully agree that if the bank is indeed aware of facts from which undue influence is to be presumed, the steps to be taken would be of the sort Hobhouse LJ describes. But in the ordinary case the facts of which the bank is aware, or must be taken to be aware, point to no more than the existence of the inevitable risk that there may have been undue influence or some other impropriety and are not facts sufficient by themselves to give rise to a presumption of undue influence. In such a case the bank does not have to take steps to satisfy itself that there is no undue influence. It must take steps to satisfy itself that the wife understands the nature and effect of the transaction.

[165] Lord Browne-Wilkinson made clear (*O'Brien*'s case [1993] 4 All ER 417 at 430, [1994] 1 AC 180 at 197) that it would only be in exceptional cases 'where a creditor has knowledge of further facts which render the presence of undue influence not only possible but probable' that a bank would, to be safe, have to insist that the wife be separately advised. In other cases it would suffice if the bank took steps 'to bring home to the wife the risk she is running by standing as surety and to advise her to take separate advice' ([1993] 4 All ER 417 at 429, [1994] 1 AC 180 at 196). He added that, as to past transactions—and each of the cases now before the House involves a past transaction—it would depend on the facts of each case whether the bank had satisfied the reasonable steps test. I would emphasise and repeat that the purpose of the steps, in the ordinary surety wife case, would be to satisfy the bank that the wife understood the nature and effect of the transaction she was entering into.

The problems

[166] The application of the *O'Brien* principles has, in the appeals now before the House, given rise to some particular problems which are to be found, also, in most of the post *O'Brien* reported cases.

Solicitors' advice

[167] In a number of cases a firm of solicitors has been acting for the husband in the transaction with the bank and has acted also for the wife in connection with the grant of the security to the bank. In many cases, the same solicitor acting for the husband and the wife has been asked by the bank to act for it in connection with the completion of the security. A number of questions arise: for instance (1) does the fact that, to the knowledge of the bank, a solicitor is acting for the wife in the security transaction entitle the bank reasonably to believe that the solicitor will have given her an adequate explanation of the nature and effect of the security document she is to sign? (2) If so, are there, in the ordinary case, ie where there is no special reason for the bank to suspect undue influence or other impropriety, any other steps that the bank ought reasonably to take? (3) If the answer to question (1) is 'Yes' and to question (2) is 'No', does the fact that the solicitor is also the husband's solicitor and is acting for the bank in arranging for completion of the security bar the bank from relying on the solicitor's role in acting for the wife? (4) In many cases the solicitor in whose offices the wife has

a signed the security document has confirmed, sometimes on the document itself and sometimes in a covering letter to the bank, that the nature and effect of the document has first been explained to the wife and that she has appeared to understand it and to be entering freely into the transaction, or to that effect. If in these cases the solicitor has in fact given no, or no adequate, explanation of the document to the wife, in what circumstances can the solicitor's knowledge of his

b failure be attributed to the bank?

[168] As to question (1), the duty of a solicitor towards his client is, in every case, dependent on the instructions, express or implied, that he has received from his client. A solicitor acting for a client in connection with a proposed transaction under which the client is to become surety or give security for the debts of another will not necessarily have instructions to advise the client about the nature

c and effect of the transaction. In most cases such instructions, if not express, would, I think, be implied; but it is at least possible that the circumstances of the solicitor's retainer would not require him to give such advice. So, in my opinion, knowledge by a bank that a solicitor is acting for a surety wife does not, without more, justify the bank in assuming that the solicitor's instructions extend to advising her about

d the nature and effect of the transaction.

[169] Normally, however, a solicitor, instructed to act for a surety wife in connection with a suretyship transaction would owe a duty to the wife to explain to her the nature and effect of the document or documents she was to sign. Exactly what the explanation should consist of would obviously depend in each case on the facts of that case and on any particular concerns that the wife might

e have communicated to the solicitor. In general, however, the solicitor should, in my opinion: (i) explain to the wife, on a worst case footing, the steps the bank might take to enforce its security; (ii) make sure the wife understands the extent of the liabilities that may come to be secured under the security; (iii) explain the likely duration of the security; (iv) ascertain whether the wife is aware of any existing indebtedness that will, if she grants the security, be secured under it; and

f (v) explain to the wife that he may need to give the bank a written confirmation that he has advised her about the nature and effect of the proposed transaction and obtain her consent to his doing so.

[170] I think the solicitor should, probably, begin by trying to discover from the wife her understanding of the proposed transaction. He, the solicitor, may

g then be in a position to remedy any misapprehensions and cure any misrepresentations.

[171] A bank, proposing to take a security from a surety wife for whom a solicitor is acting, requires, first, confirmation that the solicitor's instructions do extend to advising her about the nature and effect of the transaction. Subject to

h that confirmation, however, the bank is, in my opinion, entitled reasonably to believe that the solicitor will have advised her on the matters to which I have referred and, accordingly, that she has had an adequate explanation and has an adequate understanding of the transaction.

[172] As to question (2), there are, in my opinion, in the ordinary case and

j subject to the points about disclosure that I will make later, no other steps that the bank can reasonably be required to take. In particular the bank does not, in order to be able safely to rely on the security being offered, have to advise the wife about the wisdom of her entry into the transaction, or about the bank's opinion of the financial state or business prospects of the principal debtor.

[173] As to question (3), the fact that the solicitor is acting also for the bank in arranging for completion of the security does not, in my opinion, alter the

answers to questions (1) and (2). The solicitor's role in acting for the bank is essentially administrative. He must see that the security document is validly executed and, if necessary, see to its registration. If there are documents of title to whose custody the bank, as chargee, is entitled, the solicitor will usually have to obtain them and hold them to the bank's order. But he has no consultative role vis-à-vis the bank. His duties to the bank do not, in my opinion, in the least prejudice his suitability to advise the wife.

[174] If the solicitor is acting also for the husband, his role presents a little more difficulty. It is, after all, the existence of the risk of undue influence or misrepresentation by the husband that requires the bank to be reasonably satisfied that the wife understands the nature and effect of the transaction. If there is some particular reason known to the bank for suspecting undue influence or other impropriety by the husband, then, in my view, the bank should insist on advice being given to the wife by a solicitor independent of the husband (see Lord Browne-Wilkinson in *O'Brien's* case [1993] 4 All ER 417 at 430, [1994] 1 AC 180 at 197). But in a case in which there is no such particular reason, and the risk is no more than the possibility, present in all surety wife cases, of impropriety by the husband, there is no reason, in my opinion, why the solicitor advising the wife should not also be the husband's solicitor. In the ordinary case, in my opinion, the bank is entitled to rely on the professional competence and propriety of the solicitor in providing proper and adequate advice to the wife notwithstanding that he, the solicitor, is acting also for the husband.

[175] As to question (4), if the bank knows or has reason to suspect that the solicitor has not given the wife a proper explanation of the nature and effect of the security document, the bank should take some appropriate steps to remedy the failure. The failure of the solicitor to give the bank written confirmation that he has given the wife such an explanation will in many cases give the bank reason to suspect that he has not done so. In general, however, it will be reasonable for the bank to believe that the solicitor has properly discharged his professional duty.

[176] Mr Sher QC, counsel for five of the wives, placed some reliance on s 199(1)(ii)(b) of the Law of Property Act 1925:

'(1) A purchaser shall not be prejudicially affected by notice of ... (ii) any ... matter or any fact or thing unless ... (b) in the same transaction with respect to which a question of notice to the purchaser arises, it has come to the knowledge of his counsel, as such, or of his solicitor or other agent, as such ...'

[177] Mr Sher submitted that if a solicitor was instructed by a bank to arrange on its behalf for completion of a security to be granted by a surety wife, the solicitor was, for the purpose of any explanation or advice to be given to the wife, acting not only as the wife's solicitor but also as the bank's solicitor. That being so, the solicitor's knowledge of his own failure should, Mr Sher submitted, be attributed to the bank. Particularly, he submitted, this should be so if the solicitor's instructions from the bank had included a request that the solicitor give appropriate advice to the wife.

[178] A distinction must, in my opinion, be drawn between the case where the solicitor, as well as having instructions from the bank, is solicitor for the wife and the case where the solicitor's only instructions come from the bank and the bank is his only client. In the former case, the solicitor's duty, so far as advice to the wife is concerned, is owed to her and her alone. The fact that a request for him

a to advise her may have been made by the bank is immaterial on this point. It follows that in advising her the solicitor is not acting as the bank's solicitor and s 199(1)(ii)(b) does not apply.

[179] A different conclusion must, in my opinion, be reached if the solicitor in question never does become the wife's solicitor. The formation of a solicitor/client relationship may come about by express retainer or the retainer
b may be implied by conduct. But whichever it is, it is not a relationship which can be brought into existence by the solicitor unilaterally. In making these comments I have in mind the assumed facts in *Wallace's* case that are more fully set out below (see [249]–[257]). Shortly stated, the bank asked the solicitor to arrange for completion of the security and to advise the wife about it, the solicitor
c represented to the bank that he had advised the wife, the bank had no reason to doubt that that was so, but in fact the solicitor had given no advice or tendered any other services to the wife, other than witnessing her signature, a service for which he charged the bank, and she had had no reason to and did not regard him as acting for her. In those circumstances, the solicitor was, in my opinion, acting for the bank alone and his knowledge that no one had given the wife any
d explanation or advice about the security document could properly be attributed to the bank. But, as I have said, in cases where the solicitor has become the wife's solicitor and owes her a duty to advise her about the security document, his knowledge of his own failure to discharge that duty cannot, in my view, be attributed to the bank.

e [180] In *Royal Bank of Scotland plc v Etridge (No 2)* [1998] 4 All ER 705 at 721 (para 44) Stuart-Smith LJ set out, a number of propositions, (1) to (6), relating to legal advice to a surety wife. I respectfully agree with all these propositions, save that knowledge by a bank of special facts pointing to undue influence might require a different approach and that where the solicitor was acting only for the bank and had never become the solicitor for the wife, his knowledge of what had
f or had not taken place regarding advice to the wife might well be imputed to the bank.

[181] In the judgment in *Etridge's* case, Stuart-Smith LJ (at 715 (para 19)) expressed the view of the court as to the duty owed by a solicitor 'instructed to advise a person who may be subject to the undue influence of another'. He said:
g 'It is not sufficient to explain the documentation and ensure that she understands the nature of the transaction and wishes to carry it out ...' And: 'His duty is to satisfy himself that his client is free from improper influence, and the first step must be to ascertain whether it is one into which she could sensibly be advised to enter if free from such influence.'

h [182] These passages were cited and applied by Mance LJ in *Kenyon-Brown v Desmond Banks & Co* [2000] PNLR 266 at 273. I must respectfully dissent. The duty thus described may be applicable in a case in which the solicitor has had something or other drawn to his attention which arouses suspicion that the wife may be the victim of undue influence. In the ordinary case, however, where
j there is no more than a normal relationship of trust and confidence, financial arrangements negotiated by the husband with the bank and the wife proposing to become surety for her husband's, or his company's, debts, there will be no presumption of undue influence and no reasonable basis for suspicion of its existence. There will be a risk, a possibility, of undue influence or misrepresentation, but no more than that. The solicitor in such a case does not have a duty to satisfy himself of the absence of undue influence. His duty is accurately described as a

duty to satisfy himself that his client understands the nature and effect of the
transaction and is willing to enter into it.   *a*

Disclosure

[183] One of the issues that has arisen in several of the cases is as to the extent
of disclosure to the surety wife, or to the solicitor acting for her, that is required
of the bank.   *b*

[184] As to this, the wife's understanding of the nature and effect of the
security document she is asked to sign should, obviously, be an informed
understanding. It is necessary, it seems to me, to consider, first, the extent of the
obligation of disclosure to a would-be surety that lies generally upon the creditor
and, secondly, to consider whether any additional disclosure has to be made
where a wife is proposing to stand surety for her husband's debts.   *c*

The general law

[185] A suretyship contract is not a contract uberrimae fidei. In *Seaton v Heath,
Seaton v Burnand* [1899] 1 QB 782 at 793 Romer LJ said:

> 'The risk undertaken is generally known to the surety, and the *d*
> circumstances generally point to the view that as between the creditor and
> surety it was contemplated and intended that the surety should take upon
> himself to ascertain exactly what risk he was taking upon himself.'

[186] But although a would-be surety is, in general, expected to acquaint
himself with the risk he is undertaking, the creditor is under an obligation to *e*
disclose to the intending surety—

> 'anything that might not naturally be expected to take place between the
> parties who are concerned in the transaction, that is, whether there be a
> contract between the debtor and the creditor, to the effect that his position
> shall be different from that which the surety might naturally expect ...' *f*
> (See *Hamilton v Watson* (1845) 12 Cl & Fin 109 at 119, 8 ER 1339 at 1344, per
> Lord Campbell.)

[187] This passage from Lord Campbell's judgment in *Hamilton v Watson* was
cited by Vaughan Williams LJ in *London General Omnibus Co Ltd v Holloway* [1912]
2 KB 72 at 78, [1911–13] All ER Rep 518 at 520. Vaughan Williams LJ continued: *g*

> 'Lord Campbell, it is true, takes as his example of what might not be
> naturally expected an unusual contract between creditor and debtor whose
> debt the surety guarantees, but I take it this is only an example of the general
> proposition that a creditor must reveal to the surety every fact which under *h*
> the circumstances the surety would expect not to exist, for the omission to
> mention that such a fact does exist is an implied representation that it does
> not.' (See [1912] 2 KB 72 at 79, [1911–13] All ER Rep 518 at 520.)

[188] The general proposition expressed by Vaughan Williams LJ was somewhat
extended by King CJ in *Pooraka Holdings Pty Ltd v Participation Nominees Pty Ltd* *j*
(1989) 52 SASR 148. The duty of disclosure, said King CJ, extends to any unusual
feature surrounding the transaction between the creditor and the surety (a) of
which the creditor is or ought to be aware, (b) of which the surety is unaware,
and (c) which the creditor appreciates, or in the circumstances ought to
appreciate, might be unknown to the surety and might affect the surety's decision
to become a surety. This statement of the extent of the disclosure obligation may

a be too wide. But at least, in my opinion, the obligation should extend to unusual features of the contractual relationship between the creditor and the principal debtor, or between the creditor and other creditors of the principal debtor, that would or might affect the rights of the surety (see generally the discussion of this topic in O'Donovan and Phillips *The Modern Contract of Guarantee* (3rd edn, 1996) pp 122–131).

b
Disclosure to surety wives

[189] In general, in my opinion, there is no greater obligation of disclosure owed by a bank, or other creditor, to a surety wife than any other surety. There is, however, a difference. Where a wife is offering to stand as surety for her husband's, or his company's debts, the risk that her consent to do so may have
c been improperly procured, requires the creditor, if it is to be able safely to rely on her apparent consent, to take reasonable steps to satisfy itself that she understands what she is doing. In order to satisfy itself about this, and in order that her understanding may be an informed understanding, it may be necessary for the creditor to disclose the amount of any existing indebtedness that will be
d covered by the security. It may for the same reason be necessary for the creditor to disclose the amount of new money that is being made available to the principal debtor and will be covered by the security. The financial details to which I have referred would not, under the general law, have to be disclosed by a creditor to the would-be surety. They are details that the creditor could expect the surety, as part of the surety's risk assessment, to find out for himself. But the surety wife
e cases present their own special problems, as was recognised in *O'Brien*'s case. In the surety wife cases, and in any other cases in which a creditor is placed on inquiry as to whether the surety's apparent consent to the transaction may have been procured by some impropriety of the principal debtor, the reasonable steps the creditor should take would generally include, in my opinion, disclosing to the
f surety the financial details to which I have referred. Failure to do so would not matter, of course, if the surety already knew the details or if the creditor had reason to believe that the surety knew. I should, perhaps, add that the failure of a creditor to have disclosed these details should not, without more, be taken, in relation to past transactions, to show that the creditor had failed to take reasonable steps.

g [190] The financial details to which I have referred would, if the creditor were a bank, normally be confidential. The bank would not be entitled to disclose them without the consent of its client, the principal debtor. However, in the surety wife cases I would regard the husband's proposal that the wife stand surety for his, or his company's, debts as constituting an implied authority to the bank
h to disclose those details to the wife. Express instructions to the contrary, if given by the husband to the bank, would constitute a warning to the bank of an extra risk that the husband might be abusing his wife's trust and confidence in him. I think that the bank, before it could safely rely on the wife's apparent consent to the suretyship, would then need to insist that she receive legal advice from a
j solicitor independent of her husband.

Summary

[191] My Lords I think, given the regrettable length of this opinion, I should try and summarise my views about the principles that apply and the practice that should be followed in surety wife cases. (1) The issue as between the surety wife and the lender bank is whether the bank may rely on the apparent consent of the

wife to the suretyship transaction. (2) If the bank knows that the surety wife's consent to the transaction has been procured by undue influence or misrepresentation, or if *a* it has shut its eyes to the likelihood that that was so, it may not rely on her apparent consent. (3) If the wife's consent has in fact been procured by undue influence or misrepresentation, the bank may not rely on her apparent consent unless it has good reason to believe that she understands the nature and effect of the transaction. (4) Unless the case has some special feature, the bank's knowledge that *b* a solicitor is acting for the wife and has advised her about the nature and effect of the transaction will provide a good reason for the purposes of (3) above. That will also be so if the bank has a reasonable belief that a solicitor is acting for her and has so advised her. Written confirmation by a solicitor acting for the wife that he has so advised her will entitle the bank to hold that reasonable belief. (5) So, too, a sufficient explanation of the nature and effect of the transaction given by a *c* senior bank official would constitute good reason for the purposes of (3) above. (6) If there are any facts known to the bank which increase the inherent risk that the wife's consent to the transaction may have been procured by the husband's undue influence or misrepresentation, it may be necessary for the bank to be satisfied that the wife has received advice about the transaction from a solicitor *d* independent of the husband before the bank can reasonably rely on the wife's apparent consent. (7) If the bank has not taken reasonable steps to satisfy itself that the wife understands the nature and effect of the transaction, the wife will, subject to such matters as delay, acquiescence, change of position etc, be able to set aside the transaction if her consent was in fact procured by undue influence or misrepresentation. (8) Subject to special instructions or special circumstances, *e* the duty of a solicitor instructed to act for a wife proposing to stand as surety, or to give security, for her husband's debts is to try and make sure that she understands the nature and effect of the transaction. (9) In all surety wife cases the bank should disclose to the surety wife, or to the solicitor acting for her, the amount of the existing indebtedness of the principal debtor to the bank and the *f* amount of the proposed new loan or drawing facility. (10) Subject to (9) above, a creditor has no greater duty of disclosure to a surety wife than to any other intending surety.

[192] I am in full agreement with the analysis of the applicable principles of law and with the conclusions expressed in the opinion of my noble and learned friend Lord Nicholls of Birkenhead. I believe the analysis I have sought to give in *g* this opinion and my conclusions are consistent with them.

[193] I must now turn to the individual cases.

Royal Bank of Scotland plc v Etridge (No 2)   *h*

[194] This case comes to the House after a full trial before Judge Behrens, sitting as a judge in the Queen's Bench Division.

[195] Judge Behrens held that even if Mrs Etridge's consent to the bank's charge had been procured by the undue influence of Mr Etridge, the bank had had no notice, constructive or otherwise, of the undue influence. The Court of *j* Appeal upheld him ([1998] 4 All ER 705).

[196] The relevant facts were these. In August 1988 Mr and Mrs Etridge were living in Harewood House, Longparish, Hampshire. The property stood in Mrs Etridge's sole name. It was subject to a charge to the bank to secure the indebtedness to the bank of Anthony Thomas & Co, a company owned and controlled by Mr Etridge. A firm of solicitors, Memery Crystal, had acted for

a Mr and Mrs Etridge in connection both with the purchase and with the bank's charge.

[197] By August 1988 Mr Etridge had an overdraft facility with the bank of £100,000. He had also borrowed £195,000 from the trustees of a private trust (the Ambetta trustees). This debt was not secured on Harewood House.

[198] In August 1988 Mr and Mrs Etridge decided to sell Harewood House
b and purchase in its place the Old Rectory, Laverstoke, Hampshire. Mr Etridge was the contracting purchaser of the Old Rectory. The purchase price was £505,000. It was his and Mrs Etridge's intention that The Old Rectory would, on completion of the purchase, be conveyed to Mrs Etridge alone. Memery Crystal were instructed to act in the sale of Harewood House but another firm, Robert Gore & Co, were instructed by Mr Etridge to act in the purchase of the Old
c Rectory.

[199] The purchase of the Old Rectory was to be financed partly out of the proceeds of the sale of Harewood House and partly out of new money to be advanced by the bank. In addition, money was to be advanced by the Ambetta trustees. The financial arrangements were fairly complex and were negotiated by
d Mr Etridge. Mrs Etridge played no part in the negotiations.

[200] The sale price of Harewood House was £240,000. The net proceeds, after the Anthony Thomas & Co overdraft charged on Harewood House had been repaid, were £142,000 or thereabouts. On the day of completion of the purchase of the Old Rectory, Mr Etridge drew £261,956 odd from the bank, thereby creating an overdraft of £119,915 odd. The £261,956, plus a further
e advance of £200,000 from the Ambetta trustees, enabled the amount due on completion to be paid. The debts owing both to the bank and to the Ambetta trustees were to be secured by charges over the Old Rectory. As between the two chargees, it was agreed that the bank would have priority in respect of £100,000 and interest thereon. Next would come the debt owing to the Ambetta trustees.

f [201] On 27 September 1988, the bank had instructed Robert Gore & Co to act for the bank in connection with the charge that the bank was to be granted over the Old Rectory. The letter of instructions said:

'Re: Mrs. S. R. Etridge
Purchase of The Old Rectory, Laverstoke, Hampshire.
g We understand you act for the above and would advise that as security for existing facilities we require to take a First Legal Charge over the above property. For Land Registry purposes we are relying on the Legal Charge to the extent of £100,000. We enclose the documents detailed below and would ask that you act on our behalf in the completion of our security.

h Legal Charge
Prior to execution, please ensure the property details are correct and inserting further details as may be required. Please explain the contents and effects of the document to Mrs. Etridge, confirming she understands the same by signing the legal advice clause prior to witnessing her signature.'

j [202] Similar instructions were given to Robert Gore & Co by the Ambetta trustees.

[203] On 3 October 1988 Mr and Mrs Etridge attended the offices of Robert Gore & Co and saw Mr Ellis, an employed solicitor with the firm. Mrs Etridge signed all the documents relating to the acquisition of the Old Rectory, including the bank's charge and the Ambetta trustees' charge. The bank's charge was expressed to be a security for Mr Etridge's liabilities to the bank and was unlimited

in amount. The Ambetta trustees' charge was expressed to be a security for
Mr Etridge's liabilities to the trustees subject to a limit of £395,000. Mrs Etridge's *a*
signature was witnessed by Mr Ellis who endorsed the bank's charge with the
words: 'I hereby confirm that prior to the execution of this document I explained
the contents and effect thereof to [Mrs Etridge] who informed me that he/she
understood the same.' The Ambetta charge was endorsed with words to the
same effect.   *b*

[204] In fact, Mr Ellis gave Mrs Etridge no advice of any kind as to the nature
or content of the documents she was signing. She signed the documents without
reading them or seeking any explanation of them. Her evidence to Judge Behrens
was that she did so, trusting her husband and quite unaware that she was creating
charges over the Old Rectory. She said that she was wholly unaware of the extent
of Mr Etridge's borrowings. Judge Behrens accepted this evidence.   *c*

[205] The transfer of the Old Rectory to Mrs Etridge and the two charges
were completed on 4 October 1988.

[206] In April 1990 the bank, and in August 1991 the Ambetta trustees,
demanded repayment of their respective secured loans. Both then commenced
proceedings for, among other things, possession of the Old Rectory with a view *d*
to its sale.

[207] Mrs Etridge's defence was that her signature to the charges had been
procured by the undue influence of her husband, that the bank and the Ambetta
trustees must be taken to have had constructive notice that that was so and that
in consequence she was not bound by the charges. She contended, also, that the *e*
bank had constituted Robert Gore & Co its agents for the purpose of giving her
advice about the charges and that Mr Ellis' knowledge that he had not done so
should, therefore, be attributed to the bank.

[208] As well as defending the proceedings brought against her by the bank
and the Ambetta trustees, Mrs Etridge sued Robert Gore & Co for negligence.
The three claims were tried together.   *f*

[209] Judge Behrens held that even if there had been undue influence by
Mr Etridge in procuring Mrs Etridge to agree to the grant of the two charges,
notice of that impropriety could not be attributed either to the bank or to the
Ambetta trustees. He held that both the bank and the Ambetta trustees had been
entitled to rely on the confirmation, given by Mr Ellis by means of the endorsements *g*
on the charges, that Mrs Etridge had had the effect and contents of the charges
explained to her.

[210] The judge held, also, that 'on the evidence before me there was no
actual undue influence'. He followed this finding, however, by holding that
'subject to the manifest disadvantage point there was presumed undue influence *h*
within category 2B'. As to manifest disadvantage, he held that there was no
manifest disadvantage to Mrs Etridge in the charge granted to the bank. This was
because the liabilities secured by the charge included £100,000 advanced by the
bank to Mr Etridge to enable the purchase of the Old Rectory to be completed.

[211] The judge held, however, that there was manifest disadvantage to *j*
Mrs Etridge in the charge granted to the Ambetta trustees because only £200,000
of the £395,000 secured by the charge had been advanced to enable the purchase
of the Old Rectory to be completed.

[212] It appears, therefore, that, subject to the judge's conclusion on constructive
notice, he would have held that Mrs Etridge was bound by the bank charge but
not bound by the Ambetta trustees' charge.

a [213] As to Mrs Etridge's breach of duty claim against Robert Gore & Co, the firm admitted liability to Mrs Etridge for breach of duty but the judge was satisfied on the evidence of Mrs Etridge herself that she would have signed the two charges even if she had had a complete and full explanation of their contents and effect. So he awarded her only £2 nominal damages.

[214] On Mrs Etridge's appeal, the Court of Appeal rejected her challenge to
b the judge's finding that there had been no actual undue influence but agreed that, subject to manifest disadvantage, there was presumed undue influence within category 2B. The Court of Appeal agreed, also, that notwithstanding that the bank charge secured Mr Etridge's indebtedness to an unlimited amount, the charge was not to Mrs Etridge's manifest disadvantage. The Ambetta trustees did not challenge the judge's conclusion that their charge was to the manifest
c disadvantage of Mrs Etridge.

[215] On the constructive notice issue, too, the Court of Appeal agreed with the judge.

[216] Mrs Etridge appealed against the judge's conclusion that she was entitled only to nominal damages against Robert Gore & Co. The Court of
d Appeal dismissed her appeal on 28 April 1999 (*Etridge v Pritchard Englefield* [1999] PNLR 839).

[217] In the period during which the appeal to this House has been pending, terms of settlement have been reached between Mrs Etridge and the Ambetta trustees. So it is only her appeal in the bank's proceedings that is before the House for decision.
e [218] My Lords, the manner which first Judge Behrens and then the Court of Appeal dealt with the presumption of undue influence and with the part to be played by manifest disadvantage demonstrates, in my opinion, the tangle that the case law in this area has got into.

[219] The presumption of undue influence, whether in a category 2A case, or
f in a category 2B case, is a rebuttable evidential presumption. It is a presumption which arises if the nature of the relationship between two parties coupled with the nature of the transaction between them is such as justifies, in the absence of any other evidence, an inference that the transaction was procured by the undue influence of one party over the other. This evidential presumption shifts the onus to the dominant party and requires the dominant party, if he is to avoid a finding
g of undue influence, to adduce some sufficient additional evidence to rebut the presumption. In a case where there has been a full trial, however, the judge must decide on the totality of the evidence before the court whether or not the allegation of undue influence has been proved. In an appropriate case the presumption may carry the complainant home. But it makes no sense to find, on the one hand, that
h there was no undue influence but, on the other hand, that the presumption applies. If the presumption does, after all the evidence has been heard, still apply, then a finding of undue influence is justified. If, on the other hand, the judge, having heard the evidence, concludes that there was no undue influence, the presumption stands rebutted. A finding of actual undue influence and a finding
j that there is a presumption of undue influence are not alternatives to one another. The presumption is, I repeat, an evidential presumption. If it applies, and the evidence is not sufficient to rebut it, an allegation of undue influence succeeds.

[220] As to manifest disadvantage, the expression is no more than shorthand for the proposition that the nature and ingredients of the impugned transaction are essential factors in deciding whether the evidential presumption has arisen

and in determining the strength of that presumption. It is not a divining rod by
means of which the presence of undue influence in the procuring of a transaction
can be identified. It is merely a description of a transaction which cannot be
explained by reference to the ordinary motives by which people are accustomed
to act.

[221] In the present case, the judge's conclusion that there had been no actual
undue influence was reached after considering all the evidence. There was
evidence of the relationship between Mr and Mrs Etridge. Their relationship
was, as one would expect of a married couple living together with the family
income being provided by the husband's business activities and with financial
decisions affecting the family being taken by the husband, a relationship of trust
and confidence by her in him. But there was no evidence of abuse by Mr Etridge
of that relationship, or of any bullying of Mrs Etridge in order to persuade her to
support his decisions. Both the transactions under attack had been entered into
in part in order to provide finance for the purchase of the Old Rectory and in part
to obtain financial support for Mr Etridge in his business enterprises. Both had
elements disadvantageous to her and elements that were to her advantage. To
draw a distinction between the two charges as to inferences of undue influence
that might be drawn was, in my opinion, unreal. In my view, the judge's
conclusion that there had been no undue influence was well justified on the
evidence. That conclusion should have been an end of the case.

[222] Before your Lordships Mr Mawrey QC, counsel for Mrs Etridge, argued
that Mrs Etridge's ignorance of the nature or contents of the documents she was
signing and, in particular, her ignorance that she was charging the Old Rectory as
a security for her husband's debts, enabled her to contend that she had been
induced to sign by her husband's misrepresentation. Mr Etridge had had a duty
to explain to her the nature of the transaction. His failure to do so constituted a
misrepresentation by silence.

[223] Mr Mawrey told us that misrepresentation had always been part of
Mrs Etridge's case, and indeed it figures in her pleading. But there is no reference
to it in Judge Behrens' judgment. He made no finding on misrepresentation. Nor
did the Court of Appeal comment on the point. It is fair to conclude, therefore,
that if the misrepresentation point was argued at all below, it could only have
been very faintly. This is not surprising for the point is not sustainable. First, a
misrepresentation must, if it is to lead to an equitable or legal remedy, have led
to a false impression about some material matter being held by the victim. In the
present case Mrs Etridge had no impression at all as to the nature of the
documents she was signing. No false impression had been planted on her by
Mr Etridge. Mr Etridge's silence did not lead her to form, or to continue to hold,
any false impression. She did not bother to read the documents that were placed
before her for signature, and no one explained them to her, so she did not know
what she was signing. But she was not persuaded to sign by any misrepresentation.
Second, Judge Behrens found as a fact that if the nature and content of the
documents had been explained to her, she would still have signed. So, if there
had been any misrepresentation as to the nature and content of the documents,
it had no relevant causative effect. The misrepresentation contention is, in my
opinion, for both these reasons a hopeless one.

[224] There was, therefore, nothing, no undue influence and no
misrepresentation, to which constructive notice could attach.

[225] As to constructive notice, the bank was of course aware that Mrs Etridge
was offering her property, the Old Rectory, to secure her husband's indebtedness.

a The bank was, therefore, on notice of a risk that her consent to grant the security might have been improperly obtained by her husband. The bank had no particular reason to suspect either undue influence or misrepresentation but the risk, attendant in every case where a wife is being asked to stand surety for her husband's debts, was present.

b [226] But Mrs Etridge was, to the knowledge of the bank, being advised by Robert Gore & Co, solicitors. The solicitors confirmed to the bank, in the event falsely but the bank was not to know that that was so, that they had advised Mrs Etridge about the content and effect of the charge. That confirmation, from the bank's point of view, reduced the risk that Mrs Etridge's consent to grant the charge might have been improperly obtained. The possibility that there might have been some such impropriety could never be wholly eliminated. But the fact

c that to the bank's knowledge there were solicitors acting for Mrs Etridge, and the fact that they had told the bank that they had advised her about the content and effect of the charge, entitled the bank, in my opinion, to be satisfied that it was safe in relying on her apparent consent. There were no further steps that the bank could reasonably have been required to take.

d [227] Nor, in my opinion, can Robert Gore & Co's knowledge that they had failed to give Mrs Etridge the requisite advice be imputed to the bank. The solicitors were not the bank's agents for the purpose of advising Mrs Etridge.

[228] In my opinion, therefore, Mrs Etridge's appeal fails and should be dismissed.

e
Barclays Bank plc v Harris

[229] In this case there has not yet been a trial. Mrs Harris' appeal to your Lordships' House is against an interlocutory order striking out her defence and counterclaim and giving judgment for the bank on its claim for possession. It

f must, therefore, be assumed that the primary allegations of fact pleaded by Mrs Harris are true.

[230] Mr and Mrs Harris were in 1988 joint owners of the Old Rectory, Nether Whitacre, Coleshill, Warwickshire. They had purchased the property in 1976 for £39,000. By 1988 its value was in the region of £200,000. There were two mortgages on the property securing in total about £28,000.

g [231] Mr Harris was an industrial chemist. He carried on business through the medium of two companies. One, High Tec Powder Coatings Ltd (High Tec), carried on the business of industrial powder coatings producers and finishers. High Tec had an issued share capital of £10,000 divided into 10,000 £1 shares of which 2,499 were held by Mr Harris and 2,499 by Mrs Harris. Mr and Mrs Harris

h and their son, Peter, were directors of High Tec. But Mrs Harris took no actual part in the conduct of High Tec's business and is described in the company documents as 'Housewife'. Mr Harris had given guarantees of High Tec's liabilities to the company's bankers and to its landlords. These guarantees were not secured on the Old Rectory.

j [232] Mr Harris' other company was ST Harris (Powder Coatings Consultant) Ltd (PCC). Mr Harris' services as a powder coatings consultant were made available to clients through the medium of PCC. PCC had an issued share capital of £2, of which one £1 share was held by Mr Harris and the other by Mrs Harris. They were the directors of PCC and Mrs Harris was the company secretary. As with High Tec, she took no part in PCC's business and was described in the company documents as 'Housewife'.

[233] By 1988 High Tec was in serious financial difficulties. Mr Harris' potential liability under the guarantee he had given was £120,000. He consulted solicitors, Wragge & Co, about how to manage his personal liabilities arising from the failure of High Tec in a way that would enable him to continue to carry on business through PCC.

[234] Acting on the advice of Wragge & Co, he arranged banking facilities with Barclays Bank plc under which the bank would refinance the £28,000 secured under the existing mortgages on the Old Rectory and would provide a loan facility of £100,000 to PCC. These details were not known to Mrs Harris. In return the bank required that a guarantee, unlimited in amount, of PCC's liabilities to the bank be given by both Mr and Mrs Harris and that their liability to the bank under this guarantee be secured by a first charge over the Old Rectory. Mr Harris agreed to this.

[235] On 26 October 1988 the bank wrote to Mr Hamlett of Wragge & Co, whom the bank knew to be acting for Mr Harris, enclosing the bank's standard form of legal charge and asking Mr Hamlett to arrange to have it signed by Mr and Mrs Harris. The letter asked Mr Hamlett to confirm that the title deeds to the Old Rectory would be held to the bank's order upon repayment of the existing mortgages and added: '… under the circumstances, it would probably be easiest if you arrange to redeem the outstanding mortgages and register our charge in the usual fashion.' The letter then referred to the guarantee that Mr and Mrs Harris were to give and continued: 'I would ask you to explain the nature of the document to both parties and confirm to us that independent legal advice has been given.'

[236] On 27 October 1988 Mr and Mrs Harris went to Wragge & Co's offices and had a meeting with Mr Hamlett. Mrs Harris' pleaded case is that her husband had told her that the bank had agreed to lend PCC some money temporarily, so that he could trade his way out of his financial predicament, that she attended the solicitors' offices at the request of her husband, that Mr Hamlett interviewed them together and showed them a number of legal documents and that her husband told her he wanted her to sign, asking her to trust him. She pleads that after some discussion between Mr Hamlett and her husband that she did not understand, each of them signed the legal documents. The legal documents included a guarantee and a legal charge of the Old Rectory. The legal charge secured Mr and Mrs Harris' liabilities to the bank under the guarantee.

[237] Mrs Harris alleges in her pleading that Mr Hamlett was acting for the bank, Mr Harris and for herself (para 3(5) of her defence and counterclaim). But, as my noble and learned friend, Lord Hobhouse of Woodborough, has pointed out, her solicitor in these proceedings, Mr Holt of Evans Derry Binnion has stated in an affidavit of 28 May 1997 that 'in so far as my client is concerned Wragge & Co were not her solicitors' (para 6). Your Lordships should assume, in my opinion, that Mrs Harris' defence will be amended so as to become consistent with that statement.

[238] On 27 October 1988, Mr Hamlett wrote to the bank a letter which said, among other things: 'I have explained to Mr & Mrs Harris in detail this morning the effect of the first charge over the property and of the unlimited personal guarantee.'

[239] It appears, however, that Mr Hamlett's 27 October letter may not have been received by the bank, or, after receipt, may have gone astray. On 29 June 1989 the bank wrote to him saying that they did not appear to have received from him the confirmation that they had asked for in their letter of 26 October 1988.

a
[240] In her defence and counterclaim, Mrs Harris pleaded that her agreement to sign the guarantee and the legal charge had been obtained 'in the premises' by her husband's undue influence, or, alternatively, that it was to be presumed that it had been so obtained. She pleaded that the bank was, or should have been, aware that the transactions were manifestly disadvantageous to her and that the bank had actual or constructive notice of the undue influence. She pleaded that,
b
in the circumstances, the guarantee and the legal charge were not binding on her.

[241] As I have said, Mrs Harris' defence and counterclaim were struck out by the deputy district judge. She appealed. Her appeal was heard by Judge Alton, in the Birmingham County Court, who dismissed the appeal. The judge identified two issues, namely 'whether the bank was potentially on constructive notice ... of undue influence, presumed or actual by Mr Harris. Secondly, if so, whether it
c
took reasonable steps to negative such notice'. It was conceded, for the purpose of the strike-out application, that the relationship of trust and confidence between Mr and Mrs Harris brought the case into category 2B where undue influence was to be presumed. I doubt whether this concession was sound, for there was, I think, also a third issue that arose on the pleadings, namely, whether the facts
d
and matters pleaded by Mrs Harris, 'the premises' referred to in her defence and counterclaim, raised any presumption at all or could sustain any arguable case of undue influence. I will return to this issue.

[242] On the first of the two issues she had identified, the judge concluded that Mrs Harris had pleaded an arguable case that the bank had had constructive notice of the presumed undue influence. But as to the second issue, she concluded
e
that on the facts, either pleaded or not in dispute, the bank, in asking Wragge & Co to give appropriate advice to Mrs Harris, had taken reasonable steps to negative the constructive notice. She held, also, that Wragge & Co were not the bank's agents for any purpose other than to register the charge on the bank's behalf.

[243] The Court of Appeal agreed with the judge on both the two issues, per
f
Stuart Smith LJ:

'The solicitors were acting for Mrs Harris in the transaction and the bank were entitled to assume that they had given appropriate advice and were entitled to accept the solicitors' letter as confirmation that this had been done.' (See [1998] 4 All ER 705 at 730 (para 7).)

g
[244] In my opinion, on the premise that the solicitors were indeed Mrs Harris' solicitors, the Court of Appeal came to the correct conclusion. In reviewing their decision, however, I would start with the third issue. Was this a case in which, on Mrs Harris' pleading, there was an arguable case of undue influence? The relationship of trust or confidence was certainly present. Mr Harris conducted
h
the businesses from which the family income was derived. It was he who negotiated the financial arrangements with Barclays Bank. He did not explain the arrangements to his wife. He simply asked her to sign the legal documentation. But there is no pleaded allegation of misrepresentation. His statement, express or implied, that he would be able to trade his way out of his financial difficulties
j
may have been an expression of over optimism but cannot be, and has not been, suggested to be a misrepresentation. There was no allegation of any bullying of Mrs Harris or of any pressure on her to sign that could be characterised as excessive. She signed, without knowing what she was signing, because she trusted him. This pleaded story does not, in my opinion, raise any presumption of undue influence. It does not, in the absence of any other evidence, justify an inference that Mr Harris brought undue influence to bear in order to persuade

her to sign. Her agreement to do so is consistent with a normal, trusting,
relationship between a married couple. Since, however, it was accepted below
that, for striking out purposes, Mrs Harris could rely on there being a
presumption of undue influence, it would not be right to uphold the striking out
on this ground. The critical issue is the constructive notice issue.

[245] As to constructive notice, the bank knew that Mrs Harris was agreeing
to become surety for the debts of her husband's company, PCC. As in all such
cases the bank was, or ought to have been, aware that there was a risk of
misrepresentation or of undue influence. On the pleaded facts, the extent of the
risk was not, in my opinion, very great. There were no special features to put the
bank on inquiry. But the bank did, in order to protect itself against that risk, have
to take reasonable steps to satisfy itself that the nature and effect of the
documents she was to sign were properly explained to Mrs Harris.

[246] The bank believed that Wragge & Co were acting not only for Mr Harris
but also for Mrs Harris and would give Mrs Harris the requisite legal advice about
the documents. Mr Hamlett's letter of 27 October, if the bank received it, would
have confirmed that belief. But it does not appear that the bank's belief was
derived from anything said or done by Mrs Harris. And Mrs Harris contends that
Mr Hamlett was not her solicitor and in any event gave her no explanation about
the nature and effect of the documents. If these contentions can be made good
and if Mrs Harris does succeed in establishing undue influence it is at least
arguable that she will succeed on the constructive notice issue. In my opinion,
therefore, Mrs Harris' case must be allowed to go to trial. I would allow her
appeal.

[247] There is a further complication to which I should refer. Mrs Harris died
on 22 March 2001 while the appeal to this House was pending. Her appeal abated
in accordance with standing order X but a petition for reviver presented by
Mr Harris, her executor, was granted as of course on 9 May 2001. In the hearing
of the appeal before your Lordships no point was made as to any effect her death
or Mr Harris' executorship might have on the bank's claim for possession of the
Old Rectory or on the future course of the litigation. It may seem somewhat
incongruous for Mr Harris to be relying on his own undue influence over his wife
in order to defeat the bank's possession claim, but any difficulties or problems
must be sorted out at trial or by applications made at first instance.

Midland Bank plc v Wallace

[248] In this case, too, there has not been a full trial. The bank, having
commenced proceedings for possession of the mortgaged property, made an
application for summary judgment. Master Barratt gave Mrs Wallace leave to
defend, but Lloyd J allowed the bank's appeal and made an order for possession.
Mrs Wallace appealed. The Court of Appeal ([1998] 4 All ER 705) dismissed her
appeal.

[249] The property in question was a leasehold flat, Flat 1, 91 Priory Road,
Hampstead. Mr and Mrs Wallace were the joint registered proprietors of the flat
which was held for a term of 125 years from 25 December 1986.

[250] The flat had been acquired by Mr and Mrs Wallace without the aid of a
mortgage, but subsequently had been charged to Northern Rock Building Society
to secure an £80,000 advance to Mr Wallace partly to pay off a previous loan from
Coutts Bank and partly for his business purposes. By 1988 the Northern Rock
money had been fully utilised and Mr Wallace wanted to raise more money. The
bank agreed to advance £120,000. The advance was to be repayable on demand

a and was to be secured by an 'all moneys' legal charge over the flat. Mr Wallace accepted the bank's offer on 1 December 1988.

[251] By a letter dated 13 December 1988 the bank asked a solicitor, Mr Sidney Samson, to 'attend to the necessary formalities for us in the signing of the enclosed legal charge form by [Mr and Mrs Wallace]'. The legal charge form enclosed with the letter contained, immediately above the space for the chargors'
b signatures, the following words in bold type: '**This is an important legal document. The Bank recommends that before signing it you should seriously consider seeking the advice of a solicitor or other professional advisor.**'

[252] There was no evidence that Mr Samson had previously acted for Mr or Mrs Wallace. The inference was that Mr Samson was on the bank's panel of local solicitors willing to accept instructions to act in connection with
c conveyancing transactions between the bank and its customers.

[253] Mr and Mrs Wallace went together to a meeting with Mr Samson in his offices. In her affidavit sworn on 13 February 1996 Mrs Wallace gave her evidence of what happened at that meeting. The relevant passages were set out in para 5 of the judgment of Stuart-Smith LJ in the Court of Appeal ([1998] 4 All ER 705 at
d 735). It is not necessary for me to repeat the whole of the passages but the gist appears from the following excerpts:

e '12. ... As for the business loan itself, I was not involved at all ... Eventually I was told that I had to go to a solicitor's office to execute the Charge. I was directed to the office of Sidney Samson & Co. The firm had no connection with me ... I was there three or four minutes at most ... I signed the document as directed by a solicitor. There was no other discussion. He did not begin to tell me what I was signing or to explain to me the consequences.

13. My impression in retrospect is that the solicitor had been instructed merely to take and witness my signature ... I certainly did not regard the
f solicitor as independent as I believed that he was instructed by the Bank.'

[254] Mr and Mrs Wallace signed the legal charge at their meeting with Mr Samson in his offices. He witnessed their signatures. Beneath Mrs Wallace's signature, Mr Samson wrote: 'The same having first been explained to her and she appearing perfectly to understand it.' On Mrs Wallace's evidence this
g endorsement was untrue.

[255] On 16 December 1988 Mr Samson wrote to the bank in the following terms:

h 'In accordance with your instructions of the 13th instant, I have now seen Mr and Mrs Wallace. They have executed the documents and I have attested them stating that the documents have been explained. I enclose herewith a note of my fees.'

[256] The legal charge was dated 30 December 1988. The £120,000 was drawn down over a period between January and August 1989. The £120,000 was a loan to
j Mr Wallace alone. It was used by him to inject capital into the company, Capital Clinics Ltd, through which he ran private clinics.

[257] Later in 1989 the bank made a further loan of £106,065 to Mr and Mrs Wallace jointly. The purpose of this loan was to enable the Northern Rock's prior charge to be redeemed. In March 1994 the bank commenced proceedings for recovery of the sums due in respect of the two loans and for possession of the flat and applied for summary judgment.

[258] The question for the court was whether Mrs Wallace's affidavit disclosed an arguable defence to the bank's claim. Both before Lloyd J and before the Court of Appeal, and again before your Lordships, counsel for the bank conceded that Mrs Wallace had shown an arguable case of undue influence. For my part, I would agree that Mrs Wallace's affidavit, and in particular para 11, disclosed a sufficiently arguable case that in persuading her to sign the legal charge and in overriding her reluctance to do so Mr Wallace had abused the trust and confidence that she had in him. Accordingly, the summary judgment application turned on the constructive notice issue.

[259] As to constructive notice, the bank knew that Mr and Mrs Wallace were a married couple living together in the jointly owned flat that was to be charged to the bank. The bank knew that the £120,000 advance to Mr Wallace was to be used for his business purposes. The bank knew that the proposed charge was an 'all moneys' charge which would secure any further advances that the bank might make to Mr Wallace. In these circumstances, in my opinion, the bank was on notice of the existence of a risk that Mrs Wallace's consent to grant the charge might have been brought about by some impropriety, whether excessive pressure or misrepresentation, by Mr Wallace. The bank needed, therefore, to take reasonable steps to satisfy itself that Mrs Wallace was entering into the transaction 'freely and in knowledge of the true facts' (see *Barclays Bank plc v O'Brien* [1993] 4 All ER 417 at 431, [1994] 1 AC 180 at 198).

[260] Lloyd J decided the constructive notice issue in favour of the bank. He took the view that although Mr Samson, having accepted the instructions given him by the bank's letter of 13 December 1988, owed the bank a duty, that duty was to witness the signature of Mrs Wallace and to return to the bank the signed document, or, if she did not sign, the unsigned document. But the judge said: 'It was not, I think, any part of his function to inform the bank as to what passed between him and her by way of advice or indeed communications on her part seeking advice.' As to the endorsement that Mr Samson had written under Mrs Wallace's signature, Lloyd J said that it 'carries with it a sufficient representation that he [ie Mr Samson] had given all necessary explanation and advice to her', and added: 'in this situation the risk of her not being properly advised is one which lies between her and Mr Samson and which cannot be passed on to the bank.' The Court of Appeal agreed.

[261] I would agree that if Mr Samson had indeed been acting as Mrs Wallace's solicitor these conclusions and the reasons for them would have been unassailable. But Mrs Wallace's criticism of these conclusions has been based mainly on the proposition that Mr Samson was not her solicitor. She did not instruct him to give her any advice about the legal charge and he did not in fact give her any advice. Nor had the bank in its letter of 13 December 1988 asked Mr Samson to give her any advice about the legal charge. It had simply asked him to 'attend to the necessary formalities for us'. It is true, as the evidence stands, that Mrs Wallace never did instruct Mr Samson to give her advice and that he gave her none. It seems also to be true that Mr Samson never held himself out to Mrs Wallace as her solicitor with a duty to advise her. On her evidence, he simply witnessed her signature. Whether she noticed the endorsement he wrote beneath her signature is not clear. In my opinion, for summary judgment purposes, your Lordships must proceed on the footing that Mr Samson was not Mrs Wallace's solicitor. On whose behalf then was he acting? The answer must, in my opinion, be that he was acting on behalf of the bank from whom he received his instructions and to whom he submitted his fee note.

[262] The issue of constructive notice depends not on how Mr Samson's role appeared to Mrs Wallace, but on how his role appeared to the bank. If Mr Samson had not added the endorsement below Mrs Wallace's signature, the bank would, as I read the evidence, have had no reason to believe she had received any explanation about the legal charge. In that case the bank, on notice of the risk that Mrs Wallace's consent to the legal charge might have been improperly obtained by undue influence or misrepresentation by her husband, would have taken no steps at all to satisfy itself that her consent to the legal charge had been given 'freely and in knowledge of the true facts' (see *O'Brien's* case [1993] 4 All ER 417 at 431, [1994] 1 AC 180 at 198).

[263] Mr Samson's endorsement was, I would agree, a clear representation by him to the bank that he had acted as Mrs Wallace's solicitor for the purpose of giving her advice about the contents and effect of the legal charge. In the face of that representation, I would accept that the bank would ordinarily have been entitled to be satisfied that it could reasonably rely on Mrs Wallace's apparent consent to the transaction, evidenced by her signing of the legal charge.

[264] But Mr Samson, on the occasion when Mr and Mrs Wallace attended at his offices in order to sign the legal charge, was acting as the bank's solicitor on the bank's instructions. He was not acting as Mrs Wallace's solicitor, nor, for that matter, as Mr Wallace's. In these circumstances, in my opinion, s 199(1)(ii)(b) of the Law of Property Act 1925, comes into play. I have already set out the text of this statutory provision and discussed its implications in the type of cases that your Lordships are dealing with. On the evidence as it now stands Mr Samson knew that he had given no explanation to Mrs Wallace of the nature and effect of the legal charge. His failure was, since he was acting for the bank, the bank's failure.

[265] Accordingly, in my opinion, if the facts alleged by Mrs Wallace in her affidavit are correct the bank never shed the constructive notice imputed to it.

[266] I would, therefore, allow Mrs Wallace's appeal. The case must go to trial.

National Westminster Bank plc v Gill

[267] This is another case that comes to your Lordships' House after a full trial.

[268] Mr and Mrs Gill were, in 1988, the joint owners of 60A Queen's Park Avenue, Bournemouth, their matrimonial home. On 20 February 1989 they executed a legal charge under which the property was charged with payment of all Mr Gill's liabilities to the bank.

[269] In December 1995, after demands by the bank for repayment of sums it had advanced to Mr Gill were not met, the bank commenced proceedings for possession of the property with a view to its sale. Mrs Gill's defence to the claim was that her consent to the legal charge had been procured by Mr Gill's undue influence and that the bank had had constructive notice of the impropriety. Both the trial judge, Mr Recorder Paulusz, and the Court of Appeal ([1998] 4 All ER 705) rejected the constructive notice allegation.

[270] Mr Gill was a second hand car dealer carrying on business from home. In December 1988 he had the opportunity to acquire a garage business carried on from leasehold premises known as Gresham Garage. The purchase price was £40,000. He applied to the bank for a loan of £100,000 partly to fund the acquisition and partly to finance the garage and car sales business that he hoped to carry on from Gresham Garage.

[271] On 19 December 1988 the bank made Mr Gill a written offer of the £100,000 loan. One of the terms of the offer was that the loan be secured by a second charge of 60A Queen's Park Avenue. The bank did not have any communication with Mrs Gill about the proposed loan.

[272] On 14 February 1989 Mr Gill contracted to purchase Gresham Garage for £40,000. He paid a £4,000 deposit. Completion was due on 20 February 1989. The sum due on completion was £36,799. Solicitors, Matthew & Matthew, were acting for Mr Gill in the transaction.

[273] On 16 February 1989 the bank wrote to Matthew & Matthew and enclosed the form of legal charge, charging the matrimonial home as security for Mr Gill's liabilities to the bank, that they required Mr and Mrs Gill to sign. The letter said:

'As [the document] is in relation to the sole liabilities of Mr Gill it will be necessary for Mrs Gill to receive separate legal advice as to the nature of the document and perhaps you would confirm that this is done prior to the signing of the form.'

[274] On Monday 20 February 1989, Mr Gill told Mrs Gill that she had to go with him to Matthew & Matthew for the purpose of having their signature to documents witnessed. At the solicitors' offices they saw Mr West, a legal executive, and Mr Richard Matthew, a partner. Important evidence of what happened on this occasion was given by Mrs Gill and by Mr West and Mr Matthew. Mr Gill was not called to give evidence. Where the evidence of Mrs Gill and that of Mr West and Mr Matthew conflicted, the recorder preferred the evidence of the latter.

[275] Mrs Gill gave evidence that there had been a heated altercation between herself and her husband when she discovered that she was being asked to sign a mortgage of the matrimonial home. She said that when the document was placed before her for signature she had asked what it was and that her husband had told her he needed her signature to be able to buy the garage. She said he had told her that the bank was lending him £36,000. She disputed Mr West's evidence that he had explained the document to her and said that neither Mr West nor Mr Matthew, with whom she had a conversation in a separate room in the absence of her husband, had given her any explanation about the nature of the document that was offered for her signature. None the less, the recorder found that Mr Matthew did, while he was alone with her, give her 'a full and adequate explanation of the meaning of the document' and expressed himself as being 'satisfied that Mrs Gill did receive proper and adequate advice'. Mrs Gill told the recorder that she had had no alternative but to sign. The recorder did not accept that evidence. He did find, on the contrary, that Mr Gill had spoken enthusiastically to her about the garage and its prospects and that she shared his enthusiasm.

[276] It was, however, clear that neither Mr West nor Mr Matthew had known that the amount the bank had agreed to advance was £100,000. The amount secured by the legal charge was not expressed to be subject to any limit but the purchase price of Gresham Garage was only £40,000. So it is believable that Mrs Gill was under the misapprehension that the bank loan was to be £36,000 (£4,000 having already been paid as a deposit). It is believable also that Mrs Gill had obtained this misapprehension from what her husband had told her. The advice that, as the recorder found, Mr West and Mr Matthew gave Mrs Gill did not go beyond explaining the nature and effect of the legal charge that she was being asked to sign. Neither was in a position to offer any advice about the

a commercial advantages or disadvantages of the purchase of the garage premises and business or about the wisdom of Mrs Gill agreeing to charge the matrimonial home with her husband's indebtedness to the bank.

[277] Mr and Mrs Gill signed the legal charge on 20 February at Matthew & Matthew's offices and the solicitors then wrote to the bank in the following terms: 'We confirm that the Mortgage Documentation supplied has been *b* executed by Mr. & Mrs. Gill in accordance with your requirements and we confirm that Mrs. Gill was separately advised ...' On this evidence Mr Recorder Paulusz, although he held that the case was one in which there was a presumption of undue influence, rejected the contention that the bank should be taken to have had constructive notice of the undue influence. The Court of Appeal agreed ([1998] 4 All ER 705).

c [278] On the constructive notice point, I am in agreement with the recorder and the Court of Appeal. The case was one in which the natural trust and confidence that the bank would have expected Mrs Gill to have, and that she did in fact have, in her husband, coupled with the nature of the transaction, namely, a charge over her property as security for his debts, raised the risk that her *d* consent to the transaction might have been obtained by undue influence or misrepresentation. But the confirmation to the bank, that before signing the legal charge Mrs Gill had been separately advised by solicitors, as indeed she had been, and, by implication, that the advice had related to the nature and effect of the legal charge, entitled the bank to be satisfied that it could safely rely on her apparent consent to the transaction as being a true consent.

e [279] There is some basis in the evidence for thinking that Mrs Gill may have been induced to sign by her husband's misrepresentation that the loan agreed to be made by the bank was only £36,000. It does not appear, however, that any weight at the trial or in the Court of Appeal was sought to be placed on this misrepresentation. The emphasis seems to have been all on undue influence. *f* Whatever may have been the reason for this, it cannot, in my opinion, affect the conclusion on the constructive notice issue. The legal charge secured Mr Gill's indebtedness to the bank whatever the amount of the indebtedness might be. Matthew & Matthew's confirmation to the bank that Mrs Gill had received separate advice was an implicit confirmation that she had been advised about the meaning and effect of the document—as, indeed, the recorder found she had. *g* That advice would have included advice that the amount of the current loan might in the future be increased.

[280] I have earlier in this opinion expressed the view that in all cases the lender bank should inform the surety wife, or her solicitors, of the amount of the agreed facility and of any existing indebtedness that would be secured under the *h* proposed charge. If that had been done in the present case, it would have guarded Mrs Gill against a misapprehension about the amount of the agreed loan. But in the circumstances of this case, and in particular in view of the fact that no limit on the amount of the secured liability was expressed in the legal charge, the fact that the bank did not disclose this information does not, in my opinion, constitute *j* a failure by the bank to take reasonable steps to satisfy itself that Mrs Gill's consent had not been improperly procured.

[281] Finally, a comment on undue influence is prompted by the facts of this case. The recorder held that although there was no actual undue influence, there was a presumption of undue influence since the case fell within category 2B. The Court of Appeal recorded these findings without comment. In my opinion, these findings disclose the same error to which I have referred previously in this

opinion. By the end of the trial the recorder, having heard all the evidence, had
to decide whether or not undue influence had been established. Either the *a*
evidence did justify a finding of undue influence or it did not. On the evidence in
the case a finding of undue influence would, in my opinion, have been unthinkable.
Mrs Gill had been enthusiastic about the purchase of Gresham Garage. She knew
she was signing a legal charge under which her home became security for her
husband's debts to the bank incurred in acquiring the premises and business. She *b*
had been separately advised by a solicitor about the nature and effect of the
document she was to sign. The highest her case can be put is that she would have
liked more time to consider whether or not to sign. She said in evidence:

> 'I did sign the documents put in front of me but with time for more
> reflection, and in less urgent circumstances, with proper advice to think *c*
> about it, and time to consult a solicitor of my own, I would never have done
> so.'

This is a quite inadequate basis, in my opinion, for a finding of undue influence.
I do not think this was a case in which there was ever any evidence giving rise to
the presumption of undue influence. But, if there was, by the end of the trial the *d*
presumption had been rebutted. In my opinion, Mrs Gill's appeal must be
dismissed.

Barclays Bank plc v Coleman

[282] This, too, is a case where there has been a full trial. The mortgaged *e*
property, 52 Ashtead Road, Clapton, London E5, was purchased by Mr and
Mrs Coleman on 9 July 1986 in their joint names. It was their matrimonial home.
By a legal charge signed on 30 January 1991 they charged the property with the
repayment of sums advanced by the bank for the purpose of enabling
Mr Coleman to make some speculative property acquisitions in Uxbridge Road, *f*
Hayes, Middlesex and in Brooklyn, New York. In 1995, after the bank's demand
for payment of the outstanding debt had not been met, the bank commenced
proceedings for, among other things, possession of the property with a view to
its sale. Mrs Coleman defended the proceedings by alleging that she had
consented to the legal charge under the undue influence of her husband and that
the bank had had constructive notice of that impropriety. The trial judge, *g*
Judge Wakefield, took the view that the legal charge was not to the manifest
disadvantage of Mrs Coleman, that there was no presumption of undue influence
and that undue influence had not been established. He expressed the view, also,
that the bank had not taken reasonable steps to avoid constructive notice if there
had been any undue influence. The Court of Appeal ([2000] 1 All ER 385, [2001] *h*
QB 20) disagreed with the judge on both points, and therefore concurred with the
judge in the result. First, the court held that the transaction was to Mrs Coleman's
material disadvantage and that, in the circumstances, undue influence was to
be presumed. But they held, secondly, that constructive notice should not be
imputed to the bank. Before your Lordships Mr Jarvis QC, for the bank, has not *j*
argued against the Court of Appeal's conclusion on the undue influence issue. He
accepts that if the bank had constructive notice that Mrs Coleman's consent may
have been improperly obtained, her appeal is entitled to succeed.

[283] The relationship between Mr Coleman and Mrs Coleman is of significance.
They are Hasidic Jews. Mrs Coleman's upbringing and education in a Hasidic
community in the United States prepared her to expect and to accept a position

a of subservience and obedience to the wishes of her husband. The judge put it
thus:

> 'The upbringing and education of Mrs Coleman prepared her principally
> for marriage within her own religious community and for a life of
> subservience to the wishes of her husband. I do not mean this in any
> derogatory sense. Hers may well have been a happy state, but it was one in
b which her husband's wishes and judgment in matters of finance and business
> were to be followed without question.'

So it seems that the trust and confidence of a wife in her husband, which, notably
in relation to family finances and family business matters, is a feature of very
many marriages, is accentuated in a Hasidic marriage. It would, it seems, have
c been very difficult for Mrs Coleman to have questioned her husband's business
or financial decisions or to have declined to comply with his wishes on such
matters.

[284] In 1989 Mr Coleman, having been made redundant from his job as a
diamond cutter, began to carry on business on his own account as a property
d broker. Towards the end of 1990 he approached the bank for a loan to enable him
to purchase two commercial properties in Uxbridge Road, Hayes. He already
had some £200,000 on deposit with the bank and sought a loan from the bank to
assist him in funding a purchase price of £250,000 for the Hayes properties. At
about the same time Mr Coleman became interested in buying a half-share in an
apartment building in Brooklyn, New York. He wanted a US dollar loan from the
e bank to assist him in financing this acquisition. The bank agreed in principle to
make the loans but required a charge over 52 Ashtead Road as security.

[285] In January 1991 the bank's security department prepared the form of
legal charge and a certificate of occupancy that Mr and Mrs Coleman would be
asked to sign. Mr Coleman informed the bank that Reuben Gale & Co would
f be the solicitors for them acting in the transaction. So the bank sent the documents
to Reuben Gale & Co and Mr Coleman made an appointment for himself and his
wife to attend at Reuben Gale & Co's offices. They went to the offices on a date
somewhere between 9 and 15 January 1991. They were attended to not by a
solicitor but by a legal executive, Mr David Spring, an employee of the firm. The
legal charge was ready to be signed. Each of them signed it and Mr Spring
g witnessed each of their signatures. Mr Spring, in witnessing the signatures, signed
above a stamp bearing the legend 'D. SPRING, LEGAL EXECUTIVE, 240 STAMFORD HILL, LONDON,
N.16'. On the page following the signature page there was a typed endorsement
which read:

h   'I confirm that this document was signed in my presence and that the full
> effect of its contents have been explained to and were understood by Miriam
> Mara Coleman, and she has signed this document of her own free will.'

Mr Spring signed his name below this typed endorsement. Beneath his signature
was placed the same stamp as had appeared beneath the signatures on the
j previous page. Below this stamp Mr Spring wrote 'with R. Gale, 240 Stamford Hill,
London N.16. Solicitor.'

[286] The significance of these details is threefold. First, it would have
been clear to the bank that Mr Spring was a legal executive and not a qualified
solicitor. Second, it was clear that Mr Spring was purporting to act on behalf of
Reuben Gale & Co, the firm of solicitors whose name had been given to the bank
by Mr Coleman. Third, the endorsement entitled the bank to believe that a

sufficiently qualified person had explained the contents of the legal charge to
Mrs Coleman and that there had been no apparent reluctance on her part to sign.

[287] Mr and Mrs Coleman also signed the certificate of occupancy, showing
themselves as the only occupiers of the property. Here, too, Mr Spring counter-
signed the document in confirmation that Mr and Mrs Coleman had signed in his
presence.

[288] In fact, Mr Spring had given Mrs Coleman no explanation whatever of
the contents of the legal charge. The evidence at trial was that he had simply
asked Mr Coleman if he, Mr Coleman, had explained the documents to his wife.
The meeting had lasted only a few minutes. The bank's internal notes disclose
the bank's own understanding of what had taken place at the meeting with
Mr Spring. The relevant note reads:

> 'Prior to the signing of the ... documentation with regard to [the
> mortgaged property] Mrs Coleman attended a local firm of independent
> Solicitors, whereby she received legal advice, as to the bank's charge forms
> content. Her signature was witnessed by those solicitors who confirmed
> that the document was signed of her own free will.'

[289] Mr Coleman's property speculations for which he had sought the bank's
assistance turned out to be financially disastrous. He was unable to repay his
borrowing from the bank and proceedings by the bank for possession of
52 Ashtead Road with a view to its sale followed.

[290] Notwithstanding Mr Jarvis' concession to which I have already referred,
I should, I think, make one or two comments about the undue influence issue.
First, I agree that this was a case in which the relationship between Mr Coleman
and Mrs Coleman, in the cultural context of the Hasidic community of which
they formed a part, raised a serious question whether Mrs Coleman's consent to
the granting of the legal charge was a true consent. She gave evidence that if she
had had the content and effect of the legal charge explained to her, she might
have declined to sign it. I doubt this. The thrust of her evidence as to her
relationship with her husband was that she was bound to defer to him in the
judgment of what should or should not be done about family finances or with
family assets. It is not consistent with that evidence to suppose that a better
understanding of the nature and effect of the legal charge would have brought
her to refuse to comply with her husband's request that she sign.

[291] I think the Court of Appeal was quite right in regarding this as a case in
which there was a presumption of undue influence. But the presumption was
not, in my opinion, attributable to the 'manifest disadvantage' to Mrs Coleman
of the legal charge. The legal charge, supporting her husband's business ventures
on which he engaged in order to support his family, was no more disadvantageous
to her than any transaction in which a wife agrees to become surety in order to
support her husband's commercial activities. The presumption arose, in my
opinion, out of their relationship, in which Mrs Coleman was not merely
disinclined to second-guess her husband on matters of business, but appears to
have regarded herself as obliged not to do so. In such a case, in my opinion, the
rebuttal of the presumption would have needed legal advice from someone
independent of the husband who could have impressed upon her that she should
not sign unless she truly wanted to do so. In the circumstances, I agree with the
Court of Appeal that a presumption, or inference, of undue influence arose and
was not rebutted.

a [292] But in considering the issue of constructive notice, the question is not how the case appeared to Mrs Coleman, or to the person purporting to have given her the legal advice; it is how the case appeared to the bank. There was no evidence to show that the bank had knowledge of any greater risk of undue influence than might be present in any case in which a wife was apparently agreeing to become surety, or give security, for her husband's business debts. It

b would reasonably have appeared to the bank, from the typed endorsement on the legal charge, that Mrs Coleman had received advice from a legally qualified person acting for her, so as to enable her to understand the contents and effect of the document she was signing. The fact that the advice had been given by a legal executive and not by a qualified solicitor is not, in my opinion, material. An experienced legal executive in a firm with a conveyancing practice is well able to

c give full and adequate advice as to the contents and effect of a straightforward legal charge. The bank were entitled to believe that Reuben Gale & Co would not entrust such a task to a legal executive with insufficient experience to carry out the task properly. The bank had no reason to think that any special precautions needed to be taken in Mrs Coleman's case than would be requisite in

d any other case of a wife giving security for her husband's debts. In my opinion, the bank, having read the endorsement on the legal charge, was entitled to hold the reasonable belief that Mrs Coleman's consent to the granting of the legal charge had not been improperly obtained. There were no other steps that the bank could reasonably be required to have taken. Constructive notice of Mr Coleman's undue influence cannot, in my opinion, be imputed to the bank.

e [293] I would, therefore, dismiss Mrs Coleman's appeal.

UCB Home Loans Corp Ltd v Moore

[294] This case comes to your Lordships' House on an appeal by Mrs Moore against an order striking out her defence to UCB's claim to possession of

f Pangbourne Lodge, Tidmarsh Road, Pangbourne, Berkshire. The relevant facts, therefore, must be taken to be those pleaded by Mrs Moore, supplemented by such facts as are common ground between the parties. Mrs Moore and her husband, Mr Moore, were, in 1988, the joint owners of Pangbourne Lodge, their matrimonial home. Mr Moore carried on business through the medium of a company, Corporate Software Ltd. The company had 5,000 issued shares of

g which 2,557 were held by Mr Moore and 2,443 by Mrs Moore. They were both directors. The conduct of the business, however, was under his control and although Mrs Moore worked for the company in a secretarial and administrative capacity, she did so under her husband's direction. Mrs Moore has pleaded that she was 'accustomed to obey [Mr Moore's] directions in relation to the

h company's affairs'. It is implicit in her pleading that she reposed trust and confidence in her husband in relation to financial and business matters.

[295] In 1988 Mr Moore was seeking additional finance for the company and for that purpose enlisted the services of a Mr Zerfahs. Mr Zerfahs, who traded as Southern Assurance Services, was a registered insurance broker and had been the

j company's pension advisor for the past four years.

[296] At the insistence of Mr Moore, and induced by his representations that the proposed mortgage transaction related to a 'risk free' loan to the company, Mrs Moore signed in blank a mortgage application form. The details in this form were added without her knowledge and after she had signed. So she has pleaded.

[297] The details contained in, or added to, the signed form included the following: (i) the amount of the desired loan was £300,000; (ii) the solicitors

acting for Mr and Mrs Moore would be Quiney & Harris of 117 High Street, Wootton Bassett, Swindon; Mr Nigel Whittaker was named as the member of the firm who would be dealing with the matter; (iii) Pangbourne Lodge would be offered as security for the loan; (iv) the loan was required partly to re-finance existing borrowings charged on Pangbourne Lodge and partly for the business purposes of Corporate Software; (v) Mr Moore was managing director of Corporate Software. His annual income was £106,000; (vi) Mrs Moore was 'Secretary/PA' of Corporate Software. Her annual income was £18,000. The original amount entered on the form as Mr Moore's annual income appears to have been £36,000. The £36,000 had been altered to £106,000, a grossly inflated figure. That there had been some alteration to the original figure was apparent.

[298] The mortgage application form, carrying both Mr and Mrs Moore's signatures, was sent to UCB Home Loans Corp Ltd (UCB). UCB agreed to make the loan on the security of a first charge over Pangbourne Lodge.

[299] On 14 March 1989 Mr Zerfahs told Quiney & Harris that Mr and Mrs Moore wanted the firm to act for them in connection with the proposed transaction. Mr Zerfahs had no authority from Mrs Moore to do so. She never instructed the firm to act for her and at no stage did she meet or speak to any member of the firm about the proposed transaction.

[300] On 14 March Quiney & Harris wrote to Southern Assurance Services saying, amongst other things, that they had written to Mr and Mrs Moore thanking them for their instructions. Mrs Moore's case is that she never saw any such letter. Quiney & Harris corresponded directly with Mr Moore and had several telephone conversations with him about the proposed transaction. They never received any confirmation from Mrs Moore of their instructions to act for her.

[301] UCB, of course, believed from the contents of the mortgage application form that Quiney & Harris had been instructed by, and were acting for, both Mr and Mrs Moore. So, in a letter dated 5 May 1989, UCB asked Quiney & Harris to act for UCB in arranging for the legal charge to be executed. UCB did not ask the solicitors to give any advice to Mrs Moore. Quiney & Harris' letter to UCB in response referred to Mr and Mrs Moore as 'our clients'.

[302] The legal charge was in due course executed and the £300,000 loan was made. £154,338 odd was applied in redeeming an existing first charge over Pangbourne Lodge held by BNP Mortgages Ltd. £52,925 odd was applied in discharging the company's overdraft liability to National Westminster Bank plc. The overdraft had been secured by a second charge over Pangbourne Lodge. The balance of the £300,000 loan was paid to the company.

[303] The company was unsuccessful and went into liquidation in January 1992. In February 1994 UCB brought possession proceedings in the Reading County Court. Mrs Moore's defence alleged that her signature to the mortgage application form and her consent to the grant of the legal charge to UCB had been obtained by the undue influence of and misrepresentations made by Mr Moore. She gave further and better particulars of these allegations. UCB applied, on 30 May 1996, to strike out those parts of the defence that resisted a possession order.

[304] UCB contended that even if there had been undue influence or misrepresentation they had had no notice of it. The district judge dismissed the strike-out application. UCB appealed and Judge Holden allowed the appeal. He accepted, for the purposes of the strike-out, that Quiney & Harris had never been instructed by Mrs Moore and had given her no advice. He said: 'For the purposes of the appeal before me I must accept [Mrs Moore's] version of the facts and

a assume that there was undue influence and that she received no advice from the solicitors and did not instruct them.' But he accepted UCB's case that they had had the reasonable belief, via the mortgage application form signed by Mrs Moore, that Quiney & Harris were acting for her and would give her whatever advice she needed. He said:

b '[UCB] reasonably believed that [Mr and Mrs Moore] had their own solicitors who were dealing with the transaction and it was quite reasonable for them to assume that in carrying out that function those solicitors would give proper advice to [Mrs Moore].'

In effect, he held that constructive notice of Mr Moore's undue influence or misrepresentation could not be imputed to UCB.

c [305] The Court of Appeal agreed with Judge Holden that Quiney & Harris' knowledge that they had given Mrs Moore no advice about or explanation of the legal charge could not be imputed to UCB. They agreed that there was nothing, in the circumstances, to put UCB on inquiry: 'It was not necessary for [UCB] to give instructions to the solicitors to do what was already their duty; nor was it

d necessary to require certification that that has been done' (see [1998] 4 All ER 705 at 731 (para 6), per Stuart-Smith LJ).

[306] I have some sympathy with these conclusions but I do not think they could safely be reached on the striking out application. UCB knew that Mrs Moore was offering her share in the matrimonial home, Pangbourne Lodge, as security for the £300,000 loan to the company. But over two-thirds of the loan

e was to be applied in discharging existing indebtedness charged on Pangbourne Lodge. The balance was to go to the company in whose business Mrs Moore, as well as Mr Moore, played a part. UCB was, or should have been, aware of a risk that Mrs Moore's apparent consent might be tainted by undue influence or misrepresentation, but the risk would not have appeared to be a very great one.

f And the information that Mr and Mrs Moore had solicitors acting for them reduced the risk. It is not to the point that Mrs Moore had never instructed Quiney & Harris. UCB were not to know that that was so. They had been misled by the contents of the mortgage application form that Mrs Moore had signed in blank. It would be possible to argue that Mrs Moore, by signing in blank, had given an implied authority to her husband, or to his agent Mr Zerfahs, to

g complete the form on her behalf. It is enough, however, to conclude that UCB were entitled to take the mortgage application at its face value.

[307] But the problem is that UCB did not know what Quiney & Harris' instructions were and had no reason to assume that their instructions extended to giving Mrs Moore advice about the nature and effect of the legal charge. The

h instructions may have been no more than to agree the form of the security documents and make arrangements for them to be executed. Quiney & Harris gave UCB no indication that they had given Mrs Moore any such advice and in fact they had not done so. In my opinion, therefore, on the evidence as it now stands UCB failed to take reasonable steps to satisfy itself that Mrs Moore

j understood the nature and effect of the legal charge.

[308] Mr Sher QC, counsel for Mrs Moore, suggested that UCB should have been put on inquiry by the apparent alteration to the stated amount of Mr Moore's annual income. This, to my mind, is very much an after-the-event point. If there had been some other reason to question the genuineness of the mortgage application, the alteration of the annual amount would, I agree, have added to the suspicion. But there was no other reason and the alteration was, in

my opinion, a long way below the threshold at which an intending lender is put
on inquiry.

[309] In my opinion, however, for the reason I have given Mrs Moore's appeal
should be allowed. This case must go to trial.

Bank of Scotland v Bennett

[310] This is another case which comes to the House after a full trial. The bank
is seeking to enforce its charge over the matrimonial home, 15 Elthiron Road,
Fulham. The property was acquired by Mr and Mrs Bennett in May 1986 and
transferred into their joint names. At all material times it has been subject to a
first charge in favour of Halifax Building Society. On 5 September 1990, the
property was transferred into Mrs Bennett's sole name. The bank's charge, a
second charge, was dated 1 October 1991. The purpose of the charge was to
secure the liabilities of Mr and Mrs Bennett under a guarantee dated 12 August
1991. The guarantee guaranteed payment to the bank, up to a limit of £150,000,
of the sums owing to the bank by Galloway Seafood Co Ltd (the company).

[311] In October 1993 the bank made a formal demand for payment by the
company of the sums it owed the bank and, on failing to receive payment,
appointed receivers of the company. The sum owed by the company to the bank
was £270,000 or thereabouts. The bank followed up these steps by calling on
Mr and Mrs Bennett for payment under the guarantee of the £150,000 with
interest of £3,522 odd. Payment was not made and on 11 April 1994 the bank
commenced proceedings for payment and for possession of 15 Elthiron Road
with a view to its sale.

[312] Mrs Bennett's defence to the bank's claims was that her signature, both to
the guarantee and to the legal charge, had been procured by her husband's undue
influence and that, in the circumstances, the bank must be taken to have had
constructive notice of that impropriety. The trial judge, Mr James Munby QC,
sitting as a deputy judge in the Chancery Division ([1997] 3 FCR 193), found
in Mrs Bennett's favour on the undue influence issue. He found (at 220), first,
that Mrs Bennett had established actual undue influence:

'In my judgment the pressure and influence which, as I have found,
Mr. Bennett exerted on his wife both to procure her signature to the
guarantee and to procure her signature to the charge was undue. This is a
case in which, in my judgment, there was moral blackmail amounting to
coercion and victimization. Mrs. Bennett was not, it seems to me, acting as
a free and voluntary agent.'

On appeal, the Court of Appeal ([1999] 1 FCR 641) refused to disturb the deputy
judge's conclusion on undue influence. Chadwick LJ (at 661–662) said that to
reverse the judge's conclusion 'would ... be to give insufficient weight to the
advantage which the judge had (and which this court does not have) of hearing
the evidence given by the witness in person'.

[313] The deputy judge went on to consider, as an alternative to actual undue
influence, Mrs Bennett's case based on presumed undue influence. He held
([1997] 3 FCR 193 at 221–223) that both the guarantee and the legal charge were
manifestly disadvantageous to Mrs Bennett and that the relationship between
her and her husband was one of sufficient trust and confidence to raise a
presumption of undue influence in relation to both transactions. He held that
the presumption had not been rebutted.

[314] On this aspect of the case, Chadwick LJ ([1999] 1 FCR 641 at 662) commented on the paradox that Mrs Bennett was contending, on the one hand, that she had signed the two documents because her will to resist had been overborne by her husband but, on the other hand, that her trust and confidence in her husband was such that if he asked her to sign she would do so. The point is the same as that to which I have referred in *Coleman*'s case (see [290], above).

[315] The discussion about the presumption of undue influence was unnecessary. Once actual undue influence has been found at trial, the question whether, if the evidence had been confined to the relationship between the parties and the nature of the impugned transaction, undue influence would have been presumed and, if it would, whether it had been rebutted, becomes irrelevant. And if, after a full trial, the judge concludes that undue influence has not been established, that conclusion means either that there never was a presumption of undue influence or, if there was, that it has been rebutted.

[316] The deputy judge's and the Court of Appeal's conclusions on the undue influence issue had the result that the outcome of the case appeared to depend on the constructive notice issue. It was accepted that the bank had had no actual notice of the undue influence. Should constructive notice be imputed to the bank? The deputy judge, after considering the facts of the case, concluded that the bank had been put on inquiry as to the circumstances in which Mrs Bennett had agreed to sign the guarantee and the legal charge and had failed to take reasonable steps 'to satisfy itself that Mrs Bennett's agreement … was properly obtained' (see [1997] 3 FCR 193 at 199).

[317] On this issue the Court of Appeal disagreed. Chadwick LJ said:

'I am satisfied that the bank was entitled to take the view, on the totality of the facts known to it, that there was no real risk that Mrs Bennett's apparent consent to the transaction—and, in particular, to the charge—had been obtained by improper conduct on the part of her husband.' (See [1999] 1 FCR 641 at 672.)

Mrs Bennett's appeal to the House challenges this conclusion.

[318] I must now refer to the facts of the case relevant to the constructive notice issue. They are set out in detail in the judgments below. It is not necessary for present purposes to refer to more than the most important of them.

[319] In 1990 Mr Bennett decided to purchase a fish processing business in south-west Scotland. He caused the company, Galloway Seafood Co Ltd, to be incorporated for that purpose. The initial capital of the company was £150,000, provided as to £50,000 by Mr Bennett and £100,000 by South West Scotland Investment Fund Ltd (SWIFT). Shares in the company were issued to SWIFT, Mr Bennett and Mrs Bennett.

[320] Additional capital was needed in order to finance the purchase of the fish processing business and to provide the company with working capital. The bank agreed to allow the company overdraft facilities up to £100,000, supported by a guarantee from Mr Bennett. This guarantee, and Mr Bennett's potential liability under it, was the reason why the matrimonial home, formerly in joint names, was transferred into Mrs Bennett's sole name.

[321] Mr Bennett had solicitors acting for him in connection with the transfer of the property to Mrs Bennett. They were Dickinson, Manser & Co of Poole. Mr Parkyn, a partner, dealt with the matter. The deputy judge's judgment records telephone conversations between Mr Parkyn and Mrs Bennett regarding the transfer.

[322] Over a period from the end of 1990 to July 1991 Mr Bennett negotiated an arrangement with the bank under which the bank would increase the *a* company's overdraft facility to £380,000. Mr Bennett intended that the money would be used to build a new factory on land which the company was to purchase or lease from Dumfries and Galloway Regional Council. The company's bank overdraft was to be secured by a fixed and floating charge over the company's new factory and business and by a joint and several guarantee of the *b* company's debts to the bank, up to a limit of £150,000, to be given by Mr and Mrs Bennett. Their liability under this guarantee was to be secured by a second charge over 15 Elthiron Road. In addition, SWIFT agreed to advance £275,000 to the company. The advance was to be secured by a fixed charge over the company's new factory. Mr Bennett, SWIFT and the bank agreed that SWIFT's charge was to rank ahead of the bank's fixed and floating charges for a sum not *c* exceeding £250,000.

[323] Mr Bennett instructed Mr Parkyn to act in connection with the grant by Mrs Bennett of the second charge over 15 Elthiron Road. The instructions were given by telephone. Mr Parkyn's attendance note records:

'(3) The seafood company in Scotland is on the threshold of building a new *d* factory. (4) We can expect to hear from the Bank of Scotland in Dumfries (John Martin) who are looking for additional security of £150,000 on their home. (5) Confirmed we would be willing to act.'

It is to be noted that Mr Parkyn did not receive instructions to act in connection with the guarantee to be given by Mr and Mrs Bennett. It appears that he knew *e* nothing about that transaction. Nor did he know anything about the financial arrangements between the company, the bank and SWIFT.

[324] On 8 August 1991 Mr Parkyn received a standard form letter from the bank asking for confirmation that Mr Parkyn would act for the bank in connection with the second charge that the bank were to be granted by Mrs Bennett over *f* 15 Elthiron Road to secure the liabilities to the bank of Mr and Mrs Bennett. The letter did not indicate the nature of those liabilities. The letter said, also:

'As your firm already acts for the Mortgagor, the Bank expects that you will advise the Mortgagor on the nature and effect of the Legal Charge ... Please also stress to the Mortgagor that the Legal Charge is for all sums due by our *g* aforesaid customers.'

[325] On 13 August 1991, Dickinson, Manser & Co confirmed they were willing to act for the bank.

[326] It had been arranged that Mr and Mrs Bennett would attend at the bank's Dumfries branch in order to sign the guarantee. But, in the event, *h* Mrs Bennett was unable to keep the appointment and, instead, it was agreed that the guarantee would be sent to the bank's branch in the Haymarket, London, and would be signed there. It was signed there on 12 August 1991. Mrs Bennett received no legal advice regarding the guarantee, nor was she advised by the bank to take legal advice about it before she signed, nor did the bank have any reason *j* to suppose that she had received any legal advice about it.

[327] On 14 August 1991 Mr Parkyn wrote to Mr Bennett about the instructions he had received from the bank regarding the second charge over 15 Elthiron Road. His letter said: 'I confirm that I have now received mortgage instructions from [the bank] for an advance of £150,000 to be secured by way of a Second Charge over the above property.'

[328] The letter reveals a misunderstanding on Mr Parkyn's part of the nature of the liabilities to be secured by the second charge. The purpose of the charge was to secure the liabilities of Mr and Mrs Bennett under the guarantee, which Mr Parkyn had not seen and knew nothing about. The guarantee secured payment, up to a limit of £150,000, of the company's indebtedness to the bank.

[329] On 17 September 1991, Mr Parkyn wrote to Mr and Mrs Bennett enclosing for their signature three documents, namely, the legal charge, a declaration of occupancy, and a consent to mortgage. Presumably Mr Parkyn had been sent these documents by the bank. He gave an explanation of these documents in his letter. As to the legal charge, the letter said:

'... the Charge is intended to secure both your liabilities to the Bank however they are incurred. I would point out that whilst the facility is for £150,000, the Charge covers *all* liabilities to the Bank, whatsoever the amount.'

[330] There was, as Chadwick LJ pointed out ([1999] 1 FCR 641 at 651) nothing in the letter to suggest that Mr Parkyn was aware that the charge was to secure his clients' liabilities as guarantors of the company's indebtedness to the bank. The judge accepted Mrs Bennett's evidence that she never saw this letter.

[331] The three documents were signed by the requisite signatories on 1 October 1991. The deputy judge accepted Mrs Bennett's evidence that she did not receive any legal advice about the nature or effect of the documents and that, save as contained in the letter of 17 August 1991 that Mrs Bennett did not see, Mr Parkyn did not give any.

[332] On 1 October 1991, Dickinson, Manser & Co wrote to the bank as follows:

'We write to advise you that completion ... took place on 1st October 1991, and your instructions have been complied with ... Except as noted below, there is no matter not already disclosed to you which we should draw to your attention in connection with this matter.'

Nothing at all was 'noted below'.

[333] This letter of 1 October 1991, read in the context of the bank's letter of 8 August 1991 (referred to at [324], above), entitled the bank to suppose that Dickinson, Manser & Co had advised Mrs Bennett on the nature and effect of the legal charge.

[334] After completion of the legal charge the bank allowed the company to draw down on the £380,000 overdraft facility.

[335] It is, in my opinion, important to emphasise that there was no evidence that Mr Parkyn knew about the guarantee that Mr and Mrs Bennett had signed. Nor, therefore, was there any reason for him to be aware that the second charge of 15 Elthiron Road was securing their liabilities as guarantors of the company's debts to the bank. The evidence justifies the inference that he thought they were principal debtors. Nor was there any evidence that Mr Parkyn knew anything about the charges that the company had given to the bank and to SWIFT respectively, securing the liabilities of the company to them. And, in particular, there was no evidence that either Mr Parkyn, or Mrs Bennett, knew about the ranking agreement under which SWIFT's charge was to rank ahead of the bank's charges for an amount not exceeding £250,000.

[336] About seven months before taking the second charge over 15 Elthiron Road, the bank had received a valuation of the company's factory premises with

the proposed new factory built thereon. The valuation was well below the likely construction costs that the company would incur in building the new factory. *a* The bank did not disclose this information to Mrs Bennett or to Mr Parkyn and there is no reason to suppose that either of them was aware of it.

[337] The bank had taken no steps at all to satisfy itself that Mrs Bennett's consent to giving the guarantee had been properly obtained. So the judge concluded that constructive notice of Mr Bennett's undue influence in procuring *b* her consent to the guarantee should be imputed to the bank. He held that she was not bound by the guarantee.

[338] The bank did not appeal against this conclusion. The reason the bank did not do so was that Mr Bennett remained bound by the guarantee. The legal charge secured his liabilities to the bank as well as those of Mrs Bennett. So if the bank could uphold the legal charge against Mrs Bennett, the company's debts for *c* which Mr Bennett was liable under the guarantee would be secured by the legal charge whether or not Mrs Bennett was bound by the guarantee.

[339] As to the question whether the bank had constructive notice of Mr Bennett's undue influence in procuring Mrs Bennett to consent to the legal charge, the deputy judge would, but for the bank's omission to disclose to Mr Parkyn, or to *d* Mrs Bennett, the existence of the ranking agreement or the valuation of the company's factory premises, have regarded the bank as protected by its reasonable belief that Mrs Bennett had received appropriate legal advice about the nature and effect of the legal charge. He cited passages from the judgments in *Massey v Midland Bank plc* [1995] 1 All ER 929, *Barclays Bank plc v Thomson* [1997] 4 All ER 816, *Banco Exterior Internacional v Mann* [1995] 1 All ER 936 and *Midland* *e* *Bank plc v Serter* [1995] 3 FCR 711 and concluded, correctly in my opinion, that the fact that Dickinson, Manser & Co had been acting not only for Mrs Bennett but also for Mr Bennett and for the bank itself did not detract from the reasonableness of the bank's expectation that the solicitors would have given Mrs Bennett adequate advice about the legal charge. He said ([1997] 3 FCR 193 at 227): 'A *f* bank is in no worse position merely because, to its knowledge, the solicitor is acting both for the prospective surety and for the debtor.' And (at 229):

> 'Unless a bank is put on notice by other matters within its knowledge that the solicitors have not performed their duty to give independent advice to the surety it is as much entitled [where the solicitor is acting also for the *g* creditor] as in any other case to assume that the solicitors have been acting properly.'

I agree with both those statements.

[340] But the judge accepted (at 233) the submission made by counsel for Mrs Bennett that because the bank had failed to disclose to Mr Parkyn, or *h* to Mrs Bennett, the ranking agreement between the bank and SWIFT and had failed to disclose the disparity between the development cost and the ultimate value of the factory premises, the bank had failed 'to show that it took reasonable steps to bring home to Mrs. Bennett the risks she was running'.

[341] The judge treated the non-disclosure as a constructive notice point. His *j* reasoning, I think, proceeded in this way. (1) The bank's knowledge of the relationship between Mr and Mrs Bennett and of the nature of the transactions she was entering into, ie the guarantee and the legal charge, put the bank on notice of the risk that her agreement to the transactions might have been procured by the undue influence of her husband. (2) The bank could avoid being on constructive notice of any such impropriety by taking reasonable steps to

a   satisfy itself that Mrs Bennett understood the nature and effect of the transactions. (3) The bank's failure to disclose the material facts regarding the SWIFT ranking agreement and the value of the factory premises was a failure to take reasonable steps. (4) It was a failure to take reasonable steps because unless Mr Parkyn was given this information he could not be expected to give Mrs Bennett appropriate advice about the risks she was running.

b   [342] The Court of Appeal disagreed. Chadwick LJ ([1999] 1 FCR 641 at 671) accepted that the facts in question 'were facts which a competent advisor, advising Mrs Bennett as to the risk that the bank would need to have recourse to the security which she was providing, would need to know', but held:

c   '… the judge was wrong to hold that the bank was required to bring those facts to the notice of Mr Parkyn or his client; or … to hold that … the bank was not entitled to assume that Mr Parkyn would become aware of those facts in the course of considering what advice he needed to give to Mrs Bennett.'

[343] Chadwick LJ thought that the bank was entitled to assume that
d   Mr Parkyn would inform himself of the nature of the liabilities secured by the legal charge, and, in doing so, would become aware that 'those liabilities are themselves liabilities under a guarantee for a company's indebtedness to the bank' and that Mr Parkyn would then 'inform himself as to the company's financial position'. He continued: 'That must, at the least, involve questioning the true value of the assets in the balance sheet and understanding the ranking of
e   whatever charges have been created over those assets.'

[344] In my respectful opinion, this view of what a solicitor in the position of Mr Parkyn would inquire into and discover is unrealistic. Let it be supposed that Mr Parkyn had known about the guarantee. It is to be expected that he would have advised Mrs Bennett that the risk of the bank seeking to enforce the
f   charge so as to recover the £150,000 would depend upon the fortunes of the company. He might have asked her if she was satisfied about the company's prospects. He probably would have asked her if she knew anything about the company's existing indebtedness to the bank and the extent of its overdraft facility. If she did not know these things, he might have advised her to find out about them or have asked her if she wanted him to try and do so. But it seems to
g   me highly unlikely that he would on his own initiative have examined the company's latest balance sheet—which would probably have been well out of date—or have inquired into the balance sheet values of its assets. I think it highly unlikely that, without special instructions to do so, he would have carried out a search in order to discover what charges were registered against the company. In
h   the ordinary discharge of his duties as a solicitor advising Mrs Bennett about the nature and effect of the legal charge I do not believe he would have become aware either of the ranking agreement between the bank and SWIFT or of the valuation of the factory premises that the bank had obtained.

[345] In my opinion, however, both the deputy judge and the Court of Appeal
j   approached this question of disclosure from the wrong angle. The point was not, in my view, a constructive notice point. It was simply a disclosure point. Did the bank have an obligation to the proposed surety to disclose this information to the surety? If it did, what is the consequence of the non-disclosure?

[346] In my opinion, the ranking agreement between the company, the bank and SWIFT falls within the general proposition expressed by Vaughan Williams LJ in *London General Omnibus Co Ltd v Holloway* [1912] 2 KB 72 at 79,

[1911–13] All ER Rep 518 at 520 (see [187], above). A surety who pays off the creditor is entitled to be subrogated to the rights of the creditor in respect of the debt in question. And if the creditor, in order to discharge the debt, has recourse to security provided by the surety, the same applies. So, in the present case, if Mrs Bennett had paid the bank the £150,000, or if the bank had obtained payment by realising its security over 15 Elthiron Road, Mrs Bennett would have been entitled to the benefit of the bank's rights against the company in respect of the £150,000. These rights would have included the bank's rights under its fixed and floating charges. But those rights were subject to the ranking agreement.

[347] Moreover the ranking agreement reduced the amount of the company's assets that would be available for the payment of the company's debts to the bank and correspondingly increased the likelihood that the bank would make a call on Mr Bennett or Mrs Bennett, or both, under the guarantee and would enforce its security over 15 Elthiron Road. The ranking agreement did affect the rights of Mrs Bennett as surety.

[348] In my opinion, the bank ought to have disclosed to Mrs Bennett, or to the solicitor acting for her, the existence of the ranking agreement.

[349] The deputy judge thought that the facts regarding the valuation of the factory premises should also have been disclosed by the bank. Here, I do not agree. It is, I think, up to an intending surety to satisfy himself about the value of the principal debtor's assets or the principal debtor's credit worthiness.

[350] The bank's obligation to disclose the existence of the ranking agreement arose, in my opinion, under the general law applicable to suretyship contracts. Mr Jarvis QC, counsel for the bank, accepted that if the bank had an obligation to disclose the ranking agreement and if Mrs Bennett and Mr Parkyn were on 1 October 1991 unaware of it, Mrs Bennett was entitled to have the legal charge set aside.

[351] I would allow her appeal on this ground.

Kenyon-Brown v Desmond Banks & Co (a firm)

[352] This is the solicitors' negligence case. The solicitors, appellants before your Lordships, are Desmond Banks & Co. The proprietor of the firm, Mr Desmond Banks, acted in the matters that have given rise to this litigation.

[353] Mrs Kenyon-Brown, the respondent before the House, contends that Mr Banks acted negligently in failing to advise her properly on 12 January 1993, when she and her husband attended at his offices to sign a second legal charge of their jointly owned holiday cottage, Rock Cottage, Melplash, Bridport, to National Westminster Bank plc. The charge secured Mr Kenyon-Brown's indebtedness to the bank.

[354] In her statement of claim Mrs Kenyon-Brown pleaded that Mr Banks owed her a duty to advise her, before she signed the legal charge:

'(i) that there was a conflict of interest between the plaintiff and Mr Kenyon-Brown in respect of the proposed mortgage; and/or (ii) that the said conflict might prevent or inhibit the defendants from disclosing or explaining all aspects of the transaction to the plaintiff or from giving advice to the plaintiff which would conflict with Mr Kenyon-Brown's interests; and/or (iii) that she could and/or should obtain advice from an independent solicitor in respect of the proposed mortgage; and/or (iv) that the proposed mortgage would confer no benefit upon her; and/or (v) as to the nature and effect of the mortgage.'

a She pleaded that Mr Banks had failed to give her advice in respect of these matters, or any advice about the proposed mortgage, and that in consequence she had suffered loss.

[355] She quantified her loss as being one half of the sum of £55,000 then owing by Mr Kenyon-Brown to the bank.

[356] Mr Banks accepted in his defence that he had owed Mrs Kenyon-Brown
b a duty to advise her 'as to the meaning and effect' of the legal charge, but denied any breach of duty and denied, if there had been any breach of duty, that the breach had caused any loss. Directions were given for issues of liability to be tried before issues of damage. At trial, on the liability issues, the familiar two issues arose. What was the extent of the duty owed by Mr Banks? Had there been any breach of that duty?

c [357] The material facts can be quite shortly stated. Mr and Mrs Kenyon-Brown were directors of and shareholders in KB Insurance Brokers (London) Ltd (KB) and PM Insurance Services Ltd (PM). These companies were controlled by Mr Kenyon-Brown but Mrs Kenyon-Brown did play some part in the insurance businesses that they carried on.

d [358] In 1983 a controlling interest in each company was sold to Crusader Insurance Company Ltd (Crusader).

[359] In 1986 Mr and Mrs Kenyon-Brown purchased Rock Cottage for £50,000 with the aid of a £30,000 advance from Nationwide Building Society secured by a mortgage of Rock Cottage.

[360] In 1988 they purchased 53 Dene Road, Northwood, with the aid of
e a £30,000 advance from National Westminster Home Loans Ltd secured by a mortgage of 53 Dene Road.

[361] Both properties were in their joint names. 53 Dene Road was their home. Rock Cottage was a holiday cottage.

[362] In 1989 the opportunity to repurchase from Crusader the shares in KB and
f PM arose. As the deputy judge, Mr Peter Leaver QC, found: 'Mrs Kenyon-Brown was very much against doing so, but was overborne by her husband and very reluctantly agreed to the repurchase.'

[363] Finance was needed for the repurchase of the shares and a loan from National Westminster Bank to be secured by a second mortgage of 53 Dene Road was arranged. The loan was to be a loan to Mr Kenyon-Brown alone, not to the
g two of them jointly.

[364] Mr Banks, who had acted for Mr and Mrs Kenyon-Brown in their purchase of 53 Dene Road, and had acted previously for KB and for PM, acted for them in connection with the grant to the bank of the second mortgage of 53 Dene Road.

[365] By a letter of 13 November 1989 the bank asked Mr Banks to arrange for
h the legal charge to be signed by Mr and Mrs Kenyon-Brown and to confirm, when returning the signed document, that Mrs Kenyon-Brown had received legal advice about it. So Mr Banks arranged a meeting with her at his offices on 15 November 1989. His attendance note records the advice he gave her.

[366] Mr Banks pointed out to her that the advance was to be to
j Mr Kenyon-Brown alone, not to the two of them jointly. Mrs Kenyon-Brown responded that she trusted her husband. Mr Banks was instrumental in arranging for the sum secured by the legal charge to be limited to £150,000. No allegation has been made that in advising Mrs Kenyon-Brown on this occasion Mr Banks was in breach of the duty he owed her.

[367] The legal charge over 53 Dene Road was duly completed. It secured the liabilities to the bank of Mr Kenyon-Brown, subject to the agreed limit of £150,000.

[368] By 1992, the bank was seeking further security in respect of Mr Kenyon-Brown's indebtedness and agreement was apparently reached between it and Mr Kenyon-Brown that it would be given a second charge over Rock Cottage. By a letter of 15 December 1992 the bank sent Mr Banks the proposed form of legal charge for signature by Mr and Mrs Kenyon-Brown. The letter said: 'We shall be grateful if you will confirm that Legal Advice was given to Mrs Kenyon-Brown when the charge form is returned.'

[369] On 12 January 1993 Mrs Kenyon-Brown had a meeting with Mr Banks at his offices. His attendance note reads:

'Advised on mortgage—Jessica [Mrs Kenyon-Brown] is happy to go along with it—doesn't want me to go into it in detail—even if money is borrowed by N [Mr Kenyon-Brown] alone to buy shares in KB in his name. Dene Road already mortgage. Copy mortgage to JKB. Mrs KB appeared to understand it fully and despite the terms of my warning to be totally unconcerned that the mortgage of property jointly owned by her would benefit her husband alone and be without limit.'

[370] As indicated by the attendance note, the form of legal charge contained no limit on the amount of Mr Kenyon-Brown's liabilities to the bank that would be secured.

[371] The legal charge was duly completed and dated 12 January 1993.

[372] At the trial, Mrs Kenyon-Brown was the only witness who gave oral evidence but the deputy judge said that he did not find her evidence about the events of 15 November 1989 or 12 January 1993 persuasive. He said: 'Ultimately, I came to the conclusion that her evidence could not be relied upon.' He recorded, however, that she said that she could not contradict Mr Banks' attendance note of the 12 January 1993 meeting. He expressed his conclusions in the following passage:

'In my judgment the evidence in the present case comes nowhere near proving that the defendant was negligent in the manner of which Mrs Kenyon-Brown complains. It is for Mrs Kenyon-Brown to satisfy me, on the balance of probabilities, that the defendant failed to discharge his duty to her properly in the ways of which she complains. Mrs Kenyon-Brown has failed to satisfy me that the defendant gave no advice. Indeed the attendance note ... makes it plain that the defendant did give advice. On Miss Smith's second submission, that the defendant should, in the light of the conflict of interests, have told her to go to another solicitor, I hold that the law does not require that she [sic] should do so. While it may, in some cases be prudent for a solicitor so to advise, it will depend upon the facts of the case as to whether it was negligent or not to do so. Although Mrs Kenyon-Brown told me that she was sure that if she had been advised to go to another solicitor she would have gone, I could not accept that evidence. I form the view that Mrs Kenyon-Brown was quite clear as to what she was doing by entering into the second mortgage, and wanted to do so notwithstanding the defendant's "warning".'

[373] These conclusions might be thought to have made the prospects of an appeal unpromising. But there was an appeal and the appeal succeeded (although Wilson J dissented) ([2000] PNLR 266). The main judgment was given by Mance LJ. He based his reasoning substantially on the judgment of the Court of Appeal in *Royal Bank of Scotland plc v Etridge (No 2)* [1998] 4 All ER 705. He cited

a Stuart-Smith LJ's judgment (at 715–717 (paras 19–26)) under the heading 'Independent legal advice'. In these paragraphs Stuart-Smith LJ was considering the advice that needs to be given where a solicitor is instructed to advise a person who may be subject to the undue influence of another. I have criticised the contents of these paragraphs in an earlier section of this opinion and shall not repeat the criticism here. The duty of a solicitor always depends on the extent of
b the instructions given to and accepted by him, either expressly or by implication, by conduct or otherwise. The normal duty of a solicitor instructed to advise a would-be surety, whether a wife of the principal debtor or anyone else, about the document or documents the surety is being asked to sign, is to explain the nature and effect of the document in order to try and make sure that the surety knows
c what he or she is doing. The particular circumstances of a particular case may add to or reduce the extent of the duty owed by the solicitor. There was, in my opinion, nothing in the circumstances which resulted in Mr Banks advising Mrs Kenyon-Brown about the proposed second mortgage of Rock Cottage to add to the normal duty that I have described. Mance LJ said that since Mr Banks knew that Mrs Kenyon-Brown reposed trust and confidence in her husband (see
d the contents of the attendance note of the 15 November 1989 meeting) and that the second mortgage of Rock Cottage appeared to be entirely in Mr Kenyon-Brown's interests and was without limit of amount, he was on notice that 'there *might* be undue influence'. This is something that was never pleaded. It may be right that a solicitor who is advising a client about a transaction and has reason to suspect
e that the client is the victim of undue influence is placed under a duty to the client to try and protect her (see *Bank of Montreal v Stuart* [1911] AC 120 at 138). But if a case of that sort is to be advanced against a solicitor, it must be pleaded. A solicitor does not have reason to suspect undue influence simply because he knows a wife has trust and confidence in her husband and is proposing to give a charge over her property to support his financial position. That she is willing to do
f so is consistent with a normal relationship between spouses. Mance LJ said ([2000] PNLR 266 at 281):

> 'There is no suggestion, or likelihood in the light of Mr Banks' attendance note, that Mr Banks ascertained the amount outstanding (well in excess of
g the limit of liability in the second mortgage of 53 Dene Road), its origin and the circumstances in which it came to be outstanding, let alone the prospects of its repayment or of the additional security over Rock Cottage being called upon. Nor did he ask why Mrs Kenyon-Brown was willing to grant such additional security. Still less, therefore, did he know that her husband had
h told her that she would be bankrupted if she did not enter into the mortgage. Nor did he elicit the fact (about which she gave evidence) that she did not consider the marriage to have any long term future but wished, on the other hand, to avoid bringing it to an end until her son (aged 14 at the beginning of 1983) was older and to maintain a tolerable atmosphere at home in the
j meantime while she was living with Mr Kenyon-Brown. These are considerations which would have been central to an evaluation whether it made sense for the wife to enter into the mortgage and to a balanced decision whether to do so, made free of any undue influence by Mr Kenyon-Brown. Mr Banks did not know of them. Nor, therefore, could he either discuss them with Mrs Kenyon-Brown or, if he concluded in their light that a conflict of interest existed, suggest that she discuss them with another solicitor.'

[374] Save as to the amount of the then current indebtedness of Mr Kenyon-Brown to the bank, Mr Banks had, in my opinion, no duty or reason to make the *a* inquiries referred to. Some of the inquiries, eg eliciting the fact that Mrs Kenyon-Brown did not consider her marriage to have a long-term future, would have been an unpardonable impertinence. Mr Banks was entitled to treat Mrs Kenyon-Brown as a mature lady able to make up her own mind as to whether to allow her share in Rock Cottage to become security for her husband's debts. What he did *b* need to do, and, on the judge's findings, did do, was to try and make sure that she understood the nature and effect of the document she was being asked to sign. Wilson J, in his dissenting judgment in the Court of Appeal (at 288–289), set out, in paragraphs lettered (a) to (i) the circumstances that, in his view, determined the extent of the duty owed by Mr Banks to his client. He concluded that Mr Banks had discharged that duty. I agree and would allow this appeal.

The Harris, Wallace, Moore, Bennett and Desmond Banks & Co appeals allowed. The Etridge, Gill and Coleman appeals dismissed.

Dilys Tausz   Barrister.

a

Sarwar v Alam
[2001] EWCA Civ 1401

COURT OF APPEAL, CIVIL DIVISION
LORD PHILLIPS OF WORTH MATRAVERS MR, BROOKE AND LONGMORE LJJ

b   10, 11, 19 SEPTEMBER 2001

Costs – Order for costs – Legal expenses insurance – Before-the-event (BTE) insurance – After-the-event (ATE) insurance premium – Driver having motor vehicle insurance policy containing BTE legal expenses cover – Whether passenger entitled to recover ATE
c *premium in small personal injury claim where BTE cover available under driver's insurance policy.*

Solicitor – Practice – Costs – Before-the-event (BTE) insurance – Steps to be taken by solicitor to discover whether BTE insurance available to client – Guidance.

d   The defendant, A, possessed a motor vehicle insurance policy issued by CIS. The policy included before-the-event (BTE) legal expenses insurance, covering not only the insured but also, with the insured's consent, any passenger in the insured vehicle. The policy stated that the legal expenses insurance was administered by DAS. The latter company, which specialised in such insurance and used the services
e   of a panel of solictors' firms, was entirely separate from CIS, and the commercial relationship between them was founded on a reinsurance agreement. By virtue of that agreement, all settlements made by DAS were unconditionally binding on CIS. However, none of those matters was apparent on the face of the policy which gave the impression that DAS was merely a manager of that aspect of CIS's business. Under the policy, DAS was entitled to the full conduct and control of
f   any claim or legal proceedings, and was also entitled to appoint a legal representative where DAS regarded it as necessary. An insured person could choose an alternative legal representative only where DAS decided to commence legal proceedings or there was a conflict of interest. Any dispute as to the choice of legal representative or the handling of a claim would be referred to an independent arbitrator. In February 2000 A was driving the insured vehicle when it was
g   involved in an accident, causing minor injuries to A's passenger, S, who lived in the same household as A. S instructed solicitors to pursue a claim, and on 15 March 2000 they sent a letter before action to A. That letter was apparently not forwarded by A to his insurers. On 21 March S told his solicitors that he was not aware that any legal expenses insurance policy was available to him, and he then took out
h   after-the-event (ATE) insurance. On 3 April S's solicitors told A's insurers of the existence of the ATE policy, and in October the case was settled, without the need to commence proceedings, for £2,250 together with reasonable costs. However, A's insurers disputed the recoverability of the premium for the ATE policy by way of costs, disclosing for the first time that his motor insurance policy
j   contained a provision for legal expenses insurance which might have covered S's claim. In subsequent costs-only proceedings brought by S, the district judge refused to allow him to recover the ATE premium. That decision was affirmed on appeal by the circuit judge who held that that it was clearly desirable that unnecessary premiums were not paid by litigants, that claimants' representatives had the primary responsibility for checking whether there was any BTE insurance and that, in the context of S's claim, a sensible claimant would have used the BTE

policy rather than incur an additional insurance premium. S appealed to the
Court of Appeal.

a

Held – If, in a relatively small claim by a passenger for personal injuries arising
from a road traffic accident (ie a claim which apparently would not exceed about
£5,000), there was a reasonable possibility that the passenger was likely to blame
the driver, or the driver the passenger, it was not incumbent on the passenger to
use BTE cover if it resembled the cover provided by A's policy in the instant case.
It was not reasonable for a claimant to be required to invoke insurance cover
provided by the opponent's camp on terms such as those proffered by CIS. If
BTE insurers financed some transparently independent organisation to handle
such claims, the position might be different, but there was no such transparency
or independence in the arrangements between CIS and DAS. There were
obvious concerns as to conflict of interest in any case where a defendant was
being sued via his own policy of insurance, and it was not enough to say that any
damages recovered would be paid by a liability insurer which was a separate legal
entity from the BTE insurer. Where liability was disputed, the defendant might
well have a strong personal motivation in resisting the claim. Moreover, it was
probable that many claimants would feel uneasy in entrusting the conduct of
their claims to the insurer of the opposing party, and would distrust its advice
when adverse to their private expectations. Justice should be seen to be done,
and the rules of court should support a claimant who elected to fund his claim
from a source which was not only neutral and objective, but seen to be so.
Although as a matter of law an arbitration provision might be thought adequate
to allay a claimant's fear of receiving less than objective advice, he was entitled to
feel comfortable with the objectivity of the representative who was looking after
his claim. There was not, however, such a strong public interest in maintaining
a client's freedom of choice over the appointment of a legal advisor that that
should override the appropriateness of a claim as small as that in the instant case
being handled by a BTE insurer with or without the assistance of a panel solicitor.
The right of any citizen to be represented by a solicitor of his choice could be cut
down by circumstances, including the consideration that the cost of instructing a
solicitor of his choice (and protecting him from the risk of paying the other side's
costs) was disproportionate to the value of the proposed claim when an alternative,
reasonable, method of advancing his interests, with the help of an appropriately
qualified lawyer, was available. However, representation arranged by the insurer
of the opposing party, pursuant to a policy to which the claimant had never been
a party, and of which he had no knowledge at the time it was entered into, and
where the opposing insurer through its chosen representative reserved to itself
the full conduct and control of the claim, was not a reasonable alternative.
However careful CIS and DAS might have attempted to be, appearances mattered,
and appearances were very hostile to the notion that a passenger like S should be
obliged to go to the driver's insurers and entrust them with the full conduct and
control of his claim when he wished to sue the driver. Accordingly, the appeal
would be allowed (see [52]–[58], [61], below).

b

c

d

e

f

g

h

j

Per curiam. Proper modern practice dictates that a solicitor should normally
invite a client to bring to the first interview any relevant motor insurance policy,
household policy and stand-alone BTE policy belonging to the client and/or any
spouse or partner living in the same house as the client. It is desirable for
solicitors to develop the practice of sending a standard form letter requesting

a sight of those documents to the client in advance of the first interview. At the interview, the solicitor will also ask the client whether his liability for costs may be paid by another person, eg an employer or trade union. If (i) BTE cover is available, (ii) the motor accident claim is likely to be less than about £5,000, and (iii) there are no features of the cover that make it inappropriate (for instance, if there are a number of potential claimants and the policy cover is limited to

b around £25,000), the solicitor should refer the client to the BTE insurer without further ado. The solicitor's inquiries should be proportionate to the amount at stake, and he is not obliged to embark on a treasure hunt, seeking to see the insurance policies of every member of the client's family in case they contain relevant BTE cover which the client may use. As motor insurance often contains provision for BTE cover for a claim brought by a passenger, the solicitor should

c ordinarily ask the client passenger to obtain a copy of the driver's insurance policy, if reasonably practicable. If the solicitor sees that the BTE cover contains a stipulation that the driver should consent to its use by the passenger, he should tell the client to obtain the driver's consent before making a claim on the BTE insurer. It will be professionally inappropriate for the solicitor to do anything to

d induce the client to encourage the driver to withhold consent. If in due course there is any evidence that that has happened, the court will normally disallow both the ATE premium and any success fee claimed. Such guidance should not be treated as an inflexible code, and the overriding principle is that the claimant, assisted by his solicitor, should act in a reasonable manner. The availability of ATE cover at a modest premium will inevitably restrict the extent to which it will

e be reasonable for a solicitor's time to be used in investigating alternative sources of insurance (see [45]–[48], [50], below).

Notes

For recovery of insurance premiums by way of costs, see 41 *Halsbury's Laws* (4th
f edn reissue) para 922.

Cases referred to in judgment

Callery v Gray [2001] EWCA Civ 1117, [2001] 3 All ER 833, CA.
Callery v Gray (No 2) [2001] EWCA Civ 1246, [2001] 4 All ER 1, CA.
g *Maltez v Lewis* (2000) 19 Const LJ 65.
R v Legal Aid Board, ex p Duncan [2000] COD 159, DC.

Appeal

The claimant, Imran Sarwar, appealed with permission of Brooke LJ granted on
h 26 July 2001 from the decision of Judge Halbert at Chester County Court on 5 July 2001 dismissing his appeal from the decision of District Judge Wallace on 9 February 2001 refusing to allow Mr Sarwar to recover, as reasonable costs, the cost of an after-the-event insurance policy taken out by him in respect of a claim for personal injuries against the defendant, Muhammad Alam. The Law Society,
j the Association of Personal Injury Lawyers (APIL), the Association of British Insurers (ABI), the Forum of Insurance Lawyers (FOIL), the Motor Accident Solicitors Society (MASS), the Liability Insurers Group, the After The Event Insurers' Group (the ATE Group), DAS Legal Expenses Insurance Co Ltd (DAS) and the Trades Union Congress (TUC) participated in the appeal as interested parties with permission of Brooke LJ. The facts are set out in the judgment of the court.

Geoffrey Nice QC and Nicholas Bacon (instructed by Amelans, Didsbury) for
    Mr Sarwar.   a
Peter Birts QC and Peter Goodbody (instructed by David Higginson, Liverpool) for
    Mr Alam.
Richard Drabble QC (instructed by Solicitor to the Law Society) for the Law Society.
Stephen Irwin QC and Richard Hermer (instructed by Pattinson & Brewer) for the APIL.
John Leighton Williams QC (instructed by Barlow Lyde & Gilbert) for the ABI.   b
Anna Guggenheim QC (instructed by A E Wyeth & Co, Dartford) for the FOIL.
Benjamin Williams (instructed by Colman Tilley Tarrant Sutton, Kingston upon
    Thames) for the MASS.
Peter Birts QC (instructed by Beachcroft Wansbroughs) for the Liability Insurers
    Group.
Philip Brook Smith (instructed by Rowe Cohen, Manchester) for the ATE Group.   c
Jeremy Stuart-Smith QC (instructed by Lyons Davidson, Bristol) for DAS.
Jeremy Morgan (instructed by Russell Jones & Walker) for the TUC.

                                                                    Cur adv vult

                                                                                 d
19 September 2001. The following judgment of the court was delivered.

                                    INDEX

Part   Paragraph
  (1) Introduction   [1]
                                                                                 e
  (2) The facts of the case   [5]
  (3) The judgments in the courts below   [8]
  (4) Funding options and the solicitor's duty to the client   [11]
  (5) The intervenors in the appeal   [18]
  (6) LEI/BTE insurance   [20]   f
  (7) The practice of an LEI insurer   [27]
  (8) The CIS/DAS arrangements   [33]
  (9) The conflicting concerns about BTE cover   [39]
 (10) The appropriateness of BTE cover for small accident claims   [41]
 (11) Proper practice for a solicitor inquiring about BTE cover   [45]   g
 (12) Motor accident claims where the passenger blames the driver [52]
 (13) The concerns of the ATE Group and the TUC   [59]
 (14) How this judgment fits in with the judgment in Callery   [60]
 (15) Why we differ from the judge   [61]   h

LORD PHILLIPS OF WORTH MATRAVERS MR.

(1) *Introduction*

   [1] This case is a natural sequel to *Callery v Gray* [2001] EWCA Civ 1117, [2001] j
3 All ER 833 (*Callery*). Like *Callery*, it is concerned with a claim by a passenger
who suffered personal injuries in a road traffic accident. The passenger instructed
the same firm of solicitors as Mr Callery, and he also took out 'after-the-event'
(ATE) insurance. As in *Callery* the claim was settled for a comparatively small
sum at an early stage, without the need to institute legal proceedings. The
defendant's insurers agreed to pay costs, but disputed the recoverability of the ATE

a premium. There was no dispute as to the reasonableness of the premium, if recoverable.

[2] Here the similarities end. The disputes in *Callery* were concerned with the amount of the solicitors' success fee and with issues relating to the ATE insurance taken out by the claimant, including the amount of the ATE premium (for that issue, see *Callery v Gray (No 2)* [2001] EWCA Civ 1246, [2001] 4 All ER 1 (*Callery (No 2)*). This
b case is concerned with 'before-the-event' (BTE) insurance, which did not feature in *Callery*.

[3] Another distinguishing feature of the present case is that Mr Sarwar's claim was against the driver of the car in which he was travelling as a passenger, and not against the driver of a different car. The present dispute arose during the costs-only proceedings when Mr Alam's insurers disclosed for the first time that their
c client's motor insurance policy contained a provision for legal expenses insurance (LEI) which might have covered a claim made by a passenger in their insured's car against their insured driver. Both the district judge and the judge on appeal held that this BTE insurance was available to Mr Sarwar, and they disallowed the cost of his ATE premium on those grounds. Mr Sarwar now appeals.

d [4] Judge Halbert made his ruling in this case on 5 July 2001, between the conclusion of the hearing in *Callery* and the delivery of the judgment on 17 July. Its importance was identified during the course of the inquiry conducted by Master O'Hare in *Callery* at the request of the court, and on the last page of his report (which is annexed to the judgment in *Callery (No 2)*) he revealed that he had received a submission to the effect that Judge Halbert's decision had
e significantly altered the dynamics of the legal expenses insurance industry. The point we now have to decide did not arise for decision in either of the *Callery* judgments, but once the court became aware of it, arrangements were made to expedite the hearing of the present appeal, for which Brooke LJ granted permission, as a second appeal, on 26 July. He also granted permission for a number of
f interested parties to intervene in the appeal. Master O'Hare was invited to assist the court as an informal assessor on the appeal, and we benefited from the advice he gave us.

(2) *The facts of the case*

g [5] The facts of the case can be stated briefly. Mr Sarwar and Mr Alam live at the same address in Ashton-under-Lyne. The accident occurred on 22 February 2000 when Mr Alam drove his car out of a side road onto a main road, colliding with another car as he did so. Liability was admitted three months later. Mr Sarwar instructed Amelans who wrote a letter before action on 15 March. It appears that Mr Alam did not forward this letter to his insurers. On 21 March
h Mr Sarwar told his solicitors, on inquiry, that he was not aware that any LEI policy was available to him. He then took out an ATE policy, and on 3 April his solicitors told Mr Alam's insurers (of whose identity they were now aware) of the existence of this policy. About three weeks later they also sent them a copy of their original letter before action. On 30 October Mr Sarwar's claim was settled
j for £2,250 together with reasonable costs. On 15 November a costs-only Pt 8 claim was made pursuant to CPR 44.12A.

[6] Mr Alam possessed a motor vehicle policy issued by the Co-operative Insurance Society Ltd (CIS). Section H of this policy reads, so far as is material:

'For the purposes of this Section: (1) "We", "us" and "our" means DAS Legal Expense Insurance Company Limited, who administer this insurance

on behalf of CIS. (2) "Insured Person" means you and, with your agreement
... (ii) any passenger whilst in or on the Insured Vehicle. If any accident
occurs which results in ... (2) ... injury to an Insured Person and we accept
that there is reasonable prospect of a successful recovery against the
negligent party we will at your request: (i) negotiate to recover the Insured
Person's uninsured losses and costs (ii) pay costs and expenses incurred with
our consent together with third party costs for which the Insured Person is
responsible ... We will not ... (b) pay more than £50,000 in respect of all
claims under this Section, including the legal costs of an appeal or of
defending an appeal, arising from any one accident. If claims from more than
one Insured Person are involved the insurance will apply to the aggregate
amount and in priority to you.

Note

1. We will be entitled to the full conduct and control of any claim or legal
proceedings. 2. We will be entitled to appoint a legal representative where
we regard it as necessary. An Insured Person may choose an alternative legal
representative only where—(i) we decide to commence legal proceedings or
(ii) there is a conflict of interest. Any dispute as to the choice of legal
representative or the handling of a claim will be referred to an independent
arbitrator who will normally be the President of the Law Society. 3. An
Insured Person must not settle a claim without our agreement.'

[7] We will describe the relationship between CIS and DAS in [33]–[34], below.

(3) The judgments in the courts below

[8] District Judge Wallace held that this cover was available to Mr Sarwar, and
that the premium for the ATE policy was prima facie not allowable because it was
in effect double insurance. He considered that the BTE cover was entirely
adequate for the purposes of this action, had Mr Sarwar known about it, and he
did not think the defendant's insurers could be blamed for not mentioning the
existence of the pre-existing LEI cover when they were notified of the ATE cover,
because by that time the liability for the ATE premium had already been
incurred.

[9] Judge Halbert considered that the core of the matter centred round the
lack of any knowledge on the part of Mr Sarwar and his solicitors that any
pre-existing LEI cover existed. He said that the principal question he had to
decide was whether it was unreasonable for a claimant passenger to incur the cost
of ATE insurance without checking whether the driver's policy provided LEI
cover for his passengers. He considered that it was not reasonable to incur this
expense without making such a check. If the driver of another vehicle had hit
Mr Alam's car, it would be very obvious that Mr Alam's policy should be checked
to see if Mr Sarwar could make a claim under it, and he did not think that the fact
that the driver of the car was the defendant should change the position.

[10] The judge went on to reject the claimant's contentions on a number of
other issues which arise again for consideration on this appeal. The gist of his
decision was to the effect that it was clearly desirable that unnecessary premiums
were not paid by litigants, that the primary responsibility for checking whether
BTE insurance existed lay with those representing the claimants, and that in the
context of this case (as opposed to what he described as a 'complex or serious
case') a sensible claimant would have used the BTE policy rather than incur an
additional insurance premium.

a
(4) *Funding options and the solicitor's duty to the client*
[11] This is a challenge to the exercise of a discretion in the lower courts on an appeal in costs-only proceedings. The principles on which the lower court must approach an issue of this kind are clearly set out in CPR 44.4 and 44.5 in these terms:

b
'**44.4 Basis of assessment**
(1) ... the court will not ... allow costs which have been unreasonably incurred ...
(2) ...the court will ... (b) resolve any doubt which it may have as to whether costs were unreasonably incurred ... in favour of the paying party ...

c
44.5 Factors to be taken into account in deciding the amount of costs
(1) The court is to have regard to all the circumstances in deciding whether costs were—(a)(i) proportionately and reasonably incurred ...
(3) The court must also have regard to—(a) the conduct of all the parties ...
(b) the amount or value of any money or property involved ...'

d
[12] Material provisions of the Costs Practice Direction to CPR Pt 44 are all set out in Lord Woolf CJ's judgment in *Callery v Gray* [2001] 3 All ER 833 at [32], [33] and it is not necessary to set them out again here. 'The availability of any pre-existing insurance cover' is one of five relevant factors specifically identified in para 11.10 of the Practice Direction as appropriate to take into account in deciding whether the cost of insurance cover is reasonable, but this is not an exhaustive list. The governing rule is r 44.5(1), which imposes a duty on the court
e
to have regard to all the circumstances in deciding whether any item of costs was proportionately and reasonably incurred.
[13] As the judge rightly pointed out, the central question in this appeal is whether it was reasonable in all the circumstances for Mr Sarwar, acting on his solicitor's advice, to incur the cost of the ATE premium without making any
f
further inquiries into the possible existence of BTE cover. A solicitor's duty when he is first instructed by his client is set out in the Solicitors' Costs Information and Client Care Code 1999. This code is given teeth by rule 15 of the Solicitors' Practice Rules 1990 (as amended) which provides that:

g
'Solicitors shall: (a) give information about costs and other matters ... in accordance with a Solicitors' Costs Information and Client Care Code made from time to time by the Council of the Law Society.'

[14] Paragraph 4(j) of the care code is headed 'Client's ability to pay'. It provides, so far as is material, that:

h
'The solicitor should discuss with the client how, when and by whom any costs are to be met, and consider:—(i) whether the client may be eligible and should apply for legal aid ... (ii) whether the client's liability for their own costs may be covered by insurance; (iii) whether the client's liability for another party's costs may be covered by pre-purchased insurance and, if not, whether it would be advisable for the client's liability for another party's
j
costs to be covered by after the event insurance ... (iv) whether the client's liability for costs (including the costs of another party) may be covered by another person e.g. an employer or trade union.'

[15] We were told by Mr Drabble QC, who appeared for the Law Society, that the new code was approved by the Council of the Law Society in December 1998 at a time when the premium for ATE insurance could not be recovered from the

other side. The code is clearly concerned with the protection of the client, and
para 4(j) does not purport to impose new duties of inquiry on solicitors other
than those suggested by the fairly simple language used.

[16] Mr Cockx, who is a partner in Amelans, made a telephone attendance
note of a discussion with Mr Sarwar on 21 March 2000. The note reads:

> 'Discussing funding with client and various options available. Advising
> him of the changes due [to] the Access to Justice Act. Discussed the benefit
> of taking out a ATE policy to protect him against the payment of other side's
> costs. Client advised that he did not have the benefit of any other Legal
> Cover and wished to take out a policy with Temple Legal Protect. Will send
> out a copy.'

[17] It should be observed that Mr Cockx would have realised that he was
handling a comparatively small passenger claim in which liability was unlikely to
be in issue. He was charging £150 per hour for his time, and he noted that this
attendance consumed an hour of his time. He would have been aware of the
provisions of r 44.5, with its reference to proportionality as well as reasonableness.
He would not have had the benefit of the advice contained in the Practice
Direction to Pt 44, which had not yet been published. Furthermore, the Conditional
Fee Agreements Regulations 2000, SI 2000/692, had only been laid before
Parliament 11 days earlier and were not yet in force. Paragraph 4(2)(c) of these
regulations includes, among the matters which a legal representative must tell his
client before a conditional fee agreement (CFA) is made:

> '... whether the legal representative considers that the client's risk of
> incurring liability for costs in respect of the proceedings to which the
> agreement relates is insured against under an existing contract of insurance ...'

(5) The intervenors in the appeal

[18] We received representations on this appeal from bodies representative of
the great majority of the insurers and solicitors who have an interest in the
outcome of this appeal, and from the Trades Union Congress (TUC). In addition
to the Law Society, the intervenors included the Motor Accident Solicitors'
Society (MASS), whose 175 member firms handle about 500,000 motor accident
claims each year; the Association of Personal Injury Lawyers (APIL), whose
membership includes about 5,000 solicitors, barristers, legal executives and
academics who are predominantly concerned with injured claimants; and the
Forum of Insurance Lawyers (FOIL), whose members act predominantly or
exclusively for liability insurers.

[19] So far as insurance interests are concerned, in addition to the Association
of British Insurers (ABI), which represents over 400 insurance companies, we also
received submissions from the ATE Group (which contains 15 ATE insurance
interests) and the Liability Insurers' Group (whose members represent 88% of
the total gross premium value of the motor insurance market and about 75% of the
general liability market). The ultimate BTE insurer in this case, DAS Legal
Expenses Insurance Ltd (DAS), chose to be separately represented.

(6) LEI/BTE insurance

[20] Legal expenses insurance was first developed in Europe. Over the years
a positive view has grown up there that people have a social duty to insure

a themselves, in advance whenever possible, against life's adverse events, particularly if this result can be achieved at a modest premium. At the start LEI was offered independently of any other insurance business, but with the opening up of the insurance market in the 1980s other insurance companies wished to offer LEI as well. This meant that a closer association developed between companies which offered LEI and other general insurance providers. Concerns about possible
b conflicts of interest led to the making of an EEC Directive in 1987 and the introduction of statutory regulations pursuant to that directive in this country three years later. We will refer to the terms of these regulations in [24]–[25], below.

[21] In this country LEI has for the most part been sold with other insurance, typically motor and household policies. Its use has grown considerably over the last ten years. In *Callery* [2001] 3 All ER 833 at [18] Lord Woolf CJ noted that in
c 1998 the government disclosed that over 17 million people were now paying premiums for BTE cover at a trivial annual cost to themselves, and that the government was then keen to encourage the wider use of LEI. We were told that BTE insurance is now available in at least five main ways: (i) as part of a motor insurance policy; (ii) as part of a household insurance policy; (iii) as part of an
d employment package (or of the benefits of membership of a trade union or a professional body); (iv) as part of a credit card agreement or charge card service; or (v) by being sold directly as a stand-alone policy (for which, unless there are any unusual features, the cost is unlikely to exceed £20).

[22] The ABI told us that BTE insurance features most commonly as part of a motor insurance policy. Such insurance typically, but not invariably, includes
e cover to enable passengers in the insured vehicle to bring an action either against another driver or against their own driver. In 1999 23·5 million motor vehicles were licensed, and 9·9 million BTE motor polices were sold. This represents a 42% penetration. This market has grown significantly in the last two years, and continues to do so.

f [23] Some of the purposes of Council Directive (EEC) 87/344, on the co-ordination of laws, regulations and administrative provisions relating to legal expenses insurance (OJ 1987 L185 p 77), may be divined from two paragraphs of its preamble:

g 'Whereas, in order to protect insured persons, steps should be taken to preclude, as far as possible, any conflict of interests between a person with legal expenses cover and his insurer arising out of the fact that the latter is covering him in respect of any other class of insurance ... or is covering another person and, should such a conflict arise, to enable it to be resolved ...

Whereas the interest of persons having legal expenses cover means that the
h insured person must be able to choose a lawyer or other person appropriately qualified according to national law in any inquiry or proceedings and whenever a conflict of interests arises ...'

[24] It is unnecessary to refer to the text of the directive because so far as is material it is faithfully reproduced in the Insurance Companies (Legal Expenses
j Insurance) Regulations 1990, SI 1990/1159. Regulation 5 offered a LEI insurer three ways of conducting its business lawfully. The method adopted in the present case is described in reg 5(3) in these terms:

'The company shall entrust the management of claims under legal expenses insurance contracts to an undertaking having separate legal personality, which shall be mentioned in the separate policy or section referred to in regulation 4. If that undertaking has financial, commercial or administrative links with another insurance company which carries on one or more other classes of general insurance business, members of the staff of the undertaking who are concerned with the processing of claims, or with providing legal advice connected with such processing, shall not pursue the same or a similar activity in that other insurance company at the same time.'

[25] Regulation 4 prescribes that if LEI cover is provided under a policy relating to one or more other classes of general insurance business, it must be the subject of a separate section of the policy relating to that cover only, which must specify the nature of the LEI cover. Regulation 6, for its part, is headed 'Freedom to choose lawyer' and provides:

'(1) Where under a legal expenses insurance contract recourse is had to a lawyer (or other person having such qualifications as may be necessary) to defend, represent or serve the interests of the insured in any inquiry or proceedings, the insured shall be free to choose that lawyer (or other person).

(2) The insured shall also be free to choose a lawyer (or other person having such qualifications as may be necessary) to serve his interests whenever a conflict of interests arises.

(3) The above rights shall be expressly recognised in the policy.'

[26] It appears that the insurance ombudsman has consistently interpreted reg 6(1) as meaning that the obligation to permit the insured to select a lawyer of his choice is triggered at the time when efforts to settle a claim by negotiation have failed and legal proceedings have to be initiated.

(7) The practice of an LEI insurer

[27] The ABI showed us a statement by Mr Ross Clark, who is the underwriting and claims manager of First Assist Group Ltd (FGL). This company was formed in 1997 following the merger of two major insurance companies which had each had its own wholly-owned subsidiary handling its LEI business. FGL is one of the largest LEI providers in this country, and since March 1999 it has also been involved in ATE business to an increasing extent. In the BTE market it handles 40,000 motor uninsured loss recovery claims a year, of which 10,000 involve personal injury. He showed us his company's policy booklet, which sets out the extent of the cover provided in simple, intelligible language. FGL is separately managed from its parent, with its own employment contracts and premises, and it also undertakes independent claims handling work on LEI cases for other insurers.

[28] Mr Clark said that FGL adopts the method of conducting its business which is permitted by reg 5(c) of the 1990 regulations. This has led to FGL supporting claims made against its parent company. When legal representation is required, or when a conflict of interest arises, it is the company's practice to recommend firms of solicitors to LEI claimants. The overwhelming majority of these claimants are content to follow FGL's recommendations: they generally want appropriate representation, rather than the services of a particular solicitor.

[29] He said that the LEI insurer has a vested interest in ensuring that the cases which it funds, and for which it bears the adverse costs risk, are properly conducted. Solicitors recommended by LEI insurers are invariably firms with extensive relevant experience and substantial resources to handle the range of

a   actions introduced to them. Those firms (who are sometimes referred to as 'panel' solicitors) in turn have an interest in meeting the insurer's service standards. He was not aware of any evidence to suggest that solicitors chosen by claimants achieved better settlements for their clients than those achieved by panel solicitors. He said that the practice adopted by BTE insurers of monitoring the costs charged by the solicitors representing the claimant has the obvious

b   advantage that the cost to the paying party is generally proportionate and is kept as low as is reasonably practicable.

[30] He also observed that the need to reconcile conflicts of interest was not new to insurance companies. Nor was it limited to LEI. He said that the Norwich Union, which insures about 25% of vehicles on the road, is the largest motor vehicle insurer. He suggested that it was likely that it would be insuring both

c   the vehicles involved in an accident in just over 6% of all claims. Typical claims handling procedures would ensure that the handling of each side of the dispute was kept separate, and that the individuals responsible for handling each claim were prevented from acting together to influence its outcome. Other conflicts of interest might occur where a company insures the defence of one family member

d   against each other.

[31] FGL's experience is that substantial numbers of claims are made by passengers against their drivers, using the cover available to them under the driver's BTE policy. The company creates separate claims for the driver and each passenger and handles them independently. Mr Clark estimates that 100 accidents giving rise to uninsured loss recovery claims will produce 125 separate legal

e   claims, the extra 25 being claims made by passengers. In most cases it is readily apparent which driver is responsible for the accident.

[32] He believes that it is already well known in the market that certain motor insurers include BTE cover for all their policyholders and usually for their passengers, too. He thinks it would be very useful for BTE providers to

f   collaborate to produce a database accessible to claimants' representatives which would identify the motor policies in which BTE cover of different kinds is available. Details of this cover could perhaps be integrated in a database already used by the ABI through its website which gives comparable details in relation to the companies who are participants in a market agreement concerned with credit hire and courtesy car arrangements.

g

(8) *The CIS/DAS arrangements*

[33] Turning to the facts of the present case, we have set out in [6] above the terms of the BTE cover provided by Mr Alam's motor insurance policy. We were told that CIS first added this type of cover to their motor insurance policies in

h   September 1999, and they used DAS as their LEI provider. DAS is a specialist LEI insurer. It is an entirely separate company from CIS. It does not provide or sell any form of motor liability insurance. On the other hand, it provides both BTE and ATE legal expenses insurance. So far as BTE cover is concerned, it is the leading provider of this type of insurance in this country, providing 6·1 million

j   policies, of which 3 million are for motor legal expenses.

[34] The commercial arrangements between CIS and DAS are founded on a reinsurance agreement whereby CIS ceded to DAS by way of reinsurance 100% of the risk undertaken by CIS in the LEI section of its policies. Under this agreement CIS agreed that it would notify all legal expenses claims to DAS and that DAS should administer this insurance on CIS's behalf. It was a term of the agreement that all settlements made by DAS (as administrators of the insurance)

were unconditionally binding on CIS. As reinsurers, DAS agreed to follow the
fortunes of CIS. The agreement contained provisions whereby DAS received its
100% quota share of the premiums set out in a schedule. DAS paid CIS a
commission at an agreed rate on the profits of the business ceded, calculated in
accordance with agreed principles.

[35] None of the matters relating to DAS and its relationship with CIS that are
set out in the two preceding paragraphs of this judgment are apparent on the face
of the policy. Section H of the policy merely provides that DAS will administer
the legal expenses insurance on behalf of CIS. The reader of the policy is left with
the impression that DAS is merely a manager of this particular aspect of CIS's
business.

[36] During the course of the hearing we made a number of inquiries about
the way in which DAS conducted its business. About 80% of the motor claims
DAS handles are damage-only claims, and DAS employs about 150 in-house staff
(who include a relatively small number of lawyers) to deal with such claims. The
remaining 20%, which include personal injury claims, will typically be placed
with a panel firm of solicitors at an early stage.

[37] DAS uses the services of 52 panel firms of solicitors, with 60 offices in
England and Wales. In the part of the country with which this claim is concerned,
there are panel firms in Chester, Wrexham, Manchester and Liverpool. DAS
expects that if distance causes a problem, the solicitor would travel to see the
client. In answer to a question posed by the court, DAS says that it frequently
provides indemnity to persons for whom English is not the language of choice, as
evidenced by the appointment of interpreters for which the company pays.

[38] About seven years ago senior representatives of DAS had a meeting with
the former insurance ombudsman, at which two principles emerged, which DAS
has followed ever since. The first was that if there was a disagreement between
DAS and the insured as to the prospects of the claim, DAS would take counsel's
opinion and would follow it. The second was that reg 6(1) of the 1990 regulations
(as it now is) required freedom of choice of lawyer at and from the time that
proceedings are issued. It has been DAS's experience that very few complaints
are made about freedom to choose a lawyer. Of those that are made, the great
majority appear to DAS to have been generated by the solicitor who runs the risk
of not being instructed.

(9) The conflicting concerns about BTE cover

[39] The issues at the heart of this appeal are of great concern not only to the
immediate parties but also to all the intervenors. Liability insurers believe that if
BTE cover is available for these small motor accident claims the claimants should
use it, and should not saddle them with the cost (upheld in *Callery*) of an ATE
premium and a success fee uplift. BTE insurers wish to hold on to and expand
their business. ATE insurers are worried that if they lose business to BTE
insurers, their premiums may have to rise or they may have to go out of business
altogether. While wishing to hold the ring between the different insurance
interests which are members of the association, the ABI believes that in a case like
the present the BTE insurer should be given precedence. It believes, however,
that there is a market for both BTE and ATE insurance, which should
complement but not duplicate each other, and that each should be allowed to
develop in response to public demand.

[40] APIL and MASS both considered that ATE insurance was the appropriate
choice in a case like the present, and they were supported in this respect by the

a Law Society. FOIL was inclined to take the opposite view. The TUC was concerned that nothing should be decided which might detract from the services trade unions provide for their members through their panel solicitors. These solicitors are now assisting trade union members through collective conditional fee agreements, using either an ATE insurance policy, taken out in the member's name under s 29 of the Access to Justice Act 1999 or arrangements sanctioned by

b s 30 of that Act. The main thrust of the submissions we received from the intervenors who supported the claimant was that the instruction of a solicitor of the client's (or the client's union's) choice, backed by a suitable ATE policy, not only respects the client's entitlement to freedom of choice but is also likely to secure a better result for the client.

c (10) *The appropriateness of BTE cover for small motor accident claims*

[41] In this case we are concerned only with a relatively small personal injuries claim in a road traffic accident. We are not concerned with claims which look as if they will exceed about £5,000, and we are not concerned with any other type of BTE claim. We have no doubt that if a claimant possesses pre-existing BTE cover

d which appears to be satisfactory for a claim of that size, then in the ordinary course of things that claimant should be referred to the relevant BTE insurer.

[42] It will be recalled that in *Callery*, which was an extremely simple passenger's claim, settled for £1,500 plus costs, this court expressed concern ([2001] 3 All ER 833 at [133]) that the costs of the claim exceeded the agreed damages. In addition to disbursements of £617·50, the court allowed an ATE

e premium of £350 and an uplift on the solicitor's costs, by way of a success fee, of 20%. With the type of BTE cover with which this case is concerned (which covers both sides' costs, where necessary) the cost of processing the claim is more likely to be proportionate to the value of the claim, since there will be no uplift and no ATE premium and the cost of the BTE premium (if identifiable) is treated as an

f expense incurred in the past which is irrecoverable.

[43] We received very helpful submissions from MASS, whose members (see para [18], above) collectively have vast experience in conducting personal injury claims. The chairman of MASS told us that in her experience, formed both from her own practice and through her duties with the society, personal interviews are not ordinarily necessary to facilitate claims of this kind. MASS was

g not concerned with the idea that BTE insurers' panel solicitors, whose offices might be a considerable distance from the claimant's home, were inappropriate to handle run-of-the-mill small personal injury claims. On the other hand they considered that in larger cases, or those which raised unusual or difficult issues, it would usually be appropriate for a claimant to elect to purchase an ATE-based

h funding arrangement in preference to invoking a BTE policy, unless it could be shown that the latter was capable from the outset of providing what they described as a bespoke service adequate to the nature of the claim.

[44] In this case we are not concerned either with a larger case or with a case which raised unusual or difficult issues. A judgment concerned with those types

j of case will have to await an appeal where an issue of this kind arises directly for decision. During the course of the hearing, however, members of the court made critical observations from time to time about the size of some of the BTE insurers' panels and the possible inappropriateness in these post-Woolf days of a BTE claimant being denied freedom of choice of solicitor (at any event so far as the members of the Law Society's or some other reputable panel of approved personal injury solicitors are concerned) at the time the procedures in a pre-action protocol come to be activated. We also saw correspondence (which DAS's representatives sought to explain away) that left us uneasy about the terms on which DAS is in practice willing to allow a claimant's solicitor of choice to act for their insured. We do not have to decide any of these matters on the present appeal, however. We only mention them because Mr Leighton Williams QC, for the ABI, told us that insurers welcomed the opportunity afforded by litigation of this type to learn which business practices would be likely to be welcome to a court and which would not.

(11) *Proper practice for a solicitor inquiring about BTE cover*

[45] In our judgment, proper modern practice dictates that a solicitor should normally invite a client to bring to the first interview any relevant motor insurance policy, any household insurance policy and any stand-alone BTE insurance policy belonging to the client and/or any spouse or partner living in the same household as the client. It would seem desirable for solicitors to develop the practice of sending a standard form letter requesting a sight of these documents to the client in advance of the first interview. At the interview the solicitor will also ask the client, as required by para 4(j)(iv) of the client care code (see [14], above), whether his/her liability for costs may be paid by another person, for example an employer or trade union.

[46] If these simple steps are taken, they ought to reduce the burden and extent of the inquiries about which some of the intervenors expressed concern. The solicitor will then be able to read through the policy, and if BTE cover is available, if the motor accident claim is likely to be less than about £5,000, and if there are no features of the cover that make it inappropriate (for instance, if there are a number of potential claimants and the policy cover is only, say, £25,000), the solicitor should refer the client to the BTE insurer without further ado. The solicitor's inquiries should be proportionate to the amount at stake. The solicitor is not obliged to embark on a treasure hunt, seeking to see the insurance policies of every member of the client's family in case by chance they contain relevant BTE cover which the client might use.

[47] Now that motor insurance often contains provision for BTE cover for a claim brought by a passenger, the solicitor should ordinarily ask the client passenger to obtain a copy of the driver's insurance policy, if reasonably practicable. Whether it is reasonably practicable to comply with the solicitor's request is likely to be fact-sensitive. At one end of the spectrum is the driver who is a member of the same family or the same household (as with Mr Sarwar and Mr Alam). At the other is the unknown driver who gave a lift to a hitch-hiker who got hurt in an accident and the driver then disappeared into the night.

[48] If the solicitor sees that the BTE cover contains a stipulation, like the BTE cover in this case, that the driver should consent to its use by the passenger, the solicitor should tell the client to obtain the driver's consent before making a claim on the BTE insurer. It would be professionally inappropriate for the solicitor to do anything to induce the client to encourage the driver to withhold consent. If in due course there was any evidence that this had happened the court would normally disallow both the ATE premium and any success fee claimed. On the other hand, if the driver refuses consent for reasons of his/her own, then it is common ground that the BTE cover would not be available.

[49] So far as credit cards and charge cards are concerned, we have received no evidence of the terms of LEI cover offered by the companies marketing these cards, and we do not know how easy it is for the cardholders to avail themselves

a of such cover in a case like the present. We are inclined to think that the time taken by a solicitor in assisting a client to identify and pursue such cover would at present be likely to result in this course proving more expensive than an ATE premium in this class of case. If, at some time in the future, credit card or charge card companies decide as a matter of business practice to make the extent of any BTE cover they provide readily available to solicitors (either through one of their

b professional journals or guides or on a publicly-accessible website), then the client should also be asked to bring to the first interview any credit card or charge card belonging to him/her and/or any spouse or partner living in the same household.

[50] The guidance we have given in this part of our judgment should not be treated as an inflexible code. The overriding principle is that the claimant, assisted by his/her solicitor, should act in a manner that is reasonable. The availability of

c ATE cover at a modest premium will inevitably restrict the extent to which it will be reasonable for a solicitor's time to be used in investigating alternative sources of insurance.

[51] Mr Nice QC, for Mr Sarwar, submitted that the test of the adequacy of a solicitor's inquiries and advice should be the same as the test applied when

d determining whether a solicitor has been professionally negligent. Thus the client would either recover the cost of the premium or have a claim against his/her solicitor for breach of duty. We deprecate any attempt to equate the question of reasonableness that a costs judge has to decide with the question whether the claimant's solicitor has been in breach of duty to his/her client. If a solicitor gives advice which proves unsound, it will not necessarily follow that the

e advice was negligent. The advice will necessarily be based on information provided by the client. If the information is inadequate or inaccurate, the advice may prove to be unsound without any question of fault on the part of the solicitor.

f (12) *Motor accident claims where the passenger blames the driver*

[52] We consider—and in this respect we differ from the judge—that if there is a reasonable possibility in a passenger claim that the passenger is likely to blame the driver, or the driver the passenger, then if the BTE cover resembles the cover provided by Mr Alam's policy, it is not incumbent on the passenger to use it. The scene we were invited to consider with favour was one in which Mr Sarwar's

g solicitor was under a duty to invite his client to refer the conduct of his claim to Mr Alam's own insurers pursuant to a policy whereby those insurers, through their chosen administrators, would be entitled to 'the full conduct and control of any claim', denying him the opportunity of instructing a suitably qualified solicitor of his own choice except in the unlikely event that legal proceedings had

h to be instituted.

[53] We have no doubt that in the many cases where a passenger is content with the proposed arrangements, reputable BTE insurers endeavour to follow the practices described by Mr Ross Clark and treat each claim on its own merits in a separate compartment. It is also the case that the BTE cover in the present

j case contains an arbitration clause in the event of a dispute as to the handling of a claim. (On the other hand, it contains no mention of DAS's practice of sending the papers to independent counsel for a binding decision if the client is dissatisfied with the sum he/she is being offered.) However, in our judgment, it is not reasonable for a claimant to be required to invoke insurance cover provided by the opponent's camp on terms such as those proffered by CIS. If BTE insurers financed some transparently independent organisation to handle such claims, and made it clear in the policy that this is what they were doing, the position might *a* be different, but we do not see any such transparency or independence in the CIS/DAS arrangements.

[54] Once again, we were influenced by the submissions we received from MASS. They observed that a claimant could not be expected to rely on a BTE policy held by his opponent to fund his litigation. They added:

b

'Moreover, there are obvious concerns as to conflict of interest in any case where a defendant is being sued via his own policy of insurance. It is not enough to say that any damages recovered will be paid by a liability insurer which is a separate legal entity from the BTE insurer. Where liability is disputed, the defendant may very well have a strong personal motivation in resisting the claim (payment of an excess; loss of a no-claims bonus; a *c* stiff-necked refusal to accept the possibility that he drove carelessly—the last can generate remarkable passions). Moreover, it is probable that many claimants would feel uneasy in entrusting the conduct of their claim to the insurer of the opposing party, and would distrust its advice where adverse to their private expectations. Justice should be seen to be done, and the rules of *d* court should support a claimant who elects to fund his claim from a source which is not only neutral and objective, but is seen to be so.'

[55] We accept these submissions. Although as a matter of law an arbitration provision might be thought adequate to allay a claimant's fears of receiving less than objective advice, we consider that a claimant is entitled to feel comfortable *e* with the objectivity of the representative who is looking after his/her claim, and that the concerns which MASS identifies are reasonable concerns.

[56] We are not, however, persuaded by the Law Society's contention that there is such a strong public interest in maintaining a client's freedom of choice of legal adviser that this should override the appropriateness of a claim as small *f* as that with which we are concerned on this appeal being handled by a BTE insurer with or without the assistance of a panel solicitor. The philosophy contained in CPR 1.1(2)(c), and the express provisions of r 44.5, require the court to ensure that no costs are incurred which are not reasonable and proportionate. While we would not interpret the sensible non-exhaustive guidance given in paras 11.7–11.10 of the Costs Practice Direction as if they were the words of a *g* statute, they point the reader towards an inquiry into the availability of alternative funding arrangements which might be less expensive. The same principle is now set out in reg 4 of the 2000 regulations.

[57] In *R v Legal Aid Board, ex p Duncan* [2000] COD 159 the Divisional Court (at paras 444–468) rejected the applicant solicitors' contention that their clients had a *h* common law right to representation by the solicitor of their choice notwithstanding that they were unable to pay for the solicitor's services themselves and the limitations on the choice of a publicly-funded solicitor were prescribed by Parliament. We do not consider that it is necessary to repeat here the powerful dictum of Neuberger J in *Maltez v Lewis* (2000) 19 Const LJ 65, quoted in para 459 *j* of that judgment. It is sufficient to record that he observed that the right of any citizen to be represented by advocates and/or solicitors of his or her choice may be cut down by circumstances. One of the circumstances which may cut it down is the consideration that the cost of instructing a solicitor of the client's choice (and protecting the client from the risk of paying the other side's costs) is disproportionate to the value of the proposed claim when an alternative, reasonable,

a method of advancing the client's interests with the help of an appropriately qualified lawyer is available.

[58] On the other hand we accept Mr Drabble's submission that representation arranged by the insurer of the opposing party, pursuant to a policy to which the claimant had never been a party, and of which he/she had no knowledge at the time it was entered into, and where the opposing insurer through its chosen

b representative reserves to itself the full conduct and control of the claim, is not a reasonable alternative. Mr Birts QC, for Mr Alam, sought to persuade us that as a matter of rationality and logic there ought to be no reasonable perception that there might be a conflict of interest in the CIS/DAS arrangements when the contractual provisions of the BTE cover are studied carefully. We do not accept this submission. However careful these insurers may have attempted to be,

c appearances matter, and appearances are very hostile to the notion that a passenger like Mr Sarwar should be obliged to go to the driver's insurers and entrust them with the full conduct and control of his claim when he wishes to sue the driver.

d (13) *The concerns of the ATE Group and the TUC*

[59] We have considered carefully the submissions we received from the ATE Group and the TUC. The former was naturally anxious that we should make no decision which might prejudice the development of the fledgling ATE market and drive up ATE premiums to a level which might impede access to justice. APIL also shared this worry. The TUC, for its part, was anxious that we should

e not imperil the dedicated services trade unions and their panel lawyers offer to their members. In the context of the simple small claims with which this judgment is concerned we do not consider that either of these considerations should impel us to impose on defendants and their liability insurers a burden of costs which is disproportionate to both the value and the lack of complexity of

f the claim. We accept the submission of the Liability Insurers' Group that it is not in the interests of motorists or the general public that motor liability insurers should have to make unnecessary disbursements which raise premium costs.

(14) *How this judgment fits in with the judgment in Callery*

[60] We do not consider that there is anything in this judgment which is

g inconsistent with the judgment of this court in *Callery*. In *Callery* [2001] 3 All ER 833 at [91] Lord Woolf CJ said that the court considered that it would normally be reasonable for a CFA to be concluded and ATE cover taken out on the occasion that the claimant first instructed his solicitors. In *Callery* the court was not invited to consider the implications of the solicitors' client care code or the

h possible availability of BTE cover. If the client is able to comply with the request contained in the suggested letter which he/she receives before the first interview (see [45], above) then there is no reason why the course suggested in *Callery* should not be adopted as soon as the solicitor is satisfied that no appropriate BTE cover is available. If this inquiry cannot be satisfactorily resolved at that first

j interview the steps mentioned in para [91] of the *Callery* judgment should not be taken until such further inquiries into the availability of BTE cover as are reasonable and proportionate to the value of the claim have been concluded.

(15) *Why we differ from the judge*

[61] Finally, we remind ourselves that this court is not entitled to set aside the judgment of Judge Halbert unless we consider it was clearly wrong. While we

would wish to applaud the judge for an admirably clear judgment we consider
that he was clearly wrong when he decided that the BTE policy provided   *a*
Mr Sarwar with appropriate cover in the circumstances of this case.   We
therefore allow the appeal.

Appeal allowed. Permission to appeal to the House of Lords refused.

Melanie Martyn   Barrister.

a

Director of Public Prosecutions v Ara
[2001] EWHC Admin 493

QUEEN'S BENCH DIVISION, DIVISIONAL COURT

ROSE LJ AND SILBER J

b

21 JUNE 2001

Police – Disclosure of information – Interview – Caution – Police officer interviewing suspect without a solicitor present – Suspect making admission – Officer concluding that admission rendering suspect suitable for caution – Police refusing request by suspect's solicitor to disclose *c* *contents of interview – Non-disclosure preventing solicitor from giving informed advice on whether to accept caution – Police charging suspect – Whether police having duty to disclose contents of interview to suspect's solicitor for purpose of enabling him to advise on acceptance of caution – Whether failure to give such disclosure rendering subsequent prosecution an abuse of process.*

d

The respondent, A, was suspected of committing an assault occasioning actual bodily harm. Four days after the alleged assault, A was interviewed by a police constable at a police station with no solicitor present. In the course of that interview, A made an admission which, in the view of the constable, rendered him suitable for a caution. The constable informed A that the final decision about whether he would *e* be offered a caution rested with his supervising officer. After being released on bail, A instructed a solicitor who sought a copy of the taped interview from the police. That request was refused. Some weeks later, A and his solicitor attended at the police station where a caution was offered. A's solicitor informed the supervising officer that, as he did not have a copy of the interview, he was unable to advise his *f* client as to the issue of a caution and therefore had no option but to advise him to contest the allegation. A was then charged. At trial, A contended that the police had a duty to disclose the terms of the interview to enable an appropriate advice to be given by his solicitor as to whether or not to consent to the caution, that no such advice could be given in the absence of such disclosure and that accordingly the decision to prosecute was an abuse of process necessitating a stay of the proceedings. *g* That contention was accepted by the justices who duly granted the stay. The prosecution appealed by way of case stated.

Held – The police had a duty to supply disclosure of a previous interview to a suspect's solicitor so that the solicitor could advise the suspect whether or not to *h* consent to a caution. It was not in the public interest or in the interest of a suspect that criminal proceedings should be instituted and pursued in relation to a person whom the police were prepared merely to caution when that suspect was prepared to accept such a caution. The question of whether or not a person should accept a caution was inextricably linked with his entitlement to legal advice and to the necessary prerequisite to informed legal advice, namely that those advising a suspect *j* knew accurately the terms of the interview on the basis of which the police were prepared to issue a caution. It was the common experience of those involved in criminal cases that a suspect might have an inaccurate recollection of what he had said in the course of a police interview, even when that recollection was tested within a few days of the interview taking place. However, such a duty of disclosure did not mean that the police had a general obligation to disclose material prior to charge. That would be impracticable in many cases and highly undesirable in some, as well as being outwith the contemplation of the Police and Criminal Evidence Act 1984, the code of practice made under that Act or anything to be implied from them. *a* In the circumstances of the instant case, the failure to disclose the terms of the interview, followed by the institution and pursuit of criminal proceedings, amply justified the justices in concluding that the proceedings should be stayed as an abuse of process. Accordingly, the appeal would be dismissed (see [23]–[26], below).

b

Notes
For interviews in police stations, see 11(1) *Halsbury's Laws* (4th edn reissue) para 738.

Cases referred to in judgments
R v Croydon JJ, ex p Dean [1993] 3 All ER 129, [1993] QB 769, [1993] 3 WLR 198, DC.
R v DPP, ex p Lee [1999] 2 All ER 737, [1999] 1 WLR 1950, DC.   *c*
Wildman v DPP [2001] EWHC Admin 14, DC.

Case stated
The Director of Public Prosecutions (DPP) appealed by way of case stated from the decision of the North Surrey Justices sitting at Staines Magistrates Court on 24 January *d* 2001 granting an application by the respondent, Damian Sebastian Ara, to stay criminal proceedings againt him on the grounds of abuse of process. The facts are set out in the judgment of Rose LJ.

Richard Germain (instructed by the *Crown Prosecution Service*, Guildford) for the DPP.
Donald Broatch (instructed by *Azzopardi & Co*) for the respondent.   *e*

ROSE LJ.
  [1] There is before the court an appeal by way of case stated by the Director of Public Prosecutions. He challenges a decision of the North Surrey Justices sitting at Staines Magistrates Court on 24 January 2001 to stay proceedings against the *f* respondent defendant, for an offence of assault occasioning actual bodily harm, contrary to s 47 of the Offences Against the Person Act 1861, as an abuse of process.
  [2] The circumstances of this matter appear from the case stated. On 13 August 2000 an information was preferred by the appellant against the respondent alleging assault occasioning actual bodily harm on 8 June 2000. The justices, having heard the arguments on 24 January 2001, found the following facts. The respondent was *g* interviewed by a police constable on 12 June with no solicitor present. In the course of that interview (which was recorded) he made an admission which, in the view of that police constable, rendered him suitable for caution. At that time the officer explained to the respondent that the police might not proceed to charge, but the final decision in relation to caution would rest with a supervising officer. Thereafter on *h* that day, 12 June, the respondent was released on bail. He then instructed a solicitor.
  [3] On 21 June his solicitor wrote to the Staines police seeking a copy of the taped interview and a copy of the custody record. It is accepted before us that the respondent was entitled to a copy of the custody record and the ultimate refusal to disclose it was a breach of para C2.4 of the Code of Practice in relation to detention, treatment and questioning made under the Police and Criminal Evidence Act 1984; *j* but nothing turns on that for present purposes.
  [4] On 26 June the Staines custody inspector wrote to the respondent's solicitor declining his request. Thereafter, in writing and on the telephone, the solicitor made further requests for disclosure; none took place.
  [5] On 13 August the respondent and his solicitor attended Staines Police Station. The justices found that a caution was to be offered on that occasion on the

a   recommendation of the constable who had interviewed the respondent, subject to verification by the supervising officer. On 13 August the solicitor made it clear to the supervising officer that he did not have a record of the interview on 12 June to enable him to advise the respondent as to the issue of a caution.

[6] In consequence, the justices found, the solicitor indicated that there was no option but for him to advise the respondent to contest the allegation because he
b   could not advise the acceptance of a caution. In addition, the solicitor said that the defendant had at least 20 witnesses to establish self-defence. These events having occurred, the supervising officer proceeded to charge the respondent with assault occasioning actual bodily harm.

[7] The case rehearses the rival contentions advanced before the justices which are, in most respects, similar to the contentions which have been advanced in this
c   court. In essence, it was contended on behalf of the respondent that the police had a duty to disclose the terms of the interview to enable an appropriate advice to be given by the solicitor as to whether or not to consent to a caution. Absent disclosure, no appropriate advice could be given and, in consequence, the subsequent decision to prosecute was an abuse.

d   [8] On behalf of the prosecution it was contended that there was no duty to effect disclosure of this kind prior to charge, the relevant code of practice dealing, as it does, with matters subsequent to charge. It was also contended that disclosure would have made no difference; no formal offer of caution had been made because of the solicitor's indication of the defence reliance on self-defence. It was contended that informed consent to caution only required that the defendant should understand
e   the effect of a caution and what he would be accepting. It was also contended that the prosecution were under a duty to keep the case under review and the opportunity to dispose of it by way of caution might still have been available if an unambiguous admission had been made subsequently by the defence. Finally, it was contended that lack of disclosure did not render the subsequent proceedings an abuse necessitating
f   a stay.

[9] The justices in the case, having been referred to a number of authorities including one decision of the European Court of Human Rights and another of the European Commission of Human Rights, were of the opinion that the primary purpose of the attendance on 13 August was for a decision to be made as to a caution, or whether the respondent should be charged. They were of the view that a formal
g   offer of caution would only have been made after the supervising officer had taken account of the gravity of the matters alleged and aggravating and mitigating features and hearing the views of the interviewing officer and having been satisfied as to the existence of a reliable admission and the likelihood of consent to a caution. The justices were of the opinion that the only reason no formal caution was offered was
h   the comments by the solicitor that he, in the absence of evidence of guilt, had no option but to advise that he contest the allegation on the grounds of self-defence.

[10] The justices said that the failure to provide material to enable the solicitor to assess the prosecution case against the client prevented the solicitor from effectively participating by providing informed advice as to a caution; and informed consent,
j   the justices concluded, encompassed not only the respondent's understanding of the effect of a caution but also the reason why he should admit the offence and accept a caution as being appropriate.

[11] As a result of the lack of disclosure and the consequential inability of the respondent to receive appropriate advice, the justices concluded that the question of a caution was no longer an option. In so far as it is of any relevance, it is apparent from the endorsement of defence counsel's brief on 17 August, to which Mr Germain first drew our attention, that a caution was not going to be reconsidered. Although

that document was, of course, not before the justices, it demonstrates the
correctness of that particular conclusion on their part. The crucial conclusion of   *a*
the justices was that the failure to disclose precluded the giving of appropriate advice
and the subsequent commencement of criminal proceedings amounted to an abuse
necessitating a stay. The justices then pose two questions for the consideration of
this court, to which later I shall return.

[12] On behalf of the Director of Public Prosecutions, Mr Germain first submits   *b*
that the justices should never have ruled on the application for a stay at all, but
should have remitted the matter to the Divisional Court for consideration. For my
part, I am unable to accept that submission. Quite apart from the fact that neither
prosecution nor defence invited the justices to remit this matter for the consideration
of the Divisional Court, it does not seem to me to be one of such complexity as
would properly require the justices to remit the matter to this court rather than to   *c*
deal with it themselves.

[13] Mr Germain submits, rightly, that para E4.16 of the Code of Practice in
relation to the taping of interviews made under s 60 of the 1984 Act does not impose
a duty of disclosure prior to charge. He submits that, if a general duty of disclosure
prior to charge were to be imposed upon the police it would result in the withering   *d*
of the caution process because the police would simply not bother to caution; if
they had a general duty of disclosure, they would merely proceed to charge. The
decision as to whether to caution is always a matter for the police (see Home
Office circular 18/1994 (para 3) (cautioning of offenders)).

[14] Mr Germain submitted that the request for disclosure of the terms of the
interview did not affect the present case because the reference to the number of   *e*
witnesses capable of establishing self-defence indicates that no caution would have
been accepted by the defence. The difficulty with that submission, as it seems to me,
is that, in part, it is at variance with the findings of the justices, but, more
significantly, it does not address the impact of non-disclosure upon the ability of the
respondent's solicitor properly to advise him. Mr Germain rightly accepts that a   *f*
defendant is entitled to legal advice as to whether or not he should agree to a caution.
In my judgment, such legal advice can only be of value, if indeed it can be given at
all, if it is given with knowledge of what admissions, if any, have been made by his
client as to guilt of the offence in relation to which the possibility of a caution arises.

[15] Mr Germain rebutted the reliance on European authorities on behalf of the
respondent by reference to a judgment of Lord Woolf CJ in *Wildman v DPP* [2001]   *g*
EWHC Admin 14. In that judgment, having referred to certain European Court
authorities, Lord Woolf CJ said (at [10]) that that jurisprudence could not and should
not be applied directly to the procedures in the English jurisdiction:

'... whether access to documents is to be granted, and when it is to be granted,   *h*
must depend upon the particular domestic procedure which is being brought
into play in proceedings before the courts in this jurisdiction.'

[16] At the invitation of the court, Mr Germain commented upon *R v DPP, ex p Lee*
[1999] 2 All ER 737, [1999] 1 WLR 1950. Kennedy LJ said by reference to the
Criminal Procedure and Investigations Act 1996:   *j*

'The 1996 Act does not specifically address the period between arrest and
committal, and whereas in most cases prosecution disclosure can wait until
after committal without jeopardising the defendant's right to a fair trial the
prosecutor must always be alive to the need to make advance disclosure of
material of which he is aware (either from his own consideration of the papers

a   or because his attention has been drawn to it by the defence) and which he, as a
responsible prosecutor, recognises should be disclosed at an earlier stage.
Examples canvassed before us were—(a) previous convictions of a complainant
or deceased if that information could reasonably be expected to assist the defence
when applying for bail; (b) material which might enable a defendant to make a
pre-committal application to stay the proceedings as an abuse of process ...'
b   (See [1999] 2 All ER 737 at 749, [1999] 1 WLR 1950 at 1962.)

[17] There are references to other examples which are not presently material.
Mr Germain submitted that that passage applied only to the prosecutor and does not
apply to the police.

[18] On behalf of the respondent, Mr Broatch stressed that para (2) of the Home
c   Office circular in relation to cautioning requires that 'the offender must admit the
offence' and 'must understand the significance of the caution and give informed
consent to being cautioned'. He accepted that procedures in relation to the offering
and acceptance of a caution are not provided for by any Act or code, but, he
submitted, the 1996 Act and the Code of Practice made under it give some clue as to
the appropriate approach to disclosure in such a case. He does not seek to suggest,
d   in view of *Wildman's* case, that art 6 of the European Convention for the Protection
of Human Rights and Fundamental Freedoms (Rome, 4 November 1950; TS 71
(1953); Cmd 8969) (as set out in Sch 1 to the Human Rights Act 1998) confers an
entitlement at the pre-charge stage to the full disclosure which is appropriate before
a fair trial can be held. But, he submitted, that does not mean that there is no
e   entitlement to disclosure of any kind before charge. In support of that submission
he too relied upon a passage in the judgment of Lord Woolf CJ in *Wildman's* case.
Having referred to the custody time limits, an application to extend which was the
subject of debate in that case, Lord Woolf CJ said (at [24]):

'... it is to be hoped that in the majority of cases it is will be possible for the
f   Crown Prosecution Service to make information available to a defendant, prior
to the application being made, which will enable him or her to be satisfied as to
the propriety of the application. In so far as it is necessary for a defendant to test
any aspect of the application, then the means must be provided to enable him
or her to do that. However, formal disclosure of the sort which is appropriate
prior to the trial will not normally be necessary in regard to an application either
g   for bail or for an extension of time limits.'

[19] Mr Broatch accepted that questions as to bail and the extension of time limits
can only arise after a defendant has been charged. But, he submits, the ability of a
defendant to satisfy himself or herself 'as to the propriety of the application' affords
h   some sustenance to the argument that, in relation to the propriety or otherwise of
agreeing to accept a caution, a defendant is entitled to have disclosed to those
advising him the terms of his interview with the police. Also, submits Mr Broatch,
the entitlement to material goes substantially beyond that suggested on behalf of the
Crown which is limited to information sufficient to realise what the caution means.

[20] Mr Broatch submits that, on the facts found by the justices, the respondent
j   looked set to avoid a trial and the risk of conviction. That prospect was obstructed
because of the refusal of the police to disclose the terms of the interview. Mr Broatch
submitted that no material distinction is to be drawn between police and prosecutor
in relation to the obligation to disclose as outlined by Kennedy LJ.

[21] Mr Broatch also relied upon *R v Croydon JJ, ex p Dean* [1993] 3 All ER 129,
[1993] QB 769 and, in particular, a passage in the judgment of Staughton LJ:

'In my judgment the prosecution of a person who has received a promise, undertaking or representation from the police that he will not be prosecuted is capable of being an abuse of process. Mr Collins was eventually disposed to concede as much, provided (i) that the promisor had power to decide, and (ii) that the case was one of bad faith or something akin to that. I do not accept either of those requirements as essential.' (See [1993] 3 All ER 129 at 137, [1993] QB 769 at 778.)

[22] Mr Germain distinguished that case on the basis that, in the present case, no promise had been made to the respondent. All that had been said to him was that he could be considered for a caution, but the final decision was down to the supervising officer. The prosecution approach in the present case, Mr Broatch submitted, effectively meant: 'Accept the caution blind or be prosecuted.'

[23] The first question posed by the case stated is whether the justices were correct in deciding that there is a duty upon the police to supply disclosure of a previous interview to a suspect's solicitor in order that he could advise the suspect whether or not to consent to caution. The second question is whether, if so, they were correct in further determining that lack of such disclosure rendered the subsequent criminal proceedings such an abuse as to necessitate a stay.

[24] For my part, I would answer both those questions in the affirmative. It seems, to my mind, that it is not in the public interest or the interest of a defendant that criminal proceedings should be instituted and pursued against a defendant in relation to whom the police are prepared merely to caution when that defendant is prepared to accept such a caution. That is perhaps a statement of the obvious, because it underlies the cautioning regime. To my mind, the question of whether or not a defendant should accept a caution is inextricably linked with his entitlement, as Mr Germain concedes, to legal advice and to the necessary prerequisite for informed legal advice, that those advising know accurately the terms of the interview on the basis of which the police are prepared to issue a caution. It is the common experience of those involved in criminal cases that a suspected person may himself have an inaccurate recollection of what he said in the course of a police interview, even when that recollection is tested, as clearly it was capable of being in the present case, within a few days of the interview taking place.

[25] In my judgment, in the present case, the justices were fully entitled to conclude that the proceedings should be stayed as an abuse of process, the police having refused to disclose the terms of the interview, without which informed advice and informed consent to a caution could not properly be given. I make it clear that this does not mean that there is a general obligation on the police to disclose material prior to charge. That would, in many cases, be impracticable and, in some cases (for example where there is an ongoing investigation) highly undesirable, as well as being outwith the contemplation of the legislation, the code or anything to be implied therefrom. But, in the present case, the failure to disclose the terms of the interview followed by the institution and pursuit of a criminal trial in the circumstances described amply justified the justices in reaching the conclusion which they did. Therefore, I would dismiss this appeal.

SILBER J.
[26] I agree.

Appeal dismissed.

Dilys Tausz　　Barrister.

a
R (on the application of Beresford) v Sunderland City Council

[2001] EWCA Civ 1218

b
COURT OF APPEAL (CIVIL DIVISION)
LATHAM, DYSON LJJ AND WILSON J
16, 26 JULY 2001

Commons – Registration – Town or village green – User as of right – Publicly-owned sports arena – Whether implied permission capable of defeating claim to user as of right – Commons Registration Act 1965, s 22(1).

c

The respondent local authority was the registration authority for the purposes of registering and maintaining a register of town and village greens within its area pursuant to the Commons Registration Act 1965. Section 22(1)[a] of that Act defined

d 'Town or village green' as, inter alia, land on which the inhabitants of any locality had indulged in lawful sports and pastimes 'as of right' for not less than 20 years. The appellant, B, and other local residents submitted an application to the authority for a certain open space to be registered as a town green on the grounds that it had been so used for the relevant period. The site, which was adjacent to a park, was on publicly-owned land, had been laid out as an arena with seating

e and had been maintained initially by a development corporation and subsequently by the authority. In its decision, the authority's licensing committee referred to those facts, expressed the view that it was difficult to conceive that anyone could have imagined that the site was other than a recreational area provided for use by the public for recreation, and concluded that there had been an implied permission

f to use the land which was sufficient to defeat the claim of use 'as of right'. Accordingly, the application was dismissed, and B applied for judicial review, contending, inter alia, that an implied permission was not sufficient to defeat a claim as of right. That contention was rejected by the judge who dismissed the application. On B's appeal, she contended that there had to be some overt and contemporaneous expression of permission before a landowner could defeat a

g claim on the ground that the use was permissive, and that, as a matter of principle, the only way such expression could be given was orally or in writing. Alternatively, B contended that the committee had taken into account a number of irrelevant considerations in concluding that there had been an implied permission to use the site for lawful sports and pastimes.

h

Held – For the purposes of s 22(1) of the 1965 Act, there was no reason in principle why an implied permission could not defeat a claim to use as of right. There was a distinction between an owner's acquiescence in, or toleration of the use of, his land by others for lawful sports or pastimes, and his giving licence or

j permission for such use. In some contexts, it might be that there was little or no difference in meaning between the two concepts, but in the context of the law relating to prescription, the difference was fundamental, since use which was merely acquiesced in by the owner was prima facie 'as of right', although it might be defeated if the owner could show, inter alia, that he had permitted it.

---

a   Section 22, so far as material, is set out at [1], below

Permission involved some positive act or acts on the part of the owner, whereas passive toleration was all that was required for acquiescence. The positive act or acts might take different forms. The grant of oral or written consent was the most obvious expression of permission, but there was no reason in principle why the grant of permission should be confined to such cases. Although most cases where nothing had been said or written would properly be classified as cases of mere acquiescence, there was no reason why permission could not be inferred from an owner's overt and contemporaneous acts. In the instant case, little weight was to be attached, on its own, to the fact that the land was publicly owned, and the fact that the site was adjacent to the park was irrelevant. Notwithstanding that, to a limited extent, the committee had taken into account irrelevant considerations, they had been immaterial to its ultimate decision. That decision had been based on objectively ascertainable facts from which the committee could reasonably have concluded that there had been user by implied permission. Accordingly, the appeal would be dismissed (see [10]–[14], [26], [30], [31], [33]–[36], below).

R v Oxfordshire County Council, ex p Sunningwell Parish Council [1999] 3 All ER 385 considered.

Notes

For essential features of a town or village green, see 6 *Halsbury's Laws* (4th edn reissue) para 525.

For the Commons Registration Act 1965, s 22, see 7 *Halsbury's Statutes* (4th edn) (1999 reissue) 696.

Cases referred to in judgments

Associated Provincial Picture Houses Ltd v Wednesbury Corp [1947] 2 All ER 680, [1947] 2 KB 223, CA.
Bright v Walker (1834) 1 Cr M&R 211, [1824–34] All ER Rep 762.
Dalton v Angus & Co (1881) 6 App Cas 740, [1881-5] All ER Rep 1, HL.
De la Warr (Earl) v Miles (1881) 17 Ch D 536, [1881–5] All ER Rep 252, CA.
Gardner v Hodgson's Kingston Brewery Co Ltd [1903] AC 229, HL.
Merstham Manor Ltd v Coulsdon and Purley UDC [1936] 2 All ER 422, [1937] 2 KB 77.
Mills v Colchester Corp (1867) LR 2 CP 476.
Public Works Comrs v Angus & Co, Dalton v Angus & Co (1881) 6 App Cas 740, [1881–5] All ER Rep 1, HL.
R v Oxfordshire CC, ex p Sunningwell Parish Council [1999] 3 All ER 385, [2000] 1 AC 335, [1999] 3 WLR 160, HL.
Robson v Hallett [1967] 2 All ER 407, [1967] 2 QB 939, [1967] 3 WLR 28, DC.

Cases also cited or referred to in skeleton arguments

Mills v Silver [1991] 1 All ER 449, [1991] Ch 271, CA.
R v Secretary of State for the Environment, ex p Billson [1998] 2 All ER 587, [1999] QB 374.
R v Suffolk County Council, ex p Steed (1996) 75 P & CR 102, CA.

Appeal

The appellant, Pamela Beresford, appealed from the decision of Smith J ([2001] 1 WLR 1327) on 14 November 2000 dismissing her application for judicial review of the decision of the licensing committee of the respondent, Sunderland City Council, on 27 April 2000 rejecting an application by the appellant and three other *a* local residents for land known as the Sports Arena, adjacent to Princess Anne Park, Washington, Tyne-and-Wear, to be registered as a town green under the Commons Registration Act 1965. The facts are set out in the judgment of Dyson LJ.

b *Sheila Cameron QC* and *Douglas Edwards* (instructed by *Southern Stewart & Walker,* South Shields) for the appellant.
Philip Petchey (instructed by *Colin Langley*) for the council.

Cur adv vult

c 26 July 2001. The following judgments were delivered.

DYSON LJ (giving the first judgment at the invitation of Latham LJ).

INTRODUCTION
    [1] The appellant is a resident of Washington, Tyne-and-Wear in the administrative area of the City of Sunderland (the council). The council is *d* the registration authority for the purposes of registering and maintaining a register of town and village greens within the city pursuant to s 3 of the Commons Registration Act 1965. On 18 November 1999, the appellant, together with three other local residents, submitted an application for land known as 'the Sports Arena' adjacent to Princess Anne Park, Washington to be registered as a town green, and for the Town and Village Greens Register to be amended *e* accordingly pursuant to s 13 of the 1965 Act. On 27 April 2000, the licensing committee of the council refused the application. The sole ground on which the application was refused was that the use which was found to have been made of the Sports Arena for more than 20 years by local inhabitants was not 'as of right'. The committee decided that there had been an implied permission to use the land *f* which was sufficient to defeat the claim that there had been use 'as of right' within the meaning of the definition of 'town and village green' in s 22(1) of the 1965 Act, which is in these terms:

'"Town or village green" means land which has been allotted by or under any Act for the exercise or recreation of the inhabitants of any locality or on *g* which the inhabitants of any locality have a customary right to indulge in lawful sports and pastimes or on which the inhabitants of any locality have indulged in such sports and pastimes as of right for not less than twenty years.'

    [2] The appellant challenged that decision by judicial review. Two issues *h* were raised: (a) can an implied permission to use land defeat a claim to use of a town or village green for lawful sports and pastimes 'as of right'; and (b) if Yes, should the decision of 27 April 2000 be quashed on the grounds that it was legally flawed in one or more of the respects alleged by the appellant? Smith J answered (a) affirmatively, and (b) in the negative (see [2001] 1 WLR 1327). On behalf of *j* the appellant, Miss Cameron QC submits that both conclusions of the judge were wrong. The first issue is an issue of considerable general importance, on which there is no direct previously decided authority.

The facts
    [3] The Sports Arena lies at the northern end of Princess Anne Park and to the south of Washington town centre. Princess Anne Park is a large landscaped

parkland area. The Sports Arena is not part of the Park itself, being separated
from it by a low mound thickly planted with trees. It is a grass arena formed
within double rows of wooden benches which surround its northern, western
and southern edges. It was originally laid out by the Washington Development
Corp (WDC) in 1973–1974 using excavated soil from the shopping centre
development. In the Washington New Town Plan of 1973, the Sports Arena site
was included within an area identified as 'parkland/open space/major playing
field'. The perimeter seating (for 1,100 people) was added in 1977, and a non-turf
cricket wicket was constructed in 1979. Throughout the period of more than 20
years up to 18 November 1999, the grass was kept cut by the owners from time
to time.

[4] A handwritten draft report was submitted to the WDC's Chief Officers
Committee on 26 July 1982. This was referred to in the report prepared for the
licensing committee meeting of 27 April 2000. The draft report itself has not been
produced in evidence, although it was said in the report for the meeting of
27 April to be 'on an archived WDC file relating to the town centre'. According
to the report for the meeting of 27 April, the draft report for the meeting of 26 July
1982 referred to a 'Board paper 132/77', which stated that in the interim period,
before a sports complex could be provided, the arena was 'to be made available
for recreational sporting use and other activities on a town scale such as jazz band
parades, displays and sporting events'. There is no evidence as to what became
of the board paper, or what use was made of it by the board.

[5] In 1989, the Sports Arena site was transferred by the WDC to the
Commission for the New Towns (CNT) as part of the general disposition of assets
of the WDC on its winding-up. In 1991, certain community-related assets of the
CNT were transferred to the council. The Sports Arena was retained by the CNT
at that time since it was thought to have potential long-term commercial value.

[6] In 1996, the site was transferred by the CNT to the council. On 24 December
1998, planning permission was granted for the erection of a college of further
education on land which included the Sports Arena. As I have already said, the
application to register the site as a town green was made on 18 November 1999.

The decision of 27 April 2000

[7] The licensing committee was provided with a comprehensive report by
the director of administration. It is a model of its kind. It set out the facts clearly
and fairly, and provided an impressive exposition of the law in an area in which
there was no previous direct authority. Having set the history of the site as I have
described it, the report summarised the use to which the Sports Arena had been
put since its creation. In general terms, the site had been used as amenity open
space and a kickabout area for a period of at least 20 years. The amenity uses
included walking, football, picnics, cricket etc. Having set out in some detail the
arguments advanced in support of the application to register, and the grounds of
objection put forward by the City of Sunderland College, the report dealt with
the issues that arose. It seemed to the writer of the report that the site had been
used for lawful sports and pastimes for a period of at least 20 years prior to the
date of the application. The two questions for consideration were (a) whether the
enjoyment was by the inhabitants of the locality, and (b) whether the enjoyment
was as of right. No issue arises as to (a), and I shall say no more about it. As for (b),
the report referred to the decision of the House of Lords in *R v Oxfordshire CC, ex p
Sunningwell Parish Council* [1999] 3 All ER 385, [2000] 1 AC 335, and advised the

a committee that it was not enough to defeat a claim based on 20-year use that the use had been *tolerated* by the landowner. The report continued:

> 'In "traditional" parks which are fenced and have opening hours, enjoyment by the public (inhabitants of the locality) will be by virtue of a licence during the hours of daylight. However not all parks conform to this "traditional" model—the Princess Anne Park for example—and it would be
> *b* bizarre if these were all town and village greens. This would suggest that if it is apparent from the circumstances that the land in question has been made available to the public, and that their use has not simply been tolerated but in effect encouraged, a licence should be implied from the circumstances. It may be noted from the documents submitted with the application that the
> *c* applicants know a great deal of the history of the application site and the circumstances in which it was made available for public use. However it is not clear how far, if at all, reliance can be placed upon this material as demonstrating that the use has been by way of licence. However everyone using the site would have been aware of the perimeter seating and that the grass was kept cut. It is difficult to conceive that anyone could have imagined
> *d* that this was other than a recreational area provided for use by the public for recreation. Against this background the "implied licence" argument is strong and it is considered that on this basis the enjoyment has not been "as of right". The argument is stronger if references were to be made to the history (see section 2 above), however members are advised to treat this history with
> *e* caution as there does not appear to be any public document indicating that the land was being made available by a public authority for public use (although the 1973 New Town Plan comes close to this). This is a developing area of the law and it cannot be said that the legal position is clear. There is no authority on the implied licence argument and it may be criticised that it runs counter to the guidance of the House of Lords in the case of *Sunningwell* that
> *f* a tolerated use may be as of right. However there is clear authority for saying that a licence does not have to be communicated to the Licensees who may indeed, in ignorance of the licence, *believe* that their use is as of right. On balance in the circumstances of the present written application it is difficult to conclude that the use had been as of right.'

g [8] After hearing submissions, the committee decided to refuse the application on the following grounds:

> '(a) Members were satisfied that evidence showed the use of the Sports Arena for "lawful sports and pastimes" by the inhabitants of Washington for
> *h* a period of at least 20 years prior to the making of the application, the level of use being more than trivial or sporadic. The real issue for consideration was whether there had been permission or a licence to use the site in this way.
> (b) Having taken legal advice, members were satisfied that an implied licence would be sufficient to defeat the application, provided that there was
> *j* sufficient evidence to support the existence of a licence.
> (c) Members considered that there was evidence of an implied licence since the site is publicly owned land, specifically laid out as an arena with seating, which is adjacent to the Princess Anne Park and which has been maintained by the Council and the Washington Development Corporation before it. Members agreed with the comment in the report that "it is difficult

to conceive that anyone could have imagined that this was other than a
recreational area, provided for use by the public for recreation." The other
information contained in Section 2 of the report, whilst not in itself conclusive,
supported the view that the Sports Arena was intended for public use.'

THE FIRST ISSUE: CAN A CLAIM TO USE OF LAND 'AS OF RIGHT' BE DEFEATED BY IMPLIED
PERMISSION?

As a matter of principle

[9] Miss Cameron submits as follows. The concept of use 'as of right' connotes
use 'without force, stealth or permission' or 'nec vi, nec clam, nec precario'. There
must be some overt and contemporaneous expression of permission before a
landowner can defeat a claim based on the ground that the use was permissive,
and, *as a matter of principle,* the only way that such expression can be given is orally
or in writing. I confess that I had some difficulty in understanding the argument
that *as a matter of principle* it would be wrong to allow a claim of user 'as of right'
to be defeated by an implied grant of permission. Miss Cameron submits that, if
implied permission were capable of defeating a claim to use as of right, that
would operate unfairly against those claiming a right based on use. That is
because a landowner would be able to do nothing to prevent use of his land for
lawful sports and pastimes (or to pass and re-pass in the context of rights of way),
and yet when a claim to a prescriptive right is made, he would be able to defeat it.

[10] I cannot accept this argument. It is trite law that for user to be 'as of right',
it must be nec vi, nec clam, nec precario. As Lord Hoffmann said in *Ex p Sunningwell
Parish Council* [1999] 3 All ER 385 at 391, [2000] 1 AC 335 at 350–351 the 'unifying
element in these three vitiating circumstances was that each constituted a reason
why it would not have been reasonable to expect the owner to resist the exercise
of the right'. In the third case (nec precario), it was because he had consented to
the use. In *Dalton v Angus & Co* (1881) 6 App Cas 740 at 773, [1881–5] All ER Rep
1 at 30, Fry J (advising the House of Lords) rationalised the law of prescription as
follows:

'... the whole law of prescription and the whole law which governs the
presumption or inference of a grant or covenant rest upon acquiescence.
The Courts and the Judges have had recourse to various expedients for
quieting the possession of persons in the exercise of rights which have not
been resisted by the persons against whom they are exercised, but in all cases
it appears to me that acquiescence and nothing else is the principle upon
which these expedients rest.'

[11] Thus the law draws a distinction between (a) an owner's acquiescence in
or toleration of the use of his land by others for lawful sports or pastimes, and
(b) his giving licence or permission for such use. In some contexts, it may be that
there is little or no difference in meaning between the two concepts. But in the
context of the law relating to prescription, the difference is fundamental, since
use which is merely acquiesced in by the owner is prima facie 'as of right',
although it may be defeated if the owner can show, inter alia, that he permitted
it. It is now clearly established that mere acquiescence in or toleration of the user
by the servient owner cannot prevent the user being user as of right for purposes
of prescription (see per Lord Hoffmann in *Ex p Sunningwell Parish Council* [1999]
3 All ER 385 at 398, [2000] 1 AC 335 at 358).

a

[12] What is the essential difference in the present context between permission and acquiescence? In my view, it is that permission involves some positive act or acts on the part of the owner, whereas passive toleration is all that is required for acquiescence. The positive act or acts may take different forms. The grant of oral or written consent is the clearest and most obvious expression of permission. But there is no reason in principle why the grant of permission

b

should be confined to such cases. I can see no reason why permission may not also be inferred from an owner's acts. It may be that there will not be many cases where (in the absence of express oral or written permission) it will be possible to infer permission from an owner's positive acts. Most cases where nothing is said or written will properly be classified as ones of mere acquiescence. But suppose that (a) cricket and football pitches had been laid out and a sports pavilion built at

c

the Sports Arena; (b) the facilities had been well maintained by the various authorities that owned the site from time to time; and (c) none of the authorities issued any statement or passed any resolution expressly permitting inhabitants in the locality to use the site for purposes of sport and pastimes. Why should it not be inferred from such facts that the authorities permitted such use of the site? It

d

cannot seriously be suggested that these facts would disclose no more than acquiescence in the use of the site for the purposes of sport and pastimes. The reality is that, on such facts, the owners of the site would be showing by their overt behaviour that they were actively encouraging, and thereby permitting, the use of the site for those purposes. In principle, the position would be no different if there had been an express oral or (more likely) written grant of permission.

e

[13] I would, therefore, hold that there is no reason in principle why an implied permission may not defeat a claim to use 'as of right'. Such permission may only be inferred from overt and contemporaneous acts of the landowner.

[14] Mr Petchey relies on the fact that implied licences are known to the law in other contexts. For example, when a householder lives in a dwelling house to

f

which there is a front garden, and he does not lock the garden gate, he gives an implied licence to any member of the public who has lawful reason for doing so to proceed from the gate to the house, and inquire whether he may be admitted and to conduct his lawful business: such an implied licence may be rebutted by express refusal of it (see per Diplock LJ in *Robson v Hallett* [1967] 2 All ER 407 at

g

414, [1967] 2 QB 939 at 953–954). Mr Petchey has given other examples. In my view, it is not necessary to seek analogies from other areas of the law. It seems to me that it is obvious that a person may give permission either expressly or by implication. Whether the inference of permission is to be drawn in any particular case will depend on the facts of that case.

h

Previous authority

[15] I turn, therefore, to consider Miss Cameron's submission that the notion that a claim to use as of right may be defeated by implied permission is inconsistent with a long-established line of authority culminating in *Ex p Sunningwell Parish*

j

Council. The first case that she cited (and, she said, the most important) was *Bright v Walker* (1834) 1 Cr M&R 211, [1824–34] All ER Rep 762. This was a decision under the Prescription Act 1832 shortly after that Act came into force. As Lord Hoffmann made clear in *Ex p Sunningwell Parish Council* [1999] 3 All ER 385 at 394, [2000] 1 AC 335 at 354: 'there is no reason to believe that "as of right" [sc in s 22(1) of the 1965 Act] was intended to mean anything different from what those words meant in the 1832 and 1932 Acts.' He was referring to the Prescription Act 1832

and the Rights of Way Act 1932 respectively. Speaking of the ways in which a
claim may be defeated, Parke B said:

a

'Again, such claim may be defeated in any other way by which the same is
now liable to be defeated; that is, by the same means by which a similar
claim, arising by custom, prescription, or grant, would now be defeasible;
and, therefore, it may be answered by proof of a grant, or of a licence, written
or parol, for a limited period, comprising the whole or part of the twenty
years ...' (See (1834) 1 Cr M&R 211 at 219, [1824–34] All ER Rep 762 at 765.)

b

[16] Miss Cameron emphasises the words 'answered by proof of a grant, or of
a licence, written or parol', and submits that this is clear authority for the
proposition that the *only* way in which a claim can be defeated on the basis that
the user was *precario* is by express grant of permission orally or in writing.
Miss Cameron points out that, in his comprehensive review of the history of the
law in this area in *Ex p Sunningwell Parish Council*, Lord Hoffmann referred to
Bright's case with evident approval.

c

[17] She also relies on two passages in the first edition of *Gale on the Law of
Easements* (1839) p 121:

d

'The effect of the enjoyment being to raise the presumption of a consent
on the part of the owner of the servient tenement, it is obvious that no such
inference of consent can be drawn, unless it be shewn that he was aware of
the user, and, being so aware, made no attempt to interfere with its exercise.
Still less can such consent be implied, but rather the contrary, where he has
contested the right to the user, or where in consequence of such opposition
an interruption in the user has actually taken place. Even supposing these
defects of the user not to exist, still the effect of the user would be destroyed
if it were shewn that it took place by the express permission of the owner of
the servient tenement, for in such a case the user would not have been had
with the intention of acquiring or exercising a right. The presumption,
however, is, that a party enjoying an easement acted under a claim of right
until the contrary is shewn.'

e

f

[18] On p 125, there is a discussion of the meaning of 'nec precario' as follows:

g

'Enjoyment had under a license or permission from the owner of the servient
tenement, as has been already remarked, confers no right to the easement.
Each renewal of the license rebuts the presumption which would otherwise
arise, that such enjoyment was had under a claim of right to the easement.
Any admission, whether verbal or otherwise, that the enjoyment had been
had by permission of the owner of the servient tenement was sufficient,
before the recent statute, to prevent the acquisition of the right, however
long such enjoyment might have continued. "Si autem," says Bracton, "(seisina)
precaria fuerit et de gratia, quae tempestive revocari possit vel intempestive, ex
longo tempore non acquiritur jus". By the statute a distinction is made as to
the effect of a parol license in those cases in which the right is declared to be
absolute and indefeasible, and those in which there is no such provision. In
the former instance, although the enjoyment commenced by permission, yet
after it has continued during the requisite period (forty years in general, and
twenty in the case of lights), the right cannot be invalidated, except by proof
that the easement "was enjoyed by some consent or agreement expressly

h

j

a given or made for that purpose by deed or writing". The latter case is not affected by the statute.'

[19] Miss Cameron also relies on *Mills v Colchester Corp* (1867) LR 2 CP 476 at 486 per Willes J who said:

b 'Equally in the case of custom as in that of prescription, long enjoyments in order to establish a right must have been as of right, and therefore neither by violence nor by stealth, nor by leave asked from time to time; and of the latter character was the enjoyment relied upon in this case.'

[20] Further, she refers to *Earl De la Warr v Miles* (1881) 17 Ch D 536 at 591, 596
c [1881–5] All ER Rep 252 at 259, 262 per Brett and Cotton LJJ respectively, and *Merstham Manor Ltd v Coulsdon and Purley UDC* [1936] 2 All ER 422 at 427, [1937] 2 KB 77 at 83–84 per Hilbery J. I do not cite from these last two authorities because they contain statements of the most general nature about the need for the user not to have been pursuant to permission given by the owner. But they provide no assistance on the question whether the permission may be given
d impliedly as well as expressly.

[21] In none of the cases relied on by Miss Cameron was there an issue as to whether permission sufficient to defeat a claim to use as of right must be express, or whether it may be inferred from the circumstances of the case. It is true that in *Bright's* case (1834) 1 Cr M&R 211 at 219, [1824–34] All ER Rep 762 at 765
e Parke B did speak of 'proof of a grant, or of a licence, written or parol'. But, as always, the context is crucial. Parke B was to some extent providing a general route map of the Prescription Act 1832. He was not, however, purporting to write a thesis on every detail of the Act. In my judgment, the words relied on by Miss Cameron were not intended to be an exhaustive definition of what constitutes
f permission for the purposes of defeating a claim to use 'as of right'. The question of what kind of permission would suffice was not in issue in that case. In these circumstances, Miss Cameron seeks to build on the foundations of *Bright's* case an edifice which the context of the case and the words used by Parke B simply will not bear. It follows that the fact that Lord Hoffmann referred to *Bright's* case in *Ex p Sunningwell Parish Council* with apparent approval does not advance the
g argument.

[22] Similarly with regard to the first edition of *Gale on the Law of Easements*. The passage relied on (p 121) provides no more than an example of a situation in which acquiescence (there described as 'consent') would be defeated. Thus the author says that the effect of the user would be 'destroyed' if it were shown that
h it took place by the express permission of the owner of the servient tenement. But it cannot be inferred from this passage that the *only* way in which a claim to user as of right can be defeated on the basis that it was *precario* is where the permission was granted expressly by word or in writing. The passage (p 125) refers to 'enjoyment had under a licence or permission from the owner of the servient tenement'. It says nothing about how the grant of that permission may
j be conveyed. Similarly, it cannot be inferred from the reference to 'the effect of a parol licence' that, unless it is written, permission to defeat a claim to a prescriptive right must be given orally.

[23] In my judgment, the line of authority relied on by Miss Cameron does not support the proposition that permission may not be inferred from the facts. The only statement which at first blush appears to assist her argument is that in

Bright's case, but for the reasons that I have given, on a closer analysis, it does not in fact do so.

[24] There is one other authority which the judge considered to be inconsistent with Miss Cameron's argument, although 'inconclusively' so: *Gardner v Hodgson's Kingston Brewery Co Ltd* [1903] AC 229. In that case, the plaintiff claimed under s 2 of the 1832 Act that she and her predecessors in title had for more than 40 years been entitled to use, as of right, a way through a yard leading from her house to the public highway. She acknowledged that she had paid an annual sum of 15 shillings, but there was no conclusive evidence as to the origin of or the consideration for the payment. The defendant contended that it was for a licence to use the right of way. But there was no evidence of any agreement, oral or in writing. The House of Lords held that the plaintiff had not discharged the burden on her of establishing that the user had not been pursuant to a licence. Lord Lindley said (at 239):

'A title by prescription can be established by long peaceable open enjoyment only; but in order that it may be so established the enjoyment must be inconsistent with any other reasonable inference than that it has been as of right in the sense above explained. This, I think, is the proper inference to be drawn from the authorities discussed in the Court below. If the enjoyment is equally consistent with two reasonable inferences, enjoyment as of right is not established; and this, I think, is the real truth in the present case. The enjoyment is equally open to explanation in one of two ways, namely, by a lost grant of a right of way in consideration of a rent-charge on the plaintiff's land of 15s. a year, or by a succession of yearly licences not, perhaps, expressed every year, but implied and assumed and paid for.'

[25] The significance of this passage is that Lord Lindley was of the opinion that the payments raised an inference of a succession of yearly licences 'not perhaps expressed every year, but *implied and assumed* and paid for' (Dyson LJ's emphasis). Her claim to enjoyment as of right failed because she was not able to exclude the possibility that it had been by licence of the owner. In my view, this supports the argument that implied permission may be sufficient to defeat a claim.

[26] I conclude, therefore, that the judge was right to decide the first issue in the way that she did. There is no reason in principle why implied permission should not be relied on by an owner to defeat a claim of user as of right, and, principle pointing the way, the authorities do not suggest a different solution.

THE SECOND ISSUE: WAS THE DECISION OF 27 APRIL 2000 LEGALLY FLAWED?

[27] Miss Cameron submits that, in reaching its decision that there had been implied permission to use the site for lawful sports and pastimes, the committee took into account a number of irrelevant considerations. The factors taken into account by the committee were: (a) the site was publicly owned; (b) it was specifically laid out as an arena with seating; (c) it was adjacent to the Princess Anne Park; (d) it had been maintained by the council and the WDC before it; (e) it was difficult to conceive that anyone could have imagined that this was other than a recreational area provided for use by the public for recreation; and (f) the other information contained in s 2 of the report, whilst not in itself conclusive, supported the view that the Sports Arena was intended for public use.

[28] Before the judge, it was submitted that factors (a) and (c) were irrelevant. The judge agreed that (c) was irrelevant, but she decided that even if that factor had not been taken into account, the outcome was bound to have been the same. She rejected the argument that (a) was irrelevant, saying that the fact that the land was in public ownership was relevant when 'one is considering what conclusion a reasonable person would draw from the circumstances of user'. She said that it is well known that, unlike private landowners, local authorities as part of their normal functions provide facilities for the use of the public and maintain them at public expense.

[29] On appeal, Miss Cameron has renewed the argument that (a) and (c) were irrelevant and that the decision was flawed because, to some extent at least, it was based on them. Additionally, she argues that factor (e) was irrelevant too. Her argument is that, if one reads the second sentence of para (c) of the grounds for the decision of 27 April together with the relevant passage in the report, it is clear that the committee took into account its understanding of the state of mind of the users of the site. The subjective belief of the users is irrelevant (see *Ex p Sunningwell Parish Council* [1999] 3 All ER 385 at 393–396, [2000] 1 AC 335 at 353–356 per Lord Hoffmann). The question whether there has been use as of right must be determined objectively.

[30] I agree with the judge that the fact that the land is in public ownership is part of the relevant background for the reasons that she gives. It would have been artificial to ask the committee to ignore the fact that the site was in public ownership. It was because it was owned by successive public bodies that, on the facts of this case, the question as to whether implied permission had been given for lawful sports and pastimes arose at all. Nevertheless, I would accept that, on its own, it was a factor of little weight. There is no reason to suppose that it was regarded as an important factor by the committee. It was not identified as a relevant factor in the report that was prepared for the meeting. The same may be said of the fact that the site was adjacent to the Princess Anne Park. Mr Petchey has not sought to argue that the judge was wrong to hold that this was an irrelevant factor. But it was, at most, a peripheral point. It was not referred to in the report as a relevant factor. I do not believe that, if the committee had been told in terms that they should not take account of the fact that the land was in public ownership and was adjacent to the Princess Anne Park, their decision would have been any different.

[31] The reality of the situation is that the committee had been advised that the implied licence argument was 'strong' because of the presence of the perimeter seating and the fact that the grass was kept cut, and because no one could have imagined that this was other than a recreational area provided for use by the public for recreation. The strength of the argument was based on objectively ascertainable facts which the committee could reasonably rely on to arrive at the conclusion that this was a case of user by implied permission. I do not accept that the committee took into account the subjective beliefs of the users. Miss Cameron relies on the following two sentences from the report:

'However everyone using the site would have been aware of the perimeter seating and that the grass was kept cut. It is difficult to conceive that anyone could have imagined that this was other than a recreational area provided for use by the public for recreation.'

[32] She submits that the first sentence is directed at the subjective beliefs of the users, which are irrelevant; and that there is a clear nexus between the first

and second sentences. In other words, the second sentence suffers from the same
flaw as the first. I do not agree with this analysis. First, although it is true that the *a*
first sentence refers to the users, their awareness would have been no different
from that of any objective bystander. The second sentence makes this clear: it is
difficult to conceive of *anyone* who could have imagined that the Sports Arena
was other than a recreational area provided for use by the public for recreation.
By 'anyone', I think that the writer of the report was not confining himself to *b*
users: he meant, quite literally, anyone who knew the facts.

[33] Secondly, even if the committee did take into account the subjective
beliefs of the users, it seems to me to be very unlikely indeed that, if they had been
told in terms that they could not take those beliefs into account, they would have
arrived at a different conclusion on the implied permission issue. They had been
advised correctly that if it was 'apparent from the circumstances of the case that *c*
the land had been made available to the public, and that their use had not simply
been tolerated but in effect encouraged', then a licence should be implied from
the circumstances. In my judgment, there are no grounds for impugning this
decision. It has not been suggested that the decision was perverse in the
Wednesbury sense (see *Associated Provincial Picture Houses Ltd v Wednesbury Corp* *d*
[1947] 2 All ER 680, [1947] 2 KB 223). For the reasons that I have given, to the
limited extent that the committee did take into account irrelevant considerations,
they were immaterial to their ultimate decision.

[34] Accordingly, I would dismiss this appeal.

WILSON J.

[35] I agree.

LATHAM LJ.

[36] I also agree.

Appeal dismissed. Permission to appeal refused.

Kate O'Hanlon   Barrister.

Totty v Snowden

Hewitt v Wirral and West Cheshire Community NHS Trust

[2001] EWCA Civ 1415

COURT OF APPEAL, CIVIL DIVISION
PETER GIBSON, CHADWICK AND KAY LJJ
27, 31 JULY 2001

Particulars of claim – Service – Extension of time for service – Whether court having discretion to grant extension of time for service of particulars of claim – CPR 7.4, 7.6.

In two conjoined appeals in unrelated cases, the issue arose whether the court had discretion to grant an extension of time to a claimant who had served a claim form within the period prescribed by CPR 7.5 but who had failed to serve, within the same period, either the particulars of claim or particulars which complied with the requirements of CPR Pt 16. In the first case, both the district judge and the circuit judge had concluded that there was such a discretion under CPR Pt 3 (the court's general case management powers), and they exercised it in the claimant's favour. The defendant appealed to the Court of Appeal. In the second case, the circuit judge, reversing the district judge, concluded that there was no such discretion, and the claimant appealed. In each case, the defendant submitted that precisely the same strict regime applied to a failure to serve particulars of claim as applied, under CPR 7.6[a], to a failure to serve a claim form within the prescribed period. Rule 7.6 precluded the court, save in certain limited circumstances, from extending time to serve the claim form in cases where the application for an extension had been made after the expiry of the time prescribed for service. In contending that r 7.6 applied to the particulars of claim as well as the claim form, the defendants argued that such particulars were an integral part of the claim form and that a claim could not be served properly unless they had been served. They also contended that r 7.4(2)[b], which required the particulars of claim to be served no later than the latest time for serving a claim form, would have very little effect if it were not subject to the sanction of the regime imposed by r 7.6.

Held – The court had a discretion under CPR Pt 3 to extend time for service of the particulars of claim. Such particulars were not an integral part of the claim form. CPR 7.4 made it quite clear that the particulars of claim were treated as a separate part of the documentation normally required to commence a claim, and there was no justification for concluding, in the absence of express words to that effect, that the particulars of claim came within the provisions of r 7.6 by implication. Where there were no express words in the CPR, the court was bound to consider which interpretation would better reflect the CPR's overriding objective of dealing with a case justly. Moreover, r 7.4(2) would have effect even if it were not subject to the regime under r 7.6. A failure to comply with r 7.4 would be a factor taken into account by the court when it exercised its discretion whether to grant an extension for service of the particulars of claim. Furthermore,

---

a   Rule 7.6, so far as material, is set out at [10], below
b   Rule 7.4 is set out at [9], below

there was a perfectly sensible reason why a distinction should be drawn between
service of the claim form and service of the particulars of claim. Until the claim   *a*
form had been served, the defendant might be wholly unaware of the proceedings
and might, therefore, be deprived of the opportunity to take any steps to advance
the case. That would not be the case if the claim form had been served but the
particulars of claim were outstanding. In such circumstances, it would be open
to the defendant either to seek an order for immediate delivery of the particulars   *b*
of claim or, if it were justified, to seek to strike out the claim. Thus a very strict
regime in relation to the claim form, and a discretionary regime subject to the
overriding objective in relation to the particulars of claim, was a perfectly sensible
approach to the differing problems raised by the two types of failure to comply
with the rules as to service. It followed that the defendant's appeal in the first case
would be dismissed, while in the second case the claimant's appeal would be   *c*
allowed and the matter remitted to the court below for consideration of the
exercise of the court's discretion (see [32], [34], [36]–[41], [44], [46]–[48], below).

Vinos v Marks & Spencer plc [2001] 3 All ER 784 distinguished.

Cases referred to in judgments   *d*
Austin v Newcastle Chronicle & Journal [2001] EWCA Civ 834.
Elmes v Hygrade Food Products plc [2001] EWCA Civ 121.
Kaur v CTP Coil Ltd [2000] CA Transcript 1328.
Vinos v Marks & Spencer plc [2001] 3 All ER 784, CA.

e
Cases also cited or referred to in skeleton arguments
Biguzzi v Rank Leisure plc [1999] 4 All ER 934, [1999] 1 WLR 1926, CA.
Hannigan v Hannigan [2000] FCR 650, CA.
Jones v Telford and Wrekin Council [1999] TLR 569, CA.
Kleinwort Benson Ltd v Barbrak Ltd [1987] 2 All ER 289, [1987] AC 597, HL.   *f*
Nanglegan v Royal Free Hampstead NHS Trust [2001] EWCA Civ 127, [2001] 3 All ER
    793.

Appeals

Totty v Snowden   *g*
The defendant, Lee Snowden, appealed with permission of Tuckey LJ granted on
26 January 2001 from the decision of Judge Grenfell, sitting as a judge of the
High Court at Leeds on 13 October 2000, dismissing his appeal from the decision
of District Judge Giles on 19 July 2000 whereby he (i) declared that the particulars
of claim of the claimant, Emily Totty, should be deemed to have been served   *h*
within the period prescribed by the CPR, and (ii) dismissed Mr Snowden's
application for the claim form and particulars of claim to be set aside. The facts
are set out in the judgment of Kay LJ.

Hewitt v Wirral and West Cheshire Community NHS Trust   *j*
The claimant, Hilda Irene Hewitt, appealed with permission of Tuckey LJ granted
on 22 January 2001 from the decision of Judge Marshall Evans QC at Liverpool
County Court on 8 November 2000 allowing an appeal by the defendant, Wirral and
West Cheshire Community NHS Trust, from the decision of District Judge Jones on
7 April 2000 dismissing its application to set aside service of Mrs Hewitt's claim
form. The facts are set out in the judgment of Kay LJ.

a *Daniel Pearce-Higgins QC* and *Andrew Lewis* (instructed by *Beachcroft Wansbroughs*, Leeds) for Mr Snowden.

Michael Harrison QC and *Nicola Saxton* (instructed by *Jones Goodall*, Wakefield) for Miss Totty.

Michael Harrison QC and *Peter Foster* (instructed by *A Halsall & Co*, Birkenhead) for Mrs Hewitt.

b *Benjamin Browne QC* and *Tim Grover* (instructed by *Weightmans*, Liverpool) for the NHS Trust.

Cur adv vult

31 July 2001. The following judgments were delivered.

c
PETER GIBSON LJ.
[1] Kay LJ will give the first judgment.

KAY LJ.
[2] The issue raised by these two appeals is whether the court has a discretion *d* to grant an extension of time to a claimant who has served a claim form within the time prescribed by the CPR but who has either not served particulars of claim, or alternatively has failed to serve particulars that comply with the requirements of CPR Pt 16, within the period prescribed by CPR 7.5.

[3] The appeal in the case of *Totty v Snowden* is against a decision of Judge Grenfell *e* sitting in the Queen's Bench Division of the High Court in Leeds dated 13 October 2000, by which he rejected an appeal brought by the defendant against a decision of District Judge Giles. On 19 July 2000, District Judge Giles had declared that pursuant to his powers under CPR 3.10, the particulars of claim should be deemed to have been served within the period prescribed by the rules and refused the defendant's application for the claim form and the particulars of claim to be *f* set aside. Judge Grenfell upheld the district judge's ruling that there was a discretion to extend time and also upheld the district judge's exercise of his discretion.

[4] The appeal in the case of *Hewitt v Wirral and West Cheshire Community NHS Trust* is an appeal against a decision of Judge David Marshall Evans QC sitting in the Liverpool County Court dated 8 November 2000, by which he allowed an appeal from District Judge Jones. On 7 April 2000 District Judge Jones made an order *g* which had the effect of dismissing the defendant's application that service of the claim form be set aside and ordering the claimant to serve particulars of claim that complied with CPR 16.4 and para 4 of the Practice Direction supplementing Pt 16. Judge Marshall Evans considered the judgment of Judge Grenfell in *Totty*'s case but reached the contrary view that the court did not have a discretion to extend *h* the period of time for service of the particulars of claim. He therefore concluded that the district judge's decision was wrong.

[5] The facts underlying the appeal in *Totty*'s case are as follows. Miss Totty was severely injured in a road traffic accident on 6 June 1996. On 19 August 1999 her solicitors concluded an agreement with Mr Snowden's solicitors that Mr Snowden *j* was liable to the claimant in respect of 85% of such loss and damage as she might prove. An interim payment of £3,000 followed four days later. On 28 September 1999, the day before Miss Totty's twenty-first birthday and the expiry of the limitation period, the claim form was issued. In October 1999 there was a brief exchange of correspondence between the solicitors in which Mr Snowden's solicitors made clear that they were not prepared to consent to an order for judgment in proceedings that had not been served. On 26 January 2000, two days

before the end of the prescribed period, Miss Totty's solicitors duly served the
claim form but, having misunderstood the rules, wrote indicating that it was   *a*
their intention to serve the particulars of claim with a schedule of loss and supporting
medical evidence within 14 days. By the time they did so on 9 February 2000, the
fourteenth day after service of the claim form, the period of four months from the
issue of the claim form had elapsed and they had failed to comply with r 7.4(2).

[6] The facts relating to *Hewitt's* case are as follows. Mrs Hewitt alleges that   *b*
she suffered injury as a result of an incident which occurred on 23 August 1996 during
the course of her employment with the Wirral and West Cheshire Community NHS
Trust (the NHS Trust). She instructed solicitors to pursue her claim in about
June 1999. On 17 August 1999 the solicitors issued a claim form. It had been filled
in with little care. That part of the printed form which read 'Particulars of Claim
(attached) (to follow)' was left with neither of the alternatives deleted. Underneath   *c*
was typed:

> 'The claimant claims damages arising from an assault on her by a patient
> whilst she was employed by the defendant. The assault was the result of the
> defendant's negligence and/or failure to have sufficient regard for the claimant's
> safety whilst she was at work.'   *d*

[7] The judge concluded that it was clear that the solicitors had intended to
serve particulars of claim at a later date and that they had simply failed to delete
the word 'attached' on the form. It is common ground that the information in the
claim form did not contain the full particulars required by Pt 16 and the Practice
Direction thereto. Following problems due to service on the wrong authority,   *e*
the claim form came to the attention of the NHS Trust on 8 December 1999.
On 16 December 1999 the period for service of the particulars of claim provided
by the rules elapsed. On 12 January 2000, no particulars of claim having been
served, the defendant applied to set aside service of the claim form.

The Civil Procedure Rules 1998   *f*

[8] Part 7 provides for service of the claim form and the particulars of claim.
Rule 7.5 requires that a claim form (unless it is to be served out of the jurisdiction)
must be served 'within 4 months after the date of issue'. As already set out above,
in each case there was compliance with this requirement.

[9] Rule 7.4 provides for service of particulars of claim. It reads: *g*

> '(1) Particulars of claim must—(a) be contained in or served with the claim
> form; or (b) subject to paragraph (2) be served on the defendant by the
> claimant within 14 days after service of the claim form.
> (2) Particulars of claim must be served on the defendant no later than the
> latest time for serving a claim form ...   *h*
> (3) Where the claimant serves particulars of claim separately from the claim
> form in accordance with paragraph (1)(b), he must, within 7 days of service on
> the defendant, file a copy of the particulars together with a certificate of
> service.'

[10] Rule 7.6 provides for extending time for service of a claim form. The relevant   *j*
parts read:

> '(1) The claimant may apply for an order extending the period within
> which the claim form may be served.
> (2) The general rule is that an application to extend the time for service
> must be made—(a) within the period for serving the claim form specified by

a   rule 7.5; or (b) where an order has been made under this rule, within the
period for service specified by that order.

(3) If the claimant applies for an order to extend the time for service of the
claim form after the end of the period specified by rule 7.5 or by an order
made under this rule, the court may make such an order only if—(a) the
court has been unable to serve the claim form; or (b) the claimant has taken

b   all reasonable steps to serve the claim form but has been unable to do so; and,
(c) in either case, the claimant has acted promptly in making the application.'

Part 16 contains the requirements for the contents of the claim form and the
contents of the particulars of claim. CPR 16.2 requires the claim form to contain a
concise statement of the nature of the claim, to specify the remedy which the

c   claimant seeks and contains such other matters as may be set out in a practice
direction. Rule 16.2(2) provides: 'If the particulars of claim specified in rule 16.4 are
not contained in, or are not served with the claim form, the claimant must state
on the claim form that the particulars of claim will follow.'

[11] The required contents of the particulars of claim are specified by r 16.4.
Such particulars must include a concise statement of the facts on which the

d   claimant relies and also such other matters as may be set out in a practice
direction. By para 4 of the Practice Direction relevant to Pt 16, the particulars of
claim in a personal injuries claim must contain the claimant's date of birth and
brief details of the claimant's personal injuries. The claimant is required to attach
to the particulars of claim a schedule of loss and also a report from a medical

e   practitioner about the personal injuries which are alleged in the claim.

[12] Rule 16.8 provides that if a claim form has been issued in accordance with
r 7.2 and served in accordance with r 7.5, the court may make an order that the claim
will continue without any other statement of case. CPR Pt 3 contains the court's
case management powers. Rule 3.1(2)(a) permits the court to 'extend or shorten
the time for compliance with any rule, practice direction or court order (even if

f   an application for extension is made after the time for compliance has expired)'.
This power is, however, subject to the important qualification, 'Except where
these Rules provide otherwise'.

[13] Rule 3.10 provides:

'Where there has been an error of procedure such as a failure to comply

g   with a rule or practice direction—(a) the error does not invalidate any step
taken in the proceedings unless the court so orders; and (b) the court may
make an order to remedy the error.'

[14] In interpreting the rules and in exercising any power under the rules, the
court is required to give effect to the overriding objective (CPR 1.2). The overriding

h   objective is to deal with the case justly, which includes, so far as is practicable,
inter alia, saving expense, ensuring that the case is dealt with expeditiously and
fairly and 'allotting to [the case] an appropriate share of the court's resources, while
taking into account the need to allot resources to other cases'.

j   *Vinos v Marks & Spencer plc*

[15] The Court of Appeal considered in *Vinos v Marks & Spencer plc* [2001] 3 All ER
784 the interrelationship between CPR 7.6 and CPR Pt 3. In that case the claimant's
solicitor had failed to serve the claim form until seven days after the period of
four months provided by r 7.5(2) had elapsed. The failure was not related to any
difficulty over service and hence the claimant could not seek an extension of time
under r 7.6 after the period for service had elapsed. The contention on behalf of the

claimant was that notwithstanding that there was no possibility of an extension
under r 7.6, the court, having regard to the overriding objective, was none the a
less entitled to exercise its case management powers under Pt 3 and that r 3.10
gave the court a discretion to extend the time for serving the claim form. The
Court of Appeal rejected this argument.

[16] May LJ (at 789 (para 20)), explained the reasoning behind the decision:

> 'The meaning of r 7.6(3) is plain. The court has power to extend the time b
> for serving the claim form after the period for its service has run out "only if"
> the stipulated conditions are fulfilled. That means that the court does not
> have power to do so otherwise. The discretionary power in the rules to
> extend time periods—r 3.1(2)(a)—does not apply because of the introductory
> words. The general words of r 3.10 cannot extend to enable the court to do c
> what r 7.6(3) specifically forbids, nor to extend time when the specific
> provision of the rules which enables extensions of time specifically does not
> extend to making this extension of time.'

[17] Peter Gibson LJ (at 791 (para 26)) considered the part that the overriding
objective had to play in the matter: d

> 'The construction of the CPR, like the construction of any legislation, primary
> or delegated, requires the application of ordinary canons of construction,
> though the CPR, unlike their predecessors, spell out in Pt 1 the overriding
> objective of the new procedural code. The court must seek to give effect to
> that objective when it exercises any power given to it by the rules or e
> interprets any rule. But the use in r 1.1(2) of the word "seek" acknowledges
> that the court can only do what is possible. The language of the rule to be
> interpreted may be so clear and jussive that the court may not be able to give
> effect to what it may otherwise consider to be the just way of dealing with
> the case, though in that context it should not be forgotten that the principal f
> mischiefs which the CPR were intended to counter were excessive costs and
> delays.'

[18] That decision has been followed in a number of other decisions of the
Court of Appeal (for example, *Kaur v CTP Coil Ltd* [2000] CA Transcript 1328 and
Elmes v Hygrade Food Products plc [2001] EWCA Civ 121). The absence of a discretion g
in such matters can lead to very harsh consequences for those who act for
claimants and make relatively small mistakes in this regard in the conduct of the
litigation, but the cases clearly establish that the court has no discretion to
alleviate any such harshness, which in any event arises from a failure to observe
the rules. h

[19] In summary form, the argument advanced by the defendant in each of the
cases with which we are concerned was that precisely the same regime as applies
to failure to serve a claim form within the prescribed period applies to a failure to
serve particulars of claim. In each case the claimant contends that r 7.6 makes no
reference to particulars of claim and hence extension of the time for service of the
particulars of claim is not governed by that rule but rather falls to be considered j
under the discretionary powers contained in Pt 3.

[20] In *Totty*'s case, Judge Grenfell concluded:

> 'In my judgment, whilst the requirement under CPR 7.4(2) is mandatory,
> there is nothing that cannot be cured through CPR 3.1(2)(a). Once the claim
> form has been issued, the proceedings have commenced (r 7.2(1)). Unless

a   there is a provision such as contained within r 7.6, in my view, the court's
     management powers apply. In my judgment, the district judge was correct
     to apply r 3.10 to put right the claimant's solicitor's error and plainly
     exercised his discretion in accordance with the merits of the case and a
     correct application of r 3.9 (relief from sanctions).'

b   [21] In *Hewitt*'s case, Judge Marshall Evans explained his decision, which was
     to the opposite effect:

         'I, with some reluctance, agree with [counsel for the defendant's] submission
         that it is clear from the rules: (a) that the particulars of claim are an essential
         part of the claim form; (b) that if the particulars of claim are not contained within
         the claim form or served separately in accordance with the rules the claim form
c   is (i) defective, (ii) has not been properly served, and (iii) proceedings brought
         under the claim form have not been perfected; and (c) that if the mandatory
         requirement of service of the particulars of claim within the prescribed time
         limit is not met the validity of the claim form will lapse on the expiry of four
         months and the claimant must issue a further claim form. If this were not
d   the case there would be no sanction against a claimant who fails to comply
         with r 7.4 and Pt 16.'

     [22] He continued: 'But it does appear to me, and I conclude and hold (contrary
     to the judgment below) that this is one of the relatively few cases in which the
     CPR are utterly mandatory and prescriptive.'

e   [23] The defendant in each appeal submits that the approach of Judge Marshall
     Evans was the correct one. They support the contention that the particulars of
     claim are an integral part of the claim form and submit that for a claim to be
     commenced properly the particulars must be served otherwise the claim lapses.
     Hence the strict regime for claim forms is just as applicable to particulars of claim.

f   [24] Mr Pearce-Higgins QC on behalf of Mr Snowden draws attention to the
     fact that, unlike the old procedure, a defendant is not required to acknowledge
     service on receipt of the claim form and need take no step until the particulars of
     claim are served. He submits that this is an indication that the rules treat the
     particulars of claim as a part of the claim form and until the particulars are served
     the defendant can treat the claim form as if it had not been served.

g   [25] He further submits that the clear intent of the rules is that the claimant
     should not delay unnecessarily and against that background it is not surprising
     that the same strict regime should apply as for service of the claim form. He
     argues that to have a different approach to the particulars of claim would lead to
     uncertainty and potential delay, and that it would not be clear what the approach
h   of the court should be when called upon to exercise its discretion.

     [26] Mr Browne QC on behalf of the NHS Trust questioned what the purpose
     of including r 7.4(2) was unless it was to bring service of the particulars of claim
     within the ambit of r 7.6. The advancing of the mandatory time limit on service
     for the particulars of claim by a matter of days is of little significance unless it
j   carries with it the sanction that failure to comply will effectively bring an end to
     the proceedings.

     [27] Mr Harrison QC on behalf of each claimant not unnaturally submits that
     the approach of Judge Grenfell is the correct one.

     [28] He placed reliance upon the decision of this court in *Austin v Newcastle
     Chronicle & Journal* [2001] EWCA Civ 834. In that case the court had considered
     a case where a claim form had been served within the four-month period but the

particulars of claim had been served outside that period. The court proceeded on
the basis that r 7.6 did not apply. However, on closer examination Mr Harrison   *a*
acknowledged that the point taken in this case did not appear to have been
considered in the earlier case, and it seems that counsel and the court approached
the matter on the basis that the sole issue was whether time should be extended
under Pt 3. Mr Harrison, therefore, accepted that the case could not bind this
court but he is, at least, able to point out that it appears that the interpretation   *b*
suggested by the defendants does not even seem to have occurred to the court.

[29] Mr Harrison argues that there is no reason to read into Pt 7 an implication
that r 7.6(3) applies to the particulars of claim as well as the claim form. It would,
if it had been intended that that should be the case, have been simple for the rule
to have made specific reference to the particulars of claim. The absence of any   *c*
such express provision is consistent with an intention that the service of the claim
form should be subject to the very strict rule about late service but that late service
of particulars of claim were to be dealt with under the general discretionary powers
contained in Pt 3.

[30] Mr Harrison submits that if r 7.6 governs service of the particulars of
claim, it leads to absurd consequences. The most stark of these is that if r 7.6   *d*
applies to particulars of claim, it follows that r 3.1(2) does not since 'the rules
would provide otherwise'. Hence it would not be possible to make an application
for the exercise of the court's case management powers to extend the time for
service of the particulars of claim. Rule 7.6 makes no provision for an application
to extend the period for service of the particulars of claim. Thus the only course   *e*
open to a claimant who had served the claim form but required extra time to
serve the particulars of claim would be to apply under r 7.6(1) to extend the time
for service of the claim form. However, the claim form would already have been
served.

Conclusions   *f*

[31] It was first necessary to look at the provisions of r 7.6 in a little detail.
Rule 7.6(1) permits an application to extend the time for service of the claim
form. That provision would be wholly unnecessary were it not for the provisions
of r 7.6(3), since otherwise the general discretionary powers contained within
Pt 3 would apply. Thus those responsible for drafting the rules were singling out   *g*
the claim form for exceptional treatment. Unless the particulars of claim can
properly be viewed as an integral part of the claim form, it is a valid argument that
it is surprising that if it was intended that this exceptionally strict provision was to
apply to the claim form and to the particulars of claim, there was no express
reference to the particulars of claim in the rule and that such inclusion was left to *h*
be inferred from the rest of Pt 7.

[32] I do not accept that the particulars of claim are an integral part of the
claim form. Rule 7.4 makes it quite clear that the particulars of claim are treated
as a separate part of the documentation normally required to commence a claim.
There would be no purpose to be served in making provision for the possible   *j*
service of the claim form at an earlier time than the particulars of claim if the
particulars of claim were an essential part of the claim form, so that the latter was
of no effect without the particulars of claim. Thus I cannot accept the conclusion
of Judge Marshall Evans that the claim is 'defective' until the particulars of claim
are served or that the claim form 'has not properly been served'. Rule 16.8 would
seem to support this view since it permits the court, in an appropriate case, to

a order that a claim can proceed without any other statement of case once a claim form has been served under r 7.5.

[33] Thus in order to justify the interpretation for which the defendants contend, it would be necessary, since there are no express words to that effect, to conclude that the provisions of r 7.4, and particularly r 7.4(2), clearly imply that r 7.6 is to apply to the particulars of claim as well as to the claim form.

b [34] Rule 1.2 requires the court to have regard to the overriding objective in interpreting the rules. Where there are clear express words, as pointed out by Peter Gibson LJ in *Vinos'* case, the court cannot use the overriding objective 'to give effect to what it may otherwise consider to be the just way of dealing with the case'. Where there are no express words, the court is bound to look at which interpretation would better reflect the overriding objective. If the interpretation c sought by the defendants is right, there may well be situations in which the consequences of a relatively minor fault may result in very severe consequences for the person at fault. There may be good reasons why those consequences should follow, but it has to be appreciated that the argument advanced by the claimants does not mean they will be ignored. If the court does have a discretion, the d circumstances of the failure will fall to be considered by the court when it considers whether to exercise its discretion since discretion must be exercised having regard to the overriding objective.

[35] Further, I think that there is merit in the argument advanced by Mr Harrison as to the consequence, that he characterised as absurd, namely that since there is no power to extend the time for service of the particulars of claim e after service of the claim form, a claimant would have to apply to extend the time for service of the claim form even though the claim form had been validly served.

[36] The one argument advanced by the defendants that has caused me to hesitate in my conclusion is that if r 7.4 does not have the sanction of the regime under r 7.6, r 7.4(2) has very little effect. However, on reflection, if the claimants f are right, r 7.4(2) does have effect. In other circumstances, a person who has served his claim form has a period of 14 further days in which to serve the particulars of claim as of right, ie without the need to seek the exercise of the court's discretion. The effect of r 7.4(2) is that the claimant who chooses not to serve the claim form until the period for service has all but elapsed, loses such part of that absolute right as takes the total period beyond the prescribed limit, and is left to rely on the g exercise of the court's discretion if he wishes to extend that period. That discretion will involve considering the overriding objective, which includes ensuring that the case is dealt with expeditiously. The consideration will, therefore, start from the position that the claimant will not have complied with the requirement of r 7.4 and this will be a factor to be taken into account.

h [37] If the claimants are right in their interpretation, I consider that there is a perfectly sensible reason why a distinction could be drawn between service of the claim form and service of the particulars of claim. Until the claim form is served, the defendant may be wholly unaware of the proceedings. He may, therefore, because of his ignorance, be deprived of the opportunity to take any steps to j advance the case. The same would not be true if the claim form had been served but the particulars of claim were outstanding. In such circumstances, it would be open to a defendant either to seek an order for immediate delivery of the particulars of claim or, if it was justified, to seek to strike out the claim. Thus a very strict regime in relation to the claim form and a discretionary regime subject to the overriding objective is a perfectly sensible approach to the differing problems raised by the two types of failure to comply with the rules as to service.

[38] For these reasons, I have come to the conclusion that there is no
justification for concluding, in the absence of express words to that effect, that the
particulars of claim come within the provisions of r 7.6 by implication. Thus, I am
satisfied that the court does have a discretion to extend time in circumstances
such as those in this case.

[39] In *Totty's* case it follows that I am satisfied that Judge Grenfell was entitled
to conclude that the district judge had a discretion. There is no appeal against the
exercise of that discretion, if it exists, and accordingly in that case I would simply
dismiss the appeal.

[40] In *Hewitt's* case I consider that Judge Marshall Evans was wrong to rule
that the court had no discretion to allow an extension of time for service of the
particulars of claim. The judge did not go on and consider how he would have
exercised his discretion if he had concluded that he had such a discretion. The
appeal to the judge pre-dated current appeal rules and was, therefore, by way of
rehearing. Both parties would wish to place before the judge further evidence
relevant to the exercise of his discretion and have accordingly agreed that the
correct course, if the appeal is allowed, is for the case to be remitted to the Liverpool
County Court for consideration of the exercise of the court's discretion. In these
circumstances, I agree this would be the appropriate course and I would, therefore,
allow the appeal and remit case to the Liverpool County Court.

CHADWICK LJ.

[41] I agree.

[42] The short point raised by these appeals is whether CPR 7.4(2) has the
effect of abrogating the powers conferred on the court by CPR 3.1(2) in a case
where a claimant has issued a claim form, has served that claim form within the
period of four months after the date of issue (as required by CPR 7.5(2)), but has
not served the particulars of claim before the end of that four-month period.

[43] If r 7.4(2) is to have the effect contended for, it must be because the
subrule in some way incorporates—in relation to an application to extend time
for serving particulars of claim—the regime applicable to extensions of time for
the service of the claim form itself set out in CPR 7.6. In particular, it must be
because r 7.4(2) incorporates, in relation to an application to extend time for
serving particulars of claim in circumstances where the particulars have not been
served within the period of four months from the issue of the claim form, the
restrictions on the grant of extension of time for the service of the claim form
which are set out in r 7.6(3).

[44] In my view r 7.4(2) does not have that effect. There are, to my mind,
three reasons which compel that conclusion. First, there is no express provision
in r 7.4, or in r 7.6, which applies the limitation in r 7.6(3) to an application to
extend time for the service of particulars of claim. The consequence where
r 7.6(3) applies is draconian; so that I would expect there to be an express provision
to that effect if that consequence were intended. It is, after all, pertinent to have
in mind that r 3.1(2) begins with the words: 'Except where these Rules provide
otherwise, the court may—(a) extend or shorten the time for compliance with
any rule ...' If the CPR are to 'provide otherwise' in relation to the time for
service of particulars of claim, I would expect them to do so in clear and express
terms; as they do in relation to the time for service of the claim form itself.

[45] Second, in order to achieve the effect contended for, it is necessary to do
substantial violence to the language of r 7.6. Rule 7.6 provides a regime under
which a claimant may apply for an order extending the period in which the claim

a form may be served. In the situation in which the claim form has been served in time, the claimant does not need, or want, an order extending the period within which the claim form may be served. What the claimant wants is an order extending the period within which the particulars of claim may be served. Rule 7.6(1) does not provide for an application for such an order. Further difficulties arise in the application of Rule 7.6(3). Under that subrule—

b
> 'the court may make such an order only if—(a) the court has been unable to serve the claim form; or (b) the claimant has taken all reasonable steps to serve the claim form but has been unable to do so; and, (c) in either case, the claimant has acted promptly in making the application.'

c But where the claim form has been served in time but the particulars of claim have not been served in time, neither paras (a) nor (b) of r 7.6(3) can be satisfied. And, if neither paras (a) nor (b) can be satisfied, para (c) cannot, in terms, have any application. In order to give effect to the contention that r 7.6 applies to applications to extend time for the service of particulars of claim, it would be necessary to rewrite that rule extensively. Further, it would be necessary to *d* rewrite it in such a way that the extension of the rule applied only where time for serving particulars of claim was to be extended beyond the time limited by r 7.5 for serving the claim form. There is no reason at all why r 7.6 should apply where all that the claimant wants is an extension of the 14-day period limited by r 7.4(1)(b) which does not, of itself, take the time beyond the time limited by r 7.5. It is not at all clear to me how the Rules Committee would have dealt with the *e* point, if it had been their intention to do so. The court should be slow to imply provisions in a rule, which are not there in express terms, unless it can see, with a high degree of certainty, what the implied provisions should be.

[46] Third, there is no compelling reason of policy why the court should interpret r 7.4(2) and r 7.6 in order to cover a situation to which, on their terms, *f* they are not addressed. As Kay LJ has pointed out, there is a clear rationale for the provisions of r 7.6 in relation to the service of the claim form itself. There is no comparable rationale in relation to the service of particulars of claim, in circumstances in which the claim form has itself been served. There is no reason why that situation should not be left to be dealt with, as a matter of discretion, in the exercise of the powers conferred by r 3.1(2)(a), having regard to the overriding *g* objective. Once the claim form itself has been served, the defendant will know that there is a claim against him; and he will be in a position to invoke the assistance of the court if particulars of claim are not forthcoming within due time.

[47] For these reasons, and for the reasons given by Kay LJ, I agree with the orders which he has proposed.

h
PETER GIBSON LJ.
[48] I agree with both judgments.

Mr Snowden's appeal dismissed. Mrs Hewitt's appeal allowed.

Kate O'Hanlon   Barrister.

Re Pantmaenog Timber Co Ltd (in liquidation)
Official Receiver v Meade-King (a firm) and others
[2001] EWCA Civ 1227

COURT OF APPEAL, CIVIL DIVISION
KENNEDY AND CHADWICK LJJ
7 JUNE, 25 JULY 2001

Company – Compulsory winding up – Examination of officer of company etc – Production of documents – Directors disqualification proceedings – Official Receiver bringing directors disqualification proceedings against former director of company in compulsory liquidation – Official Receiver applying for orders for third parties to produce documents relating to company – Whether court having power to make such an order where sole purpose of application was to obtain documents for use in disqualification proceedings – Insolvency Act 1986, ss 132, 236 – Company Directors Disqualification Act 1986, s 7.

H was the former director of a company which was wound up by order of the court. On the making of that order, the Official Receiver became liquidator of the company, by virtue of his office, until some other person was appointed in his place. In cases where a winding-up order had been made by the court in England and Wales, s 132[a] of the Insolvency Act 1986 required the Official Receiver to investigate the causes of the company's failure, and to make a report to the court if he thought fit. He was also required by s 7(3)[b] of the Company Directors Disqualification Act 1986 (the Disqualification Act), if he were satisfied that the conduct of a person as director of the insolvent company had made him unfit to be concerned in the management of a company, to report that matter to the Secretary of State. It was then for the Secretary of State to decide whether it was expedient in the public interest to seek a disqualification order against that person under s 6(1) of the Disqualification Act. In a case where the company was being wound up by the court, the Secretary of State could direct, under s 7(1)(b) of the Disqualification Act, that the Official Receiver should make the application to the court for a disqualification order. In all other cases, the Secretary of State himself had to be the applicant. Following receipt of the Official Receiver's report under s 132 of the Insolvency Act, the Secretary of State decided to bring disqualification proceedings against H. After the Official Receiver commenced those proceedings, H applied for an order that the evidence in support be struck out and the proceedings dismissed, contending that insufficient evidence had been provided to support the allegations and/or to disclose a cause of action. In response, the Official Receiver sought disclosure of documents from two firms of solicitors and a firm of accountants, requesting access to their files relating to the company's affairs. The firms failed to comply with that request because H and others were claiming confidence in, or ownership of, the files. The Official Receiver then

---

a   Section 132, so far as material, provides: '(1) Where a winding-up order is made by the court in England and Wales, it is the duty of the official receiver to investigate—(a) if the company has failed, the causes of the failure ... and to make such report (if any) to the court as he thinks fit ... '
b   Section 7, so far as material, is set out at [27], below

a   issued applications for the production of the documents under s 236[c] of the
Insolvency Act, one of a series of provisions in that Act, including s 235, which
provided the Official Receiver with the investigatory powers necessary for him to
carry out his duty under s 132, notwithstanding that he might have been replaced
as liquidator. The district judge granted the applications, and H, who had been
made a party to them, appealed to the High Court, submitting that s 236 of the
b   Insolvency Act could not be invoked to obtain documents or information for use
in disqualification proceedings which had been commenced before the making of
the application under s 236. That contention was accepted by the judge who
accordingly allowed the appeal. The Official Receiver appealed to the Court of
Appeal.

c
Held – The court had no power to make an order, on an application by the
Official Receiver under s 236 of the Insolvency Act, for the production of
documents by third parties in circumstances where the sole purpose of the
application was to obtain documents for use as evidence in pending proceedings
under the Disqualification Act. Such an application fell outside the scope of s 236
d   and would therefore be an application for an improper purpose. Two reasons
compelled that conclusion. First, in a case where the company was not being
wound up by the court, the applicant in any disqualification proceedings had to be
the Secretary of State, and he was not a person who could invoke directly the
powers conferred by ss 235 and 236 of the Insolvency Act. Those powers were
e   conferred on the liquidator for the better discharge of his functions in the winding
up, not to enable the Secretary of State to obtain, indirectly, information and
documents which Parliament had not thought it necessary or appropriate to
enable him to obtain directly. There was no reason to think that Parliament
intended that the powers to obtain information and documents for use in
disqualification proceedings should be any greater in a case where the company
f   was being wound up by the court than in a case where the company was in a
voluntary winding up. Second, in a case where the company was being wound
up by the court, the function of the Official Receiver under the Insolvency Act
was to investigate the causes of failure and to report to the court. Although it was
plainly intended that the Official Receiver should be able to invoke the powers
g   under ss 235 and 236 for the purpose of discharging that function, it could not have
been intended that he should invoke those powers either for the purpose of carrying
out his role under s 7(3) of the Disqualification Act or for the purpose of obtaining
evidence for use in disqualification proceedings of which he had conduct under
s 7(1)(b) of that Act, save in so far as either purpose was incidental to the discharge
h   of his function under s 132 of the Insolvency Act. Accordingly, the appeal would
be dismissed (see [36]–[39], [41], [42], below).

Notes

For investigation by the Official Receiver, powers of the Official Receiver on an
j   inquiry into a company's dealings and reports to the Secretary of State as to the
unfitness of a person to be a director, see 7(3) *Halsbury's Laws* (4th edn) (1996
reissue) paras 2273, 2439, 2878.

For the Insolvency Act 1986, ss 132, 236, see 4 *Halsbury's Statutes* (4th edn)
(1998 reissue) 828, 904.

---

c   Section 236, so far as material, is set out [18], below

For the Company Directors Disqualification Act 1986, s 7, see 8 *Halsbury's Statutes* (4th edn) (1999 reissue) 844.

a

Cases referred to in judgments

British and Commonwealth Holdings plc (joint administrators) v Spicer & Oppenheim (a firm) [1992] 4 All ER 876, [1993] AC 426, [1992] 3 WLR 853, HL.

Castle New Homes Ltd, Re [1979] 2 All ER 775, [1979] 1 WLR 1075.

b

Cloverbay Ltd (joint administrators) v Bank of Credit and Commerce International SA [1991] 1 All ER 894, [1991] Ch 90, [1990] 3 WLR 574, CA.

NP Engineering and Security Products Ltd, Re, Official Receiver v Pafundo [1998] 1 BCLC 208, CA.

Cases also cited or referred to in skeleton arguments

c

Astra Holdings plc, Re, Secretary of State for Trade and Industry v Anderson [1998] 2 BCLC 44.

Barings plc, Re, Secretary of State for Trade and Industry v Baker [1998] 1 All ER 673, [1998] Ch 356.

First Tokyo Index Trust v Gould [1996] BPIR 406.

d

Global Info Inc, Re [1999] 1 BCLC 74.

Official Receiver v Stern [2001] 1 All ER 633, [2000] 1 WLR 2230, CA.

PFTZM Ltd, Re, Jourdain v Paul [1995] 2 BCLC 354.

Secretary of State for Trade and Industry v Hickling [1996] BCC 678.

Southbourne Sheet Metal Co Ltd, Re [1993] 1 WLR 224, CA.

e

Appeal

The Official Receiver appealed with permission of Aldous LJ granted on 11 January 2001 from the decision of Judge Weeks QC, sitting as a deputy judge of the High Court, on 14 November 2000 ([2000] All ER (D) 1815, [2001] 1 WLR 730) allowing an appeal by Andrew Thomas George Hay, the respondent to f disqualification proceedings brought by the Official Receiver under the Company Directors Disqualification Act 1986, from the orders of District Judge Frenkel made at Bristol County Court on 2 October 2000 under s 236 of the Insolvency Act 1986, requiring three professional firms, Meade-King, Wadge Rapps & Hunt and Grant Thornton, to produce within seven days documents in their possession relating to Pantmaenog Timber Co Ltd, a company in compulsory liquidation of g which Mr Hay had formerly been a director. The firms took no part in the proceedings. The facts are set out in the judgment of Chadwick LJ.

Jonathan Crow and *Bridget Lucas* (instructed by *Osborne Clarke OWA*, Bristol) for the Official Receiver.

h

Stephen Davies QC and *Hugh Sims* (instructed by *Beachcroft Wansbrough*) for Mr Hay.

Cur adv vult

25 July 2001. The following judgments were delivered.

j

CHADWICK LJ (giving the first judgment at the invitation of Kennedy LJ).

[1] These are appeals from orders made on 14 November 2000 by Judge Weeks QC, sitting as a deputy judge of the High Court in the Chancery Division, in proceedings in the liquidation of Pantmaenog Timber Co Ltd (the company) (see [2000] All ER (D) 1815, [2001] 1 WLR 730). In making those orders the judge

a allowed appeals from, and set aside, orders made on 2 October 2000 by District Judge Frenkel on applications made by the Official Receiver under s 236 of the Insolvency Act 1986 (the Insolvency Act) against two firms of solicitors and a firm of accountants. Those firms have taken no part in the proceedings and do not appear on this appeal. The effective respondent to the appeal is Mr Andrew Hay, a former director of the company against whom the Official Receiver has brought

b proceedings in which he seeks a disqualification order under s 6 of the Company Directors Disqualification Act 1986 (the Disqualification Act).

[2] The appeals fall within s 55(1) of the Access to Justice Act 1999. They are brought with the permission of this court (Aldous LJ) granted on 11 January 2001. Permission was granted on the basis that the appeals raise a point of some general importance in relation to the powers of the Official Receiver; namely, whether,

c at a time when the Official Receiver is pursuing disqualification proceedings against a former director, the court has jurisdiction to make an order, on an application made by the Official Receiver under s 236 of the Insolvency Act, requiring third parties to disclose documents and provide information to him in circumstances where the sole purpose of the application is to obtain evidence for

d use in the disqualification proceedings.

The underlying facts

[3] The company was incorporated under the Companies Act 1985 with the object of purchasing Pantmaenog Forest in the Pembrokeshire National Park from the Hay family trust. Mr Andrew Hay was one of the first directors of the

e company. The purchase was completed on 25 March 1995 by the issue to the Hay trustees of preference shares in the company. The company commenced trading shortly thereafter. It engaged Tilhill Economic Forestry Ltd to provide a forestry management service.

[4] On 16 May 1996 information was laid before the magistrates in Haverfordwest

f alleging that the company and Mr Hay had permitted the felling of trees in excess of the number allowed by the felling licence. Shortly thereafter, on 30 May 1996, Tilhill issued proceedings against the company in respect of unpaid fees. The company responded with a counterclaim alleging that Tilhill had failed to comply with instructions to obtain an adequate felling licence. On 29 April 1997 those

g proceedings were compromised on terms that Tilhill paid the sum of £6,500 to the company. In the meantime the company and Mr Hay had been convicted in the magistrates' court. Mr Hay's appeal to the Crown Court was dismissed on 29 November 1997. On 8 December 1997 he resigned as a director of the company. The company's appeal to the High Court, by way of case stated, was dismissed by consent on 28 January 1998. The company remained liable to pay £11,500 or

h thereabouts in respect of the fine and costs imposed by the magistrates.

[5] The company had ceased trading on 25 September 1997. On 16 April 1998 it sold its business to a new company, Pantmaenog Ltd, of which Mr Hay and his father, Mr Peter Hay, were directors. The purchase price, some £912,000, seems to have been applied in the redemption for cash of the preference shares which

j had been issued to the Hay trustees in 1995.

[6] On 17 June 1999 an order was made in the Bristol County Court for the winding up of the company. On the making of that order the Official Receiver became liquidator of the company by virtue of his office (see s 136(2) of the Insolvency Act). On 30 November 1999, the Registrar of Companies, who appears to have been unaware that a winding-up order had been made, caused the company's name to be struck off the register under s 652 of the 1985 Act. Upon

publication in the *Gazette* that that had been done, the company was dissolved
(see s 652(5) of that Act).   *a*

The Disqualification Act proceedings

[7] Section 6(1) of the Disqualification Act requires the court, on an application
under that section, to make a disqualification order against a director or former
director of a company which has become insolvent if satisfied that his conduct as   *b*
a director of that company makes him unfit to be concerned in the management
of a company. A disqualification order, in that context, is defined by s 1(1) of that
Act. Section 7(3) of the Disqualification Act requires the Official Receiver (in a
case where the company is being wound up by the court in England and Wales),
if it appears to him that the conditions mentioned in s 6(1) are satisfied as respects   *c*
a person who is or has been a director of that company, to report that matter to
the Secretary of State. It is for the Secretary of State to decide whether it is
expedient in the public interest that a disqualification order under s 6 of the Act
should be made against a person who is the subject of a report made under s 7(3)
(see s 7(1) of the Act). But, where the Secretary of State is of the view that a
disqualification order should be made, an application for such an order may be   *d*
made, if the Secretary of State so directs and where the company is being wound up
by the court in England and Wales, by the Official Receiver (see para (b) of s 7(1)).

[8] An application for a disqualification order under s 6 of the Disqualification
Act against Mr Hay was made by proceedings commenced in the Bristol County
Court on 29 February 2000. The application was made by the Official Receiver,   *e*
purporting to act on the direction of the Secretary of State under s 7(1)(b) of that
Act. The application, when made, was irregular in that—unknown to the Official
Receiver and, no doubt, to the Secretary of State—the company had been
dissolved some three months earlier. The effect of dissolution was that, at the
date when the application for a disqualification order was made, the company   *f*
was, strictly, no longer being wound up by the court—so that s 7(1)(b) had no
application. In the circumstances as they were at the time, the application for a
disqualification order should have been made by the Secretary of State, acting
under s 7(1)(a). But the proceedings, although irregular, were not fatally flawed.
The normal course, upon the Official Receiver and the Secretary of State becoming
aware of the dissolution, would have been to transfer the proceedings from the   *g*
county court to the High Court and to substitute the Secretary of State as
applicant in the place of the Official Receiver (see *Re NP Engineering and Security
Products Ltd, Official Receiver v Pafundo* [1998] 1 BCLC 208). An application for
transfer and substitution was, in fact, made jointly by the Official Receiver and the
Secretary of State in the present case on 4 September 2000; but, in circumstances   *h*
which I shall describe, it was not pursued.

[9] Proceedings under the Disqualification Act are subject to the Insolvent
Companies (Disqualification of Unfit Directors) Proceedings Rules 1987, SI
1987/2023. Rule 3(1) of those rules requires that, at the time when the proceedings
are issued, there must be filed in court evidence in support of the application for   *j*
a disqualification order. Where the applicant is the Official Receiver, that
evidence is in the form of a written report 'which shall be prima facie evidence of
any matter contained in it' (see r 3(2)). Rule 3(3) requires that the Official
Receiver's report shall include 'a statement of the matters by reference to which
the [respondent] is alleged to be unfit to be concerned in the management of a
company'.

[10] The application for a disqualification order against Mr Hay was supported
by a report made by the Official Receiver and dated 29 February 2000. No copy
of that report has been put before this court; but it appears from the judgment
delivered by Judge Weeks QC on 14 November 2000 ([2001] 1 WLR 730 at 733),
that the report contained three allegations of misconduct on the part of Mr Hay:
(i) causing the company to redeem the preference shares before paying the fine and
costs imposed by the magistrates; (ii) failing to ensure that adequate accounting
records were kept; and (iii) causing the company to contravene its felling licence.
The first of those matters—causing the company to redeem the preference
shares issued to the Hay trustees—took place some two years after Mr Hay had
resigned as a director of the company. As the judge put it (at 733): 'It was alleged,
implicitly if not explicitly, that Mr Hay was a de facto director after his resignation
on 8 December 1997.'

[11] Rule 6(1) of the 1987 rules provides for the respondent to an application
for a disqualification order to file in court such affidavit evidence in opposition to
the application as he wishes the court to take into consideration. Mr Hay did not
take that course. Instead he applied for an order that the Official Receiver's
evidence be struck out and that the proceedings against him be dismissed. The
grounds stated in his application were that 'the claimant does not provide
sufficient evidence to support his allegations and/or to disclose a cause of action'.
The application was supported by a witness statement, dated 16 May 2000 and
signed by a partner in the firm of Meade-King, solicitors, who had acted for the
company both in the civil proceedings brought by Tilhill and in the criminal
proceedings in the Haverfordwest Magistrates' Court. He had also acted from
time to time for Mr Hay and for his father, Mr Peter Hay.

[12] On 16 August 2000 the Bristol County Court gave notice that Mr Hay's
application to strike out the proceedings against him was listed for hearing before
Judge Weeks QC on 12 October 2000. In the circumstances to which I am about
to refer, that application has not yet been heard.

The proceedings in the liquidation

[13] As I have said, the winding-up order was made on 17 June 1999. Section 32
of the Insolvency Act provides that where an order for winding up is made by the
court in England and Wales it is the duty of the Official Receiver to investigate
the causes of failure of the company and to make a report. Over the next five
months the Official Receiver made inquiries of both Mr Hay and his father, and
also of Messrs Wadge Rapps & Hunt, the firm of solicitors who had acted on the
transfer of the Pantmaenog woodlands from the company to Pantmaenog Ltd. It
is reasonable to assume that it was as a result of a report made following those
inquiries that the Secretary of State decided that it was expedient in the public
interest that a disqualification order should be made. No immediate steps were
taken to appoint an insolvency practitioner as liquidator in the place of the
Official Receiver pursuant to s 137(1) of the Act.

[14] It appears that neither the Official Receiver nor the Secretary of State
became aware, until September 2000, that the company had been dissolved under
s 652(5) of the 1985 Act on 30 November 1999. On 1 June 2000, the Secretary of
State purported to appoint Mr M P Gerrard, a partner in Messrs Grant Thornton,
as liquidator in place of the Official Receiver. The appointment was ineffective
in law—at the time when it was made—because, for the reason which I have
already explained, the company was then no longer in the course of winding up.

But the practical effect was that the company's books and papers were transferred to Mr Gerrard.

[15] On 4 September 2000, as I have said, the Official Receiver and the Secretary of State made a joint application to transfer the disqualification proceedings to the High Court and to substitute the Secretary of State as claimant in those proceedings. Some nine days later, however, the Official Receiver had second thoughts. As the judge put it ([2001] 1 WLR 730 at 735): 'On 13 September … the official receiver changed tack.' He issued an application in his own name, and in the name of the company, to which the Registrar of Companies and the Treasury Solicitor were the only respondents, seeking an order under s 653 of the 1985 Act for the restoration of the company's name to the register. The grounds of the application, as recorded by the judge (at 735), were that 'Mr Gerrard as liquidator could then issue misfeasance proceedings seeking repayment of some £387,000'. The order was made by the district judge, without opposition, at a hearing on 2 October 2000. No notice of that hearing was given to Mr Hay. The effect of the order restoring the name of the company to the register was that the company was deemed to have continued in existence as if its name had not been struck off (see s 653(3) of the 1985 Act). By that means the initial defect in the constitution of the disqualification proceedings was cured; the Official Receiver could rely on s 7(1)(b) of the Disqualification Act.

The applications under s 236 of the Insolvency Act

[16] Faced with Mr Hay's application to strike out the disqualification proceedings the Official Receiver sought disclosure of documents from Meade-King, Wadge Rapps & Hunt and Grant Thornton. His letters to those firms, requesting access to their files relating to the company's affairs, are dated 25 and 27 July 2000. It is apparent that Mr Hay was made aware of those requests; although not by the Official Receiver. Each of the three firms replied to the Official Receiver to the effect that Mr Hay, his father, or a company with which Mr Hay was associated, AJP Management Ltd, were claiming confidence in, or ownership of, the files in their possession. The position adopted appears from a letter dated 11 September 2000 from Messrs Beachcroft Wansborough, written on behalf of AJP Management Ltd but at a time when that firm also acted for Mr Hay, to Messrs Osborne Clarke OWA, the solicitors instructed by the Official Receiver:

'It is acknowledged that some of the material on file may be susceptible to an application under section 236 of the Insolvency Act. However our client's instructions are to refuse consent to disclosure of the files save material properly relating to the business dealings and affairs of Pantmaenog and which is not otherwise protected from the duty of disclosure. In order properly to advise our client we do need to see the files ourselves. As we understand it Meade King's position is that they will not release the files to either side without agreement. Therefore as a pragmatic solution we should invite you to agree that the files should be released from Meade King to ourselves, in order that we may conduct a review and advise our client in detail on the question of disclosure. As a result of that process it may be that we are able to authorise the release of material relating to Pantmaenog that will obviate the need for litigation on this issue. We regret that our client has not authorised the disclosure of further details of the Grant Thornton advice a beyond that already disclosed. Our instructions are that the advice was provided to the trustees of the Hay family trust and not to Pantmaenog.'

[17] The suggestion that Mr Hay's advisors should see the material first, so that they could satisfy themselves what (if anything) was properly the subject of claims to confidentiality or ownership, was not acceptable to the Official Receiver and his advisors. On 26 September 2000 Osborne Clarke issued applications on
b behalf of the Official Receiver for production of documents relating to the affairs or property of the company. Those applications were heard by District Judge Frenkel on 2 October 2000, immediately after the application under s 653 of the 1985 Act for the restoration of the company to the register.

[18] Section 236 of the Insolvency Act is in these terms, so far as material:

c
'(1) This section applies as does section 234; and it also applies in the case of a company in respect of which a winding-up order has been made by the court in England and Wales as if references to the office-holder included the official receiver, whether or not he is the liquidator.

d (2) The court may, on the application of the office-holder, summon to appear before it ... (c) any person whom the court thinks capable of giving information concerning the promotion, formation, business, dealings, affairs or property of the company.

(3) The court may require any such person as is mentioned in subsection (2)(a) to (c) to ... produce any books, papers or other records in his possession
e or under his control relating to the company or the matters mentioned in paragraph (c) of the subsection.'

The effect of the opening words of s 236(1)—'This section applies as does section 234'—is that s 236 of the Act applies where a company goes into liquidation. In the context of s 234 'office-holder' includes the liquidator; but the effect of the
f second limb of s 236(1) is that that expression, in the context of s 236, also includes the Official Receiver, whether or not he is also the liquidator.

[19] The affidavits sworn by Mr Nigel Boobier, a solicitor employed by Osborne Clarke, in support of the applications for orders for the production of documents under s 236(3) of the Insolvency Act, contained a paragraph in the
g following terms:

'The Claimant [meaning the Official Receiver] is investigating in accordance with his statutory duty the business, dealings and affairs of Pantmaenog Timber Company Limited ("the Company") pursuant to Section 132 of the Insolvency Act 1986 ("the Act"). In addition, the Claimant has issued proceedings
h against some directors of the Company pursuant to the Company Directors Disqualification Act 1986.'

That paragraph may, I think, fairly be described as disingenuous. The true position appears from a passage in the judgment below:

j 'It was conceded before me that the sole purpose of seeking those orders was to obtain evidence to be used by the official receiver in the disqualification proceedings, either on Mr Hay's application to strike out or subsequently. The district judge was not told that that was the sole purpose, although he was aware that the official receiver might find the documents useful in those proceedings.' (See [2001] 1 WLR 730 at 736.)

The orders made by the district judge

[20] The district judge made the orders sought. He ordered that Meade-King—

'do within 7 days from the date of this order produce to the Claimant or his solicitors copies of all correspondence, internal memoranda, books, records, accounts, receipts, invoices and other documentation in [their] custody, possession or power which relate to the promotion, formation, business, dealings, affairs or property of Pantmaenog Timber Co Ltd, which includes documentation relating to proceedings by Tilhill Economic Forestry Ltd and dealing with a criminal prosecution both against the company.'

He ordered, further, that Meade-King make available for inspection and provide printed copies of all information stored electronically relating to those matters. Orders against Wadge Rapps & Hunt and Grant Thornton were made in similar terms; save that the documents and information to be produced by Wadge Rapps & Hunt were limited to those which related to the transfer of the Pantmaenog woodlands from the company, and the documents and information to be produced by Grant Thornton were limited to those which related to advice provided in relation to the company concerning the redemption of preference shares in the company. Each of the orders required Mr Hay to pay the Official Receiver's costs, assessed in the sum of £500.

[21] We have been provided with a note of the district judge's reasons for the orders which he made. He said this:

'I have a wide discretion under section 236 of the Insolvency Act 1986. The Official Receiver is applying for specific disclosure of documents. I am satisfied that no one can suffer any prejudice or trespass upon their legal rights of privilege or fear that other documents under the draft order being disclosed. The three applications relate to documents which either belong to or relate to the company ... Mr Hay seeks to rely on some form of oppression by the disclosure of the documents as the Official Receiver may find them useful in the company directors disqualification proceedings. I make my order with that in mind and that that might be the case. I however see nothing oppressive. The Official Receiver has to act in the public interest and if the Official Receiver seeks to introduce further evidence, it seems to me that if that puts the defendant [meaning Mr Hay] at a disadvantage then the court may adjourn the hearing to reconsider the position.'

[22] Neither Meade-King, Wadge Rapps & Hunt nor Grant Thornton attended or were represented before the district judge. Each had written to the court indicating, I think, that they were content to abide with whatever order it should make. Mr Hay had been made a party to the applications under s 236 of the Insolvency Act. He was represented by solicitors and, as I have said, the district judge made orders for costs against him.

The decision in the High Court

[23] Mr Hay appealed to the High Court, as he was entitled to do under r 7.47(2) of the Insolvency Rules 1986, SI 1986/1925. The primary submission made on his behalf—as appears from the judgment ([2001] 1 WLR 730 at 737)—was that s 236 of the Insolvency Act could not be invoked in order to obtain documents or information for use in disqualification proceedings; at least where those proceedings had been commenced before the application under s 236 was

a made. The judge (at 737 and 740) accepted that submission. He went on to say this (at 740):

> 'It follows from the concession made to me that the orders ought not to have been made in the instant case and I will set them aside. I understand that in two cases they have already been complied with and I will order the return of any documents supplied under those orders and any copies already
b   taken.'

The 'concession' to which the judge was referring in that passage was that which he had set out earlier in his judgment (at 736); namely that the sole purpose of seeking orders under s 236 of the Insolvency Act had been to obtain evidence to be used by the Official Receiver in the disqualification proceedings.

c   [24] In reaching the conclusion which he did the judge reminded himself of the observations of Lord Slynn of Hadley in *British and Commonwealth Holdings plc (joint administrators) v Spicer & Oppenheim (a firm)* [1992] 4 All ER 876 at 884–885, [1993] AC 426 at 439:

> '… it is plain that this [the power under s 236] is an extraordinary power
d   and that the discretion must be exercised after a careful balancing of the factors involved: on the one hand the reasonable requirements of the [office-holder] to carry out his task, on the other the need to avoid making an order which is wholly unreasonable, unnecessary or "oppressive" to the person concerned.'

e Lord Slynn went on, in a passage to which the judge did not refer expressly but which he plainly had in mind, to say this:

> 'The protection for the person called upon to produce documents lies, thus, not in a limitation by category of documents ("reconstituting the company's knowledge") but in the fact that the applicant must satisfy
f   the court that, after balancing all the relevant factors, there is a proper case for such an order to be made. The proper case is one where the [office-holder] reasonably requires to see the documents to carry out his functions and the production does not impose an unnecessary and unreasonable burden on the person required to produce them in the light of the [office-holder's]
g   requirements.' (See [1992] 4 All ER 876 at 885, [1993] AC 426 at 439.)

[25] It is important to keep in mind that, in the present case, the persons required to produce the documents—Meade-King, Wadge Rapps & Hunt and Grant Thornton—were not suggesting that orders under s 236 of the Act would impose unnecessary or unreasonable burdens upon them. There was no reason,
h on that ground, to refuse the orders sought. The judge based his conclusion on the premise that the first limb of Lord Slynn's test was not satisfied; that is to say, that this was not a case in which the Official Receiver needed to see the documents in order to carry out his functions. He said this:

> 'In relation to non-disqualification proceedings, the court in earlier cases
j   sought to draw a line named after an Italian river, the Rubicon. Once that line had been crossed, compulsory powers of obtaining documents were no longer available. In relation to disqualification proceedings, the line is, in my judgment, effectively drawn by the scheme of the legislation. It comes after the report under section 7(3) of the Company Directors Disqualification Act 1986, which is part of the investigative functions of the office holder and for which the period of two years is allowed, and before the initiation of the

proceedings under section 7(1), which is an entirely different function of the official receiver, if so directed by the Secretary of State. In the proceedings the Secretary of State or the official receiver has the usual methods available to any litigant of obtaining the production of documents or the attendance of witnesses. It is not necessary for him to have the special advantages of sections 235 and 236 in the proceedings because the office holder has, ex hypothesi, already reported under section 7(3). If the Secretary of State or the official receiver requires further information or papers from the liquidator, he has the specific powers conferred on him by section 7(4) of the Company Directors Disqualification Act 1986.' (See [2001] 1 WLR 730 at 739.)

[26] The crossing of the Rubicon—familiar to students of Caesar's campaign against Pompey—made its first appearance as a tool of judicial analysis in this field, I think, in the submission of Mr John Lindsay (as he then was) to Slade J in *Re Castle New Homes Ltd* [1979] 2 All ER 775 at 788, [1979] 1 WLR 1075 at 1089. It came to signify the point after which the court would not, in practice, permit a liquidator to have recourse to the powers, formerly contained in s 268 of the Companies Act 1948 and now found in s 236 of the Insolvency Act. Slade J propounded the test in *Re Castle New Homes Ltd* [1979] 2 All ER 775 at 789, [1979] 1 WLR 1075 at 1089:

'If the evidence shows that the purpose of a liquidator in seeking the examination is to achieve an advantage beyond that available to the ordinary litigant, in litigation which he has already commenced or which he has definitely decided to commence, the predisposition of the court may well be to refuse an immediate order for examination, unless the liquidator can show special grounds to the contrary. If, however, it appears from the evidence that the object of the liquidator is simply to elicit information which will enable or assist him to decide whether or not his company has a valid claim against a third party, the court will approach the liquidator's application with no such predisposition.'

By 1990, when there was an opportunity for this court to consider the point in *Cloverbay Ltd (joint administrators) v Bank of Credit and Commerce International SA* [1991] 1 All ER 894, [1991] Ch 90, 'the Rubicon test', as it had become known, had become entrenched in the practice of the Companies Court. It was disapproved by this court in the *Cloverbay* case (see the observations of Browne-Wilkinson V-C and of Nourse LJ [1991] 1 All ER 894 at 899, 903–904, [1991] Ch 90 at 101, 106 respectively). In a passage subsequently reflected in the speech of Lord Slynn in the *British and Commonwealth Holdings* case, Browne-Wilkinson V-C said this:

'The words of the [Insolvency Act] do not fetter the court's discretion in any way. Circumstances may vary infinitely. It is clear that in exercising the discretion [under s 236 of the Act] the court has to balance the requirements of the liquidator against any possible oppression to the person to be examined. Such balancing depends on the relationship between the importance to the liquidator of obtaining the information on the one hand and the degree of oppression to the person sought to be examined on the other.' (See [1991] 1 All ER 894 at 900, [1991] Ch 90 at 102.)

In so far as Judge Weeks QC was seeking to revive and apply a 'Rubicon test' in the present case—as counsel who appears for the Official Receiver on this appeal a submits that he was—the judge was in error. For my part, however, I doubt if that was in the judge's mind. I think it reasonably clear that he took the view that the conclusion which he reached was the necessary result of a process of statutory construction.

[27] Section 7(3) and (4) of the Disqualification Act, to which the judge referred in the passage of his judgment which I have set out ([2001] 1 WLR 730 at 739), are

b in these terms:

'(3) If it appears to the office-holder responsible under this section, that is to say—(a) in the case of a company which is being wound up by the court in England and Wales, the official receiver, (b) in the case of a company which is being wound up otherwise, the liquidator, (c) in the case of a company

c in relation to which an administration order is in force, the administrator, or (d) in the case of a company of which there is an administrative receiver, that receiver, that the conditions mentioned in section 6(1) are satisfied as respects a person who is or has been a director of that company, the office-holder shall forthwith report the matter to the Secretary of State.

d (4) The Secretary of State or the official receiver may require the liquidator, administrator or administrative receiver of a company, or the former liquidator, administrator or administrative receiver of a company—(a) to furnish him with such information with respect to any person's conduct as a director of the company, and (b) to produce and permit inspection of such books, papers and other records relevant to that person's conduct as such

e director, as the Secretary of State or the official receiver may reasonably require for the purpose *of determining whether to exercise, or of exercising*, any function of his under this section.' (My emphasis.)

It is clear from the words which I have emphasised that the power conferred on the Secretary of State by s 7(4) of the Act—to require an office-holder to provide

f information or to produce documents—is exercisable both before and after he has reached any decision, under s 7(1), that it is expedient in the public interest that a disqualification order under s 6 should be made. It is clear, also, that—in a case where the application for a disqualification order is to be made by the Official Receiver under s 7(1)(b), after such a decision has been reached by the Secretary of State—the Official Receiver has power, under s 7(4) of the Disqualification Act,

g to require an office-holder to provide information or to produce documents for the purpose of pursuing that application.

[28] The view which the judge took made it unnecessary for him to consider whether the orders could be challenged on the grounds that the district judge had erred in the exercise of his discretion. But he said this in the penultimate

h paragraph of his judgment (at 740):

'[Counsel] had alternative submissions as to the exercise of discretion that exists under section 236. I do not think I need to go into those submissions in any detail, but I should record some concern at the width of the orders and the fact that they were obtained on short notice and without joining all the

j parties who asserted title to the documents or rights to keep them private. The order addressed to Grant Thornton is particularly surprising because, on the face of it, it extends to advice given to anyone in relation to the company and neither Mr Peter Hay nor the Hay Trust, to whom the advice was allegedly given, was joined as a party to the application.'

Was there jurisdiction to make an order under s 236 of the Insolvency Act?

[29] As I have indicated, the question of principle raised by this appeal is whether, at a time when the Official Receiver is pursuing disqualification proceedings against a former director, the court has jurisdiction to make an order under s 236 of the Insolvency Act requiring third parties to disclose documents and provide information to him in circumstances where the sole purpose of the application is to obtain evidence for use in the disqualification proceedings.

[30] Section 236(2) of the Insolvency Act must be read in conjunction with the two sections which precede it. Section 234 gives the court power to require any person who has in his possession or control any property, books, papers or records *to which the company appears to be entitled* to deliver the property, books, papers or records to the office-holder. In that context the office-holder means the administrator, the administrative receiver, the liquidator or the provisional liquidator (as the case may be) but does not include the Official Receiver—unless, of course, he is liquidator or provisional liquidator. Section 235 imposes a duty on those who are or have been officers or employees of the company to co-operate with the office-holder; and, in particular, to give to the office-holder such information concerning the company as he may reasonably require. The obligation is enforced by a penal sanction (see s 235(5)). Section 236 reinforces ss 234 and 235; but goes one step further. It enables the court to summon before it *any person whom the court thinks capable of giving information concerning the affairs or property of the company* (see s 236(2)(c)) and to require any such person to produce books, papers or other records in his possession or under his control (whether or not such books, papers and records belong to the company or to the person summoned to appear). The power is enforceable by arrest (see s 236(5)).

[31] Sections 235 and 236 extend the meaning of 'office-holder' to include the Official Receiver (whether or not he is the liquidator of the company) in cases where the company is the subject of a winding-up order made by the court in England and Wales. In order to understand why that was thought appropriate it is necessary to have regard to ss 132 and 133 of the Act, and to ss 136 and 137.

[32] Section 132 of the Act provides that where a winding-up order is made by a court in England and Wales it is the duty of the Official Receiver to investigate, if the company has failed, the causes of the failure; and, if he thinks fit, to make a report to the court. Section 133 provides that, where a company is being wound up by the court in England and Wales, the Official Receiver may apply to the court for the public examination of any person who has been an officer of the company or has been concerned in its promotion, formation or management. Sections 235 and 236 of the Act may be seen as a further adjunct to s 132; that is to say, as providing the means (short of public examination under s 133) by which the Official Receiver can carry out the duties imposed on him by s 132.

[33] Section 136 of the Act applies, also, in cases where a company is being wound up by the court in England and Wales; save in the case where the winding-up order follows immediately upon the discharge of an administration order or where there is an existing voluntary arrangement (see s 140). In a case to which s 136 applies, the Official Receiver becomes the liquidator of the company by virtue of his office, until some other person is appointed in his place—either by the Secretary of State under s 137(1) or by the creditors or contributories under s 139. The effect of ss 235 and 236, therefore, is to provide the Official Receiver with the investigatory powers which he requires in order to carry out the duty imposed upon him by s 132, notwithstanding that he may have been replaced as liquidator of the company.

a
[34] For the purposes of the provisions of the Insolvency Act to which I have referred, the 'official receiver' in relation to a company means (subject to any direction given by the Secretary of State under s 399(6) or any appointment made under s 401(1) of the Act) the person holding the office of Official Receiver who is attached to the court in which the company is being wound up (see ss 399(1) and (4)). The same person is the 'official receiver' for the purposes of the Disqualification Act

b
(see s 21(1) of that Act).

[35] With those provisions in mind, it is easy to see why, in a case where a company is being wound up in England and Wales, s 7(3)(a) of the Disqualification Act provides that the person to consider whether the conditions mentioned in s 6(1) of the Act are satisfied as respects a person who is or has been a director of that company, and to make a report to the Secretary of State to that effect, is the Official

c
Receiver; and why s 7(1)(b) provides that the Secretary of State may direct that, in the case of a person who is or has been a director of a company which is being wound up by the court in England and Wales, the application for a disqualification order under s 6 of that Act should be made by the Official Receiver. In such a case the Official Receiver—being the Official Receiver attached to the court in which the

d
company is being wound up—is likely to be familiar with the affairs of the company and the conduct of persons in relation to it. He will have investigated the causes of failure—ex hypothesi the company will be a company which has failed (see s 6(1)(a) of the Disqualification Act and s 132(1)(a) of the Insolvency Act). He may have made a report to the court as a result of that investigation (see s 132(2) of the Insolvency Act). He will have become the liquidator (save in a case within s 140 of

e
the Act)—see s 136 of the Insolvency Act—and may still be in office as liquidator. There is obvious potential for the saving of cost and expense, in such a case, if the person who has those functions in relation to the winding up of the company is the person to make the report under s 7(3)(a) and to pursue the application for a disqualification order under s 7(1)(b) of the Disqualification Act.

f
[36] It does not follow, however, that the Official Receiver is entitled to invoke the powers conferred by ss 235 and 236 of the Insolvency Act for the purpose of carrying out the role entrusted to him by the Secretary of State under s 7(1)(b) of the Disqualification Act. The question, as the judge identified, is for what purpose have powers been conferred on the Official Receiver by s 235, and on the court by s 236; in particular, does that purpose extend to the obtaining of

g
information and documents solely for use as evidence in proceedings under the Disqualification Act. In my view the judge was right to answer that question in the negative.

[37] There are, as it seems to me, two reasons which compel that conclusion. First, in a case where the company is not being wound up by the court, the applicant

h
in any disqualification proceedings must be the Secretary of State. The Secretary of State is not a person who can invoke, directly, the powers conferred by ss 235 and 236 of the Insolvency Act. It is true that the Secretary of State can require the liquidator of the company, under s 7(4) of the Disqualification Act, to furnish him with information and to produce books and papers relating to the conduct of a

j
person against whom an application for a disqualification order has been made. That is the effect of the words '*or of exercising, any function of his under this section*' which appear in s 7(4). It was suggested in argument, by counsel for the Official Receiver, that, in the exercise of that power the Secretary of State could require the liquidator to exercise the power conferred on him under s 235 of the Insolvency Act, and could require the liquidator to make an application under s 236 of that Act. Further, it was submitted that the liquidator could properly exercise the power under s 235, or apply

to the court for an order under s 236, in order to obtain information and documents for the sole purpose of use by the Secretary of State in disqualification proceedings. In my view those contentions are misconceived. The reason, as it seems to me, is that the powers conferred by ss 235 and 236 are conferred on the liquidator for the better discharge of his functions in the winding up; and are not conferred to enable the Secretary of State to obtain, indirectly, information and documents which Parliament has not thought it necessary or appropriate to enable him to obtain directly. There is no reason to think that Parliament intended that the powers to obtain information and documents for use in disqualification proceedings should be any greater in a case where the company was being wound up by the court in England and Wales than in a case where the company was in voluntary winding up. As I have sought to explain, the role of the Official Receiver in relation to disqualification proceedings in a case where the company is being wound up by the court is attributable to considerations of convenience and cost; there is no reason to explain that role on the basis that it reflects an intention to provide enhanced powers in relation to the obtaining of information and documents.

[38] Second, in a case where the company is being wound up by the court in England and Wales, the function of the Official Receiver, under the Insolvency Act, is to investigate the causes of failure and to make a report *to the court* (see s 132 of that Act). It was plainly intended that the Official Receiver should be able to invoke the powers conferred by ss 235 and 236 for the purpose of discharging that function. Equally, as it seems to me, information which he obtains in the course of discharging his function under s 132 of the Insolvency Act is information to which he is intended to have regard, and to take into account, in making the report to the Secretary of State which s 7(3)(a) of the Disqualification Act requires. And, information which he obtains in the course of discharging his function under s 132 of the Insolvency Act is information which he is intended to use in pursuing disqualification proceedings, if that role is entrusted to him under s 7(1)(b) of the Disqualification Act. But the Official Receiver cannot have been intended to invoke the powers conferred by ss 235 and 236 of the Act either (i) for the purpose of carrying out his role under s 7(3) of the Disqualification Act—save in so far as that is incidental to the discharge of his function under s 132 of the Insolvency Act—or (ii) for the purpose of obtaining evidence for use in disqualification proceedings of which he has conduct under s 7(1)(b) of the Disqualification Act—again, save in so far as that is incidental to the discharge of his function under s 132 of the Insolvency Act. The reason is to be found in s 7(4) of the Disqualification Act. Unlike the Secretary of State—who may require information or documents under that section for the purpose of determining whether it is expedient in the public interest that a disqualification order should be made—the only purpose for which the Official Receiver could require an office-holder to provide information or documents under s 7(4) of the Disqualification Act would be that he reasonably required that information in connection with his functions under s 7(3)(a) or s 7(1)(b) of that Act. But, if those were functions in connection with which the powers conferred by ss 235 and 236 of the Insolvency Act could be invoked, s 7(4)—in so far as it applies to the Official Receiver—would be otiose. There would be ample power to obtain, under s 235(3)(c), any information which the Official Receiver required from a liquidator, administrator or administrative receiver. The inference, as it seems to me, is that Parliament included a reference to the Official Receiver in s 7(4) of the Disqualification Act because it was necessary to do so. It was thought necessary to do so, because Parliament did not contemplate that the Official Receiver would be able to invoke ss 235 and 236 of the Insolvency Act for that purpose. It is pertinent to keep in mind that the Insolvency

a Act and the Disqualification Act were enacted on the same day (25 July 1986) and form part of the same corpus of legislation.

[39] It follows that I would hold that the court has no power to make an order, on the application of the Official Receiver under s 236 of the Insolvency Act, for the production of documents in circumstances where the sole purpose of the application is to obtain documents for use as evidence in pending proceedings under the

b Disqualification Act. I prefer not to attribute that result to an absence of jurisdiction in the court; rather, it follows from the conclusion that an application made for that sole purpose is an application which falls outside the scope of the section. It is an application made for an improper purpose—in this context—and the court should not entertain it. But the distinction may be no more than semantic.

c *Conclusion*

[40] The conclusion which I have reached makes it unnecessary to consider whether the orders made on 2 October 2000 could be challenged on the grounds that the district judge had erred in the exercise of his discretion. But, for completeness, I should make it clear (i) that I share the concern of Judge Weeks QC as to the circumstances in which those orders were obtained, and as to their width, (ii) I would

d have held (if it had been necessary) that the district judge's exercise of his discretion could not stand in the circumstances that he was not informed that the sole purpose for which the orders were sought was for use as evidence in pending disqualification proceedings, and (iii), if it were a matter for the exercise of discretion in this court, I should not have thought it right to make the orders sought in the circumstances

e that there was a pending application to strike out the disqualification proceedings. That application, as it seems to me, falls to be determined on the basis of the case which the Official Receiver has advanced in his report under r 3 of the 1987 Rules. It is important to keep in mind that the purpose of that rule is to require the applicant for a disqualification order to set out the case which a respondent is called upon to meet under s 6 of the Disqualification Act.

[41] I would dismiss this appeal.

KENNEDY LJ.

[42] I agree.

Appeal dismissed. Permission to appeal refused.

Dilys Tausz   Barrister.

Poplar Housing and Regeneration Community Association Ltd v Donoghue

[2001] EWCA Civ 595

COURT OF APPEAL, CIVIL DIVISION

LORD WOOLF CJ, MAY AND JONATHAN PARKER LJJ

5 MARCH, 27 APRIL 2001

Housing – Housing association – Possession – Local authority providing defendant and her children with temporary accommodation – Authority transferring property to housing association – Defendant becoming tenant under assured shorthold periodic tenancy – Legislative provision requiring court to grant possession if notice to quit given – Housing association serving notice to quit – Whether order for possession contravening right to family life under human rights convention – Housing Act 1988, s 21(4) – Human Rights Act 1998, Sch 1, Pt I, art 8.

Human rights – Public authority – Private person performing functions of public nature – Test for determining whether private person performing public act – Human Rights Act 1998, s 6(3)(b).

A local authority granted the defendant, D, a weekly non-secure tenancy of a residential property pending a decision on whether she was intentionally homeless. In providing D with accommodation pending inquiries, the authority was complying with a statutory duty under the Housing Act 1996. Such accommodation could also be provided by a registered social landlord at the request of a local authority. The property was later transferred to the claimant, a housing association and registered social landlord created by the local authority in order to transfer to it a substantial proportion of the authority's housing stock. Accordingly D, who was the mother of three young children, became a tenant of the housing association under an assured shorthold periodic tenancy. By virtue of s 21(4)[a] of the Housing Act 1988, the court had to make an order for possession of a dwelling-house let on such a tenancy if the appropriate notice to quit had been given. There was no requirement for the court to be satisfied that it was reasonable to make such an order. After the local authority had concluded that D was intentionally homeless, the housing association served on her a proper notice to quit under s 21(4) and brought possession proceedings in the county court. At the hearing, which took place on the ordinary housing list, D contended that the making of a possession order would involve interpreting s 21(4) in a manner incompatible with the Human Rights Act 1998 since it would contravene her right to respect for her private and family life and for her home under art 8(1)[b] of the European Convention for the Protection of Human Rights and Fundamental Freedoms 1950 (as set out in Sch 1 to the 1998 Act). Article 8(2) prohibited any interference with that right by a public authority except such as was in accordance with the law and was necessary in a democratic society for, inter alia, the protection of the rights and freedoms of others. Although it had not been appreciated that D would raise such an issue, the district judge gave judgment

---

a   Section 21(4) is set out at [4], below
b   Article 8 is set out at [22], below

a immediately after considering the arguments. He rejected D's contention, holding that it would enable people who were intentionally homeless to jump the housing queue, thereby impeding the human rights of others contrary to the proviso to art 8(2). He therefore granted the possession order, but gave D permission to appeal directly to the Court of Appeal. On the appeal, D contended that the district judge should have adjourned the hearing so as to enable her to place

b before the court substantial evidence, now adduced in support of her appeal, which would have been directed, inter alia, to the question whether any breach of art 8 could be justified on the grounds set out in art 8(2). Since D was seeking a declaration of incompatibility, the Secretary of State intervened in the proceedings. He contended, as did the housing association, that the latter was not a public authority for the purposes of s 6(1)^c of the 1998 Act which made it unlawful for

c any such authority to act in a way which was incompatible with convention rights. Section 6(3)(b) provided that 'public authority' included any person certain of whose functions were of a public nature, while s 6(5) provided that, in relation to a particular act, a person was not a public authority by virtue only of sub-s (3)(b) if the nature of that act was private. The issue arose whether the performance of

d an activity by a private body was necessarily the performance of a public function if a public authority would otherwise have been under a duty to perform that activity.

Held – (1) Where it was possible for a judge to give a decision summarily in a case where there would almost certainly be an appeal, there could be substantial

e advantages in adopting that approach. It could avoid expense and delay being incurred both at first instance and in the Court of Appeal. In the instant case, the district judge had been entitled to dispose of the case as he had done. He had dealt with the art 8 issue once it had been raised before him as he had been required to do notwithstanding the language of s 21(4) of the 1988 Act. He had focused on

f art 8(2) of the convention and had decided that s 21(4) did not offend art 8 since the purpose served by it was within art 8(2). A district judge was familiar with housing issues and was perfectly entitled to apply his practical experience and common sense to an issue of that sort. It was not necessary at his level to hold a state trial into successive governments' housing policies in order to balance the public and private issues to which art 8 gave rise. A great deal of expense and

g delay had been avoided in a case which the judge was aware would be likely to come before the Court of Appeal in any event, there being no power to make a declaration of incompatibility in the county court (see [10], [26], [28], below).

(2) Section 6(3)(b) of the 1998 Act did not make a body, which had no responsibilities to the public, a public body merely because it performed acts on

h behalf of a public body which would constitute public functions if such acts were performed by that public body itself. An act could remain of a private nature even though it was performed because another body was under a public duty to ensure that the act was performed. The renting out of accommodation could certainly be an act of a private nature, and the fact that a public body might be fulfilling its

j public duty through the act of renting by a private body did not automatically change into a public act what would otherwise be a private act. What could make an act, which would otherwise be private, a public act was a feature or combination of features which imposed a public character or stamp on the act. Housing

---

c   Section 6, so far as material, is set out at [55], below

associations as a class were not standard public authorities, and such an association
would constitute a public authority only if it performed a particular function   *a*
which was a public as opposed to a private act. Whilst the activities of housing
associations need not involve the performance of public functions, in the instant
case the housing association's role, in providing accommodation for D and then
seeking possession, was so closely assimilated to that of the local authority that it
was performing public and not private functions. It therefore constituted, at least   *b*
to that extent, a functional public authority within s 6(3)(b) of the 1998 Act (see
[59], [60], [63], [65], [66], below); *Costello-Roberts v UK* (1993) 19 EHRR 112
considered.

(3) Notwithstanding its mandatory terms, s 21(4) of the 1988 Act did not
conflict with D's right to family life under art 8(1) of the convention.   *c*
Section 21(4) was necessary in a democratic society in so far as there had to be a
procedure for recovering possession of property at the end of a tenancy. The
question was whether the restricted power of the court was legitimate and
proportionate, and that was an area of policy in which the court should defer to
the decision of Parliament. Accordingly, there had been no contravention of art 8
of the convention, and the appeal would therefore be dismissed (see [72], below).   *d*

Per curiam. (1) The formal notice to the Crown, required by s 5 of the Human
Rights Act 1998 and CPR 19.4A in cases where the court is considering whether
to make a declaration of incompatibility, should always be given by the court
which will hear the proceedings. A party who seeks or acknowledges that such a
declaration may be made should give as much informal notice to the Crown as   *e*
practical of the proceedings and the issues involved. The formal and informal
notice should be given to a person named in the list published under s 17 of the
Crown Proceedings Act 1947. At the same time as the party gives informal notice
to the Crown, it should send a copy of such notice to the court and to the other
parties (see [19], below).   *f*

(2) When considering whether or not a legislative provision is compatible
with a convention right, the court should always first ascertain whether there
would be any breach of the convention in the absence of s 3^{d}of the 1998 Act,
which requires the court, so far as it is possible to do so, to read and give effect to
legislation in a way which is compatible with convention rights. If the court has   *g*
to rely on s 3, it should limit the extent of the modified meaning to that which is
necessary to achieve compatibility. Section 3 does not entitle the court to
legislate; its task is still one of interpretation, but interpretation in accordance
with the direction contained in s 3. If, in order to obtain compliance, it is
necessary to alter radically the effect of the legislation, that will be an indication   *h*
that more than interpretation is involved. The views of the parties and of the
Crown as to whether a 'constructive' interpretation should be adopted cannot
modify the task of the court; if s 3 applies, the court is required to adopt the s 3
approach to interpretation. Where, despite the strong language of s 3, it is not
possible to achieve a result which is compatible with the convention, the court is   *j*
not required to grant a declaration, and presumably in exercising its discretion as
to whether or not to grant a declaration it will be influenced by the usual
considerations which apply to the grant of declarations (see [75], [76], below).

---

d   Section 3 is set out at [74], below

Notes
a For the right to respect for private and family life, see 8(2) *Halsbury's Laws* (4th edn reissue) paras 149–152, and for the requirement to grant an order for possession of a property subject to an assured shorthold periodic tenancy after service of a proper notice to quit, see 27(1) *Halsbury's Laws* (4th edn reissue) para 975.

For the Housing Act 1988, s 21, see 23 *Halsbury's Statutes* (4th edn) (1997 reissue)
b 1082.

For the Human Rights Act 1998, ss 3, 6, Sch 1, Pt I, art 8, see 7 *Halsbury's Statutes* (4th edn) (1999 reissue) 502, 504, 524.

Cases referred to in judgment

Costello-Roberts v UK (1993) 19 EHRR 112, [1993] ECHR 13134/87, ECt HR.
c *Foster v British Gas plc* Case C-188/89 [1990] 3 All ER 897, [1991] 1 QB 405, [1991] 2 WLR 258, [1990] ECR I-3313, ECJ.
Peabody Housing Association Ltd v Green (1978) 38 P & CR 644, CA.
R v Muntham House School, ex p R [2000] LGR 255.
R v Panel on Take-overs and Mergers, ex p Datafin plc (Norton Opax plc intervening)
d [1987] 1 All ER 564, [1987] QB 815, [1987] 2 WLR 699, CA.
R v Servite Houses, ex p Goldsmith [2001] LGR 55.

Cases also cited or referred to in skeleton arguments

Abdulaziz v UK (1985) 7 EHRR 471, [1985] ECHR 9214/80, ECt HR.
Avon CC v Buscott [1988] 1 All ER 841, [1988] QB 656, CA.
e *Bristol DC v Clark* [1975] 3 All ER 976, [1975] 1 WLR 1443, CA.
Buckley v UK (1996) 23 EHRR 101, [1996] ECHR 20348/92, ECt HR.
Chapman v UK (2001) 10 BHRC 48, ECt HR.
Gillow v UK (1986) 11 EHRR 335, [1986] ECHR 9063/80, ECt HR.
Larkos v Cyprus (1999) 7 BHRC 244, ECt HR.
f *Mellacher v Austria* (1989) 12 EHRR 391, [1989] ECHR 10522/83, ECt HR.
R (on the application of Johns) v Bracknell Forest DC (21 December 2000, unreported), QBD.
R (on the application of Mahmood) v Secretary of State for the Home Dept [2001] 2 FCR 63, [2001] 1 WLR 840, CA.
g *R v DPP, ex p Kebeline, R v DPP, ex p Rechachi* [1999] 4 All ER 801, [2000] 2 AC 326, HL.
R v Secretary of State for the Home Dept, ex p Ahmed [2000] Imm AR 370, CA.
Trustees of the Dennis Rye Pension Fund v Sheffield City Council [1997] 4 All ER 747, [1998] 1 WLR 840, CA.
Wandsworth London BC v Winder [1984] 3 All ER 976, [1985] AC 461, HL.

h ### Appeal

By notice dated 19 December 2000, the defendant, Teresa Donoghue, the tenant of a residential property known as 31 Nairn Street, London E14 0LQ, appealed with permission of District Judge Naqvi granted under CPR 52.14 from his decision at Bow County Court on 5 December 2000 whereby he (i) refused to grant the
j defendant an adjournment of the possession proceedings brought against her by the claimant landlord, Poplar Housing and Regeneration Community Association Ltd (Poplar), and (ii) made an order for possession of the property under s 21(4) of the Housing Act 1988. The Secretary of State for the Environment, Transport and the Regions intervened in the appeal. The facts are set out in the judgment of the court.

Jan Luba QC and *Fiona Scolding* (instructed by *Breeze Benton & Co*) for the defendant.
Ashley Underwood and *Adrian Davis* (instructed by *Helen Sidwell, Head of Tower Hamlets Legal Services*) for Poplar.
Philip Sales and *Sarah Moore* (instructed by the *Treasury Solicitor*) for the Secretary of State.

Cur adv vult

27 April 2001. The following judgment of the court was delivered.

LORD WOOLF CJ.

The background

[1] This is an appeal from an order of District Judge Naqvi dated 5 December 2000. The judge gave permission to appeal and directed that the appeal should be heard by the Court of Appeal pursuant to CPR 52.14 on the ground that the appeal raises important points of principle and practice.

[2] The proceedings started in the Bow County Court as a straightforward claim for possession of 31 Nairn Street London E14 0LQ, of which the defendant was the tenant and which is owned by the claimant housing association, Poplar Housing and Regeneration Community Association Ltd (Poplar). On the day of the hearing, 5 December 2000, the proceedings were in the ordinary housing list. It had not been appreciated that the defendant wished to raise the issue that to make an order for possession would contravene her rights to respect for her private and family life and respect for her home contrary to art 8 of Sch 1 to the Human Rights Act 1998. Fortunately, notwithstanding the novel nature of the contention, District Judge Naqvi was in a position to consider the arguments which were advanced before him and give judgment straight away. We have a copy of that judgment and we commend the judge on the manner in which he dealt with the case.

The approach of the judge

[3] As he points out in his judgment, although this was not how the case was initially presented, the tenancy was an assured shorthold tenancy subject to s 21 of the Housing Act 1988. Section 21 deals with the recovery of possession on the expiry or termination of assured shorthold tenancies. Under the section, the court's discretion not to make an order for possession is strictly limited.

[4] Section 21(1) applies to orders for possession of dwelling houses after the coming to an end of an assured shorthold tenancy for a fixed term. The defendant did not have a fixed term tenancy. She had a periodic tenancy. Periodic tenancies are dealt with by s 21(4). Section 21(4) provides:

'Without prejudice to any such right as is referred to in subsection (1) above, a court *shall* make an order for possession of a dwelling-house let on an assured shorthold tenancy which is a periodic tenancy if the court is satisfied—(a) that the landlord or, in the case of joint landlords, at least one of them has given to the tenant a notice in writing stating that, after a date specified in the notice, being the last day of a period of the tenancy and not earlier than two months after the date the notice was given, possession of the dwelling-house is required by virtue of this section; and (b) that the date specified in the notice under paragraph (a) above is not earlier than the

a   earliest day on which, apart from section 5(1) above, the tenancy could be
      brought to an end by a notice to quit given by the landlord on the same date
      as the notice under paragraph (a) above.' (My emphasis.)

      [5] It will be observed that s 21(4) appears to be mandatory in its terms. The
      court has to make an order for possession if there is a tenancy to which the subsection
      applies and the appropriate notice has been given. There is no requirement for
b   the court to be satisfied that it is *reasonable* to make an order.

      [6] The first point taken on behalf of the defendant before the judge was that
      the notice which had been given did not comply with s 5 of the Protection from
      Eviction Act 1977. The judge held that s 5 only applied to purely common law
      notices to quit and not to statutory notices under s 21(4) of the 1988 Act. No
c   appeal has been pursued in respect of that holding.

      [7] The judge then turned his attention to the Human Rights Act argument. It
      was contended that to make an order for possession would contravene arts 6 and 8
      of the European Convention for the Protection of Human Rights and Fundamental
      Freedoms (Rome, 4 November 1950; TS 71 (1953); Cmd 8969) (as set out in Sch 1
      to the 1998 Act) and would involve interpreting s 21(4) in a manner which is not
d   compatible with the 1998 Act. The judge rejected these contentions as well. He
      said:

          'If I were to read s 21(4) of the 1988 Act in the way in which I am being
          enjoined to do, this would, in effect, enable people who were intentionally
          homeless, and that is a finding that has been already made by the local
e   authority, which has been reviewed and has not been challenged, the final
          decision having been made a year ago in November 1999, to jump the
          housing queue, that would impede the human rights of others and that is the
          proviso to art 8(2) that I have got in mind, "the protection of the rights and
          freedoms of others".'

f   [8] He did, however, postpone the date on which the order came into force
      for 42 days. This was the maximum extension which he was entitled to give. This
      was because of the defendant's exceptional personal circumstances. In addition, as
      already stated, the judge gave permission to the defendant to appeal directly to
      the Court of Appeal.

g   [9] It is the defendant's contention that the judge should have adjourned the
      hearing so as to enable her to place before the court the substantial evidence,
      which is now before this court, in support of her appeal. The evidence is directed
      to the issues of whether the housing association is a public body or performing a
      public function and whether any breach of art 8 could be justified on the grounds
      set out in art 8(2).

h   [10] In our judgment, where it is possible for a judge to give a decision
      summarily, as the judge did here, in a case where there will almost certainly be
      an appeal, there can be substantial advantages in adopting this approach. It can
      avoid expense and delay being incurred both at first instance and in the Court of
      Appeal.

j   *The facts*

      [11] The defendant moved into 31 Nairn Street in March 1998. She then had
      three children aged three, four and five. At the time of the possession proceedings
      she was expecting her fourth. The tenancy was granted by the London Borough
      of Tower Hamlets (Tower Hamlets) pursuant to its duties as the local housing

authority under s 188 of the Housing Act 1996. The tenancy was a weekly *a*
non-secure tenancy under para 4 of Sch 1 to the Housing Act 1985. This was
recorded in the written agreement dated 25 February 1998. The property was
later transferred to Poplar. Poplar was created as a housing association by Tower
Hamlets in order to transfer to it a substantial proportion of the council's housing
stock.

[12] The defendant had been provided with housing by Tower Hamlets pending *b*
a decision as to whether she was intentionally homeless. On 16 September 1999,
Tower Hamlets decided she was intentionally homeless and notified the defendant
to this effect (s 184 of the 1996 Act). The reason given was that the defendant
had left an assured shorthold tenancy to live with her sister. A review of this
decision was conducted by Tower Hamlets at the request of the defendant on
29 November 1999. The decision was confirmed. Previously the defendant would *c*
have been able, if she wished, to challenge the decision on an application for
judicial review. However, by November 1999, the procedure for challenging the
decision was by way of appeal to the county court. The defendant did not appeal.

[13] In January or February 2000, Tower Hamlets issued proceedings for
possession against the defendant. The authority then discovered that it was not *d*
the landlord and the proceedings were withdrawn. On 26 June 2000, Tower
Hamlets wrote to the defendant informing her that she was a tenant of Poplar
and was subject to an assured shorthold tenancy. On 27 June, a notice was served
by Poplar under s 21(4) of the 1988 Act. On 19 October 2000, the present proceedings
were commenced.

e

Intervention of the Secretary of State for the Environment, Transport and the Regions

[14] In this case the Secretary of State for the Environment, Transport and the
Regions (the Department) intervened in the proceedings. He was able to do so
because the defendant was seeking a declaration of incompatibility. The 1998 Act
and the CPR make provision for the Crown to intervene where a declaration that *f*
primary legislation is incompatible may be made by a court. Although the
Department has been able to intervene, the parties suggest it is unclear what are
the respective responsibilities of the parties and the court in a situation where the
Crown may want to intervene.

[15] The relevant provisions of the 1998 Act, the CPR and the Practice
Direction are as follows. The 1998 Act provides: *g*

> '4. ... (2) If the court is satisfied that the provision is incompatible with a
> Convention right, it may make a declaration of that incompatibility ...
>
> (5) In this section "court" means—(a) the House of Lords; (b) the Judicial
> Committee of the Privy Council; (c) the Courts-Martial Appeal Court; (d) in *h*
> Scotland, the High Court of Justiciary sitting otherwise than as a trial court
> or the Court of Session; (e) in England and Wales or Northern Ireland, the
> High Court or the Court of Appeal ...
>
> 5.—(1) Where a court is considering whether to make a declaration of
> incompatibility, the Crown is entitled to notice in accordance with rules of court. *j*
> (2) In any case to which subsection (1) applies—(a) a Minister of the
> Crown (or a person nominated by him) ... is entitled, on giving notice in
> accordance with rules of court, to be joined as a party to the proceedings.
>
> (3) Notice under subsection (2) may be given at any time during the
> proceedings.'

a

[16] CPR 19.4A provides:

'(1) The court may not make a declaration of incompatibility in accordance with section 4 of the [1998 Act] unless 21 days' notice, or such other period of notice as the court directs, has been given to the Crown.
(2) Where notice has been given to the Crown a Minister, or other person permitted by that Act, shall be joined as a party on giving notice to the court.'

b

[17] The Practice Direction to Pt 19 (CPR PD 19A) provides:

'6.1 Where a party has included in his statement of case—(1) a claim for a declaration of incompatibility in accordance with section 4 of the [1998 Act], or (2) an issue for the court to decide which may lead to the court considering making a declaration, then the court may at any time consider whether notice should be given to the Crown as required by that Act and give directions for the content and service of the notice. The rule allows a period of 21 days before the court will make the declaration but the court may vary this period of time.

c

6.2 The court will normally consider the issues and give the directions referred to in paragraph 6.1 at the case management conference.

d

6.3 Where a party amends his statement of case to include any matter referred to in paragraph 6.1, then the court will consider whether notice should be given to the Crown and give directions for the content and service of the notice ...

6.4(1) The notice given under rule 19.4A must be served on the person named in the list published under section 17 of the Crown Proceedings Act 1947 ... (2) The notice will be in the form directed by the court but will normally include the directions given by the court and all the statements of case in the claim. The notice will also be served on all the parties. The court may require the parties to assist in the preparation of the notice.'

e

f

[18] Paragraph 5.1B of the Practice Direction to CPR Pt 52 states:

'CPR rule 19.4A and the practice direction supplementing it shall apply as if references to the case management conference were to the application for permission to appeal. (The practice direction to Part 19 provides for notice to be given and parties joined in certain circumstances to which this paragraph applies).'

g

[19] Under these provisions what is required is reasonably clear. The difficulty which this appeal raises is when, and by whom, notice should be given to the Crown. It is desirable that a consistent practice should be adopted. However, a variety of circumstances can arise where the question of giving notice has to be considered. It is desirable, therefore, to avoid both unnecessary expense to the parties and the unnecessary involvement of the Crown, whilst at the same time ensuring that proceedings before the courts are not unduly disrupted by the requirement to give notice to the Crown.

h

j

[20] Having considered the submissions which the parties helpfully made, including submissions on behalf of the Department, we suggest that (i) the formal notice which the 1998 Act and the CPR require should always be given by the court. This is because the court will be in the best position to assess whether there is a likelihood of a declaration of incompatibility being made. (ii) So as to give the Crown as much notice as possible, whenever a party is seeking a

declaration of incompatibility or acknowledges that a declaration of incompatibility
may be made, it should give as much informal notice to the Crown as practical of   *a*
the proceedings and the issues that are involved. (iii) The formal and informal
notice to the Crown should be given to a person named in the list published
under s 17 of the Crown Proceedings Act 1947. (iv) At the same time as the party
gives notice informally to the Crown, it should send a copy of such notice to the
court so that the court is alerted to the fact that it will have to consider whether   *b*
a formal notice should be given. It should also send a copy of the notice to the
other parties. (v) In these circumstances, we are referring to the court that will
hear the proceedings. That is a trial court, at the level of the High Court or in the
case of appeals, the Court of Appeal in the case of appeals to that court and
the High Court in the case of appeals to the High Court. The county court
cannot make a declaration of incompatibility (s 4(5) of the 1998 Act).   *c*

The issues to which this appeal gives rise

[21] If it were not for contentions based on the 1998 Act, there would be no
possible basis for interfering with the judge's decision. There is no ambiguity in
the terms of s 21(4) of the 1988 Act. Poplar could not obtain possession without *d*
an order of a court but the court was required to make the order if the defendant
had a tenancy which was subject to s 21(4) and the proper notice was served
(which in this case are now not in dispute).

[22] On this appeal, as in the court below, the contentions of the defendant
depend upon art 8, coupled with art 6, of the convention set out in Sch 1 to the   *e*
1998 Act. Article 8 is in the following terms:

> '*Right to respect for private and family life*
>
> 1. Everyone has the right to respect for his private and family life, his
> home and his correspondence.   *f*
>
> 2. There shall be no interference by a public authority with the exercise of
> this right except such as is in accordance with the law and is necessary in a
> democratic society in the interests of national security, public safety or the
> economic well-being of the country, for the prevention of disorder or crime,
> for the protection of health or morals, or for the protection of the rights and *g*
> freedoms of others.'

[23] In considering art 8, it is helpful in this context to have in mind art 1 of the
First Protocol of the convention set out in Pt II of Sch 1 to the 1998 Act. Article 1
provides: 'Every natural or legal person is entitled to the peaceful enjoyment of
his possessions. No one shall be deprived of his possessions except in the public   *h*
interest and subject to the conditions provided for by law ...'

[24] Article 6 entitles the defendant to a fair trial of her right to remain in her
home. There is no question of that right being infringed. If we hold that she is
entitled to rely on art 8, it may be necessary for the case to be remitted to the
county court to determine whether it is reasonable to make an order of possession. *j*
As to art 8, it appears to us that the following issues require consideration. (1) Did
the judge adopt an appropriate procedure to determine the art 8 issue? (The
procedural issue.) (2) Is Poplar a public body or was it performing functions of a
public nature? (The public body issue.) (3) Did making an order for possession
contravene art 8? (The art 8 issue.) (4) If it did, is a declaration of incompatibility
the appropriate remedy? (The remedy issue.)

The procedural issue

a

[**25**] As already indicated, the defendant complains that the judge dealt with the art 8 issues in far too summary a manner. Poplar, on the other hand, contends, though not with much enthusiasm, that this was the only appropriate way for the judge to deal with the issue. It would have been wrong of the judge to grant an adjournment so that the defendant could place before the court the evidence that she contended was required since this would have contravened

b the clear terms of s 21(4) of the 1988 Act. Even if art 8 was contravened, the correct remedy would be to grant a declaration of incompatibility, which would be available on an appeal. It was not for the judge to interpret s 21(4) in a way which gave him a discretion to decide whether or not to make an order for possession.

c

[**26**] In general terms, we have already indicated our approval of the approach of the judge. This does not mean that we consider that the judge was not required to deal with the art 8 issue once it was raised before him. In our judgment, the judge was required to deal with the defendant's contention, notwithstanding the language of s 21(4). Section 7 of the 1998 Act provides, so far as relevant:

d

> '(1) A person who claims that a public authority has acted (or proposes to act) in a way which is made unlawful by section 6(1) may … (b) rely on the Convention right or rights concerned in any legal proceedings, but only if he is (or would be) a victim of the unlawful act.'

e

[**27**] If the defendant is right in her contentions as to the manner in which art 8 applies to her tenancy, then she is a 'victim'. Furthermore, if she is right, Poplar is a public authority. She is therefore entitled to rely on art 8 'in any legal proceedings'. The judge clearly accepted that this was the situation and that is why he set out his views as to why art 8 did not apply to her tenancy. If the defendant is

f right, the question of incompatibility will have to be considered, but unless s 21(4) is found to be incompatible, the case will have to be remitted so that a judge can, in the light of her circumstances, decide how he should exercise the discretion he would then have. This issue is therefore confined to whether the judge was entitled to decide the matter on the limited material that was then available without granting an adjournment.

g

[**28**] For reasons we have partly explained, we consider that the judge was entitled to dispose of the case as he did. He sensibly cut through the issues by accepting for the purpose of his decision that Poplar was at least performing a public function in terminating the defendant's tenancy and seeking possession and that art 8(1) therefore applied. He focused on art 8(2) and decided s 21(4) did

h not offend art 8 on the ground that the purpose s 21(4) serves is within art 8(2). A district judge is familiar with housing issues and is perfectly entitled to apply his practical experience and common sense to an issue of this sort. It is not necessary at his level to hold a state trial into successive governments' housing policies in order to balance the public and private issues to which art 8 gives rise. A great

j deal of expense and delay was avoided in a case which he was aware would be likely to come before this court in any event. (There is no power to make a declaration of incompatibility in the county court.)

[**29**] Mr Luba QC, on behalf of the defendant, advanced an argument based on the fact that the court is itself a public authority (s 6(3)(a) of the 1998 Act). However, if there is no contravention of art 8 on which the defendant is entitled to rely, this argument does not avail the defendant.

[**30**] If courts of first instance are encouraged to deal with Human Rights Act issues summarily, we appreciate, and the present appeal makes clear, that the Court of Appeal will have to be flexible in relation to its own procedures. The outcome of this appeal to a substantial extent depends upon the legislative framework. However, that legislation has to be interpreted against the factual background of how the legislation works on the ground. When it became apparent that this court was going to decide for itself the principal issues involved rather than remit the appeal, if successful, to the court below, the parties wished to place additional evidence before the court. This was done, with our agreement, after the completion of the oral argument. It inevitably meant that the preparation of this judgment was somewhat delayed.

[**31**] We are very grateful to the parties for the manner in which they have marshalled the evidence and for the further written argument which they have provided. We have considered whether we needed to hear further oral argument but have come to the conclusion that this is not necessary. The evidence, together with the written arguments, makes the positions of the parties clear. We need no further assistance in order to give our decision as to the outcome of this appeal.

The legislative framework

[**32**] In order to determine the remaining issues, it is critical to have in mind the manner in which the legislative framework, which sets out the duties which are owed to tenants in the position of the defendant, and under which a registered social landlord (RSL) such as Poplar operates, has evolved.

[**33**] The law affecting tenants of domestic accommodation has suffered from a failure to conduct a satisfactory review and consolidation of the legislation. This is despite a continuous process of amendment as the various governments of the day struggled to address the expense and chronic lack of accommodation for the less well-off members of society. The Law Commission has now been given the responsibility of remedying this situation. Until this happens, in order to understand the present legislative position, it is helpful to have the historic position in mind.

[**34**] At one time, the private sector was heavily controlled in order to mitigate the hardship caused to tenants by a shortage of housing. Rents were carefully controlled and tenants were given a substantial measure of statutory protection against eviction. So far as the private sector has been concerned, generally the policy has been to progressively reduce this control. The change of policy reflected the belief of governments that excessive control resulted in a deterioration in the quality and quantity of housing available to let in the private sector. This, it is said, has a variety of undesirable economic consequences for the public in general and the poorer members of society in particular.

[**35**] The statutory responsibility of providing for those who do not have homes was and is that of local government, acting through housing authorities. In particular, boroughs such as Tower Hamlets are subject to a range of statutory duties to provide social housing. For this purpose, as Mr Gahagan points out in his written evidence on behalf of the Department, until the 1990s, local government authorities were not only responsible for the availability of local housing, but in addition acted as social landlords with their own housing stock. However, over the last decade, a number of local housing authorities have transferred their stock of housing to RSLs. This policy is considered to have been successful and it is being expanded.

[36] Part VI of the 1996 Act governs the allocation of housing accommodation by local housing authorities. A housing authority can select someone to be a secure tenant, or an introductory tenant, or nominate someone to be an assured tenant of RSL stock. Before the housing authorities can allocate accommodation, the person to whom the accommodation is to be allocated must fulfil the qualifying requirements. For this purpose, housing authorities establish and maintain a register of qualifying persons (s 162 of the 1996 Act). Applicants have a right of review of decisions by authorities not to place them on a register or to remove them from the register. Housing authorities must also publish a scheme for determining priorities and procedures. The policy behind the 1996 Act, according to Mr Gahagan, was to create a 'single route' through the housing register into social housing and remove a perceived fast track into such housing for households accepted as statutorily homeless.

[37] Part VII of the 1996 Act places obligations on local housing authorities to assist homeless applicants. The level of assistance depends on the circumstances of the applicant and his or her household. The extent of the duty depends upon whether the applicant is or is not intentionally homeless. Assured tenancies and assured shorthold tenancies were introduced by Pt I of the 1988 Act. The regime of assured and assured shorthold tenancies applies to most new lettings of residential property in the private sector. Tenancies where the interest of the landlord belongs to a local authority are excluded from being assured tenancies (para 12 of Sch 1 to the 1988 Act).

[38] An assured shorthold tenancy is essentially a form of assured tenancy without security of tenure. Prior to the coming into force of s 96 of the 1996 Act, an assured shorthold tenancy had to be for a fixed term of not less than six months. This is no longer a requirement.

[39] Changes were introduced by the 1996 Act which, at the time of its introduction, the government made clear were intended to increase the number of properties available for private renting. Procedures were simplified. An increase in the private rented sector in fact took place subsequent to the 1996 Act coming into force. The government regards the availability of assured shorthold tenancies as contributing to a larger, better quality, and better managed, private rented sector.

[40] Mr Gahagan in his statement makes it clear that in many areas, particularly in London and the South East, demand for social housing far outweighs supply and therefore allocation must be made according to the degree of housing need and how long the applicants have been waiting. He also states:

'47. The purpose of the homelessness legislation is to provide a safety net for people who have become homeless through no fault of their own and would be vulnerable if they were not provided with temporary accommodation until a more settled housing solution becomes available. If people accepted as unintentionally homeless and in priority need were provided with accommodation with security of tenure, this would displace applicants with greater claim to scarce social housing. This would not be in the interests of public policy since it would amount to a fast track into a secure social tenancy for people accepted as statutorily homeless and would create a perverse incentive for people to apply for homelessness assistance. 48. The provision of temporary accommodation can be expensive for authorities, particularly in areas of high demand where they do not have sufficient accommodation of their own and must make arrangements with other landlords. A guiding principle underlying the legislation is that authorities are not obliged to secure accommodation, other than very briefly if the applicant has priority need, for people who have made themselves homeless intentionally. Such applicants are expected to make their own arrangements to find accommodation for themselves. 49. The interim duty to accommodate those applicants who appear to be homeless and have a priority need, pending completion of inquiries and a decision as to whether a substantive duty is owed, is a very important aspect of the safety net. It is essential to the public policy interest, however, that authorities can bring such interim accommodation to an end where they are satisfied that the applicant does not qualify for any further assistance.'

[41] The role of housing associations in providing accommodation has equally been affected by government policy.

[42] Housing associations were very much 'the legal embodiment of the voluntary housing movement' as Mr Brockway, another witness on behalf of the Department, stated. Originally, many were small local charities, though others were large entities endowed by wealthy employers or philanthropists. The legal definition of a housing association is contained in s 1(1) of the Housing Associations Act 1985. This section makes it clear that a housing association may be a charity, an industrial and provident society, or a company which does not trade for profit and which has among its objects the provision of housing accommodation. Some are fully mutual co-operative organisations. Throughout the twentieth century many housing associations were funded by grants or loans usually through local authorities. In 1964, the Housing Corporation (the Corporation) was created and thereafter most of the public funding was channelled through the Corporation. The Corporation was granted supervisory powers by the Housing Act 1974. There are now 4,000 housing associations, of which approximately 2,200 are registered with the Corporation as RSLs. Since 1988, RSLs have been required to borrow funds in the private markets to supplement public funding. To date, some £20bn has been raised outside the public sector borrowing requirement. The other major development has been the growth in the transfer of housing stock from local authorities to RSLs. Both under the previous and the present government, some 500,000 dwellings have been transferred in this way. Today, there are 1·5 million dwellings in the ownership of RSLs.

[43] Under Pt I of the 1996 Act, the Corporation is given two basic roles. These are to provide funding to RSLs and to regulate them. The funding is payable by way of grant under s 18 of the 1996 Act. Regulation covers the area of governance, finance and housing management. If performance fails, the Corporation can exercise a number of powers: it can withdraw funding, make appointments to the governing body of the RSL and remove employees or governing body members (Sch 1 to the 1996 Act).

[44] Section 170 of the 1996 Act importantly provides:

'Where a local housing authority so request, a registered social landlord shall co-operate to such an extent as is reasonable in the circumstances in offering accommodation to people with priority on the authority's housing register.'

[45] Section 213 of the 1996 Act also requires 'other bodies' to co-operate with housing authorities to assist in the discharge of their functions, subject to the request for co-operation being reasonable in the circumstances. 'Other bodies'

a includes RSLs: s 213(2)(a). Mr Brockway states that in most local authority areas, the housing authority will have nomination agreements with RSLs. These agreements enable the authority to nominate tenants, to whom the RSLs should grant tenancies, from the housing registers.

[46] Many local authorities have transferred some or all of their housing stock to one or more RSLs. This has happened so far as Poplar is concerned. Poplar

b was created for the purpose of taking over part of the housing stock of the borough of Tower Hamlets. It was a condition of Tower Hamlets receiving funding that this should happen. The funding came from the government under a scheme (the Estates Renewal Challenge Fund) designed to bring about the repair and improvement of the housing stock, the improvement of security for occupants of estates, to tackle anti-social behaviour and crime and to develop

c community initiatives. The transfer of the council stock to Poplar was only possible where there was a majority vote by tenants in favour of the transfer of the particular housing stock involved. No payment was involved for the transfer. The properties transferred were regarded as having a negative value because of their state of repair. Mr Brockway makes it clear that the government's policy

d was that the RSLs should be private sector bodies. The way they were funded was dependent on this. Mr Brockway states that as a matter of policy the Corporation has always asked RSLs to grant the most secure form of tenure available to its tenants. This will usually be achieved by granting periodic tenancies of which possession can only be achieved on discretionary grounds. Such tenancies are accepted by Mr Luba as providing the necessary protection which

e he submits is necessary to comply with art 8 of the convention. The Corporation requires that if a tenant has an assured tenancy, then an order for possession can only be sought if it is reasonable to seek the order.

[47] However, guidance has been given by the Corporation to RSLs to grant assured shorthold tenancies where special circumstances exist. Those circumstances

f include where the provision of accommodation is to be temporary, as was the position in the case of the defendant.

[48] Mr Christopher Holmes, the director of Shelter, has provided evidence for the defendant. Based on his experience, he states that in practical terms, particularly where large-scale voluntary transfers have occurred, housing associations provide the means whereby accommodation is made available to

g homeless persons. This can include interim accommodation under s 188 of the 1996 Act while the priority of an applicant is being determined and where, as in the case of the defendant, the applicant has been found to be homeless intentionally. Mr Holmes goes on to point out:

h 'To enable the statutory duties imposed on local authorities to be discharged appropriately, close co-operation with housing associations continues beyond the point where accommodation is made available. When duties come to an end and accommodation is to be recovered, notification will pass from the authority to the association and possession will be recovered in due course. In effect, the association acts as a conduit for the

j authority's decision on whether a duty arises or has come to an end.'

[49] He adds:

'Although there is no doubt that housing associations have their own constitutions and mechanisms for governance, in the practical day-to-day management of both long-term lettings and short-term provision for the

homeless, they are inextricably linked to the statutory framework imposing
duties on local authorities and associations alike.'
a

[50] He further adds:

'The complex nature of housing associations, run as they are, by unpaid
persons and with their own constitutions, is apparent. And yet the associations
are free to decide key issues regarding investment of funds and the nature of
refurbishment and development works. Although tied in with local
authorities in terms of allocations and homelessness, this does not, of itself,
alter the fundamentally private nature of associations. There are many
bodies which are required to act in accordance with public powers, duties
and functions but which remain essentially private bodies. Railtrack is an
example.'
b
c

[51] Later, having referred to Mr Brockway's approach that any RSL taking
over the stock of a housing authority will be a private sector body, Mr Holmes
adds: 'This is, of course, the case but the day-to-day management of that stock
may in my view be properly categorised as a public function in the circumstances
I have described in this statement.'
d

[52] He also refers to the fact that RSLs are subject to the scheme introduced
by s 51 of the 1996 Act for the investigation of complaints by the independent
housing ombudsman.

[53] Mr Holmes does not accept that the use of assured shorthold tenancies by
RSLs is necessary. His complaints include the fact that—
e

'More and more tenants are losing their homes on mandatory grounds.
The government's own homelessness statistics show that, between 1992 and
1999, there was an increase of nearly 63% in the number of households
accepted as homeless and in priority need following the recovery of
possession of premises let on an assured shorthold tenancy. The loss of a
shorthold is now the third most common reason for homelessness given by
persons accepted as homeless by local authorities. In some areas of high
housing demand it is the most common reason.'
f

[54] He supports his view by referring to cases which illustrate the disadvantage
of assured shorthold tenancies.
g

Public bodies and public functions

[55] The importance of whether Poplar was at the material times a public
body or performing public functions is this: the 1998 Act will only apply to Poplar
if it is deemed to be a public body or performing public functions. Section 6(1) of
the 1998 Act makes it unlawful for a public authority to act in a way which is
incompatible with a convention right. Section 6(3) states that a 'public authority'
includes 'any person certain of whose functions are functions of a public nature'.
Section 6(5) provides: 'In relation to a particular act, a person is not a public
authority by virtue only of subsection (3)(b) if the nature of the act is private.'
h
j

[56] The defendant relies on the witness statements of Mr David Cowan, a
lecturer of law at the University of Bristol (specialising in housing law and policy)
and of Professor Alder of the University of Newcastle in support of her contention
that Poplar is a public authority within s 6. Both Mr Cowan and Professor Alder
acknowledge that the questions raised are ones of importance and of some debate
in academic circles. However, Mr Cowan says it is 'tolerably clear that RSLs do

a fall within the definition of public authority under s 6(1)' as they are performing public functions.

[57] Mr Cowan says:

b 'The obligation to provide interim accommodation under Pt VII (homelessness) of the Housing Act 1996 pending inquiries is owed by the local authority to the homeless applicant. That is clearly a public function. The accommodation can be provided by an RSL (see s 206(1)(b)). An RSL which provides that accommodation is thus fulfilling a public function. Where, as here, the accommodation provided to the homeless household in satisfaction of the duty was originally owed by the local authority, but subsequently transferred to the RSL *whilst the duty was ongoing,* then the *c* public nature of a function is made all the clearer. The decision to seek possession of the property once the relevant inquiries and a decision on the homelessness application have been made are all part and parcel of that function. It is therefore clear that this case does not fall within the exemption of activities covered by s 6(5).'

d [58] We agree with Mr Luba's submissions that the definition of who is a public authority, and what is a public function, for the purposes of s 6 of the 1998 Act, should be given a generous interpretation. However, we would suggest that the position is not as simple as Mr Cowan suggests. The fact that a body performs an activity which otherwise a public body would be under a duty to perform cannot mean that such performance is necessarily a public function. A public *e* body in order to perform its public duties can use the services of a private body. Section 6 should not be applied so that if a private body provides such services, the nature of the functions are inevitably public. If this were to be the position, then when a small hotel provides bed and breakfast accommodation as a temporary measure, at the request of a housing authority that is under a duty to provide that *f* accommodation, the small hotel would be performing public functions and required to comply with the 1998 Act. This is not what the 1998 Act intended. The consequence would be the same where a hospital uses a private company to carry out specialist services, such as analysing blood samples. The position under the 1998 Act is necessarily more complex. Section 6(3) means that hybrid bodies, who have functions of a public and private nature are public authorities, but *not* *g* in relation to acts which are of a private nature. The renting out of accommodation can certainly be of a private nature. The fact that through the act of renting by a private body a public authority may be fulfilling its public duty, does not automatically change into a public act what would otherwise be a private act. See, by analogy, *R v Muntham House School, ex p R* [2000] LGR 255.

h [59] The purpose of s 6(3)(b) is to deal with hybrid bodies which have both public and private functions. It is not to make a body, which does not have responsibilities to the public, a public body merely because it performs acts on behalf of a public body which would constitute public functions were such acts to be performed by the public body itself. An act can remain of a private nature even *j* though it is performed because another body is under a public duty to ensure that that act is performed.

[60] A useful illustration is provided by the decision of the European Court of Human Rights in *Costello-Roberts v UK* (1993) 19 EHRR 112. The case concerned a seven-year-old boy receiving corporal punishment from the headmaster of an independent school. The European Court made it clear that the state cannot absolve itself of its convention obligations by delegating the fulfilment of such

obligations to private bodies or individuals, including the headmaster of an
independent school. However, if a local authority, in order to fulfil its duties, sent
a child to a private school, the fact that it did this would not mean that the private
school was performing public functions. The school would not be a hybrid body.
It would remain a private body. The local authority would, however, not escape
its duties by delegating the performance to the private school. If there were a
breach of the convention, then the responsibility would be that of the local
authority and not that of the school.

[61] The approach of Professor Alder differs from that of Mr Cowan. He
states that there is no single factor that determines whether a function is a public
function. He adds:

> 'The meaning of "public function" is not necessarily the same in the
> different contexts where the matter arises ... Analogies, particularly in
> respect to the test for determining which bodies are susceptible to judicial
> review in the Administrative Court may be helpful, given that one purpose
> of judicial review is to ensure that public bodies are subject to high standards
> of conduct the same being true of the [convention]. There is also an analogy
> with the test that is being developed in European Community law for
> determining whether a body is a public body, namely "a body, whatever its
> legal form, which has been made responsible, pursuant to a measure adopted
> by the state, for providing a public service under the control of the state and
> which has for that purpose special powers beyond those which result from
> the normal rules applicable in relations between individuals ..." (*Foster v
> British Gas plc* Case C-188/89 [1990] 3 All ER 897 at 922, [1991] 1 QB 405 at
> 427, [1990] ECR I-3313 at 3348–3349 (para 20)).'

[62] In coming to his conclusion that in this case the activities of Poplar are
within s 6, the professor relies upon the charitable status of Poplar; the fact that
Poplar is subject to the control of the Corporation; the sanctions which the
Corporation can apply; the provision of public funding to Poplar; the standards
which Poplar is required to adopt in the exercise of its powers; the control which
the Corporation can exert over the exercise of Poplar's powers; and local
authority involvement.

[63] Both the Department and Poplar dispute that Poplar is a public authority.
Mr Philip Sales helpfully adopts the distinction correctly identified by Clayton
and Tomlinson *The Law of Human Rights* (2000) vol 1, p 189 (para 5.08) between
standard public authorities, *functional* public authorities and courts and tribunals.
Mr Sales submits, and we, like Professor Alder and Mr Holmes, would agree that
housing associations as a class are not standard public authorities. If they are to
be a public authority this must be because a particular function performed by an
individual RSL is a public as opposed to a private act. The RSL would then be a
functional, or hybrid, public authority.

[64] In support of his contention, Mr Sales draws attention to the following
features of housing associations. (a) They vary vastly in size. (b) Their structure
is that of an ordinary private law entity. (c) As to regulation by the Corporation
he points to the fact that many financial institutions are regulated by the Bank of
England but this does not make them public bodies. Furthermore, the Corporation
gives each RSL freedom to decide how it achieves what is expected of it.
(d) Members of the RSL are not appointed by, or answerable to, the government
but are private individuals who volunteer their services. Even in the rare cases
where the Corporation makes appointments, the appointee owes his duty to the

a RSL. (e) In *R v Servite Houses, ex p Goldsmith* [2001] LGR 55 Moses J decided a housing association was not subject to judicial review. (f) Although an RSL is funded in part out of public funds, the major source of its income is its rental income. In any event, this is not by any means conclusive (see *Peabody Housing Association Ltd v Green* (1978) 38 P & CR 644 at 660, 662).

b [65] In coming to our conclusion as to whether Poplar is a public authority within the 1998 Act meaning of that term, we regard it of particular importance in this case that (i) while s 6 of the 1998 Act requires a generous interpretation of who is a public authority, it is clearly inspired by the approach developed by the courts in identifying the bodies and activities subject to judicial review. The emphasis on public functions reflects the approach adopted in judicial review by the courts and text books since the decision of the Court of Appeal (the judgment c of Lloyd LJ) in *R v Panel on Take-overs and Mergers, ex p Datafin plc* (*Norton Opax plc intervening*) [1987] 1 All ER 564, [1987] QB 815. (ii) Tower Hamlets, in transferring its housing stock to Poplar, does not transfer its primary public duties to Poplar. Poplar is no more than the means by which it seeks to perform those duties. (iii) The act of providing accommodation to rent is not, without more, a public d function for the purposes of s 6 of the 1998 Act. Furthermore, that is true irrespective of the section of society for whom the accommodation is provided. (iv) The fact that a body is a charity or is conducted not for profit means that it is likely to be motivated in performing its activities by what it perceives to be the public interest. However, this does not point to the body being a public authority. In addition, even if such a body performs functions that would be considered to be e of a public nature if performed by a public body, nevertheless such acts may remain of a private nature for the purpose of s 6(3)(b) and (5). (v) What can make an act, which would otherwise be private, public, is a feature or a combination of features which impose a public character or stamp on the act. Statutory authority for what is done can at least help to mark the act as being public; so can the extent f of control over the function exercised by another body which is a public authority. The more closely the acts that could be of a private nature are enmeshed in the activities of a public body, the more likely they are to be public. However, the fact that the acts are supervised by a public regulatory body does not necessarily indicate that they are of a public nature. This is analogous to the position in judicial review, where a regulatory body may be deemed public but g the activities of the body which is regulated may be categorised private. (vi) The closeness of the relationship which exists between Tower Hamlets and Poplar. Poplar was created by Tower Hamlets to take a transfer of local authority housing stock; five of its board members are also members of Tower Hamlets; Poplar is subject to the guidance of Tower Hamlets as to the manner in which it h acts towards the defendant. (vii) The defendant, at the time of transfer, was a sitting tenant of Poplar and it was intended that she would be treated no better and no worse than if she remained a tenant of Tower Hamlets. While she remained a tenant, Poplar therefore stood in relation to her in very much the position previously occupied by Tower Hamlets.

j [66] While these are the most important factors in coming to our conclusion, it is desirable to step back and look at the situation as a whole. As is the position on applications for judicial review, there is no clear demarcation line which can be drawn between public and private bodies and functions. In a borderline case, such as this, the decision is very much one of fact and degree. Taking into account all the circumstances, we have come to the conclusion that while activities of housing associations need not involve the performance of public

functions, in this case, in providing accommodation for the defendant and then
seeking possession, the role of Poplar is so closely assimilated to that of Tower
Hamlets that it was performing public and not private functions. Poplar
therefore is a functional public authority, at least to that extent. We emphasise
that this does not mean that all Poplar's functions are public. We do not even
decide that the position would be the same if the defendant was a secure tenant.
The activities of housing associations can be ambiguous. For example, their
activities in raising private or public finance could be very different from those
that are under consideration here. The raising of finance by Poplar could well be
a private function.

The art 8 issue

[**67**] To evict the defendant from her home would impact on her family life.
The effect of art 8(2) of the convention is therefore critical. The starting point is
the fact that after the order for possession was obtained, Tower Hamlets
continued to owe a limited duty to provide the defendant with assistance as a
person who was found to be intentionally homeless. This was so even though
Poplar's responsibility came to an end. If the defendant had not fallen into one of
the special categories, she would have been provided with greater security of
occupation.

[**68**] Mr Holmes recognises that the defendant could not expect security of
tenure, but he submits that there should be a residual discretion to protect the
defendant's basic human rights. He also submits that this would not in practice
give rise to undesirable consequences, to which the witnesses for the Department
refer, but this is very much a matter of judgment.

[**69**] There is certainly room for conflicting views as to the social desirability
of an RSL being able to grant assured shorthold tenancies which are subject to
s 21(4) of the 1988 Act. Mr Holmes considers the present policy mistaken.
However, in considering whether Poplar can rely on art 8(2), the court has to pay
considerable attention to the fact that Parliament intended when enacting s 21(4)
to give preference to the needs of those dependent on social housing *as a whole*
over those in the position of the defendant. The economic and other implications
of any policy in this area are extremely complex and far-reaching. This is an area
where, in our judgment, the courts must treat the decisions of Parliament as to
what is in the public interest with particular deference. The limited role given to
the court under s 21(4) is a legislative policy decision. The correctness of this
decision is more appropriate for Parliament than the courts and the 1998 Act does
not require the courts to disregard the decisions of Parliament in relation to
situations of this sort when deciding whether there has been a breach of the
convention.

[**70**] The defendant's lack of security is due to her low priority under the
legislation because she was found to be intentionally homeless. She was and
must be taken to be aware that she was never more than a tenant as a temporary
measure. In the case of someone in her position, even if she is a mother of young
children, it is perfectly understandable that Parliament should have provided a
procedure which ensured possession could be obtained expeditiously and that
Poplar should have availed itself of that procedure.

[**71**] Tenants in the position of the defendant have remedies other than under
s 21(4) which are relevant when considering art 8. There are provisions for
appeal against the decision that a person is intentionally homeless. There is the
regulatory role of the corporation and there is the ombudsman. There is also the

a fact that RSLs are subject to considerable guidance as to how they use their powers.

[72] We are satisfied, that notwithstanding its mandatory terms, s 21(4) of the 1988 Act does not conflict with the defendant's right to family life. Section 21(4) is certainly necessary in a democratic society in so far as there must be a procedure for recovering possession of property at the end of a tenancy. The
b question is whether the restricted power of the court is legitimate and proportionate. This is the area of policy where the court should defer to the decision of Parliament. We have come to the conclusion that there was no contravention of art 8 or of art 6.

The incompatibility issue

c [73] As we have decided that there is no contravention of arts 6 and 8, strictly, there is no need for us to speculate as to whether, if there had been a contravention, this would have created a situation of incompatibility. We note that if we decided that there was a contravention of art 8, the Department would prefer us not to interpret s 21(4) 'constructively' but instead to grant a declaration of incompatibility.
d However, so far, the sections of the 1998 Act dealing with interpretation and incompatibility have been subject to limited guidance and for that reason we hope it will be helpful if we set out our views even though they are strictly obiter.

[74] The relevant sections of the 1998 Act are ss 3 and 4. They are in the following terms:

e '**3.** *Interpretation of legislation.*—(1) So far as it is possible to do so, primary legislation and subordinate legislation must be read and given effect in a way which is compatible with the Convention rights.

(2) This section—(a) applies to primary legislation and subordinate legislation whenever enacted; (b) does not affect the validity, continuing operation or enforcement of any incompatible primary legislation; and
f (c) does not affect the validity, continuing operation or enforcement of any incompatible subordinate legislation if (disregarding any possibility of revocation) primary legislation prevents removal of the incompatibility.

4. *Declaration of incompatibility.*—(1) Subsection (2) applies in any proceedings in which a court determines whether a provision of primary legislation is compatible with a Convention right.
g (2) If the court is satisfied that the provision is incompatible with a Convention right, it may make a declaration of that incompatibility.

(3) Subsection (4) applies in any proceedings in which a court determines whether a provision of subordinate legislation, made in the exercise of a power conferred by primary legislation, is compatible with a Convention
h right.

(4) If the court is satisfied—(a) that the provision is incompatible with a Convention right, and (b) that (disregarding any possibility of revocation) the primary legislation concerned prevents removal of the incompatibility, it may make a declaration of that incompatibility.
j (5) In this section "court" means—(a) the House of Lords; (b) the Judicial Committee of the Privy Council; (c) the Courts-Martial Appeal Court; (d) in Scotland, the High Court of Justiciary sitting otherwise than as a trial court or the Court of Session; (e) in England and Wales or Northern Ireland, the High Court or the Court of Appeal.

(6) A declaration under this section ("a declaration of incompatibility")—(a) does not affect the validity, continuing operation or enforcement of the

provision in respect of which it is given; and (b) is not binding on the parties
to the proceedings in which it is made.'

[75] It is difficult to overestimate the importance of s 3. It applies to legislation
passed both before and after the 1998 Act came into force. Subject to the section
not requiring the court to go beyond that which is possible, it is mandatory in its
terms. In the case of legislation predating the 1998 Act where the legislation
would otherwise conflict with the convention, s 3 requires the court to now
interpret legislation in a manner which it would not have done before the 1998
Act came into force. When the court interprets legislation usually its primary
task is to identify the intention of Parliament. Now, when s 3 applies, the courts
have to adjust their traditional role in relation to interpretation so as to give effect
to the direction contained in s 3. It is as though legislation which predates the
1998 Act and conflicts with the convention has to be treated as being subsequently
amended to incorporate the language of s 3. However, the following points, which
are probably self-evident, should be noted: (a) unless the legislation would
otherwise be in breach of the convention s 3 can be ignored (so courts should always
first ascertain whether, absent s 3, there would be any breach of the convention);
(b) if the court has to rely on s 3 it should limit the extent of the modified meaning
to that which is necessary to achieve compatibility; (c) s 3 does not entitle the
court to *legislate* (its task is still one of *interpretation,* but interpretation in accordance
with the direction contained in s 3); (d) the views of the parties and of the Crown
as to whether a 'constructive' interpretation should be adopted cannot modify
the task of the court (if s 3 applies the court is required to adopt the s 3 approach
to interpretation); and (e) where despite the strong language of s 3, it is not
possible to achieve a result which is compatible with the convention, the court is
not *required* to grant a declaration and presumably in exercising its discretion as to
whether to grant a declaration or not it will be influenced by the usual considerations
which apply to the grant of declarations.

[76] The most difficult task which courts face is distinguishing between legislation
and interpretation. Here practical experience of seeking to apply s 3 will provide
the best guide. However, if it is necessary in order to obtain compliance to radically
alter the effect of the legislation this will be an indication that more than
interpretation is involved.

[77] In this case Mr Luba contends that all that is required is to insert the words
'if it is reasonable to do so' into the opening words of s 21(4). The amendment
may appear modest but its effect would be very wide indeed. It would significantly
reduce the ability of landlords to recover possession and would defeat Parliament's
original objective of providing certainty. It would involve legislating.

[78] Finally, we are prepared to grant the parties declarations if this will assist
them to seek permission to appeal. Despite this, the parties should not assume
permission to appeal will be granted. The decision whether to grant permission
or to leave the decision to grant permission to the Lords, should not be affected
by the fact that the appeal involves the 1998 Act. The House of Lords should
normally be allowed to select for itself the appeals which it wishes to hear. The
appeal is dismissed.

Appeal dismissed. Permission to appeal refused.

Kate O'Hanlon   Barrister.

R (on the application of Eliot) v Crown Court at Reading

[2001] EWHC Admin 464

b QUEEN'S BENCH DIVISION, DIVISIONAL COURT

ROSE LJ AND SILBER J

14 JUNE 2001

Criminal law – Remand in custody – Custody time limits – Extension of time limits –
c *'Good and sufficient cause' – Whether Bail Act considerations relevant when court*
considering whether there was good and sufficient cause to extend custody time limit –
Prosecution of Offences Act 1985, s 22(3).

In November 2000 the claimant, E, was committed for trial with two co-accused on
d a charge of conspiracy to defraud. A provisional trial date was fixed for May 2001.
By April 2001, when the prosecution applied for an extension of the custody time
limit, the number of defendants had increased to ten. At the time of the application,
it was expected that the trial would start some time in September 2001 and would
last for six months. The judge granted an extension until the end of September 2001
under s 22(3)[a] of the Prosecution of Offences Act 1985 which empowered the
e court to extend the time limit where it was satisfied, inter alia, that there was
good and sufficient cause to do so. The judge stated that the cause of the delay
was the fact that there would be a ten-man trial, with all the defendants pleading
not guilty, and that the court could not accommodate the trial, as far as
courtroom and judge were concerned, until September. She added that that was
f not always a good and sufficient cause for further remanding a man in custody,
but that it was in E's case. She further stated that she bore in mind the
considerations that came into play in deciding whether or not to grant E bail,
describing them as not the whole story but as something which she was entitled
to, and should, bear in mind. The judge then concluded by stating that she was
perfectly satisfied that E was somebody who should not have been granted bail
g in the first instance and that the decision to remand him in custody was entirely
right. On E's application for judicial review, the issue arose, inter alia, whether
the court was entitled to take account of Bail Act considerations on an application
to extend custody time limits.

h **Held** – Bail Act considerations were not properly to be considered when the court
addressed the question whether there was a good and sufficient cause for extending
custody time limits. The regimes were separate and different, and it was to be
hoped that Bail Act considerations would cease to be canvassed on applications
to extend custody time limits. In the instant case, however, the judge's decision
j was not fatally flawed by her reference to Bail Act considerations. She had given
two reasons for extending custody time limits, and had been entitled to grant the
extension having regard to the likely length of the trial, the number of defendants

---

a   Section 22(3), so far as material, provides: 'The appropriate court may, at any time before the expiry
     of a time limit … extend, or further extend that limit if its satisfied—(a) that there is good and
     sufficient cause for doing so … '

and the availability of a judge and courtroom. Accordingly, the application would be dismissed (see [14]–[16], [18], below).

R v Central Criminal Court, ex p Abu-Wardeh [1997] 1 All ER 159 and *R v Crown Court at Manchester, ex p McDonald, R v Crown Court at Leeds, ex p Hunt, R v Crown Court at Winchester, ex p Forbes, R v Crown Court at Leeds, ex p Wilson* [1999] 1 All ER 805 considered.

Notes
For applications for extension of custody time limits, see 11(2) *Halsbury's Laws* (4th edn reissue) para 854.

For the Prosecution of Offences Act 1985, s 22, see 12 *Halsbury's Statutes* (4th edn) (1997 reissue) 920.

Cases referred to in judgments
R v Central Criminal Court, ex p Abu-Wardeh [1997] 1 All ER 159, [1998] 1 WLR 1083, DC.

R v Crown Court at Manchester, ex p McDonald, R v Crown Court at Leeds, ex p Hunt, R v Crown Court at Winchester, ex p Forbes, R v Crown Court at Leeds, ex p Wilson [1999] 1 All ER 805, [1999] 1 WLR 841, DC.

R v Crown Court at Manchester, ex p S (23 August 1999, unreported), QBD.

R v Crown Court at Sheffield, ex p Headley [2000] 2 Cr App R 1, DC.

R v Crown Court at Worcester, ex p Norman [2000] 3 All ER 267, DC.

R v Governor of Winchester Prison, ex p Roddie [1991] 2 All ER 931, [1991] 1 WLR 303, DC.

Application for judicial review
The claimant, Peter Scott Eliot, applied for judicial review of the decision of Judge Mowat in the Crown Court at Reading on 23 April 2001 extending the custody time limit, in relation to the claimant, until the end of September 2001. The facts are set out in the judgment of Rose LJ.

Sean Enright (instructed by *Martin Murray & Associates*, Slough) for the claimant.
Michael Hick (instructed by the *Crown Prosecution Service*, Reading) for the Crown.

ROSE LJ.

[1] With permission granted by Scott Baker J, the claimant challenges a decision of Judge Mowat, on 23 April 2001, to extend custody time limits, in relation to the claimant, until the end of September 2001.

[2] The application raises two questions. First, whether Bail Act considerations (see the Bail Act 1976) are capable of giving rise to good and sufficient cause for extending custody time limits within s 22(3)(iii) of the Prosecution of Offences Act 1985. Secondly, if they are not, whether the judge's decision can effectively be challenged.

[3] The material facts can be very shortly rehearsed. The claimant is one of ten defendants who are now to be tried at the Crown Court at Reading for an offence, so far as this claimant is concerned, of conspiracy to defraud, for which he was arrested on 3 October 2000. Initially, there were two co-accused with whom he was committed for trial on 16 November 2000. At a plea and directions hearing, on 11 December, a provisional trial date was fixed for 2 May 2001. Custody time limits were due to expire on 8 March, but prior to such expiry a number of other accused were committed for trial.

a   [4] The position at the time of the application to the judge was that the trial was expected to take place some time in September 2001. But we are told by Mr Enright, for the claimant, and have no reason to doubt, that, for a variety of reasons, that may not now occur. Custody time limits were extended by the trial judge on an occasion prior to 23 April, but it is the decision on that date which is the subject of challenge. It is common ground that, as the judge indicated in the

b   course of her ruling, the likely length of the trial of these defendants, who are all, presently, pleading not guilty, is of the order of six months. The judge, as appears from her ruling, said:

'So the cause for the delay as from today to September is the fact that the position has now crystallised, we have a ten-man trial, we have all defendants

c   pleading not guilty, which we did not know until today, and the court cannot accommodate the trial, as far as courtroom and judge are concerned, until September. Now, of course, that is not always good and sufficient cause for further remanding a man in custody, but in this particular case I have come to the conclusion that it is and I bear in mind the considerations that came into play in deciding whether or not to grant him bail which, again, are not

d   the whole story, but they are something which I am entitled to, and should, bear in mind. Without rehearsing them fully, I am, as I said before, perfectly satisfied that [the claimant] is somebody who should not have been granted bail in the first instance and the decision to remand him in custody was entirely right. That being the case, I am prepared to extend the

e   custody time limit and I will say until the end of September ...'

[5] No question arises in this case in relation to due diligence and expedition. The judge was satisfied that the Crown had acted with due diligence and expedition and no attempt is made in this court to challenge that finding.

[6] The submission which Mr Enright ably makes, on behalf of the claimant,

f   is that the judge would not have ruled as she did were it not for the bail aspect of the matter. Mr Enright submits that the passage which I have read shows that the bail aspect was crucial in the judge's determination of the issue as to whether there was good and sufficient reason for extending the custody time limits. For the Crown, on the other hand, Mr Hick submits that that is not the position. The real reason advanced by the judge was the unavailability, for a trial of this potential

g   length and complexity, of a suitable courtroom and judge before September.

[7] Mr Enright's submission on the law is that, if his submission as to the proper construction of the judge's ruling is correct, her decision was fatally flawed because Bail Act considerations are not properly to be considered in relation to the extension of custody time limits. He conceded that if, on a true

h   construction of what the judge said, two separate reasons were being given by her for extending time limits, the decision would not be reviewable. That concession, as it seems to me, is rightly made, having regard, for example, to the outcome of *R v Central Criminal Court, ex p Abu-Wardeh* [1997] 1 All ER 159, [1998] 1 WLR 1083.

j   [8] So far as the propriety of taking Bail Act considerations into account is concerned, Mr Enright took the court to a number of authorities. In addition to *Ex p Abu-Wardeh*, on which he relied for the proposition that good and sufficient cause must lie in a reason for postponement of the trial, he referred to *R v Crown Court at Manchester, ex p McDonald, R v Crown Court at Leeds, ex p Hunt, R v Crown Court at Winchester, ex p Forbes, R v Crown Court at Leeds, ex p Wilson* [1999] 1 All ER 805, [1999] 1 WLR 841; *R v Crown Court at Sheffield, ex p Headley* [2000] 2 Cr App R 1;

and *R v Crown Court at Worcester, ex p Norman* [2000] 3 All ER 267. He also took
us to a judgment of Collins J in *R v Crown Court at Manchester, ex p S* (23 August
1999, unreported), which was decided four days after the decision in *Ex p Headley*,
which was not cited to Collins J.

[9] In the forefront of his submission, Mr Enright relies upon passages in the
judgment of Lord Bingham of Cornhill CJ in *Ex p McDonald* (in particular [1999]
1 All ER 805 at 808–809, [1999] 1 WLR 841 at 846), where Lord Bingham
identifies the three overriding purposes of the 1985 Act and the regulations made
thereunder, namely—

> '(1) to ensure that the periods for which unconvicted defendants are held
> in custody awaiting trial are as short as reasonably and practically possible;
> (2) to oblige the prosecution to prepare cases for trial with all due diligence
> and expedition; and (3) to invest the court with a power and duty to control
> any extension of the maximum period under the regulations for which any
> person may be held in custody awaiting trial.'

[10] Mr Enright accepted that Lord Bingham CJ ([1999] 1 All ER 805 at 810,
[1999] 1 WLR 841 at 847), in considering good and sufficient cause, referred to the
seriousness of the offence not 'of itself' being good and sufficient cause (see *R v
Governor of Winchester Prison, ex p Roddie* [1991] 2 All ER 931, [1991] 1 WLR 303);
nor the need to the protect the public (see *Ex p Abu-Wardeh*).

[11] He accepted also that in *Ex p Headley* [2000] 2 Cr App R 1 at 6, I referred to
Bail Act considerations as not 'of themselves' providing good and sufficient cause
for extending custody time limits. In *Ex p Abu-Wardeh* [1997] 1 All ER 159 at 164,
[1998] 1 WLR 1083 at 1088, Auld LJ also used the words 'in itself' by reference to
Parliament's intention not being that the original reason for custody could be a
good cause for extending custody time limits.

[12] All of those references to Bail Act considerations, 'in themselves' not being
capable of giving rise to good and sufficient cause, are of course relied on by
Mr Hick on behalf of the Crown as indicating that they may properly add weight
to other factors. But, says Mr Enright, as appears from *Ex p Norman* [2000] 3 All ER
267, in which the effect of *Ex p Headley* was summarised by Smith J (at 271) in a
judgment with which I agreed (at 273), it was said that if Bail Act considerations
were taken into account it would be wrong so to do in relation to an application
to extend custody time limits.

[13] Mr Enright stresses the passages in the judgment of Lord Bingham CJ in
Ex p McDonald, and the judgment which I gave in *Ex p Headley*, which refer to the
separate and additional protection over and above Bail Act considerations
accorded to defendants by the custody time limit regime. Mr Hick submits that
the passage relied on by Mr Enright in the judgment of Smith J was an inaccurate
summary of *Ex p Headley* and was, in any event, obiter. It is right to say that
the summary was obiter and not precisely accurate.

[14] But the question now arises as to whether Bail Act considerations are
properly to be taken into account as a factor capable of giving rise to good and
sufficient cause for extending custody time limits. In my judgment, they are not.
The regimes are separate and different. The purpose of the custody time limit
regime, as identified by Auld LJ in *Ex p Abu-Wardeh*, is one which requires a good
and sufficient cause relating to the postponement of the trial. For my part,
therefore, I accept Mr Enright's submission as to the law, namely that Bail Act
considerations are not properly to be considered when addressing the question of
whether there is good and sufficient cause. It is, therefore, to be hoped that such

a considerations will cease to be canvassed on applications to extend custody time limits.

[15] There remains the other question, which at the outset of this judgment I sought to identify, namely whether, on a true reading, the Crown Court judge's decision is fatally flawed by her reference to Bail Act considerations. In my judgment, it is not. As it seems to me, she gave two reasons for extending

b custody time limits: first, there was the unavailability of a court and judge; secondly, (and it is to be noted that she used the word 'and', not some word such as 'because' or 'by way of explanation' when dealing with the Bail Act considerations) she referred to bail considerations.

[16] In my judgment, she was entitled to reach the conclusion which she did, having regard to the features of this particular case, in terms of likely length and

c number of defendants, and the availability of a judge and courtroom for the trial.

[17] In conclusion, I stress again, without that stress being intended as a reflection upon Mr Enright whose submission as to the law, as I have indicated, I accept, that, as Lord Bingham CJ pointed out in *Ex p McDonald*, this court is likely to be very slow indeed to disturb a decision extending custody time limits made

d by a Crown Court judge (see, in particular, the passage in his judgment beginning [1999] 1 All ER 805 at 813 *b*, [1999] 1 WLR 841 at 850 *f*).

[18] For my part, for the reasons which I have given, I would refuse this application.

SILBER J.

e [19] I agree. I would also refuse this application. The regimes for custody time limits and those existing under the Bail Act 1976 are and should always be regarded as being totally different. As has been pointed out by Rose LJ, the relevant factors for each of them are different.

Application dismissed.

Dilys Tausz   Barrister.

Middlesbrough Borough Council v Safeer and others

[2001] EWHC Admin 525

QUEEN'S BENCH DIVISION, DIVISIONAL COURT

ROSE LJ AND SILBER J

26 JUNE 2001

Local authority – Powers – Powers to prosecute – Whether local authority having power to prosecute for using motor vehicle without insurance – Local Government Act 1972, s 222 – Road Traffic Act 1988, s 143 – Road Traffic Offenders Act 1988, s 4.

The appellant local authority was responsible for regulating hackney carriages and private hire vehicles within its area. Under s 4[a] of the Road Traffic Offenders Act 1988 (the Offenders Act), the authority had power to institute proceedings for the offences listed in that provision, including an offence under s 15A of the Road Traffic Act 1988 concerning safety equipment for children in motor vehicles, offences under s 17 or s 18 of that Act concerning helmets and other head-worn appliances for motor cyclists, and offences concerning dogs on roads. The list of offences in s 4 of the Offenders Act did not, however, include the offence of using a motor vehicle without insurance contrary to s 143[b] of the Road Traffic Act. The authority nevertheless brought prosecutions against the respondents for that offence. The respondents were convicted, but their appeals were allowed by the Crown Court which held that s 4 of the Offenders Act contained a complete list of offences in respect of which the local authority could bring proceedings, and that accordingly it had no right to bring prosecutions under s 143 of the Road Traffic Act. The authority appealed by way of case stated, relying on s 222[c] of the Local Government Act 1972 which empowered it to prosecute or defend or appear in any legal proceedings where it considered it expedient for the promotion or protection of the interests of the inhabitants of their area.

Held – A local authority had power, under s 222 of the 1972 Act, to institute proceedings for the offence of using a motor vehicle without insurance contrary to s 143 of the Road Traffic Act. Given the regulatory power of such an authority in respect of hackney carriages and private hire vehicles, the power to prosecute for driving without insurance was clearly apt to fall within s 222. There was nothing in the Offenders Act which stated that it contained exclusive and comprehensive powers, and s 4 of that Act did not expressly prohibit or limit the powers conferred by s 222. Nor was there any reason why s 4 should be read as being in any way an implied limitation on the powers in s 222. Furthermore, there was a sensible purpose in providing express powers in respect of the offences referred to in s 4. That section dealt primarily with offences such as the wearing of safety helmets or the use of safety equipment in cars or allowing dogs

---

a   Section 4, so far as material, is set out at [9], below

b   Section 143, so far as material, provides: '(1) ... a person must not use a motor vehicle on a road ... unless there is in force in relation to the use of the vehicle by that person such a policy of insurance ... in respect of third party risks as complies with the requirements of this Part of this Act ...

(2) If a person acts in contravention of subsection (1) above he is guilty of an offence ...'

c   Section 222, so far as material, is set out at [7], below

a on the road. In many cases, it would clearly be arguable whether action to enforce such provisions fell within the scope of a power to act in the interests of local inhabitants, as opposed to acting in the interest of a particular inhabitant. There was, however, no reason either of language or policy to read s 4 as impliedly limiting or affecting other powers of local authorities and, in particular, those in s 222 of the 1972 Act. It followed that the Crown Court had been wrong in its

b interpretation of the relevant statutes, and accordingly the matter would be remitted (see [15], [17]–[21], below).

Notes

For legal proceedings by local authorities and the express powers of local authorities to institute proceedings in respect of certain road traffic offences, see

c respectively 28 *Halsbury's Laws* (4th edn) para 1339 and 40(2) *Halsbury's Laws* (4th edn reissue) para 730.

For the Local Government Act 1972, s 222, see 25 *Halsbury's Statutes* (4th edn) (2001 reissue) 350.

For the Road Traffic Act 1988, s 143, see 38 *Halsbury's Statutes* (4th edn) (2001

d reissue) 952.

For the Road Traffic Offenders Act 1988, s 4, see 38 *Halsbury's Statutes* (4th edn) (2001 reissue) 1023.

Case referred to in judgments

Vauxhall Estates Ltd v Liverpool Corp [1932] 1 KB 733, DC.

e

Cases also cited or referred to in skeleton arguments

Associated Provincial Picture Houses Ltd v Wednesbury Corp [1947] 2 All ER 680, [1948] 1 KB 223, CA.

Barthold v Germany (1984) 7 EHRR 383, ECt HR.

f *Nottingham City Council v Amin* [2000] 2 All ER 946, [2000] 1 WLR 1071, DC.

R v Smurthwaite, R v Gill [1994] 1 All ER 898, CA.

Case stated

Middlesbrough Borough Council appealed by way of case stated from the decision of the Crown Court at Teesside on 1 November 2000 allowing an appeal by the

g respondents, Iftkhar Safeer, Asif Afzal, Raja Mohammed Asghar, Paul Robert Baxter, Bisharat Khaliq and Majid Ali, against their convictions at Teesside Magistrates' Court on 14 March 2000, 23 June 2000, 17 May 2000, 27 April 2000, 16 June 2000 and 22 May 2000 respectively, for using a motor vehicle on the road without insurance contrary to s 143 of the Road Traffic Act 1988. The question for the

h opinion of the High Court is set out at [4], below. The facts are set out in the judgment of Silber J.

Clive Lewis (instructed by *Richard Long*, Middlesbrough) for the council.
Robin Denny (instructed by *Tilly Bailey & Irvine*, Hartlepool) for the respondents.

j

SILBER J (giving the first judgment at the invitation of Rose LJ).

[1] Middlesbrough Borough Council (the council) appeal by way of case stated from a decision of the Crown Court sitting in Teesside made on 1 November 2000 by which an appeal was allowed against the decision of Teesside Magistrates' Court convicting Iftkhar Safeer, Asif Afzal, Raja Asghar, Paul Baxter, Bisharat Khaliq and Majid Ali (the respondents) of each using a motor vehicle on a road without

there being in force a policy of insurance relating to the use of that vehicle contrary *a*
to the provisions of s 143 of the Road Traffic Act 1988 (the 1988 Act).

[2] The case stated indicates that the respondents had alleged that the council
had no power to bring prosecutions under s 143 of the 1988 Act. The council,
who are now the appellants, sought to rely on s 222 of the Local Government Act
1972 and also on s 6 of the Prosecution of Offences Act 1985 as empowering them
to institute proceedings for alleged breaches of s 143 of the 1988 Act. *b*

[3] The case stated records:

> 'The Crown Court found that the resolution of this issue came down to a
> narrow point, namely whether s 4 of the Road Traffic Offenders Act 1988
> contains a complete list of offences in respect of which a Local Authority
> could institute proceedings. The Crown Court found that s 4 did contain a *c*
> complete list of offences and that the council could not rely on either s 222 of
> the Local Government Act 1972 or s 6 of the Prosecution of Offences Act 1985
> as entitling them to bring criminal proceedings for breach of s 143 of the Road
> Traffic Act 1988.'

[4] The issue on which this court is asked to give an opinion upon is the following *d*
matter of law:

> 'Namely whether in deciding the local authority did not have the right to
> prosecute for an offence of having no insurance contrary to s 143 [of the]
> Road Traffic Act 1988 and Schedule 2 of the Road Traffic Offenders Act 1988
> the Crown Court was wrong in law having regard to s 222 of the Local *e*
> Government Act 1972 and/or s 6 of the Prosecution of Offenders Act 1985.'

[5] Thus, this appeal raises an important issue on the power of local authorities
to bring prosecutions for road traffic offences.

The statutory framework *f*

[6] Local authorities are responsible for regulating hackney carriages, private
hire vehicles and generally regulating the business of carriage of persons for reward.
Thus, s 37 of the Town Police Clauses Act 1847 provides that a local authority
may licence hire carriages to ply for hire and s 48 of the Local Government
Miscellaneous Provisions Act 1976 provides for local authorities to licence private *g*
hire vehicles. In addition, a local authority cannot licence a private hire vehicle
unless it is satisfied that, inter alia, the vehicle is covered by an insurance policy
(see s 48(1)(b) of the 1976 Act).

[7] Section 222 of the 1972 Act provides, so far as is relevant to this appeal:

> '*Power of local authorities to prosecute or defend legal proceedings.*—(1) Where a *h*
> local authority consider it expedient for the promotion or protection of the
> interests of the inhabitants of their area—(a) they may prosecute or defend
> or appear in any legal proceedings and, in the case of civil proceedings, may
> institute them in their own name ...'

[8] Section 143 of the 1988 Act provides that it is an offence for a person to drive *j*
without insurance.

[9] The next relevant provision is set out in s 4(1) of the Road Traffic Offenders
Act 1988 (the RTOA) which provides:

> '(1) The council of a county ... or London Borough or the Common Council
> of the City of London may institute proceedings for an offence under section 15A

a   of the Road Traffic Act 1988 (safety equipment for children in motor vehicles) or under section 17 or 18 of that Act (helmets and other head-worn appliances for motor cyclists).'

[10] Section 4(2) and (3) of the RTOA provide that the local authority may 'institute proceedings' for various other offences which includes dogs on roads.

b
The submissions

[11] The respondents make three submissions to support the decision of the Crown Court. First, importance is attached to the distinction between, on the one hand, the activities which are authorised in s 222(1) of the 1972 Act which refers to local authorities having the power to 'prosecute or defend or appear in any c   legal proceedings', and on the other hand, s 4(1) of the RTOA which says that a council 'may institute proceedings for an offence'.

[12] Mr Denny, on behalf of the respondents, submits that there is a substantial and relevant difference between the wording as the use of the words 'may prosecute' in the 1972 Act gives a much more limited power to the local authorities than the d   words 'may institute proceedings' in s 4(1) of the RTOA. His submission is that the use of the word 'prosecute' means that it is not possible for a local authority to institute proceedings. Implicit in his submission is the fact that the word 'prosecute' must only authorise procedures that occur after proceedings have been instituted.

[13] I am unable to accept that submission. To my mind the use of the word e   'prosecute' means that the local authority is entitled to take all steps necessary to institute and pursue a prosecution. I do not accept that the word 'prosecute' has any more limited meaning than that and, in particular, I do not consider that it excludes the institution of proceedings.

[14] The second submission made by Mr Denny is that the RTOA is described f   in its preamble as being 'An Act to consolidate certain enactments relating to the prosecution and punishment' of various road traffic offences. He contends that the use of the word 'consolidate' means that it is a comprehensive code and sets out exclusively all the powers that might be given in relation to those matters.

[15] I cannot accept this because to my mind there is nothing in the title of the RTOA, or in any provisions of it, and in particular not in s 4, which states that g   those contain exclusive and comprehensive powers. The powers that are set out in s 4 of that Act are just examples of rights which are given, but are specific examples, and are not limited in any way.

[16] The third submission of the respondents is that the provisions of the RTOA impliedly repealed the provisions in s 222 of the 1972 Act. In his written h   submissions, counsel for the respondents relied on cases such as *Vauxhall Estates Ltd v Liverpool Corp* [1932] 1 KB 733 in which it was held that because a later Act was, in the words of Humphreys J (at 746), 'totally inconsistent' with an earlier Act or in the words of Avory J (at 743–744), 'so inconsistent … that the two Acts cannot stand together' there was an implied repeal of the earlier statute.

j   [17] The respondents contend that in this case the provisions in the later provision here and the RTOA reached that high threshold; I do not agree as there is no reason to believe that the provisions of s 4 of the RTOA should be regarded as exhaustive. There is no statement, expressed or implied, in s 4 of the RTOA which states that it sets out the only circumstances in which the local authority can prosecute. Thus, I conclude that s 4 has no effect on any other power previously given to the local authority to prosecute.

[18] I now turn to the submissions of Mr Lewis on behalf of the appellant council. He makes two basic submissions. The first submission is that as a matter of statutory construction, s 222 of the 1972 Act is sufficient to empower the local authority to institute criminal proceedings where they consider it expedient for the promotion of the protection of the interests of the inhabitants. As they have a regulatory power for hackney vehicles, the power to prosecute for driving without insurance is clearly apt and suitable to fall within the provisions of s 222 of the 1972 Act. He reinforces that point by saying that s 4 of the RTOA does not expressly prohibit or limit the powers conferred by s 222 of the 1972 Act. I agree with him and it is important to stress that there is nothing set out in the later Act which says that the power to prosecute is to be used solely or exclusively for the purposes set out there.

[19] The second submission of the council is that there is no reason why s 4 of the RTOA should be read as being in any way an implied limitation on the powers of s 222 of the 1972 Act which applies where a local authority is satisfied that prosecution is in the interest of the inhabitants of an area. That is a high threshold, or certainly higher than s 4 of the RTOA which does not include this constraint. In addition s 4 of the RTOA deals primarily with offences such as the wearing of safety helmets or the use of safety equipment in cars or allowing dogs on the road. It is clearly arguable, as Mr Lewis submits, in many cases whether action to enforce such provisions falls within the scope of a power to act in the interest of local inhabitants, as opposed to acting in the interest of a particular inhabitant. Thus he says, and I agree, there is a sensible purpose in providing express powers in respect of the offences referred to in s 4 of the RTOA. To my mind there is no reason, either of language or of policy, to read s 4 as impliedly limiting or effecting any other powers of the local authority and, in particular, those in s 222 of the 1972 Act.

The conclusion

[20] In answer to the question posed I would answer that by stating that the local authority did not have the right to prosecute for an offence of having no insurance contrary to s 143 of the 1988 Act and Sch 2 to the RTOA, the Crown Court erred in the light of s 222 of the 1972 Act.

ROSE LJ.

[21] I agree. The question posed by the case will therefore be answered in the affirmative. The Crown Court were wrong in their interpretation of the relevant statutes and the matter will therefore be remitted to the Crown Court.

Appeal allowed.

Dilys Tausz   Barrister.

Practice Note

a

COURT OF APPEAL, CRIMINAL DIVISION
LORD WOOLF CJ
16 OCTOBER 2001

b

Crown Court – Distribution of court business – Classification of offences – Allocation of business within the Crown Court – New directions.

LORD WOOLF CJ gave the following direction at the sitting of the court.

c
With the concurrence of the Lord Chancellor and pursuant to s 75(1) and (2) of the Supreme Court Act 1981, I direct that, with effect from 16 October 2001, the following directions shall supersede those given on 26 May 1995 ([1995] 2 All ER 900, [1995] 1 WLR 1083) as amended ([1998] 3 All ER 382, [1998] 1 WLR 1244; [2000] 1 All ER 380, [2000] 1 WLR 203).

d CLASSIFICATION

1. For the purposes of trial in the Crown Court, offences are to be classified as follows.

Class 1: (1) misprision of treason and treason felony; (2) murder; (3) genocide; (4) torture, hostage-taking and offences under the War Crimes Act 1991; (5) an offence under the Official Secrets Acts; (6) soliciting, incitement, attempt or
e
conspiracy to commit any of the above offences.

Class 2: (1) manslaughter; (2) infanticide; (3) child destruction; (4) abortion (s 58 of the Offences Against the Person Act 1861); (5) rape; (6) sexual intercourse with a girl under 13; (7) incest with a girl under 13; (8) sedition; (9) an offence under s 1 of the Geneva Conventions Act 1957; (10) mutiny; (11) piracy; (12) soliciting,
f incitement, attempt or conspiracy to commit any of the above offences.

Class 3: (1) all offences triable only on indictment other than those in classes 1, 2 and 4; and (2) soliciting, incitement, attempt or conspiracy to commit any of the above offences.

Class 4: (1) wounding or causing grievous bodily harm with intent (s 18 of the Offences Against the Person Act 1861); (2) robbery or assault with intent to rob
g
(s 8 of the Theft Act 1968); (3) soliciting, incitement or attempt to commit any of the above offences; (4) conspiracy at common law, or conspiracy to commit any offence other than those included in classes 1, 2 and 3; (5) all offences which are triable either way.

h *Cases committed, transferred, or sent for trial*

2(a). Save as provided in para 2(b) below for certain offences in class 2 and offences in class 3(1), a magistrates' court upon either (i) committing a person for trial under the Magistrates' Courts Act 1980, s 6, (ii) transferring a person under either the Criminal Justice Act 1987, s 4, or the Criminal Justice Act 1991, s 53, or,
j (iii) sending a person under the Crime and Disorder Act 1998, s 51, shall, if the offence or any of the offences is included in classes 1 or 2, specify the most convenient location of the Crown Court where a High Court judge, or, where the case is included in class 1, where a circuit judge duly approved for that purpose by the Lord Chief Justice regularly sits. These courts will be identified by the presiding judges on each circuit. Where an offence is in class 4, the magistrates' court shall specify the most convenient location of the Crown Court.

2(b). Where a presiding judge has directed that class 2 offences within the categories below, or class 3 offences, may be committed, transferred or sent from a specified magistrates' court or courts to a specified location of the Crown Court at which a High Court judge does not regularly sit, the magistrates' court shall specify that location.

- Rape
- Sexual intercourse with a girl under 13
- Incest with a girl under 13
- Soliciting, incitement, attempt or conspiracy to commit any of the above offences

3. In selecting the most convenient location of the Crown Court, the justices shall have regard to the considerations referred to in s 7 of the Magistrates' Courts Act 1980 and s 51(10) of the Crime and Disorder Act 1998, and to the location or locations of the Crown Court designated by a presiding judge as the location to which cases should normally be committed from their petty sessions area.

4. Where on one occasion a person is committed in respect of a number of offences, all the committals shall be to the same location of the Crown Court and that location shall be the one where a High Court judge regularly sits if such a location is appropriate for any of the offences.

Committals for sentence or to be dealt with

5. Where a community rehabilitation order, order for conditional discharge or a community punishment order has been made, or suspended sentence passed, and the offender is committed to be dealt with for the original offence or in respect of the suspended sentence, he shall be committed in accordance with the paragraphs below.

6. If the order was made or the sentence was passed by the Crown Court, he shall be committed to the location of the Crown Court where the order was made or suspended sentence was passed, unless it is inconvenient or impracticable to do so.

7. If he is not so committed and the order was made by a High Court judge, he shall be committed to the most convenient location of the Crown Court where a High Court judge regularly sits.

8. In all other cases where a person is committed for sentence or to be dealt with he shall be committed to the most convenient location of the Crown Court.

9. In selecting the most convenient location of the Crown Court the justices shall have regard to the locations of the Crown Court designated by a presiding judge as the locations to which cases should normally be committed from their petty sessions area.

Appeals and proceedings under the Crown Court's original jurisdiction

10. The hearing of an appeal or of proceedings under the civil jurisdiction of the Crown Court shall take place at the location of the Crown Court designated by a presiding judge as the appropriate location for such proceedings originating in the areas concerned.

Application for removal of a driving disqualification

11. Application shall be made to the location of the Crown Court where the order of disqualification was made.

Transfer of proceedings between locations of the Crown Court

a

12. Without prejudice to the provisions of s 76 of the Supreme Court Act 1981 ('Committal for trial: alteration of place of trial') directions may be given for the transfer from one location of the Crown Court to another of (i) appeals; (ii) proceedings on committal for sentence, or to be dealt with; (iii) proceedings under the original civil jurisdiction of the Crown Court where this appears

b desirable for expediting the hearing, or for the convenience of the parties.

13. Such directions may be given in a particular case by an officer of the Crown Court, or generally, in relation to a class or classes of case, by the presiding judge or a judge acting on his behalf.

14. If dissatisfied with such directions given by an officer of the Crown Court, any party to the proceedings may apply to a judge of the Crown Court who may

c hear the application in chambers.

ALLOCATION OF BUSINESS WITHIN THE CROWN COURT

General

d 1. Cases in class 1 are to be tried by a High Court judge. A case of murder, or soliciting, incitement, attempt or conspiracy to commit murder, may be released, by or on the authority of a presiding judge, for trial by a deputy High Court judge, a circuit judge or a deputy circuit judge approved for the purpose by the Lord Chief Justice.

2. Cases in class 2 are to be tried by a High Court judge unless a particular case

e is released by or on the authority of a presiding judge for trial by a deputy High Court judge, circuit judge or a deputy circuit judge. A case of rape, or of a serious sexual offence of any class, may be released by a presiding judge for trial only by a circuit judge, deputy circuit judge or recorder approved for the purpose by the senior presiding judge with the concurrence of the Lord Chief Justice.

f 3. Cases in class 3 may be tried by a High Court judge or, in accordance with general or particular directions given by a presiding judge, by a circuit judge, a deputy circuit judge or a recorder who has attended a Judicial Studies Board continuation seminar and has been duly authorised by a presiding judge.

4. Cases in class 4 may be tried by a High Court judge, a deputy High Court judge, a circuit judge, a deputy circuit judge or a recorder. A case in class 4 shall

g not be listed for trial by a High Court judge except with the consent of that judge or of a presiding judge.

5. Appeals from decisions of magistrates shall be heard by (i) a resident or designated judge, or (ii) a circuit judge, nominated by the resident or designated judge, who regularly sits at the Crown Court centre, or (iii) an experienced recorder

h specifically approved by the presiding judges for the purpose, or (iv) where no circuit judge or recorder satisfying the requirements above is available and it is not practicable to obtain the approval of the presiding judges, by a circuit judge or recorder selected by the resident or designated judge to hear a specific case or cases.

j 6. With the exception of courts operating the plea and directions scheme established under practice rules issued by the Lord Chief Justice, the following arrangements for pre-trial proceedings shall apply. (i) Applications or matters arising before trial (including those relating to bail) should be listed where possible before the judge by whom the case is expected to be tried. Where a case is to be tried by a High Court judge who is not available, the application or matter should be listed before any other High Court judge then sitting at the Crown

Court centre at which the matter has arisen; before a presiding judge; before the resident or designated judge for the centre; or, with the consent of the presiding judge, before a circuit judge nominated for the purpose. (ii) In other cases, if the circuit judge or recorder who is expected to try the case is not available, the matter shall be referred to the resident or designated judge or, if he is not available, to any judge or recorder then sitting at the centre.

7. Matters to be dealt with (eg in which a community rehabilitation order has been made or suspended sentence passed) should, where possible, be listed before the judge who originally dealt with the matter, or, if not, before a judge of the same or higher status.

Allocation of proceedings to a court comprising lay justices

8. In addition to the classes of case specified in s 74 of the Supreme Court Act 1981 ('Appeals and committals for sentence') any other proceedings apart from cases listed for pleas of not guilty which, in accordance with these directions are listed for hearing by a circuit judge or recorder, are suitable for allocation to a court comprising justices of the peace.

Transfer of cases between circuits

9. An application that a case be transferred from one circuit to another should not be granted unless the judge is satisfied that (i) the approval of the presiding judges and circuit administrator for each circuit has been obtained, or (ii) the case may be transferred under general arrangements approved by the presiding judges and circuit administrators.

10. When a resident or designated judge is absent from his centre, the presiding judges may authorise another judge who sits regularly at the same centre to exercise his responsibility.

Presiding judges' directions

11. For the just, speedy and economical disposal of the business of a circuit, presiding judges shall, with the approval of the senior presiding judge, issue directions as to the need where appropriate to reserve a case for trial by a High Court judge or deputy High Court judge and as to the allocation of work between circuit judges, deputy circuit judges and recorders and where necessary the devolved responsibility of resident or designated judges for such allocation. In such directions specific provision should be made for cases in the following categories.

(a) cases where death or serious risk to life, or the infliction of grave injury are involved, including motoring cases of this category arising from dangerous driving and/or excess alcohol;

(b) cases where loaded firearms are alleged to have been used;

(c) cases of arson or criminal damage with intent to endanger life;

(d) cases of defrauding government departments or local authorities or other public bodies of amounts in excess of £25,000;

(e) offences under the Forgery and Counterfeiting Act 1981 where the amount of money or the value of the goods exceeds £10,000;

(f) offences involving violence to a police officer which result in the officer being unfit for duty for more than 28 days;

(g) any offence involving loss to any person or body of a sum in excess of £100,000;

(h) cases where there is a risk of substantial political or racial feeling being excited by the offence or the trial;

a   (i) cases which have given rise to widespread public concern;

(j) cases of robbery or assault with intent to rob where gross violence was used, or serious injury was caused, or where the accused was armed with a dangerous weapon for the purpose of the robbery, or where the theft was intended to be from a bank, a building society or a post office;

(k) cases involving the manufacture or distribution of substantial quantities of

b drugs;

(l) cases the trial of which is likely to last more than 10 days;

(m) cases involving the trial of more than five defendants;

(n) cases in which the accused holds a senior public office, or is a member of a profession or other person carrying a special duty or responsibility to the public, including a police officer when acting as such;

c   (o) cases where a difficult issue of law is likely to be involved, or a prosecution for the offence is rare or novel.

12. With the approval of the senior presiding judge, general directions may be given by the presiding judges of the South Eastern Circuit concerning the distribution and allocation of business of all classes at the Central Criminal Court.

Kate O'Hanlon   Barrister.

Practice Direction

a

COURT OF APPEAL, CRIMINAL DIVISION

Practice – Criminal proceedings – Victim personal statements – Consideration of statements before determining sentence – Procedure.

b

1. This Practice Direction draws attention to a scheme which started on 1 October 2001, to give victims a more formal opportunity to say how a crime has affected them. It may help to identify whether they have a particular need for information, support and protection. It will also enable the court to take the statement into account when determining sentence.

c

2. When a police officer takes a statement from a victim the victim will be told about the statement and given the chance to make a victim personal statement. A victim personal statement may be made or updated at any time prior to the disposal of the case. The decision about whether or not to make a victim personal statement is entirely for the victim.

d

3. If the court is presented with a victim personal statement the following approach should be adopted. (a) The victim personal statement and any evidence in support should be considered and taken into account by the court prior to passing sentence. (b) Evidence of the effects of an offence on the victim contained in the victim personal statement or other statement, must be in proper form, that is a s 9 witness statement or an expert's report and served upon the defendant's solicitor or the defendant if he is not represented, prior to sentence. Except where inferences can properly be drawn from the nature of or circumstances surrounding the offence, a sentencer must not make assumptions unsupported by evidence about the effects of an offence on the victim. (c) The court must pass what it judges to be the appropriate sentence having regard to the circumstances of the offence and of the offender taking into account, so far as the court considers it appropriate, the consequences to the victim. The opinions of the victim or the victim's close relatives as to what the sentence should be are therefore not relevant, unlike the consequence of the offence on them. Victims should be advised of this. If despite the advice, opinions as to sentence are included in the statement, the court should pay no attention to them. (d) The court should consider whether it is desirable in its sentencing remarks to refer to the evidence provided on behalf of the victim.

e

f

g

LORD WOOLF CJ

16 October 2001

a   # Godwin v Swindon Borough Council
[2001] EWCA Civ 1478

COURT OF APPEAL, CIVIL DIVISION
PILL, MAY LJJ AND RIMER J
b   19 JULY, 10 OCTOBER 2001

Claim form – Service – Deemed day of service – Rule of procedure establishing deemed day of service of documents – Claimant serving claim form on defendant by first class post – Defendant receiving claim form within prescribed time limit but service rendered
c   *late by deeming provision – Whether deemed day of service rebuttable by evidence proving that service had actually been effected on different day – CPR 6.7(1).*

Claim form – Service – Dispensing with service – Whether court having power to dispense with service of claim form in circumstances where retrospective extension of time prohibited – CPR 6.1(b), 6.9, 7.6(3).
d

In February 2000, a few days before the expiry of the limitation period, the claimant, G, commenced proceedings for personal injury against his employer. Under CPR 7.5, G was required to serve the claim form within four months of its issue, but the court extended the time for service until 8 September 2000. G sent
e   the claim form to the employer by first class post on Thursday, 7 September, and it arrived the next day, ie the last day for service under the extension of time. However, r 6.7(1)[a] provided that a document served in accordance with the CPR 'shall be deemed to be served' on the day shown in the accompanying table. Under the provisions of that table, which covered the five methods of service other than personal service, a document served by first class post was deemed to have been served on the second day after it was posted, excluding, inter alia, a
f   Saturday or Sunday. On the basis of that provision, the employer contended that service was deemed to have taken place on Monday, 11 September (ie three days after the last day for service). The district judge accepted that contention and accordingly struck out the claim. G's appeal was allowed by the judge who held
g   that the deemed day of service was rebuttable if evidence proved that service had actually been effected on a different day. The employer appealed to the Court of Appeal, challenging that conclusion. On the appeal, the further issue arose whether, if the deemed date of service was irrebuttable, G's claim could nevertheless be saved under either r 6.1(b)[b], which provided that the rules in Pt 6 applied to service of documents except where the court ordered otherwise, or r 6.9[c], which
h   empowered the court to dispense with service of a document. In particular, the Court of Appeal considered whether r 6.9 enabled the court to dispense with service of the claim form in circumstances where the terms of r 7.6(3)[d] precluded a retrospective extension of time for serving the claim.

j   **Held** – The deemed day of service of a document under CPR 6.7(1) (Rimer J dissenting in part) was not rebuttable by evidence proving that service had

---

a   Rule 6.7 is set out at [4], below
b   Rule 6.1 is set out at [16], below
c   Rule 6.9, so far as material, provides: '(1) The court may dispense with service of a document ... '
d   Rule 7.6, so far as material, is set out at [27], below

actually been effected on a different day. The terms of that provision clearly meant that, for each of the five methods of service, the day to be derived from the table was to be treated as the day on which the document was served. Furthermore, neither r 6.1(b) nor r 6.9 could extend to enable the court to dispense with service where such a dispensation would, in substance, constitute an act specifically forbidden by r 7.6(3). If r 6.9 did so extend, it would be tantamount to giving the court a discretionary power to dispense with statutory limitation periods. Although it was not certain that an order under r 6.9 always had to be prospective, that rule did not extend to extricate a claimant from the consequences of late service of the claim form where limitation was critical and r 7.6(3) did not avail him. Accordingly (Rimer J concurring), the appeal would be allowed (see [46], [47], [50]–[52], [71], [74], [79], below); *Vinos v Marks & Spencer plc* [2001] 3 All ER 784 applied; *Infantino v MacLean* [2001] 3 All ER 802 disapproved.

Per curiam. CPR 13.3(1)ᵉ gives the court a discretion to set aside or vary a judgment entered in default of acknowledgment of service or defence if (a) the defendant has a real prospect of successfully defending the claim or (b) it appears to the court that there is some other good reason why the judgment should be set aside or varied or the defendant should be allowed to defend the claim. Subrule (1)(b) is plainly capable of extending to circumstances where the defendant had not received the claim form and particulars of claim before judgment was entered against him. The court will normally exercise that discretion in favour of a defendant who establishes that he had no knowledge of the claim before judgment in default was entered, unless it is pointless to do so (see [49], [64], [76], [77], below).

Cases referred to in judgments

Anderton v Clwyd CC (25 July 2001, unreported), QBD.
DEG-Deutsche Investitions und Entwicklungsgesellschaft mbH v Koshy [2001] EWCA Civ 79, [2001] 3 All ER 878.
Elmes v Hygrade Food Products plc [2001] EWCA Civ 121.
Forward v West Sussex CC [1995] 4 All ER 207, [1995] 1 WLR 1469, CA.
Infantino v MacLean [2001] 3 All ER 802.
International Bottling Co Ltd v Collector of Customs [1995] 2 NZLR 579, NZ HC.
Kaur v CTP Coil Ltd [2000] CA Transcript 1328.
Murphy v Ingram (Inspector of Taxes) [1974] 2 All ER 187, [1974] Ch 363, [1974] 2 WLR 782, CA.
Nanglegan v Royal Free Hampstead NHS Trust [2001] EWCA Civ 127, [2001] 3 All ER 793.
Vinos v Marks & Spencer plc [2001] 3 All ER 784, CA.

Case also cited or referred to in skeleton arguments

Clark (Inspector of Taxes) v Perks [2000] 4 All ER 1, [2001] 1 WLR 17, CA.

Appeal

The defendant, Swindon Borough Council, appealed with permission of Schiemann LJ granted on 10 April 2001 from the decision of Judge Longbotham at Bristol County Court on 19 February 2001 allowing an appeal by the claimant, Melvin Godwin, from the order of District Judge Bird on 21 December 2000

---

e   Rule 13.3 is set out at [25], below

a striking out his action for personal injury against the defendant. The facts are set out in the judgment of May LJ.

Glyn Edwards (instructed by *Wansboroughs*, Devizes) for the defendant.
David Regan (instructed by *Thompsons*, Bristol) for the claimant.

b   *Cur adv vult*

10 October 2001. The following judgments were delivered.

MAY LJ.

c [1] This is a defendant's appeal against the decision of Judge Longbotham sitting at Bristol County Court on 19 February 2001. The judge then allowed an appeal against the order of District Judge Bird on 21 December 2000 by which the district judge struck out the claimant's claim. The district judge gave permission to appeal to the circuit judge. Schiemann LJ gave permission for this second appeal. In doing so, he said that he doubted whether this appeal had a *real* prospect of
d success (his emphasis) but he said that the point was an important one upon which judicial views differ.

[2] The claimant was employed by the defendant's Highways Department as a roadman. He sustained a back injury on 26 February 1997, the day after having returned to normal duties from light duties. He claimed damages for personal
e injury against his employers by a claim form issued on 17 February 2000, shortly before the expiry of the statutory three-year limitation period. There had been a letter before action from the claimant's solicitors to the defendant in August 1997, which was promptly acknowledged. During 1998 and 1999 there was a fair amount of correspondence between the claimant's solicitors and the defendant or its
f insurers. In November 1998, the insurance company asked for a medical examination of the claimant by Mr E Smith, a consultant orthopaedic surgeon. Questions arose as to whether Mr Smith should be instructed as a single joint expert or not. The claimant was not in fact examined by Mr Smith until 3 August 2000. It is not necessary to go into details of how this delay came about, since responsibility for it is not relied upon by either party in support of their case on
g this appeal. I note that there was some disagreement about whether Mr Smith was in the event jointly instructed. The parties also considered in correspondence whether the claim form and particulars of claim might by agreement be served without the required medical report.

[3] The claim form having been issued on 17 February 2000, it was required
h by CPR 7.5(2) to be served within four months after that date. By order made on 26 May 2000, a district judge extended time for service of the proceedings to 8 August 2000. By order made on 4 August 2000, a district judge extended time for service to 8 September 2000. No point is now taken on the effectiveness of either of these orders. On 7 September 2000, the claimant posted by first class
j post to the defendant, with copies to its insurers, the claim form together with particulars of claim and a response pack, but without a medical report or schedule of loss. The letter with its enclosures were received by the defendant on 8 September 2000, the last day for service under the orders extending time. The claimant contends that service was effected within the extended time. The defendant contends that it was not because of the provisions of r 6.7(1).

[4] Rule 6.7 has as a side heading the words 'Deemed service'. The rule itself provides:

'(1) A document which is served in accordance with these rules or any relevant practice direction shall be deemed to be served on the day shown in the following table—

(Rule 2.8 excludes a Saturday, Sunday, a Bank Holiday, Christmas Day or Good Friday from calculations of periods of 5 days or less)

Method of service	Deemed day of service
First class post	The second day after it was posted
Document exchange	The second day after it was left at the document exchange
Delivering the document to or leaving it at a permitted address	The day after it was delivered to or left at the permitted address
Fax	If it is transmitted on a business day before 4 pm, on that day; or·in any other case, on the business day after day on which it is transmitted.
Other electronic method	The second day after the day on which it is transmitted

(2) If a document is served personally—
(a) after 5 p.m., on a business day; or
(b) at any time on a Saturday, Sunday or a Bank Holiday,

it will be treated as being served on the next business day.

(3) In this rule—
"business day" means any day except Saturday, Sunday or a bank holiday; and
"bank holiday" includes Christmas Day and Good Friday.'

[5] The essential submission on behalf of the defendant, which succeeded before the district judge, is that, where service is effected by one of the means provided for in the table to r 6.7(1), it is deemed to have been effected on the day provided in the second column in the table whenever in fact the document may have reached its destination or come to the attention of the receiving party. This contention found favour with the district judge, who accordingly struck out the claim. The claimant's essential submission is that the deemed day of service in the table is rebuttable if evidence proves that service was actually effected on a different day. This contention found favour with Judge Longbotham, who accordingly allowed the claimant's appeal.

[6] The district judge considered the meaning of the word 'shall be deemed'. He considered that it meant in its context that the deemed day of service is 'the date that the court is going to take as the date of service'. The main question was whether this is a rebuttable presumption. He referred to the fact that under the former Rules of the Supreme Court and County Court Rules there were deemed dates for service 'unless the contrary is shown'. Such words made clear that under those rules the presumption was rebuttable. These words do not appear in r 6.7(1). He said that this must be intentional and that it tallied with the fact that the period under the former rule had been reduced from seven days to two. He concluded that the presumption is not rebuttable.

a

[7] Judge Longbotham considered that the deemed service provisions did not displace the reality. The defendant received service within the time allowed by the rules as extended by the court orders. If the claimant had not been able to show that the defendant received the document on 8 September, then the defendant would have been deemed to have received it on 11 September, because 9 September 2000 was a Saturday and r 2.8 excludes a Saturday or Sunday (among others) from specified time periods of five days or less.

b

[8] The parties' initial written and oral submissions were fairly narrowly confined. Mr Edwards, on behalf of the appellant defendant, submitted that the use of the words 'shall be deemed to be served on the day shown in the following table' in r 6.7(1) provided for a definitive legal fiction. This has the solid advantage of certainty and everybody, in particular claimants, know where they stand. He referred to the entry in the *Oxford Companion to Law* (1980) for the word 'Deeming', which provides:

c

d

> 'A common modern kind of legal fiction. Particularly in statutes it may be provided that one thing shall be "deemed to be" another, e.g. that a dog shall be deemed to be a natural person, in which case the "deemed" thing must be treated for the purposes of the statute as if it were the thing it is statutorily deemed to be.'

[9] Mr Edwards submitted that the simple certainty afforded by this interpretation caused no injustice to claimants. On the contrary, they have the advantage of knowing for certain that, if they post a document by first class post on a Tuesday, its deemed day of service will be the following Thursday whether it was in fact delivered by then or not. If the deemed day of service were rebuttable, it would be open to a party to establish, not only that the document had arrived on the first day after it was posted (as in the present case), but also that it had arrived later than the second day after it was posted. If the deemed day of service is certain, procedural wrangles are avoided. He submits that the deemed day of service is not altered by actual knowledge, which has no place in deeming provision.

e

f

[10] Mr Edwards draws attention to CPR PD 6, para 2.2, which provides:

g

> 'Service by DX is effected, unless the contrary is proved, by leaving the document addressed to the numbered box:
> (1) at the DX of the party who is to be served, or
> (2) at a DX which sends documents to that party's DX every business day.'

h

[11] Mr Edwards submits that the use in this provision of the words 'unless the contrary is proved' shows that those responsible for drafting the rules were aware of their significance. I do not find this last submission persuasive one way or the other. Practice directions are not the responsibility of the Civil Procedure Rule Committee, whose responsibility under s 2 of the Civil Procedure Act 1997 is limited to making civil procedure rules. Practice directions are subordinate to the rules—see para 6 of Sch 1 to the 1997 Act. They are, in my view, at best a weak aid to the interpretation of the rules themselves. Further, para 2.2 of this practice direction is concerned with the fact of service by DX, not its timing.

j

[12] Mr Regan, on behalf of the claimant, emphasises the purpose of service, which is described in the glossary to the rules as being 'steps required by rules of court to bring documents used in court proceedings to a person's attention'. Mr Regan also refers to the judgment of Bingham MR in *Forward v*

West Sussex CC [1995] 4 All ER 207 at 214, [1995] 1 WLR 1469 at 1477, where he
said, with reference to the former Rules of the Supreme Court:

> 'The alternatives to personal service are allowed because they found a good
> working presumption (rebuttable, but still a good working presumption) that
> they will bring the proceedings to the notice of the defendant.'

[13] Mr Regan submits that, in the present case, the defendant had the relevant
documents formally brought to its attention before the expiry of the extended
time limit and that service was thereby effected. He submits that the function of
a 'deeming' provision is to provide for a situation where the actual circumstances
either are not known or do not need accurately to be known. He refers to various
dictionary definitions of the verb 'to deem'. He submits that 'to deem' is the
obverse of 'to know' and that you deem what you do not know. He contrasts the use
of the words 'shall be deemed' in r 6.7(1) with the words 'will be treated' in r 6.7(2).

[14] Mr Regan points to the overriding objective in r 1.1 of enabling the court
to deal with cases justly. He emphasises that one element of this is that the
court should ensure that the parties are on an equal footing. Rule 1.2 provides
that the court must seek to give effect to the overriding objective when it
exercises any power given to it by the rules or interprets any rule. It would not
be just to deprive the claimant of his claim when service was in fact effected
within the extended time limit. The court should not find an irrebuttable
presumption, contrary to the facts, which r 6.7 does not expressly provide for. He
submits that a rigid construction of the rule is unlikely to provide greater
certainty or to diminish litigation. A defendant who is able to establish that he
did not receive service by the deemed method of service is able to have any
judgment or order set aside. A rebuttable presumption would not materially
increase the extent of litigation.

[15] Since the oral hearing, two recent additional authorities have come to the
court's attention: *Infantino v MacLean* [2001] 3 All ER 802 (Douglas Brown J, 14 June
2001) and *Anderton v Clwyd CC* (25 July 2001, unreported) (McCombe J), a
judgment given after the conclusion of the oral hearing in the present appeal.
Having reserved its decision, the court drew these two authorities to the
attention of counsel and invited written submissions, for which we are grateful.
I shall refer to these two cases in more detail later in this judgment.

[16] In my judgment, r 6.7(1) has to be seen in a wider context than that which
the parties initially addressed. Part 6 contains general rules about service of
documents. It does not only apply to service of a claim form and particulars of
claim. Rule 6.1 provides:

> 'The rules in this Part apply to the service of documents, except
> where—(a) any other enactment, a rule in another Part, or a practice
> direction makes a different provision; or (b) the court orders otherwise.'

[17] Rule 6.2 provides that a document may be served by any of five methods.
These are personal service and the methods which reappear as five methods in
the table to r 6.7. Rule 6.4 provides for what constitutes personal service. This is
sufficiently exemplified for present purposes by r 6.4(3), which provides that a
document is served personally on an individual by leaving it with that individual;
and by r 6.4(4), which provides that a document is served personally on a
company or other corporation by leaving it with a person holding a senior
position within the company or corporation.

a
[18] Rule 6.3 provides that, subject to exceptions, the court will serve a document which it has issued or prepared. The exceptions include where—

'(a) a rule provides that a party must serve the document in question; (b) the party on whose behalf the document is to be served notifies the court that he wishes to serve it himself; (c) a practice direction provides otherwise

b
... (e) the court has failed to serve and has sent a notice of non-service to the party on whose behalf the document is to be served in accordance with rule 6.11.'

[19] Rule 6.3(2) provides that where the court is to serve a document, it is for the court to decide which of the methods of service specified in r 6.2 is to be used.

c Paragraph 8.1 of CPR PD 6 provides that the method used by the court will normally be by first class post.

[20] Thus, r 6.7(1) is capable of applying to any document which is to be served in accordance with the rules; it deals with all permitted methods of service other than personal service; and it applies to documents served by the court as

d well as to documents served by the parties. In practice, a large number—probably the majority—of all documents to which the rule applies are served by the court. These include, for example, nearly all orders made in a county court and claim forms and other documents issued in the Production Centre based in the Northampton County Court to which r 7.10 and the practice direction supplementing it applies. All court timetables which depend upon ascertaining a day of service of a document

e which is served other than personally have to look to r 6.7. In my view, this is a strong general argument in favour of Mr Edwards' submission that r 6.7(1) should be interpreted as providing for certainty. For example, r 26.3(1) provides that, when a defendant files a defence, the court will serve an allocation questionnaire. Rule 26.3(6) provides that each party must file the completed allocation questionnaire no later than the date specified in it, which shall be at

f least 14 days after 'the date when it is deemed to be served on the party in question'. One of the parentheses following r 26.3(7) explains that r 6.7 specifies when a document is deemed to be served. Rule 26.5(1) provides that the court will allocate the claim to a track, when every defendant has filed an allocation questionnaire, or when the period for filing the allocation questionnaires has

g expired, whichever is the sooner. This is an example of a timetable which the court has to control, where the court serves the initiating allocation questionnaire, and where the court may be required to allocate the claim to a track even though one or more of the parties has failed to file the completed allocation questionnaire or communicate with the court at all. For this purpose, the court plainly needs a

h secure base date for its timetable.

[21] I merely note for the moment that r 6.8 provides for service by an alternative method and r 6.9 provides that the court may dispense with service of a document. I will return to these provisions later in this judgment.

[22] Rule 6.10 provides that, where a rule, practice direction or court order

j requires a certificate of service, the certificate must state that the document has not been returned undelivered. It must also state the details set out in a table which follows. The table includes personal service, the five methods of service in the table to r 6.7 and service by an alternative method as provided in r 6.8. For the five methods in the table to r 6.7, the table in r 6.10 requires certification of the date for which the table in r 6.7 provides the deemed day of service. For example, for postal service, the certificate has to state the date of posting. From this, the second day after the document was posted can be ascertained as the deemed day of service.

[23] Section II of Pt 6 contains special provisions about service of the claim form. These include r 6.14, which provides:

'(1) Where a claim form is served by the court, the court must send the claimant a notice which will include the date when the claim form is deemed to be served under rule 6.7.

(2) Where the claim form is served by the claimant—(a) he must file a certificate of service within 7 days of service of the claim form; and (b) he may not obtain judgment in default under Part 12 unless he has filed the certificate of service.'

[24] The reference in sub-r (1) to the deemed date of service under r 6.7 inferentially assumes that the court will not serve the claim form by personal service. It is plain that the purpose of these provisions is that, whether the claim form is served by the court or by the claimant, the other knows the date of its service for the purpose of the timetable which that service initiates. This again, in my view, strongly suggests that the deemed day of service provided by r 6.7(1) and its table is to be regarded as fixed.

[25] For a Pt 7 claim, the details of the timetable my vary depending on, for instance, whether particulars of claim are contained in or served with the claim form (see rr 7.4 and 9.1(2)); or whether the defendant files an acknowledgment of service in accordance with Pt 10 or a defence in accordance with Pt 15 (see those Parts and r 9.2). The time periods run from service of the claim form or service of the particulars of claim (see rr 10.3 and 15.4). If the defendant fails to file an acknowledgment of service or a defence within these periods, the claimant may obtain default judgment if Pt 12 allows it (see rr 10.2 and 15.3). Under r 12.1, default judgment means judgment without trial where the defendant has failed to file an acknowledgment of service or has failed to file a defence. By r 12.3, one of the conditions which has to be satisfied before the claimant may obtain default judgment is that the time for filing one or both of these has expired. Pt 13 contains provisions for setting aside or varying default judgment entered under Pt 12. Rule 13.2 provides circumstances in which the court must set aside a judgment in default. These include where the judgment was wrongly entered because, among other things, the relevant time for doing so had not expired. Rule 13.3 provides:

'(1) In any other case, the court may set aside or vary a judgment entered under Part 12 if—(a) the defendant has a real prospect of successfully defending the claim; or (b) it appears to the court that there is some other good reason why—(i) the judgment should be set aside or varied; or (ii) the defendant should be allowed to defend the claim.

(2) In considering whether to set aside or vary a judgment entered under Part 12, the matters to which the court must have regard include whether the person seeking to set aside the judgment made an application to do so promptly.'

[26] Rule 13.5 provides:

'(1) This rule applies where—(a) the claimant has purported to serve particulars of claim; and (b) the claimant has entered judgment under Part 12 against the defendant to whom the particulars of claim were sent.

a

(2) If a claimant who has entered judgment subsequently has good reason to believe that the particulars of claim did not reach the defendant before the claimant entered judgment, he must—(a) file a request for the judgment to be set aside; or (b) apply to the court for directions.

(3) The claimant may take no further step in the proceedings for the enforcement of the judgment until the judgment has been set aside or the court

b   has disposed of the application for directions.'

[27] This appeal is, of course, centrally concerned with limitation. The relevant time period after which the present action may not be brought is three years from the date on which the cause of action accrued, that is the date of the accident. For relevant purposes, the claim is brought by issuing the claim form. This was done

c   in the present case just before the expiry of the three-year limitation period. In addition, the claim form has to be served in accordance with the rules. A failure to do so which cannot be rectified by one means or another will mean that the claim cannot proceed and often that a new claim will be statute-barred. Those who delay serving their claim to the last moment risk disaster. The general rule

d   is that a claim form must be served within four months after the date of issue—r 7.5(2). Rule 7.6 provides that the claimant may apply for an order extending the period within which the claim form may be served. The general rule is that an application to extend the time for service must be made within the currently existing period for service. Rule 7.6(3) provides:

e

'If the claimant applies for an order to extend the time for service of the claim form after the end of the period specified by rule 7.5 or by an order made under this rule, the court may make such an order only if—(a) the court has been unable to serve the claim form; or (b) the claimant has taken all reasonable steps to serve the claim form but has been unable to do so; and (c) in either case, the claimant has acted promptly in making the application.'

f

[28] In *Vinos v Marks & Spencer plc* [2001] 3 All ER 784, a claimant in a personal injury action served his claim form, particulars of claim and schedule of special damages nine days after the expiry of the four-month period in r 7.5. He applied for an extension of time for serving the claim form and for an order remedying the error which his solicitors had made. He was unable to succeed under r 7.6(3)

g   because he was unable to satisfy the relevant conditions in that subrule. His essential case was that the overriding objective of the CPR, r 1.2 and r 3.10 gave the court a discretion to extend the time for serving the claim form. This submission failed. It was held that the meaning of r 7.6(3) is plain. The court has power to extend the time for serving the claim form after the period for its service

h   has run out 'only if' the stipulated conditions are fulfilled. The general words of r 3.10 cannot extend to enable the court to do what r 7.6(3) specifically forbids, nor to extend time when the specific provision of the rules which enables extensions of time specifically does not extend to making this extension of time.

[29] In *Kaur v CTP Coil Ltd* [2000] CA Transcript 1328, again a claim form in a

j   personal injury case was served a few days after the expiry of the four-month period from its issue. The claimant was unable to meet the conditions in r 7.6(3). This court followed the reasoning in *Vinos*'s case and applied it also to the additional submission that the court might get round the difficulty by relieving the claimant from sanctions under r 3.9. Waller LJ said at para 18 of his judgment in *Kaur*'s case that even if r 3.9 was capable of application, it was in his view clear that the reasoning in *Vinos*'s case would apply as much to r 3.9 as it did to r 3.10.

[30] In *Elmes v Hygrade Food Products plc* [2001] EWCA Civ 121, the claim form in a personal injury claim was sent on the last day of the four-month period stipulated for service in r 7.5(2) to the defendants' insurers, when it should have been sent to the defendants themselves. It was served in time, but on the incorrect person. The question was whether the court had power, on the claimant's application under rr 3.10(b) and 6.8, to remedy the error by an order deeming the service to have been good service by an alternative method not permitted by the rules. The claimant's submission to this court and the court's consideration of it are in the judgment of Simon Brown LJ, with whom Penry-Davey J agreed. Simon Brown LJ said:

> '[12] Mr Porter's argument runs essentially as follows. The service of this claim on the insurers, instead of on the defendants themselves was an error of procedure within the meaning of r 3.10. So much indeed is accepted by the respondents. True it is that r 7.6 circumscribes the exercise of a discretion to extend time for service. It says nothing, however, as to the exercise of a discretion to deem service to be good. Rules 6.8 and 6.9 are the rules applicable to that situation. Those rules govern orders permitting service by an alternative method "where it appears to the court that there is good reason" and, indeed, to dispense with service altogether. It is, submits Mr Porter, sufficient "good reason" that the defendants' insurers were in fact dealing with this claim and that they would suffer no conceivable prejudice through the proceedings being served on them rather than upon their insured. The rules, accordingly, should be interpreted to give effect to the overriding objective in r 1.2. Unless, he submits, the rules unambiguously require it, claims should not fail because of a mistake which has caused no prejudice and can be corrected. Here, he submits, the rules do not unambiguously require that result. Given that the court has power to dispense altogether with service under r 6.9, it must have a lesser power to deem service upon insurers in appropriate circumstances to be good service on the insured.
>
> [13] Attractively though the argument is put and tempting though it is to try and find some way of denying the defendants the windfall of a good Limitation Act defence, thereby throwing the relevant liability upon the claimant's solicitors' insurers, I, for my part, have no doubt that it must be rejected. The fatal flaw in the argument is this. It necessarily implies that r 6.8, the rule which provides for service by an alternative method, can be applied retrospectively. If one asks what order the court is to make to rectify the mistake made here by the claimant's solicitors, it can only be an order under r 3.10 that an order for alternative service, not in fact made under r 6.8, shall be deemed to have been made. But the plain fact is that no r 6.8 order here was made and, of course, there was never an application for alternative service, let alone for an order dispensing with service. Nor, it seems to me worth observing, would it ever have been proper to make any such order in this case. Mr Porter acknowledges as much. As he observes, but for the mistake there would never have been any necessity for such an order.'

[31] Simon Brown LJ then referred to a decision of this court in *Nanglegan v Royal Free Hampstead NHS Trust* [2001] EWCA Civ 127, [2001] 3 All ER 793, where the claimant had in error served proceedings on the defendant himself instead of on his solicitor in contravention of r 6.5(4). The claimant sought to overcome that mistake by invoking respectively rr 6.1 and 6.8. Rule 6.1 was held to be too wide and general in its application to avail the claimant and r 6.8 was held,

a consistently with Simon Brown LJ's own view, to be prospective rather than retrospective in its operation. It could not be applied after the event to cure some error already made in effecting the service.

[32] The subject matter in *Infantino v MacLean* [2001] 3 All ER 802 was a complicated medical negligence claim. Mrs Infantino consulted her solicitors in April 1999. The claim form was issued on 31 August 2000, about a fortnight

b before the expiry of the limitation period. There were extensions of time for its service during which the claimant's solicitors were waiting for a protocol letter of response from Professor MacLean's solicitors. It was eventually agreed on behalf of the Medical Protection Society that there should be a further extension and that the particulars of claim would be placed in the DX system by no later than

c 26 January 2001. On that date, the claimant's solicitors wrote to the Medical Protection Society enclosing the claim form, particulars of claim and other documents. By mistake, the letter and its accompanying documents were sent to the DX number, not of the Medical Protection Society, but of the Medical Defence Union. The mistake emerged too late for service in time and service on the Medical Protection Society was effected one day late. The claimant's

d solicitors applied to the district judge for an order that the claimant should be deemed to have made proper service. The district judge granted the application, apparently granting relief from sanctions under r 3.9, although the district judge also seems to have made an order extending the claimant's time for service of the claim form and the particulars. *Vinos*'s case was cited to the district judge, but

e *Kaur*'s case was not. On appeal, Douglas Brown J held himself to be bound by these two decisions, which precluded an extension of time or relief from sanctions in these circumstances under r 3.9. The claimant, however, by respondent's notice sought an order under rr 6.1 and 6.9 dispensing with the requirement for service. It was submitted that r 6.9 gave the court a very broad power to dispense altogether with the requirements of service. It could not be

f just to penalise a claimant who had not only fully complied with the pre-action protocol but provided the defendant with the fullest possible details of her claim. An order striking out her claim could not possibly be proportionate nor could it be seen as the fair result of the court seeking to deal justly with the case.

[33] Douglas Brown J considered this court's decision in *Elmes*'s case and

g quoted in full para [13] of Simon Brown LJ's judgment, which I have set out earlier in this judgment. Douglas Brown J said that it was clear that the Court of Appeal was not considering applications and orders under rr 6.8 and 6.9 because there never was an application under either rule. It seemed from the summary of counsel's argument that the Court of Appeal was not invited to consider r 6.9 separately. Douglas Brown J

h considered that the two rules should be considered separately. Rule 6.8 replaced the provisions for substituted service in the former Rules of the Supreme Court. He said that r 6.9, on the other hand, is a new provision giving the court a general power on application to dispense with service of a document. He observed that the notes to r 6.9 in *Civil Procedure* speculate that the most likely use of r 6.9 in

j practice would be to dispense with re-service. Rule 6.9 must be read together with rules relating to the overriding objective. He then said:

> '[56] In these circumstances striking out this claim is not dealing with the case justly. It would in my view be an affront to justice, and if the rules required that result then there would be something seriously wrong with the rules. The rules, however, are not defective. Rule 6.9 enables the court to

reach a just result. If re-service can be dispensed with, so can service in the unusual circumstances of this case.   *a*

[57] The remarks of Simon Brown LJ in *Elmes*'s case, with which Penry-Davey J agreed, are obiter and although persuasive are not binding on me. The core of Simon Brown LJ's judgment on this point is that r 6.8 cannot be operated retrospectively. He appears to rule out use of r 6.9 for the same reason. The use of r 6.9 here is not strictly retrospective use. The   *b* claimant is entitled to say here, with these facts and circumstances in the court's discretion the court should exercise the power to dispense with a service. In all these circumstances I do exercise that discretion and dispense with service. He does lose a fortuitous limitation defence but there is otherwise no prejudice to the defendant on such an order being made and the matter should now proceed on the pleadings as they stand on particulars   *c* of claim and defence and no more time should be taken up on procedural wrangling.'

[34] *Anderton v Clwyd CC* (25 July 2001, unreported) is a decision of McCombe J given after the oral submissions in the present appeal. The case concerned an   *d* allegation of negligence by teachers in failing to identify learning difficulties alleged to have been suffered by the claimant at the time of her education at the council's schools. The claim form was issued on 5 July 2000, very shortly before the expiry of the limitation period, the claimant having been born on 7 July 1979. The time for service of the claim form under r 7.5(2) was to expire on 5 November 2000. There was evidence that the claim form was served by letter   *e* dated 3 November 2000. There was evidence from the defendant's solicitors that it was received on 7 November 2000. It was submitted on behalf of the claimant that by virtue of r 6.7(1) the claim form was deemed to have been served on Sunday, 5 November 2000 and was therefore served in time. It was submitted on behalf of the defendant that evidence of the date of actual service overrode any   *f* deeming provision in the rules that in any event, on the true construction of r 6.7(1), Saturdays and Sundays were to be excluded from the calculation of time; and that accordingly, the second day after the letter was posted was Tuesday, 7 November 2000. It was submitted on behalf of the claimant that r 6.7(1) did not exclude Saturdays and Sundays. If that were wrong, and if the claim form was, or must be treated to have been, served on 7 November, an order should be made   *g* under r 6.9 dispensing with the service of the claim form completely.

[35] McCombe J made findings of fact that the claim form was posted on Friday, 3 November 2000 but was only received on Tuesday, 7 November 2000. He held that he could not infer from the evidence that the posting was by first class post, so that he probably could not find that sufficient had been shown to   *h* bring the case within the deeming provisions of r 6.7(1) at all. The appeal would fail on that ground alone. On the basis, however, that he might be wrong about inferences to be drawn from the evidence, the next question was whether the fact of service occurring on a known date overrode the deeming provisions of r 6.7(1). The judge was, therefore, addressing the main issue which arises in the present   *j* appeal, but the facts of that case were the converse of those in the present appeal. In the present appeal, the claimant seeks to have the benefit of a date earlier than the deemed day of service to preserve his claim. In *Anderton*'s case, the defendant was seeking to have the benefit of a later date than the deemed day of service to defeat the claim. In that case, the defendant's submission was that for the presumption to be irrebuttable there would need to be clear words to that effect

a and that the provision was really designed to deal with a case where there was no actual evidence of when service was effected. Rule 6.7(1) is, it was submitted, merely a convenient provision to deal with the situation where a document has been served and no response is received from the party so served. That was in substance Mr Regan's submission in the present appeal. Counsel for the claimant in *Anderton*'s case pointed to the contrast between the present rule and the

b equivalent provision in the former Rules of the Supreme Court, which contained the words 'unless the contrary is shown'. McCombe J saw the force of this submission but did not think that the 'deeming' provision was to be determinative in all cases, even in the face of positive evidence to the contrary. He said:

c   '[19] I do not believe, for example, that if a claim form is served on a defendant in fact on 7 November and he then writes to the claimant to say "I have the claim form. I calculate that I must acknowledge service by 14 days from now namely 21 November", the claimant could reply, "Oh no. I posted this letter on the 3rd. You are deemed to have been served on the 5th. Therefore, your time expires on the 19th." That to my mind would be nonsensical. It would equally be nonsensical if it were not open to the

d   defendant to prove, where required, that he had never received the claim form at all and, indeed, that it had just been handed to him by a neighbour in whose letterbox it had accidentally been posted while that neighbour had been on holiday.

      [20] I think, therefore, that the presumption remains a rebuttable one and

e   that the evidence in this case does rebut any presumption that the form was served on 5 November.'

    [36] For this reason, the judge held that the appeal must fail. In the present appeal, Mr Regan relies on this decision and its reasons.

    [37] McCombe J then stated his view on the issue whether r 2.8 operated to

f exclude Saturdays and Sundays etc from the time periods provided in r 6.7(1), since this question had been fully argued before him. It was submitted that the parenthesis referring to r 2.8 is not part of the rule itself. It was also submitted that r 6.7(1) is not a rule which specifies a 'period of time for doing any act', which is the wording of r 2.8. There was also reference to a contrast between 'day' and 'business day' within r 6.7 itself. The judge considered that the drafting was

g somewhat difficult to unravel. But he concluded that the clear intention behind the reference to r 2.8 in r 6.7(1) is to indicate that Saturdays and Sundays etc should similarly be excluded from calculations of all kinds of deemed service, except those where express provision is otherwise made. Thus on the facts before him the deemed date of service was Tuesday, 7 November 2000 and for

h that reason also the appeal would fail.

    [38] McCombe J then considered the application for an order under r 6.9 dispensing with service. The application rested substantially on the decision of Douglas Brown J in *Infantino*'s case, which McCombe J considered at length. He noted that Douglas Brown J was referred to this court's decision in *Elmes*'s case,

j and McCombe J quoted extensively from that decision, including paras [12] and [13] of the judgment of Simon Brown LJ, which I have set out earlier in this judgment. McCombe J said that the court in *Elmes*'s case was clearly dealing with an application under r 6.8 only. However, it seemed to him to be clear that the court considered that equivalent considerations applied to r 6.9 and that the court had concluded that there was no power to correct the unfortunate mistake that had been made. To his mind, this must have meant that there was no power

under r 6.9 either. He referred to passages in the judgments in *Vinos's* case, and
said that for his part he would have thought that those judgments precluded an
application based upon r 6.9 in the circumstances of his case. He indicated
extreme difficulties in reconciling the decision in *Infantino's* case with either the
powerful dicta in *Elmes's* case or the rationale behind the decisions of the Court
of Appeal in *Vinos's* and *Kaur's* cases. But he said that he must follow the *Infantino*
decision, unless he was satisfied that it was plainly wrong. In the result, since that
case appeared to be the only direct authority on r 6.9, he felt duty-bound to
follow it and to hold that he did have a discretion to dispense with service in the
case before him. However, on the merits he declined to exercise it.

[**39**] In the present case, Mr Regan was not, I suspect, aware until after the oral
hearing of the decision in *Infantino's* case, and he did not initially submit in the
alternative that the court had a power which it should exercise to dispense with
service. There was however included in the appeal bundle a note of a decision of
Judge Overend in the Truro County Court on 17 May 2000, in which he held that
the deemed service provisions in r 6.7(1) were effective to displace the reality of
the receipt of the claim form by the defendant; but that there was jurisdiction to
override the provisions as to service in r 6.1(b) and even to dispense with service
altogether under r 6.9. The judge granted an application made by the claimant at
the hearing dispensing with service.

[**40**] Upon the court inviting further submissions, Mr Regan submitted that, if
the court had power to dispense with service in a case such as this, this is just the
sort of case in which it should be exercised. Mr Edwards submitted that the issue
was not properly before the court supported by an appropriate respondent's
notice.

[**41**] It is evident that there is a number of respects in which the interpretation
of the rules relating to service of documents is causing difficulty and that on
occasions different courts are reaching different conclusions on some of them.
Not all these point arise for direct decision in this appeal, but it will be helpful for
this court to give guidance which I hope will help to resolve the difficulties.

[**42**] On a preliminary matter, it is not, in my view, generally helpful to seek to
interpret the CPR by reference to the rules which they replaced and to cases
decided under former rules. I maintain what I said in *Vinos's* case [2001] 3 All ER
784 at 789 (para 17) as follows:

'Mr Lord, on behalf of the defendants, made written submissions and Mr
Peirson made oral submissions by reference to what they submit the position
would have been under the former Rules of the Supreme Court. In my
judgment, these submissions are not in point. The CPR are a new
procedural code, and the question for this court in this case concerns the
interpretation and application of the relevant provisions of the new
procedural code as they stand untrammelled by the weight of authority that
accumulated under the former rules ... There is, in my judgment, no basis
for supposing that r 7.6 in particular was intended to replicate, or for that
matter not to replicate, the provisions of former rules as they had been
interpreted.'

[**43**] It is not, therefore, I think, persuasive either way to observe that former
rules about deemed service contained the words 'unless the contrary is shown'.

[**44**] Although, as I have indicated, the date of service of a document will often
be an integral part of a timetable provided by the rules or for other reasons
important, there will be many instances in which it will be of lesser importance.

a Fixing timetables or otherwise controlling the progress of the case is part of the court's case management obligation to achieve the overriding objective (see r 1.4(2)(g)). Failure to achieve a timetable which the rules prescribe or a date fixed by an order of the court may result in the imposition of sanctions. On the other hand, there will be instances when pedantic insistence on the literal terms of a timetable will be at best a quibble and at worst positively obstructive to

b achieving substantial justice. The new procedural code of the CPR is positively packed with instances where the court has a wide discretion to manage cases to achieve substantial justice in accordance with the overriding objective. But there are some instances where the court has no discretion or only a limited discretion. It is not surprising if some of those—r 7.6(3) is an example—are rules which relate to statutory limitation. The Limitation Act 1980 contains provisions which relax in

c certain instances the otherwise guillotine effect of the statute. Section 33 of the 1980 Act is perhaps the most obvious example and ss 11 and 14A may also be seen as providing a degree of relaxation. Generally speaking, however, statutory limitation periods act as a non-discretionary guillotine. A person who serves a claim form one day after the expiry of a statutory limitation period cannot

d normally appeal to the court's discretion to relieve him from the consequences. This court's decision in *Vinos*'s case shows that, in r 7.6(3) at least, the statutory policy of the 1980 Act has generally been carried through into the CPR.

[45] The cases to which I have referred are examples of situations in which parties have, for good reason or bad, taken the risk of not serving the proceedings until the very last moment. In some instances, they have made a mistake which

e could be regarded as trivial and in the result the proceedings have been served a day or two late. Recourse has been had to a number of provisions in the rules to try to discover a discretion wider than that which r 7.6(3) provides to save a claim where the merits of the claim indicate that it should be allowed to proceed, and where the circumstances leading up to the late attempted service and mistake

f are regarded as favourable to the claimant's position. In *Infantino*'s case, the general merits were obviously strongly in favour of the claimant; less so in *Anderton*'s case. In cases such as these, however, it is necessary for the court to have a discretion. If there is a discretion, the merits can be deployed with the help of the overriding objective. However, the question whether there is a discretion

g is a matter of interpretation of the rules in the light of the overriding objective but without reference to the merits of the particular case. I maintain the view which I expressed in *Vinos*'s case [2001] 3 All ER 784 at 789–790 (para 20) as follows:

h 'Interpretation to achieve the overriding objective does not enable the court to say that provisions which are quite plain mean what they do not mean, nor that the plain meaning should be ignored. It would be erroneous to say that, because Mr Vinos' case is a deserving case, the rules must be interpreted to accommodate his particular case. The first question for this court is, not whether Mr Vinos should have a discretionary extension of time, but whether there is power under the CPR to extend the period for

j service of a claim form if the application is made after the period has run out and the conditions of r 7.6(3) do not apply. The merits of Mr Vinos' particular case are not relevant to that question ... If you then look up from the wording of the rules and at a broader horizon, one of the main aims of the CPR and their overriding objective is that civil litigation should be undertaken and pursued with proper expedition. Criticism of Mr Vinos' solicitors in this case may be muted and limited to one error capable of being represented as small; but there are statutory limitation periods for bringing proceedings. It is unsatisfactory with a personal injury claim to allow almost three years to elapse and to start proceedings at the very last moment. If you do, it is in my judgment generally in accordance with the overriding objective that you should be required to progress the proceedings speedily and within time limits. Four months is in most cases more than adequate for serving a claim form. There is nothing unjust in a system which says that, if you leave issuing proceedings to the last moment and then do not comply with this particular time requirement and do not satisfy the conditions in r 7.6(3), your claim is lost and a new claim will be statute-barred. You have had three years and four months to get things in order. Sensible negotiations are to be encouraged, but protracted negotiations generally are not.'

[46] In my judgment, although dictionaries may give various meanings for the word 'deem' in other circumstances, the provision in r 6.7(1) that 'A document … shall be deemed to be served on the day shown in the following table' and the heading to the second column in the table 'Deemed day of service' clearly mean that, for each of the five methods of service, the day to be derived from the second column is to be treated as the day on which the document is served. It is a fiction in the sense that you do not look to the day on which the document actually arrived, be it earlier or later than the date to be derived from the table. Thus in the present case, the claim form and other documents were posted a day late and the fact that they arrived earlier than the deemed day of service is no more help to the claimant than it would be help to the defendant if they had arrived later. As I say, I consider this to be the clear meaning of the words used which do not admit of the qualification necessary for the claimant's submission to succeed. This interpretation does not offend the overriding objective in cases where limitation is at issue for the reasons which I gave in *Vinos*'s case. The use of the 'deemed' in sub-r (1) and 'treated' in sub-r (2) is odd but not, in my view, of any significance one way of the other. More significant is the fact, which Mr Regan accepted, that the interpretation of r 6.7(1) has to apply not only to service by first class post, but also to the other methods of service in the table. Granted that the purpose of service is to bring the document to the attention of the person to be served, these are all methods of service other than personal service which are not bound to put the document literally into the hands of the person to be served on any particular day. All these methods of service will not achieve this unless the person to be served is there to receive the document or takes steps to do so by, for example, going to the document exchange or checking the e-mail (see CPR PD 6, para 3.3). Uncertainties in the postal system and considerations of this kind make it sensible that there should be a date of service which is certain and not subject to challenge on grounds of uncertain and potentially contentious fact. It seems to me that parties serving documents by these means are in a better position if the deemed date for service is certain than if it is open to challenge on factual grounds. This particularly applies to claimants wanting to serve a claim form at the very end of the period available to do so. The deemed day of service is finite and they will not be caught by a limitation defence where the last day for service is a Friday, if they post the claim form by first class post on the preceding Wednesday whenever it in fact arrives. Since, in my view, the deemed day of service to be derived from the table to r 6.7(1) is not rebuttable by evidence, and since, for the reasons which I shall give, the limitation consequences for a claim form which is served late are not amenable to the exercise of the court's

a discretion, a claimant who makes the kind of mistake made in the present case and in other cases to which I have referred is in no different position from a claimant who issues the claim form by mistake a day or two after the expiry of the limitation period.

[47] In my judgment, Judge Longbotham was wrong to hold otherwise in the present case, as was McCombe J in *Anderton*'s case, although that was not the *b* only basis of his decision. He was obviously correct to hold that service by *first class* post was necessary for r 6.7(1) to operate at all. Rule 6.2(1) does not permit service by any other form of post. (In theory, I suppose, an order under r 6.8 might conceivably authorise prospectively service by second class post, but then the deemed date of service would be that specified under r 6.8(3) and not that to be derived from r 6.7(1).) He was also, in my view, obviously correct to hold that *c* r 2.8 applies to the periods in r 6.7(1) for the reasons which he gave.

[48] The interpretation of r 6.7(1) which I have set out accords, in my judgment, with the general structure of other relevant rules which I referred to earlier in this judgment. It is significant that many of the documents to which r 6.7 applies will be served by the court and that the practical working of the *d* timetables by the court depends on secure dates which are not liable to be challenged by evidence of when documents actually arrive. I do not agree with Mr Regan's submission that, if r 6.7(1) provided a rebuttable presumption only, this would not be likely to give rise to significant procedural squabbles. On the contrary, it seems to me that potentially variable dates for service of documents are likely to give rise to disputes, and experience shows that many of these would assume *e* greater apparent importance than they deserve. More particularly, rr 6.10, 6.14 and 26.3(6) are examples of other rules which, in my view, are drafted on the assumption that the deemed date of service is fixed.

[49] For the large majority of stipulated time periods, the court has power under r 3.1(2) to grant discretionary extensions of time 'Except where these Rules *f* provide otherwise'. I have explained why, in my view, a person serving a document, including a claimant serving a claim form, is not disadvantaged by a deemed date of service under r 6.7(1) which is not rebuttable by evidence. The position of a person receiving a document, particularly a defendant receiving a claim form, requires further consideration in the light of considerations such as those which troubled McCombe J in *Anderton*'s case and which led him to *g* conclude that the deemed day of service was rebuttable. As to documents other than those which, if they are not responded to, may lead to default judgment, it seems to me that squabbles may occur whatever the system. Most problems will be accommodated by sensible co-operation between the parties or, failing that, by discretionary orders for extension of time, if that accords with justice. As to *h* documents which, if they are not responded to, may lead to default judgment, I have set out the relevant provisions of rr 9, 10, 15, 12 and 13 earlier in this judgment. In my judgment, Pt 13 contains appropriate provisions to deal justly with circumstances where a defendant, against whom judgment in default of acknowledgment of service or defence has been entered, at worst did not in fact *j* receive the claim form and particulars of claim before judgment was entered. Rule 13.5 is odd, in that it refers only to a claimant who has good reason to believe that particulars of claim did not reach the defendant before the claimant entered judgment. But it makes quite clear that the rules do not intend that such a defendant should be stuck with the judgment without due consideration by the court. If the judgment was wrongly entered because the conditions in r 12.3(1) or (2) and (3) were not satisfied, the court must set it aside under r 13.2. In any

other case, the court has a discretion under r 13.3(1) to set the judgment aside or
vary it. The discretion may be exercised under sub-r (a) if the defendant has a real
prospect of successfully defending the claim. That is the obverse of the relevant
part of r 24.2 and may apply whenever the defendant received the claim form and
particulars of claim. Rule 13.3(1)(b) has a disjunctive alternative, so that the court
may set aside or vary judgment entered in default if it appears to the court that
there is some other good reason why the judgment should be set aside or varied
or the defendant should be allowed to defend the claim. In my view, this is
plainly capable of extending to circumstances where the defendant has not
received the claim form and particulars of claim before judgment was entered
against him. It is not an absolute right, but does not have to depend on the
defendant having a real prospect of successfully defending the claim. The court
therefore has sufficient power to do justice in these cases and will, no doubt,
normally exercise this discretion in favour of a defendant who establishes that he
had no knowledge of the claim before judgment in default was entered unless it
is pointless to do so. The defendant, for instance, may have no defence to the
claim, but may justifiably want to have the judgment set aside on the basis that,
had he known about the claim, he would have satisfied it immediately without
having an embarrassing judgment recorded against him. There may also be
questions of costs. It is obviously open to a defendant to establish by evidence for
these purposes the date on which the claim form and particulars of claim were
received by him. That is not, in my view, precluded by my interpretation of
r 6.7(1), since the deemed day of service remains that which that rule provides.

[50] In my judgment Mr Regan was initially correct in not seeking in the
alternative to recover his client's position by applying for an order dispensing
with service under rr 6.1 or 6.9. In short, I would resolve the palpable
disagreement between Douglas Brown J in *Infantino*'s case and McCombe J in
Anderton's case in favour of McCombe J essentially for the reasons which he gave.
The heart of the matter, in my view, is that a person who has by mistake failed to
serve the claim form within the time period permitted by r 7.5(2) in substance
needs an extension of time to do so. If an application for an extension is not made
before the current time period has expired, r 7.6(3) prescribes the only
circumstances in which the court has power to grant such an extension. Just as
Vinos's case decides that the general words of r 3.10 cannot extend to enable the
court to do what r 7.6(3) specifically forbids, I do not consider that r 6.1(b) or r 6.9
can extend to enable the court to dispense with service when what would be done
is in substance that which r 7.6(3) forbids. If r 6.9 did so extend, it would be
tantamount to giving the court a discretionary power to dispense with statutory
limitation provisions. I also agree with McCombe J that the whole sense of this
court's decision in *Elmes*'s case is that what was there decided to be the effect of
r 6.8 also applies to r 6.9. I am not sure that an order under r 6.9, as distinct from
one under r 6.8, always has to be prospective. But I do consider that r 6.9 does
not extend to extricate a claimant from the consequences of late service of the
claim form where limitation is critical and r 7.6(3) does not avail the claimant.
There will be plenty of commonplace circumstances in which formal service or
re-service of a document may be pointless and where it will be sensible and
economic for the court to dispense with it.

[51] For these reasons, in my judgment Judge Longbotham's decision in the
present case was wrong. I would allow the appeal and restore the order of the
district judge.

RIMER J.

a
[52] I have read in draft the judgments of May and Pill LJJ. I too would allow this appeal. With considerable diffidence, however, I am unable to agree in all respects with their interpretation of CPR 6.7(1) and I reach the same conclusion by a different route.

[53] Rule 6.2(1) provides for five methods of serving court documents. The
b first is personal service. It is explained in r 6.4, and where it is employed there will ordinarily be little or no scope for dispute as to the fact of service. Unlike personal service, the other methods of service permitted by r 6.2(1) do not require the delivery of the document to a natural person. They instead permit service to be effected by the transmission of the document to a permitted address in one or other of various specified ways. The theory is that, once it has arrived, it will be
c likely to come to the attention of a natural person who will be a party to the proceedings (or an agent for that party), who can then take steps to respond appropriately to it. There is, however, no guarantee that, even if it does duly arrive, it will also come to the prompt attention of such a person. A claim form sent by first class post may arrive at the defendant's usual residence in the
d ordinary course of post, but if he is away on an extended holiday he may remain unaware of its arrival for weeks. In principle, though, I consider that in such a case the claimant would have properly served the claim form.

[54] Rule 6.7 is headed 'Deemed service'. May LJ has set it out, and I will repeat only the first sentence of r 6.7(1): 'A document which is served in accordance with these rules or any relevant practice direction shall be deemed to
e be served on the day shown in the following table ...' The table then sets out the 'deemed' day of service when a method other than personal service is employed. That is curiously exclusive, because personal service is a method of service 'in accordance with these rules', yet it does not receive a mention in the table. Instead, it receives a separate mention in r 6.7(2), which, in the cases there
f specified, provides that personal service effected on a particular day is instead to be 'treated' as being effected on the following business day. I do not understand why the draftsman there favoured the word 'treated' rather than 'deemed'. In my view, in the context in which they are used, they are essentially synonymous.

[55] It is r 6.7(1) that is of particular relevance. I note first that a 'deemed day
g of service' specified in the table only applies to a document 'which is *served* in accordance with these rules or any relevant practice direction ... ' In the case in which the serving party delivers the document to, or leaves it at, a permitted address, no more remains to be done in order to complete the service exercise, and the table provides that service will be deemed to have been effected on the following day. In such a case, as with personal service, there will no scope for
h doubt on the part of the serving party that he has also effected actual service of the document. In a case, however, in which he adopts any other of the tabled methods of service, he will or may be in some uncertainty as to whether the document has actually arrived. Whilst such cases may be exceptional, letters can go astray in the post or document exchange, and may either not arrive at all or
j may only arrive seriously late; and technological failures may result in faxes or e-mails not arriving. In these cases, in the absence of a response from the defendant, the serving party will be unable to prove that the document has actually arrived: he will be able to do no more than prove it was duly transmitted. In my view, however, the scheme of r 6.7(1) is that a party who duly posts or otherwise transmits his document to the other party in accordance with the rules will be regarded as having 'served' it within the meaning of the first five words of

r 6.7(1) and will then be given the benefit of the presumptions in that rule as to when it was 'deemed' to be served on the other party so as to complete the service exercise. I do not interpret those presumptions as applying only to a document which is not only duly transmitted but also arrives at its intended destination. If they did, a claimant who posts his claim form to the defendant and then never hears another word would not be able to obtain a judgment in default without being able to prove not just that the form had been duly posted, but also that it had arrived. That would usually be impossible and the rules as to proof of service do not require it.

[56] Rule 6.7(1) then provides that a document so served 'shall be deemed to be served on the day shown in the following table'. If it is sent by first class post, that is the second day after posting. In the present case, the claim form arrived on the first day after posting and it is essential to the survival of the claimant's action that he is entitled to say that the deeming provision in r 6.7(1) is rebuttable and that it has been rebutted by proof of the actual date of service. The key question is whether the court can allow evidence of fact to override a fiction.

[57] In approaching that question, I do not regard the absence from the opening sentence of r 6.7(1) of words such as 'unless the contrary is proved' as meaning that the presumption which the rule imposes must necessarily be irrebuttable. The inclusion of some such words—and such a formula was incorporated into the like provisions of the former RSC Ord 10, r 1(3)(a)—would of course remove all doubt. But whenever an apparently unqualified deeming provision is incorporated into a statute or subordinate legislation, the question whether that provision is rebuttable or not will always turn on the interpretation of the provision read in the context in which it appears. In the present case, that context is not just r 6.7. It is the CPR as a whole.

[58] In *DEG-Deutsche Investitions und Entwicklungsgesellschaft mbH v Koshy* [2001] EWCA Civ 79 at [16], [2001] 3 All ER 878 at [16], this court cited from Russell LJ's judgment in *Murphy v Ingram (Inspector of Taxes)* [1974] 2 All ER 187 at 190, [1974] Ch 363 at 370, in which he said:

'It has been remarked on high authority that in considering "deeming" provisions in statutes it is important to have in mind what appears to be the purpose of their enactment [and Russell LJ then listed three authorities] ...'

In the *DEG-Deutsche* case, Robert Walker LJ, with whose judgment Aldous LJ agreed, then proceeded to deal with the appeal on the basis that those authorities showed that the statutory hypothesis is to be carried out as far as is necessary to achieve the legislative purpose, but no further. I approach this case on that basis.

[59] The scheme of r 6.7 is that a document which has been transmitted, left or personally served in accordance with their provisions will be 'deemed' or 'treated' as actually served on a particular, identifiable day. That day will always be a business day (r 6.7 either so provides expressly, or else that is the practical effect of the words in parentheses at the beginning of the rule). If it is posted or sent by document exchange, it is deemed to arrive on the second business day after posting. In the ordinary course, it would arrive on the first day, but I infer that the extra day is provided so as to cover the case in which the document is posted or left at the document exchange after the last collection for that day. If the document is left at the permitted address, it is deemed to be served on the next day. Again, I infer that that is to cover the case in which it is left late in the day, so that fairness should treat as only served on a later day, and also to ensure that that later day is a business day. A document sent by fax will be deemed to be

a served on the same day if it is sent by 4 pm on a business day, otherwise it is deemed to have been served on the next business day. If some other electronic method is used, service is deemed to be effected on the second day after transmission. This equates that method of transmission with that by post or document exchange. Again, service is deemed to be effected on a business day following the transmission day.

b [60] In the light of these considerations, I can identify only two purposes underlying r 6.7. The first is that it is intended to fix a convenient day from which time will run during which the party served with the document is entitled to respond to it in accordance with the rules—whether by acknowledging service, serving a defence or whatever. That is obvious from the fact that service is deemed to be effected on a business day, the point of which is presumably, at least

c in part, so that time will run from the first day on which the receiving party will be able to invoke the assistance of lawyers. In that respect, the deeming provision is intended to confer an element of benefit on the recipient. The party serving the document will of course have no difficulty in identifying what the deemed day of service is. At least in some cases, however, there will or may be uncertainty

d about that on the part of the recipient. For example, a defendant receiving a claim form in the first postal delivery on Wednesday will or may not know whether it was posted at 11.55 pm on Monday or at 1.05 am on Tuesday. Nor, if he arrives at his office on Wednesday to find that a claim form has been left there, will he necessarily know whether it was left there earlier that day, or late the previous day. In those examples, he will look at r 6.7 in vain to find whether

e his time for response runs from Wednesday or Thursday. There are, therefore, imperfections in the scheme of r 6.7. But in most cases they will be unlikely to cause a problem. Documents served in accordance with that rule will usually arrive in the ordinary course of the chosen method of transmission; and if the receiving party has any doubts as to the day it is deemed to be served, he can

f always make a prompt inquiry about it and agree what it is.

[61] The other, and related, purpose of r 6.7(1) is this. In a procedural system which is so flexible as to permit service by post, document exchange, fax or other electronic method, the serving party will in most cases not know, and so will be unable to prove, that the document has actually arrived at its intended destination. Rule 6.7 plays an important role in relation to the service of claim

g forms. Most claims are undefended, in most such cases the defendant will make no response to the claim form and the claimant will want to obtain a judgment in default. A civilised system of justice will not permit him to do so unless he is able to prove that he has served the defendant and that the defendant's time for a defensive response has expired. Unless the rules positively provide for a deeming

h provision as to the fact and time of service, there will in many cases be practical difficulties in the way of a claimant proving his entitlement to judgment. Rule 6.7 is also directed at catering for this. It enables a claimant to adduce evidence from which the court will be prepared to presume that service has been effected and in turn to permit him to enter judgment.

j [62] In my view it is an obvious inference from those two purposes of r 6.7, and in particular from the first purpose, that the rule presumes that documents transmitted in accordance with it will arrive in the ordinary course of the chosen method of transmission. First of all, in most cases they *will* so arrive. Secondly, the rule cannot sensibly be interpreted as intended to fix the intended recipient's time for responding to a document which either does not arrive at all and about which he knows nothing, or which only arrives much later than the time in which it ought to arrive in the ordinary course. Such cases will be relatively rare. But there will be cases where the document, although duly transmitted in accordance with r 6.7(1), either does not arrive at all or only arrives much later than in the ordinary course. Letters do go astray or become delayed in the post. What happens if a claimant duly posts the defendant a claim form which gets lost and never arrives, or only arrives weeks later?

[63] One thing which is likely is that the claimant will enter judgment in default. He will not know that the claim form has not arrived. Nor will he know, or be able to prove, that it has. But he will be able to prove that he duly posted it and that it has not been returned undelivered. He will therefore be able to prove that it was 'served in accordance with these rules' for the purposes of r 6.7(1), and that rule will enable him to satisfy the court that it was deemed to have been served on a particular day. Time having expired for a defensive response, and there having been none, he will be entitled to judgment. But on learning of the judgment, the defendant will be likely to complain that he never received the claim form, of which he was at all times in ignorance, and so could not and did not respond to it. What can he do about it?

[64] In my judgment, it is obvious that he would be entitled to make an application to set the judgment aside under r 13.3, and would be entitled on any such application to adduce evidence that he was not *actually* served with the claim form on the day on which r 6.7 *deemed* him to have been served with it. Similarly, the claimant would probably be under an obligation to apply himself under r 13.5 to have the judgment set aside, and on that application he too would have to adduce evidence proving that the particulars of claim 'did not reach' (that is, were not actually served on) the defendant until some time after the day on which they were deemed to have been served on him. Again, if a defendant only received the claim form several days later than the deemed day of service, I consider that he would obviously be entitled to adduce evidence to that effect on any application he needed or wanted to make in support of the giving of directions as to his time for responding to it.

[65] I do not understand either of May and Pill LJJ to disagree with the essence of my observations in the preceding paragraph, and Pill LJ expressly accepts that the r 6.7(1) deeming provision is not conclusive for all purposes. In my judgment, these observations show that it is not the purpose of r 6.7 to impose a complete bar on either the claimant or the defendant from adducing evidence directed at proving that the date on which a document was *actually* served on the recipient was later than the day on which it is *deemed* to have been served on him. Despite this, I understand May LJ still to maintain the proposition that the deemed day of service to be derived from r 6.7(1) is not rebuttable by evidence. I confess that I am unable to reconcile that proposition with his acceptance that there are circumstances in which the parties can adduce evidence whose purpose is to do precisely that, namely to rebut the presumption that service was effected on the deemed day. To the extent that McCombe J in *Anderton v Clwyd CC* (25 July 2001, unreported) expressed views in line with those I have favoured, I need hardly add that I respectfully regard them as correct and agree with them.

[66] The particular point raised by this appeal is whether it is open to a claimant to prove that actual service of the claim form was effected *earlier* than the deemed day of service, and so in turn to show that the claim form was served within the time limits prescribed by r 7.5 or any extensions granted under r 7.6. The converse of that question is whether it is open to a defendant to prove that service was actually effected *later* than the deemed day of service and so prove a

a fatal non-compliance with those time limits. May LJ's view on the latter point is that it is not so open. I have at least some respectful reservations about that, but since that particular point does not arise on this appeal, I would prefer not to express any final view on it. My conclusion so far is simply that the correct approach to r 6.7 is that it is no part of its purpose to impose a total ban on either a claimant or a defendant from proving that a document was actually served *later*
b than the day on which the rule deems it to have been served. There will be cases in which evidence can be adduced in order to show just that.

[67] Turning to the particular point arising on this appeal, I have so far focused on the position of the intended recipient of the document. For reasons given, I regard it as entirely consistent with the purposes of r 6.7 that he should, at least in certain cases, be entitled to prove that he either did not receive it at all, or only
c received it later than the deemed date of service. But it does not follow that the person serving the document, in this case the claimant, is entitled to adduce evidence that it was actually served *earlier* than the deemed date of service. Whether or not he can must again depend on identifying the purposes of the deeming provision in r 6.7(1).

d [68] As to this, I have considerable difficulty with the claimant's argument. The difference between the serving party and the intended recipient is that the former has a choice as to the method of service, and as to when he effects it. If he chooses to serve his claim form personally, r 6.7(2) provides that service effected before 4 pm on Monday will be treated as effected on Monday, whereas if he serves it at 6 pm it will be treated as effected on Tuesday. I can identify no basis
e on which a claimant who chooses to serve at 6 pm could say that he had effected *actual* service on Monday so that Monday must be taken to be the day of service. The short point is that he will have deliberately adopted a method and time of service which treats service as being effected on the following business day, he must be taken to have understood that that is their effect and I can identify
f nothing in the policy underlying the rule to suggest that it did not intend him to be fixed with that effect. On the contrary, if he were to effect personal service on a non-business day, it would be contrary to their manifest purpose to allow him to claim that service must be treated as having been effected on that day: he would in that event be claiming unilaterally to deprive the defendant of a benefit as to the day of service which I interpret the rules as intending to confer on him.
g That cannot be any part of the intention or purpose underlying r 6.7. Similarly, if he chooses to leave his claim form at the defendant's office at 10 am on Monday, r 6.7(1) deems it to have been served on Tuesday. That is the consequence the rules impose on that particular method of service, and I again cannot see that it can be an implied purpose of the rules that he should be able to
h say that he had actually effected service on Monday. He might have left it there at 11.55 pm, when no one was about. The purpose of the rule is plainly in part to cater for the possibility that service might be effected late in the day, or else on a non-business day, which is why it deems it to have been effected on the following day.

j [69] If that is the right approach to those two examples of the service methods provided for by r 6.7, I cannot see that the claimant in the present case is in any different position merely because he chose to serve by first class post. Rule 6.7 must, in this respect, be interpreted uniformly. It must in my view be regarded as intended to provide the same sauce to the claimant who chooses to effect service by first class post as to the claimant who chooses to effect personal service at 3 pm on a Sunday or at 6 pm on a Monday. In this case, the claimant chose a

particular method of service under that rule, which told him in advance that the
claim form would be deemed to be served on the second day after posting. In my *a*
judgment, it is contrary to the apparent purpose of r 6.7 that he should be entitled
to say that he in fact effected service on the first day.

[70] This means that whilst I consider that, at least in some cases, it is open to
the intended recipient (and in some cases to the serving party: see r 13.5) to rebut
the presumption imposed by r 6.7 and to prove that the document was served *b*
either *later* than the deemed day, or not at all, it is not open to the party serving
the document to rebut the presumption by proving that it was served *earlier* than
that day. I do not find this a particularly odd result, because the circumstances in
which the serving party will wish to prove that the day of actual service pre-dated
that of its deemed service must be exceptional, and will ordinarily only arise in
cases in which the serving party has been negligent as to his chosen method of *c*
service.

[71] For the reasons I have given, although they differ in certain respects from
those of May and Pill LJJ, I too would allow the appeal.

PILL LJ. *d*

[72] In *International Bottling Co Ltd v Collector of Customs* [1995] 2 NZLR 579 at
584, Tompkins J accepted that 'on a matter of construction, the word "deemed"
is capable of meaning "rebuttably presumed, that is presumed until the contrary
is proved"'. I agree. However, I agree with May LJ that the expression 'deemed
to be served' in CPR 6.7(1) is not in the context of the CPR to be read as if limited
by the expression 'unless the contrary is proved'. *e*

[73] The appropriate documents were, in fact, received by the defendant on
Friday, 8 September 2000, that is on the last day for service under the orders
extending time. It is assumed that the documents were received by morning post
so that the defendant had opportunity to deal with them that day. Having been
posted by first class post on 7 September 2000, the effect of r 6.7(1) is, however, *f*
to provide that service was effected not on 8 September but, a weekend having
intervened, on 11 September 2000, that is the 'second [business] day after it was
posted' as provided by the subrule and the table which is a part of it. The
documents are to be treated as having been received on 11 September with the
result that the claim can be defeated by limitation. I reach that conclusion for the
reasons given by May LJ in his comprehensive analysis of r 6.7(1) in the context *g*
of the rules as a whole. It would not be helpful if I were to attempt to restate the
reasoning in words which would almost certainly be less persuasive.

[74] I do not reach the conclusion with the same equanimity as May LJ
however. Its effect is that the important and fundamental question whether a
claim can be defeated by a defence of limitation in a case such as the present is *h*
decided not, as under the former rules, by the facts but by the operation of a
fiction. The 'dog' in the example given in the *Oxford Companion to Law* (1980)
cited by May LJ at [8] above is in fact a dog but must be treated as a person. The
fiction, which I accept is adopted in r 6.7(1), may be justified by the importance of
certainty, even when what in law is certain is at variance with the facts, but I find the *j*
use of a fiction unattractive especially in rules designed to be comprehensible to lay
people and user-friendly, as shown for example by the heading to Pt 7: 'HOW TO
START PROCEEDINGS—THE CLAIM FORM.'

[75] The interpretation found to exist does limit the scope for factual disputes,
and that is in its favour, but it does not eliminate the possibility of such
disputes. There may still be disputes as to the day on which documents were

a posted where they are said to have been posted later than the afternoon collection from the post box, for example. Where a defendant claims not to have received the documents, there may be disputes as to whether they were posted at all.

[76] Moreover, the deeming provision is not conclusive for all purposes if May LJ's analysis of r 13.3(1)(b), with which I agree, is correct. A defendant may apply to set aside a judgment if he has not received the claim form notwithstanding

b that it is deemed to have been served on him if posted by first class post. Under r 6.7(1), the documents are treated as having been served on a particular day, even if in fact they were not, but under r 13.3(1)(b) the court is entitled to override the fiction and consider the facts.

[77] I have no difficulty with that right being available to a defendant or with the presence of a discretion in the court to set aside the judgment. I also acknowledge

c that setting aside a judgment may justly be governed by rules different from those governing limitation. Allowing a defendant to rely on the facts to set aside a judgment and not allowing a claimant to rely on the facts to establish service within a limitation period diminishes, however, the concept of 'equal footing' contemplated by r 1.1(2)(a).

d [78] As to the relevance of the views he expressed in *Vinos v Marks & Spencer plc* [2001] 3 All ER 784 to the present issue of construction, I do respectfully differ from May LJ. When a claim is to be brought, it is advisable not to wait until the last minute to bring it. That sound principle does not in my view, however, bear upon the question whether fact or fiction governs the date of service. Rule 6.7 is not to be construed on the basis that it is intended to be a sanction against

e delayed claims.

[79] I agree with the views expressed by May LJ on the effect of rr 6.1 and 6.9. I do not agree with the view tentatively expressed by Rimer J that, while it is not open to a claimant to prove service earlier than the deemed date of service, a defendant may prove that service was effected later than the deemed date of

f service. On that issue, I agree with May LJ. I have thought it right to express, with diffidence, my misgivings about the adoption in r 6.7(1) of a legal fiction but I agree that the appeal should be allowed.

Appeal allowed. Permission to appeal refused.

Kate O'Hanlon   Barrister.

Ashdown v Telegraph Group Ltd

[2001] EWCA Civ 1142

COURT OF APPEAL, CIVIL DIVISION

LORD PHILLIPS MR, ROBERT WALKER AND KEENE LJJ

1, 2 MAY, 18 JULY 2001

Copyright – Infringement – Defence – Right to freedom of expression – Whether court having to consider facts of individual case when determining whether copyright protection infringing right to freedom of expression under human rights convention – Copyright, Designs and Patents Act 1988, ss 30, 171(3) – Human Rights Act 1998, Sch 1, Pt I, art 10.

The claimant, A, was the former leader of the Liberal Democrats. During his period as party leader, A kept detailed diaries and other records of his life and political career. He treated them as confidential and kept them secure. His records included a confidential minute (the minute) made by A of a meeting attended by him, the Prime Minister and three others in October 1997 concerning the possible formation of a coalition cabinet containing two Liberal Democrats. In 1999, when it was known that A was standing down as party leader, it also became known that he was thinking of publishing his diaries. Shortly afterwards, a newspaper owned by the defendant newspaper group was given a copy of the minute by a third party, without A's knowledge or approval, and subsequently published an article which contained several verbatim quotations from the minute. A brought proceedings against the group for, inter alia, copyright infringement, and applied for summary judgment in respect of that claim. On the application, the newspaper group relied on the defence of fair dealing under s 30[a] of the Copyright, Designs and Patents Act 1988; the defence of public interest recognised or preserved by s 171(3)[b] of that Act; and various provisions of the Human Rights Act 1998, taken together with the right to freedom of expression under art 10[c] of the European Convention for the Protection of Human Rights and Fundamental Freedoms 1950 (as set out in Sch 1 to the 1998 Act). By virtue of art 10(2), the exercise of that freedom could be made subject to such restrictions as were prescribed by law and were necessary in a democratic society for the protection of the rights of others. The newspaper group contended that the court, in conforming with its duty under the 1998 Act to interpret and apply ss 30 and 171(3) of the 1988 Act in a way which preserved the newspaper group's right under art 10 of the convention, had to take account of all the individual facts to see whether restriction of the group's freedom was necessary in a democratic society. The Vice-Chancellor rejected that argument, holding that the 1998 Act had not affected the extent of the protection afforded to copyright, that the 1988 Act already struck the appropriate balance between the rights of copyright owners and the right to freedom of expression, and that accordingly it was not necessary for the court, in order to comply with art 10, to do more than apply the provisions of the 1988 Act to the relevant facts. He gave judgment for A, granted a final injunction against further infringement and directed disclosure of

---

a   Section 30, so far as material, is set out at [32], below
b   Section 171(3) is set out at [34], below
c   Article 10 is set out at [24], below

a information to enable A to exercise his right of election between damages and an account of profits. The newspaper group appealed.

Held – Rare circumstances could arise in which the right to freedom of expression guaranteed by art 10 of the convention would come into conflict with the protection afforded by the 1988 Act, notwithstanding the express exceptions to be

b found in that Act. In those circumstances, the court was bound, insofar as it was able, to apply the 1988 Act in a manner which accommodated the right to freedom of expression, and that made it necessary for the court to look closely at the facts of individual cases. The first way in which it might be possible to do that was by declining the discretionary relief of an injunction, and such a step would usually be likely to be sufficient. If a newspaper considered it necessary to copy

c the exact words created by another, there was no reason in principle why the newspaper should not indemnify the author for any loss caused to him, or alternatively account to him for any profit made as a result of copying his work. Freedom of expression should not normally carry with it the right to make free use of another's work. There was, however, the clearest public interest in giving

d effect to the right to freedom of expression in those rare cases where that right trumped the rights conferred by the 1988 Act. In such circumstances, s 171(3) of that Act permitted the defence of public interest to be raised, although it would be very rare for the public interest to justify the copying of the form of a work to which copyright attached. In the instant case, whilst there might in law have been justification for the publication of the confidential information that was

e contained in the minute, it was not arguable that there was any justification for the extent of the reproduction of A's own words. The minute had been deliberately filleted in order to extract colourful passages that were most likely to add flavour to the article and thus to appeal to the newspaper's readership. A's work product had been deployed in that way for reasons that were essentially

f journalistic in furtherance of the commercial interests of the newspaper group. It was not arguable that art 10 required that the group should be able to profit from that use of A's copyright without paying compensation. Accordingly, the appeal would be dismissed (see [45], [46], [58], [59], [82], [84], below).

Lion Laboratories Ltd v Evans [1984] 2 All ER 417, Fressoz v France (1999) 5 BHRC 654 and Hyde Park Residence Ltd v Yelland [2001] Ch 143 considered.

g Decision of Sir Andrew Morritt V-C [2001] 2 All ER 370 affirmed.

Notes

For the right to freedom of expression and for the fair dealing and public interest defences to copyright infringement, see respectively 8(2) *Halsbury's Laws* (4th edn

h reissue) paras 158–159 and 9(2) *Halsbury's Laws* (4th edn reissue) paras 338–339, 400.

For the Copyright, Designs and Patents Act 1988, ss 30, 171, see 11 *Halsbury's Statutes* (4th edn) (2000 reissue) 445, 557.

j For the Human Rights Act 1998, Sch 1, Pt I, art 10, see 7 *Halsbury's Statutes* (4th edn) (1999 reissue) 524.

Cases referred to in judgments

BBC v British Satellite Broadcasting Ltd [1991] 3 All ER 833, [1992] Ch 141, [1991] 3 WLR 174.

Bladet Tromsø v Norway (1999) 29 EHRR 125, ECt HR.

British Steel Corp v Granada Television Ltd [1981] 1 All ER 417, [1981] AC 1096, [1980] 3 WLR 774, HL.

Fraser v Evans [1969] 1 All ER 8, [1969] 1 QB 349, [1968] 3 WLR 1172, CA.

Fressoz v France (1999) 5 BHRC 654, ECt HR.

Holman v Johnson (1775) 1 Cowp 341, [1775–1802] All ER Rep 98, 98 ER 1120.

Hubbard v Vosper [1972] 1 All ER 1023, [1972] 2 QB 84, [1972] 2 WLR 389, CA.

Hyde Park Residence Ltd v Yelland [2001] Ch 143, [2000] 3 WLR 215, CA.

Jersild v Denmark (1994) 19 EHHR 1, ECt HR.

Lion Laboratories Ltd v Evans [1984] 2 All ER 417, [1985] QB 526, [1984] 3 WLR 539, CA.

Pro Sieben Media AG v Carlton UK Television Ltd [1999] 1 WLR 605, CA.

Time Warner Entertainments Co LP v Channel Four Television Corp plc [1994] EMLR 1, CA.

Tolstoy Miloslavsky v UK (1995) 20 EHRR 442, ECt HR.

Woodward v Hutchins [1977] 2 All ER 751, [1977] 1 WLR 760, CA.

Appeal

The defendant, Telegraph Group Ltd, appealed with permission of Sir Andrew Morritt V-C from his decision on 11 January 2001 ([2001] 2 All ER 370, [2001] 2 WLR 967) granting the claimant, Jeremy John Durham Ashdown, summary judgment on his claim for copyright infringement against Telegraph Group in respect of articles published in the Sunday Telegraph on 28 November 1999. The facts are set out in the judgment of the court.

Andrew Nicol QC and *James Mellor* (instructed by *Olswang*) for Telegraph Group.

Richard Spearman QC (instructed by *Bates Wells & Braithwaite*) for Mr Ashdown.

Cur adv vult

18 July 2001. The following judgment of the court was delivered.

LORD PHILLIPS OF WORTH MATRAVERS MR.

[1] This appeal raises the important question of whether the Human Rights Act 1998 has impacted on the protection afforded to owners of copyright by the Copyright, Designs and Patents Act 1988. The appellants (Telegraph Group) contend that it has. They contend that, when considering whether an actionable breach of copyright has occurred or the remedies appropriate in the event of such a breach, the court must now have regard to the right of freedom of expression conferred by art 10 of the European Convention for the Protection of Human Rights and Fundamental Freedoms (Rome, 4 November 1950; TS 71 (1953); Cmd 8969) (the convention). This, so Telegraph Group contend, requires the court to give individual consideration to the facts of each case in order to assess the impact of art 10.

[2] Sir Andrew Morritt V-C has rejected this contention (see [2001] 2 All ER 370, [2001] 2 WLR 967). He has held that the 1988 Act already strikes the appropriate balance between the rights of owners of copyright and the right of freedom of expression, and that it is not necessary, in order to comply with art 10 of the convention, to do more than apply the provisions of the 1988 Act to the relevant facts. That, in this case, he has done and, in a judgment delivered on 11 January 2001 has held that the Telegraph Group infringed the respondent's copyright. Against that judgment Telegraph Group now appeal.

The facts

a

[3] At the general election on 1 May 1997 the Labour Party won 419 seats, the Conservatives 165, the Liberal Democrats 49 and other parties 29. The scale of Labour's landslide was expected by many to put an end to any plans for formal co-operation between Labour and the Liberal Democrats and for review of the voting system (with the possible introduction of some form of proportional

b representation). In fact, however, high-level contacts continued. This case is concerned with a confidential record of a particularly important meeting held at 10 Downing Street on the evening of 21 October 1997.

[4] The record was made by the leader of the Liberal Democrats, then invariably referred to as Mr Paddy Ashdown. He has since relinquished the leadership of the Liberal Democrats and has been honoured, first with a knighthood and then with

c a life peerage. But he is not so readily recognisable as Sir Jeremy Ashdown or Lord Ashdown and it is simpler (and involves no disrespect) to refer to him as he was known at the time of the events with which the court is concerned.

[5] Since he became leader of the Liberal Democrats in 1988 Mr Ashdown had kept detailed diaries and other records of his life and political career. He treated

d these as confidential and kept them secure. If he showed them to others it was on a confidential basis. His record of the meeting on 21 October 1997 was prepared on that basis. The meeting had been attended by only five persons: apart from Mr Ashdown they were the Prime Minister, Mr Peter Mandelson, Lord Jenkins of Hillhead and Mr Jonathan Powell. Mr Ashdown dictated his minute of the meeting later that evening and it was typed by his secretary at the House of Commons.

e Only two copies were made. One was placed with Mr Ashdown's diaries and associated records in a safe in his constituency, Yeovil. The other was read by a few of his closest advisors and then was shredded.

[6] About two years later, when it was known that Mr Ashdown was standing down from the leadership of the Liberal Democrats, it also became known that

f he was thinking of publishing his diaries. He had formed this idea in about February 1999 and spent some time on sorting and editing material. His plans for publication were referred to in a radio interview called 'Resigning Issues' which was broadcast on 16 November 1999. Mr Ashdown referred to the possibility of publication in two stages because of the sensitivity of some of the material. At about this time some of Mr Ashdown's material, including the minute of the

g meeting on 21 October 1997, was shown in strict confidence to eight individuals who were representatives of newspapers or publishing houses. Considerable interest was shown but no contract was entered into before the publication by the Sunday Telegraph of which Mr Ashdown has complained.

[7] By some unknown means a copy of the minute reached the hands of the

h political editor of the Sunday Telegraph, Mr Joe Murphy. Mr Murphy's evidence was that it came from an individual who did not work for Mr Ashdown, or for the Liberal Democrats, and who thought that 'the record should be set straight'. The Sunday Telegraph did not pay for the minute. Mr Murphy knew that the minute was authentic, and that it was confidential. Indeed it is described as a 'leaked

j document' and a 'secret record' in the first and second sentences of his front-page article in the Sunday Telegraph on 28 November 1999.

[8] The Sunday Telegraph of that date published three separate items on the minute. There was the front-page article by Mr Murphy; a major story (headed exclusive and illustrated by sketches of the five participants) on pp 4 and 5; and a comment by Mr Matthew d'Ancona, a political columnist, on p 33. Mr Ashdown's counsel virtually conceded that the items on pp 1 and 33, had they stood alone,

would not have been actionable as copyright infringement. The thrust of the attack based on infringement was directed to the main story on pp 4 and 5, which contained several verbatim quotations from the minute.

[9] The full text of the minute has not been disclosed in these proceedings. The court has a redacted copy disclosing only those passages which were either quoted verbatim or closely summarised. But it is possible to see that the minute was a nine-page document and that Mr Murphy has made most use of the last four pages of it. The court was not given any precise statistics (sensibly, since infringement of copyright is not a matter of statistics) but it appears that very roughly one-quarter of the text of the main article on pp 4 and 5 consisted of verbatim or almost-verbatim reproduction of the minute, and very roughly one-fifth of the minute was reproduced in this way.

[10] As to the factual content of the articles, there was some lively reporting of what had been said by the Prime Minister, Mr Ashdown and others. An adequate picture of this can be derived from Sir Andrew Morritt V-C's summary of the political comments made by the Sunday Telegraph journalists:

'The points made by the writers are: (1) the minute confirmed that the Prime Minster had seriously intended to form a coalition cabinet by the inclusion of two Liberal Democrat Members of Parliament in place of two cabinet ministers who were Labour Members of Parliament notwithstanding the large majority he enjoyed as the result of the election in May 1997; (2) the disclosure contradicted the denials emanating from 10 Downing Street; (3) the co-operation between the Prime Minister and [Mr Ashdown] went beyond discussing a coalition cabinet and extended to assisting the Liberal Democrats to win the by-election then pending in Winchester and the Liberal Democrats toning down their criticism of the government; (4) had the members of the Labour Party known how far the Prime Minister had gone in the formation of a coalition cabinet their opposition to voting reforms in the wake of the Jenkins Report would have been a full-scale revolt.' (See [2001] 2 All ER 370 at [22], [2001] 2 WLR 967.)

[11] On 6 December 1999 Mr Ashdown commenced proceedings against Telegraph Group, the proprietor of the Sunday Telegraph, making claims for breach of confidence and copyright infringement. He was seeking injunctions and damages (or alternatively an account of profits). On 30 June 2000, after a defence had been served, Mr Ashdown applied for summary judgment under CPR Pt 24 in respect of the copyright claim only. This application was made on the basis that Telegraph Group had no real prospect of successfully defending the action, and that there was no other compelling reason for that part of the claim to go to trial (see CPR 24.2).

[12] After a two-day hearing in December 2000 Sir Andrew Morritt V-C on 11 January 2001 gave judgment against Telegraph Group on the copyright claim. He granted a final injunction against any further infringement and directed disclosure of information to enable Mr Ashdown to exercise his right of election between damages and an account of profits. However, Sir Andrew Morritt V-C gave permission to appeal and his order has been stayed pending the appeal.

Sir Andrew Morritt V-C's judgment

[13] Before Sir Andrew Morritt V-C (as in this court) it was common ground that the minute was a copyright work and that Mr Ashdown is the owner of the copyright. It was also common ground that substantial parts of the minute had

a been copied in the Sunday Telegraph for 28 November 1999, especially in the main article. Telegraph Group relied on the defence of fair dealing under s 30 of the 1988 Act; on the defence of public interest recognised or preserved by s 171(3) of the 1988 Act; and on provisions of the 1998 Act including in particular ss 3(1), 6(1) and 12(3) taken together with art 10 of the convention.

[14] After stating the facts and the issues Sir Andrew Morritt V-C observed
b that there had been no previous reported case, either at Strasbourg or in the United Kingdom, as to the interaction of freedom of expression and copyright, or any other intellectual property right. So he thought it best to consider the human rights aspect first.

[15] It had been argued on behalf of Telegraph Group that s 3(1) of the 1998 Act required the court, in interpreting and applying ss 30 and 171(3) of the
c 1988 Act, to do so in a way which preserved its right of freedom of expression under art 10. It was argued that the court had to take account of all the individual facts to see whether restriction of its freedom was necessary in a democratic society.

[16] Sir Andrew Morritt V-C accepted that art 10 could be engaged (and is
d engaged in this case) in a claim for copyright infringement. But he went on to hold:

> 'It does not follow that because art 10 is engaged the facts of each case have to be considered to determine whether the restriction imposed by the law of copyright goes further than what is necessary in a democratic society. Article
e 10(2) recognises that the exercise of the right to freedom of expression carries with it duties and responsibilities.' (See [2001] 2 All ER 370 at [13], [2001] 2 WLR 967.)

[17] He rejected the submission that scrutiny of the facts of a particular case might show that the 'exceptions, exemptions and defences' provided for in intellectual
f property legislation might need to be supplemented. Otherwise intellectual property litigation might burgeon out of control. The needs of a democratic society include the recognition of private property, including intellectual property, and the 1988 Act gives effect to the United Kingdom's obligations under the Berne Conventions of 1886 and 1971 (the Berne Convention of the International Union for the Protection of Literary and Artistic Works 1886, as revised at Paris on 24 July
g (Paris, 24 July 1971; TS 9 (1975); Cmnd 5844)).

[18] After discussing a number of cases in the European Court of Human Rights (none of which was concerned with copyright), Sir Andrew Morritt V-C restated his conclusion as follows:

h   '... art 10 cannot be relied on to create defences to the alleged infringement over and above those for which the 1988 Act provides. The balance between the rights of the owner of the copyright and those of the public has been struck by the legislative organ of the democratic state itself in the legislation it has enacted. There is no room for any further defences outside the code which establishes the particular species of intellectual property in question.'
j (See [2001] 2 All ER 370 at [20], [2001] 2 WLR 967.)

[19] Sir Andrew Morritt V-C then considered Telegraph Group's reliance on ss 30(1), 30(2) and 171(3) of the 1988 Act. He rejected the defence under s 30(1) ('Fair dealing with a work for the purpose of criticism or review') in a summary way: the articles were not criticising the minute, but the actions of the Prime Minister and the leader of the Liberal Democrats.

[20] In relation to s 30(2) ('Fair dealing ... for the purpose of reporting current events') Sir Andrew Morritt V-C acknowledged the force of Mr Ashdown's arguments that there was no reporting of 'current events'. He did not accept that Telegraph Group had no reasonable prospect of establishing the contrary. However, he considered that there was no reasonable prospect of Telegraph Group making good the defence under s 30(2), by reference to the three factors put forward in Laddie, Prescott and Vitoria *The Modern Law of Copyright and Designs* (3rd edn, 2000) vol 1, p 754 (para 20.16):

'... [(1)] whether the alleged fair dealing is ... commercially competing with the proprietor's exploitation of the ... work ... [(2)] whether the work has already been published or otherwise exposed to the public ... [and (3)] the amount and importance of the work which has been taken.'

[21] Sir Andrew Morritt V-C then turned to s 171(3) of the 1988 Act. He considered the decision of this court in *Hyde Park Residence Ltd v Yelland* [2001] Ch 143, [2000] 3 WLR 215. He concluded that it was binding authority restricting the scope of s 171(3).

[22] In relation to s 12(4) of the 1998 Act Sir Andrew Morritt V-C rejected the submission that it required the court to place extra weight on the matters specified in the subsection. He considered:

'Rather it points to the need for the court to consider the matters to which the subsection refers specifically and separately from other relevant considerations.' (See [2001] 2 All ER 370 at [34], [2001] 2 WLR 967.)

[23] He thought that it made no difference on the facts of this case. He also saw no special reason for the copyright claim to go to trial.

The rights in play

[24] Article 10 of the convention provides:

'Freedom of expression

1. Everyone has the right to freedom of expression. This right shall include freedom to hold opinions and to receive and impart information and ideas without interference by public authority and regardless of frontiers. This Article shall not prevent States from requiring the licensing of broadcasting, television or cinema enterprises.

2. The exercise of these freedoms, since it carries with it duties and responsibilities, may be subject to such formalities, conditions, restrictions or penalties as are prescribed by law and are necessary in a democratic society, in the interests of national security, territorial integrity or public safety, for the prevention of disorder or crime, for the protection of health or morals, for the protection of the reputation or rights of others, for preventing the disclosure of information received in confidence, or for maintaining the authority and impartiality of the judiciary.'

The rights granted by art 10 are generally referred to as 'freedom of expression'. But as the first paragraph makes clear, it includes the right to impart both information and ideas.

[25] The second paragraph of this article is particularly significant. In a democratic society there are many circumstances in which freedom of expression

a   must, of necessity, be restricted. In particular untrammelled exercise of freedom
of expression will often infringe the 'rights of others', both under the convention
and outside it. The right to respect for one's private life recognised by art 8 is an
example. More pertinent in the present context is the right recognised by art 1 of
the First Protocol:

b   *'Protection of property*
Every natural or legal person is entitled to the peaceful enjoyment of his
possessions. No one shall be deprived of his possessions except in the public
interest and subject to the conditions provided for by law and by the general
principles of international law.
c   The preceding provisions shall not, however, in any way impair the right
of a State to enforce such laws as it deems necessary to control the use of
property in accordance with the general interest or to secure the payment of
taxes or other contributions or penalties.'

[26] Telegraph Group submit that s 12 of the 1998 Act is of importance when
d   considering the contest between the remedies available for breach of copyright
and the right to freedom of expression. That section provides:

'(1) This section applies if a court is considering whether to grant any relief
which, if granted, might affect the exercise of the Convention right to
freedom of expression ...
e   (4) The court must have particular regard to the importance of the
Convention right to freedom of expression and, where the proceedings
relate to material which the respondent claims, or which appears to the
court, to be journalistic, literary or artistic material (or to conduct connected
with such material), to—(a) the extent to which—(i) the material has, or is
f   about to, become available to the public; or (ii) it is, or would be, in the public
interest for the material to be published; (b) any relevant privacy code.'

[27] Telegraph Group contend that Sir Andrew Morritt V-C was wrong to reject
the submission that 'must have particular regard to' indicates that the court should
place extra weight on the matters to which the subsection refers. The requirement
g   of s 2(1) of the 1998 Act to take account of the Strasbourg jurisprudence must
apply to the interpretation of the Act itself. It seems to us that s 12 does no more
than underline the need to have regard to contexts in which that jurisprudence
has given particular weight to freedom of expression, while at the same time
drawing attention to considerations which may none the less justify restricting
h   that right.
[28] The infringement of copyright constitutes interference with 'the peaceful
enjoyment of possessions'. It is, furthermore, the interference with a right arising
under a statute which confers rights recognised under international convention
and harmonised under European law (see the Berne Conventions of 1886 and
j   1971 and Council Directive (EEC) 93/98 of 29 October 1993, on harmonising the
term of protection of copyright and certain related rights (OJ 1993 L290 p 9)).
There is thus no question but that restriction of the right of freedom of expression
can be justified where necessary in a democratic society in order to protect
copyright. The protection afforded to copyright under the 1988 Act is, however,
itself subject to exceptions. Thus both the right of freedom of expression and

copyright are qualified. This appeal raises the question of how the two rights fall to be balanced, when they are in conflict.

The nature of copyright

[29] Copyright has its origins in the common law, but is now derived from the provisions of the 1988 Act. The following provisions of that Act are of particular relevance in the present case:

'**1.**—(1) Copyright is a property right which subsists in accordance with this Part in the following descriptions of work—(a) original literary, dramatic, musical or artistic works, (b) sound recordings, films, broadcasts or cable programmes, and (c) the typographical arrangement of published editions ...

2.—(1) The owner of the copyright in a work of any description has the exclusive right to do the acts specified in Chapter II as the acts restricted by the copyright in a work of that description ...

CHAPTER II ...

16.—(1) The owner of the copyright has, in accordance with the following provisions of this Chapter, the exclusive right to do the following acts in the United Kingdom—(a) to copy the work (see section 17); (b) to issue copies of the work to the public (see section 18) ...

(2) Copyright in a work is infringed by a person who without the licence of the copyright owner does, or authorises another to do, any of the acts restricted by the copyright.

(3) References in the Part to the doing of an act restricted by the copyright in a work are to the doing of it—(a) in relation to the work as a whole or any substantial part of it ...'

[30] Despite ss 2(1) and 16(2) copyright is essentially not a positive but a negative right. No provision of the 1988 Act confers in terms, upon the owner of copyright in a literary work, the right to publish it. The Act gives the owner of the copyright the right to prevent others from doing that which the Act recognises the owner alone has a right to do. Thus copyright is antithetical to freedom of expression. It prevents all, save the owner of the copyright, from expressing information in the form of the literary work protected by the copyright.

[31] It is important to emphasise in the present context that it is only the form of the literary work that is protected by copyright. Copyright does not normally prevent the publication of the information conveyed by the literary work. Thus it is only the freedom to express information using the verbal formula devised by another that is prevented by copyright. This will not normally constitute a significant encroachment on the freedom of expression. The prime importance of freedom of expression is that it enables the citizen freely to express ideas and convey information. It is also important that the citizen should be free to express the ideas and convey the information in a form of words of his or her choice. It is stretching the concept of freedom of expression to postulate that it extends to the freedom to convey ideas and information using the form of words devised by someone else. None the less there are circumstances, as we shall demonstrate in due course, where this freedom is important.

Restrictions on copyright

[**32**] Sir Andrew Morritt V-C drew attention to the fact that it is possible to identify 42 circumstances in which copying material does not infringe copyright (see [2001] 2 All ER 370 at [15], [2001] 2 WLR 967). He concluded that each of these reflected circumstances in which freedom of expression was recognised and confirmed. In effect they were circumstances where freedom of expression trumped copyright protection. Two of these call for particular consideration in the circumstances of this case. The first is the defence of fair dealing that is provided by s 30 of the 1988 Act. So far as material, that section provides:

'*Criticism, review and news reporting.*—(1) Fair dealing with a work for the purpose of criticism or review, of that or another work or of a performance of a work, does not infringe any copyright in the work …

(2) Fair dealing with a work (other than a photograph) for the purpose of reporting current events does not infringe any copyright in the work …'

[**33**] We agree that these provisions reflect freedom of expression in that, in the specific circumstances set out and provided that there is 'fair dealing', freedom of expression displaces the protection that would otherwise be afforded to copyright.

[**34**] The other restriction which requires consideration is the defence to a claim for breach of copyright that can be mounted on the basis of 'public interest'. This is not a statutory defence, but one which arises at common law, and which subsists by virtue of s 171(3) of the 1988 Act, which provides: 'Nothing in this Part affects any rule of law preventing or restricting the enforcement of copyright, on grounds of public interest or otherwise.'

[**35**] Telegraph Group argued that this provision enabled the court to give effect to the right of freedom of expression at the expense of copyright, save where it was necessary in a democratic society that freedom of expression should give way. Sir Andrew Morritt V-C rejected this submission, holding that the defence of public interest is narrowly constrained under English law. This conclusion is one to which we shall have to give detailed consideration.

Remedies for breach of copyright

[**36**] In this case Sir Andrew Morritt V-C granted Mr Ashdown an injunction restraining any further infringement of the copyright in his work. An injunction has been said to be 'a peculiarly suitable and, indeed, the normal remedy' for breach of copyright (see 9(2) *Halsbury's Laws* (4th edn reissue) para 404). It is, however, a discretionary remedy and subject to the principles governing the grant of an injunction, whether interlocutory or final, in other areas of our law.

[**37**] Compensatory relief is also available for breach of copyright. The claimant has the option of seeking damages, which will reflect the loss caused to him by the breach, or an account of the profits made by the defendant from the use of the claimant's work.

Has the 1998 Act impacted on the protection afforded to copyright?

[**38**] Sir Andrew Morritt V-C held that the 1998 Act had not affected the extent of the protection afforded to copyright. This was because he considered that the existing restrictions on that protection did all that was necessary to cater for the requirements of freedom of expression. The reasoning for this conclusion appears from the following passages of his judgment:

'[13] It does not follow that because art 10 is engaged the facts of each case have to be considered to determine whether the restriction imposed by the law of copyright goes further than what is necessary in a democratic society. Article 10(2) recognises that the exercise of the right to freedom of expression carries with it duties and responsibilities. Thus restrictions on the exercise of the right are permissible if they are (1) prescribed by law, (2) for the protection of rights of others and (3) are necessary in a democratic society. The Sunday Telegraph accepts that the provisions of the 1988 Act satisfy requirements (1) and (2). But inherent in the argument for the Sunday Telegraph is the submission that the provisions of the 1988 Act are incapable by themselves and without more of satisfying requirement (3). Indeed it was submitted in terms by counsel for the Sunday Telegraph that in every case the court should examine whether on the facts of that case it was necessary in a democratic society to provide for exceptions, exemptions and defences over and above those permitted by the legislation governing that species of intellectual property, however extensive they might be. If this is right then intellectual property litigation will burgeon out of control and the rights which the legislation apparently confers will be of no practical use except to those able and willing to litigate in all cases.

[14] I do not accept the submission. In my view the provisions of the Act alone can and do satisfy the third requirement of art 10(2) as well. The needs of a democratic society include the recognition and protection of private property. This is confirmed by the provisions of art 1 to the First Protocol. Such property includes copyright ... I can see no reason why the provisions of the 1988 Act should not be sufficient to give effect to the convention right subject only to such restrictions as are permitted by art 10(2) ...

[15] ... It is not suggested that the provisions of the 1988 Act are any more restrictive of the right of freedom of expression than those of the copyright legislation of all or most other democratic states. I can see no reason why the court should travel outside the provisions of the 1988 Act and recognise on the facts of particular cases further or other exceptions to the restrictions on the exercise of the right to freedom of expression constituted by the 1988 Act.'

[39] We have already observed that, in most circumstances, the principle of freedom of expression will be sufficiently protected if there is a right to publish information and ideas set out in another's literary work, without copying the very words which that person has employed to convey the information or express the ideas. In such circumstances it will normally be necessary in a democratic society that the author of the work should have his property in his own creation protected. Strasbourg jurisprudence demonstrates, however, that circumstances can arise in which freedom of expression will only be fully effective if an individual is permitted to reproduce the very words spoken by another.

[40] In this context, the Telegraph Group relied upon a passage in the judgment of the Strasbourg Court in *Jersild v Denmark* (1994) 19 EHHR 1 at 26 (para 31):

'At the same time, the methods of objective and balanced reporting may vary considerably, depending among other things on the media in question. It is not for this Court, nor for the national courts for that matter, to substitute their own views for those of the press as to what technique of reporting should be adopted by journalists. In this context the Court recalls that Article 10 protects not only the substance of the ideas and information expressed, but also the form in which they are conveyed.'

a [41] These words do not support a general proposition that freedom of the press includes the freedom to make use of the form of words created by another in order to convey ideas and information. *Jersild's* case was concerned with the right to use insulting language which was the creation of those using the language, not copied from another author.

[42] More pertinent is the decision of the Strasbourg Court in *Fressoz v France*
b (1999) 5 BHRC 654. Mr Fressoz was the publishing director of the French satirical weekly, *Le Canard enchaîné*. He published an article, written by Mr Roire, about the salary rise awarded to himself by the head of Peugeot at a time of industrial unrest. He illustrated the article by reproducing sections of the head of Peugeot's tax returns. Both men were successfully prosecuted in France for making unlawful use of these documents. Their case was referred to the Strasbourg
c Court, which held that art 10 had been infringed. The court observed (at 669 (para 54)):

> 'If, as the government accepted, the information about Mr Calvet's annual income was lawful and its disclosure permitted, the applicants' conviction merely for having published the documents in which that information was
d contained, namely the tax assessments, cannot be justified under art 10. In essence, that article leaves it for journalists to decide whether or not it is necessary to reproduce such documents to ensure credibility. It protects journalists' rights to divulge information on issues of general interest provided that they are acting in good faith and on an accurate factual basis
e and provide "reliable and precise" information in accordance with the ethics of journalism ...'

[43] *Fressoz's* case was not a copyright case, but it illustrates a general principle. Freedom of expression protects the right both to publish information and to receive it. There will be occasions when it is in the public interest not
f merely that information should be published, but that the public should be told the very words used by a person, notwithstanding that the author enjoys copyright in them. On occasions, indeed, it is the form and not the content of a document which is of interest.

[44] Where the subject matter of the information is a current event, s 30(2) of the 1988 Act may permit publication of the words used. But it is possible to
g conceive of information of the greatest public interest relating not to a current event, but to a document produced in the past. We are not aware of any provision of the 1988 Act which would permit publication in such circumstances, unless the mere fact of publication, and any controversy created by the disclosure, is sufficient to make them 'current events'. This will often be a
h 'bootstraps' argument of little merit, but on other occasions (such as disclosure by the Public Record Office under the 30-year rule) it may have a more solid basis.

[45] For these reasons, we have reached the conclusion that rare circumstances can arise where the right of freedom of expression will come into conflict with the protection afforded by the 1988 Act, notwithstanding the express exceptions
j to be found in the Act. In these circumstances, we consider that the court is bound, in so far as it is able, to apply the Act in a manner that accommodates the right of freedom of expression. This will make it necessary for the court to look closely at the facts of individual cases (as indeed it must whenever a 'fair dealing' defence is raised). We do not foresee this leading to a flood of litigation.

[46] The first way in which it may be possible to do this is by declining the discretionary relief of an injunction. Usually, so it seems to us, such a step will be

likely to be sufficient. If a newspaper considers it necessary to copy the exact words created by another, we can see no reason in principle why the newspaper should not indemnify the author for any loss caused to him, or alternatively account to him for any profit made as a result of copying his work. Freedom of expression should not normally carry with it the right to make free use of another's work.

Public interest

[47] In the rare case where it is in the public interest that the words in respect of which another has copyright should be published without any sanction, we have been concerned to consider why this should not be permitted under the 'public interest' exception, the possibility of which is recognised by s 171(3). Sir Andrew Morritt V-C considered that he was precluded from so holding by the decision of this court in *Hyde Park Residence Ltd v Yelland* [2001] Ch 143, [2000] 3 WLR 215. That case concerned an unusual breach of copyright—the publication by The Sun of photographs of Princess Diana and Mr Dodi Fayed, with times recorded, taken by a security video camera owned by Mr Al Fayed. The Sun claimed that it was in the public interest to publish these photographs as they gave the lie to claims being made by Mr Al Fayed that the two had enjoyed a lengthy tryst at his house in Paris.

[48] In the leading judgment, Aldous LJ started his consideration of public interest with the following observation:

'43 … The 1988 Act does not give a court general power to enable an infringer to use another's property, namely his copyright in the public interest. Thus a defence of public interest outside those set out in Chapter III of Part I of the 1988 Act, if such exists, must arise by some other route.

44 The courts have an inherent jurisdiction to refuse to allow their process to be used in certain circumstances. It has long been the law that the courts will not give effect to contracts which are, for example, illegal, immoral or prejudicial to family life because they offend against the policy of the law. In my view that inherent jurisdiction can be exercised in the case of an action in which copyright is sought to be enforced, as is made clear by section 171(3) of the 1988 Act: "Nothing in this Part affects any rule of law preventing or restricting the enforcement of copyright, on grounds of public interest or otherwise."' (See [2001] Ch 143 at 160, [2000] 3 WLR 215 at 228–229.)

[49] Aldous LJ went on to consider at length the authorities bearing on the point. His conclusion was as follows:

'64 I have pointed out earlier in this judgment that the basis of the defence of public interest in a breach of confidence action cannot be the same as the basis of such defence to an action for infringement of copyright. In an action for breach of confidence the foundation of the action can fall away if that is required in the public interest, but that can never happen in a copyright action. The jurisdiction to refuse to enforce copyright, which I believe has been recognised, comes from the court's inherent jurisdiction. It is limited to cases where enforcement of the copyright would offend against the policy of the law. The *Lion Laboratories* case (*Lion Laboratories Ltd v Evans* [1984] 2 All ER 417, [1985] QB 526) was such a case. Lion Laboratories sought to obtain an interlocutory injunction to restrain publication of documents which showed that they had suppressed information leading to or which might lead to the a wrongful conviction of motorists. The action was based upon documents which in the circumstances reeked of turpitude. As Lord Mansfield CJ said in *Holman v Johnson* ((1775) 1 Cowp 341 at 343, [1775–1802] All ER Rep 98 at 99): "No court will lend its aid to a man who founds his cause of action upon an immoral or an illegal act."

b 65 To rely upon copyright to suppress documents which could exonerate motorists convicted of drink driving or which might lead to their acquittal is, in my view, to found a cause of action upon an immoral act.

66 The circumstances where it is against the policy of the law to use the court's procedure to enforce copyright are, I suspect, not capable of definition. However it must be remembered that copyright is assignable and therefore the circumstances must derive from the work in question, not ownership of
c the copyright. In my view a court would be entitled to refuse to enforce copyright if the work is: (i) immoral, scandalous or contrary to family life; (ii) injurious to public life, public health and safety or the administration of justice; (iii) incites or encourages others to act in a way referred to in (ii).' (See [2001] Ch 143 at 167–168, [2000] 3 WLR 215 at 236.)

d
[50] Sir Andrew Morritt V-C rightly held that the narrow test of public interest identified by Aldous LJ could not extend to admit a defence to a claim for breach of copyright based only on the right of freedom of expression.

[51] In *Yelland*'s case Mance LJ, while concurring in the result, did not agree with Aldous LJ's analysis of the *Lion Laboratories* case. He held ([2001] Ch 143 at
e 172, [2000] 3 WLR 215 at 240–241):

'82 In considering the circumstances in which copyright may be overridden in the public interest, Aldous LJ treats the *Lion Laboratories* case as an action based on documents which in the circumstances reeked of turpitude, and as one where the plaintiffs were, in substance, seeking to found upon an
f immoral act. That, however, does seem to me to be too restrictive a view of the *Lion Laboratories* case on any view. That case was decided on the basis that it is not necessary to find any immoral act or "iniquity" on the part of a claimant in order to reach a conclusion that either breach of confidence or copyright is overridden. No distinction was drawn between the two in this
g connection, and Lord Denning MR's dictum in *Fraser v Evans* ([1969] 1 All ER 8 at 11, [1969] 1 QB 349 at 362) that "[iniquity] is merely an instance of just cause or excuse for breaking confidence" was applied to both: see per Stephenson LJ ([1984] 2 All ER 417 at 421, 422, 423–424, [1985] QB 526 at 535, 536, 538), and per Griffiths LJ ([1984] 2 All ER 417 at 432–433, [1985] QB 526 at 550). But that, as I have said, does not mean that the public interest in
h maintaining or overriding confidence and copyright are necessarily to be equated.

83 Whilst account must be taken of the different nature of the right involved in copyright, I prefer to state no more in this case than that the circumstances in which the public interest may override copyright are probably not capable of
j precise categorisation or definition.'

[52] Stuart-Smith LJ agreed that the appeal should be allowed for the reasons given by Aldous LJ. It does not seem to us that those reasons depended on the precise scope of the public interest exception identified by Aldous LJ. The court rejected a 'fair dealing' defence under s 30 in terms that left no scope for holding that it was in the public interest that the photographs should have been

published, however wide the scope of that test. Accordingly we have considered the *Lion Laboratories* case in order to form our own view as to the court's reasons for holding that the defendants had a public interest defence.

[53] The facts of the case can be shortly summarised. Lion Laboratories manufactured breathalyser kits widely used by the police for testing the breath of drivers suspected of being over the limit. The first and second defendants worked for Lion Laboratories. They removed without authority confidential memoranda which cast doubt on the accuracy of the breathalysers, and supplied these to a newspaper. Lion Laboratories brought proceedings for both breach of confidentiality and breach of copyright. They sought interlocutory injunctions. The Court of Appeal held that there was a serious issue to be tried as to whether the defendants had a public interest defence to each of the claims and permitted publication of specified documents.

[54] Early in the leading judgment Stephenson LJ observed:

'There is no dispute, first of all, that the documents which are the subject of this appeal are confidential, that they were taken by the first and second defendants without authority and handed over to the fourth defendants (whether for reward we do not know) and that publication would be a breach of confidence by all four defendants subject to a defence that it is in the public interest that they should be published now. Equally there is no dispute that the copyright of these documents is in the plaintiffs and to publish them would infringe the plaintiffs' copyright, subject to the same public interest being a just cause or excuse for their publication.' (See [1984] 2 All ER 417 at 421, [1985] QB 526 at 535.)

He went on to remark ([1984] 2 All ER 417 at 422, [1985] QB 526 at 536) that the trial judge had been right to make no difference between confidence and copyright for the purposes of the case.

[55] Stephenson LJ ([1984] 2 All ER 417 at 422, [1985] QB 526 at 536) made express reference to art 10 of the convention when commenting on the public interest in being informed of matters which are of real public concern. Later ([1984] 2 All ER 417 at 423, [1985] QB 526 at 537–538), he rejected the submission that the only public interest which could justify publication would be the disclosure of iniquity on the part of the plaintiffs, adopting a dictum of Lord Denning MR that iniquity 'is merely an instance of just cause or excuse for breaking confidence' (see *Fraser v Evans* [1969] 1 All ER 8 at 11, [1969] 1 QB 349 at 362).

[56] Having carefully considered Stephenson LJ's judgment, we think it clear that on the facts of the case he considered that there was a potential public interest defence to both breach of confidence and breach of copyright, and that this defence was not 'based on documents that reeked of moral turpitude'.

[57] O'Connor LJ approached the case on the basis that the gravamen of the plaintiffs' complaint was of breach of confidence and did not give separate consideration to breach of copyright. Griffiths LJ, however, made the following observations at the beginning of his judgment:

'The first question to be determined is whether there exists a defence of public interest to actions for breach of confidentiality and copyright, and, if so, whether it is limited to situations in which there has been serious wrongdoing by the plaintiffs, the so-called "iniquity" rule. I am quite satisfied that the defence of public interest is now well established in actions for breach of confidence and, although there is less authority on the point, a that it also extends to breach of copyright: see by way of example *Fraser v Evans* [1969] 1 All ER 8, [1969] 1 QB 349, *Hubbard v Vosper* [1972] 1 All ER 1023, [1972] 2 QB 84, *Woodward v Hutchins* [1977] 2 All ER 751, [1977] 1 WLR 760 and *British Steel Corp v Granada Television Ltd* [1981] 1 All ER 417, [1981] AC 1096. I can see no sensible reason why this defence should be limited to cases in which there has been wrongdoing on the part of the plaintiffs.

b I believe that the so-called iniquity rule evolved because in most cases where the facts justified a publication in breach of confidence the plaintiff had behaved so disgracefully or criminally that it was judged in the public interest that his behaviour should be exposed. No doubt it is in such circumstances that the defence will usually arise, but it is not difficult to think of instances where, although there has been no wrongdoing on the part of the plaintiff, it

c may be vital in the public interest to publish a part of his confidential information.' (See [1984] 2 All ER 417 at 432–433, [1985] QB 526 at 550.)

[**58**] In the light of these judgments, we do not consider that Aldous LJ was justified in circumscribing the public interest defence to breach of copyright as tightly as he did. We prefer the conclusion of Mance LJ that the circumstances in

d which public interest may override copyright are not capable of precise categorisation or definition. Now that the 1998 Act is in force, there is the clearest public interest in giving effect to the right of freedom of expression in those rare cases where this right trumps the rights conferred by the 1988 Act. In such circumstances, we consider that s 171(3) of the Act permits the defence of public

e interest to be raised.

[**59**] We do not consider that this conclusion will lead to a flood of cases where freedom of expression is invoked as a defence to a claim for breach of copyright. It will be very rare for the public interest to justify the copying of the form of a work to which copyright attaches. We would add that the implications of the 1998 Act must always be considered where the discretionary relief of an

f injunction is sought, and this is true in the field of copyright quite apart from the ambit of the public interest defence under s 171(3).

[**60**] We turn to consider whether a defence lies to the claim in this case under s 30 or s 171(3).

g *Section 30(1)*

[**61**] Telegraph Group submitted before us, as they had before the judge, that they had a reasonable prospect of establishing a defence under s 30(1) of the 1988 Act. Sir Andrew Morritt V-C dealt with that argument in a single paragraph of his judgment as follows:

h 'I accept, of course, that the expression "criticism and review" is of wide import (cf *Pro Sieben Media AG v Carlton UK Television Ltd* [1999] 1 WLR 605 at 614 per Robert Walker LJ). Likewise I accept that it is necessary to have regard to the true purpose of the work. Is it "a genuine piece of criticism and review or is it something else, such as an attempt to dress up the

j infringement of another's copyright in the guise of criticism, and so profit unfairly from another's work" (cf *Time Warner Entertainments Co LP v Channel Four Television Corp plc* [1994] EMLR 1 at 14 per Henry LJ). But what is required is that the copying shall take place as part of and for the purpose of criticising and reviewing the work. The work is the minute. But the articles are not criticising or reviewing the minute; they are criticising or reviewing the actions of the Prime Minister and [Mr Ashdown] in October 1997. It was

not necessary for that purpose to copy the minute at all. In my judgment the
articles do not come within s 30(1) because the purpose of copying the work *a*
was not its criticism or review.' (See [2001] 2 All ER 370 at [24], [2001] 2 WLR
967.)

We endorse this reasoning and conclusion and have nothing to add to it. Section 30(1)
can have no application to the facts of this case.   *b*

Section 30(2): current events

[62] On one of the ingredients required to establish a defence under s 30(2) of
the 1988 Act the judge found in favour of the Telegraph Group. He held that
there was a reasonable prospect of the Sunday Telegraph establishing that the *c*
copying of the minute was for the purpose of reporting current events, those
events including such matters as 'the continuing issue over the degree and nature
of actual and planned co-operation between Labour and the Liberal Democrats'
and the 'continuing saga over the role of and accuracy of information disseminated
by the Prime Minister's press office'.

[63] By a respondent's notice Mr Ashdown seeks to uphold the order below *d*
on the additional ground that the matters referred to were not in fact 'current
events' within the meaning of s 30(2). It is submitted by Mr Spearman QC, that
they were either not events at all or if they were (or arguably were) then they
were not current at the date of the publication on 28 November 1999. It is said
that an issue is not and cannot be an event and that even if the meeting itself on *e*
21 October 1997 was an event, it was no longer current by the time of publication
over two years later. On that latter aspect, Mr Ashdown seeks to distinguish the
decision in *Yelland*'s case [2001] Ch 143, [2000] 3 WLR 215 where this court held
that it was arguable that the events of 30 August 1997, leading up to the death of
the Princess of Wales and Dodi Fayed the following day, were still current a year *f*
later, though it rejected the s 30(2) defence on other grounds. Mr Spearman
emphasised that in that case, which concerned an exceptional event, the investigation
into the deaths was still continuing at the time of the publication in 1998.

[64] We find these arguments unpersuasive. As this court said in *Pro Sieben
Media AG v Carlton UK Television Ltd* [1999] 1 WLR 605 at 614, the expression *g*
'reporting current events' should be interpreted liberally. The defence provided
by s 30(2) is clearly intended to protect the role of the media in informing the
public about matters of current concern to the public. That was the approach
adopted in *Fraser v Evans* [1969] 1 All ER 8, [1969] 1 QB 349 to the predecessor of
s 30(2), and in our judgment it remains applicable to the present subsection. The *h*
meeting between the claimant, the Prime Minister and others in October 1997
was undoubtedly an event, and while it might be said that by November 1999 it
was not current solely in the sense of recent in time, it was arguably a matter of
current interest to the public. In a democratic society, information about a
meeting between the Prime Minister and an opposition party leader during the *j*
then current Parliament to discuss possible close co-operation between those
parties is very likely to be of legitimate and continuing public interest. It might
impinge upon the way in which the public would vote at the next general
election. The 'issues' identified by the Sunday Telegraph may not themselves be
'events', but the existence of those issues may help to demonstrate the continuing
public interest in a meeting two years earlier.

a [65] For present purposes all that we have to decide is whether the judge was right in holding that it was arguable that publication was for 'the purpose of reporting current events'. We are in no doubt that he was.

Fair dealing

b [66] Where part of a work is copied in the course of a report on current events, the 'fair dealing' defence under s 30 will normally afford the court all the scope that it needs properly to reflect the public interest in freedom of expression and, in particular, the freedom of the press. There will then be no need to give separate consideration to the availability of a public interest defence under s 171.

c [67] We have considered why it should ever be contrary to the public interest that a newspaper should have to pay compensation, or account for the profit made, when it makes unauthorised use of the work product of another. We have concluded that s 30 provides examples of situations where this may be justified, and that these are broadly in line with the Strasbourg jurisprudence in another area where freedom of expression has to be balanced against a justification for restricting that freedom which is recognised by art 10.

d [68] In the field of defamation, the European Court of Human Rights has recognised that the awarding of damages by a public authority for press publication of defamatory statements may infringe art 10, at least where the publication consists of balanced reporting on a matter of current public interest. The reason is that such liability may discourage the participation by the press in matters of public concern—see *Bladet Tromsø v Norway* (1999) 29 EHRR 125. In *e* *Tolstoy Miloslavsky v UK* (1995) 20 EHRR 442, where individual but not press freedom of expression was in issue, the court held that art 10 was infringed, not because damages were awarded, but because the size of the damages was disproportionate to the legitimate aim of providing reasonable compensation for injury to reputation.

f [69] The fair dealing defence under s 30 should lie where the public interest in learning of the very words written by the owner of the copyright is such that publication should not be inhibited by the chilling factor of having to pay damages or account for profits. When considering this question it is right to observe that, as damages are compensatory and not at large, they may produce a relatively mild chill.

g [70] Authority is very sparse in relation to the defence of fair dealing in the context of reporting current events (see the comment of Scott J in *BBC v British Satellite Broadcasting Ltd* [1991] 3 All ER 833 at 836, [1992] Ch 141 at 148). Sir Andrew Morritt V-C commented with approval, however, on the summary of the authors of *The Modern Law of Copyright and Designs*, vol 1, p 754 (para 20.16), *h* on the test of fair dealing in the general context of s 30. We also have found this an accurate and helpful summary and set it out for the purpose of discussion:

j 'It is impossible to lay down any hard-and-fast definition of what is fair dealing, for it is a matter of fact, degree and impression. However, by far the most important factor is whether the alleged fair dealing is in fact commercially competing with the proprietor's exploitation of the copyright work, a substitute for the probable purchase of authorised copies, and the like. If it is, the fair dealing defence will almost certainly fail. If it is not and there is a moderate taking and there are no special adverse factors, the defence is likely to succeed, especially if the defendant's additional purpose is to right a wrong, to ventilate an honest grievance, to engage in political

controversy, and so on. The second most important factor is whether the
work has already been published or otherwise exposed to the public. If it has
not, and especially if the material has been obtained by a breach of
confidence or other mean or underhand dealing, the courts will be reluctant
to say this is fair. However this is by no means conclusive, for sometimes it
is necessary for the purposes of legitimate public controversy to make use of
"leaked" information. The third most important factor is the amount and
importance of the work that has been taken. For, although it is permissible
to take a substantial part of the work (if not, there could be no question of
infringement in the first place), in some circumstances the taking of an
excessive amount, or the taking of even a small amount if on a regular basis,
would negative fair dealing.'

[71] These principles are based on a summary of the authorities before the
1998 Act came into force. They are still important when balancing the public
interest in freedom of expression against the interests of owners of copyright. It
is, however, now essential not to apply inflexibly tests based on precedent, but to
bear in mind that considerations of public interest are paramount. With that
consideration in mind, we turn to consider each of the important factors identified
in *The Modern Law of Copyright and Designs* in turn.

Commercial competition

[72] In a passage of its defence quoted by Sir Andrew Morritt V-C in his judgment
([2001] 2 All ER 370 at [25], [2001] 2 WLR 967), Telegraph Group contended that
its publication 'in no or no appreciable way competed with any publication or
publications which the claimant might issue in the future'. Sir Andrew Morritt V-C
rejected this assertion, and we consider that he was right to do so. There was
evidence, as he pointed out, that the publication in the Sunday Telegraph
destroyed a part of the value of the memoirs which it had been Mr Ashdown's
intention to sell, and which he did, in fact, sell. Equally we are in no doubt that
the extensive quotations of Mr Ashdown's own words added a flavour to the
description of the events covered which made the article more attractive to read
and will have been of significant commercial value in enabling the Sunday
Telegraph to maintain, if not to enhance, the loyalty of its readership.

Prior publication

[73] In the same passage of their defence the Telegraph Group asserted that
Mr Ashdown had already revealed some details of the matters covered in the
articles in his radio interview about 'Resigning Issues'. Sir Andrew Morritt V-C
roundly rejected this contention in his judgment:

'[Mr Ashdown] had taken great care to limit the number of people who
read it and to impose on them obligations of secrecy. Moreover the Sunday
Telegraph knew not only that the minute had not been published, indeed
Mr Murphy described it as secret, but that, as [Mr Ashdown] revealed on the
'Resigning Issues' interview, he was thinking of doing so in the not so distant
future. It is not the case that during the interview for "Resigning Issues"
[Mr Ashdown] had already disclosed the important matters covered in the
articles.' (See [2001] 2 All ER 370 at [28], [2001] 2 WLR 967.)

[74] While we endorse these conclusions, it does not seem to us that they are
wholly in point. Mr Spearman, for Mr Ashdown, argued that much of the

a   information in the minute had already been made public and that this fact made
      it even harder to justify the Sunday Telegraph publication. We consider that
      there is force in this point and will return to it in due course. What is at issue in
      a claim for breach of copyright is publication of the form of the literary work, not
      the information that it contains. It is beyond any doubt that the copyright work
      had never been published or otherwise exposed to the public before the
b   publication in the Sunday Telegraph.

          [75] At the same time, the fact that the minute was undoubtedly obtained in
      breach of confidence is a material consideration when considering the defence of
      fair dealing. Sir Andrew Morritt V-C rightly attached importance to the fact that
      the minute was secret and had been obtained by Telegraph Group without
      Mr Ashdown's knowledge or approval.

c

      The amount and importance of the work taken

          [76] Here again we consider that Sir Andrew Morritt V-C correctly found that
      this aspect of the test of fair dealing weighed against the defence of fair dealing.
      A substantial portion of the minute was copied and it is reasonable to conclude,
d   for the reasons given by Sir Andrew Morritt V-C ([2001] 2 All ER 370 at [29],
      [2001] 2 WLR 967), that the most important passages in the minute were selected
      for publication.

          [77] All these considerations point in one direction and satisfy us that
      Sir Andrew Morritt V-C was correct to conclude that if the established authorities
      fell to be applied without any additional regard to the effect of art 10 there was no
e   realistic prospect that a defence of fair dealing would be made out.

      Human rights impact

          [78] At this point, however, we believe that it is necessary to consider the
      impact of the public interest on the test of fair dealing. Are the facts of this case
f   such that, arguably, the importance of freedom of expression outweighs the
      conventional considerations set out above so as to afford the Telegraph Group a
      defence of fair dealing?

          [79] Is it arguable that it was necessary to quote verbatim the passages of
      which Mr Ashdown was the author in order to convey to the readers of the
g   Sunday Telegraph the authenticity of its reports of current events of public
      interest? Mr Nicol QC argued that it was. He contended that the subject matter
      of the article was of high public interest, concerning the potential composition of
      the government of the country. It related to an important meeting between the
      Prime Minister and other leading political figures, including Mr Ashdown. True
      it was that the basic facts in the articles may have been published already in the
h   Financial Times, the Observer and the radio interview on 'Resigning Issues'. But
      Mr Ashdown's own words gave the factual material a detail and authority which
      was novel.

          [80] There had been previous publications that gave the public much of the
      information that was contained in the Sunday Telegraph articles. An article in the
j   Financial Times dated 11 June 1999 reported that Mr Ashdown and Mr Blair had
      been 'hatching a secret project the creation of a Lab-Lib coalition'. On 26 September
      1999 the political editor of The Observer told its readers:

          'Tony Blair and Paddy Ashdown privately agreed to try to persuade Labour
          and the Liberal Democrats to go into the next election on a joint policy
          manifesto, before the LibDem leader stood down. Details of the scheme are

due to be revealed in Ashdown's diaries. Downing Street is seeking
assurances that the diaries will not be published until after the next election.   *a*
The diaries, a highly detailed account of Ashdown's top secret contacts with
Labour, are described as explosive by one senior Liberal Democrat who has
seen extracts. The source said: "They were practising a massive deception on
their respective parties".'

There were a number of other newspaper articles to similar effect.   *b*

[81] The accuracy of these accounts was challenged by Mr Blair. In these
circumstances we consider that, just as there is scope for argument that the
Sunday Telegraph's publication was the reporting of current events, so it is
arguable that the Telegraph Group were justified in making limited quotation of
Mr Ashdown's own words, in order to demonstrate that they had indeed   *c*
obtained his own minute, so that they were in a position to give an authentic
account of the meeting. In this context the last of the criteria that we have just
considered is of critical relevance. Can it be argued that the extensive reproduction
of Mr Ashdown's own words was necessary in order to satisfy the reader that the
account given of his meeting with Mr Blair was authoritative? We do not believe
that it can. The statement by the Sunday Telegraph that they had obtained a copy   *d*
of the minute coupled with one or two short extracts from it would have sufficed.

[82] There may in law have been justification for the publication of the
confidential information that was contained in the minute. That is not an issue
which is before this court. We do not, however, consider that it is arguable that
there was any justification for the extent of the reproduction of Mr Ashdown's   *e*
own words. It appears to us that the minute was deliberately filleted in order to
extract colourful passages that were most likely to add flavour to the article and
thus to appeal to the readership of the newspaper. Mr Ashdown's work product
was deployed in the way that it was for reasons that were essentially journalistic
in furtherance of the commercial interests of the Telegraph Group. We do not
consider it arguable that art 10 requires that the Group should be able to profit   *f*
from this use of Mr Ashdown's copyright without paying compensation.

[83] This appeal has been founded on the contention that Sir Andrew Morritt V-C
erred in law in holding that the Telegraph Group had infringed the 1988 Act. No
separate attack was made upon the exercise of his discretion in granting injunctive
relief. It follows that we do not need to consider whether that relief was   *g*
appropriate having regard to s 12 of the 1998 Act and art 10 of the convention.

[84] For the reasons that we have given, this appeal should be dismissed.

Appeal dismissed. Permission to appeal refused.

Kate O'Hanlon   Barrister.

a

Han and another v Commissioners of Customs and Excise

Martins and another v Commissioners of Customs and Excise

b

Morris v Commissioners of Customs and Excise

[2001] EWCA Civ 1040

c

COURT OF APPEAL, CIVIL DIVISION

POTTER, MANCE LJJ AND SIR MARTIN NOURSE

3, 4 MAY, 3 JULY 2001

d

Value added tax – Penalty – Dishonest evasion of value added tax – Whether imposition of penalty for dishonest evasion of value added tax or duty giving rise to criminal charge for purposes of fair trial provisions of human rights convention – Value Added Tax Act 1994, s 60(1) – Finance Act 1994, s 8(1) – Human Rights Act 1998, Sch 1, Pt I, art 6.

e

In three cases raising a common issue, the Commissioners of Customs and Excise imposed penalties on taxpayers for dishonest evasion of value added tax (VAT) under s 60(1)[a] of the Value Added Tax Act 1994 or dishonest evasion of duty under s 8(1)[b] of the Finance Act 1994. The legislation described such penalties, which had first been introduced in the mid-1980s and could amount to 100% of the tax evaded, as civil penalties. There were also parallel provisions for criminal proceedings against, inter alia, persons knowingly concerned in the fraudulent evasion of VAT or duty. On their appeals to the VAT and Duties Tribunal, the taxpayers contended that the imposition of those ostensibly civil penalties gave rise to criminal charges within the meaning of art 6(1)[c] of the European Convention for the Protection of Human Rights and Fundamental Freedoms 1950 (as set out in Sch 1 to the Human Rights Act 1998), and that accordingly they were entitled to the 'minimum rights' provided for by art 6(3). That contention was accepted by the tribunal on the determination of a preliminary issue. The commissioners appealed, contending, inter alia, that the classification of the penalty for dishonesty as a civil penalty should be given great weight, that civil penalties had been established as a deliberate decriminalisation of the VAT and duty penalty scheme, and that the absence of any threat of imprisonment was a powerful indicator that the penalties did not give rise to a criminal charge.

f

g

h

j

a   Section 60, so far as material, is set out at [12], below

b   Section 8, so far as material, provides: '(1) Subject to the following provisions of this section, in any case where—(a) any person engages in any conduct for the purpose of evading any duty of excise, and (b) his conduct involves dishonesty (whether or not such as to give rise to criminal liability), that person shall be liable to a penalty of an amount equal to the amount of duty evaded or, as the case may be, sought to be evaded … '

c   Article 6, so far as material, is set out at [20], [22], [23], below

Held – (Sir Martin Nourse dissenting) The imposition of civil penalties pursuant to s 60(1) of the Value Added Tax Act 1994 and s 8(1) of the Finance Act 1994 gave *a* rise to criminal charges within the meaning of art 6(1) of the convention, and accordingly a person made subject to such a penalty was entitled to the minimum rights specifically provided for in art 6(3). The European Court of Human Rights applied three criteria to determine whether a criminal charge had been imposed within the meaning of art 6, namely the classification of the proceedings in *b* domestic law; the nature of the offence; and the nature and degree of severity of the penalty which the person concerned risked incurring. So far as the first criterion was concerned, it was plain that the classification of the penalties provided for as 'civil', albeit coupled with a procedure appropriate to civil rather than criminal proceedings, could not be regarded as more than the starting point *c* where the levying and enforcement of the penalty concerned was designed to punish and deter members of the public at large in respect of dishonest conduct. Furthermore, the classification did not represent a decision on the part of the legislature to decriminalise dishonest evasion of VAT, given the parallel provisions for criminal proceedings. Rather, it created alternative regimes in respect of which Customs and Excise might none the less decide, in the course of *d* an investigation, to move from one to the other. With regard to the second criterion, the nature of the offence suspected and sanctioned by the application of civil penalties was fraud or dishonesty in respect of the tax payable, and the Customs and Excise enjoyed a discretion as to whether, on a particular set of facts, to apply a civil penalty or to prosecute. The level of criminality in cases *e* where civil penalties were applied might not differ significantly from those where criminal proceedings were taken. The contrasts between the two types of cases were procedural rather than going to the nature of the offence itself, and the European Court of Human Rights had not adopted an approach which allowed procedural features or considerations to govern or define the nature of the offence *f* under consideration. In relation to the third criterion, the weight of the European Court of Human Rights authorities, at least in the area of tax evasion, did not require that, for the purposes of any 'criminal' charge, it was necessary to demonstrate that the penalty to which the taxpayer was subject involved, or might involve, imprisonment. It was sufficient that it was substantial and that its purpose was punitive and deterrent. Those requirements had been made out in *g* the instant case. Accordingly, the appeal would be dismissed (see [26], [74]–[78], [84]–[87], [90], below.)

Öztürk v Germany (1984) 6 EHRR 409 and *Georgiou (trading as Marios Chippery) v UK* [2001] STC 80 applied.

h

Notes

For criminal charges in the context of the convention right to a fair trial, see 8(2) *Halsbury's Laws* (4th edn reissue) para 136, and for civil penalties for the dishonest evasion of duty and value added tax, see respectively 12(2) *Halsbury's Laws* (4th edn reissue) para 1216 and 49(1) *Halsbury's Laws* (4th edn reissue) para 272.   *j*

For the Finance Act 1994, s 8, see 13 *Halsbury's Statutes* (4th edn) (2000 reissue) 424.

For the Value Added Tax Act 1994, s 60, see 50 *Halsbury's Statutes* (4th edn) (2000 reissue) 123.

For the Human Rights Act 1998, Sch 1, Pt I, art 6, see 7 *Halsbury's Statutes* (4th edn) (1999 reissue) 523.

Cases referred to in judgments

1st Indian Cavalry Club Ltd v Customs and Excise Comrs [1998] STC 293, Ct of Sess.

Adolf v Austria (1982) 4 EHRR 313, [1982] ECHR 8269/78, ECt HR.

AP v Switzerland (1997) 26 EHRR 541, [1997] ECHR 19958/92, ECt HR.

Bendenoun v France (1994) 18 EHRR 54, [1994] ECHR 12547/86, ECt HR.

Brown v UK (1998) 28 EHRR CD 233, E Com HR.

Campbell and Fell v UK (1984) 7 EHRR 165, [1984] ECHR 7819/77, ECt HR.

Engel v Netherlands (No 1) (1976) 1 EHRR 647, [1976] ECHR 5100/71, ECt HR.

Garage Molenheide BVBA v Belgium Joined cases C-286/94, C-340/95, C-401/95 and C-47/96 [1998] All ER (EC) 61, [1997] ECR I-7281, ECJ.

Georgiou (trading as Marios Chippery) v UK [2001] STC 80, ECt HR.

Internationale Handelsgesellschaft mbH v Einfuhr-und Vorratsstelle für Getreide und Futtermittel Case 11/70 [1970] ECR 1125.

Johnston v Chief Constable of the Royal Ulster Constabulary Case 222/84 [1986] 3 All ER 135, [1987] QB 129, [1986] WLR 1038, [1986] ECR 1651, ECJ.

King v Walden (Inspector of Taxes) [2001] STC 822.

Lauko v Slovakia [1998] ECHR 26138/95, ECt HR.

Marks & Spencer plc v Customs & Excise Comrs [2000] STC 16, CA.

Öztürk v Germany (1984) 6 EHRR 409, [1984] ECHR 8544/79, ECt HR.

R (Greenfield) v Secretary of State for the Home Dept [2001] EWHC Admin 113, [2001] 1 WLR 1731, DC.

Cases also cited or referred to in skeleton arguments

Black-Clawson International Ltd v Papierwerke Waldhof-Aschaffenburg AG [1975] 1 All ER 810, [1975] AC 591, HL.

Customs and Excise Comrs v Peninsular and Oriental Steam Navigation Co [1992] STC 809; *rvsd* [1994] STC 259, CA.

EL v Switzerland (1997) 3 BHRC 348, ECt HR.

JJ v Netherlands (1998) 28 EHRR 168, [1999] ECHR 21351/93, ECt HR.

Kadubec v Slovakia [1998] ECHR 27061/95, ECt HR.

Matthews v UK (1999) 8 BHRC 686, ECt HR.

National & Provincial Building Society v UK (1997) 25 EHRR 127, [1997] ECHR 21319/93, ECt HR.

R v Customs and Excise Comrs, ex p Lunn Poly Ltd [1998] STC 649; *affd* [1999] STC 350, CA.

R v Ministry of Agriculture, Fisheries and Food, ex p First City Trading Ltd [1997] 1 CMLR 250.

R v Ministry of Agriculture, Fisheries and Food, ex p British Pig Industry Support Group [2000] EuLR 724.

R v W [1998] STC 550, CA.

Ravnsborg v Sweden (1994) 18 EHRR 38, [1994] ECHR 14220/88, ECt HR.

R (on the application of the Broadcasting, Entertainment, Cinematographic and Theatre Union) v Secretary of State for Trade and Industry Case C-173/99 [2001] All ER (EC) 647, ECJ.

Salabiaku v France (1988) 13 EHRR 379, [1988] ECHR 10589/83, ECt HR.

Schmautzer v Austria (1995) 21 EHRR 511, [1995] ECHR 15523/89, ECt HR.

T v Austria [2000] ECHR 27783/95, ECt HR.

Wachauf v Germany Case 5/88 [1989] ECR 2609, ECJ.

Appeal

The Commissioners of Customs and Excise appealed with permission of Aldous LJ   *a*
granted on 9 March 2001 from the decision of the Chairman of the Value Added Tax
and Duties Tribunal (Stephen Oliver QC) on 19 December 2000 ([2000] V & DR 312)
whereby, on the determination of a preliminary issue in appeals brought by the
respondent taxpayers against the imposition of civil penalties for dishonest
evasion of tax or duty, he held that the imposition of such penalties gave rise to   *b*
criminal charges within the meaning of art 6 of the European Convention for the
Protection of Human Rights and Fundamental Freedoms 1950, and that
accordingly the respondents were entitled to the 'minimum rights' provided by
art 6(3) of the convention. The facts are set out in the judgment of Potter LJ.

Kenneth Parker QC and *Timothy Ward* (instructed by the *Solicitor for the Customs and*   *c*
Excise) for the commissioners.
Eleanor Sharpston QC and *Andrew Young* (instructed by *Penningtons*) for the
respondents.

Cur adv vult

d

3 July 2001. The following judgments were delivered.

POTTER LJ.

INTRODUCTION   *e*
[1] This is an appeal by the Commissioners of Customs and Excise against a
decision of the chairman of the VAT and Duties Tribunal (Stephen Oliver QC)
(the chairman) made upon a preliminary issue, released on 19 December 2000
and certified by the tribunal pursuant to CPR PD 52, para 21.6 on 20 December
2000. The decision is reported at [2000] V & DR 312. Leave to appeal directly to
this court was granted by Aldous LJ on 9 March 2001.   *f*
[2] The decision relates to a preliminary issue raised in three appeals before
the tribunal, each of which raised a fundamental issue of law concerning the
applicability of the European Convention for the Protection of Human Rights
and Fundamental Freedoms (Rome, 4 November 1950; TS 71 (1953); Cmd 8969)
(as set out in Sch 1 to the Human Rights Act 1998) (the ECHR) to VAT and Excise
procedures, namely whether or not the imposition by the Commissioners of   *g*
Customs and Excise (the commissioners) of (ostensibly civil) penalties for alleged
dishonest evasion of tax pursuant to s 60(1) of the Value Added Tax Act 1994
(VATA) and s 8(1) of the Finance Act 1994 (FA 94) gave rise to criminal charges
within the meaning of art 6(1) of the ECHR, as each of the taxpayers contended.
[3] The chairman determined the issue in favour of the taxpayers, who are the   *h*
respondents in this appeal. The commissioners seek an order setting aside that
determination and substituting the determination by this court that the imposition
of the penalties did not give rise to criminal charges within the meaning of art 6.
[4] The importance of the question lies in the consequences which flow from
the decision of the tribunal in terms of the protection afforded to taxpayers by the   *j*
'fair trial' provisions of art 6. Where what is at issue is the 'determination ... of a
criminal charge' (see art 6(1)), various 'minimum rights' are provided for by
art 6(2) and (3) which are particularly pertinent in cases such as the present,
where penalties have been raised against non-English speakers such as Mr Yau, or
inadequate English speakers such as Mr Martins, and there are also alleged to be

a doubts in respect of the observation of the procedural safeguards which it is contended should have been available to all three respondents.

THE FACTUAL BACKGROUND

[5] The tribunal made no findings of fact. However, the following matters are not in dispute.

b
Mr Han and Mr Yau

[6] At the material time, these respondents carried on business at the Murdishaw Supper Bar in Runcorn, Cheshire, selling fish and chips and Chinese meals for consumption off the premises. Following inspection of their business records and interviews, the commissioners concluded that they had under-
c declared the VAT due and, on 25 February 1997, the commissioners issued a notice of assessment of unpaid tax in the sum of £80,767 plus interest covering the period 25 February 1991 to 31 July 1995 pursuant to s 73(1) of VATA. On 12 February 1998, that assessment was reduced to a sum of £76,455·12 plus interest, following representations by the respondents' accountants. On 26 March 1998 the
d commissioners assessed the respondents to a penalty pursuant to s 60(1) of VATA in the sum of £67,095, which represented 90% of the assessed sum. The 10% reduction was stated to be made for the respondents' 'partial assistance'.

[7] Before the tribunal Mr Han and Mr Yau challenged the 'Statement of Case' drafted by the commissioners' solicitors and they deny that they have been dishonest. They challenge the assessment of tax upon which the penalty is based.
e They do not accept that the interviews which took place were fair, contending in particular that the customs officers who carried out the interview demonstrated that they were fully aware of Mr Yau's linguistic limitations by requiring his wife to act as an interpreter. They contend that if (which is denied) there was any liability to a penalty, they were not afforded any adequate inducement or opportunity
f to co-operate with a view to mitigation of the penalty. In so far as the customs officers purport to rely on any answers allegedly given in interview, these will be challenged.

Mr and Mrs Martins

g [8] These respondents carry on a business comprising two fish and chip shops in Wantage, Oxfordshire. Following inspection of their business records and interviews, the commissioners concluded that they had under-declared output VAT. The commissioners originally assessed the respondents, pursuant to s 73(1) of VATA, in the sum of £86,202 plus interest in respect of unpaid tax. That assessment was challenged and proceedings in that respect came on before the
h tribunal on 6 October 1999 at a stage when there was no question of imposition of a penalty. However, before the tribunal, Mr Martins gave evidence that he had suppressed VAT, explaining that he was under financial pressure because his mother was dangerously ill and he needed to send money for her welfare in Portugal. He confessed to dishonesty, accepted the customs officers were right
j to raise an assessment, but disputed the quantum of the assessment which they had raised. Mr Martins speaks some English, in which language the proceedings were conducted, there being no provision for an interpreter at the tribunal. Having observed Mr Martins giving evidence, the tribunal directed that the hearing be adjourned. An officer of the commissioners who had heard Mr Martins' admission in the witness box then sought to interview him for the purposes of

issuing the penalty. Mr Martins had not been released by the tribunal as a witness in the tax assessment appeal and the officer who wished to interview him was a witness for the commissioners in those proceedings. In those circumstances, the respondents were advised that it would be inappropriate for Mr Martins to agree to such an interview by that officer.

[9] By letter dated 19 January 2000 the commissioners stated that it might be necessary in the circumstances to issue a penalty without mitigation. On 11 April 2000, the commissioners duly issued a penalty set at 90% of the quantum of tax which the commissioners estimated to be due. The tax due is denied by Mr and Mrs Martins and has yet to be determined by the tribunal in the tax assessment appeal. The respondents contend that there was no need for urgency in the determination and notification of the penalty which justified the commissioners acting as they did. Mr and Mrs Martins brought a separate appeal in respect of that penalty and it is in that appeal (rather than the tax assessment appeal which was adjourned) that the tribunal made the ruling which has given rise to the present appeal.

Mr Morris

[10] This respondent carries on business as an off-course bookmaker and is registered for the purposes of general betting duty. He is required by the Betting and Gaming Duty Act 1981 to account for general betting duty to the commissioners. The respondent's premises were visited by officers of the commissioners and he was interviewed. It appeared to the officers that betting slips had been altered and, in consequence, betting duty had been understated on the respondent's returns. By a letter dated 12 November 1998, the commissioners notified the respondent of an assessment of general betting duty in the sum of £15,304·97 in respect of the periods from 1 March 1996 to 30 April 1998. In the same letter, they notified the respondent of an assessment of penalty in the sum of £7,652 for dishonest evasion of excise duty pursuant to s 8(1) of FA 94. That sum represented a reduction of 50% of the penalty calculated to be available to reflect disclosure and co-operation given by the respondent. The respondent appealed both the assessment to unpaid tax and the imposition of the penalty. A number of factual matters are in dispute before the tribunal which go to the correctness of the procedure and the appropriateness of the penalty imposed.

THE RELEVANT STATUTORY PROVISIONS

[11] Section 73(1) of VATA provides:

> 'Where a person has failed to make any returns required under this Act ... or to keep any documents and afford the facilities necessary to verify such returns or where it appears to the Commissioners that such returns are incomplete or incorrect, they may assess the amount of VAT due from him to the best of their judgment and notify it to him.'

[12] Section 60 of VATA is headed 'VAT evasion: conduct involving dishonesty'. It provides:

> '(1) In any case where—(a) for the purpose of evading VAT, a person does any act or omits to take any action, and (b) his conduct involves dishonesty (whether or not it is such as to give rise to criminal liability), he shall be liable, subject to subsection (6) below, to a penalty equal to the amount of VAT evaded or, as the case may be, sought to be evaded, by his conduct.

a
(2) The reference in subsection (1)(a) above to evading VAT includes a reference to obtaining any of the following sums—(a) a refund any regulations made by virtue of section 13(5); (b) a VAT credit; (c) a refund under section 35, 36 or 40 of this Act or section 22 of the 1983 Act; and (d) a repayment under section 39 ...

b
(4) Statements made or documents produced by or on behalf of a person shall not be inadmissible in any such proceedings as are mentioned in subsection (5) below by reason only that it has been drawn to his attention—(a) that, in relation to VAT, the Commissioners may assess an amount due by way of a civil penalty instead of instituting criminal proceedings and, though no undertaking had been given as to whether the Commissioners will make such an assessment in the case of any person, it is

c
their practice to be influenced by the fact that a person has made a full confession of any dishonest conduct to which he has been a party and has given full facilities for investigation, and (b) that the Commissioners or, on appeal, a tribunal have power under section 70 to reduce a penalty under this section, and that he was or may have been induced thereby to make the

d
statements or produce the documents.

(5) The proceedings mentioned in subsection (4) above are—(a) any criminal proceedings against the person concerned in respect of any offence in connection with or in relation to VAT, and (b) any proceedings against him for recovery of any sum due from him in connection with or in relation to VAT ...

e
(7) On an appeal against an assessment to a penalty under this section, the burden of proof as to the matters specified in subsection (1)(a) and (b) above shall lie upon the Commissioners.'

(The burden of proof is that appropriate to civil proceedings, namely proof on the
f
balance of probabilities: see *1st Indian Cavalry Club Ltd v Customs and Excise Comrs* [1998] STC 293.)

[13] Section 70(1) of VATA provides: 'Where a person is liable to a penalty under section 60 ... the Commissioners or, on appeal, a tribunal may reduce the penalty to such amount (including nil) as they think proper.'

g
[14] Section 72 of VATA creates criminal offences in respect of the evasion of VAT as follows:

'(1) If any person is knowingly concerned in, or in the taking of steps with a view to, the fraudulent evasion of VAT by him or any other person, he shall be liable—(a) on summary conviction, to a penalty of the statutory maximum

h
or of three times the amount of the VAT, whichever is the greater, or to imprisonment for a term not exceeding 6 months or to both; or (b) on conviction on indictment, to a penalty of any amount or to imprisonment for a term not exceeding 7 years or to both ...

(3) If any person—(a) with intent to deceive produces, furnishes or sends
j
for the purposes of this Act or otherwise makes use for those purposes of any document which is false in a material particular; or (b) in furnishing any information for the purposes of this Act makes any statement which he knows to be false in a material particular or recklessly makes a statement which is false in a material particular, he shall be liable—(i) on summary conviction, to a penalty of the statutory maximum ... or to imprisonment for a term not exceeding 6 months or to both; or (ii) on conviction on indictment,

to a penalty of any amount or to imprisonment for a term not exceeding
7 years or both.'

[15] Section 8 of FA 94 sets out a similar statutory regime in respect of civil
penalties for the evasion of excise duty as is imposed by s 60 of VATA and
provisions analogous to those set out in s 70(1) of VATA also apply under FA 94.
Section 8(1) of FA 94 creates liability in identical terms to s 60(1) of VATA; s 8(2)
includes within that liability the obtaining of various repayments, reliefs etc; such
differences of wording as exist are immaterial to this appeal.

[16] Appeal lies to the VAT and Duties Tribunal in respect of both the
assessment of unpaid tax and the imposition of a civil evasion penalty.

THE HUMAN RIGHTS ACT 1998 AND ARTICLE 6 OF THE ECHR
[17] Article 6 of the ECHR is a 'Convention right' within the meaning of s 1 of
the Human Rights Act 1998.

[18] Section 2(1) of the 1998 Act provides:

'A court or tribunal determining a question which has arisen in connection
with a Convention right must take into account any—(a) judgment, decision,
declaration or advisory opinion of the European Court of Human Rights ...
whenever made or given, so far as, in the opinion of the court or tribunal, it
is relevant to the proceedings in which that question has arisen.'

[19] Section 3(1) of the 1998 Act imposes the interpretative obligation that: 'So
far as it is possible to do so, primary legislation and subordinate legislation must
be read and given effect in a way which is compatible with the Convention
rights.'

[20] Article 6(1) of the ECHR provides, so far as relevant:

'In the determination of his civil rights and obligations or of any criminal
charge against him, everyone is entitled to a fair and public hearing within a
reasonable time by an independent and impartial tribunal established by
law.'

[21] Thus, a finding that the imposition of a penalty gives rise to a criminal
charge is the threshold condition for application of the substantive provisions of
art 6 to the civil penalty procedures under s 60 of VATA and s 8 of FA 94. If
applicable, there are implicit in the fair trial provisions of art 6(1) rights which
include a right to silence and a privilege against self-incrimination.

[22] Article 6(2) enshrines the presumption of innocence in criminal matters
as follows: 'Everyone charged with a criminal offence shall be presumed innocent
until proved guilty according to law.'

[23] Article 6(3) provides further 'minimum rights' for those facing criminal
charges:

'Everyone charged with a criminal offence has the following minimum
rights: (a) to be informed promptly, in a language which he understands and
in detail, of the nature and cause of the accusation against him; (b) to have
adequate time and facilities for the preparation of his defence; (c) to defend
himself in person or through legal assistance of his own choosing or, if he has
not sufficient means to pay for legal assistance, to be given it free when the
interests of justice so require; (d) to examine or have examined witnesses
against him and to obtain the attendance and examination of witnesses on his
behalf under the same conditions as witnesses against him; (e) to have the

a   free assistance of an interpreter if he cannot understand or speak the language used in court.'

[24] Unlike certain other convention rights, such as art 8 (right to privacy) or art 10 (freedom of expression), which are qualified rights admitting of derogation in particular cases or categories of cases, the fair trial guarantee contained in art 6 does not admit of such derogation.

b   [25] Since s 2(1) of the 1998 Act requires the court or tribunal to take into account the Strasbourg case law of the European Court of Human Rights when determining a question which has arisen in connection with a convention right, that case law provides the starting point for the domestic court or tribunal's deliberations and the court or tribunal has a duty to consider such case law for the purposes of making its adjudication. It is not bound to follow such case law
c   (which itself has no doctrine of precedent) but, if study reveals some clear principle, test or autonomous meaning consistently applied by the Strasbourg Court and applicable to a convention question arising before the English courts, then the court should not depart from it without strong reason.

[26] It is not in dispute between the parties that the Strasbourg case law makes
d   clear that the concept of a 'criminal charge' under art 6 has an 'autonomous' convention meaning (see *Engel v Netherlands (No 1)* (1976) 1 EHRR 647 at 677–678 (para 81)). There are effectively three criteria applied by the Strasbourg Court in order to determine whether a criminal charge has been imposed (see *Engel's* case and more recently *AP v Switzerland* (1997) 26 EHRR 541 at 558 (para 39)). They are:
e

(a) the classification of the proceedings in domestic law;

(b) the nature of the offence; and

(c) the nature and degree of severity of the penalty that the person concerned risked incurring.

f
The Strasbourg Court does not in practice treat these three requirements as analytically distinct or as a 'three-stage test', but as factors together to be weighed in seeking to decide whether, taken cumulatively, the relevant measure should be treated as 'criminal'. When coming to such decision in the course of the court's 'autonomous' approach, factors (b) and (c) carry substantially greater
g   weight than factor (a).

[27] In addressing this court, the submissions of the parties have been limited to the question of the importation of the principles of the ECHR, and in particular the application of art 6, through the medium of the 1998 Act. However, it is right to record that Miss Sharpston QC has reserved her position to argue elsewhere
h   that this is a case where the rights guaranteed by the ECHR are required to be applied by direct application of Community law. In this connection she points out that art 22(8) of the Sixth Council Directive (EEC) 77/388 on the harmonisation of the laws of the member states to turnover taxes—common system of value added tax: uniform basis of assessment (OJ 1977 L145, p 1) provides:

j   'Member States may impose other obligations which they deem necessary for the correct collection of the tax and for the prevention of evasion, subject to the requirement of equal treatment for domestic transactions and transactions carried out between Member States by taxable persons and provided that such obligations do not, in trade between Member States, give rise to formalities connected with the crossing of frontiers.'

[28] She submits that, whilst the power of member states under that directive is discretionary, the exercise of such powers (which in the United Kingdom is embodied inter alia in the provisions at issue in this case) is circumscribed by the general principles of Community law.

[29] In this connection, Miss Sharpston relies upon the observation in *Internationale Handelsgesellschaft mbH v Einfuhr-und Vorratsstelle für Getreide und Futtermittel* Case 11/70 [1970] ECR 1125 at 1134 (para 4) that—

'respect for fundamental rights forms an integral part of the general principles of law protected by the Court of Justice. The protection of such rights, whilst inspired by the constitutional traditions common to the Member States, must be ensured within the framework of the structure and objectives of the Community.'

[30] In this context, the general principles of Community law include respect for the ECHR and, in particular, art 6 rights: see *Johnston v Chief Constable of the Royal Ulster Constabulary* Case 222/84 [1986] 3 All ER 135 at 156, [1987] QB 129 at 147, [1986] ECR 1651 at 1682 (para 18): and cf the observations of the Court of Justice of the European Communities in *Garage Molenheide BVBA v Belgium* Joined cases C-286/94, C-340/95, C-401/95 and C-47/96 [1998] All ER (EC) 61 at 82–83, [1997] ECR I-7281 at 7329 (paras 46–49) in relation to the application of the principle of proportionality as a fundamental principle of Community law to the national measures adopted by a member state in the exercise of its powers relating to VAT.

[31] However, Miss Sharpston also recognises that in *Marks & Spencer plc v Customs & Excise Comrs* [2000] STC 16, this court has made clear that, once a member state has correctly implemented a Community directive, an individual may not assert any right directly arising under it. Thus the question whether the penalties in issue are properly to be regarded as civil or criminal involves essentially the same question and process of interpretation of VATA and FA 94 as arise under the 1998 Act, namely whether the relevant provisions are open to interpretation in a manner which upholds convention rights or whether the provisions of the legislation are so clearly incompatible with convention rights that it is not possible so to interpret them.

[32] The essence of the commissioners' case on this appeal has been that, having regard to the three factors mentioned at [26] above, the chairman ought to have concluded that the imposition of the penalties did not give rise to criminal charges and that, in failing to do so, he erred in law. The respondents contend that the chairman properly recognised and correctly applied those criteria in coming to his decision, which they invite this court to endorse.

THE DECISION BELOW

[33] The decision of the chairman was set out at length and with great care. He first reviewed the civil and criminal penalty provisions under domestic law (see [11]–[15] above). He referred to their history and the fact that, until the introduction by the Finance Act 1985 of the civil penalty code which was the precursor of s 60 of VATA, the VAT offence code had provided solely for criminal offences, both in respect of regulatory matters and for fraud. The civil penalty code was introduced as a result of, and broadly for the reasons to be found in, the *Report of the Committee on Enforcement Powers of the Revenue Departments* (Cmnd 8822 (1983)) (the Keith Report), from which the chairman quoted. He then referred to the three *Engel v Netherlands* criteria (see [26] above) and proceeded to examine the civil penalties imposed under s 60 in the light of those criteria.

[**34**] Having done so he set out his conclusion, as follows:

'As I read the *Ozturk* decision (*Öztürk v Germany* (1984) 6 EHRR 409), the proper approach is to regard none of the *Engel* criteria (*Engel v Netherlands (No 1)* (1976) 1 EHRR 647) as determinative; instead, all the relevant factors are to be weighed and the decision reached accordingly. Features that together weigh most heavily on the criminal charge side are the punitive and deterrent characteristics of the section 60 and the section 8 penalties coupled with the amounts of those penalties. In this connection I have not found the possibility of mitigation as indicative one way or the other. It would be irrational if the non-co-operative taxpayer, for example, were to have Convention rights under Article 6.1 while the co-operative taxpayer, whose offence had been as serious but had earned mitigation, should be denied Convention rights. On that basis I think that the penalties are properly to be classed as "criminal charges" for the purpose of Article 6.1. Thus the Appellants have, on the reasoning in the cases taken into account so far, established that they have Convention rights entitling them to have the penalty assessment determined as criminal charges.' (See [2000] V & DR 312 at 319 (para 19).)

[**35**] The chairman then went on to say that his conclusion was in line with a recent decision of the Strasbourg Court in *Georgiou (trading as Marios Chippery) v UK* [2001] STC 80. In that case the court declined to admit to a full hearing an application based on alleged violation of art 6, on the grounds that it was, on the merits, 'manifestly ill-founded'. However, the court stated (at 88):

'The criteria for establishing whether a "criminal charge" has been determined are the domestic classification of the "offence", the nature of the "offence", and the nature and degree of severity of the potential and actual penalty ... The court notes that the penalty proceedings in the present case were classified as civil, rather than criminal, in domestic law. However, as in *Bendenoun v France* ((1994) 18 EHRR 54 at 74–76 (paras 44–48)), the penalty was intended as a punishment to deter re-offending, its purpose was both deterrent and punitive and the penalty itself was substantial. These factors taken together indicate that the penalty imposed in the present case was a "criminal charge" within the meaning of art 6(1).'

[**36**] Those observations related to penalties imposed by Customs and Excise under s 13 of FA 94, the predecessor of s 60 of VATA. Having cited them, the chairman concluded:

'The *Georgiou* decision is directly on point as regards both the penalty provisions with which this appeal is concerned. I am not of course bound by it but I am nonetheless required by section 2 of the [1998 Act] to take it into account, which I have done. The penalties in question are "criminal charges" within Article 6.1 ECHR; the implications of their being so will depend on the circumstances of the particular case.' (See [2000] V & DR 312 at 319 (para 21).)

THE KEITH REPORT

[**37**] As already mentioned, the genesis of the VAT civil penalty code is to be found in the 1983 Keith Report, to which both parties have referred us.

[**38**] At the time of the inquiry, the VAT offence code was set out in s 38 of the Finance Act 1972. It provided solely for criminal offences and no civil penalties were provided for fraud or negligent acts or omissions of a lesser kind. The offence code was intended to be comprehensive and covered both offences of

fraudulent or reckless actions in relation to payment of VAT and for offences of strict liability in relation to matters of regulation, such as the keeping and producing of records, the furnishing of VAT returns and the payment of outstanding tax (regulatory matters). The code also included the power to compound the criminal proceedings ie to settle such proceedings out of court on such terms as Customs and Excise thought fit, usually the payment of a sum in respect of the arrears of tax plus an amount intended to penalise the taxpayer. Where proceedings were not compounded, they proceeded before the criminal courts, either summarily or on indictment, the imposition of penalties on conviction (within statutory maxima) being a matter for those courts.

[39] The Keith Report noted this position. Such arrangements were contrasted with those available to the Inland Revenue in respect of tax, where civil penalties were provided, both for regulatory matters and a wide range of offences such as neglect and fraud, on proof to the civil standard. Criminal proceedings under the 'mainstream' criminal law were taken only in respect of 'heinous' cases of fraud. The report recorded that the general thrust of the representations to it was that it was strongly desirable that there should be harmonisation of offence arrangements for VAT and direct taxes, most witnesses taking the Inland Revenue's scheme, with or without amendment, as their favoured model (pp 384–385 (paras 18.2.1–18.2.2)). Paragraph 18.3.3 (p 389) of the Keith Report recorded that:

'The Department told us that, given acceptance of the need for a regulatory sanction, they would certainly envisage a system of civil sanctions, operating in much the same way as that of the Inland Revenue, with the civil penalties structured as were the existing criminal ones, and with Departmental internal procedures for selection of cases unchanged.'

[40] In dealing with the suggestion of the introduction of a single penalty code, the Keith Report recorded as follows (pp 390–391 (para 18.3.7)):

'Turning to the question of the introduction of penalties for civil fraud, to run in parallel with the bringing and compounding of criminal proceedings, Customs and Excise told us that to run the two systems together would undoubtedly give much greater flexibility in dealing with fraud or near fraud. It would afford welcome assistance in dealing with those cases where there were indications of fraud but where it was not possible to obtain proof to the criminal standard. At present those cases finished as simple unpenalised assessments and represented a loss to the Exchequer in delayed receipt of tax and cost of investigation. The proposal would therefore help the Department to deploy their resources effectively in the light of changing circumstances. It might well be that, in time, the need to compound criminal proceedings would be reduced, though Customs and Excise did not think that the need would wither away entirely.'

[41] Because the system of civil penalties would depend on encouraging the co-operation of the taxpayer, the department expressed the view that it would be necessary to make provision along the lines of s 105 of the Taxes Management Act 1970 so as to secure the admissibility of any evidence induced by such encouragement in the situation where an investigation started as a civil enquiry but turned into a serious case requiring criminal treatment (p 392 (para 18.3.12)). This reservation is now reflected in s 60(4) of VATA.

[42] The Keith Report went on to consider the position in relation to the 'regulatory matters' referred to at [33] above. It recommended the abolition of

a the criminal sanction for all such regulatory matters, with the substitution of a system of civil penalties in lieu. In this respect it recommended the enlargement of the VAT offence code by the enactment of a civil default of 'gross negligence'.

[43] So far as fraud and dishonesty were concerned, the Keith Report noted (p 398 (para 18.4.11)) that the requirement that fraud had to be provable to the criminal standard before penalties could be exacted meant that many large
b understatements arising through demonstrable lack of care, but short of fraud provable to that standard, went unpenalised. It continued as follows (pp 399–400 (para 18.4.16)):

'We have noted ... the high resource cost of the investigation of fraud to the criminal standard, and the understandable constraints this imposes on
c the investigation of the smaller frauds. We recognise the need for effective criminal sanctions to deal with the more serious frauds, and we make proposals below to improve the VAT offence code in this sense. However ... while more than 80 per cent of VAT fraud cases are now compounded, because of the entirely criminal character of the VAT offence code all VAT fraud cases have to be investigated and reported to the criminal standard,
d even if at an early stage it can be identified that the case is one that is likely to be compounded. By comparison, the Inland Revenue offence code providing civil penalties for fraud, buttressed by inducement provisions, allows a "civil" form of investigation and settlement, with the burden of criminal investigation being taken up only in those cases identified from the
e outset or in their course as sufficiently heinous to justify prosecution. In those cases where "civil" investigation techniques suffice to secure evidence of the true extent of the fraud, the process is an economical one, at least by comparison with the cost of a comparable criminal investigation. The investigation of acts of dishonesty in relation to tax matters in a "civil" style, reinforced by inducements, rather than as criminal offences under the
f Judge's Rules, was generally welcome to our witnesses and we heard no consistent body of criticism of the lower civil burden of proof in such cases as being unfair to the taxpayer ... *We conclude that a new default should be introduced into VAT law and we use the term "civil fraud" to distinguish it from similar dishonest conduct, "fraud", prosecuted in the criminal courts. As we discuss*
g *also at Chapter 19.2.9, the difference in terminology marks the difference in the investigatory techniques and sanctions applied, rather than a difference in the essential nature of the conduct.'* (My emphasis.)

[44] Later, in relation to criminal penalties in VAT, the Keith Report stated (p 401 (para 18.4.20)):
h
'... we ... accept the need for effective criminal sanctions to deal with the more serious cases of fraud. We reject the view that criminal offences should not be created by revenue statutes: on the contrary, we think it desirable that the VAT offence code should be comprehensive, embracing both civil and criminal penalties applying to the entire range of defaulting conduct
j commonly encountered. On this basis we now discuss the criminal offences and penalties which should be provided under the VAT offence code.'

The Keith Report then went on to propose (p 407 (para 18.4.38)):

'In the case of dishonest conduct investigated as civil fraud, we propose ... that the penalty attaching should be capable of mitigation from 100 per cent down to 50 per cent, but no lower, as a means of encouraging the cooperation of the taxpayer in the investigation process. Where an investigation disclosing such a default is not concluded by a settlement, assessments should be made to recover the tax undeclared, interest thereon and a penalty calculated at such rate between 50 per cent and 100 per cent as Customs and Excise consider warranted by the cooperation received. A trader should have the right to dispute all those elements assessed, by appealing to the VAT Tribunal. The Tribunal should be entitled to adjudicate on any or all of the following matters, where these are disputed, in a single hearing: (a) the assessment or the amount of the assessment of tax, on the normal grounds, (b) whether the fault amounts to a civil fraud on the balance of probabilities ... (c) the amount of interest, (d) the rate of penalty the Tribunal considers appropriate in the circumstances within the range of 50 per cent to 100 per cent of the culpable tax.'

[45] In relation to the choice between the use of civil penalties or criminal proceedings in relation to offences involving dishonesty, the Keith Report made no recommendation, but stated (p 411 (para 18.4.50)):

'In our view the relative use of civil or criminal investigation techniques is a matter for Customs and Excise to regulate, weighing the competing calls on their resources, the nature of the frauds suspected and the extent to which civil or criminal investigation techniques are capable of turning up sufficient admissible evidence to satisfy the respective burdens of proof for criminal or civil proceedings. Whether investigators should switch from the civil to the criminal mode, or vice versa, in the course of an investigation, as may happen now in direct tax investigations, seems to us also essentially a matter for the Department, in the light of experience and the views of courts and Tribunals as to fairness to the accused in the circumstances of a particular case.'

THE RELEVANT FEATURES OF THE VAT CIVIL PENALTY CODE

[46] Section 60 of VATA was enacted pursuant to the Keith Report recommendations for a civil penalty code for VAT offences; however, the recommendation that mitigation of the penalty imposed for offences involving dishonesty should not exceed 50% was not followed, s 70 of VATA permitting reduction to such amount (including nil) as the commission should think proper.

[47] Following the recommendations of the Keith Report, s 13 of the 1985 Act introduced a penalty for evasion of VAT where it could be shown that a taxpayer's conduct involved dishonesty, the terms of which are now embodied in s 60 of VATA. Section 14 of the Finance Act 1986 introduced a provision allowing the recovery of the penalty from directors and managing officers where it could be shown that the facts giving rise to the penalty was attributable to their dishonesty. That is now s 61 of VATA. Section 8(1) of FA 94 introduced the power to issue a civil evasion penalty for evasion of excise duty involving dishonesty.

[48] Before us the parties have emphasised various features of the civil penalty code introduced by VATA. In the following list, the commissioners emphasise points (1) to (4), while the respondents emphasise points (5) to (10).

(1) Section 60(4)(a) of VATA expressly refers to 'an amount due by way of a civil penalty'.

a (2) Such penalties were provided for as a deliberate decriminalisation of the VAT and duty penalty scheme.

(3) They are alternatives to criminal penalties which are available in more serious cases.

(4) The taxpayer is dealt with by means of a civil procedure, subject to the lower burden of proof (balance of probability) and avoids the stigma of a criminal
b conviction.

(5) The penalties require a finding of dishonesty.

(6) There is no ascertainable legal distinction or touchstone of liability as between treatment of a taxpayer under the civil penalty provisions of s 60 and his prosecution under s 72 of VATA. Despite the invitation of the court, neither counsel was able to think of circumstances (apart from the evidence necessary to
c satisfy the burden of proof) in which establishment of liability under s 60 could not equally suffice for a prosecution under the provisions of s 72.

(7) The distinction in application depends upon the discretion of Customs and Excise, which in turn depends upon internal criteria relating to the seriousness of the case, the availability of resources and the likelihood of obtaining a conviction
d in criminal proceedings, bearing in mind the different burden of proof.

(8) The function of the civil penalties is not compensatory. They are imposed in addition to the assessed liability for tax or duty and the interest recoverable thereon.

(9) The function of the penalties is one of punishment and deterrence vis-à-vis
e the individual taxpayer and general deterrence so far as taxpayers at large are concerned.

(10) The penalties (subject to mitigation) are substantial, being 100% of the tax evaded or sought to be evaded.

THE PRACTICE IN ADMINISTERING THE CODE

f [49] Following the introduction of civil evasion penalties, Customs and Excise continued to investigate cases of dishonest evasion which it regarded as aggravated or serious with a view to criminal proceedings in cases where the VAT evaded was at least £25,000 in total over the previous three years; or where the evasion involved one or more businesses whose activities were solely or primarily bogus or undertaken as a systemic fraud against tax; or where, during the
g course of an investigation for a civil offence, the taxpayer continued in a deliberate intent to deceive; or where the offence was perpetrated by lawyers, accountants or other advisors of businesses in respect of VAT matters, current or former tax officials, or persons who occupied a prominent position in the field of law or government; or where the evasion was executed in conjunction with other
h criminal activities; or where there had been a previous VAT or Customs and Excise offence which had resulted in imposition of a penalty, compounding of proceedings or a criminal conviction. However, following revision of its prosecution policy with effect from 1 September 2000, Customs and Excise focused criminal investigation and prosecution activity on the most serious cases of VAT evasion
j where a strong deterrent message is required and it is considered that the use of civil penalties would not achieve this. It is no longer the policy to prosecute solely on the basis of the amount of revenue involved and the civil penalty procedure may now be used in cases involving several hundred thousand pounds of VAT avoided. This is regarded as a more cost-effective use of resources in most cases of dishonest evasion. In July 2001, the prosecution policy was further revised to focus Customs and Excise investigation and prosecution activity on tackling

major and persistent offenders, conviction of whom is deemed likely to have
strong deterrent effect and to result in custodial sentences.

[50] So far as civil evasion penalties are concerned, after undertaking whatever
preliminary investigations are considered appropriate, an officer will interview
the taxpayer and secure any other available evidence, including the relevant
records of the business. Before the interview commences, a copy of VAT Notice
730 ('Civil Evasion Penalty Investigations: Statement of Practice') is handed to
the taxpayer and, if present, his or her representative. The officer will ensure that
the taxpayer understands the content of the notice, which outlines the approach
of Customs and Excise to reaching an agreement on the undeclared VAT and
how the taxpayer can reduce any penalty imposed by co-operating in the
investigation. The notice informs the taxpayer that he can reduce the penalties
significantly by promptly disclosing full details of his true liability and by the
extent to which he co-operates over the whole enquiry. So far as disclosure is
concerned, he is told that early and truthful admission at interview of the extent
of the arrears and why they arose will attract a considerable reduction. He is also
told that he can receive a further major reduction if he supplies information
promptly, attends interviews, answers questions honestly and accurately, and
gives the relevant facts to establish his true liability. He is told that, in various
circumstances, reductions from the full penalty figure will normally be made up
to certain maximum percentages specified, namely up to 40% for an early and
truthful explanation as to why the arrears arose and their true extent, up to 25%
for co-operation in substantiating the true amount of the arrears, and up to
10% for attending interviews and producing records and information as required.
Thus the maximum reduction generally obtainable is 75% of the tax under-declared
though, in exceptional circumstances, consideration may be given to a further
reduction. Customs and Excise term this method of dealing with the taxpayer the
'inducement' procedure.

[51] The officer does not formally caution the taxpayer. He will explain that
the investigation is not being conducted with a view to prosecution for VAT
evasion, that the taxpayer is not obliged to co-operate in the customs
investigation and that it is a decision for him to decide whether or not to speak to
the investigation officers or assist in the investigation generally. Officers are able
to compel the disclosure of documents and other material by virtue of their
powers under Sch 11, para 7(2) of VATA which gives them the power to require
the production of documents relating to supplies of goods or services, and
acquisitions or importations which are made in the course or furtherance of
business. Where a trader refuses to produce records on request, it is customs
policy to remind him of his legal obligations and serve a form of notice demand
to produce specified records. If the taxpayer fails to comply with such a notice,
he is in breach of the VAT regulatory provisions and is liable to a regulatory civil
penalty under s 69(3) of VATA.

[52] Once the investigation is complete, a decision is made as to whether
dishonesty has been established and whether and in what amount a penalty will
be imposed.

[53] Once the taxpayer has received notice of the penalty he has a right of
appeal to the VAT and Duties Tribunal, which appeal is governed by the civil
procedures set out in the Value Added Tax Tribunals Rules, SI 1986/590.

[54] By way of contrast, if, under the prosecution policy criteria, Customs and
Excise consider that a criminal investigation with a view to prosecution is
appropriate, and there is sufficient evidence to demonstrate reasonable grounds

a to suspect fraud prior to approaching the taxpayer, procedures appropriate to a criminal investigation will be followed. Customs investigators have powers to obtain search warrants and access orders and to arrest suspects, which powers are not available in a civil case. In addition, they conduct interviews in accordance with the requirements of the Police and Criminal Evidence Act 1984 (PACE), which normally take place in the presence of the taxpayer's solicitor and are

b conducted under caution without use of, or reference to, the inducement procedure.

THE STRASBOURG CASE LAW

[**55**] We have been referred to a number of decisions of the Strasbourg Court. In *Adolf v Austria* (1982) 4 EHRR 313, the applicant was the subject of a complaint

c of assault, the police being instructed to investigate whether a punishable offence had been committed. Such an investigation constituted the commencement of criminal proceedings. The Austrian District Court, at the request of the public prosecutor, terminated the proceedings without a hearing on the grounds that the conditions of s 42 of the Penal Code had been met, namely, that the degree of

d guilt was slight, the act had only trifling consequences and that punishment was not necessary as a deterrent. The court, while finding that there had on the facts been no violation of the applicant's rights under art 6 of the ECHR, held unanimously that art 6 was applicable to the District Court proceedings. It held (at 322–323 (para 30)) that, in ascertaining whether there was a 'criminal charge' for the purposes of art 6(1), or whether the applicant was 'charged with a criminal

e offence' for the purposes of art 6(2) and (3):

> 'These expressions are to be interpreted as having an "autonomous" meaning in the context of the Convention and not on the basis of their meaning in domestic law. The legislation of the State concerned is certainly relevant, but it provides no more than a starting-point in ascertaining
>
> *f* whether at any time there was a "criminal charge" against Mr. Adolf or he was "charged with a criminal offence". The prominent place held in a democratic society by the right to a fair trial favours a "substantive", rather than a "formal", conception of the "charge" referred to by Article 6; it impels the Court to look behind the appearances and examine the realities of the
>
> *g* procedure in question in order to determine whether there has been a "charge" within the meaning of Article 6. In particular, the applicant's situation under domestic legal rules in force has to be examined in the light of the object and purpose of Article 6, namely the protection of the rights of the defence.'

h The court went on to say (at 324 (para 33)):

> 'As regards the concept of a non-punishable act, it is clearly in line with the title and text of section 42 ... Nevertheless, non-punishable or unpunished criminal offences do exist and Article 6 of the Convention does not distinguish between them and other criminal offences; it applies whenever a person is
>
> *j* "charged" with any criminal offence.'

[**56**] In *Engel v Netherlands* (*No 1*) (1976) 1 EHRR 647, the Strasbourg Court considered the application of the concept of a 'criminal charge' in respect of various penalties imposed upon the applicants for offences against military discipline in a military court. In holding that art 6 was applicable, the court observed (at 677 (para 80)):

'All the Contracting States make a distinction of long standing, albeit in
different forms and degrees, between disciplinary proceedings and criminal
proceedings. For the individual affected, the former usually offer substantial
advantages in comparisons with the latter, for example as concerns the
sentences passed. Disciplinary sentences, in general less severe, do not
appear in the person's criminal record and entail more limited consequences.
It may nevertheless be otherwise; moreover, criminal proceedings are
ordinarily accompanied by fuller guarantees.'

The court stated that the autonomous concept of a 'criminal charge' was still
applicable in the context of disciplinary proceedings. Limiting itself to 'the sphere
of military service' it repeated (at 678 (para 82)) that the categorisation under the
law of the respondent state—

'provides no more than the starting point. The indications so afforded
have only a formal and relative value and must be examined in the light of
the common denominator of the respective legislation of the various
Contracting States.'

It went on to state that 'the very nature of the offence is a factor of greater import'
and continued (at 678–679 (para 82)) that it was necessary also to—

'take into consideration the degree of severity of the penalty that the
person concerned risks incurring. In a society subscribing to the rule of law,
there belong to the "criminal" sphere deprivations of liberty liable to be
imposed as punishment, except those which by their nature, duration or
manner of execution cannot be appreciably detrimental. The seriousness of
what is at stake, the traditions of the Contracting States and the importance
attached by the Convention to respect for the physical liberty of the person
all require that this should be so.'

[57] In *Öztürk v Germany* (1984) 6 EHRR 409 the Strasbourg Court was concerned
with a case in which the applicant had been charged with a traffic offence, which,
under German law, was regarded as 'regulatory' only, having been 'de-criminalised'
under a scheme in relation to road traffic offences. A regulatory offence was defined
(at 413 (para 18)) as—

'an unlawful ... and reprehensible ... act, contravening a legal provision
which made the offender liable to a fine [within prescribed limits]. The
amount of the fine being fixed in each case by reference to the seriousness of
the offence, the degree of misconduct attributable to the offender and ... [for
minor offences] the offender's financial circumstances ...'

If, however, the act constituted both a regulatory and a criminal offence, only the
criminal law was applicable. None the less, because no criminal penalty was
imposed, the act could be punished as a 'regulatory offence'. If, without having
established inability to pay, the person concerned had not paid the fine in due
time, the person might be made the subject of a detention order under the Code
of Criminal Procedure.

[58] The court recognised that the legislation in question marked an
important stage in the history of the reform of German criminal law but stated
none the less that—

'according to the ordinary meaning of the terms, there generally come
within the ambit of the criminal law offences that make their perpetrator

a liable to penalties intended, *inter alia*, to be deterrent and usually consisting of fines and of measures depriving the person of his liberty. In addition, misconduct of the kind committed ... continues to be classified as part of the criminal law in the vast majority of the Contracting States ... [where] such misconduct, being regarded as illegal and reprehensible, is punishable by criminal penalties.' (See (1984) 6 EHRR 409 at 423 (para 53).)

b
The court (at 423–424 (para 53)) went on to observe that the penalties imposed—

'retained a punitive character, which is the customary distinguishing feature of criminal penalties. The rule of law infringed by the applicant has, for its part, undergone no change of content. It is a rule that is directed, not c towards a given group possessing a special status—in the manner, for example, of disciplinary law—, but towards all citizens in their capacity as road-users; it prescribes conduct of a certain kind and makes the resultant requirement subject to a sanction that is punitive. Indeed, the sanction—and this the Government did not contest—seeks to punish as well as to deter ...
d Above all, the general character of the rule and the purpose of the penalty, being both deterrent and punitive, suffice to show that the offence in question was, in terms of Article 6 of the Convention, criminal in nature.'

[59] In *Bendenoun v France* (1994) 18 EHRR 54, the applicant was a French national resident in Switzerland who was prosecuted and fined by the French customs and e tax authorities in the French administrative courts, being later sentenced to imprisonment for tax evasion by the French criminal courts. In relation to the administrative proceedings he complained of violation of his art 6 rights. The French government maintained that the proceedings did not relate to a criminal charge, because tax surcharges imposed on the applicant bore all the hallmarks of an administrative penalty within the meaning of the court's case law. None the f less, the Strasbourg Court held (at 75–76 (para 47)) that art 6 applied because:

'In the first place, the offences with which Mr Bendenoun was charged came under Article 1729(1) of the General Tax Code. That provision covers all citizens in their capacity as taxpayers, and not a given group with a g particular status. It lays down certain requirements, to which it attaches penalties in the event of non-compliance. Secondly, the tax surcharges are intended not as pecuniary compensation for damage but essentially as a punishment to deter reoffending. Thirdly, they are imposed under a general rule whose purpose is both deterrent and punitive. Lastly, in the instant case the surcharges were very substantial amounting to 422,434 FF in respect of h Mr Bendenoun personally and 570,398 FF in respect of his company; and if he failed to pay, he was liable to be committed to prison by the criminal courts. Having weighed the various aspects of the case, the Court notes the predominance of those which have a criminal connotation. None of them is decisive on its own, but taken together and cumulatively they made the j "charge" in issue a "criminal" one within the meaning of Article 6(1) which was therefore applicable.'

[60] *Bendenoun v France* is a case upon which the respondents strongly rely. They point out that all four elements relied upon by the Strasbourg Court in that case are present in the instant cases save for the fact that the applicant in *Bendenoun's* case was liable to be committed to prison for non-payment. However, that is not a

requirement which has been regarded as essential in subsequent decisions of the
Strasbourg Court.   *a*

[61] In *AP v Switzerland* (1997) 26 EHRR 541, fines had been imposed on the
applicants in respect of tax evasion by their late husband and father, pursuant to
provisions of Swiss law which permitted such a procedure. The court upheld the
plea of the applicants on the basis that it is a fundamental rule of criminal law that
criminal liability does not survive the person who has committed the criminal act.   *b*
However, in dealing with the applicability of art 6 it stated (at 558 (para 39)):

> 'The Court reiterates that the concept of "criminal charge" within the
> meaning of Article 6 is an autonomous one. In earlier case law the Court has
> established that there are three criteria to be taken into account when it is
> being decided whether a person was "charged with a criminal offence" for   *c*
> the purposes of Article 6. These are the classification of the offence under
> national law, the nature of the offence and the nature and degree of severity
> of the penalty the person concerned risks incurring.'

Having held that the fines were, in the opinion of the court, 'not inconsiderable'
the court went on to state (at 558–559 (paras 41–42)):   *d*

> 'As regards the nature of the offence, it is noted that tax legislation lays
> down certain requirements, to which it attaches penalties in the event of
> non-compliance. The penalties, which in the present cases take the form of fines,
> are not intended as pecuniary compensation for damage but are essentially
> punitive and deterrent in nature ... As regards the classification of the   *e*
> proceedings under national law, the Court attaches weight to the finding of
> the highest court in the land, the Federal Court, in its judgment in the
> present case, that the fine in question was "penal" in character and depended
> on the "guilt" of the offending taxpayer.'

[62] The court in *AP v Switzerland* was concerned with a case where the tax   *f*
evasion was punishable by a substantial fine; however, the offender was not
subject to any process of imprisonment in default. Subsequently, in *Lauko v
Slovakia* [1998] ECHR 26138/95 the court was again concerned with a minor
offence which the Constitutional Court of Slovakia described as—

> 'characterised, in general, by a wrongful breach of law or legal obligations   *g*
> in different spheres of public administration which represents a minor
> danger to the society. Because of its character, a minor offence is not subject
> to examination by a court ... the examination of minor offences falls within
> the competence of administrative authorities.' (See [1998] ECHR 26138/95
> (para 16).)   *h*

The applicant's offence fell to be dealt with under the Code of Civil Procedure,
subject to review by a court in cases of a fine exceeding SKK 2,000. In holding that
art 6(1) applied, the Strasbourg Court noted (para 56) that the offence was not
characterised under domestic law as 'criminal', but observed (para 57) that
indications furnished by the domestic law have only relative value (see Öztürk's   *j*
case). So far as the nature of the offence was concerned, the court observed that
the legal rule infringed by the applicant was directed to all citizens and not
towards a given group possessing a special status. It also noted the fine and order
for costs imposed and observed (para 58): 'The fine imposed on the applicant was
intended as a punishment to deter reoffending. It has a punitive character, which

a is the customary distinguishing feature of criminal penalties' referring to Öztürk's case and *AP v Switzerland* in this respect.

[63] The Strasbourg Court did not proceed further to close examination of the nature and degree of severity of the penalty risked by the appellant, stating as follows (para 58):

b 'The Government contended ... that the minor offence in issue had several features which distinguished it from offences within the realm of the criminal law *stricto sensu*. However the elements relied on by the Government such as the fact that the commission of the offence is not punishable by imprisonment and is not entered on the criminal record are not decisive of the classification of the offence for the purpose and applicability of Article 6(1) (see *Öztürk v*

c *Germany* (1984) 6 EHRR 409 at 423–424 (para 53)). In sum, the general character of the legal provision infringed by the applicant together with the deterrent and punitive purpose of the penalty imposed on him, suffice to show that the offence in question was, in terms of Article 6 of the Convention, criminal in nature. Accordingly, there is no need to examine it also in the light of the third criterion stated above ... The relevant lack of

d seriousness of the penalty at stake cannot deprive an offence of its inherently criminal character (see *Öztürk v Germany* (1984) 6 EHRR 409 at 424 (para 54)).'

[64] Finally, in *Georgiou's* case, the Strasbourg Court ruled that a civil penalty imposed for dishonest evasion of VAT pursuant to s 13(1) of the 1985 Act (the terms of which were identical to s 60 of VATA) amounted to a criminal charge

e within the meaning of art 6(1) (see [35] and [36] above).

DISCUSSION

The application of the case law above cited

f [65] It seems clear from the case law above cited that in considering the three criteria routinely applied by the Strasbourg Court for the purpose of determining whether the applicant is the subject of a 'criminal charge', the first criterion, namely the categorisation of the allegation in domestic law, is no more than a starting point for the classification, and is not decisive of the nature of the allegation. If the offence the subject of the allegation is not criminalised by the

g national law, the court determines whether it is none the less criminal in character for the purposes of art 6 of the ECHR by proceeding to the second and third criteria, namely the nature of the offence and the severity of the penalty which it invokes. As stated in *Lauko's* case, the second and third criteria are alternative rather than cumulative. However, that is not an approach which

h appears to have been adopted in practice and, as also stated in *Lauko's* case, a cumulative approach may be adopted where the analysis of each criterion does not lead to a clear conclusion (see *Bendenoun's* case).

[66] Under the second criterion, the court considers whether or not, under the law concerned, the 'offence' is one which applies generally to the public at large or

j is restricted to a specific group. If the former, then despite its 'de-criminalisation' by the national law, it is apt to be regarded as criminal. Further, if a punitive and deterrent penalty is attached, it is likely to be regarded as criminal in character, even in cases where the penalty is in the nature of a fine rather than imprisonment. On the other hand, where the offence is limited to a restricted group, as is generally the case in relation to disciplinary offences, the court is unlikely to classify a charge under the applicable disciplinary or regulatory code as criminal, at least unless it involves or may lead to loss of liberty.

[67] In the context of disciplinary proceedings, the Strasbourg Court has placed great emphasis on the seriousness of the penalty or imprisonment attached to the offence as the touchstone for holding the proceedings criminal rather than disciplinary: see *Engel's* case and see *Campbell and Fell v UK* (1984) 7 EHRR 165, a case concerning a serious prison disciplinary offence resulting in an award of 570 days' loss of remission. The latter case was distinguished by the Divisional Court in the recent decision of *R (Greenfield) v Secretary of State for the Home Dept* [2001] EWHC Admin 113, [2001] 1 WLR 1731, in a case where the maximum penalty which could be awarded for the prison disciplinary offence in question was 42 additional days, and was wholly different in kind from the penalty which might have been imposed for an equivalent criminal charge. It is plain that the imposition of a substantial fine in disciplinary proceedings will not in itself render charges criminal in nature: see *Brown v UK* (1998) 28 EHRR CD 233, in which it was held that the fact that a £10,000 fine was imposed by the Solicitors' Complaints Tribunal did not attract the provisions of art 6. However, outside the context of disciplinary proceedings, and in particular, in the field of tax evasion, it appears that a substantial financial penalty which is imposed by way of punishment and deterrence will suffice (see *Bendenoun's* case and *Georgiou's* case).

[68] Finally, it is to be observed that the treatment of the categorisation of the allegation in domestic law merely as a starting point marginalises, and indeed largely renders irrelevant, the rationale underlying a national law which seeks to decriminalise conduct which would otherwise be treated, or generally regarded, as criminal in nature. The trend of the Strasbourg decisions, exemplified in *Bendenoun's* case and *Georgiou's* case, has been to fasten upon and emphasise the applicability of the second and third criteria, despite the view reflected in the opinions of the dissenting judges in *Öztürk's* case to the effect that decriminalisation, at least of 'minor offences', may work in the general interests of individuals by elimination of the moral judgment and the drawbacks customarily connected with criminal proceedings: see in particular the dissenting opinion of Judge Bernhardt, with which Judge Thor Vilhjalmsson also agreed. Equally the Strasbourg Court has ignored the observations of Judge Matscher that differences in the conceptions which underlie criminal and 'regulatory' offences and, in particular, differences in their legal effects whether of substance or procedure, affect their very nature and that excessively broad interpretation of the concept of 'criminal' and 'civil' for the purpose of extending the guarantees included in art 6 is not an appropriate solution.

[69] The view last stated has throughout informed the submissions of Mr Parker QC for the commissioners. However, his submissions, and the counter-arguments of Miss Sharpston QC for the respondents, may best be elaborated in relation to the three criteria.

The classification of the proceedings in domestic law

[70] In seeking to show that the chairman erred in his application of the three criteria and in following the Strasbourg decision in *Georgiou's* case, Mr Parker has submitted: (1) That the classification of the penalty for dishonesty as a civil penalty (both impliedly, by contrast with s 72 of VATA, and expressly in the language of s 60(4)(a) of that Act) should be accorded great weight. (2) Justification for such classification and the procedures associated with it is to be found in the plain

a intention of the legislature to decriminalise most of the VAT and duties penalty
system, and to provide an alternative to criminal prosecution and punishment for
the most serious cases of dishonesty. (3) The statutory regime for civil penalties
is fair, beneficial to the taxpayer and supported by the sound public policy
rationale propounded in the Keith Report, which apparently had the support of
the various interest groups which made submissions to it, including the traders
b subject to such regime. (4) Creation of the civil penalties scheme was not an
exercise in reclassification of a type which the court in Öztürk's case (1984)
6 EHRR 409 at 421 (para 49) feared that 'might lead to results incompatible with
the object and purpose of the Convention'; it involved the creation of an
alternative regime which in less 'serious' cases of dishonest evasion replaced
criminal procedures with a civil process regulated by the 1986 rules. Those rules
c set out procedures akin to those in ordinary civil litigation in relation to statements
of case, defence and reply (rr 7 and 8), particulars (r 9), directions (r 11),
amendments (r 14), extension of time (r 19), disclosure (r 20), witness statements
(r 21), witness summonses (r 22), procedure at hearing (r 27) and evidence (r 28),
which proceedings regulate the ultimate determination of liability by a tribunal
d whose decision does not involve the status or stigma of a criminal conviction.

[71] Miss Sharpston for the respondents accepts that the penalties imposed
upon them are described in each of the relevant statutory schemes with the
epithet 'civil'. However, she submits: (1) That the term 'civil penalty' does not
necessarily exclude a construction that such penalty is in fact criminal *in nature*,
any more than a term such as 'fixed penalty' excludes certain road traffic offences
e from being criminal in nature. (2) She relies upon the extract from the Keith
Report quoted in italics at [43] above as showing that the difference in the *nature*
of the dishonest conduct invoking a civil process under s 60 of VATA or
prosecution under s 72 of VATA is non-existent. While there is a difference in the
investigatory techniques and the penalties to which the taxpayer is subject, there
f is no difference in the essential nature of the 'charge'. She relies on the recognition
in para 18.4.50 (p 411) of the Keith Report (see [45] above) that the relative use
made of the civil and criminal modes of procedure is essentially a matter to be left
to the experience and views of the commissioners and so, subject to changing
policy guidelines, it has remained. (3) Miss Sharpston relies upon the clear view
of the Strasbourg Court that the domestic classification is in no sense
g determinative and asserts that it is also clear that the essential nature of the
conduct in respect of which the penalty is imposed remains criminal, albeit s 60
of VATA introduces a more summary and convenient method of disposal for the
discretion and for the benefit of Customs and Excise, whether or not it may also
be regarded as 'beneficial' to the taxpayer.

h

The nature of the offence

[72] Mr Parker accepts that the penalties under s 60 have features which the
Strasbourg Court has held militate in favour of a finding that a penal measure is
criminal in nature. He accepts that it is appropriate to regard the s 60 provisions
j as applying in principle to all citizens qua taxpayers and not to a restricted group.
He further accepts that the function of the penalties is not to compensate
Customs and Excise but one of punishment and deterrence, albeit the penalty is
calculated by reference to the amount of unpaid tax, subject to reduction for
mitigation. Finally, he accepts that the penalties require a finding of 'dishonesty'
which is generally regarded as a matter for criminal sanction and would
generally, subject to the discretion of Customs and Excise, be amenable to

prosecution under s 72. None the less, he submits that both VATA and FA 94
plainly envisage that the circumstances giving rise to a penalty need *not* be treated
as giving rise to a criminal charge. Miss Sharpston relies upon the very matters
conceded by Mr Parker. She also makes the point that the absence of a rule
imposing imprisonment in the event of non-payment of a tax penalty does not
indicate that a 'criminal charge' is not involved: see the views of the Strasbourg
Court in *Öztürk's* case, *Lauko's* case and *Georgiou's* case. She submits that the very
substantial nature of the penalties able to be imposed, albeit subject to the criteria
for mitigation applied by Customs and Excise, constitute a substantial
punishment for an offence of dishonesty.

The nature and degree of severity of the penalty

[73] Mr Parker relies upon the absence of any risk of imprisonment. He
submits that the principal concern in *Engel's* case was that, in a society subscribing
to the rule of law, deprivations of liberty liable to be imposed as a punishment
belong to the 'criminal sphere' (see (1976) 1 EHRR 647 at 678–679 (para 82),
quoted at [56] above). Thus the absence of any threat of imprisonment in the
instant cases is a powerful indicator that the penalties do not give rise to a
criminal charge. He also submits that the maximum penalty to which the court
should have regard should not be the figure of 100% of the tax due, because the
starting point for the tribunal's deliberation is the level of the penalty actually
imposed, taking into account mitigation. Miss Sharpston asserts that the Strasbourg
jurisprudence has moved on since *Engel's* case and that the subsequent decisions
demonstrate that the scale of the penalties involved in the instant cases, whether
before or after mitigation, and bearing in mind their penal and deterrent (as
opposed to compensatory) effect, are sufficiently burdensome to render the
change criminal under the third criterion. She also submits that it is the exposure
of the taxable person at the time of charge, namely to 100% of the tax alleged to
have been evaded, which the court should take into account.

[74] I am reluctantly persuaded that the submissions for the respondents must
prevail, as they prevailed before the chairman below. I am reluctant, because in
my view the rationale for the VAT civil penalties scheme was convincingly
propounded in the Keith Report as a just balance between the legitimate interests
of Customs and Excise in improving the collection of a tax in relation to which
widespread evasion was prevalent, and the interests of the taxpayer in avoiding
the travails of a criminal prosecution and the stigma of conviction of a criminal
offence of dishonesty in cases of deliberate evasion. It also represented a sensible
rationalisation of the schemes for collecting tax and penalising evasion as
between Customs and Excise on the one hand and the Inland Revenue on the
other. Nor am I aware of any widespread dissatisfaction or allegations of injustice
in relation to the procedures followed since the adoption of the Keith Report
recommendations by legislation. I am nonetheless persuaded by what I regard as
the clear state of the Strasbourg case law in relation to a case of this kind.

[75] So far as the first criterion is concerned, it is plain that the classification of
the penalties provided for as 'civil', albeit coupled with a procedure appropriate
to civil rather than criminal proceedings, cannot be regarded as more than the
starting point where the levying and enforcement of the penalty concerned is
designed to punish and deter members of the public at large in respect of
dishonest conduct. Furthermore, the classification does not represent a decision
on the part of the legislature to decriminalise dishonest evasion of VAT, given the
parallel provision under s 72(1) of VATA for the criminal prosecution of any

a person knowingly concerned in the fraudulent evasion of VAT and, under s 72(3), of any person acting fraudulently in the respects therein set out. This, rather, creates alternative regimes in respect of which Customs and Excise may none the less decide in the course of an investigation to change from one to the other. The provisions of art 6 of the ECHR, however, are concerned to protect a potential defendant to criminal proceedings from an early stage, and the nature and consequences of the 'charge' may affect the degree of co-operation which he is

b prepared to afford in the course of an investigation.

[76] So far as the second criterion is concerned, the nature of the offence suspected and sanctioned by the application of civil penalties is fraud/dishonesty in respect of the tax payable or actually payable, whether under ss 60 or 72 of VATA, and Customs and Excise enjoy a discretion as to whether, on a particular

c set of facts, to apply a civil penalty or to prosecute. As observed by the chairman:

> 'Cases where section 60 penalties are in issue usually involve allegations of dishonest and systemic suppressions of sales or use of fictitious invoices over a number of accounting periods ... To those of us with judicial experience of criminal proceedings, the level of criminality alleged against the appellant
> *d* does not appear significantly different from that involved in Crown Court fraud trials.' (See [2000] V & DR 312 at 315 (para 7).)

He went on to observe (at 315–316 (para 7)):

> 'The essential contrasts are these. The appeal before the Tribunal is quicker
> *e* and less demanding on the Commissioners' resources. The standard of proof is lower. Criminal proceedings do not apply. Instead the procedure is regulated by the VAT Tribunal Rules 1986. In particular, the Tribunal has a broad discretion in respect of the evidence it may admit under rule 28. The imposition of a penalty does not give rise to a criminal record and loss of liberty is not a possibility.'

f

[77] While the essential contrasts to which the chairman referred are highly desirable from the point of view of the efficient collection of tax and (as I have already observed) there is no reason to suppose they lead to widespread unfairness, they are procedural in nature rather than going to the nature of the offence itself. The Strasbourg Court does not adopt an approach which allows procedural
g features or considerations to govern or define the nature of the offence under consideration. Yet those are the features upon which Mr Parker has been obliged principally to place reliance under criterion (a). His submissions under criterion (b) have consisted principally of concessions.

[78] So far as the third criterion, the nature and degree of the penalty, is
h concerned, again the weight of Strasbourg authority is in favour of the respondents in the sense that, in the area of tax evasion at least, such authority does not require that, for the purposes of a 'criminal' charge, it is necessary to demonstrate that the penalty to which the taxpayer is subject involves, or may involve, imprisonment. It is sufficient that it is substantial and its purpose is
j punitive and deterrent. It seems to me that those requirements are made out in the case of these respondents.

[79] Since first drafting this judgment, I have had drawn to my attention the decision of Jacob J in *King v Walden (Inspector of Taxes)* [2001] STC 822 in which, applying the criteria as considered in the Strasbourg authorities to which I have referred, and persuaded by the analysis and reasoning of the chairman in this case, he held that the system for imposition of penalties for fraudulent or negligent

delivery of incorrect tax returns or statements is 'criminal' for the purposes of
art 6(2) of the ECHR. In doing so, he plainly went further than the decision in
this case, the reasoning in which is largely premised upon penalties in respect of
dishonesty. However, whereas the conclusions of Jacob J go further than those
which I have expressed, they are not inconsistent with them.

THE IMPLICATIONS OF THE APPLICATION OF ARTICLE 6

[80] As the chairman made clear (see [2000] V & DR 312 at 320 (para 22)), the
issue in this appeal affects a large number of appellants to the tribunal, whose
appeals await its outcome. In that respect, it should be made clear that the appeal
in this case concerns a decision upon a preliminary point of a *general* nature.
Although I have set out the bare facts of the respondents' appeals to the tribunal,
each appeal gives rise to *individual* points of procedure, in respect of which
objection is taken or certain legal consequences are said to follow which have not
been argued before this court, or indeed below. Each will call for an individual
ruling by the tribunal in the light of this court's decision. The same will be true
of the substantial number of cases awaiting disposal which have apparently raised
a yet wider variety of points said to arise on the basis that art 6 applies, not simply
to the imposition of penalties for dishonest evasion under s 60, but in relation to
other penalties, in particular under s 63 of VATA ('Penalty for misdeclaration or
neglect resulting in VAT loss for one accounting period equalling or exceeding
certain amounts').

[81] So far as s 63 is concerned, it is plain that little guidance will be afforded
by this decision. Section 63 is no more than a regulatory provision which, unlike
dishonest evasion under s 60, gives rise to no apparent criminal offence, whether
under the general law or any other provision of VATA. Further, the penalty is
limited to 15% of the VAT which would have been lost if the inaccuracy in the
return made by the taxpayer had not been discussed.

[82] We have been informed that, whereas a variety of points await disposal,
the commissioners' principal concern relates to their desire to make continued
use of the 'inducement' procedure as a method of obtaining the co-operation of
the taxpayer for the purpose of establishing the amount of tax evaded and
imposing a civil penalty discounted upon the basis of the degree of co-operation
received. It is envisaged that Customs and Excise may be vulnerable to the
tribunal excluding as inadmissible evidence obtained during an interview, or
subsequently, as a result of supplying to the taxpayer the statement of practice in
VAT Notice 730. If such rulings were to become widespread it would
significantly affect the ability of Customs and Excise successfully to defend
appeals and would threaten the basis of the whole of the civil evasion penalty
regime. Arguments have apparently already been 'flagged' to the effect that the
inducement procedure may amount to a breach of the right to silence and the
right against self-incrimination. Whether this is correct has not been argued
before us. However, I would only observe that the fears of the commissioners
seem to me likely to prove unfounded in this respect.

[83] It appears that the inducement procedure, at least as refined in December
2000, makes explicit to the taxpayer, in addition to the information supplied in
VAT Notice 730, that the civil evasion investigation is not being conducted with
a view to prosecuting the trader for VAT evasion, that the trader is not obliged to
co-operate in the Customs investigation, and it is entirely a decision for the trader
to decide whether or not to speak to the investigating officer or assist generally in
the Customs investigation. It must be remembered that the requirements of

a   art 6(1) in relation to a fair trial, together with what has been held to be the implicit recognition of a right to silence and a privilege against self-incrimination, are of a general nature and are not prescriptive of the precise means or procedural rules by which domestic law recognises and protects such rights.

[84] It by no means follows from a conclusion that art 6 applies that civil penalty proceedings are, for other domestic purposes, to be regarded as criminal *b*   and, therefore, subject to those provisions of PACE and/or the codes produced thereunder, which relate to the investigation of crime and the conduct of criminal proceedings *as defined by English law*. Any argument as to whether and how far that Act and the codes apply is one which will have to be separately considered if and when it is advanced. In this context, however, the specific provisions of s 60(4) of VATA are plainly of considerable importance. I would merely add my *c*   view that, if matters are made clear to the taxpayer on the lines indicated at [83] above at the time when the nature and effect of the inducement procedure are also made clear to him (whether by VAT Notice 730 or otherwise), it is difficult to see that there would be any breach of art 6. It also seems to me that, even if PACE were applicable, it is most unlikely that a court or tribunal would rule *d*   inadmissible under ss 76 or 78 of that Act any statements made or documents produced as a result, at any rate in the absence of exceptional circumstances. On the other hand, it follows from this decision that a person made subject to a civil penalty under s 60(1) of VATA will be entitled to the minimum rights specifically provided for in art 6(3).

e   CONCLUSION

[85] For the reasons above stated, I would dismiss this appeal.

MANCE LJ.

[86] The preliminary issue before us is whether the imposition of penalty *f*   assessments on the respondent taxpayers under s 60 of the Value Added Tax Act 1994 amounted to criminal charges for the purposes of art 6 of the European Convention for the Protection of Human Rights and Fundamental Freedoms (Rome, 4 November 1950; TS 71 (1953); Cmd 8969) (as set out in Sch 1 to the Human Rights Act 1998) (the ECHR). The VAT and Duties Tribunal was, by s 6(1) of the 1998 Act, required to act compatibly with the rights provided by art 6, *g*   and so is this court. I have had the advantage of reading in draft the judgments of both Potter LJ and Sir Martin Nourse, who express opposing views as to the correct answer to the preliminary issue. For the same reasons as those given by Potter LJ, I consider that Mr Stephen Oliver QC, the chairman of the VAT and Duties Tribunal, was correct in answering the issue affirmatively (see [2000] *h*   V & DR 312).

[87] Under s 2 of the 1998 Act the tribunal and this court are not bound by, but are obliged to take into account, the Strasbourg case law, when determining such an issue. The effect of the case law is in my view to point unequivocally towards the answer given by the tribunal below and by Potter LJ in his judgment. I refer *j*   in particular to the cases of *Öztürk v Germany* (1984) 6 EHRR 409 (a case, like the present, of a domestically 'decriminalised' offence), *Bendenoun v France* (1994) 18 EHRR 54, *AP v Switzerland* (1997) 26 EHRR 541, and *Georgiou (trading as Marios Chippery) v UK* [2001] STC 80, cited more fully in the judgment of Potter LJ. While I appreciate that there are contrary arguments which might have found favour in the European Court of Human Rights, and did find favour in some minority judgments there, I do not consider that it is appropriate now to place

this country's jurisprudence out on a limb in an area where that court has sought *a*
explicitly to develop an autonomous international test.

[88] The classification of a case as criminal for the purposes of art 6(3) of the
ECHR, using the tests established by the Strasbourg jurisprudence, is a classification
for the purposes of the ECHR only. It entitles the defendant to the safeguards
provided expressly or by implication by that article. It does not make the case
criminal for all domestic purposes. In particular, it does not, necessarily, engage *b*
protections such as those provided by the Police and Criminal Evidence Act 1984.
The submissions before us did not address this point, or, indeed, the subject of
burden of proof (although I note that no objection was even raised to a civil
burden in *Georgiou*'s case). As Mr Stephen Oliver and Potter LJ have both observed,
the precise implications under the ECHR of classification of any case as criminal *c*
for the purposes of the ECHR will have to be worked out on a case-by-case basis.

[89] The present decision might be thought to be detrimental to a sensible
policy of decriminalisation, although any stigma which might attach to convention
criminality has evidently been outweighed in the respondent taxpayers' thinking by
the perceived benefits of protections afforded during investigation and determination
of any claims to penalties. I think that it is perhaps unfortunate that the case law *d*
cited to us does not enable, and the present preliminary issue does not allow, any
more detailed analysis or conclusions with respect to the effects of treating the
present offences as criminal for convention purposes. But I remain to be convinced
that our decision will seriously undermine or disrupt the general nature of existing
procedures. *e*

[90] I agree accordingly that the appeal should be dismissed.

SIR MARTIN NOURSE.

[91] The function of the Commissioners of Customs and Excise, like that of
the Commissioners of Inland Revenue, is the assessment and collection of *f*
revenues due to the Crown. In the vast majority of cases they find that taxpayers
co-operate with them in the performance of that function, if not with enthusiasm,
at least candidly and promptly. In a minority of cases they encounter inefficiency,
negligence, deliberate indifference or even fraudulent evasion. In such cases it
becomes part of their function to enforce the payment of the unpaid tax. Only to
that extent can they be said to be a law enforcement agency. Even then enforcement *g*
is, in reality, a part of the process of collection.

[92] Until 1985 the VAT offence code provided solely for criminal offences,
both for regulatory matters and for fraud, though offences of alleged fraud were
in the great bulk of cases dealt with by monetary settlement, not prosecution, by
means of compounding. But in February 1983 there was submitted to the then *h*
Chancellor of the Exchequer the *Report of the Committee on Enforcement Powers of
the Revenue Departments* (Cmnd 8822) (the Keith Report) under the chairmanship
of Lord Keith of Kinkel, a Lord of Appeal in Ordinary. Chapter 18 of that report
was entitled 'The VAT offence code: the case for change', and it is from para
18.2.1 (p 384) that my summary of the position before 1985 is taken. It continued: *j*

'These arrangements stand in contrast to those of the Inland Revenue side,
where civil penalties are provided both for regulatory matters and for a wide
range of offences such as neglect and fraud on proof to the civil standard; and
where criminal proceedings under the mainstream criminal law are taken
only in respect of "heinous" cases of fraud.'

a

[93] At paras [37]–[45] of his judgment Potter LJ has dealt in greater detail with the VAT offence code before 1985 and set out or referred to the key passages in ch 18 of the Keith Report. Repetition is unnecessary. It is desirable only to emphasise two points and to make a third. First, the committee, having noted (p 389 (para 18.3.4)) the strong feelings of some traders and representative bodies about VAT regulatory prosecution, recommended (p 397 (para 18.4.9)) that the criminal sanction for regulatory matters in VAT should be abolished. Second, in para 18.4.16

b

(p 400) of the report the committee said:

c

'The investigation of acts of dishonesty in relation to tax matters in a "civil" style, reinforced by inducements, rather than as criminal offences under the Judges' Rules, was generally welcome to our witnesses and we heard no consistent body of criticism of the lower civil burden of proof in such cases as being unfair to the taxpayer.'

Third, the Keith Report was evidently the product of a full and careful investigation into the system of enforcing the payment of unpaid tax conducted by a committee whose abilities and combined experience well fitted them to undertake that task.

d

[94] The statutory provisions enacted pursuant to the recommendations of the Keith Committee are now found in the Value Added Tax Act 1994 (VATA) in relation to VAT and in the Finance Act 1994 (FA 94) in relation to excise duty. As Potter LJ has explained, it is only necessary to refer to VATA, the material provisions of which are fully set out in his judgment. The most important of them are ss 60(1) and 72(1). Section 60 is headed 'VAT evasion: conduct involving dishonesty'. So far

e

as material, sub-s (1) provides:

'In any case where—(a) for the purpose of evading VAT, a person does any act or omits to take any action, and (b) his conduct involves dishonesty (whether or not it is such as to give rise to criminal liability), he shall be liable … to a penalty equal to the amount of VAT evaded or, as the case may be,

f

sought to be evaded, by his conduct.'

[95] Section 72 is headed 'Offences'. Subsection (1) provides:

'If any person is knowingly concerned in, or in the taking of steps with a view to, the fraudulent evasion of VAT by him or any other person, he shall

g

be liable—(a) on summary conviction, to a penalty of the statutory maximum or of three times the amount of the VAT, whichever is the greater, or to imprisonment for a term not exceeding 6 months or to both; or (b) on conviction on indictment, to a penalty of any amount or to imprisonment for a term not exceeding 7 years or to both.'

h

[96] It is to be observed that liability to a penalty under s 60(1) depends on conduct, for the purpose of evading VAT, involving dishonesty, whether or not the conduct is such as to give rise to criminal liability. Under s 72(1) criminal liability depends on a person being knowingly concerned in, or in the taking of steps with a view to, the fraudulent evasion of VAT by himself or any other

j

person. The wording of these two provisions shows that Parliament contemplated the possibility of a person's conducting himself dishonestly for the purpose of evading VAT, but without being guilty of the fraudulent evasion of VAT. Although counsel on both sides were unable to suggest hypothetical facts which would establish liability under s 60(1) but fall short of establishing it under s 72(1), it would be most unwise to assume that there could not be conduct, for example deliberate indifference, where that would turn out to be the case.

[97]   At paras [49]–[54] of his judgment Potter LJ has given a detailed account
of the commissioners' practice in administering the post-1985 enforcement code.   *a*
Of particular importance is the inducement procedure explained at [50]. In
essence, that is a procedure which, by offering the taxpayer reductions in the
penalty, enlists his co-operation in the assessment and collection of the tax due.
Thus it exemplifies the true function of the commissioners, demonstrating that
the punishment of dishonest taxpayers is subsidiary to it.   *b*

[98]   It is against this background that we must decide the question whether
the imposition of penalties pursuant to s 60(1) of VATA (equally pursuant to
s 8(1) of FA 94) gives rise to criminal charges within the meaning of art 6(1) of the
European Convention for the Protection of Human Rights and Fundamental
Freedoms (Rome, 4 November 1950; TS 71 (1953); Cmd 8969) (as set out in Sch 1
to the Human Rights Act 1998) (the ECHR) which, so far as material, provides: *c*

> 'In the determination of his civil rights and obligations or of any criminal
> charge against him, everyone is entitled to a fair and public hearing within a
> reasonable time by an independent and impartial tribunal established by
> law.'
                                                                                  d
Implicit in the right to a fair trial, so the European Court of Human Rights has held,
are rights to disclosure and to silence and a privilege against self-incrimination.

[99]   In deciding the question we must apply the 1998 Act, for whose purposes
art 6 is one of 'the Convention rights'; see s 1(1)(a). So far as material, s 2(1)
provides:
                                                                                  e
> 'A court or tribunal determining a question which has arisen in connection
> with a Convention right must take into account any—(a) judgment, decision,
> declaration or advisory opinion of the European Court of Human Rights ...'

Reference has also been made to s 3(1) of that Act, which provides that, so far as
possible, primary and subordinate legislation must be read and given effect in a   *f*
way which is compatible with the convention rights. However, since no question
on the meaning of the United Kingdom legislation has arisen, that provision
would seem to have no application to this case.

[100]   We are required to take into account the decisions of the Strasbourg
Court. We cannot make our own decision without doing so and, in taking them
into account, we must give them due weight, even though the doctrine of stare   *g*
decisis does not apply. But it is important to emphasise that that doctrine is
inapplicable, not only between decisions of the Strasbourg Court and those of our
own courts, but also between decisions of the Strasbourg Court themselves.
While a line of Strasbourg decisions may, as they have in defining a 'criminal
charge' for the purposes of art 6(1), evince a current of opinion as to the relative   *h*
importance of the criteria to be taken into account, allowance must always be
made for cases where reason and common sense demand that it should be
re-examined.

[101]   All the Strasbourg decisions from *Engel v Netherlands (No 1)* (1976)
1 EHRR 647 to *AP v Switzerland* (1997) 26 EHRR 541 hold that three criteria are   *j*
to be taken into account in determining whether a criminal charge has been
imposed by a contracting state. They are, first, the classification of the proceedings
in domestic law; second, the nature of the offence; third, the nature and degree
of severity of the penalty that can be imposed. While it is said that these criteria
are not in practice treated as analytically distinct or as a three-stage test but as
factors to be weighed together, the more recent decisions demonstrate a

a tendency to reduce the first of them to a position of relative unimportance, even
to a point where it seems to have been paid no more than lip service. The reason
for this, as it appears, is the tension between the classification of the proceedings
in the domestic law of the contracting state and the 'autonomous Convention
meaning' which the Strasbourg Court has held must be given to the expression
'criminal charge' (see e g *Adolf v Austria* (1982) 4 EHRR 313 at 322 (para 30)).

b [102] In a number of respects the key decision for our purposes is *Öztürk v
Germany* (1984) 6 EHRR 409, where it was held that the imposition of a penalty for
a minor traffic offence which the German legislature had removed from the sphere
of the criminal law and had reclassified as a regulatory offence was nevertheless a
criminal charge for the purposes of art 6(1). In giving judgment, the court, after
reaffirming the autonomous ECHR meaning of the expression 'criminal charge'
c and the three criteria to be taken into account, acknowledged it to be clear that
the offence in question had been removed from the sphere of the criminal law by
the German legislation. The judgment continues (at 422 (paras 51–52)):

d 'Whilst the Court thus accepts the Government's arguments on this point,
it has nonetheless not lost sight of the fact that no absolute partition
separates German criminal law from the law on "regulatory offences", in
particular where there exists a close connection between a criminal offence
and a "regulatory offence". Nor has the Court overlooked that the provisions
of the ordinary law governing criminal procedure apply by analogy to
"regulatory" proceedings, notably in relation to the judicial stage, if any, of
e such proceedings ... In any event, the indications furnished by the domestic
law of the respondent State have only a relative value. The second criterion
stated above—the very nature of the offence, considered also in relation to
the nature of the corresponding penalty—represents a factor of appreciation
of greater weight.'

f The court went on to hold that the nature of the offence and the penalty that
could be imposed (a regulatory fine which, though less burdensome than a penal
fine, had retained a punitive character) were such as to render the imposition of
the penalty a criminal charge.

[103] It appears that *Öztürk*'s case is the only case in which the Strasbourg
g Court has had to consider the imposition of penalties for offences which a
contracting state has removed from the sphere of the criminal law. The court
said (at 420–421 (para 49)):

'The Convention is not opposed to States, in the performance of their task
as guardians of the public interest, both creating or maintaining a distinction
h between different categories of offences for the purposes of their domestic
law and drawing the dividing line, but it does not follow that the classification
thus made by the States is decisive for the purposes of the Convention. By
removing certain forms of conduct from the category of criminal offences
under domestic law, the law-maker may be able to serve the interests of the
j individual as well as the needs of the proper administration of justice, in
particular in so far as the judicial authorities are thereby relieved of the task of
prosecuting and punishing contraventions—which are numerous but of
minor importance—of road traffic rules. The Convention is not opposed to
the moves towards "decriminalisation" which are taking place—in extremely
varied forms—in the member States of the Council of Europe. The Government
quite rightly insisted on this point. Nevertheless, if the Contracting States

were able at their discretion, by classifying an offence as "regulatory" instead
of criminal, to exclude the operation of the fundamental clauses of Articles 6
and 7, the application of those provisions would be subordinated to their
sovereign will. A latitude extending thus far might lead to results incompatible
with the object and purpose of the Convention.'

[104] Although the decision in *Öztürk's* case went the other way and despite
the observations I have quoted from para 52 of the judgment (at 422), it is natural
to assume that the court's acknowledgment, in para 49 (at 420–421), that the
ECHR is not opposed to moves towards decriminalisation was intended to allow
for some flexibility in the importance to be attached to the first of the three
criteria. It is notable that in his dissenting opinion Judge Bernhardt said (at
437–438):

'... I agree with the present judgment and the settled case law of this Court
that the qualification of certain notions and procedures under national law
cannot be the final word. The autonomy of the Convention and its
provisions excludes any unilateral qualification which cannot be reviewed.
But this does not mean that the national qualification is without any
importance. We are here concerned with the difficult and precarious task of
drawing the borderline between the qualification by the national legal
system and the national margin of appreciation, on the one hand, and the
autonomy of the Convention provisions, on the other.'

The value of those general observations is not diminished by their having been
expressed in a dissenting opinion. I would add that, even if the doctrine of stare
decisis had been applicable, *Öztürk's* case would plainly have been distinguishable
from the present case.

[105] The respondents have relied on other decisions of the Strasbourg Court,
in particular on *Bendenoun v France* (1994) 18 EHRR 54. They have been considered
in the judgment of Potter LJ. With one exception, they do not require further
reference. Amongst other things, they hold that a penalty intended not to
compensate for damage, but to punish and deter, is characteristic of a criminal
charge and, further, that it is unnecessary for the penalties available to include
deprivation of liberty. The exception is *Georgiou (trading as Marios Chippery) v UK*
[2001] STC 80, which the chairman of the VAT and Duties Tribunal, Mr Stephen
Oliver QC, said was directly in point (see [2000] V & DR 312). That is correct in
so far as it was a decision under what is now s 60(1) of VATA. However, the court
did not have the benefit of the full and careful arguments that we have heard from
Mr Kenneth Parker QC, for the commissioners, and Miss Eleanor Sharpston QC,
for the respondents and, in regard to the first criterion, it simply noted that the
proceedings were classified as civil, rather than criminal, in our domestic law. In
my view *Georgiou's* case is not a decision to which, for present purposes, weight
need be given.

[106] I turn to consider the penalties imposed by s 60(1) of VATA in relation
to each of the three criteria.

(1) The classification of the proceedings in United Kingdom law

The penalties are expressed to be civil in nature and their imposition is subject
to an automatic right of appeal to a civil tribunal whose proceedings are governed
by the Value Added Tax Tribunals Rules, SI 1986/590. The introduction of s 60(1)
was part of a deliberate and carefully considered decriminalisation of all regulatory

and some more serious VAT offences. The more serious offences were not wholly decriminalised. Fraudulent evasion of VAT remains a criminal offence. The practice, now well established, of the commissioners in imposing penalties under s 60(1), in particular the inducement procedure, is part and parcel of their function of assessing and collecting revenues due to the Crown. The punitive and deterrent effect of the penalty system is subsidiary thereto. The system is fair, beneficial to the taxpayer and in the public interest. The imposition of a penalty does not give the taxpayer a criminal record.

(2) The nature of the offence

[107] On behalf of the commissioners Mr Parker accepted that there are certain features of the penalties which the Strasbourg decisions have identified as showing that their imposition gives rise to a criminal charge. First, they apply in principle to all citizens qua taxpayers, not just to a limited class. Second, the function of the penalties is not to compensate for the tax unpaid but to punish and deter dishonest taxpayers. Third, the imposition of the penalties requires a finding of dishonesty. While it is true that weight has been given to these features by the Strasbourg decisions, the second of them entails a very superficial view of the present case. Though the penalties are punitive and deterrent in the sense that they are not compensatory, they have the more profound and realistic function of assisting the collection of unpaid tax.

(3) The nature and the degree of severity of the penalty

[108] No sentence of imprisonment can be imposed under s 60(1). The maximum penalty is the amount of the VAT evaded or sought to be evaded. But it is subject to reduction by means of the inducement procedure. In the cases before the court there have been reductions of 10% in two of them and of 50% in the third. While a reduction of, say, 50% in a case where the amount of the tax evaded is large will still result in a penalty of considerable amount, it can hardly be said to be disproportionate to the amount of the tax evaded.

[109] What ought to be the approach of an English court to the question we have to decide? In relation to the second and third criteria the penalties are not so serious as to require their imposition to be treated, without more, as a criminal charge. Everything seems to depend on whether it is open to us to attribute a greater importance to the first criterion than has been the tendency of the more recent Strasbourg decisions. In my judgment it is. We were consistently told by those who advocated the incorporation of the ECHR in our law that it would enable our courts to make a beneficial contribution to its jurisprudence. In my opinion that contribution ought to start with a recognition of the widely differing traditions and institutions of the contracting states. What ought to be treated as a criminal charge in some of them may not need to be so treated in others. In this country we have, since 1689, developed a system of civil administration in which the executive, being subject to review by the courts, acts responsibly and fairly towards the individual citizen, the protection of whose rights is an integral part of the system.

[110] The assessment and collection of revenues due to the Crown is an important part of our civil administration. The VAT penalty system is fair, beneficial to the taxpayer and in the public interest. The rights of the taxpayer are already adequately protected. It would be folly, in the name of an abstraction, to introduce a further and unnecessary protection, whose practical consequence

would be to impair the efficiency of the system at no advantage to the taxpayer. *a*
For my part, I decline to do so.

[111] I would allow the appeal and make whatever declaration is appropriate
to reflect the view I have expressed.

Appeal dismissed.

Kate O'Hanlon   Barrister

a # R (on the application of the Inland Revenue Commissioners) v Crown Court at Kingston

[2001] EWHC Admin 581

b

QUEEN'S BENCH DIVISION, DIVISIONAL COURT

KENNEDY LJ AND STANLEY BURNTON J

3, 4, 24 JULY 2001

c

Crown Court – Practice – Application for dismissal of charges – Prosecution case depending on documentary evidence – Applicant applying for dismissal of charge on grounds that jury could not properly convict – Judge concluding that prosecution evidence not giving rise to necessary inferences as to applicant's guilt or to inferences that were compelling – Whether judge usurping role of jury – Criminal Justice Act 1987, s 6.

d

J, a partner in a well-known firm of accountants, played a major role in advising on, and implementing, a tax-saving scheme for one of the firm's clients. If operated legitimately, the scheme would have been tax-effective. However, the Revenue alleged that various transactions supposedly carried out under the scheme were fictitious, existing only on paper and manufactured for the purpose

e of defrauding it. J was charged with conspiracy to defraud the Revenue, but denied any knowledge of the alleged frauds. He applied for the charges to be dismissed pursuant to s 6[a] of the Criminal Justice Act 1987, which required the judge, on such an application, to dismiss a charge 'if it appears to him' that the evidence against the applicant would not be sufficient for a jury properly to

f convict him. The judge considered a number of documents relied upon by the prosecution to establish that J did have the requisite knowledge. In a brief ruling, he stated that, on studying each document in its context and taking into account the way in which J had dealt with each matter that raised suspicion, it became clear that a great deal of the prosecution evidence pointed specifically away from

g his guilt. The judge concluded that most of the evidence did not enable the necessary inference to be drawn from the primary facts except in one or two cases, that even in those cases the general inferences were not compelling and that there were no inferences which a reasonable man would unerringly find compelling. He therefore ruled that, taken as a whole, it would not be safe to

h leave the case to the jury. On its application to the Divisional Court for judicial review of the judge's decision, the Revenue did not contend that his ruling was perverse, but instead submitted that he had applied an incorrect test to the documentary evidence. In particular, the Revenue contended that the judge had usurped the role of the jury by deciding for himself the correct inference to be

j drawn from a document rather than considering whether an inference of guilt

---

a Section 6, so far as material, provides: '(1) Where notice of transfer has been given, any person to whom the notice relates, at any time before he is arraigned ... may apply ... to the Crown Court ... for the charge, or any of the charges, to be dismissed; and the judge shall dismiss a charge ... if it appears to him that the evidence against the applicant would not be sufficient for a jury properly to convict him ...'

was capable of being drawn. It further contended that the judge had failed to give
adequate reasons for his decision.   *a*

Held – (1) The test to be applied on an application to dismiss charges was that
prescribed by s 6 of the 1987 Act, namely did it appear to the judge that the
evidence would not be sufficient for a jury properly to convict the defendant?
That section clearly required the judge to take into account the whole of the   *b*
evidence against a defendant and to decide whether he was satisfied that it was
sufficient for a jury properly to convict the defendant. It was not appropriate for
the judge to view any evidence in isolation from its context and other evidence,
any more than it was appropriate to derive a meaning from a single document or
the other connected documents before the court. Moreover, the judge was not   *c*
bound to deal with the application under s 6 by assuming that a jury might make
every possible inference capable of being drawn from a document against the
defendant. Section 6 expressly provided that the judge would decide not only
whether there was any evidence to go to a jury, but whether that evidence was
sufficient for a jury properly to convict. That exercise required the judge to assess
the weight of the evidence. That was not to say that the judge was entitled to   *d*
substitute himself for the jury. The question for him was not whether the
defendant should be convicted on the evidence put forward by the prosecution,
but the sufficiency of that evidence. Where the evidence was largely documentary,
and the case depended on the inferences or conclusions to be drawn from it, the
judge had to assess the inferences or conclusions that the prosecution proposed   *e*
to ask the jury to draw from the documents, and decide whether it appeared to
him that the jury could properly draw those inferences and come to those
conclusions. A judge's conclusion as to the weight to be given to any evidence
and his conclusion that the evidence against the defendant was or was not
sufficient for a jury properly to convict him could only be impugned if they could   *f*
be shown to be conclusions that no reasonable judge could have reached.
Moreover, the words in s 6(1), 'if it appears to [the judge]', made it clear that
Parliament intended the judge to have a wide margin of appreciation in that
respect. It followed in the instant case that the Revenue's challenge could
succeed only if it established that the judge's decision was perverse. Looking at
the evidence as a whole, it could not be said that the judge's decision was perverse *g*
(see [16]–[18], [35], below).

(2) When giving reasons a judge, even in a case dealt with in considerable
detail, was not obliged in his ruling to consider every document referred to and
to summarise his conclusions on it. In any event, it could only be in a very
exceptional case that the Divisional Court would remit a case to the Crown Court   *h*
for the judge to give further reasons. It should do so only if there were strong
grounds for believing that the judge's decision was one that he could not properly
have arrived at. However, if it were established that his decision was one not
properly open to him, there would be no point in requiring the judge to elaborate
on his reasons; his decision could be quashed immediately. In the instant case,   *j*
the judge's reasons, though extremely brief, made clear the facts that he had
taken into account in coming to his decision and his conclusion that the
documentary evidence was insufficiently unequivocal to enable a jury properly
to convict. Accordingly, the application would be dismissed (see [36], [37],
below).

Notes
a For applications to the Crown Court for the dismissal of charges, see 11(2) *Halsbury's Laws* (4th edn reissue) para 863.

For the Criminal Justice Act 1987, s 6, see 12 *Halsbury's Statutes* (4th edn) (1997 reissue) 999.

b **Cases referred to in judgment**
Associated Provincial Picture Houses Ltd v Wednesbury Corp [1947] 2 All ER 680, [1948] 1 KB 223, CA.
Euro Hotel (Belgravia) Ltd, Re [1975] 3 All ER 1075.
R v Central Criminal Court, ex p Director of Serious Fraud Office [1993] 2 All ER 399, [1993] 1 WLR 949, DC.
c *R v Oxford City Magistrates, ex p Berry* [1987] 1 All ER 1244, [1988] QB 507, [1987] 3 WLR 643, DC.

Application for judicial review
The claimant, the Commissioners of Inland Revenue, applied for judicial review
d of the decision of Judge Hucker in the Crown Court at Kingston on 26 October 2000 allowing an application by the interested party, Robin Wayne John, for the dismissal, under s 6 of the Criminal Justice Act 1987, of charges against him of conspiracy to defraud the Revenue. The facts are set out in the judgment of the court.

e *Richard Sutton QC, Mark Lucraft* and *Michelle Nelson* (instructed by the *Solicitor to the Inland Revenue*) for the Revenue.
Alun Jones QC and *Hugo Keith* (instructed by *Simons Muirhead & Burton*) for Mr John.

Cur adv vult

f 24 July 2001. The following judgment of the court was delivered.

STANLEY BURNTON J.

Introduction
g [1] In these proceedings the Commissioners of Inland Revenue seek an order to quash the ruling of Judge Hucker at the Crown Court at Kingston dismissing, pursuant to s 6 of the Criminal Justice Act 1987, all of the charges against the interested party, Robin Wayne John. The charges in question were of conspiracy to defraud the Revenue, and related to a tax-saving scheme operated at the instigation of, and principally for the benefit of, Ian Leaf.
h [2] The distinction between lawful tax avoidance and illegal tax evasion is well known. Tax-saving schemes that involve transactions having little or no commercial benefit apart from the scheme are a common feature of commercial life. In the absence of statutory criminal prohibitions, the transactions involved in the scheme and the scheme itself are lawful. Whether the scheme is effective
j depends on the provisions of the tax legislation in question. Tax saving crosses the border from lawful to criminal when it involves the deliberate and dishonest making of false statements to the Revenue. A criminal scheme may involve the dishonest bringing into existence or use of documents evidencing transactions that never took place, or the creation and use of documents that contain some other misrepresentation of fact, such as the date when they were executed or

came into effect. The Inland Revenue allege that the scheme used by Mr Leaf on the advice and with the knowing participation of Mr John was such a criminal scheme.

[3] During the period covered by the charges, Mr John was a partner of Ernst & Young, the well-known firm of accountants, and was based in London. He specialised in advising on tax-saving schemes. Ian Leaf was resident in Switzerland. He ran a company in Rolle, Switzerland, the name of which was, ironically, Prudential SA. He was a client of Ernst & Young.

[4] The scheme to which the charges relate involved the purchase by companies controlled by Mr Leaf of companies (referred to as 'targets') registered in England the assets of which were solely, or almost solely, cash, and which had substantial corporation tax liabilities. The price paid for a target reflected its tax liabilities as well as its cash assets. The scheme involved, among other steps, that relevant members of the group of companies into which the target passed should be resident in the United Kingdom for a certain period, and in Guernsey at other times; that after acquisition the target should engage in large-scale profitable trading on the foreign exchange market; that it should borrow very large sums from an independently-owned bank, thereby incurring proportionately large liabilities for interest; and the declaration of substantial dividends by the target justified by its profits on its foreign exchange dealings. The apparent result of the implementation of the scheme was to eliminate the tax liabilities of the target companies, or even apparently to entitle them to repayment of large sums previously paid in respect of their tax liabilities. The amounts involved during the operation of the scheme were enormous: the total tax which was not paid to the Inland Revenue or repaid by it exceeded £60m.

[5] The target companies were renamed by Mr Leaf after their acquisition. There were three groups of target companies that feature in this case. (There were others, but it is unnecessary to mention them in this judgment.) Each company in a group was given a name common to other companies in that group. The three groups were the Kinetic, the Yorkstone and the Zenith groups. In each group there was a Holdings company (eg Kinetic Holdings Ltd) that held the shares of the subsidiary companies in the group; an Investments company (eg Kinetic Investments Ltd) and a Subsidiaries company (eg Kinetic Subsidiaries Ltd). They were purportedly lent enormous sums of money by Allied Bank Corp (ABC), a bank incorporated in Nauru controlled by Mr Leaf; they purportedly prepaid interest to ABC on their borrowings; and they purportedly traded on a huge scale in foreign exchange through other Leaf companies, Guild Corp Ltd (GCL) and Gilt-Edged Investments Ltd (GIL), acting as their trading advisers and brokers.

[6] The Inland Revenue allege that Mr John advised and played a major part in establishing the tax-saving scheme in question. For the purposes of this application, they accept that the scheme was tax-efficient: that is to say, that if the various transactions involved in it had been properly carried out, the tax liabilities of the targets would have been lawfully reduced or eliminated, and in appropriate circumstances repayments of tax would have become due. However, they allege that the transactions involved in the scheme, or at least certain essential ones, were not carried out at all: they were fictions or shams. In fact, they allege, there were no large loans from a bank to the targets: the bank in question was a company controlled by Mr Leaf that did not have at its disposal assets of the size required by the scheme as it was purportedly implemented. In fact, they allege, there was no foreign exchange dealing, only the creation of contract notes and

a statements of account in the names of Guild and Gilt that were used to represent to the Inland Revenue that there had been such trading.

[7] In addition, the Inland Revenue allege that the residence of the targets did not move as required by the scheme: at all times they were controlled by Mr Leaf, through directors resident in Guernsey who acted as his nominees to conceal the true centre of management of the target companies, on which the place of their residence for the purposes of the relevant tax liabilities depended. They also
b allege that the date of the purported transfer of management and control of the companies to Guernsey was retrospectively and dishonestly changed by the replacement of original board minutes (which were destroyed to avoid detection of the alteration) with a written resolution of the board purporting to have been passed on 1 December 1992 evidencing a decision to transfer management and
c control on that date. In fact, they allege, the board did not pass such a resolution on that date or at all: it had previously decided, on the instructions of Mr Leaf, to transfer management and control to Guernsey at an earlier date, as had been evidenced by the replaced and destroyed original minutes. The substitute written resolution of the board of Kinetic Subsidiaries, bearing the date 1 December 1992,
d came into existence after 22 February 1993 and was submitted to the Inland Revenue on 14 May 1993.

[8] Mr Leaf is in custody in Italy as a result of proceedings to extradite him to London. For the purposes of the present application, it has been assumed that the Inland Revenue allegations against him are well founded, i e that the transactions apparently carried out by the target companies were in fact shams, fictions
e existing on paper only that were manufactured for the purpose of defrauding the Revenue, and that the Guernsey directors did act as his nominees, so that, contrary to what was represented to the Inland Revenue, the true centre of management and control of the targets following their acquisition was Switzerland; and that these shams and deliberate misrepresentations were orchestrated by,
f and carried out for the benefit of, Mr Leaf. If these frauds did occur, the Revenue lost a very substantial sum as a result of the fraud of Mr Leaf and those who knowingly participated in his fraud. In this judgment we refer to these alleged and assumed frauds; but nothing in this judgment should be taken to indicate that the Inland Revenue proved them to us, or as in any way prejudging the prosecution case against Mr Leaf.
g

The judge's ruling on the application to dismiss

[9] Mr John accepts that he played a major role in advising on the tax-saving scheme and in implementing it. However, he denies that he knew that the transactions carried out by the target companies after their acquisition by Mr Leaf
h were not genuine, or that false documents were being submitted to the Inland Revenue. For the purposes of the application made on his behalf to Judge Hucker, the only real issue was whether the prosecution had shown that a jury could properly conclude that Mr John knew that he was assisting in the perpetration of frauds on the Revenue. His knowledge was the central, indeed the only live, issue.

j [10] The hearing of Mr John's application for dismissal took four days. The judge was taken to numerous documents and to the witness statements relied on by the prosecution to establish Mr John's knowledge of and participation in the fraudulent scheme. In his ruling, Judge Hucker stated:

> '7. It is necessary before considering the development of the defence submission to consider the basis of the prosecution case and set it out in outline.

8. There is one area from which it clearly does not emanate, and that is
the statements of witnesses included in the transfer. I am wholly satisfied *a*
about this and will spend no further time considering them—save to note
that at first blush it is difficult, (to put it no higher) to understand why a
number of the prosecution witnesses do not find themselves in the same
position as Mr John.'

[11] The judge then described the tax-saving scheme and the fraud, and *b*
continued:

'9. Robin John advised in relation to the scheme at the outset, and then as
is clear from the documentation, advised on the format and style of many of
the supporting documents for the fraud—contract notes, loan agreements,
and even the appearance of bank statements.' *c*

He then listed a number of documents that he regarded as representing
individually and in total the high point of the prosecution case, and a group of
documents that the Crown said went directly to fraud. In his conclusions, he
stated as follows:
d
'16. At the outset of my consideration of this case, and having read the
skeleton arguments in full, the witness statements and the very full "Statement
of Evidence" prepared by Mr Sutton and his two junior counsel—it seemed to
me that I would be indicating that there would be more than sufficient
inferences to be drawn, of a compelling nature, that would point to criminal
conduct in most, if not *all* transfer charges—sufficient to be tried by a jury. *e*
17. However, even prior to hearing Mr Jones and during Mr Sutton's
opening on the dismissal application there began to emerge lurking doubts.
The more slowly each document was studied and put into context—even
when accompanied by an expert commentary by Mr Sutton, what was once
a clear landscape seemed to cloud over, or at least become misty. At this *f*
juncture I asked questions as to what did either this or that really mean?
There can be little doubt that many ordinary sensible people (oft quoted in
legal contexts—both civil and criminal in different ways) could look at the
history of this case and concentrating specifically on Robin John, and
assessing the financial figures that genuinely read like telephone numbers
could have their *suspicions* raised to an extent that might be perceived as *g*
conclusive proof of guilt.
18. It is when Mr Jones dealt with each matter point by point—head on,
that it became clear that a great deal of the prosecution evidence points
specifically *away* from guilt. Very often the closer each point is examined the
clearer this point becomes. *h*
19. For example:
19.1 Why should only one advisor not be alerted to potential fraud
and/or dishonesty when other reputable advisors were not?
19.2 Why should Mr John only be one of many—kept in separate
compartments and held at arms' length? *j*
19.3 Why should the advice tendered be open to examination by other
advisors—or really anybody else generally?
19.4 Why should *future* advice tendered to wholly independent directors
of high probity and integrity—when all they had to do was to pick up a
phone and speak to the Inland Revenue or the police *or* their own solicitors

a or accountants? In my judgment nobody acting fraudulently or dishonestly upon the scale as alleged in this case would *dare* to casually fax the material I have seen, to be studied by any passing person. (There were no confidential markings, envelopes or codes used for critical material. Further, any partner in Ernst & Young could have had access.)

b 19.5 Why should Mr John risk a whole series of chartered or certified accountants starting an investigation of their own volition e g J Lewis ...?

20. I conclude that my preliminary view of this case against Robin John, was mistaken and that most of the evidence does not provide the necessary inference to be drawn from primary facts except in one or two cases ... *and even here* the general inferences to be drawn are not compelling. Further there are no inferences which a reasonable man would, unerringly find

c compelling. Taken as a whole, it would not be safe to leave the transfer case to a jury. They could *only* convict on the basis of speculation and prejudice. I allow the application to dismiss.'

[12] It was not in issue before us that this court has jurisdiction to review a decision of a Crown Court judge on an application under s 6 of the 1987 Act on the

d normal grounds for judicial review. However, only in exceptional circumstances should this court interfere with a decision by a trial judge under s 6. In *R v Central Criminal Court, ex p Director of Serious Fraud Office* [1993] 2 All ER 399 at 407, [1993] 1 WLR 949 at 958, Woolf LJ said:

e 'I would however emphasise that I do not anticipate the courts being prepared as a matter of discretion to give leave to make a s 6 application except in the exceptional case. The jurisdiction should clearly only be exercised in extremely limited circumstances. In this contention I would draw particular attention to the comments of May LJ in *R v Oxford City Justices, ex p Berry* [1987] 1 All ER 1244 at 1248, [1988] QB 507 at 512–513 with

f regard to the judicial review of a decision of the justices to commit a defendant for trial. Normally the assessment of the judge of the merits of the proceedings should be regarded as conclusive. In accord with the normal approach to judicial review it will not be part of the function of this court to second guess the judge who has heard the application.'

g Pill J agreed that 'the jurisdiction should be exercised only in extremely limited circumstances' (see [1993] 2 All ER 399 at 409, [1993] 1 WLR 949 at 960).

[13] The Inland Revenue submit that the judge erred in three essential respects: in disregarding the evidence contained in the witness statements; in applying an incorrect test to the documentary evidence; and in failing to give adequate

h reasons for his decision. They have not expressly submitted that the judge reached a conclusion that no reasonable tribunal correctly applying the law could have arrived at: ie they have not alleged that his ruling was perverse. While defending the judge's approach to the evidence, Mr Jones submitted that in substance Mr Sutton was seeking to appeal the judge's decision, and to have a

j rehearing of the application to dismiss, a procedure which goes beyond the powers of a reviewing court.

The witness statements

[14] The witness statements before the judge evidenced the lack of genuine foreign exchange trading and the absence of genuine loans to the targets by ABC.

They also evidenced that the Guernsey directors of the target companies were reputable persons who had in fact acted in accordance with Mr Leaf's wishes. *a* The statements evidenced the role of Mr John in advising on the tax-saving scheme and its implementation. However, none of the witness statements evidenced that Mr John had known that any transactions purportedly carried out by the targets were fictitious or that he had known of facts from which his knowledge of the fraud could be inferred. The prosecution case as to his knowledge of the fraudulent nature *b* of the scheme as carried out by Mr Leaf depends on the documentary evidence put before the court. Given that the issue before the judge was Mr John's knowledge of the fraud, he was right to say, as he did in para 8 of his ruling, that the prosecution case did not emanate from the witness statements. There is nothing in the first point.

c

The judge's approach to the documentary evidence

[15] Mr Sutton criticised the judge for failing to distinguish between direct documentary evidence and circumstantial evidence. He submitted that the judge treated all of the evidence as circumstantial, leading to inferences, instead of direct, which it was. Furthermore, in relation to inferences, Mr Sutton submitted *d* that the judge erred in deciding for himself what was the correct inference to draw from a document rather than considering whether an inference of guilt was capable of being drawn, and dealing with the application for dismissal on the basis that it was for the jury to decide whether or not that was the correct inference to draw in this case. Paragraph 5.6 of Mr Sutton's skeleton for this court stated:

e

'The judge's task at dismissal is to determine whether the inferences that the prosecution asks the jury to draw are capable of being sustained in the light of all the evidence. If they are, it is for the jury to decide whether they are prepared to draw those inferences.'

In his submissions to us, he contended that it was not for the judge to weigh up *f* inferences and probabilities as he did in para 19 of his ruling, and that that was to usurp the function of the jury.

[16] We do not think that the judge did err in these respects. The judge did not treat the documentary evidence as circumstantial. The documentary evidence contained no admission of fraud by Mr John, and nothing that indisputably *g* informed him of the frauds committed by Mr Leaf or showed knowledge of or knowing participation in the frauds. The prosecution case depends on the inferences to be drawn from the documents, as the judge rightly stated. The test to be applied by the judge on the application to dismiss was that prescribed by s 6: did it appear to him that the evidence against Mr John would not be sufficient for a jury properly to convict him? In our view, the statute clearly requires the judge *h* to take into account the whole of the evidence against a defendant, and to decide whether he is satisfied that it was sufficient for a jury properly to convict the defendant. This is what the judge did. On an application under s 6, it is not appropriate for the judge to view any evidence in isolation from its context and other evidence, any more than it is appropriate to derive a meaning from a single *j* document or from a number of documents without regard to the remainder of the document or the other connected documents before the court. We reject the argument that the judge was bound to deal with the application under s 6 by assuming that a jury might make every possible inference capable of being drawn from a document against the defendant. Section 6 expressly provides that the

a judge will decide not only whether there is any evidence to go to a jury, but whether that evidence is sufficient for a jury properly to convict. That exercise requires the judge to assess the weight of the evidence. This is not to say that the judge is entitled to substitute himself for the jury. The question for him is not whether the defendant should be convicted on the evidence put forward by the prosecution, but the sufficiency of that evidence. Where the evidence is largely *b* documentary, and the case depends on the inferences or conclusions to be drawn from it, the judge must assess the inferences or conclusions that the prosecution propose to ask the jury to draw from the documents, and decide whether it appears to him that the jury could properly draw those inferences and come to those conclusions.

[17] Mr Sutton also submitted that the judge erred in law in failing to give *c* proper weight to the evidence and in concluding that the case could not be safely left to the jury. As mentioned in the previous paragraph, on an application under s 6, it is for the judge to determine the weight to be given to the evidence against the defendant. His conclusion as to the weight to be given to any evidence, and his conclusion that the evidence against the defendant is or is not sufficient for a *d* jury properly to convict him, can only be impugned if they can be shown to be conclusions that no reasonable judge could have come to. This court cannot interfere if the decision of the judge was within the range of decisions open to a reasonable judge properly directing himself as to the law. Moreover, the words in s 6(1) 'if it appears to (the judge)' make it clear that Parliament intended the judge to have a wide margin of appreciation in this respect (cf *Ex p Director of the* *e* *Serious Fraud Office*).

[18] It follows that this application can succeed only if the Inland Revenue can establish that the judge's decision was perverse, ie unreasonable in the *Wednesbury* sense (see *Associated Provincial Picture Houses Ltd v Wednesbury Corp* [1947] 2 All ER 680, [1948] 1 KB 223). As mentioned above, this is a burden they *f* have not expressly taken on themselves. We agree with Mr Jones that the Inland Revenue's submissions seek to classify the judge's decision as to the inferences that a jury could properly draw from the documentary evidence as errors of law. We none the less propose to consider the documentary evidence and the question whether the judge was entitled to come to his conclusion.

g *The documentary evidence*

[19] We do not propose to discuss all of the numerous documents referred to in the course of argument, let alone the very large number of documents in the so-called core bundles placed before us, the very great majority of which were never referred to. We shall confine ourselves to those which in our view are the *h* most significant.

[20] Before coming to the documents, some general comments are called for. The first relates to the use of so-called 'nominee' directors, usually in offshore jurisdictions. (The expression 'nominee director' is to be avoided, since it confuses directors who are nominated by shareholders, and who properly carry out *j* their responsibilities as directors, and those who are appointed by shareholders and only do as they are instructed by the person who appointed them.) It is a feature of modern commercial life that many companies have their place of residence in offshore jurisdictions purely in order to avoid tax which would be payable if the company were located in the United Kingdom. Corporate residence depends on the location of the central management and control of the company. Inevitably,

persons who live onshore wish to own companies that reside offshore. For this
purpose, they may arrange for the appointment of directors of the company who *a*
themselves reside in the offshore jurisdiction in question. Notwithstanding the
ultimate 'foreign' ownership of the shares of the company, it will be resident for
tax purposes in the offshore jurisdiction in question if the appointed directors
genuinely determine its affairs in that jurisdiction. If, however, they simply obey
the instructions of the ultimate owner of the company's shares who remains in *b*
another jurisdiction, the central management and control, and therefore the
residence of the company for the purposes of its tax liabilities, will be the location
of the ultimate owner of its shares. The difficulty here is to distinguish between
the situation in which the directors act as mere ciphers, simply doing as they are
told by the ultimate owner of the company, and the situation in which the
directors have explained to them by the ultimate owner of the company's shares *c*
that certain transactions are in the interests of the company, and decide on the
basis of the information given to them that the company should enter into them.
In the latter situation, the company can genuinely claim to be resident offshore;
in the former situation, its offshore residence is not genuine, but a false sham.
The line between them is a very nice one, as the Inland Revenue no doubt *d*
appreciates, and as do those involved in the minimising of tax by locating
companies in offshore jurisdictions, including the professional directors of offshore
companies. That line features large in the case against Mr John. It may be
impossible for someone who is not present at the board meetings of a company,
and who is not told how the board in fact takes its decisions, to know on which
side of the line the company operates. It is not alleged that Mr John attended *e*
board meetings of the target companies in Guernsey or that he was informed by
their directors how they took their decisions.

[21] It is also necessary to comment on the use of pre-prepared minutes of
board meetings. Minutes of both board and general company meetings are often
drafted in advance of the meetings to which they relate. There is nothing *f*
improper in the use of such drafts, provided the meeting does deal with the
business before it in the manner indicated in the draft, and that, in the case of a
board meeting, the directors present do have the discussions and make the
decisions indicated by the draft. It is one thing for directors to take into account
the wishes of the ultimate shareholder of their company or the advice of its
advisors, as indicated by a draft resolution; it is another for them to act without *g*
regard to the company's interests or their own judgment, but solely because they
are instructed to do so by their ultimate shareholder.

[22] The prosecution allege that the Guernsey residents who were appointed
as directors of the target companies at the instigation of Mr Leaf were mere
ciphers, acting solely on the instructions of Mr Leaf, and known to be so by *h*
Mr John; and that Mr John was a knowing party to the false representations made
to the Inland Revenue as to the place of residence of the companies. For this
purpose they rely on the document that causes us the greatest concern in this
case. It is one of the documents referred to by the judge as one of a group that
the Crown said went directly to fraud. It is a note of a meeting in February 1993 *j*
at which Mr John was present, sent to him by Ms Reiter of Prudential by fax dated
22 February 1993. Mr John is referred to in the note by his initials, RWJ. Mr John
certainly received the note, since he annotated it in his handwriting. In it,
Guernsey was referred to as GSY; a question mark was used as a wild card. The
relevant part of the note is as follows, with italics added by us:

'1. GENERAL

... b. *Transfer of control: RWJ/MRJ/CER agreed that the existing date on which Kinetic, Yorkstone and Zenith purportedly moved their control to GSY is incorrect, as it took place prior to the end of the relevant accounting period and creates a problem for group relief (see 1d for details). It was agreed that the control of KIL, KSL, YIL, YSL, ZIL and ZSL should move to the end of the respective accounting periods.* RWJ suggested leaving the control transfer of KHL, YHL and ZHL on their original dates. The problem is that it would hard for ?IL and ?SL to say that they are not controlled from GSY if ?HL is so controlled and they have the same sole director. RWJ suggested that ?IL and ?SL might appoint new directors to rebut that presumption. However, on reflexion (sic), an attempt retrospectively to appoint new Directors would seem equally as artificial, particularly as they were not mentioned in the subsequently filed Annual Returns, as to try to claim that Garvey managed GCL's operations as of 1.1.92.

Therefore we propose the following:

i *to transfer the control of ?HL, ?IL and ?SL on the same date, being the first day of the new accounting period.* We will therefore not need to appoint supplemental directors for ?IL and ?SL.

ii For the future, we should follow RWJ's memo of April 1992 by transferring control of ?SL to GSY immediately after acquisition. RWJ to reconfirm that it is acceptable to transfer the control of ?HL and ?IL to GSY prior to purchasing ?SL.

iii We should leave all appointments and resignations of directors unchanged (ie leave the GSY company as sole director). *However, we should change the text of existing board minutes in order to clarify that the date of the transfer of control took place after the end of the accounting period and to confirm the place where these meetings occurred (ie not in Guernsey).* RWJ to confirm that if the meetings took place eg in Sark, the IR might argue that control was not in the UK, but will not be able to argue that the companies were controlled by GSY.

The result of this is substantially to reduce the number of artificial steps. *RWJ to confirm that copies of all superceded minutes currently kept by Ernst & Young (EYG) and or the directors will be returned to us uncopied. CER will then liase with W Hunter from EYG for details.*

c. UK trading: RWJ/MRJ/CER discussed abandoning UK trading through Guild Corporation Ltd (GCL), that is dispensing with the services of Mr Garvey altogether and, except for Kinetic and Yorkstone where contract notes already went out, reversing the GCL transactions ...

Therefore we propose the following:

i. Mr Garvey will not have been a manager of GCL prior to 1.1.93. However, his appointment as director from 1.1.93 will remain valid.

ii. We will not try to deny the existence of previous GCL activities. We believe that it would be difficult for the IR to argue that this was not UK trading as GCL is a UK company and will accept tax liability on its profits ...

v. For the future, we should make sure that the UK activity is more substantive. This means e.g. transfer a small amount of money to a real broker who will execute a significant volume of commodities trading. RWJ to assist.'

[23] The passages we have italicised certainly are capable of leading to the inference that those present at the meeting proposed to bring into existence board minutes of the companies in question that falsely represented that they had decided to transfer control to Guernsey at the end of their respective accounting periods, when in fact the directors had already decided to and had transferred control during their accounting periods. The inference of dishonesty is supported by the express concern that copies of the existing board minutes be destroyed. That paragraph of the note was annotated by Mr John 'Do (it) yourself'. The proposal was ultimately implemented not by the creation of board minutes, but by the submission by at least one of the companies, via its auditors, to the Inland Revenue of a written resolution of the board. The inference of dishonesty also receives support from the reason reportedly given for not backdating the appointment of new directors of the Investment and Subsidiary companies, namely that the companies had submitted annual returns that did not mention their appointments: ie the backdating of the appointments might be noticed. Those at the meeting similarly seem to have contemplated the backdating of the appointment of Mr Garvey as manager of GCL to a date prior to the true date of his appointment.

[24] The reference in the last sentence of the above extract to 'a real broker' may be innocuous: it may contrast that real broker with GCL and GIL who, at least prior to Mr Garvey's appointment, had no broker on their staff and therefore could only trade in foreign exchange if they in turn employed a 'real' broker.

[25] However, this document has to be read in the context of earlier documents that show that Mr John was informed that there had been or was genuine trading in foreign exchange, that he was concerned that there should be genuine trading and that he was equally concerned that the Guernsey directors should be men of known integrity. In his draft report on the scheme, sent to Mr Leaf on 6 March 1992, Mr John advised Mr Leaf:

'It is important that the directors of Target have the necessary blend of seniority and experience to rebut any suggestion that they are merely ciphers. To this end we suggest that in addition to (say) a partner from the St Peter Port Office of Ernst & Young, that Mr Leaf is also a director of the company, and that such decisions as are required for the company are actually taken in Guernsey.'

There were further discussions of the proposed directors in Mr John's fax to Mr Leaf of 8 May 1992 and in Mr Leaf's fax to Mr John of 28 May 1992:

'Stephen (Harlow, of E&Y Guernsey) has fortunately proposed an ex-manager of Standard Chartered: whilst he is perhaps not quite of the same calibre as the first chap, he is equally not a typical nominee.'

[26] The directors appointed to the target companies included Mr David Le Maitre, who had been principal in Ernst & Young Guernsey and who signed a number of the misleading resolutions of the companies. He is a prosecution witness whose honesty has not been questioned. Two other directors who signed relevant minutes, Mr Mallett and Mr Willis, are also prosecution witnesses of unquestioned honesty. The point is made by Mr Jones, on behalf of Mr John, that Mr John was entitled to expect the directors of the targets to act honestly, and only to sign a revised minute if it gave a true account of the business conducted at the meeting to which it related. On this basis, it is suggested that Mr John must

a   have thought that the original minutes, evidencing a decision to transfer control during an accounting period, misstated what had been decided at the meetings in question. The original minutes were to be destroyed, it is suggested, to avoid the practical problems involved in having two inconsistent sets of minutes in existence rather than for fear of discovery that the later minute was a backdated alteration of history.

b   [27] Mr Sutton also relied on Mr John's fax to Mr Leaf of 6 March 1992 as showing that Mr John was aware that the transactions envisaged by the scheme would be shams, and certainly was alive to the possibility that they might be shams. Mr John stated:

c   '1. I would draw your attention to the point in the general comments about whether these are real transactions. When you start to look at the numbers involved for a company with significant tax capacity, your borrowings add up to a total that looks significant, even in relation to the national debt. This being so, it rather begs the question "did they happen". Despite the level of documentation, and I appreciate that I am not familiar

d   with the banking and investment arrangements you have, but the question which springs to my mind, and no doubt to that of the Inland Revenue, in that on such large sums of money even a very small margin would be a great deal, and the bank would have to allocate a considerable amount of capital: indeed not that many banks could accommodate the transactions. In this

e   case there is a suspicion that the transaction is a sham and whilst I am not suggesting that this is the case there is certainly a prima facie case for suggesting it. This being so, the simplicity of procedure 3 and to some extent procedure 4 makes it rather too easy for the Revenue to take the point. At least on procedures 1 and 2 money is being borrowed by one person and then lent to another and the other person uses it for a securities trade. Whilst not

f   providing complete protection to the accusation that they are sham transactions, it certainly does not make it any worse. In view of this I think that you might be better to stick with procedures 1 and 2 even though it does involve an extra company.'

[28] However, in the draft report enclosed with that fax, Mr John advised:

g   'The temptation for the arrangements under consideration is that given the enormous sums required for borrowing, capitalisation etc, money does not actually pass between Bank, Funding, Target etc to save on transmission difficulties etc. If money does not actually pass between the parties then arguably, (say), Funding has not had the use of the money. It was held in

h   Re Euro Hotels (Belgravia) Ltd ([1975] 3 All ER 1075) that for a payment to amount to "interest of money" there must in general be a sum by reference to which the "interest" is to be ascertained, due to the person entitled to the interest. It will be readily appreciated that if funds are not genuinely advanced, then any payment will not constitute interest for tax purposes. In

j   addition, the potential for attack under (s 787 of the Income and Corporation Taxes Act 1988] arises, as discussed at 6.6 above. We strongly recommend that funds genuinely flow from the bank through the companies, evidenced by documentation at the relevant banks concerned.'

[29] In a fax dated 29 April 1992, Mr Leaf informed Mr John:

'There are some four or five companies which have commenced securities trading under the previous procedures, but none of which have come to the end of their first accounting period since acquisition ... Could you please let me have a check list of information you require and/or steps to be taken in order to export these companies to Guernsey as soon as possible.'

This fax is relied on by Mr Jones as justifying an honest belief by Mr John that genuine trading had and did thereafter take place. He also took us to a fax dated 8 May 1992 from Mr John referring to the agent in the United Kingdom genuinely concluding contracts on behalf of the Guernsey companies, and to a fax from Mr Leaf to Mr John dated 5 January 1993 stating:

'Switch from currency trading to option trading. As you know, we were keen for this to start from the beginning of January and would not want to get it wrong.'

[30] The prosecution also allege that the payments of interest in advance by the target companies to ABC were a sham, and that Mr John must have known it. Mr Sutton referred to the commercial improbability of paying interest in advance on loans not yet drawn down, the actual amount of which might not be as anticipated. However, in a fax to Mr Leaf of 12 May 1992, Mr John stated:

'I have discussed the concept of paying interest in advance, rather than in arrears, with Counsel on previous occasions and I am happy that it is effective in obtaining relief for tax purposes although I am aware that the Inland Revenue do not like interest being paid in advance but I remain of the view that there is nothing they can do about it. This is a point you may wish to confirm with Milton Grundy (the well-known tax counsel) particularly as you may welcome his further comments on the points set out below.'

[31] Mr Leaf did indeed refer the question of payment of interest in advance to Milton Grundy (see the fax dated 18 May 1992 from Poppi SA to Mr Grundy [not reproduced]). In the light of these documents, the payment of interest in advance and Mr John's knowledge of it are not indicative of his participation in a fraud.

[32] Mr Sutton relied on a memorandum of a meeting between Mr John and Ian Tredinnick that took place on 4 December 1992 as showing that Mr John was aware that transactions were being invented after their purported date. Ian Tredinnick worked for Mr Leaf. He too was a chartered accountant. The prosecution accept that he acted honestly. It is therefore difficult to regard the memorandum of their meeting as evidence of the carrying out of a fraudulent conspiracy. In any event, the memorandum does not provide the prosecution with the evidence they claim. It is true that it refers to finalising GIL transactions to 30 June 1992; but it also states, in an underlined sentence:

'The company should be carrying on a genuine trade—so that the revenue is not to be treated as a capital gain or interest income for tax purposes.'

[33] The last matters to which we refer are the contracts between the trading target companies and GCL and GIL purporting to appoint one or other of those companies as broker to carry out foreign exchange dealing on behalf of the trading target companies, and the contracts of loan between ABC and target companies. It is clear from the documents that Mr John advised on the terms of

a these agreements during 1992 and early 1993. In a fax dated 25 January 1993, he was told that a draft agreement would form part of the documents to be sent to the Inland Revenue. When executed, these contracts were given dates in January and February 1992, before they had been drafted. In other words, they were backdated, presumably for the purpose of representing to the Inland Revenue that they had been entered into on those dates rather than, as was the fact, about a year later. Copies of some at least of these contracts were submitted to the
b Inland Revenue, with no explanation that they had been backdated.

[34] The defence's answer to this point is that the scheme was ongoing, and that Mr John was concerned to draft documents applying to trading and borrowings by target companies to be acquired in the future rather than to transactions that had already apparently occurred. We add that as far as we have seen, no document
c shows unequivocally that Mr John knew that the contracts were or had been backdated, as opposed to their being given retrospective effect.

Conclusion on the evidence

[35] When we look at the evidence as a whole, we are clear that it cannot be
d said that the judge's decision was perverse or one that he could not reasonably have arrived at. We do not say that we should necessarily have made the same decision. The view he took of the note of the meeting attended by Mr John, enclosed with Ms Reiter's fax of 22 February 1993, referred to at [22] above, was more charitable than we would have taken. But that is a far thing from saying that the view he took of the evidence as a whole was not one he was entitled to
e take.

Inadequate reasons

[36] Lastly, Mr Sutton submitted that the reasons given by the judge were inadequate, so that the prosecution were unable to discern why he had rejected
f their case. The reasons given by the judge for his ruling were brief in the extreme. However, we do not think that the judge, even in a case dealt with in as much detail as this, was obliged in his ruling to consider every document referred to and to summarise his conclusions on it. His reasons made clear the facts that he had taken into account in coming to his decision and his conclusion that the documentary evidence was insufficiently unequivocal to enable a jury properly
g to convict Mr John. In any event, it can only be in a very exceptional case that this court would remit a case such as this to the Crown Court for the judge to give further reasons. We should only do so if there were strong grounds for believing that his decision was one that he could not properly have arrived at. However, if it was established that his decision was one not properly open to him, there
h would be no point in requiring the judge to elaborate on his reasons: his decision could be quashed immediately.

Conclusion

[37] For the reasons set out above, there are no grounds for interfering with
j the judge's decision. The application for judicial review of his decision will be dismissed.

[38] We add that in a case such as this, depending essentially on documents and the inferences to be drawn from them, and involving a considerable number of documents, we should have been considerably assisted if the prosecution had supplied us with a document specifying the propositions alleged by them to be

established by the documents in the case, and identifying the documents, or the
passages in long documents, relied upon for each of those propositions. A more *a*
analytical approach would have enabled us to deal with this case far more
efficiently.

Application dismissed.

Dilys Tausz   Barrister.

Delaware Mansions Ltd and another v Westminster City Council

[2001] UKHL 55

HOUSE OF LORDS

LORD STEYN, LORD BROWNE-WILKINSON, LORD COOKE OF THORNDON, LORD CLYDE AND LORD HUTTON

3, 4 APRIL, 25 OCTOBER 2001

Nuisance – Right to sue – Continuing nuisance – Roots of defendant's tree desiccating ground beneath property and causing structural cracking – Claimant acquiring freehold of property after cracks occurring and carrying out reasonable remedial work – Whether reasonable remedial expenditure recoverable by current owner in respect of pre-transfer damage arising from continuing nuisance.

The respondent authority was the owner of a tree growing in the footpath of the highway some four metres from the front boundary of a property consisting of several blocks of flats held under long leases. During 1989 cracks began to appear in the structure, and structural engineers were instructed. In a brief report delivered to the landlord in March 1990 (the March report), the engineers concluded that the cracking had been caused by the roots of the tree and recommended the tree's removal or, if that were not possible, the underpinning of the property. In April 1990 the landlord agreed to sell the freehold reversion to the appellant, F Ltd, and the sale was completed in June 1990. There was no assignment of any right of action against the authority in respect of the tree. The authority's attention was first drawn to the problem in August 1990 when it was sent a copy of the March report. No reply or immediate action resulted. After a more detailed survey was carried out in December 1990 and January 1991, an architect endorsed the view that the worst cracking had resulted from foundation damage, that remedial steps were urgently required and that underpinning was necessary. At a site meeting in January 1991, the authority agreed to carry out root pruning, but it was made clear by F Ltd that underpinning works would nevertheless have to proceed. Remedial work, including the insertion of piles, commenced in January 1992 and was completed in July 1992 at a cost of almost £571,000. If the tree had been removed, underpinning would not have been necessary, and the cost of repair to the property would only have been £14,000. In a subsequent action for damages, F Ltd sought to recover from the authority the much greater sum that it had spent in carrying out the remedial work. At trial, the judge concluded that the ground beneath the property had become desiccated as a result of the activities of the tree roots and that F Ltd had acted reasonably in executing the works once the authority had declined to remove the tree. He nevertheless dismissed the claim, holding that all or almost all of the structural damage had occurred no later than March 1990 (ie before the transfer of the freehold to F Ltd), and that only the previous landlord could sue in respect of that damage. The judge's decision was reversed by the Court of Appeal which held that F Ltd could recover on the basis of there being a continuing nuisance. The authority appealed to the House of Lords.

Held – Where there was a continuing nuisance of which the defendant knew or ought to have known, reasonable remedial expenditure could be recovered by the

owner who had had to incur it. The answer to the issue was to be found by applying
the concepts which underlay much modern tort law and, more particularly, the law a
of nuisance, namely reasonableness between neighbours (real and figurative) and
reasonable foreseeability. The label nuisance or negligence was of no real
significance. The concern of the common law lay in working out the fair and just
content and incidents of a neighbour's duty rather than affixing a label and
inferring the extent of the duty from it. If, however, reasonableness between b
neighbours was the key to the solution of the problem, it could not be right to
visit the authority or owner responsible for a tree with a large bill for
underpinning without giving them notice of the damage and the opportunity of
avoiding further damage by removal of the tree. Defendants were therefore
entitled to notice and a reasonable opportunity of abatement before liability for
remedial expenditure could arise. Should they elect to preserve a tree for c
environmental reasons, they could fairly be expected to bear the cost of underpinning
or reasonably necessary remedial works. The party on whom the cost had fallen
could recover it, even though there might be elements of hitherto unsatisfied
pre-proprietorship damage or protection for the future. In the instant case, there
had been a continuing nuisance during F Ltd's ownership until at least the d
completion of the underpinning and the piling. It did not matter that further
cracking of the superstructure might not have occurred after March 1990. The
encroachment of the roots was causing continuing damage to the land by
dehydrating the soil and inhibiting rehydration. Damage consisting of impairment of
load-bearing qualities of residential land was itself a nuisance. Cracking in the
building was consequential. Having regard to the proximity of the tree to the e
property, a real risk of damage to the land was foreseeable on the part of the
authority. The latter had had ample notice and time before the underpinning.
Accordingly, the authority was liable, and the appeal would therefore be
dismissed (see [1], [2], [29], [31], [33], [34], [38]–[40], below).

Goldman v Hargrave [1966] 2 All ER 989, *Masters v London Borough of Brent* [1978] f
2 All ER 664 and *Solloway v Hampshire CC* (1981) 79 LGR 449 considered.

Notes

For continuing nuisances, see 34 *Halsbury's Laws* (4th edn reissue) para 90.

Cases referred to in opinions
g

*Butler v Standard Telephones and Cables Ltd, McCarthy v Standard Telephones and
    Cables Ltd* [1940] 1 All ER 121, [1940] 1 KB 399.
Cambridge Water Co v Eastern Counties Leather plc [1994] 1 All ER 53, [1994] 2 AC
    264, [1994] 2 WLR 53, HL.
Darley Main Colliery Co v Mitchell (1886) 11 App Cas 127, [1886–90] All ER Rep 449, h
    HL.
Davey v Harrow Corp [1957] 2 All ER 305, [1958] 1 QB 60, [1957] 2 WLR 941, CA.
Goldman v Hargrave [1966] 2 All ER 989, [1967] 1 AC 645, [1966] 3 WLR 513, PC.
Hunter v Canary Wharf Ltd, Hunter v London Docklands Development Corp [1997] 2 All ER
    426, [1997] AC 655, [1997] 2 WLR 684, HL. j
Hurst v Hampshire CC (1997) 96 LGR 27, CA.
Job Edwards Ltd v Birmingham Navigations Co [1924] 1 KB 341, CA.
Leakey v National Trust for Places of Historic Interest or Natural Beauty [1980] 1 All ER
    17, [1980] QB 485, [1980] 2 WLR 65, CA.
Lemmon v Webb [1894] 3 Ch 1; *affd* [1895] AC 1, [1891] All ER Rep 749, HL.

a   *Masters v London Borough of Brent* [1978] 2 All ER 664, [1978] QB 841, [1978] 2 WLR 768.

McCombe v Read [1955] 2 All ER 458, [1955] 2 QB 429, [1955] 1 WLR 635.

Middleton v Humphries (1912) 47 ILT 160.

Morgan v Khyatt [1964] 1 WLR 475, PC.

Overseas Tankship (UK) Ltd v The Miller Steamship Co Pty, The Wagon Mound (No 2)
b   [1966] 2 All ER 709, [1967] 1 AC 617, [1966] 3 WLR 498, PC.

Proprietors of Strata Plan No 14198 v Cowell (1989) 24 NSWLR 478, NSW SC.

Richmond (City of) v Scantelbury [1991] 2 VR 38, Vic SC.

Rylands v Fletcher (1868) LR 3 HL 330, [1861–73] All ER Rep 1, HL.

Sedleigh-Denfield v O'Callaghan [1940] 3 All ER 349, [1940] AC 880, HL.

c   *Solloway v Hampshire CC* (1981) 79 LGR 449, CA.

Sparham-Souter v Town and Country Developments (Essex) Ltd [1976] 2 All ER 65,
        [1976] QB 858, [1976] 2 WLR 493, CA.

Stratford Theater Inc v Town of Stratford (1953) 140 Conn 422, Conn SC.

Thompson v Gibson (1841) 7 M&W 456, [1834–42] All ER Rep 623, Exch Ct.

d   *West Leigh Colliery Co Ltd v Tunnicliffe & Hampson Ltd* [1908] AC 27, [1904–7] All ER
        Rep 189, HL.

Whitehouse v Fellowes (1861) 26 JP 40.

Appeal

e   The defendant, Westminster City Council (Westminster), appealed with permission of the Appeal Committee of the House of Lords given on 12 January 2000 from the order of the Court of Appeal (Beldam, Pill and Thorpe LJJ) on 21 July 1999 ([2000] BLR 1) allowing an appeal by the second plaintiff, Flecksun Ltd, the owner of the freehold of a property known as Delaware Mansions, Delaware Road, Maida Vale, London W9, from the order of Mr Recorder Derek Wood QC,

f   sitting as an Official Referee in the Queen's Bench Division of the High Court on 3 March 1998 ((1998) 88 BLR 99), dismissing an action for damages for, inter alia, nuisance brought against Westminster by Flecksun and the first plaintiff, Delaware Mansions Ltd, the management company owned by the tenants of the property, in respect of damage caused to the property by the roots of a tree owned by Westminster. The first plaintiff took no part in the proceedings before

g   the Court of Appeal and the House of Lords. The facts are set out in the opinion of Lord Cooke of Thorndon.

Richard Mawrey QC and *Adrian Cooper* (instructed by *Vizard Oldham*) for
        Westminster.

h   *Michael Pooles QC* and *Simon Wilton* (instructed by *Beachcroft Wansbroughs*) for
        Flecksun.

Their Lordships took time for consideration.

j   25 October 2001. The following opinions were delivered.

LORD STEYN.

[1] My Lords, since the opinion of Lord Cooke of Thorndon in this case is the last which he will deliver in the House of Lords, it is appropriate to pay tribute to his massive contribution to the coherent and rational development of the law in New Zealand, in England and throughout the common law world. His opinion

in the case before the House is characteristically lucid and compelling. For the reasons he has given I would also dismiss the appeal.

LORD BROWNE-WILKINSON.

[2] My Lords, I have had the advantage of reading in draft the speech of my noble and learned friend Lord Cooke of Thorndon. I agree with it and for the reasons which he has given I, too, would dismiss this appeal.

LORD COOKE OF THORNDON.

[3] My Lords, this case raises an issue, on which there is surprisingly little authority in English law, about the recoverability of remedial expenditure incurred after encroachment by tree roots. By writ and statement of claim issued in the Queen's Bench Division, Official Referees' Business, on 7 June 1995, two plaintiffs claimed damages and interest from the Westminster City Council (Westminster) as highways authority for the area including the property affected and as owner of a London plane tree growing in the footpath of the highway, Delaware Road in Maida Vale, some four metres from the front boundary of the property. The first plaintiff was Delaware Mansions Ltd (Delaware), a management company owned by the tenants of Delaware Mansions, which consist of 19 blocks divided into 167 flats, occupying the whole of the north-eastern side of the road. The second plaintiff was Flecksun Ltd (Flecksun), a wholly-owned subsidiary of Delaware. Flecksun had in 1990 acquired the freehold of Delaware Mansions from the original owners and developers, the Church Commissioners.

[4] The case came before Mr Recorder Derek Wood QC, sitting as an Official Referee ((1998) 88 BLR 99). He dismissed the claims of both plaintiffs, while making a number of findings of fact favourable to them. They appealed to the Court of Appeal ([2000] BLR 1), but Delaware did not pursue its appeal, nor has it taken any part in the hearing in your Lordships' House, so the House is not required to consider whether it had standing to sue. The appeal of Flecksun came before a Court of Appeal consisting of Beldam, Pill and Thorpe LJJ. For reasons given by Pill LJ in a judgment delivered on 21 July 1999 the court allowed Flecksun's appeal, with the effect that Flecksun was to recover judgment for £835,430·92 (being the expenditure claimed, £570,734·98, including removal costs of the leaseholders, plus interest). By leave granted by an Appeal Committee, Westminster appeals to this House.

The history and the issue

[5] The flats are held by the individual tenants under long leases granted by the Church Commissioners. On 5 April 1990 the Church Commissioners agreed to sell their freehold reversion to Flecksun for £1. The sale was completed by registered transfer on 25 June 1990. There was no express assignment of any right of action against Westminster respecting the plane tree, and it has not been argued that there was an implied one. It is common ground that the nominal consideration was not influenced by the effect of the plane tree on the property.

[6] The plane tree was probably planted at the time when the Maida Vale estate, including Delaware Mansions, was developed by the Church Commissioners in the early years of the twentieth century. It is now almost as high as the five-storey brick Delaware Mansions. It stands, somewhat isolated from other smaller trees, approximately between flats numbers 73 to 82 and 83 to 92. As found by the trial judge, damage by cracking came to be caused by the roots of the tree, through causing desiccation and shrinkage of the London clay soil, to blocks 9, 10, 11 and 12.

a   The dates of the cracking have assumed importance, I think disproportionate, in the argument of the case. It is not disputed that Westminster owns and controls the tree, one of no less than 7,000 street trees (half of them London planes) within its jurisdiction. The trees are regularly inspected by an officer of the council, and tree-pruning is carried out by contractors. Westminster's records show that in 1983 the contractors were told to trim the crown of this tree by 50% and in 1986

b   by 25%. From the mid-1970s the tree had been allowed to develop a large crown. About that time severe tree-pruning went out of fashion; people liked to see a more bushy effect; with lighter pruning the demand of the foliage for water increased and roots grew more extensively.

[7] During 1989, a year of drought, Delaware's then managing agents (Chestertons) began to receive reports from residents in blocks 9 to 12 that cracks

c   were appearing in the structure. In December 1989 the agents instructed structural engineers, the Cairns Smith Partnership (CSP), to make a report on the cracking. In a report delivered to the Church Commissioners on 5 March 1990, CSP concluded that the cracking had been caused by the roots of the tree, and recommended that it be removed. If removal was not possible, they recommended underpinning. It

d   will be noted that this was before the transfer agreement between the Church Commissioners and Flecksun, but it was a brief rather than a detailed report. It was evidently not seen by Westminster at that stage.

[8] After the transfer of the freehold to Flecksun, another firm of managing agents took over. They requested Mr F G Finch, a qualified architect specialising in the refurbishment of London properties, to look into the damage in more

e   detail and collaborate with CSP. In December 1990 and January 1991 CSP conducted a more detailed survey of the cracking and concurrently Finch Associates presented a comprehensive report. Mr Finch endorsed the view that the worst cracking had resulted from foundation damage, that remedial steps were urgently required, and that underpinning was necessary. After considering

f   much expert and other evidence the judge made a finding ((1998) 88 BLR at 112), which again has become prominent in the case, that—

'all or almost all of the structural damage which is the subject-matter of the plaintiffs' claim had occurred as a result of the 1989 drought not later than March 1990. If, which is not certain, some further cracking took place in the

g   superstructure after that date, that cracking in my judgment was the further consequence of the 1989 to early 1990 damage to the foundations.'

[9] The attention of Westminster appears first to have been drawn to the problem when on 14 August 1990 (that is to say, a month and three weeks after

h   the transfer) Chestertons sent to Westminster CSP's March report. No reply or immediate action resulted, but eventually, to quote the judge (at 112), it was agreed shortly after 3 January 1991 at a site meeting that root pruning would be carried out—

'by cutting a trench approximately 300mm wide and 1 metre deep along the

j   back edge of the pavement, and then back-filling the trench with a PVC liner to reduce re-growth. It was also made clear by the plaintiffs at this meeting that the underpinning works proposed by CSP would nevertheless have to proceed and, as part of those works, a further trench would be cut at basement level. It was not and never has been admitted by Westminster that the structural damage described by CSP had in fact been caused by tree roots.'

[10] Subsequently soil consultants were engaged by CSP and their representative (Mr Quarrell) gave evidence, as did an arboriculturist (Dr Biddle) and a consulting engineer (Mr Butcher) engaged by Westminster. There was a strong conflict of expert evidence at the trial. In the end the judge found on the balance of probabilities that the ground beneath blocks 10 and 11, and to a lesser extent blocks 9 and 12, had become desiccated as a result of the activities of roots belonging to the plane tree in front of block 11. He also made (at 117–118) the following findings, which are of undoubted importance:

'In October 1991 root pruning was carried out and a pavement-level root barrier inserted as previously agreed by Westminster. But the plaintiffs adhered to the advice of CSP, and occupiers of some of the basement flats began to move out to enable CSP's programme of underpinning works to be carried out. This work started in January 1992. On 6 March 1992 and again on 9 April 1992 the contractors found tree roots beneath the foundations to Blocks 10 and 11. These findings powerfully corroborate the evidence of tree roots and desiccation put forward by Mr Quarrell, and they necessitated the insertion of piles instead of underpinning in the locations affected. The work was completed in July 1992 at a total cost to the plaintiffs (including the removal costs of the leaseholders) of £570,734.98. Westminster agree that this sum was in fact incurred, and that it was a fair and reasonable sum for the works which were actually carried out and for the other heads of expenditure which were in fact incurred. Mr Butcher however stated that in his opinion the scope and extent of the works was excessive if and insofar as they were brought about by the roots of this tree. He could accept that structural works to the stairwells to Blocks 10 and 11 were justified. He challenged the need to extend those works beyond those areas, suggesting that the additional work which he was unable to accept was carried out for the sake of protecting the building against possible future damage rather than repairing the damage which had occurred up to that date. Mr Cairns [giving evidence for the plaintiffs] explained to me that this was a matter of professional judgement. He agreed that a line had to be drawn somewhere, and in cross-examination Mr Butcher accepted that Mr Cairns' scheme was a reasonable one, even though he did not agree with it. In my judgment the costs incurred by the plaintiffs were properly and reasonably incurred and, if a legal cause of action can be established, would be recoverable from Westminster.'

[11] It is common ground, as recorded in the joint statement of facts and issues before your Lordships, that this amounts to a finding that the claimants acted reasonably in executing the extent of works undertaken. It has not been contended for Westminster that the work done for the council in October 1991 was sufficient both to remedy the existing damage from the roots and to safeguard against future damage from the same source. Instead the argument has been that all the existing damage had occurred before Flecksun acquired the freehold and that only the Church Commissioners could sue for that damage (subject to any limitation defence); and that Flecksun could only sue for fresh damage if and when it occurred. That argument was accepted by the trial judge. The Court of Appeal held, however, that Flecksun could recover on the basis that there was a continuing nuisance. Their reasoning is encapsulated in the following passage in the judgment of Pill LJ ([2000] BLR 1 at 4–5), the reference to *Hunter*

a   being to *Hunter v Canary Wharf Ltd, Hunter v London Docklands Development Corp*
    [1997] 2 All ER 426 at 441, [1997] AC 655 at 695:

        '22. Thus where there is a continuing nuisance, the owner is entitled to a
        declaration, to abate the nuisance, to damages for physical injury and to an
        injunction. He is in my judgment, and on the same principle, entitled to the
b   reasonable cost of eliminating the nuisance if it is reasonable to eliminate it.
        This does not offend against Lord Lloyd's formulation in *Hunter* which was
        not intended to define the remedies of an owner subject to a nuisance by
        encroachment.
        23. A nuisance is present during [Flecksun's] ownership; acceptance of
        the need for remedial work establishes that. The actual and relevant damage
c   is the cost of the necessary and reasonable remedial work. Underpinning has
        been held to be a reasonable way of eliminating the nuisance and the owner
        can recover the cost of doing it. There is no need to prove further physical
        damage resulting from the nuisance.'

d   *English cases on encroaching roots*
    [12] There are dicta in the reports to the effect that, in the law of nuisance,
    root encroachment into a neighbouring property is similar to bough encroachment
    over the property. For instance in *Lemmon v Webb* [1894] 3 Ch 1, where it was
    held that a neighbour could lop boughs overhanging his property without notice
    to the owner of the tree, provided that he could do so without entering the
e   owner's land, Lindley, Lopes and Kay LJJ (at 14, 16 and 24 respectively) all said
    that a similar right of abatement by cutting applied to encroaching roots. That,
    though, is of no help on damages. Evidently there are only a handful of reported
    cases decided in England on damages for root encroachment. Counsel had found
    only seven before the present case. I shall refer briefly to each of them.
f   [13] The first such case is as late as 1939: *Butler v Standard Telephones and Cables
    Ltd, McCarthy v Standard Telephones and Cables Ltd* [1940] 1 All ER 121, [1940] 1 KB
    399, a judgment of Lewis J. The plaintiffs' houses were damaged by the roots of
    trees on the defendant's adjoining land burrowing under the walls of the houses
    and causing the soil to shrink through abstraction of moisture. Underpinning of
    one of the affected houses had not prevented later settlement. The damages were
g   agreed subject to the determination of the issue of liability, so the decision
    provides no help on damages. On liability the judge found for the plaintiffs,
    following dicta in *Lemmon's* case and an Irish decision (*Middleton v Humphries*
    (1912) 47 ILT 160).
    [14] The next case was *McCombe v Read* [1955] 2 All ER 458, [1955] 2 QB 429, a
h   judgment of Harman J. The main point decided was that an injunction will lie to
    restrain a continuing nuisance to property caused by encroachment of tree roots.
    Damages were also claimed, including the cost of a not wholly successful
    underpinning. The judge said that the latter cost was accepted, and that as regards
    later damage the plaintiff could only recover if he could prove continuing damage
j   from the same nuisance, in which event he could claim the damage accruing up
    to the date of judgment. An inquiry as to damage was ordered.
    [15] *Davey v Harrow Corp* [1957] 2 All ER 305, [1958] 1 QB 60 reached the Court
    of Appeal (Lord Goddard CJ, Jenkins and Morris LJJ). The judgment of the court
    was delivered by Lord Goddard CJ. It was a standard case of cracking of walls due
    to root penetration, except that at first instance it had been found that the plaintiff
    had not proved that the offending trees, since cut down, were on the defendant's

land rather than his own. The judge assessed damages, if they had been recoverable, at £1,000, and no question of quantum was argued on appeal. Further evidence established, however, that in fact the trees were on the land of the defendant, so the appeal was allowed. Lord Goddard CJ regarded it as established that encroachment by roots was a nuisance and that, if damage was caused, an action on the case would lie. For the defendant an argument was that the plaintiff had to show that the trees were planted and not self-sown, and that no action could be maintained where the damage was caused by natural growth or natural causes. Lord Goddard CJ rejected that distinction:

> 'The nuisance consists in allowing the trees to encroach from the land of their owner into that of his neighbour. The owner must keep his trees in, just as he may not allow filth to escape from his premises on to that of his neighbour ...' (See [1957] 2 All ER 305 at 309, [1958] 1 QB 60 at 71.)

[16] *Morgan v Khyatt* [1964] 1 WLR 475 was an appeal to the Privy Council from the New Zealand Court of Appeal. Roots from thirsty pohutukawa trees on the defendant's property had damaged a concrete wall and drains therein leading from the plaintiff's house. The trial judge had awarded the plaintiff damages for repair costs, and an injunction. This was upheld by the Court of Appeal and again by the Judicial Committee, subject to a minor modification in the terms of the injunction. Viscount Simonds, who presided, is reported (at 476) to have said during the argument that the Court of Appeal were right in following *Davey's* case, which the Board thought rightly decided. But the judgment of the Board, delivered by Lord Evershed, is (at 477) consistent with a requirement of knowledge on the part of the defendant:

> 'As regards the law applicable in such a case as the present, their Lordships can feel no doubt that it was correctly applied by both courts in New Zealand. It is sufficient, therefore, for present purposes to say that it has in their Lordships' opinion long been established as a general proposition that an owner of land may make any natural use of it; but also (and by way of qualification of the general rule) that if an owner of land grows or permits the growth on his land in the natural way of trees whose roots penetrate into adjoining property and thereby cause and continue to cause damage to buildings upon that property, he is liable for the tort of nuisance to the owner of that adjoining property. It was found both by Leicester J. and by the Court of Appeal in New Zealand that such were the facts in the present case; that is to say, that the roots of Morgan's four pohutukawa trees had penetrated into the adjoining property now owned by the respondent and to his knowledge had long been damaging the wall and drains therein and would (unless somehow prevented) inevitably and increasingly continue so to do.'

[17] *Masters v London Borough of Brent* [1978] 2 All ER 664, [1978] QB 841, a decision of Talbot J, is the English case closest to the present on the facts. The plaintiff's father had a leasehold interest in a house in which he lived with the plaintiff and the plaintiff's wife. The roots of a lime tree planted in the pavement in front of the house encroached on the land and caused subsidence undermining the foundations of the house by extracting moisture from the subsoil. The defendant local authority accepted that this was an actionable nuisance; the question of the date at which the authority knew or should have known this is not discussed in the judgment. The plaintiff and his father took the advice of a building company as to the necessary works (described at one point in the judgment as

a repairs) but at that stage could not afford the cost. The father transferred the leasehold to the plaintiff to enable the plaintiff to raise a mortgage to pay for the remedial work. He did so and sued the local authority for the cost of the work. He was met by the same argument as is advanced for Westminster in the present case: that the damage had occurred before he acquired the proprietary interest. But Talbot J accepted that there was a continuing actionable nuisance affecting the land *b* both during the father's ownership and during the plaintiff's ownership. He said that there was in fact, not in theory, continuing damage:

> 'Where there is a continuing nuisance inflicting damage on premises, those who are in possession of the interest may recover losses which they have borne whether the loss began before the acquisition of the interest or *c* whether it began after the acquisition of the interest. The test is: what is the loss which the owner of the land has to meet in respect of the continuing nuisance affecting his land?' (See [1978] 2 All ER 664 at 669, [1978] QB 841 at 848.)

[18] In the present case the trial judge declined to follow *Masters'* case and *d* criticised Talbot J's reasoning in principle, although accepting that the case might have been correctly decided on its own special facts. The argument for Westminster is that it was wrong. The argument for Flecksun is that it was right but that it is not necessary for the House to uphold it in order for the respondent to succeed. The Court of Appeal thought it unnecessary to hear submissions on *Masters'* case.

e [19] Whether the defendant's liability is strict had not been expressly examined in the cases up to this point. It did arise in *Solloway v Hampshire CC* (1981) 79 LGR 449, another Court of Appeal decision (Stephenson and Dunn LJJ and Sir David Cairns). This decision was much influenced by the circumstance that in the meantime a differently constituted Court of Appeal had held in *Leakey v National Trust for Places of Historic Interest or Natural Beauty* [1980] 1 All ER 17, [1980] QB *f* 485 (a case relating to falls of earth from a mound that had built up on the defendant's land) that the duty arising from a nuisance which is not brought about by human agency does not arise unless and until the defendant has, or ought to have had, knowledge of the existence of the defect and the danger thereby created. In turn *Leakey's* case had been influenced by the well-known authorities *Sedleigh-Denfield v O'Callaghan* [1940] 3 All ER 349, [1940] AC 880 and *g* *Goldman v Hargrave* [1966] 2 All ER 989, [1967] 1 AC 645, to which I will return a little later.

[20] *Solloway's* case I see as a significant case for present purposes. In 1967 the plaintiff bought a house built in 1922. About eight metres from the front there was growing in the pavement a horse chestnut tree owned by the defendant *h* highway authority. In 1966, a year of a second successive very hot summer with drought conditions, cracks appeared in the walls. The cause was root dehydration. The damage had to be rectified by underpinning costing £5,656. Although the subsoil in the area was almost entirely plateau gravel with clay underneath, the subsoil of the plaintiff's house had outcrops of clay which were of such a nature *j* that, even without the drought, the roots would have reached them and caused damage by dehydration. The plaintiff recovered the rectification cost at first instance before Stocker J. The council's appeal was allowed, however, on grounds relating to unforeseeability and the scope of the responsible authority or owner's duty. Each member of the Court of Appeal gave a separate judgment, albeit on broadly similar lines, Dunn and Stephenson LJJ expressing regret at having so to decide.

[21] The starting point in the judgments in *Solloway*'s case was acceptance that since *Leakey*'s case a reasonably foreseeable risk of damage by encroachment had to be established. On that point Dunn LJ (who gave the first judgment) thought that there was no more than a vague possibility. Sir David Cairns was of the same mind. Stephenson LJ was willing to assume that there was a real risk, reasonably apparent to the defendant's engineers if they had thought about it. But all three appellate judges thought that the cost and inconvenience to the local authority of taking any effective steps to remove or reduce it would have been quite out of proportion to the risk. As Dunn LJ put it ((1981) 79 LGR 449 at 458):

> 'In my view there is no reason to suppose that many of the houses in Shirley Avenue could be eliminated from this risk. We were told that there is an avenue of trees all along that road and the evidence was that pockets of clay might exist anywhere in Shirley Avenue. All the householders, it seems to me, would have to be approached, not only in Shirley Avenue but in any other street in Hampshire where there are trees adjacent to houses.'

It was said also that it would all have been of great inconvenience to householders, and that the widespread examination of subsoils by the sinking of boreholes would have caused alarm affecting market values.

[22] The last case in the line of English decisions cited is *Hurst v Hampshire County Council* (1997) 96 LGR 27. This is of no present assistance as it turned on whether a highway authority had a sufficient interest in trees growing on the verge of the highway to be liable in nuisance for root damage, a point not in dispute in the present case.

Other nuisance cases

[23] None of the roots cases in the line just reviewed was concerned with the argument that remedial expenditure is not recoverable by the current owner for pre-transfer damage, except *Masters'* case, which is against the argument. On behalf of Westminster, however, counsel relied on other cases of nuisance, notably *Whitehouse v Fellowes* (1861) 26 JP 40 (negligently constructed drain causing flooding of adjoining land); *Darley Main Colliery Co v Mitchell* (1886) 11 App Cas 127, [1886–90] All ER Rep 449 (successive subsidences from working of coal by lessees of seams under plaintiff's land); and *West Leigh Colliery Co Ltd v Tunnicliffe & Hampson Ltd* [1908] AC 27, [1904–7] All ER Rep 189 (also a case of subsidence through working of minerals). While these are cases of longstanding authority, care is needed in identifying precisely what was decided in each.

[24] In *Whitehouse*'s case the issue was one of time limitation. A statute prescribed a limit of three months. Did time run from the negligent work or the resultant flooding? The decision was for the latter alternative, on the ground that there was a continuing nuisance giving rise to a fresh cause of action on each occasion of damage. No question of remedial expenditure arose.

[25] In the *Darley Main* case the issue was again limitation. In 1868 the working of the coal had caused a subsidence of the plaintiff's cottages for which the defendants had accepted liability and made satisfaction by repairing the cottages. In 1882 further subsidence and further injury to the cottages occurred. It was brought about when the owner of adjoining land worked coal there, but the defendants admitted that if they had left sufficient support under the plaintiff's land that working would have done no harm. By a majority, Lord Blackburn dissenting, the House of Lords held that the original excavating lessees were responsible for permitting a continuing nuisance, for each incident of damage

a   from which a fresh cause of action arose. Again the measure of damages was not discussed; they were to be assessed by an arbitrator.

[26] In the *West Leigh* case the issue was somewhat different. It was whether depreciation in the value of the surface owner's property brought about by the apprehension of future damage could be recovered. The House of Lords held not, Lord James of Hereford dubitante. Lord Loreburn LC said ([1908] AC 27 at

b   34, [1904–7] All ER Rep 189 at 193) that to allow recovery once and for all of the entire diminution in the value of the property would be inconvenient and capricious in its results. The plaintiff was held entitled to recover the cost of repairs to his wall, plus nevertheless an allowance for the depreciation of its value as a damaged and repaired structure (see [1908] AC 27 at 32–33, [1904–7] All ER Rep 189 at 190 per Lord Ashbourne).

c   [27] Thus none of the authorities chiefly relied upon for Westminster has focused on the content of remedial expenses, whether by distinguishing between pre- and post-proprietorship damage or between making good existing damage and safeguarding against future damage. The same is true of two authorities on which Mr Recorder Wood relied, namely *Thompson v Gibson* (1841) 7 M&W 456, [1834–42]

d   All ER Rep 623 and *Sparham-Souter v Town and Country Developments (Essex) Ltd* [1976] 2 All ER 65 at 68–70, [1976] QB 858 at 867–868 per Lord Denning MR.

Reasonableness as a criterion

[28] It seems to me therefore that any decision which your Lordships may give in this case must to some extent break new ground in English law. One point

e   at least is clear. Double recovery could not be permitted. But there is no question of that in the present case, nor was there in *Masters v London Borough of Brent* [1978] 2 All ER 664, [1978] QB 841. The Church Commissioners here had not incurred the remedial expenditure; and on the authority of the *West Leigh* case, on which Westminster rely, they could apparently not have recovered depreciation in the

f   market value of their property resulting from apprehension of future damage.

[29] Beyond that I think that the answer to the issue falls to be found by applying the concepts of reasonableness between neighbours (real or figurative) and reasonable foreseeability which underlie much modern tort law and, more particularly, the law of nuisance. The great cases in nuisance decided in our time have these concepts at their heart. In *Sedleigh-Denfield v O'Callaghan* [1940] 3 All ER

g   349, [1940] AC 880, the House of Lords held that an occupier of land 'continues' a nuisance if, with knowledge or presumed knowledge of its existence (in that case a defective grating giving rise to flood damage), he fails to take reasonable means to bring it to an end when he has reasonable time to do so. In *Overseas Tankship (UK) Ltd v The Miller Steamship Co Pty, The Wagon Mound (No 2)* [1966]

h   2 All ER 709 at 719, [1967] 1 AC 617 at 644, the Privy Council, approaching the case under the rubrics of both nuisance and negligence, said per Lord Reid: 'If it is clear that the reasonable man would have realised or foreseen and prevented the risk, then it must follow that the appellants are liable in damages.'

[30] Once more, in *Goldman v Hargrave* [1966] 2 All ER 989 at 995–996, [1967]

j   1 AC 645 at 663, the Privy Council per Lord Wilberforce, as to an occupier's duty to take reasonable steps to prevent the spreading of a fire caused by lightning striking a tree, said, and likewise not discriminating between nuisance and negligence (see [1966] 2 All ER 989 at 991–992, [1967] 1 AC at 656–657):

'So far it has been possible to consider the existence of a duty, in general terms; but the matter cannot be left there without some definition of the scope of his duty. How far does it go? What is the standard of the effort required? What is the position as regards expenditure? It is not enough to say merely that these must be "reasonable" since what is reasonable to one man may be very unreasonable, and indeed ruinous, to another: the law must take account of the fact that the occupier on whom the duty is cast has, ex hypothesi, had this hazard thrust upon him through no seeking or fault of his own. His interest, and his resources, whether physical or material, may be of a very modest character either in relation to the magnitude of the hazard, or as compared with those of his threatened neighbour. A rule which required of him in such unsought circumstances in his neighbour's interest a physical effort of which he is not capable, or an excessive expenditure of money, would be unenforceable or unjust. One may say in general terms that the existence of a duty must be based upon knowledge of the hazard, ability to foresee the consequences of not checking or removing it, and the ability to abate it. Moreover in many cases, as for example in Scrutton LJ's hypothetical case of stamping out a fire [see *Job Edwards Ltd v Birmingham Navigations Co* [1924] 1 KB 341 at 357], or the present case, where the hazard could have been removed with little effort and no expenditure, no problem arises; but other cases may not be so simple. In such situations the standard ought to be to require of the occupier what it is reasonable to expect of him in his individual circumstances. Thus, less must be expected of the infirm than of the able-bodied: the owner of small property where a hazard arises which threatens a neighbour with substantial interests should not have to do so much as one with larger interests of his own at stake and greater resources to protect them: if the small owner does what he can and promptly calls on his neighbour to provide additional resources, he may be held to have done his duty: he should not be liable unless it is clearly proved that he could, and reasonably in his individual circumstance should, have done more. This approach to a difficult matter is in fact that which the courts in their more recent decisions have taken.'

[31] In both *The Wagon Mound (No 2)* and *Goldman's* case the judgments, which repay full rereading, are directed to what a reasonable person in the shoes of the defendant would have done. The label nuisance or negligence is treated as of no real significance. In this field, I think, the concern of the common law lies in working out the fair and just content and incidents of a neighbour's duty rather than affixing a label and inferring the extent of the duty from it.

[32] Even in the field of *Rylands v Fletcher* strict liability (see (1868) LR 3 HL 330, [1861–73] All ER Rep 1) the House of Lords in *Cambridge Water Co v Eastern Counties Leather plc* [1994] 1 All ER 53, [1994] 2 AC 264 has stressed the principles of reasonable user and reasonable foreseeability (see the speech of Lord Goff of Chieveley [1994] 1 All ER 53 at 71–72, [1994] 2 AC 264 at 299–301). It was the absence of reasonable foreseeability of harm of the relevant type that excluded liability in that case.

[33] Approaching the present case in the light of those governing concepts and the judge's findings, I think that there was a continuing nuisance during Flecksun's ownership until at least the completion of the underpinning and the piling in July 1992. It matters not that further cracking of the superstructure may not have occurred after March 1990. The encroachment of the roots was causing continuing damage to the land by dehydrating the soil and inhibiting rehydration. Damage consisting of impairment of the load-bearing qualities of residential land is, in my view, itself a nuisance. This is consistent with the opinions of Talbot J

a in *Masters'* case [1978] 2 All ER 664, [1978] QB 841 and the Court of Appeal in the instant case, although neither Talbot J nor Pill LJ analysed specifically what they regarded as a continuing nuisance. Cracking in the building was consequential. Having regard to the proximity of the plane tree to Delaware Mansions, a real risk of damage to the land and the foundations was foreseeable on the part of Westminster, as in effect the judge found. It is arguable that the cost of repairs to b the cracking could have been recovered as soon as it became manifest. That point need not be decided, although I am disposed to think that a reasonable landowner would notify the controlling local authority or neighbour as soon as tree root damage was suspected. It is agreed that if the plane tree had been removed, the need to underpin would have been avoided and the total cost of repair to the building would have been only £14,000. On the other hand the judge c has found that, once the council declined to remove the tree, the underpinning and piling costs were reasonably incurred, despite the council's trench.

[34] It is at this point that I see *Solloway v Hampshire CC* (1981) 79 LGR 449 as important as a salutary warning against imposing unreasonable and unacceptable burdens on local authorities or other tree owners. If reasonableness between d neighbours is the key to the solution of problems in this field, it cannot be right to visit the authority or owner responsible for a tree with a large bill for underpinning without giving them notice of the damage and the opportunity of avoiding further damage by removal of the tree. Should they elect to preserve the tree for environmental reasons, they may fairly be expected to bear the cost of underpinning or other reasonably necessary remedial works; and the party on e whom the cost has fallen may recover it, even though there may be elements of hitherto unsatisfied pre-proprietorship damage or protection for the future. But, as a general proposition, I think that the defendant is entitled to notice and a reasonable opportunity of abatement before liability for remedial expenditure can arise. In this case Westminster had ample notice and time before the f underpinning and piling, and is in my opinion liable.

'A world elsewhere'

[35] Although counsel evidently preferred a more insular approach, it can be useful to remember that there is a common law world elsewhere which may provide some help, particularly on issues where English law is not yet settled. g Without undertaking extensive research, it is not difficult to find some support for the views already expressed in Australasian and United States jurisprudence.

[36] In Fleming *The Law of Torts* (9th edn, 1998) p 498 there is the following passage:

h   'Abatement is a privilege, not a duty. An ancient ruling has it that it "destroys any right of action in respect of the nuisance". But as now interpreted, it means no more than that the act of abatement has the effect of removing the nuisance so that the claimant is not entitled to future damages. He may, however, recover damages for past injury. And although some dicta assume that the cost of removing the nuisance is also irrecoverable, it has been held j   that this does not preclude reimbursement for the cost of mitigating future damage.'

For the last sentence three decisions are cited in a footnote, two of them in roots cases, namely *Proprietors of Strata Plan No 14198 v Cowell* (1989) 24 NSWLR 478 and *City of Richmond v Scantelbury* [1991] 2 VR 38 at 48. It is of interest that in *Cowell's* case in the Supreme Court of New South Wales, Hodgson J said (at 488):

'In a case such as this, as a general rule, I think it is highly desirable that persons in the position of the defendants be given notice of this kind, and thus have a fair opportunity to abate the nuisance themselves before large sums of money are spent on such works as building barrier walls.'

The judge went on to excuse the failure to give notice in that particular case, on the ground that it would have made no difference to the inactivity of the defendant. He also found that the defendant was not liable until it (knowingly) adopted a continuing nuisance which had not been reasonably foreseeable. On the particular facts he disallowed the cost of underpinning but allowed the cost of other remedial works.

[37] In *Prosser and Keeton on Torts* (5th edn, 1984) p 640 there is this:

'Also, in addition to the depreciation measure of damages, the plaintiff in a nuisance case may recover the reasonable cost of his own efforts to abate the nuisance or prevent future injury. For example, where a sewer line backed up and overflowed into the plaintiff's theater, the plaintiff hired a contractor to re-lay lateral sewer lines to avoid the problem in the future, and the contractor's charges being reasonable, the plaintiff was allowed to recover them. Such decisions seem correct, though it should also be noted that to the extent the plaintiff is in fact able to abate the nuisance by his own efforts, or to the extent it is abatable by injunction, permanent damages are not assessed.'

The sewer case cited is *Stratford Theater Inc v Town of Stratford* (1953) 140 Conn 422. Two other cases are cited.

[38] In the end, in my opinion, the law can be summed up in the proposition that, where there is a continuing nuisance of which the defendant knew or ought to have known, reasonable remedial expenditure may be recovered by the owner who has had to incur it. In the present case this was Flecksun. Accordingly I would dismiss the appeal with costs.

LORD CLYDE.

[39] My Lords, I have had the advantage of reading in draft the speech of my noble and learned friend Lord Cooke of Thorndon. I agree with it and for the reasons which he has given I, too, would dismiss this appeal.

LORD HUTTON.

[40] My Lords, I have had the advantage of reading in draft the speech of my noble and learned friend Lord Cooke of Thorndon. I agree with it and for the reasons which he has given I, too, would dismiss this appeal.

Appeal dismissed.

Dilys Tausz   Barrister.

a # Igwemma v Chief Constable of Greater Manchester Police
[2001] EWCA Civ 953

b COURT OF APPEAL, CIVIL DIVISION
KENNEDY AND RIX LJJ
6, 20 JUNE 2001

c *Jury – Answers – Finality – Civil proceedings – Jury answering questions in civil action and being discharged by judge – Jury remaining in court while judge clarifying outcome of case for benefit of claimant – Jury foreman realising jury had misunderstood question – Judge permitting jury to alter answer – Whether judge in civil proceedings having discretion to allow discharged jury to alter answer given by them – Guidance on exercise of discretion.*

d The claimant, I, was arrested by a police constable after being involved in a fracas with two brothers. He was taken to a police station and charged with conduct likely to cause a breach of the peace, but the prosecution was later discontinued. I subsequently brought an action against the defendant chief constable for false imprisonment and malicious prosecution. At trial, four questions were put to the jury. The fourth question was: 'Has the claimant proved that it is more likely *e* than not that after he had interviewed [the brothers] at the police station [the constable] did not honestly believe that the claimant had committed a breach of the peace?' The jury answered that question in the affirmative. As a result, the claim for malicious prosecution succeeded, although the claim for false imprisonment failed because of the jury's answer to the other questions. The judge then told the *f* jury that he had to consider an outstanding question of law and that they could sit and listen, but that they were free to leave since their function was finished. The jury stayed. Counsel for I then asked the judge to explain the situation to his client. The judge responded by saying that he had won on one claim and lost on the other. At that point, the jury foreman told the judge that the jury thought that they might have misunderstood the questions since they had believed, in *g* relation to the fourth question, that the claimant was the police. After clarifying the meaning of that question, the judge asked the jury to retire. When they returned four minutes later, they answered the fourth question in the negative. I appealed, contending that the judge had erred in law or in the exercise of his discretion by permitting the jury to alter the answer that they had initially *h* returned to the fourth question.

Held – A judge in civil proceedings could allow an alteration to be made in a verdict which had been returned, or an answer which had been given, even after the jury had been discharged, provided that the interests of justice made it *j* appropriate for him to do so. In deciding whether or not the interests of justice favoured that course, the judge first had to look carefully at the time which had elapsed since the original verdicts or answers had been returned. Secondly, he had to consider why it was said to be appropriate to seek further assistance from the jury. It would, for example, be easier to seek further assistance from a jury where the jury itself raised the possibility of a misunderstanding in circumstances where there was scope for misunderstanding, as opposed to the situation where there seemed to be no misunderstanding and no obvious scope for misunderstanding or other apparent acceptable reason to alter what had already been said. Thirdly, the judge had to consider whether the jury might have been persuaded to change its view by anything said or done since it gave its original verdicts or answers, especially if anything had emerged which would not normally be heard by a jury during a contested trial. There was, however, no rule prohibiting a jury, once discharged, from returning a verdict which was the result of further debate. A conclusion to the contrary would be an unnecessary fetter on judicial discretion. If there had been a misunderstanding which could only be eliminated by some further debate, it was right for the judge to allow such debate. In the instant case, the judge had been entitled to proceed as he had done, and accordingly the appeal would be dismissed (see [33]–[35], [46], [47], [50], [51], below).

Notes
For jury once discharged, see 26 *Halsbury's Laws* (4th edn reissue) para 448.

Cases referred to in judgments
R v *Alowi* (8 March 1999, unreported), CA.
R v *Andrews* (1986) 82 Cr App Rep 148, CA.
R v *Aylott* [1996] 2 Cr App Rep 169, CA.
R v *Bills* [1995] 2 Cr App Rep 643, CA.
R v *Carter* [1964] 1 All ER 187, [1964] 2 QB 1, [1964] 2 WLR 266, CCA.
R v *Follen* [1994] Crim LR 225, CA.
R v *Maloney* [1996] 2 Cr App Rep 303, CA.
R v *Parkin* (1824) 1 Mood CC 45, CCR.
R v *Russell* (1984) 148 JP 765, CA.
R v *Steadman* (13 January 1994, unreported), CA.
R v *Vodden* (1853) Dears CC 229, 169 ER 706, CCR.

Appeal
The claimant, Joseph Igwemma, appealed with permission of Potter LJ granted on 22 June 2000 from the decision of Judge Tetlow at Manchester County Court on 29 March 2000 allowing the jury to alter the answer to a question put to it in the trial of the claimant's action for false imprisonment and malicious prosecution against the defendant, the Chief Constable of Greater Manchester Police, even though he had already discharged the jury. The facts are set out in the judgment of Kennedy LJ.

Leslie Thomas (instructed by *Jackson & Cantor*, Liverpool) for the claimant.
Michael Smith (instructed by *Weightmans*, Manchester) for the defendant.

Cur adv vult

20 June 2001. The following judgments were delivered.

KENNEDY LJ.
[1] This appeal concerns the decision of a trial judge to permit a jury hearing a civil action, after it had answered all four questions asked of it, to reconsider its answer to the fourth question and then to return a different answer to that question.

Facts

a

[2] For the purposes of the appeal the facts can be briefly stated. The claimant, Mr Igwemma, owned a building at Chorley Old Road, Bolton. On the ground floor there was a shop, and on the first and second floors there were two flats, let to tenants. On 1 April 1996 Mr Paul Eckersley, the tenant of the second floor flat, decided to move out. He was assisted by his brother Neil, and they opened a rear

b door on the ground floor. That activated a burglar alarm. The claimant and his brother-in-law, Chris Smith, went to see what was happening, and there was then an incident involving the landlord on the one side and the tenant and his brother on the other side. The police were called, and Pc Parker was one of the two police officers who arrived. He arrested the claimant, who was taken to the police station and handed over to the custody officer, Sgt Kenyon. The claimant

c was charged with conduct likely to cause a breach of the peace, and was detained for a time. The prosecution was later discontinued, and the claimant brought proceedings against the chief constable for false imprisonment and malicious prosecution. He claimed that Pc Parker failed properly to investigate when he first arrived, and jumped to the wrong conclusion as to the cause of the trouble.

d He further claimed that the officer continued to detain him when he knew from his inquiries that the claimant should be released.

Trial

[3] At the trial four questions were formulated for the consideration of the jury. They were as follows:

e

'(1) Has the defendant proved that it is more likely than not that Pc Parker honestly believed that the claimant would commit a breach of the peace if he did not arrest the claimant? (2) Has the defendant proved that it is more likely than not that Pc Parker informed the claimant that he was under arrest when he arrested the claimant? (3) Has the defendant proved that it is more

f likely than not that Pc Parker informed the claimant of the reason for his arrest when he arrested the claimant? (4) Has the claimant proved that it is more likely than not that after he had interviewed the Eckersleys at the police station Pc Parker did not honestly believe that the claimant had committed a breach of the peace?'

g [4] In retrospect it can be said that it might have been better if the questions had referred to 'Mr Igwemma' rather than the 'claimant', and if the references to 'he' and 'Pc Parker' in question (4) had been transposed.

[5] When directing the jury the judge made it clear that questions (1) to (3) related to false imprisonment, where the burden of proof lay upon the defendant,

h whereas question (4) related to malicious prosecution, where the burden of proof was upon the claimant. There is no criticism of the conduct of the trial up to the point at which the jury answered all four questions in the affirmative. However, it is worth noting that after retiring and before answering the four questions the jury did send a note to the judge which asked: 'Can we as a group state that

j (a) procedures were not followed when Mr Igwemma was incarcerated, locked up; (b) treated unfairly as a result of?'

[6] Apparently that question was asked when the jury had already reached conclusions in relation to the four questions they had been asked to consider, but had not yet revealed their conclusions. After considering the note with counsel the judge answered the jury's question in the negative and then, having obtained confirmation that the jury was ready to answer the four questions they had been

asked to consider, those questions were put to the jury and the foreman answered
each question in the affirmative, and stated that the decisions were unanimous.
The jury's own question does not appear for present purposes to be of any
relevance.

[7] As the judge pointed out, the effect of the jury's answers was that the claim
of false imprisonment failed, but the allegation of malicious prosecution succeeded,
and it became a matter for the judge to assess damages. There was a further issue
arising out of the claimant's detention at the police station, and the judge said to
the jury:

> 'There is the one issue which you were deprived of because it was not an
> issue before you and that is the question of whether the detention in the
> police station—whether he should have been released after he had been
> charged at 12.15 or whether the custody sergeant was right on what he had
> to keep him there. That is curiously a question of law for me. If you want
> to sit and listen to it all you are very welcome to do that or if you want to go
> you are free to go, you need not be unanimous on that, I can tell you that
> now. So sit and listen, you are entitled to, you have, as it were, brought in
> the answers, this is another part of the matter, but you are finished in your
> function so entirely as you like to do. If you want to go feel free to do, if you
> want to stay, stay. You do not have to be unanimous on that.'

[8] Counsel for the claimant then asked for a couple of minutes to discuss the
position with his client, saying, 'I am fairly certain that he did not actually
understand what has happened in the last few minutes'. The judge said:

> 'No, he may not do. He has won on one, he has lost on t'other, it is as
> simple as that, unless the jury have got it wrong themselves. Yes, you want
> to stay?'

[9] The final question was apparently addressed to the jury, and a juror then
said something which the shorthand writer has been unable to decipher, after
which the exchanges continued as follows:

> 'Judge: Did you give me the wrong answer?
> The Foreman: I think maybe that we misunderstood the four questions.
> Judge: Oh, right. I just wondered—can I explain it, the way you said yes
> to the last question, the burden on the claimant ...
> The Foreman: We were led to believe that the claimant was—on the
> fourth question—was the police.
> Judge: It is not the police, it is the claimant.
> The Foreman: That is what we were led to believe.
> Counsel for the defendant: I am sorry, I am afraid it is probably the fact
> that I did not put claimant and defendant at the top of the sheet when the
> questions were drafted but the claimant is Mr Igwemma and the defendant
> in respect of all the questions is the police.
> Judge: Well you understood the defendant was the police?
> The Foreman: On three parts we realised ...
> Judge: Well, just a minute, I had better ask you to retire. The fourth
> question is: "Has Mr Igwemma proved it is more likely than not after he had
> interviewed the Eckersleys at the police station that Pc Parker did not
> honestly believe that the claimant had committed a breach of the peace?" Do
> you want to just retire for a moment just to clarify that? Because yes,

a   obviously if—at the moment—let me put it this way, by answering yes to the fourth, if that is what you meant, that means that Mr Igwemma—Pc Parker did not believe that he was guilty of a breach of the peace after he had interviewed the Eckersleys. Now if that is not what you mean—retire for a moment and see what it is, but the claimant is Mr Igwemma anyway. So you are happy about the first three, that is all right?

b   The Foreman: Yes.

    Judge: Good.'

[10] The jury then retired again and when they returned four minutes later the transcript reads:

c   'Judge: Ladies and Gentlemen of the Jury, you have now sorted it out have you?

    The Foreman: Yes we have.

    Judge: I think what I am going to do is I will ask the clerk to ask question 4 again and then get the answer whichever way it is.

d   The Clerk: Question 4 is "Has the claimant proved that it is more likely than not that after he had interviewed the Eckersleys at the police station PC Parker did not honestly believe that the claimant had committed a breach of the peace?" What is your answer?

    The Foreman: No.

    Judge: And that is the answer of you all?

e   The Foreman: That is the answer of us all.

    Judge: Thank you very much indeed. Well thank you very much for bringing that to our attention otherwise it would have—that is all right, that is all right. I apologise probably on behalf of the drafter and myself for not making it clear. It can be very confusing, it is easy for us we are used to the phraseology, so do not feel embarrassed at all.'

f

[11] Mr Thomas, who has appeared for the claimant before us, but who did not appear in the court below, takes three points in relation to the facts. First, he points out that after the jury returned their original answers they were in effect discharged. That I accept. They were told that they were finished in their function and were free to go. Secondly, Mr Thomas points out that even when

g   the jury knew the effect of their answers initially they expressed no unease until the judge, when seeking to encapsulate the effect of the jury's answers for the benefit of the claimant, added 'unless the jury have got it wrong themselves'. At that point, Mr Thomas submits, the judge wrongly opened the door to further consideration by the jury of their existing decision. I accept that the judge's

h   suggestion that the jury may have got it wrong was unfortunate, but it may well have been prompted by some visible jury unease. A few minutes later, in the absence of the jury, the judge said that it was clear that the man in the back row was unhappy, so it is difficult to accept that the judge's suggestion was of any particular significance, and even if it was it can only have encouraged members

j   of the jury to say something which patently some of them, at least, wanted to say. No one even now suggests that the judge was pressing the jury to reach a different conclusion. Thirdly Mr Thomas submits that when the jury foreman said 'I think that maybe we misunderstood the four questions', the judge wrongly focused only on question (4). Mr Smith, for the defendant, believes that the foreman may actually have said 'we misunderstood the fourth question'. In the absence of agreement between counsel I cannot so read the transcript, but I note

that counsel who appeared for the claimant in the court below did not suggest
that the jury should be invited to reconsider questions (1) to (3), and before
sending the jury out for the last time the judge prudently obtained the foreman's
confirmation that the jury was content with the answers given in relation to
questions (1) to (3). I therefore conclude that whatever the foreman may have
said initially, the jury never sought to re-open their answers to those earlier
questions.

Ground of appeal

[12] The sole ground of appeal is that:

> 'The learned judge erred in law and further or in the alternative in the
> exercise or purported exercise of his judicial discretion, by permitting the
> jury to alter the answers it had initially returned to the questions posed of it,
> when having received the verdict of the jury he permitted the jury to further
> discuss the consequences of their verdict after the verdict was announced by
> the foreman of the jury in open court.'

[13] On 11 April 2000 the trial judge refused permission to appeal on the basis
that the matter was within the proper exercise of his discretion, and permission
to appeal was granted by the single Lord Justice on 22 June 2000.

Law

[14] There is no civil procedure rule which lays down what is to happen when,
as in this case, almost immediately after giving its decision a civil jury indicates
that it is unhappy with what has been said. So far as counsel have been able to
ascertain there is no statutory provision and there is no decided case which bears
directly upon the point, but it is worth bearing in mind the overriding objective
of the Civil Procedure Rules set out in CPR 1.1, which is to enable the court to
deal with cases justly, with no unnecessary expenditure on costs.

[15] Both counsel submit, and I accept, that some assistance can be gained
from authorities in the criminal field. In *R v Parkin* (1824) 1 Mood CC 45 the
Court of Crown Cases Reserved considered a case of larceny where the defendant
contended that he had found a stolen bank note long after it was stolen. The jury
said they found the defendant guilty of having the note in his possession, but how
he got it they could not say. The judge asked if they thought he might have found
it, one juror said 'Yes' and the judge said that amounted to an acquittal and a
verdict of not guilty was recorded. The judge admonished the defendant and
ordered the bank note to be given to the prosecutor. Some jurors then, within
three or four minutes of the verdict of not guilty being recorded, said they did not
agree with the answer which had been given, and that the juror who gave it had
no authority to answer as he did. The judge asked the jury to retire again, and
the jury then returned a verdict of guilty. The Court of Crown Cases Reserved
held (at 46–47) that 'the mistake in the verdict might be corrected'.

[16] *R v Vodden* (1853) Dears CC 229, 169 ER 706 was another decision of the
Court of Crown Cases Reserved in relation to a charge of larceny. Both the Clerk
of the Peace and the Chairman of Quarter Sessions understood the jury spokesman
to have returned a verdict of not guilty, but when the prisoner was discharged other
jurors said the verdict was guilty. The prisoner was returned to the dock, and all
12 jurors then said the verdict was guilty, including the original spokesman, who
said that was what he had originally said. A verdict of guilty was recorded, and
Pollock CB said that the court was all of the opinion that the conviction was right:

a 'The mistake was corrected within a reasonable time and on the very occasion on which it was made.'

[17] In *R v Carter* [1964] 1 All ER 187, [1964] 2 QB 1 the two appellants were alleged to have held a razor to the face of a man in order to rob him. There was an issue as to the use of the razor, and prosecuting counsel finally submitted that if the jury was not satisfied about its use they could acquit of the offence charged,
b and find the defendants guilty of the lesser offence of aggravated robbery. In summing up the judge did not expressly leave that alternative to the jury. When a verdict of not guilty was returned the defendants were discharged. The foreman then explained that the jury wished to convict of the lesser charge. In the Court of Criminal Appeal Lord Parker CJ said:

c   '... a verdict is not complete until a jury has dealt with all the possible verdicts on the indictment, and, if a judge discharges a prisoner before the jury have completed their verdict, in the view of this court that discharge is a complete nullity.' (See [1964] 1 All ER 187 at 188, [1964] 2 QB 1 at 6.)

[18] So in both of the nineteenth-century cases and in *R v Carter*, what appeared
d to be a verdict of not guilty was changed into one of guilty when it emerged within a short space of time that the original verdict did not represent the real intentions of the jury. Furthermore in *R v Carter* the court was able to overcome the difficulty created by the fact that the defendants had been discharged.

[19] It seems that none of the three authorities to which I have referred thus far were cited to the Court of Appeal (Criminal Division) in *R v Russell* (1984)
e 148 JP 765, a decision on which Mr Thomas now places some reliance. In that case the defendant was charged with obstructing a police officer contrary to s 23(4) of the Misuse of Drugs Act 1971. The jury was given a majority direction, and when brought back to court about two hours later, at 3.16 pm, was still unable to reach a decision. The judge then told the jury that there was no need
f to rush, but indicated that he would bring the jury back to court at about 4 pm unless they reached a decision before then. The jury was in fact brought back to court at 4.07 pm, and when asked if they had reached a verdict on which at least 10 of them agreed, the foreman said 'No'. The members of the jury were not asked if they were likely to reach a verdict and were simply discharged. A few minutes later the jury bailiff came into court and said that the jury wanted more
g time. The court was reconvened at 4.15 pm, and the judge permitted the jury to deliberate further. At 4.40 pm they returned a verdict of guilty. Popplewell J, giving the judgment of the court, said (at 768):

'The primary point that is taken in this appeal is that once the jury has been
h   discharged by the Assistant Recorder no agreement by his counsel to the continuation of the trial could put the matter right. That argument is not founded on any authority that counsel could have been able to find. Counsel for the prosecution, in helpful address to the court, has submitted that once the jury have been told that they are discharged from reaching a verdict in the matter that is the end of that particular trial, and that any subsequent
j   proceedings are a nullity because the jury, having been discharged, are *functus officio*. In our judgment, that is a good argument. When the jury returned the Assistant Recorder should have asked them whether there was any sensible prospect of their reaching agreement if they had more time.'

[20] In her note on the decision ([1984] Crim LR 425 at 426), Professor Birch is critical, pointing out how much seems to have been hung on the fact that the jury

had been discharged, a matter which (albeit in relation to the defendants) was not found to be an insuperable obstacle in *R v Carter* [1964] 1 All ER 187, [1964] 2 QB 1.

[21] Eighteen months later another division of the Court of Appeal (Criminal Division), presided over by Lord Lane CJ, considered the appeal of *R v Andrews* (1986) 82 Cr App Rep 148. The appellant and his wife were charged with cruelty to a five-year-old child. The jury convicted the wife of positive acts of cruelty, but in relation to the appellant returned a verdict of not guilty. A police officer gave evidence of the wife's antecedent history and her counsel began to address the court. The jury then passed a note to the court which read: 'We thought we had found Paul Andrews guilty of wilful neglect, what happens now?' About ten minutes had elapsed since the verdict of not guilty had been returned. The judge then accepted an amended verdict de bene esse, and in the Court of Appeal Simon Brown J, having referred to the two nineteenth-century cases, said (at 154–155):

'It seems to this Court, both on those two authorities and as a matter of general principle, that the position in law is as follows: where the jury seeks to alter a verdict which has been pronounced by the foreman, the judge has a discretion whether to allow the alteration to be made. In exercising that discretion he will, it goes without saying, take into account all the circumstances of the case; in particular the important considerations will be the length of time which has elapsed between the original verdict and the moment when the jury express their wish to alter it, the probable reason for the initial mistake, the necessity to ensure that justice is done not only to the defendant but also to the prosecution. The fact that the defendant has been discharged from custody is one of the factors but is not necessarily fatal to the judge's discretion to alter the verdict to one of guilty. If the jury has been discharged and *a fortiori* if they have dispersed, it might well be impossible for the judge to allow the verdict to be changed. That however it is unnecessary to decide upon the instant appeal. Clearly if there were any question of the jury's verdict being altered as a result of anything they heard after returning their initial verdict, then there could be no question of allowing a fresh verdict to be returned.'

[22] In *R v Follen* [1994] Crim LR 225 a jury which had been given a majority direction said that there were no counts on which at least ten of them were agreed, and that there was no realistic prospect of verdicts if more time were allowed. They were then discharged, and the judge indicated that there would have to be a fresh trial. That was all somewhat surprising, because shortly before being brought back into court the jury had sent a note to the judge indicating that ten of them were agreed in relation to one unspecified count. There was then a disturbance in the public gallery, and some disturbance in the jury box. The judge's impression was that there had been a misunderstanding, so he asked the jury to retire again. A few minutes later they came back into court, and indicated that ten of them were agreed in relation to one count, a count of buggery, of which they then convicted. In the Court of Appeal both *R v Russell* (1984) 148 JP 765 and *R v Andrews* (1986) 82 Cr App Rep 148 were considered, and Watkins LJ said:

'We do not doubt that there is no fixed rule of principle or of law to the effect that it inevitably follows that once a judge has made an order discharging a jury from returning a verdict there cannot arise some circumstance which permits

a a judge to set aside that order and thereby to allow the jury further consideration
of the responses they have made to questions asked of them as to their
verdicts either by the clerk of the court or by the judge himself or both. But
in our view it is only in the very rare circumstances that that might be done.'

[23] In that case the Court of Appeal concluded that the judge was wrong to
b set aside the discharge and the appeal was allowed.

[24] *R v Bills* [1995] 2 Cr App Rep 643 is the next authority on which Mr Thomas
relies. In that case the jury acquitted the defendant of wounding with intent to do
grievous bodily harm, but convicted him of unlawful wounding. They remained
in the jury box whilst the court was told of his previous convictions, and they
were then discharged. A juror then told the usher that the foreman had given the
c wrong verdict. The jury was reassembled and asked to explain. Through their
foreman they indicated that they had intended to convict of the more serious
charge, and the judge accepted that verdict. In the Court of Appeal *R v Follen* was
referred to, and Russell LJ said (at 647):

d   'In our judgment it cannot be gainsaid that the jury, before returning the
verdict which the judge accepted and upon which he sentenced the appellant,
had heard material which they had no right to hear in the trial process,
namely previous convictions of the appellant. We bear in mind in
determining whether to quash the section 18 verdict that the original verdict
returned was plain and unequivocal. We do not understand how there could
e   have been any misunderstanding as suggested by the foreman. The summing-up
had been clear, and there was no indication of dissent when the section 20
verdict was announced. Wherever the truth lies, of course this appellant is
understandably convinced that the truth lies in the jury hearing his previous
convictions. We are satisfied that the verdict under section 18 is an unsafe
f   and unsatisfactory verdict. The judge should not have permitted it to be
returned in the particular circumstances of this case.'

[25] Mr Thomas submits that in the present case the original answers were
plain and unequivocal, the judge's direction had been clear, and there was no
immediate indication of dissent when the answers were given.

g [26] The next decision to which we were referred is *R v Aylott* [1996] 2 Cr App
Rep 169. Together with a co-accused, Clarke, Aylott was charged on an indictment
which alleged murder, with manslaughter as an alternative. After being given a
majority direction the jury sent a note to the judge which contained voting
figures, so the judge did not show the note to counsel. When brought back to
h court the jury indicated that even if allowed more time they were unlikely to
agree to the requisite extent. What they did not indicate clearly was that they
were only in disagreement as to one part of the indictment. They were then
discharged. The judge rose and went to his room, and almost at once he was told
by the court clerk or by an usher that the jury had reached a verdict. Having
j discussed the situation with counsel he concluded that he may have misunderstood
the note. He then received a second note from the jury which read:

      'As directed we have viewed the two defendants separately. The case of
Aylott we have reached a unanimous verdict. The case of Clarke we have
reached a unanimous verdict on the first count, but are hung on the second
count the alternative charge of manslaughter.'

[**27**] That note was considered with counsel. When they returned to court the jury indicated, in answer to a question from the judge, that they had reached their *a* conclusion in relation to Aylott before sending any note, and since being discharged they had spoken to no one outside their number. Aylott was then convicted of murder, Clarke was acquitted, and in Clarke's case, the jury being unable to agree in relation to the alternative count of manslaughter, he was discharged. In the Court of Appeal the authorities were extensively considered, *b* and Pill LJ said (at 177):

'In the judgment of this Court it is open to the Court to uphold the conduct of a judge who has discharged a jury and later taken a verdict from them. There is no fixed rule of principle or of law to the effect that once a jury have been discharged from returning a verdict there cannot arise some circumstance *c* which permits a judge to set aside the order of discharge. The discharge in the present case was based on a fundamental mistake. When discharged by the judge, the jury had reached verdicts. The judge was entitled, in the circumstances, to proceed to consider the question and to take the verdicts, in effect setting aside the discharge which he himself had ordered. As in [*R v Steadman* (13 January 1994, unreported)], it was plain in this case that the jury *d* had remained together and had not spoken to anyone outside their number. We have considered whether there is a principle underlying the cases to which we have been referred. The principle which emerges, in our view, is the fundamental concern of the courts to ensure that proceedings are fair and do justice in a particular case. Fairness is important to defendants and also to *e* the public.'

[**28**] The appeal was dismissed. Mr Smith, for the defendant before us, invites our attention to the last sentence which I have cited.

[**29**] In *R v Maloney* [1996] 2 Cr App Rep 303, when a jury which had received a majority direction returned its verdict, the clerk of the court omitted to ask how *f* many of them agreed and how many dissented. Section 17(3) of the Juries Act 1974 provides:

'The Crown Court shall not accept a verdict of guilty ... unless the foreman of the jury has stated in open court the number of jurors who respectively agreed to and dissented from the verdict.' *g*

[**30**] The jury was allowed to go, and the omission was then spotted. After the weekend the jury was reassembled and answered the question which should have been put to them on the previous Friday. In the Court of Appeal it was pointed out that prior to the passing of the Criminal Justice and Public Order Act 1994 dispersal of the jury would have been fatal, but on the Monday no further *h* deliberation was required. The foreman simply said in the presence of the other jurors what the position had been when the verdict was returned, so as to enable the court to accept the verdict, and the appeal was dismissed.

[**31**] The most recent decision of which we are aware is *R v Alowi* (8 March 1999, unreported). The appellant had faced an indictment containing seven *j* counts. The jury convicted of counts 4 to 7 and was given a majority direction in relation to counts 1 to 3. Later the jury sent a note which led the judge to believe that no agreement was likely in relation to counts 1 and 3. They were brought back to court and they convicted on count 2. They were not asked if, given time, they would be able to return verdicts on counts 1 and 3. They were simply discharged from returning verdicts on those counts. There was some inconclusive discussion

a between the judge and counsel about what would happen next, and the jury returned to their room to collect their belongings. They also took the opportunity to continue their discussions. They told the court clerk what they were doing, and he told the judge. He decided to set aside his order discharging the jury, and they then convicted on count 1. They were unable to agree in relation to count 3. In the Court of Appeal Judge LJ said:

b   ' … it is necessary to revert to first principles. In our judgment those are clear. Once the judge has discharged the jury, normally speaking, it is functus officio. The principle is not absolute or immutable, and there are some very limited circumstances where the judge is permitted to set aside the order and seek further assistance from the jury, either to provide their
c   verdict or to explain some aspects of it. Counsel submitted that this was a matter in effect of broad discretion. The judge had to exercise careful judgment but he was entitled to set aside the discharge if, following discharge, first, he was satisfied that there were no extraneous reasons which may have affected the jury's further consideration of the case, that nothing
d   was said in court which might have affected their deliberations, and that there was no reason to believe that anything had happened to the jury physically in the sense that there was any ground for concern about whether they had properly remained together and gone straight back to their jury room to resume their discussions. We recognise the force of those points, and no doubt in a case where the discretion is being exercised they form a
e   sensible basis for a judge's consideration about how to reach his decision, in the light of all the particular features of the individual case. What we have done however is to consider the authorities which bear on the point where, exceptionally, the jury was permitted to return a verdict after it had been discharged by the judge. These occasions are very limited indeed. If, before
f   discharge, the jury has in fact reached verdicts, and they have been discharged accidentally without being invited to deliver their verdicts, then the judge is entitled to set aside the discharge and accept the verdicts which the jury have already reached. That seems to us to be well demonstrated by the cases of *R v Carter*, *R v Aylott*, and *R v Steadman*. Similarly where the court has made a procedural error in the taking of majority verdicts and, let it be
g   noted in the context of a majority verdict of guilty, and the mistake was rectified, there was no problem in setting aside the discharge. The jury were invited to return to court and give the court the precise figures on which the majority verdicts had been based—*R v Maloney*. But it is clearly established by *R v Russell* and again *R v Follen* that once discharged the jury cannot return
h   a verdict which is the result of further debate. For that purpose the verdict is a nullity and so far as *R v Follen* is concerned, the verdict was set aside because there had been discussion in court in the presence of the jury about a possible retrial. In our judgment, looking at the facts of this case overall, the jury was discharged; having been discharged they listened to discussions
j   in open court about the possible consequences of the verdicts which they had reached; they then returned to their room; they continued discussing the outstanding counts without any of the normal arrangements which apply to a jury in retirement, and having discussed these matters at some length, they then returned to court and returned verdicts which they had been discharged from giving. We do not think that it was open to the judge to set aside the order discharging the jury from further considering those counts. This was

not a case in which a jury were simply recording verdicts which they had in
truth already reached.'

Submissions and conclusions

[**32**] Mr Thomas submits that where a verdict has been returned it can be
revisited where there has been a plain and obvious mistake. Whether it should
be revisited depends on the time lapse before the jury raises any complaint,
whether that complaint has been instigated by anyone else, whether during that
interval the jury has heard anything it should not have heard, and whether there
is any good and obvious reason for the jury's apparent change of mind. Mr Thomas
further submits that, despite the weight of authority to the contrary, once the
jury is discharged the trial is at an end, and no fresh verdict can be received.

[**33**] Mr Smith submits that what matters is the integrity of the trial process,
whether there is any real risk that the jury has changed its mind as a result of
things said or done after it has delivered its original verdict. The object should be
to achieve justice without too much weight being attached to the formal step of
discharging the jury.

[**34**] In my judgment it is important not to lose sight of what, in any jury trial,
criminal or civil, the court is attempting to achieve. The object is to do justice
between the parties, without unnecessary delay or expense. The function of the
jury is to make findings in relation to those issues which the jury are asked to
resolve, and it is important that the jury's findings should then be effectively
transmitted to and understood by the court. If there has been, or may have been,
some misunderstanding, that must be investigated and put right, if that can be
done without injustice to either party. So, in one sense, a judge does have a wide
discretion. He can allow an alteration to be made in a verdict which has been
returned or an answer which has been given, even after the jury has been
discharged, but only where the interests of justice make it appropriate for him to
do so. In considering whether or not the interests of justice favour that course
the judge will necessarily look carefully at: (1) The time that has elapsed since the
original verdicts or answers were returned. (2) Why it is said to be appropriate to
seek further assistance from the jury. It will, for example, be easier to seek further
assistance from a jury where, as here, the jury itself raises the possibility of a
misunderstanding in circumstances where there was scope for misunderstanding, as
opposed to the situation where there seems to be no misunderstanding and no
obvious scope for misunderstanding or other apparent acceptable reason to alter
what has already been said. (3) Whether the jury may have been persuaded to
change its view by anything said or done since it gave its original verdicts or
answers, especially if anything has emerged which would not normally be heard
by a jury during a contested trial.

[**35**] In the present case the timescale was short, and, despite the clear
direction, the possibility of a misunderstanding was implicit in question (4). That
there may have been a misunderstanding was raised by the jury before its
members separated and before they had heard anything they should not have
heard. In those circumstances, in my judgment, the judge was fully entitled to set
aside the discharge and to allow the jury to deliberate further under properly
controlled circumstances, in order to enable them to give the answer they wished
to give to question (4) in the first place. In *R v Alowi* it was said, obiter, that 'once
discharged the jury cannot return a verdict which is the result of further debate'.
The authorities relied upon do not seem to me to support that wide proposition,
which in my judgment is an unnecessary fetter on the judicial discretion. If there

a has been a misunderstanding it can only be eliminated by at least some further debate, and that, as it seems to me, is all that happened here. That is why, in my judgment, it was right for the judge to proceed as he did, and in consequence it was right for us to dismiss this appeal.

RIX LJ.

b [36] I agree. I gratefully adopt Kennedy LJ's statement of the facts and review of the authorities in the criminal field. I add some thoughts of my own because of the importance and interest of the issue raised by this appeal.

[37] It is interesting to observe how the authorities have proceeded cautiously from stage to stage, but also how, with the exception of *R v Russell* (1984) 148 JP 765, the courts have not in general regarded the discharge of the jury (or of the
c defendant) as an insuperable difficulty.

[38] The essential basis of the jurisdiction to accept a corrected verdict appears to be that a mistake has occurred which the jury itself identifies and wishes to put right. But mistakes come in different forms. In the earliest case which has come to light, that of *R v Parkin* (1824) 1 Mood CC 45, the mistake appears to have been
d that the judge mistook the single juror who said 'Yes' as answering for the jury as a whole. The jury retired and may well have continued their deliberations. In that case the verdict had been given, or at any rate taken, without the jury's authority. In the next case, *R v Vodden* (1853) Dears CC 229, 169 ER 706, the mistake was a simple one of mishearing (or possibly a slip of the foreman's tongue). The mistake was corrected, even though the defendant had been
e discharged, but nothing appears to have been made of that. Pollock CB said:

'We do not think the Court is called upon to say at what interval of time a correction should be made. All we do is to say that in the present case the interval was not too long. Nothing has been done but what daily takes place in the ordinary transactions of life; namely, a mistake is corrected within a
f reasonable time, and on the very spot on which it was made.' (See (1853) Dears CC 229 at 231, 169 ER 706 at 707.)

[39] In *R v Carter* [1964] 1 All ER 187, [1964] 2 QB 1, the mistake was one of omission: the jury had determined on a verdict on an alternative count, but had not been asked for it. The court held that in the circumstances the verdict that
g had so far been taken was incomplete and that the defendant's discharge was therefore a nullity. The discharge had been relied on as rendering the trial over and the jury and judge as functus officio. That theory, however, begged the practical question: if the verdict was incomplete and the trial was not over, then the discharge was itself founded on a mistake and could be treated as a nullity.

h [40] *R v Russell* was the first case in which the discharge of the jury was relied on as an insuperable barrier. In the absence of citation of any previous authority the court accepted the submission that it was, and that anything thereafter was a nullity. The court did not consider what might have been the position if the jury's discharge had not been an insuperable bar. However, the decision was
j rendered in ignorance of *R v Carter*, which was dealing with an analogous argument derived from the discharge of the defendant, and has not stood the test of time: see *R v Follen* [1994] Crim LR 225, *R v Bills* [1995] 2 Cr App Rep 643, *R v Aylott* [1996] 2 Cr App Rep 169, *R v Maloney* [1996] 2 Cr App Rep 303 and *R v Alowi* (8 March 1999, unreported). In the first of those cases Watkins LJ said that there is no fixed rule of principle or of law to the effect that the discharge of the jury can never be set aside, and in *R v Aylott* and *R v Maloney* that dictum was acted upon.

[41] Immediately subsequent to *R v Russell*, however, came *R v Andrews* (1986) 82 Cr App Rep 148, another case where the defendant rather than the jury had *a* been discharged. There is no mention of *R v Russell*, nor even of *R v Carter*, which would have been directly in point, but on the basis of *R v Parkin* (1824) 1 Mood CC 45 and *R v Vodden* (1853) Dears CC 229, 169 ER 706 the court held (at 154) that 'where the jury seeks to alter a verdict which has been pronounced by the foreman, the judge has a discretion whether to allow the alteration to be made'. *b* It was another case where the jury had determined to convict on an alternative count on which a verdict had not been taken. Nothing very much appears to have been made of the defendant's discharge, which Simon Brown J said (at 154) was not fatal to the judge's discretion but was 'one of the factors' for him to take into account. However, Simon Brown J expressly reserved the case where a jury had been discharged. *c*

[42] It was just such a case that next came forward for consideration in *R v Follen*. There the jury could not agree on a verdict, and were then discharged. It was only following a disturbance in the public gallery and after or coincident with that some dissension among the jurors that the judge took it upon himself to ask the jury to retire again to consider their verdict. They returned with a verdict of *d* guilty. That verdict was set aside, not because the proceedings after the jury's discharge were a nullity (it was in response to such a submission based on *R v Russell* that Watkins LJ said that there was no fixed rule to that effect), but because the court was not satisfied that there had been any mistake on the jury's part in their original answer that they were unable to reach even a majority verdict. Given the absence of any mistake on the part of the jury and the obvious concern *e* that the jury had been influenced by the disturbance in the gallery, the verdict of guilty was unsafe. The case is briefly reported in [1994] Crim LR 225, but we have been able to consult the full transcript.

[43] *R v Bills* [1995] 2 Cr App Rep 643 was another case in which the jury had been discharged, the court accepted that there was nevertheless a discretion to *f* accept a further verdict from the jury, but that verdict was quashed. There the jury purported after discharge to convict on a charge of wounding with intent even though they had originally acquitted the defendant on that charge and had convicted on only the lesser alternative of unlawful wounding. As in *R v Follen*, the court was not satisfied that a mistake had occurred. Russell LJ said (at 647): 'We do not understand how there could have been any misunderstanding as *g* suggested by the foreman.' Again, there was concern that the jury had been influenced by subsequent events, namely hearing about the defendant's previous convictions.

[44] *R v Aylott* was the first case in which exercise of the discretion to accept a new verdict even after the jury's discharge was upheld at the appeal stage. It was *h* a case of mistake, in the sense of a misunderstanding between jury and court. The judge thought that the jury were saying that they were unable to bring in any verdict: in fact they had already determined that Aylott's co-defendant was guilty of murder, and that Aylott was not guilty of murder. The only matter on which they were unresolved was whether Aylott was guilty or not of the alternative *j* offence of manslaughter. When almost immediately after their discharge that mistake was brought to light, the jury's true verdict was taken. Pill LJ reasoned that, as the discharge itself had proceeded on a fundamental mistake, it could be set aside. He also emphasised that the principle emerging from the authorities which he had reviewed was the court's fundamental concern for fairness and justice.

a

[45] Within a few months of the decision in *R v Aylott* it was joined by another case in which a new verdict after the jury's discharge was upheld on appeal, namely *R v Maloney*. It is interesting to note that the court in *R v Maloney* did not have *R v Aylott* cited to it, so that it proceeded by considering the authorities afresh. The problem in *R v Maloney* was (so far) unique in that it did not proceed from any mistake on the jury's part or from any misunderstanding of the jury's answers, nor was it the jury which drew attention in due course to the problem.

b

What happened was that after the jury had returned a majority verdict of guilty the clerk of the court forgot to ask the foreman for the numbers of the majority and the dissent. Under statute that verdict was therefore vitiated. The judge and counsel realised the error too late to recall the jury, and, since it was a Friday evening, the jury could not be reassembled until the following Monday, when a

c

verdict of eleven to one was recorded. It was held that the discharge of the jury was no bar to rectification of their verdict, and that in the circumstances not even the jury's dispersal nor the intervention of the weekend upset the validity of what had been done. Of course, it was not so much a case of the verdict being rectified, as of it being completed. The case perhaps illustrates the good sense of stating a

d

rule which permits the justice of the particular cause to be achieved in preference to a formal rule of nullity; and also demonstrates how difficult it is to state any principle, such as that essayed at the beginning of para [38] above, without allowing for exceptions.

[46] Finally, in *R v Alowi* the court on appeal quashed a verdict of guilty where the judge had allowed the jury to continue their discussions even after he had

e

discharged them from returning a verdict on a particular count which they had then been unable to resolve. It appears that the judge had been under the misapprehension that they had no hopes of resolving it. On appeal it was held that although, if it was a matter of discretion, there was force in a submission that in the circumstances of the case the judge had exercised such a discretion

f

lawfully, nevertheless the verdict was a nullity. Kennedy LJ has set out a full extract from the judgment of Judge LJ. I would merely emphasise the passages where Judge LJ said:

> 'But it is clearly established by *R v Russell* and again *R v Follen* that once discharged the jury cannot return a verdict which is the result of further debate. For that purpose the verdict is a nullity ... We do not think it was

g

> open to the judge to set aside the order discharging the jury from further considering those counts. This was not a case in which a jury were simply recording verdicts which they had in truth already reached.'

[47] In the present case, there is I think no question of further consideration of

h

a verdict not yet arrived at. I will revert to this below. It may be that, properly understood, *R v Alowi* is a decision on its facts. Nevertheless, I think it right to say, in agreement with Kennedy LJ, that the nullity rule propounded in *R v Alowi*, although narrower than the blanket rule stated in *R v Russell*, is not justified on the authorities, and that the true rule, and the better rule, is that ultimately it is

j

all a matter of discretion.

[48] I would accept that the case where the jury has arrived at a decision which is misstated or misunderstood, and which simply needs to be rectified, if that can properly be done without unfairness or injustice, is more straightforward; and that the case where a jury has *failed* to reach a decision before discharge and where the jury must therefore deliberate further if their true decision is to be rendered is more open to attack. Nevertheless, I would not for myself exclude

the latter case under a formal rule of nullity, but would prefer, if that is consistent with the authorities, to look to fairness and justice and to the integrity of the trial process and of the jury's role within that as my touchstones. Thus, take the following example. A jury is misunderstood to be indicating that it cannot resolve the charge laid before it. Prior to it being discharged, however, the misunderstanding is clarified and the jury is asked to retire again. In principle there is nothing wrong with that. Now suppose, however, that the jury was discharged immediately before the misunderstanding came to light. Provided that the jury had heard nothing in the interim, on the basis that it had laid aside its office, which it should not have done, then I do not see why the trial must be aborted. Take another example. A foreman states a verdict under the mistaken belief that all jurors were agreed with it. It immediately becomes obvious that that was not the case. I do not see why the trial cannot continue: the unauthorised verdict is simply set aside, and the jury retires to continue its incomplete deliberations. Now again suppose, however, that the jury was discharged immediately before this mistake came to light. The discharge is a factor, but I do not see why an automatic rule of nullity must be interposed. In as much as the jury's discharge is a formal impediment to anything further being done in the name of the jury, the authorities indicate that, if the merits demand it, the discharge can be set aside.

[49] Do the authorities permit such a view? I believe that they do. Starting with *R v Follen*, both the cases which quash the disputed verdicts (*R v Follen* and *R v Bills*) and those which uphold them (*R v Aylott* and *R v Maloney*) state a rule of discretion, not of nullity. *R v Russell* is not in its terms authority for a narrow rule of nullity that a jury once discharged cannot return a verdict which is the result of further debate (although on the facts the jury had been discharged from returning a verdict before going on to reach one), even if it could be reinterpreted to that effect. *R v Follen* does not proceed on the basis that further debate is necessarily a nullity, only that for a judge to set aside his discharge of the jury is 'something which cannot be lightly undertaken ... only a very rare circumstance can bring that about'.

[50] In any event, as indicated above, I do not consider the present case to be one where the jury did deliberate further. The foreman indicated that the jury had made a mistake in dealing with the fourth question, but did not want to revisit the first three. When the jury retired again, they were only gone for a period of four minutes. In as much as there was any further discussion between the jurors, I am satisfied that it must have been solely for the purpose of clarifying that they had always intended in truth to answer question four as 'No' rather than 'Yes'. Otherwise it is very difficult to believe that a complete reconsideration of question four, leading to a volte-face, could have been achieved in such a short period.

[51] In such circumstances the authorities indicate that the guiding principle must be that of fairness and justice, or what can be called the interests of justice. Second only to that, or indeed as part and parcel of that principle, is the consideration that the integrity of the trial process and of the jury's role in that process should not be compromised. Among the leading factors to take into account in giving effect to those principles is whether the court is satisfied that some plain or obvious mistake or misunderstanding has occurred, and thus whether there is some satisfactory explanation for it. Save in an exceptional case such as *R v Maloney*, it is for the jurors themselves to raise the issue of their mistake or of the court's misunderstanding of them, and to do so as promptly as

a possible. If the court is not satisfied that a mistake or misunderstanding has occurred, if the court is concerned that rather the jury is revisiting a matter they have already decided, then it will not be right to exercise its discretion in favour of permitting a further verdict. For these purposes, it will always be relevant to ask whether the jury may have been influenced by anything that they may have seen or heard since they gave their original decision, a fortiori if such new matter

b would have been inadmissible for the purposes of trial. Particularly in a civil case, the factor of costs cannot be divorced from the interests of justice. Discharge of the jury will always be a relevant factor, and may of course lead to events which would compromise the integrity of the process or of the jury's role in it: but, other things being equal, the mere fact of discharge of the jury is not critical.

[52] I agree that on the facts of the present case the application of these
c principles supports the exercise of the judge's discretion to permit the jury to rectify its mistake. I see no reason to interfere in the exercise of that discretion. The appeal must therefore be dismissed.

Appeal dismissed.

Dilys Tausz   Barrister.

R v Allen (No 2)

[2001] UKHL 45

HOUSE OF LORDS

LORD BINGHAM OF CORNHILL, LORD NICHOLLS OF BIRKENHEAD, LORD STEYN, LORD
HUTTON AND LORD SCOTT OF FOSCOTE

11–14 JUNE, 11 OCTOBER 2001

*Income tax – Emoluments from office or employment – Living accommodation –
Benefits in kind – Director – Shadow director – Whether shadow director having same
liability to tax as director in respect of provision of living accommodation and benefits
in kind – Income and Corporation Taxes Act 1988, s 168(8).*

The defendant, A, was charged on several counts of cheating the public revenue.
In relation to five of those counts (the shadow director counts), the Crown
alleged that A had concealed the provision of living accommodation and benefits
received from offshore companies for which he was liable to income tax as a
shadow director. Under the Income and Corporation Taxes Act 1988, the
provision of such accommodation and benefits to a company director by reason
of his office was to be taxed as emoluments of his office. Section 168(8)[a] of the
1988 Act provided, in its concluding part, that 'director' included any person in
accordance with whose directions or instructions the directors of the company
were accustomed to act. A was convicted on all counts. He appealed, contending,
inter alia, that as a shadow director he was not liable to tax in respect of the
provision of living accommodation and benefits in kind. The Court of Appeal
dismissed the appeal. On further appeal to the House of Lords, A contended, inter
alia, that in many cases the link between the services rendered to the company by
the alleged shadow director and the provision of living accommodation or
benefits alleged to be emoluments would be tenuous or non-existent, and that
there was a valid distinction between taxing benefits flowing from the holding of
a real office or employment and taxing a benefit which, in reality, was attributable
not to an office or employment but to a person's direct or indirect ownership of
a company.

Held – It was the intention of Parliament in enacting the concluding part of
s 168(8) of the 1988 Act that accommodation and benefits in kind received by a
shadow director were to be taxed in the same way as those received by a director.
Whilst in some cases the link between the services provided by a shadow director
and the accommodation or benefits which he received from the company might
be tenuous, there would be many cases where the services of a shadow director
were as valuable as those of an actual director and there would be no valid
distinction between such services. If A's arguments were correct, it would be
simple for a person who was a director in all but name to avoid the charge to tax.
Accordingly, the convictions on the shadow director counts were safe, and the
appeal would be dismissed (see [1]–[3], [19], [36], [39], below).

Per curiam. Since the state is entitled, for the purpose of collecting income tax,
to require a citizen to inform it of his income and to enforce penalties for failure

---

a   Section 168, so far as material, is set out at [13], below

a   to do so, a notice under s 20(1)[b] of the Taxes Management Act 1970 requiring
    information cannot constitute a violation of the right against self-incrimination
    under art 6 of the European Convention for the Protection of Human Rights and
    Fundamental Freedoms 1950 (as set out in Sch 1 to the Human Rights Act 1998)
    (see [1]–[3], [30], [39], below); *Saunders v UK* (1997) 2 BHRC 358 distinguished.

b   **Notes**
    For the meaning of director for the purposes of tax liability for benefits in kind,
    see 23 *Halsbury's Laws* (4th edn reissue) para 727.
        For the Income and Corporation Taxes Act 1988, s 168, see 44 *Halsbury's
    Statutes* (4th edn) (1996 reissue) 284.

c   **Cases referred to in opinions**
    Brown v Stott (Procurator Fiscal, Dunfermline) [2001] 2 All ER 97, [2001] 2 WLR 817,
        PC.
    Edwards (Inspector of Taxes) v Clinch [1981] 3 All ER 543, [1982] AC 845, [1981]
        3 WLR 707, HL.
d   *Funke v France* (1993) 16 EHRR 297, [1993] ECHR 10828/84, ECt HR.
    Ibrahim v R [1914] AC 599, [1914–15] All ER Rep 874, PC.
    R v Baldry (1852) 2 Den 430, CCR.
    R v Barker [1941] 3 All ER 33, [1941] 2 KB 381, CCA.
    R v Dimsey (No 2) [2001] UKHL 46, [2001] 4 All ER 786.
e   *R v Lambert* [2001] UKHL 37, [2001] 3 All ER 577, [2001] 3 WLR 206.
    R v Sang [1979] 2 All ER 1222, [1980] AC 402, [1979] 3 WLR 263, HL.
    R v Warwickshall (1783) 1 Leach 263.
    Saunders v UK (1997) 2 BHRC 358, ECt HR.
    Secretary of State for Trade and Industry v Deverell [2000] 2 All ER 365, [2001] 1 Ch
f   340, [2000] 2 WLR 907, CA.
    Sheffield v UK (1998) 5 BHRC 83, ECt HR.
    Sporrong v Sweden (1982) 5 EHRR 35, [1982] ECHR 7151/75, ECt HR.
    Taxpayer, Re (1993, unreported) Special Commissioners' Decision F1 3099/93 and
        3100/93.
g

    Appeal
    The appellant, Brian Roger Allen, appealed with leave of the Appeal Committee
    of the House of Lords given on 10 October 2000 from the decision of the Court
    of Appeal (Laws LJ, Moses J and Judge Crane) on 7 July 1999 ([1999] STC 846,
h   [2000] QB 744) dismissing his appeal against his conviction before Judge Hordern
    and a jury in the Crown Court at Knightsbridge on 19 February 1998 on 13 counts
    of cheating the public revenue of income and corporation tax. The Court of
    Appeal certified that points of law of general public importance, set out at [9] and
    [11], below, were involved in its decision. The facts are set out in the opinion of
    Lord Hutton.
j

    Alan Newman QC and *James Kessler* (instructed by *Gouldens*) for the appellant.
    David Milne QC, Peter Rook QC, Jonathan Fisher and *Rupert Baldry* (instructed by the
        Solicitor of Inland Revenue) for the Crown.

    ---

    b   Section 20, so far as material, is set out at [24], below

Their Lordships took time for consideration.

11 October 2001. The following opinions were delivered.

LORD BINGHAM OF CORNHILL.

[1]   My Lords, I have had the benefit of reading in draft the opinion of my noble and learned friend, Lord Hutton, with which I am in full agreement. For the reasons he gives I would dismiss this appeal.

LORD NICHOLLS OF BIRKENHEAD.

[2]   My Lords, I have had the advantage of reading in draft the speech of my noble and learned friend, Lord Hutton. For the reasons he gives I too would dismiss this appeal.

LORD STEYN.

[3]   My Lords, I have read the opinion of my noble and learned friend, Lord Hutton. For the reasons he gives I would also dismiss the appeal.

LORD HUTTON.

[4]   My Lords, the appellant, Brian Roger Allen, was charged before Judge Hordern and a jury in the Crown Court at Knightsbridge on 13 counts of cheating the public revenue of income tax and corporation tax. He was convicted on 19 February 1998 on all counts and on 20 February he was sentenced to 13 concurrent terms of seven years' imprisonment. A confiscation order was made against him pursuant to s 71 of the Criminal Justice Act 1988 in the sum of £3,137,165 with a consecutive term of seven years' imprisonment in default.

[5]   Each of the first seven counts charged the same offence of cheating the public revenue of corporation tax by concealing and/or otherwise failing to disclose the existence of profits made by an offshore company, which was managed and controlled by the appellant in the United Kingdom. Count 1 was as follows:

> '*STATEMENT OF OFFENCE*
>
> Cheating Her Majesty the Queen and the Commissioners of Inland Revenue, contrary to common law.
>
> *PARTICULARS OF OFFENCE*
>
> BRIAN ROGER ALLEN, between 1 January 1980 and 31 March 1992, with intent to defraud and to the prejudice of Her Majesty the Queen and the Commissioners of Inland Revenue, cheated Her Majesty the Queen and the Commissioners of Inland Revenue of public revenue, namely corporation tax, by concealing from and/or otherwise failing to disclose to the Commissioners of Inland Revenue for the purposes of the Taxes Acts the existence of profits made by an offshore company, namely Meldrette Investments Ltd, which was managed and controlled by him in the United Kingdom during the said period.'

Counts 2 to 7 charged the same offence in relation to six different offshore companies.

[6]   Counts 8, 9, 10, 12 and 13 charged the same offence of cheating the public revenue of income tax by delivering and/or causing to be delivered a tax return for a particular year showing income which was false, misleading and deceptive,

a   in that it omitted to declare all the income and benefits which the appellant
received during that period. Count 8 was as follows:

'STATEMENT OF OFFENCE
Cheating Her Majesty the Queen and the Commissioners of Inland
Revenue, contrary to common law.

b

PARTICULARS OF OFFENCE
BRIAN ROGER ALLEN, on or about 3 April 1992, with intent to defraud and
to the prejudice of Her Majesty the Queen and the Commissioners of
Inland Revenue, cheated Her Majesty the Queen and the Commissioners
c   of Inland Revenue of public revenue, namely income tax, by delivering
and/or causing to be delivered to an inspector of taxes a tax return for the
year 1989/1990 showing income for the year to 5 April 1989 in respect of
himself which was false, misleading and deceptive in that it omitted to
declare all the income and benefits which he received during the said period.
        Particulars of omitted income and benefits are—income and benefits
d   received from: (i) Peche D'Or Investments Ltd; (ii) Meldrette Investments Ltd.'

Count 9 related to the year 1990/1991, count 10 related to the year 1991/1992,
count 12 related to the year 1992/1993 and count 13 related to the year 1994/1995.
Counts 9 and 10 related to the omission of income and benefits received from
(i) Peche D'Or Investments Ltd (Peche D'Or) and (ii) Meldrette Investments Ltd
e   (Meldrette). Count 12 related to the omission of income and benefits received
from (i) Peche D'Or, (ii) Meldrette and (iii) Berkshire Investments Ltd. Count 13
related to the omission of income and benefits received from Peche D'Or.
    [7] The Crown's case against the appellant on counts 1 to 7 was that he had
dishonestly concealed the fact that he managed and controlled in the United
f   Kingdom the businesses of the respective companies specified in those counts in
order to give the false impression that the companies were not resident in the
United Kingdom so as to avoid corporation tax being charged against those
companies. The Crown's case against the appellant on counts 8 to 10 and 12 to
13 was that the appellant concealed the provision of living accommodation and
benefits received from the offshore companies for which he was liable to income
g   tax as a shadow director. Count 11 was as follows:

'STATEMENT OF OFFENCE
Cheating Her Majesty the Queen and the Commissioners of Inland
Revenue, contrary to common law.

h

PARTICULARS OF OFFENCE
BRIAN ROGER ALLEN, on or about 3 April 1992, with intent to defraud and
to the prejudice of Her Majesty the Queen and the Commissioners of
Inland Revenue, cheated Her Majesty the Queen and the Commissioners
j   of Inland Revenue of public revenue, namely income tax, by delivering
and/or causing to be delivered to an Inspector of Taxes a schedule of assets
as at 31 January 1991 in respect of his assets and the assets of his minor
children which was false, misleading and deceptive in that it omitted to
disclose divers assets which were owned by him.
        Particulars of the omitted assets are—his beneficial interest in shares issued by
offshore companies, his beneficial interest in properties held in the names

of offshore companies, and his beneficial interest in bank accounts held in the United Kingdom and in Jersey in the names of offshore companies.'

[8] The appellant appealed against his convictions to the Court of Appeal on a number of grounds, and his appeal was dismissed and the convictions affirmed (see [1999] STC 846, [2000] QB 744). One ground of appeal advanced before the Court of Appeal, and rejected by it, was that under s 739(2) of the Income and Corporation Taxes Act 1988 (ICTA) the income of the offshore companies was deemed to be the income of the appellant and that the income was also deemed not to be the income of those companies. In consequence, none of the companies was liable to any corporation tax as the income was not their income and, therefore, the appellant's dishonesty could not have caused any loss to the Revenue and he could not be guilty of the offence of cheating the Revenue.

[9] In respect of this issue the Court of Appeal certified the following point of law:

'Whether s 739(2) of the Income and Corporation Taxes Act 1988 has either of the additional effects, in relation to income which it requires to be deemed to be income of an individual ordinarily resident in the United Kingdom: (a) of requiring, for corporation tax purposes, that same income to be deemed not to be the income of a company incorporated outside the United Kingdom whose income it actually is; (b) of requiring for income tax purposes, that same income to be deemed not to be the income of the person (whether an individual or a company) resident or domiciled outside the United Kingdom whose income it actually is.'

[10] The appellant's appeal was heard together with the appeal of Dermot Jeremy Dimsey who had administered on behalf of the appellant the offshore companies (and their bank accounts) specified in the indictment against the appellant and who had been convicted of the offence of conspiracy to cheat the public revenue. On the appellant's appeal before this House his counsel, Mr Newman QC, adopted the argument of counsel for Dimsey, Mr Venables QC, on the s 739(2) point. For the reasons given in the speech of my noble and learned friend Lord Scott of Foscote in *R v Dimsey (No 2)* [2001] UKHL 46, [2001] 4 All ER 786, with which I am in full agreement, I would reject the appellant's ground of appeal in relation to s 739(2).

The shadow director point

[11] Another ground of appeal advanced before the Court of Appeal and rejected by it was that as a shadow director the appellant was not liable to tax in respect of the provision of living accommodation and benefits in kind. In respect of this issue the Court of Appeal certified the following point of law:

'Whether s 145 and/or s 154 of the Income and Corporation Taxes Act 1988 impose a charge to tax under Schedule E in respect of relevant benefits received from a company by an individual who, while having no actual office or employment with that company, none the less falls within the extended meaning of "director" under section 168(8) of the Act.'

[12] Under the provisions of Chs I and II of Pt V of ICTA where, by reason of his employment, a person is provided with living accommodation or he or members of his family or household are provided with benefits in kind, the value of the accommodation or the cash equivalent of the benefits is to be treated as emoluments of his employment for the purposes of Schedule E.

[13] Section 145(1) in Ch I provides, in relation to the provision of living accommodation:

'Subject to the provisions of this section, where living accommodation is provided for a person in any period by reason of his employment ... he is to be treated for the purposes of Schedule E as being in receipt of emoluments of an amount equal to the value to him of the accommodation for the period, less so much as is properly attributable to that provision of any sum made good by him to those at whose cost the accommodation is provided.'

Section 145(8) provides:

'For the purposes of this section ... (b) the expressions "employment", "family or household", "director", "full-time working director", "material interest" and (in relation to a body corporate) "control" shall be construed in accordance with subsections (2), (4) and (8) to (12) of section 168 as if this section were included in Chapter II of this Part.'

Section 154(1) in Ch II provides in relation to benefits in kind:

'Subject to section 163, where in any year a person is employed in employment to which this Chapter applies and—(a) by reason of his employment there is provided for him, or for others being members of his family or household, any benefit to which this section applies; and (b) the cost of providing the benefit is not (apart from this section) chargeable to tax as his income, there is to be treated as emoluments of the employment, and accordingly chargeable to income tax under Schedule E, an amount equal to whatever is the cash equivalent of the benefit.'

Section 167(1) sets out the employment to which Ch II relates:

'This Chapter applies—(a) to employment as a director of a company (but subject to subsection (5) below), and (b) to employment with emoluments at the rate of £8,500 a year or more.'

Section 168 provides:

'(1) The following provisions of this section apply for the interpretation of expressions used in this Chapter.
(2) Subject to section 165(6)(b), "employment" means an office or employment the emoluments of which fall to be assessed under Schedule E; and related expressions shall be construed accordingly ...
(8) Subject to subsection (9) below, "director" means—(a) in relation to a company whose affairs are managed by a board of directors or similar body, a member of that board or similar body; (b) in relation to a company whose affairs are managed by a single director or similar person, that director or person; and (c) in relation to a company whose affairs are managed by the members themselves, a member of the company, and includes any person in accordance with whose directions or instructions the directors of the company (as defined above) are accustomed to act.
(9) A person is not under subsection (8) above to be deemed to be a person in accordance with whose directions or instructions the directors of the company are accustomed to act by reason only that the directors act on advice given by him in a professional capacity.'

Schedule E set out in s 19 in Pt I of ICTA provides, in paras 1 and 5:

> '1. Tax under this Schedule shall be charged in respect of any office or employment on emoluments therefrom which fall under one or more than one of the following Cases—Case I: any emoluments for any year of assessment in which the person holding the office or employment is resident and ordinarily resident in the United Kingdom, subject however to section 192 if the emoluments are foreign emoluments (within the meaning of that section) and to section 193(1) if in the year of assessment concerned he performs the duties of the office or employment wholly or partly outside the United Kingdom; Case II: any emoluments, in respect of duties performed in the United Kingdom, for any year of assessment in which the person holding the office or employment is not resident (or, if resident, not ordinarily resident) in the United Kingdom, subject however to section 192 if the emoluments are foreign emoluments (within the meaning of that section); Case III: any emoluments for any year of assessment in which the person holding the office or employment is resident in the United Kingdom (whether or not ordinarily resident there) so far as the emoluments are received in the United Kingdom; and tax shall not be chargeable in respect of emoluments of an office or employment under any other paragraph of this Schedule ...
>
> 5. The preceding provisions of this Schedule are without prejudice to any other provision of the Tax Acts directing tax to be charged under this Schedule and tax so directed to be charged shall be charged accordingly.'

[14] The argument of the Crown can be briefly summarised as follows. A director of a company is treated by ss 167(1) and 168(2) as being in 'employment' for the purposes of Ch II of Pt V, even if he is not actually employed by the company. Therefore, the effect of s 167(1)(a) is that the Chapter applies to a director who has no actual employment. The effect of the concluding part of s 168(8) is that for the purposes of the Chapter and, in particular, for the purposes of s 168(2), a shadow director is treated as holding the office of director. Accordingly, the appellant as a shadow director was chargeable under Schedule E in respect of the value of the living accommodation and benefits in kind received from the companies.

[15] Mr Kessler, junior counsel for the appellant, advanced two main arguments. The first argument was that in *Edwards (Inspector of Taxes) v Clinch* [1981] 3 All ER 543 at 546, [1982] AC 845 at 861, Lord Wilberforce stated that the word 'office' must 'connote a post to which a person can be appointed, which he can vacate and to which a successor can be appointed'. Therefore, a shadow director does not hold an office. Section 168(8) states that a 'director' includes a shadow director, but it should not be read as deeming a shadow director to hold an office. The purpose of s 168(8) was to avoid the repetition of the words 'director or deemed director' when the word 'director' is used numerous times in Ch II. The purpose was not to extend the meaning of other words such as 'office'.

[16] The second argument was that even if the effect of the concluding part of s 168(8) is that a shadow director has an 'office', he does not have 'employment' within the meaning of s 168(2) because he does not have an office 'the emoluments of which fall to be assessed under Schedule E'. Two reasons were advanced in support of this argument. The first was that, in respect of the deemed office of a director, it is not one the emoluments of which fall to be assessed under Schedule E. On this point the Crown's argument was circular because it assumed this

a requirement to be satisfied in order that the emoluments can be regarded as falling to be assessed under Schedule E. The second reason was that the charge which the Crown seeks to impose is one to which para 5 of Schedule E relates and that paragraph does not impose a territorial limitation. In consequence, the Crown's argument would result in a charge to tax without territorial limitations so that shadow directors throughout the world provided with living accommodation or
b benefits would be caught, which cannot have been the legislative intention. Mr Kessler relied on the acceptance of this argument by a Special Commissioner, Dr John Avery Jones, who, in respect of the equivalent section in the Finance Act 1977 to s 145, stated in *Re Taxpayer* (1993, unreported) Special Commissioners' Decision F1 3099/93 and 3100/93:

c   'As we have seen, the definition of employment has the effect of providing a territorial limitation; if the employment is within that limitation, s 33 deems there to be Schedule E emoluments unrelated to any Case of Schedule E. If one could use the deemed emoluments under the section to complete the circle in the definition of employee and make the section apply, there would
d   be no territorial limitation to the section and all employees in the world provided with living accommodation would be caught. This cannot have been intended. This seems to me to be a compelling reason why one cannot use the deemed emoluments to make the section apply.'

[17] Mr Kessler supported his two arguments on the construction of the statutory provisions by a third argument of a more general nature relating to the
e undesirable and anomalous consequences of the construction contended for by the Crown. He submitted that it is a worldwide practice to use companies as a vehicle to hold wealth. It is normal practice for persons resident but not domiciled in the United Kingdom to hold assets situated in the United Kingdom via an offshore company for the object of mitigating inheritance tax. In order to
f make the disposal of a foreign home easier, it is also normal practice for persons resident and domiciled in the United Kingdom to hold that home via an offshore company. The judgment of Morritt LJ in *Secretary of State for Trade and Industry v Deverell* [2000] 2 All ER 365, [2001] 1 Ch 340 gives a wide meaning to the words in s 22(4) of the Company Directors Disqualification Act 1986 which are very similar to the concluding words of s 168(8), so that a person is regarded as a shadow
g director if the properly appointed directors surrender their discretion and give effect to directions or instructions from that person.

[18] In consequence on the Crown's argument, the scope of the living accommodation and benefit in kind provisions would be very wide. Mr Kessler further submitted that in many cases the link between the services rendered to
h the company by the alleged shadow director and the provision of living accommodation or benefits alleged to be emoluments would be tenuous or non-existent. There is a valid distinction between taxing benefits flowing from the holding of a real office or employment subject to charge under Schedule E and taxing a benefit which is not in reality attributable to an office or employment but
j is attributable to a person's direct or indirect ownership of a company.

[19] My Lords, I am unable to accept this argument. It is clear that it was the intention of Parliament that living accommodation and benefits in kind provided by a company for a director should be taxed as emoluments received by him from his office. Whilst in some cases the link between the services provided by a shadow director and the accommodation or benefits which he receives from the company may be tenuous, there will be many cases where the services of a

shadow director are as valuable as those of an actual director and there would be
no valid distinction between the services provided by a director and those   *a*
provided by a shadow director. If the appellant's arguments were correct it
would be simple for a person who is a director in all but name to avoid the charge
to tax under ss 145 and 154. In my opinion, it was the intention of Parliament in
enacting the concluding part of s 168(8) that accommodation and benefits in kind
received by a shadow director should be taxed in the same way as those received *b*
by a director, and I consider that the statutory provisions relied upon by the
Crown are effective to achieve that purpose.

[20] I am unable to accept Mr Kessler's first argument on the construction of
the provisions. Under the concluding part of s 168(8) a shadow director is taken
to be a director and, therefore, under ss 167(1)(a) and 168(2) he is employed in the
office of a director if the emoluments of that office can be regarded as falling to *c*
be assessed under Schedule E. Taking account of the intention of Parliament in
enacting the concluding part of s 168(8) that a distinction should not be drawn
between directors and shadow directors, I consider that Mr Kessler's circularity
argument does not enable a shadow director to escape the charge to tax. In my
opinion Mr Milne QC, for the Crown, was correct in submitting that there is a *d*
statutory circularity built into the provisions, so that as a shadow director is to be
regarded as a director it follows that living accommodation and benefits received
by him should be treated as emoluments falling to be assessed under Schedule E.

[21] I am also unable to accept Mr Kessler's second argument in relation to
territorial limitations. He submitted that the tax imposed by ss 145(1) and 154(1) *e*
was charged under para 5 of Schedule E, which did not contain a territorial
limitation, and not under one of the three Cases set out in para 1. However, para 5
relates to other provisions of the Tax Acts directing tax to be charged 'under this
Schedule' (my emphasis). The concluding words of para 1 state: 'tax shall not be
chargeable in respect of emoluments of an office or employment under any other
paragraph of this Schedule.' Therefore, when another provision of a Tax Act *f*
directs that benefits are to be charged to tax as emoluments under Schedule E,
I consider that those emoluments will fall within para 1 and are not to be regarded
as falling within para 5. A territorial limitation is contained within each of the three
cases in para 1, and, accordingly, a territorial limitation is present in respect of the
tax imposed by ss 145(1) and 154(1). Accordingly, I would hold that the appellant *g*
was rightly convicted as a shadow director and that the convictions on counts 8, 9,
10, 12 and 13 are safe.

Self-incrimination

[22] The Crown's case against the appellant on count 11 was that in a schedule
of assets provided by him to the Revenue during the course of a Hansard *h*
investigation into his affairs he omitted to list his beneficial interest in shares
issued by offshore companies. Before the Court of Appeal, as a ground of appeal,
the appellant criticised part of the judge's summing up on the issue whether
certain trust deeds were a sham. This ground of appeal was rejected by the Court
of Appeal and the ground has not been renewed before this House.   *j*

[23] However, with the leave of the House, the appellant was permitted to
argue a new point relating to art 6 of the European Convention for the Protection
of Human Rights and Fundamental Freedoms (Rome, 4 November 1950; TS 71
(1953); Cmd 8969) (as set out in Sch 1 to the Human Rights Act 1998). This
argument consisted of two parts and can be briefly summarised as follows. First,
under s 20(1) of the Taxes Management Act 1970 the Revenue requested the

a appellant to provide certain information, and then, under the Hansard procedure, the Revenue both threatened and induced the appellant to produce the schedule of assets to which count 11 related. In consequence, the appellant's right to a fair trial under art 6 was violated because his right not to incriminate himself was breached. Secondly, although the trial and conviction of the appellant took place before the relevant sections of the 1998 Act came into force on 2 October
b 2000, the appellant was entitled, pursuant to ss 7(1)(b) and 22(4) of that Act, to rely in an appeal heard after 2 October 2000 on rights conferred by the convention and incorporated into English law by the Act. The House heard the submissions of the parties before it gave judgment on 5 July 2001 in *R v Lambert* [2001] UKHL 37, [2001] 3 All ER 577, [2001] 3 WLR 206. In *R v Lambert* the House held that the 1998 Act did not operate retrospectively to make unsafe, by reason of a breach of
c art 6, a conviction prior to 2 October 2000 which was safe under English law at the time the conviction took place. Therefore, on that ground the appellant's argument in respect of his conviction on count 11 must fail. However, as the issue whether there was a violation of the appellant's rights under art 6 was fully argued, and as the point is one of general importance, I propose to express my
d opinion on it.

[24] As I have stated, the Crown's case against the appellant on count 11 related to the schedule of assets referred to in that count in which the appellant omitted to specify his very substantial interests in offshore companies. Section 20 of the 1970 Act provides:

e '(1) Subject to this section, an inspector may by notice in writing require a person—(a) to deliver to him such documents as are in the person's possession or power and as (in the inspector's reasonable opinion) contain, or may contain, information relevant to—(i) any tax liability to which the person is or may be subject, or (ii) the amount of any such liability, or (b) to
f furnish to him such particulars as the inspector may reasonably require as being relevant to, or to the amount of, any such liability ...

(7) Notices under subsection (1) or (3) above are not to be given by an inspector unless he is authorised by the Board for its purposes; and—(a) a notice is not to be given by him except with the consent of a General or
g Special Commissioner; and (b) the Commissioner is to give his consent only on being satisfied that in all the circumstances the inspector is justified in proceeding under this section.'

Section 98(1) of the 1970 Act provides:

h 'Subject to the provisions of this section and section 98A below, where any person—(a) has been required, by a notice served under or for the purposes of any of the provisions specified in the first column of the Table below, to deliver any return or other document, to furnish any particulars, to produce any document, or to make anything available for inspection, and he fails to
j comply with the notice, or (b) fails to furnish any information, give any certificate or produce any document or record in accordance with any of the provisions specified in the second column of the Table below, he shall be liable, subject to subsections (3) and (4) below—(i) to a penalty not exceeding £300, and (ii) if the failure continues after a penalty is imposed under paragraph (i) above, to a further penalty or penalties not exceeding £60 for each day on which the failure continues after the day on which the penalty

under paragraph (i) above was imposed (but excluding any day for which a penalty under this paragraph has already been imposed).'

[25] On 9 May 1991 the appellant was served with a notice pursuant to s 20(1) of the 1970 Act. The notice required a variety of information, including requirement 6, which stated: 'I require a certified statement of all your assets and liabilities as at 31 January 1991.' The appellant failed to comply with the notice and he received a summons, dated 13 August 1991, to appear before the General Commissioners:

'IN THE DIVISION OF LEEDS

To Mr B R Allen of The Warleys, Hammerpond Road, Plummer Plain, Horsham, West Sussex

INFORMATION has been laid this day by Mr G W Young of Inland Revenue, Special Office one of Her Majesty's Inspectors of Taxes that— 1. you were served for the purposes of s 20(1) of the Taxes Management Act 1970 with a notice dated 9 May 1991 requiring you to deliver to Mr A R Maxwell one of Her Majesty's Inspectors of Taxes, not later than 31 July 1991 the following document(s)—Per schedule attached. 2. you have failed to comply with the notice thereby rendering yourself liable under the provisions of s 98(1) of the Taxes Management Act 1970 to a penalty not exceeding fifty pounds.

YOU ARE THEREFORE hereby summoned to appear before the Commissioners for the general purposes of the Income tax for the above-named Division sitting at 29 Park Place, Leeds on the 3rd day of September next at the hour of 2 o'clock in the afternoon to answer the information and to be further dealt with according to law.

Dated the 13th day of August 1991

Your attention is drawn to the statutory provisions overleaf and in particular to those relating to penalties.'

This summons was signed by two of the commissioners for the general purposes of the income tax for the division.

[26] The appellant still failed to comply with the s 20(1) notice and, at a meeting between the appellant and his accountant and officials of the Revenue, the officials adopted what is termed 'the Hansard procedure' whereby one of the officials formally read out to the appellant the reply of the Chancellor of the Exchequer (177 HC Official Report (6th series) written answers col 882) to a parliamentary question on 18 October 1990 which was in the following terms:

'The practice of the board of Inland Revenue in cases of fraud in relation to tax is as follows: 1. The board may accept a money settlement instead of instituting criminal proceedings in respect of fraud alleged to have been committed by a taxpayer. 2. It can give no undertaking that it will accept a money settlement and refrain from instituting criminal proceedings, even if the taxpayer has made a full confession and has given full facilities for investigation of the facts. It reserves to itself full discretion in all cases as to the course it pursues. 3. Nevertheless, in considering whether to accept a money settlement or to institute criminal proceedings, its decision is influenced by the fact that the taxpayer has made a full confession and has given full facilities for investigation into his affairs and for examination of such books, papers, documents or information as the board may consider necessary.'

a At this meeting further questions relating to his financial affairs were also put to the appellant. Subsequently, the appellant provided answers to the various questions put to him, and, in compliance with requirement 6 of the s 20(1) notice, he delivered to the Revenue the schedule of assets referred to in count 11.

[27] Mr Newman, on behalf of the appellant, submitted that in obtaining from the appellant the schedule of assets upon which the prosecution case was based b the Revenue had breached his right to a fair trial under art 6 because the appellant had been compelled under threat of penalty to incriminate himself by providing the schedule of assets. Mr Newman also submitted that the appellant had been subjected to an inducement to provide the schedule by the assurance implicit in the Hansard statement that if the taxpayer makes a full confession criminal proceedings would not be instituted against him.
c
[28] In support of his submission relating to self-incrimination, Mr Newman relied on the judgment of the European Court of Human Rights in *Funke v France* (1993) 16 EHRR 297 at 326 (para 44) in which it was held that the right to a fair trial given by art 6(1) includes the right 'to remain silent and not to contribute to incriminating itself'. Mr Newman also relied strongly on the judgment of the d Court of Human Rights in *Saunders v UK* (1997) 2 BHRC 358. In that case the Secretary of State for Trade and Industry appointed inspectors to investigate the affairs of Guinness plc pursuant to ss 432 and 442 of the Companies Act 1985. During the course of that investigation Mr Saunders made statements to the inspectors in reply to questions from them. Mr Saunders was subject to legal e compulsion to give evidence to the inspectors. He was obliged under ss 434 and 436 of the 1985 Act to answer the questions put to him by the inspectors in the course of the interviews which they conducted with him. A refusal by him to answer the questions put to him could have led to a finding of contempt of court and the imposition of a fine or committal to prison for up to two years, and it was no defence to proceedings consequent on a refusal that the questions were of an f incriminating nature. In the course of the subsequent criminal trial in which he was charged with offences relating to an illegal share support operation, the transcripts of Mr Saunders' answers to the inspectors, whether directly self-incriminating or not, were used against him by the prosecution in a manner which sought to incriminate him. Mr Saunders lodged an application with the European g Commission of Human Rights complaining that the use at his trial of statements made by him to the inspectors under their compulsory powers deprived him of a fair hearing in violation of art 6(1) of the convention. Both the Commission of Human Rights and the Court of Human Rights upheld Mr Saunders' complaint. In its judgments the Court of Human Rights stated ((1997) 2 BHRC 358 at 373–376):

h   '68. The Court recalls that, although not specifically mentioned in art 6 of the convention, the right to silence and the right not to incriminate oneself are generally recognised international standards which lie at the heart of the notion of a fair procedure under art 6. Their rationale lies, inter alia, in the protection of the accused against improper compulsion by the authorities j   thereby contributing to the avoidance of miscarriages of justice and to the fulfilment of the aims of art 6 ... The right not to incriminate oneself, in particular, presupposes that the prosecution in a criminal case seek to prove their case against the accused without resort to evidence obtained through methods of coercion or oppression in defiance of the will of the accused. In this sense the right is closely linked to the presumption of innocence contained in art 6(2) of the convention.

69. The right not to incriminate oneself is primarily concerned, however, with respecting the will of an accused person to remain silent ... In the present case the Court is only called upon to decide whether the use made by the prosecution of the statements obtained from the applicant by the inspectors amounted to an unjustifiable infringement of the right. This question must be examined by the Court in the light of all the circumstances of the case. In particular, it must be determined whether the applicant has been subject to compulsion to give evidence and whether the use made of the resulting testimony at his trial offended the basic principles of a fair procedure inherent in art 6(1) of which the right not to incriminate oneself is a constituent element.

70 ... the government have emphasised, before the Court, that nothing said by the applicant in the course of the interviews was self-incriminating and that he had merely given exculpatory answers or answers which, if true, could serve to confirm his defence. In their submission only statements which are self-incriminating could fall within the privilege against self-incrimination.

71. The Court does not accept the government's premise on this point since some of the applicant's answers were in fact of an incriminating nature in the sense that they contained admissions to knowledge of information which tended to incriminate him ... In any event, bearing in mind the concept of fairness in art 6, the right not to incriminate oneself cannot reasonably be confined to statements of admission of wrongdoing or to remarks which are directly incriminating. Testimony obtained under compulsion which appears on its face to be of a non-incriminating nature—such as exculpatory remarks or mere information on questions of fact—may later be deployed in criminal proceedings in support of the prosecution case, for example to contradict or cast doubt upon other statements of the accused or evidence given by him during the trial ...

74. Nor does the Court find it necessary, having regard to the above assessment as to the use of the interviews during the trial, to decide whether the right not to incriminate oneself is absolute or whether infringements of it may be justified in particular circumstances. It does not accept the government's argument that the complexity of corporate fraud and the vital public interest in the investigation of such fraud and the punishment of those responsible could justify such a marked departure as that which occurred in the present case from one of the basic principles of a fair procedure. Like the Commission, it considers that the general requirements of fairness contained in art 6, including the right not to incriminate oneself, apply to criminal proceedings in respect of all types of criminal offences without distinction from the most simple to the most complex. The public interest cannot be invoked to justify the use of answers compulsorily obtained in a non-judicial investigation to incriminate the accused during the trial proceedings. It is noteworthy in this respect that under the relevant legislation statements obtained under compulsory powers by the Serious Fraud Office cannot, as a general rule, be adduced in evidence at the subsequent trial of the person concerned. Moreover the fact that statements were made by the applicant prior to his being charged does not prevent their later use in criminal proceedings from constituting an infringement of the right.'

[29] My Lords, the present case is one which relates to the obligation of a citizen to pay taxes and to his duty not to cheat the Revenue. It is self-evident that

a   the payment of taxes, fixed by the legislature, is essential for the functioning of
     any democratic state. It is also self-evident that to ensure the due payment of
     taxes the state must have power to require its citizens to inform it of the amount
     of their annual income, and to have sanctions available to enforce the provision
     of that information. In the United Kingdom this power is contained in the
     provisions of the 1970 Act. Section 8(1) provides:

b   'For the purpose of establishing the amounts in which a person is
         chargeable to income tax and capital gains tax for a year of assessment, and
         the amount payable by him by way of income tax for that year, he may be
         required by a notice given to him by an officer of the Board—(a) to make and
         deliver to the officer, on or before the day mentioned in subsection (1A)
c   below, a return containing such information as may reasonably be required
         in pursuance of the notice, and (b) to deliver with the return such accounts,
         statements and documents relating to information contained in the return,
         as may reasonably be so required.'

     Section 93 provides:

d   '(1) This section applies where—(a) any person (the taxpayer) has been
         required by a notice served under or for the purposes of section 8 or 8A of
         this Act (or either of those sections as extended by section 12 of this Act) to
         deliver any return, and (b) he fails to comply with the notice.
         (2) The taxpayer shall be liable to a penalty which shall be £100.
e   (3) If, on an application made to them by an officer of the Board, the
         General or Special Commissioners so direct, the taxpayer shall be liable to a
         further penalty or penalties not exceeding £60 for each day on which the
         failure continues after the day on which he is notified of the direction (but
         excluding any day for which a penalty under this subsection has already been
f   imposed).'

     Further subsections make provision for additional penalties if the taxpayer still
     fails to make a return.
         [30] The tax return for the year ended 5 April 2001 sent to every individual
     taxpayer contains the following notice on its first page:

g   'This Notice requires you by law to send me a Tax Return for the year from
         6 April 2000 to 5 April 2001. Give details of all your income and capital gains
         using this form and any supplementary Pages you need … Make sure your
         Tax Return, and any documents I ask for, reach me by 30 September 2001 if
         you want me to calculate your tax, OR collect any tax you owe (less than
h   £2,000) through your PAYE code for 2002–2003, OR 31 January 2002 at the
         latest, or you will be liable to an automatic penalty of £100. Make sure your
         payment of any tax you owe reaches me by 31 January 2002, or you will have
         to pay interest and perhaps a surcharge. Any Tax Return may be checked.
         Please remember that there are penalties for supplying false information.'

j   It is clearly permissible for a state to enact such provisions and there could be no
     substance in an argument that there is a violation of art 6(1) if the Revenue
     prosecuted a citizen for cheating the Revenue by furnishing a standard tax return
     containing false information. Similarly, in the present case, viewed against the
     background that the state, for the purpose of collecting tax, is entitled to require
     a citizen to inform it of his income and to enforce penalties for failure to do so,
     the s 20(1) notice requiring information cannot constitute a violation of the right

against self-incrimination. The present case is, therefore, clearly distinguishable from *Saunders v UK* on that ground. As Lord Bingham of Cornhill stated in *Brown v Stott (Procurator Fiscal, Dunfermline)* [2001] 2 All ER 97 at 115, [2001] 2 WLR 817 at 836:

> 'The jurisprudence of the European Court very clearly establishes that while the overall fairness of a criminal trial cannot be compromised, the constituent rights comprised, whether expressly or implicitly, within art 6 are not themselves absolute. Limited qualification of these rights is acceptable if reasonably directed by national authorities towards a clear and proper public objective and if representing no greater qualification than the situation calls for ... The court has also recognised the need for a fair balance between the general interest of the community and the personal rights of the individual, the search for which balance has been described as inherent in the whole of the convention (see *Sporrong v Sweden* (1982) 5 EHRR 35 at 52–53 (para 69); *Sheffield v UK* (1998) 5 BHRC 83 at 94 (para 52)).'

[31] In respect of his argument that there had been a breach of art 6(1) because the delivery of the schedule of assets had been 'involuntary', having been induced by a promise implicit in the Hansard statement that the appellant would not be prosecuted if he furnished the required information, Mr Newman relied on the decision of the Court of Appeal *R v Barker* [1941] 2 KB 381, [1941] 3 All ER 33. In that case at an interview a Revenue official read an earlier version of the Hansard statement to the taxpayer and his accountant, the appellant Barker. This statement differed from the later statement made in October 1990 because it stated ([1941] 2 KB 381 at 382) that where the taxpayer voluntarily disclosed the fact of his past frauds and furnished full information to the Revenue 'the board will not institute criminal proceedings, but will accept the pecuniary settlement'. After the statement had been read to them, the appellant and the taxpayer produced to the Revenue official two ledgers which had been fraudulently prepared to induce the Revenue authorities to believe that the irregularities amounted to £7,000 in all. At a later interview two further ledgers and working papers were produced which showed that the earlier ledgers were incomplete and had been brought into existence to deceive the Revenue. Subsequently, a letter was written which made it clear that the full amount of the irregularities was about £10,400. The appellant and the taxpayer were prosecuted and convicted of the offences of conspiring to cheat the Revenue and of having delivered false statements of account with intent to defraud.

[32] Before the Court of Appeal, counsel for the appellant argued that the statement read from Hansard was partly a promise or an inducement, and the appellant had produced the books or documents as a result of the promise, inducement or threat. Consequently, his action was not free and voluntary and the books or documents should not have been admitted in evidence. This argument was accepted by the Court of Appeal and Tucker J stated:

> 'The court ... does not desire to question that there may be cases in which evidence can be given of facts the existence of which have come to the knowledge of the police as the result of an inadmissible confession. But in the present case the promise or inducement which was implied in this extract from Hansard expressly related to the production of business books and records, and the court is of opinion that if, as a result of a promise, inducement or threat, such books and documents are produced by the person or persons to whom the promise or inducement is held out, or the

threat made, those documents stand on precisely the same footing as an oral or a written confession which is brought into existence as the result of such a promise, inducement or threat. The result is that, in the opinion of the court, these vital documents and books, namely, the ledgers and the working papers of the appellant, were wrongly admitted in evidence and in those circumstances the conviction of the appellant cannot stand.' (See [1941] 2 KB 381 at 384–385.)

The effect of this decision was reversed by s 105 of the 1970 Act (which replaced an earlier and similar provision) and which provides:

'(1) Statements made or documents produced by or on behalf of a person shall not be inadmissible in any such proceedings as are mentioned in subsection (2) below by reason only that it has been drawn to his attention that—(a) pecuniary settlements may be accepted instead of a penalty being determined, or proceedings being instituted, in relation to any tax, (b) though no undertaking can be given as to whether or not the Board will accept such a settlement in the case of any particular person, it is the practice of the Board to be influenced by the fact that a person has made a full confession of any fraudulent conduct to which he has been a party and has given full facilities for investigation, and that he was or may have been induced thereby to make the statements or produce the documents.

(2) The proceedings mentioned in subsection (1) above are—(a) any criminal proceedings against the person in question for any form of fraudulent conduct in connection with or in relation to tax, and (b) any proceedings against him for the recovery of any tax due from him, and (c) any proceedings for a penalty or on appeal against the determination of a penalty.'

[33] Section 76(4) of the Police and Criminal Evidence Act 1984 provides:

'The fact that a confession is wholly or partly excluded in pursuance of this section shall not affect the admissibility in evidence—(a) of any facts discovered as a result of the confession; or (b) where the confession is relevant as showing that the accused speaks, writes or expresses himself in a particular way, of so much of the confession as is necessary to show that he does so.'

Cross and Tapper on Evidence (8th edn, 1995) p 535, footnote 4, comment unfavourably on *R v Barker* and say:

'The extremely unsatisfactory case of *R v Barker* [1941] 2 KB 381, [1941] 3 All ER 33 which appeared to assimilate false accounts with a confession of false accounting, and which was overturned on its facts by Finance Act 1942, s 34 (see now Taxes Management Act 1970, s 105), appears to be inconsistent with s 76(4)(a) as a matter of law, and can be supported now only upon the basis of the judge's discretion, see Lord Diplock in *R v Sang* ([1979] 2 All ER 1222 at 1229, [1980] AC 402 at 435).'

[34] My Lords, I am unable to accept Mr Newman's submission and to follow the reasoning of the Court of Appeal in *R v Barker*. In that case the court stated ([1941] 2 KB 381 at 385):

'... those documents stand on precisely the same footing as an oral or a written confession which is brought into existence as a result of such a promise, inducement or threat.'

In my respectful opinion this is not so. When the Crown relies on an oral or written confession made by the accused and puts it in evidence it does so because it considers that the confession is true. When the courts have excluded a confession because it was involuntary, having been obtained by an inducement, they have done so on the ground that it was unsafe to rely on the confession as being true. As Lord Sumner explained in *Ibrahim v R* [1914] AC 599 at 610–611, [1914–15] All ER Rep 874 at 878:

'... the rule which excludes evidence of statements made by a prisoner, when they are induced by hope held out, or fear inspired, by a person in authority, is a rule of policy. "A confession forced from the mind by the flattery of hope or by the torture of fear comes in so questionable a shape, when it is to be considered as evidence of guilt, that no credit ought to be given to it" (*R v Warwickshall* (1783) 1 Leach 263). It is not that the law presumes such statements to be untrue, but from the danger of receiving such evidence judges have thought it better to reject it for the due administration of justice (*R v Baldry* (1852) 2 Den 430 at 445).'

[35] However, in *R v Barker* and in this case the respective accused did not give information contained in the documents and the schedule, respectively, which the Crown claimed was true, both accused gave false information and were prosecuted for giving that false information. To the extent that there was an inducement contained in the Hansard statement, the inducement was to give true and accurate information to the Revenue, but the accused in both cases did not respond to that inducement and instead of giving true and accurate information gave false information. Therefore, in my opinion, the appellant's argument in this case that he was induced by the hope of non-institution of criminal proceedings held out by the Revenue to provide the schedule and that its provision was, therefore, involuntary is invalid. If, in response to the Hansard statement, the appellant had given true and accurate information which disclosed that he had earlier cheated the Revenue and had then been prosecuted for that earlier dishonesty, he would have had a strong argument that the criminal proceedings were unfair and an even stronger argument that the Crown should not rely on evidence of his admission, but that is the reverse of what actually occurred.

[36] Accordingly, I would dismiss the appellant's appeal.

LORD SCOTT OF FOSCOTE.

[37] My Lords, one of the grounds of appeal argued on behalf of the appellant was that under s 739(2) of the Income and Corporation Taxes Act 1988 the income of the offshore companies (referred to in the judgment of the Court of Appeal ([1999] STC 846 at 857, [2000] QB 744 at 756)) was deemed to be the income of the appellant and that the income must, therefore, be deemed not to be the income of the companies (see my noble and learned friend Lord Hutton's opinion, at [8] above).

[38] As Lord Hutton has explained at [10], above, counsel for the appellant, Mr Newman QC, dealt with the s 739(2) point before your Lordships by adopting the argument on that point advanced before your Lordships by counsel for Dimsey. In a separate opinion which I have prepared for the purposes of Dimsey's appeal, I have set out my reasons for rejecting his ground of appeal based on s 739(2) (see *R v Dimsey (No 2)* [2001] UKHL 46, [2001] 4 All ER 786). For the same reasons I would reject Allen's s 739(2) ground of appeal.

a [**39**] Accordingly, for those reasons and for the reasons given by my noble and learned friend, Lord Hutton, with which I am in full agreement, I too would dismiss this appeal.

Appeal dismissed.

Kate O'Hanlon Barrister.

R v Dimsey (No 2)

[2001] UKHL 46

HOUSE OF LORDS

LORD BINGHAM OF CORNHILL, LORD NICHOLLS OF BIRKENHEAD, LORD STEYN, LORD HUTTON AND LORD SCOTT OF FOSCOTE

11–14 JUNE, 11 OCTOBER 2001

Income tax – Avoidance – Transfer of assets abroad – Income payable to persons resident or domiciled out of the United Kingdom – Statutory provision deeming income of foreign transferee to be that of transferor – Whether provision relieving foreign transferee of normal liability to pay tax on its income – Income and Corporation Taxes Act 1988, s 739(2).

The appellant, D, provided financial services to clients. Those services included setting up offshore companies for persons resident in the United Kingdom and the administration of those companies. D set up three such companies for C, a United Kingdom resident. Following a Revenue investigation into C's tax affairs, D was charged on one count of conspiring with C and the latter's solicitor to cheat the public revenue. At trial, the Revenue alleged, inter alia, that the defendants had attempted to cheat it of corporation tax due from the three offshore companies. The defendants were convicted. D appealed against conviction, relying, inter alia, on s 739(2)[a] of the Income and Corporation Taxes Act 1988, an anti-tax avoidance provision first enacted in 1936, which deemed the income of a foreign transferee to be that of the tax avoider/transferor. D contended that, since the income of the companies was deemed to be C's income for income tax purposes, that income had to be deemed not to be that of the companies; that therefore those companies had not been liable to pay corporation tax on their profits; and that accordingly there could be no offence of conspiring to cheat the Revenue of the corporation tax payable by them. The Court of Appeal rejected that contention and dismissed the appeal. D appealed to the House of Lords.

Held – On the true construction of s 739(2) of the 1988 Act, a foreign transferee of assets was not relieved of his normal liability to pay tax on his income. The legislative history of s 739 and other relevant provisions of the 1988 Act, a comparison of s 739(2) with other tax avoidance provisions and the tax avoidance purpose of s 739 all suggested that the correct approach was to confine the effect of s 739 to the transferor, and to decline to treat as real the consequences that would follow the deemed state of affairs if the deemed state of affairs were real. Accordingly, in the instant case the three offshore companies were liable to corporation tax, and the appeal would be dismissed (see [1]–[4], [40], [41], [60], [72], [73], below).

Per curiam. Section 739(2) of the 1988 Act, construed so as to deem the transferee's income to be the income of the transferor but leaving the liability of the transferee to pay tax on its income unaffected by the deeming provision,

---

a   Section 739, so far as material, is set out at [6], below

a complies with the right to the peaceful enjoyment of possessions under art 1[b]of the First Protocol to the European Convention for the Protection of Human Rights and Fundamental Freedoms 1950 (as set out in Sch 1 to the Human Rights Act 1998) (see [1]–[4], [71], below).

Notes

b For prevention of avoidance of income tax in respect of transfer of assets abroad, see 23 *Halsbury's Laws* (4th edn reissue) para 1565.

For the Income and Corporation Taxes Act 1988, s 739, see 44 *Halsbury's Statutes* (4th edn) (1996 reissue) 1132.

Cases referred to in opinions

c *Gasus Dosier-und Fördertechnik GmbH v Netherlands* [1995] 20 EHRR 403, [1995] ECHR 15375/89, ECt HR.

Howard de Walden (Lord) v IRC [1942] 1 All ER 287, [1942] 1 KB 389, CA.

IRC v Garvin [1981] STC 344, [1981] 1 WLR 793, HL.

Marshall (Inspector of Taxes) v Kerr [1993] STC 360, CA; *rvsd* [1994] 3 All ER 106,
d   [1995] 1 AC 148, HL.

National & Provincial Building Society v UK [1997] STC 1466, [1997] ECHR 21319/93, 21449/93, 21675/93, ECt HR.

R v Allen (No 2) [2001] UKHL 45, [2001] 4 All ER 768.

R v Lambert [2001] UKHL 37, [2001] 3 All ER 577, [2001] 3 WLR 206.

e *Vestey v IRC (Nos 1 and 2)* [1979] 3 All ER 976, [1980] AC 1148, [1979] 3 WLR 915, HL.

Appeal

The appellant, Dermot Jeremy Dimsey, appealed with leave of the Appeal Committee of the House of Lords given on 10 October 2000 from the decision of
f the Court of Appeal (Laws LJ, Moses J and Judge Crane) on 7 July 1999 ([1999] STC 846, [2000] QB 744) dismissing his appeal against his conviction before Judge Addison and a jury in the Crown Court at Guildford on 21 March 1997 of conspiracy to cheat the public revenue. The Court of Appeal certified that the following point of law of general public importance was involved in its decision:
g 'Whether s 739(2) of the Income and Corporation Taxes Act 1988 has either of the additional effects, in relation to income which it requires to be deemed to be income of an individual ordinarily resident in the United Kingdom (a) of requiring, for corporation tax purposes, that same income to be deemed not to be the income of a company incorporated outside the United Kingdom whose
h income it actually is; (b) of requiring for income tax purposes, that same income to be the income of the person (whether an individual or a company) resident or domiciled outside the United Kingdom whose income it actually is.' The facts are set out in the opinion of Lord Scott of Foscote.

Robert Venables QC, Peter Doyle, Timothy Lyons and *Amanda Hardy* (instructed by
j   Saunders & Co) for the appellant.

David Milne QC, Peter Rook QC, Jonathan Fisher and *Rupert Baldry* (instructed by the Solicitor of Inland Revenue) for the Crown.

---

b   Article 1 is set out at [62], below

Their Lordships took time for consideration.

a

11 October 2001. The following opinions were delivered.

LORD BINGHAM OF CORNHILL.

[1] My Lords, I have had the advantage of reading in draft the opinion of my noble and learned friend, Lord Scott of Foscote. For the reasons he gives I would *b* answer the certified question as he proposes and dismiss the appeal.

LORD NICHOLLS OF BIRKENHEAD.

[2] My Lords, I have had the advantage of reading in draft the speech of my noble and learned friend, Lord Scott of Foscote. For the reasons he gives I too would dismiss this appeal.

c

LORD STEYN.

[3] My Lords, I have read the opinion of my noble and learned friend, Lord Scott of Foscote. For the reason he gives I would also dismiss the appeal.

d

LORD HUTTON.

[4] My Lords, I have had the benefit of reading in draft the speech of my noble and learned friend, Lord Scott of Foscote, with which I am in full agreement. For the reasons he gives I too would dismiss this appeal.

e

LORD SCOTT OF FOSCOTE.

[5] My Lords, s 18 of the Finance Act 1936 enacted important and far-reaching provisions designed to counter tax avoidance by the transfer of assets abroad. Various amendments and additions to the original provisions have been made since then but the broad scheme established in 1936 remains in force. The current provisions are to be found in ss 739 to 746 of the Income and Corporation *f* Taxes Act 1988.

[6] Subsection (1) of s 739, which in s 18 of the 1936 Act took the form of a preamble, expresses the purpose of the statutory provisions:

> '... the following provisions of this section shall have effect for the purpose of preventing the avoiding by individuals ordinarily resident in the United *g* Kingdom of liability to income tax by means of transfer of assets by virtue or in consequence of which, either alone or in conjunction with associated operations, income becomes payable to persons resident or domiciled outside the United Kingdom.'

h

Subsection (2) contains the principal provision whereby the tax avoidance consequences of the transfer abroad are sought to be negated:

> 'Where by virtue or in consequence of any such transfer, either alone or in conjunction with associated operations, such an individual has, within the meaning of this section, power to enjoy, whether forthwith or in the future, *j* any income of a person resident or domiciled outside the United Kingdom which, if it were income of that individual received by him in the United Kingdom, would be chargeable to income tax by deduction or otherwise, that income shall, whether it would or would not have been chargeable to income tax apart from the provisions of this section, be deemed to be income of that individual for all purposes of the Income Tax Acts.'

a [7] The potential breadth of this provision was cut back by the decision in your Lordships' House in *Vestey v IRC (Nos 1 and 2)* [1979] 3 All ER 976, [1980] AC 1148. It was held that the provision (then s 412(1) of the Income Tax Act 1952) applied only to the individual or individuals who had sought to avoid tax by transferring assets abroad and did not apply to individuals simply because they might become the recipients of income or capital derived from those assets. A tax liability was

b later imposed by s 45 of the Finance Act 1981 (now s 740 of the 1988 Act) on the actual recipients of income or capital derived from the transferred assets.

[8] My Lords, the issue on this appeal is a short one. It is whether s 739(2), deeming the income of the foreign transferee to be the income of the tax avoider/transferor, impels the corollary that that income is, for tax purposes, to be deemed not to be the income of the foreign transferee.

c [9] This issue does not arise out of a dispute between the Revenue and a foreign transferee as to the tax liability of the latter. This should not be thought surprising. Foreign transferees are in general chosen by tax avoiders for their invulnerability to tax demands by the Revenue. They do not submit tax returns and then engage in disputations with the Revenue as to the extent of their liability.

d This issue arises out of criminal proceedings taken against the tax avoider and his associates. I must explain how it comes about.

The facts

[10] The appellant, Dermot Jeremy Dimsey, is resident in Jersey. Via a Jersey

e company, DFM Consultants Ltd, the appellant provides financial services to clients. These services include setting up offshore companies for persons resident in the United Kingdom and the administration of these companies. One of the appellant's clients was a Mr Chipping, a resident in the United Kingdom. Mr Chipping became involved as an intermediary in the supply of avionic equipment to South Africa.

f On Mr Chipping's instructions the appellant formed two offshore companies, Thomlyn Supplies Ltd (Thomlyn) and Glenville Supplies Ltd (Glenville) to deal with the South African contracts that Mr Chipping had obtained. Mr Chipping was the beneficial owner of the shares in, and was in control of, the two companies.

[11] The South African contracts were signed by the appellant in Jersey on behalf of the companies. The profits made by Thomlyn were £664,057, and by

g Glenville were £582,000 (see the judgment of the Court of Appeal given by Laws LJ [1999] STC 846 at 854, [2000] QB 744 at 751). The appellant arranged for the issue of credit cards in the names of the two companies, but for the personal use of Mr Chipping. He arranged for the payment by the companies of liabilities incurred through Mr Chipping's use of these cards for personal expenditure.

h [12] The appellant set up a third offshore company, Lantau Investments Ltd (Lantau), for Mr Chipping. Lantau was not a trading company but was used as a receptacle for some of the profits derived from the South African contracts. A flat in England for the use of a member of Mr Chipping's family was acquired by Lantau.

j [13] In September 1993 the Revenue began an investigation into Mr Chipping's tax affairs. The appellant assisted Mr Chipping in providing false and misleading information to the Revenue regarding the three offshore companies, the South African contracts and certain bank accounts that Mr Chipping held in Jersey. A solicitor in England, Mr Da Costa, had been retained by Mr Chipping to act for him in the Inland Revenue investigation. He, too, played a part in the provision of this false and misleading information.

[14] In due course the Revenue commenced criminal proceedings against
Mr Chipping, Mr Da Costa and the appellant. There were eleven counts. All bar   *a*
one, count 10, were counts under which Mr Chipping alone was accused of cheating
the Revenue. He pleaded guilty to counts 1 to 8, which related to undeclared
taxable income for the years 1986/1987 to 1993/1994 and to income and benefits
derived from Thomlyn, Glenville and Lantau. He was convicted at trial on the
other two counts of cheating the public revenue. One of these counts related to   *b*
£200,000 odd, which had been paid by Thomlyn and/or Glenville to Lantau as,
in effect, nominee for Mr Chipping. The other count charged Mr Chipping with
cheating the Revenue of corporation tax by concealing the existence of profits
made by the offshore companies.

[15] Count 10, the only count under which the appellant and Mr Da Costa
were charged, alleged a conspiracy contrary to s 1(1) of the Criminal Law Act 1977.   *c*
The alleged conspirators were Mr Chipping, Mr Da Costa and the appellant. The
particulars were that the three accused—

> 'Between 1 January 1993 and 8 July 1994, conspired together, with intent
> to defraud and to the prejudice of Her Majesty the Queen and the
> Commissioners of Inland Revenue, to cheat Her Majesty the Queen and   *d*
> the Commissioners of Inland Revenue of public revenue by failing to make
> full and complete disclosure to the Commissioners of Inland Revenue of:
> (i) [Mr Chipping's] worldwide assets and liabilities; (ii) income and benefits
> which had derived from offshore companies which he, [Mr Chipping],
> managed and controlled, namely [Glenville, Lantau, Thomlyn]; (iii) profits   *e*
> made by the said offshore companies which he [Mr Chipping] managed and
> controlled; (iv) interest received by [Mr Chipping] which was derived from
> bank accounts held at the Royal Trust Bank (Jersey) Ltd.'

[16] Particular (i) was deleted during the course of the trial. Particular (ii)
related only to the sum of £200,000 odd that had been paid to Lantau and to the   *f*
sums charged to the Thomlyn and Glenville credit cards. Particular (iv) related
to interest on the Jersey bank accounts. The Revenue has conceded that a
conviction could not be upheld on the basis of particular (iv) alone.

[17] Particular (iii) is, for present purposes, the most important. At the trial
the Revenue ran their case under particular (iii) on the footing that the
conspirators had attempted to cheat the Revenue of corporation tax due from the   *g*
three offshore companies. These companies, it was said, were liable to corporation
tax because they were resident in the United Kingdom. They were resident in the
United Kingdom because the management and control of their respective businesses
took place in the United Kingdom. The profits of the three companies were,
therefore, liable to attract corporation tax. There was no mention at the trial of   *h*
s 739 of the 1988 Act. No one took the point that under s 739 the income of each
of the three companies was deemed to be the income of Mr Chipping. This point
only emerged in the Court of Appeal.

[18] The jury convicted all three defendants on count 10. Mr Doyle, one of
the junior counsel for the appellant, has pointed out that it is not possible to know   *j*
which of the particulars constituted the basis on which the jury brought in their
verdict of guilty. It may well have been particular (iii) alone. Accordingly, if a
conviction based on particular (iii) cannot be upheld, the conviction, he submits,
is unsafe.

[19] My Lords, this submission is, in my opinion, well-founded. Particular (i)
has been withdrawn, particular (iv) cannot suffice on its own and particular (ii)

a concentrated on Mr Chipping's personal tax liability. The appellant's evidence was that he had had nothing to do with Mr Chipping's personal tax returns or tax liabilities and had advised Mr Chipping to obtain expert tax advice. It is quite possible that the jury accepted this evidence and convicted the appellant on the basis of particular (iii) alone. It must follow that if a conviction on the basis of particular (iii) cannot be upheld, the appellant's conviction cannot stand.

b [20] Mr Chipping, who had pleaded guilty to eight counts and had been convicted on all three counts, was sentenced to three years' imprisonment. He has not appealed. Mr Da Costa was sentenced to 12 months' imprisonment. He, too, has not appealed. The appellant was sentenced to 18 months' imprisonment. He alone has appealed. He had served the sentence before his appeal came to be heard in the Court of Appeal.

c

The issues

[21] Before the Court of Appeal and before this House, the appellant's appeal has been based upon the proposition that the three offshore companies were not in law liable to pay United Kingdom corporation tax on their profits. If the *d* companies were not in law liable to pay corporation tax, there could be no such thing as an offence of cheating, or conspiring to cheat, the Revenue of corporation tax payable by the companies. This must be right.

[22] Mr Rook QC, counsel for the Revenue, has pointed out that count 10 refers to 'public revenue', not to 'corporation tax'. If the income of the companies is, under s 739, deemed to have been the income of Mr Chipping for income tax *e* purposes, then the concealing of that income would be depriving the Revenue of 'public revenue', ie income tax payable by Mr Chipping, whether or not corporation tax was payable by the companies. Mr Rook's point is, in my opinion, correct but it cannot avail the Revenue on this appeal. The prosecution was conducted at trial on the footing that corporation tax payable by the companies *f* was the 'public revenue' of which the three accused had conspired to cheat the Revenue. The appellant, and presumably the other two accused, defended the case on the basis on which it was prosecuted. In bringing in a verdict of guilty, the jury must have been satisfied that each of the accused had had the requisite mens rea in relation to a conspiracy to cheat the Revenue of tax payable by the companies. If the Revenue's case had been based on conspiracy to cheat the Revenue of tax *g* which, under s 739, was payable by Mr Chipping, the questions put to and evidence given by the appellant might have been different. The jury's view as to whether the appellant had the intention requisite for guilt might have been different. It is, in my opinion, too late for the prosecution to alter the basis of its case. It cannot now attempt to uphold the conviction on a basis not explored at *h* trial. If it is right that, in law, the three offshore companies were not liable to pay United Kingdom corporation tax, the appellant is, in my opinion, entitled to succeed in his appeal.

[23] There were two grounds on which it was argued before the Court of Appeal that a conviction on the conspiracy count based on particular (iii) should *j* be set aside.

[24] It was argued, first, that the trial judge misdirected the jury as to the correct test for determining whether Thomlyn, Glenville and Lantau were resident in the United Kingdom. Residence in the United Kingdom was, of course, a necessary condition of their liability to corporation tax. In giving the judgment of the court, Laws LJ set out the relevant passages from the judge's summing up, summarised the law and concluded that there had been no misdirection.

[25] The second ground was the s 739 point. As I have said, this point was raised for the first time before the Court of Appeal. This was not the Revenue's fault. It was not until the course of the trial that the Revenue first became aware that Mr Chipping was the beneficial owner of the shares in the three offshore companies and that s 739 might apply. That is why, at trial, the Revenue concentrated, in regard to particular (iii), on the companies' liability to corporation tax. In the Court of Appeal the s 739 point was raised by counsel for the appellant, not by the Revenue. It was submitted on behalf of the appellant that s 739(2) applied, with the result that the income of each of the offshore companies was deemed for income tax purposes to be the income of Mr Chipping. So, it was submitted, it followed that the income must be deemed not to be the income of the companies. If that were right, then none of the companies could be liable to corporation tax in respect of that income. The Revenue accepted that, having regard to the facts that had emerged at trial, s 739(2) did apply, but did not accept that the section required that the companies' income be deemed not to be theirs for tax purposes. The Court of Appeal agreed with the Revenue and dismissed the appeal.

[26] The Court of Appeal certified the s 739 point as a point of law of general public importance but refused leave to appeal. Leave to appeal to this House on the s 739 point was granted by an Appeal Committee. The appellant, at the commencement of the hearing of the appeal, sought leave to appeal also on the corporate residence point. Your Lordships declined, however, to entertain an appeal on this point. As is pointed out in the Revenue's case, there was no dispute between the parties as to the correct test in law of corporate residence. The only question was whether that test had been accurately reflected in the judge's summing up. That issue had been fully considered in the Court of Appeal.

[27] No mention had been made in the Court of Appeal of the European Convention for the Protection of Human Rights and Fundamental Freedoms (Rome, 4 November 1950; TS 71 (1953); Cmd 8969) (as set out in Sch 1 to the Human Rights Act 1998). The hearing in the Court of Appeal took place in 1999 before the incorporation of the convention into domestic law under the 1998 Act. The relevant sections of the 1998 Act came into effect on 2 October 2000. With the leave of the Appeal Committee, the appellant was permitted to base an argument on art 1 of the First Protocol to the convention.

[28] There are, therefore, two issues before your Lordships. The first is whether under s 739(2) of the 1988 Act the income of the three offshore companies, which is deemed to be the income for income tax purposes of Mr Chipping, must also be deemed not to be the income of the companies. The second issue only arises if the companies' income, notwithstanding that under s 739(2) it is deemed to be the income of Mr Chipping for tax purposes, remains for tax purposes the income of the companies. The issue is whether this state of affairs is inconsistent with the right to property guaranteed by art 1 of the First Protocol to the convention.

[29] I should add that both in the Court of Appeal and before your Lordships' House the appellant's appeal has been heard together with an appeal brought by Brian Roger Allen, another of the appellant's clients. The s 739 point arises on both appeals. And Mr Allen, like the appellant, has raised before the House a convention point, albeit a different convention point from the appellant's First Protocol point. I have had the advantage of reading in draft the opinion of my noble and learned friend Lord Hutton in *R v Allen (No 2)* [2001] UKHL 45, [2001] 4 All ER 768. The remarks about retrospectivity and *R v Lambert* [2001] UKHL 37, [2001] 3 All ER 577, [2001] 3 WLR 206 made by my noble and learned friend in

a his opinion ([2001] 4 All ER 768 at [23]) apply also to the convention point raised by the appellant. If the appellant's conviction was safe before the incorporation of the convention into domestic law, it has not ceased to be safe because of that incorporation.

The section 739 issue

b [30] The thrust of the submission made by Mr Venables QC, on behalf of the appellant, is that the deeming provision in s 739(2) must be carried through to what he contends is its logical conclusion. He cites Peter Gibson LJ who, in *Marshall (Inspector of Taxes) v Kerr* [1993] STC 360 at 366, said:

c '... I take the correct approach in construing a deeming provision to be to give the words used their ordinary and natural meaning, consistent so far as possible with the policy of the Act and the purposes of the provisions so far as such policy and purposes can be ascertained; but if such construction would lead to injustice or absurdity, the application of the statutory fiction should be limited to the extent needed to avoid such injustice or absurdity, unless such application would clearly be within the purposes of the fiction.

d I further bear in mind that because one must treat as real that which is only deemed to be so, one must treat as real the consequences and incidents inevitably flowing from or accompanying that deemed state of affairs, unless prohibited from doing so.'

e [31] So, Mr Venables submits, one must treat as real the statutory deeming required by s 739(2). The income of the transferee is deemed to be that of the transferor. One must then treat as real the consequences and incidents flowing from or accompanying that deemed state of affairs. If the income were the income of the transferor it would not be the income of the transferee.

[32] This approach to s 739(2) is, Mr Venables submits, fortified by a presumption *f* against double taxation and a presumption that Parliament intends taxation according to law and not according to administrative fiat.

[33] As to double taxation, if the Revenue are right in their submissions on this appeal, then Mr Chipping is liable under s 739(2) to income tax on the companies' income and the companies are liable to corporation tax on the same income. In *g* the course of the hearing before your Lordships, Mr Milne QC, counsel for the Revenue, gave an assurance on behalf of his clients that in seeking to recover income tax against a transferor under s 739(2) credit would always be given for any tax that had been paid on the same income by the transferee, and vice versa. But, as Lord Wilberforce remarked in *IRC v Garvin* [1981] STC 344 at 350, [1981] 1 WLR 793 at 799, the avoidance of double taxation 'should be a right and not *h* merely a privilege'.

[34] As to taxation according to law and not according to administrative fiat, this House in *Vestey v IRC (Nos 1 and 2)* [1979] 3 All ER 976 at 985, [1980] AC 1148 at 1172 rejected the Revenue's contentions that every beneficiary was taxable on the whole of the trust income regardless of whether he or she had received any, that *j* 'there is no duty on the commissioners to collect the whole of this [tax] from any one beneficiary', and that '[the commissioners] are entitled, so long as they do not exceed the total, to collect from selected beneficiaries an amount decided upon by themselves'. Lord Wilberforce said:

'I accept ... that they cannot, in the absence of clear power, tax any given income more than once. But all of this falls far short of saying that so long as they do not exceed a maximum they can decide that beneficiary A is to bear so much tax and no more, or that beneficiary B is to bear no tax.' (See [1979] 3 All ER 976 at 985, [1980] AC 1148 at 1173.)

[35] However, the issue before your Lordships is one of construction of s 739(2). If the section, on its true construction, does leave the transferee liable to be taxed on its actual income notwithstanding that that income is the deemed income on which the transferor is liable to be taxed then, subject to the Human Rights Act point, that is that. The issue, of course, only arises in relation to income of a transferee on which the transferee is liable to pay United Kingdom tax. But on the premise that the three offshore companies were resident in the United Kingdom at the material time, it is common ground that, leaving aside s 739(2), they would have been liable to pay corporation tax on their profits (see s 6 of the 1988 Act). And the income each company received in the tax year in question would have had to be brought into the computation of its taxable profits.

[36] Section 739(2) is expressed to deem the transferee's income to be the income of the transferor 'for all purposes of the Income Tax Acts'. Section 831(1) of the 1988 Act has separate definitions of 'the Corporation Tax Acts' and 'the Income Tax Acts' and the Court of Appeal concluded, accepting a submission made by counsel on behalf of the Revenue, that the deeming provision did not affect the liability to corporation tax of transferee companies: 'In short (as was submitted by Mr Brennan, junior counsel for the Crown) the deeming provision does not affect corporation tax' (see [1999] STC 846 at 865, [2000] QB 744 at 764 per Laws LJ).

[37] There is a possible implication in this language that, in the view of the Court of Appeal, the deeming provision would affect the income tax liability of a transferee who was not a company but an individual. Suppose the case of a transferee, resident and domiciled abroad, to whom assets have been transferred as part of a tax avoidance scheme and where the tax avoider has power to enjoy income of the transferee so as to attract s 739(2). For as long as the transferee remains non-resident the present problem does not arise. The transferee is not liable to pay United Kingdom tax on income generated abroad. But suppose, whether through inadvertence or by design, the transferee becomes resident in the United Kingdom. What would be the tax liability of the transferee in respect of the income which, under s 739(2), is deemed to be the income of the transferor 'for all the purposes of the Income Tax Acts'? Is it the case that the transferee, if a company, would have to bring that income into its computation of profits for corporation tax purposes but, if a non-corporate individual, would not be liable to income tax in respect of that income?

[38] I am unable to accept that a distinction between the position of a transferee company and a transferee who is an individual can accord with what Parliament intended. The contrary view requires that the deeming words in s 739(2) be read as follows: 'shall ... for all purposes of the Income Tax Acts be deemed to be the income of that individual and not the income of any other individual'. This wording would, I think, justify drawing a distinction between a transferee company and a transferee who is an individual.

[39] By contrast, Mr Venables, for the appellant, would have the deeming words read: 'shall ... for all tax purposes be deemed to be the income of that individual and not the income of any other person'. This reading would prevent any

a distinction being drawn between the liability of a company transferee to corporation tax and the liability of an individual transferee to income tax.

[40] Mr Milne, on the other hand, would simply leave the words as enacted and confine the deeming provision to its literal meaning. He would, that is to say, confine its effect to the transferor and decline to treat as real the consequences that would follow the deemed state of affairs if the deemed state of affairs were b real (see *Marshall (Inspector of Taxes) v Kerr* [1993] STC 360 at 366).

[41] In my opinion, the legislative history of s 739 and the other provisions in Ch III of Pt XVII of the 1988 Act, the comparison of s 739(2) with other tax avoidance provisions, and the tax avoidance purpose of s 739 all suggest that Mr Milne's approach is the right one.

c *The legislation*

[42] The original enactment was s 18 of the Finance Act 1936. Subsection (1) of s 18 was the ancestor of s 739(2). When the 1936 Act was enacted, and until 1965 when corporation tax was introduced, companies paid income tax, not corporation tax. A distinction between company transferees and individual transferees d based upon the reference to 'the Income Tax Acts' would not have been possible under s 18, or, indeed, until 1965. The deeming provision would either have exonerated from liability to tax the income of all transferees or of no transferees.

[43] By the time corporation tax was introduced, in 1965, s 18 of the 1936 Act had become s 412 of the Income Tax Act 1952. Companies were still liable to income tax on their income. There was still no distinction that could be drawn e as to the effect of the deeming provision on the tax liability of company transferees compared with individual transferees.

[44] No amendment was made to s 412(1) when, in 1965, corporation tax was introduced and companies were no longer liable to income tax on their income. It is not possible to suppose that Parliament, in introducing corporation tax, f intended, without any mention or discussion, to draw a distinction between the effect of the s 412(1) deeming provision as between company transferees and individual transferees.

[45] Section 412 of the 1952 Act was replaced by s 478 of the Income and Corporation Taxes Act 1970. The deeming provision in sub-s (1) was in the same terms as in its statutory predecessors. Section 478 of the 1970 Act was in turn g replaced by s 739 of the 1988 Act.

[46] This legislative history makes it impossible, in my opinion, to attribute to Parliament any intention that there should be a distinction between the effect of the deeming provision on the liability to tax of a company transferee and its effect on the liability to tax of an individual transferee. In my opinion, therefore, either h s 739(2) exonerates both company transferees and individual transferees from liability to tax on their income or it exonerates none of them.

[47] Section 18 was not the only provision in the 1936 Act that sought to combat tax avoidance. Section 21 dealt with settlements made by a settlor on his children. Subsection (1) provided that any income of a settlement paid to or for j the benefit of an unmarried infant child of the settlor 'shall ... be treated for all the purposes of the Income Tax Acts as the income of the settlor ... *and not as the income of any other person*' (my emphasis).

[48] Confronted by the express words in s 21(1), 'and not as the income of any other person', it seems to me very difficult, if not impossible, to argue that those words, or something similar, which are notably absent from s 18(1) should be an

implied addition to s 18(1). A comparison between s 18(1) and s 21(1) suggests strongly that the omission of any such words from s 18(1) was deliberate.

[49] Section 24 of the Finance Act 1938 fortifies the point. The section deals with the case where an owner of securities has transferred to someone the right to receive interest payable in respect of the securities while himself remaining the owner of the securities. Subsection (1), which provides in para (a) that the interest 'shall be deemed to be the income of the owner', provides also, in para (c), that the interest 'shall not be deemed to be the income of any other person'. Section 730 of the 1988 Act reproduces the deeming provisions originally to be found in s 24 of the 1938 Act. Paragraphs (a) and (c) are to all intents and purposes in the same terms as in the 1938 Act.

[50] In other statutory deeming provisions, too, there is express reference to the tax liability of persons other than the person at whom the deeming provision is principally aimed. Section 660 of the 1988 Act deals with short-term dispositions. Subsection (1) provides that the income of the property thus disposed of—

'shall be deemed for all the purposes of the Income Tax Acts to be the income of the person, if living, by whom the disposition was made, and not to be the income of any other person.'

[51] The wording in these tax avoidance provisions strongly supports, in my opinion, Mr Milne's approach to the deeming provision in s 739(2).

The double taxation point

[52] Mr Venables submitted that it was to be presumed that Parliament did not intend the same income to be taxed twice, once in the deemed hands of the transferor and also in the actual hands of the transferee. This is, to my mind, a submission of weight but it is not a conclusive one. It is apparent that the draftsman of the legislation did give thought to the need to avoid double taxation. Subsection (6) of s 18 of the 1936 Act incorporated the provisions of Sch 2 to the 1936 Act. Paragraph 1 of Sch 2 said:

'Tax at the standard rate shall not be charged by virtue of the principal section in respect of income which has borne tax at the standard rate by deduction or otherwise ...'

[53] This provision would have dealt with the case where the transferee's income included income sourced in the United Kingdom and from which tax had already been deducted at source. But the words 'or otherwise' show that the provision would have covered, also, any case in which the transferee had paid tax on its income. It is worth repeating that in 1936 income tax was payable by individuals and by companies. This provision, too, did not distinguish between individual transferees and company transferees. It did not need to.

[54] In 1965, when companies became liable to corporation tax, the provision should, I think, have been amended so as to prevent a transferor being charged tax on deemed income where the transferee had paid corporation tax on the actual income. Section 480(1) of the 1970 Act replaced s 413(1) of the 1952 Act, which had replaced para 1 of Sch 2 to the 1936 Act. All were in the same terms. Section 743(1) of the 1988 Act provided:

'Income tax at the basic rate shall not be charged by virtue of section 739 in respect of income which has borne tax at the basic rate by deduction or otherwise.'

a [55] The provision, like its predecessors, caters for the deduction of tax at source. It would cater also for a case where the transferee, being an individual, had paid tax at the basic rate (or, now, the lower rate or Schedule F ordinary rate) on the income in question. But it does not cover, expressly at any rate, the case of a company transferee that has paid corporation tax on the income. It seems to me clear that this must be the result of an inadvertent oversight. If the point ever
b arose for decision I would be attracted by the view that s 743(1) should be construed so as to cover income which had been included in the computation of profits on which a company had paid tax. That construction would, in my opinion, accord with the Parliamentary intention. But it is not necessary to decide the point now. All that is necessary is to notice that Parliament did pay attention to possible double taxation and the possibility that the income of the s 739 transferee
c might have borne tax. Section 743(1) and its statutory predecessors show, in my opinion, that s 739(2) is not intended to exclude the normal tax liability that would lie on a transferee in respect of its income.

[56] Section 743(1), like its predecessors, is looking at the double taxation problem from the point of view of the transferor on whom the liability to pay tax
d on deemed income is being imposed. There is no comparable provision protecting the transferee in a case where, under s 739(2), the transferor has paid tax on his deemed income.

[57] This, however, is more a theoretical point than a real one. It is in practice highly unlikely that United Kingdom tax can be recovered from a s 739 transferee. Transferees are chosen by tax avoiders in order to avoid United Kingdom tax.
e Non-resident and foreign domiciled transferees are likely to be chosen. They do not submit tax returns to the Revenue. In the present case it is only because Mr Chipping, the transferor, so involved himself in the affairs of his offshore companies that they became resident in the United Kingdom that their liability to corporation tax arose.

f [58] Accordingly, the double taxation possibilities that the Revenue's case undoubtedly leaves theoretically open do not seem to me to carry weight in considering the correct construction of s 739(2).

[59] This conclusion does not seem to me to detract in the least from the principles expressed by this House in *Vestey v IRC (Nos 1 and 2)* [1979] 3 All ER 976,
g [1980] AC 1148. The Revenue's contention in *Vestey v IRC* was that each of the beneficiaries, none of whom was a transferor, was caught by s 412(1) of the 1952 Act and liable to tax on the whole of the income of the trustees, the transferees. The situation for which the Revenue was contending was not simply one of double taxation. It was one of multiple taxation. The Revenue was contending for an administrative discretion which would enable them to assess one or more
h of the beneficiaries in such sums as they, the Revenue, thought fit, subject only to the limitation that the total income of the trustees should not be taxed more than once. This was the context which led Lord Wilberforce to say:

'Taxes are imposed upon subjects by Parliament. A citizen cannot be taxed
j unless he is designated in clear terms by a taxing Act as a taxpayer and the amount of his liability is clearly defined. A proposition that whether a subject is to be taxed or not, or that, if he is, the amount of his liability is to be decided (even though within a limit) by an administrative body, represents a radical departure from constitutional principle. It may be that the Revenue could persuade Parliament to enact such a proposition in such terms that the courts would have to give effect to it; but unless it has done so, the courts,

acting on constitutional principles, not only should not, but cannot validate
it.' (See [1979] 3 All ER 976 at 984–985, [1980] AC 1148 at 1172.)

[60] None of this, in my opinion, bites in the present case. There is no doubt
about the liability, in principle, of companies resident in the United Kingdom to
corporation tax. There is no constitutional problem. The question is whether
Parliament, in imposing the s 739 tax liability on tax avoiders, intended thereby
to relieve the transferees of their normal liability to tax on their income, the
income which forms the basis of the tax liability imposed on the tax avoider.
Vestey v IRC does not, in my opinion, assist in answering this question. I would
answer the question in the negative. Section 739(2), on its true construction, does
not, in my opinion, relieve transferees of their normal liability to pay tax on their
income.

The Human Rights Act 1998

[61] Mr Milne accepted that the 1988 Act must now be construed, so far as it
is possible to do so, in a way compatible with convention rights (see s 3 of the
Human Rights Act 1998).

[62] Article 1 of the First Protocol to the convention says:

'Every natural or legal person is entitled to the peaceful enjoyment of his
possessions. No one shall be deprived of his possessions except in the public
interest and subject to the conditions provided for by law and by the general
principles of international law.

The preceding provisions shall not, however, in any way impair the right
of a State to enforce such laws as it deems necessary to control the use of
property in accordance with the general interest or to secure the payment of
taxes or other contributions or penalties.'

[63] Mr Lyons, the other junior counsel for the appellant, has submitted that
a construction of s 739(2) that would leave the transferor liable to tax on its
deemed income and the transferee liable to tax on its actual income, leaving it to
the discretion of the Revenue which liability to seek to enforce and to what
extent, would be inconsistent with this article.

[64] In *Gasus Dosier-und Fördertechnik GmbH v Netherlands* [1995] 20 EHRR 403
at 435 (para 62), the European Court of Human Rights said this about art 1:

'According to the Court's well-established case law, the second paragraph
of Article 1 of [the First Protocol] must be construed in the light of the
principle laid down in the Article's first sentence. Consequently, an
interference must achieve a "fair balance" between the demands of the
general interest of the community and the requirements of the protection of
the individual's fundamental rights. The concern to achieve this balance is
reflected in the structure of Article 1 as a whole, including the second
paragraph: there must therefore be a reasonable relationship of
proportionality between the means employed and the aim pursued.'

[65] Mr Milne submitted that such element of discretion as the Revenue
enjoyed in deciding whether to pursue the transferee for tax on its actual income
or the transferor for tax on the deemed income was proper, as a matter of public
policy, in order to enable tax to be collected. Section 739 is, after all, a provision
designed to combat tax avoidance.

a [66] *Lord Howard de Walden v IRC* [1942] 1 All ER 287, [1942] 1 KB 389 is in point. The taxpayer appealed against an assessment to income tax and surtax made against him in respect of income deemed to be his under s 18 of the 1936 Act. The taxpayer had power to enjoy only a small part of the income of the transferee companies but he was assessed to tax in respect of the whole of their income. The Court of Appeal declined to accept the invitation of the taxpayer's
b counsel to construe the section so as to limit the charge to tax to the benefit which the taxpayer had actually obtained. Lord Greene MR said:

> '... even if the only alternative to the construction of counsel for the appellant is the second of the three constructions, we are not prepared to say that it is necessarily as unjust as he contends. The section is a penal one, and
c whatever its consequences may be, they are intended to be an effective deterrent to practices which the legislature considers to be against the public interest. For years a battle of manoeuvre has been waged between the legislature and those who are minded to throw the burden of taxation off their own shoulders on to those of their fellow-subjects ... It would not shock us in the least to find that the legislature has determined to put an end
d to the struggle by imposing the severest of penalties. It scarcely lies in the mouth of the taxpayer who plays with fire to complain ...' (See [1942] 1 All ER 287 at 289, [1942] 1 KB 389 at 397.)

e [67] In *National & Provincial Building Society v UK* [1997] STC 1466 the Court of Human Rights had to consider the effect of art 1 of the First Protocol on legislation which retrospectively validated certain regulations which had been held to be invalid and which had imposed a tax liability on building societies in respect of past interest payments. The court, in holding there had been no violation of the convention, said (at 1486 (para 76)):

f > 'Having regard to a contracting state's margin of appreciation in the tax field and to the public interest considerations at stake, it could not be said that the decisions taken by Parliament to enact these measures with retrospective effect were manifestly without reasonable foundation or failed to strike a fair balance between the demands of the general interest of the community and the protection of the rights of the applicant societies.'

g [68] In considering the implications of art 1 in a s 739 case, it is necessary, in my opinion, to distinguish between the position of the tax avoider/transferor and that of the transferee. The tax avoider/transferor has a tax liability imposed upon him. The income of the transferee is deemed to be his for tax purposes. The tax avoider cannot, however, be taxed on income of the transferee which has already
h borne tax (see s 743(1) and [48]–[51], above). There is no element of administrative discretion involved here.

[69] The tax liability being imposed on the tax avoider does not depend on his having actually received any benefit from the income or assets of the transferee. The liability may be regarded as having a penal character and as intended to
j discourage United Kingdom residents from seeking to avoid tax by transferring assets abroad. The imposition of such a tax liability is, in my opinion, well within the margin of appreciation allowed to member states in respect of tax legislation.

[70] What about the transferee? The transferee will usually be resident abroad and will not be liable to pay United Kingdom tax on its income generated abroad. If, however, in any tax year the transferee becomes resident in the United

Kingdom, it will have the normal tax liability of any other United Kingdom
resident. Recovery by the Revenue of the tax may be difficult if the transferee,   *a*
although resident, has no assets in the United Kingdom, and I imagine that in
such cases the Revenue would usually not try to do so but instead would prefer
to recover tax under s 739(2) from the transferor. I do not follow, however, how
this state of affairs could possibly be represented as constituting an infringement
of the transferee's art 1 rights.   *b*

[71] In my opinion, s 739(2), construed so as to deem the transferee's income
to be the income of the transferor, the tax avoider, for income tax purposes but
so as to leave the liability of the transferee to pay tax, income tax or corporation
tax as the case may be, on its income unaffected by the deeming provision, is well
within the margin of appreciation allowed to member states in respect of
tax legislation. The public interest requires that legislation designed to combat tax   *c*
avoidance should be effective. That public interest outweighs, in my opinion, the
objections, mainly theoretical, that Mr Venables has taken to the effect of s 739(2)
construed as I would construe it. There is nothing, in my opinion, in art 1 of the
First Protocol that requires a different construction of s 739(2) in order to render
it convention-compliant.   *d*

Conclusion

[72] For the reasons I have given, the three offshore companies, resident in the
United Kingdom through Mr Chipping's activities as the jury must have found,
were in law liable to corporation tax. It follows that there was no legal impediment
standing in the way of a conviction of the appellant, and the others, of the offence   *e*
of conspiring to cheat the Revenue of corporation tax payable by the three
companies.

[73] I would, therefore, dismiss this appeal.

Appeal dismissed.

Kate O'Hanlon   Barrister

a

Farley v Skinner
[2001] UKHL 49

HOUSE OF LORDS

b LORD STEYN, LORD BROWNE-WILKINSON, LORD CLYDE, LORD HUTTON AND LORD SCOTT
OF FOSCOTE

18, 19, 21 JUNE, 11 OCTOBER 2001

Contract – Damages for breach – Non-pecuniary damages – Claimant considering
c *purchase of tranquil country property and instructing surveyor to report on aircraft noise*
– Surveyor negligently reporting that property unlikely to be affected by aircraft noise –
Claimant buying property and subsequently discovering that it was significantly
affected by such noise – Claimant staying in property but bringing contractual claim
against surveyor for non-pecuniary damages – Whether non-pecuniary damages only
available in cases where object of entire contract was to give pleasure, relaxation or
d *peace of mind – Whether such damages recoverable only in cases where promisor*
guaranteed achievement of those ends.

The claimant, F, was interested in buying a property in the countryside, some 15
miles from an international airport, which he hoped would offer him peace and
e tranquillity in his retirement. He engaged the defendant surveyor to inspect the
property, specifically instructing him to investigate, in addition to the usual
matters to be expected of a surveyor on such an inspection, whether the property
was seriously affected by aircraft noise. Those instructions were accepted by the
surveyor who subsequently reported that it was unlikely that the property would
suffer greatly from such noise. F duly purchased the property and spent a
f considerable sum modernising and refurbishing it. After he moved in, F discovered
that the property was indeed affected by aircraft noise, particularly at those times
of the day when he was most likely to wish to enjoy the property's amenities.
F decided not to sell the property, but brought an action against the surveyor for
breach of his contractual duty of care, seeking damages for diminution in value
of the property and compensation for non-pecuniary damage. The judge
g concluded that the surveyor had been negligent, that F would not have
purchased the property if his instructions had been properly carried out and that
he had made the best of a bad job by not moving out. On the basis of those
conclusions, the judge made an award of £10,000 on F's claim for non-pecuniary
damage, although he rejected the primary claim for diminution in value of the
h property. On the surveyor's appeal, the Court of Appeal held, by a majority, that
the judge's award of non-pecuniary damages was contrary to principle.
Accordingly, the appeal was allowed, and F appealed to the House of Lords. In
seeking to uphold the Court of Appeal's decision, the surveyor contended that
the exceptional category of cases in which the court could award non-pecuniary
j damages for breach of contract was restricted to those cases where the object of
the entire contract was to give pleasure, relaxation or peace of mind; that that
exceptional category did not extend to a breach of a contractual duty of care, even
if imposed to secure pleasure, relaxation and peace of mind, but was instead
confined to cases where the promisor guaranteed achievement of such an object;
and that F had forfeited any right to recover non-pecuniary damages by staying
in the property.

Held – Where a surveyor gave a specific contractual undertaking to investigate a
matter important for the buyer's peace of mind, the buyer was in principle
entitled to recover non-pecuniary damages for breach of that undertaking. There
was no reason in principle or policy why the scope of recovery in the exceptional
category of cases should depend on the object of the contract as ascertained from
all its constituent parts. Rather, it was sufficient that a major or important object
of the contract was to give pleasure, relaxation or peace of mind. Similarly, a
claim for non-pecuniary damages was not barred merely because the surveyor
undertook only to exercise reasonable care rather than to guarantee the achievement
of a result. Although contractual guarantees of performance and promises to
exercise reasonable care were fundamentally different, that difference between
an absolute and relative contractual promise did not require a distinction in
respect of the recovery of non-pecuniary damages. There was no reason why only
those claimants who negotiated guarantees might recover non-pecuniary damages
for a breach of contract. It would be a singularly unattractive result if a professional
person, who undertook a specific obligation to exercise reasonable care to investigate
a matter judged and communicated to be important by his customer, could
please himself whether or not to comply with the wishes of the promisee which,
as embodied in the contract, formed part of the consideration for the price. Nor
had any legal principle been put forward to justify the contention that F's
decision to stay put—found by the judge to have been reasonable—divested him
of his claim for non-pecuniary damages. Accordingly, the appeal would be allowed,
and the judge's award of damages restored, even though it appeared to be at the
very top end of what could possibly be regarded as appropriate damages in such
a case (see [15], [24]–[26], [28], [29], [31], [32], [39], [41]–[45], [51], [53], [56], [61],
[110], [111], below).

*Ruxley Electronics and Construction Ltd v Forsyth, Laddingford Enclosures Ltd v
Forsyth* [1995] 3 All ER 268 applied; *Watts v Morrow* [1991] 4 All ER 937 explained
and distinguished; *Knott v Bolton* (1995) 45 Con LR 127 overruled.

Per Lord Steyn. Awards of non-pecuniary damages should be restrained and
modest. It is important that logical and beneficial developments in the law should
not contribute to the creation of a society bent on litigation (see [28], below).

Notes

For damages for loss of amenity arising from breach of contract, see 12(1)
Halsbury's Laws (4th edn reissue) paras 957–961.

Cases referred to in opinions

Addis v Gramophone Co Ltd [1909] AC 488, [1908–10] All ER Rep 1, HL.
Atkins (G W) Ltd v Scott (1991) 46 Con LR 14, CA.
Bailey v Bullock [1950] 2 All ER 1167.
Cassell & Co Ltd v Broome [1972] 1 All ER 801, [1972] AC 1027, [1972] 2 WLR 645, HL.
Cook v S [1967] 1 All ER 299, [1967] 1 WLR 457, CA.
Diesen v Samson 1971 SLT (Sh Ct) 49.
Hadley v Baxendale (1854) 9 Exch 341, [1843–60] All ER Rep 461, 156 ER 145.
Hamlin v Great Northern Rly Co (1856) 1 H & N 408, 156 ER 1261.
Hayes v James & Charles Dodd (a firm) [1990] 2 All ER 815, CA.
Heron II, The, Koufos v C Czarnikow Ltd [1967] 3 All ER 686, [1969] 1 AC 350, [1967]
    3 WLR 1491, HL.
Heywood v Wellers (a firm) [1976] 1 All ER 300, [1976] QB 446, [1976] 2 WLR 101, CA.

a   *Hobbs v London and South Western Rly Co* (1875) LR 10 QB 111, [1874–80] All ER
          Rep 458.
    Jackson v Chrysler Acceptances Ltd [1978] RTR 474, CA.
    Jackson v Horizon Holidays Ltd [1975] 3 All ER 92, [1975] 1 WLR 1468, CA.
    Jarvis v Swans Tours Ltd [1973] 1 All ER 71, [1973] QB 233, [1972] 3 WLR 954, CA.
    Johnson v Gore Wood & Co (a firm) [2001] 1 All ER 481, [2001] 2 WLR 72, HL.
b   *Knott v Bolton* (1995) 45 Con LR 127, CA.
    Livingstone v Rawyards Coal Co (1880) 5 App Cas 25, HL.
    Panatown Ltd v Alfred McAlpine Construction Ltd [2000] 4 All ER 97, [2001] 1 AC 518,
          [2000] 3 WLR 946, HL.
    Perry v Sidney Phillips & Son (a firm) [1982] 3 All ER 705, [1982] 1 WLR 1297, CA.
c   *R v Investors Compensation Scheme Ltd, ex p Bowden* [1994] 1 All ER 525, [1994]
          1 WLR 17, DC; *rvsd* [1995] 1 All ER 214, [1995] QB 107, [1994] 3 WLR 1045,
          CA; *rvsd* [1996] 1 AC 261, [1995] 3 All ER 605, [1995] 3 WLR 289, HL.
    Radford v De Froberville [1978] 1 All ER 33, [1977] 1 WLR 1262.
    Robinson v Harman (1848) 1 Exch 850, [1843–60] All ER Rep 383, 154 ER 363, Exch.
    Rookes v Barnard [1964] 1 All ER 367, [1964] AC 1129, [1964] 2 WLR 269, HL.
d   *Ruxley Electronics and Construction Ltd v Forsyth, Laddingford Enclosures Ltd v Forsyth*
          [1995] 3 All ER 268, [1996] AC 344, [1995] 3 WLR 118, HL; *rvsg* [1994] 3 All ER
          801, [1994] 1 WLR 650, CA.
    *Victoria Laundry (Windsor) Ltd v Newman Industries Ltd (Coulsdon & Co Ltd, third
          party)* [1949] 1 All ER 997, [1949] 2 KB 528, CA.
    Wapshott v Davis Donovan & Co [1996] PNLR 361, CA.
e   *Watts v Morrow* [1991] 4 All ER 937, [1991] 1 WLR 1421, CA.

Appeal

The plaintiff, Graham Farley, appealed with permission of the Appeal Committee
of the House of Lords given on 12 December 2000 from the decision of the Court
f   of Appeal (Stuart-Smith and Mummery LJJ, Clarke LJ dissenting) on 6 April 2000
((2000) 73 Con LR 70) allowing an appeal by the defendant, Michael Skinner,
from the order of Judge Peter Baker QC, sitting as a judge of the High Court, on
27 May 1999 awarding the plaintiff damages of £10,000 for non-pecuniary damage
in his action against the defendant for breach of a contractual duty of care in
respect of a survey of a property known as Riverside House, Blackboys, East
g   Sussex. The facts are set out in the opinion of Lord Steyn.

Martin Spencer (instructed by *Irwin Mitchell*, Leeds) for the plaintiff.
Mark Simpson and *Spike Charlwood* (instructed by *Williams Davies Meltzer*) for the
          defendant.
h

Their Lordships took time for consideration.

11 October 2001. The following opinions were delivered.

j   **LORD STEYN.**
      [1] My Lords, the central question is whether a buyer who employed a surveyor
to investigate whether a property in the countryside was seriously affected by
aircraft noise may in principle recover non-pecuniary damages against the surveyor
for the latter's negligent failure to discover that the property was so affected. The
trial judge answered this question in the affirmative. A two-member Court of
Appeal disagreed on it. The point was then re-argued before a three-member

Court of Appeal ((2000) 73 Con LR 70). By a majority the Court of Appeal
reversed the decision of the trial judge and ruled that there was no right to   *a*
recover non-pecuniary damages in such cases. The second Court of Appeal was
deluged with authorities. So was the House on the present appeal. The hearings
of what was a comparatively simple case took up an exorbitant amount of time.
This circumstance underlines the importance, in the quest for coherent and just
solutions in such cases, of simple and practical rules.   *b*

I. *Riverside House, aircraft noise and the surveyor*

[2] In 1990 the plaintiff, a successful businessman, contemplated retirement.
He owned a flat in London, a house in Brighton and a property overseas. He
wanted to buy a gracious country residence. He became interested in a beautiful
property known as Riverside House in the village of Blackboys in Sussex which   *c*
was situated some 15 miles from Gatwick International Airport. The property is
in the heart of the countryside. There is a stream running through the middle of
it. The property has a croquet lawn, tennis court, orchard, paddock and swimming
pool. Although the attractive house required modernisation and refurbishment, it
appeared to be ideal for the plaintiff. There was, however, one question mark over   *d*
the transaction. For the plaintiff a property offering peace and tranquillity was the
raison d'être of the proposed purchase. He wanted to be reasonably sure that the
property was not seriously affected by aircraft noise.

[3] The plaintiff engaged as his surveyor the defendant, who had been in
practice as a sole practitioner for some years. The surveyor had to investigate the
usual matters expected of a surveyor who inspects a property. In addition the   *e*
plaintiff also specifically asked the surveyor to investigate, amongst other things,
whether the property would be affected by aircraft noise. The plaintiff told the
surveyor that he did not want a property on a flight path. The surveyor accepted
these instructions.

[4] On 17 December 1990 the surveyor sent his report to the plaintiff. From   *f*
the plaintiff's point of view it was a satisfactory report. About aircraft noise the
surveyor reported:

'You have also asked whether you felt the property might be affected by
aircraft noise, but we were not conscious of this during the time of our
inspection, and think it unlikely that the property will suffer greatly from   *g*
such noise, although some planes will inevitably cross the area, depending
on the direction of the wind and the positioning of the flight paths.'

Comforted by this reassuring report the plaintiff decided to buy the property.
The purchase price was £420,000 (which included £45,000 for chattels). The
purchase was completed on 28 February 1991.   *h*

[5] In the next few months the plaintiff caused the house to be modernised and
refurbished at a total cost of about £125,000. During this period he was unaware
that there was a significant problem associated with aircraft noise. On 13 June 1991
the plaintiff and his partner (who had a 32·74% beneficial interest) moved in.
Since 1991 they had lived there three to four days a week for seven to nine months   *j*
of the year.

[6] After he moved in the plaintiff quickly discovered that the property was
indeed affected by aircraft noise. In fact, the property was not far away from a
navigation beacon (the Mayfield Stack) and at certain busy times, especially in the
morning, the early evening, and at weekends, aircraft waiting to land at Gatwick
would be stacked up maintaining a spiral course around the beacon until there

a was a landing slot at the airport. Aircraft frequently passed directly over, or nearly over, the position of the house. The impact of aircraft noise on the tranquillity of the property was marked. The property was undoubtedly affected by aircraft noise.

[7] It is common ground that the plaintiff's enjoyment of the property was diminished by aircraft noise at those times when he was enjoying the amenities of the property outdoors and aircraft were stacked up, maintaining their spiral b course around the beacon, waiting for a landing slot at the airport. Nevertheless, after initial vacillation, the plaintiff decided not to sell the property and he does not presently intend to do so.

II. *The proceedings in the High Court*

c [8] In due course the plaintiff claimed damages against the surveyor. The action came for trial before Judge Peter Baker QC sitting as a judge of the Queen's Bench Division in May 1999. The action was resolutely defended by the surveyor on all aspects of the claim. The judge accepted the plaintiff's account of his instructions to the defendant. I have already set out the instructions. The judge had to consider whether the defendant had been negligent. It was clear that the d surveyor could have discovered the true position by checking with Gatwick. He did not do so. The judge found that the surveyor had been negligent and that, if the surveyor had carried out his instructions properly, the plaintiff would not have bought the property. The judge's conclusions on this aspect are not challenged on the appeal before the House.

e [9] The principal claim was one for a diminution of value of the property by reason of the negative effect of aircraft noise. The judge found that the purchase price coincided with the open market value of the property after taking into account aircraft noise. He accordingly dismissed the principal claim. There is also no challenge to this part of the judgment at first instance.

[10] The judge then had to consider the plaintiff's claim for non-pecuniary f damage. He accepted the evidence of Mr Attwood, a sound expert. The report of this expert summarised the general effect of the aircraft noise on Riverside House as follows:

'On a subjective basis, the aircraft noise, with its particular character, is out of keeping with the nature of the area around the house. The grounds are in g a very beautiful setting with many specimen trees and with a stream running through the middle. The outlook is also very beautiful. Essentially, this house and garden are in the heart of the countryside. The noise from the aircraft, flying overhead, represents a very significant intrusion into the peace of this setting ... It is the opinion of the author that the aircraft noise h represents a very significant nuisance to anyone trying to enjoy the amenity of the grounds at Riverside House.'

The judge approached the claim in accordance with the law as stated in *Watts v Morrow* [1991] 4 All ER 937, [1991] 1 WLR 1421. He upheld the plaintiff's claim:

j 'Here I think one must bear in mind that this was a specific contract dealing, inter alia, with noise so far as the defendant is concerned, and I was impressed by the account that Mr Farley gave of a number of matters. Firstly, he is particularly vulnerable because he has a habit, practice, of being an early riser and of wishing, when clement weather conditions prevail as even in this country [they] occasionally do, to sit outside on his terrace, or wherever, and enjoy the delightful gardens, the pool and the other amenities which is made pretty

intolerable, he says, and I accept from his point of view between, say, the
hours of 6 o'clock and 8 o'clock in the morning which is the time when he
would be minded to do this. Likewise, pre-dinner drinks are not made the
better for the evening activity in the sky not far away. That he is not a man,
if I may say so, with excessive susceptibilities is shown by the fact that he did
his best to grit his teeth and put up with it but, as he ultimately said, "Why
should I when I had endeavoured to cover this particular point in the
instructions that I had given to a professional man whom I had paid to do
this?" He finds it a confounded nuisance, and this is a matter that, of course,
he will be stuck with. It is not a case of something like drains or dry rot or
what have you that he can do anything about. Short of buying Gatwick and
closing it down, this is a matter that will continue.' (My emphasis.)

For what he described as the discomfort that had been sustained by the plaintiff
the judge awarded £10,000.

[11] Immediately after this judgment was given counsel for the defendant invited
the judge to deal specifically with one of his arguments, viz that the plaintiff's
claim must be rejected because he had decided not to move house. The judge
dealt with this point as follows:

'Bingham LJ said in *Watts v Morrow* [1991] 4 All ER 937 at 959, [1991]
1 WLR 1421 at 1445: "If, on learning of the defects which should have been
but were not reported, a purchaser decides (for whatever reason) to retain
the house and not move out and sell, I would question whether any loss he
thereafter suffers, at least in the ordinary case, can be laid at the door of the
contract-breaker." Dealing with that, in my judgment this is not an ordinary
case because if you look how matters worked out, Mr Farley, not knowing
at the time of the defect of which he should have been informed, on my
judgment, thereafter incurred vast expense in altering the house to get it to
a much higher standard. I think the sum of £100,000-odd was mentioned. It
was a very large sum. It seems to me, he not learning of the matters which
I find in my judgment in this case until much later than he incurred that
expense, it seems to me it would be putting too high a burden to say that he
should then have decided to move and to get away from the nuisance, if
I may so describe it. That nuisance being, for obvious reasons, not one that
one can do anything about. It is not a structural defect that can be remedied,
and that therefore he made the best of a bad job and stayed. I think in my
judgment with the greatest deference, what Bingham LJ was saying was, in
my view obiter. He should not be penalised for not having done that. Thank
you for reminding me of that matter.'

The judge's decision on the claim for non-pecuniary damages therefore stood.

III. *The proceedings in the Court of Appeal*

[12] The surveyor appealed to the Court of Appeal. In November 1999 the
matter came before Judge and Hale LJJ. The issue was whether as a matter of law
the judge was entitled to make the award of non-pecuniary damages. The members
of the court disagreed. Judge LJ thought that the judge's decision was correct and
he would have dismissed the appeal. Hale LJ took the opposite view and would
have allowed the appeal. For her the insuperable obstacle was that the surveyor

a had not guaranteed a result but had only undertaken a duty to exercise reasonable care. In the result the matter had to be re-argued.

[13] In March 2000 the matter came before a three-member Court of Appeal ((2000) 73 Con LR 70). In separate judgments the majority (Stuart-Smith and Mummery LJJ) held that the award of non-pecuniary damages was contrary to principle and allowed the appeal. In a detailed and powerful judgment Clarke LJ

b dissented. Stuart-Smith LJ concluded that the judge made the award on the ground that the breach of contract caused physical inconvenience and discomfort to the plaintiff. He found that the evidence did not justify this conclusion. He further held that the case fell beyond the reach of the exceptional category where the very object of the contract is to provide pleasure, relaxation, or peace of mind. He did so essentially for two separate reasons. First, in his view (at 79) the

c particular obligation to investigate aircraft noise was 'simply one relatively minor aspect of the overall instructions'. Secondly (at 82), there was not 'an obligation to achieve a result' but a mere obligation to exercise reasonable care. Mummery LJ agreed with Stuart-Smith LJ and reinforced his reasoning by reference to policy considerations of incommensurability, subjectivity and difficulties of proof involved

d in claims for mental distress flowing from breach of contract.

IV. *The law*

[14] The judgments in the Court of Appeal and the arguments before the House took as their starting point the propositions enunciated by Bingham LJ in

e *Watts v Morrow*. In that case the Court of Appeal had to consider a claim for damages for distress and inconvenience by a buyer of a house against his surveyor who had negligently failed to report defects in the house. Bingham LJ observed:

'(1) A contract-breaker is not in general liable for any distress, frustration, anxiety, displeasure, vexation, tension or aggravation which his breach of

f contract may cause to the innocent party. This rule is not, I think, founded on the assumption that such reactions are not foreseeable, which they surely are or may be, but on considerations of policy. (2) But the rule is not absolute. Where the very object of a contract is to provide pleasure, relaxation, peace of mind or freedom from molestation, damages will be awarded if the fruit

g of the contract is not provided or if the contrary result is procured instead. If the law did not cater for this exceptional category of case it would be defective. A contract to survey the condition of a house for a prospective purchaser does not, however, fall within this exceptional category. (3) In cases not falling within this exceptional category, damages are in my view recoverable for physical inconvenience and discomfort caused by the breach

h and mental suffering directly related to that inconvenience and discomfort. If those effects are foreseeably suffered during a period when defects are repaired I am prepared to accept that they sound in damages even though the cost of the repairs is not recoverable as such. But I also agree that awards should be restrained, and that the awards in this case far exceeded a

j reasonable award for the injury shown to have been suffered.' (See [1991] 4 All ER 937 at 959–960, [1991] 1 WLR 1421 at 1445; numbering introduced by me.)

As Stuart-Smith LJ (at 76–81) pointed out in the present case, the propositions of Bingham LJ have often been cited and applied.

[15] But useful as the observations of Bingham LJ undoubtedly are, they were never intended to state more than broad principles. In *Cassell & Co Ltd v Broome* [1972] 1 All ER 801 at 836, [1972] AC 1027 at 1085 Lord Reid commented:

> '... experience has shown that those who have to apply the decision (*Rookes v Barnard* [1964] 1 All ER 367, [1964] AC 1129) to other cases and still more those who wish to criticise it seem to find it difficult to avoid treating sentences and phrases in a single speech as if they were provisions in an Act of Parliament. They do not seem to realise that it is not the function of ... judges to frame definitions or to lay down hard and fast rules. It is their function to enunciate principles and much that they say is intended to be illustrative or explanatory and not to be definitive.'

Bingham LJ would have had this truth about judicial decision-making well in mind. So interpreted the passage cited is a helpful point of departure for the examination of the issues in this case. Specifically, it is important to bear in mind that *Watts v Morrow* was a case where a surveyor negligently failed to discover defects in a property. The claim was not for breach of a specific undertaking to investigate a matter important for the buyer's peace of mind. It was a claim for damages for inconvenience and discomfort resulting from breach. In *Watts v Morrow* therefore there was no reason to consider the case where a surveyor is in breach of a distinct and important contractual obligation which was intended to afford the buyer information confirming the presence or absence of an intrusive element before he committed himself to the purchase.

V. *Recovery of non-pecuniary damages*

[16] The examination of the issues can now proceed from a secure foothold. In the law of obligations the rules governing the recovery of compensation necessarily distinguish between different kinds of harm. In tort the requirement of reasonable foreseeability is a sufficient touchstone of liability for causing death or physical injury: it is an inadequate tool for the disposal of claims in respect of psychiatric injury. Tort law approaches compensation for physical damage and pure economic loss differently. In contract law distinctions are made about the kind of harm which resulted from the breach of contract. The general principle is that compensation is only awarded for financial loss resulting from the breach of contract (*Livingstone v Rawyards Coal Co* (1880) 5 App Cas 25 at 39 per Lord Blackburn). In the words of Bingham LJ in *Watts v Morrow* [1991] 4 All ER 937 at 959, [1991] 1 WLR 1421 at 1445, as a matter of legal policy 'a contract-breaker is not *in general* liable for any distress, frustration, anxiety, displeasure, vexation, tension or aggravation which his breach of contract may cause to the innocent party' (my emphasis). There are, however, limited exceptions to this rule. One such exception is damages for pain, suffering and loss of amenities caused to an individual by a breach of contract (see *McGregor on Damages* (16th edn, 1997) pp 56–57 (para 96)). It is not material in the present case. But the two exceptions mentioned by Bingham LJ, namely where the very object of the contract is to provide pleasure (proposition (2)) and recovery for physical inconvenience caused by the breach (proposition (3)), are pertinent. The scope of these exceptions is in issue in the present case. It is, however, correct, as counsel for the surveyor submitted, that the entitlement to damages for mental distress caused by a breach of contract is not established by mere foreseeability: the right to recovery is dependent on the case falling fairly within the principles governing the special exceptions. So far there is no real disagreement between the parties.

VI. *The very object of the contract: the framework*

[17] I reverse the order in which the Court of Appeal considered the two issues. I do so because the issue whether the present case falls within the exceptional category governing cases where the very object of the contact is to give pleasure, and so forth, focuses directly on the terms actually agreed between the parties. It is concerned with the reasonable expectations of the parties under the specific terms of the contract. Logically, it must be considered first.

[18] It is necessary to examine the case on a correct characterisation of the plaintiff's claim. Stuart-Smith LJ thought ((2000) 73 Con LR 70 at 79) that the obligation undertaken by the surveyor was 'one relatively minor aspect of the overall instructions'. What Stuart-Smith and Mummery LJJ would have decided if they had approached it on the basis that the obligation was a major or important part of the contract between the plaintiff and the surveyor is not clear. But the Court of Appeal's characterisation of the case was not correct. The plaintiff made it crystal clear to the surveyor that the impact of aircraft noise was a matter of importance to him. Unless he obtained reassuring information from the surveyor he would not have bought the property. That is the tenor of the evidence. It is also what the judge found. The case must be approached on the basis that the surveyor's obligation to investigate aircraft noise was a major or important part of the contract between him and the plaintiff. It is also important to note that, unlike in *Addis v Gramophone Co Ltd* [1909] AC 488, [1908–10] All ER Rep 1, the plaintiff's claim is not for injured feelings caused by the breach of contract. Rather it is a claim for damages flowing from the surveyor's failure to investigate and report, thereby depriving the buyer of the chance of making an informed choice whether or not to buy resulting in mental distress and disappointment.

[19] The broader legal context of *Watts v Morrow* must be borne in mind. The exceptional category of cases where the very object of a contract is to provide pleasure, relaxation, peace of mind or freedom from molestation is not the product of Victorian contract theory but the result of evolutionary developments in case law from the 1970s. Several decided cases informed the description given by Bingham LJ of this category. The first was the decision of the sheriff court in *Diesen v Samson* 1971 SLT (Sh Ct) 49. A photographer failed to turn up at a wedding, thereby leaving the couple without a photographic record of an important and happy day. The bride was awarded damages for her distress and disappointment. In the celebrated case of *Jarvis v Swans Tours Ltd* [1973] 1 All ER 71, [1973] QB 233, the plaintiff recovered damages for mental distress flowing from a disastrous holiday resulting from a travel agent's negligent representations (compare also *Jackson v Horizon Holidays Ltd* [1975] 3 All ER 92, [1975] 1 WLR 1468). In *Heywood v Wellers (a firm)* [1976] 1 All ER 300, [1976] QB 446, the plaintiff instructed solicitors to bring proceedings to restrain a man from molesting her. The solicitors negligently failed to take appropriate action with the result that the molestation continued. The Court of Appeal allowed the plaintiff damages for mental distress and upset. While apparently not cited in *Watts v Morrow, Jackson v Chrysler Acceptances Ltd* [1978] RTR 474 was decided before *Watts v Morrow*. In the *Chrysler Acceptances* case the claim was for damages in respect of a motor car which did not meet the implied condition of merchantability in s 14 of the Sale of Goods Act 1893. The buyer communicated to the seller that one of his reasons for buying the car was a forthcoming touring holiday in France. Problems with the car spoilt the holiday. The disappointment of a spoilt holiday was a substantial element in the award sanctioned by the Court of Appeal.

[20] At their Lordships' request counsel for the plaintiff produced a memorandum based on various publications which showed the impact of the developments already described on litigation in the county courts. Taking into account the submissions of counsel for the surveyor and making due allowance for a tendency of the court sometimes not to distinguish between the cases presently under consideration and cases of physical inconvenience and discomfort, I am satisfied that in the real life of our lower courts non-pecuniary damages are regularly awarded on the basis that the defendant's breach of contract deprived the plaintiff of the very object of the contract, viz pleasure, relaxation, and peace of mind. The cases arise in diverse contractual contexts, e g the supply of a wedding dress or double glazing, hire purchase transactions, landlord and tenant, building contracts, and engagements of estate agents and solicitors. The awards in such cases seem modest. For my part what happens on the ground casts no doubt on the utility of the developments since the 1970s in regard to the award of non-pecuniary damages in the exceptional categories. But the problem persists of the precise scope of the exceptional category of case involving awards of non-pecuniary damages for breach of contract where the very object of the contract was to ensure a party's pleasure, relaxation or peace of mind.

[21] An important development for this branch of the law was *Ruxley Electronics and Construction Ltd v Forsyth, Laddingford Enclosures Ltd v Forsyth* [1995] 3 All ER 268, [1996] AC 344. The plaintiff had specified that a swimming pool should at the deep end have a depth of 7 ft 6 ins. The contractor failed to comply with his contractual obligation: the actual depth at the deep end was the standard 6 ft. The House found the usual 'cost of cure' measure of damages to be wholly disproportionate to the loss suffered and economically wasteful. On the other hand, the House awarded the moderate sum of £2,500 for the plaintiff's disappointment in not receiving the swimming pool he desired. It is true that for strategic reasons neither side contended for such an award. The House was, however, not inhibited by the stance of the parties. Lord Mustill and Lord Lloyd of Berwick justified the award in carefully reasoned judgments which carried the approval of four of the Law Lords. It is sufficient for present purposes to mention that for Lord Mustill ([1995] 3 All ER 268 at 277, [1996] AC 344 at 360) the principle of pacta sunt servanda would be eroded if the law did not take account of the fact that the consumer often demands specifications which, although not of economic value, have value to him. This is sometimes called the 'consumer surplus': see Harris, Ogus and Philips 'Contract Remedies and the Consumer Surplus' (1979) 95 LQR 581. Lord Mustill rejected the idea that 'the promisor can please himself whether or not to comply with the wishes of the promisee which, as embodied in the contract, formed part of the consideration for the price'. Lord Keith of Kinkel and Lord Bridge of Harwich agreed with Lord Mustill's judgment and with Lord Lloyd's similar reasoning. Labels sometimes obscure rather than illuminate. I do not therefore set much store by the description 'consumer surplus'. But the controlling principles stated by Lord Mustill and Lord Lloyd are important. It is difficult to reconcile this decision of the House with the decision of the Court of Appeal in the present case. I will in due course return to the way in which the majority attempted to distinguish the *Ruxley Electronics* case. At this stage, however, I draw attention to the fact that the majority in the Court of Appeal ((2000) 73 Con LR 70 at 79) regarded the relevant observations of Lord Mustill and Lord Lloyd as obiter dicta. I am satisfied that the principles enunciated in the *Ruxley Electronics* case in support of the award of £2,500 for a breach of respect of the provision of a pleasurable amenity have been authoritatively established.

a VII. *The very object of the contract: the arguments against the plaintiff's claim*

[22] Counsel for the surveyor advanced three separate arguments each of which he said was sufficient to defeat the plaintiff's claim. First, he submitted that even if a major or important part of the contract was to give pleasure, relaxation and peace of mind, that was not enough. It is an indispensable requirement that the object of the entire contract must be of this type. Secondly, he submitted that *b* the exceptional category does not extend to a breach of a contractual duty of care, even if imposed to secure pleasure, relaxation and peace of mind. It only covers cases where the promiser guarantees achievement of such an object. Thirdly, he submitted that by not moving out of Riverside House the plaintiff forfeited any right to recover non-pecuniary damages.

c [23] The first argument fastened onto a narrow reading of the words 'the very object of [the] contract' as employed by Bingham LJ in *Watts v Morrow* [1991] 4 All ER 937 at 960, [1991] 1 WLR 1421 at 1445. Cases where a major or important part of the contract was to secure pleasure, relaxation and peace of mind were not under consideration in *Watts v Morrow*. It is difficult to see what the principled justification for such a limitation might be. After all, in 1978 the Court of Appeal *d* allowed such a claim in the *Chrysler Acceptances* case in circumstances where a spoiled holiday was only one object of the contract. Counsel was, however, assisted by the decision of the Court of Appeal in *Knott v Bolton* (1995) 45 Con LR 127 which in the present case the Court of Appeal treated as binding on it. In *Knott's* case an architect was asked to design a wide staircase for a gallery and impressive entrance hall. He failed to do so. The plaintiff spent money in *e* improving the staircase to some extent and he recovered the cost of the changes. The plaintiff also claimed damages for disappointment and distress in the lack of an impressive staircase. In agreement with the trial judge the Court of Appeal disallowed this part of his claim. Reliance was placed on the dicta of Bingham LJ in *Watts v Morrow* [1991] 4 All ER 937 at 959–960, [1991] 1 WLR 1421 at 1445.

f [24] Interpreting the dicta of Bingham LJ in *Watts v Morrow* narrowly, the Court of Appeal in *Knott's* case ruled that the central object of the contract was to design a house, not to provide pleasure to the occupiers of the house. It is important, however, to note that *Knott's* case was decided a few months before the decision of the House in the *Ruxley Electronics* case. In any event, the technicality of the reasoning in *Knott's* case, and therefore in the Court of Appeal judgments in the *g* present case, is apparent. It is obvious, and conceded, that if an architect is employed only to design a staircase, or a surveyor is employed only to investigate aircraft noise, the breach of such a distinct obligation may result in an award of non-pecuniary damages. Logically the same must be the case if the architect or surveyor, apart from entering into a general retainer, concludes a separate *h* contract, separately remunerated, in respect of the design of a staircase or the investigation of aircraft noise. If this is so the distinction drawn in *Knott's* case and in the present case is a matter of form and not substance. David Capper 'Damages for Distress and Disappointment—The Limits of *Watts v. Morrow*' (2000) 116 LQR 553 at 556 has persuasively argued:

j
'A ruling that intangible interests only qualify for legal protection where they are the "very object of the contract" is tantamount to a ruling that contracts where these interests are merely important, but not the central object of the contract, are in part unenforceable. It is very difficult to see what policy objection there can be to parties to a contract agreeing that these interests are to be protected via contracts where the central object is

something else. If the defendant is unwilling to accept this responsibility he or she can say so and either no contract will be made or one will be made but including a disclaimer.'

There is no reason in principle or policy why the scope of recovery in the exceptional category should depend on the object of the contract as ascertained from all its constituent parts. It is sufficient if a major or important object of the contract is to give pleasure, relaxation or peace of mind. In my view *Knott's* case was wrongly decided and should be overruled. To the extent that the majority in the Court of Appeal relied on *Knott's* case their decision was wrong.

[25] That brings me to the second issue, namely whether the plaintiff's claim is barred by reason of the fact that the surveyor undertook an obligation to exercise reasonable care and did not guarantee the achievement of a result. This was the basis upon which Hale LJ after the first hearing in the Court of Appeal thought that the claim should be disallowed. This reasoning was adopted by the second Court of Appeal and formed an essential part of the reasoning of the majority. This was the basis on which they distinguished the *Ruxley Electronics* case. Against the broad sweep of differently framed contractual undertakings, and the central purpose of contract law in promoting the observance of contractual promises, I am satisfied that this distinction ought not to prevail. It is certainly not rooted in precedent. I would not accept the suggestion that it has the pedigree of an observation of Ralph Gibson LJ in *Watts v Morrow* [1991] 4 All ER 937 at 956–957, [1991] 1 WLR 1421 at 1442: his emphasis appears to have been on the fact that the contract did not serve to provide peace of mind, and so forth. As far as I am aware the distinction was first articulated in the present case. In any event, I would reject it. I fully accept, of course, that contractual guarantees of performance and promises to exercise reasonable care are fundamentally different. The former may sometimes give greater protection than the latter. Proving breach of an obligation of reasonable care may be more difficult than proving breach of a guarantee. On the other hand, a party may in practice be willing to settle for the relative reassurance offered by the obligation of reasonable care undertaken by a professional man. But why should this difference between an absolute and relative contractual promise require a distinction in respect of the recovery of non-pecuniary damages? Take the example of a travel agent who is consulted by a couple who are looking for a golfing holiday in France. Why should it make a difference in respect of the recoverability of non-pecuniary damages for a spoiled holiday whether the travel agent gives a guarantee that there is a golf course very near the hotel, represents that to be the case, or negligently advises that all hotels of the particular chain of hotels are situated next to golf courses? If the nearest golf course is in fact 50 miles away a breach may be established. It may spoil the holiday of the couple. It is difficult to see why in principle only those plaintiffs who negotiate guarantees may recover non-pecuniary damages for a breach of contract. It is a singularly unattractive result that a professional man, who undertakes a specific obligation to exercise reasonable care to investigate a matter judged and communicated to be important by his customer, can in Lord Mustill's words in the *Ruxley Electronics* case [1995] 3 All ER 268 at 277, [1996] AC 344 at 360: '... please himself whether or not to comply with the wishes of the promisee which, as embodied in the contract, formed part of the consideration for the price.' If that were the law it would be seriously deficient. I am satisfied that it is not the law. In my view the distinction drawn by Hale LJ and by the majority in

a the Court of Appeal between contractual guarantees and obligations of reasonable care is unsound.

[26] The final argument was that by failing to move out the plaintiff forfeited a right to claim non-pecuniary damages. This argument was not advanced in the Court of Appeal. It will be recalled that the judge found as a fact that the plaintiff had acted reasonably in making 'the best of a bad job'. The plaintiff's decision *b* also avoided a larger claim against the surveyor. It was never explained on what legal principle the plaintiff's decision not to move out divested him of a claim for non-pecuniary damages. Reference was made to a passage in the judgment of Bingham LJ in *Watts v Morrow* [1991] 4 All ER 937 at 959, [1991] 1 WLR 1421 at 1445. Examination showed, however, that the observation, speculative as it was, did not relate to the claim for non-pecuniary damages (see the criticism of *c* Professor M P Furmston 'Damages—Diminution in Value or Cost of Repair?—Damages for Distress' (1993) 6 JCL 64 at 65). The third argument must also be rejected.

[27] While the dicta of Bingham LJ are of continuing usefulness as a starting point, it will be necessary to read them subject to the three points on which I have *d* rejected the submissions made on behalf of the surveyor.

VIII. *Quantum*

[28] In the surveyor's written case it was submitted that the award of £10,000 was excessive. It was certainly high. Given that the plaintiff is stuck indefinitely with a position which he sought to avoid by the terms of his contract with the *e* surveyor I am not prepared to interfere with the judge's evaluation on the special facts of the case. On the other hand, I have to say that the size of the award appears to be at the very top end of what could possibly be regarded as appropriate damages. Like Bingham LJ in *Watts v Morrow* [1991] 4 All ER 937 at 960, [1991] 1 WLR 1421 at 1445 I consider that awards in this area should be restrained and *f* modest. It is important that logical and beneficial developments in this corner of the law should not contribute to the creation of a society bent on litigation.

IX. *Conclusion*

[29] In agreement with the reasoning of Clarke LJ I would therefore hold that the decision of the majority in the Court of Appeal was wrong. I would also reject *g* the subsidiary written argument of counsel for the surveyor that the plaintiff was not entitled to his costs at trial.

X. *Inconvenience and discomfort*

[30] It is strictly unnecessary to discuss the question whether the judge's decision *h* can be justified on the ground that the breach of contract resulted in inconvenience and discomfort. It is, however, appropriate that I indicate my view. The judge had a great deal of evidence on aircraft noise at Riverside House. It is conceded that noise can produce a physical reaction and can, depending on its intensity and the circumstances, constitute a nuisance. Noise from aircraft is exempted from *j* the statutory nuisance system and in general no action lies in common law nuisance by reason only of the flight of aircraft over a property (see s 6(1) of the Civil Aviation Act 1982 and McCracken, Jones, Pereira and Payne *Statutory Nuisance* (2001) para 10.33). The existence of the legislation shows that aircraft noise could arguably constitute a nuisance. In any event, aircraft noise is capable of causing inconvenience and discomfort within the meaning of Bingham LJ's relevant proposition. It is a matter of degree whether the case passes the threshold. It is

sufficient to say that I have not been persuaded that the judge's decision on this
point was not open to him on the evidence which he accepted. For this further
reason, in general agreement with Clarke LJ, I would rule that the decision of the
Court of Appeal was wrong.

XI. *Disposal*

[31] I would allow the appeal and restore the judge's decision.

LORD BROWNE-WILKINSON.

[32] My Lords, I have had the advantage of reading in draft the speeches of my
noble and learned friends, Lord Steyn and Lord Scott of Foscote. For the reasons
they have given I too would allow the appeal.

LORD CLYDE.

[33] My Lords, in December 1990 the appellant plaintiff, Graham Farley, was
interested in buying a house at Blackboys, East Sussex. The trial judge described
it as a beautiful house in a beautiful setting. It had a terrace, a croquet lawn, a
tennis court, an orchard, a paddock and a swimming pool. The property is not
very far from Gatwick Airport. He engaged the respondent defendant, a surveyor,
to inspect and report on the property. He also asked him to report on certain
specific matters, including whether the property would be affected by aircraft
noise. The defendant did so, but it is now accepted that his report was negligent
in relation to the aircraft noise. The plaintiff relied on the report and bought the
property. Considerable work required to be done to the house and some time
passed before the plaintiff was able to move in. He then discovered the extent of
the aircraft noise. Had the defendant made an adequate investigation of the
aircraft noise he would have ascertained the true position and the plaintiff would
not have bought the property. His enjoyment of the amenity of the property
outside the house has been diminished by aircraft noise. He has not sought to sell
the property and does not intend to do so. He claims damages for the impairment
to his use and enjoyment of the property caused by aircraft noise.

[34] Much weight in the argument was placed upon the observations of
Bingham LJ in *Watts v Morrow* [1991] 4 All ER 937 at 959–960, [1991] 1 WLR 1421
at 1445. Having expressed the general rule that a contract-breaker is not in
general liable for the distress and suchlike which may follow upon the breach,
Bingham LJ continued:

> 'But the rule is not absolute. Where the very object of a contract is to
> provide pleasure, relaxation, peace of mind or freedom from molestation,
> damages will be awarded if the fruit of the contract is not provided or if the
> contrary result is procured instead. If the law did not cater for this
> exceptional category of case it would be defective. A contract to survey the
> condition of a house for a prospective purchaser does not, however, fall
> within this exceptional category. In cases not falling within this exceptional
> category, damages are in my view recoverable for physical inconvenience
> and discomfort caused by the breach and mental suffering directly related to
> that inconvenience and discomfort.'

In the ordinary case, accordingly, damages may be awarded for inconvenience,
but not for mere distress; but where the contract is aimed at procuring peace or
pleasure, then, if as a result of the breach of contract that expected pleasure is not

a realised, the party suffering that loss may be entitled to an award of damages for the distress.

[35] It would detract from the importance of this summary in *Watts v Morrow* if the words used were to be treated as written in stone and subjected to the kind of analysis which might be more appropriate to a conveyancing document. The expression 'physical inconvenience' may be traced at least to the judgment of

b *Hobbs v London and South Western Rly Co* (1875) LR 10 QB 111 at 122, [1874–80] All ER Rep 458 at 463, where in that case damages were awarded for the inconvenience suffered by the plaintiffs for having to walk between four and five miles home as a result of the train on which they had taken tickets to Hampton Court travelling instead to Esher. They had tried to obtain a conveyance but found that there was none to be had. A further claim was made for the

c consequences of an illness which the wife contracted as a result of the walk but that was refused by the Court of Appeal as too remote. The railway company paid into court £2 as being ample to cover the cost of a conveyance. They resisted a larger award for inconvenience, relying on the observations of Pollock CJ in *Hamlin v Great Northern Rly Co* (1856) 1 H & N 408 at 411, 156 ER 1261 at 1262 to

d the effect a plaintiff could recover whatever damages naturally resulted from the breach of contract, 'but not damages for the disappointment of mind occasioned by the breach of contract'. Cockburn CJ referred ((1875) LR 10 QB 111 at 115, [1874–80] All ER Rep 458 at 460) to the claim which was allowed as one for 'personal inconvenience'. Blackburn J referred ((1875) LR 10 QB 111 at 120, [1874–80] All ER Rep 458 at 462) to it as an 'inconvenience'. Mellor J ((1875) LR

e 10 QB 111 at 122, [1874–80] All ER Rep 458 at 463) contrasted matters of 'real physical inconvenience' with matters 'purely sentimental'. Archibald J observed ((1875) LR 10 QB 111 at 124): 'The case is not one of mere vexation, but it is one of physical inconvenience, which can in a sense be measured by money value ...' It does not seem to me that there is any particular magic in the word 'physical'.

f It served in *Hobbs'* case to emphasise the exclusion of matters purely sentimental, but it should not require detailed analysis or definition. As matter of terminology I should have thought that 'inconvenience' by itself sufficiently covered the kinds of difficulty and discomfort which are more than mere matters of sentimentality, and that 'disappointment' would serve as a sufficient label for those mental reactions which in general the policy of the law will exclude.

g [36] In *Hobbs'* case the defendants were prepared to compensate the plaintiffs for the cost of a conveyance, even although they had not been able to find any. In the present case the defendant would be prepared to pay for the costs of sale and removal if the plaintiff had decided to sell because of the noise. It is said by the respondent that since he has decided to keep the house he is not entitled to

h any damages at all. But in *Hobbs'* case the plaintiffs were entitled to damages in respect of the inconvenience. It is hard to understand why a corresponding result should not follow here. That an award may be made in such circumstances is to my mind in line with the thinking of this House in *Ruxley Electronics and Construction Ltd v Forsyth, Laddingford Enclosures Ltd v Forsyth* [1995] 3 All ER 268,

j [1996] AC 344. In that case there was a breach in the performance of a contract to provide a pleasurable amenity, a swimming pool. The cost of rebuilding it to conform to the required specification was an unreasonable and inappropriate measure of the damages. The House restored the judge's original award of general damages for loss of amenity. So also here, where the plaintiff has decided to remain in the property despite its disadvantage, he should not be altogether deprived by the law of any compensation for the breach of contract. It may be noticed in passing that in *Hobbs'* case the damages awarded for the inconvenience were substantially more than the cost of the conveyance. In the present case it seems that the cost of removal, for which at an earlier stage the plaintiff was claiming, far exceeded the sum awarded for inconvenience. But those differences do not affect the principle.

[37] The judge found that the plaintiff was not a man of excessive susceptibility and he refers to the inconvenience he was suffering as 'real discomfort'. I do not consider it appropriate to explore the detail of the inconvenience as being 'physical', either because it impacts upon his eardrums, or because it has some geographical element, such as the relative locations of the aircraft and the property, or the obviously greater audibility of their movements when the plaintiff is seeking to enjoy the amenity of the terrace and the gardens than when he is inside the house. In my view the real discomfort which the judge found to exist constituted an inconvenience to the plaintiff which is not a mere matter of disappointment or sentiment. It is unnecessary that the noise should be so great as to make it impossible for the plaintiff to sit at all on his terrace. Plainly it significantly interferes with his enjoyment of the property and in my view that inconvenience is something for which damages can and should be awarded.

[38] As I have already noted the plaintiff's claim has been not for disappointment at the absence of the expected pleasure but for inconvenience. The claim related to the use and enjoyment of the property, but I do not understand this as intended to include injury to his personal feelings. The judge quoted from the headnote to *Watts v Morrow* [1991] 1 WLR 1421 at 1422, where the summary is given in these terms: '(2) That in the case of the ordinary surveyor's contract general damages were recoverable only for distress and inconvenience caused by physical consequences of the breach of contract ...' That formulation is no doubt prompted by such passages in the judgment of Ralph Gibson LJ ([1991] 4 All ER 937 at 957, 958, [1991] 1 WLR 1421 at 1442, 1443) 'distress caused by physical consequences' and 'the physical consequence of such a breach'. But elsewhere he uses the expression 'physical discomfort or inconvenience resulting from the breach' (see [1991] 4 All ER 937 at 955, [1991] 1 WLR 1421 at 1440) and the language of Bingham LJ ([1991] 4 All ER 937 at 959–960, [1991] 1 WLR 1421 at 1445) which I have already quoted is in like terms. But it seems plain that the judge was proceeding upon the basis that this was an ordinary surveyor's contract and the award which he sought to make was intended to be within the guidance which *Watts v Morrow* gave him on that approach. That is to say that it was not an award falling within the exceptional category noted in *Watts v Morrow*. He recorded that the plaintiff found the noise to be a 'confounded nuisance', but the award which he made was intended to meet the 'real discomfort' which he found the plaintiff to be suffering. It seems to me that he decided the case as an ordinary example of inconvenience following on a breach of contract. In my view he was entitled to make an award on that basis. While the judge thought that the award would be regarded by the plaintiff as almost derisory I would regard it as almost erring on the side of generosity. But I would not interfere with it. In my view the appeal can be allowed on the foregoing basis.

[39] But it is possible to approach the case as one of the exceptional kind in which the claim would be for damages for disappointment. If that approach was adopted so as to seek damages for disappointment, I consider that it should also succeed.

[40] It should be observed at the outset that damages should not be awarded, unless perhaps nominally, for the fact of a breach of contract as distinct from the

a consequences of the breach. That was a point which I sought to stress in *Panatown Ltd v Alfred McAlpine Construction Ltd* [2000] 4 All ER 97, [2001] 1 AC 518. For an award to be made a loss or injury has to be identified which is a consequence of the breach but not too remote from it, and which somehow or other can be expressed and quantified in terms of a sum of money. So disappointment merely at the fact that the contract has been breached is not a proper ground for an

b award. The mere fact of the loss of a bargain should not be the subject of compensation. But that is not the kind of claim which the plaintiff is making here. What he is seeking is damages for the inconvenience of the noise, the invasion of the peace and quiet which he expected the property to possess and the diminution in his use and enjoyment of the property on account of the aircraft noise.

[**41**] The critical factor on this approach, as it seems to me, is that the plaintiff

c made the specific request of the defendant to discover whether the property might be affected by aircraft noise. It is suggested that because this point was wrapped up together with a number of other matters in the instructions given by the plaintiff it cannot be regarded as constituting the 'very object' of the contract. But that approach seems to me simply to be playing with words. What is referred

d to as a breach of contract is often a breach of a particular provision in a contract. The effect of that breach may affect the continued existence of the other terms of the contract, so as to bring the whole to an end. But the point which is the focus of concern is a particular provision in the whole agreement. I can see no reason for distinguishing the present case from a situation where the plaintiff had instructed the defendant simply to advise on the matter of aircraft noise, having

e already obtained a survey report covering all the other matters. The defendant's argument gained some support from *Knott v Bolton* (1995) 45 Con LR 127 where the Court of Appeal regarded the failure to provide the wide staircase and gallery which the clients had particularly requested as the main object of the contract with the architects was held to be the designing of the house, not the giving of

f pleasure in respect of the staircase and the gallery. In so far as the court proceeded on the basis that the contract could only be regarded as a whole I consider that it was mistaken. The approach involves a very literal reading of the passage in *Watts v Morrow*, to which I have already referred.

[**42**] What was said in *Watts v Morrow* must be seen in the context of the case. It is instructive to refer to a passage in the judgment of Ralph Gibson LJ with

g which Bingham LJ was expressly in complete agreement. He said of the proposition that the contract in that case was a contract whose subject matter was to provide peace of mind or freedom from distress:

'That, with respect, seems to me to be an impossible view of the ordinary

h surveyor's contract. No doubt house buyers hope to enjoy peace of mind and freedom from distress as a consequence of the proper performance by a surveyor of his contractual obligation to provide a careful report, but there was no express promise for the provision of peace of mind or freedom from distress and no such implied promise was alleged. In my view, in the case of the ordinary surveyor's contract, damages are only recoverable for distress

j caused by physical consequences of the breach of contract.' (See [1991] 4 All ER 937 at 956–957, [1991] 1 WLR 1421 at 1442.)

The present case is not an 'ordinary surveyor's contract'. The request for the report on aircraft noise was additional to the usual matters expected of a surveyor in the survey of a property and could properly have attracted a extra fee if he had spent extra time researching that issue. It is the specific provision relating to the peacefulness of the property in respect of aircraft noise which makes the present case out of the ordinary. The criterion is not some general characteristic of the contract, as, for example, that it is or is not a 'commercial' contract. The critical factor is the object of the particular agreement.

[43] The defendant, following something of the thinking in the second hearing before the Court of Appeal in the present case, sought to take from the passage in the judgment of Ralph Gibson LJ in *Watts v Morrow* [1991] 4 All ER 937 at 956–957, [1991] 1 WLR 1421 at 1442 support for an argument that while damages for distress might be granted in the case of a breach of a warranty for the provision of peace and quiet, an award should not be permitted where the case is one of a failure to exercise reasonable skill and care in the performance of a contractual obligation to provide information. I am not persuaded that that can fairly be taken from the passage in question nor that the alleged consequence follows from the distinction. There would be no sufficient logic in allowing damages for inconvenience where the travel agent warrants that the client will have peace and quiet on the beach at Brighton and refusing damages where he negligently advises his client that that beach would be a place to find peace and quiet. Nor does it seem to me that the distinction is one supported by precedent. On the contrary *Heywood v Wellers (a firm)* [1976] 1 All ER 300, [1976] QB 446 was a case of negligent advice by a solicitor where an award for the consequent distress was made.

[44] The object of the request to consider the risk of aircraft noise was very plainly to enable the plaintiff to determine the extent of the peace and quiet which he could enjoy at the property. It would be within the contemplation of the defendant that if the noise was such as to interfere with the occupier's peaceful enjoyment of the property the plaintiff would either not buy it at all or live there deprived of his expectation of peace and quiet. Each of these consequences seems to me to flow directly from the breach of contract so as to enable an award of damages to be made on one or other basis. The present case can in my view qualify as one of the exceptional cases where a contract for peace or pleasure has been made and breached, thereby entitling the injured party to claim damages for the disappointment occasioned by the breach.

[45] For the foregoing reasons I would allow the appeal and restore the judge's award.

LORD HUTTON.

[46] My Lords, I have had the advantage of reading in draft the speech of my noble and learned friend Lord Steyn and I gratefully adopt his account of the facts of the case and of the issues to which they give rise and I can therefore proceed to state my opinion on those issues. I consider first the question whether the plaintiff is entitled to recover damages to compensate him for the annoyance and nuisance from aircraft noise to which the defendant's breach of contract exposed him, the judge having found that the plaintiff would not have bought the house if the defendant, as he should have done under the contract, had advised him of the true position in relation to aircraft noise. I propose to consider this issue on the assumption (contrary to the opinion which I express later) that the annoyance and nuisance from aircraft noise did not constitute physical inconvenience and discomfort.

The principle, and the exception to it, stated in Watts v Morrow

a   **[47]** It is clearly established as a general rule that where there has been a breach of contract damages cannot be awarded for the vexation or anxiety or aggravation or similar states of mind resulting from the breach. The principle was stated by Bingham LJ in *Watts v Morrow* [1991] 4 All ER 937 at 959, [1991] 1 WLR 1421 at 1445:

b   'A contract-breaker is not in general liable for any distress, frustration, anxiety, displeasure, vexation, tension or aggravation which his breach of contract may cause to the innocent party. This rule is not, I think, founded on the assumption that such reactions are not foreseeable, which they surely are or may be, but on considerations of policy.'

c   This general principle has recently been approved by this House in *Johnson v Gore Wood & Co (a firm)* [2001] 1 All ER 481, [2001] 2 WLR 72. The principle has particular application to commercial cases and in *Johnson*'s case Lord Cooke of Thorndon observed ([2001] 1 All ER 481 at 516, [2001] 2 WLR 72 at 108) that: 'Contract-breaking is treated as an incident of commercial life which players in
d   the game are expected to meet with mental fortitude.' But the principle is not applicable in every case and in *Watts v Morrow* [1991] 4 All ER 937 at 960, [1991] 1 WLR 1421 at 1445 Bingham LJ went on to state that there was an exceptional category of cases which he described as follows:

e   'Where the very object of a contract is to provide pleasure, relaxation, peace of mind or freedom from molestation, damages will be awarded if the fruit of the contract is not provided or if the contrary result is procured instead. If the law did not cater for this exceptional category of case it would be defective. A contract to survey the condition of a house for a prospective purchaser does not, however, fall within this exceptional category.'

f   Bingham LJ then stated:

           'In cases not falling within this exceptional category, damages are in my view recoverable for physical inconvenience and discomfort caused by the breach and mental suffering directly related to that inconvenience and discomfort.'

g   Cases such as *Jarvis v Swans Tours Ltd* [1973] 1 All ER 71, [1973] QB 233, where a travel company in breach of contract fails to provide the holiday for which the plaintiff has paid and damages are awarded for mental distress, inconvenience, upset, disappointment and frustration, are examples of this exception to the
h   general principle.

     [48] In addition, the speeches of Lord Mustill and Lord Lloyd of Berwick (with which Lord Keith of Kinkel and Lord Bridge of Harwich agreed) in *Ruxley Electronics and Construction Ltd v Forsyth, Laddingford Enclosures Ltd v Forsyth* [1995] 3 All ER 268, [1996] AC 344 established that in some cases the plaintiff, notwithstanding that he suffers no financial loss, should be compensated where
j   the defendant is in breach of a contractual obligation. In that case a contractor contracted to build a swimming pool for a householder in his garden. The contract specified that the pool should have a maximum depth of 7 ft 6 ins but, as built, the maximum depth was only 6 ft. The trial judge found that the pool as constructed was perfectly safe to dive into and that the shortfall in depth had not

decreased the value of the pool. The judge held that the householder was entitled
to damages of £2,500 for loss of amenity and rejected his claim for the cost of
reinstatement which would have involved demolition of the existing pool and the
reconstruction of a new one, on the ground that the cost of reinstatement was an
unreasonable claim in the circumstances. The Court of Appeal held ([1994] 3 All ER
801, [1994] 1 WLR 650) that the householder was entitled to recover the cost of
reinstatement amounting to £21,560. This House held that reinstatement would
be unreasonable and the expense of the work involved would be out of all
proportion to the benefit to be obtained. But the speeches of Lord Mustill and
Lord Lloyd are important in relation to the present case because they considered
the entitlement of a party to a building contract to recover damages for breach of
contract where he was not entitled to the cost of reinstatement and where the
breach had not caused diminution in the market value of the property. Their
conclusion was that in such a case justice required that reasonable damages
should be awarded. Lord Mustill stated:

> 'It is a common feature of small building works performed on residential
> property that the cost of the work is not fully reflected by an increase in the
> market value of the house, and that comparatively minor deviations from
> specification or sound workmanship may have no direct financial effect at all.
> Yet the householder must surely be entitled to say that he chose to obtain
> from the builder a promise to produce a particular result because he wanted
> to make his house more comfortable, more convenient and more conformable
> to his own particular tastes; not because he had in mind that the work might
> increase the amount which he would receive if, contrary to expectation, he
> thought it expedient in the future to exchange his home for cash. To say that
> in order to escape unscathed the builder has only to show that to the mind
> of the average onlooker, or the average potential buyer, the results which he
> has produced seem just as good as those which he had promised would make
> a part of the promise illusory and unbalance the bargain. In the valuable
> analysis contained in *Radford v De Froberville* [1978] 1 All ER 33 at 42, [1977]
> 1 WLR 1262 at 1270 Oliver J emphasised that it was for the plaintiff to judge
> what performance he required in exchange for the price. The court should
> honour that choice. Pacta sunt servanda. If the appellant's argument leads
> to the conclusion that in all cases like the present the employer is entitled to
> no more than nominal damages, the average householder would say that
> there must be something wrong with the law.' (See [1995] 3 All ER 268 at
> 276–277, [1996] AC 344 at 360.)

And he stated that in some cases—

> 'and in particular those where the contract is designed to fulfil a purely
> commercial purpose, the loss will very often consist only of the monetary
> detriment brought about by the breach of contract. But these remedies are
> not exhaustive, for the law must cater for those occasions where the value of
> the promise to the promisee exceeds the financial enhancement of his
> position which full performance will secure. This excess, often referred to in
> the literature as the "consumer surplus" (see e g the valuable discussion by
> Harris, Ogus and Phillips, "Contract Remedies and the Consumer Surplus"
> (1979) 95 LQR 581) is usually incapable of precise valuation in terms of money,
> exactly because it represents a personal, subjective and non-monetary gain.
> Nevertheless where it exists the law should recognise it and compensate the

a promisee if the misperformance takes it away.' (See [1995] 3 All ER 268 at 277, [1996] AC 344 at 360–361.)

[49] In his speech Lord Lloyd referred ([1995] 3 All ER 268 at 289, [1996] AC 344 at 374) to the general rule that in claims for breach of contract the plaintiff cannot recover damages for his injured feelings and referred to the exception to this rule, as exemplified in the holiday cases, that a plaintiff may recover damages
b for his disappointment where the object of a contract is to afford pleasure. He stated that this was the principle which the trial judge had applied and he held that the judge had been entitled to award £2,500 to the householder on the ground that the contract was one 'for the provision of a pleasurable amenity', and in the event the householder's pleasure was not as great as it would have been if the
c pool had been 7 ft 6 ins deep. He then stated:

> 'That leaves one last question for consideration. I have expressed agreement
> with the judge's approach to damages based on loss of amenity on the facts
> of the present case. But in most cases such an approach would not be
> available. What is then to be the position where, in the case of a new house,
d the building does not conform in some minor respect to the contract, as, for
> example, where there is a difference in level between two rooms, necessitating
> a step? Suppose there is no measurable difference in value, and the cost of
> reinstatement would be prohibitive. Is there any reason why the court
> should not award by way of damages for breach of contract some modest
e sum, not based on difference in value, but solely to compensate the buyer for
> his disappointed expectations? Is the law of damages so inflexible, as I asked
> earlier, that it cannot find some middle ground in such a case? I do not give
> a final answer to that question in the present case. But it may be that it would
> have afforded an alternative ground for justifying the judge's award of
> damages. And if the judge had wanted a precedent, he could have found it
f in Sir David Cairns's judgment in *G W Atkins Ltd v Scott* ((1991) 46 Con LR
> 14), where, it will be remembered, the Court of Appeal upheld the judge's
> award of £250 for defective tiling. Sir David Cairns said (at 23): "There are
> many circumstances where a judge has nothing but his common sense to
> guide him in fixing the quantum of damages, for instance, for pain and
> suffering, for loss of pleasurable activities or for inconvenience of one kind
g or another."' (See [1995] 3 All ER 268 at 289–290, [1996] AC 344 at 374.)

[50] Whilst the *Ruxley Electronics* case was concerned with the proper measure of damages for breach of a construction contract, I consider that the principle stated in it can be of more general application and that, as Lord Mustill stated
h ([1995] 3 All ER 268 at 277, [1996] AC 344 at 360), there are some occasions 'where the value of the promise to the promisee exceeds the financial enhancement of his position which full performance will secure' and for which the law must provide a remedy. In my opinion the present case falls within the ambit of this principle as the defendant in breach of contract failed to alert the plaintiff to the
j presence of aircraft noise with the result that the plaintiff bought a house which he would not have bought if he had been made aware of the true position.

[51] Counsel for the defendant submitted that even if it were right to extend the exception as exemplified by the holiday cases to other cases, nevertheless the exception must be confined to cases where, in the words of Bingham LJ in *Watts v Morrow* [1991] 4 All ER 937 at 960, [1991] 1 WLR 1421 at 1445, 'the very object of a contract' is to provide the benefit which the promisee regards as being of particular

importance to him. This argument was accepted by Hale LJ in the first hearing
before the Court of Appeal and by Stuart-Smith and Mummery LJJ in the second   *a*
hearing. I am unable to accept this submission because I can see no reason in
principle why, if a plaintiff who has suffered no financial loss can recover damages
in some cases if there has been a breach of the principal obligation of the contract,
he should be denied damages for breach of an obligation which, whilst not the
principal obligation of the contract, is nevertheless one which he has made clear to   *b*
the other party is of importance to him. It is clear from the speech of Lord Mustill
in the *Ruxley Electronics* case [1995] 3 All ER 268 at 277, [1996] AC 344 at 360 that
he considered that a householder may obtain damages for comparatively minor
deviations from specification or sound workmanship which do not cause any
diminution in the value of the house. And it is clear that in that case the obligation
to build a pool 7 ft 6 ins deep as opposed to 6 ft deep could not be regarded as the   *c*
principal obligation or the very object of the contract.

[52] In *Knott v Bolton* (1995) 45 Con LR 127 the defendant architect was given
instructions to include in his design of a house a wide staircase with a gallery area
and an imposing and impressive entrance hall and he failed to carry out these
instructions. The plaintiffs sought to recover general damages for the disappointment   *d*
and distress they suffered by reason of this failure, but their claim was rejected by
the trial judge and the Court of Appeal. In a judgment delivered some months
before the decision of the House in the *Ruxley Electronics* case, Russell LJ laid
emphasis (at 129) on the words 'the very object of [the] contract' in Bingham LJ's
judgment in *Watts v Morrow* [1991] 4 All ER 937 at 960, [1991] 1 WLR 1421 at 1445
and stated: *e*

> 'One or two comments upon that passage are apposite. In my judgment
> the words "the very object of a contract" are crucial within the context of the
> instant case. The very object of the contract entered into by Mr Terence
> Bolton was to design for the Knotts their house. As an ancillary of that of   *f*
> course it was in the contemplation of Mr Bolton and of the Knotts that
> pleasure would be provided, but the provision of pleasure to the occupiers
> of the house was not the very object of the contract and there was nothing
> in the contractual relationship between Mr Bolton and the Knotts to indicate
> that he in any sense warranted or expressed himself to be contractually
> bound to provide for the Knotts the pleasure of occupation. Of course the   *g*
> pleasure of their occupation was an ancillary of the object of the contract, but
> it was not the very object of the contract.'

I consider, with respect, that in that case the Court of Appeal was led into error by
concentrating too much on the concept of the provision of pleasure—the correct
approach would have been to have taken the view later expressed by Lord Mustill   *h*
in his speech in the *Ruxley Electronics* case [1995] 3 All ER 268 at 276–277, [1996]
AC 344 at 360 and to have held that the plaintiffs were entitled to recover some
reasonable damages because they were entitled to say that they chose to obtain
from the architect a promise to produce a particular design in order to make the
house conform to their own particular tastes and wishes. Accordingly I consider   *j*
that the decision of the Court of Appeal in *Knott*'s case should not be followed.

[53] I further consider that there is no valid distinction between a case where
a party promises to achieve a result and a case where a party is under a contractual
obligation to take reasonable care to achieve a result. Suppose a case where a
householder's enjoyment of his garden is spoilt by an unpleasant smell from a
septic tank at the bottom of the garden and he employs a company to clean out

a   the tank. If the contract constituted a promise by the company to clean out the tank and it failed to do so, with the result that the smell continued, I think that in accordance with the principle stated by Lord Mustill in the *Ruxley Electronics* case [1995] 3 All ER 268 at 277, [1996] AC 344 at 360–361 the householder would be entitled to recover a modest sum of damages for the annoyance caused by the continuation of the smell. But if the contract provided that the company would

b   exercise reasonable care and skill to clean out the tank and due to its negligence the tank was not cleaned out, I consider that the householder would also be entitled to damages.

[54] Whilst I do not accept the submission advanced on behalf of the defendant that, where there is no pecuniary loss, damages can only be recovered where the claim is for breach of an obligation which is the very object of the contract, I think

c   that (other than in building contract cases where the principle stated by Lord Mustill in the *Ruxley Electronics* case [1995] 3 All ER 268 at 277, [1996] AC 344 at 360–361 gives direct guidance) there is a need for a test which the courts can apply in practice in order to preserve the fundamental principle that general damages are not recoverable for anxiety and aggravation and similar states of mind caused by

d   a breach of contract and to prevent the exception expanding to swallow up, or to diminish unjustifiably, the principle itself. It will be for the courts, in the differing circumstances of individual cases, to apply the principles stated in your Lordships' speeches in this case, and the matter is not one where any precise test or verbal formula can be applied but, adopting the helpful submissions of counsel for the

e   plaintiff, I consider that as a general approach it would be appropriate to treat as cases falling within the exception and calling for an award of damages those where: (1) the matter in respect of which the individual claimant seeks damages is of importance to him, and (2) the individual claimant has made clear to the other party that the matter is of importance to him, and (3) the action to be taken in relation to the matter is made a specific term of the contract. If these three

f   conditions are satisfied, as they are in the present case, then I consider that the claim for damages should not be rejected on the ground that the fulfilment of that obligation is not the principal object of the contract or on the ground that the other party does not receive special and specific remuneration in respect of the performance of that obligation.

g   [55] Counsel for the defendant submitted that the award of damages of £10,000 was manifestly excessive as it constituted compensation for the inconvenience and annoyance from the aircraft noise which the plaintiff would continue to suffer for an indefinite period in the future. In support of this submission counsel relied on the observation of Bingham LJ in *Watts v Morrow* [1991] 4 All ER 937 at

h   959, [1991] 1 WLR 1421 at 1445:

'If, on learning of the defects which should have been but were not reported, a purchaser decides (for whatever reason) to retain the house and not move out and sell, I would question whether any loss he thereafter suffers, at least in the ordinary case, can be laid at the door of the contract-

j   breaker.'

Therefore counsel submitted that the damages should have been restricted to compensation for inconvenience and annoyance suffered for one year, that being a reasonable time during which the plaintiff could have moved house; after the period of a year, the inconvenience and annoyance suffered by the plaintiff could not be regarded as caused by default of the defendant.

[56] I am unable to accept that submission. I consider that in the circumstance
of this case where the plaintiff had expended a considerable sum of money in   *a*
improving the house before he was aware of the defendant's failure to inform
him of aircraft noise, and where he would have had to incur very considerable
expense in selling and buying a new house and moving to it, it was reasonable for
him to decide to stay in the house, even though that involved putting up with the
noise, and I think that the trial judge was right to reject the defendant's argument   *b*
on this point.

Physical inconvenience and discomfort

[57] The second principal issue which arises on this appeal is whether, as a
separate ground, the plaintiff is entitled to recover damages because the aircraft
noise constituted physical inconvenience and discomfort which he suffered as a   *c*
consequence of the defendant's breach of contract. The authorities cited and
analysed by Clarke LJ in his judgment make it clear, as he observes (2000) 73 Con LR
70 at 89, that damages are recoverable for physical inconvenience and that it is
not necessary to establish any kind of physical injury or loss. Thus in *Hobbs v
London and South Western Rly Co* (1875) LR 10 QB 111 at 117, Cockburn CJ stated: *d*
'I think there is no authority that personal inconvenience, where it is sufficiently
serious, should not be the subject of damages to be recovered in an action of this
kind.' Mellor J stated (at 122–123):

> 'I quite agree with my Brother Parry, that for the mere inconvenience,
> such as annoyance and loss of temper, or vexation, or for being disappointed   *e*
> in a particular thing which you have set your mind upon, without real
> physical inconvenience resulting, you cannot recover damages ... where the
> inconvenience is real and substantial arising from being obliged to walk
> home, I cannot see why that should not be capable of being assessed as
> damages in respect of inconvenience.'   *f*

And Archibald J stated (at 124):

> 'The case is not one of mere vexation, but it is one of physical inconvenience,
> which can in a sense be measured by money value, and the parties here had
> the firm measure of that inconvenience in the damages given by the jury.'   *g*

[58] I also consider that Barry J in *Bailey v Bullock* [1950] 2 All ER 1167 at
1170–1171 and Beldam LJ in *Wapshott v Davis Donovan & Co* [1996] PNLR 361 at
378 were right to emphasise that there is a distinction between mere annoyance
or disappointment at the failure of the other party to carry out his contractual
obligation and actual physical inconvenience and discomfort caused by the   *h*
breach. Therefore the judge was entitled to award damages to the plaintiff for the
annoyance caused to him by the aircraft noise if the noise constituted physical
inconvenience and discomfort.

[59] In his careful judgment the judge expressly referred to one head of
damages discussed in *Watts v Morrow* and cited part of the headnote which states: *j*

> '... in the case of the ordinary surveyor's contract general damages were
> recoverable only for distress and inconvenience caused by physical
> consequences of the breach of contract ... such damages should be a modest
> sum for the amount of physical discomfort endured ...' (See [1991] 1 WLR
> 1421 at 1422.)

a Therefore the judge clearly had in mind that damages could only be awarded for physical inconvenience and discomfort. He subsequently stated that the plaintiff had sustained 'real discomfort'. The fact that the judge also stated that the plaintiff found the noise 'a confounded nuisance' does not, in my opinion, mean that the noise could not be regarded as a physical inconvenience and discomfort. No doubt as Mr Hobbs walked home after midnight with his wife and children

b the four or five miles from Esher station through the drizzling rain he thought that the walk was a confounded nuisance, but that did not disentitle him from recovering damages for physical inconvenience and discomfort.

[60] The aircraft noise was something which affected the plaintiff through his hearing and can be regarded as having a physical effect upon him, and on the evidence which was before him I consider that it was open to the judge to find

c that the plaintiff suffered physical inconvenience and discomfort.

[61] I agree with Judge and Clarke LJJ that on first impression the award of £10,000 damages appears to be a very high one, but I also agree with them that this is a very unusual case where the inconvenience and discomfort caused to the plaintiff will continue, and on further consideration I do not consider that it

d would be right for an appellate court to set aside the award as being excessive. Therefore I would allow the appeal and restore the order of the judge.

LORD SCOTT OF FOSCOTE.

[62] My Lords, this is a case with simple facts, a short question and, in my
e respectful opinion, a simple answer.

[63] The plaintiff, Mr Farley, wanted to purchase a house in the country. Riverside House at Blackboys, Sussex was on the market. It seemed to fit the bill. It was, however, 15 miles or so from Gatwick Airport. Mr Farley was anxious that his rural retreat should not be affected by aircraft noise. He instructed Mr Skinner, the defendant, who is a chartered surveyor, to inspect the property

f and report on its general and structural condition. He asked Mr Skinner, also, to report on whether, in view of the proximity of the property to Gatwick Airport, the property would be affected by aircraft noise. Mr Skinner accepted these instructions. On 17 December 1990 Mr Skinner provided Mr Farley with a detailed 38-page report. The report contained, on p 35, a paragraph about aircraft noise.

g The paragraph indicted Mr Skinner's opinion that it was 'unlikely that the property will suffer greatly from such noise'.

[64] Unfortunately, Mr Skinner had made inadequate inquiries about aircraft noise and, in particular, had not discovered that within a few miles from the property was the Mayfield Stack, an area where aircraft waiting to land at Gatwick were directed to circle until the airport was ready to receive them and from

h where their route to the airport frequently passed over or near to Blackboys.

[65] It was found by the trial judge, and is accepted before your Lordships, that Mr Skinner's failure to find out about the Mayfield Stack and to draw its implications to Mr Farley's attention was an inadequate contractual response to his instructions

j about aircraft noise.

[66] In short, Mr Skinner was in breach of contract. His client, Mr Farley, is entitled in principle to be compensated in damages for the breach.

[67] Mr Farley gave evidence that if he had received from Mr Skinner the information about aircraft noise to which he, Mr Farley, was contractually entitled, he would not have purchased Riverside House. This evidence was accepted by the judge. But, in the event, in reliance on the contractually inadequate information

about aircraft noise that he had received from Mr Skinner, Mr Farley purchased
the property.

[68] Having purchased the property, Mr Farley put in hand fairly extensive
works of modernisation and renovation. It was only after these had been carried
out that he moved in and took up residence. It was then that he discovered that
the property was affected by aircraft noise. The degree of discomfort caused by
noise is always to some extent subjective. There was evidence that many, perhaps
most, of the residents in the area were not troubled by the noise. But Mr Farley
was.

[69] He gave evidence that it interfered with his enjoyment of a quiet,
reflective breakfast, a morning stroll in his garden or pre-dinner drinks. The trial
judge having heard the evidence, concluded that 'real discomfort ... has been
sustained by Mr Farley in this case'.

[70] It is accepted by Mr Simpson, counsel for Mr Skinner, that if Mr Farley,
on becoming aware of the extent of the aircraft noise, had decided to resell,
Mr Skinner would have been liable to compensate him at least for the costs of
reselling. But, having had the house modernised and renovated to his taste, and
no doubt having become attached to the house, Mr Farley decided not to sell.
But none the less, feeling that he ought to be compensated for Mr Skinner's
breach of contract, he commenced an action for damages.

[71] He claimed damages on the footing that the true value of the property,
affected by the aircraft noise, was substantially less than the price he had paid. On
this issue, however, the judge concluded that the aircraft noise that upset
Mr Farley did not result in any diminution in the value of the property.

[72] Mr Farley claimed damages on the footing, also, that: 'The plaintiff's use
and enjoyment of the property has been impaired by aircraft noise.' The judge
held that Mr Farley was entitled to damages for impairment of use and
enjoyment and awarded him £10,000.

[73] Mr Skinner appealed. The issue on appeal was whether, in law, Mr Farley
was entitled to contractual damages for impairment of his enjoyment of Riverside
House. My noble and learned friend, Lord Steyn, has described the course of
proceedings in the Court of Appeal and it suffices for me to say that two Lords
Justices held that he was, three held that he was not, and it is now for your
Lordships to resolve the issue.

[74] The reason why such an apparently straightforward issue has caused such
division of opinion is because it has been represented as raising the question
whether and when contractual damages for mental distress are available. It is
highly desirable that your Lordships should resolve the present angst on this
subject and avoid the need in the future for relatively simple claims, such as
Mr Farley's, to have to travel to the appellate courts for a ruling.

[75] In my opinion, the issue can and should be resolved by applying the
well-known principles laid down in *Hadley v Baxendale* (1854) 9 Exch 341,
[1843–60] All ER Rep 461 (as restated in *Victoria Laundry (Windsor) Ltd v Newman
Industries Ltd (Coulsdon & Co Ltd, third party)* [1949] 1 All ER 997, [1949] 2 KB 528)
in the light of the recent guidance provided by Bingham LJ in *Watts v Morrow*
[1991] 4 All ER 937, [1991] 1 WLR 1421 and by this House in *Ruxley Electronics and
Construction Ltd v Forsyth, Laddingford Enclosures Ltd v Forsyth* [1995] 3 All ER 268,
[1996] AC 344.

[76] The basic principle of damages for breach of contract is that the injured
party is entitled, so far as money can do it, to be put in the position he would have
been in if the contractual obligation had been properly performed. He is entitled,

a that is to say, to the benefit of his bargain (see *Robinson v Harman* (1848) 1 Exch 850 at 855, [1843–60] All ER Rep 383 at 385).

[77] In the *Ruxley Electronics* case builders had agreed to construct a swimming pool with a diving area 7 ft 6 ins deep. The pool when constructed had a depth of only 6 ft. The cost of rebuilding the pool to the contractual depth would have been £21,560. But the trial judge, having heard the evidence, concluded that the pool *b* owner did not have the intention of using the damages to reconstruct the pool. He found also that the residential property of which the pool formed part had suffered no diminution in value by reason of the lack of one foot of depth in the pool's diving area. None the less the pool owner claimed the £21,500 as damages. The builders, on the other hand, contended that, on the facts as found, the pool owner had suffered no loss and the damages should be nil. The trial judge *c* accepted neither contention but instead awarded the £2,500 expressed as compensation for 'a loss of amenity brought about by the shortfall in depth' (see [1995] 3 All ER 268 at 280, [1996] AC 344 at 363). The Court of Appeal ([1994] 3 All ER 801, [1994] 1 WLR 650) set aside the £2,500 award and substituted an award of the cost of rebuilding, ie the £21,560. This House restored the trial *d* judge's order.

[78] Lord Mustill referred ([1995] 3 All ER 268 at 276, [1996] AC 344 at 360) to situations where, in the carrying out of building works on residential property, there had been minor deviations from the contractual specifications but where the deviations had not reduced the value of the property below the value it would have had if the work had been properly carried out. He went on:
e

'Yet the householder must surely be entitled to say that he chose to obtain from the builder a promise to produce a particular result because he wanted to make his house more comfortable, more convenient and more conformable to his own particular tastes; not because he had in mind that the work might *f* increase the amount which he would receive if, contrary to expectation, he thought it expedient in the future to exchange his home for cash. To say that in order to escape unscathed the builder has only to show that to the mind of the average onlooker, or the average potential buyer, the results which he has produced seem just as good as those which he had promised would make a part of the promise illusory and unbalance the bargain. In the valuable *g* analysis contained in *Radford v De Froberville* [1978] 1 All ER 33 at 42, [1977] 1 WLR 1262 at 1270 Oliver J emphasised that it was for the plaintiff to judge what performance he required in exchange for the price. The court should honour that choice. Pacta sunt servanda. If the appellant's argument leads to the conclusion that in all cases like the present the employer is entitled to *h* no more than nominal damages, the average householder would say that there must be something wrong with the law.' (See [1995] 3 All ER 268 at 276–277, [1996] AC 344 at 360.)

Lord Lloyd of Berwick, to the same effect, said:

j 'What is then to be the position where, in the case of a new house, the building does not conform in some minor respect to the contract, as, for example, where there is a difference in level between two rooms, necessitating a step? Suppose there is no measurable difference in value, and the cost of reinstatement would be prohibitive. Is there any reason why the court should not award by way of damages for breach of contract some modest sum, not based on difference in value, but solely to compensate the buyer for

his disappointed expectations? Is the law of damages so inflexible ... that it
cannot find some middle ground in such a case? I do not give a final answer   *a*
to that question in the present case. But it may be that it would have afforded
an alternative ground for justifying the judge's award of damages.' (See
[1995] 3 All ER 268 at 289, [1996] AC 344 at 374.)

[79] The *Ruxley Electronics* case establishes, in my opinion, that if a party's
contractual performance has failed to provide to the other contracting party   *b*
something to which that other was, under the contract, entitled, and which, if
provided, would have been of value to that party, then, if there is no other way
of compensating the injured party, the injured party should be compensated in
damages to the extent of that value. Quantification of that value will, in many
cases be difficult and may often seem arbitrary. In the *Ruxley Electronics* case the   *c*
value placed on the amenity value of which the pool owner had been deprived
was £2,500. By that award, the pool owner was placed, so far as money could do
it, in the position he would have been in if the diving area of the pool had been
constructed to the specified depth.

[80] In the *Ruxley Electronics* case the breach of contract by the builders had not
caused any consequential loss to the pool owner. He had simply been deprived   *d*
of the benefit of a pool built to the depth specified in the contract. It was not a
case where the recovery of damages for consequential loss consisting of vexation,
anxiety or other species of mental distress had to be considered.

[81] In *Watts v Morrow* [1991] 4 All ER 937, [1991] 1 WLR 1421, however, that
matter did have to be considered. As in the present case, the litigation in *Watts v*   *e*
Morrow resulted from a surveyor's report. The report had negligently failed to
disclose a number of defects in the property. The clients, who had purchased the
property in reliance on the report, remedied the defects and sued for damages.
The judge awarded them the costs of the repairs and also general damages of
£4,000 each for 'distress and inconvenience' (see [1991] 4 All ER 937 at 940, [1991]
1 WLR 1421 at 1424). As to the cost of repairs, the Court of Appeal substituted   *f*
an award of damages based on the difference between the value of the property
as the surveyor's report had represented it to be and the value as it actually was.
Nothing, for present purposes, turns on that. As to the damages for 'distress and
inconvenience' the Court of Appeal upheld the award in principle but held that
the damages should be limited to a modest sum for the physical discomfort   *g*
endured and reduced the award to £750 for each plaintiff. Bingham LJ ([1991]
4 All ER 937 at 959–960, [1991] 1 WLR 1421 at 1445) in an important passage, set
out the principles to be applied where contractual damages for distress and
inconvenience are claimed:

> 'A contract-breaker is not in general liable for any distress, frustration,   *h*
> anxiety, displeasure, vexation, tension or aggravation which his breach of
> contract may cause to the innocent party. This rule is not, I think, founded
> on the assumption that such reactions are not foreseeable, which they surely
> are or may be, but on considerations of policy.
>
> But the rule is not absolute. Where the very object of a contract is to   *j*
> provide pleasure, relaxation, peace of mind or freedom from molestation,
> damages will be awarded if the fruit of the contract is not provided or if the
> contrary result is procured instead. If the law did not cater for this
> exceptional category of case it would be defective. A contract to survey the
> condition of a house for a prospective purchaser does not, however, fall
> within this exceptional category.

a   In cases not falling within this exceptional category, damages are in my
     view recoverable for physical inconvenience and discomfort caused by the
     breach and mental suffering   directly related to that inconvenience and
     discomfort.'

     [82] In the passage I have cited, Bingham LJ was dealing with claims for
b   consequential damage consisting of the intangible mental states and sensory
     experiences to which he refers. Save for the matters referred in the first paragraph,
     all of which reflect or are brought about by the injured party's disappointment at
     the contract-breaker's failure to carry out his contractual obligations, and recovery
     for which, if there is nothing more, is ruled out on policy grounds, Bingham LJ's
     approach is, in my view, wholly consistent with established principles for the
c   recovery of contractual damages.

     [83] There are, however, two qualifications that I would respectfully make to
     the proposition in the final paragraph of the cited passage that damages 'for
     physical inconvenience and discomfort caused by the breach' are recoverable.

     [84] First, there will, in many cases, be an additional remoteness hurdle for the
d   injured party to clear. Consequential damage, including damage consisting of
     inconvenience or discomfort, must, in order to be recoverable, be such as, at the
     time of the contract, was reasonably foreseeable as liable to result from the
     breach (see *McGregor on Damages* (16th edn, 1997) pp 159–160 (para 250)).

     [85] Second, the adjective 'physical', in the phrase 'physical inconvenience and
     discomfort', requires, I think, some explanation or definition. The distinction
e   between the 'physical' and the 'non-physical' is not always clear and may depend
     on the context. Is being awoken at night by aircraft noise 'physical'? If it is, is
     being unable to sleep because of worry and anxiety 'physical'? What about a
     reduction in light caused by the erection of a building under a planning
     permission that an errant surveyor ought to have warned his purchaser-client
f   about but failed to do so? In my opinion, the critical distinction to be drawn is not
     a distinction between the different types of inconvenience or discomfort of which
     complaint may be made but a distinction based on the cause of the inconvenience
     or discomfort. If the cause is no more than disappointment that the contractual
     obligation has been broken, damages are not recoverable even if the disappointment
     has led to a complete mental breakdown. But, if the cause of the inconvenience
g   or discomfort is a sensory (sight, touch, hearing, smell etc) experience, damages
     can, subject to the remoteness rules, be recovered.

     [86] In summary, the principle expressed in the *Ruxley Electronics* case should
     be used to provide damages for deprivation of a contractual benefit where it is
     apparent that the injured party has been deprived of something of value but the
h   ordinary means of measuring the recoverable damages are inapplicable. The
     principle expressed in *Watts v Morrow* should be used to determine whether and
     when contractual damages for inconvenience or discomfort can be recovered.

     [87] These principles, in my opinion, provide the answer, not only to the issue
     raised in the present case, but also to the issues raised in the authorities which
j   were cited to your Lordships.

     [88] In *Hobbs v London and South Western Rly Co* (1875) LR 10 QB 111, [1874–80]
     All ER Rep 458 the claim was for consequential damage caused by the railway
     company's breach of contract. Instead of taking the plaintiff, his wife and two
     children to Hampton Court, their train dumped them at Esher and they had to
     walk five miles or so home in the rain. The plaintiff's wife caught a cold as a result
     of the experience. The plaintiff was awarded damages for the inconvenience and

discomfort of his and his family's walk home but his wife's cold was held to be too remote a consequence. The plaintiff's recovery of damages attributable, in part, to the discomfort suffered by his wife and children was in accordance with principle. The contractual benefit to which he was entitled was the carriage of himself and his family to Hampton Court. It was reasonable in my opinion, to value that benefit, of which he had been deprived by the breach of contract, by reference to the discomfort to the family of the walk home. This was, in my view, a *Ruxley Electronics* case.

[89] *Jarvis v Swans Tours Ltd* [1973] 1 All ER 71, [1973] QB 233 was a case in which the plaintiff had contracted for a holiday with certain enjoyable qualities. He had been given a holiday which lacked those qualities. His holiday had caused him discomfort and distress. The trial judge awarded him £31·72, one half of the price of the holiday. This must, I think have been the value attributed by the judge to the contractual benefit of which the plaintiff had been deprived. But on the plaintiff's appeal against so low an award, the Court of Appeal allowed him £125.

[90] Somewhat different reasons were given by the three members of the court. Lord Denning MR said:

> 'In a proper case damages for mental distress can be recovered in contract … One such case is a contract for a holiday, or any other contract to provide entertainment and enjoyment. If the contracting party breaks his contract, damages can be given for the disappointment, the distress, the upset and frustration caused by the breach.' (See [1973] 1 All ER 71 at 74, [1973] QB 233 at 237–238.)

The reference in this passage to the 'contract for a holiday, or any other contract to provide entertainment and enjoyment' is consistent with an intention to compensate the plaintiff for the contractual benefit of which he had been deprived. The reference, however, to 'the disappointment, the distress' etc reads like a reference to consequential damage.

[91] Edmund Davies LJ based his decision on the defendant's failure 'to provide a holiday of the contractual quality' (see [1973] 1 All ER 71 at 75, [1973] QB 233 at 239). He held that the amount of damages was not limited by the price for the holiday. He said ([1973] 1 All ER 71 at 76, [1973] QB 233 at 239): 'The court is entitled, and indeed bound, to contrast the overall quality of the holiday so enticingly promised with that which the defendants in fact provided.' He regarded the plaintiff's vexation and disappointment as relevant matters to take into account in 'determining what would be proper compensation for the defendants' marked failure to fulfil their undertaking'. This was a *Ruxley Electronics* approach. Stephenson LJ based his decision on the 'reasonable contemplation of the parties … as a likely result of [the holiday contract] being so broken' (see [1973] 1 All ER 71 at 76, [1973] QB 233 at 240). He said ([1973] 1 All ER 71 at 77, [1973] QB 233 at 240–241) that where there are contracts 'in which the parties contemplate inconvenience on breach which may be described as mental: frustration, annoyance, disappointment' damages for breach should take that inconvenience into account. This was a *Watts v Morrow* approach.

[92] *Jackson v Horizon Holidays Ltd* [1975] 3 All ER 92, [1975] 1 WLR 1468 was a case brought by another disappointed holidaymaker. He had booked a holiday for himself, his wife and children. Its quality turned out to be substantially below contractually justified expectations. The plaintiff recovered £1,100 damages as compensation not only for his own discomfort but also for the discomfort experienced by his wife and children. In my opinion, the justification for such an

a award is that the plaintiff was entitled to be compensated for the value of the contracted benefit of which he had been deprived. This case, like *Jarvis'* case [1973] 1 All ER 71 at 76, [1973] QB 233 at 239 per Edmund Davies LJ, and like *Hobbs'* case, is a *Ruxley Electronics* type of case.

[93] *Knott v Bolton* (1995) 45 Con LR 127 is, in my opinion, inconsistent with the *Ruxley Electronics* case and should now be regarded as having been wrongly b decided. The plaintiffs had been deprived of the wide staircase and gallery and baronial entrance hall to which they were contractually entitled and had to put up with lesser facilities. A value should, in my opinion, have been placed on the benefit of which they had been deprived.

[94] In *Heywood v Wellers (a firm)* [1976] 1 All ER 300, [1976] QB 446 a firm of solicitors was sued for failure to provide adequate legal services to the plaintiff in c connection with proceedings to protect her from molestation by an ex-boyfriend. The failure had the result that the plaintiff continued to suffer molestation. She was awarded damages as compensation for the vexation, anxiety and distress that the continuing molestation had caused her. This, in my opinion, is a clear example of compensation for consequential loss within the reasonable contemplation of d the parties at the time of the contract as liable to be caused by the solicitors' failure to deal properly with the anti-molestation proceedings.

[95] Contrast *Cook v S* [1967] 1 All ER 299, [1967] 1 WLR 457 and *Hayes v James & Charles Dodd (a firm)* [1990] 2 All ER 815, both solicitors' negligence cases where it was claimed that the solicitors' failure to provide the services to which the plaintiffs had been contractually entitled had caused the plaintiffs anguish, e distress and vexation.

[96] In *Cook's* case Lord Denning MR said:

'... if anything goes wrong with the litigation owing to the solicitor's negligence ... It can be foreseen that there will be injured feelings; mental f distress; anger, and annoyance. But for none of these can damages be recovered.' (See [1967] 1 All ER 299 at 303, [1967] 1 WLR 457 at 461.)

As Bingham LJ pointed out in *Watts v Morrow* [1991] 4 All ER 937 at 959, [1991] 1 WLR 1421 at 1445, these damages are ruled out on public policy grounds.

[97] In *Hayes'* case [1990] 2 All ER 815 at 824 Staughton LJ said that contractual g damages for mental distress were, as a matter of policy, limited to certain classes of case and that the classes 'should not ... include any case where the object of the contract was not comfort or pleasure, or the relief [from] discomfort, but simply carrying on a commercial activity with a view to profit'. So he disallowed the claim for damages for anguish and vexation.

h [98] In my opinion, the distinction between commercial contracts and other contracts is too imprecise to be satisfactory. I think the decision of Staughton LJ was plainly correct for the reason that the commercial character of the contract required a negative answer to the question whether the anguish and vexation caused by the breach and for which recovery was sought was within the reasonable contemplation of the parties at the time of the contract (see also Lord Reid's point j in *The Heron II, Koufos v C Czarnikow Ltd* [1967] 3 All ER 686 at 690, [1969] 1 AC 350 at 383 that the loss in question should, to be recoverable, be 'not very unusual and easily foreseeable').

[99] In *Perry v Sidney Phillips & Son (a firm)* [1982] 3 All ER 705, [1982] 1 WLR 1297, contractual damages for distress and discomfort caused to the plaintiff by having to live for a while in a house with a leaking roof and defective drains were

awarded as compensation for a surveyor's negligent failure to draw attention to these defects in his report. The Court of Appeal adopted a foreseeability approach. *a*

[100] In *R v Investors Compensation Scheme Ltd, ex p Bowden* [1994] 1 All ER 525 at 537, [1994] 1 WLR 17 at 28, decided after *Watts v Morrow* had been reported, Mann LJ said: 'Unless the very object of the contract is as stated by Bingham LJ (*Watts v Morrow* [1991] 4 All ER 937 at 960, [1991] 1 WLR 1421 at 1445), then a contract breaker is not liable to compensate for mental and physical distress *b* consequent upon his breach of contract.'

[101] This statement is not, in my opinion, accurate. It concentrates only on the first part and ignores the second part of Bingham LJ's proposition. I agree with Mann LJ that a contract relating to the investment of money is not such a contract as Bingham LJ had in mind as a contract 'the very object' of which is to provide pleasure etc. But if a breach of any contract has caused physical *c* inconvenience or discomfort that is within the recognised rules of remoteness and mental distress is a part of that inconvenience or discomfort, it would, in my opinion, in principle be recoverable.

[102] Mr Simpson referred to *Johnson v Gore Wood & Co (a firm)* [2001] 1 All ER 481, [2001] 2 WLR 72, which he said was indistinguishable from the present case. *d* The case raised a number of difficult issues which have nothing whatever to do with the present case but the case did involve also a claim for damages for mental distress caused by solicitors' negligence. The alleged negligence was the solicitors' failure to advise Mr Johnson, the client, about various financial matters. Mr Johnson claimed, among other heads of damage, damages 'for the mental distress and anxiety which he has suffered' as a result of the alleged negligence. Lord Bingham *e* of Cornhill ([2001] 1 All ER 481 at 505, [2001] 2 WLR 72 at 96) cited the first two paragraphs of the passage from his own judgment in *Watts v Morrow* [1991] 4 All ER 937 at 959–960, [1991] 1 WLR 1421 at 1445 that I have cited at [81], above. He referred to the *Ruxley Electronics* case and said ([2001] 1 All ER 481 at 505, [2001] 2 WLR 72 at 97): 'It is undoubtedly true that many breaches of contract cause *f* intense frustration and anxiety to the innocent party.'

[103] He did not, however, think that Mr Johnson's claim for damages for mental distress and anxiety came within the established principles for the recovery of such damages.

[104] The decision in *Johnson*'s case is, in my view, plainly distinguishable from the present. It was not, in my view, remotely arguable that Mr Johnson's alleged *g* mental distress was a consequence that, at the time he retained the solicitors, was reasonably in the contemplation of the parties as liable to result from a breach.

[105] It is time for me to turn to the present case and apply the principles expressed in the *Ruxley Electronics* case and *Watts v Morrow*. In my judgment, Mr Farley is entitled to be compensated for the 'real discomfort' that the judge *h* found he suffered. He is so entitled on either of two alternative bases.

[106] First, he was deprived of the contractual benefit to which he was entitled. He was entitled to information about the aircraft noise from Gatwick-bound aircraft that Mr Skinner, through negligence, had failed to supply him with. If Mr Farley had, in the event, decided not to purchase Riverside House, *j* the value to him of the contractual benefit of which he had been deprived would have been nil. But he did buy the property. And he took his decision to do so without the advantage of being able to take into account the information to which he was contractually entitled. If he had had that information he would not have bought. So the information clearly would have had a value to him. Prima facie, in my opinion, he is entitled to be compensated accordingly.

a   [107] In these circumstances, it seems to me, it is open to the court to adopt a *Ruxley Electronics* approach and place a value on the contractual benefit of which Mr Farley has been deprived. In deciding on the amount, the discomfort experienced by Mr Farley can, in my view, properly be taken into account. If he had had the aircraft noise information he would not have bought Riverside House and would not have had that discomfort.

b   [108] Alternatively, Mr Farley can, in my opinion, claim compensation for the discomfort as consequential loss. Had it not been for the breach of contract, he would not have suffered the discomfort. It was caused by the breach of contract in a causa sine qua non sense. Was the discomfort a consequence that should reasonably have been contemplated by the parties at the time of contract as liable to result from the breach? In my opinion, it was. It was obviously within the

c   reasonable contemplation of the parties that, deprived of the information about aircraft noise that he ought to have had, Mr Farley would make a decision to purchase that he would not otherwise have made. Having purchased, he would, having become aware of the noise, either sell, in which case at least the expenses of the resale would have been recoverable as damages, or he would keep the

d   property and put up with the noise. In the latter event, it was within the reasonable contemplation of the parties that he would experience discomfort from the noise of the aircraft. And the discomfort was 'physical' in the sense that Bingham LJ in *Watts v Morrow* [1991] 4 All ER 937 at 960, [1991] 1 WLR 1421 at 1445 had in mind. In my opinion, the application of *Watts v Morrow* principles entitles Mr Farley to damages for discomfort caused by the aircraft noise.

e   [109] I would add that if there had been an appreciable reduction in the market value of the property caused by the aircraft noise, Mr Farley could not have recovered both that difference in value and damages for discomfort. To allow both would allow double recovery for the same item.

     [110] Whether the approach to damages is on *Ruxley Electronics* lines, for
f   deprivation of a contractual benefit, or on *Watts v Morrow* lines, for consequential damage within the applicable remoteness rules, the appropriate amount should, in my opinion, be modest. The degree of discomfort experienced by Mr Farley, although 'real', was not very great. I think £10,000 may have been on the high side. But in principle, in my opinion, the judge was right to award damages and I am not, in the circumstances, disposed to disagree with his figure.

g   [111] For the reasons I have given and for the reasons contained in the opinion of my noble and learned friend, Lord Steyn, I would allow the appeal and restore the judge's order.

Appeal allowed.

Dilys Tausz   Barrister.

Khan v Chief Constable of West Yorkshire Police

[2001] UKHL 48

HOUSE OF LORDS

LORD NICHOLLS OF BIRKENHEAD, LORD MACKAY OF CLASHFERN, LORD HOFFMANN, LORD HUTTON AND LORD SCOTT OF FOSCOTE

28 JUNE, 11 OCTOBER 2001

Race relations – Discrimination – Victimisation – Police sergeant bringing racial discrimination proceedings against chief constable in respect of rejection of application for promotion to inspector – Sergeant applying for similar post with another force while proceedings pending – Chief constable refusing to provide reference sought by other force for fear of prejudicing position in pending proceedings – Whether refusal constituting victimisation 'by reason that' sergeant had brought discrimination proceedings – Race Relations Act 1976, s 2(1)(a).

K, a detective sergeant of Indian origin, was a long-serving member of the West Yorkshire police force. Over the years, he made a number of unsuccessful applications for promotion to the rank of inspector. Following the last such rebuff, K brought industrial tribunal proceedings for racial discrimination against the appellant chief constable, alleging that he had been treated less favourably, on grounds of race, than other applicants contrary to the Race Relations Act 1976. While the proceedings were pending, K applied to another police force for an inspector's post. That force asked the West Yorkshire police for a reference. Such a reference would normally have been given, but the force's solicitor advised the chief constable that it would be inappropriate to provide a reference for K because the pending litigation raised issues that would be relevant to the reference. Acting on that advice, the West Yorkshire police informed the other force that the chief constable was unable to comment on K's application for fear of prejudicing his position in the discrimination proceedings. K subsequently amended his claim to add a claim under s 2(1)(a)[a] of the 1976 Act for discrimination by way of victimisation, based on the refusal to provide a reference. Under s 2(1)(a), a person (the discriminator) discriminated against another person (the person victimised) in any circumstances relevant for the purposes of any provision of the Act if he treated the person victimised less favourably than in those circumstances he treated or would have treated other persons, and did so 'by reason that' the person victimised had brought proceedings against the discriminator under the Act. K's claim for direct discrimination failed, but his claim for victimisation succeeded. The chief constable's appeal was dismissed by the Employment Appeal Tribunal. That decision was in turn affirmed by the Court of Appeal which held that K had been treated less favourably than other employees for whom a reference had been sought, and that the less favourable treatment had been by reason of his having performed an act protected by s 2(1) of the 1976 Act, namely the bringing of discrimination proceedings. The chief constable appealed to the House of Lords.

a Section 2, so far as material, is out at [16], below

a **Held** – Where an employer, acting honestly and reasonably, took steps to preserve his position in pending proceedings for racial discrimination, those steps would not have been taken 'by reason that' the proceedings had been commenced, and accordingly they would not constitute discrimination by way of victimisation within the meaning of s 2(1)(a) of the 1976 Act. Such a conclusion accorded with the spirit and purpose of the Act. Moreover, the statute

b accommodated that approach without any straining of language. An employer who conducted himself in that way was not doing so because of the fact that the complainant had brought discrimination proceedings. He was doing so because, currently and temporarily, he needed to take steps to preserve his position in the outstanding proceedings, ie the reason for the employer's action was the existence of the proceedings, not their commencement. The act protected by

c s 2(1)(a) could not have been intended to prejudice an employer's proper conduct of his defence, so long as he acted honestly and reasonably. Acting within that limit, he could not be regarded as discriminating by way of victimisation against the employee who brought the proceedings. In the instant case, K had been treated less favourably than other employees since the West Yorkshire police ordinarily provided references for members of the force who were seeking new

d employment. However, it was necessary to look further than that. The industrial tribunal had failed to do so, and had therefore fallen into error. Accordingly, the appeal would be allowed (see [21], [30], [31], [34], [42], [44]–[47], [52], [59], [61], [76], [78]–[81], below).

Cornelius v University College of Swansea [1987] IRLR 141 approved.

e

Notes

For discrimination by way of victimisation, see 13 *Halsbury's Laws* (4th edn reissue) para 402.

For the Race Relations Act 1976, s 2, see 7 *Halsbury's Statutes* (4th edn) (1999

f reissue) 119.

Cases referred to in opinions

Aziz v Trinity Street Taxis Ltd [1988] 2 All ER 860, [1989] QB 463, [1988] 3 WLR 79, CA.

Brown v TNT Express Worldwide (UK) Ltd [2001] ICR 182, CA.

g *Cornelius v University College of Swansea* [1987] IRLR 141, CA.

De Souza v Automobile Association [1986] ICR 514, CA.

James v Eastleigh BC [1990] 2 All ER 607, [1990] 2 AC 751, [1990] 3 WLR 55, HL.

Kirby v Manpower Services Commission [1980] 3 All ER 334, [1980] 1 WLR 725, EAT.

Ministry of Defence v Jeremiah [1979] 3 All ER 833, [1980] QB 87, [1979] 3 WLR 857,

h CA.

Nagarajan v London Regional Transport [1999] 4 All ER 65, [2000] 1 AC 501, [1999] 3 WLR 425, HL; *rvsg* [1998] IRLR 73, CA.

R v Birmingham City Council, ex p Equal Opportunities Commission [1989] 1 All ER 769, [1989] AC 1115, [1989] 2 WLR 520, HL.

j

Appeal

The Chief Constable of West Yorkshire appealed with permission of the Appeal Committee of the House of Lords given on 25 October 2000 from the order of the Court of Appeal (Lord Woolf MR, Hale LJ and Lord Mustill) on 24 February 2000 ([2000] ICR 1169) dismissing his appeal from the decision of the Employment Appeal Tribunal (Judge Peter Clark, P Dawson and RN Straker) on 28 July 1998 dismissing his appeal from (i) the decision of an industrial tribunal sitting at Leeds, promulgated on 22 April 1997, upholding the claim brought against the chief constable by the respondent, Det Sgt Raham Noor Khan, for racial discrimination by way of victimisation under s 2(1)(a) of the Race Relations Act 1976, and (ii) the tribunal's decision, promulgated on 30 July 1997, awarding Sgt Khan £1,500 for injury to his feelings. The facts are set out in the opinion of Lord Nicholls of Birkenhead.

David Bean QC, David Jones and *Joanna Moody* (instructed by *Sharpe Pritchard,* agents for *Ajaz Hussain,* Wakefield) for the chief constable.

John Hand QC and *Melanie Tether* (instructed by *Russell Jones & Walker,* Leeds) for Sgt Khan.

Their Lordships took time for consideration.

11 October 2001. The following opinions were delivered.

LORD NICHOLLS OF BIRKENHEAD.

[1] My Lords, Det Sgt Raham Noor Khan is a long-serving member of the West Yorkshire constabulary. He is of Indian origin. He has lived in England for over 30 years. He joined the force in 1975, and was promoted to the rank of sergeant in 1985. Sergeant Khan is a most capable and thorough police officer, but his supervising officers perceived a weakness. Over the years he made a number of unsuccessful applications for promotion to the rank of inspector. He was told by his supervising officers that his managerial style and team leadership skills were seen to be a problem.

[2] On 31 May 1996 Sgt Khan tried again. He made another application for promotion. The overall assessment of his work was 'very good'. But Chief Insp Sidney did not support the application. In her promotion assessment dated 5 June 1996 she said that Sgt Khan 'has an identified weakness in the area of communication/personnel style which adversely affects his team leadership skills'. This further application by Sgt Khan was unsuccessful.

[3] Sergeant Khan was not satisfied with this outcome. He was of the view that his failure to obtain promotion was not based on a fair assessment of his merits and abilities. The real reason was his racial origin. On 1 September 1996 he made an application to an industrial tribunal. He named the chief constable and four senior officers as respondents. He claimed that his failure to obtain promotion, and the failure by these officers to support his application, constituted racial discrimination. The officers had treated him less favourably than other applicants, and had done so on grounds of race. The application was resisted.

[4] In the following month, October 1996, Sgt Khan responded to an advertisement in the *Police Review* magazine. He applied to the Norfolk Police Force for an appointment to the post of inspector. The Norfolk Police Force asked the West Yorkshire force for a reference. They asked that Sgt Khan's chief officer should give his observations and recommendations on Sgt Khan's suitability for the post. They also asked for copies of Sgt Khan's last two staff appraisals.

[5] In the ordinary course such a request would have caused no difficulty. But Sgt Khan's claim in the industrial tribunal had not yet been heard. Because of the pending claim for racial discrimination the West Yorkshire police sought internal

a legal advice from the force's solicitor, Mr Ajaz Hussain. Acting on that advice, on 24 October 1996 the West Yorkshire personnel officer replied:

> 'Sergeant Khan has an outstanding industrial tribunal application against the chief constable for failing to support his application for promotion. In the light of that, the chief constable is unable to comment any further for fear of prejudicing his own case before the tribunal.'

b

Thus, West Yorkshire made no observations or recommendations on Sgt Khan's application, nor were copies of his staff appraisals sent to the Norfolk police. In short, Sgt Khan was not given a reference.

[6] On 9 January 1997 Sgt Khan amended his pending claim in the industrial
c tribunal. He added a claim against the West Yorkshire chief constable for victimisation, because of the refusal by the West Yorkshire police to provide him with a reference. This claim gives rise to the issue now before the House.

[7] The claims for direct discrimination and victimisation were heard at the Leeds Industrial Tribunal over six days, from February 1997 onwards. The tribunal announced its decision on 22 April 1997. The claim for direct discrimination failed.
d Sergeant Khan was not treated less favourably, and even if less favourable treatment had been found, it would not have been on the grounds of race. The claim for victimisation, based on the failure to provide a reference, succeeded.

[8] Meanwhile, Sgt Khan's promotion transfer application was considered by the Norfolk police. He underwent assessment, which he passed. But he was
e unsuccessful at interview on 10 March 1997.

[9] On 30 July 1997, after a further hearing, the industrial tribunal announced its decision on the appropriate remedy for West Yorkshire's victimisation of Sgt Khan. The tribunal found that even if Sgt Khan had obtained a glowing reference as distinct from no reference, because of his performance at interview
f he would not have succeeded. So the tribunal made no award for financial loss, but they awarded Sgt Khan £1,500 compensation for injury to feelings.

[10] An appeal by the West Yorkshire police was dismissed by the Employment Appeal Tribunal on 28 July 1998. A further appeal to the Court of Appeal ([2000] ICR 1169) was dismissed by that court, comprising Lord Woolf MR, Hale LJ and Lord Mustill, on 24 February 2000.

g
[11] Plainly, in October 1996 West Yorkshire police found themselves in a position of considerable difficulty. The subject matter of the request for a reference for Sgt Khan was the very matter awaiting adjudication in the industrial tribunal. The Norfolk Police Force were seeking the views of the West Yorkshire force on Sgt Khan's suitability for promotion to the rank of inspector. But the views
h of Sgt Khan's supervising officers on this matter, expressed as recently as June 1996, were being challenged by Sgt Khan as racially discriminatory. Those views, he said, constituted unlawful racial discrimination. That issue remained to be decided. That being so, the chief constable could hardly be expected to repeat those selfsame views to another potential employer while that serious challenge
j against the authors of those views remained outstanding. Repetition of those views at that time could justifiably have been castigated as irresponsible behaviour by the chief constable, as well as possibly leading to a further allegation of direct racial discrimination. Such conduct by the chief constable could prejudice his case before the industrial tribunal. It would also mean that if the discrimination claim were to succeed, the chief constable would be at risk of being censured for his aggravation of the wrong done to Sgt Khan by members

of the West Yorkshire police, and the amount of compensation increased
accordingly.   *a*

[12] But, according to Sgt Khan, that is the course the chief constable should
have followed. The chief constable, it was submitted, should have given Sgt Khan
a reference along the lines:

> 'Sergeant Khan recently applied for internal promotion to the rank of   *b*
> inspector. That application was not supported, and I enclose copies of his
> last two appraisals. By way of observations on, and recommendations for,
> Sergeant Khan's suitability for the post you have advertised, the chief
> constable reiterates what Chief Insp Sidney said in an assessment for
> promotion form dated 5 June 1996, a copy of which is enclosed. As a result
> of that application not being supported Sgt Khan has commenced   *c*
> proceedings against the chief constable of this force alleging he has been
> discriminated against on the grounds of his race.'

Thus, according to the submissions advanced on behalf of Sgt Khan, the chief
constable should have repeated to the Norfolk police the very views which were
being challenged in pending judicial proceedings as evidence of unlawful racial   *d*
discrimination. By failing to do so, the argument runs, the chief constable was
himself guilty of discrimination by way of victimisation.

[13] This is a surprising proposition. To my mind it has only to be spelled out
for it to be apparent that this cannot be right.
                                                                                 e

THE STATUTORY PROVISIONS

[14] I turn to the statutory provisions. The Race Relations Act 1976 provides
that discrimination in certain fields is unlawful. The fields include employment,
education, planning, trade unions and trade associations. Part II of the Act
concerns discrimination in the employment field. Section 4 renders it unlawful   *f*
to discriminate against applicants for employment or employees in the ways, or
circumstances, described in the section. In the case of employees, the circumstances
listed in s 4(2) are (a) in the terms of employment the employer affords the
employee, or (b) in the way he affords, or refuses to afford, him access to
opportunities for promotion or other benefits, or '(c) by dismissing him, or
subjecting him to any other detriment'. I accept Sgt Khan's claim that the refusal *g*
to provide a reference for him constituted a detriment within the meaning of
s 4(2)(c) even though, as matters turned out, this did not cause him any financial
loss. Provision of a reference is a normal feature of employment.

[15] Sections 1 and 2 explain what is meant by discrimination. Discrimination
means either racial discrimination, as defined in s 1, or discrimination by way of *h*
victimisation, as defined in s 2. Section 1 defines the two familiar types of racial
discrimination. Direct discrimination, in sub-s (1)(a), occurs if on racial grounds
one person treats another less favourably than he treats or would treat other persons
in circumstances relevant for the purposes of the Act. Indirect discrimination is
defined in s 1(1)(b).   *j*

[16] The primary object of the victimisation provisions in s 2 is to ensure that
persons are not penalised or prejudiced because they have taken steps to exercise
their statutory rights or are intending to do so. The structure of s 2 is similar to
the structure of s 1(1)(a), but with an important difference. Racial discrimination, in
s 1(1)(a), is discrimination on the grounds of race. Discrimination by victimisation,
in s 2, is discrimination on one of the grounds, colloquially known as the protected

a acts, described in s 2. Section 2(1) defines discrimination by way of victimisation as follows:

> 'A person ("the discriminator") discriminates against another person ("the person victimised") in any circumstances relevant for the purposes of any provision of this Act if he treats the person victimised less favourably than in those circumstances he treats or would treat other persons, and does so by
>
> b reason that the person victimised has—(a) brought proceedings against the discriminator or any other person under this Act; or (b) given evidence or information in connection with proceedings brought by any person against the discriminator or any other person under this Act; or (c) otherwise done anything under or by reference to this Act in relation to the discriminator or
>
> c any other person; or (d) alleged that the discriminator or any other person has committed an act which (whether or not the allegation so states) would amount to a contravention of this Act, or by reason that the discriminator knows that the person victimised intends to do any of those things, or suspects that the person victimised has done, or intends to do, any of them.'

d [17] Section 2(2) provides an exception. Section 2(1) does not apply to treatment of a person by reason of any allegation made by him if the allegation was false and not made in good faith. In the present case the industrial tribunal rejected a contention that Sgt Khan's allegations of racial discrimination were not made in good faith.

e [18] Difficulties have arisen in the application of this definition of victimisation and the like definition in s 4 of the Sex Discrimination Act 1975. The difficulties have been most apparent in cases where the employer's impugned conduct was his response to a protected act but he was not racially or gender motivated. I must first refer briefly to the principal authorities. They are illustrative of the problems.

f
THE AUTHORITIES
[19] In *Kirby v Manpower Services Commission* [1980] 3 All ER 334, [1980] 1 WLR 725 an employee at a job centre was demoted because he had disclosed confidential information about possible contraventions of the race relations legislation. The Employment Appeal Tribunal held this was not victimisation

g within s 2. Slynn J, delivering the judgment of the tribunal, said ([1980] 3 All ER 334 at 340, [1980] 1 WLR 725 at 732) that the relevant question was whether the employers had treated the complainant less favourably than they would have treated someone in their employment who gave away confidential information whatever its kind. So Mr Kirby's claim failed, because the Manpower Services

h Commission would have treated in the same way any employee who gave away confidential information whatever its nature.
[20] *Aziz v Trinity Street Taxis Ltd* [1988] 2 All ER 860, [1989] QB 463 was a decision of the Court of Appeal, comprising Slade, Neill and Mann LJJ. Mr Aziz was a member of a taxi drivers' association. He collected evidence with a view

j to pursuing a racial discrimination claim against the association, by secretly recording conversations with other members. He was expelled for doing so, and he brought a victimisation claim. Slade LJ, delivering the judgment of the court, disapproved the test applied in *Kirby*'s case. He held that by expelling Mr Aziz the association had treated him less favourably than other members. But, to constitute victimisation, the motive which caused the alleged discriminator to treat the complainant less favourably than others must be a motive consciously connected with the race relations legislation (see [1988] 2 All ER 860 at 871, [1989] QB 463 at 485). Mr Aziz's claim therefore failed, because the fact that the recordings were made by reference to the Act had not influenced the association in expelling Mr Aziz. Any member who made undisclosed recordings of conversations relating to the activities of the association in a controversial context would have been treated in the same way.

[21] Next, in order of time, is the decision of the Court of Appeal in the present case. Lord Woolf MR held ([2000] ICR 1169 at 1177) that Sgt Khan had been treated less favourably by being refused a reference. It was necessary to compare the way other employees in relation to whom a reference was requested would normally be treated with the way Sgt Khan was treated. Further, Sgt Khan was treated less favourably by reason of having done a protected act. If it had not been for the proceedings brought under the Act a reference would have been provided.

[22] Finally, in *Brown v TNT Express Worldwide (UK) Ltd* [2001] ICR 182 the employee requested an afternoon off work to consult his advisor about a racial discrimination claim he had brought against his employer. The claim was due for hearing in an employment tribunal the following week. The employer refused permission, although requests for time off for personal reasons were normally granted. Despite this, the employee left work to keep his appointment, whereupon he was dismissed. Mr Brown's victimisation claim succeeded. The Court of Appeal, comprising Peter Gibson and Mantell LJJ and Sumner J, rejected the employer's contention that the appropriate comparator was an employee who had brought proceedings against the employer but not under the 1976 Act.

VICTIMISATION

(1) *The relevant circumstances*

[23] Victimisation occurs when, in any circumstances relevant for the purposes of any provision of the Act, a person is treated less favourably than others because he has done one of the protected acts. Thus, the definition of victimisation has, essentially, three ingredients. The first is 'in any circumstances relevant for the purposes of any provision of this Act'. This is a reference to circumstances in respect of which discrimination is unlawful under the Act. For instance, under s 4(2) it is unlawful for an employer to discriminate against an employee by dismissing him. If an employee brings a victimisation claim based on his dismissal, the relevant circumstances are his dismissal by his employer. In the present case Sgt Khan is treated as employed by the chief officer of police of West Yorkshire (see s 16 of the Act). The relevant circumstances are that, while employed, Sgt Khan requested a reference when seeking new employment and his request was refused.

(2) *Less favourable treatment*

[24] The second ingredient in the statutory definition calls for a comparison between the treatment afforded to the complainant in the relevant respect with the treatment he affords, or would afford, to other persons 'in those circumstances'.

[25] As appears from my summary of the authorities, different views have emerged on the correct way to identify the 'others', or the comparators or control group, as they are usually known. One approach is that, to continue with my example, if an employee is dismissed the control group comprises the other

a employees. The complainant was less favourably treated because he was
   dismissed and they were not. There may be good reasons for this difference in
   treatment but, on this approach, that is a matter to be taken into account at the
   third stage when considering why the employer afforded the employee less
   favourable treatment. This was the approach adopted in *Aziz's* case. It was
   the approach adopted at all levels in the present case. Sergeant Khan was treated
b less favourably than other employees, because references are normally provided
   on request and Sgt Khan was refused a reference. It was also the approach
   adopted in *Brown's* case.

   [26] The other approach is that when considering whether a complainant was
   treated less favourably there should be factored into the comparison features
   which make the situation of the complainant and the control group fairly
c comparable. The control group should be limited to employees who have not
   done the protected act but whose circumstances, in the material respects, are
   fairly comparable. This approach was adopted by the Employment Appeal
   Tribunal in *Kirby's* case and by the Court of Appeal in *Nagarajan v London Regional
   Transport* [1998] IRLR 73 at 76 (para 13) (this point was not the subject of the
d subsequent appeal to your Lordships' House (see [1999] 4 All ER 65, [2000] 1 AC
   501)).

   [27] There are arguments in favour of both approaches. On the whole I see
   no sufficient reason for departing from the former approach, adopted by Slade LJ
   in *Aziz's* case [1988] 2 All ER 860 at 869, [1989] QB 463 at 483. The statute is to
   be regarded as calling for a simple comparison between the treatment afforded to
e the complainant who has done a protected act and the treatment which was or
   would be afforded to other employees who have not done the protected act.

   [28] Applying this approach, Sgt Khan was treated less favourably than other
   employees. Ordinarily West Yorkshire provides references for members of the
   force who are seeking new employment.

f
   (3) *'by reason that'*

   [29] Contrary to views sometimes stated, the third ingredient ('by reason that')
   does not raise a question of causation as that expression is usually understood.
   Causation is a slippery word, but normally it is used to describe a legal exercise.
   From the many events leading up to the crucial happening, the court selects one
g or more of them which the law regards as causative of the happening. Sometimes
   the court may look for the 'operative' cause, or the 'effective' cause. Sometimes it
   may apply a 'but for' approach. For the reasons I sought to explain in *Nagarajan's*
   case [1999] 4 All ER 65 at 70–72, [2000] 1 AC 501 at 510–512, a causation exercise
   of this type is not required either by s 1(1)(a) or s 2. The phrases 'on racial
h grounds' and 'by reason that' denote a different exercise: why did the alleged
   discriminator act as he did? What, consciously or unconsciously, was his reason?
   Unlike causation, this is a subjective test. Causation is a legal conclusion. The
   reason why a person acted as he did is a question of fact.

   [30] A situation, closely comparable to that in the present case, arose in *Cornelius v
j University College of Swansea* [1987] IRLR 141. This was a decision of the Court of
   Appeal, comprising Donaldson MR, and Fox and Bingham LJJ. Like the present
   case, *Cornelius'* case concerned steps taken by employers to preserve their position
   pending the outcome of proceedings. A college declined to act on an employee's
   transfer request or to operate their grievance procedure while proceedings under
   the 1975 Act, brought by the employee against the college, were still awaiting

determination. Giving the only reasoned judgment, Bingham LJ said (at 145–146 (para 33)):

> 'There is no reason whatever to suppose that the decisions of the Registrar and his senior assistant on the applicant's requests for a transfer and a hearing under the grievance procedure were influenced in any way by the facts that the appellant had brought proceedings or that those proceedings were under the Act. The existence of proceedings plainly did influence their decisions. No doubt, like most experienced administrators, they recognised the risk of acting in a way which might embarrass the handling or be inconsistent with the outcome of current proceedings. They accordingly wished to defer action until the proceedings were over. But that had ... nothing whatever to do with the appellant's conduct in bringing proceedings under the Act. There is no reason to think that their decision would have been different whoever had brought the proceedings or whatever their nature, if the subject matter was allied. If the appellant was victimised, it is not shown to have been because of her reliance on the Act.'

Two strands are discernible in this passage. One strand is that the reason why the officers of the college did not act on the complainant's two requests was the *existence* of the pending proceedings, as distinct from the complainant's conduct in *bringing* the proceedings. They wished to defer action until the proceedings were over. The second strand is that the college decisions had nothing to do with the complainant's conduct in bringing proceedings against the college *under the 1975 Act*. The decisions would have been the same, whatever the nature of the proceedings, if the subject matter had been allied to the content of the employee's requests.

[31] Mr Hand QC, for Sgt Khan, submitted that *Cornelius'* case was wrongly decided. I do not agree. Employers, acting honestly and reasonably, ought to be able to take steps to preserve their position in pending discrimination proceedings without laying themselves open to a charge of victimisation. This accords with the spirit and purpose of the Act. Moreover, the statute accommodates this approach without any straining of language. An employer who conducts himself in this way is not doing so because of the fact that the complainant has brought discrimination proceedings. He is doing so because, currently and temporarily, he needs to take steps to preserve his position in the outstanding proceedings. Protected act (a) ('by reason that the person victimised has—(a) brought proceedings against the discriminator ... under this Act') cannot have been intended to prejudice an employer's proper conduct of his defence, so long as he acts honestly and reasonably. Acting within this limit, he cannot be regarded as discriminating by way of victimisation against the employee who brought the proceedings.

[32] Mr Hussain's evidence was that giving a reference as asked might have compromised the chief constable's handling of the case brought against him. An adjudication by the industrial tribunal in favour of Sgt Khan would mean that the chief constable had put forward a reference which proved to be inconsistent with the outcome of the proceedings. There was the unacceptable prospect that the chief constable would give a reference upon the opinion of his senior officers which was later rejected by a judicial body. The chief constable would not have been placed in this dilemma had the industrial tribunal hearing been concluded. Meanwhile the only course of action open to the chief constable was to bring the outstanding proceedings to the attention of the Norfolk force and leave it at that.

a [33] Mr Hussain's evidence was also that he did not believe his advice to the chief constable would have been any different whatever the nature of the pending proceedings. One of the examples he gave was of a civilian employee, dismissed as a consequence of dishonesty, seeking a reference before the determination of a pending unfair dismissal claim. Mr Hussain's evidence was not challenged before the tribunal.

b [34] The approach of the industrial tribunal was, in effect, that there was no need to look further once it was seen that the West Yorkshire force ordinarily provided a reference and copies of the previous appraisals and that the only difference in this case was Sgt Khan's commencement of proceedings under the Act: '... it is clearly the respondents' case that that, and that alone, gave them good cause to react the way that they did ...' With all respect to the tribunal,
c I think there was a need to look further, for the reasons I have given. In not doing so the tribunal fell into error. I would allow this appeal.

LORD MACKAY OF CLASHFERN.

[35] My Lords, the facts giving rise to this appeal are fully set out in the speech
d of my noble and learned friend Lord Nicholls of Birkenhead and I need not repeat them.

[36] I turn to the statutory provisions under which this appeal rises. The Race Relations Act 1976 provides that discrimination in certain fields is unlawful. The fields include employment, education, planning, trade unions and trade associations. Part II of the Act concerns discrimination in the employment field. As a preliminary,
e I refer to s 16 which provides that for the purposes of Pt II of the Act, the holding of the office of constable shall be treated as employment by the chief officer of police as respects any act done by him in relation to a constable. In the circumstances of this case, therefore, Sgt Khan is treated as employed by the chief officer of police of West Yorkshire in respect of that chief officer's actions in relation to
f Sgt Khan. Section 4 of the Act deals with discrimination by employers:

> '*Discrimination against applicants and employees.*—(1) It is unlawful for a person, in relation to employment by him at an establishment in Great Britain, to discriminate against another—(a) in the arrangements he makes for the purpose of determining who should be offered that employment; or
g (b) in the terms on which he offers him that employment; or (c) by refusing or deliberately omitting to offer him that employment.
>
> (2) It is unlawful for a person, in the case of a person employed by him at an establishment in Great Britain, to discriminate against that employee— (a) in the terms of employment which he affords him; or (b) in the way he
h affords him access to opportunities for promotion, transfer or training, or to any other benefits, facilities or services, or by refusing or deliberately omitting to afford him access to them; or (c) by dismissing him, or subjecting him to any other detriment.'

It will be seen that the statute provides that discrimination is unlawful in a variety
j of circumstances set out in this section.

[37] It was said that the type of discrimination involved in the present appeal was under s 4(2)(c) subjecting Sgt Khan to any other detriment. Detriment has been widely defined (see *De Souza v Automobile Association* [1986] ICR 514). I think it would also be possible to place this case under s 4(2)(b) in relation to access to other benefits, the benefit in the present instance being that of a reference when an employee applies to another prospective employer. We were informed that

there was no specific mention of references in the relevant statutes including the employment statutes but I think the word 'benefits' would be wide enough to include them.

[38] So far then Sgt Khan's case rests on the assertion that the Chief Constable of the West Yorkshire Police has dealt with him unlawfully in respect that being a person employed by him at an establishment in Great Britain, the chief officer discriminated against him in the way he refused to afford him access to the benefit of references or by subjecting him to any other detriment. We now have to ascertain what is meant by discrimination in the context of s 4(2) and for that the relevant provision is s 2 which provides:

> 'Discrimination by way of victimisation.—(1) A person ("the discriminator") discriminates against another person ("the person victimised") in any circumstances relevant for the purposes of any provision of this Act if he treats the person victimised less favourably than in those circumstances he treats or would treat other persons, and does so by reason that the person victimised has—(a) brought proceedings against the discriminator or any other person under this Act; or (b) given evidence or information in connection with proceedings brought by any person against the discriminator or any other person under this Act; or (c) otherwise done anything under or by reference to this Act in relation to the discriminator or any other person; or (d) alleged that the discriminator or any other person has committed an act which (whether or not the allegation so states) would amount to a contravention of this Act, or by reason that the discriminator knows that the person victimised intends to do any of those things, or suspects that the person victimised has done, or intends to do, any of them.'

Section 2(1) does not apply to treatment of a person by reason of any allegation made by him if the allegation was false and not made in good faith. The industrial tribunal in the present case held that sub-s (2) did not apply to the proceedings raised by Sgt Khan and accordingly sub-s (1) does apply to him. I refer, as my noble and learned friend has done, to the matters referred to in paras (a), (b) and (d) as the protected acts.

[39] In order that discrimination by way of victimisation under s 2 should occur it is necessary that there should be 'circumstances relevant for purposes of any provision of this Act'. Secondly, it is necessary that the discriminator treats the person victimised less favourably than in those circumstances he treats or would treat other persons; and, thirdly, it is necessary that he does so by reason that the person victimised has done one of the protected acts. In my view, in order to ascertain who are the 'other persons' with whom comparison should be made in any particular case one must identify the circumstances relevant for the purposes of any provision of the Act in which the discrimination is said to have occurred and then to consider how other persons in those circumstances have been treated.

[40] Obviously in the present case the circumstances include the fact that Sgt Khan is to be treated as employed by the chief officer of the West Yorkshire police at an establishment in Great Britain. Assuming, as I have done, that the request for a reference is an access to a benefit I think it can be said that the circumstances relevant for the purposes of this act include also in this case the circumstance of Sgt Khan's application for a reference. If the case is treated as a subjection of Sgt Khan to any other detriment I do not see reference to any other circumstance than that he is employed at an establishment in Great Britain. If one now goes back to s 2, in my

a view the circumstances relevant for the purposes of any provision of this Act which are at issue in this case is the simple fact that Sgt Khan is treated for the purposes of this Act as employed by the chief officer of the West Yorkshire police at an establishment in Great Britain and that he is so employed and has made an application for the benefit of a reference.

b [41] On this basis the other persons with whose treatment the treatment of Sgt Khan must be compared are persons employed at the same establishment in Great Britain as Sgt Khan, namely, in the West Yorkshire police, and who have applied for a reference when seeking employment with another employer.

[42] The refusal of a reference to Sgt Khan when it is common ground that generally a reference would be given is in my view sufficient to demonstrate that in the circumstances relevant for the purposes of s 4 of the Act, Sgt Khan has been *c* treated less favourably than other persons.

[43] The third requirement for discrimination under s 2 is that it has occurred by reason that the person victimised has done one of the protected acts. In this case, therefore, the question is was Sgt Khan refused a reference by reason that he had brought proceedings against the chief officer of police under this Act? It is *d* clear that Sgt Khan had brought proceedings against the chief officer of police under this Act but the requirement is that the less favourable treatment must be accorded by reason that he has done so.

[44] The advice of the solicitor advising the chief officer was laid fully before the industrial tribunal and no challenge was made of it. It was to the effect that because there was pending litigation raising issues which were relevant to the *e* reference it would be inappropriate for the chief officer to give a reference. In my opinion in these circumstances the chief officer having acted in accordance with that perfectly understandable advice did not treat Sgt Khan less favourably than he would have done others applying for a reference by reason that Sgt Khan had brought proceedings under the Act.

f [45] It is clear that if the proceedings had been terminated when the request for a reference was made the obstacle to giving it would have been removed and I have no doubt that the chief officer has clearly established that in the present case he did not refuse a reference by reason that Sgt Khan had raised proceedings against him under the Act.

[46] In my opinion this analysis leads to a workable approach to the statutory *g* provisions and is in accordance with the purpose of the statute as described by Bingham LJ in *Cornelius v University College of Swansea* [1987] IRLR 141 at 145 (para 31). For these reasons I agree that the appeal should be allowed.

LORD HOFFMANN.

h [47] My Lords, I have had the advantage of reading in draft the speech of my noble and learned friend Lord Nicholls of Birkenhead with which I agree.

[48] The appeal raised three points. First, when s 2(1) of the Race Relations Act 1976 speaks of the person victimised being treated 'less favourably than in those circumstances he treats or would treat other persons', who are these *j* hypothetical other people and what are the hypothetical circumstances? Mr Khan says that one should suppose a police officer like himself who had asked for a reference and appraisals but had not done 'the protected act', ie brought proceedings under the Act. Such a person would have not have been denied a reference. The West Yorkshire police say that in addition to supposing that he had not brought proceedings under the Act, one should also suppose that he had brought proceedings on some other ground, e g for libel or constructive dismissal.

Such a person would also not have been given a reference. I agree with my noble and learned friend Lord Nicholls of Birkenhead, the Employment Appeal Tribunal and the Court of Appeal ([2000] ICR 1169) that the first view is correct.

[49] The purpose of the statute is that a person should not be victimised because he has done the protected act. It seems to me no answer to say that he would equally have been victimised if he had done some other act and that doing such an act should therefore be attributed to the hypothetical 'other persons' with whom the person victimised is being compared. Otherwise the employer could escape liability by showing that his regular practice was to victimise anyone who did a class of acts which included but was not confined to the protected act.

[50] The requirement that doing the protected act must have been the reason for the less favourable treatment is adequate to safeguard an employer who acted for a different and legitimate reason. On the other hand, it will rightly provide no defence for an employer who can only say that although his reason was indeed the doing of the protected act, it formed part of a larger class of acts to which he would have responded in the same way.

[51] The second question is whether Mr Khan was actually treated less favourably than someone who had not brought proceedings would have been. The chief constable says that it is not enough that he was treated differently. His treatment must be worse. This is an objective question and if one looks at the matter objectively, he was better off without a reference. If he had been given one, it would have contained an express statement that his application for promotion was not supported. In that case, the Norfolk constabulary would not even have asked him to an assessment. As it was, he at least got through to interview.

[52] This was not a point taken in the industrial tribunal, the Employment Appeal Tribunal or the Court of Appeal. It seems to have surfaced as a result of remarks made at the hearing of the application for leave to appeal before the Appeal Committee. It is attractive but I think that upon analysis it is wrong. There is a distinction between the question of whether treatment is less favourable and the question of whether it has damaging consequences. Mr Khan, with full knowledge of what Chief Insp Sidney's assessment contained, wanted it to be sent to Norfolk. His request was refused when a similar request by someone else would have been granted. That seems to me to be less favourable treatment which the tribunal found caused injury to Mr Khan's feelings. The fact that he was actually invited to an assessment showed that the less favourable treatment caused him no economic loss but does not prevent it from having been less favourable.

[53] The point is allied to the question of whether, assuming that there was discrimination under s 2(1), Mr Khan was subjected to 'detriment' within the meaning of s 4(2)(c). Being subjected to detriment (or being treated in one of the other ways mentioned in s 4(2)) is an element in the statutory cause of action additional to being treated 'less favourably' which forms part of the definition of discrimination. A person may be treated less favourably and yet suffer no detriment. But, bearing in mind that the employment tribunal has jurisdiction to award compensation to injury to feelings, the courts have given the term 'detriment' a wide meaning. In *Ministry of Defence v Jeremiah* [1979] 3 All ER 833 at 841, [1980] QB 87 at 104 Brightman LJ said that 'a detriment exists if a reasonable worker would or might take the view that the [treatment] was in all the circumstances to his detriment'. Mr Khan plainly did take the view, at any rate in October 1996, that not having his assessment forwarded was to his

a detriment and I do not think that, in his state of knowledge at the time, he can be said to have been unreasonable.

[54] That brings me to the third and most difficult question, which is whether Mr Khan was treated less favourably 'by reason that' he had 'brought proceedings … under this Act' (s 2(1)(a)). This raises a question of causation: was the fact that he brought proceedings a *reason* why the West Yorkshire police treated him less *b* favourably.

[55] Of course, in one sense the fact that he had brought proceedings was a cause of his being treated less favourably. If he had not brought proceedings, he would have been given a reference. In some contexts, a causal link of this kind will be enough. For example, in *R v Birmingham City Council, ex p Equal Opportunities Commission* [1989] 1 All ER 769, [1989] AC 1115 the question was whether the *c* council had treated a girl less favourably 'on the ground of her sex', contrary to s 1 of the Sex Discrimination Act 1975. The House of Lords decided that her sex did not have to be the reason why the council had decided to treat her in that way. It was sufficient that she would have been treated differently if she had been a boy (see also *James v Eastleigh BC* [1990] 2 All ER 607, [1990] 2 AC 751).

d [56] There are parallels between the purposes of ss 1 and 2 of the 1976 Act (and between the corresponding ss 1 and 4 of the 1975 Act): see *Nagarajan v London Regional Transport* [1999] 4 All ER 65, [2000] 1 AC 501. But the causal questions which they raise are not identical. As Mr Hand QC, who appeared for Mr Khan, readily accepted, one cannot simply say that Mr Khan would not have been treated less favourably if he had not brought proceedings. It does not follow that *e* his bringing proceedings was a reason (conscious or subconscious) why he was treated less favourably. In *Nagarajan's* case Lord Steyn said that s 2—

'contemplates that the discriminator had knowledge of the protected act and that such knowledge caused or influenced the discriminator to treat the victimised person less favourably than he would treat other persons … But *f* … it does not require the tribunal to distinguish between conscious and subconscious motivation.' (See [1999] 4 All ER 65 at 78, [2000] 1 AC 501 at 519–520.)

[57] This is not at all the same thing as saying that but for the protected act, he *g* would not have been treated in the way he was. The difference emerges very clearly from the judgment of Bingham LJ in *Cornelius v University College of Swansea* [1987] IRLR 141. Mrs Cornelius was an employee of the university who made a complaint of sex discrimination to an industrial tribunal. While the proceedings were pending she applied for a transfer to another post and to be heard under the university's grievance procedure. A senior assistant registrar replied that no *h* action could be taken on the transfer until the outcome of the proceedings was known. The registrar himself wrote to say that a grievance hearing was inappropriate while the industrial tribunal proceedings were pending. Mrs Cornelius claimed that this was victimisation. She said that the registrar's letter indicated that but for her commencement of proceedings, her application for a transfer and a grievance *j* hearing would have been considered in the normal way.

[58] Bingham LJ (at 145 (para 33)) rejected the complaint for the following reasons:

'There is no reason whatever to suppose that the decisions of the Registrar and his senior assistant on the applicant's requests for a transfer and a hearing under the grievance procedure were influenced in any way by the facts that

the appellant had *brought* proceedings or that those proceedings were under
the Act. The *existence* of proceedings plainly did influence their decisions. No
doubt, like most experienced administrators, they recognised the risk of
acting in a way which might embarrass the handling or be inconsistent with
the outcome of current proceedings. They accordingly wished to defer
action until the proceedings were over. But that had, so far as the evidence
shows, nothing whatever to do with the appellant's conduct in *bringing*
proceedings under the Act. There is no reason to think that their decision
would have been different whoever had brought the proceedings or
whatever their nature, if the subject matter was allied.' (My emphasis.)

[59] This decision, with which I respectfully agree, shows that once proceedings
have been commenced, a new relationship is created between the parties. They
are not only employer and employee but also adversaries in litigation. The
existence of that adversarial relationship may reasonably cause the employer to
behave in a way which treats the employee less favourably than someone who
had not commenced such proceedings. But the treatment need not be,
consciously or unconsciously, a response to the commencement of proceedings.
It may simply be a reasonable response to the need to protect the employer's
interests as a party to the litigation. It is true that an employee who had not
commenced proceedings would not have been treated in the same way. Under s 1,
one would have needed to go no further. Under s 2, however, the commencement
of proceedings must be a reason for the treatment and in *Cornelius'* case it was not.

[60] A test which is likely in most cases to give the right answer is to ask
whether the employer would have refused the request if the litigation had been
concluded, whatever the outcome. If the answer is no, it will usually follow that
the reason for refusal was the existence of the proceedings and not the fact that
the employee had commenced them. On the other hand, if the fact that the
employee had commenced proceedings under the Act was a real reason why he
received less favourable treatment, it is no answer that the employer would have
behaved in the same way to an employee who had done some non-protected act,
such as commencing proceedings otherwise than under the Act.

LORD HUTTON.

[61] My Lords, I have had the advantage of reading in draft the speeches of my
noble and learned friends Lord Nicholls of Birkenhead and Lord Hoffmann.
I agree with them and for the reasons which they give I, too, would allow this
appeal.

LORD SCOTT OF FOSCOTE.

[62] My Lords, the relevant facts and the history of the proceedings in this case
have been set out in the opinions of my noble and learned friends, Lord Nicholls
of Birkenhead and Lord Hoffmann. I need not repeat them save to the extent
necessary to explain the conclusions I have reached.

[63] The problem is as to the proper application to the facts of the case of s 2(1)
of the Race Relations Act 1976. Section 2(1) provides, so far as is relevant to this
case:

'A person ("the discriminator") discriminates against another person ("the
person victimised") in any circumstances relevant for the purposes of any
provision of this Act if he treats the person victimised less favourably than in
those circumstances he treats or would treat other persons, and does so by

a reason that the person victimised has—(a) brought proceedings against the discriminator or any other person under this Act ...'

[64] Sergeant Khan, an officer in the West Yorkshire police, had applied for promotion to the rank of inspector. But a staff appraisal made by a senior officer, while in some respects complimentary, had referred to perceived weaknesses in his team leadership skills and he was informed that his application for promotion
b would not be supported by his supervising officers. Sergeant Khan then made an application under the 1976 Act alleging that his chief constable had discriminated against him on the grounds of his race in failing to support him for promotion.

[65] While Sgt Khan's discrimination claim was still pending, he made an application to the Norfolk Police Force for appointment as an inspector in that
c force. The Norfolk Police Force requested a reference from the West Yorkshire Police Force. Sergeant Khan's personnel officer replied to the request in these terms:

'Sergeant Khan has an outstanding industrial tribunal application against the chief constable for failing to support him for promotion [to the rank of
d inspector]. In the light of that, the chief constable is unable to comment any further for fear of prejudicing his own case before the tribunal.'

[66] Sergeant Khan then added a s 2(1) victimisation claim to his race discrimination claim.

[67] The two claims were heard together. The race discrimination claim
e failed; the victimisation claim succeeded.

[68] Sergeant Khan's application to the Norfolk police was not, in the event, adversely affected by the West Yorkshire Police Force's refusal to give him a reference. Indeed, the reverse was the case. Although his application was not in the end successful, it progressed further than it would have done had he received
f a reference on the same lines as the appraisals which had led to the failure of his application for promotion to inspector in his own police force.

[69] In these circumstances Sgt Khan's s 2(1) victimisation claim raises the following issues: (1) In considering whether Sgt Khan was treated by West Yorkshire Police Force less favourably than other persons, with whom is Sgt Khan to be compared? (2) What is the test of whether the treatment complained of was
g less favourable than the treatment that would have been accorded to the comparators? (3) What is the test to determine whether the complainant has been treated in the manner complained of 'by reason that' he has done the protected act?

h (1) *The comparators*

[70] In the submissions to your Lordships various comparators were suggested.

[71] One suggestion was that the treatment accorded to Sgt Khan should be compared to the treatment that would have been accorded to other officers of the West Yorkshire police who had brought discrimination proceedings against their
j employers. This cannot be right. It would enable an employer to justify victimising an employee who had brought proceedings under the Act by asserting that he would similarly victimise every employee who brought proceedings under the Act.

[72] Another suggestion was that the treatment accorded to Sgt Khan should be compared to the treatment that would have been accorded to other officers who had brought employment-related proceedings, but not race discrimination proceedings, against their employer. This cannot be right either. It would enable

employers to victimise employees who brought race discrimination proceedings
against them provided they, the employers, were prepared similarly to victimise
any employee who had the temerity to sue them for anything.

[73] A third suggestion was that the treatment accorded to Sgt Khan should be
compared to the treatment that would have been accorded to an officer in a
position the same in all respects as Sgt Khan's save only that this hypothetical
officer had not done the protected act, ie, in this case, had not brought race
discrimination proceedings. This, in my opinion, is the correct comparator. It
provides to employees who do one or other of the protected acts specified in
s 2(1) the protection that Parliament must have intended them to have.

[74] In *Aziz v Trinity Street Taxis Ltd* [1988] 2 All ER 860 at 869, [1989] QB 463
at 483 Slade LJ said:

'In our judgment, for the purpose of the comparison which s 2(1) makes
requisite, the relevant circumstances do not include the fact that the
complainant has done a protected act.'

I agree. I would add that, save for the fact that the complainant has done a
protected act, the relevant circumstances include all the circumstances in which
the alleged discriminator treated the complainant in the manner complained of.
The Court of Appeal in the present case came, I think, to much the same
conclusion (see [2000] ICR 1169 at 1180 per Lord Woolf MR).

(2) Was Sgt Khan treated 'less favourably'?

[75] He was certainly treated differently. If it had not been for the pending
race discrimination proceedings the request by the Norfolk Police Force for a
reference would have been complied with. But did the chief constable's refusal
to provide the reference constitute treatment that was less favourable to Sgt Khan
than if the reference had been provided? The reference would, after all, have
been seriously damaging to Sgt Khan's prospects of obtaining the appointment
that he had applied for.

[76] It cannot, in my opinion, be enough for s 2(1) purposes simply to show
that the complainant has been treated differently. There must also be a quality in
the treatment that enables the complainant reasonably to complain about it. I do
not think, however, that it is appropriate to pursue the treatment and its
consequences down to an end result in order to try and demonstrate that the
complainant is, in the end, better off, or at least no worse off, than he would have
been if he had not been treated differently. I think it suffices if the complainant
can reasonably say that he would have preferred not to have been treated
differently. In the present case Sgt Khan wanted the reference to be given. He
knew it would be likely to contain adverse remarks that would be damaging to
the prospects of his application. But he wanted a reference to be given. And in
normal circumstances, it would have been given. In these circumstances he was,
in my opinion, entitled to regard himself as having been treated 'less favourably'
in that the reference was withheld.

(3) The causation point

[77] Was the reference withheld 'by reason that' Sgt Khan had brought the race
discrimination proceedings? In a strict causative sense it was. If the proceedings had
not been brought the reference would have been given. The proceedings were a
causa sine qua non. But the language used in s 2(1) is not the language of strict
causation. The words 'by reason that' suggest, to my mind, that it is the real

a   reason, the core reason, the *causa causans*, the motive, for the treatment complained of that must be identified.

[78] In *Cornelius v University College of Swansea* [1987] IRLR 141 Bingham LJ put his judicial finger on the critical distinction for s 2(1) purposes between the bringing of discrimination proceedings and the existence of the proceedings. He said (at 145 (para 33)):

b   'There is no reason whatever to suppose that the decisions of the Registrar and his senior assistant on the applicant's requests for a transfer and a hearing under the grievance procedure were influenced in any way by the facts that the appellant had brought proceedings or that those proceedings were under the [Sex Discrimination Act 1975]. The existence of proceedings plainly did

c   influence their decisions … They … wished to defer action until the proceedings were over. But that had, so far as the evidence shows, nothing whatever to do with the appellant's conduct in bringing proceedings under the Act.'

[79] In the present case, it is clear that the refusal to provide the reference was

d   attributable to the existence of the race discrimination proceedings that Sgt Khan had brought. But was the reason for the refusal that Sgt Khan had brought the proceedings? The answer to this question is, in my opinion, apparent from the evidence given by Mr Hussain, force solicitor for West Yorkshire police, in his written statement. He explained that he had advised that 'the provision of a reference … might compromise the chief constable and other respondents'

e   handling of the case against them as brought by the applicant' and said: 'The chief constable would not have been placed in this dilemma had the industrial tribunal hearing been concluded.' He said also:

f   'I do not believe my advice would have been any different had there been other litigation *extant* against an officer or employee for whom a reference had been requested.' (My emphasis.)

Mr Hussain was not cross-examined on this evidence which makes clear that a request for a reference for Sgt Khan would have been complied with once the litigation had concluded. The evidence establishes that the reason for the refusal of the reference was not that Sgt Khan had brought the proceedings but that the

g   proceedings were still on foot and might be prejudiced by the content of the reference if it were given.

[80] In the Court of Appeal ([2000] ICR 1169 at 1178–1179) Lord Woolf MR referred to Bingham LJ's conclusion in *Cornelius'* case that the complainant had failed to show that the college's treatment of her was because she had brought

h   proceedings against the college under the Sex Discrimination Act 1975, but did not go on to apply the same reasoning to the present case. In my respectful opinion this was an error. I would allow the appeal in the present case on the ground that Sgt Khan has failed to show that the reason for the chief constable's refusal to comply with the Norfolk Police Force's request for a reference about

j   him was that he had brought the race discrimination claim. The reason, on the evidence, was that the proceedings were pending. This conclusion, in my opinion, makes sense of the legislation and its purpose. It does not stand in the way of the success of a s 2(1) victimisation claim where, on the evidence, the conclusion is justified that the employer's reason for singling out the complainant for less favourable treatment is that the complainant has brought the proceedings. It does enable justice to be done to an employer who, as in the present case, would otherwise be placed by the pendency of the proceedings in an unacceptable Morton's fork, forced to choose between conduct which risked *a* a s 2(1) complaint and conduct which risked an aggravated damages award if the race discrimination claim should succeed.

[81] Like my noble and learned friends whose opinions I have read and with which I agree, I would allow the appeal and set aside the award of damages to Sgt Khan.

Appeal allowed.

Celia Fox   Barrister.

Petrotrade Inc v Texaco Ltd

a

COURT OF APPEAL, CIVIL DIVISION

LORD WOOLF MR, CLARKE AND LATHAM LJJ

23 MAY 2000

b

Costs – Order for costs – Indemnity costs – Power to award indemnity costs where defendant failing to beat claimant's Pt 36 offer – Principles governing exercise of power – CPR 36.21.

c *Interest – Damages – Award of interest – Enhanced interest – Power to award enhanced interest on damages and costs where defendant failing to beat claimant's Pt 36 offer – Principles governing exercise of power – CPR 36.21.*

(1) CPR 36.21[a] applies where at trial a defendant is held liable for more than the
d proposals contained in a claimant's Pt 36 offer, or the judgment against the defendant is more advantageous to the claimant than those proposals. It requires the court, unless it considers it unjust to do so, (i) to order interest on the whole or any part of any sum of money (excluding interest) awarded to the claimant at a rate not exceeding 10% above base rate for some or all of the period starting with the latest date on which the defendant could have accepted the offer without
e needing the permission of the court, and (ii) to order that the claimant is entitled to costs on the indemnity basis from that date and interest on those costs not exceeding 10% above base rate. That power does not produce penal consequences since an order for indemnity costs does not enable a claimant to receive more costs than he has actually incurred and an order for costs, even when made on an
f indemnity basis, does not compensate a claimant for having to come to court to bring proceedings. Rather, the power is a means of achieving a fairer result for a claimant. If a defendant involves a claimant in proceedings after an offer has been made and, in the event, the result is no more favourable to the defendant than that which would have been achieved if the claimant's offer had been accepted without the need for proceedings, the message of r 36.21 is that, prima facie, it is
g just to make an order for indemnity costs and for interest to be awarded at an enhanced rate (see p 855 *b* to *d*, p 856 *b d e g h*, p 859 *h*, and p 860 *b e*, below).

(2) CPR 36.21 applies only where a defendant is held liable at trial, and accordingly does not apply where he is held liable on an application for summary judgment. In such cases, however, the court has a wide discretion as to both
h interest and costs, and the making and refusal of a Pt 36 offer is a highly material factor in deciding how those discretions should be exercised. It is possible for the court, when exercising its general jurisdiction as to interest, to give a higher rate of interest than the going rate, and it is important that the courts bear that in mind, otherwise claimants may be tempted not to obtain summary judgment in
j cases where it can be obtained with the objective of obtaining higher rates of interest at the conclusion of a trial. The award of interest should not exceed the 10% referred to in r 36.21, and the court will have to take into account all the circumstances in considering whether it will be just to make an order for enhanced interest. If a claim is small, enhanced interest has to be at a higher rate than if the

---

a   Rule 36.21 is set out at p 855 *b* to *g*, below

claim is large, otherwise the additional advantage for the claimant will not be
achieved (see p 855 *g h*, p 858 *c e g*, p 859 *h j*, and p 860 *b d e*, below).   *a*

Case referred to in judgment

Little v George Little Sebire & Co [1999] TLR 798, CA.

Appeal and cross-appeal   *b*

The claimant, Petrotrade Inc, brought proceedings for breach of contract against
the defendant, Texaco Ltd, to recover the unpaid part of the price of 6,000 metric
tons of gasoil that the claimant had supplied to the defendant. The latter had
refused to pay the whole of the price on the ground that the gasoil did not comply
with the contractual specification. On 11 December 1998 Langley J gave
summary judgment for the claimant in the sum of $US140,66·75 plus interest, but   *c*
his decision was reversed on 6 May 1999 by the Court of Appeal (Kennedy, Otton
and Clarke LJJ). The lead judgment was delivered by Clarke LJ. On 21 December
1999, following the service of amended points of claim on 16 August 1999,
Langley J granted the claimant summary judgment under CPR Pt 24 in the same
sum (plus interest) as in his previous judgment, but refused to award it enhanced *d*
interest and indemnity costs. The defendant appealed with permission of the judge
against the order for summary judgment, while the claimant cross-appealed against
the judge's refusal to award enhanced interest and indemnity costs. The facts, so
far as material to the cross-appeal, are set out in the judgment of Lord Woolf MR.

Sara Cockerill (instructed by *Hill Taylor Dickinson*) for the defendant.   *e*
Michael Nolan (instructed by *Davies Johnson & Co*, Plymouth) for the claimant.

Clarke LJ, with whom Latham LJ and Lord Woolf MR agreed, delivered a
judgment dismissing the defendant's appeal. The following judgments were then
delivered in relation to the claimant's cross-appeal, with the paragraph numbering *f*
running continuously from the judgments given on the appeal.

LORD WOOLF MR.

53. The cross-appeal is as to Langley J's decision on 21 December 1999.
Langley J refused to award the claimant enhanced interest and costs on an
indemnity basis, despite the fact that the claimant had made a CPR Pt 36 offer *g*
which was lower than the amount of the judgment in favour of the claimant.

54. The particular significance of the cross-appeal is that it is the first
opportunity which this court has had to consider the general approach to be
adopted by a court where a defendant is ordered to pay a sum in excess of a
claimant's offer under Pt 36.   *h*

55. Part 36 is one of the cornerstones of the reforms of procedure made by the
CPR. Part 36 makes significant changes to the previous practice and procedure
relating to payments into and out of court under what was RSC Ord 22. The first
of these changes is that offers to settle can be made before as well as after the
commencement of proceedings. In the case of both, the court is required to take *j*
into account an offer when making any order as to costs (see r 36.10). Secondly,
offers to settle can be made by any party to the proceedings. In particular, as in
this case, they may now be made by a claimant.

56. A Pt 36 offer may relate to the whole claim, to part of it or to any issue that
arises in the proceedings (see r 36.5(2)). In addition a Pt 36 offer is not confined
to money claims. However, if a defendant's offer includes an offer to settle a money

a claim, a payment into court is required once proceedings have started (see r 36.3). There are procedural requirements which have to be complied with, otherwise the offer will not strictly speaking constitute a Pt 36 offer. This does not prevent a party making an offer in whatever manner that party chooses, but if that offer is not in accordance with Pt 36, 'it will only have the consequences specified' in Pt 36 'if the court so orders' (r 36.1).

b   57. This appeal is primarily concerned with r 36.21. The terms of that rule are:

> '(1) This rule applies where at trial—(a) a defendant is held liable for more; or (b) the judgment against a defendant is more advantageous to the claimant, than the proposals contained in a claimant's Part 36 offer.

c
> (2) The court may order interest on the whole or part of any sum of money (excluding interest) awarded to the claimant at a rate not exceeding 10% above base rate for some or all of the period starting with the latest date on which the defendant could have accepted the offer without needing the permission of the court.

d
> (3) The court may also order that the claimant is entitled to—(a) his costs on the indemnity basis from the latest date when the defendant could have accepted the offer without needing the permission of the court; and (b) interest on those costs at a rate not exceeding 10% above base rate.

> (4) Where this rule applies, the court will make the orders referred to in paragraphs (2) and (3) unless it considers it unjust to do so.

e
> (Rule 36.12 sets out the latest date when the defendant could have accepted the offer)

> (5) In considering whether it would be unjust to make the orders referred to in paragraphs (2) and (3) above, the court will take into account all the circumstances of the case including—(a) the terms of any Part 36 offer;

f
> (b) the stage in the proceedings when any Part 36 offer or Part 36 payment was made; (c) the information available to the parties at the time when the Part 36 offer or Part 36 payment was made; and (d) the conduct of the parties with regard to the giving or refusing to give information for the purposes of enabling the offer or payment into court to be made or evaluated.

> (6) The power of the court under this rule is in addition to any other power

g it may have to award interest.'

    58. It will be noted that the opening words of r 36.21 are: 'This rule applies *where at trial*' (my emphasis). Those words are not to be ignored. They mean that the rule does not apply where, as in this case, summary judgment is given under

h CPR Pt 24. Rule 24.1 sets out a procedure by which the court may decide a claim or a particular issue 'without a trial'. This may seem surprising, but it is to be borne in mind that a court always has the power to order costs on an indemnity basis. The court also has the general power to award interest at such a rate as it considers just. Furthermore, if proceedings are disposed of summarily this will

j normally be at an early stage in the proceedings so that questions of costs and interest will not be as significant as they would otherwise be.

    59. The provisions of r 36.21(2) and (3) are important because without them Pt 36 offers would be of no value to a claimant. Rule 36.21(2) and (3) create the incentive for a claimant to make a Pt 36 offer. It is for this reason that para (4) of the rule is worded in terms which requires the court to make the orders referred to in paras (2) and (3) 'unless it considers it unjust to do so'.

60. It should be appreciated, even in cases to which para (4) applies, that the court retains a considerable discretion as to the period during which and the rate *a* at which interest should be payable.

61. The reason for r 36.21 not applying where there is no trial is probably a decision of the Rules Committee that paras (2) and (3) should not apply to proceedings which are a form of debt collecting. By making a Pt 36 offer, a claimant could put himself in a position where indemnity costs and enhanced *b* interest orders could be made when it would not be appropriate.

62. However, it would be wrong to regard the rule as producing penal consequences. An order for indemnity costs does not enable a claimant to receive more costs than he has incurred. Its practical effect is to avoid his costs being assessed at a lesser figure. When assessing costs on the standard basis the court will only allow costs 'which are proportionate to the matters in issue' and 'resolve *c* any doubt which it may have as to whether costs were reasonably incurred or reasonable and proportionate in amount in favour of the paying party'. On the other hand, where the costs are assessed on an indemnity basis, the issue of proportionality does not have to be considered. The court only considers whether the costs were unreasonably incurred or for an unreasonable amount. The court will then *d* resolve any doubt in favour of the receiving party. Even on an indemnity basis, however, the receiving party is restricted to recovering only the amount of costs which have been incurred (see CPR 44.4 and 44.5).

63. The ability of the court to award costs on an indemnity basis and interest at an enhanced rate should not be regarded as penal because orders for costs, even when made on an indemnity basis, never actually compensate a claimant for *e* having to come to court to bring proceedings. The very process of being involved in court proceedings inevitably has an impact on a claimant, whether he is a private individual or a multi-national corporation. A claimant would be better off had he not become involved in court proceedings. Part of the culture of the CPR is to encourage parties to avoid proceedings unless it is unreasonable for them to *f* do otherwise. In the case of an individual, proceedings necessarily involve inconvenience and frequently involve anxiety and distress. These are not taken into account when assessing costs on the normal basis. In the case of a corporation, corporation senior officials and other staff inevitably will be diverted from their normal duties as a consequence of the proceedings. The disruption this causes to a corporation is not recoverable under an order for costs. *g*

64. The power to order indemnity costs or higher rate interest is a means of achieving a fairer result for a claimant. If a defendant involves a claimant in proceedings after an offer has been made, and in the event, the result is no more favourable to the defendant than that which would have been achieved if the claimant's offer had been accepted without the need for those proceedings, the *h* message of r 36.21 is that, prima facie, it is just to make an indemnity order for costs and for interest at an enhanced rate to be awarded. However, the indemnity order need not be for the entire proceedings nor, as I have already indicated, need the award of interest be for a particular period or at a particular rate. It must not however exceed the figure of 10% referred to in Pt 36. *j*

65. There are circumstances where a just result is no order for costs or no interest even where the award exceeds an offer made by a claimant. Rule 36.21 does no more than indicate the order which is to be made by the court unless it considers it is unjust to make that order. The general message of r 36.21, when it applies, is that the court will usually order a higher rate of interest than the going rate. As to what the additional rate of interest should be, it is not possible to give

specific guidance. Reference for general guidance has to be made to the terms of r 36.21 and, in particular, to the provisions of para (5).

66. Having made those remarks, I turn shortly to the facts of the appeal in so far as they are relevant to the question of costs and interest. The important starting point is the fact that Petrotrade Inc, the claimant, made a Pt 36 offer on 25 March 1999. That offer was in the sum of $US 7,000 less than the sum actually recovered by the claimant. Although that offer was made by the claimant before *b* the CPR came into force on 26 April 1999, it was still a matter which a court would be entitled to take into account in exercising its discretion as to costs. I accept the submission of Mr Nolan that it is a relevant circumstance, though the offer is not technically a Pt 36 offer.

67. Because the claimant was concerned as to whether an offer made prior to *c* the commencement of the CPR would be effective, on 26 April 1999 a further offer was made by them in the same terms. It is significant to note that the judgment of the Court of Appeal on the first appeal by the defendant (to which Clarke LJ referred in his judgment on this appeal) was given on 6 May 1999, almost precisely 12 months ago. This was followed by amended points of claim *d* which were served by the claimant on 16 August 1999. The next relevant date is 21 December 1999 when the second judgment in favour of the claimant was given by Langley J.

68. The offers to which I have referred are contained in two letters from the claimant's solicitors to the defendant's solicitors of 25 March 1999 and 26 April 1999 in the following terms.

e 69. 25 March 1999:

> 'Dear Sirs
>
> We note that this action will fall within the transitional arrangements for the new Civil Procedure Rules and therefore come under Practice Direction *f* 51. Having taken instructions from our client, and in an effort to resolve this matter, our clients are prepared to make a formal "offer of settlement" in accordance with part 36 of the Practice Directions. Our client is prepared to accept the sum of US$142,942.15, inclusive of interest up to the date of this offer, and costs. This offer takes into account any counterclaim. In the event that this offer is not accepted, we reserve the right to bring a copy of this *g* letter to the Court's attention on the issues of interest and costs. This offer is open for 21 days from the date of this letter. After 21 days, the offer may only be accepted if liability for costs is agreed or with the permission of the Court.'

70–71. 26 April 1999:

h
> 'Dear Sirs,
>
> Without prejudice to the offer contained in our letter of 25th March, in the event Part 36 offers in settlement are not effective prior to 26th April, we hereby repeat the offer contained in our letter of 25th March. Our client is prepared to accept the sum of US$142,942.15, inclusive of interest up to the *j* date of this offer, and costs. This offer takes into account any counterclaim. In the event that this offer is not accepted, we reserve the right to bring a copy of this letter as well as that of 25th March to the Court's attention on the issues of interest and costs.'

72. Both the offers were followed by a summary judgment granted by Langley J. In accordance with what I have said earlier in this judgment, because they were

summary judgments means that the terms of r 36.21 did not apply. It is still necessary, however, to consider whether, if r 36.21 did or did not apply to the judgment, this is a case where the judge in the exercise of his discretion should have made an indemnity order for costs or an order in relation to interest which would be above the normal rate.

73. So far as interest is concerned in commercial cases, the going rate is now 1% above base rate. That was the rate of interest which the judge awarded, adjusted for the sum involved being in dollars. In the ordinary way, in the Commercial Court, the practice of awarding interest at the going rate should continue, notwithstanding the CPR's introduction, until the present practice is shown to be no longer appropriate.

74. Although r 36.21 has no application, where an offer is made by a claimant in the present circumstances, it is possible for the court, when exercising its general jurisdiction as to interest, to give a higher rate of interest than the going rate. It is important that courts bear this in mind otherwise claimants might be tempted not to obtain summary judgment in cases where it could be obtained with the objective of obtaining higher rates of interest at the conclusion of a trial. That would be entirely contrary to the whole ethos and policy of the CPR. I am confident that if it was shown this had occurred, the court would use its powers to ensure that a claimant did not benefit by any such tactic.

75. If it is accepted that a court has power to depart from the going rate because of a claimant's offer, the question then arises as to what additional interest it would be appropriate to offer? Quite clearly it should not exceed the 10% referred to in r 36.21. The court would have to take into account all the circumstances in considering whether it would be just to make an order of enhanced interest. Those include the matters which are set out in r 36.21(5).

76. Looking at the facts of this case, it is relevant that no one suggests that the defendant was otherwise than bona fide in disputing the claim. It may have been wrong as to its assessment of the legal position but it is not a situation where the conduct of the proceedings justifies any specific criticism. If there is cause to criticise a party, then, in accord with the policy of the CPR, I would not say that this would justify increasing the rate of enhanced interest to punish that party. It would, however, mean because the party had behaved in that way, the party had forfeited the opportunity of achieving a reduction in the rate of additional interest payable. This is not the position.

77. The amount of the claim is also a relevant factor. If a claim is small, enhanced interest has to be at a higher rate than if the claim is large, otherwise the additional advantage for the claimant will not be achieved. In this case the sum involved was neither particularly large nor particularly modest. The conclusion that I would come to is that, if the matter was one for my discretion at first instance, I would award in the region of 4% above base rate for the appropriate period.

78. In considering the appropriate period in this case, I would have taken into account the fact that the claimant had not advanced their case in a satisfactory manner. I would take that course not because of any pleading error but because of the requirement that a claimant should provide the other parties with the information which they need in order to evaluate the offer which has been made.

79. So far as pleading points are concerned, we were helpfully referred to the decision of Mr David Foskett QC, sitting as a deputy High Court judge in the case of *Little v George Little Sebire & Co* [1999] TLR 798. In that case Mr Foskett

a indicated that the court should take as the starting point 10% above base. This is not an approach I would endorse. However, he also said:

> '2.6 If one accepts for this purpose the premise that, as originally pleaded, the claim arising from scheme 2 would have failed, there are, it seems to me, two relevant questions when it comes to the issue of costs. (1) If it had been pleaded correctly, would it have succeeded? (2) If it had been pleaded
b correctly, would the defendant's attitude to the litigation have changed?'

80. Mr Foskett then answered those questions respectively, 'Yes' and 'No'. This is the approach the court should have adopted here where they can be answered similarly. I would have taken that into account in deciding the period of interest which would be appropriate. Having regard to the history described by Clarke LJ
c in his judgment on the appeal, the appropriate period for enhanced interest which I would regard as right in this case would have been 12 months.

81. Turning to the question of indemnity orders for costs, I would also have made an order for indemnity costs commencing after the judgment was given by Clarke LJ in the Court of Appeal on the first occasion. I would have regarded it
d as appropriate to have said in this case that from about the time of the first Pt 36 offer by the claimant, indemnity costs should be ordered.

82. In my remarks so far, I have indicated the order I would have made, but that does not dispose of the cross-appeal. The question arises as to whether it can appropriately be said that, on the arguments which were advanced before him in the court below, the judge erred in the exercise of his discretion. The argument
e before the judge was wholly different from the argument which has been advanced in this court. In particular, the applicability of r 36.21 was not raised. It seems to me that it would be wrong to interfere with a judge's decision on questions of discretion as to costs where the judge has not had placed before him the arguments which would, perhaps, have compelled him to take a different
f view.

83. The fact that the court has power to make the orders to which I have referred in this judgment should not be used as justification for appeals on questions of costs where the judge has done his best, as I believe the judge did in this case, to come to the right answer as a matter of discretion on the material which was before him.
g 84. Accordingly, while I have given what I hope is some indication as to the approach to be taken to questions such as those canvassed before us in the future, in this case I have come to the conclusion that the cross-appeal should be dismissed.

h CLARKE LJ.
85. I agree with the judgment and order of Lord Woolf MR, and wish to add only a few words of my own. In a case to which CPR 36.21 does not apply because the defendant is not held liable 'at trial' within the meaning of r 36.21(1)(a), I do not think it is appropriate to apply the subsequent paragraphs
j of that rule as if the rule did apply. However, the court has a wide discretion as to both interest and costs. I entirely agree that the making and refusal of a Pt 36 offer is a highly material factor in deciding how those discretions should be exercised.

86. Although, as so often, everything will depend on the circumstances of the case, justice will ordinarily require that factor to be reflected in both the order for costs and in the award of interest. In the instant case I entirely agree with the

approach outlined by Lord Woolf MR. In particular I agree with the period of
12 months to which he referred on the footing that the 12 months began at about   *a*
the time of the previous judgment of the Court of Appeal. I further agree with
the order proposed.

LATHAM LJ.

87. I also agree. I would associate myself with what Clarke LJ has indicated   *b*
about the length of the period in question and I would take the beginning of the
appropriate period for enhanced interest to be about May of last year.

88. As far as the issue of principle is concerned in relation to the application of
the matters set out in CPR 36.21 to situations where a case is disposed of other
than at trial, I would merely add that it is clear from r 44.3(4) that the CPR itself
acknowledges that the court should have regard to a Pt 36 offer in the situation   *c*
such as this. Rule 44.3(4) reads:

> 'In deciding what order (if any) to make about costs, the court must have
> regard to all the circumstances, including—(a) the conduct of all the parties;
> (b) whether a party has succeeded on part of his case, even if he has not been
> wholly successful; and (c) any payment into court or admissible offer to   *d*
> settle made by a party which is drawn to the court's attention (whether or
> not made in accordance with Part 36).'

89. It seems to me that, by analogy, it is right for the court to take into account
the fact of an offer under Pt 36 in a situation where r 36.21 does not strictly apply.

90. For those reasons, I agree with Lord Woolf MR and Clarke LJ and agree   *e*
with the orders proposed.

Appeal and cross-appeal dismissed.

James Wilson   Barrister (NZ).

McPhilemy v Times Newspapers Ltd and others (No 2)

[2001] EWCA Civ 933

COURT OF APPEAL, CIVIL DIVISION

SIMON BROWN, CHADWICK AND LONGMORE LJJ

12, 20 JUNE 2001

Costs – Order for costs – Indemnity costs – Power to award indemnity costs where defendant failing to beat claimant's Pt 36 offer – Purpose of power – CPR 36.21(3).

Interest – Damages – Award of interest – Enhanced interest – Power to award enhanced interest on damages and costs where defendant failing to beat claimant's Pt 36 offer – Whether power to be exercised in relation to jury awards in defamation cases – CPR 36.21(2).

In May 1996 the claimant, M, brought an action for libel against the defendants in relation to allegations made in a newspaper article. In December 1999, 21 days before the trial was due to begin, M made an offer under CPR Pt 36, offering to settle the case in return, inter alia, for a payment of £50,000 damages for the hurt and distress caused to him by the article. Under Pt 36, the defendants had 21 days to accept that offer without requiring the permission of the court. They failed to do so, and at trial the jury awarded M general damages of £145,000. In cases where, at trial, a defendant was held liable for more than the proposals contained in a claimant's Pt 36 offer, CPR 36.21[a] required the court, unless it considered it unjust to do so, (i) to order interest on the whole or any part of the sum of money awarded to the claimant at a rate not exceeding 10% above base rate for some or all of the period starting with the latest date on which the defendant could have accepted the offer without needing the permission of the court (r 36.21(2)), and (ii) to order that the claimant was entitled to costs on the indemnity basis from that date (r 36.21(3)(a)) and to interest on those costs not exceeding 10% above base rate (r 36.21(3)(b)). M duly made an application under r 36.21 for enhanced interest and indemnity costs, but the judge concluded that it would have been unjust to make an order under either para (2) or (3). In giving his reasons for refusing to award enhanced interest, the judge relied on the fact that a jury's award in a libel action traditionally took account of everything down to the moment of verdict, including aggravation caused by the defendant's conduct of the trial. In respect of his refusal to award indemnity costs, the judge referred, inter alia, to the proximity of the trial when the offer had been made. He also stated that an order for the payment of costs on the indemnity basis carried some stigma, was bound to be interpreted as an indication of the court's disapproval of a defendant's conduct and might be thought to carry punitive overtones. M appealed.

Held – (1) An order for indemnity costs under CPR 36.21(3) was not penal and carried no stigma or implied disapproval of the defendant's conduct. It was clear from the structure and language of r 36.21, that an order for the payment of costs

---

a   Rule 36.21 is set out at [2], below

on an indemnity basis from the latest date when the defendant could have
accepted the offer without needing the permission of the court was the order
which the court could be expected to make in a case where a claimant who had
made a Pt 36 offer was, nevertheless, obliged to proceed to trial—because the
defendant had not accepted the offer—and then beat his own offer at trial. In those
circumstances, it was only where the court considered that such an order would be
unjust that it was permitted to refuse an order for the payment of costs on an
indemnity basis. Properly understood, the making of such an order in a case to
which r 36.21 applied indicated only that the court, when addressing the task
which it was set by that rule, had not considered it unjust to make the order for
indemnity costs for which the rule provided. It followed that the basis on which
the judge had exercised his discretion was flawed, and the Court of Appeal was
therefore required to form its own view on the question whether it would be
unjust to make the orders under r 36.21(2) and (3) (see [9]–[11], [27], [28], below);
Petrotrade Inc v Texaco Ltd [2001] 4 All ER 853 applied.

(2) Although the court had to take into account the stage of the proceedings
at which a Pt 36 offer was made, the fact that such an offer had been made in the
month before the trial could not of itself and without more be a reason for
holding that it was unjust to make orders under CPR 36.21(2) and (3). It was
important to keep in mind that the orders for which those paragraphs provided
had effect only from the latest date when the defendant could have accepted the
offer without needing the permission of the court. Although there might be
circumstances where it would be unjust to make the orders because the offer was
made so late that a defendant had no proper opportunity to consider it, or
because the costs already incurred were such that there was little to be saved by
bringing the proceedings to an end at that stage, that was not the position in the
instant case. The fact that the offer had been made at a late stage of proceedings
did not support the conclusion that it would be unjust to make the orders under
r 36.21(2) and (3) (see [12], [27], [28], below).

(3) The power to award interest at an enhanced rate under CPR 36.21(2) should
not be used to award interest in a case where it had to be assumed that the jury,
in reaching their award, had taken into account the anxiety, inconvenience and
distress of defamation proceedings. In such circumstances, an order to pay
interest on the amount of the award, in respect of any period prior to its date,
would risk introducing an element of double compensation and cross the boundary
which separated compensation from punishment. Accordingly, it would be
inconsistent with the purpose of the power conferred by para (2), namely to
enable the court, in a case to which r 36.21 applied, to redress the element of
perceived unfairness, otherwise inherent in the legal process, which arose from
the fact that damages, costs and statutory interest would not compensate the
successful claimant for the inconvenience, anxiety and distress of having to resort
to and pursue proceedings which he had sought to avoid by an offer to settle (see
[17]–[21], [27], [28], below).

(4) In contrast, an order under CPR 36.21(3) for indemnity costs did not give
rise to a risk of double compensation. The purpose of the power under para (3)(a)
was to enable the court to address the perceived unfairness arising from the fact
that an award of costs on the standard basis would almost invariably lead to the
successful claimant recovering less than the costs which he had to pay to his
solicitor. In reaching their award of damages, the jury were not concerned with
costs, and there was no reason to think that their award took any account of the
probable shortfall if costs were subsequently ordered on the standard basis. It

a followed in the instant case that there was no injustice in making an order under r 36.21(3)(a) that M was entitled to his costs on an indemnity basis from the latest date when the Pt 36 offer could have been accepted without the permission of the court. Nor was there any injustice, in principle, in an order under para (3)(b) for the payment of interest on costs which would be made the subject of the order under para (3)(a). The purpose of the power to award interest on costs under that

b paragraph was to redress the element of perceived unfairness which arose from the general rule that interest was not allowed on costs paid before judgment. Accordingly, the court would order payment of interest at 4% over base rate on the costs to which the order applied, from the date on which the work had been done or liability for disbursements had been incurred. However, paras (2) and (3) were not intended to confer on the court powers to vary the rate at which interest

c was payable on a judgment debt. Thus the court had no power to make an order under para (2) for the payment of interest on the amount of the jury's award in respect of any period after judgment, or under para (3)(b) for the payment of interest on costs in respect of any such period. It followed that M's appeal would be allowed to the extent indicated (see [22]–[25], below).

d
Cases referred to in judgments

Hunt v R M Douglas (Roofing) Ltd [1988] 3 All ER 823, [1990] 1 AC 398, [1988] 3 WLR 975, HL.

Petrotrade Inc v Texaco Ltd [2001] 4 All ER 853, CA.

Thomas v Bunn, Wilson v Graham, Lea v British Aerospace plc [1991] 1 All ER 193,

e [1991] 1 AC 362, [1991] 2 WLR 27, HL.

Wall v Lefever [1998] 1 FCR 605, CA.

Cases also cited or referred to in skeleton arguments

All-In-One Design & Build Ltd v Motcomb Estates Ltd [2000] TLR 260.

f *Ford v GKR Construction Ltd* [2000] 1 All ER 802, [2000] 1 WLR 1397, CA.

Maltez v Lewis (1999) 16 Const LJ 65.

Phonographic Performance Ltd v AEI Rediffusion Music Ltd [1999] 2 All ER 299, [1999] 1 WLR 1507, CA.

Tanfern Ltd v Cameron-MacDonald [2000] 2 All ER 801, [2000] 1 WLR 1311, CA.

g
Cross-appeal

By writ issued on 3 May 1996 the claimant, Sean McPhilemy, a journalist and managing director of Box Productions Ltd, sought damages for libel from the defendants, Times Newspapers Ltd, Liam Clarke and Andrew Neil, in relation to an article published in the Sunday Times on 9 May 1993 concerning a television

h programme, 'The Committee', produced by Box Productions and broadcast on Channel 4 on 2 October 1991, which had alleged the existence in Northern Ireland of a committee known as 'The Central Co-ordinating Committee' (The Committee) whose members were alleged to be co-conspirators in the assassination of suspected Republicans by Loyalist paramilitary organisations. The article

j claimed that the programme was a hoax and suggested that the quality of its sources was so poor that no respectable broadcaster would have considered putting it out. On 21 December 1999 the claimant made, under CPR Pt 36, an offer to settle the action for, inter alia, a payment of £50,000 damages for the hurt and distress caused by the article. At a pre-trial review on the same day, he produced a document, purporting to be a notice under CPR Pt 14, stating that for the purpose of the proceedings he did not challenge the matters pleaded in para 10A of the defendants' particulars of justification—namely that 'none of those identified ... has ever conspired to commit any murders and are not members of *a* any organisation such as The Committee described in the programme'—and that he did not put the defendants to proof of the same. However, that notice was subsequently withdrawn following a ruling by Eady J. On 30 March 2000, following a 38-day trial before Eady J and a jury and five days of jury deliberations, judgment was given for the claimant, on the jury's unanimous verdict, for *b* general damages of £145,000. In giving their verdict, the jury found (1) that the article was defamatory of the claimant, (2) that the defendants had not proved on the balance of probabilities that there was no such Committee as described in the programme, (3) that they had not proved that the claimant had deliberately set out to mislead viewers as to the case put forward in the programme for the existence of The Committee, (4) that they had not proved on the balance of *c* probabilities that the claimant had had been reckless as to the truth of the programme's allegations concerning the existence or activities of The Committee and (5) that they had not succeeded in proving that the article had been substantially accurate. The defendants appealed against the jury's award with permission of Eady J on the ground that the jury's second finding had been *d* perverse, while the claimant cross-appealed against the judge's refusal to make orders, under CPR 36.21(2) and (3), for the payment of enhanced interest on the award and for indemnity costs. On 12 June 2001 the Court of Appeal ([2001] EWCA Civ 871, [2001] All ER (D) 90 (Jun)) dismissed the defendants' appeal and then proceeded to hear argument on the cross-appeal. The facts, so far as material to the cross-appeal, are set out in the judgment of Chadwick LJ.	*e*

James Price QC and Matthew Nicklin (instructed by Bindman and Partners) for the claimant.
Andrew Caldecott QC and Caroline Addy (instructed by H₂O Henry Hepworths) for the defendants.

f

Cur adv vult

20 June 2001. The following judgments were delivered.

CHADWICK LJ (giving the first judgment at the invitation of Simon Brown LJ). *g*
[1] The underlying facts which have given rise to these proceedings are set out in the judgment of Simon Brown LJ on the principal appeal. It is unnecessary for me to rehearse them. For the reasons which we gave on 12 June 2001, we dismissed the appeal of Times Newspapers Ltd and others (to whom, for convenience, I will refer in this judgment collectively as The Times or the defendants) against *h* the order made by Eady J on 31 March 2000. We have now heard argument on the claimant's cross-appeal against so much of that order as dismissed his application under CPR 36.21. It is to that cross-appeal that the judgment which I now give relates.
[2] CPR Pt 36 contains rules about offers to settle and the consequences—in particular, the consequences in relation to costs—where an offer to settle is made *j* in accordance with its provisions. Rule 36.21 is in these terms:

'(1) This rule applies where at trial—(a) a defendant is held liable for more; or (b) the judgment against a defendant is more advantageous to the claimant, than the proposals contained in a claimant's Part 36 offer.

(2) The court may order interest on the whole or part of any sum of money (excluding interest) awarded to a claimant at a rate not exceeding 10% above base rate for some or all of the period starting with the latest date on which the defendant could have accepted the offer without needing the permission of the court.

(3) The court may also order that the claimant is entitled to—(a) his costs on the indemnity basis from the latest date when the defendant could have accepted the offer without needing the permission of the court; and (b) interest on those costs at a rate not exceeding 10% above base rate.

(4) Where this rule applies, the court will make the orders referred to in paragraphs (2) and (3) unless it considers it unjust to do so …

(5) In considering whether it would be unjust to make the orders referred to in paragraphs (2) and (3) above, the court will take into account all the circumstances of the case including—(a) the terms of any Part 36 offer; (b) the stage in the proceedings when any Part 36 offer or Part 36 payment was made; (c) the information available to the parties at the time when the Part 36 offer or Part 36 payment was made; and (d) the conduct of the parties with regard to the giving or refusing to give information for the purposes of enabling the offer or payment into court to be evaluated.

(6) Where the court awards interest under this rule and also awards interest on the same sum and for the same period under any other power, the total rate of interest may not exceed 10% above base rate.'

In that context and for the purposes of paras (2) and (3) of the rule, 'the latest date [on which/when] the defendant could have accepted the offer without needing the permission of the court' is prescribed by CPR 36.12. Where the offer is made not less than 21 days before the start of the trial, it means the date not later than 21 days after the offer was made.

[3] It follows that, in a case where the claimant who has made a Pt 36 offer (which has not been accepted) is successful at trial, the court is required to consider whether the defendant has been held liable for more than the amount for which the claimant has offered to settle, or whether the judgment against the defendant is more advantageous to the claimant than the proposals contained in the offer to settle. If the outcome of the trial is that, to adopt the phrase commonly used in this context, the claimant has 'beaten' his own Pt 36 offer, then r 36.21 applies and the court is required to make an order for the payment of interest under para (2), and for the payment of costs under para (3), unless it considers it unjust to do so (see para (4)).

[4] The offer relied upon by the claimant in the present case is contained in a letter dated 21 December 1999 which was sent by his solicitors to the solicitors acting for The Times. The terms of settlement proposed in that letter were as follows:

'1. A payment of £50,000 damages to our client for the hurt and distress caused by the article; 2. damages for the financial losses incurred by our client to be assessed if not agreed; 3. a retraction and apology to be placed prominently in the pages of the Sunday Times in appropriate terms to be agreed with us on our client's behalf; 4. a statement in open court; 5. an undertaking not to repeat the libel; 6. all costs incurred up to the date of receipt of notice of acceptance of the offer as per rule 36.14.'

The letter concluded with a statement that those proposals were intended as a Pt 36 offer; that the offer would remain open for acceptance for a period of 21 days; and that the offer related to the whole of the claim in the action. The period of 21 days from 21 December 1999 came to an end on 11 January 2000.

[5] CPR 36.5 sets out the requirements, as to form and content, which must be satisfied if proposals are to be treated as comprised in a Pt 36 offer for the purposes, inter alia, of r 36.21. It was not suggested before the judge—and it has not been submitted in this court—that those requirements were not satisfied. Nor has it been suggested that the other requirements in para (1) of r 36.21 were not satisfied. It is accepted that the fact that the claimant was awarded £145,000 by the jury in respect of general damages, as against the amount (£50,000) which he had offered to accept in the letter of 21 December 1999, suffices to satisfy sub-para (a) of that paragraph. It is unnecessary, therefore, to consider whether the judgment was more advantageous to the claimant than, for example, the lesser amount of general damages coupled with a retraction and an apology would have been. This is not a case in which it is said that sub-para (b) of r 36.21(1) has any relevance.

[6] It follows, therefore, that the judge was required to make orders under paras (2) and (3) of r 36.21 unless satisfied that it was unjust to do so. The judge was satisfied that it would be unjust to make an order under para (2) for the payment of interest on the general damages awarded by the jury. He explained why he took that view in a short passage of the judgment which he gave on 30 March 2000:

'It is traditionally the case that the jury's award in libel takes account of everything down to the moment of their verdict, including any aggravation caused by the defendant's conduct of the trial. Accordingly, it has never been the case that damages for libel carry interest. It seems to me that it would be unjust to award interest on the sums fixed by the jury, whether from 13 January or at all. Special damages might well be treated differently in this respect, but that does not arise today.'

He was satisfied, also, that it would be unjust to make an order under para (3) of r 36.21 for indemnity costs. He referred to 'the unique circumstances of this case'. He expressed doubt whether, as a matter of construction, there was power under sub-para (b) of para (3) to make an order for the payment of interest on costs unless the costs themselves were the subject of an order under sub-para (a) of that paragraph. But, if there were power to do so, that is to say, power to order the payment of interest on costs which were to be assessed on the standard basis, he did not think it appropriate to exercise that power.

[7] There is no doubt that the question whether or not it was unjust to make orders under paras (2) and (3) of r 36.21 was a question for the judge to determine in the exercise of his discretion. In exercising that discretion he was obliged to take into account all the circumstances of the case; including, in particular, the specific matters referred to in para (5) of that rule. If the judge took into account the matters which he ought to have taken into account, and left out of account matters which he ought not to have taken into account, it would be wrong in principle for this court to interfere with his decision. It could only do so if satisfied that the decision was so perverse that the judge must have fallen into error. This court must respect the judge's exercise of the discretion which has been entrusted to him. The court must resist the temptation to substitute its own view for that of the judge unless satisfied that his discretion has been exercised on a basis which is

a wrong in law; or that the conclusion which he has reached is so plainly wrong that his exercise of the discretion entrusted to him must be regarded as flawed.

[8] I turn, then, to examine the basis upon which the judge reached his conclusion that it would be unjust to make any order under paras (2) and (3) of r 36.21. He identified four reasons which may be summarised as follows: (i) the proximity of the trial when the offer was made; (ii) the fact that the defendants b were funding the preparations for trial of the claimant's action, in particular, in connection with the compilation and copying of the trial bundles; (iii) what the judge described as 'an unusual public interest element', in that the defendants were taking on the burden of proving that the committee of alleged conspirators did not exist; and (iv) the fact, described by the judge as being 'of great significance', that the Pt 36 offer, contained in the letter of 21 December 1999, required the c defendants to publish a retraction and apology in their newspaper and also to join in a statement in open court. But, having identified, and elaborated upon, those reasons, the judge said:

d   'The question is whether in these unusual circumstances I consider that it would be unjust to follow the modern presumption in favour of indemnity costs, which still carries something of a stigma and is bound to be interpreted as an indication of the court's disapproval of the defendant's conduct.'

That passage reflected an observation earlier in the judgment, that an order for indemnity costs 'might be thought to carry punitive overtones'.

e   [9] In my view the judge was wrong to take into account—as, plainly, he did—his belief that an order for the payment of costs on the indemnity basis made under r 36.21(3) implied disapproval by the court of a defendant's conduct; carried some stigma; or could properly be regarded as punitive. It is, to my mind, clear from the structure and language of r 36.21, and, in particular, from para (4) of that rule, that an order for the payment of costs on an indemnity basis (from f the latest date when the defendant could have accepted the offer without needing the permission of the court) is the order which the court can be expected to make in a case where a claimant who has made a Pt 36 offer is, nevertheless, obliged to proceed to trial, because the defendant does not accept the offer, and then beats his own offer at trial. In those circumstances, it is only where the court considers g that such an order would be unjust that it is permitted to refuse an order for the payment of costs on an indemnity basis. To make the order carries no implied disapproval of the defendant's conduct; nor any stigma. Properly understood, the making of such an order in a case to which r 36.21 applies indicates only that the court, when addressing the task which it is set by that rule, has not considered it unjust to make the order for indemnity costs for which the rule provides.

h   [10] In *Petrotrade Inc v Texaco Ltd* [2001] 4 All ER 853 this court explained why an order for the payment of indemnity costs, made under r 36.21, should not be regarded as penal. Lord Woolf MR, with whom the other members of the court (Clarke and Latham LJJ) agreed, said (at 856):

j   '62. However, it would be wrong to regard the rule as producing penal consequences. An order for indemnity costs does not enable a claimant to receive more costs than he has incurred. Its practical effect is to avoid his costs being assessed at a lesser figure. When assessing costs on the standard basis the court will only allow costs "which are proportionate to the matters in issue" and [will] "resolve any doubt which it may have as to whether costs were reasonably incurred or reasonable and proportionate in amount in favour of the paying party". On the other hand, where the costs are assessed on an indemnity basis, the issue of proportionality does not have to be *a* considered. The court only considers whether the costs were unreasonably incurred or for an unreasonable amount. The court will then resolve any doubt in favour of the receiving party. Even on an indemnity basis, however, the receiving party is restricted to recovering only the amount of costs which have been incurred (see CPR 44.4 and 44.5). *b*

63. The ability of the court to award costs on an indemnity basis and interest at an enhanced rate should not be regarded as penal because orders for costs, even when made on an indemnity basis, never actually compensate a claimant for having to come to court to bring proceedings. The very process of being involved in court proceedings inevitably has an impact on a claimant, whether he is a private individual or a multi-national corporation. A *c* claimant would be better off had he not become involved in court proceedings. Part of the culture of the CPR is to encourage parties to avoid proceedings unless it is unreasonable for them to do otherwise. In the case of an individual, proceedings necessarily involve inconvenience and frequently involve anxiety and distress. These are not taken into account when assessing costs *d* on the normal basis. In the case of a corporation, corporation senior officials and other staff inevitably will be diverted from their normal duties as a consequence of the proceedings. The disruption this causes to a corporation is not recoverable under an order for costs.

64. The power to order indemnity costs or higher rate interest is a means of achieving a fairer result for a claimant. If a defendant involves a claimant *e* in proceedings after an offer has been made, and in the event, the result is no more favourable to the defendant than that which would have been achieved if the claimant's offer had been accepted without the need for those proceedings, the message of r 36.21 is that, prima facie, it is just to make an indemnity order for costs and for interest at an enhanced rate to be awarded. *f* However, the indemnity order need not be for the entire proceedings nor, as I have already indicated, need the award of interest be for a particular period or at a particular rate. It must not however exceed the figure of 10% referred to in Pt 36.'

The guidance contained in those paragraphs was not available until the end of *g* May 2000; in particular, it was not available to Eady J on 30 March 2000, when he made his order in the present case.

[11] It follows that this is a case in which the basis on which the judge exercised his discretion can now be seen to have been flawed. The judge thought, wrongly, that the order for indemnity costs which he was invited to make under *h* r 36.21 was punitive in nature; and would be seen as indicating some measure of disapproval of the defendants' conduct which he did not regard as merited and which he did not intend. Those considerations were unfounded and should have been left out of account. This, then, is a case in which this court is entitled, indeed, bound, to set aside the view reached by the judge; and to form its own view on the question whether it would be unjust to make the orders for which *j* paras (2) and (3) of r 36.21 provide.

[12] The Times, as respondents to this cross-appeal, rely on the factors identified by the judge and to which I have already referred. First, it is said that the Pt 36 offer was made at a very late stage in the proceedings. It was, in fact, made just 21 days before the trial was due to begin (on 11 January 2000); although, in the event, the commencement of the trial was postponed, for other

a reasons, until 25 January 2000. It is plain that the stage of the proceedings at which a Pt 36 offer is made is a factor which a court must take into account; see para (5)(b) of r 36.21. But, as it seems to me, the fact that the offer is made in the month before the trial cannot, of itself and without more, be a reason for holding that it is unjust to make orders under paras (2) and (3) of that rule. It is important to keep in mind that the orders for which those paragraphs provide have effect

b only from the latest date when the defendant could have accepted the offer without needing the permission of the court. So, in a case (such as the present) where the Pt 36 offer is made more than 21 days before the start of the trial, orders under paras (2) and (3) cannot relate to costs incurred or interest accruing before 12 January 2000. They cannot relate to any period before the offer was made; and they allow, necessarily, for a period of at least 21 days following the

c offer, during which The Times had the opportunity to consider whether or not to accept the offer or to seek clarification of its terms. It is not difficult to imagine circumstances in which it would be unjust to make orders under paras (2) and (3) of r 36.21 because the offer was made so late that a defendant had no proper opportunity to consider it; but, making due allowance for the intervention of the

d Christmas holidays and millennium celebrations, I am not persuaded that that was the position in the present case. Nor is it difficult to imagine circumstances in which it might be unjust to make orders under those paragraphs because the offer was made so late that the costs already incurred were (in proportion to the costs yet to be incurred) such that there was little to be saved by bringing the proceedings to an end at that stage. But, again, that is not this case. In my view,

e the fact that the offer was made at a late stage in the proceedings, although a factor which the court must take into account, does not support the conclusion, in the present case, that it would be unjust to make orders under paras (2) and (3) of r 36.21.

[13] Second, it is said that it was unjust to make orders under r 36.21 in the

f circumstances that the defendants' solicitors had taken upon themselves the burden of preparing the bundles for trial. For my part, although we were told that there was a limited concession below that the point had some relevance, I find that submission difficult to understand. It was not pressed in argument before us; and I need say little about it. It is sufficient, I think, to point out that, because the defendants' solicitors took upon themselves the burden of preparing bundles for

g trial, there can be little or no element in the claimant's costs (whether assessed on the standard or on the indemnity basis) which can relate to the preparation of bundles; and that, if the defendants' solicitors had not taken that burden upon themselves, then an amount equivalent to the costs which they incurred in carrying out that exercise would have been incurred by the claimant's solicitors

h and would have been recoverable from the defendants under an order for costs in the event (which happened) that the claimant succeeded in the action. The most that can be said, as it seems to me, is that The Times have had to pay their own solicitors, sooner and on an 'own client' basis, for work for which they would otherwise have had to reimburse the claimant, later and on a standard

j basis. I cannot think that that factor should lead to the conclusion that it would be unjust to make orders under paras (2) and (3) of r 36.21.

[14] Third, The Times rely upon what they describe as 'public interest and the problems of acceptance'. Their submissions elide what the judge regarded as distinct points: (a) that there was an unusual public interest element in the sense that The Times were taking on the burden of proving that the supposed Committee of conspirators referred to in the programme and in the claimant's book did not

exist; and (b) that the offer in the letter of 21 December 1999 required The Times to publish a retraction and apology, and to join in a statement in open court. In relation to those points the judge said:

> 'Had the defendants accepted the offer suddenly put before them on 21 December the overwhelming inference to be drawn from that by interested observers would be ... that the supposed members of The Committee did not have the resolve to come to court and face their accuser. That might have been reasonably thought by the Sunday Times to be unfair to the individuals concerned and also to be contrary to public interest in having a full and open resolution of these issues. Fourthly, and of great significance, the offer of 21 December required the defendants to publish a retraction and apology in their newspaper and also to join in a statement in open court. In the light of the defendants' strongly held views about the programme and the evidence to be adduced at trial from the alleged Committee members, it is inconceivable that they would have consented to take those steps.'

[15] It is necessary to have in mind that the Pt 36 offer was made at a time when the claimant was seeking, by means of the Pt 14 notice which was served on the same day, to litigate his defamation claim on the basis that he did not challenge the assertion, in para 10A of The Times' particulars of justification, that the supposed Committee did not exist. At the pre-trial review on 21 December 1999 the claimant sought an order that the alleged members of The Committee should not be called to give evidence; on the basis that there was no longer an issue to which their evidence could relate. In those circumstances, as it seems to me, the claimant could not have insisted on any published retraction or apology, or on any statement in open court, which did not, in terms, make it clear that, far from the supposed members of The Committee being unwilling to face their accuser (as the judge put it), it was the claimant who did not wish to challenge the evidence which they were expected to give. I accept, of course, that if the claimant had sought to insist on a retraction and apology, or on a statement in open court, which did not make that clear, then it might well have been unjust to make orders under paras (2) and (3) of r 36.21 on the basis that the offer was one which (with hindsight) should have been accepted. But the terms of the retraction and apology which the claimant sought, or would have been prepared to accept, were never explored. Those matters were never explored because The Times chose not to respond to the offer letter of 21 December 1999. It was unreal to expect that Mr McPhilemy would, himself, make a statement withdrawing the allegations which he had made; and, in those circumstances, The Times was determined to have a decision on the question whether or not the supposed Committee did exist. Had the terms of the retraction and apology which the claimant would have been prepared to accept (or could have been prevailed upon to accept) in order to settle these proceedings been explored, the position might now appear in a different light. But the opportunity to expose the offer as one which The Times could not, in fairness to the alleged members of The Committee, accept was not taken; and, in those circumstances, I am not persuaded that the compromise of this defamation action which was on offer on 21 December 1999 could not have been presented to interested and informed observers in such a way as to make it clear that any inference that the alleged Committee members were unwilling to face the claimant in court would be wholly unfounded.

[16] Nor am I persuaded that there was any public interest to be served in insisting on a trial in order to have 'a full and open resolution of these issues'.

To take the view that a defamation action between a journalist and a newspaper—in which the real issue was whether the journalist had acted honestly and responsibly on the basis of the information which he claimed to have received from his sources, and to which the alleged Committee members were not parties—was a suitable vehicle for 'a full and open resolution' of the question whether there was, in Northern Ireland at the relevant time, something approaching an institutional conspiracy amongst so-called Loyalists to assassinate Republicans was, as it seems to me, misconceived from the outset. In making that observation I intend no criticism of the decision to permit the issue to be raised by The Times as an element in the defence of justification. I do no more than point out that, whatever decision the jury reached if the issue was left to them, it was never likely that there would have been 'a full and open resolution' of matters which were never capable of being fully resolved in private litigation of this nature.

[17] There is, however, force in the final point advanced on behalf of The Times; that is to say, that it is established practice, in defamation cases, for the court to refuse to direct the payment of interest, in respect of any period prior to the date of the award, on the amount of the jury's award. The justification for that practice is that the amount of the jury's award takes account of everything down to the date of the award, including, in particular, the strain and distress caused to the claimant by the conduct of the trial and the fact that the claimant has had to wait for payment of the compensation to which he has ultimately been held entitled. It is said that it would be unjust to order the payment of interest, under para (2) of r 36.21, on any part of the jury's award in the present case, at least in respect of any period prior to the date of the award, because it has to be assumed: (i) that the award itself includes an element which reflects the loss to the claimant equivalent to the actual or notional cost of being kept out of the monetary compensation, which (on the hypothesis that the libel had been established) he should have had immediately after the libel was published, by the delay occasioned by legal proceedings and a trial; and (ii) that the award itself takes account of the anxiety and distress of the proceedings and trial to which Lord Woolf MR referred in the *Petrotrade* case. To order the payment of interest under para (2), in respect of any period prior to the date of the award, would involve double compensation.

[18] I find that final point persuasive. In order to explain why, it is necessary, I think, to return to an examination of the purposes for which the powers in paras (2) and (3) of r 36.21 have been conferred.

[19] It is plain, as Lord Woolf MR pointed out in the *Petrotrade* case, that paras (2) and (3) of r 36.21, in conjunction with para (4), are intended to provide an incentive to a claimant to make a Pt 36 offer. The incentive is that a claimant who has made a Pt 36 offer (which is not accepted) and who succeeds at trial in beating his own offer stands to receive more than he would have received if he had not made the offer. Conversely, a defendant who refuses a Pt 36 offer made by a claimant and who fails to beat that offer at trial is at risk of being ordered to pay more than he would have been ordered to pay if the offer had not been made. But those incentives have to be set in the context that, as this court emphasised in the *Petrotrade* case, r 36.21 is not to be regarded as producing penal consequences. The powers conferred by the rule, to order indemnity costs or a higher rate of interest, are intended to provide 'a means of achieving a fairer result for a claimant' (see para 64 in Lord Woolf MR's judgment ([2001] 4 All ER 853 at 856), to which I have already referred). Exercise of the powers cannot achieve 'a fairer result' if it leads to the claimant receiving more than can properly be regarded as a full and complete recompense for having to resort to, to pursue and to endure

the strain and anxiety of legal proceedings. An exercise of the powers which led
to the claimant receiving more than could properly be regarded as compensation,   *a*
in that enlarged sense, would, necessarily in my view, be penal in nature. It could
only be supported on the basis that there was a need to punish the defendant by
requiring him to pay an amount which went beyond any amount needed to
compensate the claimant. But, subject to the limitation that the powers are
intended to be used in order to achieve a fairer result for the claimant and not to   *b*
punish the defendant, it is plain that they are to be used in order to redress
elements, otherwise inherent in the legal process, which can properly be regarded
as unfair.

[20] Two of those elements—which many would regard as obviously unfair—
were identified by Lord Woolf MR in the *Petrotrade* case. First, an award of costs
on the standard basis will, almost invariably, lead to the successful claimant   *c*
recovering less than the costs which he has to pay to his solicitor. So, although
he has been successful, he is out of pocket. Costs on an indemnity basis should
avoid that element of unfairness. Second, neither costs on an indemnity basis nor
interest awarded under s 35A of the Supreme Court Act 1981 will compensate the
successful claimant for the inconvenience, anxiety and distress of proceedings or   *d*
(where the claimant is a corporation) the disruption caused by the diversion of
senior management from their normal duties. Interest at an enhanced rate, that
is to say at a rate which is higher than the rate which would otherwise be ordered,
under s 35A of the 1981 Act, may redress that element of unfairness. It is
pertinent to note that para (6) of r 36.21 expressly recognises that the court may
make an order for the payment of interest under para (2) notwithstanding that it   *e*
also orders the payment of interest on the same sum and for the same period
under some other power—of which the power under s 35A of the 1981 Act is an
obvious example. Paragraph (6) imposes an overall limit of 10% above base rate.

[21] I conclude, therefore, that the power to award interest under para (2) of
r 36.21 at an enhanced rate—that is to say, at a rate higher than the rate (if any)   *f*
which would otherwise be chosen under s 35A of the 1981 Act—is conferred in
order to enable the court, in a case to which r 36.21 applies, to redress the element
of perceived unfairness, otherwise inherent in the legal process, which arises
from the fact that damages, costs (even costs on an indemnity basis) and statutory
interest will not compensate the successful claimant for the inconvenience,   *g*
anxiety and distress of having to resort to and pursue proceedings which he had
sought to avoid by an offer to settle on terms which (as events turned out) were
less advantageous to him than the judgment which he achieved. But, if that is the
purpose for which the power has been conferred, then it should not be used to
award interest in a case where it must be assumed that the anxiety, inconvenience
and distress of defamation proceedings have already been taken into account by   *h*
the jury in reaching their award. To order the payment of interest on the amount
of the award, in respect of any period prior to the date of the award, would be to
risk introducing an element of double compensation. It would be to risk crossing
the boundary which separates compensation from punishment.

[22] An order, under para (3) of r 36.21, for the payment of costs on an   *j*
indemnity basis does not give rise to a risk of double compensation. The purpose
for which the power to order the payment of costs on an indemnity basis is
conferred, as it seems to me, is to enable the court, in a case to which r 36.21
applies, to address the element of perceived unfairness which arises from the fact
that an award of costs on the standard basis will, almost invariably, lead to the
successful claimant recovering less than the costs which he has to pay to his

a solicitor. The jury, in reaching their award of damages, are not concerned with costs; and there is no reason to think that their award takes any account of the probable shortfall if costs are subsequently ordered on the standard basis. In my view, therefore, there is no injustice in making an order, under para (3)(a) of r 36.21, that the claimant is entitled to his costs on the indemnity basis from the latest date when The Times could have accepted his Pt 36 offer without needing

b the permission of the court. In the present case that date is 11 January 2000.

[23] Nor do I see any injustice, in principle, in an order under para (3)(b) of r 36.21 for the payment of interest on the costs which are the subject of the order which I would make under para (3)(a). The purpose for which the power to order interest on costs under that paragraph is conferred is, I think, plain. It is to redress, in a case to which r 36.21 applies, the element of perceived unfairness

c which arises from the general rule that interest is not allowed on costs paid before judgment (see *Hunt v R M Douglas (Roofing) Ltd* [1988] 3 All ER 823 at 833, [1990] 1 AC 398 at 415). So, in the ordinary case, the successful claimant who has made payments to his own solicitor on account of costs in advance of the trial will be out of pocket even if he obtains, at the trial, an order for costs on an indemnity

d basis. He will get interest on his costs from the date of the order (whether he has actually paid them or not); but he will get nothing to compensate him for the cost of money (or the loss of the use of money) which he has had to bear before trial in relation to payments which he has made on account of costs. An order under para (3)(b) of r 36.21 enables the court to achieve a fairer result in that respect. Accordingly, having regard to the point which, as it seems to me, para (3)(b) is

e intended to meet, I would order payment of interest at a rate which reflects (albeit generously) the cost of money, say, 4% over base rate; and I would direct that interest runs, on the costs to which the order applies, from the date upon which the work was done or liability for disbursements was incurred.

[24] I have not yet addressed the question whether it would be right to order

f interest after judgment, either (i) under para (2) of r 36.21, on the award of damages, or (ii) under para (3)(b) of that rule, on the costs which I would make the subject of an order under para (3)(a). In my view paras (2) and (3)(b) of r 36.21 are not intended to confer on the court powers to vary the rate at which interest is payable on a judgment debt pursuant to s 17 of the Judgments Act 1838. An

g order for costs is a judgment debt for the purposes of the 1838 Act (see *Thomas v Bunn, Wilson v Graham, Lea v British Aerospace plc* [1991] 1 All ER 193, [1991] 1 AC 362). The power to fix the rate at which interest is payable on judgment debts has been conferred on the Lord Chancellor by s 44 of the Administration of Justice Act 1970 and is exercisable by him with the concurrence of the Treasury. I can see no reason why Parliament should have intended to confer on the courts—

h indirectly through rules made by the Civil Procedure Rules Committee under s 1(1) of the Civil Procedure Act 1997—power to vary in individual cases a rate fixed under the 1970 Act; nor any reason why a power to fix the rate at which interest is payable on judgment debts could be required for the purpose of 'securing that the civil justice system is accessible, fair and efficient' (see s 1(3) of

j the 1997 Act). Nor can I see why a party who fails to pay a judgment debt, which (ex hypothesi) the court has ordered that he should pay, should pay more, or less, interest on that debt because, in the litigation which has led to that order, the other party has, or has not, made an offer to which r 36.21 applies. The point was not addressed at any length in the argument on the cross-appeal; but, for my part, I am not persuaded that the court has power to make an order under para (2) of r 36.21 for the payment of interest on the amount of the jury's award in respect of any period after judgment; or to make an order under para (3)(b) for the payment of interest on costs in respect of any period after judgment.

[25] It follows, therefore, that I would allow the cross-appeal to the extent which I have indicated. I would direct that the claimant is entitled to his costs on the indemnity basis from 12 January 2000 (which is the date for which he contends); and to interest on those costs at the rate of 4% above base rate from the date upon which the work was done or liability for a disbursement was incurred until 30 March 2000, that being the date of judgment. Interest thereafter, on damages and costs, will be payable at the judgment rate, under s 17 of the 1838 Act, in the ordinary course.

[26] I should add that I have had the advantage of reading, in advance, the judgment which Simon Brown LJ is to hand down. I agree with him, for the reason which he gives, that the costs of the principal appeal should be paid by The Times on the indemnity basis.

LONGMORE LJ.

[27] I agree with the judgments of both the other members of the court.

SIMON BROWN LJ.

[28] I agree with all that Chadwick LJ has said with regard to the claimant's cross-appeal and with the order he proposes. The judge below, without the benefit of this court's judgment in *Petrotrade Inc v Texaco Ltd* [2001] 4 All ER 853, wrongly directed himself that an indemnity costs order under CPR 36.21 is of a penal nature and implies condemnation of the defendant's conduct and so would be unjust unless the defendants have behaved unreasonably in continuing the litigation after the offer. That misunderstands the rationale of the rule. It is not designed to punish unreasonable conduct but rather as an incentive to encourage claimants to make, and defendants to accept, appropriate offers of settlement. That incentive plainly cannot work unless the non-acceptance of what ultimately proves to have been a sufficient offer ordinarily advantages the claimant in the respects set out in the rule. Given that in a defamation action it would generally be unjust to award interest on the damages, let alone at an enhanced rate, it becomes even more important that a r 36.21 order is made as to costs, irrespective of whether or not the claimant is represented under a conditional fee arrangement. Otherwise the rule will simply become ineffective in this area of litigation, an area where to my mind it should play a prominent part.

[29] When dismissing the principal appeal, we left over for decision whether Times Newspapers Ltd should pay the claimant's costs of that appeal on a standard or an indemnity basis. Clearly rather more of a stigma attaches to an indemnity costs order made in this context than in the context of a r 36.21 offer, although even then no moral condemnation of the defendants' lawyers is necessarily implied (see *Wall v Lefever* [1998] 1 FCR 605 at 617). In my judgment, however, an indemnity costs order is certainly appropriate in the circumstances of The Times' appeal here: as our judgments on that appeal make plain, to have permitted the defendants to argue their case on perversity must inevitably have brought the administration of justice into disrepute among right thinking people. I understand Chadwick and Longmore LJJ to agree with this view. We accordingly dismiss the principal appeal with costs on an indemnity basis.

Cross-appeal allowed in part.

Dilys Tausz   Barrister.

a # LG Caltex Gas Co Ltd and another v China National Petroleum Corp and another

[2001] EWCA Civ 788

b COURT OF APPEAL, CIVIL DIVISION

LORD PHILLIPS OF WORTH MATRAVERS MR, PILL AND KEENE LJJ

14, 15 MAY 2001

c Arbitration – Award – Setting aside award – Jurisdiction – Jurisdiction to make award – Respondents claiming not to be parties to contracts containing arbitration clauses – Whether parties having made ad hoc submissions to arbitrator on question of jurisdiction – Whether appellants entitled to challenge arbitration awards – Arbitration Act 1996, s 67.

The appellant companies had made claims in excess of about $US 40m arising out
d of a series of agreements made in 1995 with the respondents and others for
co-operation in a project for the importation and marketing of liquid petroleum
in southern China. Two sets of arbitration proceedings were commenced in 1997
before the same sole arbitrator pursuant to a supply agreement dated 18 October
1995 and a charterparty dated 17 October 1995, both of which provided for
non-institutional arbitration in London. The respondents reserved their position
e with respect to jurisdiction, contending that they were not party to the alleged
contracts and that the arbitration agreements were not binding on them. By two
awards dated 24 May 1999, the arbitrator held that the respondents were not
parties to or bound by either the supply agreement or the charterparty. The
appellants challenged both awards pursuant to s 67[a] of the Arbitration Act 1996,
f on the basis that the awards concerned the arbitrator's jurisdiction and that, by
virtue of s 67, the court had the final say on matters of jurisdiction. The judge
ordered the trial of various preliminary issues and held, inter alia, (i) that the
parties had made ad hoc submissions to the arbitrator by exchange of
communications in writing on the issue of whether the respondents were parties
to the contracts, and that therefore s 67 did not apply; and (ii) that the awards
g were not awards as to substantive jurisdiction for the purposes of s 67(1)(a),
which provided that a party to arbitral proceedings might apply to the court to
challenge an award of the arbitral tribunal as to its substantive jurisdiction, as the
awards made were awards on the merits. The appellant companies appealed.

h **Held** – (1) Section 67(1)(a) entitled a party to challenge an award of an arbitrator
made as to his substantive jurisdiction. However, if it was shown that the award
was made under a separate agreement that the arbitrator should rule on that
matter, such a challenge would fail. In the instant case, the judge had erred in
concluding that the parties had made ad hoc submissions on the question of
j whether the respondents were parties to the contract. Although parties sometimes
proceeded to conduct an arbitration without appreciating that the dispute fell
outside the scope of the arbitration clause under which the arbitrator had been
appointed, and in such circumstances the courts had, in the past, held that such
conduct evidenced the conclusion of an ad hoc agreement, that was not so in the

---

a   Section 67, so far as material, is set out at [15], below

instant case. The parties had been represented by experienced commercial solicitors conversant with the provisions of the 1996 Act and the issue of jurisdiction had been appreciated from the outset. Had the solicitors wished to conclude an ad hoc agreement to address that issue, they would have done so expressly. In the event, the conduct of the solicitors accorded with what one would have expected of solicitors paying regard to the provisions of the 1996 Act, and no ad hoc agreement enlarging the scope of the arbitrator's jurisdiction had been concluded. It followed that the appellants were not precluded from challenging the awards under s 67 on that ground (see [63]–[68], [81]–[83], below).

(2) Notwithstanding that the arbitrator's awards took the form of awards on the merits, the entirety of his reasons for the awards were relevant to the issue of jurisdiction and did not address any matter which extended beyond the issue of jurisdiction. It followed that although the award had purported to make a finding as to liability, as to which the arbitrator had no jurisdiction, it had implicitly determined that the respondents were not party to any arbitration agreements and that the arbitrator had no substantive jurisdiction. In those circumstances the appropriate course was to treat the awards as awards in relation to the arbitrator's substantive jurisdiction, which he had jurisdiction to make under s 30 of the Act, rather than as awards on the merits, which he had no jurisdiction to make. On that basis, it followed that s 67(1)(a) applied to the awards. Moreover, s 73 of the Act was no bar to the relief sought by the appellants, since they were not making any of the objections to which that section applied, and accordingly the appeal would be allowed (see [71]–[83], below).

Notes

For the powers of the court in relation to the award, see Supp to 2 *Halsbury's Laws* (4th edn reissue) paras 690–713.

For the Arbitration Act 1996, s 67, see 2 *Halsbury's Statutes* (4th edn) (1999 reissue) 607.

Cases referred to in judgments

Almare Societa di Navigazione SpA v Derby & Co Ltd, The Almare Prima [1989] 2 Lloyd's Rep 376.

Brown (Christopher) Ltd v Genossenschaft Oesterreichischer Waldbesitzer Holzwirtschafts-bertriebe Registrierte Genossenschaft Mit Beschrankter Haftung [1953] 2 All ER 1039, [1954] 1 QB 8, [1953] 3 WLR 689.

Heyman v Darwins Ltd [1942] 1 All ER 337, [1942] AC 356, HL.

Westminster Chemicals & Produce Ltd v Eichholz and Loeser [1954] 1 Lloyd's Rep 99.

Cases also cited or referred to in skeleton arguments

Allied Vision Ltd v VPS Film Entertainment GmbH [1991] 1 Lloyd's Rep 392.

AT & T Corp v Saudi Cable Co [2000] 2 All ER (Comm) 625, CA.

Azov Shipping Co v Baltic Shipping Co [1999] 1 All ER 476.

Cia Maritima Zorroza SA v Sesostris SAE, The Marques de Bolarque [1984] 1 Lloyd's Rep 652.

Dalmia Dairy Industries Ltd v National Bank of Pakistan [1978] 2 Lloyd's Rep 223, CA.

Egmatra AG v Marco Trading Corp [1999] 1 Lloyd's Rep 862.

Exmar BV v National Iranian Tanker Co, The Trade Fortitude [1992] 1 Lloyd's Rep 169.

Finzel, Berry & Co v Eastcheap Dried Fruit Co [1962] 1 Lloyd's Rep 370; *affd* [1962] 2 Lloyd's Rep 11, CA.

a *Halki Shipping Corp v Sopex Oils Ltd* [1998] 2 All ER 23, [1998] 1 WLR 726, CA.
   Inco Europe Ltd v First Choice Distribution (a firm) [2000] 1 All ER (Comm) 674,
      [2000] 1 WLR 586, HL.
   Oil Products Trading Co Ltd v SA Société de Gestion D'Entreprises Coloniales (1934)
      150 LT 475.
   Rustal Trading Ltd v Gill & Duffus SA [2000] 1 Lloyd's Rep 14.
b *Willie (Charles M) & Co (Shipping) Ltd v Ocean Laser Shipping Ltd, The Smaro* [1999]
      1 Lloyd's Rep 225.

Appeal

The appellants, LG Caltex Gas Co and Contigroup Companies Inc, appealed with
the permission of Aikens J from his decision on 19 January 2001 whereby he
c determined preliminary issues and held that the appellants could not challenge,
pursuant to s 67 of the Arbitration Act 1996, arbitration awards made on 24 May
1999 by the arbitrator, Mr Bruce Harris, whereby he declared that the respondents,
China National Petroleum Co and China Petroleum Technology & Development
Corp, were not parties to the contracts relied upon by the appellants. The facts
d are set out in the judgment of Lord Phillips of Worth Matravers MR.

Angus Glennie QC, Lawrence Akka and *Toby Landau* (instructed by *Holman Fenwick*
   & Willan) for the appellants.
Michael Collins QC (instructed by *Zaiwalla & Co*) for the respondents.

e **LORD PHILLIPS OF WORTH MATRAVERS MR.**
   [1] This is an appeal by LG Caltex Gas Co (LG Caltex) and Contigroup
Companies Inc (Conti), from a judgment of Aikens J, dated 19 January 2001, in
favour of the respondents, China National Petroleum Co (CNPC) and China
Petroleum Technology & Development Corp (CPTDC). Permission to appeal
f was granted by Aikens J because this case raises new and important points in
relation to ss 67 and 73 of the Arbitration Act 1996.
   [2] The appeal relates to two sets of arbitration proceedings, which have been
heard together and which raise identical issues. The sole arbitrator involved is
Mr Bruce Harris, a commercial arbitrator of great experience. Each set of
proceedings involves a claim by one of the appellants against both respondents
g for damages of breach of a contract containing an arbitration clause. In each case
the respondents deny being party to the contract in question.
   [3] The issue of whether the respondents were parties to the contracts is the
principal bone of contention between them and the appellant. That issue bears
simultaneously on two questions, the first procedural and the second substantive.
h (1) Are the respondents party to arbitration agreements which give Mr Harris
jurisdiction to determine the substance of the disputes? (2) Are the respondents
liable in damages for breach of contract?
   [4] After a lengthy hearing Mr Harris has made two final awards dated 24 May
1999 in which he has held that the respondents are not party to the contracts in
j question.
   [5] The appellants contend that these awards are, in substance, rulings by
Mr Harris that he has no jurisdiction and that these rulings are susceptible to
challenge in the court by virtue of the provisions of the 1996 Act. The
respondents contend that the awards determine the substantive issues of whether
they are liable under the contracts. They further contend that Mr Harris had
jurisdiction to make a final determination of these issues, not by reason of the

arbitration clauses in the contracts, but because in the course of the arbitration proceedings they reached agreement with the appellants that Mr Harris should *a* determine these central issues. These alleged agreements have been referred to as 'ad hoc' agreements, although, as I shall explain in due course, that expression can have more than one meaning.

[6] Aikens J has ruled that the respondents are correct and that it is not open to the appellants to challenge Mr Harris' findings that the respondents were not *b* party to the contracts on which the appellants' claims are founded. The challenges to Mr Harris' awards came before Aikens J in the form of applications under s 67 of the 1996 Act to have the awards set aside. Aikens J skilfully case-managed the applications by identifying four preliminary issues and directing argument upon them. This appeal requires a review of the analysis made by the judge of these issues. *c*

[7] At the heart of the dispute is the question of the impact of the 1996 Act on English procedure where the jurisdiction of an arbitrator is in issue. I propose to consider the position before 1996 before turning to the relevant provisions of the 1996 Act.

d

THE POSITION BEFORE 1996

[8] Nearly 50 years ago Devlin J, with characteristic clarity, described the position of arbitrators facing challenge to their jurisdiction in *Brown (Christopher) Ltd v Genossenschaft Oesterreichischer Waldbesitzer Holzwirtschaftsbertriebe Registrierte Genossenschaft Mit Beschrankter Haftung* [1953] 2 All ER 1039 at 1042–1043, [1954] 1 QB 8 at 12–13: *e*

'It is clear that at the beginning of any arbitration one side or the other may challenge the jurisdiction of the arbitrator. It is not the law that arbitrators, if their jurisdiction is challenged or questioned, are bound immediately to cease to act, and to refuse to act, until their jurisdiction has been determined by some court which has power to determine it finally. Nor is it the law that *f* they are bound to go on without investigating the merits of the challenge and determine the matter in dispute leaving the question of their jurisdiction to be held over until it is determined by some court which had power to determine it. They might then be merely wasting their time and everybody else's. They are not obliged to take either of those courses. They are entitled *g* to inquire into the merits of the issue whether they have jurisdiction or not, not for the purpose of reaching any conclusion which will be binding on the parties, because that they cannot do, but for the purpose of satisfying themselves, as a preliminary matter, whether they ought to go on with the arbitration or not. If it became abundantly clear to them that they had no *h* jurisdiction as, for example, it would be if the submission which was produced was not signed, or not properly executed, or something of that sort, then they might well decide not to proceed with the hearing. They are entitled, in short, to make their own inquiries in order to determine their own course of action, but the result of that inquiry has no effect whatsoever on the rights of the parties. That is plain, I think, from the burden that is put *j* on a plaintiff who is suing on an award. He is obliged to prove not only the making of the award but that the arbitrators had jurisdiction to make the award. The principle omnia praesumuntur does not apply to proceedings of arbitration tribunals or, indeed, to the proceedings of inferior tribunals of any sort. There is no presumption that merely because an award has been made that, therefore, it is a valid award. It has to be proved by the party who *a* sues on it that it was made by the arbitrators within the terms of their authority, that is, with jurisdiction. Jurisdiction has to be proved affirmatively. If the plaintiff takes on himself the burden of proving the award and fails to prove that the arbitrators had jurisdiction, of course, his action fails and it is irrelevant whether the arbitrators thought or did not think that they had jurisdiction. Their finding is of no value to him. But if he proves that the

b arbitrators did have jurisdiction then he succeeds and his success is not destroyed because the arbitrators themselves went into the matter and came to the same conclusion which, ex hypothesi, was the right one. In short, any view that is expressed by the arbitrators expressly or impliedly in the award, any finding, if it can be called a finding, that they had jurisdiction, does not make the award any better and likewise does not make it any worse.'

c
[9] An arbitration agreement is often contained in the contract that sets out the substantive rights and obligations of the parties. Where a respondent denies that he is party to such a contract, that challenge raises simultaneously (1) the procedural issue of whether the arbitrator has jurisdiction; and (2) the substantive issue of whether the respondent is liable for breach of contract.

d [10] Before 1996, if the arbitrator in an award in favour of a claimant held that the disputed contract bound the respondent, the respondent could challenge that finding in court, although it purported to resolve both the issue of jurisdiction and the issue of liability. Equally, if the arbitrator held that he had no jurisdiction because the respondent was not party to the contract, the claimant could

e challenge that finding in court. The editors of the second edition of Mustill & Boyd *Commercial Arbitration* (1989) pp 108–109 explained the position:

'… it has in the past always been accepted in England that an arbitrator cannot make a binding award as to the initial existence of the contract, and that he cannot foreclose the question by making an award which takes it for

f granted. For if in truth no contract was ever made, then the arbitration provisions of the supposed contract never bound the parties; and an arbitrator appointed under those provisions could have no authority to act. So, although an arbitrator, faced with a dispute about whether a contract ever came into existence or if it did, whether a party to the arbitration was a party to the agreement, can and often should consider and rule upon it, his

g ruling does not bind the parties, and may always be reopened by the Court.'

[11] *Heyman v Darwins Ltd* [1942] 1 All ER 337, [1942] AC 356 is the principal authority which supports that text.

[12] There was no need for the respondent to await the issue of the award

h before challenging the jurisdiction of the arbitrator. It was common practice for a respondent to apply to the Commercial Court for a declaration that he was not bound by the alleged arbitration agreement, which usually produced the result that the arbitration was stayed pending a decision of the court on the jurisdictional issue. The desirability of avoiding the delay caused to the arbitral

j process in such circumstances was one of the primary reasons for the changes made by the 1996 Act.

[13] It was always possible for the parties to agree that the arbitrator should determine whether or not the contract containing the arbitration clause had been validly concluded. Such an agreement constituted an independent arbitration agreement conferring on the arbitrator jurisdiction to resolve the issue which he would not otherwise have had. Where a respondent took part in an arbitration

raising issues which fell outside the jurisdiction of the arbitrator, the court would
normally infer that the parties had agreed that the arbitrator had jurisdiction to
resolve the issues that were in dispute: see for example *Westminster Chemicals &
Produce Ltd v Eichholz and Loeser* [1954] 1 Lloyd's Rep 99 and *Almare Societa di
Navigazione SpA v Derby & Co Ltd, The Almare Prima* [1989] 2 Lloyd's Rep 376.

THE 1996 ACT

[14] As I have stated, some of the provisions of the 1996 Act were designed to
prevent the process of the arbitration being delayed pending resolution of issues
of jurisdiction by the court. The following provisions are relevant to this appeal.
Section 1:

'The provisions of this Part are founded on the following principles, and
shall be construed accordingly—(a) the object of arbitration is to obtain the
fair resolution of disputes ...'

Section 4:

'(1) The mandatory provisions of this Part are listed in Schedule 1 and
have effect notwithstanding any agreement to the contrary.

(2) The other provisions of this Part (the "non-mandatory provisions")
allow the parties to make their own arrangements by agreement but provide
rules which apply in the absence of such agreement.'

[15] The sections which follow, save s 30, are all mandatory provisions.
Section 30:

'(1) Unless otherwise agreed by the parties, the arbitral tribunal may rule
on its own substantive jurisdiction, that is, as to—(a) whether there is a valid
arbitration agreement, (b) whether the tribunal is properly constituted, and
(c) what matters have been submitted to arbitration in accordance with the
arbitration agreement.

(2) Any such ruling may be challenged by any available arbitral process of
appeal or review or in accordance with the provisions of this Part.'

Section 31:

'(1) An objection that the arbitral tribunal lacks substantive jurisdiction at
the outset of the proceedings must be raised by a party not later than the time
he takes the first step in the proceedings to contest the merits of any matter
in relation to which he challenges the tribunal's jurisdiction. A party is not
precluded from raising such an objection by the fact that he has appointed or
participated in the appointment of an arbitrator.

(2) Any objection during the course of the arbitral proceedings that the
arbitral tribunal is exceeding its substantive jurisdiction must be made as
soon as possible after the matter alleged to be beyond its jurisdiction is raised.

(3) The arbitral tribunal may admit an objection later than the time
specified in subsection (1) or (2) if it considers the delay justified.

(4) Where an objection is duly taken to the tribunal's substantive
jurisdiction and the tribunal has power to rule on its own jurisdiction, it
may—(a) rule on the matter in an award as to jurisdiction, or (b) deal with
the objection in its award on the merits. If the parties agree which of these
courses the tribunal should take, the tribunal shall proceed accordingly.

a   (5) The tribunal may in any case, and shall if the parties so agree, stay
proceedings whilst an application is made to the court under section 32
(determination of preliminary point of jurisdiction).'

Section 32:

b   '(1) The court may, on the application of a party to arbitral proceedings
(upon notice to the other parties), determine any question as to the
substantive jurisdiction of the tribunal. A party may lose the right to object
(see section 73).

    (2) An application under this section shall not be considered unless—(a) it
is made with the agreement in writing of all the other parties to the
proceedings, or (b) it is made with the permission of the tribunal and the
c   court is satisfied—(i) that the determination of the question is likely to
produce substantial savings in costs, (ii) that the application was made
without delay, and (iii) that there is good reason why the matter should be
decided by the court.'

d   Section 67:

    '(1) A party to arbitral proceedings may (upon notice to the other parties
and to the tribunal) apply to the court—(a) challenging any award of the
arbitral tribunal as to its substantive jurisdiction; or (b) for an order declaring
an award made by the tribunal on the merits to be of no effect, in whole or
e   in part, because the tribunal did not have substantive jurisdiction. A party
may lose the right to object (see section 73) ...'

Section 73:

    '(1) If a party to arbitral proceedings takes part, or continues to take part,
in the proceedings without making, either forthwith or within such time as
f   is allowed by the arbitration agreement or the tribunal or by any provision
of this Part, any objection—(a) that the tribunal lacks substantive
jurisdiction, (b) that the proceedings have been improperly conducted,
(c) that there has been a failure to comply with the arbitration agreement or
with any provision of this Part, or (d) that there has been any other
g   irregularity affecting the tribunal or the proceedings, he may not raise that
objection later, before the tribunal or the court, unless he shows that, at the
time he took part or continued to take part in the proceedings, he did not
know and could not with reasonable diligence have discovered the grounds
for the objection.'

h   THE FACTS
    [16] This appeal turns largely on the implications of the conduct of the parties
in the light of the provisions which I have just read. Accordingly, it is necessary
to set out the facts in detail. Those facts have been carefully stated by Aikens J in
his judgment and I shall gratefully incorporate them at this stage with some
j   minor adaption.

The parties to the arbitrations and the proceedings
    [17] LG Caltex was known in 1995 as Hoyu Energy Co Ltd. It was concerned
with projects for buying and selling liquid petroleum gas (LPG). The appellant,
Conti (formerly Continental Grain Co), was, in 1995, the disponent owner of the
LPG vessel 'Al Berry'.

[18] The two respondents are separate legal entities created under the laws of
the People's Republic of China. The relationship between them was one of many
issues in the two arbitrations.

The alleged contracts

[19] In 1995 negotiations took place in China between the appellants, the
respondents and other companies, to promote a project to import and market
LPG in southern China. As a result of these negotiations, on 6 September 1995 a
'Memorandum of Understanding' was signed between LG Caltex and other
companies. The appellants say that the respondents were signatories to that
memorandum. The memorandum envisaged that an LPG terminal would be
built at Maoming in Southern China. But whilst this was being done storage
facilities for the imported LPG would be provided by ocean vessels. The LPG
would then be transferred to coastal tankers. The memorandum provided that
LG Caltex would negotiate purchase contracts for 40,000 mt of LPG per month
for carriage to and delivery at Maoming. LG Caltex was to be responsible for the
carriage. LG Caltex was to pay for the purchases but was to be reimbursed by
other parties to the memorandum.

[20] These provisions in the memorandum gave rise to the two alleged
contracts which were the subject of the two arbitrations before Mr Harris.
(1) The first alleged contract was a purported charterparty dated 17 October 1995,
but allegedly entered into on 18 October 1995. By this charter Conti chartered the
LPG vessel 'Al Berry' to 'China Petroleum Technology & Development
Corporation, a subsidiary of China National Petroleum Corporation of Beijing', as
charterers. The charter provided that the vessel was to act as a floating storage off
Shuidong, Guadong province. The allegation of the appellants was that this
charter bound CPTDC and also CNPC as the principals of CPTDC. (2) The
second alleged contract was a purported supply contract dated 18 October 1995.
This was between LG Caltex (called Hoyu Energy Co Ltd in the documents)
as sellers of LPG and Asia Pacific Petrochemicals Co Ltd as buyers. The
document envisaged the supply of a minimum of 40,000 mt of LPG per month
for a 12-month period between October 1995 to September 1996, for delivery to
one floating storage vessel off Shuidong. Under this document CPTDC was to
provide certain guarantee letters for each shipment of LPG. In the arbitrations
the appellants alleged that this contract bound both CPTDC and CNPC as the
principals of CPTDC and both were responsible for certain obligations under the
contract.

[21] Both these 'contracts' contained a clause providing for English law. The
'Supply Contract' provided for disputes to be settled by arbitration in London. The
'charterparty' provided for disputes to be settled by arbitration in London if either
party should elect it in place of the English courts.

The history of the arbitrations

[22] On 26 September 1997 Holman Fenwick & Willan (HFW), solicitors for the
appellants, wrote to both respondents asking them to concur in the appointment of
an arbitrator to deal with disputes that HFW said had arisen under the
'charterparty'. Mr Harris and two other potential arbitrators were suggested. On
the same date HFW also wrote to the two respondents giving notice that there
were disputes under the 'supply agreement' and also seeking their concurrence
in the appointment of a single arbitrator. The same three names were put
forward. Linklaters initially responded on behalf of CPTDC only in relation to

a the 'charterparty', but responded on behalf of both respondents in relation to the 'supply agreement'. However, after some correspondence, by 28 November 1997 Linklaters had agreed, on behalf of both respondents, to the appointment of Mr Harris as the sole arbitrator in relation to both the 'charterparty' and the 'supply contract' disputes. In each case this agreement was stated to be 'without prejudice to our clients' rights as to jurisdiction which we reserve'.

b [23] Mr Harris asked the two sides to give him 'thumbnail sketches' of the disputes between them. HFW did so on behalf of the appellants in a letter dated 20 November 1997. They indicated that it was the appellants' case that CNPC were parties to both contracts, even though CNPC was not named in either of them. HFW asserted that CNPC were the principals of CPTDC. HFW indicated that 'the precise relationships between [the two companies] may be issues in
c dispute'.

[24] Linklaters set out the respondents' summary in a letter dated 28 November 1997. They indicated that CPTDC would dispute liability under the 'charterparty', saying that the person who signed for CPTDC (Mr Ma) was drunk at the time and was induced to sign by representatives of LG Caltex. Linklaters' letter also denied
d that CPTDC was a party to any 'supply contract' with Conti. Linklaters said that CNPC denied it was party to either of the two 'contracts'. They said that CNPC was not the principal of CPTDC.

[25] On 8 December 1997 Linklaters paid the respondents' share of Mr Harris' appointment fee. In a covering letter (not copied to HFW), Linklaters said that 'this is without prejudice to CNPC's position regarding any challenge to
e jurisdiction'. There was no mention of CPTDC's position.

[26] On 6 March 1998 the appellants served their claim submissions in each of the arbitrations. They submitted that both CNPC and CPTDC were parties to and bound by the alleged contracts.

[27] In March the parties responded to questions that Mr Harris had raised in
f December 1997 about the relationship between the two arbitrations proceeding before him and a further ICC arbitration concerning other alleged agreements between the parties and others as well. HFW said, in a letter dated 26 March 1998, that jurisdictional challenges had been made in the ICC arbitration, but 'no such challenge has yet been indicated in the two arbitrations before you'. This was not strictly true as Linklaters had stated throughout that CNPC contended it
g was not a party to either contract; and in the 'thumbnail sketch' Linklaters had indicated that CPTDC would submit that it was not a party to the 'charterparty' because its signatory did not have authority to bind CPTDC as he was drunk at the time and had been induced to sign by representatives of LG Caltex.

[28] In Linklaters' response they reiterated the reservation of CNPC. They
h also stated 'with respect to the two ad hoc arbitrations before you, we have indicated that our clients are willing for them to proceed and be heard concurrently'. In his judgment Aikens J emphasised the words 'ad hoc'.

[29] On 15 May 1998 the respondents served their defence submissions in relation to both the 'supply contract' and the 'charterparty'. In each of those
j submissions it is stated in paras 1.1 and 1.2 that neither respondent was a party to either 'contract'. Paragraph 1.2 of each submission denies that there is (in either case) a valid agreement to arbitrate.

[30] In a letter to Mr Harris dated 15 May 1998 which accompanied the defence submissions, Linklaters invited Mr Harris to address 'jurisdictional matters by way of a preliminary issue hearing'. HFW responded to this suggestion in a long letter dated 9 June 1998. They said that if the jurisdictional issues were

to be properly investigated, then it would entail a detailed examination of the
facts concerning the original agreement of the parties (as alleged by the appellants); *a*
the part played by the representative of CPTDC in this; the parties' subsequent
conduct and the relationship between CPTDC and CNPC. HFW submitted that the
jurisdictional issues were therefore not suitable for preliminary issues. They
suggested that 'the questions of jurisdiction are dealt with by the Tribunal in its
award on the merits of each case: cf s 31(4) of the Arbitration Act 1996'. *b*

[31] Linklaters replied to this on 18 June 1998. They recognised that the issue
of whether CPTDC had entered into a 'valid agreement to arbitrate' in relation
to each 'contract' was one that involved 'exploration of facts which would
duplicate evidence at a hearing on the merits of the claim'. So that suggestion
was not pursued. But the point on whether CNPC was bound by the contracts *c*
was still urged. However, Mr Harris ruled that there should be no preliminary
issues in his letter of 22 June 1998.

[32] The parties therefore continued their preparations for full hearings in both
arbitrations. On 29 October 1998 Linklaters' retainer on behalf of the respondents
was terminated. In a letter dated 29 October 1998 to Mr Harris (copied to HFW), *d*
Mr Wang Jiajie, counsel for CPTDC and CNPC, stated that CPTDC's view was
that the arbitrator had no jurisdiction to decide the issue of whether the
'charterparty' bound CPTDC. He also stated that because CNPC had not signed
either 'contract' then 'there is not any arbitration clause between CNPC and any
parties'.

[33] Zaiwalla & Co (Zaiwalla) were instructed by the respondents on *e*
2 November 1998. They expressed concern over the issue of whether Mr Harris
was properly able to continue as the sole arbitrator in both cases. Then on
9 November 1998 Zaiwalla wrote to Mr Harris (with a copy to HFW) stating that
the respondents were withdrawing their consent to him acting as a sole arbitrator.
The reason given was '[Mr Harris'] failure to disclose that [he] did not possess any *f*
legal qualifications'.

[34] On 25 November 1998 the respondents applied to the court for a
declaration that the appointment of Mr Harris was void, because it had been
vitiated by a mistake as to his qualifications. Mance J heard the applications on
1 December and gave judgment dismissing them on 4 December 1998. *g*

[35] Zaiwalla wrote to Mr Harris on 4 December, suggesting that he should
still resign as the applications had put him in an embarrassing position. In the
same letter Zaiwalla again raised the argument that CPTDC was not a party to
the 'charterparty contract', so that the first issue in that case was whether there
was 'ever a valid London Arbitration Clause'. In a fax dated 7 December 1998 *h*
from Beijing, Zaiwalla also suggested that the issue of whether there were any
valid agreements between the parties should be taken as a preliminary point in
court under s 32 of the Act.

[36] HFW's response the same day was that these points had already been
aired and the arbitrator had declined to order any preliminary issues. Their letter *j*
continued:

'By asking the arbitrator to determine the preliminary questions, your
clients indicated that they were content for these matters to be dealt with
subject to any rights of appeal or review under the Arbitration Act 1996, by
the arbitrator.'

[37] Mr Harris declined to give his consent to the court hearing a preliminary issue on whether there were binding contracts between the parties. He pointed out that the hearings before him were due to take place in five weeks' time.

[38] Zaiwalla replied to Mr Harris on 8 December 1998, reporting that their clients had instructed them to take part in the arbitration hearings before him, but 'under reserve and without prejudice to all their contentions in respect of which they expressly reserve their position'. That fax was copied to HFW. In a further fax to HFW on the same date, Zaiwalla reiterated that they would participate in the arbitrations before Mr Harris 'under reserve'. Zaiwalla made a suggestion, clearly intended to be 'without prejudice', that if the tribunal were expanded, or a substitute for Mr Harris were found, then their reserves would be dropped. HFW rejected this suggestion. Thereafter all letters from Zaiwalla were marked 'under reserve'.

[39] The hearings before Mr Harris started on 15 March 1999. Mr Mark Strachan QC, who appeared for the respondents, stated at the very start of the hearing that the respondents appeared 'under reserve'. He continued:

> 'The respondents say that they were not parties to either of the two agreements which are now being arbitrated for the reasons which are set out in detail in the defence submissions and I do not propose therefore to elaborate them but simply to state our position that we are here under reserve for those reasons.'

The hearings before Mr Harris took 15 days, on various dates between 15 March and 29 April. Mr Harris produced his two awards and detailed reasons (running to 41 pages and 111 paragraphs) on 24 May 1999.

[40] This concludes my adoption of the facts set out in the judgment below.

THE AWARDS

[41] Each award was headed 'FINAL AWARD' and included the following recital:

> '... the parties agreed that I, the undersigned Bruce Harris of 104 Ledbury Road, London W11 2AH should be appointed sole arbitrator. The agreement of CNPC and CPTDC was given without prejudice to their right to contend that I had no jurisdiction, since they argued that they had not signed and/or were not bound by the said contract. The arbitration was throughout conducted on the basis that CNPC and CPTDC's position as to my jurisdiction was reserved.'

The award in relation to the supply contract said:

> 'I award AND DECLARE that CNPC and CPTDC were not bound by the alleged contract and are accordingly under no liability to LG Caltex in respect of it or the claims advanced under it.'

The award in relation to the charterparty said:

> 'I award AND DECLARE that CNPC and CPTDC were not bound by the alleged charter and are accordingly under no liability to Conti in respect of it or the claims advanced under it.'

The joint reasons to the awards recorded:

> 'The respondents in both arbitrations appeared under reservations as to my jurisdiction in two respects. In the first place, they contended that they

were not parties to the relevant contracts and thus not parties to any   a
arbitration agreements.'

The reasons ended:

'For the reasons given in paras 1 to 69 above, I declare that the respondents
were not bound by the contracts relied upon in these references and are thus
under no liability to the claimants.'   b

[42] These lengthy reasons dealt and dealt exclusively with whether the
respondents were party to the respective contracts.

THE FOUR PRELIMINARY ISSUES
[43] The four preliminary issues that Aikens J directed should be tried before   c
him were as follows:

'(1) Whether the tribunal's awards are awards as to its "substantive
jurisdiction" within the meaning of s 67(1)(a) of the Act; (2) whether the
applicants, although contending that the tribunal had substantive
jurisdiction on the basis that the parties had entered into contracts   d
incorporating valid arbitration agreements (namely the supply contract and
the charterparty), may apply for an order pursuant to s 67(1)(b) of the Act,
declaring that the awards made by the tribunal are of no effect; (3) whether
the parties concluded an ad hoc arbitration agreement which was binding on
all parties and which conferred jurisdiction on the tribunal to determine
whether the respondents were parties to the supply contract and charterparty,   e
and if so whether the applicants are precluded from bringing any challenge
under s 67 for that reason; (4) whether in relation to the s 67 challenge, the
applicants have in any event lost the right to object pursuant to s 73 of the Act.'

                                                                          f
THE SIGNIFICANCE OF THE THIRD ISSUE
[44] Aikens J took the view that if the parties had concluded what he described
as an ad hoc agreement to arbitrate the issue of whether there were binding
contracts, that agreement rendered Mr Harris' decision on that point one which
fell within his jurisdiction under the ad hoc agreement. In that event, all
questions of whether Mr Harris had jurisdiction would fall away and his award   g
on the point would be binding and not susceptible to challenge under s 67. Thus,
the question of whether or not an ad hoc agreement was concluded was of critical
importance. The nature of the agreement that Aikens J intended to describe by
the phrase 'ad hoc' is apparent from the following paragraph of his judgment:

'48. The way to avoid any challenge to the jurisdiction of an arbitrator to   h
make a binding award on the initial existence of a contract under the old law
was to enter into an ad hoc agreement for him to do so. That agreement
conferred authority to decide the issue and the result bound the parties,
subject to any statutory rights to appeal on a point of law or otherwise to
challenge the award. An ad hoc submission to an arbitrator was simply an   j
agreement between two parties that an arbitrator would determine an
existing dispute between them that was not already the subject of an existing
arbitration agreement. An ad hoc agreement was often made without any
formalities. It might be concluded from an exchange of letters or faxes or
even be construed from the conduct of the parties in the course of an existing
reference to an arbitration tribunal: see e g ... The Almare Prima ... In

considering whether an ad hoc agreement was made, the court had to decide what was the objective intention of the parties, just as it does in relation to any other type of contract.'

[45] The type of ad hoc agreement described by Aikens J is one whereby the parties confer jurisdiction on the arbitrator to resolve the substantive dispute between them. In the present case, the respondents contended that they had *b* concluded an ad hoc agreement in relation to one issue only, albeit the central issue, namely, whether the respondents were party to the two contracts on which the appellants founded their claims for damages. An answer to that question, favourable to the appellants in respect of either claim, would not of itself entitle them to any relief. It would, however, determine the central issue in the *c* substantive dispute in their favour. It would also establish that Mr Harris had jurisdiction to entertain their claim for damages. Thus the ad hoc agreement alleged in each case was an agreement purporting to confer on Mr Harris jurisdiction to determine whether he had substantive jurisdiction.

[46] Mr Angus Glennie QC, for the appellants, argued before Aikens J, and *d* again before us, that: (1) it was unlikely that the parties would conclude such an agreement when s 30 of the 1996 Act already recognised Mr Harris' competence to rule on his own jurisdiction; and (2) such an agreement could not deprive the parties of their right to challenge before the court any finding Mr Harris made as to his jurisdiction. Section 67 of the 1996 Act was a mandatory provision which could not be excluded by agreement.

e [47] Aikens J's response to this submission appears from the following passage from the following paragraphs of his judgment:

> '54. If there is a dispute about the jurisdiction of the arbitrator to decide an issue, then the arbitrator can rule upon the point (ss 30 and 31(4)(a)), or the court can do so as a preliminary issue in certain circumstances (s 32). The *f* arbitrator's decision can then be challenged (s 67(1)(a), but subject to s 73). That regime may mean that parties would be less concerned to ensure that the arbitrator has jurisdiction at the outset, because he can rule on it and the matter can easily be reviewed by the court. But the Act does not stop the parties from making an ad hoc submission on a particular issue (such as *g* whether a contract was concluded) if it appears that the jurisdiction of the arbitrator to decide a particular point is in issue and the parties wish to ensure that his jurisdiction cannot be impugned. There is no prohibition in the Act. The fact that both ss 31 and 67 of the Act are "mandatory" provisions, so cannot be excluded by agreement between the parties, does not prevent parties from enlarging the existing jurisdiction of an arbitrator by an ad hoc *h* submission. The only issue in each case is whether, objectively construed, the communications of the parties have resulted in an ad hoc submission.
>
> 55. Therefore I have concluded that, under the regime of the Act, it is perfectly possible for parties to make an ad hoc submission to an arbitrator on an issue that is not covered by an existing arbitration agreement. In this *j* case that means that an ad hoc submission would be found (if at all) in the relevant correspondence between the solicitors prior to the hearings before Mr Harris.'

[48] In this passage Aikens J did not focus on the point that the alleged ad hoc agreement was one under which Mr Harris was to rule on his own jurisdiction; nor did he explain why s 67(1)(a) had no application to a ruling on jurisdiction made

pursuant to an ad hoc agreement. He simply spoke in general terms of enlarging the existing jurisdiction of the arbitrator by an ad hoc submission.

[49] It would be strange if s 67(1)(a) had the result that parties to a dispute could not by agreement confer on an arbitrator jurisdiction to make a final and binding award on the issue of whether they had concluded an earlier arbitration agreement, conferring on the arbitrator jurisdiction to adjudicate on the substantive dispute between them. Such a result would seem in conflict with the principle set out in s 1(b) of the 1996 Act. If the parties had appointed someone other than Mr Harris to resolve the issue of whether the respondents were party to the contracts, there would be no basis for challenging his ruling. Why should the parties not be entitled to confer on Mr Harris the power to make a ruling that would be equally definitive?

[50] The answer to the conundrum is, I suggest, as follows. Section 67(1)(a) entitles a party to challenge an award of an arbitrator as to his substantive jurisdiction. However, if it is shown that the award is made under a separate agreement that he should rule on that matter, the challenge will fail. Thus, in the instant case, there has been no bar to the appellants' right to challenge in court Mr Harris' awards. Before Aikens J that challenge has failed because of the finding of the ad hoc agreement.

ISSUE 3

Was there an ad hoc submission on the issue of whether the parties were bound by the two contracts?

[51] Aikens J thought it logical to address this issue first. I agree and shall follow his example. It is not possible to analyse the judge's reasoning on this issue without first setting it out in full. It was as follows:

'63. The position up to the time the respondents' defence submissions were served in May 1998 is as follows. (1) The applicants asserted (in correspondence and in their claim submissions) that CPTDC and CNPC were parties to two contracts with the applicants. They also asserted that those two contracts contained arbitration clauses whose scope was wide enough to cover the claims on the contracts that the applicants wished to make against the respondents. The applicants gave notice of arbitration in relation to disputes under both contracts in their letters of 26 September 1997. At all times after that HFW made it clear that they wished the arbitrator to decide the issue of which respondent was bound by the two contracts. The applicants therefore made a kind of "offer" (in writing) to conclude an ad hoc submission to Mr Harris of this issue. (2) On behalf of the respondents Linklaters agreed to the appointment of Mr Harris in relation to disputes under both contracts, but expressly reserved the position of both the respondents as to the jurisdiction of the arbitrator in their letters on 21 October and 10 November 1997. (3) The respondents' "thumbnail sketch" letter of 28 November 1997 clearly stated their case that CNPC was not a party to either contract and that CPTDC was not a party to the charterparty contract. The paragraphs dealing with the supply contract are more equivocal but they certainly do not admit that CPTDC was a party to such a contract. (4) That position was maintained until Linklaters received the claim submissions on 9 March 1998. Linklaters then wrote their letter of 19 March 1998 to HFW. This asked for six months (until 9 September 1998) in which to prepare the respondents' defences. The letter states that it is "without prejudice to CNPC's rights to challenge the jurisdiction of the tribunal which we fully reserve". Nothing is stated about CPTDC's position. (5) HFW responded in their letter of 26 March, stating that in the ICC arbitration there had been a challenge by CNPC and CPTDC to the validity of the underlying agreements "and therefore the jurisdiction of the Tribunal". HFW also stated that in the ICC arbitration CNPC had said it was not a party to any agreement. But, HFW continued: "no such challenge has yet been indicated in the two arbitrations before you". As I have already pointed out, that is not the case, strictly speaking ... However the letter does go on to acknowledge that because the defences have not been pleaded the issues between the parties had not yet crystallised. (6) In their response on 30 March, Linklaters reiterated the reservation of CNPC to the jurisdiction of the tribunal, fully reserving its position. Later on the same page Linklaters make the contradictory remark that "with respect to the two ad hoc arbitrations before you, we have indicated that our clients are willing for them to proceed and be heard concurrently".

65. Mr Siberry submitted that by the time HFW received Linklaters' letter of 30 March 1998 there was an ad hoc submission. I cannot accept this contention. It seems clear that the parties had not fully analysed the issue of the jurisdiction of Mr Harris at this stage. Linklaters had clearly reserved the rights of CNPC to challenge the jurisdiction of Mr Harris and had denied that CNPC was party to either contract. As to CPTDC's position, Linklaters had made it clear in previous correspondence that CPTDC's case was that it was not bound by the charterparty. That stance was not withdrawn in the letter of 30 March. Indeed Linklaters make the point that they needed more time to see what the issues were. That leaves the position of CPTDC on the "supply contract". There again Linklaters said that they needed more time to find out what the issues were.

66. Linklaters did not have to make any formal objection to the substantive jurisdiction of Mr Harris until (at the latest) they took the first step in the proceedings to contest the merits of whether the respondents were party to the two "contracts". That point would be when the defence submissions were served. Therefore it is unlikely that it would be possible to construe from the correspondence an agreement that the issue of whether the respondents were party to the two "contracts" had been submitted ad hoc to Mr Harris. In my view the court cannot readily infer that the parties have agreed to make an ad hoc submission to an arbitrator by virtue of their correspondence and conduct if the issue which would be the subject of the ad hoc submission has not been squarely identified by the parties. That issue did not fully emerge until the defence submissions of the respondents, served on 15 May.

67. What was the position after the defence submissions were served? (1) At the same time as the defence submissions were served Linklaters sent a letter of 15 May inviting Mr Harris to address "jurisdictional matters by way of a preliminary issue hearing". The letter focused particularly on the position of CNPC, although in the pleading the jurisdiction point is made on behalf of both respondents. In my view the letter and the pleadings together indicated that Linklaters were prepared that Mr Harris should have jurisdiction to decide the issue of whether the respondents were party to the two contracts. (2) HFW resisted the idea of preliminary issues, but in their letter of 9 June 1998 suggested that the questions of jurisdiction be dealt with

in Mr Harris' awards on the merits. That indicates that HFW remained
content that Mr Harris should have jurisdiction to decide the "central issue"
of whether the respondents were bound by the two contracts. (3) Linklaters
accepted HFW's suggestion in relation to CPTDC in their response on 18
June 1998. But they pursued the idea of a preliminary issue on whether
CPTDC, as agent, could bind CNPC, as principal, to the two contracts.
Mr Harris ruled against that idea in his fax of 22 June 1998. (4) Thereafter,
in the period 23 June to 27 July 1998, there was correspondence between
Linklaters and HFW on the procedural steps and timetable that would lead
to the two arbitration hearings before Mr Harris. Linklaters did not make
any further reservations as to the jurisdiction of Mr Harris and neither did
HFW. (5) On 23 July 1998 there was a directions hearing before Mr Harris.
On 27 July 1998 he sent a fax to the two solicitors to confirm the directions
that had been agreed or determined at the hearing on 23 July 1998. The
directions aimed at hearings which it was proposed would take place in
January 1999.

68. It seems to me that, by the time of Mr Harris' fax of 27 July 1998 at the
latest, the parties had, through their solicitors, made an ad hoc submission to
Mr Harris of the issue of whether the respondents were parties to and bound
by the two "contracts". That submission was an arbitration agreement
within s 5(2)(b) of the Act, because it was an agreement made "by exchange
of communications in writing" between Linklaters, HFW and Mr Harris.
Viewed objectively the correspondence indicates that the parties had
decided and agreed that Mr Harris should have jurisdiction to determine the
issue of whether the respondents were party to the two "contracts".

69. Thereafter until Linklaters' retainer was terminated, the parties
continued with preparations for the full hearing before Mr Harris of the
"central issue" of whether the respondents were party to and bound by the
contracts. No question of any reservations concerning Mr Harris' jurisdiction
was raised by either side.

70. After Zaiwalla were instructed there were challenges to Mr Harris'
position as arbitrator. From early December 1998 Zaiwalla stated that the
respondents would only participate in the arbitrations before Mr Harris
"under reserve".

71. But if, as I have concluded, the parties had already conferred
jurisdiction on Mr Harris to consider the central question of whether the
respondents were party to the two "contracts", then the respondents could
not thereafter unilaterally withdraw the authority of Mr Harris to determine
that issue.'

[52] I agree with the judge that the parties had not concluded an ad hoc
agreement prior to the service of the defence submissions on 15 May. But there
are one or two aspects of his analysis of the negotiations prior to that date that
indicate, I believe, that he was going off track.

[53] In para 63(1) of his judgment, the judge described the fact that HFW at all
times 'made it clear that they wished the arbitrator to decide the issue of which
the respondent was bound by the two contracts' as the making of 'a kind of
"offer" in writing' to conclude an ad hoc submission to Mr Harris of this issue.
I do not agree. HFW's stance did no more than reflect the fact that HFW wished
Mr Harris to deal with the jurisdiction issue in accordance with s 30 of the 1996
Act. That is not to say that HFW might not have been more than ready to

a conclude an ad hoc agreement had they believed this to be on the cards. But had they intended to suggest such a course, they would surely have done so in terms which made the nature of their proposal clear.

[54] In para 63(6) the judge described as 'contradictory' to Linklaters' challenge to Mr Harris' jurisdiction their remark 'with respect to the two ad hoc arbitrations before you, we have indicated that our clients are willing for them to *b* proceed and be heard concurrently'. The judge believed that this remark was contradictory because of the significance he attached to the words 'ad hoc'.

[55] The authors of the 21st edition of *Russell on Arbitration* (1997) para 2-024 make the following comment on the meaning of these words:

c 'The expression "ad hoc", as in "ad hoc arbitration" or "ad hoc submission" is used in two quite different senses: an agreement to refer an existing dispute; and/or an agreement to refer either future or existing disputes to arbitration without an arbitration institution being specified to supervise the proceedings, or at least to supply the procedural rules for the arbitration. This second sense is more common in international arbitrations.'

d
[56] The judge clearly thought that Linklaters intended the words to have the former meaning; ie that they were contemplating separate submissions to Mr Harris in relation to the disputes about jurisdiction. It is clear from the second reference that Linklaters made in their letter to the ad hoc proceedings that they were giving the phrase its latter meaning. I quote 'with respect to the question *e* raised in your fax of 1 December 1997 regarding the concurrent ICC and ad hoc proceedings'.

[57] So it seems to me that the judge approached the negotiations after 15 May on the false premise that both parties were toying with the possibility of a special agreement under which Mr Harris would be given jurisdiction to determine *f* conclusively the issue of his own jurisdiction.

[58] The judge concluded that the terms of the defence submissions, coupled with Linklaters' letter of 15 May, indicated that Linklaters were prepared to agree that Mr Harris should have jurisdiction to decide the issue of whether the respondents were party to the two contracts. I do not agree with this conclusion.

g
[59] If Linklaters had been content that Mr Harris should rule definitively on the question of whether the respondents were party to the contracts, there would have been no point in their preserving any challenge to his jurisdiction at all. They could simply have agreed 'ad hoc' that Mr Harris should have jurisdiction to determine all issues between the parties. In the event, however, the defence submissions challenged specifically both the contracts and the agreements to *h* arbitrate. Linklaters' invitation to Mr Harris in their letter of 15 May to address jurisdictional matters by way of preliminary hearing, was at odds with the suggestion that they were prepared to agree that Mr Harris should have jurisdiction to determine the central issue between the parties. Linklaters' stance from their letter of 28 November 1987, agreeing to the appointment of Mr Harris *j* down to the termination of their retainer on 29 October 1998, was entirely consistent with the procedure that would ordinarily follow from the provisions of the 1996 Act. Absent agreement to the contrary, Mr Harris was bound to rule on his own jurisdiction pursuant to s 30. But it would be open to either party to challenge his ruling pursuant to s 67. Linklaters reserved their right to make such a challenge and, up to 18 June 1998, made it quite plain that jurisdiction was a live issue.

[60] Mr Michael Collins QC, for the respondents, referred to a suggestion by
Linklaters in their 18 June letter, that the issue of whether CNPC was a party to
the contracts could be determined as a preliminary issue and thus conclude major
issues on both arbitrations 'once and for all'. He suggested that that indicated that
Linklaters were expecting Mr Harris' ruling on the jurisdiction issue to be
determinative.

[61] While I follow the argument, I do not consider that the use of this phrase
demonstrates that Linklaters were proposing an ad hoc agreement which would
result in Mr Harris making a final determination of the central issue. Linklaters'
letter of 18 June repeatedly made the point that the respondents were
maintaining their challenge to Mr Harris' jurisdiction. Their attitude is not
consistent with the suggestion that the respondents were prepared to agree to
Mr Harris making a binding ruling on the central issue.

[62] Mr Collins did not suggest that the correspondence that followed the 18
June letter up to the time that Linklaters' retainer was withdrawn contained
anything of relevance. On instructions he submitted, however, that significance
could be attached to correspondence from Zaiwalla, once they had replaced
Linklaters. I reject that suggestion. The issue is whether or not an ad hoc
agreement had been concluded before Zaiwalla came on the scene. Nothing
written by Zaiwalla bears on that issue.

[63] So far as HFW were concerned, Aikens J held that their letter of 9 June
1998 suggesting that Mr Harris rule on jurisdiction in an award dealing with the
merits indicated that 'HFW remained content that Mr Harris should have
jurisdiction to decide the "central issue" of whether the respondents were bound
by the two contracts'. I do not find that HFW's letter contained any suggestion
of an ad hoc agreement that Mr Harris should make a binding ruling on
jurisdiction. On the contrary, HFW referred expressly to the provisions of s 31(4)
of the 1996 Act when discussing the manner in which Mr Harris should deal with
the jurisdiction issue.

[64] While it is not strictly relevant to the objective determination of what the
parties agreed, it is quite plain that it never occurred to HFW that they had
concluded an ad hoc agreement with Linklaters that Mr Harris should have
jurisdiction to decide the jurisdiction issue. Thus, when Zaiwalla sought at a late
stage to get the jurisdiction issue referred to the court pursuant to s 32 of the 1996
Act, HFW wrote on 7 December 1998:

> 'In a letter dated 18 June 1998 Linklaters raised a number of jurisdictional
> matters which they thought appropriate for the termination as preliminary
> issues by the Arbitrator. That relating to CPTDC was: "Was CPTDC a party
> to a valid Agreement to Arbitrate?" The other preliminary questions
> identified by Linklaters in that letter is not relevant to the matters you have
> now raised. The question was considered by Mr Harris and by fax message
> dated 22 June he concluded that there were insufficient grounds for a hearing
> of any preliminary issues. By asking the Arbitrator to determine the
> preliminary questions, your clients indicated that they were content for
> these matters to be decided, subject to any rights of appeal or review under
> the Arbitration Act 1996, by the Arbitrator. The Arbitrator determined that
> the issues should be heard as part of the main hearing. Your clients appeared
> until now to have accepted this. Pleadings and preparation have proceeded
> on that basis.'

a [65] Nor is there any hint in Mr Harris' awards or reasons that he derived any part of his jurisdiction from an ad hoc agreement concluded between the solicitors after the statement of defence had been served, or indeed at any time. He recorded in each award the respondents' contention that he had no jurisdiction, adding that the arbitration was, throughout, conducted on the basis that the respondents' position as to his jurisdiction was reserved.

b [66] Had Mr Harris understood that the parties had concluded an ad hoc agreement enlarging the scope of his jurisdiction, I have no doubt that he would have referred to this in his awards. This conclusion is reinforced by a letter dated 30 October 1998, from Mr Harris to the respondents, which Zaiwalla placed before us after the hearing. In this, Mr Harris wrote:

c 'Under the 1996 Arbitration Act, which applies to this case, I have power to rule on my own jurisdiction, and the parties have agreed that I should do so.'

[67] This demonstrates Mr Harris' understanding that he was proceeding, with the agreement of the parties, to exercise the power conferred by s 30.

d [68] Sometimes parties proceed to conduct an arbitration without appreciating that the dispute falls outside the arbitration clause under which the arbitrator has been appointed. In such circumstances, the courts have in the past held that their conduct evidenced the conclusion of an ad hoc agreement. That is not this case. The parties have been represented by experienced commercial solicitors conversant with the provisions of the 1996 Act. The issue of jurisdiction has been
e appreciated from the outset. Had the solicitors wished to conclude an ad hoc agreement to address that issue, they would have done so expressly. In the event, their conduct accorded with that which one would expect of solicitors paying due regard to the provisions of the 1996 Act. Aikens J erred in concluding that this conduct gave rise to an ad hoc agreement.

f ISSUE 1

Are Mr Harris' awards ones as to his 'substantive jurisdiction' within s 67(1)(a)?

[69] I am deviating from the course taken by the judge in considering this question next. The issue here is whether Mr Harris' awards were awards as to his
g substantive jurisdiction to which s 67(1)(a) applies, or awards on the merits to which s 67(1)(b) applies. Aikens J held that they were the latter. His reasons were principally those set out in the following passage from his judgment:

'78. In my view they are not such awards. My reasons, briefly, are as follows. (1) Section 67(1) draws a distinction between an award as to the
h substantive jurisdiction of a tribunal and an award on the merits. This reflects the distinction made in s 31(4) of the Act. That section provides that where a party has taken an objection to the jurisdiction of an arbitral tribunal, then the tribunal can deal with the matter in one of two ways. Either it rules on the matter in an award on jurisdiction or it deals with the
j jurisdiction challenge in its award on the merits. (2) Therefore the Act contemplates that an award of a tribunal "as to its substantive jurisdiction" will specifically address that point and will not go on to deal with the merits of the underlying dispute between the parties. If the award goes on to deal with the merits, then it ceases to be an award as to the tribunal's substantive jurisdiction for the purposes of ss 31 and 67; it becomes an award on the merits instead. (3) Whether an award is one as to the substantive jurisdiction

of the Tribunal must depend on the correct construction of the wording of
the award itself. If the award contains reasons then those should also be
considered in order to decide whether the award itself is "as to [the]
substantive jurisdiction" of the Tribunal. (4) In this case the recitals of the
two awards note that the respondents contended that the arbitrator did not
have jurisdiction to determine the issue of whether they were bound by the
two "contracts". But in the body of the two awards there is no reference to
any jurisdictional issue. Mr Harris' awards both state that he awards and
declares that the respondents were not bound by the alleged contracts and
so are under no liability to LG Caltex in respect of the contracts or claims
made under them. The awards therefore deal with "the merits". To my
mind that simply precludes them from being awards as to the substantive
jurisdiction of Mr Harris.'

Here again I differ from the conclusion of the judge. My reasons are as follows.

[70] Section 31(4) provides that a tribunal, when faced with an objection to his
jurisdiction, may (a) rule on the matter in an award as to jurisdiction or (b) deal
with the objection in its award on the merits. The latter option is, however, only
one that will be open to the tribunal where it concludes that it has jurisdiction. In
that event it will be open to the tribunal to exercise that jurisdiction and deal with
the merits. Where, however, the tribunal rules that it has no jurisdiction, it is
axiomatic that it cannot then make an award on the merits. The position is
correctly stated by Mr Veeder QC in Albert Jan van den Berg (ed) *International
Handbook on Commercial Arbitration* (1993) p 50:

'If the tribunal rules that it has jurisdiction, it will proceed to resolve the
merits of the parties' dispute. If the tribunal rules that it has no jurisdiction,
it cannot of course proceed to an award on the merits.'

[71] This position is reflected by the provisions of s 67(1). Where an arbitrator
makes an award holding that he has no jurisdiction, that award will be open to
challenge under s 67(1)(a). Section 67(1)(b) can have no application to an award
in which the arbitrator holds that he has no substantive jurisdiction, for it
provides for a challenge on the ground that the tribunal did not have substantive
jurisdiction. Section 67(1)(b) can only apply to the situation where the arbitrator
holds that he has substantive jurisdiction and proceeds to make an award on the
merits. The nature of Mr Harris' awards must be determined in the light of the
above considerations.

[72] Mr Harris' awards have, as Aikens J found, the form of awards on the
merits. This is because they declare in each case, after the finding that the
respondents are not bound by the alleged contract, that they are accordingly
under no liability. Implicitly, each award determined that the respondents were
not party to any arbitration agreement and that Mr Harris had no substantive
jurisdiction.

[73] The correct form of awards ruling on jurisdiction should have ended 'are
accordingly not party to any arbitration agreement so that I have no substantive
jurisdiction in this matter', or words to like effect. Such awards would have
carried the implication that the respondents were under no liability to the
claimants.

[74] The issue of jurisdiction was before Mr Harris. His correct course was to
rule on it pursuant to s 30 of the 1996 Act. He ruled on it implicitly. The entirety
of his reasons were relevant to the issue of jurisdiction; they did not address any

a matter which extended beyond the issue of jurisdiction. Mr Harris' awards purported to make a finding as to liability. He had no jurisdiction to make that finding.

[75] In these circumstances, I consider the appropriate course is to treat Mr Harris' awards as awards in relation to his substantive jurisdiction which he was competent to make under s 30 rather than as awards on the merits which he b had no jurisdiction to make. That approach has regard to the substance of the awards in that it reflects their legal effect.

[76] For these reasons, I hold that the provisions of s 67(1)(a) apply to Mr Harris' awards. It follows that issue 2 does not arise, and it remains to deal with issue 4.

c
ISSUE 4

Have the appellants lost the right to challenge Mr Harris' lack of jurisdiction by virtue of s 73?

[77] Aikens J held that the provisions of s 73 did indeed preclude the appellants d from challenging Mr Harris' lack of jurisdiction, assuming, contrary to his finding, that there was no ad hoc agreement. The essence of his reasoning is in the following passages of his judgment:

'74. (1) Once the respondents had pleaded in their defence submissions that they were not party to or bound by the two contracts and that there e were no valid arbitration agreements, then in the absence of any subsequent ad hoc submission to Mr Harris of the issue of whether the respondents were a party to the two "contracts", Mr Harris could not have had jurisdiction to determine that issue.

(2) If the applicants had wished to object that Mr Harris had no f jurisdiction to decide the issue of whether the respondents were a party to the two "contracts" they could have done so at that point. Under s 31(1) of the Act, the applicants could have objected at any time up to the point at which they took the first step in the proceedings to contest the merits of the matter in relation to which the applicants challenged (or could have challenged) the tribunal's jurisdiction. In the context of this case that must g mean up [to] the point when the applicants served their points of reply, which is when they challenged the merits of the respondents' submission that were not a party to the two "contracts".

(3) But the applicants and HFW did not take the point, either then or at any later stage during the arbitration proceedings before Mr Harris, that he h lacked substantive jurisdiction to determine the issue of whether the respondents were party to the two "contracts". This is hardly surprising as the applicants' argument was that the contracts were binding on the respondents and they contained valid arbitration clauses.

(4) But the effect of this lack of protest means that the applicants must j lose their right to assert now that Mr Harris lacked jurisdiction to decide the issue.'

[78] It seems to me that this reasoning is founded on a false premise. The premise is that Mr Harris made awards on the merits which the appellants are now seeking to challenge on the grounds of want of jurisdiction. On my analysis the position is much more simple.

[79] Mr Harris has ruled that he has no substantive jurisdiction. The appellants seek to challenge that ruling pursuant to s 67(1)(a). In these circumstances s 73 has no application. The appellants are not making any of the objections to which that section applies. For these reasons, I differ from the judge's conclusion that s 73 is a bar to the relief that the appellants seek.

[80] The issue of whether the respondents were party to the two contracts was a central issue in the dispute as to liability. The appellants were urging that Mr Harris had jurisdiction to determine liability. Mr Harris, after a hearing that lasted three weeks, has decided the central issue against them. Because that issue was also the issue that determines jurisdiction, the appellants are now able to reopen it. The judge considered this result unjust. I am not persuaded that it is. Where an issue on which jurisdiction turns is also an issue relevant to liability, each party will be in a position, subject to making any necessary reservations, to reopen that issue before the court if the arbitrator's ruling on jurisdiction goes against them. In this instance it is the appellants who have profited from this situation.

[81] For the reasons I have given, I would allow this appeal.

PILL LJ.

[82] I agree.

KEENE LJ.

[83] I also agree.

Appeal allowed.

Kate O'Hanlon   Barrister.

a

R v Looseley
Attorney General's Reference (No 3 of 2000)
[2001] UKHL 53

b HOUSE OF LORDS

LORD NICHOLLS OF BIRKENHEAD, LORD MACKAY OF CLASHFERN, LORD HOFFMANN, LORD HUTTON AND LORD SCOTT OF FOSCOTE

25–27 JUNE, 25 OCTOBER 2001

c *Criminal law – Trial – Stay of proceedings – Abuse of process – Entrapment – Circumstances in which criminal proceedings to be stayed or evidence excluded on grounds of entrapment – Whether English law on entrapment complying with right to fair trial under human rights convention – Police and Criminal Evidence Act 1984, s 78 – Human Rights Act 1998, Sch 1, Pt I, art 6.*

d The English law on entrapment has not been modified by the right to a fair trial under art 6[a] of the European Convention for the Protection of Human Rights and Fundamental Freedoms 1950 (as set out in Sch 1 to the Human Rights Act 1998). Under English law, entrapment is not a substantive defence to criminal proceedings, but where a defendant can show entrapment the court may stay the proceedings as an abuse of process or exclude evidence pursuant to s 78[b] of the Police and

e Criminal Evidence Act 1984. Of those two remedies, the grant of a stay, rather than the exclusion of evidence at the trial, should, as a matter of principle, normally be regarded as the appropriate response in a case of entrapment. A prosecution founded on entrapment is an abuse of the court's process. Police conduct which brings about state-created crime is unacceptable and improper,

f and to prosecute in such circumstances is an affront to the public conscience. In deciding whether conduct amounts to state-created crime, the overall consideration is whether, having regard to all the circumstances of the case, the conduct of the police or other law enforcement agency is so seriously improper as to bring the administration of justice into disrepute. Circumstances of particular relevance are the nature of the offence, the reason for the particular police operation, and the

g nature and extent of police participation in the crime. The greater the inducement held out by the police, and the more forceful or persistent the police overtures, the more readily may a court conclude that the police have overstepped the boundary. It will not, however, normally be regarded as objectionable for the police to behave as would an ordinary customer of a trade, whether lawful or

h unlawful, being carried on by the defendant. The latter's criminal record is unlikely to be relevant unless it can be linked to other factors grounding reasonable suspicion that the defendant is currently engaged in criminal activity. Such an approach is consistent with the jurisprudence of the European Court of Human Rights on art 6 of the convention in the context of entrapment (see [16],

j [19], [25]–[30], [33], [35], [36], [71], [72], [100], [104], [109], [117], [118], [128], below).

R v Latif, R v Shahzad [1996] 1 All ER 353, *Teixeira de Castro v Portugal* (1998) 4 BHRC 533 and *Nottingham City Council v Amin* [2000] 2 All ER 946 considered.

---

a   Article 6, so far as material, is set out at [122], below
b   Section 78, so far as material, is set out at [87], below

Notes

For the convention right to a fair trial and for entrapment, see respectively 8(2) *a*
Halsbury's Laws (4th edn reissue) para 134 and 11(1) *Halsbury's Laws* (4th edn
reissue) para 48.

For the Police and Criminal Evidence Act 1984, s 78, see 17 *Halsbury's Statutes*
(4th edn) (1999 reissue) 236.

For the Human Rights Act 1998, Sch 1, Pt I, art 6, see 7 *Halsbury's Statutes* (4th *b*
edn) (1999 reissue) 523.

Cases referred to in opinions

Amato v The Queen [1982] 2 SCR 418, Can SC.
Bennett v Horseferry Road Magistrates' Court [1993] 3 All ER 138, [1994] 1 AC 42,
   [1993] 3 WLR 90, HL.   *c*
Brannan v Peek [1947] 2 All ER 572, [1948] 1 KB 68, DC.
Brown v Stott (Procurator Fiscal, Dunfermline) [2001] 2 All ER 97, [2001] 2 WLR 817,
   PC.
Browning v J W H Watson (Rochester) Ltd [1953] 2 All ER 775, [1953] 1 WLR 1172,
   DC.   *d*
Connelly v DPP [1964] 2 All ER 401, [1964] AC 1254, [1964] 2 WLR 1145, HL.
DPP v Marshall [1988] 3 All ER 683, DC.
Ealing London Borough v Woolworths plc [1995] Crim LR 58, DC.
Hampton v US (1976) 425 US 484, US SC.
Khan v UK (2000) 8 BHRC 310, ECt HR.
Lüdi v Switzerland (1992) 15 EHRR 173, ECt HR.   *e*
Nottingham City Council v Amin [2000] 2 All ER 946, [2000] 1 WLR 1071, DC.
Police v Lavalle [1979] 1 NZLR 45, NZ CA.
R v Ameer, R v Lucas [1977] Crim LR 104.
R v Birtles [1969] 2 All ER 1131n, [1969] 1 WLR 1047, CA.
R v Burnett [1973] Crim LR 748, CA.   *f*
R v Chalkley, R v Jeffries [1998] 2 All ER 155, [1998] QB 848, [1998] 3 WLR 146, CA.
R v Foulder [1973] Crim LR 45.
R v Gill [1989] Crim LR 358, CA.
R v Keane [1994] 2 All ER 478, [1994] 1 WLR 746, CA.
R v Khan (Sultan) [1996] 3 All ER 289, [1997] AC 558, [1996] 3 WLR 162, HL.
R v Latif, R v Shahzad [1996] 1 All ER 353, [1996] 1 WLR 104, HL.   *g*
R v Lawrence, R v Nash (1993) Independent, 31 January, CA.
R v Mack [1988] 2 SCR 903, Can SC.
R v McCann (1971) 56 Cr App R 359, CA.
R v McEvilly, R v Lee (1973) 60 Cr App R 150, CA.
R v Mealey, R v Sheridan (1974) 60 Cr App R 59, CA.   *h*
R v Sang [1979] 2 All ER 1222, [1980] AC 402, [1979] 3 WLR 263, HL.
R v Shannon [2001] 1 WLR 51, CA.
R v Smurthwaite, R v Gill [1994] 1 All ER 898, CA.
Ridgeway v The Queen (1995) 184 CLR 19, Aust HC.
Sherman v US (1957) 356 US 369, US SC.   *j*
Soering v UK (1989) 11 EHRR 439, [1989] ECHR 14038/88, ECt HR.
Sorrells v US (1932) 287 US 435, US SC.
Taunton Deane BC v Brice (1997) 31 Licensing Review 24, DC.
Teixeira de Castro v Portugal (1998) 4 BHRC 533, ECt HR.
US v Russell (1973) 411 US 423, US SC.
Williams v DPP [1993] 3 All ER 365, DC.

_a_ **Appeal and reference**

R v Looseley

Grant Spencer Looseley appealed with leave of the Appeal Committee of the House of Lords given on 14 February 2001 from the order of the Court of Appeal (Roch LJ, Smith and Moore-Bick JJ) on 13 April 2000 dismissing his appeal against

_b_ his conviction in the Crown Court at Guildford on 5 January 2000 on three counts of supplying or being concerned in the supply of a class A drug. The appellant had pleaded guilty following a ruling by Judge Bassingthwaighte on 27 October 1999 whereby he (i) refused to stay the proceedings as an abuse of the process of the court, and (ii) refused to exclude the evidence of an undercover police officer. The Court of Appeal certified that a point of law of general public importance, set

_c_ out at [76], below, was involved in its decision. The facts are set out in the opinion of Lord Hutton.

A-G's Reference (No 3 of 2000)

On 23 November 2000 the defendant appeared for trial in the Crown Court at

_d_ Derby on two counts of supplying or being concerned in supplying a class A drug. The proceedings against him were stayed by Judge Appleby QC on the ground that undercover police officers had incited the defendant to commit the offences. The next day, the judge lifted the stay, the prosecution offered no evidence and verdicts of not guilty were entered. Following the defendant's acquittal, the Attorney General referred to the Court of Appeal, under s 36 of the Criminal Justice

_e_ Act 1972, a point of law, set out at [80], below, for that court's consideration. The Court of Appeal (Kennedy LJ, Curtis and Hughes JJ) gave its opinion on 17 May 2001 ([2001] EWCA Crim 1214, [2001] 2 Cr App R 472), and on the application of the Attorney General referred the point to the House of Lords for its consideration. The facts are set out in the opinion of Lord Hutton.

_f_
Patrick O'Connor QC and _Michael Cousens_ (instructed by _Castle Partnership_, Guildford) for Looseley.
David Perry and _Christopher Hehir_ (instructed by the _Crown Prosecution Service_) for the Crown in Looseley's appeal.
Ben Emmerson QC, Alastair Munt and _Danny Friedman_ (instructed by _Rickards &_

_g_ _Cleaver_, Alfreton) for the acquitted person in the Attorney General's reference.
David Perry and _Duncan Penny_ (instructed by the _Crown Prosecution Service_) for the Attorney General.

Their Lordships took time for consideration.

_h_
25 October 2001. The following opinions were delivered.

LORD NICHOLLS OF BIRKENHEAD.
    [1] My Lords, every court has an inherent power and duty to prevent abuse of
_j_ its process. This is a fundamental principle of the rule of law. By recourse to this principle courts ensure that executive agents of the state do not misuse the coercive, law enforcement functions of the courts and thereby oppress citizens of the state. Entrapment, with which these two appeals are concerned, is an instance where such misuse may occur. It is simply not acceptable that the state through its agents should lure its citizens into committing acts forbidden by the law and then seek to prosecute them for doing so. That would be entrapment. That

would be a misuse of state power, and an abuse of the process of the courts. The unattractive consequences, frightening and sinister in extreme cases, which state conduct of this nature could have are obvious. The role of the courts is to stand between the state and its citizens and make sure this does not happen.

[2] These propositions, I apprehend, are not controversial. The difficulty lies in identifying conduct which is caught by such imprecise words as lure or incite or entice or instigate. If police officers acted only as detectives and passive observers, there would be little problem in identifying the boundary between permissible and impermissible police conduct. But that would not be a satisfactory place for the boundary line. Detection and prosecution of consensual crimes committed in private would be extremely difficult. Trafficking in drugs is one instance. With such crimes there is usually no victim to report the matter to the police. And sometimes victims or witnesses are unwilling to give evidence.

[3] Moreover, and importantly, in some instances a degree of active involvement by the police in the commission of a crime is generally regarded as acceptable. Test purchases fall easily into this category. In *DPP v Marshall* [1988] 3 All ER 683 a trader was approached in his shop in the same way as any ordinary customer might have done. In breach of his licence he sold individual cans of lager to plain clothes police officers. In *Nottingham City Council v Amin* [2000] 2 All ER 946, [2000] 1 WLR 1071 a taxi was being driven in an area not covered by its licence. The driver accepted plain clothes police officers as fare-paying passengers. Police conduct of this nature does not attract reprobation even though, in the latter case, the roof light on the taxi was not illuminated. The police behaved in the same way as any member of the public wanting a taxi in the normal course might have done. Indeed, conduct of this nature by officials is sometimes expressly authorised by Act of Parliament. The statute creating an offence may authorise officials to make test purchases, as in s 27 of the Trade Descriptions Act 1968.

[4] Thus, there are occasions when it is necessary for the police to resort to investigatory techniques in which the police themselves are the reporters and the witnesses of the commission of a crime. Sometimes the particular technique adopted is acceptable. Sometimes it is not. For even when the use of these investigatory techniques is justified, there are limits to what is acceptable. Take a case where an undercover policeman repeatedly badgers a vulnerable drug addict for a supply of drugs in return for excessive and ever increasing amounts of money. Eventually the addict yields to the importunity and pressure, and supplies drugs. He is then prosecuted for doing so. Plainly, this result would be objectionable. The crime committed by the addict could readily be characterised as artificial or state-created crime. In the absence of the police operation, the addict might well never have supplied drugs to anyone.

[5] I shall return later to the knotty problem of defining, or identifying, the limits of acceptable 'proactive' conduct by the police. First I must consider where English law now stands on the overall question of entrapment.

The remedy for entrapment

[6] Common law countries differ in the nature of the remedy provided in entrapment cases. In the United States entrapment is a substantive defence in the Federal courts. This is based on a presumption of legislative intent. 'Congress could not have intended that its statutes were to be enforced by tempting innocent persons into violations' (see *Sherman v United States* (1957) 356 US 369 at 372). The issue therefore is one for decision by the jury. The Canadian Supreme Court has adopted a different approach. In Canada the remedy is by way of stay of

proceedings (see *R v Mack* [1988] 2 SCR 903). In Australia a third approach has found favour. In *Ridgeway v The Queen* (1995) 184 CLR 19 the High Court declined to follow the Canadian route. A stay is regarded as inappropriate once it is accepted that entrapment is not a substantive defence. But a trial judge has a discretion to exclude evidence of an offence where its commission was brought about by unlawful or improper conduct on the part of law enforcement officers. Likewise, in New Zealand the court has an inherent jurisdiction to exclude evidence so as to prevent an abuse of process by the avoidance of unfairness (see *Police v Lavalle* [1979] 1 NZLR 45).

[7] The judicial response to entrapment in this country before *R v Sang* [1979] 2 All ER 1222, [1980] AC 402 can be summarised as follows. Entrapment attracted expressions of judicial disapproval, notably by Lord Goddard CJ in *Brannan v Peek* [1947] 2 All ER 572 at 574, [1948] 1 KB 68 at 72, and Lord Parker CJ in *R v Birtles* [1969] 2 All ER 1131n, [1969] 1 WLR 1047 at 1049, but it did not furnish a substantive defence (see *R v McEvilly, R v Lee* (1973) 60 Cr App R 150 and *R v Mealey, R v Sheridan* (1974) 60 Cr App R 59). Although not constituting a defence, in some cases judges excluded evidence in entrapment cases (*R v Foulder* [1973] Crim LR 45, *R v Burnett* [1973] Crim LR 748 and *R v Ameer, R v Lucas* [1977] Crim LR 104). Entrapment was regarded as a mitigating factor in, for instance, *R v McCann* (1971) 56 Cr App R 359.

[8] In *R v Sang* your Lordships' House affirmed the Court of Appeal decisions of *R v McEvilly* and *R v Mealey*. The House treated it as axiomatic that entrapment does not exist as a substantive defence in English law. Lord Diplock ([1979] 2 All ER 1222 at 1226, [1980] AC 402 at 432) noted that many crimes are committed by one person at the instigation of others. The fact that the counsellor or procurer is a policeman or a police informer, although it may be of relevance in mitigation of penalty for the offence, cannot affect the guilt of the principal offender: '… both the physical element (actus reus) and the mental element (mens rea) of the offence with which he is charged are present in his case.' Likewise, Lord Fraser of Tullybelton ([1979] 2 All ER 1222 at 1238, [1980] AC 402 at 446) observed that all the elements, factual and mental, of guilt are present and no finding other than guilty would be logically possible. The degree of guilt may be modified by the inducement and that can appropriately be reflected in the sentence. Lord Fraser famously added that when Eve, taxed with having eaten forbidden fruit, replied 'the serpent beguiled me', her excuse was at most a plea in mitigation and not a complete defence.

[9] In *R v Sang* the House also decided that, leaving aside admissions and confessions, the court is not concerned with how evidence was obtained. It is no ground for the exercise of a trial judge's discretion to exclude evidence that the evidence was obtained as the result of the activities of an agent provocateur, or by other unfair or improper means. That would be to let in the defence of entrapment by the back door. *R v Foulder, R v Burnett* and *R v Ameer* were wrongly decided. Entrapment is a mitigating factor and no more. Lord Scarman ([1979] 2 All ER 1222 at 1243, [1980] AC 402 at 451) stated that the true relevance of official entrapment into the commission of crime is upon the question of sentence, when its mitigating value may be high.

[10] The decision in *R v Sang* has not escaped criticism. For present purposes it is sufficient to note that the reasoning of their Lordships was directed at the question whether entrapment constitutes a substantive defence or is a cause for excluding evidence at the trial. But, as already noted, entrapment raises another and anterior issue, an issue of an altogether different dimension, quite distinct

from the question of the defendant's guilt or the actual conduct of the trial. Entrapment assumes the defendant did the proscribed act, with the necessary intent, and without duress. But when entrapment occurs, the commission of the offence by the defendant has been brought about by the state's own agents. This is the crucially important difference between cases of entrapment and other cases of instigated crime. In *R v Sang* their Lordships were not called upon to consider whether a judge has power to stay criminal proceedings when law enforcement officers have acted in this way. Implicitly, however, they rejected the availability of this judicial remedy in entrapment cases. Lord Scarman said so expressly. He observed that a court is in duty bound to protect itself against abuse of its process, which 'is not this case' (see [1979] 2 All ER 1222 at 1245, [1980] AC 402 at 455).

[11] In this field English criminal law has undergone substantial development over the comparatively short period of 20 years since *R v Sang* was decided. The first development has been statutory. The decision in *R v Sang* on the admissibility of evidence obtained unfairly has been reversed by Parliament, by s 78 of the Police and Criminal Evidence Act 1984. Under s 78 the court now has power to exclude evidence on which the prosecution proposes to rely if, having regard to all the circumstances, the court considers the admission of the evidence would have such an adverse effect on the fairness of the proceedings that the court ought not to admit it. The circumstances to which the court is to have regard include, expressly, the circumstances in which the evidence was obtained.

[12] The phrase 'fairness of the proceedings' in s 78 is directed primarily at matters going to fairness in the actual conduct of the trial; for instance, the reliability of the evidence and the defendant's ability to test its reliability. But, rightly, the courts have been unwilling to limit the scope of this wide and comprehensive expression strictly to procedural fairness. In *R v Smurthwaite, R v Gill* [1994] 1 All ER 898 at 902, Lord Taylor of Gosforth CJ stated that s 78 has not altered the substantive rule that entrapment does not of itself provide a defence. The fact that the evidence was obtained by entrapment does not of itself require the judge to exclude it. But, in deciding whether to admit the evidence of an undercover police officer, the judge may take into account matters such as whether the officer was enticing the defendant to commit an offence he would not otherwise have committed, the nature of any entrapment, and how active or passive was the officer's role in obtaining the evidence. I do not understand Auld LJ to have been expressing a contrary view in *R v Chalkley, R v Jeffries* [1998] 2 All ER 155 at 178–180, [1998] QB 848 at 874–876. *R v Chalkley* was not an entrapment case. Most recently in *R v Shannon* [2001] 1 WLR 51 at 68 (para 39), Potter LJ, as I read his judgment, accepted that evidence may properly be excluded when the behaviour of the police or prosecuting authority has been such as to justify a stay on grounds of abuse of process.

[13] Next, the common law also has developed since the decision in *R v Sang*. In *Bennett v Horseferry Road Magistrates' Court* [1993] 3 All ER 138, [1994] 1 AC 42 your Lordships' House held that the court has jurisdiction to stay proceedings and order the release of the accused when the court becomes aware there has been a serious abuse of power by the executive. The court can refuse to allow the police or prosecuting authorities to take advantage of such an abuse of power by regarding it as an abuse of the court's process. Lord Griffiths ([1993] 3 All ER 138 at 151, [1994] 1 AC 42 at 62) echoed the words of Lord Devlin that the courts 'cannot contemplate for a moment the transference to the executive of the responsibility for seeing that the process of law is not abused' (see *Connelly v DPP* [1964] 2 All ER 401 at 442, [1964] AC 1254 at 1354). The judiciary should accept

a a responsibility for the maintenance of the rule of law that embraces a willingness to oversee executive action and to refuse to countenance behaviour that 'threatens either basic human rights or the rule of law' (see [1993] 3 All ER 138 at 150, [1994] 1 AC 42 at 62).

[14] In *Bennett's* case the defendant claimed he had been forcibly abducted and brought to this country to face trial in disregard of extradition laws. It was not an

b entrapment case. But in *R v Latif, R v Shahzad* [1996] 1 All ER 353, [1996] 1 WLR 104 the House confirmed that the same principle is applicable in entrapment cases (see [1996] 1 All ER 353 at 361, [1996] 1 WLR 104 at 112–113 per Lord Steyn).

[15] These statutory and common law developments have been reinforced by the Human Rights Act 1998. It is unlawful for the court, as a public authority, to act in a way which is incompatible with a convention right. Entrapment, and the

c use of evidence obtained by entrapment ('as a result of police incitement'), may deprive a defendant of the right to a fair trial embodied in art 6 of the European Convention for the Protection of Human Rights and Fundamental Freedoms (Rome, 4 November 1950; TS 71 (1953); Cmd 8969) (as set out in Sch 1 to the 1998 Act): see the decision of the European Court of Human Rights in *Teixeira de*

d *Castro v Portugal* (1998) 4 BHRC 533.

[16] Thus, although entrapment is not a substantive defence, English law has now developed remedies in respect of entrapment: the court may stay the relevant criminal proceedings, and the court may exclude evidence pursuant to s 78 of the 1984 Act. In these respects *R v Sang* has been overtaken. Of these two remedies the grant of a stay, rather than the exclusion of evidence at the trial,

e should normally be regarded as the appropriate response in a case of entrapment. Exclusion of evidence from the trial will often have the same result in practice as an order staying the proceedings. Without, for instance, the evidence of the undercover police officers the prosecution will often be unable to proceed. But this is not necessarily so. There may be real evidence, or evidence of other

f witnesses. Exclusion of all the prosecution evidence would, of course, dispose of any anomaly in this regard. But a direction to this effect would really be a stay of the proceedings under another name. Quite apart from these practical considerations, as a matter of principle a stay of the proceedings, or of the relevant charges, is the more appropriate form of remedy. A prosecution founded on entrapment would be an abuse of the court's process. The court will not permit the prosecutorial

g arm of the state to behave in this way.

[17] I should add that when ordering a stay, and refusing to let a prosecution continue, the court is not seeking to exercise disciplinary powers over the police, although staying a prosecution may have this effect. As emphasised earlier, the objection to criminal proceedings founded on entrapment lies much deeper. For

h the same reason, entrapment is not a matter going only to the blameworthiness or culpability of the defendant and, hence, to sentence as distinct from conviction. Entrapment goes to the propriety of there being a prosecution at all for the relevant offence, having regard to the state's involvement in the circumstance in which it was committed.

j [18] A further point of principle should be noted. As observed by Auld LJ in *R v Chalkley* [1998] 2 All ER 155 at 178, [1998] QB 848 at 874, a decision on whether to stay criminal proceedings as an abuse of process is distinct from a determination of the forensic fairness of admitting evidence. Different tests are applicable to these two decisions. Accordingly, when considering an application by a defendant to exclude evidence under s 78, courts should distinguish clearly between an application to exclude evidence on the ground that the defendant should not be tried at all and an application to exclude evidence on the ground of procedural fairness. Sometimes a defendant may base his application under s 78 on both grounds. Then the court will need to reach a separate decision on each ground.

Entrapment and the limits of acceptable police conduct

[19] As already noted, the judicial response to entrapment is based on the need to uphold the rule of law. A defendant is excused, not because he is less culpable, although he may be, but because the police have behaved improperly. Police conduct which brings about, to use the catchphrase, state-created crime is unacceptable and improper. To prosecute in such circumstances would be an affront to the public conscience, to borrow the language of Lord Steyn in *R v Latif* [1996] 1 All ER 353 at 361, [1996] 1 WLR 104 at 112. In a very broad sense of the word, such a prosecution would not be fair.

[20] But what is *meant* by 'state-created crime'? What is the legal concept underlying oft-repeated expressions such as lure, incite, or instigate? What is the distinction, of relevance in the commission of a crime, which these phrases are seeking to draw? If an undercover policeman asks a known drug supplier for drugs, is he 'luring' the unsuspecting supplier into committing a crime? If not, why not? What does 'lure' mean in this context? By what criteria is a trial judge to distinguish the acceptable from the unacceptable?

[21] Questions such as these have generated extensive overseas judicial utterances and also academic literature, both in this country and abroad. The several suggested answers have different emphases and, to a limited extent, different practical consequences. Underlying some of the learning is the notion that expressions such as 'state-created crime' and 'lure' and 'incite' focus attention on the role played by the police in the formation of the defendant's intent to commit the crime in question. If the defendant already had the intent to commit a crime of the same or a similar kind, then the police did no more than give him the opportunity to fulfil his existing intent. This is unobjectionable. If the defendant was already presently disposed to commit such a crime, should opportunity arise, that is not entrapment. That is not state-created crime. The matter stands differently if the defendant lacked such a predisposition, and the police were responsible for implanting the necessary intent.

[22] Reasoning such as this, especially in the United States, is a prominent feature of the juridical analysis of why some police conduct is acceptable and other conduct is not. But, even leaving aside the difficulty that predisposition is an inherently speculative inference of fact, this analysis is inadequate as a tool. In particular, taken to its logical conclusion this analysis means that whenever the defendant's predisposition to commit the crime is established there cannot be a defence of entrapment. In the United States the law seems to have been taken this distance (see *Hampton v US* (1976) 425 US 484 at 489–490 per Rehnquist J). But surely it is going too far to say that a person who is ready and willing to commit a certain kind of crime can never be entrapped into committing it. As Lamer J observed in *R v Mack* [1988] 2 SCR 903 at 954, it is always possible that, notwithstanding a person's predisposition, in the particular case it was the conduct of the police which led the defendant into committing the crime. In other words, the existence or absence of predisposition in the individual is not the criterion by which the acceptability of police conduct is to be decided. Predisposition does not make acceptable what would otherwise be unacceptable conduct on the part of the police or other law enforcement agencies. Predisposition does not negative misuse of state power.

[23] Accordingly, one has to look elsewhere for assistance in identifying the
limits to the types of police conduct which, in any set of circumstances, are
acceptable. On this a useful guide is to consider whether the police did no more
than present the defendant with an unexceptional opportunity to commit a crime.
I emphasise the word unexceptional. The yardstick for the purpose of this test
is, in general, whether the police conduct preceding the commission of the offence
was no more than might have been expected from others in the circumstances.
Police conduct of this nature is not to be regarded as inciting or instigating crime,
or luring a person into committing a crime. The police did no more than others
could be expected to do. The police did not create crime artificially. McHugh J
had this approach in mind in *Ridgeway v The Queen* (1995) 184 CLR 19 at 92, when
he said:

> 'The State can justify the use of entrapment techniques to induce the
> commission of an offence only when the inducement is consistent with the
> ordinary temptations and stratagems that are likely to be encountered in
> the course of criminal activity. That may mean that some degree of deception,
> importunity and even threats on the part of the authorities may be
> acceptable. But once the State goes beyond the ordinary, it is likely to
> increase the incidence of crime by artificial means.'

[24] This is by no means the only factor to be taken into account when assessing
the propriety of police conduct. The investigatory technique of providing an
opportunity to commit a crime touches upon other sensitive areas. Of its nature
this technique is intrusive, to a greater or lesser degree, depending on the facts.
It should not be applied in a random fashion, and used for wholesale 'virtue-testing',
without good reason. The greater the degree of intrusiveness, the closer will the
court scrutinise the reason for using it. On this, proportionality has a role to play.

[25] Ultimately the overall consideration is always whether the conduct of the
police or other law enforcement agency was so seriously improper as to bring
the administration of justice into disrepute. Lord Steyn's formulation of a prosecution
which would affront the public conscience is substantially to the same effect (see
R v Latif [1996] 1 All ER 353 at 361, [1996] 1 WLR 104 at 112). So is Lord Bingham
of Cornhill CJ's reference to conviction and punishment which would be deeply
offensive to ordinary notions of fairness (see *Nottingham City Council v Amin* [2000]
2 All ER 946 at 949, [2000] 1 WLR 1071 at 1076). In applying these formulations
the court has regard to all the circumstances of the case. The following comments
may be made on some circumstances which are of particular relevance.

[26] *The nature of the offence.* The use of proactive techniques is more needed
and, hence, more appropriate, in some circumstances than others. The secrecy and
difficulty of detection, and the manner in which the particular criminal activity is
carried on, are relevant considerations.

[27] *The reason for the particular police operation.* It goes without saying that the
police must act in good faith and not, for example, as part of a malicious vendetta
against an individual or group of individuals. Having reasonable grounds for
suspicion is one way good faith may be established, but having grounds for suspicion
of a particular individual is not always essential. Sometimes suspicion may be
centred on a particular place, such as a particular public house. Sometimes random
testing may be the only practicable way of policing a particular trading activity.

[28] *The nature and extent of police participation in the crime.* The greater the
inducement held out by the police, and the more forceful or persistent the police
overtures, the more readily may a court conclude that the police overstepped the

boundary: their conduct might well have brought about commission of a crime by a person who would normally avoid crime of that kind. In assessing the weight to be attached to the police inducement, regard is to be had to the defendant's circumstances, including his vulnerability. This is not because the standards of acceptable behaviour are variable. Rather, this is a recognition that what may be a significant inducement to one person may not be so to another. For the police to behave as would an ordinary customer of a trade, whether lawful or unlawful, being carried on by the defendant will not normally be regarded as objectionable.

[29] *The defendant's criminal record.* The defendant's criminal record is unlikely to be relevant unless it can be linked to other factors grounding reasonable suspicion that the defendant is currently engaged in criminal activity. As Frankfurter J said, past crimes do not forever outlaw the criminal and open him to police practices, aimed at securing repeated convictions, from which the ordinary citizen is protected (see *Sherman v US* (1957) 356 US 369 at 383).

The Human Rights Convention

[30] The question raised by *A-G's Reference (No 3 of 2000)* is whether, in a case involving the commission of an offence by an accused at the instigation of undercover police officers, the judicial discretion conferred by s 78 of the 1984 Act or the court's power to stay proceedings as an abuse of the court has been modified by art 6 of the convention and the jurisprudence of the European Court of Human Rights. I would answer that question in the negative. I do not discern any appreciable difference between the requirements of art 6, or the Strasbourg jurisprudence on art 6, and English law as it has developed in recent years and as I have sought to describe it.

[31] The case of *Teixeira de Castro v Portugal* (1998) 4 BHRC 533 concerned a conviction for trafficking in heroin, based mainly on statements of two police officers. The European Court held that the necessary inference from the circumstances was that these officers had 'exercised an influence such as to incite the commission of the offence'. The court concluded there had been a violation of the applicant's right to a fair trial under art 6(1). The court's statement of principle (at 540 (para 36)), is not divergent from the approach of English law. I agree with the observations of my noble and learned friend Lord Hoffmann on the court's application of that principle to the facts of that case.

[32] For these reasons, and those given by my noble and learned friends Lord Hoffmann and Lord Hutton, I would make the orders Lord Hutton proposes on these two appeals.

LORD MACKAY OF CLASHFERN.

[33] My Lords, I have had the advantage of reading in draft the speeches prepared by my noble and learned friends, Lord Nicholls of Birkenhead, Lord Hoffmann and Lord Hutton. I agree with the orders that Lord Hutton proposes in these two appeals, and with the reasons my noble and learned friends have given for so doing.

[34] I consider that the detailed analysis of particular circumstances which would justify ordering a stay or which would not do so will be helpful in reaching a conclusion but no two cases are likely to be exactly the same in all their circumstances. I would wish to stress that the ultimate question for the tribunal facing a case in which entrapment is alleged is whether, in the words of my noble and learned friend, Lord Nicholls, the state through its agents had lured the accused into committing an act or acts forbidden by law for which the state is now

a seeking to prosecute him. I agree that it is difficult in advance to give a precise and exhaustive definition of what the question means but after the facts have been either agreed or proved, and the helpful illustrations given by my noble and learned friends are taken into account, the tribunal must decide the case by applying the general principle on which these illustrations are based and whose meaning they elucidate.

b **LORD HOFFMANN.**

[35] My Lords, the question in both of these appeals is whether the English law concerning entrapment is compatible with the convention right to a fair trial. In my opinion it is. I have had the advantage of reading in draft the reasons of Lord Nicholls of Birkenhead for reaching the same conclusion. I agree with them.

c ENGLISH LAW ON ENTRAPMENT

[36] Entrapment occurs when an agent of the state—usually a law enforcement officer or a controlled informer—causes someone to commit an offence in order that he should be prosecuted. I shall in due course have to refine this description d but for the moment it will do. In *R v Latif, R v Shahzad* [1996] 1 All ER 353 at 361, [1996] 1 WLR 104 at 112 Lord Steyn said that English law on the subject was now settled. It may be summarised as follows. First, entrapment is not a substantive defence in the sense of providing a ground upon which the accused is entitled to an acquittal. Secondly, the court has jurisdiction in a case of entrapment to stay the prosecution on the ground that the integrity of the criminal justice system e would be compromised by allowing the state to punish someone whom the state itself has caused to transgress. Thirdly, although the court has a discretion under s 78 of the Police and Criminal Evidence Act 1984 to exclude evidence on the ground that its admission would have an adverse effect on the fairness of the proceedings, the exclusion of evidence is not an appropriate response to entrapment. The question f is not whether the proceedings would be a fair determination of guilt but whether they should have been brought at all. I shall briefly enlarge upon these three points.

(a) *Not a defence*

[37] The fact that the accused was entrapped is not inconsistent with his having g broken the law. The entrapment will usually have achieved its object in causing him to do the prohibited act with the necessary guilty intent. So far as I know, the contrary view is held only in the Federal jurisdiction of the United States. It is unnecessary to discuss the cogent criticisms which have been made of this doctrine, notably by Frankfurter J in his dissenting judgment in *Sherman v US* (1957) 356 US h 369, because it has never had any support in authority or academic writing in this country. Indeed, the majority judgment of Rehnquist J in *US v Russell* (1973) 411 US 423 at 433, which describes the criticisms as 'not devoid of appeal' suggests that its survival in the Federal jurisdiction owes more to stare decisis and its perceived constitutional and pragmatic advantages than to its intellectual coherence.

j (b) *The jurisdiction to stay proceedings*

[38] The court's assertion of such a jurisdiction is of recent origin. It was not even discussed as a possible response to entrapment by the Law Commission in its *Criminal Law Report on Defences of General Application* (Law Com No 83) (1977), which dealt with entrapment at pp 32–53. Nor was it mentioned by the House of Lords in *R v Sang* [1979] 2 All ER 1222, [1980] AC 402, when it was decided that

the court had no discretion to exclude evidence on the ground that the offence
had been procured by entrapment or that the evidence had been unfairly obtained. *a*
It seems fairly clear, however, that if anyone had suggested such a jurisdiction, it
would have been emphatically rejected. Lord Diplock dismissed the notion of a
discretion to exclude evidence of an offence procured by entrapment as a 'procedural
device' to evade the rule that entrapment was not a substantive defence. He
would almost certainly have taken the same view of a stay of proceedings, as *b*
Mason CJ, Deane and Dawson JJ later did in their joint judgment in *Ridgeway v The
Queen* (1995) 184 CLR 19 at 40. The House in *R v Sang* said that the only
constitutionally proper way in which the court could mark its disapproval was by
admonishing the police (as Lord Goddard CJ had done in *Brannan v Peek* [1947]
2 All ER 572 at 574, [1948] 1 KB 68 at 72 and *Browning v J W H Watson (Rochester) Ltd*
[1953] 2 All ER 775 at 779, [1953] 1 WLR 1172 at 1177) and by imposing a light or *c*
nominal sentence. It was for the police authorities to take disciplinary action
or prosecute policemen or informants who took part in the crime.

[39] This disclaimer of court responsibility for convicting a person who was
on trial in consequence of an abuse of state power was not to everyone's taste.
The Canadian Supreme Court, when it came to consider the matter, thought that *d*
it was not good enough. In *Amato v The Queen* [1982] 2 SCR 418 at 462–463,
Estey J said:

> '... the repugnance which must be experienced by a court on being
> implicated in a process so outrageous and shameful on the part of the state
> cannot be dissipated by the registration of a conviction and the imposition *e*
> afterwards of even a minimum sentence. To participate in such injustice up
> to and including a finding of guilt and then to attempt to undo the harm by
> the imposition of a lighter sentence, so far from restoring confidence in the
> fair administration of justice, would contribute to the opposite result.'

These views accorded with much of what was said by Frankfurter J in his *f*
dissenting judgment in *Sherman v US*. They were subsequently elaborated by
Lamer J, speaking for the unanimous Supreme Court of Canada, in *R v Mack*
[1988] 2 SCR 903. A stay should be granted not because the accused was not
guilty or because he could not receive a fair trial or to discipline the police but to
protect the integrity of the criminal justice system. *g*

[40] The case which eventually took English law down the same path was
Bennett v Horseferry Road Magistrates' Court [1993] 3 All ER 138, [1994] 1 AC 42, in
which the House of Lords decided that a criminal court had power to inquire into
allegations that the accused had been kidnapped abroad by authorities acting in
collusion with the United Kingdom police and, if it found them proved, had a *h*
discretionary jurisdiction to stay the proceedings. Lord Griffiths said that the
jurisdiction was necessary to enable the courts to refuse to countenance behaviour
which threatened basic human rights or the rule of law. The stay is sometimes
said to be on the ground that the proceedings are an abuse of process, but
Lord Griffiths described the jurisdiction more broadly and, I respectfully think, *j*
more accurately, as a jurisdiction to prevent abuse of executive power.

[41] It was on the authority of *Bennett's* case that the House decided in *R v Latif*
that in principle a stay could be granted on the grounds of entrapment. Lord Steyn
([1996] 1 All ER 353 at 361, [1996] 1 WLR 104 at 112) said that the court should
exercise the jurisdiction when 'Weighing countervailing considerations of policy
and justice', the judge considers that the bringing of the prosecution 'amounts to

a an affront to the public conscience'. I shall try later to analyse in more detail what this means.

(c) *The s 78 discretion*

[42] The s 78 discretion enables the judge to safeguard the fairness of the trial. But the entrapped defendant is not ordinarily complaining that the admission of *b* certain evidence would prejudice the fairness of his trial. He is saying that whatever the evidence, he should not be tried at all. The appropriate remedy, if any, is therefore not the exclusion of evidence but a stay of the proceedings. The distinction was clearly made by the Law Commission in its 1977 report at para 5.29, by Andrew Choo in *Abuse of Process and Judicial Stays of Criminal Proceedings* (1993) pp 164–166 and by Potter LJ in *R v Shannon* [2001] 1 WLR 51.

c   [43] On the other hand, if the court is not satisfied that a stay should be granted and the trial proceeds, the participation of state agents in the commission of the crime may well be relevant to the exercise of the discretion under s 78. As Potter LJ pointed out in *R v Shannon* (at 68), the question at that stage is not whether the proceedings should have been brought but whether the fairness of *d* the proceedings will be adversely affected by, for example, admitting the evidence of the agent provocateur or evidence which is available as a result of his activities:

'So, for instance, if there is good reason to question the credibility of evidence given by an agent provocateur, or which casts doubt on the *e* reliability of other evidence procured by or resulting from his actions, and that question is not susceptible of being properly or fairly resolved in the course of the proceedings from available, admissible and "untainted" evidence, then the judge may readily conclude that such evidence should be excluded.'

f   [44] This question of whether the proceedings should be stayed on the grounds of entrapment should logically be decided before the proceedings have begun. But sometimes proceedings are not conducted entirely logically and an application to exclude evidence under s 78 may be in substance a belated application for a stay. If so, it should be treated as such and decided according to *g* the principles appropriate to the grant of a stay.

THE EUROPEAN JURISPRUDENCE

[45] These appeals raise the question of whether the exercise of the power to stay proceedings as affirmed in *R v Latif* is sufficient to satisfy the right to a fair trial under art 6 of the European Convention for the Protection of Human Rights *h* and Fundamental Freedoms (Rome, 4 November 1950; TS 71 (1953); Cmd 8969) (as set out in Sch 1 to the Human Rights Act 1998). It is clear from the decisions of the European Court of Human Rights, which must be taken into account under s 2(1)(a) of the 1998 Act, that the right is not confined to a fair determination of the question of guilt. It is also a right not to be tried at all in circumstances in *j* which this would amount to an abuse of state power.

[46] This appears most clearly from the decision in *Teixeira de Castro v Portugal* (1998) 4 BHRC 533 at 541 (para 39) in which the court decided that 'right from the outset, the applicant was definitively deprived of a fair trial' because his conviction was for a drugs offence which had been 'instigated' by two police officers. This is the situation of entrapment in which, in an appropriate case, an English court would order a stay of proceedings under the principle in *R v Latif*.

But Mr O'Connor QC, who appeared for Mr Looseley in his appeal and
Mr Emmerson QC, who appeared for the acquitted person in the Attorney
General's reference, both submitted that the principles upon which the power to
order a stay was exercised in England did not satisfy the requirements of the
convention as stated in *Teixeira de Castro*'s case. In order to examine this
submission, I must first analyse the current English law and then consider
whether it is consistent with what the European Court has decided.

THE APPLICATION OF THE ENTRAPMENT DOCTRINE IN ENGLAND

[47] At the highest level of abstraction, the English principles are easy to state.
The court is concerned with whether there has been an abuse of executive
power, something which is, as Lord Steyn said in *R v Latif, R v Shahzad* [1996]
1 All ER 353 at 361, [1996] 1 WLR 104 at 112, an affront to the public conscience
or, as Estey J said in *Amato v The Queen* [1982] 2 SCR 418 at 446, whether the
court's participation in such proceedings would bring the administration of
justice into disrepute. But to leave the matter entirely at that level would incur
the criticism, levelled by Lord Diplock in *R v Sang* [1979] 2 All ER 1222 at 1226,
[1980] AC 402 at 431, that 'What is unfair, what is trickery in the context of the
detection and prevention of crime, are questions which are liable to attract highly
subjective answers' or the reproach of Rehnquist J that the court was claiming a
'"chancellor's foot" veto over law enforcement practices of which it did not
approve' (see *US v Russell* (1973) 411 US 423 at 435).

[48] The objections to entrapment are certainly more specific than a generalised
fastidiousness about police practices. The theme which runs through all discussions
of the subject is that the state should not instigate the commission of criminal
offences in order to punish them. But what counts for this purpose as instigation?
An examination of the authorities demonstrates, in my opinion, that one cannot
isolate any single factor or devise any formula that will always produce the
correct answer. One can certainly identify a cluster of relevant factors but in the
end their relative weight and importance depends upon the particular facts of the
case.

[49] Limited assistance can therefore be gained from distinctions which
restate the question rather than provide a criterion for answering it. For example,
it has been said that a policeman or paid informer should not act as an agent
provocateur; an expression used to signify practices employed by foreigners
unacquainted with English notions of decency and fair play (see *Report of the Royal
Commission on Police Powers and Procedure* (Cmd 3297) (1929) para 104). But what
exactly is an agent provocateur? The Royal Commission said that he was 'a
person who entices another to commit an express breach of the law which he
would not otherwise have committed, and then proceeds or informs against him
in respect of such offence'. This is helpful so far as it goes, but one still has to say
what amounts to enticing and what it means to say that the breach of the law
would not otherwise have been committed. In other words, the definition
assumes but does not define the standards of decency and fair play with which the
activity of the agent provocateur is contrasted.

CAUSING AND PROVIDING AN OPPORTUNITY

[50] Many cases place emphasis upon the question of whether the policeman
can be said to have caused the commission of the offence, rather than merely
providing an opportunity for the accused to commit it with a policeman rather
than in secrecy with someone else. There is no doubt that this will usually be a

a most important factor deciding whether or not the police have overstepped the line between legitimate crime detection and unacceptable crime creation. But a note of caution must be sounded. First, as Lord Steyn said in *R v Latif* [1996] 1 All ER 353 at 360, [1996] 1 WLR 104 at 111, it is important but not necessarily decisive. Other factors, some of which I shall mention in a moment, may have to be taken into account as well. Secondly, a good deal will depend upon what is
b accepted as evidence that the accused would have committed the offence with someone else.

[51] A good example of a straightforward application of the distinction between causing the commission of the offence and providing an opportunity for it to be committed is the case of *Nottingham City Council v Amin* [2000] 2 All ER 946, [2000] 1 WLR 1071. Mr Amin owned a taxi which was not licensed to ply for
c hire in Nottingham. Two plain clothes policemen who saw him driving down a street in Nottingham in the middle of the night flagged him down. He stopped and upon request agreed to take them to the destination which they named. When they arrived, the policemen paid the fare and then charged him with the offence of plying for hire without a licence.

d [52] The stipendiary magistrate excluded the evidence of the policemen under s 78 of the 1984 Act on the ground that they had been agents provocateurs. The prosecutor appealed. As I have already indicated, I think that the use of s 78 was on any view inappropriate. The accused was not saying that the admission of the evidence would prejudice the fairness of his trial. His case was that he should not have been charged with an offence which the policemen had induced him to
e commit. The proper remedy, if any, would have been a stay of proceedings. But the point is academic because the Court of Appeal treated the case as if it had concerned an application for a stay and applied the same principles.

[53] Lord Bingham of Cornhill CJ observed ([2000] 2 All ER 946 at 948, [2000] 1 WLR 1071 at 1075) that to call the policemen agents provocateurs was to
f express the magistrate's conclusion rather than his reasoning. The question was whether they could properly be so described. This depended on whether the case fell on one side or the other of a line which Lord Bingham CJ formulated in the following terms:

g   'On the one hand, it has been recognised as deeply offensive to ordinary notions of fairness if a defendant were to be convicted and punished for committing a crime which he only committed because he had been incited, instigated, persuaded, pressurised or wheedled into committing it by a law enforcement officer. On the other hand, it has been recognised that law enforcement agencies have a general duty to the public to enforce the law and
h   it has been regarded as unobjectionable if a law enforcement officer gives a defendant an opportunity to break the law, of which the defendant freely takes advantage, in circumstances where it appears that the defendant would have behaved in the same way if the opportunity had been offered by anyone else.' (See [2000] 2 All ER 946 at 950, [2000] 1 WLR 1071 at 1076–1077.)

j
[54] In referring to whether the defendant would have behaved in the same way if the opportunity had been offered by anyone else, Lord Bingham CJ obviously did not mean only that the defendant would have responded in the same way to someone who was not a policeman. Since the defendant in such cases ex hypothesi does not know that he is dealing with a policeman, such a condition would invariably be satisfied. What he meant was that the policemen

behaved like ordinary members of the public in flagging the taxi down. They did
not wave £50 notes or pretend to be in distress.

[55] The test of whether the law enforcement officer behaved like an ordinary
member of the public works well and is likely be decisive in many cases of
regulatory offences committed with ordinary members of the public, such as
selling liquor in unlicensed quantities (*DPP v Marshall* [1988] 3 All ER 683) selling
videos to children under age (*Ealing London Borough v Woolworths plc* [1995] Crim
LR 58) and operating a private hire vehicle without a licence (*Taunton Deane BC v
Brice* (1997) 31 Licensing Review 24). But ordinary members of the public do not
become involved in large scale drug dealing, conspiracy to rob (*R v Mealey, R v
Sheridan* (1974) 60 Cr App R 59) or hiring assassins (*R v Gill* [1989] Crim LR 358,
R v Smurthwaite, R v Gill [1994] 1 All ER 898). The appropriate standards of behaviour
are in such cases rather more problematic. And even in the case of offences
committed with ordinary members of the public, other factors may require a
purely causal test to be modified.

SUSPICION AND SUPERVISION

[56] In the case of some regulatory offences, the effective administration of
the law may require enforcement officers to have the power to make random
tests. But normally it is not considered a legitimate use of police power to provide
people not suspected of being engaged in any criminal activity with the opportunity
to commit crimes. The only proper purpose of police participation is to obtain
evidence of criminal acts which they suspect someone is about to commit or in
which he is already engaged. It is not to tempt people to commit crimes in order
to expose their bad characters and punish them.

[57] This point was made very clearly by Buxton J in the *Taunton Deane* case
when Mr Brice complained that two council employees had tempted him to carry
them for reward in his unlicensed vehicle by offering the opportunity of a long
and lucrative journey. The judge attached importance to the fact that the council
were carrying out a bona fide investigation into complaints about Mr Brice's
activities:

'That decision [to use entrapment] was not made for an ulterior motive or
in the hope of persuading someone who was not breaking the law to start
doing so, but rather to see whether or not evidence was available upon
which a prosecution could properly be mounted.'

[58] These facts may be contrasted with the example given by Lamer J in *R v
Mack* [1988] 2 SCR 903 at 957 of the police officer who 'decides that he wants to
increase his performance in court'. To this end, he plants a wallet with money in
an obvious location in a park and keeps watch. This is unacceptable behaviour
because the policeman is preying on the weakness of human nature to create
crime for an improper purpose.

[59] The principle that the police should prevent and detect crime, not
employ themselves in creating it, requires some modification of the causal test.
In the case of the planted wallet, the policeman has not 'incited, instigated,
persuaded, pressurised or wheedled' the hapless offender into stealing it. He has
provided him with an opportunity of which he has taken free advantage.
Nevertheless, for a different reason, the policeman's conduct is an abuse of state
power which the judicial branch of government should not countenance.

[60] Closely linked with the question of whether the police were creating or
detecting crime is the supervision of their activities. To allow policemen or

a controlled informers to undertake entrapment activities unsupervised carries great danger, not merely that they will try to improve their performances in court, but of oppression, extortion and corruption. As we shall see, the European Court in *Teixeira de Castro v Portugal* (1998) 4 BHRC 533 attached great importance to the fact that the police were not acting in the course of an officially authorised investigation.

b [61] The need for reasonable suspicion and proper supervision are both stressed in the *Undercover Operations Code of Practice* issued jointly by all United Kingdom police authorities and HM Customs and Excise in response to the Human Rights Act 1998. It deals with the employment of 'undercover officers', 'test purchasers' and 'decoys'. Undercover officers are defined as specially trained law enforcement officers working incognito 'under direction in an authorised *c* investigation' to infiltrate an existing conspiracy, arrest suspected criminals or counter a threat to national security. Test purchasers are appropriately trained law enforcement officers who seek 'by means of authorised activity, to establish the nature and/or availability of a commodity or service, the possession, supply or use of which involves an offence'. Test purchasers are used mainly in the drug *d* trade. Decoys are officers who place themselves passively in a position to become a victim of crime for the purpose of arresting the offender.

[62] Undercover officers may be used only in connection with national security or serious crime and in cases in which the desired result cannot reasonably be achieved by other means (see para 2.2). Authorisation must be given by an assistant chief constable or a commander in the Metropolitan or City of London *e* Police.

[63] The use of a test purchaser must be authorised by a superintendent in the police or National or Scottish Crime Squads and para 3.2 states that the authorising officer must be satisfied that a test purchase is—

f   'required in support of an investigation into a criminal offence concerning the possession, supply or use of a commodity or service and that reasonable grounds have been established prior to the deployment of a test purchaser to suspect that such an offence is being committed …'

[64] The authorising officer must also be satisfied that the desired result of the test purchase cannot reasonably be achieved by other means and a note for *g* guidance (note 3A) emphasises:

'Test purchase should not be used as a speculative means of search for the existence of a commodity or service where no other reasonable grounds exist to suspect that criminal offences have been or are being committed.'

h [65] The requirement of reasonable suspicion does not necessarily mean that there must have been suspicion of the particular person who happens to have committed the offence. The police may, in the course of a bona fide investigation into suspected criminality, provide an opportunity for the commission of an offence which is taken by someone to whom no suspicion previously attached. *j* This can happen when a decoy (human or inanimate) is used in the course of the detection of crime which has been prevalent in a particular place. Lamer J in *R v Mack* [1988] 2 SCR 903 at 957 gave the example of the police planting a handbag in a bus terminal where numerous thefts have recently taken place. A real example in England was *Williams v DPP* [1993] 3 All ER 365, in which the police were investigating thefts from vehicles in Essex. They left an unattended transit van with the back door open and cartons of cigarettes visible. When the appellants stole the cigarettes, they were arrested. Although the judgment contains (at 369) some reference to causal reasoning ('they were tricked into doing what they wanted to do'), I do not think that in such a case causation provides a sufficient answer. If the trick had been the individual enterprise of a policeman in an area where such crime was not suspected to be prevalent, it would have been an abuse of state power. It was justified because it was an authorised investigation into actual crime and the fact that the defendants may not have previously been suspected or even thought of offending was their hard luck.

THE NATURE OF THE OFFENCE

[66] The provision in the Code of Practice which requires the authorising officer to be satisfied that the desired result of deploying an undercover officer or test purchaser cannot reasonably be achieved by other means shows that the justification for such methods will partly depend upon the nature of the offence. Consensual offences such as dealing in unlawful substances or offences with no immediate victim like bribery or offences which victims are reluctant to report are the most obvious candidates for such methods. So is the infiltration of conspiracies. But the fact that the offence is a serious one is not in itself a sufficient ground for the police to ignore the provisions of the code or the courts to condone their actions by allowing the prosecution to proceed.

PREDISPOSITION

[67] The United States Federal doctrine that entrapment is a ground for acquittal does not protect a person who was 'predisposed' to commit the offence. Predisposition is regarded as showing that the defendant had the necessary guilty intent and was not lured by entrapment into committing an offence which would not otherwise have occurred to him. Predisposition may be proved by, among other things, previous convictions or similar fact evidence. The prospect of such matters going before the jury explains why the defence is rarely invoked in Federal criminal prosecutions. The result is that people with criminal records are fair game for entrapment.

[68] Since the English doctrine assumes the defendant's guilt and is concerned with the standards of behaviour of the law enforcement officers, predisposition is irrelevant to whether a stay should be granted or not. The facts which lead the police to suspect that crimes are being committed and justify the use of an undercover officer or test purchaser may also point to the accused and show predisposition. But that is a coincidence. The fact that, for example, the accused has previous convictions is in English law neither necessary nor sufficient. Suspicion may attach to a person who has previously escaped conviction and, contrariwise, the fact that a person has been previously convicted may provide no ground for suspecting a current course of criminality which would justify the use of covert operations. Nor is the fact that a person is a drug addict and therefore likely to know a supplier a sufficient ground in itself for tempting him to move altogether outside his usual way of life and act as intermediary in the supply of a substantial quantity of drugs. Such persons may be particularly vulnerable to unfair pressures of this kind. It may be possible to justify them for the purpose of securing the prosecution and conviction of the supplier but not the prosecution and conviction of the intermediary.

ACTIVE AND PASSIVE

[69] The need for an authorised and bona fide investigation into suspected criminality is sufficient to show that the question of entrapment cannot be

a answered simply by asking whether the defendant was given an opportunity to commit the offence of which he freely availed himself. This is important but not enough. The matter is more complicated and other factors have to be taken into account. Likewise, I do not think that even the causal question can be answered by a mechanical application of a distinction between 'active' and 'passive' conduct on the part of the undercover policeman or informer. In cases in which the offence

b involves a purchase of goods or services, like liquor or videotapes or a taxi ride, it would be absurd to expect the test purchaser to wait silently for an offer. He will do what an ordinary purchaser would do. Drug dealers can be expected to show some wariness about dealing with a stranger who might be a policeman or informer and therefore some protective colour in dress or manner as well as a certain degree of persistence may be necessary to achieve the objective. And it

c has been said that undercover officers who infiltrate conspiracies to murder, rob or commit terrorist offences could hardly remain concealed unless they showed some enthusiasm for the enterprise. A good deal of active behaviour in the course of an authorised operation may therefore be acceptable without crossing the boundary between causing the offence to be committed and providing an

d opportunity for the defendant to commit it.

[70] Likewise it seems to me that when Lord Bingham CJ in *Nottingham City Council v Amin* [2000] 2 All ER 946 at 950, [2000] 1 WLR 1071 at 1077, said that the accused should not be 'incited, instigated, persuaded, pressurised or wheedled' into committing the offence, he was not intending each of those verbs to be given a disjunctive and technical meaning. He was intending to evoke a more general

e concept of conduct which causes the defendant to commit the offence as opposed to giving him an opportunity to do so. No doubt a test purchaser who asks someone to sell him a drug is counselling and procuring, perhaps inciting, the commission of an offence. Furthermore, he has no statutory defence to a prosecution. But the fact that his actions are technically unlawful is not regarded

f in English law as a ground for treating them as an abuse of power (see *R v Latif, R v Shahzad* [1996] 1 All ER 353, [1996] 1 WLR 104 and compare *Ridgeway v The Queen* (1995) 184 CLR 19).

[71] In summary, therefore, the principles of English law on which a stay of proceedings may be granted on grounds of entrapment involve the consideration of a number of aspects of the behaviour of the law enforcement authorities, some

g of which I have examined in detail, and deciding whether the involvement of the court in the conviction of a defendant who had been subjected to such behaviour would compromise the integrity of the judicial system.

TEIXEIRA DE CASTRO v PORTUGAL

h [72] My Lords, these principles are in my opinion entirely consistent with the decision of the European Court in *Teixeira de Castro v Portugal* (1998) 4 BHRC 533. Both the Commission and the court stressed the fact that the policemen, although not acting unlawfully, were not authorised to use undercover operations. Unlike the case of *Lüdi v Switzerland* (1992) 15 EHRR 173, no investigation had been

j opened by a judge and there was no judicial or other supervision of the officers. Although the United Kingdom technique for authorising and supervising such operations (as described in the Code of Practice) is very different from the judicial supervision in continental countries, the purpose is the same, namely to remove the risk of extortion, corruption or abuse of power by policemen operating without proper supervision. The European Court obviously had these risks very much in mind when it condemned the methods used to prosecute Mr de Castro.

[73] The court also recorded that the 'competent authorities', that is to say, the authorities who would normally be expected to authorise such an investigation, had no good reason to suspect that Mr de Castro was a drug trafficker. Nor had the police themselves heard of him until an intermediary told them that he was a person who might be able to supply heroin. They immediately drove to his house in the middle of the night, said that they wanted to buy PTE 200,000 worth of heroin and produced a roll of banknotes. Mr de Castro obtained the heroin from an intermediary and, apart from the intermediary's suggestion that he might be able to supply, there was no other evidence that he had been dealing in heroin.

[74] My Lords, every case depends upon its own facts but there is nothing in the general principle applied by the European Court or the cluster of factors to which it attached importance which suggests any difference from the current English approach to entrapment. The contrary submission depends upon an excessively literal and technical analysis of some of the language used by the court. So, for example, the court said (at 541 (para 38)) that 'the two police officers did not confine themselves to investigating Mr Teixeira de Castro's criminal activity in an essentially passive manner, but exercised an influence such as to incite the commission of the offence.'

[75] This sentence is relied upon for the proposition that even in an authorised undercover operation, the officer must take no active step such as offering to buy an illegal substance. Such conduct amounts to 'incitement' of the offence. I do not believe that the court intended to lay down such a rigid and prescriptive rule. The description of the policemen's conduct must be seen as one of the various factors which led to the court's conclusion that there had been an abuse of police power which denied the defendant a fair trial.

THE CERTIFIED QUESTIONS

[76] This brings me to the certified questions in the two appeals before the House. First, *R v Looseley*, in which the certified question was:

'Should the judge have refused to admit the evidence of the undercover police officer "Rob" because the role played by "Rob" went beyond observation and involved asking the appellant to supply him with heroin, a request to which, on the judge's findings, the appellant readily agreed.'

[77] The facts of the case are stated in the speech of my noble and learned friend, Lord Hutton, and I need not repeat them. The factors to which I attach importance are the following. First, Rob was acting in the course of an authorised undercover operation arising out of concern about the supply of class A drugs in the Guildford area. Secondly, the Wooden Bridge public house was reasonably suspected to be a focal point for the trade. Thirdly, having obtained the defendant's telephone number from someone at the public house as a potential source of supply, Rob telephoned and asked him in general terms whether he could 'sort us out a couple of bags', to which the defendant said 'Yes'. Rob might just as well have said, 'Are you by any chance a heroin dealer?' and received an affirmative reply.

[78] From that point, it seems to me, Rob and his superiors who were controlling his operations had reasonable cause to suspect that the defendant was a dealer. The subsequent offer to purchase was in the course of a legitimate undercover purchase and not calculated to cause him to do anything which he would not have done in response to a similar request from any customer. I attach

a little importance to the fact that he 'readily agreed' to sell. This seems to me to be neutral, because the question is not so much his behaviour but that of the police. It means only that the police did not have to take any steps to persuade him which might have taken them across the boundary between giving him the opportunity to commit the offence and causing him to do so. The facts are in my opinion miles away from *Teixeira de Castro*'s case, and I think that the judge was

b right to reject the application to exclude Rob's evidence under s 78 of the 1984 Act and should for the same reasons have refused an application for a stay.

[79] Mr O'Connor QC also submitted that the telephone call to the defendant and the request for drugs were an infringement of the right to respect for his private life under art 8 of the convention. I regard this submission as unsustainable. The defendant was on his own admission in the business of dealing in drugs. He

c responded willingly to solicitation. The policeman did not invade his privacy any more than a customer who walks into a shop. The fact that the business was unlawful and this particular solicitation was from a policeman does not make it a breach of his human rights (see *Lüdi v Switzerland*). I would therefore answer the certified question No and dismiss the appeal.

d [80] In *A-G's Reference (No 3 of 2000)* the question referred to the House by the Court of Appeal is:

'In a case involving the commission of offences by an accused at the instigation of undercover police officers, to what extent, if any, have: (i) the judicial discretion conferred by s 78 of the Police and Criminal Evidence Act 1984;

e and (ii) the power to stay the proceedings as an abuse of the court; been modified by art 6 of the European Convention on Human Rights and the jurisprudence of the European Court of Human Rights?'

[81] To this question I would give the same answer as the Court of Appeal, namely that no modification is required. But, like my noble and learned friend

f Lord Hutton, I respectfully disagree with the Court of Appeal's view that the judge was wrong to stay the proceedings. In my opinion he was entitled to reach the view that he should. On the statements before him, which by consent he was invited to accept as true, the defendant had never dealt in heroin. He was induced to procure heroin for the undercover officer by the prospect of a profitable trade

g in smuggled cigarettes. The judge was entitled to take the view that even if this was an authorised operation, the police had caused him to commit an offence which he would not otherwise have committed.

LORD HUTTON.

h [82] My Lords, the issue which arises in these two cases is what conduct by undercover police officers in obtaining evidence against a drugs dealer will constitute entrapment of such a nature that either a prosecution based on that evidence will be stayed as an abuse of process or the evidence will be excluded under s 78 of the Police and Criminal Evidence Act 1984.

j [83] The two cases before the House have been heard together. One case is the appeal of Grant Spencer Looseley against his conviction at Guildford Crown Court on three counts of supplying or being concerned in supplying to another a class A controlled drug (heroin). The other case is a reference brought by the Attorney General pursuant to s 36 of the Criminal Justice Act 1972 and consequent on the acquittal of a defendant charged on two counts of supplying or being concerned in supplying to another a class A controlled drug (heroin).

The appeal of Looseley

[84] The prosecution case was that the appellant and another defendant named Harris had supplied heroin to an undercover police officer known as 'Rob'. In 1999 police in Guildford mounted an undercover operation because of their concern about the trade in class A drugs in that area. One focus of the operation was a public house where a man provided Rob with the appellant's first name and telephone number and suggested to him that he should telephone the appellant if he wished to obtain drugs. Rob telephoned the appellant and said to him, 'Hello, mate, can you sort out us a couple of bags?', and the appellant replied, 'Er yes, I'll sort you out, mate'. The appellant then gave the officer directions to his flat. The officer went to the flat, and a price of £30 for half a gram of heroin was agreed. The appellant and Rob then drove to the flat of Harris in Rob's car. The appellant left the car taking £30 from Rob. He returned a few moments later saying that he had 'the stuff'. The appellant and Rob then returned to the appellant's flat where the appellant took a small package from his mouth, opened it, took a small quantity of the substance in the package for himself, and gave the remainder to Rob. On analysis the package was found to contain 152 mg of heroin at 100% purity. This transaction was the subject of count 2 of the indictment.

[85] Four days later Rob again telephoned the appellant, who agreed to 'sort him out'. Rob and the appellant met at the public house. They then drove in Rob's car to a theatre in Guildford. The appellant left the car, once again taking £30 of the officer's money with him. When he returned he handed a cling-film ball to Rob. They then went to the appellant's flat, where the appellant took a small amount from the cling-film ball and returned the remainder to Rob. On this occasion the wrap was found, when analysed, to contain 132 mg of heroin at 70% purity. This transaction was the subject of count 3 of the indictment.

[86] Three days later Rob once again went to the appellant's flat and asked if the appellant could supply him with a gram of heroin. The appellant spoke to someone by telephone. Rob and the appellant went to another address. The appellant took £60 from the officer, and returned with a cling-film wrap. The appellant told Rob that this was only half the amount but the remainder would be ready in an hour. In fact, although the officer returned to the appellant's flat several times that afternoon, no further drugs were supplied to him. The wrap that he did receive was found, on analysis, to contain 224 mg of heroin at 100% purity. This transaction was the subject of count 4 of the indictment.

[87] At the trial in the Crown Court it was submitted as a preliminary issue to the trial judge, Judge Bassingthwaighte, that the indictment ought to be stayed as an abuse of the process of the court or, alternatively, that the evidence of Rob should be excluded pursuant to the discretion conferred on the judge by s 78(1) of the 1984 Act which provides:

> 'In any proceedings the court may refuse to allow evidence on which the prosecution proposes to rely to be given if it appears to the court that, having regard to all the circumstances, including the circumstances in which the evidence was obtained, the admission of the evidence would have such an adverse effect on the fairness of the proceedings that the court ought not to admit it.'

[88] There was a voir dire and the judge heard evidence from Rob and from Det Insp Marjoram, the officer in charge of the operation which gave rise to the indictment. On the conclusion of the voir dire the judge delivered his ruling in which he declined either to stay the indictment as an abuse of process or to

a exclude the evidence in the exercise of his discretion under s 78 of the 1984 Act. In the course of his ruling the judge referred to a number of English authorities and also to the judgment of the European Court in *Teixeira de Castro*'s case. The judge said:

b 'I do not understand from any of the cases to which I have referred (*Teixeira de Castro v Portugal* (1998) 4 BHRC 533 included) that there is a discernible principle that evidence obtained as a result of undercover observation or infiltration is inadmissible. The guiding principle seems to be as identified in the English cases, that the commission of offences should come about without the prompting of undercover officers in the sense that they provoke or incite the commission of offences which would not *c* otherwise have occurred without their intervention ... In *Texeira de Castro's* case it also seemed of importance to the court that the applicant was not known to be involved in the drugs scene, possibly because he had no convictions for drug offences. The court seems to suggest that incitement thus became more of a consideration because it involved someone not known to be involved in that world, and I shall return to that issue in due *d* course ... While I bear the provisions of art 6 of the convention in mind, I also remind myself that the concept of proportionality referred to in the case of *Soering v UK* (1989) 11 EHRR 439, indicates that it is inherent to the whole of the convention that there is a search for the fair balance between the demands of the general interests of the community and the requirements of *e* the protection of the individual's human rights.'

Referring to *Teixeira de Castro*'s case the judge said:

'The court's finding is conclusively expressed at para 39 of the report ((1998) 4 BHRC 533 at 541). It is based upon the fact that in the court's opinion the officers instigated an offence which would not have occurred *f* without their intervention. That is the essence of the ruling, and while I note comments about officers being active and passive, which our own Court of Appeal have also made, I do not take it as expressed in *Teixeira de Castro*'s case that simply because an undercover officer may behave actively that conduct is prohibited and may not found a prosecution. Active conduct is not of *g* course necessarily the same as incitement. Certainly, however, caution is expressed, and rightly expressed, about undercover officers moving from passive to active roles, but I take *Teixeira de Castro*'s case to say that what must occur in all such situations is an assessment of all the relevant circumstances, just as the Court of Appeal has said in England and Wales. As I have said *h* already, what distinguishes this case both from *R v Lawrence, R v Nash* (1993) Independent, 31 January and from *Teixeira de Castro*'s case is that a course of offending is revealed: not just one offence.'

And:

j 'It therefore seems to me that the European Court, looking at all the surrounding circumstances, saw the possibility that Teixeira, a man of relevant good character, was persuaded into just one drug procurement, possibly against his better judgment, possibly tempted for gain, and that he was therefore incited into the commission of an offence which would otherwise never have occurred to him. The court saw the involvement of the undercover officers in that context. What occurred here was that these two defendants—both at least known drug users, both the subject of drugs intelligence and both then discovered and contacted only after infiltration of the local drugs scene—then supplied heroin on a continuing basis to an undercover officer. Admittedly, that officer presented himself as an ideal customer so far as a drug dealer is concerned, but I do not consider that he did anything other than present himself in that condition. I find it difficult, underlining the fact that I am here considering all the surrounding circumstances, to assess that conduct as incitement.'

[89] Following this ruling the appellant changed his pleas on counts 2 to 4 to guilty and the sentencing of the appellant was postponed until a date to be fixed.

[90] The appellant appealed against his conviction to the Court of Appeal and the appeal was dismissed. In delivering the judgment of the Court of Appeal Roch LJ stated:

'30. In our judgment the law is clear, and the law is consistent with the European Convention on Human Rights and the judgment of the European Court of Human Rights, namely that if an accused person's involvement in an offence is due to that person being incited by a law enforcement officer to commit the offence, or by that person being trapped into committing the offence by a law enforcement officer, then the evidence of that law enforcement officer should be excluded by the trial judge exercising his power under s 78 of the Police and Criminal Evidence Act 1984. In many cases were such a ruling to be made the case against the accused would not be able to proceed further. On the other hand, if the law enforcement officer has done no more than give an accused the opportunity to break the law, of which the accused has freely taken advantage in circumstances where it appears that the accused would have behaved in the same way if the opportunity had been offered by anyone else, then there is no reason why the officer's evidence should be excluded and the accused's trial should proceed with that evidence being admitted. No doubt there will be cases, of which this was one, where such a ruling will lead to a change of plea. 31. On which side of that line evidence of a law enforcement officer will fall is primarily a question of fact for the trial judge to decide when making his ruling. It is of significance that in *Teixeira de Castro v Portugal* (1998) 4 BHRC 533 in the judgment of the European Court this appears (at 540 (para 34)): "The court reiterates that the admissibility of evidence is primarily a matter for regulation by national law and as a general rule it is for the national courts to assess the evidence before them. The court's task under the convention is not to give a ruling as to whether statements of witnesses were properly admitted as evidence, but rather to ascertain whether the proceedings as a whole, including the way in which evidence was taken, were fair ..."'

The Court of Appeal certified the following point of law of general public importance for the opinion of the House:

'Should the judge have refused to admit the evidence of the undercover police officer "Rob" because the role played by "Rob" went beyond mere observation and involved asking the appellant to supply him with heroin, a request to which, on the judge's findings, the appellant readily agreed?'

A-G's Reference (No 3 of 2000)

[91] The defendant (the acquitted person) appeared in the Crown Court at Derby before Judge Appleby QC charged on one count with the offence of

a supplying to another a class A controlled drug (heroin) and on a second count with the offence of being concerned in supplying to another a class A controlled drug (heroin).

[92] The circumstances in which it was alleged the offences were committed were summarised as follows by Judge Appleby in his ruling:

b 'Police officers see a man called S and they ask him if he wants to buy—these are undercover officers—some [contraband] cigarettes and so on. He went with them to where the defendant ... is. S goes to the car where [the defendant] was. Cigarettes are handed over. There is a conversation about cigarettes and the conversation is to do with cigarettes. Thereafter the conversation with the defendant is: "Can you sort out any brown?" Later on c many, many conversations with the defendant, offering cigarettes and persuading him, within reason initially, to provide them with a class A drug. Eventually the defendant obtains drugs from another source. It is on record that he said at one stage: "I'm not really into heroin myself."'

It is also relevant to record that when interviewed by the police after his arrest the d acquitted person said that he had had 'nothing at all' to do with heroin, and that he was 'not interested' in it, but that he had become involved because two men had approached him, offering to sell him cheap cigarettes. He said that the officers 'were getting me cheap fags, so as far as I was concerned a favour for a favour'.

e [93] At the commencement of the trial the defence applied both for the exclusion of the evidence of the undercover police officers under s 78 of the 1984 Act and for a stay of the prosecution as an abuse of process. The trial judge approached the matter as an application for a stay on grounds of abuse of process and granted the stay. On the next day the trial judge lifted the stay, the prosecution offered no evidence and verdicts of not guilty were entered.

f [94] In his ruling, after summarising the facts in the passage which I have already set out, Judge Appleby said:

'An elaboration of those facts by Mr Munt on behalf of the defence, admitted facts, makes it absolutely clear to me that in this case these officers went further than was permissible and in fact incited and procured this g defendant to commit an offence he would not otherwise have committed.'

The judge then set out passages from the judgment of the European Court in *Teixeira de Castro v Portugal* (1998) 4 BHRC 533 and continued:

h 'The judgment of the European Court of Human Rights goes on to say (at 541 (para 39)): "In the light of all these considerations, the court concludes that the two police officers' actions went beyond those of undercover agents because they instigated the offence and there is nothing to suggest that without their intervention it would have been committed." I repeat those words, and with considerable hesitation and reluctance in the light of all the j considerations, I come to the conclusion that the police officers in this case and their actions went beyond those of undercover agents because they instigated the offence and there is nothing to suggest that without their intervention it would have been committed. And because of that, on the basis of that court's decision, the intervention of the officers and its use in the criminal proceedings, these criminal proceedings, would mean that right from the outset the applicant would be deprived of a fair trial.'

[95] On the acquittal the Attorney General referred the following point of law to the Court of Appeal for its opinion:

'In a case involving the commission of offences by an accused at the instigation of undercover police officers, to what extent, if any, have: (i) the judicial discretion conferred by s 78 of the Police and Criminal Evidence Act 1984; and (ii) the power to stay the proceedings as an abuse of the court; been modified by art 6 of the European Convention on Human Rights and the jurisprudence of the European Court of Human Rights?'

[96] In delivering the judgment of the Court of Appeal ([2001] EWCA Crim 1214, [2001] 2 Cr App R 472) Kennedy LJ stated (at [35]):

'In considering in a case of this type an application either to stay or to exclude evidence pursuant to section 78 the Court will be concerned both with the freedom of action of the accused and with the propriety or otherwise of the actions of the undercover officers. In most cases the principal question will be whether the officers did no more (whether by active or passive means) than to afford the accused the opportunity to offend, of which he freely took advantage in circumstances where it appears that he would have behaved in a similar way if offered the opportunity by someone else or whether, on the other hand, by means of unworthy or shameful conduct, they have persuaded him to commit an offence of a kind which otherwise he would not have committed. That approach is in our judgment consistent, without modification, with Article 6. *Teixeira de Castro* must be considered on its own facts in the setting of Portuguese criminal procedure. It will not always be easy in a particular case to say whether the accused freely accepted an opportunity and would have acted similarly if it had been presented by someone else.'

At the conclusion of his judgment, referring to the decision of Judge Appleby, Kennedy LJ stated (at [48]):

'The judge did not hear evidence and thus did not reach any conclusions of primary fact. He reached the conclusion he did with evident reluctance. He formed the view that the decision in *Teixeira de Castro* robbed him of the power to make any decision other than he did, and created a situation where the only test to be applied was whether the officer was acting as an *agent provocateur* in the sense that he was enticing the accused to commit that particular offence which he did. In that we are satisfied he fell into error. He further appears to have directed himself that the accused's proven history of dealing on some scale in Class B drugs was of no relevance. Since his disposition to commit the offence in the absence of persuasion by the officers was directly relevant, that was a misdirection, as Mr Emmerson only faintly disputed. If, on the facts we have recited, the judge had asked himself whether the undercover officers had done more than give the accused an opportunity to break the law of which the accused had freely taken advantage then, in our judgment, he would have answered that question in the negative, and he would not have ruled as he did.'

Having delivered its judgment the Court of Appeal referred the point of law to the House for its opinion.

The issue

a [97] The problem which arises where there has been entrapment by police officers is one which has been considered by appellate courts in many jurisdictions. It is apparent from the authorities to which I am about to refer that the approach of the English courts has been to consider whether the prosecution should be stayed as an abuse of process or whether the evidence obtained by the police

b officers should be excluded on the ground of unfairness. As the authorities cited by my noble and learned friends, Lord Nicholls of Birkenhead and Lord Hoffmann, show, in the United States entrapment is held to be a substantive defence, in Canada a stay of proceedings is granted, and in Australia evidence obtained by unlawful or improper conduct on the part of law enforcement officers is excluded on the grounds of public policy.

c [98] In *R v Latif, R v Shahzad* [1996] 1 All ER 353, [1996] 1 WLR 104 Lord Steyn in his speech, with which the other members of the House agreed, considered the circumstances in which the conduct of law enforcement officers should cause a prosecution to be stayed for abuse of process. It had been established by this House in *R v Sang* [1979] 2 All ER 1222, [1980] AC 402 that entrapment is not a

d substantive defence under English law, in the sense that it does not have the effect that no crime is committed by the alleged principal offender as, notwithstanding the entrapment, he has the mens rea and commits the actus reus to constitute the offence. After recognising this and commenting that it was not the end of the matter Lord Steyn stated the dilemma in this way:

e   'If the court always refuses to stay such proceedings, the perception will be that the court condones criminal conduct and malpractice by law enforcement agencies. That would undermine public confidence in the criminal justice system and bring it into disrepute. On the other hand, if the court were always to stay proceedings in such cases, it would incur the reproach that it is failing to protect the public from serious crime.' (See [1996] 1 All ER 353

f   at 360, [1996] 1 WLR 104 at 112.)

The answer which Lord Steyn gave was as follows:

   'The weaknesses of both extreme positions leaves only one principled solution. The court has a discretion: it has to perform a balancing exercise

g   … the judge must weigh in the balance the public interest in ensuring that those that are charged with grave crimes should be tried and the competing public interest in not conveying the impression that the court will adopt the approach that the end justifies any means.' (See [1996] 1 All ER 353 at 360, 361, [1996] 1 WLR 104 at 112, 113.)

h On the facts before the House in that case Lord Steyn said:

   'The conduct of the customs officer was not so unworthy or shameful that it was an affront to the public conscience to allow the prosecution to proceed. Realistically, any criminal behaviour of the customs officer was venial compared to that of Shahzad. In these circumstances I would reject

j   the submission that the judge erred in refusing to stay the proceedings.' (See [1996] 1 All ER 353 at 361, [1996] 1 WLR 104 at 113.)

[99] In *Nottingham City Council v Amin* [2000] 2 All ER 946, [2000] 1 WLR 1071 a taxi driver licensed by the local authority was hailed by two plain clothes police officers while driving in an area not covered by his licence. He stopped and took the two officers to the address they requested in return for a fare. He was

prosecuted for using his taxi to ply for hire when he had not previously obtained
a licence to operate in that area. At the hearing of the prosecution the stipendiary
magistrate ruled that having regard to the effect of art 6 of the European
Convention for the Protection of Human Rights and Fundamental Freedoms
(Rome, 4 November 1950; TS 71 (1953); Cmd 8969) (as set out in Sch 1 to the
Human Rights Act 1998) the evidence of the police officers, whom he described
as agents provocateurs, should be excluded from evidence under s 78 of the 1984
Act. On appeal by the local authority the Divisional Court allowed the appeal and
remitted the case to the magistrate with a direction to convict. Lord Bingham of
Cornhill CJ stated:

> 'On the one hand, it has been recognised as deeply offensive to ordinary
> notions of fairness if a defendant were to be convicted and punished for
> committing a crime which he only committed because he had been incited,
> instigated, persuaded, pressurised or wheedled into committing it by a law
> enforcement officer. On the other hand, it has been recognised that
> law enforcement agencies have a general duty to the public to enforce the
> law and it has been regarded as unobjectionable if a law enforcement officer
> gives a defendant an opportunity to break the law, of which the defendant
> freely takes advantage, in circumstances where it appears that the defendant
> would have behaved in the same way if the opportunity had been offered by
> anyone else.' (See [2000] 2 All ER 946 at 950, [2000] 1 WLR 1071 at
> 1076–1077.)

[100] Therefore the approach taken by the English cases is that it is necessary
to balance the competing requirements that those who commit crimes should be
convicted and punished and that there should not be an abuse of process which
would constitute an affront to the public conscience. In carrying out this
balancing exercise it will be necessary for the court in each individual case to take
into account a number of factors. These factors have been discussed in the
speeches of my noble and learned friends, Lord Nicholls and Lord Hoffmann, and
I am in full agreement with the views which they express. I further consider, with
respect, that the approach to be taken by a court and the matters to be considered
are well set out in the dissenting judgment of McHugh J in the High Court of
Australia in *Ridgeway v The Queen* (1995) 184 CLR 19 at 92 (save that, in my
opinion, a prosecution should not be permitted to proceed when the evidence
had been obtained by threats):

> 'I do not think that it is possible to formulate a rule that will cover all cases
> that arise when an accused person seeks to stay a prosecution on the ground
> that the offence was induced by or was the result of the conduct of law
> enforcement authorities. The ultimate question must always be whether the
> administration of justice will be brought into disrepute because the processes
> of the court are being used to prosecute an offence that was artificially
> created by the misconduct of law enforcement authorities. That question
> should be determined after considering four matters: (1) Whether conduct
> of the law enforcement authorities induced the offence. (2) Whether, in
> proffering the inducement, the authorities had reasonable grounds for
> suspecting that the accused was likely to commit the particular offence or
> one that was similar to that offence or were acting in the course of a bona
> fide investigation of offences of a kind similar to that with which the accused
> has been charged. (3) Whether, prior to the inducement, the accused had

a the intention of committing the offence or a similar offence if an opportunity arose. (4) Whether the offence was induced as the result of persistent importunity, threats, deceit, offers of rewards or other inducements that would not ordinarily be associated with the commission of the offence or a similar offence.'

b [101] In balancing the relevant factors the English courts have placed particular emphasis on the need to consider whether a person has been persuaded or pressurised by a law enforcement officer into committing a crime which he would not otherwise have committed, or whether the officer did not go beyond giving the person an opportunity to break the law, when he would have behaved in the same way if some other person had offered him the opportunity to commit a

c similar crime, and when he freely took advantage of the opportunity presented to him by the officer.

[102] In considering the distinction (broadly stated) between a person being lured by a police officer into committing an offence so that it will be right to stay a prosecution, and a person freely taking advantage of an opportunity to commit an offence presented to him by the officer, it is necessary to have in mind that a

d drugs dealer will not voluntarily offer drugs to a stranger, unless the stranger first makes an approach to him, and the stranger may need to persist in his request for drugs before they are supplied. Therefore, in my opinion, a request for drugs, even if it be persistent, need not be regarded as luring the drugs dealer into committing a crime with the consequence that a prosecution against him should

e be stayed. If a prosecution were not permitted in such circumstances the combating of the illegal sale of drugs would be severely impeded, and I do not consider that the integrity of the criminal justice system would be impaired by permitting a prosecution to take place. In my opinion a prosecution should not be stayed where a police officer has used an inducement which (in the words of McHugh J in *Ridgeway*'s case (1995) 184 CLR 19 at 92) 'is consistent with the

f ordinary temptations and stratagems that are likely to be encountered in the course of criminal activity'. This is in conformity with the approach taken by the United States Supreme Court in *Sorrells v US* (1932) 287 US 435 at 441–442 where the court stated:

g 'It is well settled that the fact that officers or employees of the Government merely afford opportunities or facilities for the commission of the offence does not defeat the prosecution. Artifice and stratagem may be employed to catch those engaged in criminal enterprises … The appropriate object of this permitted activity, frequently essential to the enforcement of the law, is to reveal the criminal design; to expose the illicit traffic, the prohibited

h publication, the fraudulent use of the mails, the illegal conspiracy, or other offences, and thus to disclose the would-be violators of the law. A different question is presented when the criminal design originates with the officials of the Government, and they implant in the mind of an innocent person the disposition to commit the alleged offence and induce its commission in order

j that they may prosecute.'

See also *US v Russell* (1973) 411 US 423 at 435–436.

Section 78 of the Police and Criminal Evidence Act 1984

[103] There is one further observation which I wish to make in respect of the English authorities. In many of the cases where the issue of entrapment has been

considered no detailed consideration has been given to the question whether the prosecution should be stayed as being an abuse of process or whether the evidence should be excluded under s 78 of the 1984 Act on the ground that its submission would have such an adverse effect on the fairness of the proceedings that the court ought not to admit it. However in *R v Shannon* [2001] 1 WLR 51 the Court of Appeal gave consideration to the relationship between entrapment and s 78 and Potter LJ (at 68 (para 39)) stated in relation to s 78:

> '... the ultimate question is not the broad one: is the bringing of proceedings fair (in the sense of appropriate) in entrapment cases. It is whether the fairness of the proceedings will be adversely affected by admitting the evidence of the agent provocateur or evidence which is available as the result of his action or activities. So, for instance, if there is good reason to question the credibility of evidence given by an agent provocateur, or which casts doubt on the reliability of other evidence procured by or resulting from his actions, and that question is not susceptible of being properly or fairly resolved in the course of the proceedings from available, admissible and "untainted" evidence, then the judge may readily conclude that such evidence should be excluded. If, on the other hand, the unfairness complained of is no more than the visceral reaction that it is in principle unfair as a matter of policy, or wrong as a matter of law, for a person to be prosecuted for a crime which he would not have committed without the incitement or encouragement of others, then that is not itself sufficient, unless the behaviour of the police (or someone acting on behalf of or in league with the police) and/or the prosecuting authority has been such as to justify a stay on grounds of abuse of process.'

I am in agreement with this analysis which accords with the statement of Lord Steyn in *R v Latif, R v Shahzad* [1996] 1 All ER 353 at 360–361, [1996] 1 WLR 104 at 112:

> 'If the court concludes that a fair trial is not possible, it will stay the proceedings. That is not what the present case is concerned with. It is plain that a fair trial was possible and that such a trial took place. In this case the issue is whether, despite the fact that a fair trial was possible, the judge ought to have stayed the criminal proceedings on broader considerations of the integrity of the criminal justice system.'

[104] Therefore I consider that if a defendant wishes to rely on entrapment he should normally do so by applying before the proceedings begin for a stay on the ground of abuse of process. If his application is refused it will still be open to him to seek to exclude the evidence under s 78 on the kind of ground stated by Potter LJ. But I agree with my noble and learned friend, Lord Hoffmann, that if a later application to exclude evidence under s 78 is, in substance, an application to stay on the ground of entrapment, a court should apply the principles applicable to the grant of a stay.

The judgment of the European Court of Human Rights in Teixeira de Castro v Portugal

[105] The European Court sets out the facts:

> '9. In connection with an operation monitoring drug trafficking, two plain clothes officers of the Public Security Police (the PSP) from the Famaliçao police station approached an individual, VS, on a number of occasions. He

a was suspected of petty drug trafficking in order to pay for drugs—mainly hashish—for his own consumption. They hoped that through VS they would be able to identify his supplier and offered to buy several kilograms of hashish from him. Unaware that they were police officers, VS agreed to find a supplier. However, despite being pressed by the two officers, he was unable to locate one. 10. Shortly before midnight on 30 December 1992 the

b two officers went to VS's home saying that they were now interested in buying heroin. VS mentioned the name of Francisco Teixeira de Castro as being someone who might be able to find some. However, he did not know the latter's address and had to obtain it from FO. All four then went to the applicant's home in the purported buyers' car. The applicant came outside at FO's request and got into the car where the two officers, accompanied by

c VS, were waiting. The officers said that they wished to buy 20g of heroin for PTE 200,000 and produced a roll of banknotes from the Bank of Portugal. 11. Mr Teixeira de Castro agreed to procure the heroin and, accompanied by FO, went in his own car to the home of another person, JPO. The latter obtained three sachets of heroin, one weighing 10g and the other two 5g

d each, from someone else and, on his return, handed them over to the applicant in exchange for a payment, which, though the precise figure is not known, exceeded PTE 100,000. 12. The applicant then took the drugs to VS's home. VS had in the meantime returned there and the two police officers were waiting outside. The deal was to take place in the house. The officers went inside at VS's invitation; the applicant then took one of the

e sachets out of his pocket whereupon the two officers identified themselves and arrested the applicant, VS and FO, shortly before 2 am. They searched all three and found the applicant to be in possession of another two sachets of heroin, PTE 43,000 in cash and a gold bracelet.' (See (1998) 4 BHRC 533 at 535–536.)

f [106] The applicant, Mr Teixeira de Castro, was prosecuted before a criminal court in Portugal which convicted him and sentenced him to six years imprisonment. The applicant appealed to the Supreme Court in Portugal against his conviction but the Supreme Court dismissed his appeal. Before the European Court the applicant complained that he had not had a fair trial in violation of art 6(1) of the

g convention in that he had been incited by plain clothes police officers to commit the offence of which he was later convicted. The European Court upheld the applicant's complaint and held that there had been a violation of art 6(1).

   [107] The court stated (at 540):

h '36. The use of undercover agents must be restricted and safeguards put in place even in cases concerning the fight against drug trafficking. While the rise in organised crime undoubtedly requires that appropriate measures be taken, the right to a fair administration of justice nevertheless holds such a prominent place ... that it cannot be sacrificed for the sake of expedience. The general requirements of fairness embodied in art 6 apply to proceedings

j concerning all types of criminal offence, from the most straightforward to the most complex. The public interest cannot justify the use of evidence obtained as a result of police incitement.'

The essence of the reasoning of the court (at 541) is:

   '38. In the instant case it is necessary to determine whether or not the two police officers' activity went beyond that of undercover agents. The court

notes that the government have not contended that the officers' intervention
took place as part of an anti-drug trafficking operation ordered and supervised
by a judge. It does not appear either that the competent authorities had good
reason to suspect that Mr Teixeira de Castro was a drug trafficker; on the
contrary, he had no criminal record and no preliminary investigation concerning
him had been opened. Indeed, he was not known to the police officers, who
only came into contact with him through the intermediaries, VS and FO ...
Furthermore, the drugs were not at the applicant's home· he obtained them
from a third party who had in turn obtained them from another person ...
Nor does the Supreme Court's judgment of 5 May 1994 indicate that, at the
time of his arrest, the applicant had more drugs in his possession than the
quantity the police officers had requested thereby going beyond what he had
been incited to do by the police. There is no evidence to support the
government's argument that the applicant was predisposed to commit
offences. The necessary inference from these circumstances is that the two
police officers did not confine themselves to investigating Mr Teixeira de
Castro's criminal activity in an essentially passive manner, but exercised an
influence such as to incite the commission of the offence. Lastly, the court
notes that in their decisions the domestic courts said that the applicant had
been convicted mainly on the basis of the statements of the two police
officers. 39. In the light of all these considerations, the court concludes that
the two police officers' actions went beyond those of undercover agents
because they instigated the offence and there is nothing to suggest that
without their intervention it would have been committed. That intervention
and its use in the impugned criminal proceedings meant that, right from the
outset, the applicant was definitively deprived of a fair trial. Consequently,
there has been a violation of art 6(1).'

[108] In my opinion the principle stated by the court is that the fairness of a
trial is violated if the crime for which the defendant is prosecuted has been incited
or instigated by police officers: thus the court concluded its reasoning, by stating:

'... the two police officers' actions went beyond those of undercover
agents because they instigated the offence and there was nothing to suggest
that without their intervention it would have been committed. That
intervention and its use in the impugned criminal proceedings meant that,
right from the outset, the applicant was definitively deprived of a fair trial.
Consequently, there has been a violation of art 6(1).'

[109] Accordingly I consider that the approach of the English courts and of
McHugh J in Ridgeway's case is in no way inconsistent with the ratio decidendi of
the European Court in Teixeira de Castro's case. As Lord Bingham of Cornhill CJ
stated in Nottingham City Council v Amin [2000] 2 All ER 946 at 950, [2000] 1 WLR
1071 at 1076–1077, there would be a violation of the concept of fairness 'if a
defendant were to be convicted and punished for committing a crime which he
only committed because he had been incited, instigated, persuaded, pressurised
or wheedled into committing it by a law enforcement officer'.

[110] In some cases in England the argument has been advanced by counsel
for the defence that the European Court has laid down as a principle that unless
the police officers act 'in an essentially passive manner' they have incited the
commission of the offence and that, in consequence, there must be a breach of
art 6(1). Defence counsel point to the penultimate sentence in para 38 of the

judgment in *Teixeira de Castro*'s case ((1998) 4 HRRC 533 at 541) in support of this submission. Thus in *Amin*'s case [2000] 2 All ER 946 at 953, [2000] 1 WLR 1071 at 1080, Lord Bingham CJ described counsel for the defendant as advancing the following argument:

> 'None the less, Mr Beloff is entitled to, and does, attach significance to the precise language which the court uses in para 38 of the judgment. He submits that the two police constables in Nottingham did not confine themselves to investigating the respondent's criminal activity and did not do so in an "essentially passive manner". Accordingly he submits that they are to be regarded, in the light of that authority, as having instigated the offence or incited it and so as having acted as agents provocateurs so as to render the proceedings as a whole unfair, there being no other significant evidence against the respondent.'

Lord Bingham CJ rejected this argument, stating:

> 'While I for my part am willing to accept that, on a precise and literal reading of the court's language, Mr Beloff is entitled to make that submission, I am wholly unwilling to accept the far-reaching proposition which he bases on it. It seems to me that that conclusion has to be understood in the context of the whole argument before the court on that occasion and on the special facts of that case. It is true that in the present case the criminal activity alleged was much more minor. It is also true that the facts are much simpler and that they simply cannot lend themselves to the construction that this respondent was in any way prevailed upon or overborne or persuaded or pressured or instigated or incited to commit the offence. The question for the stipendiary magistrate was whether, on the facts which he found, the admission of this evidence had such an adverse effect on the fairness of the proceedings that he should exclude it, or whether (to put the test in a different way) the effect of admitting it was to deny the respondent a fair trial. In my opinion the only possible answer to both questions was No.' (See [2000] 2 All ER 946 at 953–954, [2000] 1 WLR 1071 at 1080–1081.)

In my respectful opinion Lord Bingham CJ was right to conclude that some of the wording of para 38 was based on the special facts of that case and it is relevant to observe that in its judgments the court has often emphasised that it is concerned with the particular facts of the case before it (see *Brown v Stott (Procurator Fiscal, Dunfermline)* [2001] 2 All ER 97 at 115, [2001] 2 WLR 817 at 836 per Lord Bingham).

[111] The particular facts which the court emphasises in para 38 included the following: (a) the police officers' intervention did not take place as part of an anti-drug trafficking operation ordered and supervised by a judge; (b) the competent authorities had no good reason to suspect that Mr Teixeira de Castro was a drug trafficker; he had no criminal record and no preliminary investigation concerning him had been opened; (c) there was no evidence to suggest that Mr Teixeira de Castro was predisposed to commit offences.

[112] Therefore I am of opinion that the court did not intend to state as a general principle that there was a breach of art 6 of the convention whenever police officers gave a person an opportunity to break the law and he took advantage of that opportunity in circumstances in which it appeared that he would have behaved in the same way if some other person had given him the opportunity to commit a similar crime. In my opinion if a person freely takes advantage of an opportunity to break the law given to him by a police officer, the police officer is

not to be regarded as inciting or instigating the crime in the context of the
prohibition of entrapment. The conduct of the police officer should not be viewed
as constituting incitement or instigation where, as McHugh J states in *Ridgeway v
The Queen* (1995) 184 CLR 19 at 92, that conduct is 'consistent with the ordinary
temptations and stratagems that are likely to be encountered in the course of
criminal activity', and I do not consider that the judgment of the court lays down
a principle to the contrary.

[113] In the case of *R v Looseley*, as appears from his ruling, the judge considered
that tape recordings which were played to him gave a degree of support to the
contention of the prosecution that Looseley was an active and current drugs
dealer. The undercover police officer made contact with Looseley in the course
of an undercover police operation concerning the supply of drugs in the
Guildford area. A senior police officer had authorised the operation and had
overseen its progress. The judge found that the undercover officer had presented
himself to Looseley as an ideal customer for a drugs deal, but the judge also found
specifically that he did not go beyond that portrayal and that he presented himself
exactly as someone in the drugs world would expect to see a heroin addict. There
then arose a relationship between Looseley and the officer during which
Looseley supplied him with heroin on more than one occasion. The judge found
that there was evidence to show that Looseley was steeped in the drug culture
and encouraged the officer, whom he probably saw as a lucrative customer, to
take more heroin from him.

[114] The judge's conclusion in the light of the facts before him was that,
whilst the officer presented himself as an ideal customer so far as a drugs dealer
was concerned, the officer did not do anything other than present himself as such,
and accordingly the conduct of the officer did not constitute incitement. In my
opinion the judge's assessment, which he made in the course of a lucid and
careful ruling, was one which he was fully entitled to make.

[115] A further argument was advanced by Mr O'Connor QC on behalf of
Looseley that the request to him for drugs by the police officer was a violation of
his right to respect for his private life under art 8 of the convention. I consider for
the reasons given by my noble and learned friend, Lord Hoffmann, that that
argument is without substance. Accordingly I would answer the certified question
in the negative and would dismiss Looseley's appeal.

[116] In the case giving rise to the Attorney General's reference I respectfully
differ from the view taken by the Court of Appeal and I consider that the judge
was right to rule that the prosecution should be stayed on the ground that the
police officers had instigated the offence. It was clear on the facts that the reason
why the acquitted person had supplied heroin to the officers was because they
repeatedly offered to supply, and did supply to him, cut-price cigarettes and he
wished to continue to benefit from that supply. When he was interviewed by the
police after his arrest he said that he was not interested in heroin, but that he had
become involved because two men had approached him offering to sell him
cheap cigarettes. He said it was 'a favour for a favour'. Therefore the officers did
more than give him the opportunity to commit the offence of supplying
heroin—they instigated the offence because they offered him inducements that
would not ordinarily be associated with the commission of such an offence.

[117] I would answer the point of law referred by the Attorney General by
stating that in relation to the exercise of the judicial discretion conferred by s 78
of the 1984 Act and the exercise of the power to stay proceedings as an abuse of
process of the court, the principles of English law as set out in the authorities to

a which reference has been made in this speech are in conformity with art 6 of the convention and the jurisprudence of the European Court and do not require modification.

LORD SCOTT OF FOSCOTE.

b [118] My Lords, I have had the advantage of reading in advance the opinions of my noble and learned friends, Lord Hoffmann, Lord Nicholls of Birkenhead and Lord Hutton, and am in complete agreement with their analysis of the nature of an entrapment defence in criminal proceedings.

[119] In *R v Sang* [1979] 2 All ER 1222, [1980] AC 402 this House made clear that there was no defence of 'entrapment' known to English law (see [1979] 2 All ER 1222 at 1226, 1235, [1980] AC 402 at 432, 443 per Lord Diplock and *c* Lord Salmon respectively). If 'defence' is restricted to meaning a contention that if accepted would negative guilt, the proposition that there is no defence of entrapment remains as true today as it was in 1980. If the act done by an individual constitutes the actus reus of the crime and the individual has the requisite mens rea it is no defence for him to say that he did the act at the *d* invitation or instigation or with the encouragement of someone else. And if the 'someone else' turns out, unbeknownst to the individual at the time, to be a police officer or some other representative of the executive, the ingredients necessary to constitute the commission of the offence are as much present as they would be if the 'someone else' had no connection at all with the authorities.

e [120] Neither s 78 of the Police and Criminal Evidence Act 1984 nor art 6 of the European Convention for the Protection of Human Rights and Fundamental Freedoms (Rome, 4 November 1950; TS 71 (1953); Cmd 8969) (as set out in Sch 1 to the Human Rights Act 1998) has elevated 'entrapment' to the status of a defence in the sense described above. Section 78 gives the court a discretion to exclude evidence if 'the evidence would have such an adverse effect on the fairness *f* of the proceedings that the court ought not to admit it'. Where evidence has been obtained by entrapment this condition for its exclusion may in some cases be satisfied. Where the evidence is excluded the consequence in some cases may be that the prosecution cannot succeed. But the entrapment circumstances that will have brought about this result will not have constituted a defence in the sense described above.

g [121] The entrapment circumstances may in some cases be such that a prosecution would be 'an affront to the public conscience' (Lord Steyn in *R v Latif, R v Shahzad* [1996] 1 All ER 353 at 361, [1996] 1 WLR 104 at 112) or 'deeply offensive to ordinary notions of fairness' (Lord Bingham of Cornhill CJ in *Nottingham City Council v Amin* [2000] 2 All ER 946 at 950, [2000] 1 WLR 1071 at *h* 1076). In cases of that sort the court has an inherent jurisdiction to stay the prosecution (see *Bennett v Horseferry Road Magistrates' Court* [1993] 3 All ER 138, [1994] 1 AC 42). A successful application to stay a prosecution on the ground of entrapment enables the accused to escape from the charge. But the entrapment still cannot be properly described as a defence. It does not negative any of the *j* ingredients requisite for guilt. The court's decision to allow the accused to go free is based upon its disapproval of the behaviour of the police officers, not upon the prosecution's failure to establish those ingredients.

[122] Article 6 of the convention entitles an accused to a fair trial 'In the determination … of any criminal charge against him'. This restates what was already English law. It is a fundamental principle of English law that the court is under the duty to ensure the accused a fair trial (see *R v Sang*). The fairness of a

trial may be compromised if the prosecution is allowed to rely on evidence
obtained by unfair means. The court's discretion under s 78 of the 1984 Act to
exclude evidence (see *R v Khan (Sultan)* [1996] 3 All ER 289, [1997] AC 558)
provides the remedy in domestic law and, in my opinion, enables the domestic
law to accord with what is required for compliance in this area with art 6 (see
Khan v UK (2000) 8 BHRC 310).

[123] In *Teixeira de Castro v Portugal* (1998) 4 BHRC 533, the European Court
of Human Rights considered entrapment in the context of art 6. The facts of the
case and the relevant paragraphs of the court's judgment are set out in the
opinion of my noble and learned friend, Lord Hutton. I need not repeat them.
The court concluded (at 541 (para 39)) that the intervention of the police officers
and their instigation of the offence with which the accused had been charged
'meant that, right from the outset, the applicant was definitively deprived of a fair
trial' and that, consequently, there had been a violation of art 6(1).

[124] My Lords, I confess that I have found it rather difficult to follow why the
facts recited in the European Court's judgment rendered the trial unfair. But, on
the footing that in the particular circumstances of that case it would have been
unfair to Mr de Castro to allow the prosecution to put in evidence the facts that
had followed the police officers' intervention and instigation, the application in
English law of s 78 would have produced the same result.

[125] It is, in my opinion, important to keep clear and distinct, whether under
domestic law or for art 6 purposes, matters which constitute a defence properly
so called and matters which may provide a reason for excluding particular
evidence. It is well established that documents and information held by the
prosecution which may prove the accused's innocence should be disclosed (see
R v Keane [1994] 2 All ER 478, [1994] 1 WLR 746). If the prosecution is unwilling
to disclose them, for example because they may disclose the identity and place in
danger an informant, the prosecution will usually have to be abandoned. But
documents and material which relate only to the question whether the admission
of particular evidence would be unfair need not lead to so stark a conclusion. In
considering whether police officers had sufficient existing grounds for suspecting
an individual of involvement in crime in order to justify their undercover
involvement in the commission of the offence charged, the police should not, in
my opinion, be expected to disclose the source of their suspicions if to do so
would reveal the identity of an informant or prejudice their ability to obtain
similar information in the future. Entrapment allegations in resisting a prosecution
must not be allowed to achieve the status of a true defence. Otherwise the balance
to which my noble and learned friend, Lord Hutton, referred at [100], above,
would, I fear, tilt unacceptably towards those who commit crimes and to the
detriment of the public at large.

[126] I agree with my noble and learned friends that for the reasons they have
given the certified question in the Looseley case should be answered No and that
the appeal should be dismissed.

[127] In the case giving rise to the Attorney General's reference I am less clear
that the police officers' conduct was such as to require the s 78 discretion to be
exercised so as to exclude the evidence of the undercover police officers. I doubt
whether the conduct of the police officers was out of the line of what might have
been expected of many purchasers of contraband cigarettes. The inducements
offered to the accused in order to persuade him to supply heroin do not seem to
me to correspond with what would be necessary to cause the prosecution to be
an affront to the public or to offend ordinary notions of fairness. This was,

a however, a matter for the discretion of the trial judge, and it may be that his value judgment was one that he was entitled to reach.

[128] I respectfully agree with the answer proposed by Lord Hutton to the point of law referred by the Attorney General.

Looseley's appeal dismissed. Order accordingly on the Attorney General's reference.

Kate O'Hanlon   Barrister.

R (on the application of Lichniak) v Secretary of State for the Home Department

R v Lichniak

R (on the application of Pyrah) v Secretary of State for the Home Department

R v Pyrah

[2001] EWHC Admin 294

QUEEN'S BENCH DIVISION, DIVISIONAL COURT AND COURT OF APPEAL (CRIMINAL DIVISION)

KENNEDY LJ, GARLAND AND RICHARDS JJ

3, 4 APRIL, 2 MAY 2001

Criminal law – Court of Appeal – Jurisdiction – Appeal against sentence – Sentence fixed by law – Court imposing on claimants mandatory life sentences for murder – Claimants seeking judicial review of sentences as incompatible with rights under human rights convention – Whether Court of Appeal having jurisdiction to hear matter as appeal against sentence – Criminal Appeal Act 1968, s 9(1) – Supreme Court Act 1981, s 29(3) – Human Rights Act 1998, s 3(1).

Sentence – Life imprisonment – Mandatory life sentence – Murder – Whether mandatory life sentence for murder incompatible with human rights in cases where convicted person posing no foreseeable risk to public at time of sentence – Murder (Abolition of Death Penalty) Act 1965, s 1 – Human Rights Act 1998, Sch 1, Pt I, arts 3, 5.

The claimants, L and P, were convicted of separate murders, and were sentenced to imprisonment for life as required by s 1[a] of the Murder (Abolition of Death Penalty) Act 1965. The trial judges were of the view that the claimants were unlikely to present any danger to the public upon release and that there was no likelihood of re-offending. The period of detention necessary to meet the requirements of retribution and general deterrence was fixed at eleven years in L's case and eight years in P's case. The claimants applied for judicial review of the decisions to impose life sentences, contending that such sentences should not be imposed where, at the time of sentencing, there was no foreseeable risk of the offender being a danger to the public after he had served the penal element of the sentence, and that a mandatory life sentence violated two provisions of the European Convention for the Protection of Human Rights and Fundamental Freedoms 1950 (as set out in Sch 1 to the Human Rights Act 1998), namely the right to liberty in art 5[b], because such a sentence was arbitrary, and the prohibition against inhuman or degrading treatment or punishment under art 3[c], because it was disproportionate. At the hearing, in which the court sat both as a

---

a Section 1, so far as material, is set out at [1], below
b Article 5, so far as material, is set out at [2], below
c Article 3 is set out at [1], below

a Divisional Court and as the Court of Appeal (Criminal Division), the Secretary of State contended that neither court had jurisdiction to hear the challenges. In particular, he argued that the Divisional Court was precluded by s 29(3)^d of the Supreme Court Act 1981 from hearing the applications because a challenge to a sentence was a matter relating to trial on indictment, and that the Criminal Division of the Court of Appeal could not be vested with jurisdiction to hear

b appeals by the claimants against sentence because s 9(1)^e of the Criminal Appeal Act 1968 precluded an appeal to the Court of Appeal against any sentence fixed by law.

Held – (1) Although a decision to impose a mandatory life sentence following conviction was plainly a matter relating to trial on indictment, the court, by

c sitting as a division of the Court of Appeal, had jurisdiction to entertain the instant cases as appeals against sentence since they raised arguable issues as to the compatibility of s 1 of the 1965 Act with the convention. Section 3(1)^f of the 1998 Act required the court to read and give effect to s 9(1) of the 1968 Act in a way which was compatible with convention rights. If a statutory provision which

d required the imposition of a sentence of life imprisonment was incompatible with the convention then, at least until Parliament had had the opportunity to consider its response to the court's declaration of incompatibility, the sentence was not fixed by law for the purposes of s 9(1); alternatively the exclusion of sentences fixed by law was itself subject to an implied exception where the statutory provision fixing the sentence was incompatible with the convention

e (see [12], [13], below).

(2) A mandatory sentence of life imprisonment for murder was not incompatible with either art 3 or art 5 of the convention. Such a sentence was, in reality, an indeterminate one, and there would rarely be imprisonment for life. In other cases, the penal element having been decided upon at an earlier stage,

f when that element had been served the Secretary of State might, if recommended to do so by the Parole Board, after consultation with the Lord Chief Justice and the trial judge, release the prisoner on licence. In practice, the Secretary of State referred cases to the board for consideration, and if a prisoner had been released on licence and was recalled he would have the opportunity to have his recall

g considered by the board. That was all part of what was involved in the mandatory life sentence. It could not be labelled inhuman or degrading. There was sufficient individualised consideration of the offender's case within the context of the sentence. Thus it was open to Parliament, acting within its discretionary area of judgment, to retain the sentence without violating art 3. As for art 5, it was not

h for the court, within the context of that provision, to review the appropriateness of the original sentence. Even if that were wrong, a sentence could not be arbitrary when in each case the application of the sentence was individualised, and everyone knew that it would be individualised from the moment it was imposed. Accordingly, the appeals would be dismissed (see [42], [47], [51], below);

j

---

d Section 29(3) provides: 'In relation to the jurisdiction of the Crown Court, other than its jurisdiction in matters relating to trial on indictment, the High Court shall have all jurisdiction to make orders of mandamus, prohibition or certiorari as the High Court possesses in relation to the jurisdiction of an inferior court.'

e Section 9, so far as material, is set out at [10], below

f Section 3(1) provides: 'So far as it is possible to do so, primary legislation and subordinate legislation must be read and given effect in a way which is compatible with the Convention rights.'

Weeks v UK (1987) 10 EHRR 293, *Wynne v UK* (1994) 19 EHRR 333 and *V v UK, T v UK* (1999) 30 EHRR 121 considered.

a

Notes

For the supervisory jurisdiction of the High Court over the Crown Court, the prohibition on inhuman and degrading treatment and the right to liberty, and appeal against sentence following trial on indictment, see respectively 1(1) *Halsbury's Laws* (4th edn reissue) para 142, 8(2) *Halsbury's Laws* (4th edn reissue) paras 124, 127 and 11(2) *Halsbury's Laws* (4th edn reissue) para 1355.

b

For the Murder (Abolition of Death Penalty) Act 1965, s 1, see 12 *Halsbury's Statutes* (4th edn) (1997 reissue) 314.

For the Criminal Appeal Act 1968, s 9, see 12 *Halsbury's Statutes* (4th edn) (1997 reissue) 381.

c

For the Supreme Court Act 1981, s 29, see 11 *Halsbury's Statutes* (4th edn) (2000 reissue) 1066.

For the Human Rights Act 1998, s 3, Sch 1, Pt I, arts 3, 5, see 7 *Halsbury's Statutes* (4th edn) (1999 reissue) 502, 522.

d

Cases referred to in judgment

Bromfield v UK (1 July 1998, unreported), E Com HR.
Brown v Stott (Procurator Fiscal, Dunfermline) [2001] 2 All ER 97, [2001] 2 WLR 817, PC.
Costello-Roberts v UK (1993) 19 EHRR 112, ECt HR.
DPP v Crown Court at Manchester [1993] 2 All ER 663, [1994] 1 AC 9, [1993] 2 WLR 846, HL.

e

Doody v Secretary of State for the Home Dept [1993] 3 All ER 92, [1994] 1 AC 531, [1993] 3 WLR 154, HL.
Equal Opportunities Commission v Secretary of State for Employment [1994] 1 All ER 910, [1995] 1 AC 1, [1994] 2 WLR 409, HL.

f

Håkansson and Sturesson v Sweden (1990) 13 EHRR 1, ECt HR.
Hussain v UK (1996) 22 EHRR 1, ECt HR.
R v Basra (1989) 11 Cr App R (S) 527, CA.
R v DPP, ex p Kebeline, R v DPP, ex p Rechachi [1999] 4 All ER 801, [2000] 2 AC 326, [1999] 3 WLR 972, HL.
R v Offen [2001] 2 All ER 154, [2001] 1 WLR 253, CA.

g

R v Parliamentary Comr for Standards, ex p Al Fayed [1998] 1 All ER 93, [1998] 1 WLR 669, CA.
R v Secretary of State for the Home Dept, ex p Stafford [1998] 4 All ER 7, [1999] 2 AC 38, [1998] 3 WLR 372, HL.
R v Smith [1987] 1 SCR 1045, Can SC.

h

Sillery v R (1981) 35 ALR 227, Aust HC.
Smalley Crown Court at Warwick [1985] 1 All ER 769, [1985] AC 622, [1985] 2 WLR 538, HL.
Soering v UK (1989) 11 EHRR 439, ECt HR.
State v Vries [1997] 4 LRC 1, Nam HC.

j

Thynne v UK (1990) 13 EHRR 666, ECt HR.
V v UK, T v UK (1999) 30 EHRR 121, ECt HR.
Van Droogenbroeck v Belgium (1982) 4 EHRR 443, ECt HR.
Weeks v UK (1987) 10 EHRR 293, ECt HR.
Woodson v North Carolina [1976] 428 US 286, US SC.
Wynne v UK (1994) 19 EHRR 333, ECt HR.

a **Applications for judicial review and appeals against sentence**

R (on the application of Lichniak) v Sec of State for the Home Dept; R v Lichniak
The claimant, Daniella Lichniak, applied for judicial review of, alternatively
appealed against, the sentence of life imprisonment imposed on her under s 1 of
the Murder (Abolition of Death Penalty) Act 1965 following her conviction for
b murder in the Crown Court at Cardiff on 11 July 1990 after a trial before Ognall J
and a jury. The facts are set out in the judgment of the court.

R (on the application of Pyrah) v Sec of State for the Home Dept; R v Pyrah
The claimant, Glyn Pyrah, applied for judicial review of, alternatively appealed
against, the sentence of life imprisonment imposed on him under s 1 of the
c Murder (Abolition of Death Penalty) Act 1965 following his conviction for murder
in the Crown Court at Bristol on 26 January 1998 after a trial before Brian Smedley J
and a jury. The facts are set out in the judgment of the court.

Edward Fitzgerald QC and *Phillippa Kaufmann* (instructed by *Bhatt Murphy*) for the
d   claimants/appellants.
David Pannick QC and *Mark Shaw* (instructed by the *Treasury Solicitor*) for the
    Secretary of State and the Crown.

Cur adv vult

e 2 May 2001. The following judgment of the court was delivered.

KENNEDY LJ.
    [1] Each of these claimants seeks judicial review of a decision to impose a
mandatory sentence of life imprisonment following their separate convictions for
f murder. They contend that s 1 of the Murder (Abolition of Death Penalty) Act
1965 is incompatible with arts 3 and 5 of the European Convention for the
Protection of Human Rights and Fundamental Freedoms (Rome, 4 November 1950;
TS 71 (1953); Cmd 8969) (as set out in Sch 1 to the Human Rights Act 1998).
Section 1(1) of the 1965 Act so far as material provides that 'a person convicted of
murder shall ... be sentenced to imprisonment for life'. Article 3 of the
g convention reads: 'No one shall be subjected to torture or to inhuman or
degrading treatment or punishment.'
    [2] Article 5 so far as material reads:

    '1. Everyone has the right to liberty and security of person. No one shall
h   be deprived of his liberty save in the following cases and in accordance with
    a procedure prescribed by law: (a) the lawful detention of a person after
    conviction by a competent court ...'

    [3] Permission to apply for judicial review was granted by Scott Baker J on
23 January 2001 when he also ordered that this court sit both as a Divisional
j Court and as the Court of Appeal (Criminal Division), which we have done.

CIRCUMSTANCES OF OFFENCES

(A) *Lichniak*
    [4] In January 1990, when she was 29 years of age, Daniella Lichniak was living
with a man named Thomas. In the words of the trial judge, Thomas—

'used her to go with him in his car to a local public house, and there to
challenge the deceased man to a fight. She took a large carving knife from
the car and while the two men were grappling with each other she fatally
stabbed the deceased. Steven Thomas was also charged with murder, but
acquitted by the jury on the basis that he was not party to a joint venture to
use the knife.'

At her trial the jury had to consider the issues of intent and diminished responsibility.
There was evidence that she was suffering from a chronic depressive anxiety state
sometimes causative of sudden panic attacks. The judge in his report to the
Secretary of State after the trial said:

'I have no doubt that while the jury (in my view) rightly rejected her
defence of diminished responsibility, she was in a state of chronic anxiety
stress induced in part by the demands of four (including two very young)
children, as well as a fairly stormy relationship with Thomas, with whom she
had lived for 12 years and who had fathered all the children. I think that she
became highly emotional on this occasion and took the knife and killed on
an impulse—hence Thomas' acquittal.'

[5] Mr Fitzgerald QC submitted that there is evidence that she was a 'battered
wife' and, more important for present purposes, that she never did present any
ongoing danger to society. The trial judge said: 'She has no previous convictions,
and I do not believe that upon release she is likely to commit offences of a kind
making her a public danger.'

[6] We see no reason to question that assessment. In her case the period of
detention necessary to meet the requirements of retribution and general
deterrence was fixed at eleven years. She served that period, and is now in an
open prison awaiting a review of her case by the Parole Board.

(B) *Pyrah*

[7] In October 1996 Pyrah, who was then 41 years of age, had been drinking
heavily. He heard and saw in the street a fracas which involved a woman being
assaulted and pushed to the floor. Medical evidence indicated that he was
sensitive to that kind of situation because as a child he had seen his mother being
treated violently. He went up to the woman's assailant and punched him,
knocking him to the ground. He then kicked him. The first and fatal kick was
described as being like a penalty kick, and the injury sustained proved fatal. The
trial judge described the incident as a tragic event, and said in his report to the
Secretary of State: 'In my view he does not present any danger to the community
and there is no likelihood of him re-offending.'

[8] Subsequent medical reports have tended to confirm that assessment, which
we see no reason to question. In his case the period necessary to meet the
requirements of retribution and general deterrence was fixed at eight years.

THE BASIC SUBMISSION

[9] Mr Fitzgerald's basic submission is that now that all mandatory life
sentences are recognised to fall into two parts, namely first a penal element to
meet the requirements of retribution and general deterrence (fixed by the Home
Secretary after considering the views of the trial judge and the Lord Chief Justice)
and, secondly, a subsequent period of detention justified on preventive grounds, life
sentences should not be imposed where at the time of sentencing there is no
foreseeable risk of the defendant being a danger to the public after he or she has

a served the penal element of the sentence. Referring to the convention, Mr Fitzgerald argues that the mandatory life sentence has no clear penological objective. It violates art 5 because it is arbitrary, and art 3 because it is disproportionate. Before we turn to look at these submissions in more detail we must say something about the jurisdiction of this court.

b JURISDICTION

[10] Everyone agrees that the issues now raised need to be addressed, but there is a problem as to jurisdiction. Section 9(1) of the Criminal Appeal Act 1968 provides:

c 'A person who has been convicted of an offence on indictment may appeal to the Court of Appeal against any sentence (not being a sentence fixed by law) passed on him for the offence ...'

[11] Plainly on the face of it the sentence for murder is fixed by law, namely by s 1 of the 1965 Act, so it is not easy to see how we, sitting as a division of the Court of Appeal, can be vested with jurisdiction to hear an appeal against sentence.

d [12] The obvious alternative is the jurisdiction of the Divisional Court to hear an application for judicial review, but s 29(3) of the Supreme Court Act 1981 makes it clear that the jurisdiction of the Divisional Court in relation to the Crown Court relates only to matters other than the latter court's jurisdiction 'in matters relating to trial on indictment'. Although the Crown Court is not named by either claimant as defendant, the decision under challenge in each case is the

e decision to impose a mandatory life sentence following conviction, which is plainly a matter relating to trial on indictment (see *Smalley v Crown Court at Warwick* [1985] 1 All ER 769 at 779, [1985] AC 622 at 642, approved in *DPP v Crown Court at Manchester* [1993] 2 All ER 663 at 669, [1994] 1 AC 9 at 20). Furthermore, as Mr Pannick QC for the Secretary of State pointed out, the only relevant

f decision other than the one identified by the claimants would seem to be the decision of Parliament in 1965 and there is no challenge to that. If there were it would fall foul of what in *R v Parliamentary Comr for Standards, ex p Al Fayed* [1998] 1 All ER 93 at 94, [1998] 1 WLR 669 at 670 was described by Lord Woolf MR as the court's 'self-denying ordinance in relation to interfering with proceedings of Parliament'. It would also now encounter the problem that whereas s 6(1) of the

g Human Rights Act 1998 makes it unlawful for a public authority to act in a way which is incompatible with a convention right, s 6(3) makes it clear that for the purposes of s 6 Parliament is not a public authority. On the other hand there is a question whether a declaration of incompatibility could be made under s 4 without identifying an unlawful act under s 6. In *Equal Opportunities Commission v Secretary*

h *of State for Employment* [1994] 1 All ER 910 at 919, [1995] 1 AC 1 at 26 Lord Keith of Kinkel accepted that a declaration of incompatibility could be made in relation to primary legislation in judicial review proceedings brought by a person with a sufficient interest. That of course was in relation to an EC issue and was before Parliament enacted the 1998 Act, and in *R v DPP, ex p Kebeline, R v DPP,*

j *ex p Rechachi* [1999] 4 All ER 801 at 836, [2000] 2 AC 326 at 371 Lord Steyn emphasised the importance of human rights challenges in relation to criminal matters taking place 'in the criminal trial or on appeal'.

[13] For present purposes we are satisfied that the most attractive route to jurisdiction is to have resort to s 3(1) of the 1998 Act which requires us to read and give effect to s 9(1) of the 1968 Act in a way which is compatible with convention rights. If a statutory provision which requires the imposition of a sentence of life

imprisonment is incompatible with the convention then, at least until Parliament
has had the opportunity to consider its response to the court's declaration of *a*
incompatibility, the sentence is not for the purposes of s 9(1) of the 1968 Act fixed
by law; alternatively the exclusion of sentences fixed by law is itself subject to an
implied exception where the statutory provision fixing the sentence is incompatible
with the convention. Accordingly we hold that this court, sitting as a division of
the Court of Appeal, has jurisdiction to entertain these matters as appeals against *b*
sentence, since they raise arguable issues as to the compatibility of s 1 of the 1965
Act with the convention. We in each case extend time and grant permission to
appeal. That makes it unnecessary to consider further what if any jurisdiction we
might have as a Divisional Court to entertain proceedings for judicial review.

THE POLITICAL HISTORY   *c*
[14] Mr Fitzgerald submits that over the years since the abolition of capital
punishment the justification put forward for mandatory life imprisonment in
relation to offences of murder has changed. Originally it was directly related to
the gravity of the crime. All murders were said to be so heinous that the offender
must forfeit his liberty for the rest of his life. If it was restored to him, that could
only be a matter of grace, and he would have to remain on licence lest it proved *d*
unwise to have released him. But that approach is and always has been untenable
because everyone knows that some crimes which do not attract mandatory
sentences of life imprisonment are more heinous than many murders, and many
murders, such as so-called mercy killings, are not offences calling for condign
punishment—as can be seen from the varying judicial recommendations as to the *e*
period of imprisonment to be served to meet the requirements of retribution and
general deterrence. If life means life, then it is arbitrary and disproportionate, so
it has come to be regarded as an indeterminate sentence, part penal and part
preventative, for which there is no justification in circumstances where the
offender is not expected to be a danger if released after he has served the penal
element of his sentence, and this more modern approach, Mr Fitzgerald *f*
contends, offends against the long-standing principle of domestic law that an
indeterminate sentence should be 'reserved for cases where the defendant is
someone in respect of whom there is some relevant feature which cannot be
determined at the time when the judge is passing the sentence'. That was said by
Lord Lane CJ in *R v Basra* (1989) 11 Cr App R (S) 527 at 529 in relation to *g*
discretionary life imprisonment, but, Mr Fitzgerald submits, the principle is of
general application.
[15] Before us the defendant still relies on a statement made by Mr Kenneth
Baker as Home Secretary in the House of Commons on 25 June 1991 (193 HC
Official Report (6th series) cols 867–868) when he said: *h*

'At the core of the crime of murder is the intentional taking of another
person's life—killing someone, with an intent to kill or to do grievous bodily
harm. It is all very well to talk about mercy killings or so-called domestic
murders, but the fact remains that in each case another person's life has been
intentionally taken away. It is a crime where there can never be any *j*
possibility of the victim recovering or receiving redress or compensation. It
is a crime of dreadful finality. I believe that the public perceive, rightly, a
distinction between the seriousness of murder and that of other crimes. This
justifies a unique penalty for those who commit it. The public have a right
to expect that Parliament and the criminal justice system will take effective
steps to punish those who commit this crime and to protect the public from

a   offenders who have shown themselves capable of intentionally taking another person's life.'

[**16**] By way of contrast, in 1993 the Committee on the Penalty for Homicide, chaired by Lord Lane, summarised its first six conclusions thus:

b   '(1) The mandatory life sentence for murder is founded on the assumption that murder is a crime of such unique heinousness that the offender forfeits for the rest of his existence his right to be set free.

(2) That assumption is a fallacy. It arises from the divergence between the legal definition of murder and that which the lay public believes to be murder.

c   (3) The common law definition of murder embraces a wide range of offences, some of which are truly heinous, some of which are not.

(4) The majority of murder cases, though not those which receive most publicity, fall into the latter category.

(5) It is logically and jurisprudentially wrong to require judges to sentence all categories of murderer in the same way, regardless of the particular

d   circumstances of the case before them.

(6) It is logically and constitutionally wrong to require the distinction between the various types of murder to be decided (and decided behind the scenes) by the Executive as is, generally speaking, the case at present.'

[**17**] In 1993 Mr Michael Howard, as Home Secretary, said that before any

e   mandatory life sentence prisoner was released on licence he would consider—

'Not only (a) whether the period served by the prisoner is adequate to satisfy the requirements of retribution and deterrence and, (b) whether it is safe to release the prisoner, but also (c) the public acceptability of early release.'

f   We are told by Mr Pannick that (c) has never been a determining factor, but the present Secretary of State follows the policy of his predecessors.

[**18**] Mr Fitzgerald also referred us to a large body of material, including the parliamentary debates underlying s 1 of the 1965 Act and later reports. JUSTICE, in a written intervention, provided the court with a history of the mandatory life

g   sentence, critiques of it, and the wider context of the position in other jurisdictions. We have taken all that material into account but do not consider it necessary to lengthen this judgment by a repetition of it.

GENERAL APPROACH

[**19**] Mr Fitzgerald submits that under art 5 of the convention the basic

h   principle is that no one should be deprived of their liberty in an arbitrary fashion, and that if a life sentence is imposed where there is no objective justification for that sentence then the sentence is both arbitrary and disproportionate. Under art 3 a sentence which is manifestly disproportionate can be an 'inhuman and degrading' punishment.

j   [**20**] For the defendant Mr Pannick's response is that these issues have been addressed by the European Court of Human Rights in *V v UK, T v UK* (1999) 30 EHRR 121, where the appellants had been sentenced to be detained during Her Majesty's pleasure. That too is a sentence which is automatically imposed where a defendant of the prescribed age is convicted of murder. It is imposed irrespective of the circumstances of the offence and of the offender. Some offenders may present no risk of future offending, and may have committed an offence less grave

than other offences which do not require a mandatory indeterminate sentence
from which the offender will only be released after serving a tariff period, when it
is considered that he may safely be released, and on the basis that thereafter he
will be at risk of recall for the rest of his life. In other words, Mr Pannick submits,
for present purposes the cases of T and V are indistinguishable on their facts, and
this court is required by s 2(1) of the 1998 Act to take into account the decisions
of the European Court. Mr Fitzgerald submits that in V v UK, T v UK there was
an important distinction, in that the two boys could not be regarded as presenting
no danger if released at the end of their tariff period, and that is something which
we must examine more closely in due course.

[21] Mr Pannick goes on to submit that there was a very good reason why the
European Court decided V v UK, T v UK as it did—namely because an indeterminate
sentence (whether it be mandatory life imprisonment or detention during Her
Majesty's pleasure) allows for and involves in practice an individualised
assessment of tariff, risk and recall, so that it is neither degrading nor arbitrary. It
may be that an assessment should not be made by the executive, but that is not
something for consideration in this case.

[22] One of the authorities on which Mr Fitzgerald places considerable
reliance is the recent decision of this court in R v Offen [2001] 2 All ER 154, [2001]
1 WLR 253 which concerned sentences of life imprisonment imposed after
conviction of a second 'serious offence' within the meaning to be ascribed to
those words by s 2(5) or (6) of the Crime (Sentences) Act 1997. Such a sentence
must be imposed save where there are 'exceptional circumstances', and the court
held that those words must be so construed as not to contravene the prohibition
on inhuman and degrading treatment, or arbitrary and disproportionate punishment,
to be found in arts 3 and 5 of the convention. The government's intention was
that the public should receive proper protection from persistent violent or sex
offenders, and the court gave effect to that intention by indicating that in every
case judges must assess the risk to the public, and use the words 'exceptional
circumstances' to ensure that no offender is sentenced to life imprisonment who
does not constitute a significant risk to the public. Mr Pannick submits, rightly,
that in R v Offen the court was not concerned with mandatory life sentences, and
he submits that they are different because Parliament has decided that in the case
of murder, by reason of the gravity of the offence, the punishment is to be an
indeterminate sentence during which consideration will be given to tariff and
risk, and after release there will be liberty only subject to licence. In rare cases a
life sentence may mean life in prison, but such cases are very rare. So whereas in
R v Offen this court was seeking to further the purposes of Parliament, Mr Pannick
submits that if Mr Fitzgerald's submissions are accepted we will be frustrating the
clear intention of Parliament as to what the sentence should be in the case of
murder, and also producing a curious distinction between our view of the
legislation in relation to mandatory sentences in the case of adults, and the
opinion of the European Court in relation to mandatory sentences in the case of
young offenders.

[23] Mr Pannick further submits that there are three principles established
under the convention to which we must have regard. First, the relevant
provisions of the convention require a balance between the interests of the
applicant and those of the community. In Soering v UK (1989) 11 EHRR 439 a
West German national was seeking to avoid extradition to Virginia to face a
charge of capital murder, and in its judgment the court said (at 468 (para 89)):

a   '... inherent in the whole of the Convention is a search for a fair balance between the demands of the general interest of the community and the requirements of the protection of the individual's fundamental rights.'

[24] Secondly, the European Court in its approach to the convention does not concentrate on formal procedures, but looks at the realities. In *Van Droogenbroeck v*
b   *Belgium* (1982) 4 EHRR 443, a case concerned with detention of a recidivist, the court said (at 456 (para 38)) 'one must look beyond the appearances and the language used and concentrate on the realities of the situation'. Here, Mr Pannick submits, the claimants are putting too much weight on the language used when a judge sentences a defendant to life imprisonment, and not concentrating on the realities of the situation.

c   [25] Thirdly, Mr Pannick reminds us that in *Brown v Stott (Procurator Fiscal, Dunfermline)* [2001] 2 All ER 97 at 114, [2001] 2 WLR 817 at 834 Lord Bingham of Cornhill said:

d   'Judicial recognition and assertion of the human rights defined in the convention is not a substitute for the processes of democratic government but a complement to them. While a national court does not accord the margin of appreciation recognised by the European Court as a supra-national court, it will give weight to the decisions of a representative legislature and a democratic government within the discretionary area of judgment accorded to those bodies.'

e   Other members of the Privy Council made observations to the same effect. That, he submits, is of particular relevance to a controversial issue of policy which has been the subject of repeated consideration by Parliament. In his reply Mr Fitzgerald reminded us of an additional principle, that decisions of the European Court and Commission are made on their particular facts rather than
f   reviewing national law in abstracto (see *Håkansson and Sturesson v Sweden* (1990) 13 EHRR 1 at 11 (para 46)). Decisions need to be read with that in mind.

PREVIOUS LITIGATION

[26] Mr Pannick submits that this case is the latest in a series of cases in
g   England and in Strasbourg which have challenged various aspects of the requirement that a life sentence be imposed after a conviction for murder. Each challenge has failed because on each occasion the courts have said that Parliament is entitled to maintain its statutory requirement. In *Doody v Secretary of State for the Home Dept* [1993] 3 All ER 92, [1994] 1 AC 531 the House of Lords upheld the right of the Secretary of State to set the tariff, Lord Mustill recognising
h   ([1993] 3 All ER 92 at 103, [1994] 1 AC 531 at 556) that the old reasoning in favour of life imprisonment as the appropriate sentence for a grave crime is 'much weakened now that the indeterminate sentence is at a very early stage formally broken down into penal and risk elements'. He further recognised that the discretionary and mandatory life sentences may now be converging, and continued:
j
'It may be—I express no opinion—that the time is approaching when the effect of the two types of life sentence should be further assimilated. But this is a task for Parliament, and I think it quite impossible for the courts to introduce a fundamental change in the relationship between the convicted murderer and the state, through the medium of judicial review.' (See [1993] 3 All ER 92 at 105, [1994] 1 AC 531 at 559.)

[27] As Mr Fitzgerald points out, that was said before the convention became part of English law, but the European Court did refer to *Doody*'s case, and to the distinction between discretionary and mandatory life sentences, when deciding the next case in the series to which Mr Pannick refers, namely *Wynne v UK* (1994) 19 EHRR 333. There the applicant, having been convicted of murder and having served the tariff element of his life sentence, was complaining under art 5(4) of the absence of any provision to have the continued lawfulness of his detention reviewed by a court. In *Thynne v UK* (1990) 13 EHRR 666 the European Court had recognised that right in the case of discretionary life prisoners, but in its decision in *Wynne*'s case the court said ((1994) 19 EHRR 333 at 346 (para 33)):

'This view was taken because of the very nature of the discretionary life sentence which, unlike the mandatory sentence, was imposed not because of the inherent gravity of the offence but because of the presence of factors which were susceptible to change with the passage of time, namely mental instability and dangerousness. A clear distinction was drawn between the discretionary life sentence which was considered to have a protective purpose and a mandatory life sentence which was viewed as essentially punitive in nature.'

[28] The submission was made to the court that the two types of sentence had tended to converge, but the court said (at 347 (para 35)):

'However, the fact remains that the mandatory sentence belongs to a different category from the discretionary sentence in the sense that it is imposed automatically as the punishment for the offence of murder irrespective of considerations pertaining to the dangerousness of the offender. That mandatory life prisoners do not actually spend the rest of their lives in prison and that a notional tariff period is also established in such cases—facts of which the Court was fully aware in [*Thynne v UK* (1990) 13 EHRR 666]—does not alter the essential distinction between the two types of life sentence.'

[29] In para 36 (at 347) the court expressly adhered to its previous finding that—

'as regards mandatory life sentences, the guarantee of Article 5(4) was satisfied by the original trial and appeal proceedings and confers no additional right to challenge the lawfulness of continuing detention or re-detention following revocation of the life sentence.'

[30] Of course, as Mr Fitzgerald points out, the court was there concerned with art 5(4) and whether Wynne was entitled to a review of his continued detention, but if it was realistically possible to attack the mandatory life sentence on the grounds now advanced it is a little surprising that the opportunity was not taken to do so. Mr Fitzgerald also points out that Wynne had been convicted of manslaughter after his release on licence under the original sentence for murder. How his dangerousness was assessed when he was originally sentenced to life imprisonment we do not know, but if an assessment was made it does not seem to have been regarded as critical by any one.

[31] The third decision in Mr Pannick's series was *R v Secretary of State for the Home Dept, ex p Stafford* [1998] 4 All ER 7, [1999] 2 AC 38 where the House of Lords was concerned with a mandatory life sentence prisoner who had been recalled after committing non-violent offences whilst on licence. Counsel pointed out that many discretionary life sentence prisoners had committed offences more serious than those serving mandatory life sentences, and yet they were entitled to

a judicial review by the Parole Board of their continuing detention. As Lord Steyn said:

> 'Counsel's argument is in reality an appeal for a more rational system. The appeal to symmetry was rejected by the House of Lords in *Doody v Secretary of State for the Home Dept* [1993] 3 All ER 92 at 105, [1994] 1 AC 531 at 559. And *b* in *Wynne v UK* (1994) 19 EHRR 333 the European Court of Human Rights held that the post-tariff phase of the detention of a mandatory life sentence prisoner does not attract the safeguards of art 5(4) of the European Convention on Human Rights. As matters stand at present the duality is embedded into our law by primary legislation.' (See [1998] 4 All ER 7 at 15, [1999] 2 AC 38 at 49.)

c
[32] Again Mr Fitzgerald submits that may have been so in July 1998, when *Ex p Stafford* was decided, but the incorporation of the convention has effected a radical change. The difficulty with that argument is of course that for the European Court incorporation was and is of no significance, which brings us to the final case in Mr Pannick's series, *V v UK, T v UK* (1999) 30 EHRR 121 to which *d* we have already referred, and to which we will return. There reliance was placed both on art 3 and on art 5(1) and we now turn to look at the two articles separately.

[33] Mr Fitzgerald submits that the mandatory life sentence is inhuman and degrading by reason of its disproportionality, in that it orders lifelong detention, *e* is imposed irrespective of the individual circumstances of the offender or of the crime, is imposed on offenders of widely differing culpability, imposes a far greater punishment on those convicted of murder even in circumstances where the borderline between murder and manslaughter has only just been passed, and serves no useful penological purpose.

f ARTICLE 3
[34] In *Costello-Roberts v UK* (1993) 19 EHRR 112, a case about corporal punishment in a school, the European Court stated (at 133 (para 30)):

> '... in order for punishment to be "degrading" and in breach of Article 3, the humiliation or debasement involved must attain a particular level of *g* severity and must in any event be other than that usual element of humiliation inherent in any punishment. Indeed Article 3, by expressly prohibiting "inhuman" and "degrading" punishment, implies that there is a distinction between such punishment and punishment more generally. The assessment of this minimal level of severity depends on all the circumstances *h* of the case. Factors such as the nature and context of the punishment, the manner and method of its execution, its duration, its physical and mental effects and, in some instances, the sex, age and state of health of the victim must all be taken into account.'

j [35] In *V v UK, T v UK* (1999) 30 EHRR 121 the European Court considered whether that article could be invoked in relation to the sentence of detention during Her Majesty's pleasure passed on the two boys. It recorded the Commission's acceptance of the case for the government, saying (at 182 (para 95)):

> '[The Commission] referred to [*Hussain v UK* (1996) 22 EHRR 1] where the Court held that the sentence of detention during Her Majesty's pleasure was primarily preventative, attracting the guarantees of Article 5(4). It could not,

therefore, be said that the applicant had forfeited his liberty for life or that his detention gave rise to a violation of Article 3.'

[36] Mr Fitzgerald submits that the reference to *Hussain's* case is significant because in that case, which also concerned a sentence of detention during Her Majesty's pleasure, the court had said (at 24 (para 53)):

'. . an indeterminate term of detention for a convicted young person, which may be as long as that person's life, can only be justified by considerations based on the need to protect the public.'

[37] The same point was repeated by the court in *V v UK, T v UK* (1999) 30 EHRR 121 at 183 (para 96). Thus the context, submits Mr Fitzgerald, is an indeterminate sentence for which the only justification is preventive.

[38] In *V v UK, T v UK* the court expressed its conclusion in relation to art 3, saying (at 183 (para 98)):

'The Court recalls that States have a duty under the Convention to take measures for the protection of the public from violent crime. It does not consider that the punitive element inherent in the tariff approach itself gives rise to a breach of Article 3, or that the Convention prohibits States from subjecting a child or young person convicted of a serious crime to an indeterminate sentence allowing for the offenders continued detention or recall to detention following release where necessary for the protection of the public.'

[39] As Mr Pannick points out, there is nothing there to suggest that the sentence will only be legitimate if at the time of sentencing it is envisaged that the offender will present an ongoing risk. Indeed para 99 (at 183) begins:

'The applicant has not yet reached the stage in his sentence where he is able to have the continued lawfulness of his detention reviewed with regard to the question of dangerousness ...'

[40] That would tend to suggest that so far as the European Court was concerned any assessment of dangerousness that may or may not have been made at the time of sentence was of no significance. Overall, the court's conclusions are expressed in terms that indicate no objection under art 3 to a mandatory indeterminate sentence for murder.

[41] The only other decision to which we need refer in relation to art 3 is the decision on admissibility of the European Commission in *Bromfield v UK* (1 July 1998, unreported). There the applicant, aged 20, had been sentenced to custody for life after being convicted of murder. Dealing with his complaint in relation to art 3, para 2 of the decision states:

'The Commission recalls that there is no incompatibility with the convention in the imposition of a life sentence as a security or retributive measure in a particular case or in a decision to keep a recidivist or habitual offender at the disposal of the government (*Weeks v UK* (1987) 10 EHRR 293). While in the cases concerning detention during Her Majesty's pleasure, the court commented that a sentence pursuant to which young persons forfeited their liberty for the rest of their lives might raise issues under art 3 of the convention (see e g *Hussain v UK* (1996) 22 EHRR 1), the Commission considers that these remarks apply to sentences of life imprisonment imposed on children under the age of 18 to whom special considerations *a* apply. It does not find that the imposition of a mandatory sentence of life imprisonment in respect of the offence of murder committed by young adults between the ages of 18 and 21 discloses treatment or punishment prohibited by art 3 of the convention.'

b [42] In our judgment the weight of the jurisprudence is overwhelming. Whatever one may think about the desirability of a change of policy, it cannot be accepted that a mandatory sentence of life imprisonment for murder is incompatible with art 3. In reality, as Mr Pannick points out, the sentence is an indeterminate one—rarely will there be imprisonment for life. In other cases the penal element having been decided upon at a earlier stage, when that element has been served the Secretary of State may, if recommended to do so by the Parole *c* Board, after consultation with the Lord Chief Justice and the trial judge if available, release the prisoner on licence (see s 29 of the Crime (Sentences) Act 1997). In practice the Secretary of State does refer cases to the Parole Board for consideration, and if a prisoner has been released on licence and is recalled he will have the opportunity to have his recall considered by the Parole Board (see s 31 of the 1997 Act). That is all part of what is involved in the mandatory life *d* sentence, and in reality such a sentence, which includes the policy applied in relation to it, cannot be labelled inhuman or degrading. There is sufficient individualised consideration of the offender's case within the context of the sentence. Thus it is open to Parliament, acting within its discretionary area of judgment, to retain the sentence without violating art 3.

e
ARTICLE 5
[43] We turn now to the complaint in relation to art 5. Mr Fitzgerald submits that to have an indeterminate sentence for all murders is arbitrary. In some cases a lesser determinate sentence would suffice because culpability and the needs of retribution and deterrence can be evaluated at the end of the trial, and there is no *f* discernible risk to warrant an indeterminate sentence. Furthermore, as such a sentence is at least in theory the most severe sentence available to an English judge it should not be imposed as a matter of course for murders where the gravity of the offence is less than the gravity of other crimes. It is arbitrary to impose a sentence that can neither be justified on preventive grounds nor *g* justified on the basis of retributive proportionality.
[44] This broad argument was considered by the European Court in *V v UK, T v UK* (1999) 30 EHRR 121. The Commission had accepted the government's submission that the indeterminate sentences imposed in that case were not unlawful or arbitrary, pointing out that—

h 'Its purpose was to enable consideration to be given to the specific circumstances of the applicant's case, so that he would be detained only for so long as was necessary with regard to the need for punishment, rehabilitation and the protection of the community.' (See (1999) 30 EHRR 121 at 184 (para 103).)

j [45] The court continued (at 184–185):

'104. The Court observes that the applicant was detained following conviction by a competent court; in other words, his detention falls within the scope of Article 5(1)(a) of the Convention. There can be no question but that the sentence of detention during Her Majesty's pleasure is lawful under English law and was imposed in accordance with a procedure prescribed by law. Moreover, it cannot be said that the applicant's detention is not in conformity with the purposes of the deprivation of liberty permitted by *a* Article 5(1)(a), so as to be arbitrary.

105. It follows that there has been no violation of Article 5(1) of the Convention in the present case.'

[46] Mr Pannick submits that if a sentence of detention during Her Majesty's pleasure which has to be imposed without regard to the circumstances of the *b* offence or of the offender is not arbitrary, bearing in mind the convention's proper concern for the young, how can it be said that in the case of an adult a mandatory sentence of life imprisonment is arbitrary? Its purpose, he submits, is to punish the offender by subjecting him to an indeterminate sentence under which he will only be released when he has served the tariff part of his sentence, *c* and when it is considered safe to release him, and even then for the rest of his life he will be liable to be recalled. That is not merely the effect of the sentence, it is the sentence. Continued application of the life sentence regime to the offender is entirely in conformity with the purpose of that sentence. For that reason, it cannot be arbitrary so as to be in breach of art 5.

[47] In so far as Mr Fitzgerald submits that where there is not a discernible risk *d* of re-offending it is wrong to impose an indeterminate sentence, Mr Pannick responds by saying that such a submission falls outside the scope of art 5. In *Weeks v UK* (1987) 10 EHRR 293, a case concerned with the lawfulness of detention after recall, the European Court said (at 312 (para 50)) that 'it is not for the Court, within the context of Article 5, to review the appropriateness of the *e* original sentence'. Even if that be wrong, Mr Pannick submits, and we accept, that a sentence cannot be arbitrary for an adult when an equivalent sentence has been found not to be so in the case of a young offender, and when in each case the application of the sentence is individualised, and everyone knows that it will be individualised from the moment it is imposed. Although, as Mr Fitzgerald pointed out, decisions of the European Court are related to their own particular *f* facts, the process of reasoning displayed by the European Court is of assistance, as illustrated by both counsel during the course of this case. The reasoning in the decided cases tells strongly against the claimant's case on art 5.

OTHER JURISDICTIONS

[48] Mr Fitzgerald drew our attention to the decision of the United States *g* Supreme Court in *Woodson v North Carolina* (1976) 428 US 286, a death penalty case, but, as the court itself observed (at 305):

'Death, in its finality, differs more from life imprisonment than a one hundred year prison term differs from one of only a year or two. Because of *h* that qualitative difference, there is a corresponding difference in the need for reliability in the determination that death is the appropriate punishment in a specific case.'

[49] That passage makes the point that where fundamental rights are differently expressed (as in the United States Constitution) and the background *j* and issues in dispute are different, the decisions of a non-European Court may be of limited assistance, especially when, as is in the present case, the relevant issues have been copiously considered both here and in Strasbourg. For that reason we find it unnecessary to refer to the two decisions of the Inter-American Commission on Human Rights which we were invited to consider. The same applies to the decision of the High Court of Namibia in *State v Vries* [1997] 4 LRC 1

a and to the decision of the High Court of Australia in *Sillery v R* (1981) 35 ALR 227, which turned on a question of statutory interpretation.

[**50**] In *R v Smith* [1987] 1 SCR 1045 the Canadian Supreme Court held that a minimum sentence of seven years for importing narcotics constituted cruel and unusual punishment, and thus contravened s 12 of the Canadian Charter of Rights and Freedoms, but, as Mr Pannick points out, there is a significant difference

b between such a sentence and an indeterminate sentence, the application of which is individualised as regards fixation of tariff, assessment of risk, and the liability to recall.

CONCLUSION

[**51**] The arguments put forward by Mr Fitzgerald are persuasive in favour of

c a change of policy, and may carry weight in a political debate, but in our judgment, as the law now stands, they do not enable this court to allow these appeals against sentence on the basis that the mandatory sentences imposed were incompatible with the convention. We therefore dismiss these appeals.

Appeals dismissed. Court certifying that a point of law of general public importance was involved in its decision, namely 'Whether s 1(1) of the Murder (Abolition of Death Penalty) Act 1965 is incompatible with arts 3 and/or 5 of the European Convention on Human Rights'.

Dilys Tausz   Barrister.

1 November 2001. The Appeal Committee of the House of Lords gave leave to appeal.

Liverpool Roman Catholic Archdiocese Trustees Incorporated v Goldberg (No 2)

a

CHANCERY DIVISION

EVANS-LOMBE J

12–16, 19–23, 26–30 MARCH, 2–6 APRIL, 6 JULY 2001

b

Practice – Evidence – Expert witness – Admissibility – Expert witness having long-standing friendship with party proposing to call him – Whether relationship between expert and party rendering expert's evidence inadmissible.

c

The claimant brought proceedings for professional negligence against G, a barrister specialising in tax. At trial, G wished to rely on the expert evidence of F, another tax barrister in the same set of chambers as G and a friend of many years standing. In his expert report, F stated that he did not believe that his relationship with G would affect his evidence, but he accepted that his personal sympathies were engaged to a greater degree than would probably be normal with an expert witness. The issue therefore arose whether F's relationship with G precluded him from giving expert evidence on G's behalf.

d

Held – Where it was demonstrated that a proposed expert witness had a relationship with the party calling him which a reasonable observer might think *e* was capable of affecting the expert's views so as to make them unduly favourable to that party, his evidence should not be admitted however unbiased his conclusions might probably be. The question was one of fact, namely the extent and nature of the relationship between the proposed witness and the party. In the instant case, F's admission made him unsuitable to be called as an expert witness *f* on the public policy ground that justice had to be seen to be done as well as done. Accordingly, F's evidence, though otherwise qualifying as expert evidence, would not be admitted (see [12]–[14], below).

Notes

For expert evidence generally, see 17 *Halsbury's Laws* (4th edn) para 83.

g

Cases referred to in judgment

Barings plc (in liq) v Coopers & Lybrand (a firm), Barings Futures (Singapore) Pte Ltd (in liq) v Mattar (9 February 2001, unreported), Ch D.

National Justice Cia Naviera SA v Prudential Assurance Co Ltd, The Ikarian Reefer *h* [1993] 2 Lloyds's Rep 68; *rvsd* [1995] 1 Lloyd's Rep 455, CA.

Midland Bank Trust Co Ltd v Hett, Stubbs & Kemp (a firm) [1978] 3 All ER 571, [1979] Ch 384, [1978] 3 WLR 167.

Prudential Assurance Co Ltd v McBains Cooper (a firm) [2001] 2 All ER 1014, [2000] 1 WLR 2000, CA.

j

Whitehouse v Jordan [1981] 1 All ER 267, [1981] 1 WLR 246, HL.

Action

The claimant, Liverpool Roman Catholic Archdiocese Trustees Incorporated, claimed damages for professional negligence from the defendant, David Goldberg QC. During the trial, the claimant challenged the admissibility of expert a evidence to be given on the defendant's behalf by Michael Flesch QC, but Evans-Lombe J decided to deal with the issue in his judgment in the action. The facts, so far as material to the question of the admissibility of Mr Flesch's evidence, are set out in the judgment.

Michael Briggs QC and *Giles Goodfellow* (instructed by *McCormicks*, Leeds) for the
b claimant.
Andrew Simmonds QC and *David Owen* (instructed by *Linklaters*) for the defendant.

Cur adv vult

6 July 2001. The following judgment was delivered.
c

EVANS-LOMBE J.
[1] This case concerns a claim by the corporate trustee of the Roman Catholic Archdiocese of Liverpool against the defendant for professional negligence in the advice that he gave with relation to the trustee's tax affairs between November
d 1989 and October 1996. The hearing concluded on 6 April of this year when I reserved judgment. I circulated a draft of that judgment to the parties on 6 June. I did this so that the parties should have an opportunity to correct minor errors, and also at the parties' request to deal with a particular point in the case. The day fixed for the formal handing down of the judgment was 3 July. However on the evening before that day I received a joint application by both parties asking me
e not to hand down my judgment because they had arrived at an agreement which would settle the issues between them.
[2] It is well established by authority going back a considerable time that parties to civil litigation may settle their dispute by agreement and withdraw a case from a judge at any stage up to the moment when he has started to deliver
f judgment. There are certain public law exceptions to this general rule. See *Prudential Assurance Co Ltd v McBains Cooper (a firm)* [2001] 2 All ER 1014, [2000] 1 WLR 2000, a decision of the Court of Appeal.
[3] That case goes on to decide that where, as very often happens today, a judge has circulated a draft judgment to the parties for whatever purpose, at a time when the dispute between them remains unsettled, the process of giving
g judgment has started, and the judge retains a discretion to continue that process by handing down his judgment even though all parties to the litigation have asked for him not to do so. In that case the Court of Appeal refused to interfere with the decision of a judge, who had circulated a draft of his judgment to the litigants before him, to give judgment against their wishes on the ground that
h there were important points in the case which his judgment decided as to which there was a public interest that his decision should be known.
[4] In the present case I have concluded, in the exercise of the same discretion, that I should not hand down the entirety of my judgment. I was informed that a condition of the settlement between the parties before me was that judgment
j would not be given. The course which I have chosen therefore means that that settlement will take effect saving the time and expense involved in appeals, by either party, for which I would have been minded to give permission.
[5] I do however think that I should deal with one question which arose in the course of the case and in respect of which I received submissions. This question concerns the admissibility as expert evidence of the evidence of Mr Flesch QC called on behalf of the defendant. This is a procedural question of some general

importance and does not concern the merits of the parties' cases with which I had
to deal.

[6] In a judgment given on 2 March of this year at a pre-trial review ([2001]
TLR 187) Neuberger J dealt with an application to rule Mr Flesch's evidence
inadmissible on the grounds, first, that his close relationship with the defendant
(they had known each other for 28 years and were good friends, they are also in
the same chambers) rendered Mr Flesch incapable of fulfilling the role of an
expert witness, and, secondly, that his evidence amounted to no more than
saying what he would have done and advised in the defendant's position. In the
result Neuberger J stood the application over to trial. On the way he expressed
the opinion that—

'the fact that Mr Flesch has had a close personal relationship, and a close
professional relationship with the defendant in the sense that they had been
friends and in the same chambers for a long time, does not mean as a matter
of law, or even as a matter of fact, that Mr Flesch is incapable of fulfilling the
functions described by Lord Wilberforce and Cresswell J [in *Whitehouse v
Jordan* [1981] 1 All ER 267, [1981] 1 WLR 246 and *National Justice Cia Naviera
SA v Prudential Assurance Co Ltd, The Ikarian Reefer* [1993] 2 Lloyds's Rep 68
respectively].'

[7] With some diffidence I would draw attention to a recent judgment of my
own in *Barings plc (in liq) v Coopers & Lybrand (a firm), Barings Futures (Singapore)
Pte Ltd (in liq) v Mattar* (9 February 2001, unreported) which dealt with the
admissibility of expert evidence. In that judgment I expressed the view that the
question of whether particular evidence was admissible as expert evidence was to
be decided in two stages. The first stage was an examination of whether the
evidence in question qualified as admissible expert evidence, and the second stage
was an inquiry whether, if so, it should actually be admitted as of assistance to the
court. The first stage turns on whether the evidence comes within the provisions
of s 3 of the Civil Evidence Act 1972. The authorities show that to qualify as
expert evidence within s 3, the party seeking to call the evidence must satisfy the
court of the existence of a body of expertise governed by recognised standards or
rules of conduct capable of influencing the court's decision on any of the issues
which it has to decide and that the witness to be called has a sufficient familiarity
with and knowledge of the expertise in question to render his opinion potentially
of value in resolving any of those issues.

[8] The second stage turns on the nature of the evidence sought to be given.
Thus, where the question is one of law, expert evidence will be excluded because
that is within the expertise of the court and expert evidence does not assist (see
Midland Bank Trust Co Ltd v Hett, Stubbs & Kemp (a firm) [1978] 3 All ER 571, [1979]
Ch 384). Neuberger J expressed the view that part of Mr Flesch's evidence was
likely to be held inadmissible under this head.

[9] The question of the admissibility of Mr Flesch's evidence was raised early
in the trial. I decided that I would not then rule on its admissibility but deal with
that question in the course of my judgment. It was, however, accepted that large
sections of his expert's report would not be relied upon because they dealt with
points of law. The surviving parts of the report were directed primarily to
Mr Flesch's experience of dealing with the Revenue in the course of negotiations
to settle back tax claims and the proper tactics to be employed in attempting to
settle such a claim without recourse to litigation. Mr Flesch was called and was
cross-examined.

a [10] Mr Flesch's evidence qualified as that of an expert within s 3 but, in my judgment, the court should disregard it on the ground that Mr Flesch was unable to fulfil the role of an expert witness because of his close relationship with the defendant.

[11] In his report, having described that relationship, Mr Flesch said this:

b 'I do not believe that this (i e the relationship) will affect my evidence. I certainly accept that it should not do so but it is right that I should say that my personal sympathies are engaged to a greater degree than would probably be normal with an expert witness.'

[12] It seems to me that this admission rendered Mr Flesch's evidence unacceptable as the evidence of an expert on grounds of public policy that justice
c must be seen to be done as well as done. This is clear from the passage in the speech of Lord Wilberforce in *Whitehouse*'s case [1981] 1 All ER 267 at 276, [1981] 1 WLR 246 at 256–257 cited by Neuberger J where he says:

'While some degree of consultation between experts and legal advisers is entirely proper, it is necessary that expert evidence presented to the court
d should be, *and should be seen to be*, the independent product of the expert, uninfluenced as to form or content by the exigencies of litigation.' (My emphasis.)

The role of an expert witness is special owing, as he does, duties to the court which he must discharge notwithstanding the interest of the party calling him
e (see per Cresswell J in *The Ikarian Reefer* [1993] 2 Lloyds's Rep 68).

[13] I accept that neither s 3 nor the authorities under it expressly exclude the expert evidence of a friend of one or the parties. However, in my judgment, where it is demonstrated that there exists a relationship between the proposed expert and the party calling him which a reasonable observer might think was
f capable of affecting the views of the expert so as to make them unduly favourable to that party, his evidence should not be admitted however unbiased the conclusions of the expert might probably be. The question is one of fact, namely the extent and nature of the relationship between the proposed witness and the party.

[14] With great respect to the preliminary views expressed by Neuberger J, it
g seems to me that Mr Flesch's admission of the nature and the closeness of his relationship with the defendant made him unsuitable, on grounds of public policy, to be called as an expert witness in support of the defendant's case and his evidence, although it would otherwise have qualified within s 3, should not be admitted.

Judgment accordingly.

Celia Fox   Barrister.

Bank of China v NBM LLC and others a

QUEEN'S BENCH DIVISION (COMMERCIAL COURT)
DAVID STEEL J
14 JUNE, 5 JULY 2001

b

Practice – Pre-trial or post-judgment relief – Freezing order – Worldwide freezing order
– Pre-trial order – Extra-territorial effect of order – Protection of third parties – Proviso
protecting third parties in respect of assets outside the jurisdiction – Appropriate terms.

The claimant brought proceedings in New York against various defendants, c
seeking damages for alleged misappropriation of its funds. Although none of the
defendants were domiciled in England and Wales, the claimant obtained from
the English court a worldwide freezing order in support of the New York
proceedings. That order required the defendants to produce affidavits of assets,
but none of them complied. Notice of the order was given to the applicant, UBS,
a foreign bank which was subject to the jurisdiction of the English court by virtue d
of having a London branch. UBS was not a party to the proceedings and had not
been named in the original order, but was served because two of the defendants
allegedly had an historical relationship with it in Zurich and the Cayman Islands.
After being served, UBS informed the claimant that it had a number of concerns
regarding the extent to which the order purported to freeze assets held with any e
of its branches outside the jurisdiction. In particular, UBS explained that accounts
held at its Swiss branches were subject to Swiss law; that, in the absence of an
order from a Swiss court, those branches were obliged to operate the accounts
according to their clients' instructions; that a failure to do so might result in
liabilities under Swiss law, while it might be contended that the operation of such
accounts in accordance with Swiss law might amount to a breach of the freezing f
order. It was eventually agreed to amend the order to provide that, in respect of
assets outside the jurisdiction, nothing in the order prevented UBS or its
subsidiaries from complying, inter alia, with what it reasonably believed to be its
obligations under the criminal law of the country or state in which those assets
were situated. UBS subsequently applied for a further variation to the order, g
replacing the proviso with another providing that, in respect of assets outside the
jurisdiction, nothing in the order prevented UBS or its subsidiaries from
complying with what it reasonably believed to be its obligations, contractual or
otherwise, under the laws and obligations of the country or state in which those
assets were situated or under the proper law of any account in question. The
claimant contended, inter alia, that the court should be reluctant to allow a third h
party bank to distribute assets simply because it reasonably believed that it had to
comply with a defendant's directions.

Held – Where the court granted a freezing order in respect of assets outside the
jurisdiction, it should include in the order, unless it was inappropriate to do so, a j
proviso that nothing in it prevented an affected third party or its subsidiaries from
complying with what they reasonably believed to be their obligations, contractual or
otherwise, under the laws and obligations of the country or state in which those
assets were situated or under the proper law of any account in question. Banks
which were domiciled or otherwise present within the jurisdiction should not be
required to decide whether to act in conflict with the terms of the freezing order

a   or in conflict with its duties to its customer under local law. Such an approach
was consistent with the interests of comity. Moreover, in maintaining a fair
balance between the interests of a claimant and the interests of a third party, the
court always had to bear in mind the risk associated with exercising an exorbitant
jurisdiction, a risk that might be of particular prejudice to third parties. In the
instant case, the absence of any defendant within the jurisdiction and the
b   consequent inability to enforce the obligation to produce an affidavit of assets
rendered the proviso sought by UBS all the more desirable. A third-party bank
should not be exposed to the risks of refusing to comply with the terms of its
mandate. Nor should a court order be made a necessary precondition to compliance.
Accordingly, the application would be granted (see [13], [18]–[21], below).
Baltic Shipping v Translink Shipping Ltd [1995] 1 Lloyd's Rep 673 followed.
c

Notes
For freezing orders (formerly called Mareva injunctions) over assets outside the
jurisdiction and the protection of third parties, see 3(1) *Halsbury's Laws* (4th edn
reissue) paras 331, 334.
d
Cases referred to in judgment
Babanaft International Co SA v Bassatne [1989] 1 All ER 433, [1990] Ch 13, [1989]
2 WLR 232, CA.
Baltic Shipping v Translink Shipping Ltd [1995] 1 Lloyd's Rep 673.
Crédit Suisse Fides Trust SA v Cuoghi [1997] 3 All ER 724, [1998] QB 818, [1997]
e   3 WLR 871, CA.
Derby & Co Ltd v Weldon (No 2) [1989] 1 All ER 1002, [1990] Ch 65, [1989] 2 WLR
412, CA.

Application
f   The Union Bank of Switzerland AG (UBS) applied for a variation to a freezing
order granted to the claimant, the Bank of China, on 13 March 2001 under s 25 of
the Civil Jurisdiction and Judgments Act 1982 in support of proceedings brought
by the claimant in New York against NBM LLC and 21 other defendants,
including the fifteenth and sixteenth defendants, John Chou and Sherry Liu. The
facts are set out in the judgment.
g

Thomas Keith (instructed by *Clifford Chance*) for UBS.
Susan Prevezer QC (instructed by *Coudert Brothers*) for the claimant.

Cur adv vult

h
5 July 2001. The following judgment was delivered.

DAVID STEEL J.
[1] This application comes at an apposite moment in that it coincides with a
review of the provisions of the CPR applicable to the Commercial Court,
j   including the prescribed form of freezing orders.
[2] The applicant is Union Bank of Switzerland AG (UBS), a third-party bank
on whom a worldwide freezing order has been served. The aim of the application
is to obtain a variation of that order in the following terms:

'It is further ordered and directed that nothing in this order shall, in respect
of assets located outside England and Wales, prevent UBS AG or its

subsidiaries from complying with: 1. What it reasonably believes to be its obligations, contractual or otherwise under the laws and obligations of the *a* country or state in which those assets are situated or under the proper law of any bank account in question; and 2. Any orders of the courts of that country or state, provided reasonable notice of any application for such an order by UBS AG or of any of its subsidiaries (to the extent such notice is permitted by the criminal law of such country or state) is given to the *b* claimant's solicitors.

[3] Indeed it is submitted that such a provision should be included in the standard form of freezing order (subject of course to variation or amendment in a particular case).

[4] The background can be summarised very briefly. The worldwide freezing *c* order was granted on 13 March 2001 under s 25 of the Civil Jurisdiction and Judgments Act 1982 in support of substantive proceedings underway in New York. Those proceedings involve claims for damages relating to alleged misappropriation by the defendants of some $34m from the claimant.

[5] None of the defendants are domiciled in this jurisdiction but within the United States or the Cayman Islands. The only assets identified in the order were *d* stocks of metal or credit balances held by GNI Ltd or Maple Investment Ltd. The order required each of the defendants to disclose the nature and whereabouts of their assets and thereafter to confirm that information on affidavit. None of the defendants have complied with these disclosure obligations.

[6] UBS is a foreign corporation but with a London branch. UBS is not a party *e* to the proceedings and is not named in the freezing order. However a copy of the freezing order was notified to UBS on 16 March 2001. The justification for such notification appears to derive from an affidavit of the deputy general manager of the claimant in which he deposes:

'I believe that the defendant Chou and S Liu had a historical relationship *f* with the Union Bank of Switzerland in Zurich, Switzerland. The enquiry agents also reported that the defendants Chou and S Liu had a historical relationship with the Union Bank of Switzerland in the Cayman Islands.'

[7] The covering letter from the claimant's solicitors by which notification of the freezing order was effected made this observation: *g*

'In regard to assets in other jurisdictions we would draw your attention to the relevant part of the guidance notes which provide that the order applies to persons subject to the jurisdiction of the High Court who have been given notice of this order at their place of business within this jurisdiction and are able to prevent acts or omissions outside the jurisdiction which constitute or *h* assist in a breach of the injunction. You will no doubt wish to take your own advice on the matter, but it seems to us on the face of the injunction that, to the extent that UBS is able to instruct or request its overseas branches, subsidiaries or its associated institutions to freeze any accounts held by any of the respondents, this should be done.' *j*

[8] The reaction of UBS was to despatch a letter which was a variation of a standard form of response to notification of injunctions of like kind. Dated 16 March, it stated as follows:

'We have a number of concerns regarding the extent to which the order purports to freeze assets held with any branches of UBS AG outside of the

a
jurisdiction. For example, accounts held at branches of UBS AG in Switzerland are subject to Swiss law and our Swiss colleagues are obliged to operate such accounts according to their clients instructions, in the absence of an order of a Swiss court. Therefore, in the event that the order obtained seeks to restrain assets held at Swiss branches of UBS AG, the bank is placed in an impossible position as failure to operate any Swiss accounts in

b
accordance with Swiss law may be a breach of such law and may result in liabilities thereunder. However, a claimant may contend that operation of such accounts in accordance with Swiss law may amount to a breach of an order such as that obtained by your client. It is clearly inappropriate for an innocent third party to be placed in this position. We refer you to *Baltic Shipping v Translink Shipping Ltd* [1995] 1 Lloyd's Rep 673. For the reasons set

c
out in that case we invite you to consent to a variation in the terms in the present order.'

[9] Following extensive exchanges between the solicitors for the parties, a partial amendment was agreed to the order in the following terms:

d
'It is further ordered and directed that nothing in this order shall, in respect of assets located outside England or Wales, prevent UBS AG or any of its subsidiaries from complying with: 1. What it reasonably believes to be its obligations under the criminal law of the country or state in which those assets are situated, and 2. Any orders of the courts of that country or state

e
provided reasonable notice of any application for such an order by UBS or any of its subsidiaries (to the extent of such notice is permitted by the criminal law of such country or state), is given to the claimant's solicitors.'

[10] This variation to the order was agreed without prejudice to the entitlement of the applicant to seek a further amendment along the lines indicated at the

f
beginning of this judgment.

[11] The applicant's submissions can be summarised as follows. (i) Albeit the freezing order contains the standard *Derby v Weldon* proviso (see *Derby & Co Ltd v Weldon (No 2)* [1989] 1 All ER 1002, [1990] Ch 65), this is of little assistance to the applicant since by virtue of its London branch it is subject to the jurisdiction. Indeed it is submitted that the terms of the proviso add to the applicant's

g
uncertainty since it is quite unclear whether for instance a subsidiary within the jurisdiction would be regarded as able to prevent acts or omissions on the part of its parent outside the jurisdiction. (ii) This court has made it plain that it regards the risk of double jeopardy thereby imposed upon a third-party bank as justifying the inclusion of the very variation which the applicant seeks. (iii) Whilst the

h
suggested terminology has not been included in the standard form, it is the experience of the applicant that on request the variation has invariably been accepted following despatch of the form of the letter sent on 16 March. (iv) The inclusion of such a provision is all the more appropriate in circumstances such as the present where none of the defendants are domiciled within the jurisdiction.

j
Thus, if as has duly occurred none of the defendants have complied with their obligation to give disclosure as to their assets, there is in fact an impasse because the claimants are unable to apply to the court for a committal order. (v) Whilst the applicant cannot point to any specific difficulty occasioned to them by the terms of this particular freezing order the explanation is or at least may be that they are unable to be more explicit without finding themselves in breach of relevant provisions as to confidentiality and/or secrecy in other jurisdictions.

[12] The claimant submits as follows. (i) The fact that the standard form of freezing order does not include the terms of the proviso sought by UBS despite recommendations to the contrary is itself instructive. (ii) The problem of double jeopardy would only arise in the civil context if UBS were required to do something both by a court in this country and a court abroad. (iii) Given the nature of the case made against the defendants by the claimant which gave rise to the justification for a worldwide freezing order, the court should be reluctant to allow a third-party bank to distribute assets simply because it reasonably believes it must comply with the directions of one or more defendants themselves. (iv) In any event it was not suggested that the applicant bank was in fact faced with any practical difficulty absent the additional proviso nor was it clear what confidentiality or secrecy laws were likely to be breached. (v) The bank was protected by an indemnity in its favour and the freezing of a bank account held by a customer could not constitute any significant interference with its business.

[13] As a matter of general principle it is in my judgment important that a freezing order should be clear and unequivocal so that both the parties to it and any third party knows exactly where they stand. In particular banks which are domiciled or otherwise present within the jurisdiction should not be required to decide whether to act in conflict with the terms of the freezing order or in conflict with its duties to its customer under local law. Such an approach in my judgment is consistent with the interests of comity as elaborated on in *Babanaft International Co SA v Bassatne* [1989] 1 All ER 433, [1990] Ch 13.

[14] In his end of year statement as judge in charge of the Commercial Court on 30 July 1993 Saville J, no doubt fully aware of the practical implications of the decision in the *Babanaft International* case and the decision of the Court of Appeal in *Derby & Co Ltd v Weldon (No 2)*, said this:

> 'A problem emerged earlier this year which was of great concern to those banks which are subject to the jurisdiction of both the English court and the courts of the country or countries where they may be holding assets of the defendant which are made the subject of a worldwide Mareva. Certain countries may not recognise or give effect to ex parte orders made in this jurisdiction and indeed may make inconsistent orders. In such cases third-party banks can be put in an impossible position, being required to do something by a court in this country and the opposite by a court abroad. The *Derby v Weldon* proviso does not seem to help as it does not apply to persons who are subject to the jurisdiction which of course is the case with most major banks. To solve this problem of double jeopardy we would suggest in appropriate cases that something along the lines of the following provision be added to the order.'

The judge then set out the proviso in the terms which are being sought in the present application.

[15] In *Baltic Shipping v Translink Shipping Ltd* [1995] 1 Lloyd's Rep 673, an application in precisely similar terms to that which is before the court was made by a third-party bank. The principal submission made on behalf of the claimant on the facts of that case was that the proviso suggested by the bank gave the bank too much protection. The conclusion of Clarke J (at 678–679) was to this effect:

> 'The bank is not a party to these proceedings. It should be given all reasonable protection. It is not in principle desirable for a bank to have to rely upon the undertaking in damages ... I do not think that the bank should

a
have to run the risk that it would be in breach of its contract under the law
of Noumea for it to pay out pending an application by the plaintiff to the
local Court. That approach appears to me to be consistent with the general
approach of the Courts in the cases to which I have referred ... In general
plaintiffs should recognise this difficulty and apply to the local Court as soon
as they possibly can, either at the same time or as soon as may be after a

b
world-wide *Mareva* has been granted. It appears to me that if the bank's
proviso is adopted the plaintiff has reasonable protection because the bank
can only act on reasonable belief. In forming that belief it will have to act on
the information available to it. So if in a particular case the plaintiff has the
powerful opinion of a lawyer to the effect that there would be no breach of
local law if a payment out were to be made then the bank will have to take

c
the opinion into account in forming its belief. If the belief is not reasonable
then the bank will be at risk.'

[16] The judge went on to conclude that in general and 'subject to the facts of
the particular case' it would be desirable that a proviso along the lines of that

d
proposed in Saville J's end of year statement should be included in the standard
Mareva.

[17] It is fair to say that the facts of the *Baltic Shipping* case are very different
from the present case. There was a post-judgment freezing order in respect of a
specific bank account. The claimant was aware of the existence of the bank
account and had failed to take reasonable steps to protect himself within the

e
foreign jurisdiction.

[18] But these factual distinctions do not in my judgment affect the principle.
In maintaining a fair balance between the interests of the claimant and the
interests of the third-party bank the court must always bear in mind the risk
associated with exercising an exorbitant jurisdiction, a risk which may be of

f
particular prejudice to third parties.

[19] I recognise that the recommendations of Saville J and indeed of Clarke J
were not adopted by the Rules Committee. The present Commercial Court
Guide (August 1999) echoes its predecessor in saying (para F19.10):

g
'As regards freezing injunctions in respect of assets outside the jurisdiction
of the English Courts, the standard wording in relation to effects on third
parties may in some cases appropriately incorporate wording to enable
overseas branches of banks or similar institutions which have offices within
the jurisdiction to comply with what they reasonably believe to be their
obligations under the laws of the country where the assets are located or

h
under the proper law of the relevant banking or other contract relating to
such assets.'

[20] As presently advised I would prefer the view that such a provision should
be included unless inappropriate, rather than only included if appropriate. On the

j
facts of the present case, the absence of any defendant within the jurisdiction and
the consequent inability to enforce the obligation to produce an affidavit of assets
renders the proviso all the more desirable (see *Crédit Suisse Fides Trust SA v Cuoghi*
[1997] 3 All ER 724 at 730, [1998] QB 818 at 827). A third-party bank should not
be exposed to the risks of refusing to comply with the terms of its mandate.
Further, a court order should not be made a necessary precondition to
compliance.

[21] It follows in my judgment that the proviso urged upon the court by the applicant, UBS, should be included. Furthermore, it is appropriate for the Rules Committee to reconsider whether it should be included in the standard form annexed to CPR Pt 25.

Order accordingly.

James Wilson   Barrister.

a R (on the application of Saadi and others) v Secretary of State for the Home Department

[2001] EWHC Admin 670, [2001] EWCA Civ 1512

b
QUEEN'S BENCH DIVISION (ADMINISTRATIVE COURT)

COLLINS J

21, 22 JUNE, 7 SEPTEMBER 2001

c
COURT OF APPEAL, CIVIL DIVISION

LORD PHILLIPS OF WORTH MATRAVERS MR, SCHIEMANN AND WALLER LJJ

2, 3, 19 OCTOBER 2001

Immigration – Asylum seeker – Detention pending decision on claim – Secretary of State implementing new policy on detention of asylum seekers whose claims could be
d *decided quickly – Policy providing for short period of detention in reception centre pending decision – Claimants being detained under new policy and challenging lawfulness of detention – Whether detention infringing claimants' right to liberty under human rights convention – Immigration Act 1971, Sch 2, para 16(1) – Human Rights Act 1998, Sch 1, Pt I, art 5(1).*

e
The claimants, four Iraqi Kurds, arrived in the United Kingdom in December 2000 and claimed asylum. They were detained at a reception centre which had been established under a policy announced on behalf of the Secretary of State in March 2000 in response to the growing number of claims for asylum. That policy had been implemented under the power of immigration officers, contained in
f para 16(1)[a] of Sch 2 to the Immigration Act 1971, to detain a person who had arrived in the United Kingdom pending his examination and a decision to give or refuse him leave to enter. Its aim was to enable a significant number of asylum applications to be decided within about seven days by ensuring that applicants were available for an early interview or subsequent queries, had access to proper advice and were readily available for service of the decision. The policy applied
g to applicants of certain nationalities (including Iraqi Kurds) whose claims appeared to be capable of being dealt with quickly. The detention criteria identified various classes of applicant whose claims would be unsuitable for consideration at the reception centre, including those who were considered likely to abscond. The claimants, none of whom had been detained for more than ten days,
h challenged the lawfulness of their detention in judicial review proceedings. The judge concluded that the claimants had been detained in order to enable their applications to be determined speedily, and that such detention was permissible under the provisions of the 1971 Act. He further held, however, that the claimants' detention infringed their right to liberty under art 5(1)[b] of the
j European Convention for the Protection of Human Rights and Fundamental Freedoms 1950 (as set out in Sch 1 to the Human Rights Act 1998) since it did not fall within the exception to that right provided by art 5(1)(f), namely the lawful arrest or detention of a person to prevent his effecting an unauthorised entry into

---

a   Paragraph 16(1) is set out at [2], below (Collins J's judgment)
b   Article 5, so far as material, is set out at [25], below (Collins J's judgment)

the country or of a person against whom action was being taken with a view to deportation. Accordingly, the applications were allowed, and the Secretary of State appealed.

Held – The Secretary of State's policy, and the detention of asylum seekers in accordance with that policy, was lawful both under the 1971 Act, viewed in isolation, and under art 5 of the convention. As a matter of domestic law, there could be no doubt that the claimants' detention fell within the express statutory powers of immigration officers contained in the 1971 Act, and it was impossible to condemn as irrational the policy of subjecting to a short period of detention, designed to ensure that the regime operated without dislocation, those asylum seekers whose applications appeared susceptible to rapid resolution. A short period of detention, in conditions suitable for asylum seekers as opposed, for example, to convicted prisoners, was not an unreasonable price to pay in order to ensure the speedy resolution of the claims of a substantial proportion of the influx of asylum seekers. As regards the convention, art 5(1)(f) had been intended to preserve the right of member states to decide whether to allow aliens to enter their territories on any terms whatsoever. The jurisprudence of the European Court of Human Rights contemplated that it would be lawful to confine aliens in a centre of detention pending deportation or in an international zone for the time that was inevitably needed to organise the practical details of the alien's repatriation or while his application for leave to enter the territory in order to be afforded asylum was considered, provided always that confinement was accompanied by suitable safeguards and that it was not prolonged excessively. The test of proportionality required by art 5(1)(f) required the court simply to consider whether the process of considering an asylum application, or arranging a deportation, had gone on too long to justify the detention of the person concerned, having regard to the conditions in which the person was detained and any special circumstances affecting him or her. Applying that test, no disproportionality had been demonstrated in the instant case. Accordingly, the claimants' detention was lawful and the appeal would therefore be allowed (see [7], [26]–[28], [30], [40], [64]–[66], [69], below (Court of Appeal judgment)).

Chahal v UK (1996) 1 BHRC 405 and *Amuur v France* (1996) 22 EHRR 533 considered.

Note

For detention of persons liable to examination and removal, see 4(2) *Halsbury's Laws* (4th edn reissue) para 119, and for the right to liberty and the immigration exception to that right, see 8(2) *Halsbury's Laws* (4th edn reissue) paras 127, 133.

For the Immigration Act 1971, Sch 2, para 16, see 31 *Halsbury's Statutes* (4th edn) (2000 reissue) 134.

For the Human Rights Act 1998, Sch 1, Pt I, art 5, see 7 *Halsbury's Statutes* (4th edn) (1999 reissue) 522.

Cases referred to in judgments

A v Australia (1997) 4 BHRC 210, UN HRC.

A-G for Canada v Cain, A-G for Canada v Gilhula [1906] AC 542, [1904–7] All ER Rep 582, PC.

Abdulaziz v UK (1985) 7 EHRR 471, [1985] ECHR 9214/80, ECt HR.

Ali v Switzerland (1998) 28 EHRR 304, [1998] ECHR 24881/94, E Com HR and ECt HR.

a *Amuur v France* (1996) 22 EHRR 533, [1996] ECHR 19776/92, ECt HR.
Bozano v France (1986) 9 EHRR 297, ECt HR.
Chahal v UK (1996) (1995) 23 EHRR 413, E Com HR, 1 BHRC 405, ECt HR.
General Medical Council v Spackman [1943] 2 All ER 337, [1943] AC 627, HL.
NC v Italy [2001] ECHR 24952/94, ECt HR.
R v Governor of Durham Prison, ex p Singh [1984] 1 All ER 983, [1984] 1 WLR 704.

b *R v Secretary of State for the Home Dept, ex p Brezinski, R v Secretary of State for the
Home Dept, ex p Glowacka* (19 July 1996, unreported), QBD.
R v Secretary of State for the Home Dept, ex p Daly [2001] UKHL 26, [2001] 3 All ER
433, [2001] AC 532, [2001] 2 WLR 1622.
R v Secretary of State for the Home Dept, ex p Khan [1995] 2 All ER 540, CA.

c *R v Secretary of State for the Home Dept, ex p Mahmood* [2001] 2 FCR 63, [2001]
1 WLR 840, CA.
R v Special Adjudicator, ex p B [1998] Imm AR 182.
*R (on the application of Samaroo) v Secretary of State for the Home Dept, R (on the
application of Sezek) v Secretary of State for the Home Dept* [2001] EWCA Civ 1139,
(2001) Times, 18 September.

d *R (on the application of Sezek) v Secretary of State for the Home Dept* [2001] EWCA Civ
795, (2001) Times, 20 June.
Tan Te Lam v Superintendent of Tai A Chau Detention Centre [1996] 4 All ER 256,
[1997] AC 97, [1996] 2 WLR 963, PC.
Tomasi v France (1992) 15 EHRR 1, [1992] ECHR 12850/87, ECt HR.
Winterwerp v Netherlands (1979) 2 EHRR 387, [1979] ECHR 6301/73, ECt HR.

e *Zamir v UK* (1983) 40 DR 42, E Com HR.

Cases also cited or referred to in skeleton arguments
Akhtar v Governor of Pentonville Prison [1993] Imm AR 424, CA.
Belgian Linguistic Case (No 2) (1968) 1 EHRR 252, [1968] ECHR 1474/62, ECt HR.

f *Bouamar v Belgium* (1987) 11 EHRR 1, [1987] ECHR 9106/80, ECt HR.
Bozano v France (1986) 9 EHRR 297, [1986] ECHR 9990/82, ECt HR.
Brogan v UK (1988) 11 EHRR 117, [1988] ECHR 11209/89, ECt HR.
Brown v Stott (Procurator Fiscal, Dunfermline) [2001] 2 All ER 97, [2001] 2 WLR 817, PC.
Ceský v Czech Republic (2000) 33 EHRR 8, [2000] ECHR 33644/96, ECt HR.
Ciulla v Italy (1989) 13 EHRR 346, [1989] ECHR 11152/84, ECt HR.

g *De Jong v Netherlands* (1984) 8 EHRR 20, [1984] ECHR 8805/79, ECt HR.
Deweer v Belgium (1980) 2 EHRR 439, [1980] ECHR 6903/75, ECt HR.
Dougoz v Greece (2001) 10 BHRC 306, ECt HR.
Fox v UK (1990) 13 EHRR 157, [1990] ECHR 12244/86, ECt HR.
Gundem v Turkey (2001) 32 EHRR 17, ECt HR.

h *Guzzardi v Italy* (1980) 3 EHRR 333, [1980] ECHR 7367/76, ECt HR.
Hill (Gary) v Chief Constable of the South Yorkshire Police [1990] 1 All ER 1046, [1990]
1 WLR 946, CA.
IRC v Rossminster Ltd [1980] 1 All ER 80, [1980] AC 952, HL.
Ireland v UK (1978) 2 EHRR 25, [1978] ECHR 5310/71, ECt HR.

j *Karanakaran v Secretary of State for the Home Dept* [2000] 3 All ER 449, CA.
Kemmache v France (No 3) (1994) 19 EHRR 349, [1994] ECHR 17621/91, ECt HR.
Kurt v Turkey (1998) 5 BHRC 1, ECt HR.
Litwa v Poland [2000] ECHR 26629/95, ECt HR.
Lynas v Switzerland (1976) 6 DR 141, E Com HR.
Mahmod, Re [1995] Imm AR 311, IAT.
McVeigh v UK (1981) 5 EHRR 71, E Com HR.

Quinn v UK [1997] EHRLR 167, ECt HR.

R v A (No 2) [2001] UKHL 25, [2001] 3 All ER 1, [2001] 2 WLR 1546.

R v Governor of Brockhill Prison, ex p Evans (No 2) [2000] 4 All ER 15, [2001] 2 AC 19, HL.

R v Governor of Richmond Remand Centre, ex p Asghar [1971] 1 WLR 129, DC.

R v Naillie; R v Kanesarajah [1993] 2 All ER 782, [1993] AC 674, HL.

R v Secretary of State for the Home Dept, ex p Canbolat [1997] Imm AR 281, DC; *affd* [1998] 1 All ER 161, [1997] 1 WLR 1569, CA.

R v Secretary of State for the Home Dept, ex p Robinson [1997] 4 All ER 210, [1998] QB 929, CA.

R v Secretary of State for the Home Dept, ex p Yassine [1990] Imm AR 354.

R v Uxbridge Magistrates' Court, ex p Adimi, R v Secretary of State for the Home Dept, ex p Sorani, R v Crown Prosecution Service, ex p Sorani, R v Secretary of State for the Home Dept, ex p Kaziu [1999] 4 All ER 520, [2001] QB 667, DC.

R (on the application of Yiadom) v Secretary of State for the Home Dept Case C-357/98 [2001] All ER (EC) 267, ECJ.

Raimondo v Italy (1994) 18 EHRR 237, ECt HR.

Sanchez-Reisse v Switzerland (1986) 9 EHRR 71, [1986] ECHR 9862/82, ECt HR.

Soering v UK (1989) 11 EHRR 439, [1989] ECHR 14038/88, ECt HR.

Vilvarajah v Secretary of State for the Home Dept [1990] Imm AR 457, CA.

Weeks v UK (1987) 10 EHRR 293, [1987] ECHR 9787/82, ECt HR.

X v UK (1977) 12 DR 207, E Com HR.

X v UK (1981) 4 EHRR 188, [1981] ECHR 7215/75, ECt HR.

Applications for judicial review

The claimants, Shayan Baram Saadi, Zhenar Fazi Maged, Dilshad Hassan Osman and Rizgan Mohammed, applied for judicial review of the lawfulness of their detention at the Oakington Reception Centre in December 2000, pending a decision on their claims for asylum, in accordance with the policy of the respondent, the Secretary of State for the Home Department, announced in Parliament on 16 March 2000. The facts are set out in the judgment.

Rick Scannell and *Duran Seddon* (instructed by *Wilson & Co*) for the claimants.

David Pannick QC, Neil Garnham QC and *Michael Fordham* (instructed by the *Treasury Solicitor*) for the Secretary of State.

Cur adv vult

7 September 2001. The following judgment was delivered.

COLLINS J.

[1] The three claims involving four claimants which have been heard together before me raise the question whether detention at what is called the Oakington Reception Centre is lawful. The claimants are Kurds from Iraq. They arrived in this country in December 2000 and claimed asylum. It was decided that their claims should be considered at Oakington and that therefore they should be detained there for up to ten days while interviews and other inquiries were made. Each was then released from detention. It was common ground that their release was no bar to the continuation of the judicial review proceedings since the lawfulness of the detention was material to a possible claim for damages and in any event was an issue which needed to be determined.

[2] Powers to detain those seeking entry to or who are to be removed from the United Kingdom are contained in Sch 2 to the Immigration Act 1971.

a Paragraph 2 entitles an immigration officer to examine any person arriving in the United Kingdom to determine whether he should be given leave to enter and para 16(1) provides:

'A person who may be required to submit to examination under paragraph 2 above may be detained under the authority of an immigration officer pending his examination and pending a decision to give or refuse him leave to enter.'

b

Paragraphs 8, 9 and 10 enable an immigration officer (or, if certain conditions which I need not detail are fulfilled, the Secretary of State) to remove those refused leave to enter or illegal entrants and para 16(2) (as substituted by the Immigration and Asylum Act 1999) provides:

c

'If there are reasonable grounds for suspecting that a person is someone in respect of whom directions may be given under any of paragraphs 8 to 10 ... that person may be detained under the authority of an immigration officer pending—(a) a decision whether or not to give such directions; (b) his removal in pursuance of such directions.'

d

Paragraph 21(1) enables an immigration officer to grant temporary admission to the United Kingdom to any person liable to be detained. Section 4 of the 1999 Act (which came into force on 11 November 1999) enables the Secretary of State to provide or arrange for the provision of 'facilities for the accommodation of persons' temporarily admitted to the United Kingdom or released from detention or granted bail under the Immigration Acts. And para 21 of Sch 2 to the 1971 Act has been amended by para 62 of Sch 14 to the 1999 Act by the addition of sub-paras (2A) to (2E). Subparagraphs (2) to (2E) now read as follows:

e

'(2) So long as a person is at large in the United Kingdom by virtue of this paragraph, he shall be subject to such restrictions as to residence, as to his employment or occupation and as to reporting to the police or an immigration officer as may from time to time be notified to him in writing by an immigration officer.

f

(2A) The provisions that may be included in restrictions as to residence imposed under sub-paragraph (2) include provisions of such a description as may be prescribed by regulations made by the Secretary of State.

g

(2B) The regulations may, among other things, provide for the inclusion of provisions—(a) prohibiting residence in one or more particular areas; (b) requiring the person concerned to reside in accommodation provided under section 4 of the Immigration and Asylum Act 1999 and prohibiting him from being absent from that accommodation except in accordance with the restrictions imposed on him.

h

(2C) The regulations may provide that a particular description of provision may be imposed only for prescribed purposes.

(2D) The power to make regulations conferred by this paragraph is exercisible by statutory instrument and includes a power to make different provision for different cases.

j

(2E) But no regulations under this paragraph are to be made unless a draft of the regulations has been laid before Parliament and approved by a resolution of each House.'

I shall have to consider those powers and their scope in due course.

[3] Before March 2000, when the opening of Oakington was announced, the
Home Office policy on the use of detention was set out in a White Paper *a*
published in 1998 and entitled: *Fairer, Faster and Firmer—A Modern Approach to
Immigration and Asylum* (Cm 4018) in these terms (para 12.3):

'The Government has decided that, whilst there is a presumption in favour
of temporary admission or release, detention is normally justified in the *b*
following circumstances.
  • where there is a reasonable belief that the individual will fail to keep the
terms of temporary admission or temporary release;
  • initially, to clarify a person's identity and the basis of their claim; or
  • where removal is imminent. In particular, where there is a systematic *c*
attempt to breach the immigration control, detention is justified wherever
one or more of those criteria is satisfied.'

In *R v Special Adjudicator, ex p B* [1998] Imm AR 182, Kay J referred to the policy
on detention prior to the 1998 White Paper. It was that detention should only be
used where there was no alternative and as a last resort. It does not appear that *d*
the 1998 White Paper was intended to change that policy. In para 12.11 it was
made clear that detention should be for the shortest possible time and para 12.7
required that written reasons should be given at the time of the detention. Thus,
prior to the Oakington regime, detention was in effect to be limited to those cases
where there was a concern that the individual might abscond or otherwise fail to
comply with any terms of temporary admission, where there was a need to *e*
discover what was an individual's true identity (for example, where false
documents were presented), or where removal was imminent.
[4] On 16 March 2000 the minister (Mrs Barbara Roche) announced a change
in a written answer to a parliamentary question. She said:
f

'Oakington Reception Centre will strengthen our ability to deal quickly with
asylum applications, many of which prove to be unfounded. In addition to the
existing detention criteria, applicants will be detained at Oakington where it
appears that their application can be decided quickly, including those which
may be certified as manifestly unfounded. Oakington will consider applications *g*
from adults and families with children, for whom separate accommodation
is being provided, but not from unaccompanied minors. Detention will
initially be for a period of about seven days to enable applicants to be
interviewed and an initial decision to be made. Legal advice will be available
on site. If the claim cannot be decided in that period, the applicant will be
granted temporary admission or, if necessary in line with existing criteria, *h*
moved to another place of detention. If the claim is refused, a decision about
further detention will similarly be made in accordance with existing criteria.
Thus, detention in this latter category of cases will normally be to effect
removal or where it has become apparent that the person will fail to keep in
contact with the Immigration Service.' (See 346 HC Official Report (6th series) *j*
written answers col 263.)

In a statement which has been put before me on behalf of the Secretary of State,
Mr Ian Martin, an inspector in the Immigration and Nationality Directorate
(IND) in the Home Office, has explained what he describes as the thinking behind
Oakington in these terms (para 10):

a
'This was to be a centre at which asylum applications would be decided quickly, within about seven days. In order to achieve that objective for significant numbers of applicants, an intensive consideration and decision process was required. In particular, it was considered essential that applicants should be available for an early interview and to submit any further representations that may be judged necessary. It was also considered

b
important that they should be readily available for the decision to be served. The Home Office's experience is that many applicants, particularly those whose applications are likely to be unfounded, are unwilling to comply with fast-track asylum procedures. In the government's view, the aim of considering and deciding asylum claims within about seven days for substantial numbers of applicants were best achieved by requiring applicants to reside at

c
Oakington, under existing immigration detention powers.'

[5] It is thus apparent that a decision to detain at Oakington is not based on any considerations whether the applicant in question may abscond or otherwise fail to comply with terms of temporary admission. Indeed, the overriding or, as Mr Martin puts it, the governing criterion is whether the claim appears capable

d
of being decided quickly. To assist immigration officers in deciding on suitability, a list of nationalities has been drawn up which can justify consideration at Oakington because they are expected to be simple to deal with. Those lists are amended from time to time and in some cases they are limited to particular individuals within certain nationalities. Asylum seekers from Iraq are included,

e
but the description in the list reads as follows: 'Iraq—must speak Sorani, only Kurds from autonomous area, usually from Sulaymaniya, Dohuk and Irbil and their provinces but please phone for further advice.' In a letter of 19 October 2000 to the Refugee Legal Centre (RLC), the Home Office approach to Kurds from Iraq was explained in these terms:

f
'As you know, it has been decided to process through Oakington ... those Iraqi asylum applicants whose claims appear straightforward i e Kurds from the Kurdish Autonomous Area in Northern Iraq who claim they are at risk because of their membership of one of the Kurdish political parties.'

This was part of a correspondence in which the RLC were asserting that Iraqi

g
Kurds were not simple cases and should not therefore qualify for consideration at Oakington.

[6] The guidance on suitable cases for Oakington as might be expected identifies those which are to be regarded as unsuitable. Those are:

'• any case which does not appear to be one in which a quick decision can

h
be reached.
• any case, which has complicating factors, or issues, which are unlikely to be resolved within the constraints of the Oakington process model.
• age dispute cases, other than those where there is clear and irrefutable documentary evidence that the applicant is aged over 18 years.

j
• disabled applicants, save but the most easily manageable.
• any person who has special medical needs, save but those which can be managed within a GP surgery environment.
• any person who gives reason to believe that they might not be suitable for the relaxed Oakington regime.
• any person whose detention would be contrary to published detention criteria.

Apart from the final category, there may be very good reasons for accommodating someone who falls into one of the unsuitable categories from time to time and this document should be considered merely as a statement of intent.'

The 'published detention criteria' are set out in para 38.8 of the Operational Enforcement Manual. They include persons 'where there is independent evidence that they have been tortured'. In addition, at para 38.3.1 Oakington is specifically referred to and the list of those unsuitable for it is set out. There is a significant qualification to the penultimate entry in the list to which I have already referred. In 38.3.1 this reads: '... any person who gives reason to believe that they might not be suitable for the relaxed Oakington regime, including those who are considered likely to abscond.'

[7] It is therefore clear that detention at Oakington is based on two criteria only. First, is the applicant a national of a listed country and, if so, does he have the relevant characteristics (if any) which show that his claim is likely to be able to be dealt with quickly and, more particularly, within the seven to ten-day timescales allowed for? Secondly, is there any reason why he is otherwise unsuitable for detention at Oakington? Not only are the pre-existing criteria for detention irrelevant but they are a contra-indication. Someone who may abscond would not be suitable. This has led Mr Scannell to submit that detention at Oakington is for administrative convenience. It is desirable that the applicant be available for interview and to answer any subsequent queries and that can best be achieved by detaining him to ensure his presence. It is also desirable that he should have access to proper advice and representatives and that is also provided for at Oakington through the RLC and the Immigration Advisory Service. In addition, interpreters are available at all material times. The justification is expressed by Mr Martin in these terms:

'In this way, the Oakington procedure is intended to help facilitate the entry into the United Kingdom of those who are entitled to do so and to prevent the entry (and facilitate the removal) of those who are not entitled to enter and would be making an unauthorised entry.'

[8] I am bound to say that I have considerable sympathy with Mr Scannell's submission. The detention of the individual is not because he has done anything which might usually be considered as a justification for depriving him of his liberty but because his application can more easily be dealt with speedily and so the rate of disposal generally can be improved. As long ago as 1943 Lord Atkin observed that convenience and justice were often not on speaking terms (see *General Medical Council v Spackman* [1943] 2 All ER 337, [1943] AC 627). However, even if the detention is dictated by an administrative convenience, it may still be lawful, particularly if the advantages to immigration control and decision-making in general can be regarded as a proper justification for it. Mr Pannick QC does not accept that it is proper to regard the Oakington regime as detention for administrative convenience. In any event, he suggests that to try to label it is unhelpful. I must look to see whether the power that undoubtedly exists is being used for a proper purpose. If it is, the immigration officers can decide, guided by the Secretary of State, when it is to be used. The purpose is set out in para 16 of Sch 2 to the 1971 Act. It is undoubtedly being used for that purpose. Thus, whatever pejorative descriptions may be used, detention is lawful, certainly in terms of domestic law without considering the impact of the

a European Convention for the Protection of Human Rights and Fundamental Freedoms (Rome, 4 November 1950; TS 71 (1953); Cmd 8969) (as set out in Sch 1 to the Human Rights Act 1998) (the European Convention).

[9] Before going further, I should deal with the circumstances of the claimants before me. The material facts in each case can be stated shortly.

b (i) *Dr Saadi*

Shayan Saadi is a doctor of medicine. He arrived at Heathrow on 30 December 2000 and immediately claimed asylum. His claim was based on the contention that he had worked for the Iraqi Workers' Communist Party and, in the course of his duties at a hospital, he had treated three members of that party who had been injured in an attack by the Patriotic Union of Kurdistan (PUK). This had resulted

c in his arrest and detention by the PUK and had led to his decision to flee. The documents produced show that the immigration officer dealing with his claim contacted Oakington, since his claim appeared to qualify, and Oakington agreed to take him, but there was no room for him there until 2 January 2001. He was therefore granted temporary admission until then, when he was detained and

d taken to Oakington. Following an interview, his asylum claim was refused on 8 January and on 9 January he was granted temporary admission. On 5 January, the RLC wrote to IND requesting his release on the ground that his detention was unlawful. The main matter relied on, which I shall deal with when I have recited the facts of all the claims, was that Iraqi Kurds should not be dealt with at Oakington because their applications could not properly be regarded as simple.

e

(ii) *Zhenar Maged*

Mr Maged arrived at Dover on 6 December 2000. He was found hiding in a lorry together with a number of other illegal entrants. He claimed asylum on the basis that he had acted against the interests of the PUK, of which he was a

f member, and so feared persecution by them. He was dealt with at Oakington and on 16 December 2000 his claim was refused. On 9 December the RLC wrote requesting his release and reasons for his detention in much the same terms as in the case of Dr Saadi. He has been granted temporary admission.

g (iii) *Dilshad Osman*

Mr Osman arrived hidden in a lorry with four others at Dover on 4 December 2000. He claimed asylum at Croydon where he may have been referred by the authorities at Dover. It is not entirely clear on the evidence how he came to apply at Croydon rather than at Dover. In any event, he was referred to Oakington and his claim was based on the contention that he was a PUK activist who lived in

h Makhwar, a town under Iraqi government administration. His application was refused on 11 December 2000 and he was granted temporary admission on 12 December. On 7 December the RLC wrote a letter requesting his release (and that of his fellow claimant Mr Mohammed) in similar terms to those in the other cases.

j

(iv) *Rizgan Mohammed*

Mr Mohammed arrived hidden in a lorry on the same day as Mr Osman. His application for asylum was based on fear of persecution by the Islamic Movement of Iraqi Kurdistan which he, as a member, was suspected of having in some way betrayed. He says he claimed asylum at Dover but was referred to Croydon because no interpreter was available. His claim was dealt with at Oakington and

was refused on 11 December 2000. He was granted temporary admission on
12 December. The RLC letter requesting his release was in similar terms to those
in the other cases.

[10] It is to be noted that Messrs Maged, Osman and Mohammed were all
illegal entrants who, but for their asylum claims, would have been removed as
such. Dr Saadi on the other hand arrived openly at Heathrow and sought leave
to enter as a refugee. The distinction may be important when I come to consider
the impact of art 5 of the European Convention.

[11] One complaint which has been made in each of these cases is that none of
the claimants was told why he was being detained. I have already mentioned the
requirement that written reasons should be given at the time of the detention.
A form IS91R headed 'Reasons for Detention and Bail Rights' is provided to
immigration officers. It must be filled out and handed to the person who is to be
detained. At the material time, it stated that detention was being ordered under
powers contained in the Immigration Acts and continued: 'Detention is only used
when there is no reasonable alternative available. It has been decided that you
should remain in detention because ...' There then follow five reasons ((a) to (e))
against which are boxes which should be ticked. The five reasons are: (a) you are
likely to abscond if given temporary admission or release; (b) there is insufficient
reliable information to decide on whether to grant you temporary admission or
release; (c) your removal from the United Kingdom is imminent; (d) you need to
be detained whilst alternative arrangements are made for your case; (e) your
release is not considered conducive to the public good. The form continues: 'This
decision has been reached on the basis of the following factors ...' There are then
13 factors with boxes to be ticked if a particular one applies. They include the
absence of 'enough close ties to make it likely that you will stay in one place',
a previous failure to comply with conditions or a previous absconding, a use of
deception, a failure to give satisfactory answers to an immigration officer, a failure
to produce satisfactory evidence of identity, nationality or lawful basis to be in the
United Kingdom and unsatisfactory character, conduct or associations. I have
referred to all those that could conceivably be relevant in the circumstances of
cases such as those which are before me.

[12] Mr Martin says that a 'structural problem' arose during 2000 regarding
the content of the form IS91R 'concerning the options of its language to cover
Oakington detention'. It apparently took the Home Office three months to
realise that the wording was clearly not appropriate for Oakington detention
which depended on nothing more than that the individual in question came from
a country on the relevant list because his claim could, it was believed, be processed
quickly. So on 7 June 2000 it was said in the general orders to immigration
officers: 'We are currently reviewing the IS91R reasons for detention form. The
revised form, which will be issued shortly, will take account of the revised
Oakington criteria.' Nothing seems to have been done since the Operational
Enforcement Manual records on 21 December 2000 that the form was currently
being revised and that the revised version would be issued shortly. When
Mr Martin made his statement on 12 April 2001, the form had still not been
revised, but an addendum had been attached with effect from 2 February 2001
which reads:

> 'Reason for Detention
> I have decided that you should be detained because I am satisfied that your
> application may be decided quickly using the fast track procedures established
> at Oakington Reception Centre. In reaching this decision I have taken into

a account that, on initial consideration, it appears that your application may be one which can be decided quickly.'

[13] It is, says Mr Martin, a matter of regret that the form lagged behind the change in policy. I would use much stronger language. It is a disgrace. To include the Oakington reason for detention would have been simple and why it took nearly 11 months to produce the addendum is difficult to understand. The result

b was that immigration officers had to give the detainee information which may well have been inaccurate. Mr Martin says:

'... the existing version of the form was the only one available to the immigration officers who dealt with these claimants. No doubt this will have presented a dilemma to officers. Given the availability of Oakington

c and the known criteria as to suitability, I strongly suspect that the old form IS91R was being used by ticking boxes which were considered to be present as additional factors in a case, or at least were the closest fit from a range of choices which did not readily encompass the new Oakington policy.'

d The form clearly indicated that detention was only used where there was no reasonable alternative. All the reasons and factors reflect some possible misconduct by the detainee or the need for him to be cared for by detention. As Mr Martin concedes, it was wholly inappropriate for Oakington detention and it is, for example, difficult to follow what reason could conceivably have been close to fitting Dr Saadi's case. Unfortunately, the copy of the IS91R which should have

e been retained on the file has disappeared and so I do not know, nor does Dr Saadi, why it was said he should be detained.

[14] The vice of this is that reasons will be on file which are not accurate. The applicant may be branded as a possible absconder or be said to have committed some other misdemeanour and this will be on his file and may be held against him in future. Furthermore, the law requires that a person be informed why he is

f being detained and the information must be accurate.

[15] As I have said, Dr Saadi's IS91R is missing. In Mr Maged's case, none of the boxes (a) to (e) is ticked, but box 6 of the factors upon which the decision has been reached, which reads 'You have not produced satisfactory evidence of your identity, nationality or lawful basis in the U.K.', has been ticked. That is said to

g have been appropriate, but it was not the reason why detention was ordered and we do not know what oral explanation was given to Mr Maged. In Mr Osman's case, the immigration officer has ticked boxes (a) and (b) and relied on lack of close ties, use of deception and failure to produce satisfactory evidence of identity etc. In Mr Mohammed's case, only box (b) has been ticked and the factors relied on are use of deception and failure to produce satisfactory evidence of identity

h etc. The answer to the RLC's letters of 7 December states:

'Your client has been detained at Oakington on the basis of this restatement of detention criteria at Oakington Reception Centre. The determining officer concluded that it appeared that your client's application could be decided quickly on the basis of various factors including your client's nationality.

j The fact that your client's individual circumstances were considered by the determining officer in reaching his decision to detain in accordance with current detention policy indicates that all relevant factors were taken into account.'

Mr Martin accepts that there is a 'tension' between what is said in the letter and the IS91R.

[16] The use of inappropriate forms and the giving of reasons for detention on
those forms which may not have been wholly accurate do not affect the　*a*
lawfulness of the detention. The real reason was the new Oakington process. If
that was lawful, the disgraceful failure to prepare proper forms cannot render it
unlawful. In any event, it may be that in the cases of the illegal entrants the
immigration officers could properly rely on at least the absence of identification
and the clandestine entry as factors justifying detention even if, had Oakington　*b*
not been used, temporary admission would have been granted. I do not need to
go into the matter further since Mr Scannell has not sought to argue that the
muddle about reasons renders the detentions unlawful.

[17] It was suggested that to regard Iraqi Kurds as appropriate to be dealt with
at Oakington was wrong. Reliance was placed on a United Nations Commissioner
for Refugees letter of 27 November 2000 which indicated that the volatile　*c*
political climate and shifting alliances in Northern Iraq made the assumption that
the Kurdistan Democratic Party and the PUK could provide protection in their
respective areas unsustainable. The letter assumed that Oakington was to be used
where claims were likely to be decided to be manifestly unfounded. That
assumption was incorrect; indeed, none of the claimants' applications has been　*d*
regarded as manifestly unfounded. Naturally, some applications will be referred
to Oakington because it is believed that they are manifestly unfounded. Such
cases can often be dealt with quickly. The Home Office has explained why it
believed that Kurds from northern Iraq could often be processed quickly. I do not
think that Mr Scannell has come anywhere near establishing that that view was
irrational. The fact that a claim can be and is processed speedily does not mean　*e*
that it is not properly considered. All claims should be processed as quickly as
possible and all that is being done at Oakington is to choose those which seem
likely to be able to be processed more quickly than others.

[18] Complaint has been made that the screening process is inadequate so that
some who should not be detained (for example, because they have suffered torture　*f*
in the past) may be. At an early stage (usually on the second day), the detainee is
seen by a legal representative. If anything is then raised which shows that he
should not be detained, it can be put to the authorities and release should follow.
If it does not, an immediate application for habeas corpus can be made. In any
event, Mr Martin has indicated that suitability is kept under review and the
instructions are that anyone who turns out to be unsuitable should not be kept at　*g*
Oakington.

[19] Mr Scannell has submitted that detention is arbitrary because, due to the
limited numbers that can be accommodated, it is a matter of chance whether an
individual goes to detention at Oakington or gets temporary admission to have
his application dealt with in a different fashion. The criteria for admission to　*h*
Oakington are not themselves arbitrary. Certain nationalities are listed because
and only because the view has been taken that they are likely to be able to be
processed quickly. Thus any discrimination is not unlawful, since the decision
that nationality should be adopted as a criterion is objectively justifiable. The fact that
there is limited room at Oakington cannot create arbitrariness. To suggest that a　*j*
regime such as Oakington cannot be instituted until there is room for all those
who might qualify is absurd.

[20] Mr Scannell has submitted that the powers to detain contained in the
Immigration Act 1971 require that individual consideration be given to each
detainee's circumstances and that a person be detained only if it is reasonably
necessary to detain him. The desirability of speedy decision-making cannot itself

a [24] It seems to me that the detention of the claimants was lawful in that it was permitted by the provisions of the 1971 Act as amended. The remaining question to be answered, and the one which is of fundamental importance, is whether the Human Rights Act 1998 and the application of art 5 of the European Convention renders the detention unlawful. Mr Pannick submitted that that was the only real issue in the cases. I agree.

b [25] Article 5, so far as material, reads as follows:

'1. Everyone has the right to liberty and security of person. No one shall be deprived of his liberty save in the following cases and in accordance with a procedure prescribed by law ... (f) the lawful arrest or detention of a person to prevent his effecting an unauthorised entry into the country or of a person c against whom action is being taken with a view to deportation or extradition ...
4. Everyone who is deprived of his liberty by arrest or detention shall be entitled to take proceedings by which the lawfulness of his detention shall be decided speedily by a court and his release ordered if the detention is not lawful.'

d It is to be noted that art 5(4) is not dealing with bail. In *Zamir v UK* (1983) 40 DR 42 at 59 (para 109) the European Commission of Human Rights said:

'... this right [sc under art 5(4)] must be seen as independent of the possibility of applying to a court for release on bail. In any event the Commission observes that the applicant's solicitor asked the Home Office e that the applicant be released in a letter dated 11 October 1978 and, further, requested that the applicant be admitted to bail in the application for *habeas corpus* ...'

And in *Chahal v UK* (1996) 1 BHRC 405 at 432 (para 127) the European Court of Human Rights said:

f '... it is clear that art 5(4) does not guarantee a right to judicial review of such breadth as to empower the court, on all aspects of the case including questions of pure expediency, to substitute its own discretion for that of the decision-making authority. The review should, however, be wide enough to bear on those conditions which are essential for the "lawful" detention of a g person according to art 5(1) ...'

Paragraph 22(1B) of Sch 2 to the 1971 Act prevents any application for bail being made by a person detained under para 16(1) pending examination unless seven days have elapsed since the date of his arrival in the United Kingdom. Otherwise, the right to apply for bail is unrestricted and art 5(4) is met by the right to apply h for habeas corpus or judicial review of the lawfulness of the detention. And once any examination is concluded (which will normally be on day five) bail can in all cases, at least in theory, be applied for.

[26] The question is whether the detention at Oakington is permitted by art 5(1)(f). The conditions set out in art 5(1) are designed to ensure that there can j be no arbitrary deprivation of liberty and must be given a narrow interpretation (see *Winterwerp v Netherlands* (1979) 2 EHRR 387 at 401 (para 37)). In *NC v Italy* [2001] ECHR 24952/94 (para 41) the European Court of Human Rights stated that it did not suffice that the deprivation of liberty was executed in conformity with national law; it must also be necessary in the circumstances. *Tomasi v France* (1992) 15 EHRR 1 concerned the detention of the applicant for four years and seven months before his eventual acquittal on serious charges. A risk of

absconding was relied on to justify at least part of the detention. The court
pointed out (at 52 (para 98)) that there had been a failure to give reasons why the *a*
risk was decisive and to counter any risk by measures such as lodging securities
or keeping the applicant under court supervision. The court in these cases is
indicating that measures short of detention must be considered and rejected
before detention can be justified even if the conditions in art 5(1) permitting
detention appear to be met. Otherwise, the detention would not be lawful. But *b*
these cases do not necessarily help Mr Saadullell since they were not concerned with
art 5(1)(f), to which different considerations apply, as will become apparent.

[27] The European Convention is of course an international document aimed
at countries with differing systems of law. Thus it cannot be construed like an
English statute even though it is incorporated into domestic law by way of a
schedule to the 1998 Act. But the words have been carefully chosen and effect *c*
must be given to them and to the purpose which dictated their use. Thus it is
clear that art 5(1)(f) is looking at two different stages. The first part is concerned
with the control of those who are seeking to enter a state and the second with
those whom a state is seeking to remove. Thus the reference to the prevention
of an unauthorised entry must in my view cover a person who seeks leave to *d*
remain as well as one who is seeking leave to enter. Equally action may include
the making of investigations to see whether removal should follow.

[28] It is clear from *Chahal*'s case that detention with a view to removal can be
justified under art 5(1)(f) even though there is no danger of absconding. The court
said ((1996) 1 BHRC 405 at 430):

e

'112. The Court recalls that it is not in dispute that Mr Chahal has been
detained "with a view to deportation" within the meaning of art 5(1)(f) …
Article 5(1)(f) does not demand that the detention of a person against whom
action is being taken with a view to deportation be reasonably considered
necessary, for example to prevent his committing an offence of fleeing; in
this respect art 5(1)(f) provides a different level of protection from art 5(1)(c). *f*
Indeed, all that is required under this provision is that "action is being taken
with a view to deportation". It is therefore immaterial, for the purposes of
art 5(1)(f), whether the underlying decision to expel can be justified under
national or convention law. 113. The Court recalls, however, that any
deprivation of liberty under art 5(1)(f) will be justified only for as long as *g*
deportation proceedings are in progress. If such proceedings are not prosecuted
with due diligence, the detention will cease to be permissible under
art 5(1)(f) …'

Mr Chahal had been detained for almost five years. None the less, the court
found that there was no breach of art 5. In R (*on the application of Sezek*) *v Secretary* *h*
of State for the Home Dept [2001] EWCA Civ 795, (2001) Times, 20 June, the Court
of Appeal adopted the same approach. Peter Gibson LJ said (at [13]):

'From the right to liberty and security is expressly excepted the case of a person
against whom action is being taken with a view to deportation. Article 5(1)(f) has
been construed strictly, as the jurisprudence relating to that provision *j*
demonstrates … There is nothing in the convention nor any authority to
support counsel's assertion that Mr Sezek's detention is incompatible with
art 5(1)(f) if other ways of preventing him absconding are available.'

[29] *Amuur v France* (1996) 22 EHRR 533 concerned the first part of art 5(1)(f).
The applicants arrived at Orly airport and claimed asylum. They were held at the

a airport and a nearby hotel, part of which had been converted to be used as a holding area, for 20 days and then, following refusal of leave to enter, removed to Syria, via which they had travelled to France. The court unsurprisingly decided that they had been deprived of liberty and so fell within the protection of art 5 and that the failure to allow access to legal or other advice for 15 days made the deprivation of liberty not compatible with art 5(1). The European Court of b Human Rights said (at 556–557 (para 43)):

'Holding aliens in the international zone does indeed involve a restriction upon liberty, but one which is not in every respect comparable to that which obtains in centres for the detention of aliens pending deportation. Such confinement, accompanied by suitable safeguards for the persons concerned, c is acceptable only in order to enable States to prevent unlawful immigration while complying with their international obligations, particularly under the 1951 Geneva Convention ... and the European Convention on Human Rights. States' legitimate concerns to foil the increasingly frequent attempts to get round immigration restrictions must not deprive asylum seekers of the protection afforded by these Conventions.'
d

[30] It is clear that the detention of a person seeking entry and falling within the first part of art 5(1)(f) must be to prevent that person effecting an unauthorised entry. The language of art 5(1)(f) makes that clear. Thus detention cannot be justified on the ground that it may speed up the process of determination of applications generally and so may assist other applicants. Equally, it is plain that e detention cannot be justified on the basis that it might deter others from seeking to enter by making false claims for asylum. Indeed, Mr Pannick did not seek to suggest that any such policy could be lawful. It would clearly not be lawful. But he does submit that because without a favourable decision on the asylum claim entry cannot be authorised, detention is justified. The investigation will prevent f an unauthorised entry and so detention as part of the process is permissible. I cannot accept that submission. It flies in the face of any sensible reading of art 5(1)(f) and is in my view incompatible with the approach of the court in *Amuur's* case in the passage cited at [29] above. Once it is accepted that an applicant has made a proper application for asylum and there is no risk that he will abscond or otherwise misbehave, it is impossible to see how it could reasonably be said that g he needs to be detained to prevent his effecting an unauthorised entry. He is doing all that he should to ensure that he can make an authorised entry. If his application is refused, further consideration may be given to whether he should be detained under the second part of art 5(1)(f), but the fact that all these claimants were then granted temporary admission underlines the reality that h there was considered to be no danger of any of them effecting an unauthorised entry.

[31] Mr Pannick then submits that they are properly to be regarded as covered by the second part of art 5(1)(f) because they will be removed unless their asylum claims are allowed. A person who arrives and seeks leave to enter cannot properly j be regarded as someone 'against whom action is being taken with a view to deportation' (in this context, deportation merely means removal). Even if action is extended to include investigation, the investigation is to see whether he should be permitted to enter. In any event, it is not compatible with asylum seekers' rights under the Geneva Convention Relating to the Status of Refugees (Geneva, 28 July 1951; TS 39 (1953); Cmnd 9171) (as amended by the 1967 Protocol Relating to the Status of Refugees (New York, 31 January 1967; TS 15 (1969); Cmnd 3906)) to

regard the investigation of claims for asylum in all cases as being action with a
view to deportation. The question is not whether they should be removed but   *a*
whether they should be permitted to enter. Thus there can be no doubt that
Dr Saadi at least did not fall within either part of art 5(1)(f) of the European
Convention.

[32] It is suggested that illegal entrants are in a different position. Whether or
not they are depends on the facts of a particular case. Thus where an illegal *b*
entrant is caught and removal is to be effected, a claim for asylum to stop such
removal cannot prevent the second part of art 5(1)(f) applying. Equally the same
will apply where removal is ordered and that triggers an asylum claim. *Chahal v
UK* was such a case. But it has been recognised that refugees may well be
compelled to obtain entry to a safe country by illegal means and such illegal entry
should not necessarily be held against them. If a person enters by unlawful   *c*
means, for example hidden in a lorry, but does so with a view to claiming asylum,
and claims asylum on arrival or within such time after arrival as is reasonable, he
is not dealt with on the basis that he is to be removed but on the basis that he is
applying to enter. That reflects the factual situation in the cases of Messrs Maged,
Osman and Mohammed. It was never suggested to them that they were to be   *d*
removed or that action was being taken with a view to their removal. The action
being taken was with a view to determining whether they should be allowed to
remain and so to enter. If an illegal entrant only claims asylum when discovered,
the situation may be different and the approach of the Court of Appeal in *R v
Secretary of State for the Home Dept, ex p Khan* [1995] 2 All ER 540 may justify *e*
detention under the second part of art 5(1)(f).

[33] It is wholly artificial to regard the detention as within the second part of
art 5(1)(f). It is not. It is therefore not possible to justify the detention since it
does not fall within art 5(1)(f) and is accordingly unlawful.

[34] That conclusion means that it becomes unnecessary to consider whether *f*
the detention was arbitrary so as to render it not lawful and so not within
art 5(1)(f). However, the matter has been fully argued and, in case these cases go
further, I should deal with the point. If the detention is covered by the second
part of art 5(1)(f), there will be no question of arbitrariness. So much is clear from
Chahal's case and *Sezek*'s case. Action with a view to removal justifies detention
and the only situation in which such detention will be unlawful is if it is for an *g*
unreasonable time or in unreasonable circumstances. Neither consideration applies
to these claims.

[35] Mr Pannick submitted that the same principle must apply to the first part
of art 5(1)(f). Once it is established that the detention is covered by either part of
art 5(1)(f), no more need be established to show that it is lawful. In order to *h*
justify detention under the first part it is necessary to show that it is to prevent the
detainee effecting an unlawful entry. If that is the purpose, it is submitted that it
is unnecessary to determine whether other means short of detention could achieve
that purpose. Under the second part, nothing is to be achieved by the detention;
it is justified by action being taken with a view to removal. But under the first *j*
part the detention is designed to prevent the detainee effecting an unauthorised
entry. This is much closer to art 5(1)(c) and so the approach set out in *Tomasi*'s
case and *Winterwerp*'s case would seem to be more appropriate. When detention
is used to ensure that an individual does or does not do something, it is surely
required that it be established that that result cannot reasonably be achieved by
means other than detention. Otherwise, the detention could properly be said to

a be arbitrary and thus to contravene the fundamental objective of art 5 and the right to liberty.

[36] Thus far I have assumed that *Chahal's* case will apply to the detention if the second part of art 5(1)(f) is applicable. But I am not persuaded that *Chahal's* case does apply. It is in my judgment necessary to identify the reason for the detention. It is clear that it is in order that there should be speedy
b decision-making of a substantial number of applications: that indeed is the evidence from Mr Martin which is before me. The minister said in a news release announcing Oakington's opening:

'Speeding up the asylum process is a major objective in our reform of the asylum system. People who come to the United Kingdom may be fleeing
c terrible persecution and it is important that their claims are dealt with swiftly, so that rather than being stuck in an administrative limbo they are able to get on with rebuilding their lives. Oakington will enable us to deal quickly with the straightforward asylum claims. It is in everyone's interest that both genuine and unfounded asylum seekers are quickly identified.
d Genuine asylum seekers can be given the support they need to integrate with society. And those with unfounded claims can be sent home quickly thereby sending a strong signal to others thinking of trying to exploit our asylum system.'

I certainly (and I suspect most people) would not quarrel with the sentiments
e expressed, although it is perhaps somewhat ironic that none of the claimants can at present be returned to northern Iraq since there is no means of getting them there except via Baghdad and, for obvious reasons, they cannot be returned there. But, desirable though it is that there should be speedy decisions, that cannot necessarily justify detention. Even assuming that either part of art 5(1)(f) applies,
f the reality is that the claimants were not detained because of that but because of the belief that speedy resolution of their applications could not otherwise be achieved.

[37] Accordingly, as it seems to me, it is necessary to show that detention was indeed required to achieve that purpose. That is because it is clear that none of the claimants would have been detained but for the fact that they qualified for the
g Oakington fast-track procedure and had to be detained to enable that procedure to be carried out. They were not detained because they might otherwise effect an unauthorised entry or because action was being taken with a view to their removal from the United Kingdom. While that may be a justification for a finding that art 5(1)(f) applies (and, for the purposes of this part of my judgment,
h I am assuming that it is) it was not the reason for or the immediate cause of the detention. That being so, it is in my view, consistently with the right to liberty enshrined in art 5, necessary to decide whether detention was indeed proportionate. If it was not, it was arbitrary and so not lawful.

[38] I recognise the care which must be exercised before I could consider it
j proper to intervene and the margin of discretion to be allowed to the Secretary of State as the decision-maker. The principles have been helpfully set out in a very recent decision of the Court of Appeal in *R* (*on the application of Samaroo*) *v Secretary of State for the Home Dept, R* (*on the application of Sezek*) *v Secretary of State for the Home Dept* [2001] EWCA Civ 1139, (2001) Times, 18 September. After considering relevant authorities, in particular *R v Secretary of State for the Home Dept, ex p Mahmood* [2001] 2 FCR 63, [2001] 1 WLR 840 and *R v Secretary of State*

for the Home Dept, ex p Daly [2001] UKHL 26, [2001] 3 All ER 433, [2001] AC 532, Dyson LJ said (at [35]):

> 'Accordingly, the function of the court in a case as this is to decide whether the Secretary of State has struck the balance fairly between the conflicting interests of Mr Samaroo's right to respect for his family on the one hand and the prevention of crime and disorder on the other. In reaching its decision, the court must recognise and allow to the Secretary of State a discretionary area of judgment. In considering the particular factors to which the court will have regard in deciding to what extent (if at all) to defer to the opinion of the Secretary of State, I have been assisted by the discussion at para 3.26 (p 75) of *Human Rights Law and Practice* (1999), of which Lord Lester of Herne Hill QC and David Pannick QC are the general editors. They identify the following factors. (a) The nature of the convention right: is the right absolute or (as in the case of art 8) does it require a balance to be struck? The court is less likely to defer to the opinion of the decision-maker in the former case than the latter. (b) The extent to which the issues require consideration of social, economic or political factors. The court will usually accord consideration deference in such cases because it is not expert in the realm of policy-making, nor should it be because it is not democratically elected or accountable. (c) The extent to which the court has special expertise, for example in relation to criminal matters. (d) Where the rights claimed are of especial importance, a "high degree of constitutional protection" will be appropriate. The European Court of Human Rights has recognised as being of especial importance rights to freedom of expression and access to the courts.'

It is necessary to seek a fair balance between the human rights of the individual and the interests of the community at large. Article 5 defines the circumstances in which deprivation of liberty may be permitted with precision. In some cases, things may have happened (e g a conviction by a competent court or action being taken with a view to removal) which justify detention. In such cases, it will be easier to establish that the detention was lawful. In others, detention is to achieve or to prevent something. In such cases, there is a need to show that detention was reasonably required to achieve or to prevent that thing.

[39] I entirely accept that the presence of the applicant, his attendance at interview and his availability both to consult his representative and for any further questioning which may be considered necessary is vital. The system will not otherwise operate successfully. I accept, too, that interviews may frequently for different reasons need to be rescheduled, sometimes at short notice, and so presence at all material times is required. Mr Martin says that only by detention can that be achieved.

[40] The Immigration and Asylum Act 1999 has conferred the powers (now in sub-paras (2A) to (2E) of para 21 of Sch 2 to the Immigration Act 1971) to impose conditions on temporary admission. Conditions are a feature of bail in criminal cases and one such condition may be a condition of residence. So there can be a condition of residence at a true reception centre (rather than the euphemistic and somewhat misleading description of Oakington). There can be a requirement to attend at interview as and when required and a condition that the applicant is available at particular times (for example, during normal working hours). It can be made clear that a failure to co-operate or to abide by the requirements of availability will be likely to result in the rejection of the claim under para 340 of the Immigration Rules. It will be difficult for an appellant in such circumstances to

a persuade an adjudicator or the Immigration Appeal Tribunal that his claim is well-founded if he failed without excuse (for it would be difficult to establish any excuse) to co-operate.

[**41**] It is said that if there were no locks applicants would leave (not because they were going to abscond; they would not be at Oakington if there was a concern that they might abscond). They might then not be available: perhaps they would
b miss the bus or it would be running late. Perhaps their watches might stop. Most applicants would have no resources; they would need none since board and lodging would be provided. It seems to me that in those circumstances they would be unlikely to leave—there would be no incentive to do so. I do not of course suggest that it would be right to require a 24-hour presence: that would be akin to house arrest and might well be regarded as detention. But that is not
c necessary to achieve the objective of the system.

[**42**] Mr Scannell has suggested that in reality detention was decided on because of concerns by those who lived near Oakington that asylum seekers would cause problems if allowed to leave the centre. The local planning authority was consulted in accordance with the system in operation where development by
d government which does not require formal planning permission is concerned. This culminated in a proposed condition in the following terms:

> 'No detainee shall normally be allowed to leave the Centre without the provision of transport or an escort although persons granted temporary admission to the United Kingdom from the Centre will normally be offered
e transport to connect with rail or bus services but may make their own arrangements (Reason: to minimise the risk of prejudicing public order and to allay public concern about the possible effect of significant numbers of strangers without support within the local community).'

This, it appears, was accepted by the Home Office. It is said that it appears to be
f inconsistent with the statement made in October 1999, when the Oakington proposal was being publicised, that: 'In certain circumstances applicants would be able, with prior approval, to leave without escort for specific purposes and periods.' Mr Martin explains that that was intended to deal with such matters as a need for medical attention which could not be provided at the centre. He draws
g attention to an answer to a question in Parliament on 3 April 2000 which makes that point. He categorically denies that a concern that local public opinion would not accept anything other then detention played any part in the decision that detention was needed. In the light of that, I do not think it would be right for me to accept that Mr Scannell's suggestion is correct. Nor should I rely on such public concerns as a reason for finding that detention was proportionate. I should say
h that both counsel accepted that in considering proportionality I was entitled to rely on matters which supported the Home Office view even if not relied on by them, but I should be very slow to do so.

[**43**] I recognise that, as Mr Martin has said, ministers have considered whether a use of the power to impose conditions would have achieved the desired result
j and have decided that it would not. But I have also had put before me extracts from *Hansard*. In a debate on what is now s 4 of the 1999 Act on 2 November 1999, Lord Williams of Mostyn, the government spokesman, said:

> 'I turn now to the second element of the amendment; it is not about the use of detention or the regime proposed at Oakington. The point of the amendment is to give greater flexibility in the use of temporary admission. We would

then be able to develop reception facilities at which those given temporary
admission were required to reside, but were free to come and go during the *a*
day if they wished ... It is not 24-hour detention; it is an intermediate stage
... We want to be able to ensure that applicants remain at the accommodation
overnight—again, I say this without any doubt that it is a proper thing to
say—and to be able to say to them, "We require you to be present at this
designated accommodation at certain times because that is when your *b*
interviews will occur". There is nothing wrong with that. In fact, it is a
sensible way to behave. One must apply proportionality in more than one
way.' (See 606 HL Official Report (5th series) col 736.)

Why should that not be effective to achieve what Oakington sets out to achieve?
Surely measures short of detention should be tried first and detention should be *c*
regarded as the last resort.

[44] I have hesitated long before concluding that the arguments put forward
by Mr Pannick based on Mr Martin's evidence do not persuade me that my view
is wrong. I am satisfied that detention is not proportionate. I have, of course,
considered all the material put before me and I do not find it necessary to extend *d*
this judgment by going into greater detail. Essentially, it boils down to a concern
that applicants would leave the centre if there were no locks and therefore their
presence for interview or questioning could not be guaranteed. Those concerns
seem to me to be based on assumption and speculation rather than on substance.

[45] As I hope will be clear, I am not saying that to detain those who come to
this country seeking asylum is necessarily unlawful. It will be very easy to justify *e*
detention of illegal entrants, particularly those who have shown that they have
single-mindedly set out to get here. Many will have spent what for them and
those who supported them were large sums of money to be assisted by agents,
who are in reality in the main criminals preying on those who, whether for
economic reasons or because they face at worst persecution and at best probably *f*
discrimination and certainly a miserable existence, wish to make a life for
themselves in this country. Their desire to settle here at all costs may be ample
justification for forming the view that if not detained they will effect an
unauthorised entry, particularly, of course, if they are not fleeing persecution and
so are not likely to succeed in establishing that they are refugees. Equally, I am
not saying that no one detained at Oakington is lawfully detained. In the majority *g*
of cases, once the decision is made (often to refuse leave to enter) temporary
admission is granted. But it is envisaged that in some cases detention will
continue and in those, there would have been reason to detain beyond the need
for a speedy decision on their claim for asylum.

[46] What I have decided is that to be lawful detention must be justified for *h*
the individual under art 5(1)(f). Thus the reasons for and the purpose behind a
person's detention are all-important. In these cases, the claimants have not been
detained because they might otherwise effect an unauthorised entry or because
action is being taken to remove them; it is because it is considered necessary to
achieve a speedy decision in the interests of the general administration in relation *j*
to asylum claims. Indeed, the grant of temporary admission on refusal of the
claims at a time when the likelihood of absconding is, one would have thought,
greater shows that concerns that an unauthorised entry might otherwise be
effected cannot have been the reason for detention. The reason for the detention
of each individual is what is important. In these cases, it is to enable there to be
speedy determination of their applications. It is that that renders the detentions

a in these cases unlawful. The same may well apply to many, perhaps most, Oakington cases. But that is because and only because the Home Office has chosen to make it clear that the sole reason why most applicants are detained at Oakington is because of the advantages it provides in ensuring speedy decisions. Otherwise, the applicants would be granted temporary admission and would not be detained.

[47] For the reasons I have given, I am satisfied that the detention of all the
b claimants was not lawful. I will hear counsel on the appropriate relief to be granted.

Applications allowed. Permission to appeal granted.

James Wilson   Barrister (NZ).
c

Appeal

The Secretary of State appealed. Permission was given to Liberty, Justice and the Aire Centre to intervene by way of written submissions.

d Lord Goldsmith QC A-G, David Pannick QC and Michael Fordham (instructed by the Treasury Solicitor) for the Secretary of State.
Rick Scannell and Duran Seddon (instructed by Wilson & Co) for the claimants.

Cur adv vult

e 19 October 2001. The following judgment of the court was delivered.

LORD PHILLIPS OF WORTH MATRAVERS MR.

[1] On 7 September Collins J, sitting in the Administrative Court, gave judgment in favour of four Kurds who had come to this country to seek asylum. They had
f been detained for a period not exceeding ten days in Oakington Reception Centre. Collins J held that this detention was unlawful because it violated the right to liberty enshrined in art 5 of the European Convention for the Protection of Human Rights and Fundamental Freedoms (Rome, 4 November 1950; TS 71 (1953); Cmd 8969) (as set out in Sch 1 to the Human Rights Act 1998) (the European Convention). If he is correct a cornerstone of the government's
g current procedure for processing applications for asylum is removed. The Secretary of State appeals against that decision. The appeal raises an issue of principle of importance not only in this jurisdiction, but in other states who are signatories to the European Convention and who are having to cope with an unprecedented flood of asylum seekers. We have allowed to intervene, by way
h of a joint written submission, Liberty, Justice and the Aire Centre.

[2] Collins J's judgment sets out the background facts with admirable clarity and relieves us of the need to attempt to duplicate that exercise.

[3] Over recent years applications for asylum to this and other countries have been escalating. Here the average monthly number of applications from July to
j September 1999 was nearly 7,000. This was 60% higher than the figure for the previous year. This appeal involves claimants from Iraq. In relation to that country, claims in 1997 averaged 90 per month, in 1998, 110 per month, in 1999, 150 per month and, in the first months of 2000, 280 per month. There are a number of reasons for this. Internal conflicts carrying with them well-founded fears of persecution for minorities are unhappily prevalent in a number of states. At the same time conflicts between states, harsh treatment falling short of persecution, and the

marked disparity in living conditions, standards of living and social benefits in different countries have led many to seek to emigrate as refugees when their *a* plight, though often miserable, is not such as to entitle them to refugee status.

[4] Coping with the huge number of asylum seekers poses heavy administrative problems. It is desirable that those who are entitled to asylum should have their status recognised as quickly as possible, so that they can enjoy the benefits that we accord to refugees. It is current government policy that those who are not *b* entitled to asylum should be removed, unless there are special circumstances which make it appropriate to grant them exceptional leave to remain. Again it is desirable that the status of these be determined as quickly as possible. To this end the government has sought to introduce a fast-track procedure which involves the detention of some applicants for a period of about a week in order to ensure speedy and efficient processing of their applications. It is the legality of that *c* procedure which is in issue. The claimants contend that it is contrary to our domestic law, as it was before the 1998 Act incorporated the European Convention. They further contend that it violates the convention. Collins J rejected the former submission but upheld the latter. Both are advanced before us.

[5] It is artificial, but convenient, to consider English domestic law and the *d* European Convention separately. Collins J adopted that course, and we propose to do the same. We shall start, as did he, with domestic law. The power of the executive to detain immigrants has long been governed by statute. At the time that both the European Convention and the Geneva Convention Relating to the Status of Refugees (Geneva, 28 July 1951; TS 39 (1953); Cmnd 9171) (as amended *e* by the 1967 Protocol Relating to the Status of Refugees (New York, 31 January 1967; TS 15 (1969); Cmnd 3906)) were agreed, the detention of aliens was governed by the Aliens Order 1920, SR & O 1920/448, made under the Aliens Restriction Acts 1914 and 1919. Aliens landing without leave were liable to be detained until removed (see 1 *Halsbury's Laws* (3rd edn) para 992). These statutory provisions were replaced by the Immigration Act 1971. Collins J has set out the *f* provisions of that Act which authorise detention of a person pending a decision to give or refuse him leave to enter, or alternatively the grant of temporary admission (see Collins J's judgment at [2]). The power to grant temporary admission only exists in relation to a person who is liable to be detained. Thus, as a matter of statutory interpretation the power to detain persists up to the time that the *g* decision to grant or refuse leave to enter is taken.

[6] As an alternative to temporary admission, bail may be granted to a person detained. The application for bail is made to an immigration officer or adjudicator, and the grant of bail is an administrative, not judicial act. Bail cannot be granted to a person detained pending examination unless seven days have elapsed since *h* the arrival of that person in the United Kingdom.

[7] Having regard to the statutory provisions considered above, there can be no doubt that the detention of the claimants at Oakington for a maximum of ten days fell within the express statutory powers of the immigration officers. That is not, of course, the end of the matter. Express statutory powers can be limited by *j* implication. The lawful exercise of those powers can also be restricted, according to established principles of public law, by government policy and the legitimate expectation to which such policy gives rise. The issue in relation to domestic law is whether the detention of the claimants infringed any such implicit restriction.

[8] The power to detain conferred by para 16(1) of Sch 2 to the 1971 Act is expressed to be 'pending his examination and pending a decision to give or refuse

a him leave to enter'. Read literally, the only limit on the power is a temporal one. It persists until the decision is taken to give or refuse leave to enter.

[9] For the claimants, Mr Scannell argued that the purpose for which the power was given was the conduct of the examination of the asylum seeker. He further argued that detention was only authorised in as much as it was necessary to achieve that purpose. Where an applicant was prepared voluntarily to submit to

b examination there was no necessity and thus no power to detain. Detention would be justified where, for instance, there were reasonable grounds for apprehending that the applicant might abscond.

[10] Collins J did not accept this argument. He held that the purpose was clearly set out in para 16(1), and that, in particular, para 16(1) enabled a person to be detained 'pending a decision to give or refuse him leave to enter'. We agree.

c The wording of the paragraph is clear. It empowers detention not for the purpose of examination or for the purpose of deciding whether to give or refuse leave to enter, but 'pending' those events. The purpose of the power to detain is simply to prevent a person entering without leave.

[11] Mr Scannell argued that this could be achieved by the grant of temporary

d admission. Under s 11 of the 1971 Act, temporary admission is deemed not to constitute entry. Mr Scannell submitted that where there was no risk that an applicant would not co-operate with the immigration authorities, he could not properly be detained but had to be granted temporary admission.

[12] As a matter of statutory interpretation, this contention is manifestly unsound.

e It amounts to contending that there is no power to detain where temporary admission can be granted. Yet the power to grant temporary admission only exists in relation to a person who is 'liable to be detained'.

[13] It does not follow that there is no implied limitation on the power to detain pending examination and the decision whether or not to grant leave to enter.

f A similar power to detain is conferred on the Secretary of State 'pending the making of a deportation order' (see para 2(2) of Sch 3 to the 1971 Act). In *R v Governor of Durham Prison, ex p Singh* [1984] 1 All ER 983 at 985, [1984] 1 WLR 704 at 706 Woolf J held that although this power was not subject to any express limitation of time it was impliedly limited to such period as was reasonably necessary to enable the machinery of deportation to be carried out. As Collins J

g recorded, this principle was approved by the Privy Council in *Tan Te Lam v Superintendent of Tai A Chau Detention Centre* [1996] 4 All ER 256, [1997] AC 97.

[14] Collins J concluded that the only limitation on the power to detain pending examination and the decision whether to grant or refuse leave to enter is that the detention must be for a reasonable time. For the Secretary of State, the

h Attorney General supported this conclusion. He argued that the power to detain persisted for so long as was reasonably necessary to conduct the examination and to reach a decision whether or not to grant leave to enter. As a matter of statutory interpretation we accept this submission. Were it not correct, the power to grant temporary admission would also be liable to come to an end before an examination

j could reasonably be completed and a decision whether to grant or refuse leave to enter reasonably be taken.

[15] We are not aware that it has ever been the policy of the Secretary of State that applicants for leave to enter should be detained pending the decision of their applications, however long that might take. A more liberal policy has been adopted whereby he has approved the exercise of the power to grant temporary admission in place of detention. If the basis upon which immigration officers are

detaining asylum seekers at Oakington is in conflict with this policy, then, under
established principles of public law, they are acting unlawfully.   *a*

[16] Collins J has set out in his judgment details of the Home Office policy on
detention set out in the 1998 White Paper entitled *Fairer, Faster and Firmer—A
Modern Approach to Immigration and Asylum* (Cm 4018). Under that White Paper
the Home Office adopted as a matter of policy principles that Mr Scannell has
unsuccessfully contended they were bound to apply as a matter of law. Initial   *b*
detention would last no longer than was necessary to clarify a person's identity and
the nature of their claim. Thereafter they would be granted temporary admission
unless there was reason to believe that they would not comply with the terms of
that admission.

[17] Had this policy persisted, the claimants would have had an unanswerable
claim. Home Office policy changed, however, on 16 March 2000. On that day   *c*
the minister, Mrs Barbara Roche, announced a new and additional criterion for
detention. A detention facility would be provided at Oakington. Detention
would enable the examination of applicants for asylum and the decision whether
or not to grant them this to proceed with much greater expedition. Detention at
Oakington would be restricted to about seven days. Asylum applicants would be   *d*
selected for detention at Oakington only where it seemed likely that it would be
possible to reach a decision on their applications within that period. If this proved
a false hope, they would be given temporary admission or, if necessary, removed
for detention elsewhere in accordance with existing criteria.

[18] There was much debate before Collins J and before us as to whether it
was necessary to detain applicants in order to achieve the expedition that was the   *e*
object of the new policy. Mr Scannell sought to make out a case that this was not
even the Secretary of State's motive for the detention. Rather, he submitted, it
was to assuage concerns of those living in the vicinity of Oakington at the prospect
of large numbers of asylum seekers wandering around the locality, concerns that
might have resulted in effective opposition to the grant of planning permission   *f*
for the centre.

[19] This suggestion was categorically denied by Mr Ian Martin, an inspector
in the Immigration and Nationality Directorate in the Home Office and Oakington
Project Manager, who submitted no less than four statements on behalf of the
Secretary of State. Having considered the evidence Collins J dismissed the allegation
that the Secretary of State's decision to detain applicants at Oakington was   *g*
attributable to this ulterior motive. We consider that he was right to do so.

[20] It is the case for the Secretary of State that detention at Oakington is necessary
if the expedition of processing asylum claims that will result in resolving them
within a week is to be achieved. The question arises as to whether this case is
made out. Collins J did not consider that this question was relevant when considering   *h*
whether detention fell within the powers conferred by the 1971 Act, putting any
question of the 1998 Act on one side. He held that the detention fell within those
powers because it was 'pending' the decision of whether or not to grant leave to
enter and it could not be argued that seven to ten days was an excessive period
to consider an application for asylum. As to this last point we agree. In this context it   *j*
is particularly significant that para 22(1B) of Sch 2 to the 1971 Act expressly provides
that bail cannot be granted to a person detained pending examination unless seven
days have elapsed since the arrival of that person in the United Kingdom.

[21] Collins J considered whether it was necessary to detain applicants in
order to consider their applications with the desired expedition in the context of
the test of proportionality under the 1998 Act. He expressed scepticism about the

a Secretary of State's case. He suggested that stringent conditions of residence, albeit falling short of a 24-hour presence, might well suffice and that applicants would have no incentive to leave the premises and would be unlikely to do so. He described concerns expressed by Mr Martin as 'based on assumption and speculation rather than on substance'.

b [22] At the end of the day, Collins J did not have to decide the issue because he held that detention for the sole purpose of effecting a speedy determination of applications was not permitted by art 5(1)(f) of the European Convention and was therefore an unlawful infringement of liberty under art 5. None the less he expressed the view that, if art 5(1)(f) applied, the detention was disproportionate.

c [23] We have yet to consider the effect of the European Convention, but we are not persuaded that the question of whether it is necessary to detain asylum seekers in order to process them speedily is irrelevant from the viewpoint of domestic law. If the policy reason for detention is that this is necessary in order to effect speedy processing of applications for asylum and, in fact, it is not necessary for this purpose, then the decision to detain may be open to attack on the ground of irrationality.

d [24] The Attorney General drew attention to lengthy sections of two of Mr Martin's statements dealing with this issue. We quote some relatively short extracts from these:

e 'The view of the Home Office is as follows: that blanket restrictions would not be as effective to ensure that applicants would remain at Oakington; that the reality is that individuals would leave the premises if not formally detained; and that this would indeed undermine the speed and effectiveness of the process which are its very objective. There is a difference between, on the one hand, directing applicants to stay at Oakington and not to leave and, on the other hand, taking measures to prevent them from doing so. In the view of the Home Office, in order to achieve the purpose of ensuring that applicants remain at Oakington, it is necessary to take steps to prevent them from leaving ... If applicants absented themselves, even temporarily, this would present substantial difficulties for the processing of cases. It would affect the absent applicants' own cases. It would stand also to have a detrimental knock-on effect on the efficient operation of the decision making process for others ... These are not easy questions and a balance has to be struck. In introducing the Oakington regime the Home Office was of the clear view that the presence of applicants on site at all times was necessary for the proper and effective working of the fast-track regime. I would add from experience that in my view the applicants' continued presence on site does indeed play a vital part in achieving the objectives for which Oakington was introduced ... Careful thought has been given, and is given on an ongoing basis, as to how to make the detention as short as possible while achieving the objectives of substantive decision-making within seven to ten days. The Secretary of State's view is that it is necessary for the applicant to be available on site beyond day three.'

[25] The Attorney General submitted that the court should accept this evidence as demonstrating that detention is reasonably necessary to achieve the expedition for which the Secretary of State is aiming. He further submitted that it is the Secretary of State who has responsibility for the arduous task of handling the thousands of immigrants seeking asylum in this country and that it is for the Secretary of State and

not the court to decide what measures are necessary. The Secretary of State and his officials have experience which the court does not enjoy.

[26] We share the doubts expressed by Collins J as to whether detention is really necessary to ensure effective and speedy processing of asylum applications. But in expressing these doubts we are conscious that we are doing that for which Collins J criticised Mr Martin. We are indulging in assumption and speculation. It is not in doubt that, if asylum applications are to be processed within the space of seven days, the applicants are necessarily going to have to be subjected to severe restraints on their liberty. In one way or another they will be required to be present in a centre at all times when they may be needed for interviews, which it is impossible to schedule to a pre-determined timetable. Would applicants voluntarily submit to such a regime, if not detained? Many no doubt would, but it is impossible to condemn as irrational the policy of subjecting those asylum seekers whose applications appear susceptible to rapid resolution to a short period of detention designed to ensure that the regime operates without dislocation.

[27] This is not a conclusion that we have reached easily. Asylum seekers are detained at Oakington only if it seems likely that their applications can be resolved within a week. But they must also be persons who are not expected to attempt to abscond or otherwise misbehave. At first blush it seems extreme to detain those who are unlikely to run away simply to make it easier to process their claims. But the statistics that we have set out at the start of our judgment cannot be ignored. As Lord Williams of Mostyn observed in debate in the House of Lords on 2 November 1999, faced with applications for asylum at the rate of nearly 7,000 per month, 'no responsible government can simply shrug their shoulders and do nothing' (see 606 HL Official Report (5th series) col 733). A short period of detention is not an unreasonable price to pay in order to ensure the speedy resolution of the claims of a substantial proportion of this influx. In the circumstances such detention can properly be described as a measure of last resort.

[28] In this context we would emphasise one further point. The Attorney General pointed out not merely that detention was for a short period but that it was in conditions appropriate for asylum seekers as opposed, for example, to convicted prisoners. This point seems to us to be of some importance in identifying what is really at issue in this case. The circumstances at Oakington involve a degree of deprivation, but it is the fact of detention to which objection is made rather than the living conditions in the centre. Mr Scannell accepts that if temporary admission had been granted, it would have been appropriate to make this subject to stringent conditions as to residence. The regime that such conditions would have involved would not have differed greatly from that at Oakington, save that applicants would not have been physically prevented from leaving the premises. The issue is whether the additional element of detention can lawfully be imposed. We have concluded that under domestic law it can.

[29] Mr Scannell had a further objection to the practice of detaining applicants at Oakington. He contended that it was arbitrary, because Oakington is not large enough to contain all who would satisfy the criteria for admission to it. Whether an applicant is sent to Oakington or not is thus, to a degree, a matter of chance. Collins J rejected this submission, and so do we. The criteria governing the selection of those who are sent to Oakington are clear and rational. We agree with the judge that the fact that there is limited room at Oakington, so that not

a   all who would qualify to go there can be accommodated, does not result in arbitrariness.

[**30**] For these reasons we agree with the conclusion of Collins J that the detention of the claimants fell within the power conferred on immigration officers by the 1971 Act and that, considered solely from the viewpoint of domestic legislation, the policy of the Secretary of State was lawful. As Collins J observed, the critical

b   issue is whether the 1998 Act renders it unlawful.

[**31**] The human right in play in these proceedings is the right to liberty. Article 5 of the European Convention provides: '1. Everyone has the right to liberty and security of person. No one shall be deprived of his liberty save in the following cases and in accordance with a procedure prescribed by law ...' There follows a list of exceptions to the right to liberty. These include: '... (f) the lawful

c   arrest or detention of a person to prevent his effecting an unauthorised entry into the country or of a person against whom action is being taken with a view to deportation or extradition.'

[**32**] At the heart of this part of the appeal is an issue as to what is meant by 'unauthorised entry'. The case of the Secretary of State is simple. Unauthorised

d   entry is an entry which has not been authorised. Under international law, every state has the right to decide who may enter its territory. When an alien sets foot on the territory of a state, that state can do two things. It can authorise entry, with or without restrictions, or it can refuse entry. Unless and until it authorises entry, the alien will, if he or she moves within the territory, be effecting unauthorised entry.

e   Article 5(1)(f) recognises the right of a state to prevent this by detaining the person seeking to enter.

[**33**] Collins J rejected this submission. He held:

'Once it is accepted that an applicant has made a proper application for asylum and there is no risk that he will abscond or otherwise misbehave, it is

f   impossible to see how it could reasonably be said that he needs to be detained to prevent his effecting an unauthorised entry. He is doing all that he should to ensure that he can make an authorised entry.' (See Collins J's judgment at [30].)

g   [**34**] Mr Scannell submitted that this analysis was correct. We put to him that this meant that art 5 required a state to grant temporary admission into its territory to any applicant for asylum who is not expected to abscond or otherwise misbehave for as long as is necessary to resolve that person's application for asylum. After reflecting, he agreed with this and reduced his submissions on the point to writing. He did so in the context of our domestic legislation.

h

'There can be no dispute but that both "leave" (s 4 of the 1971 Act) and "temporary admission" are forms of lawful authority for a person who is subject to immigration control to be present in the United Kingdom. This provides the inevitable and necessary context in which to examine the

j   meaning of art 5(1)(f) in these cases. There can therefore be no question that the grant of leave or the grant of temporary admission constitute an "unauthorised entry" simply because they are both "authorised". The grant of temporary admission is a form of "entry" within the meaning of art 5(1)(f). Seen as such, in respect of asylum seekers who will not "abscond or otherwise misbehave", there is indeed an obligation upon the Secretary of

State to grant such temporary admission since it cannot be said that detention will be "to prevent his effecting an unauthorised entry".'

[35] The conclusions that the intervenors invited us to draw were to similar effect:

'7.2 Where a foreigner exercises the international humanitarian right to seek asylum and does so in compliance with national law provisions for claims to enter the territory, he or she is not seeking unauthorised entry, and should not in principle and without more be subject to a deprivation of liberty. While a restriction of liberty may be appropriate in such cases, a deprivation should be reserved only for cases where there is evidence of absconding or of non-co-operation with determination procedures. Detention must be a rational response to the facts of the case rather than born out of administrative convenience. On ordinary principles and consistently with the case law of the European Court of Human Rights, the permissible limbs for detention under art 5(1)(f) must be narrowly construed. 7.3 Thus there must be a rational connection between the detention and the enumerated limbs under art 5(1)(f). Where an asylum seeker makes a claim in compliance with national law procedures for entry, he or she is not to be regarded as unlawfully present nor as seeking unauthorised entry, and detention thus cannot prevent that which in law is not being sought. Detention cannot be permitted under the first limb.'

[36] The European Convention is a living instrument and when interpreting it and considering the Strasbourg jurisprudence, it is necessary to bear in mind that its effect may change in step with changes in the standards applied by the member states. As a starting point, however, it seems to us sensible to consider the position in 1951, when the convention was agreed. In agreeing to art 5, were member states binding themselves to grant to aliens a licence to enter their territories and to enjoy liberty, albeit subject to some restrictions, within them, pending the determination of applications for a more formal authority to enter? We do not believe that they were. The right of a state to determine whether aliens should enter its territory was a firmly entrenched principle of public international law.

[37] In *A-G for Canada v Cain, A-G for Canada v Gilhula* [1906] AC 542 at 546, [1904–7] All ER Rep 582 at 584–585, Lord Atkinson, when giving the decision of the Privy Council, said:

'One of the rights possessed by the supreme power in every State is the right to refuse to permit an alien to enter that State, to annex what conditions it pleases to the permission to enter it, and to expel or deport from the State, at pleasure, even a friendly alien, especially if it considers his presence in the State opposed to its peace, order, and good government, or to its social or material interests: Vattel, *Law of Nations*, book 1, s. 231; book 2, s. 125.'

[38] The eighth edition of *Oppenheim's International Law*, published in 1955, vol 1, pp 675–676 (para 314), stated: 'The reception of aliens is a matter of discretion, and every State is by reason of its territorial supremacy competent to exclude aliens from the whole, or any part, of its territory.'

[39] We have no reason to believe that the signatories to the European Convention intended to make inroads into that discretion for those awaiting a decision on an application for leave to enter. The problem of what to do about large numbers of asylum seekers, some of whose applications require many months

a to process, was not a live one at the time. We were told by counsel that even at the time that the 1971 Act was passed, applications for asylum were running at the rate of only around 200 a year, and it is significant that that Act makes no express reference to applicants for asylum. The same edition of *Oppenheim* comments (p 677 (para 316)):

b   'Now the so-called right of asylum is certainly not a right possessed by the alien to demand that the State into whose territory he has entered with the intention of escaping prosecution in some other State should grant protection and asylum. For such State need not grant such demands. The Constitutions of a number of countries expressly grant the right of asylum to persons persecuted for political reasons, but it cannot yet be said that such a *c*   right has become a "general principle of law" recognised by civilised States and as such forming part of International Law.'

[40] Our conclusion is that the exception to the right to liberty in art 5(1)(f) was intended to preserve the right of the member states to decide whether to allow aliens to enter their territories on any terms whatsoever. Article 5(1)(f) *d* carried, initially at least, the meaning for which the Secretary of State contends.

[41] In *Abdulaziz v UK* (1985) 7 EHRR 471 at 497 (para 67) the European Court of Human Rights observed:

'Moreover, the court cannot ignore that the present case is concerned not only with family life but also with immigration and that, as a matter of well-established international law and subject to its treaty obligations, a State *e*   has the right to control the entry of non-nationals into its territory.'

[42] In the field of immigration, the court gives considerable weight to the right of states to control immigration. It has, however, on occasion held that this right is subordinated to the right to family life.

f   [43] It is possible that the approach of the court to the position of asylum applicants has changed over the years as more states have agreed to recognise the right to asylum and the volume of asylum seekers has grown. So far as general principles of international law are concerned the position has not changed. The current edition of 18(2) *Halsbury's Laws* (4th edition reissue), reissued in 2000, states in paras 983 and 984: 'In customary international law a state is free to refuse *g* the admission of aliens to its territory, or to annex whatever conditions it pleases to their entry ... a state may expel an alien from its territory at its discretion.'

[44] Turning more specifically to asylum seekers, in the second edition of Goodwin-Gill on *The Refugee in International Law* (1996) p 250, the author refers to a plenary session of the Executive Committee of the United Nations Committee *h* on Human Rights in 1986 which recognised that:

'... if necessary, detention may be resorted to only on grounds prescribed by law to verify identity; to determine the elements on which the claim to refugee status or asylum is based; to deal with cases where refugees or asylum seekers have destroyed their travel and / or identity documents or have used fraudulent *j*   documents in order to mislead the authorities of the State in which they intend to claim asylum; or to protect national security or public order.'

[45] The intervenors referred us to Communication no 560/1993 of the United Nations Human Rights Committee, *A v Australia* (1997) 4 BHRC 210, expressing views under art 5(4) of the Optional Protocol of the International Covenant on Civil and Political Rights (New York, 16 December 1966; TS 6

(1977); Cmnd 6702) in relation to the detention of boat people by Australia. In relation to the issue of whether detention was arbitrary under the covenant, the committee commented (at 229):

> '9.2. … that the notion of "arbitrariness" must not be equated with "against the law" but be interpreted more broadly to include such elements as inappropriateness and injustice. Furthermore, remand in custody could be considered arbitrary if it is not necessary in all the circumstances of the case, for example to prevent flight or interference with evidence: the element of proportionality becomes relevant in this context. The state party however, seeks to justify the author's detention by the fact that he entered Australia unlawfully and by the perceived incentive for the applicant to abscond if left in liberty. The question for the Committee is whether these grounds are sufficient to justify indefinite and prolonged detention. 9.3. The Committee agrees that there is no basis for the author's claim that it is per se arbitrary to detain individuals requesting asylum. Nor can it find any support for the contention that there is a rule of customary international law which would render all such detention arbitrary. 9.4. The Committee observes however, that every decision to keep a person in detention should be open to review periodically so that the grounds justifying the detention can be assessed. In any event, detention should not continue beyond the period for which the state can provide appropriate justification. For example, the fact of illegal entry may indicate a need for investigation and there may be other factors particular to the individuals, such as the likelihood of absconding and lack of co-operation, which may justify detention for a period. Without such factors detention may be considered arbitrary, even if entry was illegal.'

[46] The intervenors also placed before us some information, hastily obtained, of the way asylum seekers are treated in certain Western European countries. While these demonstrated the use of reception centres, and restrictions on freedom of movement, they did not evidence a practice of detaining asylum seekers. The Attorney General told us that the adequacy of this information was in issue as his instructions were that at least some Western European countries did detain asylum seekers.

[47] Having regard to the various matters referred to above, it would have been possible for the European Court of Human Rights to restrict the ambit of the operation of art 5(1)(f) of the European Convention, in so far as it considered that its terms permitted the court to do so. We turn to the jurisprudence to see to what extent it supports the claimants' contention that the right to detain recognised by art 5(1)(f) does not now apply to aliens seeking leave to enter, provided always that they demonstrate that they will comply with such lesser restrictions as may be placed upon them by the immigration authorities. That jurisprudence is sparse. There are two important decisions; the Secretary of State relied on one and the claimants on the other.

[48] In *Chahal v UK* (1996) 1 BHRC 405 Mr Chahal alleged that a number of articles of the European Convention had been violated, including art 5(1). He was a Sikh separatist leader whom the Home Secretary was seeking to deport on the ground that he was a threat to national security. Deportation proceedings were protracted over a period of some five years. During the whole of this period Mr Chahal was held in detention. One of the issues before the court was whether this deprivation of liberty was permitted under the terms of art 5(1)(f).

a   [49] In giving its opinion the European Commission of Human Rights ((1995) 23 EHRR 413 at 447 (para 119)) made the following statement of principle:

> '... the Commission considers that, in principle, the first applicant has been lawfully detained under Article 5(1)(f) of the Convention as a "person against whom action is being taken with a view to deportation". It would be unduly
b
> narrow to interpret Article 5(1)(f) as confined to cases where the person is detained solely to enable the deportation order to be implemented. The words of the provision are broad enough to cover the case where the person is originally detained with a view to deportation, but challenges that decision or claims asylum, and continues to be detained pending determination of that challenge or claim. The first applicant was detained with a view to
c
> deportation in August 1990. The deportation order was made in July 1991. The applicant continues to be detained for the purpose of giving effect to that order. The fact that implementation of the decision to deport was suspended while the Secretary of State considered the asylum request and reconsidered the request after the judicial review proceedings, does not affect the purpose or lawfulness of the detention.'
d

[50] The commission went on to conclude that the detention was not justified under art 5(1)(f) because the deportation proceedings had not been pursued, as they should have been, with due expedition.

[51] The European Court of Human Rights did not agree with this conclusion.
e   Before considering the facts, it also made observations of principle which are important in the present context ((1996) 1 BHRC 405 at 430):

> '112. The Court recalls that it is not in dispute that Mr Chahal has been detained "with a view to deportation" within the meaning of art 5(1)(f) ... Article 5(1)(f) does not demand that the detention of a person against whom
f
> action is being taken with a view to deportation be reasonably considered necessary, for example to prevent his committing an offence or fleeing; in this respect art 5(1)(f) provides a different level of protection from art 5(1)(c). Indeed, all that is required under this provision is that "action is being taken with a view to deportation". It is therefore immaterial, for the purposes of art 5(1)(f), whether the underlying decision to expel can be justified under
g
> national or convention law. 113. The Court recalls, however, that any deprivation of liberty under art 5(1)(f) will be justified only for as long as deportation proceedings are in progress. If such proceedings are not prosecuted with due diligence, the detention will cease to be permissible under art 5(1)(f).'

h   [52] The court, after considering the facts, concluded that the domestic procedures had been conducted with due diligence. It went on to observe, however (at 431):

> '118. It also falls to the Court to examine whether Mr Chahal's detention was "lawful" for the purposes of art 5(1)(f), with particular reference to the
j
> safeguards provided by the national system. Where the "lawfulness" of detention is in issue, including the question whether "a procedure prescribed by law" has been followed, the convention refers essentially to the obligation to conform to the substantive and procedural rules of national law, but it requires in addition that any deprivation of liberty should be in keeping with the purpose of art 5, namely to protect the individual from arbitrariness. 119. There is no doubt that Mr Chahal's detention was lawful under

national law and was effected "in accordance with a procedure prescribed by law" ... However, in view of the extremely long period during which *a* Mr Chahal has been detained, it is also necessary to consider whether there existed sufficient guarantees against arbitrariness.'

[53] The court went on to consider evidence relating to the question of whether Mr Chahal was, indeed, a risk to national security and concluded that (at 432 *h* (para 122)):

'... there were at least prima facie grounds for believing that if Mr Chahal were at liberty, national security would be put at risk and thus, that the Executive had not acted arbitrarily when it ordered him to be kept in detention.'

c

[54] We would make the following observations about this decision. First, it is inconsistent with any contention that the justification for detaining a person with a view to deportation is that this is necessary to prevent absconding or other misbehaviour. Secondly, it demonstrates that detention with a view to deportation can only be justified if the deportation proceedings are pursued with due *d* diligence. Thirdly, it suggests that, even where deportation proceedings are proceeding with due diligence, if they continue for an exceptional length of time some justification for detention needs to be advanced if the detention is not to constitute arbitrary treatment.

[55] *Chahal's* case involved consideration of the second limb of art 5(1)(f)—detention with a view to deportation. It was referred to by the commission in *Ali v* *e* *Switzerland* (1998) 28 EHRR 304 at 310 (para 39) to support the proposition that:

'The Commission recalls that Article 5(1) of the Convention requires only that "action is being taken with a view to deportation". It is therefore immaterial, for the purposes of Article 5(1)(f), whether the underlying decision to expel can be justified under national or Convention law.'   *f*

[56] In that case the deportation order that had been made could not be enforced and the commission decided that in those circumstances detention could not be considered to be of a person 'against whom action is being taken with a view to deportation'.

[57] The Attorney General argued that a general principle was to be derived *g* from *Chahal's* case that was applicable to the whole of art 5(1)(f). This was that detention did not have to be *necessary* for the particular process that was in train, whether this was consideration of an application for leave to enter or deportation. Provided that the process was being pursued with due diligence and was not proving unduly protracted, detention could be justified. He argued that it would *h* be quite extraordinary if detention could be justified where a deportation order was made before an application was made for asylum, but not where the deportation order would follow as a matter of course if the asylum application failed.

[58] Mr Scannell argued that a different approach applied where applicants *j* had asked for asylum against whom there was no order for deportation. That approach he suggested was demonstrated by the decision in *Amuur v France* (1996) 22 EHRR 533. In that case, asylum seekers from Somalia were held in the international zone of Paris–Orly airport and a nearby hotel for 20 days. No impediment was placed in the way of their leaving the country, but they did not do so and were finally deported to Syria, having been refused leave to enter

France. The restraints to which they were subjected were contrary to French
domestic law. France was thus not in a position to contend that this was 'lawful'
detention under art 5(1)(f) of the European Convention. France argued, however,
that because the applicants were free to leave the country, they had not been
deprived of their liberty.

[59] The court concluded (at 558 (para 49)) that 'holding the applicants in
the transit zone of Paris–Orly Airport was equivalent in practice, in view of the
restrictions suffered, to a deprivation of liberty. Article 5(1) is therefore applicable
to the case'.

[60] The restrictions referred to included being placed under strict and constant
police surveillance, having no legal and social assistance—particularly with a
view to completing the formalities relating to an application for political refugee
status—and no court review of the length of or necessity for their confinement.

[61] In the course of considering whether the applicants had experienced
deprivation of liberty, the court said (at 556–557):

> '42. … In order to determine whether someone has been "deprived of his
> liberty" within the meaning of Article 5, the starting point must be his
> concrete situation, and account must be taken of the whole range of criteria
> such as the type, duration, effects and manner of implementation of the
> measure in question. The difference between deprivation of and restriction
> upon liberty is merely one of degree or intensity, and not one of nature or
> substance. 43. Holding aliens in the international zone does indeed involve
> a restriction upon liberty, but one which is not in every respect comparable
> to that which obtains in centres for the detention of aliens pending
> deportation. Such confinement, accompanied by suitable safeguards for the
> persons concerned, is acceptable only in order to enable States to prevent
> unlawful immigration while complying with their international obligations,
> particularly under the 1951 Geneva Convention Relating to the Status of
> Refugees and the European Convention on Human Rights. States' legitimate
> concern to foil the increasingly frequent attempts to get round immigration
> restrictions must not deprive asylum seekers of the protection afforded by
> these Conventions. Such holding should not be prolonged excessively,
> otherwise there would be a risk of it turning a mere restriction on liberty—
> inevitable with a view to organising the practical details of the alien's
> repatriation or, where he has requested asylum, while his application for
> leave to enter the territory for that purpose is considered—into a deprivation
> of liberty. In that connection account should be taken of the fact that the
> measure is applicable not to those who have committed criminal offences
> but to aliens who, often fearing for their lives, have fled from their own
> country. Although by the force of circumstances the decision to order holding
> must necessarily be taken by the administrative or police authorities, its
> prolongation requires speedy review by the courts, the traditional guardians
> of personal liberties. Above all, such confinement must not deprive the
> asylum seeker of the right to gain effective access to the procedure for
> determining refugee status.'

[62] Mr Scannell's submissions, and indeed the conclusion of Collins J, turn
largely on this passage. Mr Scannell submitted that the court were equating
'unauthorised entry' in art 5(1)(f) with 'unlawful immigration' and that 'unlawful
immigration' was equivalent to 'getting round immigration restrictions'. Thus,

an applicant who was prepared to abide by any restrictions imposed by the immigration authorities could not lawfully be detained pursuant to art 5(1)(f). a

[63] It is not appropriate to treat a passage in a judgment of the European Court of Human Rights as if it were a statutory provision and to resort to minute textual analysis for this purpose. At the same time, it is not easy to derive general principles from a passage that we have found far from clear.

[64] The court is expressly comparing 'mere restriction on liberty', which does b not infringe art 5, with 'deprivation of liberty', which does. Yet the examples of what constitutes 'mere restriction of liberty' look very like 'lawful detention to prevent unauthorised entry, or while action is being taken with a view to deportation', which is permitted by art 5(1)(f). It seems to us that the court contemplates that it will be lawful to confine aliens in a centre of detention c pending deportation or in an international zone for the time that is inevitably needed to organise the practical details of the alien's repatriation or while his application for leave to enter the territory in order to be afforded asylum is considered, provided always (1) that confinement is accompanied by suitable safeguards and (2) that it is not prolonged excessively.

[65] It is significant that the court treats together both detention of the person d seeking to enter and detention of the person awaiting deportation. *Amuur's* case must be read with the later decision in *Chahal's* case. It seems to us that the court is considering as lawful detention pending the consideration of an application for leave to enter or the making of arrangements for deportation and not applying a test of whether the detention is necessary in order to carry out those processes. e The inroad that we believe that the European Court of Human Rights has made into the right of immigration authorities to detain aliens pending consideration of the applications for leave to enter, or their deportation, is that these processes must not be unduly prolonged. It is in relation to the duration of detention that the question of proportionality arises.

[66] Although Collins J held that detention at Oakington did not fall within f art 5(1)(f) at all, he went on to consider proportionality. In so doing the test that he applied was whether detention was proportionate to the need to process applicants speedily. He decided that it was not because he was not satisfied that it was necessary to achieve that object. We consider that the test of proportionality required by art 5(1)(f) requires the court simply to consider whether the process g of considering an asylum application, or arranging a deportation, has gone on too long to justify the detention of the person concerned having regard to the conditions in which the person is detained and any special circumstances affecting him or her. Applying that test no disproportionality is demonstrated in this case.

[67] The Secretary of State has determined that, in the absence of special h circumstances, it is not reasonable to detain an asylum seeker for longer than about a week, but that a short period of detention can be justified where this will enable speedy determination of his or her application for leave to enter. In restricting detention to such circumstances he may well have gone beyond what the European Court of Human Rights would require. We are content that he j should have done so. The vast majority of those seeking asylum are aliens who are not in a position to make good their entitlement to be treated as refugees. We believe, none the less, that most right-thinking people would find it objectionable that such persons should be detained for a period of any significant length of time while their applications are considered, unless there is a risk of their absconding or committing other misbehaviour.

a   [68] We started this judgment by remarking that it was artificial to consider English domestic law and the European Convention separately. The Human Rights Act 1998 has made that convention part of the constitution of the United Kingdom, but the convention sets out values which our laws have reflected over centuries. The need, so far as possible, to interpret and give effect to statutory provisions in a matter which is compatible with convention rights is now a *b*   mandatory discipline, but it is not a novel approach.

[69] The policies that have constrained, and still constrain, the exercise of the statutory power to detain aliens who arrive on our shores do not result from any conscious application of art 5 of the European Convention. They result from a recognition, that is part of our heritage, of the fundamental importance of liberty. The deprivation of liberty with which this appeal is concerned falls at the bottom end of the scale of interference with that right. It is right, none the less, that its legitimacy should have received strict scrutiny. Our conclusion is that it is lawful. This appeal is, accordingly, allowed.

Appeal allowed. Permission to appeal granted.

Kate O'Hanlon   Barrister.

Colley v Council for Licensed Conveyancers

[2001] EWCA Civ 1137

COURT OF APPEAL, CIVIL DIVISION

SIR ANDREW MORRITT V-C, MAY AND DYSON LJJ

27, 28 JUNE, 17 JULY 2001

Appeal – Right of appeal – Statutory appeal – Whether rule of procedure imposing general requirement for permission to appeal in statutory appeals – Administration of Justice Act 1985, s 26(7) – CPR 52.3(1) – CPR PD 52, para 17.2.

The appellant, C, was a licensed conveyancer. Following various complaints about the professional services that C had provided to his clients, the respondent regulatory body made two orders against him under its statutory powers. Section 26(7)[a] of the Administration of Justice Act 1985 Act provided that a person who was subject to such orders could appeal to the High Court. C served appellant's notices in respect of both orders. At that stage, it was assumed by the parties that permission to appeal was required by CPR 52.3(1)(a)[b], even though that provision applied in its express terms only to appeals from a judge in the county court or High Court, not to appeals from tribunals. A High Court judge granted limited permission to appeal from the first order, but refused permission to appeal from the second. On C's application for permission to appeal to the Court of Appeal from the judge's orders, the issue arose, inter alia, whether the CPR did in fact require permission to be given for an appeal to the High Court under s 26(7) of the 1985 Act or indeed for any statutory appeal to that court. In contending that such permission was required, the regulatory body relied on para 17.2[c] of CPR PD 52, the practice direction supplementing CPR Pt 52 which dealt with appeals in general. Para 17.2 provided that Pt 52 applied to statutory appeals with certain amendments, none of which referred to or bore upon the question of permission to appeal. It was therefore contended that para 17.2 applied to statutory appeals, with appropriate modification, the requirement for permission to appeal imposed by r 52.3(1)(a), notwithstanding that Section III of PD 52, which made special provision about a long list of largely statutory appeals, expressly stated that it did not amend or remove any right of appeal. C contended, inter alia, that there was no power to impose by means of a practice direction a requirement for permission to appeal in statutory appeals, even though r 52.3(1)(b) provided that an appellant required permission to appeal as provided by the relevant practice direction. That provision was followed by a note in parenthesis, stating that other enactments could provide that permission was required for particular appeals.

Held – On its true construction, para 17.2 of CPR PD 52 did not impose a requirement for permission to appeal in statutory appeals where the right of

---

a Section 26, so far as material, is set out at [12], below
b Rule 52.3(1) is set out at [29], below
c Paragraph 17.2 is set out at [35], below

a appeal was otherwise unrestricted. Although a requirement for permission to appeal in statutory appeals could be imposed by a practice direction, such a requirement was not imposed by the general words of para 17.2. The wording of r 52.3(1)(b), particularly the words in parenthesis, was more consistent with the requirement that the practice direction should make specific provision for particular appeals. PD 52 did not do so, and para 17.2 could not introduce a requirement for permission

b without some interpolation. Whilst such an interpolation might be justified if PD 52 were otherwise consistent, it was not permissible if it would thereby introduce inconsistency. The introduction of a general requirement would give rise to substantial inconsistencies with Section III. The intrinsic nature of the appeals to which that section applied, and the tribunals from which they could be brought, differed. In some of them permission to appeal was expressly required

c by the statute conferring the right of appeal, while in other cases the relevant statute was silent about the need for permission. It followed that the rule and the practice direction required, if not individual provision for individual rights of appeal, at least quite explicit provision for all statutory appeals. Accordingly, in the instant case permission to appeal was not required for C's appeal to the High

d Court under s 26(7) of the 1985 Act, and those parts of the judge's orders granting or refusing such permission would be set aside (see [43], [48]–[52], [56], below).

Notes

e For statutory appeals, see 37 *Halsbury's Laws* (4th edn reissue) para 1523.

    For the Administration of Justice Act 1985, s 26, see 11 *Halsbury's Statutes* (4th edn) (2000 reissue) 1264.

Cases referred to in judgment

f *R v Secretary of State for the Home Dept, ex p Daly* [2001] UKHL 26, [2001] 3 All ER 433, [2001] 2 WLR 1622, HL.

    R v Secretary of State for the Home Dept, ex p Simms [1999] 3 All ER 400, [2000] 2 AC 115, [1999] 3 WLR 328, HL.

Application for permission to appeal

g William George Colley, a licensed conveyancer, applied for permission to appeal from the orders of Blofeld J on 24 October 2000 whereby he (i) granted Mr Colley only limited permission to appeal from the order of the Disciplinary and Appeals Committee of the respondent regulatory body, the Council for Licensed Conveyancers, on 5 June 2000 that a direction given to Mr Colley by the Council's

h Investigating Committee should be treated for the purposes of enforcement as if it were contained in an order of the High Court, and (ii) refused Mr Colley permission to appeal from the order of the Council's Disciplinary and Appeals Committee on 15 August 2000 suspending his practising licence for six months and directing him to pay a contribution to the costs of pursuing the complaints

j made against him. The facts are set out in the judgment of the court.

Murray Hunt (instructed by *Strachan Visick*) for Mr Colley.

Jeremy David Cook (instructed by *Reynolds Porter Chamberlain*) for the Council.

Cur adv vult

17 July 2001. The following judgment of the court was delivered.

a

SIR ANDREW MORRITT V-C.

Introduction

[1] The appellant, Mr Colley, is a licensed conveyancer. The respondent, the Council for Licensed Conveyancers (the Council), is the statutory body entrusted *b* by Parliament with the regulation of the provision of conveyancing services by those who are not solicitors. Various complaints to the Council about the professional services provided by Mr Colley to his clients gave rise to two orders dated respectively 5 June 2000 (the June decision) and 15 August 2000 (the August decision). Mr Colley wished to challenge them.

[2] Mr Colley's first attempt was by way of judicial review. On 1 September *c* 2000 Owen J refused Mr Colley permission to apply on the ground that s 26(7) of the Administration of Justice Act 1985 conferred on Mr Colley a statutory right of appeal to the High Court which he had not used. So, on 13 September 2000, Mr Colley served appellant's notices in respect of both decisions. He sought extensions of time within which to do so but not permission to appeal generally. *d* Those applications came before Blofeld J on 24 October 2000. At that stage it was assumed by all parties that permission to appeal was required pursuant to CPR 52.3. Blofeld J granted limited permission to appeal from the June decision but refused permission to appeal from the August decision.

[3] Mr Colley was dissatisfied with this outcome. He took the view, following *e* the further reflection of his advisers, that permission to appeal was not required to enable him to challenge in the High Court both the June decision and the August decision. Accordingly on 7 November 2000 Mr Colley served appellant's notices in respect of the two orders of Blofeld J. In respect of both decisions he seeks permission to appeal and an order setting aside the order of Blofeld J on the footing that his right of appeal is unrestricted. *f*

[4] Permission to appeal was refused on paper by Sir Murray Stuart-Smith on 20 December 2000. The application was renewed in court before Schiemann and Sedley LJJ on 15 February 2001. They adjourned it to come on after notice had been given to the Council. The written argument of counsel for Mr Colley dated 21 February 2001 in support of Mr Colley's application raised the additional point that Owen J was wrong to have considered that the statutory right of appeal *g* extended to the June decision as well as the August decision. He submitted that the application and appeal in respect of the June decision should proceed by way of judicial review under CPR Pt 54. In addition he sought to amend his appellant's notice relating to the June decision to raise two points additional to those for which Blofeld J had given permission. He sought similar relief relating to the *h* August decision. Finally he contended that if permission is required then it should be granted unconditionally by this court. The written argument of counsel for the Council dealt with each of these issues. In addition he drew our attention to the provision in s 26(8) of the 1985 Act that the decision of the High Court on an appeal under that section is final. *j*

[5] Thus there are five issues: (1) whether the right of appeal conferred by s 26(7) of the 1985 Act applies to the June decision; (2) whether permission to appeal is required for an appeal under that section in respect of the August decision and, depending on the outcome of issue (1), the June decision; (3) whether Mr Colley should have permission to amend his appellant's notices; (4) whether Mr Colley should be granted unrestricted permission to appeal in respect of both decisions;

a and (5) whether the provision in s 26(8) of the 1985 Act that the decision of the High Court on an appeal under that section is final has any and if so what effect on such order as we would otherwise make.

[6] The inter partes hearing commenced before Dame Elizabeth Butler-Sloss P and Keene LJ on 25 June 2001. They thought that at least the second issue should be considered by a court comprising three judges. Accordingly the hearing was
b adjourned and recommenced before us on 27 June 2001. We heard argument from both parties on the first issue that day. We concluded, and so informed the parties, that the statutory right of appeal conferred by s 26(7) of the 1985 Act did extend to the June decision. We then heard argument on the second issue in relation to both the June decision and the August decision. It was agreed that,
c whatever the outcome of the second issue, the third and fourth did not call for any decision from us. In the case of the third issue, questions of amendment must be for the judge before whom the appeal ultimately comes. In the case of the fourth issue, s 54(4) of the Access to Justice Act 1999 precludes any appeal from the decision of Blofeld J on whether or not permission to appeal, if required, should be granted. Accordingly what follows are our reasons for concluding that the
d statutory right of appeal conferred by s 26(7) of the 1985 Act extends to the June decision and our decision on the second and fifth issues.

The facts

[7] Before turning to those matters we should briefly refer to the underlying
e facts. The June decision related to the alleged conduct of Mr Colley when acting for a Mrs Barker in connection with her purchase of a leasehold flat in Bournemouth. The lease to her did not contain any express right of access from the front door of the building over the hallway to the front door of her flat. When she came to sell her lease in 1998 the purchaser was not prepared to rely on such implied rights as might exist. In consequence Mrs Barker spent £500 in obtaining an express grant.
f Mrs Barker complained to the Council. The matter was referred to the Investigating Committee who directed Mr Colley to pay £500 to Mrs Barker and to repay to her certain fees she had paid. The direction was not complied with and the Council preferred a complaint to the Disciplinary and Appeals Committee which, on 5 June 2000, made the June decision. The decision, made under a specific
g statutory provision to which we will refer in due course, was that the direction of the Council given by its Investigating Committee should be treated for the purposes of enforcement as if it were contained in an order of the High Court. In addition Mr Colley was ordered to pay to the Council £4,112·50 towards their costs of pursuing the complaint.

h [8] The August decision arose out of complaints made by the Council in connection with the sale of Mr and Mrs Wheeler's house in Poole. The allegations were to the effect that Mr Colley continued to act for Mr and Mrs Wheeler and Mr and Mrs Carter when a conflict of interest had arisen in that Mr Colley was also instructed by Mr and Mrs Carter in connection with the prospective purchase of
j the property at a lower price than that offered by the second prospective purchasers, Mr and Mrs Phippin; that he failed properly to protect their interests and failed to comply with an oral undertaking he had given. The Disciplinary and Appeals Committee found these charges proved. By their order made on 15 August 2000 they suspended Mr Colley's practising licence for six months and directed him to pay a contribution to their costs of pursuing the complaints of £19,933·75.

[9] We should also mention that the grounds relied on by Mr Colley in his
applications for judicial review related more to the composition of the various   *a*
committees by whom the charges against Mr Colley were heard than the
underlying merits of the complaints. We understood that Mr Colley also contended
in relation to the June decision that Mrs Barker enjoyed sufficient implied rights
and in relation to the August decision that there was in fact no conflict of interest.

b

The statutory right of appeal

[10] The first issue requires a close consideration of the provisions of Pt II of
the 1985 Act dealing with licensed conveyancing and s 53 of, and Sch 8 to, the
Courts and Legal Services Act 1990 by which they were amended and extended.

[11] One of the purposes of the 1985 Act was to regulate the provision of   *c*
conveyancing services by persons who are not solicitors but are licensed in
accordance with Pt II of that Act. The Council was established by s 12
in accordance with the provisions set out in Sch 3 as a licensing and disciplinary
body for those providing such services. By s 13 the Council is required to make
rules for the education and training of those seeking to practise as licensed
conveyancers. Sections 14 to 19 deal with applications for, the grant of and the   *d*
suspension or termination of such licenses. By s 20 the Council is required to
make rules as to professional practice, conduct and discipline of licensed
conveyancers and ss 21 to 23 deal with financial requirements as to insurance,
accounting for clients' money and interest thereon.

[12] Sections 24 to 26 deal with disciplinary proceedings. The process involves   *e*
a preliminary investigation by an Investigating Committee (IC), in accordance
with s 24, followed by a hearing before a Disciplinary and Appeals Committee
(DAC), in accordance with s 25. Section 26, as originally enacted and so far as
material, provided:

'(1) Where on the hearing of any allegation the Discipline and Appeals   *f*
Committee are satisfied that a licensed conveyancer—(a) has been convicted
as mentioned in section 24(1)(a)(i) of an offence which renders him unfit to
practise as a licensed conveyancer; (b) has, while holding a licence in force
under this Part, failed to comply with any condition to which that licence
was subject; or (c) has failed to comply with any rules made by the Council
under this Part, the Committee may, if they think fit, make one or more of   *g*
the orders referred to in subsection (2).

(2) Those orders are—(a) an order revoking any licence held by the
licensed conveyancer; (b) an order directing that the licensed conveyancer
shall be disqualified (either permanently or during a specified period) from
holding a licence under this Part; (c) an order suspending any licence held by   *h*
the licensed conveyancer; (d) an order that any such licence shall have effect
subject to such conditions as may be specified in the order; (e) an order
directing the payment by the licensed conveyancer of a penalty not exceeding
£3,000, to be forfeited to Her Majesty; (f) an order that the licensed
conveyancer be reprimanded by the Council; (g) an order requiring the   *j*
licensed conveyancer to pay the costs incurred in bringing against him the
proceedings before the Committee or a contribution towards those costs,
being a contribution of such amount as the Committee consider reasonable.

(3) Where, on the hearing of any allegation or complaint, it appears to the
Committee that the professional services provided by a licensed conveyancer
in connection with any matter in which he or his firm had been instructed by

a a client were in any respect not of the quality that could reasonably have been expected of him as a licensed conveyancer the Committee may, if they think fit—(a) determine that the fees to which the licensed conveyancer or his firm shall be entitled in respect of those services shall be limited to such amount as may be specified in their determination; and (b) by order direct him to comply, or to secure compliance, with such one or more of the

b following requirements as appear to them to be necessary in order to give effect to their determination, namely—(i) a requirement to refund the whole or part of any amount already paid by or on behalf of the client in respect of the fees of the licensed conveyancer or his firm in respect of those services; (ii) a requirement to remit the whole or part of those fees; (iii) a requirement to waive, whether wholly or to any specified extent, the right to recover

c those fees ...

(7) A person against whom an order is made by the Committee by virtue of subsection (1) may appeal to the High Court, and on any such appeal the High Court may make such order as it thinks fit.

(8) The decision of the High Court on an appeal under subsection (7) shall

d be final.'

[13] It will be noted that sub-s (3) provided for inadequate professional services to be dealt with in accordance with the procedure under sub-s (1). Consequently a complaint to that effect leading to an order under sub-s (2) was within the statutory right of appeal conferred by sub-s (7).

e [14] Part II of the 1990 Act deals with the extension of conveyancing services. Section 53 contains a number of provisions applying to the Council earlier provisions of the Act. Section 53(7) calls attention to the fact that Sch 8 makes further provision in connection with the powers given to the Council by the 1985 Act in relation to licensed conveyancers including amendments of Pt II of the

f 1985 Act. One of the amendments was the repeal of s 26(3) of the 1985 Act. Subsection (7) authorises the Lord Chancellor to modify any of the provisions of Pt II of the 1985 Act in connection with the provisions made by that section and by Sch 8. So far as relevant, s 53(9) provides:

g 'Subject to any provision made by this section, Schedule 8 or any order made by the Lord Chancellor under subsection (8), the provisions of Part II of the Act of 1985 shall, with the necessary modifications, apply with respect to—(a) any application for an advocacy, litigation or probate licence; (b) any such licence; (c) the practice of any licensed conveyancer which is carried on by virtue of any such licence; (d) rules made by the Council under Schedule 8;

h (e) the management and control by licensed conveyancers (or by licensed conveyancers together with persons who are not licensed conveyancers) of bodies corporate carrying on businesses which include the provision of advocacy, litigation or probate services; and (f) any other matter dealt with by this section or Schedule 8, as they apply with respect to the corresponding matters dealt with by Part II of that Act.'

j
[15] Schedule 8 to the 1990 Act contains a number of provisions dealing with qualification regulations and rules of conduct, the application for and issue of licences and their revocation and suspension. Part II of the Schedule is entitled 'Amendments of Provisions Relating to the Powers of the Council etc'. Paragraph 12 contains powers of delegation. Paragraph 13 deals with the Council's power of intervention. Paragraphs 14 to 18 are concerned with inadequate

professional services. Paragraph 14 authorises the Council to take any of the steps
mentioned in para 15 with respect to a licensed conveyancer—   *a*

> 'where it appears to it that the professional services provided by him in
> connection with any matter in which he or his firm has been instructed by a
> client have, in any respect, not been of the quality which it is reasonable to
> expect of him as a licensed conveyancer.'
>   *b*

[16] The steps referred to in para 15 are directions with regard to limiting the
costs charged by the licensed conveyancer, securing, at his expense, rectification
of any error or omission of his and the payment of compensation to his client.
Thus the regime for dealing with inadequate professional services was separated
from s 26(1) of the 1985 Act. Paragraph 17 provides:
                                                                                          c

> '(1) If a licensed conveyancer fails to comply with a direction given under
> this Part of the Schedule, any person may make a complaint in respect of that
> failure to the Discipline and Appeals Committee; but no other proceedings
> whatever shall be brought in respect of it.
>   (2) On the hearing of such a complaint the Discipline and Appeals
> Committee may, if it thinks fit (and whether or not it makes any order under   *d*
> section 26(2) of the Act of 1985), direct that the direction be treated, for the
> purpose of enforcement, as if it were contained in an order made by the High
> Court.'

[17] It will be noted that the June decision was made in exercise of the power
conferred by para 17(2). That is what the DAC said they were doing both to   *e*
Mr Colley at the outset of the hearing and in the formal order they made. Indeed
the requirement that Mr Colley pay £500 to Mrs Barker could only have been
made under para 15 of the 1990 Act.

[18] It is in these circumstances that counsel for Mr Colley submits that the
statutory right of appeal does not extend to the June decision. He submits that *f*
s 26(7) applies only to an order made by virtue of sub-s (1) in relation to a
complaint properly brought under that subsection. He contends that the
proceedings in which the June decision was made was a complaint under para 17(1)
of Sch 8 to the 1990 Act, not one falling within s 26(1) of the 1985 Act.

[19] Counsel for the Council contends that the relevant provisions of the 1985
Act and the 1990 Act must be read together. He submits that a failure to comply *g*
with a direction is a breach of the rules and so comes within s 26(1). He points
out that the 1990 Act made comparable provision for solicitors' inadequate
professional services and provided unambiguously for a statutory right of appeal.

[20] In reply counsel for Mr Colley points out that Mr Colley was not charged
under s 26(1). He submits that no assistance is derived from the different   *h*
provisions dealing with solicitors. He suggests that the two regimes, that is s 26
of the 1985 Act and paras 14 to 17 of Sch 8 to the 1990 Act, run on parallel lines
and do not meet.

[21] In our view it is plain that the statutory right of appeal does apply to the
June decision. Before the changes made by the 1990 Act inadequate professional *j*
services were dealt with in accordance with s 26. As such, the statutory right of
appeal necessarily applied. We see no reason why, when making separate
provision for such matters in Sch 8, Parliament should have intended that the
challenge to such an order should thereafter be by way of judicial review.
Paragraph 17(2) recognises that the same conduct may lead to an order under
s 26(2) as well as a direction under para 17(1). It would be absurd if the method

a of challenging the two orders in court should differ, one being by way of judicial review and the other by way of appeal.

[**22**] In our view the solution is provided by s 53(9). We have quoted the subsection in full in [14] above. If one rewrites the subsection, substituting the specific for the general, it provides:

b   '... the provisions of Part II of the Act of 1985 [s 26(7)] shall, with the necessary modifications, apply with respect to ... (f) any other matter dealt with by this section or Schedule 8 [a direction under para 17(2)], as they apply with respect to the corresponding matters [s 26(1) and (2)] dealt with by Part II of that Act.'

c [**23**] Counsel for Mr Colley submitted that there was no sufficient correspondence between s 26(1) and (2) of the 1985 Act and para 17 of Sch 8 to the 1990 Act. He also suggested that if this is what Parliament had intended it would have made more specific provision than this. We reject both those submissions. The two provisions plainly correspond because inadequate professional services with which para 17 is concerned were formerly dealt with under s 26 because of the

d terms of sub-s (3). Given that correspondence the provision is sufficiently specific even if not immediately apparent.

[**24**] For all these reasons we conclude that the statutory right of appeal provided in s 26(7) is exercisable in respect of a direction made under para 17(2). Accordingly an appeal from the June decision lies to the High Court. It follows that we reject the submission of counsel for Mr Colley that Owen J was wrong

e when he refused to permit Mr Colley to proceed by way of judicial review.

Permission to appeal

[**25**] Consequently, the second issue, whether or not the right of appeal is exercisable only with permission, arises in respect of both the June decision and

f the August decision. The outcome of this issue will affect not only the rights of Mr Colley in this case but the rights of all those seeking to exercise any statutory right of appeal to the High Court.

[**26**] The right of access to a court is of fundamental constitutional importance. It is scarcely necessary to refer to authority for that obvious proposition. Lord Bingham of Cornhill stated in *R v Secretary of State for the Home Dept, ex p Daly*

g [2001] UKHL 26 at [5], [2001] 3 All ER 433 at [5], [2001] 2 WLR 1622 that important rights, including the right of access to a court, calling for appropriate legal protection, may be curtailed only by clear and express words, and then only to the extent reasonably necessary to meet the ends which justify the curtailment. For present purposes, it seems to us that access to a court means that those who

h need the assistance of a court to assert their legal rights and obtain remedies to which they are in law entitled are able to start proceedings in an appropriate court to that end. Having started the proceedings, they are entitled to have the court determine them according to law.

[**27**] The civil justice system in this jurisdiction has for over 100 years had a

j structure for appeals and there are rights of appeal against most first instance decisions. There are some instances where rights of appeal are limited by statute. Until fairly recently, leave or permission to appeal was not required for many classes of appeal. It has, at least in modern times, always been necessary to obtain leave to appeal to the House of Lords. In courts below the House of Lords, there have been progressive moves to introduce a requirement for leave or permission to appeal. It is unnecessary to trace the full history. By way of example, s 7 of the

1990 Act inserted s 18(1A) of the Supreme Court Act 1981, which empowered
what became RSC Ord 59, r 1B. This rule was added by the Rules of the Supreme
Court (Amendment) 1993, SI 1993/2133 and amended by the Rules of the
Supreme Court (Amendment) SI 1995/2206. It prescribed classes of case in which
leave to appeal to the Court of Appeal was required. From 1 January 1999, the
requirement for permission to appeal to the Court of Appeal was extended so that
permission was required for all appeals except appeals against committal orders,
refusals to grant habeas corpus and secure accommodation orders made under
s 25 of the Children Act 1989.

[28] The current provisions start with s 54 of the 1999 Act. So far as relevant
that section provides:

'(1) Rules of court may provide that any right of appeal to—(a) a county
court, (b) the High Court, or (c) the Court of Appeal, may be exercised only
with permission ...
(4) No appeal may be made against a decision of a court under this section
to give or refuse permission (but this subsection does not affect any right
under rules of court to make a further application for permission to the same
or another court).
(5) For the purposes of this section a right to make an application to have
a case stated for the opinion of the High Court constitutes a right of appeal.'

[29] The rule now governing appeals is CPR 52.3(1). That provides, so far as
relevant:

'An appellant or respondent requires permission to appeal—(a) where the
appeal is from a decision of a judge in a county court or the High Court,
except where the appeal is against—(i) a committal order; (ii) a refusal to
grant habeas corpus; or (iii) a secure accommodation order made under
section 25 of the Children Act 1989; or (b) as provided by the relevant practice
direction. (Other enactments may provide that permission is required for
particular appeals).'

[30] CPR Pt 52 then provides that an application for permission to appeal may
be made to 'the lower court' or to the appeal court. CPR 52.1(3)(c) defines 'lower
court' to mean 'the court, tribunal or other person or body from whose decision
an appeal is brought'. CPR 52.3(4) provides that if the appeal court refuses
permission to appeal without a hearing, the person seeking permission may
request the decision to be reconsidered at a hearing. CPR 52.3(6) provides that
permission to appeal will only be given where '(a) the court considers that the
appeal would have a real prospect of success; or (b) there is some other compelling
reason why the appeal should be heard'. There are other parts of CPR Pt 52
(mainly CPR 52.3, 52.4 and 52.5) which make provision for or allude to the need
for permission to appeal.

[31] The definition of the 'lower court' makes clear that the rule is intended to
apply, or be capable of applying, to appeals from tribunals and other persons or
bodies from whose decision an appeal is brought. Leaving tribunals and these
others aside for a moment and concentrating on appeals within the civil court
system, it might be said that the existence or otherwise of a system of appeal and
the details of its operation do not impinge on the right of access to a court. The
right of access is accommodated by the right to bring proceedings at first instance
and to have them determined according to law. Rights of appeal are not so much
rights of access to a court, as rights to have the opportunity of persuading a higher

a court that the first instance decision is wrong. There are instances where Parliament expressly provides that there shall be no right of appeal from particular kinds of decision. But the entrenched system of appeals enabling dissatisfied litigants to appeal at least once to a higher court recognises the possibility that on occasions first instance decisions may be unjustly wrong and provides a means of putting them right.

b   [32] The imposition of a requirement for permission to appeal may curtail rights of appeal, but the nature and extent of the curtailment will depend on the criteria adopted for giving or refusing permission and the procedural arrangements for seeking it. As to the latter, CPR 52.3(4) entitles a person seeking permission to ask for the decision to be reconsidered at a hearing. As to the criteria for giving or refusing permission, under CPR 52.3(6) the court has to consider that the
c appeal would have a real prospect of success or that there is some other compelling reason why the appeal should be heard. There is thus a filter to stop proposed appeals which have no real prospect of success and where there is no other compelling reason why the appeal should be heard. Although, of course, this filter may be described as a restriction on a person's right of appeal, there is,
d in our judgment, no restriction on the applicant's access to the court at all—on the contrary, they have the positive right to come to court and argue their case. There is no substantial restriction—and certainly no intrinsically unjust restriction—on the right of appeal, since there is, in our view, no reason in justice why a person should be entitled to occupy the time of the court, and put opposing parties to expense and trouble, in conducting appeals which have no real prospect
e of success and where there is no other compelling reason why the appeal should be heard.

   [33] Although, as we have indicated, the definition of 'lower court' in CPR 52.1(3) indicates that the rule may apply to appeals to a court from tribunals, CPR 52.3(1) does not in terms impose a requirement for permission to appeal on such appeals.
f CPR 52.3(1)(b) is drafted to enable the relevant practice direction to provide for permission to appeal to be required in circumstances other than those covered by CPR 52.3(1)(a). In the context, this plainly includes statutory appeals, since appeals within the court system itself are covered by sub-sub-para (a). The parenthesis draws attention to 'particular appeals' for which other enactments may provide that permission is required.
g   [34] We should also refer to provisions in the Civil Procedure Act 1997. Section 1(2) provides that Sch 1 is to have effect. Paragraph 6 of that Schedule states: 'Civil Procedure Rules may, instead of providing for any matter, refer to provision made or to be made about that matter in directions.' Practice Directions are defined by s 9(2) as 'directions as to the practice and procedure of
h any court within the scope of Civil Procedure Rules'.

   [35] The practice direction associated with CPR Pt 52, PD 52, provides, in para 17.2: 'Part 52 applies to statutory appeals with the following amendments.' The amendments are to points of detail in the procedure which do not refer to or bear upon the question of permission to appeal. Section III of this practice
j direction makes special provisions about a long list of very largely statutory appeals. The section is not exhaustive and does not create, amend or remove any right of appeal. The lists, although not exhaustive, give a vivid idea of the large number of statutory appeals to which this practice direction applies. The special provisions in Section III mainly concern time limits and persons who have to be served. In no instance do the special provisions include a requirement for permission to appeal which is not already required by the statutes in question.

[**36**] Paragraph 18 of the practice direction applies to appeals by way of case stated. As with para 17, it applies subject to any provision about a specific category of appeal in any enactment and to Section III of PD 52. Paragraph 18.2 provides that CPR Pt 52 applies to appeals by way of case stated subject to amendments which follow. The amendments include, in para 18.3, that the procedure for applying to the Crown Court or a magistrates' court to have a case stated for the opinion of the High Court is set out in the Crown Court Rules 1982, SI 1982/1109 and the Magistrates' Courts Rules 1981, SI 1981/552 respectively. There is thus preserved for cases stated what is in broad substance a species of permission to appeal. Thus para 18.3 of PD 52 must, in our view, be taken to modify, for cases stated, the provisions in CPR Pt 52 relating to permission to appeal.

[**37**] In refusing permission to appeal on the papers Sir Murray Stuart-Smith evidently considered that the effect of para 17.2 of PD 52 was to apply the provisions of CPR 52.3(1)(a), with the necessary modifications, to statutory appeals. Counsel for Mr Colley submits that he was wrong to have done so.

[**38**] The issue, therefore, is whether the very general words of para 17.2 of PD 52—that CPR Pt 52 applies to statutory appeals with a small handful of amendments which do not modify those parts of CPR Pt 52 which provide for permission to appeal—is sufficient to impose a requirement for permission to appeal on all statutory appeals where otherwise the right of appeal was unrestricted.

[**39**] Counsel for Mr Colley, submits that the restriction of a hitherto unfettered right of appeal by the imposition of a requirement for permission to appeal constitutes a restriction on the proposed appellant's right of access to a court. Such rights may be curtailed only by clear and express words, and then only to the extent reasonably necessary to meet the ends which justify the curtailment. The clear and express words need to have parliamentary scrutiny and authority. As Lord Hoffmann said in *R v Secretary of State for the Home Dept, ex p Simms* [1999] 3 All ER 400 at 412, [2000] 2 AC 115 at 131:

'... the principle of legality means that Parliament must squarely confront what it is doing and accept the political cost. Fundamental rights cannot be overridden by general or ambiguous words. This is because there is too great a risk that the full implications of their unqualified meaning may have passed unnoticed in the democratic process. In the absence of express language or necessary implication to the contrary, the courts therefore presume that even the most general words were intended to be subject to the basic rights of the individual.'

[**40**] Counsel for Mr Colley submits that s 54(1) of the 1999 Act does not enable rules of court to provide that a statutory right of appeal from a tribunal may be exercised only with permission; that CPR 52.3(1) does not impose a requirement for permission to appeal for statutory appeals from tribunals; that a requirement for permission to appeal for statutory appeals from tribunals cannot lawfully be imposed by a practice direction because practice directions are not subject to any parliamentary scrutiny; and that para 17.2 of PD 52 does not, properly understood, impose any such requirements. Counsel for the Council makes submissions to the contrary for each of these regressive submissions.

[**41**] In our judgment, s 54(1) of the 1999 Act clearly empowers the making of rules imposing a requirement for permission to appeal which include statutory appeals to a court. The language is clear and, not least by the use of the word

a 'any', entirely apt to include appeals of this kind. We accept the submission of counsel for Mr Colley that a statutory appeal to a court is the first opportunity for bringing the question before a court. But, as we have indicated, we do not consider that a requirement for permission to appeal under the procedure and with the criteria provided in Pt 52 is properly described as a restriction on access to a court.

b [42] In addition to the plain wording of s 54(1) read as a whole, there are, in our view, other indications that the section extends to statutory appeals. First, a 'right of appeal to … a county court' is, if anything, more apt to cover an appeal from a tribunal to a county court than an appeal within the county court, as from a district judge to a circuit judge, although this is obviously also covered. The same point applies, with somewhat less force, to 'any right of appeal to the High Court'. Before the introduction of the rule and practice direction with which this appeal is concerned, civil appeals to the High Court within the civil justice system were not as extensive as they now are. Second, s 54(5) provides that, for the purposes of the section, a right to make an application to have a case stated for the opinion of the High Court constitutes a right of appeal. Thus, a statutory appeal by case stated comes within s 54(1); it would be very odd if other statutory appeals did not do so also.

[43] We do not accept the submission of counsel for Mr Colley that there is no power to impose a requirement for permission to appeal in statutory appeals by means of a practice direction. Sections 1 and 2 of the 1997 Act give the Civil Procedure Rules Committee power to make rules of court generally governing the practice and procedure to be followed in the Civil Division of the Court of Appeal, the High Court and county courts. As we have already noted, s 1(2) of the 1997 Act provides that Sch 1 is to have effect. Paragraph 6 of Sch 1 provides: 'Civil Procedure Rules may, instead of providing for any matter, refer to provision made or to be made about that matter by directions.' CPR 52.3(1)(b) does just that. It follows that there is explicit parliamentary authority in these provisions of the 1997 Act and in s 54(1) of the 1999 Act for a requirement for permission to appeal in statutory appeals to be imposed by a practice direction.

[44] Further, since the parliamentary authority in s 54(1) plainly authorises the imposition of a need for permission to appeal for any or all statutory appeals, the principle of legality to which Lord Hoffmann referred in *Ex p Simms* has been achieved. Parliament has squarely confronted what it was doing and, at the more detailed level, has scrutinised the statutory instrument which says that a requirement for permission to appeal may be provided by the Practice Direction. The same applies to the procedure and criteria for the giving or refusing permission.

h [45] We have found the final submission of counsel for Mr Colley much more difficult. Paragraph 17.2 of PD 52 provides in terms that CPR Pt 52 applies to statutory appeals with certain amendments. The amendments are limited and do not by their terms affect the issue. The amendments do not include any relevant changes to CPR 52.3, 52.4 or 52.5, and so the general provisions relating to permission to appeal are not expressly excluded by amendment. There is a tension between the principle stated by Lord Bingham in *Ex p Daly,* that the right of access to a court may only be curtailed by clear and precise words, and the provision of CPR 1.2 that the court must seek to give effect to the overriding objective when it interprets any rule.

[46] There are, in our view, persuasive 'overriding objective' considerations to the effect that a requirement for permission to appeal generally is salutary,

necessary and just and that what now applies almost universally within the civil court system should apply also to statutory appeals. There is a structure broadly equivalent to permission to appeal retained in para 18 of PD 52 for cases stated. Accordingly, there is a persuasive case that para 17.2 of PD 52 is to be read as imposing a requirement for permission to appeal for statutory appeals, and that this is achieved as a matter of construction by applying CPR 52.3(1)(a) to them with appropriate modification.

[47] The contrary submission, advanced by counsel for Mr Colley, is that the words of para 17.2 of PD 52 cannot be read as providing for a requirement for permission to appeal. The provision is circular. CPR 52.3(1)(b) empowers—if, contrary to the submission of counsel for Mr Colley, it does—the requirement to be provided by the Practice Direction, but the Practice Direction does not do so. The Practice Direction provides that CPR Pt 52 is to apply to statutory appeals, but CPR Pt 52 does not impose a requirement for permission to appeal for statutory appeals. The broader submission is that the Practice Direction would need to impose the requirement explicitly, which it does not; and that it could not properly do so without making provision for each statutory appeal individually. Such individual treatment would be necessary to comply with Lord Bingham's requirement that any curtailment of this kind can only be achieved by clear and express words.

[48] As is indicated by the lists and provisions in Section III of PD 52, it applies to a large number of diverse statutes which give a right of appeal to a court. They cover widely different people and circumstances and the intrinsic nature of the appeals and the tribunals from which they may be brought differ. In four of the cases set out in the table of statutory appeals to the High Court contained in para 20 of PD 52, permission to do so is expressly required by the statute conferring the right of appeal. In 22 cases the statute conferring the right is silent about any need for permission, though in three of them permission is expressly required for any further appeal from the High Court to the Court of Appeal. One of the cases covered by Section III is that of contempt of court which, by CPR 52.3(1)(a), is specifically exempted from any requirement of permission to appeal. Specific provision for obtaining permission for appeals from the tribunal direct to the Court of Appeal is made in a number of paragraphs (21.6, 21.8, 21.10) in terms which are not the same as the general provisions of Section I of PD 52. In the case of an appeal from the decision of the Pensions Appeal Tribunal to the High Court, the relevant Act requires permission to appeal. Paragraph 22.5 of PD 52 contains detailed provision as to how such permission is to be obtained. This is inconsistent with general requirements for permission to appeal and the procedure for doing so having been prescribed by Section I of PD 52.

[49] The wording of CPR 52.3(1)(b), in particular the words in parenthesis, is more consistent with a requirement that the Practice Direction should make specific provision for particular appeals; and this Practice Direction does not do so. As we have pointed out, para 17.2 cannot introduce a requirement for permission without some interpolation. Whilst such an interpolation might be justified if the Practice Direction were otherwise consistent, it is not permissible if it would thereby introduce inconsistency. For the reasons indicated in [48] above, we consider that the introduction of a general requirement in accordance with Section I would give rise to substantial inconsistencies with Section III.

[50] In these circumstances, we do not consider that either the rule or the Practice Direction are to be read as intending or achieving the result for which the Council contends by the general words in para 17.2 of PD 52. In our view,

a the rule and Practice Direction require if not individual provision for individual rights of appeal at least quite explicit positive provision for all statutory appeals.

[51] For all these reasons we accept the submission of counsel for Mr Colley that permission to appeal is not required for his appeals to the High Court pursuant to s 26(7) of the 1985 Act from either the June decision or the August decision.

b

Permission to amend/grant of permission to appeal

[52] As we have already indicated, neither of these issues now arise. It will be for the judge before whom the appeals ultimately come to decide whether Mr Colley should be permitted to amend his notices of appeal in the form now sought or in any other form. If, contrary to our decision on the second issue,
c permission to appeal is required, the jurisdiction to decide whether to grant it is conferred exclusively on the lower court or the High Court. An appeal to the Court of Appeal against the refusal or limited grant of permission to appeal is excluded by s 54(4) of the 1999 Act. In the event that we have concluded that there is no need to obtain permission, the jurisdiction of this court is not excluded
d by that subsection.

The effect of s 26(8) of the 1985 Act

[53] We have already set out the terms of this subsection in [12] above. The question is whether the assumption by Blofeld J that permission was required and the consequential refusal of unlimited permission to appeal from either decision
e was a 'decision of the High Court on an appeal' under s 26(7) of the 1985 Act. If it was, then this court has no jurisdiction to intervene. At the conclusion of the oral argument on all the other points, we invited counsel to submit further written argument on this point. We are grateful for the further written submissions they provided to us.

f [54] The decision whether or not to grant permission when it is required is not appealable because of the provisions of s 54(4) of the 1999 Act. It is therefore unnecessary to reach any final conclusion whether it would also be a decision on the appeal for the purposes of s 26(8). Our inclination would be to hold that it would be because it is a consideration of the merits of the underlying dispute and, depending on the outcome, may be conclusive. The point may be important in
g the context of art 6 of the European Convention for the Protection of Human Rights and Fundamental Freedoms (Rome, 4 November 1950; TS 71 (1953); Cmd 8969) (as set out in Sch 1 to the Human Rights Act 1998).

[55] But the judge's assumption, fostered by both parties, that permission to appeal was required was neither a 'decision' nor a consideration of the merits of
h the underlying dispute. As such the jurisdiction of this court to consider the issue whether permission to appeal is required was not, in our view, excluded by s 26(8). Nor, rightly, did the Council object to Mr Colley taking in this court a point—that permission to appeal is not needed—not taken on his behalf in the court below. In these circumstances we see no impediment to the grant of such
j declarations or orders as are now needed to secure the prompt hearing by a High Court judge of Mr Colley's appeals from both the June decision and the August decision.

Conclusion

[56] Subject to any further argument on the form of order, we consider that we should declare that (1) the right of appeal conferred by s 26(7) of the 1985 Act

applies to the June decision as well as to the August decision; and (2) CPR Pt 52
and its associated Practice Direction do not require a prospective appellant under
that subsection to obtain any permission to appeal. In addition we will set aside
those parts of the orders of Blofeld J as granted or refused permission to appeal.
We will grant permission to appeal to the extent necessary to enable us to make
those declarations and orders. We will direct that Mr Colley's appeals be fixed for
hearing in the High Court as soon as is reasonably possible.

Permission to appeal granted and appeal allowed.

Melanie Martyn   Barrister.

a   # R (on the application of Quintavalle) v Secretary of State for Health

[2001] EWHC Admin 918

b   QUEEN'S BENCH DIVISION (ADMINISTRATIVE COURT)

CRANE J

31 OCTOBER, 1, 15 NOVEMBER 2001

Medical treatment – Human fertilisation – Embryo – Cell nuclear replacement –
c   *Whether organism created by cell nuclear replacement falling within statutory*
definition of embryo – Human Fertilisation and Embryology Act 1990, s 1(1).

The Chief Medical Officer's Expert Group published a report reviewing the potential to benefit human health of developments in cell nuclear replacement
d   (CNR), a form of cloning that did not normally involve fertilisation. Instead, a nucleus from one cell was transplanted into an unfertilised egg, with the cell subsequently being treated to encourage it to grow and divide, forming first a two-cell structure and then developing in a similar way to a normal embryo. The report recommended allowing research using embryos, whether created by in vitro fertilisation or CNR, to increase understanding about human disease, subject to
e   the control of the Human Fertilisation and Embryology Act 1990. It clearly assumed that organisms produced by CNR constituted embryos within the meaning of s 1(1)[a] of the 1990 Act, which provided that 'embryo' meant a live human embryo where 'fertilisation is complete'. The government accepted the report's recommendations and similarly proceeded on the basis that organisms
f   produced by CNR were embryos and subject to the Act. That view was challenged in judicial review proceedings by the director of an association which was opposed to human cloning. He sought a declaration that human embryos created by CNR fell outside the definition in s 1(1), contending that an embryo which had not been produced by fertilisation could not be an embryo 'where fertilisation is complete'. The Secretary of State argued for a purposive interpretation of s 1,
g   submitting that the organism produced by CNR was morphologically and functionally indistinguishable from an embryo produced by fertilisation, that the essential concept was that of a live human embryo and that s 1(1) should be read as if the words were 'a live human embryo where [if it is produced by fertilisation] fertilisation is complete'.

h
Held – An organism created by CNR without fertilisation was not an embryo within the meaning of s 1(1) of the 1990 Act. Although such an organism was naturally described as an embryo, at least when the two-cell stage was reached, the words of s 1(1) could not be stretched to cover organisms produced by CNR,
j   involving no fertilisation. The insertion into s 1(1) of the words 'if it is produced by fertilisation' would involve an impermissible rewriting and extension of the definition. It followed that organisms produced by CNR were not subject to regulation under the 1990 Act, and a declaration would be granted accordingly (see [43], [60], [62], below).

a   Section 1(1) is set out at [1], below

Notes

For the meaning of embryo, see 30 *Halsbury's Laws* (4th edn reissue) para 59 n1.   *a*
    For the Human Fertilisation and Embryology Act 1990, s 1, see 28 *Halsbury's Statutes* (4th edn) (2001 reissue) 290.

Cases referred to in judgment

Airedale NHS Trust v Bland [1993] 1 All ER 821, [1993] AC 789, [1993] 2 WLR 316,   *b*
    Fam D, CA and HL.
Gillick v West Norfolk and Wisbech Area Health Authority [1985] 3 All ER 402, [1986]
    AC 112, [1985] 3 WLR 830, HL.
R v Comr for Local Administration, ex p Croydon London BC [1989] 1 All ER 1033, DC.
R v Secretary of State for Foreign Affairs, ex p World Development Movement Ltd [1995]
    1 All ER 611, [1995] 1 WLR 386, DC.   *c*
R v Secretary of State for the Home Dept, ex p Ruddock [1987] 2 All ER 518, [1987]
    1 WLR 1482.
Royal College of Nursing of the UK v Dept of Health and Social Security [1981] 1 All ER
    545, [1981] AC 800, [1981] 2 WLR 279, QBD, CA and HL.

   d

Cases also cited or referred to in skeleton arguments

A (children) (conjoined twins: surgical separation), Re [2000] 4 All ER 961, [2001] Fam
    147, CA.
R v Customs and Excise Comrs, ex p Lunn Poly Ltd [1999] STC 350, CA.
R v HM Treasury, ex p Smedley [1985] 1 All ER 589, [1985] QB 657, CA.

   e

Application for judicial review

The claimant, the Pro-Life Alliance, acting through its director, Bruno Quintavalle, applied by way of judicial review for a declaration that organisms created by cell nuclear replacement were not embryos within the meaning of s 1(1) of the Human Fertilisation and Embryology Act 1990 contrary to the assumption of the   *f* defendant, the Secretary of State for Health, in his official response in August 2000 to recommendations in a report of the Chief Medical Officer's Expert Group published in June 2000. The facts are set out in the judgment.

Gerald Barling QC and *Martin Chamberlain* (instructed by *Brown Cooper*) for the
    claimant.   *g*
James Eadie (instructed by the *Solicitor for the Department of Health*) for the defendant.

Cur adv vult

15 November 2001. The following judgment was delivered.   *h*

CRANE J.

    [1] The central issue in this application for judicial review is whether the organism created by cell nuclear replacement (CNR), an organism often referred to as an 'embryo', falls within the definition of 'embryo' in s 1(1) of the Human Fertilisation and Embryology Act 1990. Section 1(1) reads: *j*

    '*Meaning of "embryo", "gamete" and associated expressions.*—(1) In this Act, except where otherwise stated—(a) embryo means a live human embryo where fertilisation is complete, and (b) references to an embryo include an egg in the process of fertilisation, and, for this purpose, fertilisation is not complete until the appearance of a two cell zygote.'

a It is common ground that the CNR process does not involve fertilisation. It involves a procedure commonly known as cloning. To avoid begging the question, I shall not refer to the organism created by CNR as an 'embryo' in this judgment.

The history of these proceedings

[2] In June 2000 a report was published, *Stem Cell Research: Medical Progress with*
b *Responsibility* (the Donaldson report), by the Chief Medical Officer's Expert Group 'reviewing the potential of developments in stem cell research and cell nuclear replacement to benefit human health'. Its principal recommendation was (at para 5.10):

'Research using embryos (whether created by *in vitro* fertilisation or cell
c nuclear replacement) to increase understanding about human disease and disorders and their cell-based treatments should be permitted, subject to the controls in the Human Fertilisation and Embryology Act 1990.'

[3] Although the Donaldson committee did not discuss whether as a matter of law the definition in s 1(1) covered organisms produced by CNR, it is clear that
d this was assumed, as the recommendation implies. The assumption is further made clear by the following passage (at para 4.17):

'However, although these embryos [sc organisms produced by CNR] differ in the method of their creation, they are undoubtedly human embryonic life, which, given the right conditions, could develop into a human being.'
e
The assumption is confirmed by para 2.26 and box 9 at para 2.29.

[4] In August 2000 the government published its response, *Government Response to the Recommendations made in the Chief Medical Officer's Expert Group Report* (Cm 4833) (the 2000 response), accepting the recommendations. In the foreword to
f the response it indicated an intention of bringing forward legislation to implement them and noted that regulations necessary to extend the purposes for which embryos may be used for research were 'affirmative'. It referred to organisms produced by CNR as 'embryos created by cell nuclear replacement'. The response proceeded on the basis that these were embryos and subject to the Act.

[5] Pro-Life Alliance describes itself as an association committed to campaigning
g for absolute respect for innocent human life and is opposed inter alia to human cloning. It has been permitted to make submissions in at least one previous case and there has been no objection to its standing to make the present application. In referring to the claimant I mean Pro-Life rather than its director, whose name appears on the application.

h [6] On 7 November 2000 the claimant applied for permission to apply for judicial review. It sought a declaration that human embryos created by CNR are not within the definition in the Act. It also sought a declaration that the Secretary of State had no power to make regulations in this connection. In fact the Human Fertilisation and Embryology (Research Purposes) Regulations 2001, SI 2001/188,
j were made on 24 January 2001. The claimant does not now contend that they are ultra vires, because they merely extended the purposes for which a licence for research may be issued, without purporting to alter the definition of an 'embryo'.

[7] On 26 January 2001 the application for permission was listed for oral hearing. At the suggestion of Sullivan J it was ordered that the application for permission and any related issues, together with the substantive hearing of the matter, be listed together. They were eventually listed before me on 31 October 2001.

[8] Pursuant to directions the claimant produced a set of scientific propositions, on which the defendant commented. Expert evidence was filed on both sides. *a* For the claimant, Dr Gulam Bahadur, Head of Fertility and Reproductive Medicine Laboratories at University College, London, and University College London Hospital Trust; and Professor David Prentice, Professor of Life Sciences at Indiana State University and Adjunct Professor of Medical and Molecular Genetics at Indiana University School of Medicine, USA. For the defendant, there *b* are statements from Professor Allan Templeton, Professor of Obstetrics and Gynaecology at the University of Aberdeen, and from Professor Ian Wilmut, Head of Gene Expression and Development at the Roslin Institute in Midlothian and an honorary Professor at Edinburgh University.

[9] Very shortly before the hearing the defendant indicated an intention of applying to cross-examine the claimant's expert witnesses and to file further evidence *c* and for the inevitable consequential adjournment. I heard those applications on the afternoon of 30 October. I refused an adjournment and did not grant the other applications, although without finally refusing them. In the event my initial view that cross-examination and further evidence were inappropriate and unnecessary was confirmed during the hearing. I have read the experts' illuminating *d* statements with interest and noted that there are differences of opinion on some matters, but I have not identified any differences that would make it difficult for me to resolve this application. Cross-examination in judicial review cases is rare. Both these applications by the defendant are refused.

[10] During the course of the hearing, having heard sufficient of the arguments, I gave permission to apply for judicial review.   *e*

[11] The matters requiring consideration are these. (1) Should permission be refused on the ground of delay? I have already indicated that I was not refusing permission on that ground, but would give my reasons in my judgment. (2) Has the court jurisdiction in the circumstances to grant judicial review and, if it does, should the court in its discretion exercise that jurisdiction? (3) The central issue as *f* already described. (4) The claimant has argued in the alternative that if the defendant's contentions on the central issue are correct and hence CNR is subject to the Act, s 3(3)(d) of the Act would render CNR unlawful. The claimant has indicated an intention to amend to seek a declaration accordingly.

Fertilisation and cell nuclear replacement   *g*

[12] The expert evidence describes the processes in detail, but for present purposes they can be shortly described.

[13] In the ovary the egg is a diploid germ (or reproductive) cell. It is described as 'diploid' because its nucleus contains a full set of 46 chromosomes. By the process of meiotic division the nucleus divides into two parts. Only one of these, *h* a pronucleus containing only 23 chromosomes (described as 'haploid'), plays any further part in the process. Fertilisation begins when the male germ cell, the sperm, whose pronucleus contains 23 chromosomes, meets the haploid female germ cell and is a continuous process taking up to 24 hours. As part of the process the male and female pronuclei fuse to form one nucleus with a full complement *j* of 46 chromosomes, a process known as syngamy. The one-cell structure that exists following syngamy is the zygote. After several hours the cell divides to create a two-cell zygote. At this stage it is generally referred to as an embryo. At about 15 days after fertilisation a heaping-up of cells occurs which is described as the 'primitive streak'.

[14] Fertilisation may of course take place in the normal way or in vitro.

[15] CNR is a process by which the nucleus, which is diploid, from one cell is
a transplanted into an unfertilised egg, from which (in the process I am considering)
the nucleus has been removed. The nucleus is derived from either an embryonic
or a foetal or an adult cell. The cell is then treated to encourage it to grow and
divide, forming first a two-cell structure and then developing in a similar way to
an ordinary embryo.

b   [16] CNR is a form of cloning. Clones are organisms that are genetically identical
to each other. When CNR is used, if the embryo develops into a live individual,
that individual is genetically identical to the nucleus transplanted into the egg.
There are other methods of cloning, for example, embryo splitting, which may
occur naturally or be encouraged. Identical twins are the result of embryo splitting.

      [17] The famous Dolly the sheep was produced by CNR. Live young have since
c been produced by CNR in some other mammals. It has not yet been attempted
in humans.

      [18] As I have indicated, CNR of the kind under consideration does not normally
involve fertilisation. There are techniques that involve both cell nuclear replacement
and fertilisation, but I am not considering those. In most circumstances at least,
d such techniques will fall within s 1(1) of the Act, because fertilisation is involved.

The history of the legislation

      [19] I am invited by both parties to consider the history before and after the
passing of the Act.

e   [20] The story begins with the publication in 1984 of the *Report of the Committee
of Inquiry into Human Fertilisation and Embryology* (Cmnd 9314), chaired by Dame
Mary Warnock (the Warnock report). The report recommended the setting up
of a licensing authority to regulate both research and certain infertility services.
It recommended that human embryos should be afforded some protection in law
and that certain procedures should be prohibited by the criminal law.

f   [21] In its discussion of cloning, the Warnock report referred (at p 73) to
nucleus substitution:

      '12.14. Another technique, which has sometimes been referred to as
      cloning, but which may more accurately be described as nucleus substitution
g   would raise more fundamental questions. These would occur if it became
      possible to remove the nucleus from a fertilised human egg and, without
      detriment to its subsequent development, replace it with the nucleus taken
      from an adult human. This process would open the way for the creation of
      "carbon copy clones". It has been suggested that one day it might be possible
      to produce immunologically identical organs for transplantation purposes to
h   replace a diseased organ, for example a kidney. The cloned replacement
      organ would be grown in an embryo in which the nucleus has been replaced
      by one taken from the person for whom the replacement organ was
      intended.'

j   [22] It is to be noted that the Warnock report was referring to the removal of
the nucleus from a *fertilised* human egg.

      [23] The Warnock report also recommended that since the appearance of the
primitive streak marks the beginning of individual development of the embryo,
no live human embryo may be kept alive, if not transferred to a woman, nor used
as a research subject beyond 14 days after fertilisation (ignoring any time when
the embryo may have been frozen).

[24] Following a consultation paper, the government published a White Paper *Human Fertilisation and Embryology: A Framework for Legislation* (Cm 259) in November 1987. The government decided to set up a licensing authority.

[25] The White Paper said:

'7. Before setting out the detail of the proposed legislation, it is important to define what is meant by the term "embryo". One common definition of an embryo is the product of conception from fertilisation to the end of the eighth week of development. The Warnock Committee regarded the embryonic stage as the six weeks immediately following fertilisation ... 8. The Government proposes that legislation should apply to embryos created in vitro (ie. by mixing sperm and eggs together in a dish), from the point at which fertilisation is completed. The start of cell division would be taken to be proof that the process of fertilisation has ended. The legislation would apply to these embryos up to the time at which they are transferred to a woman's uterus. This would mean that, if research were permitted, the use of embryos which were not transferred to a woman would be controlled throughout the time they were held outside the body.'

[26] The government proposed that if research was permitted, the authority would not be able to give a licence for the use of embryos beyond 14 days or after the appearance of the primitive streak, whichever was the earlier.

[27] About nuclear substitution, the White Paper said:

'38. Similar concerns [to those about modifying an embryo's genetic structure] arise from fears that it will one day be possible to produce artificially two or more genetically identical individuals by nucleus substitution (sometimes known as cloning). The Warnock Report (paragraph 12.11 [on cloning] and 12.14) described techniques by which such results might theoretically be achieved, although there is no knowledge of such work being carried out artificially with human embryos. The Bill will make such practices a criminal offence.'

[28] The Act followed. No evidence about the progress of the legislation through Parliament has been introduced. The Human Fertilisation and Embryology Authority (the authority) was set up by the Act.

[29] On 27 February 1997 a paper entitled 'Viable offspring derived from fetal and adult mammalian cells' by Professor Wilmut (one of the experts in this case) and others, was published in *Nature* ((1997) 385 *Nature* 810). The paper revealed the birth of lamb number 6LL3, now famous as Dolly the sheep. Not only did she achieve popular fame; her birth following CNR using an adult sheep cell represented a very significant scientific development. There had in fact been earlier births of sheep in 1996, following CNR, but using a sheep embryo as a donor source.

[30] Much discussion of cloning followed, including, importantly for present purposes, the possible use of CNR on human organisms for research purposes, not intended to lead to the birth of a human being. The House of Commons Science and Technology Committee published a report in March 1997 entitled *The Cloning of Animals from Adult Cells* (HC Paper 373 (1996–97)). The government published its response to that report in December 1997 (*The Cloning of Animals from Adult Cells: Government Response to the Fifth Report of the House of Commons Select Committee on Science and Technology 1996–97 Session* (Cm 3815)). In December 1998 a report entitled *Cloning Issues in Reproduction, Science and Medicine* was

a   published jointly by the Human Genetics Advisory Commission and the
    authority. There followed the Donaldson report.

Delay
    [31] By CPR 54.5(1), the claim form 'must be filed—(a) promptly; and (b) in
    any event not later than 3 months after the grounds to make the claim first arose'.
b   [32] In my judgment the grounds to make the claim first arose when the 2000
    response was published. I shall give my reasons later for concluding that the
    2000 response provides grounds for judicial review. The report of March 1997
    could not be the subject of judicial review, for reasons of Parliamentary privilege.
    In any event, neither that report, nor the response of December 1997, nor the
    report of December 1998 contained any firm indication of action of a kind that
c   could be the subject of judicial review. In my judgment the claimant has acted
    with reasonable promptness.
    [33] In any event, it is open to the court to deal with applications made late if
    the applicant has behaved sensibly and reasonably or the matters raised are of
    general importance (see *R v Comr for Local Administration, ex p Croydon London BC*
d   [1989] 1 All ER 1033 at 1046 per Woolf LJ, *R v Secretary of State for the Home Dept,
    ex p Ruddock* [1987] 2 All ER 518 at 522, [1987] 1 WLR 1482 at 1486 per Taylor J,
    and *R v Secretary of State for Foreign Affairs, ex p World Development Movement Ltd*
    [1995] 1 All ER 611 at 627, [1995] 1 WLR 386 at 402 per Rose LJ). On those
    principles, if I am wrong in my views about the absence of delay, I am satisfied
e   that I should deal with the application on its merits.

Jurisdiction and discretion
    [34] It is submitted on behalf of the defendant that the jurisdiction to grant a
    declaration does not arise in relation to the contents of the 2000 response or
    alternatively that such a jurisdiction should not be exercised.
f   [35] The claimant relies on *Gillick v West Norfolk and Wisbech Area Health Authority*
    [1985] 3 All ER 402, [1986] AC 112. Lord Bridge of Harwich ([1985] 3 All ER 402
    at 1126–1127, [1986] AC 112 at 193) referred to the decision in *Royal College of
    Nursing of the UK v Dept of Health and Social Security* [1981] 1 All ER 545, [1981] AC
    800, where both the Royal College of Nursing (RCN) and the department sought
g   declarations as to the lawfulness of a circular issued by the department which was
    said by the RCN to give advice that was unlawful. No technical question of
    jurisdiction was taken. Lord Bridge continued:

        'Against this background it would have been surprising indeed if the courts
        had declined jurisdiction. But I think it must be recognised that the decision
h   (whether or not it was so intended) does effect a significant extension of the
        court's power of judicial review. We must now say that if a government
        department, in a field of administration in which it exercises responsibility,
        promulgates in a public document, albeit non-statutory in form, advice
        which is erroneous in law, then the court, in proceedings in appropriate form
j   commenced by an applicant or plaintiff who possesses the necessary locus
        standi, has jurisdiction to correct the error of law by an appropriate declaration.
        Such an extended jurisdiction is no doubt a salutary and indeed a necessary
        one in certain circumstances, as the *Royal College of Nursing* case itself well
        illustrates. But the occasions of a departmental non-statutory publication
        raising, as in that case, a clearly defined issue of law, unclouded by political,
        social or moral overtones, will be rare. In cases where any proposition of law

implicit in a departmental advisory document is interwoven with questions
of social and ethical controversy, the court should, in my opinion, exercise   *a*
its jurisdiction with the utmost restraint, confine itself to deciding whether
the proposition of law is erroneous and avoid either expressing ex cathedra
opinions in areas of social and ethical controversy in which it has no claim to
speak with authority or proffering answers to hypothetical questions of law
which do not strictly arise for decision.' (See [1985] 3 All ER 402 at 427, [1986]   *b*
AC 112 at 193.)

[36] I was also referred to the remarks of Lord Goff of Chieveley in *Airedale
NHS Trust v Bland* [1993] 1 All ER 821 at 864, [1993] AC 789 at 862 about the
desirability of matters relating to the medical profession being determined by
declaratory relief rather than being left for decision ex post facto in criminal   *c*
proceedings. Those were not judicial review proceedings, but proceedings in the
Family Division for a declaration relating to withdrawal of treatment from a
patient.

[37] The claimant seeks to rely on Parliamentary statements that the
government had received advice to the effect that the Act and in particular the   *d*
definition in s 1 applied to organisms produced by CNR. Leaving aside questions
of Parliamentary privilege, I do not consider it appropriate to take those into
account. Opinions expressed by government ministers about the meaning of an
Act of Parliament, wherever expressed, appear to me to be well outside the
jurisdiction contemplated by Lord Bridge.

[38] However, the 2000 response was a definitive government response to a   *e*
proposal that new purposes of research be permitted not only on embryos
undoubtedly within that definition but also on organisms produced by CNR, on
the assumption that those are within the definition in the Act. The 2000 response
proposed regulations based on that assumption. Sullivan J was told, as I have
been, that the authority has stated that it will not issue licences under the   *f*
regulations until these proceedings are resolved. It has set out that in a published
bulletin. The question of law is not merely hypothetical. There is no indication
that researchers are proposing to carry out CNR without waiting for a licence and
hence there is no suggestion that criminal offences are likely. Indeed, if the
claimant is correct, researchers may create organisms by CNR without reference
to the Act, although they might face criminal proceedings on the basis of a   *g*
contention that such creation is prohibited by s 3(3)(d) of the Act. I shall consider
that subsection later and I take the view that it does not prohibit CNR as presently
under consideration. Nevertheless the point might be tested in criminal proceedings.
As in some medical cases, it is undesirable that responsible researchers, and
indeed the authority, are left in doubt or that the matter be tested in ex post facto   *h*
criminal proceedings.

[39] The defendant argues that the claimant's stance is illogical, in that the
claimant opposes cloning and the creation and use of embryos for research on
principle and the effect of a declaration would be that CNR is not subject to any
statutory or regulatory control. The defendant argues that the claimant's motive is   *j*
to force these issues back onto the Parliamentary agenda, when the government
have in fact announced that they propose to introduce primary legislation to put
the coverage of the Act beyond doubt as far as reproductive cloning is concerned.

[40] It may well be that the claimant's motives include those suggested. It is
not for the court to influence the Parliamentary agenda. However, no objection
has been taken to the standing of the claimant. If they have raised a legitimate

a concern about the meaning of s 1—and I consider that they have—the court has and should exercise jurisdiction. Although, in Lord Bridge's words, the issue has 'political, social and moral overtones', I shall confine myself to the proposition of law said to be erroneous. I shall avoid expressing opinions in areas of social and ethical controversy, except to echo the submissions of both parties that these are matters of profound social and ethical importance.

b
The central issue

[41] The claimant now accepts that the organism produced by CNR is 'live' and 'human' for the purposes of the definition.

[42] During the hearing there has been discussion about whether the organism produced by CNR is properly described as an 'embryo' as a matter of scientific c language. The defendant submits that it is morphologically and functionally indistinguishable from an embryo produced by fertilisation. The claimant has pointed to certain differences of structure. They point to the fact that on currently available data from animal experiments only a tiny percentage of such organisms will result in live births. The defendant replies that this difference is largely the d result of the present state of scientific expertise. The claimant also points out that some scientific opinion refers to the organisms as 'reconstructed embryos'.

[43] Ultimately, however, it is conceded, in my view correctly, that the organism produced by CNR is naturally described as an 'embryo', at least when the two-cell stage is reached. That is consistent with the expert evidence before the court. If the definition in s 1(1) had ended at the word 'embryo', without the e following words and without s 1(1)(b), I should have held that the organism fell within the definition.

[44] The claimant relies on the following words and submits simply that an embryo that has not been produced by fertilisation cannot be an 'embryo where fertilisation is complete'.

f   [45] The defendant argues for a purposive construction of s 1(1). It argues that the essential concept is 'a live human embryo'. The subsection should be read as if the words were, in effect, 'a live human embryo where [if it is produced by fertilisation] fertilisation is complete'.

[46] Assistance in construing s 1(1)(a) is to be obtained from other parts of the Act.

[47] The effect of s 1(1)(b) is to extend the protection given to an embryo back g in time before fertilisation is complete. Fertilisation is for this purpose not complete until the appearance of the two-cell zygote. But for the purposes of the Act an egg 'in the process of fertilisation' is an embryo. In other words, once the process of fertilisation, which is a process over a period of time, begins, the egg is an 'embryo' for the purposes of the Act.

h   [48] It is argued on behalf of the claimant that the organism produced by CNR is not properly referred to as a 'zygote'. They correctly point to the Greek origin of the word in the root zyg- (ζευγ), carrying the meaning of two things being yoked together, but the derivation of a word often does not govern its present meaning. However, they also correctly point to definitions of 'zygote' in scientific j dictionaries published in 2000, which assume fertilisation. I accept that although the organism developing from CNR has similarities to a zygote, it is not, at least so far, settled scientific practice to refer to it as a zygote. Professor Templeton goes no further than saying: 'In my opinion, the one cell structure can appropriately be described as a zygote.'

[49] In my view, even if the defendant's central submission were correct, s 1(1)(b) would not apply to the organism produced by CNR. Nothing is 'in the process of

fertilisation'. It follows that there could be doubt whether that organism was an 'embryo' prior to the two-cell stage. Professor Wilmut, for example, refers to the organism as a 'reconstructed embryo', 'a term used by biologists to describe embryos created using CNR usually at the one or two-cell stage'. It may well be that responsible researchers would treat the organism as subject to control from an earlier stage, by analogy with s 1(1)(b). However, they would not be obliged to do so unless it became settled scientific practice to refer to the organism as an 'embryo' before the two-cell stage. The very fact that an area of doubt would result is in itself an argument against the defendant's construction of s 1.

[50] The remainder of s 1 reads:

'(2) This Act, so far as it governs bringing about the creation of an embryo, applies only to bringing about the creation of an embryo outside the human body; and in this Act—(a) references to embryos the creation of which was brought about *in vitro* (in their application to those where fertilisation is complete) are to those where fertilisation began outside the human body whether or not completed there, and (b) references to embryos taken from a woman do not include embryos whose creation was brought about *in vitro*.
(3) This Act, so far as it governs the keeping or use of an embryo, applies only to keeping or using an embryo outside the human body.
(4) References in this Act to gametes, eggs or sperm, except where otherwise stated, are to live human gametes, eggs or sperm but references below in this Act to gametes or eggs do not include eggs in the process of fertilisation.'

[51] Subsections (2)(a) and (4) clearly assume a process of fertilisation. The other parts of these subsections would generally have less relevance to an organism produced by CNR, but that is not necessarily decisive in deciding the central issue.

[52] I turn to the important s 3:

'(1) No person shall—(a) bring about the creation of an embryo, or (b) keep or use an embryo, except in pursuance of a licence.
(2) No person shall place in a woman—(a) a live embryo other than a human embryo, or (b) any live gametes other than human gametes.
(3) A licence cannot authorise—(a) keeping or using an embryo after the appearance of the primitive streak, (b) placing an embryo in any animal, (c) keeping or using an embryo in any circumstances in which regulations prohibit its keeping or use, or (d) replacing a nucleus of a cell of an embryo with a nucleus taken from a cell of any person, embryo or subsequent development of an embryo.
(4) For the purposes of subsection (3)(a) above, the primitive streak is to be taken to have appeared in an embryo not later than the end of the period of 14 days beginning with the day when the gametes are mixed, not counting any time during which the embryo is stored.'

[53] Subsections (1), (2) and (3)(b) and (c) cause no difficulty of application if an organism produced by CNR is an embryo, although subsection (2)(b) would have no relevance.

[54] Subsection (3)(a) must be read with sub-s (4). These provisions were inserted in the light of the Warnock committee's recommendations. The claimant submits that sub-s (4) of s 3, a deeming provision, is definitive on the question when the primitive streak appears. It is submitted that since sub-s (4) cannot apply to an organism produced by CNR, the organism would be denied (as far as the Act is concerned) the protection intended for an embryo not only after the 14-day

a period, but after the appearance of the primitive streak. I accept that sub-s (4) cannot be read in a way that would apply to an organism produced by CNR. However, the defendant submits that although sub-s (4) prohibits licences permitting keeping or use after 14 days, sub-s (3)(a) prohibits licences permitting keeping or use after the appearance of the primitive streak even if that should occur earlier. The latter construction is consistent with the proposal in the White Paper. Partly for that reason, I prefer this construction. It follows that a licence

b issued in relation to an organism produced by CNR would have to comply with sub-s (3)(a). Whether the licence included reference to any 14-day period would be a matter for the authority.

[55] Subsection (3)(d) raises important issues. It was clearly inserted in the light of the concern expressed by the Warnock committee and adopted by the White

c Paper. Its effect is to prevent the licensing of nuclear substitution where the egg has been fertilised. That is because such an egg is an 'embryo' by reason of s 1(1)(b) and this conclusion is not affected by s 1(4) because there is no reference in s 3(3)(d) to an 'egg'. However, s 3(3)(d) does not in terms prevent the licensing of CNR in the sense with which I am concerned, because the egg has not been

d fertilised.

[56] The claimant relies strongly on s 3(3)(d). It is argued that if CNR in the present sense had been known to the Warnock committee, the concern of the committee about cloning would have applied equally to CNR in both senses. It is further argued that if Parliament had been aware of this kind of CNR, the prohibition in the section would have extended to both kinds.

e [57] Mr Eadie on behalf of the defendant argues that the court should not speculate about what the Warnock committee, or Parliament, would have said about CNR of the present kind. However, he concedes that somewhat similar ethical considerations arise in relation to nuclear substitution in fertilised and unfertilised eggs, although it might be argued that there is an ethical distinction. I cannot

f accept his argument that I should take note of the fact that the regulations have been the subject of affirmative resolutions. I am construing the Act. I cannot take into account the views expressed by Parliament in 2001. Scientific knowledge has moved on. Not only has nuclear substitution proved to be possible in animals, but it has become clear that CNR has potential for research purposes that was not known in 1990. I do not think that I should speculate about whether, if Parliament

g had known about both types of CNR, it would have prohibited both. Nor do I think that I should speculate about whether either or both might have been permitted for research purposes only, but not reproductive purposes, which is what is now proposed. I remind myself that I am interpreting what Parliament in fact enacted in the Act, not what it would or might have enacted if the scientific

h advances of 1997 had been known then.

[58] Section 12 of the Act requires certain conditions in every licence granted by the authority. Among those are the provisions of Sch 3, requiring consents to the use of gametes (eggs or sperm) or embryos. The provisions are tightly drawn to require effective consent to such use and to permit the withdrawal of such

j consent. If the defendant's construction of s 1 is correct, consent would be required from the woman whose egg was used for CNR, but not from the person whose cell was used for transplanting into the denucleated egg. Such a person would be the person 'cloned' by the process, that is, the organism produced would be genetically identical to that person. The claimant submits that this result cannot have been intended. The defendant points out that the authority could require such consent.

Conclusions

[**59**] The defendant argues for a purposive interpretation of s 1. The argument is a powerful one. The Warnock committee was appointed to examine the social, ethical and legal implications of recent, and potential developments in the field of human assisted reproduction. Its report was, in the light of knowledge at the time, comprehensive. Had the discoveries of 1997 been known, they would have been considered. Similarly the White Paper and the Act itself was clearly intended to provide comprehensive control, either by prohibition or licensing, of human reproduction. The parties differ about whether CNR would have fallen under the licensing provisions or under the prohibition in s 3(3)(d), but it is inconceivable that Parliament would have ignored CNR.

[**60**] The claimant nevertheless argues that the words of s 1(1) cannot be stretched to cover organisms produced by CNR, involving no fertilisation. Its argument is in my view supported by the way in which the provisions of s 3(3)(d) and Sch 3 are worded. I place less weight on the fact that ss 1(1)(b) and 3(4) would not apply and that the authority would be left to make decisions in areas not explicitly covered by the Act.

[**61**] I decline any invitation to attempt to rewrite any of the sections of the 1990 Act to make them apply by analogy to organisms produced by CNR.

[**62**] I accept the defendant's argument that the reason for inserting in s 1(1)(a) the words 'where fertilisation is complete' and the following words in s 1(1)(b) was to define the moment at which the Act's protection applied to the organism. Nevertheless the words are there. The question is whether to insert the additional words is permissible: 'a live human embryo where [if it is produced by fertilisation] fertilisation is complete'. With some reluctance, since it would leave organisms produced by CNR outside the statutory and licensing framework, I have come to the conclusion that to insert these words would involve an impermissible rewriting and extension of the definition.

[**63**] The claimant's alternative argument about s 3(3)(d) of the Act does not arise. However, even if I had accepted the defendant's interpretation of s 1(1), I should not have interpreted s 3(3)(d) in the way claimed.

[**64**] I shall grant a declaration broadly in the terms sought in para 45(1) of the grounds. However, I think it may be appropriate to refer to the appropriate paragraphs of the 2000 response itself rather than of the Donaldson report. I invite submissions on the point and the preparation of an appropriate draft.

Application allowed. Declaration granted in the following terms: 'Human embryos created by the cell nuclear replacement technique that involves the insertion of the nucleus of a human somatic cell into an unfertilised egg (oocyte) which has had its nucleus removed (ie has been enucleated) are not "embryos" within the meaning of s 1 of the Human Fertilisation and Embryology Act 1990 and, therefore, are not subject to regulation under that Act.' Permission to appeal granted.

Dilys Tausz   Barrister.